THE GREAT E C T HOAX

L O H

E N E

C V R

T U A

R L P

O S Y

I

V

E

(Manufacturer Fraud and Deception)

<u>VOLUME I of II</u>

Douglas G Cameron

The Great Electro Convulsive Therapy Hoax Volume I

(Manufacturer Fraud and Deception)

Douglas G Cameron

Cover art
By Donna Zoe Grabow

ISBN: 979-8-9881280-0-7

Brave New World Publishing LLC
17350 State Hwy 249
Ste 220 # 15783
Houston TX 77064

DEDICATION

To all my fellow human beings who have suffered at the cruel hands of the mental health system
and
To my three children Doug, Scott, and Chris who grew up watching me write this book for over thirty years of their lives

Table of Contents

PART V

Those who suppress history doom humankind to repeat it.

Abstract

In spite of an article the author published in Journal of Mind and Behavior (Cameron 1994), delineating the preponderant power of modern day Brief Pulse (BP) devices compared to Sine Wave (SW), there yet lingers the misconception that modern day BP-“ECT” devices are lower in Energy Output (EO) or power than SW devices. This manuscript will explain why this misperception persists, how and why BP advocates have covered up the preponderant power of BP devices misleading the American Public and the FDA for more than forty years, why the “ECT” of today is not the ECT grandfathered in, in 1976, but something else entirely, and how and why the entire concept of convulsion as therapy is based upon sixty years of fraud. This manuscript explains in detail how the so-called new and improved BP machines, in lieu of diminishing in power, first doubled and then quadrupled in power without public awareness, how manufacturers have disparately and fraudulently interpreted never before examined national and international standards, and how modern machines' have invisibly quintupled electrical titration per individual age category with the latest Brief Pulse generation. In sum, this manuscript examines fraudulent safety studies, misleading MRI studies, why “ECT” is no longer “ECT,” but ENR (Electro Neurotransmission Reduction), the true goal of so-called “ECT,” why it is no surprise that the most revealing MRI study ever performed reveals gross reduction in neuro-connections following “ECT,” and finally what the correlation is between neurotransmission reduction and the increase in device power with each new Brief Pulse device generation.

Introduction

In spite of a 1994 article (Cameron 1994) published in the Canadian *Journal of Mind and Behavior* clearly showing the preponderant power of modern day Brief Pulse (BP) devices compared to the older Sine Wave (SW) devices, research and media articles, and even Surgeon General reports continue to assume that modern day BP is a lower Energy device and thus safer than the previous SW models. (Fink 1997; Fodero, 1993; Food and Drug Administration, 1986B, p.13; Food and Drug Administration, 1990, September 5, p.36581; Kellner, 1994, February 2; National Institute of Mental Health and Center for Mental Health Services, 1994; Sackeim, 1991, p.234; Satcher, August 16,1999; Stone, 1994; Weiner, 1979, 1980; Welch, 1982). This manuscript explains why this longstanding misperception persists, why it is totally incorrect, how manufacturers have deliberately cultivated this falsehood, and the consequences to the world at large. This book clearly exposes how and why for decades manufacturers have deceived the American Public, the FDA, the ERA (European Regulatory Agency), the IEC (International Electrotechnical Commission), and even practicing physicians via manufacturer cover-ups regarding the true power of their devices, devices delivering suprathreshold dosages under the false guise of minimal stimulus output. In short, this manuscript patently, and for the first time, depicts the historical evolution of the initial minimal stimulus, lower Energy Output (EO) Brief Pulse devices (as opposed to SW) devices—compared to the much more powerful Brief Pulse devices in use today, BP devices surreptitiously and conspiratorially manufactured not only to equal but to surpass the well-known damaging outputs of Sine Wave in almost every age category. These "modern-day" Brief Pulse devices are designed to deliver, deliberately and premeditatedly, excessive, damaging, suprathreshold dosages of electricity all in order to make the procedure "work." In brief, Volume I discloses for the first time how modern day BP devices more than double in power immediately following the close of the first FDA investigation of ECT in 1982 while Volume II discloses how a third generation of souped-up BP devices subsequently quadruples in power about 1995--all without public awareness. Indeed, manufacturers go to great lengths to convince the public of the exact opposite. In addition, Volume I and II explain how the quadrupling of power is concomitant with quadrupled threshold output per individual recipient--again sans public awareness and again while manufacturers simultaneously disseminate misleading information regarding the "minimal stimulus" power of modern day Brief Pulse devices. Revealed in Volume I is the history of how manufacturers on a world-wide basis have furtively misinterpreted standards in order to make damaging outputs "legal," and in Volume II how manufacturers have dispensed with regulations altogether. Too, Volume I reveals how almost all "safety studies" for "the newer 'ECT'" BP devices have been performed at minimal stimulus output far below the clinically applied pre-set doses utilized by all modern day manufacturers and why none of these studies have detected the patently identifiable damage which occurs following "ECT. " Indeed, the actual manufacturer goal of so-called "ECT" substantiated by the actual power of these devices is set forth here for the first time ever. In sum, all manufacturer secrets regarding the composition, and so the true power and purpose of these devices is revealed in Volume I and II for first time in the long history of this sordidly deceptive process, most specifically, the increasing power of each new device generation with the express goal of destroying a greater and greater percentage of neuronal connections.

But let me be even clearer regarding the books' thesis of fraud. Once Congress granted the FDA power to condone or condemn medical devices in 1976, "ECT" became scrutinized for the first time since the machine's invention in 1938. As a result, manufacturers introduced the Brief Pulse device as a safer alternative to Sine Wave utilized from 1938 to 1976 (and beyond as we shall observe). In short, Brief Pulse was introduced as an improvement over SW by virtue of its capacity to administer "convulsive therapy" with half the electrical energy of SW while still inducing the same so-called "adequate" seizures. In this way, cognitive dissonance, namely, long term memory complaints would be addressed, the chief objection to the SW device. Once the investigation was over, however, and as we shall witness, manufacturers furtively began increasing the power of Brief Pulse, first equaling and then surpassing SW in power. Manufacturers cover up the true power of these devices, but also attempt to justify “moderate” increases first by claiming UL (Unilateral) "ECT" "dose-sensitive," requiring twice the electricity needed to induce an adequate seizure to be effective. Manufacturers then claim both BL (Bilateral) and UL "ECT" require twice the electricity needed to induce an adequate seizure to be effective in that both BL and UL “ECT” double in resistance (Impedance) over a course of "treatments." In this way, UL ECT requires four times threshold while BL ECT requires twice threshold to remain effective at the end of a "treatment course." So powerful did Brief Pulse devices become, however, that manufacturers have been forced to hide the actual power increases which soared well over the so-called "justification increases" as we shall see. Thus, in that it has always been excessive electricity, electricity well over that required to induce an adequate seizure that has been associated with cognitive dissonance reflective of brain damage, manufacturers have been forced to cover up the true power of these devices. The truth is, these devices do not work with adequate seizure at all. Instead, they work as they have always worked, past and present, as a result of adequate amounts of electricity. In brief, manufacturers have been forced to cover up the power of their devices in that excessive electricity damages the brain resulting in long term memory dysfunction. In sum, these machines must damage the brain in order to "work," a fact of which manufacturers are only too well aware.

Volume I and II of *The Great Electroconvulsive Therapy Hoax* exposes for the first time ever, in detail, the true power emissions of these machines. Finally, I wish to apologize for the necessity of mathematical proofs throughout the texts. However, long experience has taught me that without these irrefutable proofs, advocates of these devices will simply label these findings --"anecdotal." Feel free, if you are not mathematically inclined, therefore, to skim over these proofs and go directly to the facts found in the narration and the various charts and graphs revealing detailed power. For those who need these proofs such as regulatory experts, attorneys, physicians, on the other hand, that is, who must verify my results, I welcome your perusal.

PART I

SECTION I: TWO ERAS

Chapter 1

The BP ERA

It is important to understand there have been two basic "ECT" Eras in America (and throughout the world) - the first shall be coined *the SW (Sine Wave) Era*,[1] occurring from about 1940 to 1976 (in the United States), and the second, *the BP (Brief Pulse) Era*, occurring from 1976 to the present.

Because Brief Pulse devices are composed of intermittent as opposed to continuous electrical output and Constant Current in lieu of Constant Voltage, the Brief Pulse device is capable of inducing seizures at less than half the Energy Output (EO) of standard SW, which comparatively, induces seizures at suprathreshold or excessive dosages of electricity. [2] Modern safety and efficacy studies of "ECT" typically compare BP to SW, studies only initiated following Paul Blachley's resurrection [3] of BP devices via MMECTA[4] Corporation in 1973 (Blachley, 1976a; Carney and Sheffield; Sackeim and Weiner, 1993, p.53; Weaver et al. , 1977). This was closely followed by FDA's 1976 emergence as an investigatory medical device agency via the 1976 Medical Device Amendment to the Food, Drug, and Cosmetic Act (Rice, 1982, p.66).

Blachley's original aim in resurrecting the less powerful minimal stimulus potential of a BP or Brief Pulse device, was to considerably shorten the entire procedure by using an extremely intensive form of "ECT" -- multiple convulsions per single anesthetic setting (American Psychiatric Association Task Force on ECT 1978, p.81; Blachley and Gowing,1966).[5] The reduced output Brief Pulse "ECT" device was to be used to compensate for Blachley's more intensive "Multiple Monitored 'ECT.' " Even so, since several convulsions or electroshocks administered per single anesthetic setting can induce status epilepticus not always visible to the naked eye, monitoring seizure activity via an adjunctive EEG scan proved cautionary, thus Blachley dubbed his new Brief Pulse "ECT" device "MMECTA" -- "Multiple Monitored Electro-Convulsive Therapy Apparatus" (Blachley,

---

[1] BP was first utilized in the 40s and 50s, but was discarded as ineffective (Cameron, 1994; Impastato et al., 1957). The great majority of all clinically applied "ECT" up to 1976; therefore, was Standard SW.

[2] Utilizing UL electrode placement and narrower pulse widths, BP is actually capable of one forth the EO of SW to induce adequate convulsions (Grahn, Jerhrich, Couvillon, and Moench, 1977), while utilizing BL placement, one half (and actually less) than that of SW (Weiner 1979; 1980). In fact, earlier BP devices (Liberson, 1948), were able to induce adequate seizures at even lower outputs.

[3] W.T. Liberson first experimented with Brief Pulse as early as 1948 (Liberson, 1948). The experiments were eventually abandoned due to inefficacy (Cameron, 1994).

[4] MM stands for Multiple Monitored; MECTA eventually dropped the double M.

[5] Standard "ECT" must be comparatively suprathreshold to be effective. Reduced intensity of the "ECT" procedure to threshold level, therefore, is always compensated by an intensity increase in some other aspect or aspects of the operation - increased power of the machine, wider electrode placement, greater number of procedures, reduced spacing of treatments, multiple treatments in one setting, etc.; otherwise, efficacy becomes insignificant. Had Blachley applied multiple procedures in a single anesthetic setting utilizing the comparatively suprathreshold dosages of Standard SW instead of BP or the suprathreshold BP machines which followed, he may have regressed his recipients to infant-like states (American Psychiatric Association Task Force on ECT 1978; Glueck, Reiss, and Bernard, 1957).

1976a). Though Blachley's technique proved too dangerous to continue, more traditional advocates of what was to become the modern Brief Pulse era, appreciated that the interrupted constant current of the MMECTA Brief Pulse device did indeed induce "adequate" seizures at one third to one half the EO (Energy Output) of Medcraft's powerful Standard SW device -- the B-24-III (Department of Health and Human Services, 1982a, pp. G3-G4; Grahn et al, 1977; Weiner, 1979; Weiner, 1980) just as the inventor of Brief Pulse, W. T. Liberson (1945; 1946; 1948) had determined a quarter of a century earlier.

Based upon the alleged therapeutic benefit of adequate seizure alone, then, Blachley's "new" Brief Pulse device, resurrected from the original 1948 experiments of W. T. Liberson, initiated the modern BP era, re-igniting avid interest in Liberson's original lower dosage Brief Pulse device. Whatever the motivation for Blachley's 1976 reintroduction of the Brief Pulse device then, the re-emergence of an instrument which could considerably reduce the electricity required to induce a grand mal convulsion appeared to engender new hope for increased safety with electroshock, just as early pioneers Wilcox (1948) and Liberson (1946) had been inspired to believe years earlier. Convinced that the lowest possible electrical dosage--that is--the lowest EO (Energy Output) possible to induce adequate seizures--would prove safer and just as effective as SW, modern advocates of Brief Pulse, just as originators Wilcox with his direct current and Liberson, with his early intermittent or brief pulse current had been. In short, modern advocates of Brief Pulse aspired to permanently reduce or even eliminate memory damage from the ECT process by dramatically reducing the amount of electricity needed to induce the same adequate seizure. Just as Liberson and Wilcox had hoped years earlier then, perhaps the resurrected Brief Pulse device, based on pure convulsion theory alone, would in the modern era prove safer and just as effective as SW after all, enabling the ECT procedure to at long last be administered with much less harm to its recipients, specifically, without long-term brain or memory damage.

Though clinical literature has appeared all throughout the history of "ECT" touting the "ECT" procedure the practical application of convulsion theory (Ottoson, 1960; American Psychiatric Association Task Force on ECT, 1978; Department of Health and Human Services, 1982a; Fink 1997; Weiner, 1980; Welch et al, 1982; MECTA Corporation,1993), in fact, twenty-five years prior to FDA's Congressional authorization to scrutinize U. S. medical devices in 1976, well before Blachley's resurrected BP device in 1973, true minimal stimulus ECT devices such as Brief Pulse had been discarded as ineffective. In short, true lower Energy Output minimal stimulus or true "ECT" devices had been manufactured and utilized in the late 1940s and early 1950s (as noted above), both in the U. S. (Impastato et al. , 1957) and abroad, all totally capable of inducing the same grand mal convulsions as SW. Unfortunately, they had ultimately proved ineffective compared to higher Energy Output SW devices and so had eventually failed on the marketplace (Cameron, 1994, p.189; Delmas-Marsalet, 1942; Grahn, Jerhrich, Couvillon, and Moench, 1977). Indeed, while shock advocates continue to claim "electroconvulsive therapy" to be based on the therapeutic benefit of adequate convulsion alone, a theory indicating minimal stimulus efficacy so long as the "adequate seizure" is induced, in actual fact, manufacturers have long known that the adequate seizure induced with reduced output or close to minimal electrical stimulus is ineffective. Certainly, while "ECT" advocates continued and continue to claim that so-called "electroconvulsive therapy devices" are based on convulsion theory or the so-called therapeutic effect of grand mal seizure, the so-called "electro-convulsive therapy devices" SW devices utilized during the SW Era from 1940 to 1976 were not actually electroconvulsive therapy devices at all, but rather what we shall later deem with detail, ENR or Electro Neurotransmission Reduction devices--machines actually based on adequate amounts of electricity. [6] Clearly then, in light of Wilcox and Liberson's minimal stimulus or true "electroconvulsive therapy devices" of the past, SW devices are not "electro convulsive therapy" devices at all in that they are not based on minimal stimulus electricity, but rather high intensity doses of electricity, particularly in the younger age categories. SW machine efficacy, in short, is not, nor ever has been based on adequate seizure--but rather, adequate dosages of electricity (Cameron, 1994; Grahn,1977; Impastato et al. , 1957; Robin and Tissera, 1982; Wilcox, 1946). [7] Put another way, the efficacy of the extremely powerful and destructive SW device [8] renowned for long term memory damage, was plainly exposed as electro-dependent by Wilcox's much less intensive DC (Direct Current) experiments of the early and mid-1940s (Wilcox, 1946;

---

[6] See Cameron, 1994. ECT (Electro Convulsive Therapy) devices = minimal stimulus convulsion devices. ENR (Electro Neurotransmission Reduction) devices = suprathreshold or adequate electricity devices.

[7] In the author's opinion, deliberate cultivation of a false theory in order to administer a similar appearing, but necessarily destructive procedure is the heart of the case for fraud, both in the SW era from at least 1950 to 1976, as well as the BP era, from 1976 to the present, as we shall see.

[8] Due to simple convenience, SW uses unmodified wall current requiring no alteration whatsoever.

Friedman, Wilcox, and Reiter, 1942) as well as Liberson's early experiments with Brief Pulse. Indeed, SW devices were exposed as electro-dependent both by early SW comparisons to Liberson's BP devices in the late 1940s (Liberson, 1949) and again by even later SW comparisons to Blachley's lower energy BP device in the 1970s (Blachley, 1974; Weiner, 1979; 1980), both of which could induce the same grand mal seizures as SW, but at much lower electrical outputs. SW then, plainly emits suprathreshold or excessive dosages of electricity (with respect to the eliciting of grand mal convulsions) in most age categories compared to true minimal stimulus devices or what are actually "ECT" devices such as Unidirectional or Brief Pulse devices set at or close to minimal stimulus output (Wilcox 1946; Cameron, 1994; Grahn, 1977; Weiner, 1979, 1980). In brief, SW clearly emits unnecessarily excessive dosages of electricity to induce so-called adequate grand mal seizures (Alexander, 1953, p.64; Sulzbach, Tillotson, Guillemin, and Sutherland, 1943) in most age categories. On the other hand, these excessive electrical dosages are necessary, as we shall see, to make the procedure "work" (Beale, 1994; Cameron, 1994; Impastato et al. , 1957; Petrides and Fink, 1997; Robin and Tissera, 1982; Sackeim, 1991, pp.233-234; Weiner, 1997, p.9). By the same token, the minimal stimulus experiments of the 1940s and 50s[9] along with the re-introduction of Liberson's Brief Pulse apparatus through Blachley in 1973, clearly show that grand mal seizures induced with minimal stimulus are ineffective as we shall see. In fact, as we shall clearly observe, lower energy devices such as Liberson's and Blachley's Brief Pulse which can induce the same adequate grand mal seizures as SW, expose "convulsion therapy" as myth by their necessary replacement with higher output devices. Manufacturers, in fact, have long known that adequate seizures induced with reduced output or what is actually minimal electrical stimulus are ineffective. In sum, but well known only to manufacturers, "convulsive therapy" simply does not "work."

Medcraft's Sine Wave vs Brief Pulse

The most enduring of the SW instruments amongst U. S. manufacturers - and by no mere coincidence one of the most powerful U. S. apparatuses[10] - was and is Medcraft's B-24 Sine Wave device, capable since 1950 of administering up to 200 Joules of electricity including glissando [11] (Department of Health and Human Services, 1982a, pp. G3-G4; Medcraft Corporation,1984). [12] [13] In fact, by about 1978, immediately ensuing FDA's and MMECTA's (near simultaneous) emergence, Medcraft Corporation suddenly found itself the single remaining SW "ECT" device manufacturer in America (Grahn et al. , 1977). [14] Totally unchecked from its' onset, in spite of tens of thousands of memory complaints [15] (Cameron, 1997; Frank, 1978; Friedberg, 1976; Janis, 1950; Rice, 1982), Medcraft, for more than twenty-five years (1947 to 1976) had bumped up against few, if any regulatory obstacles. Amazingly, even at the publication of this manuscript (2023), the same Medcraft SW instrument, the Medcraft B-24, continues to be marketed and applied in the field today, in spite of the now recognized destructive potential of SW devices in general. [16]

---

[9] Minimal stimulus devices had been tried and discarded in the 40s and 50s due to inefficacy (Cameron, 1994).

[10] Perhaps the only American SW device to exceed the power of Medcraft's B-24, was Ruben Reiter's Molac II (Cameron, 194; Impastato et al., 1957; Grahn, 1977) manufactured until about 1978, just before the first FDA hearings in 1979.

[11] Glissando is the gradual gliding up to a certain output in order to avoid precipitous impact.

[12] The device is still being manufactured by Medcraft at the date of this publication.

[13] One passage within the Medcraft 510K pre-market application to the FDA claims that at 100Ω, the device can emit up to 289J. Rarely; however, would such a low Impedance occur.

[14] By 1975, there were only two remaining SW Manufacturers in America - the Ruben Reiter Company and Medcraft. By 1978, there was only one. Opponents of "ECT" had no idea how close they had come to abolishing shock by 1978.

[15] The greatest culpability lies with manufacturers. However, before regulatory agencies such as the FDA which was empowered in 1976, a large measure of culpability lies with the APA (American Psychiatric Association) which could have ordered the procedures halted had it so desired. APA must or certainly should have been aware of failed minimal stimulus experiments from 1940 to 1957 and concomitantly the suprathreshold application of Standard SW devices. Another culpable agency is NIMH (National Institute of mental Health), created in 1948 to further research into this and other areas and which should also have been aware of the failure of minimal stimulus and thus the fact that convulsive theory is false. Forced compliance of persons falling under the unfortunate label of "mental patient" simply took precedence over any concerns for individual safety.

[16] Medcraft, perhaps the cagiest and quietest of the manufacturers, has long avoided public contact and attention and thus culpability. Not only did Medcraft avoid sending any direct representative to communicate with the FDA beginning in 1979, but is the single device manufacturer to retain a policy of refusing to share their instruction manuals without actual purchase of the device.

So why did "ECT" advocates choose the Brief Pulse device for presentation to the FDA in 1976? Perhaps, it was because with the re-introduction of Liberson's Brief Pulse device in 1973, Blachley, Weiner, and other modern day Brief Pulse advocates, finally recognized the injustice of the terrible memory loss which had been inflicted upon those who had suffered at the hands of SW instruments for so long. Perhaps these advocates truly hoped to elicit adequate, but effective convulsions to address depression at greatly reduced dosages of electricity, proving the Brief Pulse device one of the most critically scientific and humane breakthroughs of the twentieth century! Perhaps too, Weiner, Welch, Sackeim, Coffey and other modern day advocates of Brief Pulse, were either not cognizant of or remained unconvinced of the failed experiments with minimal stimulus conducted by early researchers Liberson and Wilcox during the 1940s and 50s and so, beginning about 1976, began to repeat these early experiments with minimal stimulus Brief Pulse, confident of more successful results (Cameron, 1994). [17] Perhaps then, with the reintroduction of the new and improved Brief Pulse device, these modern day Brief Pulse advocates sincerely desired to protect recipients of "ECT" from unnecessary brain damage and its resultant memory dysfunction (Weiner, 1979; Weiner, 1980). Perhaps, they reasoned, that in prior years, earlier devices utilizing minimal stimulus electrical dosing such as Brief Pulse, hadn't been afforded a genuine opportunity so that utilization of Blachley's resurrected lower dosage Brief Pulse device, might mark a new beginning for ECT yet, indeed, marking the first time in almost twenty-five years that true ECT would be administered with actual minimal stimulus output. Thus, the reintroduced Brief Pulse device would not be utilized for intensive multiple monitored "ECT" as Blachley had envisioned (Blachley, 1976a; Blachley, and Gowing, 1966), but as a "conventional" ECT apparatus (Monitored Electro Convulsive Therapy Apparatus) standardly applied every other day for several weeks. Indeed Brief Pulse seemed to revitalize the hope that convulsion theory--induction of adequate seizures alone with the much safer minimal electrical stimulus output of Brief Pulse--would finally prove that "ECT" could be administered both safely and effectively after all. Anticipating a more humane treatment and immense improvement then, Blachley's company name now evolved from MMECTA (Multiple Monitored ECT Apparatus) to simply "MECTA" (Monitored ECT Apparatus).

[17] This is not likely. Weiner (1988) has a museum of the older instruments and has written extensively on the subject.

Chapter 2

FDA Scrutiny of Medical Devices; Contract with Utah Biomedical Test Lab

On the other hand, as alluded to above, an important event took place in 1976, which may have influenced and, in fact, compelled manufacturers to precipitously proffer a dramatic and tangible new improvement. In May of 1976, - under the new Medical Device Amendment to the Food, Drug, and Cosmetic Act (Rice, 1982, p.66) - the FDA (Food and Drug Administration) forthwith became newly authorized by Congress to scrutinize all new medical devices.

That very same year (1976), almost immediately following Congressional passage of "the Act" (Medical Device Amendment), FDA contracted with a private company, the Utah Biomedical Test Laboratory (UBTL) to investigate the safety and performance (efficacy) requirements for the extremely controversial ECT device (Food and Drug Administration, 1978, November 28, p.55729; Department of Health and Human Services, 1982a, pp. A40-A41). After all, the device was being reviewed amidst the onslaught of thousands of long-term memory complaints. The purpose of the investigation by Grahn et al.'s UBTL is explained by Utah below.

> This document presents the results of '. . . Safety and Performance [Efficacy] Requirements' for Electroconvulsive Therapy Devices. " The objectives of this task are: 1.) To analyze and document available information related to safety and performance characteristics recommendations as to which safety and performance characteristics of electroconvulsive therapy devices are essential for minimizing patient and operator hazards [18] [and] . . .3.) To present the results of this study in a comprehensive final report. (Grahn et al. , 1977, p.1)

Reviewing over thirty-five years of clinical literature -- circa 1940 to 1976 -- replete with professional papers espousing convulsion theory as valid, including claims of both safety and efficacy at threshold (that is, efficacy of adequate seizures induced by minimal stimulus [Ottoson, 1960]), Utah Biological Test Laboratory (UBTL) speedily concluded that a performance Standard assuring reasonable safety and efficacy for ECT could indeed be written If based around induction of the adequate seizure alone.

> [C]urrently, there is only one application of ECT instruments and that is to produce seizures. (Ibid, p.15)

[18] There are two general categories regarding safety of "ECT" devices. One is the normal safety standards with respect to any electrical equipment in general to guard against accidental electrical shock through short-circuiting requiring grounding of wires, etc., perhaps more for the benefit of the operator than the recipient. Manufacturers often brag they are in compliance with IEC and other standards (in this respect) - which indeed they are. The second category, which applies uniquely to "ECT" is concerned with the total amount of current and energy output through the brain which can be administered without damaging the recipient, or at least reducing the risk as much as possible. No agency, including IEC has any established standard regarding this concept, as we shall see and so the standard has been left to the industry, which tends to avoid any limitation as we shall also see. Nevertheless, Utah plainly recognized that machines inducing convulsion with true minimal stimulus cause the least amount of risk and so should be able to be standardized. On the other hand, excessive electricity, through any number of experiments, including EEG, cognitive studies, MRI, animal, autopsy, etc. has quite clearly shown to produce cognitive damage.

Not surprisingly, the indicatory machine parameters provided by UBTL clearly called for true minimal stimulus output via true minimal stimulus devices; specifically, the newly reintroduced and newly touted -- Brief Pulse device. Officially adopted by the FDA in 1978, the UBTL Report not only favored minimal stimulus parameters to meet medical device criteria of simultaneous efficacy and reasonable safety, but strongly identified hazardous treatment with "suprathreshold dosing" of electricity (generally defined as electrical dosing in unnecessary excess of that required to produce an adequate seizure).

With the new and improved Brief Pulse device in mind, the UBTL final report (Grahn, Jerhrich, Couvillon, and Moench, 1977) concluded that the development of a safety and performance Standard based upon known safety and efficacy data, was indeed both indicated and feasible. Indeed, in 1978, this view was accepted by the FDA's Neurological Devices Advisory Panel, and by the FDA itself (Federal Register 11-28-78, pp.55729-30; Department of Health and Human Services, 1982a, p. A41).

Thus, based mostly upon the clinical literature up to 1976 incorporative of the promised reduced electrical parameters of Brief Pulse, in conjunction with a new modern Brief Pulse archetype submitted by a seemingly new company, "Custom Systems Associates Inc." soon renamed "MECTA Incorporated," Utah enthusiastically recommended true minimal stimulus devices based upon classical convulsion theory (Grahn et al. , 1977, p.41). In brief, it was the newly reintroduced Brief Pulse device, a device which had not been utilized or manufactured for over twenty-five years, which was alone deemed capable of achieving the official grandfathered in goal and definition of "electroconvulsive therapy"-- *minimal stimulus production of adequate seizures.* Thus, based upon findings such as those below, Utah's and, in turn, the FDA's express aim and expectation of an equally effective "ECT device," but with greatly enhanced safety compared to SW, was the greatly reduced output of the newly reintroduced Brief Pulse device, ushering in the new Brief Pulse Era.

> The essence of the treatment is the convulsion or seizure, not the electrical stimulation of the brain. (Grahn et al. , 1977, p.2)
>
> [. . .] Ottoson. . [1960][19] . . . has conducted one of the best controlled studies reported on memory impairment versus stimulus intensity. In two patient populations, grand mal seizures were evoked by supraliminal [suprathreshold] and liminal [threshold] stimulation. In a previous facet of this overall study conducted with same degree of rigor and control, Ottosson found that an increase in the stimulus intensity, which apparently does not change the seizure discharge, possibly gives a more rapid therapeutic response, but does not change the final degree of improvement or the number of treatments required to reach it. A double blind memory test procedure was conducted and pre- and post-treatment test scores compared. The conclusion was that an increase of stimulus intensity, which apparently does not change the EEG picture of the seizure, results in significantly increased memory disturbance. The results indicate that the major part of the memory disturbance due to ECT, in contrast to its therapeutic effect and its influence on the post-seizure cerebral electrical activity, may be accounted for by effects of electrical stimulation other than seizure activity. (Ibid, p.26)
>
> In 1971, Weaver et al. issued a report on their studies of stimulus parameters in ECT (Weaver et al. , 1971). . . . [T]he authors' contention is that significantly less energy is required to induce a seizure with the [brief] pulse waveform . . . than with 60 Hz sinewaves. (Ibid, p.30)

Utah Favors Brief Pulse

Ironically, Grahn et al. representing Utah Biomedical Test Laboratory had not only rediscovered (in the literature) and reported the forgotten minimal stimulus studies performed between 1940 and 1957 (Cameron, 1994), but had rediscovered slightly later European studies of safer "liminal" (threshold) versus "supraliminal" (suprathreshold) dosages of electricity, including a number of EEG studies pointing to morbidity and brain

[19] Ottosson in 1960 (Ottosson, 1960) did report conflicting reports of efficacy regarding AC-SW versus BP. While American manufacturers suppressed the lack of efficacy of adequate seizure alone, reverting back to unsafe AC-SW devices, Europeans migrated toward half SW- half BP in an attempt to compromise efficacy with safety. Eventually, European Manufacturers revert to more powerful devices as well. Nevertheless, this is further proof that American Manufacturers knew full well true convulsion theory based upon minimal stimulus is invalid, and also knew that supraliminal or suprathreshold stimulation is universally dangerous. Ottosson's report is also indicative that both APA and BP Manufacturers in 1976, knew of the inefficacy of unmodified BP but chose to suppress this information as well in order to give the false impression that ECT, utilizing BP, could be administered both safely and effectively.

damage as a result of electrical dosages beyond that required to induce an adequate seizure. These studies specifically alluded to damage caused by the higher EO SW devices, which, along with the new MECTA Brief Pulse device newly re-introduced in 1976, were the only two "ECT" machines manufactured in the United States at this time. Grahn reports:

> The consensus [in the literature from 1940 to 1976] appears to be that the exact stimulus waveform parameters used to produce a seizure are unimportant as long as the stimulus produces a grand mal seizure (Ibid, p.22). This belief is supported by studies conducted early in the history of ECT that concluded that the energy levels necessary to produce a convulsion are far below the levels at which irreversible brain damage occurs. (Grahn et al. , 1977, p.22) [20]

> He [Liberson] claimed that the therapeutic response [21] [22] was at least as good as the conventional AC [sine wave alternating current] technique . . . . With BST [brief stimulus technique or brief pulse], Liberson noted less memory disturbance. (Grahn et al. , 1977, p.24)

In short, as already noted, Utah recommended minimal stimulus Brief Pulse over the extraneous outputs emitted by SW and a standard written around Brief Pulse.

In brief, both the SW literature and SW manufacturers' brochures, i.e. Medcraft (Medcraft Corporation, 1984), had up until 1976 described the "ECT" procedure (forcibly administered to thousands) as "convulsive therapy," the alleged sole goal of which was the induction of adequate grand mal seizures (defined as seizures between fifteen and twenty-five seconds or more in duration) with the least amount of electricity. Through comparative studies of Blachley's newly resurrected Brief Pulse device to SW, however, Utah correctly identified and reported the Medcraft B-24 SW device as a suprathreshold instrument compared to Brief Pulse. Utah also correctly concluded that both Brief Pulse and Sine Wave devices were capable of inducing equally adequate grand mal seizures. Subsequently, both Utah and thus the FDA, quite naturally determined that the safety of "ECT" devices could be greatly improved through the use of Brief Pulse alone; moreover, that a standard could and should be written based around a minimal stimulus mandate using the reintroduced Brief Pulse device as the preferred instrument. Utah, and thus the FDA, further concluded that the most reduced energy output possible regarding the induction of so-called adequate seizures should be mandated by the standard. Logically then, in that both Brief Pulse and SW could induce adequate seizures, adherence to such a standard eliminating SW would increase safety (via reduced output) while maintaining equal efficacy

---

[20] According to the literature Grahn (et al.) researched, "equivalent therapeutic results can be obtained from convulsions produced by injection of drugs or inhalation of chemicals" (Grahn et al, 1977, p.22) leading Grahn et al. to mistakenly conclude that adequate convulsion alone is the agent involved in so-called "therapeutic efficacy." While SW Manufacturers such as Medcraft were almost certainly aware since at least 1950 that convulsion theory had been clearly disproven through the failure of minimal stimulus devices from 1940-1957 (Cameron, 1994), in that the failure of minimal stimulus went unreported in the literature, Utah would have been unaware of this fact. In all procedures utilizing drugs and inhalants, though one common denominator is indeed convulsion, the other often overlooked common variable is that in all cases, the drug, inhalant, or other agent utilized is potentially brain damaging. Raw assault of the brain through toxic agents, especially wherein injury occurs, is commonly accompanied by convulsions. The famous team of English Researchers, Robin and Tissera, would come to this same conclusion in 1982 when they showed efficacy was clearly related not to the convulsion - but to electricity (Robin and Tissera, 1982). There is little doubt, that, though covered up by the "ECT" industry, the BP era from 1976 to the present, through the necessity of suprathreshold dosing clearly proves that adequate convulsion alone is of no therapeutic value. The false idea that a convulsion is therapeutic may be the greatest medical hoax of the twentieth and twentieth centuries.

[21] Perhaps one hint regarding clinician's definition of "efficacy" is in Cerletti's original goal of the consequent "tranquility" he observed in pigs, resulting in their passively submitting to their throats being cut. Bayles's description of the results of BST (Brief Pulse) compared to SW, is that with BST, along with greater awareness and less confusion as a result of less trauma to the brain, patients were also "seemingly more apprehensive" (Bayles, Busse, and Ebaugh, 1950; Grahn et al., 1977, p.25). This was partly due to a lack of anesthesia. Apparently what clinicians and institutional caregivers sought was not greater awareness resulting in greater apprehension, but rather the organic passivity following brain trauma and brain damage.

[22] Though institutional caregivers have been replaced in many instances by family members caring for elderly parents in their own homes, family members can seek the same goal as did the institutional caregivers of the past - organic passivity resulting in manageability. Organic passivity may then be twisted into or justified as an antidepressant effect for the "consumer" which actually can, for a period, occur following damage to the brain. In fairness to NAMI members, however, a myriad of studies put forth by manufacturer affiliated advocates, as well as manufacturers themselves, have falsely assured family members of the complete safety of the procedure.

(Department of Health and Human Services, 1982a, p. A41)]. In sum, from 1976 forward, Utah and thus FDA expected ECT machines to induce adequate seizures with the most minimal electrical stimulus possible and so with what should be Brief Pulse alone. Outputs in excess of minimal stimulus were clearly depicted as unnecessarily enhancive of risk.

> A number of early investigators felt that 60 Hz alternating current [Sine Wave] was not the optimum stimulus for ECT. . . [These experiments] suggest that neurostimulation is most effectively achieved (with narrow pulses [*Brief Pulse* and thus reduced electrical output)]. (Grahn et al. , 1977, p.23)

Based upon the most minimal electrical stimulus possible to induce grand mal seizures, then, Utah and thus FDA favored Brief Pulse, specifically suggesting a maximum parameter of the 81 Joules already demonstrated by MECTA Corporation via the introduction of its' new 81J Brief Pulse archetype, the early MECTA "C" (Grahn et al. , 1977, 51-52). Indeed, the early 81J MECTA "C" and even the slightly later 108J MECTA "C" scrutinized by Utah between 1976-1977, utilized an impressively low maximum output to induce grand mal seizures, far below that of the alleged 145-200J maximum of Medcraft's B-24 SW apparatus (Department of Health and Human Services, 1982a, G3). Brief Pulse was also well below German and English made SW and partial SW machines also investigated and reported by Utah (Grahn et al. , 1977). Most noteworthy was Utah's explicit claim that MECTA's new Brief Pulse instrument was capable of inducing the same "adequate seizures" at one quarter (Grahn et al., 1977, 52) the Energy Output of Medcraft's B-24 Sine Wave instrument, specifically identified as having at least a 145 Joule ceiling at a 200 Ohm Impedance (Grahn et al. , P.51-52), a 170 Joule ceiling at 170 Ohms (Department of Health and Human Services, 1982a, A46) and a 200J ceiling at a lesser unspecified Impedance. Thus, the long history of memory complaints with "ECT," including written accounts to FDA during the 1976-1982 hearings depicting hundreds of crippling "ECT" experiences, in conjunction with Utah's comparisons of SW to Brief Pulse, and even research submitted to FDA by MECTA asserting the superiority of the reduced Energy Output Brief Pule device, compelled FDA to conclude that the damaging effects of ECT (specifically memory damage) could be dramatically diminished via the use of the new reduced output Brief Pulse device alone and that a standard could and should be written to that effect. It was the Utah study and recommendation as well as the MECTA "C" archetype, in short, which, in spite of numerous objections from past recipients, influenced FDA Panelists to permit the continuation of so-called "electroconvulsive therapy" with "electroconvulsive therapy devices" subsequent to 1976. Based on the research Utah had conducted in conjunction with the new evidence of Brief Pulse superiority submitted by MECTA and APA spokesperson Richard Weiner, therefore, FDA permitted the continuation of "ECT" contingent upon a standard requiring minimal stimulus and thus minimal stimulus devices comparable to the MECTA "C" Brief Pulse by MECTA. It was with this conclusion that FDA ultimately closed the public hearings on ECT in 1982. FDA contingencies for ongoing use of "ECT," consequently, plainly included development of the improved lower energy Brief Pulse device along with the promise of a new APA (American Psychiatric Association) Standard, centered around BP's reduced output MECTA "C," a standard FDA gave manufacturers ample time and leniency to finalize. In short, the resultant 1982 APA Standard written in main by Weiner limiting output to 110 Joules, persuaded FDA to allow the controversial continuation of "ECT. " Unfortunately, the 1982 APA Standard did not become mandatory at this point in that Weiner, representing all extant manufacturers during this period, convinced the FDA that the standard could be further refined and improved with but a little more time.

Utah as the Bridge from the SW Era of the past to the BP Era of the future

Thus, the Utah Lab, through its 1976 literature review had clearly identified, quite correctly and for the first time in twenty five years, the B-24 and other SW devices as suprathreshold instruments [23] compared to Brief Pulse. Convinced of BP's potential for simultaneous efficacy and safety which indeed seemed a most logical and cogent determination, Utah submitted its findings to the FDA which accepted its tentative recommendations. In short, Utah recommended Brief Pulse to the FDA in order to guarantee the most minimal (and thus safest) electrical stimulus possible to elicit the same adequate (and so allegedly similarly effective) seizures as SW, a

---

[23] Utah never uses the word "suprathreshold" a later invention, but does use "excessive" and "considerably above minimum duration needed to induce a seizure" (Grahn et al., 1977, p 24).

determination FDA believed would significantly improve the safety of "ECT." According to Utah's exhaustive journal and literature review then, the single goal of ECT should be the induction of the "therapeutic adequate convulsion" with the least amount of electricity possible to achieve that goal, meaning the development and utilization of Brief Pulse alone, indeed a device such as the MECTA "C," making the Utah Report the determining bridge traversing the past-present chasm from the Sine Wave era (1940-1976) of the past to the "much safer" Brief Pulse era (1976 - present) of the future. In short, the Utah Study forced the ECT industry to adopt and develop Brief Pulse in lieu of SW with a promise to ultimately write and recommend adoption of a standard in accordance with Weiner's unofficial 1982 APA Standard.

SW Manufacturers Implicated

Ironically, though perhaps not intended, the Utah study indirectly, though unknowingly, insinuated fraud and deception on the part of all SW device manufacturers (including Medcraft) prior to and up through 1976. That is, in uncovering the reduced output experiments of the 40s and 50s, Utah had unwittingly implicated SW manufacturers in several areas. First, SW manufacturers had quite falsely implied or claimed in their brochures and other advertisements during the entirety of the SW period that their various SW contraptions were (and are) minimal stimulus and thus electroconvulsive therapy devices. [24] Utah did this by pointing out literature containing early examples of Brief Pulse and direct current experiments juxtaposed with SW. Because both Medcraft and Reiter were in business in the United States during the period of early minimal stimulus experimentation, both must or should have been aware that their SW devices were electro-dependent (in lieu of convulsion dependent) in nature. Certainly they must have known that their devices were not minimal stimulus devices. After all, Medcraft had actually increased the power of its SW device to more successfully market the B-24, while the Reiter company had discarded its direct current lower energy device for the extremely powerful Molac II. Thus, the Utah study indirectly accuses the SW industry of fraudulent (and certainly misleading) claims regarding minimal stimulus and even in deeming their machines "ECT" devices based on "convulsion theory. " In claiming SW devices minimal stimulus and thus “convulsive therapy devices” while manufacturers clearly knew they were not, meant that not only were SW manufacturers mislabeling their devices, but that SW manufacturers continued to maintain as true, the plainly debunked theory of “convulsion therapy” (Cameron, 1994). Clearly "convulsion therapy" had been disproved through Wilcox and Liberson's failed minimal stimulus experiments, but which manufacturers such as Medcraft and Reiter apparently secreted or ignored, thereby misinforming the public. Just as SW manufacturers from 1940-1976 suppressed this information, however, Medcraft (just as modern day Brief Pulse manufacturers do today) continues to imply that the B-24 SW is a minimal stimulus and thus an "Electro Convulsive Therapy" device (Medcraft Corporation, 1984).

Early manufacturers such as Medcraft and Reiter, would certainly have been aware of minimal stimulus devices such as Reiter's own Direct Current device as well as Liberson's minimal stimulus BP devices manufactured between 1940 and 1957, machines capable of inducing equally adequate grand mal seizures at greatly reduced energy outputs. But while Utah re-discovered these experiments, they failed to understand why these lower output devices had not sold and so had been discarded during the early era. Indeed, because the failure of convulsion alone had not been reported in the literature, Utah had no way of comprehending that these early experiments had actually proved convulsion theory or the theory of adequate convulsion incorrect. Utah also had no way of knowing that both Medcraft and Reiter had deceitfully prolonged "convulsion theory" as valid in order to continue selling their electro-dependent devices, devices which successfully facilitated the very effective management of “mental patient” inmates through the deliberately terrifying perpetration of convulsion invoking, memory damaging, doses of electricity, typically without anesthesia, a terror-inducing strategy, the aim and effect of which were strikingly similar to the gravely dreaded lobotomy--management and control. Sadly, with no report regarding the early minimal stimulus experiments as the debunking of convulsion theory, "convulsion theory" continued to justify the application of SW in managing large patient populations. Indeed, SW devices were in great demand by SW-Era institutions, the manufacturers of which continued to make SW devices, unlike the early, experimental minimal stimulus BP devices (Cameron, 1994). Unfortunately, the Utah study offers no explanation regarding the continued use of raw SW in the U. S. following the failure of

---

[24] There were a number of SW manufacturers from 1940-1976 (Cameron, 1994). Medcraft, in fact, continues to imply that the B-24 SW is a minimal stimulus and thus an Electro Convulsive Therapy device (Medcraft Corporation, 1984).

adequate convulsion revealed by the much lower output Direct Current and Brief Pulse devices of the 1940s and 1950s, never speculating on what plainly appears to have been a cover-up. In short, Utah failed to question why these minimal stimulus devices--if capable of both greater safety and equal efficacy--had been discarded twenty-five years earlier and SW devices allowed to devolve back into the "unnecessary" suprathreshold dosing they then continued to utilize up to the FDA investigation beginning in 1976. Indeed, the failure of reduced output devices appears to have been the very inconvenient truth--that "convulsion therapy" has no therapeutic value and that standard SW devices actually worked through fear as well as damage to the brain via what were actually excessive dosages of electricity. In short, literature disseminated after 1950 written or inspired by SW manufacturers asserting the validity of "convulsion theory," was not only misleading, but fraudulent.

In that the literature does not specifically elaborate on this failure, therefore, Utah never speculates why these early minimal stimulus devices miscarried. In spite of this oversight, however, as a result of reviewing the literature, authors of the 1976-1977 Utah study, logically and naturally endorsed the new BP instrumentation with its' unique capacity to induce so-called "adequate seizures" at much lower electrical output than SW. Based wholly upon the mistaken notion of convulsion theory, therefore, and the fact that Brief Pulse could induce adequate seizures at less than half the output of SW, Utah logically recommended the utilization of Brief Pulse devices in lieu of SW, concluding that a standard could indeed be written around Brief Pulse minimal stimulus induced adequate seizures. Thus, the resultant 1982 APA Standard written by Weiner (under pressure from the FDA) in accordance with Utah's recommendations of minimal stimulus Brief Pulse output, becomes the touchstone against which more and more powerful modern day Brief Pulse instruments [25] (as seen in this manuscript) can be compared for both safety and efficacy. Indeed, it is the 1982 APA Standard which makes it possible to evaluate power and deception regarding subsequent modern day BP devices within the modern day Brief Pulse Era. Only two U. S. devices as noted, the 81J--108J MECTA "C" Brief Pulse device and the 200J B-24 SW device--were being manufactured at the time of the FDA investigation between 1976 and 1982. Both devices could induce equally adequate seizures, but the Brief Pulse device could induce them at half (or less) the electrical output of SW. There is no doubt that FDA anticipated and expected the lower energy Brief Pulse device to supplant the more dangerous higher energy SW device FDA assumed would soon become obsolete. Based upon Utah's recommendations, in brief, in accordance with the 1982 APA Standard squarely aimed at insuring the substitution of the reduced energy Brief Pulse device for the higher energy SW device, the Brief Pulse device became celebrated in the press as the "new and improved 'ECT' " device. In short, FDA's insistence on the development of an American Standard for ECT devices stipulating the lower output Brief Pulse to induce adequate seizures, seemed to assure FDA, which in turn sought to assure the American public, of the procedure's "new and improved" safety. [26] Stated differently, in that Brief Pulse could induce the same adequate seizures as SW and thus was presumed equally efficacious, it was assumed the higher Energy SW device, the Medcraft B-24, would soon be eliminated and ultimately prohibited albeit the actual decision to eliminate sine wave appears to have been left to the manufacturers. Indeed, as already noted, manufacturers, via Weiner, actually produced the "1982 APA Standard" during the FDA investigation even as the manufacturers' (via Weiner) pledge to the FDA future lower EO with exclusively Brief Pulse devices.

Thus, it was with the emergence of the FDA in 1976 as a new scrutinizer of medical devices, and the FDA investigation of the "ECT device" that the Utah Study with FDA adopted recommendations published in 1977, facilitated the writing and publishing of the 1982 APA Standard, the result of which reveals, albeit implicitly, the first great cover-up involving SW devices amidst the SW Era from 1950 to 1976. Remarkably, moreover, the second great cover-up, regarding the BP Era (from 1976 to the present) begins. It is mainly this second cover-up regarding the power of modern-day Brief Pulse devices, upon which this present manuscript elaborates.

In Summary

In summary, the Utah study -- or more specifically -- the 1976-1982 FDA investigation of ECT and "ECT" devices exposes SW as unnecessarily suprathreshold, re-kindling interest in the minimal stimulus Brief Pulse

---

[25] The Utah Study was obtained by the author through a Freedom of Information Request from the Food and Drug Administration.

[26] Perhaps the FDA's blind trust of the APA and manufacturers in developing BP as well as a BP Standard is attributable to the fact that that minimal stimulus BP and comparatively suprathreshold SW devices are capable of inducing equally adequate seizures. The false notion of their equal efficacy based, in turn, upon the totally false notion that adequate convulsion is the therapeutic agent, allowed FDA to assume there could be no reason for manufacturers or the APA to prevaricate.

experiments that had occurred between 1940 and 1957 (Cameron, 1994). Certain assumptions are clearly established--if a series of adequate convulsions constitutes the "ECT" procedure, then anything above minimal stimulus is unnecessary, in short, any amount of electricity over and above that required to induce an adequate seizure is unnecessary and so unnecessarily damaging. Only minimal stimulus, that is, the least amount of electricity necessary to induce a so-called adequate seizure can be deemed even relatively safe (or at least, as safe as the "treatment" can be made). Based on the information provided, then, Utah implicitly defines and reaffirms "convulsion theory" as inherent to the ECT procedure itself, a fact presumed in virtually all ECT literature up to 1977 (and which the Utah study itself never appears to question). In short, "ECT" is entirely posited on the premise of "convulsion theory," that is, the so-called adequate grand mal seizure being therapeutic in nature. [27] The gist of Utah's findings, therefore, forced the ECT industry to begin supplanting SW with Brief Pulse devices such as the MECTA "C," and to begin anew with the serious development of lower energy BP devices regulated by an official standard limiting the output of "ECT" devices accordingly. Newly under FDA auspices, consequently, unlike the unenforced low energy output discoveries [28] of the 1940s and 1950s -- modern day BP devices would be regulated by the newly written 1982 APA Standard, to be further refined for finalization by the American Psychiatric Association Task Force on ECT. This modern Standard -- which was to guarantee the most minimal stimulus electrical output possible to induce the "adequate" grand mal seizure and which defines "ECT" as the induction of adequate seizures with the least amount of electricity possible, would be the consumer's guarantee of reasonable safety under the then recent 1976 "Medical Device Act" newly mandated by Congress. By default, this meant stipulating the induction of adequate convulsions with the most minimal of electrical stimuli for which the lower energy Brief Pulse device was to be the sole instrument for all future "ECT. " With the induction of adequate seizures, therefore, which the Brief Pulse device could equally induce (compared to SW) but at a much lower electrical dose, enhanced safety seemed virtually guaranteed. Equal efficacy as a result of equally induced "adequate" seizures was presupposed.

In fact, Utah was even more inspired by the prospect of UL "ECT" efficacy which required even less electricity, half that of BL ECT.

> Today it has been established that unilateral ECT applied to the nondominant hemisphere will produce less post-seizure confusion and amnesia than bilateral electrode placement . . However, there is divided opinion over the clinical efficacy of the two forms of treatments. For the same therapeutic effect, more unilateral treatments <u>may</u> [underlining is Utah's] be required, but this difference, if real, appears to be small. (Grahn et al.1977, p.9)
>
> The use of the unilateral placement of electrodes (on the nondominant hemisphere) and, to a lesser extent, pulse-type stimuli are mainly to reduce the confusion and amnesia effects of ECT. (Ibid, p.17) [29]

Manufacturers eventually stave off this logic, however, by declaring UL "ECT" "dose sensitive" requiring twice the output of BL "ECT. " Thus, according to modern BP manufacturers, UL and BL "ECT" require the same "dosage" of electricity to be effective.

Adequate Seizures Alone Ineffective. Convulsion Theory False

After delving into the ECT literature, Grahn et al. , authors of the 1976 Utah study, determined that: " . . . studies conducted early in the history of ECT . . . conclude . . . that the energy levels necessary to produce a convulsion are far below the levels at which irreversible brain damage occurs. " As noted elsewhere, the team was referring to early low dosage BP and unidirectional (that is, direct as opposed to alternating) current experiments conducted between 1940 and 1957 by Wilcox, Friedman, Liberson and others, many of which are cited or referenced in the Utah Report. These early experiments clearly demonstrated to Utah that reduced

---

[27] The assumption that "convulsion theory" is valid is the one great error about which the Utah report, through no fault of its own, is mistaken (Cameron, 1994).

[28] "Discoveries" refers to the findings that BP could induce adequate seizures with a fraction of the output of SW.

[29] Unilateral ECT, discovered by Wilcox, as well as Liberson's minimal stimulus Brief Pulse device, failed to elicit the results sought by clinicians and so the techniques failed on the marketplace (Cameron, 1994; Impastato et al., 1957).

electrical dosage reduces morbidity (long term memory dysfunction suggestive of brain damage) and the degree of reduced morbidity is in direct proportion to the degree of reduced electrical stimulus. Moreover, these same early works cite minimal stimulus devices as effective. [30] In fact, although successfully inducing adequate seizures, such (minimal stimulus) devices, that is, those aiming at adequate seizure alone, are ineffective as we shall see (Cameron 1994). Perhaps fearing negative publicity, SW manufacturers such as Medcraft, which also experimented with early reduced stimulus devices, never reported or divulged the failure of these minimal stimulus experiments regarding failed efficacy. Conversely, manufacturers such as Medcraft never reported the unfortunate need for excessive electrical dosing (via SW) in lieu of adequate seizure alone to make the procedure "work. " That is, Medcraft never reported the need for suprathreshold dosing in order to make the procedure "effective." Perhaps Medcraft failed to report these early known factors in that Medcraft understood that a direct relationship between high or suprathreshold electrical dosing and efficacy is highly suggestive of a damage-efficacy relationship, a factor which would have negatively affected the sale of SW machinery had it been published during the SW or any other era. In short, the failure of minimal stimulus and so adequate convulsion was never identified. Because the ultimate failure of these minimal stimulus or ECT devices (Ibid) - including Liberson's early Brief Pulse experiments - was never adequately reported in the literature (Ibid), Utah, relying upon the recorded documentation within various scholarly journals, all of which continued to espouse convulsion theory as valid, never questioned the efficacy of the reduced energy BP apparatus resurrected by MECTA. In fact, because the literature continued to claim convulsion theory valid, just as the early originators of minimal stimulus devices, Liberson, Wilcox, and Friedman initially assumed, the Utah investigators who rediscovered these lost experiments, began to share the same enthusiastic conclusion as early researchers. In short, Utah believed that since both minimal stimulus and suprathreshold SW devices could induce equivalent grand mal convulsions, they produced equivalent therapeutic results. [31] Indeed, because Liberson, Friedman, Wilcox and SW manufacturers all abdicated their responsibility to report the failure of convulsion theory, that is, the clear failure of adequate seizure alone to produce a therapeutic effect, the failure of convulsion as therapy, which would have facilitated the abandonment of "ECT" or convulsion theory altogether, this crucial piece of information went unrecorded in the literature. Certainly, the unfortunate fact that "convulsion" alone is ineffective and that suprathreshold electrical damage is required to make the procedure work was promptly hushed up, no doubt to keep the industry alive. As a result, as we shall shortly begin to see, the falsehood of the "therapeutic seizure," repeats itself during the modern day BP Era (1976 - present) over a second forty-five to fifty year span continuing through to the date of this publication. [32]

More Detail of the Early Cover-up and Utah's Erroneous Assumption

Early researchers (quoted in the Utah Report) experimented with lower energy, minimal stimulus devices around which Grahn et al. (1977) form their assumptions. For example, in addition to Liberson's Brief Pulse apparatus conceived in the 1940s, other early researchers, as noted, such as psychiatrists Friedman and

---

[30] In that there were few if any publications to the contrary, Utah had no reason to assume that low dosage electrically induced adequate convulsions were ineffective, an assumption which would prove to be a costly blunder both to the pocketbook and brains of the American Public. It is a false assumption initially fueled by total manufacturer disregard for the safety or rights of "mental patients," particularly before 1975. But it was an assumption propelled forward into the post 1976 era by the unfortunate medical device exception that previously utilized medical devices could be grandfathered in without premarket approval and without a written standard unlike FDA scrutiny required of all entirely new medical devices. The assumption that medical devices used for a period of years before 1976 were acceptable to the American public and therefore safe and should be grandfathered in, is a critically major loophole in the ACT of 1976 which did not take into consideration forced mental health "treatment" up to and following that period, and which for many years had and still does include forced "ECT." Married to this blunder is the important fact that only after 1975, did mental health commitments in America even begin to be based upon danger to self or others (U.S. Supreme Court--O'Conner v Donaldson, 1975). Commitments based on any other principles were finally deemed unconstitutional. Consequently, grandfathering treatments from medical devices unconstitutionally forced upon tens of thousands of recipients should have been excluded from the ACT and "ECT" devices should have been forced to undergo ordinary FDA scrutiny before being foisted upon new generations of the unwitting American public.

[31] Utah, just as Liberson, Wilcox and Friedman, erroneously believed that it was the adequate convulsion that produced the "therapeutic" results.

[32] The failure of both reduced dosage techniques (UL and BP) to be effective has once again led to the cover-up of suprathreshold devices in the BP Era, beginning from 1976.

Wilcox, also in the 1940s, co-collaborated with electrical engineer Ruben Reiter to devise some of the first reduced output direct current devices. Such devices utilized a much less powerful Direct Current (DC) in lieu of Alternating Current (SW), as noted, to achieve equivalent grand mal seizures.

> In 1942, Friedman . . . employed a unidirectional stimulus waveform . . . Friedman [also] adopted an unusual electrode placement [unilateral electrode placement [33]]. . . Besides therapeutic results comparable to the more conventional form of ECT [sine wave] . . , Friedman claimed that the convulsive threshold [with UL and unidirectional current] was a fraction of that required by alternating apparatus and that confusion, disorientation and memory defects were absent. (Ibid, p.23-24)
>
> In 1949, Pacella stated the rationale for investigating different electrical stimulus parameters. His four reasons were (1) to increase the therapeutic effect (2) to minimize the electrical energy consistent with maximum therapeutic effect (3) to minimize undesirable complications, and (4) to minimize post-seizure confusion and memory disturbances . . . . (Grahn et al. , 1977, p.22-23)

Though successfully inducing equivalent grand mal seizures with greatly reduced morbidity, believing their devices as effective as the higher energy output SW devices, early researchers were disappointed to find that clinicians in the field found the devices ineffective (Impastato, Berg, and Gabriel, 1957). In fact, practitioners continued their demand for the more powerful SW devices with alternating current, a detail never openly discussed in the literature and so, via the history of "ECT," can only be deduced. Plainly, though, minimal stimulus devices failed on the marketplace, and by 1957, the last of the Ruben Reiter Direct Current minimal stimulus devices was permanently discarded, silently replaced by an exceptionally powerful suprathreshold AC-SW device, the Molac II (Cameron, 1994; Impastato et al. , 1957). Instead of reporting the failure of minimal stimulus (and therefore convulsion theory in general), then, manufacturers such as the Rueben Reiter Company, which continued to market SW devices, persisted in touting the validity of convulsion theory, knowingly and falsely advertising their powerful suprathreshold SW apparatuses as minimal stimulus or "ECT" devices. Tellingly, the Molac II SW persevered another twenty years on the marketplace until in 1976, the FDA became officially authorized by Congress to begin scrutinizing medical devices. While the Rueben Reiter Company folded, however, Medcraft and Medcraft's B-24 SW device persisted, persisting to this day.

Ignorant of the true history of minimal stimulus devices, therefore, but impressed by early minimal stimulus experiments and so with Blachley's new MECTA Brief Pulse device, Utah, in 1977, emphasizes to FDA Liberson's early minimal stimulus experiments with Brief Pulse.

> In 1944, Liberson . . . published his observations on the use of the brief stimulus [Brief Pulse] technique . . . He concluded from his experiments on stimulus parameters that the duration of the individual pulses of 60 Hz sinewaves and [even] Friedman's stimulus (i.e., about 8ms) was considerably above the minimum duration needed to induce a convulsion. (Grahn et al. , 1977, p.24)

Indeed, as already noted, in experimenting with BP or systematically interrupted current, Liberson had discovered that even Friedman's reduced DC-SW device was unnecessarily suprathreshold regarding the eliciting of adequate seizures (Liberson, 1945b; 1946; 1948). It is these particular findings -- early minimal stimulus experiments, particularly with BP -- following Utah's review of the literature corroborated by MECTA's newly resurrected Brief Pulse device, which, in 1976, for the first time in over a quarter century (and perhaps for the first time publicly), implicitly exposed the Medcraft B-24 as an unnecessarily suprathreshold instrument, forcing the "ECT" industry to re-evaluate Brief Pulse as a possible substitute for Sine Wave. Unaware that early minimal stimulus experiments between 1940 and 1957 ultimately resulted in failure, and, in fact, had proved convulsion theory false (Cameron, 1994) -- Utah unfortunately missed the significance of Medcraft's 1950

---

[33] Unilateral electrode placement was yet another early discovery (Cameron, 1994) permitting even greater reduction of current (and thus of interest to Utah), and was thereby (unknown to Utah) even less effective than minimal stimulus BL electrode placement. Modern day manufacturers soon exploited the concept of UL by administering the same amount of electricity (which required half as much to induce a seizure) for UL as for BL, thus applying the first suprathreshold dosing with BP in the modern BP Era. The rationale for suprathreshold dosing with UL, was that UL, unlike BL, ECT is "dose sensitive," a false theory used over and over again by manufacturers as a justification for enhancing electrical output. The true reason for enhancing BP, of course, is minimal stimulus is not effective with wither UL or BL in that convulsion theory is false. This fact has been known by the industry in general since about 1950.

supplanting of the early 1940s and 1950s Brief Pulse experiments with powerful SW devices. Nor was Utah aware of the little known fact that around 1950, a year during which minimal stimulus devices were being introduced generally, a powerful Medcraft SW model was replaced not by a minimal stimulus or some other reduced output device, but by an even more powerful SW device in order to increase efficacy--the Medcraft B-24 still in existence today--this in spite of increased (albeit unreported) morbidity. [34] [35] Indeed, Utah (and thus the FDA) missed the import of Medcraft's enhanced B-24-III SW device and the Reuben Reiter Company's enhanced Molac II SW device, the latter company of which, between 1949 and 1957, had engineered the first minimal stimulus reduced output devices utilizing Direct Current (Cameron, 1994). Unaware of the apparent want of efficacy and so the wholesale discarding of Reiter minimal stimulus devices in 1957 (Impastato et al. , 1957), Utah failed to connect the lack of efficacy issue with the disappearance of minimal stimulus at that time along with the concomitant manufacturing of both the B-24-III and the extremely powerful Molac II Alternating Current SW device. Indeed, the Molac II continued to be manufactured from 1957 to 1976, right up to the very year (1976) as mentioned above, FDA was granted Congressional authority to investigate and assess medical devices generally for both safety and efficacy (Cameron, 1994; Impastato, Berg, and Gabriel, 1957). [36] It seems untenable that by 1976, neither the Reuben Reiter Company, nor Medcraft, major manufacturers of U. S. SW devices for about a quarter century at that time, could have been unaware that early minimal stimulus devices, (i.e. unidirectional SW, unmodified Brief Pulse, and even unilateral electrode placement at threshold) -- had proven ineffective twenty to twenty-five years earlier (Cameron, 1994). Nor does it seem possible that ECT historian, electrical engineer, and psychiatrist Richard Weiner, spokesperson for all "ECT" manufacturers before the FDA from 1976 to 1982, including MECTA and Medcraft (Department of Health and Human Services, 1982a; Ibid, 1982b; Ibid, 1982c), and even for the American Psychiatric Association for the years FDA publicly investigated ECT, could have been unaware of the failure of the adequate seizure with early BP experiments (Department of Health and Human Services, 1982a; Ibid, 1982b; Ibid, 1982c).

Utah Report Continued

While the early Brief Pulse experiments and the introduction of the MECTA "C" Brief Pulse formed the hopeful conclusions from which Utah and the FDA took their inspiration, in fact, the early Brief Pulse devices had failed on the marketplace. Nevertheless, it was due to the alleged equal therapeutic response of minimal stimulus BP experiments reiterated by Utah in its' literature overview compared to SW from 1940 to 1976, that Utah and thus the FDA which had sponsored, funded, and adopted the Utah findings, became convinced that Brief Pulse minimal stimulus induced seizures produce less memory disturbance (which it does) with equal efficacy (which it does not). Obviously, these conclusions made the "new and improved" Brief Pulse device alone, the obvious choice for the ongoing use of ECT. [37] [38] Neither manufacturers nor the APA did anything to discourage the Utah-FDA conclusion -- instead promising the development of BP minimal stimulus devices such as the prototypical MECTA "C" in coordination with a forthcoming Standard based on the 1982 APA Standard, limiting output to newly reduced, in fact, minimal stimulus emissions. What choice, but to agree did the "ECT" industry have, after all? An admission of minimal stimulus inefficacy meant admitting to the debunking of convulsion theory itself; moreover, that damaging doses of electricity were not only necessary, but the very "treatment"

---

[34] Medcraft has been improperly claiming since at least 1950, that the B-24 is a minimal stimulus device. From a recent Medcraft flyer describing the B-24 SW, "Many clinicians believe that successful therapy requires consistent delivery of current at minimal energy levels necessary to effect proper treatment. The B-24-III is designed with features that assure precise levels of output from treatment to treatment" (Medcraft Corporation, 1984). Medcraft discarded an early BP experiment of its own about 1950.

[35] Medcraft has been manufacturing the same B-24 for the last fifty years to the date of this publication.

[36] The Molac II, criticized by Grahn et al. for being too powerful and having no timer, was discontinued about 1977 about the time FDA began to investigate.

[37] Attempting to make their SW devices marketable at any cost, manufacturers' neglect to report the failure of the adequate seizure alone led to a twenty-five year cover-up by SW Manufacturers. The SW Era cover-up, falsely portraying convulsion theory as valid along with deceptive claims of minimal stimulus, lasted from about 1950 to 1976. The industry has never been held accountable.

[38] Crucial to the SW Era cover-up is the fact that few, if any rights, existed for mental patients during the SW Era. This enabled manufacturers to bypass patient satisfaction - or rather dissatisfaction - and please only the institutions which bought their devices, the sole goal of which was management of inmate population.

itself. Thus, both advocates of the procedure and manufacturers went along with emphasizing Brief Pulse for future "treatment" in that Brief Pulse could induce equally adequate convulsion, with but half the output of SW.

Indeed, Utah, as noted, cites numerous minimal stimulus findings such as the ones below, to which no manufacturer, including Medcraft objected:

> In 1950, Bayles . . published the results of a comparative study between the square pulse technique of Liberson (BST) [Brief Stimulus Technique or Brief Pulse] and 60 Hz sinewave stimulus. Bayles cites that the BST stimulus approximates . . . the pulse requirements shown necessary for stimulating isolated peripheral nerves with minimal energy . . . . Experimental and clinical use of the BST stimulus showed that convulsions could be produced using only one-tenth to one-fifth [39] of the current required when using 60 Hz sinewave. Based upon trials in 112 patients, Bayles concluded that the outstanding difference between the results of the two techniques was the considerable difference in confusion and disorientation. The BST patients were more alert, more in contact, less vague, and seemingly more apprehensive. This observation [was] coupled with the similarity of clinical effectiveness . . . . (Grahn et al. , 1977, p.25)

Utah, In short, clearly voiced its support for the numerous forgotten or suppressed minimal stimulus experiments, particularly with Brief Pulse which claimed equal efficacy like the one above, but without understanding -- much less why -- these experiments had failed. Again, the reason for Utah's erroneous conclusions is apparent. The failure of minimal stimulus is never reported in the literature. Manufacturers, and specifically, SW manufacturers kept the failure of minimal stimulus and, therefore, the failure of convulsion theory itself, a secret (Cameron, 1994).

Indeed, as already noted, Utah reported not only on American minimal stimulus experiments, but also European experiments similarly correlating reduction in electricity with the elimination of memory dysfunction as well as "equal efficacy. " Reporting on the 1960 Ottoson study in Scandnavia, Utah comments:

> [. . .] Ottosson . . [1960][40] . . . has conducted one of the best controlled studies reported on memory impairment versus stimulus intensity. In two patient populations, grand mal seizures were evoked by supraliminal [suprathreshold] and liminal [threshold] stimulation. In a previous facet of this overall study conducted with same degree of rigor and control, Ottosson found that an increase in the stimulus intensity, which apparently does not change the seizure discharge, possibly gives a more rapid therapeutic response, but does not change the final degree of improvement or the number of treatments required to reach it. A double blind memory test procedure was conducted and pre- and post-treatment test scores compared. The conclusion was that an increase of stimulus intensity, which apparently does not change the EEG picture of the seizure, results in significantly increased memory disturbance. The results indicate that the major part of the memory disturbance due to ECT, in contrast to its therapeutic

---

[39] It is important to realize that Liberson, Friedman, and Wilcox were able to induce adequate seizures with dramatically less energy output than SW devices such as the B-24 by Medcraft and this has been known since the mid-forties. Even the MECTA BP device introduced to Utah in 1976 was not the most minimal stimulus device possible, in that even briefer pulses had been originally utilized by Liberson to successfully induce adequate seizures. Moreover, Bayles' and Liberson, Friedman, and Wilcox utilized unilateral electrode placement in their experiments, reducing energy output even further. The point is that neither the early devices nor unilateral electrode placement, in spite of reports of therapeutic efficacy, obtained the clinical results looked for in the field. Consequently, the devices gradually increased in power until they were eventually, once again, replaced by the much more powerful suprathreshold SW devices, making it clear that electrical dosage - not adequate convulsion is responsible for "efficacy." Incredibly, the failure of the adequate convulsion theory went virtually unreported to the American public. Certainly SW manufacturers were and are aware of this history and in describing their devices as convulsive therapy or minimal stimulus devices, and thus "ECT" devices (which they are not) SW manufacturers have been and continue to commit fraud.

[40] A few years later, Ottosson in 1960 (Ottosson, 1960) did report conflicting reports of efficacy regarding AC-SW versus BP. While American manufacturers suppressed the lack of efficacy of adequate seizure alone, reverting back to unsafe, possibly brain damaging AC-SW devices, Europeans migrated toward half SW- half BP in an attempt to finesse efficacy with safety. Eventually, European manufacturers reverted to the more powerful devices as well. Nevertheless, American manufacturers knew or should have known full well that convulsion theory based upon minimal stimulus is invalid, and that supraliminal or suprathreshold stimulation is universally dangerous. Ottosson's report is also suggestive that both APA and BP manufacturers in 1976, knew of the inefficacy of minimal stimulus BP, but chose to suppress this information in order to give the false impression that ECT, utilizing the "new and improved" BP device, could be administered both safely and effectively.

> effect and its influence on the post-seizure cerebral electrical activity, may be accounted for by effects of electrical stimulation other than seizure activity. (Grahn et al. , 1977, p.26)

Clearly, early experimenters both in Europe and America similarly hoped or believed memory dysfunction could be reduced or eliminated via the reduction of current to true threshold levels of electricity - without sacrificing efficacy. The assumption was based upon the discovery that the same adequate seizures (using BP and/or unidirectional devices) can indeed be induced at much lower electrical dosages than had been being previously utilized (with SW). Nevertheless, while memory dysfunction does indeed decrease with decreasing electrical stimulation, "efficacy," as the marketeers of these early minimal stimulus devices had soon learned, also decreases. In fact, a so-called adequate seizure alone may not be effective at all (Robin and Tissera,1982; Sackeim, 1991, p.233-234), a fact which painfully manifests itself via six decades of what appear to be elaborate manufacturer cover-ups regarding the necessity of enhanced machine devices with enhanced electrical dosing in order to achieve efficacy, cover-ups which span both the SW and BP eras. Suppression of both the early and later minimal stimulus results indicate that for more than seventy years to date, both SW and Brief Pulse manufacturers have knowingly concealed that both efficacy and damage are associated with increased electrical dosing. In short, manufacturers have covered up the fact that efficacy and damage are inextricably related (Breggin, 1979; Cameron, 1994; Friedberg, 1977; Sterling, 2000). On the other hand, Utah, citing extensively from the earliest experiments with minimal stimulus, makes the same honest but erroneous assumption as the earliest hopeful minimal stimulus researchers, that is, the spurious supposition that it is adequate seizures -- not adequate electrical dosages -- that produce the looked for effect. Indeed, based upon convulsion theory--that grand mal seizures are somehow therapeutic, it logically follows that machines or wave-forms utilizing greatly reduced electrical output, but which elicit the same adequate seizures should produce the same efficacious results as the higher dose SW devices. The thinking of both early researchers and Utah, of course, was that by eliminating the intensive electrical doses known to cause memory damage, the therapeutic effect could be isolated and that memory damage could then be minimized or even eliminated. Because the failure of these early experiments was never reported by these same early researchers, however, most of whom were associated with SW manufacturers who wanted to continue marketing their extremely "effective" devices in spite of damaging recipients' memories, SW instruments continued to be manufactured. Long term memory damage was simply ignored or rationalized away (as it is today), and SW machines were spuriously reported as "minimal stimulus" or "ECT" devices based on "adequate convulsion" alone. [41]

Below, Utah cites the 1968 Valentine study which conducted similar research of early Brief Pulse, again assuming the same alleged efficacy and hope not only with reduced output using BP, but with unilateral (one sided) electrode placement requiring even less Energy Output.

> A controlled comparative study on both stimulus waveform and electrode placement was conducted by Valentine et al. in 1968 [Valentine et al. , 1968]. . [42] . . . If one assumes a constant resistive patient impedance of 200 ohms, then the energy doses are about 30 Joules for the pulse stimulus and 160[43] Joules for the sinewave stimulus. The authors reported no considerable differences between the groups, but post treatment confusion and memory disturbance were significantly reduced by the use of the pulse current and the unilateral electrode application. (Grahn et al. , 1977, p.28)

---

[41] Considered a "throw-away population," so-called "mental patients" had almost no rights at this time so that abuse of this nature was rampant.

[42] Note that there are virtually no more comparative studies of threshold to suprathreshold in America after 1957. The Valentine study is British.

[43] The resistances here are misleading. The average resistance for SW would be somewhat higher, thus lowering the Energy Output. In fact, Blachley et al., (1976?) later report an average of about 145 Joules for SW and even this may be exaggerated. Nevertheless, even today's second generation BP devices, rather than emitting an average of about 30 Joules as reported above, emits an average of about 140 Joules.30J is based upon the mean between the minimum allowable impedance reported to Utah by MECTA in 1976 (Blachley, Denny and Fling, 1976?, Grahn et al., 1977, p.35) resulting in about 30 Joules (Grahn et al., 1977, p.28; Valentine et al., 1968; see also Thymatron chart), and the maximum impedance - 555.5 ohms - reported by Somatics Inc. for their second generation device the Thymatron DG (see Somatics' manual; see also chart) resulting in about 252 Joules. Note the equivalent average of standard SW and modern day BP.

Thus, Utah continually and comprehensively cites studies asserting the equal efficacy of Brief Pulse minimal stimulus with SW and "equally effective unilateral electrode placement" [44] with dramatically reduced electrical dosing and so far less memory, i.e. brain damage. Utah, in its naivety then, enthusiastically reports its findings of reduced energy output devices with particular emphasis upon Brief Pulse. The already mentioned 1971 Weaver Study below cited in Utah's 1976 report to the FDA is cited below:

> In 1971, Weaver et al. issued a report on their studies of stimulus parameters in ECT (Weaver et al. , 1971). . . . [T]he authors' contention is that significantly less energy is required to induce a seizure with the [brief] pulse waveform . . . than with 60 Hz sinewaves. (Ibid, p.30)

Utah's redundant focus on the comparatively reduced energy output of BP relative to SW, i.e. 30 Joules versus 160 Joules, to induce equally adequate seizures and thus equally effective results is thematic. Studies, such as these which initially excited early researchers, in short, newly persuaded Utah and thus its sponsor, the FDA, that a reasonable standard incorporating the Congressional mandate of simultaneous safety and efficacy newly using minimal stimulus output could be written. Incredibly, neither Medcraft, MECTA, Somatics (a newly emerging Brief Pulse company) nor the APA Task Force, did anything to inform, correct, or discourage the false notion that equally adequate seizures induced with much less power and electricity are equally effective. [45] As we shall shortly see, beginning about 1982, modern day BP manufacturers begin to hide from the FDA, the American public, and even practicing physicians, the inevitably increasing power of their modern day BP devices -- secreting the fact that modern day Brief Pulse soon equals and then surpasses SW in both power and electrical doses administered in almost all age categories. Brief Pulse manufacturers do so, of course, for the same reason SW manufacturers did so in the past, to make their machines "effective. " In short, just as SW manufacturers did formerly, modern day Brief Pulse manufacturers do today, hide the fact that the dream of a reduced output device based on the myth of the "adequate convulsion," is a scientific falsehood.

Utah Study Continued - Extant SW Devices Vs the MECTA BP Device

The second part of the Utah study investigates the Medcraft B-24 (Alternating Current) SW device and the Molac II (Alternating Current [46]) SW device, the former still being manufactured and the latter manufactured right up to the time of the Utah investigation. Utah compares these devices to the resurrected MECTA BP device (the MECTA "C") newly submitted to the FDA, as noted, by the then new Custom Systems Associates (Grahn et al. , p.33) or what soon became known as "MECTA. " Once again, neither Reiter's Molac II (SW) nor Medcraft's B-24 (SW) compare to the MECTA BP device (proffered for FDA scrutiny during its investigation of "ECT") regarding increased safety by virtue of BP's reduced energy output. Utah continues to make the mistake of assuming SW and BP equally effective in that both kinds of devices induce equally adequate grand mal seizures. It is in this capacity then, that Utah continues [47] to expose SW as unnecessarily suprathreshold (to induce an adequate convulsion), leading up to what should have certainly been the final demise of SW, and the requisite use of minimal stimulus BP only - just as Utah recommends in its' conclusion.

In fact, shortly after the publication of Grahn's Utah Report in 1977, the demise of SW seemed so certain that the (Ruben) Reiter Company not only ceased manufacturing the Molac II, but folded entirely, ceasing to exist as a company. Important statements by Utah regarding SW devices such as the ones cited below criticizing these machines, facilitated the demise of the Reiter SW manufacturer.

---

[44] It was Utah's emphasis on UL placement (along with BP stimulus) that forced the APA and the ECT Industry to emphasize both UL and BP. While BP eventually (surreptitiously) surpassed SW in power, the efficacy and utilization of UL is also mythological. Not only did UL quickly become deemed "dose sensitive" requiring at least double threshold dosing to be "effective," but UL continues to be comparatively underutilized relative to BL. UL at threshold, just as BL at threshold, is relatively ineffective - both axioms of which have been known for at least fifty years (Cameron, 1994).

[45] Had these entities informed FDA that efficacy could not be achieved without suprathreshold dosing associated with memory dysfunction and; consequently, damage, FDA may have banned the procedure as early as 1976.

[46] Alternating current, particularly with respect to SW, is much more powerful than Direct Current. The AC (Alternating Current) is noted simply to differentiate devices such as the Molac II and Medcraft's B-24 from early SW experiments with Direct Current utilized in an attempt to elicit minimal stimulus (Friedman, 1942; Cameron, 1994; Wilcox, 1946).

[47] Early experimenters between 1940 and 1957 both in America and Europe showed that SW was unnecessarily suprathreshold to induce "adequate" seizures(Cameron, 1994).

> There is an investigation of two widely used ECT instruments conducted by Davies et al. in a 1971 paper [(Davies, Detre, Egger, Tucker, and Wyman, 1971)]. They. . . report on the Molac II and also the Medcraft B-24 manufactured by Medcraft, Inc. . . . The authors were led to this investigation when a literature review on ECT for a textbook on psychiatric treatment disclosed no publications documenting that ECT devices meet the manufacturer's specifications and claims. [48] (Grahn et al. , 1977, p.32)

> Davies et al. found that it was extremely difficult to apply the stimulus for fractions of a second [with the SW devices]. This finding is important if one adheres to the authors' philosophy that it is good clinical practice to give minimal effective doses of any treatment. (Grahn et al. , 1977, p.32)

Davies findings of "no publications documenting that ECT devices meet the manufacturer's specifications and claims" refers to the false minimal stimulus claims of SW manufacturers' Medcraft and Reiter throughout the entirety of the SW Era. The second citation informs the reader that minimum stimulus is virtually impossible to administer on either SW machine in that neither machine lends itself to fractions of a second. In short, neither SW machine is precise enough to administer true minimal stimulus in any age category.

Grahn et al. (Utah) then go on to cite hopeful passages from an unpublished Blachley study (founder of MECTA Corporation) concerning the new MECTA BP device, the MECTA "C":

> The last device-related paper was sent to the UBTL [Utah Biological Test Laboratory] project Scientist by Custom Systems Associates, Inc. [MECTA], when they were queried for information on their ECT device [Blachly, Denny, and Fling, unpublished (1976)]. The authors express the opinion that ECT devices have not evolved significantly from their crude beginnings, and in the design of the MECTA unit - the only perceived parameter was patient safety. Areas of concern were: (1) minimum stimulus energy . . . . [49] (Grahn et al. , p.33-34)

> Pulse width can be varied from 0.15 [**and Duration**] to 2.0 seconds in six steps. The minimum and maximum stimulus energies [of MECTA's BP device] are about 0.6 and 81 Joules,[50] respectively. The resultant impedance measurement is compared to a present range of values. If it is outside this range, the stimulus current cannot be applied. (Ibid)

Thus, based on the passage above, what was probably the earliest MECTA "C" BP device introduced to Utah (and thus the FDA) in 1976, was limited to 81 Joules maximum, a vast improvement over the 145-200J B-24 SW device by Medcraft. [51] Utah was further impressed that this prototypical MECTA "C" BP device had optional settings for brief pulses as succinct as .15 milliseconds, allowing adequate seizures at more or less

---

[48] SW manufacturers falsely claimed their devices were minimal stimulus or "convulsive therapy" apparatuses.

[49] While Blachley et al. express concerns over safety and so criticizing Standard SW apparatuses, the MECTA device (initially deemed MMECTA - Multiple Monitored Electroconvulsive Therapy Apparatus) was originally resurrected for multiple shocks per single anesthetic setting - not safer application for "standard ECT." It is with some degree of deception, then, that Blachley et al. present the device to Utah as a device for administering "standard ECT" which is one shock per anesthetic setting. Blachley fails to mention the original purpose - multiple shocks per anesthetic setting. This information might have been important in tipping off Utah that true minimal stimulus is ineffective unless compensated electrically (Cameron, 1994) or through various application techniques, i.e. larger number of treatments or multiple treatments per single anesthetic setting.

[50] If this is the MECTA "C" device, maximum dosage is about 108 Joules, later reported by Weiner in 1982 (Department of Health and Human Services, 1982a). The device reported by MECTA to Utah in 1976 appears to have been averaged with a 300 Ohm maximum, and so 81 Joules maximum. It is also possible that the device reported to Utah had a limiter of 300 ohms and by 1982, the device had become more powerful, expanding to about 410 ohms.

[51] Based on the figures above, the (probable early) MECTA "C" device appears to have utilized about 240 volts of electricity and had a 300 ohm maximum impedance ceiling. Blachley may have used an average of 300 ohms to figure minimal and maximal Energy Output, thus deriving .6 and 81 Joules respectively. The later MECTA "C" device was capable of 108 Joules, followed by the MECTA D-1 with an Impedance override, as we shall see.

the most minimal energy output possible. [52] The following passage is a continuation of Utah's commentary of the above unpublished 1976 Blachley study submitted (by Blachley) to Utah regarding the early MECTA "C. " Utah reported:

> Blachley et al. compared stimulus energy doses available from their device to energy doses from sinewave (Medcraft's B-24] and 1/4 sinewave [European] instruments. Within the "normally used limits for stimulus," the MECTA devices supply about 10 Joules while the sinewave and 1/4 sinewave devices supply 145 Joules and 32 Joules respectively. . . . . [53] Blachley et al. conclude with the belief that there is no magic in the use of 60 Hz sinewave stimuli and its' use is a serious mistake. Anyone investigating stimulus energy should realize that rapid rising, narrow pulses at low frequency should be used to reduce the delivered energy. (Blachley, Denney, and Fling, unpublished; Grahn et al. , 1977, p.34)

BP Machines Begin to Grow In Power

Passages like the one above, "corroborating" both the precision and the "efficacy" of minimal stimulus BP as late as 1976 and 1977, convinced Utah, FDA, the public at large, and even many clinicians that the greatly reduced energy output of the resurrected BP device, could induce adequate seizures at "a tiny fraction of the energy output of the older [SW] devices" (Kellner, 1994, February 2) and so would greatly improve the safety of "ECT. " Tellingly, the (probable) early 81J "C" device reported to Utah by MECTA in 1976, had by about 1980 (Weiner, 1980) transitioned to the later, slightly more enhanced 108J MECTA "C" device utilizing about 328 volts of electricity to overcome an Impedance ceiling of about 410 ohms [54] (Glen, and Weiner, 1983, pp 33-34). This later model "C" device, while yet purportedly half the output of SW (Department of Health and Human Services, 1982a, pp. E20, G3-G4) nevertheless represented a stealthy unnoticed upward creeping in power from 81 Joules to 108 Joules maximum for BP which would prove prescient. [55] Indeed, the increase in output from 81J to 108J suggests that MECTA may already have begun experimenting with increased electrical dosing, a practice which would eventually result in BP devices equaling and then surpassing SW in power in almost every age category, as we shall see. In fact, while both MECTA "Cs" could yet induce seizures at greatly reduced output relative to SW in almost every age category, MECTA soon developed the "D-1" with "Impedance override," for allegedly "difficult cases. " Voltage may have increased to a probable 400V increasing cumulative output to about 140 maximum Joules and so with the capacity to overcome a probable 520Ω Impedance as we shall also see. While the override was allegedly for difficult or exceptionally recalcitrant cases only (regarding the inducing of adequate seizures), in fact, the higher output made higher individual dosing probable in all age groups and in all cases. The MECTA "D-1" BP device could now deliver a cumulative maximum output of about 140 Joules which meant the device had gone from a 1.1 fold threshold or 1.1 MTTLOI (Multifold Threshold Titration Level Output Intensity) in all age categories to a 1.4 MTTLOI. While the MECTA C and D-1 BP devices could yet induce adequate seizures at lower outputs than SW in most age categories (Blachley, Denney, and Fling, unpublished; Grahn et al. , 1977, p.34), what neither MECTA nor Blachley revealed (to FDA) in their reporting ten Joules as "the normally used limits for [BP] stimulus" (Blachley, Denney, and Fling, unpublished; Grahn et al. , 1977, p.34)--seeming to mean about ten joules above threshold--was that minimal stimulus or

[52] Unidirectional BP devices can induce adequate seizures at the most minimal stimulus possible. Even BP manufacturers, coming to realize that such low electrical dosages -- in spite of adequate seizures -- were highly ineffective, hypothesized that bidirectional current might cause "possible polarization problems" (Blachley et al., 1974; Grahn et al., 1977, p.30; Tresise and Stenhouse, 1968). This provided the rationale for SW manufacturers and then modern day BP manufacturers to utilize machines initially, twice the power necessary to induce a grand mal seizure. To the author's knowledge, there is no legitimate study indicating unidirectional current more problematic than bidirectional (Grahn et al., 1977, p.30). Indeed, unidirectional current is safer by virtue of reduced electricity.

[53] Blachley et al. may be saying that SW can be off by as much as 145J above threshold, half-SW 32J above threshold, and BP 10J above threshold, indicating that Brief Pulse is superior in that it emits the least amount of energy output over threshold.

[54] Voltage and resistance are based upon parameters given in Glen and Weiner, (1983) and Ohm's law. These parameters, however, are most probably a depiction of the earlier 81J MECTA "C." The 108J MECTA "C" had a slightly higher Voltage (about 400V) and could overcome a slightly higher Impedance (of about 402 ohms).

[55] The B-24 device can emit up to 200J, but only under remote circumstances requiring extremely low and unpredictably low Impedances necessarily in the youngest age category.

just above minimal stimulus dosing was becoming less and less utilized by BP manufacturers in actual clinical practice. For example, by 1985, three years following the end of the FDA investigation of "ECT" devices, newer second generation BP devices manufactured by MECTA and eventually two other BP manufacturers, Somatics and Elcot, unbeknownst to all but manufacturers, skyrocketed in power to about 250 Joules (Cameron, 1994) or a 2.5 MTTLOI in all age categories while third generation BP devices manufactured about 1995 would eventually double that as we shall soon see. In brief, with every increase in overall power, what the author has deemed MTTLOI (Multifold Threshold Titration Level Output Intensity) has increased simultaneously, the significance of which we shall soon observe. Perhaps, slight cumulative output increases as early as 1980 and 1982 did not concern FDA in that no matter how powerful BP machines became, manually titrated dosing could yet be set to induce adequate seizures at consistently decreased electrical dosages compared to SW. In short, there seemed to be no reason for concern as FDA assumed manufacturers sought the same reduction in power to elicit adequate seizures as FDA and Utah. Moreover, the new BP manufacturers via numerous published studies by manufacturer-affiliated "experts," persevered in suggesting that BL (bilateral) ECT continued to be administered at threshold (or just above). Neither FDA nor Utah ever questioned the efficacy of the adequate seizure. As a result, Utah, and thus the FDA remained enamored of convulsion theory and thus of Brief Pulse generally--that is--the efficacy of the adequate seizure and so minimal stimulus output with the only device capable of it--Brief Pulse. Unreported was the fact that manufacturers' increasing machine outputs signaled commensurately increasing MTTLOIs in all age categories in an effort to make BP devices as "effective" as SW, an issue which completely escaped the attention of the regulators. This is not surprising in that--as we shall see--manufacturers have gone to great extremes to camouflage this information. On the other hand, even a new more powerful 140J first generation Brief Pulse device as opposed to the MECTA C's 108J maximum and as opposed to SW capable of a 200J maximum (albeit in disparate age categories),[56] [57] should have been cause for alarm.

Utah Continued (BP Machines Begin to Grow In Power)

While the powerful Medcraft B-24 SW--not an ECT but an ENR device as we will learn--has remained virtually unchanged for almost 70 years to date, BP ECT devices, from 1976 forward, similarly begin to slowly, almost imperceptibly, creep up in electrical output. Though power was at first directly, then indirectly reported, manufacturers rationalized away the first power enhancements as outputs used only for "rare, exceptionally high" impedances. Indeed, manufacturers and manufacturer-affiliated "experts" continued to assert to FDA and physicians alike that the most common form of "ECT," BL (bilateral) "ECT" was always administered and always effective at just above threshold output.

In any case, unbeknownst to regulatory agencies and the general public, by 1982, BP devices were already equaling SW devices in cumulative output (though in disparate age categories) and by 1985, had begun to surpass SW devices in output (though again in disparate age categories) in most age categories as we shall see. In fact, second generation MECTA Brief Pulse devices soon became capable of a never to be reported 259 Joules of electricity (as opposed to 200J SW devices) with a potential of about 450 Volts and the capacity of overcoming an Impedance ceiling of about 562 ohms (Cameron, 1994). Certainly, the devolving MECTA SR1 and 2 routinely emitted 2.5 times minimal stimulus dosing even with BL "ECT" recipients and so 5.0 times minimal stimulus with UL "ECT" recipients, none of which was known until as late as 1994, never revealed by manufacturers or physicians associated with manufacturers, but by a very few independent researchers, studies both rarely mentioned or typically misconstrued (Cameron, 1994; Beale et al. ,1994). Indeed, BP device enhancements and concomitant electrical dosage increases per all age groups with second generation BP devices, as we shall see, appear hidden from the FDA, the public in general, and even from practicing clinicians. In fact, it is directly due to the evasive and deceptive reporting methodologies by Brief Pulse device manufacturers that todays' powerful Brief Pulse mechanisms continue to remain associated with their now totally unmerited reputation of delivering doses of electricity at a fraction of the energy output of SW.

[56] As will be explained in more detail later, SW devices, unlike BP devices, cannot simply be set to emit their maximum potentials of 200J, but are instead dependent upon the Resistance of the human skin and skull, in essence, age. Because resistance low enough to allow 200J is rare, the typical maximum on SW may be about 145J.

[57] While SW devices may typically emit a 145J maximum and The D-1 could emit a circa 140J maximum, the maximum for SW would necessarily be in a much younger age category than BP.

Instead, manufacturers continue to exploit the FDA sponsored Utah Report which praised the prototypical MECTA "C" Brief Pulse device proffered to the FDA around 1976. For example, under a section called "Problem Areas," the 1976-77 Utah study lauds Blachley's initial BP device, logically identifying high output SW devices as problematic:

> At least one researcher [(Blachley, 1976b)] has identified the need for new neuropatholoical studies on the effects of ECT . . . . Consistent with this cautious view is the concern of a number of investigators over the high stimulus energies available from ECT devices and the use of energy inefficient [SW] waveforms. (Grahn et al. , 1977, p.35)

Thus, the Utah report consistently called attention to the danger of SW's unnecessarily excessive output (energy inefficient waveforms) and the need for the safer BP device utilizing minimal stimulus energy to induce "adequate" seizures, even conducting a 1976 survey amongst users (of "ECT" devices). Utah clearly defined "ECT" and the "ECT device" in concluding:

> [T]here is only one clinical application for these devices and that is to produce a grand mal convulsion in a patient with a mental illness. (Ibid, p.37)

Utah's definition for "ECT" is clearly a device utilizing the least amount of electricity possible to induce an adequate seizure. Indeed, based upon past and present literature as well as information disseminated by the manufacturers themselves that "ECT" depends upon induction of the adequate convulsion alone, Utah's continuous assumption (as well as many professionals today) solidified the FDA's conviction that the suprathreshold dosing of SW often manifesting long-term memory dysfunction (Impastato, 1957) was an unnecessary hazard which could be resolved via minimal stimulus adequate seizures induced by the resurrected Brief Pulse device. In fact, only minimal stimulus devices, machines designed to induce adequate convulsions alone (grand mal seizures of twenty-five seconds or more in length) with the least amount of electricity possible can be deemed ECT or Electro Convulsive Therapy devices. In contrast, devices deliberately designed to emit several times the EO required to induce a grand mal convulsion or which inherently emit several times the dosing necessary to induce an "adequate" seizure and, in fact, depend upon electricity for their effect, are not adequate seizure or ECT devices at all, but like SW devices, "adequate electrical dosage" apparatuses. Adequate electrical dosage devices, whether SW or BP (as the phrase implies), are designed to produce not adequate convulsions, but adequate doses of electricity--in short, advertently designed suprathreshold instruments this manuscript has deemed ENR (Electro Neurotransmission Reduction) devices, as will be discussed in more detail as the manuscript progresses. Certainly, the "ENR" procedure is a totally variant procedure than that of "ECT" with a totally different aim. Whereas the goal of the ECT device is to induce an adequate seizure, the goal of the ENR device is to induce adequate amounts of electricity, suggesting that the adequate or grand mal convulsion is of only secondary or possibly no importance at all. Indeed, if ENR machines emitting suprathreshold doses -- into which all modern day BP machines eventually devolve -- are necessary in order to make the procedure "work," not only does "reasonable safety" disappear with the lower energy output advantage of BP, but the "ECT" procedure disappears and an entirely different one emerges, one that is entirely diverse from that depicted both by manufacturers and information provided to the FDA via the Utah investigation. This is critical in that it is the ECT device and the ECT procedure alone that forms the basis for Utah's recommendations and FDA's decision to permit the continuation of the procedure into the Brief Pulse era from 1976 forward. In sum, the decision to allow the continuation of "ECT" or "Electro Convulsive Therapy" after 1976 is based solely upon the induction of the adequate convulsion alone and that upon the least amount of electricity possible. Conversely, "ECT" is in no way based upon an adequate amount of electricity well over seizure threshold for its effect. In that the process and aim of ENR (and the ENR device) is totally unlike the process and aim of the "electro convulsive therapy" and thus the "ECT" device wholly based upon "convulsion theory," the opposing devices must be differentiated, the one from the other. In brief, FDA must see the modern day ENR device as a new and undefined apparatus requiring pre-market approval before such an apparatus can be marketed. [58] In essence, it is not ENR which is described or grandfathered in, in 1978, but rather, "ECT. " Passing off ENR devices as ECT devices which do not qualify under the

[58] Being new devices applying a "new" treatment - the grandfather clause within "the Act" permitting devices already in existence to continue being marketed without pre-market approval - should be disallowed for the new kind of devices.

grandfathered criteria is fraud. The fact that ENR devices were labeled as "ECT" devices throughout much of the SW Era does not make ENR devices ECT devices, any more than deeming ENR devices "ECT" devices throughout the majority of the Brief Pulse era today justifies the existence of these new devices without FDA approval. Both are fraudulent . Both are deceptive.

Suprathreshold Efficacy with Memory Dysfunction Vs Minimal Stimulus Inefficacy with Less Memory Dysfunction

Numerous pieces of evidence should have tipped Utah off that "ECT" only works via some kind of damage to the brain in that when memory damage occurs with higher energy output, the device seems to "work" whereas when memory damage is reduced with lower energy output, the device doesn't seem to "work." For example, on a Utah Users Survey (1976-77), Utah asked general clinicians, almost all of whom used Medcraft or Reiter [SW] devices to comment on efficacy. Here's what Utah found:

> [R]espondents stated that the ECT instruments they used were very reliable and on the most part seemed satisfied with their performance. . . . Overall, device reliability does not appear to be a problem. (Ibid, p.38, 39)

Thus, efficacy of SW devices was not problematic. Instead, users of SW equipment were mostly concerned by memory or brain damage with SW and so the possibility of reducing output. Utah found that:

> More comments were related to stimulus energy than any other single aspect of ECT devices. Psychiatrists expressed a need for automatic timing of stimulus duration . . . a means of measuring patient impedance so that minimum stimulus energy may be delivered, . . . safe limits on maximum voltage and current . . . , a means to deliver the minimum energy necessary to produce a "complete" seizure, and more controlled studies on stimulus parameters to minimize energy. (Ibid, p.38)

Revealingly, then, like FDA and Utah, clinicians themselves were convinced of the efficacy of adequate seizures alone [59] and thus lower output in order to reduce memory dysfunction. In short, they too, appear to be misinformed. Again, this is due both to the same corrupted literature reviewed by Utah and to spurious information regarding the "adequate convulsion" which continues to be disseminated both by the older SW manufacturers and the newer BP manufacturers. Because early manufacturers understood the inefficacy of minimal stimulus via the early minimal stimulus experiments twenty-five years earlier, manufacturers had begun building more and more powerful SW devices. Administering physicians, on the other hand, even amidst the last of the SW era, appear to be uninformed of the debunking of convulsion theory between 1940 and 1950, and so go on patiently awaiting new and improved, true minimal stimulus devices. Even as late as 1976, then, Utah found that the main concern of SW expressed by administering clinicians wasn't efficacy, but safety--the desire for true minimal stimulus devices along with a standard to minimize memory damage and so the means to identify and be assured of the smallest electrical dosage possible to induce the adequate seizure. Administering physicians themselves, in short, continued to take for granted the validity of convulsion theory.

From Utah's passages above, then, we may deduce that practitioners of SW were not concerned with efficacy (whether in terms of patient management or some other criteria) but rather memory dysfunction, which remained all too prevalent a concern with SW. [60] In short, as late as 1976, most authors, researchers, and clinicians taught new physicians via the literature and as medical mentors to believe in "convulsion theory" or "efficacy of the adequate seizure," logically assuming that EO in excess of that required to induce the adequate seizure should be reduced in order to reduce memory dysfunction. Moreover, we can assume from clinicians'

---

[59] Clinicians themselves have been misinformed by manufacturers regarding convulsion theory, so-called convulsion therapy, and the premise upon which the devices work.

[60] This is by far the most serious and common complaint by recipients of the procedure. In fact, at least half of all "ECT" recipients believe they have suffered some degree of memory or brain damage as a result of "ECT" (Cameron, 1994; Janis, 1950; Squire, 1986; Squire and Chace, 1975; Squire and Slater, 1983; Squire, Slater and Miller, 1981) and Marilyn Rice believed the number was actually 100%.

responses that in spite of SW manufacturers' many spurious claims of minimal stimulus, these administering physicians were and are all too familiar with hundreds complaints of memory damage with SW. It can be no surprise then, that clinicians too, were much in favor of the new and improved minimal stimulus Brief Pulse device, and that such a new and improved device was thought to be imminent. In short, based on the Utah Report, based on clinicians' common experiences regarding memory complaints with SW, and based on the well-known fact that output surpassing that required to induce the adequate seizure has long been identified with increased memory dysfunction, Brief Pulse, with its' "new-found" capacity to induce adequate grand mal seizures with greatly reduced output (compared to SW), appeared to be the future of the ECT industry, that Brief Pulse appeared to be the answer if the "ECT" procedure, now overseen by the FDA, was to continue forward into the last quarter of the twentieth century. Compelled by the newly authorized FDA (strongly influenced by the Utah Report) therefore, MECTA 's much less powerful but allegedly "equally efficacious," newly resurrected Brief Pulse prototypical MECTA "C" device seemed to be the wave of the future. Just as it initially had meant to practitioners in the 1940s (Cameron, 1994), the 1976 newly resurrected Brief Pulse device appeared to Utah, the FDA, and users (clinicians) in the field as the most hopeful, the most progressive, and the most forward leaning solution.

Utah's "User's Survey" (1976-77)

Ironically, while SW can induce dangerously high outputs in the younger age categories, SW may fail to induce convulsion in the older age categories due to increasing resistance resulting in a diminishing current. Consequently, SW practitioners almost certainly had (and have) to use full power for older recipients (even administering multiple treatments in one setting), as a result of which burns sometimes emanate. Brief Pulse, on the other hand uses increasing Voltage in cases of greater resistance and so maintains the speed of the current at any age, a subtle indication, paradoxically, of the much greater prescient power of Brief Pulse as opposed to SW (and thus BP's potential abuse). Nevertheless, we once again hear Utah's long familiar concerns of high stimulus intensity and duration with SW, for which it once again recommends BP due to its' touted lower stimulus energy in inducing adequate seizures.

> High stimulus energies are sometimes required to induce seizures in patients with high convulsive thresholds. . . . Because ECT is given to elderly patients . . . and these individuals are likely to have both a higher convulsive threshold and skin resistance, considerable energy may be required to produce a seizure with concomitant reddening or burning of the skin beneath the electrodes. . . . [S]ince pulse-stimulus [BP] devices can induce seizures with significantly less energy than 60 Hz sinewave instruments, the convulsive threshold also depends upon stimulus waveform. Therefore the increased stimulus energy dose required to induce a seizure in a patient having a high convulsive threshold is more likely to produce burns if a 60 Hz stimulus is used. (Ibid, pp 39-40)

More Machine Detail Regarding Medcraft and Reiter--Knowing Deception

Of the three extant U. S. manufacturers of "ECT" equipment at the time of the FDA investigation in 1976 - (1) Reuben Reiter, Sc. D. , Inc. , (2) Medcraft Inc. , and (3) Customs Systems Associates Inc. (MECTA) - both Reiter and Medcraft had been producing SW devices for twenty and twenty-five years respectively (Grahn et al. , 1977, p 41) while the third manufacturer, Customs Systems Associates, Inc. or MECTA, was the newly formed company, whose device conveniently emulated Liberson's lower energy BP device originally manufactured in the 1940s (1945b; 1948). What Utah and FDA did not know, of course, was that by the 1950s, these lower EO devices had been discarded as ineffective and so unmarketable (Cameron, 1994). In any case, as has been emphasized, Liberson's Brief Pulse device was again being reintroduced to the FDA around 1976 (Grahn et al, 1977), not coincidentally, the year FDA received its newfound Congressional authorization to scrutinize all medical devices and the beginning of its investigation of the very controversial and much criticized "ECT" device.

As noted above, the Reuben Reiter Company had been the first producer of reduced output SW devices via a much less powerful direct current version (as opposed to alternating current) in an early effort to reduce memory dysfunction reflective of what most clinicians took to be some sort of damage due to excessive currents (Wilcox, 1946). Tellingly, however, by 1957, the Reuben Reiter Company had totally given up on the reduced output experiment in lieu of its much more marketable, much more in demand, much more powerful AC SW device--the Molac II (Impastato et al. , 1957). [61] Thus the Reiter Company cannot repudiate that in the 40s and 50s, the company itself deemed its own reduced energy device ineffective, and was thereby rejected by practitioners as unmarketable. Nor can the company be exculpated of knowing that alternating current SW devices had been producing serious, universal memory dysfunction (Janis, 1950) since at least the 1940s (Breggin, 1979; Friedberg, 1976; 1977). The truth is, Reiter simply ignored memory dysfunction in order to profit from their much higher output device, in fact, producing for sale, the powerful Molac II, which, in spite of memory grievances, the company continued to manufacture for the next twenty years. [62]

Neither, as noted, can Medcraft Incorporated be absolved, a company which had begun manufacturing standard SW devices around 1945. Almost certainly as a result of the failed minimal stimulus BP experiments of W. T. Liberson (Cameron, 1994; Liberson, 1948) and the failed DC (direct current) reduced experiments of P. H. Wilcox (Wilcox, 1946; Cameron, 1994, Impastato et al. , 1957), and finally, the lack of demand for one of their own reduced output devices, Medcraft, instead of diminishing output to minimize memory dysfunction, increased the power of its antecedent SW device circa 1950 to the much more powerful (much criticized) B-24-III SW device. [63] After all, Medcraft was forced to contend with Reiter's extremely powerful Molac II and wished to remain competitive (Department of Health and Human Services, 1982c, pp. G3-G4;1982a; Grahn et al. , 1977; Medcraft Corporation, 1984). Indeed, Medcraft has been manufacturing "ECT" devices since the 1940s, the period inclusive of the early experimental reduced output devices (1940-1957) so that by 1957 and probably much earlier, Medcraft could not have avoided awareness of the suprathreshold nature of the B-24-III SW device compared to the numerous earlier failed reduced energy devices. Like Reiter, Medcraft simply ignored the inevitable memory dysfunction caused by its B-24 in order to compete with Reiter and so remain profitable. Certainly, both the Molac II and the B-24 SW were notorious for creating long-term memory dysfunction complained of by thousands of recipients recorded throughout the literature (Janis, 1950), complaints which had led to the minimal stimulus experiments initially. Indeed then, it was the Utah study, sponsored by the FDA, which re-discovered these minimal stimulus experiments of the 1940s and 1950s. In fact, from the Utah Report, we learn that Medcraft had formerly produced a rarely mentioned apparatus of its own during the reduced output period, called the Mark II FA-1 (Grahn et al. , 1977, p.43-44). While the Mark II FA-1 was capable of powerful AC-SW (standard SW) similar to Medcraft's B-24, significantly, the Mark II FA-1 was also capable of a much less powerful, unidirectional current (DC) similar to early minimal stimulus devices manufactured by Wilcox in the 1940s, as well as half sine-wave, akin to devices once manufactured in Europe, all in order to reduce memory dysfunction long associated on both continents with standard SW (Grahn et al. , 1977, pp.44-47). The longevity of the Medcraft history concomitant with the production of the Medcraft Mark II FA-1 [64] [65] clearly indicates Medcraft's awareness prior (to the Utah study) that: (1) SW devices such as the B-

---

[61] Utah mentions the Reiter Model SOS and also a Reiter model CW47, neither of which seemed to be any longer manufactured at the time Utah reviewed the literature about 1976. The company's originator, P.H. Wilcox may have kept these models for his own personal collection, but they had long since become "obsolete." Indeed, by 1976, almost all practitioners or "Users" were employing either the Medcraft B-24-III, or the Molac II (Grahn et al., 1977).

[62] The company dissolved the year FDA began its investigation into ECT, critical of SW.

[63] Medcraft has continued to manufacture and market the B-24 (now deemed the B-24 III) up to the date (2023) of this publication (Medcraft, 1984).

[64] The Mark II FA-1 was nothing but a variation of the B-24, but with optional reduced output functions. Both had the same minimal and maximal voltages of between 70 and 170 volts and both contained the "glissando" feature for the gradual rise in voltage as opposed to a sudden jolt, allegedly to reduce fractures (Grahn et al., 1977, pp.43-44), but only the Mark II FA-1 contained the optional reduced output features. The early American unidirectional devices as well as the European half-SW devices, contained features that were obviously added due to their superiority over American AC-SW regarding reduced memory dysfunction - but proved, like early BP experiments -much less effective.

[65] By 1976, Medcraft may have anticipated an FDA mandatory switch to a reduced energy output device in which case Medcraft could have reproduced the Mark II FA-1, which while not currently marketed, was yet within Medcraft's purview to do so if the indeed FDA demanded reduced output. The potential resurgence of the Mark II FA-1 may have been one reason Medcraft did not disband like the Ruben Reiter Company. Soon, however, MECTA resurrected BP, superior to AC and half-SW in its capacity to induce adequate

24-III were known suprathreshold instruments compared to BP and other reduced output devices such as AC and half SW (Friedman, 1942), (2) that the Medcraft B-24 III is not an ECT device (based on minimal stimulus, adequate seizure, or convulsion theory) as Medcraft has long touted in Medcraft brochures and manuals [66] (Medcraft Corporation, 1984), (3) that the B-24 is, in fact, an adequate electrical dosage device, (4) that reduced output devices are ineffective compared to higher output devices such as the B-24-III or Molac II, (5) and finally, that the inherent outcome of these powerful SW devices with their excessive electrical dosing is increased long term memory dysfunction (Janis, 1950), a clear manifestation of what even SW manufacturers thought to be some sort of damage to the brain (Friedberg, 1977). In short, by 1957, and certainly by 1976, Medcraft had to have been aware that minimal stimulus devices are ineffective, that "convulsion theory" based on the minimal stimulus induction of the adequate seizure had been thoroughly debunked (Cameron, 1994; Impastato et al. , 1957), and finally that so-called "ECT" efficacy is inextricably related to the necessity of excessive electrical dosages related to long-term memory dysfunction and so very likely, some sort of then unidentified damage to the brain. [67] As revealed by Utah, any number of studies both before (Impastato et al. , 1957) and following (Squire and Zouzounis, 1986) the 1976 ingression of FDA as inspector of medical devices, corroborate the failure of the adequate seizure alone as well as increased memory damage as a result of excessive dosages of electricity, information known to SW manufacturers since at least the 1950s. Medcraft's awareness of these facts is evident in its supplanting of the reduced output Mark II FA-1 with the B-24-III SW while Reiter's awareness is evident in its supplanting of its reduced energy output DC device with the much more powerful Molac II AC-SW. Thus, both Medcraft and the Ruben Reiter company were aware of the scarcity of sales regarding reduced output devices compared to the B-24-III SW and the Molac II AC-SW. Indeed, both companies were also aware of the early elimination of minimal stimulus due to inefficacy. Answering to no regulatory body, Medcraft chose the steadfast fifty year production and marketing of the Medcraft B-24-III SW from 1950 to date (2023) while the Reuben Reiter Company chose the production of the Molac II from at least 1957 to 1976. Moreover, that modern day Brief Pulse manufacturers have never demanded elimination of Medcraft's continued use of the B-24 SW device into the modern Brief Pulse era bears testimony that neither SW nor modern day Brief Pulse devices are any longer ECT devices dependent upon convulsion to make them work, but rather adequate electricity devices as we shall see. Because of the historical elimination of reduced output and particularly minimal stimulus devices in both the SW and modern day Brief Pulse eras, both kinds of manufacturers which falsely claim minimal stimulus, we can be certain that both manufacturer types were and are aware of the detrimental effects of the suprathreshold outputs of the other, that is, the suprathreshold outputs that both types of machines—SW and BP-- currently emit. In turn, both types of manufacturers are or should be aware of the inefficacy of the adequate convulsion, that is, the complete failure of ECT or minimal stimulus induced adequate seizures. In brief, SW and modern day BP manufacturers have long known that their devices were and are electro-dependent, that these machines were and are not based on adequate seizure, but adequate amounts of electricity and that as such, these devices are not "ECT" devices at all, but ENR devices, devices now understood to "work" by electrically overloading brain circuitry to reduce neural connectivity, as we shall see. Indeed, as we shall observe in detail, modern day Brief Pulse apparatuses, just like SW devices, are actually ENR mechanisms. That is, modern Brief Pulse devices, like SW devices of old, have once again devolved into electro-dependent mechanisms designed to electrically overload brain circuitry grossly reducing connectivity. Neither SW, as we have seen, nor modern Brief Pulse apparatuses, as we shall see, therefore, are "ECT" devices at all.

---

seizures with the most minimal energy output. As a result, American manufacturers, including Medcraft as we shall see, began switching to BP.

[66] Based on supraliminal electrical dosage--not adequate seizure--the Medcraft B-24-III is actually an ENR—not an ECT device.

[67] When the aim of the procedure is convulsion, minimal electric current acts only as a catalyst. When suprathreshold electrical dosage takes the lead, convulsion becomes incidental, a mere side effect of the new preponderant aim – reduced neurotransmitter connectivity through "adequate" doses of electricity in lieu of "adequate convulsion." While manufacturers may argue the validity of convulsion theory based on the fact that subliminal dosages or sub-convulsive activity is ineffective, so adequate seizure alone is also ineffective. The truth is, after fifty years with no regulatory oversight, manufacturers knew full well that there was absolutely no evidence whatsoever that convulsions have any therapeutic benefit except inducing fear and population control; indeed, there had much evidence adequate convulsions alone are not therapeutically effective. Brain damage; however, the result of toxic assaults to the brain, e.g., excessive dosages of electricity, result in both a temporary euphoric apathy (Breggin) and often what may be the more important aim—greater patient manageability.

Failure to Acknowledge

The actual experimentation, production, and discarding of minimal stimulus or reduced output devices by both Reuben Reiter, Sc. D. , Incorporated, and Medcraft Incorporated, implicates these manufacturers [68] in what appears to be fraud and deception during the greater part of the SW Era wherein SW manufacturers knowingly misrepresent and mislabel SW devices as "minimal stimulus" and "convulsive therapy" as do Brief Pulse manufacturers today. Indeed, the later SW devices just as the later BP devices are actually electrical dosage (ENR) devices for the underlying purpose of altering behavior via electrical impairment of the brain for a provisionally protracted period of time, although supposedly used for depression and other "forms of mental illnesses"). In any case, both the modern SW and the modern BP device are "ENR" in lieu of "ECT" devices in that neither later SW devices nor later BP devices depend upon the least amount of electricity possible to induce as adequate convulsion. Rather both the SW device and the modern BP device are totally dependent upon adequate amounts of electricity to achieve their looked for effects. The results, reduced connectivity (invariably resulting in long-term memory impairment) reflective of brain injury are clearly proved in the Perrin study as we shall see. Adequate convulsion or ECT devices, in contrast, have little or no "therapeutic" value, whereas, the "effect" of adequate dosage or ENR devices cannot be extricated from impairment and, indeed, actually depend upon it. Because there was no FDA creating safety and efficacy requirements during the SW era, adequate dosage devices were fraudulently, willfully, and knowingly used by SW manufacturers to injure or impair literally hundreds of thousands of recipients against their wills. In that mental institutions seem to have been the main purchasers of such devices during this era, their primary function was to master and control inmate populations. [69] Modern BP devices have a similar function though not necessarily confined to institutions.

Based on the early history of reduced output devices in the 1940s and the 1950s and the history of SW generally, both Medcraft and the Reiter Company, in 1976, omitted to inform FDA and Utah of what both manufacturers were well aware -- that adequate seizures alone are ineffective. This awareness should have led to the later suspicion that neither would Blachley's resurrection of Liberson's minimal stimulus BP device be effective and that, just like SW, BP devices introduced in 1976 for the FDA would have to be dramatically enhanced in power immediately following FDA scrutiny in order to achieve the looked for effect. Like SW, moreover, American BP manufacturers, represented by Richard Weiner, must have known or at least suspected that enhanced power would almost certainly negate the safety advantage of BP's reduced output advantage regarding the long complained of memory dysfunction due to brain damage. Both SW and BP manufacturers, in short, failed to inform FDA that which was never disclosed to the public during the SW era -- long term memory dysfunction, the direct manifestation of brain damage due to excessive electrical dosing is inextricably related to "efficacy" (whether this be the temporary blunting of depression or behavioral modification); that the treatment is, in fact, electrical damage to the brain (Breggin, 1979). Moreover, both failed to disclose that convulsion theory had long ago been debunked by earlier reduced output experiments so that "ECT" machines would again have to devolve into ENR or adequate electrical dosage devices in order to make the treatment "work. "

History of Forced Treatment and Absence of Mental Patient Rights

The history of unscrutinized gadgets, surgery, and other "therapies" incorporating insidiously injurious agents for the sole purpose of "controlling" mental patient inmates - was (and is) the direct result of insufficient safeguards for persons confined to mental institutions resulting in what was (and in many states yet is[70]) --

---

[68] MECTA, as well as APA Representative Richard Weiner must have been aware of the early discarding of BP as ineffective.

[69] It was not until 1975, one year before "the ACT" authorizing FDA to approve new medical devices, that the U.S. Supreme Court in O'Conner versus Donaldson recognized "danger to self or others" as the only constitutional criteria for commitment. Perhaps it was the rationale that mental patients are dangerous and need controlling - and the fact that the real aim of lobotomy - like electroshock - was to manage inmates, making them more co-operative, compliant, and thereby "less dangerous" - that APA turned a deaf ear to the cries of thousands of injured ECT recipients during the SW era. A deaf ear was also turned to the minimal stimulus failures corroborative of the necessity of suprathreshold dosing and so memory dysfunction and brain damage in order to effect change. Indeed, the 1950 Janis study revealed long-term memory dysfunction affecting virtually 100% of recipients treated with standard SW.

[70] The majority of states within the U.S. still retain laws permitting forced "ECT" treatments.

forced "treatment. "[71] The total absence of informed consent during the SW era, concomitant with the institutions' desire to manage inmate populations appears to have resulted in the unscrutinized dissemination of false, erroneous, and/or deceptive information regarding "ECT" and any number of other perfidious and inhumane procedures, but which from a management standpoint, are seen as "effective procedures. " Not surprisingly, as we have seen, misleading information regarding so-called "electroconvulsive therapy" and so-called "electroconvulsive therapy devices" can be traced back to manufacturers whose abiding interest in profit, and thus reluctance to discard an "effective treatment" (from the institutions' perspective) has resulted in the ongoing seventy year cover-up of which this treatise is the subject.

Utah Reports on European-Made Devices

The 1976-77 FDA sponsored Utah study, as we have seen, reported not only on American devices, but on the English manufacturer, Ectron Ltd. and the German Company, Siemens AG. By 1976, the year the FDA began investigating "ECT" via Utah Biomedical Test Laboratory, the English manufacturer, Ectron was producing four different types of "ECT" devices, while the German Company, Siemens AG, was manufacturing the so-called Konvulsator 2077. These English and German made devices offered practitioners a number of options -- including sub-convulsive stimulation as well as various types of current for so-called "convulsive therapy" (involving the less powerful unidirectional current [DC]) [72] as well as the more powerful bidirectional (AC) current. The main feature of European devices at this time entailed a half-sine wave, half-pulse characteristic requiring more output (to create an adequate seizure) than pure Brief Pulse, but far less energy output than the pure AC-SW which American manufacturers had produced and marketed all throughout the SW Era. Both the English and the German companies had begun producing their variegated devices in the 1960s, following the failed minimal stimulus experiments of Delmat-Marselet in Europe (1942), Ottosson's inaccurate [73] conclusions regarding the alleged validity of convulsion theory and minimal stimulus efficacy (1960), followed the failed reduced output experiments of Americans Wilcox, Friedman, and Liberson (Impastato, Berg, and Gabriel, 1957). Inherent in the constitution of these moderately early European half-SW, half -pulse devices, was the conspicuous acknowledgement that while unmitigated SW caused devastating memory dysfunction,[74] true minimal stimulus or adequate seizure devices were relatively ineffective. European devices around 1976, then, reflect an attempted compromise between efficacy and safety.

In spite of such attempts to salvage the memory of "ECT" recipients via moderately reduced output; however, the earlier and later history of European reduced output devices is similar to that of the earlier and later American experiments also designed to reduce output. While like American manufacturers which continued to claim their increasingly powerful apparatuses "convulsive therapy" instruments, European manufacturers, too, at a certain point, began utilizing more and more powerful devices to achieve efficacy

---

[71] The so-called anti-depressant rationale has almost totally replaced the more preponderant and unsavory aim of management and control, creating the illusion of a patient-satisfied and patient-oriented procedure. In point of fact, management and control from a third party perspective may yet be the preponderant sociological aim of so-called "ECT," particularly when it is forced. Tellingly, much of the "ECT" in the modern Brief Pulse age is administered to persons sixty-five years and older often living with their adult children or in some sort of care facility. It is these adult children, who - taking the place of institutional caregivers of old – who often seek to manage their plaintive and troublesome, aging parents through "ECT." Moreover, it is often these adult children seeking personal asylum from plaintive and aging parents, who are the greatest advocates of the procedure, in short, another third party perspective.

[72] Unidirectional currents (DC) are inherently less powerful than bi-directional currents (AC); however, this can be misleading. Unidirectional current devices can utilize very long Durations as well as high Voltages in order to enhance Charge and cumulative output.

[73] History has shown that Ottosson was incorrect in his assessment of the procedure's efficacy at threshold or minimal stimulus. Like many early researchers' who sincerely believed in "convulsion theory" Ottosson was excited and inspired by the notion that so-called "adequate seizures" could be induced with relatively non-harmful low dosages of electricity.

[74] Advocates of ECT/ENR devices often claim the only difference between SW and BP is the disorientation and confusion time following the procedure, both of which allegedly, equally clear up in time. Such a claim is patently untrue, contradicting the findings of Wilcox, Liberson, Janis, and many others. Such claims attempt to play down the seriousness of permanent brain damage (Andre, 1991; Breggin, 1979; Cameron, 1997; Friedberg, 1976; Janis, 1950) as a result of suprathreshold electroshock. If reduced energy output did not result in dramatic long-term differences in memory dysfunction, the history of ECT/ENR would hardly be riddled with years of experiments attempting to preserve both an intact brain and efficacy - such long-term results of which clearly show the mutual exclusivity of the two conditions. In short, most unfortunately, efficacy is inextricably linked to brain damage.

(Cameron, 1994). Thus, in spite of similarly successful experiments to induce adequate grand mal seizures at reduced doses of electricity, device manufacturers both in Europe (and evidently Asia) appear to have gradually begun eliminating ineffective, albeit, safer adequate seizure devices in favor of increasingly more powerful adequate electrical dosage machines capable of enhanced (suprathreshold) outputs. The implicit conclusion on both continents appears to be that that both safety and efficacy cannot co-exist with this procedure; consequently, both In America and Europe, safety is eventually sacrificed for efficacy, even as manufacturers continue to claim their devices "convulsive therapy apparatuses" based on the adequate convulsion. In short, manufacturers on both continents ubiquitously cover up enhanced and enhancing power, as we shall see in detail later on with respect to both American and English devices. Unfortunately, while the history of English and American BP devices are examined in this manuscript, other device manufacturers do *not* come within the purview of this report. Even so, we can intelligently extrapolate from both the American and English histories the main dilemma of "ECT" as failed attempts to administer the procedure both safely and efficaciously due to the frustratingly inextricable relationship between efficacy and damage. In short, the invariable necessity of adequate doses of electricity in lieu of adequate seizures is required to make the procedure "work. "

In that the suppressed axiom regarding the inefficacy of adequate convulsion, in turn connoting convulsion theory as spurious, has been born out on both American and Western European continents as we shall see in much greater detail later, it is safe to assume that Eastern European as well as Asian manufacturers of "ECT" devices have been plagued with the same dilemma and so have had to resort either to the use of standard SW or the same gross enhancing of Brief Pulse devices over time. Axiomatically then, all modern day manufacturers of "effective" devices which label their machines "convulsive therapy" and/or "minimal stimulus" apparatuses suggesting memory improvement as a result of reduced output compared to SW, unfailingly make the same false or deceptive claims. The mere existence of early minimal stimulus devices both in Europe and America in an attempt to decrease morbidity through reduced dosages of electricity followed by the same recrudescent increasing of power over time - suggest that like American companies, Eurasian companies as well are fully aware that the so-called "ECT" procedure requires morbidity producing suprathreshold electrical dosing in order be "effective. " Conversely, manufacturers world-wide are similarly aware that convulsion theory itself is bogus.

Succinctly then, similar patterns of enhancement exist in both SW and BP eras on both continents. In short, rather than abandoning the procedure entirely and so folding corporately, all modern day English, European, and American manufacturers have instead introduced what appear to be incipient energy reducing devices (usually Brief Pulse) which are then furtively enhanced over time to first equal then surpass the power of SW devices generally. That SW devices are replaced by Brief Pulse for greater recipient safety via reduced outputs and so are greatly improved devices, then, is blind illusion on a world-wide basis. Because "efficacy" and "minimal stimulus" are aphoristically and mutually contradictory, English BP devices (and others), just as American BP devices as we shall see, eventually begin to incorporate the same pre-fixed suprathreshold electrical dosing as American-made BP devices in order to achieve "efficacy.

Chapter 3

1978 FDA Proposal to Reclassify ECT Devices from Class III to Class II

Contingent upon Utah's recommendation to the FDA that an ECT device Standard could be written based on adequate convulsion theory, that is, based upon the assumption that equally adequate and, therefore, equally effective grand mal convulsions could be induced with the greatly reduced outputs of Brief Pulse (compared to SW), the FDA Neurological Device Classification Panel (FDA Advisory Panel) on November 28, 1978, announced that upon completion and acceptance of said written Standard, the "ECT" device would be placed in Class II.

The notion that an American Standard could be written assuring the public of reasonable safety and efficacy, thereby qualifying the "ECT" device for Class II status, is evidence of FDA's conclusion that ECT devices modified to minimal stimulus output (for inducing adequate seizures) might be considered a reasonably safe venture -- that is -- wherein benefit outweighs risk. The procedure, contingent upon said improvements, would then be able to continue into the last quarter century of the twentieth century and beyond as a viable medical procedure. Within the "November, 1978" public announcement to re-classify devices into Class II; therefore, FDA scheduled a public hearing for "May 29, 1979" with public comments due "January 29, 1979. " [75] Both manufacturers and interested public parties were invited. Based upon the FDA Advisory Panel's recommendations (deemed the "FDA Neurological Device Classification Panel"), as well as professional and public commentary to be heard, and finally upon information already made available primarily through the Utah Biomedical Test Laboratory investigation--a separate non-FDA Panel of salaried experts would decide upon the appropriate classification of the "ECT" device. The vote was to take place immediately following the May 29, 1979 public meeting. The initial announcement published in the Federal Register November 11, 1978, soliciting public commentary on ECT and announcing the upcoming public hearing "May 29, 1979" included the following important commentaries by the FDA Advisory Panel, already recommending Class II for "ECT" devices in lieu of the more relegated Class III in which it presently abided. The Register read:

The Neurological Device Classification Panel, an FDA advisory committee, made the following three recommendations:

> 1) Identification: An electroconvulsive therapy device is a device used for treating severe psychiatric disturbances, e. g. , severe depression, by inducing in the patient a major seizure by applying a brief intense electrical current to the patient's head. (Food and Drug Administration, 1978, November 28)

The initial terse statements above made by the FDA advisory panel, imply electric current administered for no other purpose than the induction of a major motor seizure, indicating convulsion--not electricity--as the sole therapeutic agent. Succinctly then, the Panel's sentence reads: "An electroconvulsive therapy device is a device used for treating severe psychiatric disturbances . . . by inducing in the patient a major seizure . . . by applying a brief intense electrical current. " "Brief" implies Brief Pulse, but also as "minimal" a current as possible in order to induce the so-called "adequate seizure. " Thus, the FDA Advisory Panel also implicitly defines "ECT"

---

[75] It was at this point that Marilyn Rice, founder of "Committee For Truth In Psychiatry," composed of shock survivors who had experienced long-term memory dysfunction as a result of the procedure, formed to oppose Class II classification.

as minimal electrical stimulus to induce an adequate seizure, a depiction which becomes even clearer in the next commentary. Certainly there is no discussion of electrical dosage beyond that necessary to elicit the "adequate seizure. "

> 2) Recommended classification: Class II (performance Standards). The Panel recommends that establishing a performance Standard for this device be a high priority. (Food and Drug Administration, 1978, November 28, p.55729)

FDA Panel recommendation that: “[E]stablishing a performance Standard for this device [must] be a high priority” is not surprising as Class II medical devices include those for which a specific performance Standard for safety and efficacy has been or can be written. We should keep in mind that the FDA Panel based its recommendations on the Utah report, which failed to recognize that the therapeutic efficacy of adequate seizure is ineffective. Thus, the Advisory Panel’s main concern, as we shall see, is defining and assuring both efficacy and safety through a regulatory standard, that is, publicly guaranteeing both efficacy and reasonable safety, distinctly crucial components of the original Congressional mandate granting FDA approval or disapproval of any medical or neurological device.

Class II, then, implies reasonable efficacy and safety of machines via the specific defining limits and safeguards of a specific Standard. Breaching the Standard means breaching the regulatory boundaries guaranteeing reasonable safety and efficacy.

Class III on the other hand, the class into which devices are initially placed and the Class in which the "ECT" device yet remains, may include devices with no specifically definable safety parameters and, in fact, which may have no criteria other than their having been in continual use before and up to 1976, the year Congress newly authorized FDA to approve new medical devices. The practice of permitting the marketing of devices merely because they were in use before and continuing up to 1976 is known as “grandfathering. ” Thus, all so-called "ECT" devices were “grandfathered” into Class III in 1976 and suspended there until FDA could more fully investigate. Class I, of course, generally contains those devices with a proven history of both safety and efficacy, further corroborated by a written standard approved by FDA confirming the safety and efficacy to which the device must conform. The following, then, is the third recommendation of the FDA Neurological Device Classification Panel along with the stipulations required for the transitioning of "ECT" devices from Class III to Class II:

> 3) Summary of reasons for recommendation: The Panel recommends that electroconvulsive therapy (ECT) devices be classified into Class II (performance Standards) because the devices must be capable of providing the correct amount of current to the patient to induce a seizure without unnecessarily injuring the patient. The Panel believes that general controls will not provide sufficient control over these characteristics. Although the use of this device involves a substantial risk to the patient, the Panel believes that the benefit of the treatment outweighs the risks involved if the patients are selected carefully and the devices are designed and used properly. The Panel believes that a Standard will provide reasonable assurance of the safety and effectiveness of the device and that there is sufficient information to establish a Standard to provide such assurance. (Food and Drug Administration, 1978, November 28, p.55729)

Persuaded by the Utah Report (which had rediscovered early EEG studies comparing BP to SW) clearly identifying the excessive dosing of SW as the cause of increased memory morbidity, the FDA advisory Panel manifestly recommended the writing of a specific Standard delineating maximum electrical parameters. This maximum would more or less prohibit output exceeding that required to induce the “therapeutic” grand mal seizure. In that the data submitted (to Utah) by MECTA in 1976 described Brief Pulse as reducing the amount of Energy Output required to induce the “necessary” seizure by as much as four fold, the FDA Panel's recommendation is strongly indicative of the development and utilization of Brief Pulse, and so use of the least amount of electricity necessary to induce an adequate seizure. By implication, the Panel recommends the discarding of SW. The recommended Standard, therefore, was to safeguard recipients via the most minimal stimulus possible to invoke adequate “therapeutic seizures,” and this, of course, meant exclusive use of the Brief Pulse device. Thus, the “benefit . . . outweighs . . . risks” phrase stipulating “devices . . . . designed and used properly,” based on “a Standard [that] will provide reasonable assurance of [both] . . . safety and effectiveness" can be interpreted as a Standard guaranteeing minimal stimulus output to induce adequate or "therapeutic seizures. " Moreover, the Panel is not satisfied with "general controls" but rather a Standard delineating specific parameters. The Panel's fourth recommendation or statement below makes clear that the Utah Study is the chief basis for the FDA recommendation:

> 4) Summary of data on which the recommendation is based: The Panel members based their recommendation on their personal familiarity with the use of this [ECT] device and on information provided by Dr. Allen R. Grahn of the Utah Biomedical Test Laboratory. Dr. Grahn conducted a study under contract to the FDA on ECT devices and presented the results of his study to the Panel. . . Dr. Grahn's study was based on a review of the scientific literature, information provided by ECT manufacturers, and a survey of ECT users. He pointed out that the optimum electrical characteristics of ECT devices have not been determined but that a reliable therapeutic result may be achieved using a variety of device electrical designs. (Food and Drug Administration, 1978, November 28, p.55729)

In short, the FDA Panel assumes equal therapeutic results with a variety of waveforms and instruments so long as a "therapeutic seizure" is induced. Significantly, as noted above, comparative EEG studies conducted before 1976, re-discovered by and referenced in the Utah Report (Proctor and Goodwin, 1943), identify the production of delta and theta waves indicative of brain damage as a result of the more powerful SW; whereas, minimal stimulus instruments such as Brief Pulse depict dramatic reductions in the neuropathological production of these waves. Certainly, as already noted, based on the Utah data, the obvious choice is Brief Pulse requiring the least amount of energy to obtain the "necessary" seizure, resulting, of course, in the clear reduction -- if not complete elimination -- of brain trauma and very possibly brain damage.

To summarize then, FDA, via Utah, was clearly under the impression that safety could only be reasonably guaranteed through the use of the most minimal stimulus output possible to induce the alleged requisite seizure, and that only a specific Standard guaranteeing the least amount of electricity possible could provide a Congressionally mandated "reasonable assurance of . . [both] safety and effectiveness. " The Panel (via Utah and other input) was thereby convinced that the reduced energy levels of Brief Pulse enhance safety, that reduced energy levels are capable of inducing equally "adequate" and therefore equally "therapeutic" seizures, and finally that "adequate seizure" alone (not electricity) is the basis of "ECT. " Data submitted to Utah by MECTA Corporation depicting Brief Pulse induced seizures at one forth the output of SW was fully supported both by APA spokesperson Richard Weiner, and by EEG studies rediscovered by Utah delineating reduced brain trauma and memory dysfunction (very possibly indicative of brain damage). These factors logically convinced FDA that a specific Standard stipulating a specific minimal stimulus metric or maximum output (with Brief Pulse) was both feasible and imperative in assuring that the procedure could be administered safely enough to become a "reasonable risk," that is, that the risk-benefit ratio would be a reasonable one. Central to FDA's conviction, of course, because it was based on both seemingly reliable data and convulsion theory in general, was FDA's inherent, unquestioned assumption that adequate convulsion alone is the therapeutic factor so that the machine could be improved via a Standard requiring the least amount of electricity necessary to induce it. [76] The next FDA (Panel) recommendation informed readers of the specific risks.

> 5) Risks to health: . . . Brain damage: Excessive (or improper control of the applied) electrical current may produce injury to the brain. . . . Cardiac arrhythmia: The therapeutic convulsions may be accompanied by irregular heartbeat or cardiac arrest. . . . Memory loss: The patient may suffer amnesia after the treatment. (Food and Drug Administration, 1978, November 28, p.55729)

---

[76] APA via Richard Weiner and a handful of manufacturer-affiliated psychiatrists continue from 1976 forward mostly through NIMH grants - performing and expanding these same precedential comparative studies between SW and BP in order to confirm and establish the relative safety of BP. Unfortunately, as we shall see, while BP manufacturers surreptitiously enhance electrical parameters surpassing SW for clinical use, Weiner and others knowingly continue to conduct comparative safety studies with BP set at minimal stimulus output. Moreover, neither Weiner, the APA, nor any Manufacturer - including Medcraft - bother to indicate to the FDA or Utah that although minimal stimulus BP had been attempted by Liberson from about 1945 to about 1950, the failed results of all reduced output experiments from 1940 to 1957, including Liberson's BP experiments, had exposed convulsion theory as false.

By 1978, then, through Proctor and Goodwin's comparative EEGs (1943) and a myriad of other data regarding memory dysfunction (Janis 1950), FDA clearly recognized the need for minimal stimulus devices such as Brief Pulse and that unnecessarily enhanced SW current, that is, excess energy output superfluous to that required to induce adequate seizures as a result of which unnecessary brain trauma is produced, very possibly indicative of brain damage, should be eliminated. Based on all the data then, the FDA conclusion appears to have been a “no-brainer. ” What benefit could there be, after all, in utilizing electrical dosages in excess of that needed to induce adequate seizures? What benefit could there be in taking a totally unnecessary risk? What benefit in needlessly occasioning injury? Brief Pulse then, with its' mechanical capacity to induce the same grand mal seizures at greatly reduced energy output, resulting in minimal delta and theta brain wave activity (Proctor and Goodwin, 1943), was key to FDA's conviction that a Standard could and should be composed, insuring the most minimal electrical stimulus possible to induce the “necessary” seizures. It seemed obvious, then, that such a standard to this effect would greatly improve the procedure, a procedure which could be just as effectively administered with a much lower energy output than SW and so with a much greater degree of safety. Unmistakably, it was the re-introduction and potential utilization of MECTA's reduced Energy Output Brief Pulse device, the reduction in output of which was corroborated by the APA Task Force, which FDA believed would fulfill the FDA's new Congressional stipulation for reasonable assurance of safety and efficacy. In fact, given the destructive nature of SW, supplanting SW with minimal stimulus Brief Pulse appeared to be the sole condition upon which FDA approved the continuation of the ECT procedure beyond the 1976-1982 hearings. To be reclassified into Class II, moreover, would simply require a standard guaranteeing the condition of minimal stimulus induced adequate seizures with Brief Pulse. In sum then:

The (FDA Advisory) Panel believed that a Standard would provide reasonable assurance of safety and effectiveness of the "ECT" device and that there was now sufficient information to establish a Standard to provide just such assurance (Food and Drug Administration, 1978, November 28, p.55729).

The task of writing the American Standard for ECT would be handed to APA Task Force Chairman and manufacturer spokesperson, Richard Weiner. The standard, it appeared, would be the crucial fulcrum about which the procedure would continue into the last quarter of the twentieth century, and without which the "ECT" procedure might well have been doomed. Thus "ECT" would continue under Class III status until such time that the promised standard actually materialized. Indeed, a standard did emerge about 1982 at the end of the public hearing series some four years later, since known as the "1982 APA Standard for ECT. "

Chapter 4

1978 American Psychiatric Association ECT Task Force Report 14

As noted above, it is important to apprehend that once the FDA, through the Medical Device Amendments Act of 1976, had been appointed by Congress to scrutinize and approve all new medical devices before marketing, that many previously existing devices -- that is -- devices existing before and up through 1976, went into a kind of limbo category deemed “Class III. ” Such devices could continue to be marketed, but only under FDA scrutiny. “Grandfathered” devices, placed in Class III, as already noted, included those for which no standard had been written or for which no standard could be written. Those Class III devices for which an FDA approved standard had been written (insuring benefit surpassing risk) were to be upgraded to Class II, or possibly Class I (devices of proven safety and efficacy wherein the benefit appears to unequivocally surpass risk). But performance standard or no, manufacturers of previously existing devices (or devices comparable to those produced and ongoing prior to 1976) could, via “grandfathering,” continue marketing their devices sans standard until such time a written standard could be written and approved, or until such time manufacturers submitted “pre-market approvals” for FDA approbation. Thus, even grandfathered devices for which no performance standard had been or could be written and so remained in Class III, would, like new devices, have to submit a so-called “pre-market approval. ” “Pre-market approval” for “grandfathered” devices, however, was based on much less stringent criteria than devices created post 1976. In fact, the only real criterion was that such devices had to have been marketed and utilized prior to 1976. The term "pre-market approval” then, is both ironic and misleading in that “grandfathered” devices could continue to be marketed even without "pre-market approval. " Moreover, even with “pre-market approval,” these devices were supposed to remain in Class III until FDA could approve a written standard.

Following its’ new mandate to scrutinize medical devices, FDA almost immediately began investigating “ECT” via an independent party, Utah Biomedical Test Laboratory. Subsequently, FDA scheduled a public hearing for the “ECT” device in 1979. To prepare for the hearing, the APA (American Psychiatric Association), with the cooperation of "ECT" manufacturers, formed a 1978 APA Electroconvulsive Therapy Task Force which assumed the FDA charge of writing an American Psychiatric Association Standard for "ECT," hopefully in time for the 1979 public hearing, a standard which would eventually be known as the "1982 APA Standard for 'ECT. ' " While the 1978 Electroconvulsive Therapy Task Force Report (No.14; 17) did not complete the written Standard it eventually did pen following the hearing, the initial Report appears to have been formulated and submitted to the FDA with an eye toward convincing FDA that a standard could, indeed, be written, one incorporating both the safety and efficacy criteria an acceptable standard called for. In short, the Report maintained that a standard could be written in that ECT, effective at minimal stimulus as the earlier literature (reviewed by the Utah Report) had maintained, could limit a device (Brief Pulse) to about 100 joules or minimal stimulus, justifying a Class II category status. Not surprisingly, however, the 1978 APA Task Force Report encouraged the FDA to place the device into Class II even before the promised standard could be completed.

As discussed above, the criteria by which a performance standard for “ECT” was to be written had already been officially framed by the 1976-77 Utah Report in its’ official determination of ECT as “convulsive therapy. ” As such, and as the standard eventually bears out, Utah clearly expected the performance standard to insure the least amount of stimulus possible to induce "adequate convulsions. " With no other choice, then—a standard for ECT had to conform to FDA criteria of “benefit outweighing risk,” minimal stimulus criteria confirmed by Utah which the 1978 APA ECT Task Force Report (with Weiner at its head) were forced to adjudicate "valid." That is, in its report, APA fully acknowledged "convulsive therapy" as the inducing of so-called "adequate convulsions" with the least amount of electricity possible. In that, according to the literature reviewed by Utah, electricity had no role other than the elicitation of the adequate seizure itself, electrical output in excess of that required to induce the adequate seizure was clearly deemed undesirable. Thus, the APA Task Force was tasked with writing a Standard insuring minimal stimulus (just as Utah suggested), almost certainly around the newly reintroduced Brief Pulse device. The following are critical excerpts from the FDA-adopted Utah Report and FDA panel with which the APA Task Force on ECT was forced to agree.

> Blachley et al. conclude with the belief that there is no magic in the use of 60 Hz sinewave stimuli and its' use is a serious mistake. Anyone investigating stimulus energy should realize that rapid rising, narrow pulses at low frequency should be used to reduce the delivered energy. (Blachley, Denney, and Fling, unpublished; Grahn et al. , 1977, p.34)
>
> Consistent with this cautious view is the concern of a number of investigators over the high stimulus energies available from ECT devices and the use of energy inefficient [SW] waveforms. (Grahn et al. , 1977, p.35)
>
> [T]here is only one clinical application for these devices and that is to produce a <u>grand</u> <u>mal</u> convulsion in a patient with a mental illness. (Ibid, p.37)
>
> More comments were related to stimulus energy than any other single aspect of ECT devices. Psychiatrists expressed a need for . . . a means of measuring patient impedance so that minimum stimulus energy may be delivered, [and expressed a need for] a means to deliver the minimum energy necessary to produce a "complete" seizure . . . . (Ibid, p.38)
>
> Although the use of this device involves a substantial risk to the patient, the Panel believes that the benefit of the treatment outweighs the risks involved if . . . the devices are designed and used properly. The Panel believes that a Standard will provide reasonable assurance of the safety and effectiveness of the device and that there is sufficient information to establish a Standard to provide such assurance. (Food and Drug Administration, 1978, November 28, p.55729)

In that Utah (and thus the FDA) had inadvertently exposed the Medcraft device as a suprathreshold apparatus compared to Brief Pulse, the 1978 Task Force Report was compelled to write the standard around Blachley's re-introduction of the BP minimal stimulus machine resurrected from the 1940s -- specifically MECTA's new Brief Pulse "C" limited first to 81 and then to 110 maximum joules, allegedly half that of SW.

In was in this way, therefore, that the 1978 APA Electroconvulsive Therapy Task Force was compelled by Utah in turn compelled by FDA to make Brief Pulse the vanguard, the promise, and the loadstone for the so-called "new and improved" ECT device for what was to become the new Brief Pulse Era. It was in this way also that FDA compelled the 1978 APA Task Force to confirm the officially grandfathered in definition of "electro-convulsive therapy" as the induction of adequate seizures alone with the least amount of electricity possible. The standard would thereby have to incorporate the improved safety aspect of "ECT," that is, the guarantee of "minimal stimulus" to induce these "adequate convulsions. " In short, the "new and improved" procedure -- minimal stimulus induced adequate convulsions in lieu of the unnecessarily excessive electricity emitted by SW -- was prototypically epitomized by MECTA's new resurrected minimal stimulus BP device with greatly reduced electrical parameters fully capable of inducing adequate seizures with half the output of SW in all age categories--the MECTA "C. "

Indeed, The 1978 APA Report affirms that the ECT procedure administered by the "ECT machine" must be based on the convulsive therapy theory defined by von Meduna, as well as Wilson, Liberson, Ottoson, and others. The principle assumed was that so long as adequate seizures can be induced, the efficacy is the same regardless of the output. Based on this principle, memory disturbing electrical excess appeared eliminable. Vital and inherent in the definition of ECT both in the Utah and the APA Task Force Reports, therefore, and thus within the context of ECT's purpose, aim, and theory is the total elimination of excessive - or - what is presently defined as - suprathreshold -- dosages of electricity meaning any electrical output over that required to assure an “adequate seizure.” Electrical output over that required to induce the adequate seizure, in short, is identified by the Utah Report, the FDA Panel on ECT, the 1978 APA ECT Task Force Report, and all classical theorists of ECT from 1940 to 1978 as unacceptable, undesirable, and unnecessary. Phrased differently, suprathreshold unnecessarily excessive electrical output is specifically and clearly identified by all these sources as that beyond which an adequate seizure can be induced. All clearly purport to agree that it is the excessive doses of electricity (emitted by SW), in sum, which produce the undesirable morbidity in the form of memory dysfunction and very possibly brain damage and so were looked to be eliminated by the “new and improved Brief Pulse “ECT” device in turn based on a new American Standard. Both the direct and indirect definition of ECT by all sources then, is a machine which induces an adequate seizure with the least amount of Energy Output possible. It is this definition of minimal stimulus in conjunction with the induction of an adequate seizure then, which defines the "ECT" process as well as the ECT apparatus.

Although the 1978 Task Force, chaired by Richard Weiner was formed to create a Standard based on these findings, no American Standard was forthcoming within the 1978 APA Task Force Report itself. Nevertheless, contained within the 78’ APA Task Force Report are a number of important commentaries promising the emergence of minimal stimulus Brief Pulse and even the affirmation of the efficacy of minimal stimulus UL placement reducing electrical output even further all to be incorporated in an upcoming standard. The 1978 Task Force Report proclaims:

> [A]ll available evidence supports the contention that memory loss is an undesirable side effect of ECT, not related to therapeutic efficacy. (American Psychiatric Association Task Force on ECT 1978, p.57)
>
> [F]ollowing the development of right unilateral ECT . . , it became clear that this mode of convulsive therapy results in markedly less memory impairment than conventional bilateral ECT . . . . Yet right unilateral ECT is clinically as effective, or nearly as effective, as bilateral ECT . . . . (American Psychiatric Association Task Force on ECT, 1978, p.57)
>
> [C]linial reports emphasize a small difference in the clinical response between unilateral and bilateral electrode placements, asserting that unilateral ECT is slower and requires one or two additional seizures for equal efficacy. (American Psychiatric Association Task Force on ECT, 1978, p.81)

The APA Task Force consequently planned a new series of comparative studies to confirm the greater safety and equal efficacy of the new and improved Brief Pulse device seemingly leading to standardization of minimal stimulus. In turn, such a Standard for "ECT" assuring public safety wherein benefit would clearly outweigh risk, would ultimately lead to FDA approval and so a category graduation from Class III to at least Class II. Endorsed by the American Psychiatric Association, therefore, the new and improved Brief Pulse machines, circumscribed by an upcoming Standard ensuring minimal stimulus with the induction of adequate seizures and so “equally effective” (to SW), appeared to make the newer safer “ECT” a shoe-in for its continuation into the next quarter century and beyond, even seemingly guaranteeing a promotion from Class III to Class II.

Not surprisingly, then, the APA Task Force theme of the reduced dosage Brief Pulse device inducing equally adequate seizures with equal efficacy is replete throughout the Task Force's 1978 document. Under pressure from both the FDA and public outcries of memory dysfunction from the older SW devices, the APA Task Force, though unwilling to relinquish SW outright, began to disenfranchise itself from the seemingly archaic SW instrument, instead, adopting the new Brief Pulse device which could deliver equally adequate seizures, but at just above threshold, one half the EO (Energy Output) of SW. In short, the Report contained what appeared to be an acknowledgement, albeit somewhat begrudgingly, of the greater safety and equal efficacy attributed to the reduced output Brief Pulse device. For example, the Task Force reported:

> Impairment in memory functions may . . . be reduced by modifying parameters of the electric current . . These technical aspects are still under investigation but if their promise is fulfilled, current [amperage] type may be an additional parameter to reduce adverse effects. (American Psychiatric Association Task Force on ECT, 1978, p.81)

Thus the 1978 APA Task Force Report endorsed the equal efficacy of minimal stimulus induced seizures with Brief Pulse as well as the efficacy of unilateral electrode placement requiring even less electrical output than BL electrode placement, an endorsement of great import in persuading the FDA that the newer safer parameters of Brief Pulse were indeed viable and that a standard could indeed be written around this greatly reduced output instrument. With such a device and the development of these contingencies, ECT could and would resume as a safer more viable medical treatment. The definition of the "Electro Convulsive Therapy" device that is "grandfathered in" is thus an apparatus capable of inducing adequate convulsions (twenty-five seconds or more in length) with the least possible amount of electricity. It goes without saying that electricity is the catalyst in ECT, not the treatment; that is, that convulsion alone is the so-called therapeutic feature of ECT. The fact that previous machines had been using much more electricity than that needed to induce the adequate seizure meant that machines could go from ENR back to ECT devices. Transforming ENR back to ECT, in short, meant greatly reducing electrical output, indeed, using the most minimal stimulus possible to induce adequate seizures. Brief Pulse ECT seemed to mean there would be little or no mitigation regarding the emphasis of convulsion itself, and so little or no extraneous complications due to unnecessarily excessive electricity, namely, devastating memory loss, clearly associated with too much power.

Shortly following the publication and submission of the 1978 APA Task Force Report and just prior to the 1979 FDA decision to keep the devices in Class III until a standard could be written and adopted espousing Brief Pulse minimal stimulus output, Richard Weiner, the head of the 1978 APA Task Force Report on ECT published these statements in the *American Journal of Psychiatry*:

> [B]rief pulse stimulus . . . initially used in the 1940s has only recently come into common clinical practice with the development of the . . . MECTA ECT device. . . . Unlike sine wave, which varies in amplitude continuously over time, brief pulse stimuli consist of short pulses of current . . . . Because of this, generalized seizures can usually be evoked with about one-third the total amount of electrical energy required with sine wave stimuli . . . . This is important in view of the fact that acute cognitive deficits and EEG abnormalities may be related to the amount of electrical energy delivered by the ECT device. (Weiner, 1979, p.1513)

Regarding unilateral electrode placement, requiring even less electricity to induce an adequate seizure, Weiner asserts in the same article that:

> A reduction in the severity of acute organic impairment has been reported with the incorporation of certain refinements in ECT technique, chiefly unilateral nondominant electrode placement and brief pulse stimuli. (Weiner, 1979, p.1515)

Thus, in both the 1978 APA Task Force Report and the American Journal of Psychiatry in 1979 in the very midst of the first FDA investigation of ECT, Weiner clearly implies that adequate convulsion alone, the induction of which requires no more than true minimal stimulus output by a true minimal stimulus device (such as Brief Pulse), comprises the therapy, the parameters of which should eliminate suprathreshold outputs. Moreover, Weiner confirms both independently and in the 1978 Task Force Report the looked for efficacy of UL (Unilateral) electrode placement requiring half the electrical energy of BL (Bilateral) ECT. Indeed, UL electrode placement is accepted in both the Utah and the 1978 Task Force Reports as equally effective as BL ECT, but by virtue of even greater reduced output, and so the most "cognitively advantageous. "

Time and time again then, "Convulsive Therapy" is either directly or indirectly defined for and by Utah, the FDA, and the APA as "adequate seizure alone" so that machine improvement lay in reduced electrical output to induce so-called "adequate seizures. " According to all authoritative sources at this time then, electricity plays no part other than catalyzing the "therapeutic seizure"; which is to say that seizure, not electricity, is the treatment, that seizure alone, not electricity produces the "therapeutic effect. " Moreover, all important agencies seem to agree that the degree of electricity above that required to induce the necessary seizure is directly proportional to the degree of cognitive dissonance. In that the seizure alone is the treatment and in that the electricity plays no part other than catalyzing the adequate seizure, all official entities agree at this juncture that the most minimal stimulus possible should be utilized to induce the "adequate seizure" in order to have both an effective treatment and to eliminate the cognitive consequences caused by excessive electricity. Finally, all three seem to agree that the most cognitively advantageous form is UL ECT in conjunction with the most cognitively advantageous device, the Brief Pulse apparatus, the combination of which requires the least amount of electricity possible to induce the so-called adequate seizure, and so appears to be the means by which all future "ECT" might be administered.

The 1978 APA Report, then, affirms both the direct and indirect definition of “Electroconvulsive Therapy” grandfathered in by the FDA as "the induction of adequate seizure with the most minimal amount of electricity possible.” [77] The fact that ECT is allegedly based on convulsive theory in turn based on adequate seizure alone (and not electricity) is absolutely crucial in differentiating "ECT" from a totally unrelated procedure with an entirely different goal we can now identify as ENR (Electro Neurotransmission Reduction), requiring excessive or suprathreshold electrical dosages in order to work. [78] In short, ECT is seizure dependent, ENR electro-dependent. One theoretically works by seizure alone, the other by electricity and quite possibly electricity alone. It is this critical difference which differentiates "ECT" administered with the BP device at minimal stimulus and with UL electrode placement and around which a standard is said to have been writeable from “ENR. ” ECT seeks to eliminate the excessive electrical dosages administered by the SW devices of the past, that is, from ENR, based on adequate amounts of electricity aimed, as we shall see, at reducing neurotransmitters in the brain. Indeed, ENR, unlike ECT, advertently administers excessive electrical dosages administered by both SW and the later BP devices as we shall see. In any case, it is the grandfathered in definition of ECT -- minimal stimulus induced adequate seizures -- which in 1976 inspires the Utah influenced FDA to replace the older SW devices with the "new and improved" Brief Pulse device for all future "ECT" procedures and with which Weiner and the APA Task Force agree. Finally, it is the grandfathered in definition of "ECT" as "convulsive therapy" or the "therapeutic seizure" alone which convinces Utah, the FDA, and seemingly the APA that from 1976 forward, the new and improved device known as Brief Pulse should alone be used to administer "ECT" as it can so with much greater safety than what was erroneously thought to be an "ECT" device of the past. In short, the SW machine which had been administering unnecessarily high energy outputs in the now antiquated SW Era had actually been an a ENR device soon to be supplanted by Brief Pulse which can actually administer the ECT, the FDA had grandfathered in by definition, in 1976.

It is "ECT" alone then, ECT as described by Utah, the FDA, and the "1978 APA Task Force on ECT," that is grandfathered in, in 1976--not ENR. That is, it is "ECT" based on the adequate convulsion which was expected of all past devices and which was now expected of all future devices -- not “ENR” based upon adequate or suprathreshold dosages of electricity. Clearly, Utah's and FDA's acknowledged definition and goal of "ECT" is induction of the adequate seizure alone, certainly not reduction of neurotransmitters via electrical damage to the brain as a result of "adequate" or excessive doses of electricity. In fact, the acknowledged goal of ECT by all three entities is clearly the elimination of all possible brain damage by the administering of the most minimal electrical energy possible via the "new and improved" Brief Pulse apparatus and preferably with UL electrode placement decreasing output even further. Moreover, the American standard was to be written accordingly.

More Comparison of "ECT" to "ENR"

"ENR," Electro Neurotransmission Reduction, a procedure requiring adequate amounts of electricity through the temporal lobes to deliberately damage neurotransmitters in order to reduce the number of transmissions in the brain--has never been delineated as such in any professional paper -- and is, in fact, vigorously denied by advocates of “ECT,” including manufacturers. Nevertheless, this is the procedure knowingly or unknowingly administered by SW machines from about 1940 to 1976, and, as we shall later see, knowingly administered by

---

[77] The APA Report could not very well have concluded otherwise. With the independent lab’s conclusions taken directly from the literature, a denial of minimal stimulus efficacy would have been to deny the validity of convulsion therapy itself, and to label the literature from 1957 to 1976 erroneous or fraudulent regarding Medcraft’s B-24-III. The only rational direction the ECT Task Force could take was to confirm the literature and thus the validity of minimal threshold output, mildly attacking Medcraft’s B-24 as an unintentional suprathreshold instrument. With the anti-psychiatry movement hot on the heels of the long criticized procedure, Weiner’s APA Task Force may have felt compelled to move toward the new and improved Brief Pulse instrument based on minimal stimulus convulsions. Enter MECTA.

[78] When the agent-inducing force (electricity) becomes the treatment itself or even a necessary part of the treatment involving efficacy, then the new treatment is not merely a variation of the original, but an entirely different procedure - in this case no longer convulsive therapy induced by electricity, but rather adequate electrical dosage in which electricity is involved in efficacy. As a result, the convulsion may or may not play a part and, in fact, may be simply be incidental, i.e. a side-effect of ENR (Robin and Tissera, 1982).

Brief Pulse manufacturers from about 1982 to the present. Thus, "ENR" - a treatment based upon excessive or suprathreshold dosages of electricity -- that is -- adequate or multifold threshold dosages of electricity uses a very different means and has a very different aim than the "Electro Convulsive Therapy" grandfathered in, in 1976, a procedure according to the literature based on "convulsion theory," the aim of which is induction of the "adequate seizure" alone, supposedly to counteract depression. While ECT academics often claim the exact mechanism of ECT is unknown, it has been theorized that the seizure releases certain chemicals which counteract depression, at least for a time. In any case, the clear aim of ECT is the induction of the minimal stimulus induced "adequate seizure. " Thus, it is "ECT" alone which is delineated in past and current studies, in the Utah Study (accepted by the FDA), by manufacturers, and finally, by 1978 APA Task Force Report. Clearly, what is deemed "Electro Convulsive Therapy" is based on classical convulsion theory ideally requiring just enough electricity to induce the adequate convulsion and no more. ECT, in short, is the attempt to induce the "adequate seizure" alone with the least amount of electricity possible, this single description and definition of which throughout the literature, is grandfathered in under the FDA in 1976, and which is subsequently confirmed by the APA. That the complement of "adequate seizure"-- "minimal stimulus"-- is the Utah, FDA, and APA depiction of both ECT itself and improved "safety" throughout the FDA hearings cannot be overstated. Indeed its opposite, that which is not ECT, ENR, is the hazardous practice of emitting unnecessarily "excessive output" or suprathreshold dosages of electricity -- doses in calculated excess of that required to induce the adequate seizure for the purpose of eliminating neural connections. Inducing adequate seizures with the least amount of electrical energy possible, then, is both the definition of and justification for "ECT" continuing as a viable procedure subsequent to 1976, the refinement of and adherence to minimal stimulus, the sole validation for a standard and the device's recommended placement into Category II. That suprathreshold dosing is not merely a variation of ECT, but rather an entirely different procedure with an entirely different aim becomes overtly manifest via Utah's, FDA's, and APA's redundant delineation of "ECT" both as the employment of convulsion theory based on the induction of adequate seizure alone, and by the diametrically opposed depictions of safe versus hazardous within these same reports, in short, minimal stimulus versus suprathreshold dosing. Not only do Utah, FDA, and by compulsion, APA all agree in 1978 that the Congressional conformation to a reasonable risk -benefit ratio with "ECT" must incorporate minimal stimulus induced adequate seizures with Brief Pulse, but the literature too, indicates the refinement of and so increased safety of "ECT" via just above threshold convulsions versus suprathreshold outputs, the latter of which consistently identifies SW as both hazardous and unnecessary. Indeed, all four American manufacturers, Medcraft, MECTA, Somatics, and Elcot (now defunct) adamantly deny any description of their devices as electro-dependent, all insisting their devices are built upon the validity of convulsion theory or the so-called therapeutic benefit of the "adequate seizure" alone. That manufacturers not only regularly lied regarding minimal stimulus during the entirety of the SW era, but that manufacturers of modern-day Brief Pulse devices similarly prevaricate and rationalize today is highly indicative, as we shall see, that ECT--minimal stimulus induced adequate seizures is, in fact, ineffective, as all manufacturers know. Consequently, just as it was "ENR" administered by the SW devices of the past, it is "ENR" which is administered by the Brief Pulse devices of today. Conversely, it is "ECT," not "ENR" which is described during the SW Era of the past, thus "ECT" alone which was grandfathered into the new BP Era. Once again then, despite the ENR devices extant today, it is "ECT" which continues to be spuriously depicted by current Brief Pulse manufacturers. Clearly, "ENR" or the use of electro-dependent devices requiring adequate dosages of electricity for the express purpose of damaging thousands of neurotransmitters is not "Electro Convulsive Therapy. " ENR is clearly not ECT based on convulsion theory or the so-called adequate convulsion. Nor has "ENR" or electro-dependent devices ever been described in the literature as a therapy. [79] In any case, it is certainly not ENR which was "grandfathered in," in 1976, but ECT alone.

Anti-Psychiatry

In the early 1970s, a new movement was born--the anti-psychiatry movement, mainly centered around the outcome and abuse of so-called "ECT. " Out of this movement, a challenge was issued based on numerous documented memory complaints and the exhaustive advocacy by Californian Leonard Roy Frank, editor of

---

[79] A few experimental subliminal, non-convulsive devices appeared in the 1950s which were apparently neither harmful nor effective. These early subliminal devices were neither ECT nor ENR apparatuses.

Madness Network News, (Frank, 1978), a founding member of NAPA (Network Against Psychiatric Abuse) as well as Marilyn Rice and her Committee For Truth in Psychiatry consisting of hundreds of self-deemed "shock survivors" (Cameron, 1979),[80] together with a handful of responsible physicians and PHDs such as John Friedberg (Friedberg, 1977), Peter Breggin (Breggin, 1979), Lee Coleman (Coleman, 1984), Peter Sterling, Robert Grimm, and others. This movement, together with the 1976 Congressional mandate to scrutinize all Neurological Devices, put tremendous pressure on the "ECT" industry as a whole. For the industry to survive; therefore, the old "ECT" (actually "ENR") had to be eliminated, at least superficially, [81] and the "new and improved ECT" ushered in. From about 1978 forward, the industry had to promise, in essence, that forthwith, only true "ECT" would be permitted, and so came the inauguration of the "new and improved" BP Era.

Not coincidentally, thanks to FDA's new 1976 role of monitoring all medical devices, a new ECT era was ushered in. Indeed, most device manufacturers felt "ECT" could only re-enter the market-place with the "new and improved, kinder and gentler" "ECT" devices -- namely Brief Pulse. [82] As we shall see, however, the BP Era eventually devolves into the second great cover-up (the first, the total mischaracterization of SW as an "ECT" or minimal stimulus device and thus the complete cover-up of SW as what we now know to be ENR). Because the lie of convulsive therapy remained intact before, throughout, and following the 1976-1982 FDA hearings on ECT, manufacturers, in order to continue marketing ECT devices at all, were first made to produce true ECT devices, and then, when they fail to work, forced to carry forth the cover-up into the latter part of the twentieth and beginning of the twenty first centuries, as we shall see. In short, both non-professionals and medical professionals alike were and continue to be misinformed that ECT, via the reduced EO Brief Pulse device, is administered with much less output and so much less risk than the older more destructive SW devices and that seizures are induced at half - if not one third - the Energy Output of SW. Indeed, both manufacturers and the APA continue to assure both professionals and non-professionals alike that the new BP apparatuses induce equally effective seizures with much lower output than SW so that "ECT" has been vastly improved over that which it was. [83] In fact, as we shall see, manufacturers have progressively and surreptitiously enhanced the newly resurrected Brief Pulse devices beginning about 1982, just as SW devices of old were enhanced. Indeed, the longstanding lie of the minimal stimulus induced therapeutic seizure has remained unexposed--until now. In short, as we shall see, both the SW devices of the past and the most modern day Brief Pulse devices of the present, are not the ECT devices they are claimed to be, but rather, once again, have devolved into ENR devices. As we shall see, the so-called ECT device, just as ECT itself, is a totally illusory procedure.

---

[80] Following Rice's death, Committee for Truth in Psychiatry was taken over by Linda Andre, author of *Doctors of Deception—What They Don't Want You to Know about Shock Treatment* (Andre L., 2009).

[81] Academically, it was Friedberg's (Friedberg, 1976; 1978) and Breggin's brilliant research (Breggin, 1979), inspired by lay scientists Marilyn Rice (Rice, 1982) and Leonard Roy Frank (1979) - both injured geniuses from shock, which sounded or should have sounded the death knoll for SW devices in America. Sociologically, it should also be mentioned that CCHR (Citizen's Commission On Human Rights), through unrelenting criticism of "ECT," also aided in what should have been the demise of SW in America and were present during the 1982 hearings before the FDA.

[82] It is quite possible that Medcraft's B-24 continued to be clinicians main instrument of choice for another five or more years, until the introduction of the BP souped-up pre-calibrated devices beginning in 1982.

[83] At first, both BL and UL ECT electrode placement were declared equally effective (Malitz et al., 1986).

Chapter 5

1979 FDA Public Hearing on ECT

In promising a new American standard oriented around the development of the "new and improved" BP device, the electroshock industry had already won the major battle against "ECT" critics in winning the fight for FDA approval for the ongoing existence of the procedure itself. (Both SW and the resurrected BP device were deemed "ECT" devices and so allowed "grandfathering.") Less crucial, but still important, was the re-classification of the Brief Pulse device from Class III (most dangerous; tenuous; unproven, grandfathered; unstandardized; etc.) to Class II (safer; standardized, etc.), based upon a promised minimal stimulus standard. On May 29, 1979, FDA held the first public hearing on "ECT" inviting general commentary from manufacturers and professionals, as well as the lay public. Following the hearing, a separate non-FDA Panel of salaried experts was to determine whether or not the machine would be reclassified (Food and Drug Administration, 1978, November 28, p.55729; Food and Drug Administration, 1979, May 29). Based upon the Utah recommendation that a standard insuring both safety and efficacy could indeed be written, the FDA Neurological Device Classification Panel (the FDA advisory committee) had already issued their recommendation that the device be grouped with Class II (Food and Drug Administration, 1978, November 28, p.55729). Class III, the lowest classification, of course, includes grandfathered-in medical devices for which it is not yet discernible that an FDA approvable standard ensuring reasonable safety and efficacy parameters can be or has been written. Regardless of classification, however, manufacturers of "ECT" devices, through the grandfathering loophole (and because FDA via Utah and the APA had become convinced a standard could in time be written), would be allowed to continue manufacturing and marketing their apparatuses even without an FDA approved standard. Manufacturers needed only apply for "pre-market approval" in order to continue marketing their devices, a process good for up to 30 months [84] of delay (Food and Drug Administration, 1979, May 29, p.77, 127) whereas in the meantime, devices would be allowed to retail.

In main, FDA's new investigatory duty endowed FDA with the responsibility of forcing manufacturers of all new medical devices to provide proof of reasonable safety and efficacy, ensured by a specific acceptable standard, before marketing their devices. Conversely, FDA was to prohibit any new devices for which potential for harm unreasonably exceeded potential for benefit, and so for which no approvable standard could be written. Although older pre-1976 "ECT" devices could be investigated by the same criteria as the newer devices, due to the "grandfathering" clause, the process for disallowing any device which appears to have been in existence before 1976 became a much more tenuous undertaking and procrastination worked on the side of the manufacturers. On the other hand, while the FDA could not disallow "ECT" devices simply for having no standard (because of their pre-1976 existence), the FDA Advisory Panel's recommendation that Brief Pulse ECT be grouped into Class II was entirely based on the strong contingency that "establishing a performance Standard for this device be a high priority" (Food and Drug Administration, 1978, November 28, p.55729). The following are verbal excerpts from the 1979 Public hearing.

---

[84] Paradoxically, pre-market approval for grandfathered devices needed only consist of proof that the device in question was comparable to devices marketed before 1976 (Congressional authorization of the FDA to scrutinize medical devices). On the other hand, pre-market approval attained in this manner without a written approved standard, and without conforming to the FDA criteria for safety and efficacy required of all new medical devices, might yet have to remain in Class III. In fact, this was exactly the case with "ECT" devices, which, because there is yet no approved standard, remains in Class III to this day.

Dr. Mark L. Dyken - *(Chairperson Neurological Section: Respiratory and Nervous Systems Devices Panel, Voting participant - Advisory Committee)* - "[T]he charge of this committee today is simply . . . to address the question, 'Does sufficient information exist for the establishment of a performance Standard to provide reasonable assurance of the device's safety and effectiveness. ' [D]r. Munzer will again review very simply what Class II means and what our charge is, concerning this classification. "

Dr. Robert F. Munzer, Ph. D. (FDA) - ". . . The . . . [question] is 'Can the safety and effectiveness of this device with respect to the persons for whom it is intended . . . be reasonably assured by means of a Standard?' From the House Report there is a statement: 'The key concept -- the safety and effectiveness of a device -- are to be determined 'weighing any probable benefit against any probable risk of injury or illness from such use' - makes it clear that the . . . legislation recognizes that products having the power to be useful in the healing arts also have the potential to do harm, and that the determination of safety and effectiveness is to carefully balance these considerations. Regulation cannot eliminate all risks, but rather must eliminate those risks which are unreasonable in relation to the benefits derived. " [85] (Food and Drug Administration, 1979, May 29, pp.97-99)

Following FDA Panelist Munzer's statement above, APA presented its' arguments proposing Class II placement of (Brief Pulse) ECT devices prior to submission of a written standard -- that is -- based on the mere promise of a specific standard to be proffered within a very few months (Ibid, pp.76-77). Numerous lay individuals and entities, including Marilyn Rice and her advocacy group, *Committee For Truth In Psychiatry*, an organization of deeply disgruntled "ECT" survivors concerned over devastating memory dysfunction as a result of the procedure, and an issue over which Rice had become convinced, pertained to one hundred percent of "ECT" recipients, argued passionately for leaving the device in Class III. Heavily influenced by new information submitted from new BP manufacturer MECTA Corporation (originally - Custom Systems, Incorporated) maintaining that BP, by virtue of its ability to induce adequate seizures with much lower energy output dramatically improving the procedure's safety (particularly regarding memory) (Grahn et al. , 1977), the Utah investigatory team and thus the FDA, had already concluded that a standard for reasonable safety and efficacy could indeed be written (Grahn et al. , 1977). Based upon Utah's findings, it seemed clear to the FDA and in turn those individuals and panelists attending the 1979 FDA Hearing, that a "new and improved" ECT device with a "reasonably assured" degree of safety was possible simply by supplanting the higher electrical energy output of SW devices with the lower electrical energy output of BP devices. Concerns of high output expressed by the advocacy organization, *Public Citizen*, are addressed by FDA Panelist Veale.

Mr. Veale (FDA Panelist) - "I presume . . . your basic concern is the amount of energy supplied. . . . The wave form itself has a great bearing on the energy that is supplied. . . Am I correct in saying that what you are concerned about is not applying more energy than is necessary?"

Mr. Leflar (Public Citizen Health Research Group) - "Correct. " (Food and Drug Administration, 1979, May 29, pp.51-52)

---

[85] Utah-FDA appear to have had no notion that hazardous and efficacious electrical energy dosages might be one and the same so that a standard providing for simultaneous safety and efficacy could never be written. Indeed, it is for this very reason that even forty-five years later to date beginning with Congressional authorization for FDA scrutiny of "ECT" in 1976, that there is no official standard for "ECT." Indeed it is for this reason manufacturers have altogether avoided submission of a standard for FDA scrutiny. Moreover, it is for this reason, too, that the American Psychiatric Association - in spite of numerous promises to the contrary, has avoided and delayed into oblivion for more than forty-five years to date – FDA submission of a simple specific Energy Output and Dosage Standard (minima and maxima) for BP devices. While there is an unofficial default standard upon which manufacturers base their Brief Pulse devices, as we shall later see, it is a standard which would or should never pass FDA scrutiny for simultaneous safety and effectiveness.

Picking up his cue from the FDA adopted Utah report, Richard Weiner, Chairman of the1978 APA Task Force on ECT, indeed encouraged the FDA Panel to consider the improved safety of the "new and improved" BP device versus the higher output SW:

> Dr. Weiner - "[O]bviously the use of a briefer, narrower pulse width allows one to induce a generalized seizure with a lower total amount of energy . . . Well, their [the Utah Report; FDA Advisory Panel] conclusion was that performance Standards could be written. " (Food and Drug Administration, 1979, May 29, p.81)
>
> I would think that as soon as the draft of the report [that is --the APA recommended Standard] is available, it would probably have some effect in terms of Clinicians. I might mention that the use of lower energy devices - this [BP] device from Custom Systems, Incorporated [MECTA] is selling very well, and is replacing the other [higher energy SW] machines. It is still used less than the other machines, but I think it soon will overtake the Reiter [Molac II (SW)], and may already have. I do not have enough data and the Reiter is no longer being sold. (Ibid, p.83)
>
> It is very difficult to separate dosage from wave form, because the amount of dosage is related to the type of wave form that you use. The studies that have compared over the years -- brief pulse versus sine wave forms -- have found that acutely there is less confusion and less acute signs of impairment with the low energy stimulus. (Food and Drug Administration, 1979, May 29, p.88)

Unbeknownst to the FDA at the time of these 1979 hearings, MECTA, as hitherto noted, had already moved to a slightly more powerful BP machine than the device submitted in 1976 to the Utah-FDA investigatory team of Grahn and associates (Grahn et al. , 1977; Weiner, 1979; 1980). The device originally submitted, most probably the initial MECTA "C" is described by Grahn and associates as having an energy output ceiling of 81 Joules and a narrow pulse width capable of inducing seizures at one quarter the Energy Output of Medcraft's B-24 SW. The B-24, on the other hand, and as reported by Utah, had an energy output ceiling of 145 Joules deliverable in a shorter span of time (Grahn et al. , 1977), thereby utilizing much greater energy output to induce the same "adequate seizure. " [86]

In fact, known only to MECTA and affiliates, the initial 81J MECTA "C" device, may have already proven ineffective. By 1979, therefore, MECTA had already created a later model MECTA "C" (for BL Brief Pulse minimal stimulus) with an enhanced 108J ceiling as well as a wider pulse width potential, resulting, in increased dosing, now one-half (not one quarter) the Energy Output of SW (Department of Health and Human Services, 1982c, pp. G3-G4; Grahn et al. , 1977; Weiner, 1979; 1980). [87] In light of the Utah-FDA conclusion that forthcoming BP apparatuses offer greater safety by virtue of lower Energy Output, the decreasing power discrepancy between Medcraft's B-24 SW and the later MECTA "C" (going from one-fourth the power of SW to one half the power of SW), might have been of interest to FDA, a fact which went unreported by MECTA, Weiner, and the American Psychiatric Association until 1982, virtually the conclusion of the formal FDA investigation into "ECT" (Department of Health and Human Services, 1982c, pp. G3-G4). Significantly, MECTA BP devices, as we shall see, from 1982 forward, begin creeping stealthily upwards in terms of power.

Vital to the enhanced safety of BP's lower energy output and FDA's endorsement of Brief Pulse in 1976 and 1979, is, of course, the FDA Advisory Panelists' unquestioned assumption that the "ECT" procedure works solely by virtue of the adequate seizure and that the BP device at just above threshold is just as effective as SW which delivers much higher outputs. In responding to Dr. Stevens' comments below then, APA ECT Task Force Chairman, electrical engineer, and manufacturer spokesperson--psychiatrist Richard Weiner, encourages the idea of Brief Pulse efficacy at just above convulsion threshold.

> Dr. Stevens - "I would like to make a comment in this connection. This problem has not been addressed -- this issue of energy -- how much energy should be imposed. It is difficult to quantitate. The problem is that if you do not give enough [output] to cause a convulsion -- the

[86] Weiner later asserts that the SW device emits 200 maximum Joules.

[87] Of course, the one quarter output figure was already dubious in that 4 x 81 = 324J, not 145J or even 200J.

convulsion is the therapeutic phenomenon, regardless of how it gets there -- then the patient has what is called a missed convulsion. It has no therapeutic effect whatsoever . . . . So the Clinician has to decide whether he wants to give perhaps a little excess -- which may be harmful -- or not enough -- and have a missed convulsion -- which is very undesirable. That is the doctor's dilemma in this predicament. Am I correct, Dr. Weiner?" (Food and Drug Administration, 1979, May 29, p.90)

Dr. Weiner - "The important therapeutic factor in ECT is the production of a generalized seizure, at least electrographically. . . . All one needs [is] to have a seizure which has sufficient duration [*25 seconds or more*], so one does need to give enough stimulus energy, in whatever form it is, to produce a grand mal seizure of sufficient length on electrographic criteria. " (Ibid)

Plainly, due to Utah's research followed by corroborative testimony from Weiner consistent with those conclusions, the 1979 FDA Panelists were under the firm impression that grand mal seizure alone is the therapeutic agent responsible for the efficacy of "ECT. " In terms of safety, then, as verified by Weiner (several paragraphs) above, the logical aim is adequate grand mal seizure with the most minimal electrical dosage or energy output reasonably possible, the coming standard of which, as noted, was to assure this dynamic. Virtually nothing is suggested by manufacturers or professionals in the 1979 FDA Hearings (or in the Utah Report) indicating the need for multi-fold suprathreshold dosages of electricity to achieve efficacy with either bilateral or unilateral "ECT. " [88] [89] Utah's Report incorporative of numerous rediscovered comparative EEG studies contrasting minimal stimulus (administered with the reduced output experimental devices of the past) with suprathreshold dosing (using standard SW), unequivocally convinced FDA Panelists that Energy Output in excess of that required to induce the "adequate seizure" is both unnecessary and potentially harmful, that the aim of ECT is just enough energy to induce the adequate seizure and no more. Indeed, Weiner, representing both the APA and the manufacturers,[90] gives the FDA Panelists no reason to believe otherwise, thereby bolstering the unquestioned "maxim" regarding the efficacy of the adequate seizure with just above threshold output using Brief Pulse. Moreover, Weiner fails to report to the FDA the moderate enhancement of the MECTA "C" (Weiner, 1979; 1980); neither does he report any efficacy issues associated with the earlier, less powerful model "C" in spite of the capacity of both models to induce the same adequate grand mal seizure.

Instead, the *1978 APA Task Force Report on ECT,* (American Psychiatric Association Task Force on ECT, 1978; Welch et al, 1982) the Utah Report, and Weiner's personal testimony before the FDA (1979 Panelists), all uniformly confirm the notion that "ECT" is effective at just above seizure threshold, so long as the seizures are "adequate. " Minimal stimulus efficacy (the least amount of power required to induce the adequate convulsion) at this time, appears to include not only BL (Bilateral) ECT but also UL (Unilateral) ECT, the latter of which is capable of inducing adequate seizures at half the electrical dosage or Energy Output as that of BL ECT. All these factors convince FDA panelists an enforceable future Standard guaranteeing both safety and efficacy for future consumers, is both writeable and forthcoming,[91] in turn impelling the FDA decision to perpetuate "ECT" generally, in spite of previous consumer complaints. The obvious hope is that the Brief Pulse device, a much more efficient and precise instrument than SW, could induce these adequate seizures with greatly reduced output, thereby eliminating memory confusion, potential brain damage, and recipient complaints. In the following personal testimony from APA Task Force Chairman Richard Weiner regarding BP versus SW, Weiner attempts a dash of gray. Although the Panel clearly understands seizures can be induced with BP at far lower outputs than SW, it is at this point in the hearing that Weiner creates misgivings and confusion in asserting that although UL electrode placement results in dramatic reduction of memory loss compared to BL (even apparently with Brief Pulse), no specific wave form [BP over SW] can be definitively recommended at this time so that more studies would be needed (Ibid, p.89).

---

[88] Over the next twenty years, Brief Pulse manufacturers slowly begin acknowledging the need for suprathreshold dosing, first with UL, then with BL in order to make the procedure effective. The author maintains that manufacturers and other proponents of the procedure understood or should have understood this fact at the time of the 1979 hearings.

[89] By 1995, as we shall see, BP devices are surreptitiously delivering a circa five times threshold output for BL "ECT" (two and one half times threshold in terms of charge), and circa ten times threshold output for UL "ECT."

[90] No manufacturers appear at the public hearings.

[91] It was the line of reasoning that BP was effective at minimal stimulus which seduced the FDA into granting tremendous leniency and time to the APA to develop a Standard. To this date, no Standard has been forthcoming.

> Dr. Weiner - "[T]he studies that have kind of looked more carefully at memory aspects a little further down the road than just the first couple of days have found it difficult to separate the two [waveforms - BP versus SW]. [92] Now, that has been different in terms of electrode placement -- unilateral versus bilateral electrode placement -- where clearly, if you look a week down the road, there is still a marked difference in the level of impairment, with less impairment present with the unilateral electrode placement. " (Ibid, p.88)

In light of all the evidence, the assertion that it is difficult to separate the two waveforms with respect to memory appears counterintuitive. Does Weiner make this statement because he is representing both MECTA (the BP manufacturer) and Medcraft (the one remaining SW manufacturer)? Or is Weiner's statement foreboding of much more powerful future Brief Pulse devices, which because of their necessarily increasing power over time, as we shall see, eventually lose their cognitive advantage over SW? In short, does Weiner know something the panelists don't? Noteworthy too, is the fact that no manufacturer representative appears at the 1979 FDA public hearing. Richard Weiner represents them all. Consequently, it is Richard Weiner, APA Task Force Chairman on ECT, whose responsibility it becomes to create the first American Standard for ECT. [93] Panelist Chairman Dr. Munzer Ph. D. publicly notes:

> Chairman Munzer: - "We sent out invitations to all the manufacturers of ECT equipment, but none of them have . . come. " (Food and Drug Administration, 1979, May 29, p.73) [94]

Immediately following Munzer's observation, APA Task Force Chairman Richard Weiner, M. D. , Ph. D. , is introduced to the Panel. It is Richard Weiner then, who acts as spokesperson for both manufacturers and the APA, and who, as Chairman of the APA Task Force on ECT, is assigned the role of generating the first American Standard for ECT, conflicting roles which Weiner continues to play for the next forty-five years following this, the first FDA hearing on ECT up to the date of this publication (2023). Arguing on behalf of APA and manufacturers [95] that devices should be placed in Class II (in lieu of Class III), Weiner informs FDA Panelists that he is indeed working on the required Standard, but for some reason, in spite of what should have been a fairly straightforward regulatory brief, Weiner claims the task cannot be completed for another several years, surprising for an industry in a seeming hurry to become legitimized by a Class II or even Class I rating.

> Dr. Weiner - I am addressing this panel in my capacity as Chairperson of the Task Force on the Development of Safety and Performance Standards for ECT Devices of the American Psychiatric Association, which is at work on the development of Standards for ECT devices in collaboration with the American National Standards Institute [ANSI] . . . . (Ibid, p.73)

---

[92] This statement may be designed to suggest that memory damage is reversible with both SW and BP devices, an irresponsible and untenable implication in total contradiction to the 1950 Janis study (Janis, 1950) as well as later studies by Squire (Squire and Zouzounis, 1986; Squire and Slater, 1983; Squire and Chace, 1975). In order to prove BP safer than SW, Weiner will perform numerous NIMH funded anterograde memory tests unlike the retrograde memory tests of Janis and Squire, both of which validated long term permanent memory loss and loss of personal experiences. Though Weiner does not directly express his convictions before Marilyn Rice or the FDA Panelists, Weiner had by this time already published his opinion that memory complaints are mere hysteria (Weiner, 1979; 1980), an unsubstantiated theme with which Weiner and a handful of manufacturer-related "ECT" academics would flood the literature for the next twenty-five years (Fink, 1978; 1979; Cameron, 1994). As we shall later see, almost all of Weiner's safety tests with Brief Pulse, including prospective memory measurements, are performed at minimal stimulus only, in direct contradiction to clinically applied BP dosages later discovered to be suprathreshold.

[93] With the FDA hearings, the Reiter Company decided to permanently close its doors.

[94] Manufacturers have not addressed the FDA panel in any FDA public hearing to date. Their sole representative and spokesperson appears to be Richard Weiner of the APA. Manufacturers of "ECT" devices may not have survived FDA scrutiny without the very clever, anomalous mathematical machinations of APA Representative, Richard Weiner, as we shall see.

[95] Weiner's dual role as manufacturer spokesperson, in essence—lobbyist, and APA chairman of the APA Task Force on ECT should have been seen as a conflict of interests. Nevertheless, the Panel entrusted Weiner and the Task Force with the charge of creating the first American Standard for ECT.

> Dr. [Ann] Barnet [Panel Consultant] - . . . Do you know when the Task Force might be ready to suggest some Standards?. .
>
> Dr. Weiner - . . . I quoted a figure of two years. I would hope before that time we would have a draft available. Of course, this has to go through various kinds of consensus procedures to be acknowledged as a national Standard, and we are going to be working with the American National Standards Institute [ANSI] in that capacity. (Ibid, p.82-83)

Nevertheless, Weiner assures the Panel, a standard can be written:

> Dr. Weiner - "Our [APA] Task Force . . . is in unanimous agreement that sufficient information is or shortly will be available . . . to arrive at a recommended Standard which will act to influence both manufacturers and users [doctors] of ECT equipment towards maximizing the design and use with respect to safety considerations. (Food and Drug Administration, 1979, May 29, p.76)

When the Panel questions Weiner about specific electrical parameters, Weiner remains vague:

> Dr. Weiner - The extent to which we [will] be able to get specific is hard to tell . . . .
>
> Dr. Wald - Well, after forty years of use there still seems to be quite a bit of controversy as to what is best, whatever best may be. Do you think you are able to bring it all to the point that you know now what is best?
>
> Dr. Weiner - I think we will be able to bring it to a point where we can bring a greater focus, both on the part of the manufacturers and the Users [doctors], on safety and performance aspects of the devices. That I think we can do. In terms of coming up with an optimal set of parameters, and all sorts of parameters, I do not think we can do that. (Food and Drug Administration, 1979, May 29, p.84)

Suspicion is cast upon Weiner's refusal to depict specific electrical parameters and so whether or not a Standard can indeed be written.

> Dr. Frances Conley M. D. (voting Panelist) - . . . There is no mention of power sources, forces, amperage, voltage, anything of this sort. . . . I do not know how you can build a machine without having some idea of where your starting parameters are and what is going to determine your parameters.
>
> Dr. Wald - I also wonder if even markings on the machine are rated in terms of energy or just numbers, 1, 2, 3, 4, 5. [96] I have not seen evidence that there is sufficient data to write a Standard for the device.
>
> Dr. Wepsic - One of the things that bothers me is the fact that no manufacturer of these devices is here, nor has there been any comment that they have been in touch with the panel to discuss their equipment, how it is used, what the parameters are and what they are looking for in terms of use of the device. (Food and Drug Administration, 1979, May 29, p.106)

Dr. Stevens comments on the non-specific description of BP devices, making the viable point:

> Dr. Stevens - . . . I do not think that at the end of ten years there will be any more significant information, and by significant I mean as far as determining what parameters should be used

[96] At the time MECTA's second generation SR 1 and 2 series emerged in 1983, the power dial contained 256 increments. While not identified as such, the increments almost certainly stand for actual Energy Output in joules of which the second generation MECTA device is fully capable (Cameron, 1994).

for the treatment of patients, so I think the argument of, 'Let us wait and get more information,' would project us into infinity . . .. [97] (Ibid, p.109-110)

FDA continues to press APA Representative Weiner regarding the relationship between lower energy and a specific - not a general - standard.

Mr. Veale [FDA] - . . . Presumably what you would want to see in a premarket approval application is some justification for this particular device that they are promoting and want to sell, some justification of why they think this device is safe and why they think it is effective. And that justification would be in terms of studies that have been done on the device, studies that have been done on the energy that the device uses and the clinical reports on the device. . . . What you may well find is that the data that you get in premarket approval applications is the data that you have before you now. . ..

Dr. Shelley Chou M. D. [FDA Panelist] - I am just wondering in my own mind who is going to come up with some data to answer the questions that Mr. Leflar this morning came up with.

Mr. Veale - The questions regarding energy?

Dr. Chou - Regarding energy and wave form and all that.

Dr. John L. Lacy, Ph. D. [FDA Panel Consultant] - Well, I imagine the first thing is that we are going to have the report of the APA Task Force. . ..

Here Weiner begins to backtrack, promising a specific Standard.

Dr. Weiner - I do not anticipate just a general Standard of the type that Grahn suggested [Grahn et al. , 1977 (Utah Report)]. I will let that much out. I think we can be more specific about that. Exactly what we are going to recommend, there is no way I can say that. But I think the information is there. The members of the task force, I will say, are leaning towards recommending, now . . . , going into the literature survey, recommending for a brief pulse stimulus. But we are going to try and be open-minded and look and see if we can justify this as well as we think we can. But I am sorry if I gave the impression that we are just interested in writing a general Standard . . ..

Mr. Veale [FDA] - The Utah report mentioned something about energy limits of .6 to 81 Joules. [98] Aside from the actual values, do you think you will be coming up with minima and maxima?

Dr. Weiner - Oh, certainly. We drew up the things that we are going to go into . . . and these included the wave forms, the voltage, the currents, the total energy, the pulse width, the inter-pulse interval, the size of the electrodes, the location of the electrodes, the means in which the electrodes were coupled to the skin. We are going to look into this very, very carefully and we are going to come up with some recommendations.

Mr. Veale - As far as wave form is concerned, I believe the basic argument has always centered around sine wave versus square [brief] pulse.

---

[97] In spite of Weiner's indication that specific parameters are not possible, FDA's demand for specific metrics regarding electrical energy or dosage ceilings were actually quite reasonable. In fact, as we shall later see, manufacturers of present day devices successfully hide important parameters, including output energy in joules which might expose the modern day BP device as anything but minimal stimulus and, therefore, a hazardous device, the constitution of which strongly implicates electricity - not convulsion - as the agent responsible for both efficacy and long-term memory dysfunction.

[98] Note how the FDA, based on the Utah Report, believes BP devices will be limited to somewhere around 81 Joules, the limits of the prototypical MECTA "C" originally presented to the FDA, but which had already been replaced with a later 108J MECTA "C." Later BP devices, as we shall see, will far exceed the 108J MECTA "C."

Dr. Weiner - Right. (Ibid, 130-133)

FDA now presses for a deadline.

> Mr. Veale - There are several factors in how long it would be before . . an FDA regulation Standard would be effective. One is how long it would take committee to develop it, and I understand that is estimated to be one to two years, something like that.
>
> Dr. Weiner - My best guess now is between one and two years, yes. [99]
>
> Mr. Veale - Once it is developed, then the process that the FDA has to go through to adopt it could take - - How long do you estimate it would take?
>
> Dr. Block [FDA] - . . . We want the task force to develop a Standard; we would like then to get consensus throughout all interested parties, which would then lead to an American National Standard. . . . Now, that whole consensus process could take, I would say, up to two years. The minimal consensus, going through APA, might only take several months.
>
> Dr. Wald Ph. D. [FDA Panelist] - After it is written.
>
> Dr. Block [FDA] - Right. After you have your first draft. In other words, the first draft would then go through APA. So I would say you are probably talking, before you get an American National Standard, of perhaps a total of three years, whereas you might have a draft within, say one year to 18 months. [100] (Ibid, p.137)

In fact, there is no question that minimal stimulus Brief Pulse results in a dramatic reduction of memory loss. What Weiner, representing both the APA Task Force on ECT and the ECT manufacturers does not share with the Panel is that which Weiner himself, MECTA, and Medcraft must all have at least suspected, that neither bilateral nor unilateral minimal stimulus induced adequate seizures are “therapeutically” effective, that ECT itself—based on the so-called "therapeutic seizure" is a myth. Indeed, the only procedure that is "effective," as time will tell, is "ENR," Electro Neuro-Transmitter Reduction which only "works" through adequate amounts of electricity well over threshold. This, however, is information which neither Weiner nor the manufacturers wish to reveal. That the effect depends upon doses of electricity suspected of damaging the brain means that by its very nature, what is actually "ENR" can never be administered "safely," particularly with respect to memory. As such, unbeknownst to FDA, manufacturers would never allow a standard to be written limiting ECT to minimal stimulus, or if written, manufacturers would never allow its adoption. To do so, would spell the end of the "ECT" industry. This is because "ECT" is not "ECT" at all, but rather "ENR" as we shall ultimately see.

Indeed, not until 1990, do manufacturers make clear their declaration that Brief Pulse unilateral “ECT” at just above threshold, is ineffective,[101] that it is to be deemed "dose-sensitive" and so must be administered at twice threshold to be “effective. ” Moreover, while manufacturers will continue to maintain that BL ECT is effective at just above threshold, manufacturers will eventually justify administering even BL "ECT" at twice threshold and more, as we shall observe. In truth, as noted above, both BL and UL minimal stimulus induced seizures are and always have been ineffective, a fact established as early as 1950 during the experimental phase of the SW Era (Cameron, 1994) of which both Weiner and U. S. manufacturers must have been aware. But because manufacturers of the SW era suppressed this information in order to continue selling their brain

---

[99] Weiner and the Task Force, pressed by the FDA, finally submit an ECT Standard in 1982, the last year of the FDA public hearings.

[100] While the APA does submit a standard to the FDA in 1982, to date, no American Standard has ever been recorded by ANSI, nor has APA ever submitted or applied for an American Standard with ANSI (Sackeim, 1991, p.235). Neither did the APA Task Force push for adoption of the submitted standard, instead choosing to delay for further “refinement.” There is a distinct advantage for manufacturers’ avoidance of specific standards. Without such specifics, it is difficult for the FDA to demand pre-market approval which by definition need comply to a set standard. (Food and Drug Administration, 1979, May 29, p.128). Meanwhile all manufacturers continue marketing their devices fifty years later via “grandfathering.”

[101] By 1994, as we shall see, it will be equally “discovered” that bilateral “ECT” induced adequate seizures at just above threshold is also ineffective, a fact which should have been understood by SW manufacturers from at least 1957 as well as BP manufacturers who were allegedly improving, via reduced output, the excessive electrical dosing of SW (Cameron, 1994; Impastato et al., 1957).

stultifying SW devices, modern Brief Pulse manufacturers have had to suppress this information yet again for the entirety of the Brief Pulse Era, now some forty-five years later.

Unfortunately, neither Utah nor the FDA were aware of these facts in 1979, so that their conclusions at the end of the 1976-1982 FDA hearings that improvements were possible via the reduced output BP waveform and via unilateral electrode placement, both of which could supposedly render equally adequate seizures, were never to come to fruition. Improvement through reduced output Brief Pulse and UL ECT, however, were firmly and optimistically seeded in Panelists' minds, all of whom were determined to modernize "ECT" with a new standard limiting electrical output to just above threshold output with Brief Pulse. And so, while Weiner and the APA Task Force were compelled to write such a standard, a standard mandating minimal stimulus Brief Pulse outputs to be deemed "the 1982 APA Standard for ECT," as we shall see, not surprisingly, adoption of this standard will be continually deferred and so ultimately never officialized. Moreover, FDA cannot know what Weiner and the manufacturers already knew, that true minimal stimulus is, in fact, ineffective with both BL and UL electrode placement even though both produce adequate seizures. Neither can FDA know that modern Brief Pulse manufacturers will work to totally suppress these facts with numerous deceptive reporting stratagems covering up the true future power of modern day Brief Pulse apparatuses. Finally, FDA cannot know that Brief Pulse manufacturers under Weiner will tirelessly work to surreptitiously circumvent the 1982 APA Standard foisted upon manufacturers in 1982, as we shall observe.

Thus, while the standard both Utah and the FDA looked for would never be accepted by the manufacturers and so would never be officially adopted by the FDA with manufacturer approval, manufacturers' promise to write such a standard via their leader, Richard Weiner, enabling BP manufacturers and even Medcraft, the one remaining American SW manufacturer, to circumvent FDA censure. So successful are Weiner's upcoming delay tactics together with manufacturers' spurious reporting methods as we shall see, BP manufacturers not only survive FDA scrutiny under the 1976-1982 FDA hearings, but like the SW manufacturers of the previous era, continue on from 1976 to the present in a near unregulated manner. Extremely reminiscent of the manner in which SW manufacturers evaded scrutiny from 1950 to 1976, surviving the early experimental failures of UL and BP minimal stimulus occurring between 1942 and 1957, so manufacturers of what are soon to become extremely powerful Brief Pulse devices emitting outputs far above threshold, manage to avoid detection of their machines' excessive power. In each respective era then, repression of the debunking of convulsion theory generally, spurious reporting, non-reporting, and fictitious claims of minimal stimulus, successfully combine to camouflage simple, crucial information which, revealed to authorities, would make clear the impossibility of "safety" regarding the "ECT" procedure generally-- with either SW or with Brief Pulse. The inability to adhere to a standard requiring minimal stimulus induced adequate seizures and so the impossibility of guaranteeing a reasonably safe procedure, is plainly due to the inextricable necessity of having machines based on adequate doses of electricity well above threshold in order to damage the brain (Breggin) in the form of neurotransmitter death, very probably leading, if revealed, to abandonment of the procedure altogether [102] [103] or if not abandonment, to the procedure's use in a far more limited fashion.

Following the 1979 hearing, the voluntary panel of experts formed by the FDA were tasked with voting whether to move the device into Class II or retain it in Class III. Suspicious of a non-specified standard, that is, a standard which might prove too general, and what some suspected to be the avoidance of a standard altogether, the Panel of experts wisely decided to retain the device in Class III until an acceptable standard could be written, submitted, and officially adopted. That the device continues to remain in Class III even today speaks volumes.

---

[102] Whereas BP manufacturers have successfully delayed the submission of a specific standard for over forty-five years, covering up the increasing electrical energy of their devices, SW manufacturers, not having to contend with the FDA during the past or the modern era, have simply ignored the existence of lower energy devices capable of inducing the same adequate seizures as SW but which manufacturers know to be ineffective. Indeed, during the SW era, SW manufacturers simply claimed their devices minimal stimulus or "ECT" devices in that there was no FDA to regulate them. The re-introduction of BP in 1976, although BP had been utilized more than twenty five years earlier - as well as the ensuing mathematical cover-up, is a direct result of FDA intervention demanding lower Energy Output devices.

[103] It has been fully understood by device manufacturers for almost fifty years that so-called adequate convulsions have no therapeutic value whatsoever and that hazardous or brain damaging electrical dosages must be applied for efficacy. The procedure cannot be made safe in that efficacy and damage are one and the same (see Breggin).

Chapter 6

FDA "Invites" APA to Develop a Standard

Based upon the UBTL-FDA[104] investigation and the Advisory Panel's conclusions, APA had little choice but to agree with the FDA's "invitation" to develop the proposed standard (Department of Health and Human Services, 1982a, p. A41). Consequently, the newly formed 1978-79 APA Task Force was forced to define and write regulatory language for ECT as it was described in the literature (reviewed by Utah) and as Medcraft and other manufacturers had (misleadingly) been describing it for at least twenty-five years. In short, "electro convulsive therapy" relies on the therapeutic effect of electrically induced adequate seizures alone wherein electricity's only alleged role is in inducing the adequate seizure. Based on convulsion theory, in brief, adequate seizures induced with lower EO Brief Pulse should have been just as effective as adequate seizures induced by the much more powerful SW apparatus. (Utah had successfully identified SW as suprathreshold compared to BP [105] [106].) Facing possible loss of the procedure entirely, the 1979 APA Task Force on ECT, therefore, obligated itself to writing a standard identifying minimal stimulus parameters via utilization of the reduced output Brief Pulse device, a device capable of inducing the same adequate seizures at one-quarter to one third to one half the EO of Medcraft's B-24 SW device (Weiner, 1979).

In a letter dated July 9, 1979, slightly more than one month following the 1979 FDA Public Hearing for ECT device classification, the Medical Director of the American Psychiatric Association, Melvin Sabshin M. D. wrote the following comments to the 1979 Acting Commissioner of Food and Drug Administration, Sherwin Gardner.

> Melvin Sabshin M. D. - "The main points of contention respecting waveform parameters concern square wave [low energy BP] versus sine wave stimulus waveform shape . . . There have been numerous studies of stimulus waveform shape in both animals and humans spanning a period of over thirty-five years. These studies have shown that brief duration stimulus waveforms produce less acute central nervous system (CHS) side effects and do not compromise therapeutic efficacy. The appropriate range of clinically relevant stimulus parameters for this form of stimulus has likewise been investigated and reported. . . . Public investigations have shown that the therapeutic response to ECT is derived from the induction of generalized brain seizure activity, and not from the electrical stimulus. CNS [Central Nervous System] side effects, on the other hand, [may be] related to both the seizure and the stimulus. For these reasons, the use of low-energy stimuli is indicated, as described above. It is also

---

[104] Utah Biomedical Test Laboratory - Food and Drug Administration

[105] Utah apparently never questioned why, by 1957, minimal stimulus devices had been discarded (Cameron, 1994); simply, that the psychiatric literature - even after 1957 - continued to label and describe even the SW procedure as "convulsive therapy" (Medcraft, 1984). In this regard, much of the literature from 1950 to 1976 - a substantial amount of which may have been written or influenced by nondisclosed psychiatrists associated with manufacturers (Cameron, 1994) - as well as information within manufacturers' brochures (Medcraft, 1984) – appears to be spurious, mislabeled and even fraudulent.

[106] Apparently, Utah-FDA had no idea that manufacturers' labeling of SW as "convulsive therapy" had become a convenient and highly deceptive cover-up - that minimal stimulus was even by 1950 determinedly and scrupulously avoided, and that the harmful procedure being applied – what we now know to be ENR - was applied knowingly to recipients in order to achieve "efficacy."

> clear that devices should be limited in energy output to that necessary to induce seizures in nearly all patients. " (American Psychiatric Association, 1979, July 9)

Richard Weiner, Chairman of the 1978-79 APA Task Force, entrusted by the FDA with the task of actually creating the American Standard, confirmed Sabshin's comments in an academic publication dated December of 1979. Weiner acknowledges:

> With brief pulse stimuli, seizures can be induced with a smaller amount of electrical energy than with sine wave stimuli because the flow of the current with brief pulses is intermittent . . . yet the two types of waveforms have similar efficacy. . .. Studies comparing the memory deficits associated with minimally versus markedly suprathreshold electrical stimuli provide evidence that the intensity of the electrical stimulus is . . involved. . . . Generalized seizures can usually be evoked [with the MECTA ECT device] with about one-third the total amount of electrical energy required with sinewave stimuli. . . . This is important in view of the fact that acute cognitive deficits and EEG abnormalities may be related to the amount of electrical energy delivered by the ECT device. (Weiner, 1979, pp.1151, 1153)

A Standard limiting electroconvulsive therapy to BP, then, assuring the induction of adequate seizures with low electrical dosage, while at the same time maintaining the efficacy of SW, seemed to guarantee future recipients of effective treatment together with the reduction or even elimination of cognitive deficits, specifically long-term memory damage. Such an American Standard would seemingly give surety to both the safety and the efficacy of "ECT. "

Chapter 7

Power Enhancements Begin

Conflictingly, Weiner, had become the "ECT" spokesperson to FDA both for the extant manufacturers and the APA. Within months of the FDA's 1979 decision to retain the ECT device in Class III until a safety standard could be written and within months of APA Chairman Weiner's promise to the FDA to complete an American standard specifically limiting output to minimal stimulus with Brief Pulse, Richard Weiner, presiding officer of the *APA Task Force on the Development of a Safety and Performance Standard for Electroconvulsive Therapy Devices*, published a new paper, "ECT and Seizure Threshold: Effects of Stimulus Waveform and Electrode Placement" (Weiner 1980). In the paper, Weiner utilizes the slightly more powerful MECTA "C" BP device noted earlier. Rather than the earlier 81J MECTA "C" BP Device presented by MECTA for the Utah-FDA investigatory report published in 1977 (Grahn et al, 1977), by 1980, MECTA had begun marketing a slightly later model with increased pulse width also known as the MECTA "C,"[107] a device capable not of 81 Joules, but of 108 maximum Joules[108] (Weiner, 1980). In lieu of seizures induced at only one third to one quarter the power of SW, the newer more powerful MECTA device now induced seizures at allegedly half the Energy Output of Medcraft's B-24 (Department of Health and Human Services, 1982a , pp. G3-G4). The fact that even at the time of the 1979 Hearings, MECTA had already begun enhancing the power of its' 81J MECTA BP device with the knowing support of psychiatrist-electrical engineer Richard Weiner, and that this information was not volunteered to the FDA either by MECTA or Weiner until about 1982, is prescient. That the earlier less powerful device, in spite of its' ability to induce the same adequate seizures, may not have been as effective, would, no doubt, as noted, have been of critical interest to the FDA, particularly regarding FDA's new obligation to the public to insure both safety and efficacy wherein benefit exceeds risk. Note instead, that both the APA and Weiner (1980) publicly stated to the FDA that the new Brief Pulse device was effective at minimal stimulus, thereby "validating" convulsion theory, creating the clear impression that a standard assuring the least amount of electricity to induce adequate seizures could indeed be written. Even if FDA had noted the telltale enhancement, however, what FDA could not have predicted was that this was to be the first in a long surreptitious series of Brief Pulse enhancements which would never be reported and have never been reported to date either to the FDA or the American public. But we shall examine this in much greater detail a little later in the manuscript.

---

[107] None of the lettered series are actually identified in these reports. Nevertheless, it is possible to identify them as such through the described electrical parameters.

[108] Such increases in power, if noted at all, were, until very recently, ascribed to exceptional cases in which a seizure could purportedly not be obtained.

Chapter 8

1982 Public Hearing on ECT: *Antipsychiatry Movement Continued:*

Armed with the Utah investigation, FDA, as noted earlier, called for a public hearing in 1982. To make matters even worse for manufacturers, Ken Kesey, a few years before, had released his near fatal novel, *One Flew Over the Cuckoo's Nest* (Kesey, 1962) exposing and deposing shock for exactly what it was during the SW Era - a horribly insidious instrument, often applied without anesthetic, used most often to manage institutionalized patients. The novel, followed by the movie premiering in 1977, was thus an important, brutally raw and deadly accurate portrayal of institutional life and the role played by "shock therapy." The book's classical significance rivals Sinclair Lewis's portrayal of big business via his novel *Babbitt* (Lewis) or Upton Sinclair's portrayal of unregulated big business via his novel, *The Jungle.* (Sinclair). Every man, woman, and teenager in America instantly recognized as authentic, the cruel portrayal of the mental institutions of the 1950s and their mission to control "patients" through electroshock shock and psychosurgery. No amount of counter-propaganda on the part of the "ECT" industry depicting the practice of "ECT" as a medical procedure has ever been able to wholly erase from public awareness that era's shameful enactment of man's inhumanity to man. It was a time, after all, when "mental patients" had no rights whatsoever. Moreover, it was still well before the Supreme Court decision declaring involuntary commitment of an individual neither dangerous to one's self or others, unconstitutional (O'Connor v. Donaldson 1975). Kesey's novel, the 1975 Supreme Court decision and the 1977 movie, *One Flew Over the Cuckoo's Nest,* played a key role in forcing society and the "mental health" industry to re-examine not only psychosurgery, but "ECT" and how it was used institutionally. [109] In fact, it helped force the "ECT" industry to at least begin using anesthesia, and at least attempt to introduce a "new and improved ECT" far less harmful than SW. Indeed, it was the 1976 Congressional mandate to approve new medical devices such as "ECT" which kickstarted ECT's meaningful scrutiny.

Hand in hand with the . . . *Cuckoo's Nest* "fiction," an embarrassing new movement - the anti-psychiatry movement emerged - making itself known through protests, books, rallies, television, radio, scientific articles, and even state referendums. Many of these groups and individuals, victims of the procedures and the ravages of institutional life, found, for the first time in history, the courage to speak out against the cruelty and barbarism of their institutional experiences, in particular, forced "ECT," many of them maimed authors with first-hand knowledge (Farmer, 1973; Frank, 1978; Field, 1964; Cameron, 1979; Chamberlin, 1977; Gotkin and Gotkin, 1974; Andre, 1982; 2009; Rice 1982; Lapon 1986). The "Movement," as it came to be called, which also included a handful of courageous physicians and professionals (Coleman, Sterling, Friedberg, Szasz, Grimm, Breggin) was replete with individuals who began exposing the results of so-called "ECT" (and other forms of psychiatric "treatment") in, perhaps, an even more menacing manner than *Cuckoo's Nest* - through their own immediate experiences in the form of personal testimony and letters to the FDA and other governing bodies.

---

[109] Practitioners, at least, began anesthetizing recipients.

Moreover, APA and the manufacturers fully realized they would encounter this movement at the FDA 1982 public hearing and perhaps on an ongoing basis. [110] [111] [112]

Medcraft, the one remaining manufacturer from the past, by itself could never have withstood the onslaught of movement leaders appearing before the FDA Neurological Device Panel. Nor could Medcraft have defended the Energy Output levels its B-24 SW utilized. Written testimony from articulate victims, well-known anti-psychiatry leaders - Ken Donaldon, Lenny Lapon, George Ebert, Joy Rose, Marilyn Rice, Mary Redfield (alias Ellen Field), Lenny Lapon, Marjorie Faeder, Jeanne Lindsay, (Janet Gotkin was scheduled to appear but couldn't attend), and Don Johnson - many of whom had written and published books and all of whom provided hard-hitting heartbreaking testimonials of their experiences with "ECT," crushed any idea that the procedure was "safe. " In fact, not a single "ECT" recipient appeared to defend the procedure. Too, Ted Chabasinski's famous Berkeley referendum banning "ECT" from the Berkeley city limits occurred in 1982, toward the end of the FDA investigation with much national publicity. There could be no defense and indeed APA didn't even try. Only one argument could keep "ECT" alive - a "new and improved" device, one that had not victimized those currently testifying. Thus, the new reduced output Brief Pulse inducing adequate convulsions at just above threshold with half the EO of the Medcraft device became the essence of the APA justification for continuing the procedure beyond the FDA investigation. Not surprisingly, crafty Medcraft never publicly appeared and tellingly, continues to make the same device today. Almost no one realized that Medcraft was the single SW device manufacturer left in the U. S. at the time, in essence the only manufacturer left which had produced "ECT" devices before 1976. Had the anti-psychiatry movement realized the sparseness of their opponents, they might have descended upon the Connecticut based company with loud and persistent protests.

Pro-movement groups opposing reclassifying ECT into a safer category included Robert Leflar, attorney for the advocacy group, Public Citizen funded by Ralph Nader, who spoke of the many reports of memory loss, and Linda Purdue of Citizens Commission on Human Rights who testified that ECT is " only . . . effective and reliable in producing . . . erasure of memory." Purdue quoted Californian psychiatrist Frank Jobody that "the manifestation of . . . damage to the temporal lobes and other parts of the brain is amnesia . . . . " However, only one actual ECT recipient was allowed to testify and that was Marilyn Rice. In fact, amongst all the experts, it was former researcher and ECT recipient, New Yorker, Marilyn Rice alone, who understood the true nature of what was happening with the ECT apparatus and who fully understood the importance of blocking its legitimization as a Class II or even Class I device for the upcoming generations. In short, it was chiefly Rice's testimony which prevented the device's rise from Class III to Class II or even Class I. Here is part of her testimony:

> Let me take a moment to explain who I am. I am a former economist, accountant, and statistician, now retired due to brain and mouth damage. The mouth damage comes from insane dentistry. The brain damage is due to electric shock. The connection is that I became so debilitated and depressed over what was being done to my mouth . . . that I fell Into the hands of the psychiatrists. . . . I might say that 25 years of expertise in my own field was . . .

---

[110] Susan Foote, a Berkeley professor and tough consumer specialist hired for a time by FDA within whose city of Berkeley, a temporary ban on shock would soon be temporarily enacted, in 1982, lent an ear to consumer complaints and so voiced distrust for the APA-shock industry marriage, expressing dismay at APA's appearing before the FDA in lieu of manufacturers. No manufacturer representative, other than Weiner, made an appearance.

[111] In 1986, two former shock recipients, Cameron and Loper, led a successful legislative attempt to outlaw forced "ECT" in Texas, ultimately prohibiting the procedure for minors under sixteen and requiring a signature for each individual treatment from any who "volunteered" for the procedure. Other dramatic examples are replete throughout the history.

[112] The classical and effective strategy against the validity of such claims is to call all such complainers, "Scientologists." While it is true Scientologists, as a group, have long opposed bio-psychiatry and certainly "ECT," the anti-psychiatry movement did not spring from Scientology, but rather is the natural child of suppression, torture, and the unconscionable condition of rightlessness. To be clear, during the SW era, most "ECT" in the U.S. (and elsewhere) had been administered against the will of the individual. Both the negative publicity of *Cuckoo's Nest,* the anti-psychiatry movement, exposure by Scientology, new laws enabling the right to refuse in a few states, and finally the 1976 FDA investigation, forced the "ECT" industry to remake the image of "ECT." To combat the anti-psychiatry movement in general, spokespersons for the "ECT" industry resorted to denial of long term memory loss, labeling all memory complaints, hysteria, drug related, or repercussions of mental illness, and calling all who oppose "ECT "Scientologists." In fact, APA was forced at long last to require anesthesia for all "ECT" procedures, and to support the resurrection of the "new and improved ECT"--in short--Brief Pulse.

> knocked out. But I certainly did not forget how to conduct research. And it is as an expert on electric shock, not just as a pitiful shock patient, that I would like to make the following remarks. The objective of this Panel's concern with electroconvulsive therapy, ECT, is to assure the safety of the electrical devices used to trigger convulsions. Safety, in this context, means mainly safety to memory. It is the long-run effect upon memory that is causing so much worry about this treatment. For an ECT device to be safe, the shock it delivers should not permanently wipe out or dim years of the patient's past. . . . What is in dispute is the condition of the patient's memory in the long run. Patients report that the recovery of memory is not complete. Almost any ex-patient will say that his memory of the past remained forever dimmed, with the dimming amounting to erasure of many events, of the years most recently preceding the shocks. The better educated will describe the dimming and erasure of the knowledge they possessed prior to the shocking. Psychiatrists, on the other hand, in person and in their literature, insist that memory fully returns after convulsive therapy. Article after article, book after book, proclaims as much with authors emphatically quoting each other to prove it. . . . Who Is lying? Is it the doctors, or is it the patients? . . . I would recommend that ECT devices be classified in Class III . . . not because I believe that any measure of control over shock machines will change the overall memory effect of ECT, but because [and here she quotes Public Citizen] 'The announcement of the Class III designation and surrounding publicity would have an educative effect; . . . dissemination of [this] information would cut back on present abuse of ECT. '

FDA consultant Dr Ann Barnet inquires of Rice:

> Dr Ann Barnet: Did your research lead you to believe that the amount of energy delivered to the patient has anything to do with the long-term effects on memory?
>
> Rice: It convinces me it has not. This question was gone into very thoroughly in the early 15 years, say, of shocking: 'Could we not set off a fit with lesser amperage, or better wave forms?' They definitely could, but with less therapeutic efficacy. It was always that way. It seemed to take a certain amount of brain damage to get a certain amount of therapeutic effect.
>
> Now ultimately . . . there were about 20 studies that are very germane to this question. . . . finally they came out with the pragmatic rule that 20 gentle shocks by the better type of electrical form equaled 12 ordinary shocks. . . . So at that point, there had just been enough experimentation. [113] Now many years have passed and it seems that that has been forgotten. And it seems that somebody may be wanting to spend a lot of money opening up the same question. But I would recommend that anyone who wants to go into that question should first sit down with the studies that have been made, and then see if they want to do it all over . . . 'He who does not learn by history is bound to repeat it. '

Rice's words would prove prophetic. In studying the same psychiatric literature, she had clearly seen what even Utah had failed to observe and what Weiner and company refused to acknowledge—that minimal stimulus was ineffective and the new machines would begin increasing in electrical power once again harming recipients in order to make the procedure "effective. " Rice's insight, however, failed to inspire FDA to object to Weiner's and Utah's claim that MECTA had re-discovered the new and improved reduced output device everyone was looking for. On the other hand, Rice was instrumental in getting the FDA to remain wary of placing the device in Class II without the actual adoption of a specific standard compelling the minimal stimulus output the prototypical MECTA "C" exemplified to the FDA. Thus, while Rice could not stop the FDA from allowing "ECT" to persist after 1976, Rice had predicted that repeating the experiments of the 40s and 50s with Brief Pulse and other less powerful devices would eventually lead to the same tragic injuries manufacturers of the earlier SW era had known were required of this flawed "treatment. " With her acute logic, in any case, Rice had helped

---

[113] The indication is "they" stopped making the "gentle" machines.

influence the FDA to remain cautious of the promise of a "new and improved" device and to leave the device in Class III until a standard regulating output was actually written, adopted, and enforced.

Thus, it was, in main, the psychiatric survivor movement in conjunction with FDA scrutiny, that forced the waning "ECT" industry, under the auspices of Weiner and the APA, to act quickly and in co-operation with one another to write an American standard. Leary that the anti-psychiatry movement might otherwise achieve a ban, the ECT industry via their spokesperson Richard Weiner had been forced to convince the FDA that a truly reduced output device had arrived in the form of Brief Pulse which could actually replace SW. Moreover, it had to do so by actually writing and presenting a regulatory standard to that effect.

Chapter 9

Richard Weiner's 1982 Petition To Reclassify

By the time the 1982 public hearings were held, MECTA had switched yet again from the more powerful 108J MECTA "C" Brief Pulse device to a newer even more powerful circa 140J MECTA "D" Brief Pulse device. The "D" was similar to the later "C" except that the "D" now incorporated "Impedance Override. " In lieu of automatically limiting output to a maximum Impedance, the limiting mechanism could now be overridden. This enabled the machine to induce not a 108J maximum, but now up to 140 maximum Joules, nevertheless, an improvement over SW. This, however, did not keep Weiner, (as he had in 1979 and as does MECTA and other manufacturers even today), from under-reporting the Energy Output of the newest MECTA device in his 1982 "Petition to Reclassify. " Although MECTA now utilized the 140J "D" device, Weiner reported to the FDA only 100 maximum Joules for the Brief Pulse device (Department of Health and Human Services, 1982a, G4), similar to the 108J "C" device. In that the Medcraft B-24 SW device was capable of emitting 200J (in rare circumstances), Brief Pulse at a 100J (and even at a 108J) maximum, could still be touted as half the power of SW.

For the 1982 public hearings, the APA (American Psychiatric Association), via Weiner's newly submitted "Petition To Reclassify . . . " formally petitioned FDA to reclassify the "ECT" machine from Category III (unrated and unsafe) to Category I, (provably safe neurological devices with standards), in essence, unreserved FDA approval for both safety and efficacy wherein benefit unquestionably exceeds risk (Department of Health and Human Services, 1982a). Following the May 28th,1976 Medical Device Amendments Act, the Congressional mandate authorizing FDA to scrutinize all new Neurological devices, (Department of Health and Human Services, 1982c, p.121), "ECT" devices, as previously noted, had been automatically grandfathered into Category III (Food and Drug Administration, 1979, September 4). Thus, following the 1979 FDA public hearing, "ECT" continued to remain in category III until APA could submit a convincing standard regulating excessive output and subsequently attain FDA approval. As of May, 1976, then, previous neurological devices were allowed to continue on the American Marketplace unfettered, even without a pre-market application and even without a written Standard, bypassing the normal FDA approval process wherein benefit must be shown to exceed "reasonable" risk. Thenceforward, of course, that is, subsequent to 1976, manufacturers of new medical devices were required to submit industry Standards based on proven results before being marketed. Thus, by an unpropitious and unwise caveat in the law pertaining to previously utilized ongoing devices, "ECT" manufacturers enjoyed the unearned privilege of their apparatuses being "grandfathered in" (Department of Health and Human Services, 1982c, pp.121; 211-212). Had a pre-marketing statement based on reasonable risk, in turn based on a written performance standard been required for "ECT" devices (in lieu of "grandfathering" or merely having to present evidence that current devices were comparable to those previously manufactured), had there been no exception in the law regarding previously utilized devices, or had the so-called "ECT" machine not been in continual use before and up to FDA authorization to scrutinize all new

Neurological devices, "ECT" devices might possibly have never erupted onto the U. S. marketplace (Cameron, 1979; Department of Health and Human Services, 1982c, p.223). [114] [115]

With the caveat in place, however, manufacturers of devices before 1976, even those manufacturers marketing machines with no approved standard whatsoever, needed only apply for pre-market approval by a May 28, 1982 deadline (Food and Drug Administration, 1979, September 4, p.51776). Moreover, while the pre-market approval was supposed to be based on safety and efficacy testing, if such testing could not be provided, manufacturers had the option of simply showing their current devices comparable to previously manufactured devices. [116] Because Medcraft (the single remaining U. S. SW manufacturer) was yet producing the same (and so "comparable") instrument it had in the 1950s, Medcraft soon realized that as long as its device was "effective," the FDA could not demand even the simplest proof of safety for its B-24 SW apparatus, a gadget which had been unrestrictedly, coercively, and terroristically employed against US citizenry for almost forty consecutive years (Department of Health and Human Services, 1982c, p.223; Cameron, 1997; Hotchner, 1966; Redman, 1961; Cameron 1979,1997; Chamberlin, 1977; Farmer, 1973; Frank, 1978, Gotkin and Gotkin, 1974; Redman, 1961, Lapon, 1986; Andre, 1989; Plath, 1971; Susko, 1991). Thus, in spite of receiving hundreds of complaints regarding SW memory devastation as well as ample criticism from any number of consumer organizations, FDA could do nothing to prevent Medcraft from continuing to market its device. The only hope for regulation lay in the adoption of a written standard circumscribing electrical output to minimal stimulus or about 100 maximum joules via Brief Pulse instrumentation.

Regardless of the fact that SW devices had for years been universally utilized for management of institutionalized patients, and had a reputation with those on the receiving end of it as a ghastly and fearful instrument, (Cameron, 1979,1997; Frank, 1978), and finally in spite of Utah's uncovering of numerous comparative studies showing much greater cognizant deficiency and even brain damage with SW as opposed to minimal stimulus Brief Pulse, Medcraft made no attempt whatsoever to improve the safety of the B-24 by reducing what were obviously unnecessarily suprathreshold doses of electricity. Medcraft only knew that as long as no standard was adopted, FDA could not prohibit it from marketing its previously extant device. Indeed, a few clinicians were known to prefer the SW device specifically for the cognitive deficiency it inflicted (Breggin, 1979, pp.178-182; Fink, 1957; Fink, Kahn, and Green, 1958). [117] In that the clientele for SW devices had in large been institutions interested in managing mental patients who had no self-preservation rights whatsoever, marketing the procedure to “consumers” or demonstrating actual “safety” had never before been a marketing priority for Medcraft. Indeed, although it could not compete with Brief Pulse regarding safety, and although Medcraft did create a sort of Brief Pulse device for which there has never been much demand (as we shall see), because there was yet a market for SW, Medcraft offered no improvements to its B-24 SW (by reducing output) other than encouraging the use of anesthesia. In light of the reduced output, more humane device, MECTA had exhibited to the FDA via It prototypical MECTA "C," modern day validity of SW as a caring or even valid "medical device" -- not merely a human cattle prod -- proved difficult, if not impossible. The MECTA "C" Brief Pulse, after all, could allegedly do the same job at half the output, and so half the memory damage. In conclusion, Medcraft did nothing. All they did or could do was wait for the death knell of SW in the form of the new American standard. On the other hand, perhaps Medcraft knew something FDA did not.

---

[114] The spirit of the grandfathering clause was that if a device had been in use for a period of time before 1976, and if the device was still in use, the device had proved itself time-tested. However, no provision had been made for a device applied against the will of a marginal population for almost forty years. Congress certainly needs an exception for such caveats. In short, if there are too many complaints, or if force was commonly used, simultaneous safety and efficacy should be shown before a machine’s continued utilization as if it were a new device.

[115] At the date of this publication, the device remains in Class III and no performance Standard has ever been submitted by manufacturers for FDA adoption.

[116] That this device should have been allowed by the Congress of the United States of America amidst the moans of thousands of U.S. citizens crying for redress and complaining of permanent memory loss (Department of Health and Human Services, 1982c, p.232), comprises a kind of legal travesty for which there can be no common-sense defense.

[117] The theory then and now regarding “ECT,” though rarely acknowledged today, is behavioral modification as a result of surgically altering the brain (Fink, 1957; Fink et al., 1958).

Richard Weiner and the Re-birth of "ECT"

"ECT" nearly died a natural death. The only U. S. SW manufacturer remaining -- Medcraft -- extant longer than any other SW manufacturer in US history,[118] hung on under overwhelming adversity (Department of Health and Human Services, 1982c, p.223), virtually the only "ECT" device persisting in the psychiatric arsenal. Yet even as the anti-psychiatry movement began breathing a sigh of relief, institutions in need of this managerial device, bitterly complained. Without these instruments of control, clinicians became disgruntled, family members, incensed. After all, from the perspective of those not on the receiving end of this powerful behavior modifier-- "it worked!" Drugs, they held, were not always "effective" -- or too slow. With the unpopularity and gradual demise of lobotomy, moreover, "ECT" had become the new mainstay of a coercive unregulated mental health industry heavily dependent upon shock or the mere threat of it as its sledge, a simply irreplaceable sledge. Conversely, from the perspective of the thousands of "ECT" recipients who had been subjected to it, almost all of whom had received forced unanesthetized "ECT" during the SW era, the memory devastating "ECT" device was nothing less than insidious (Frank). Moreover, the bitter anti-psychiatry struggle against "ECT" had not been without influence. By 1976, the year of the first FDA "ECT" investigation and in many ways, the beginning of a new patient rights movement, "ECT," like lobotomy, had become totally entombed in the dark reputation its' barbaric history so richly deserved (Department of Health and Human Services,1982c, pp.230-231).

With new FDA scrutiny, then, were ECT to continue post FDA scrutiny, a "new and improved" apparatus had to replace the old one; safety advances had to be asserted. In short, the ECT industry had now been forced to re-make its image. To do this, as we have seen, manufacturers resurrected Brief Pulse from the 1940s along with the then novel universal policy of providing "ECT" recipients with anesthesia. (Cameron 1994; Liberson 1948; Blachley, 1976a). Once Brief Pulse had been resuscitated, the incipient Brief Pulse company MECTA, just as SW manufacturers of the past had done, anxiously reached out to the protective arms of the APA, as did, problematically enough, the one remaining U. S. SW manufacturer - Medcraft (Department of Health and Human Services, 1982c, p.223).

Richard Weiner, an electrical engineer-psychiatrist engaged in aiding MECTA with its new and improved BP device, emerged as the industry's neo-modern champion and defender -- a new-sprung hero of the bio-psychiatry movement, now suddenly the foremost patron of and spokesperson for the re-emergence of the "new and improved" Brief Pulse device. In short, Weiner agreed to take on the task of representing both the APA (Department of Health and Human Services, 1982b, p.3) and the "ECT" manufacturers to the FDA in hopes of saving, improving, and re-making the image of "ECT" for a new era in which patient rights had quite precipitously become, at least, somewhat significant (Department of Health and Human Services, 1982a; 1982c, p.222).[119]

Highly credentialed, Weiner's intentions did not appear malevolent. Indeed, there seemed to be every indication he was sincere in his efforts to build a new and improved apparatus (p.13), a kinder, gentler device (p.13; Department of Health and Human Services, 1982a, pp. G3-G4) empathizing with those thousands of US (and Eurasian) citizens who had heretofore been damaged with the archaic SW instruments of the past. Promising to write a standard enforcing the use of the lower energy Brief Pulse device, Weiner seemed to be seeking the elimination of SW altogether, along with its memory damaging tribulations. In fact, all the evidence indicated that Weiner was an avid believer in minimal stimulus (p. A20, A45; Department of Health and Human Services, 1982c, p.236), a true Ottossonian[120] (Department of Health and Human Services, 1982a, A40-A41; Ottosson, 1960), one who sincerely believed in the revitalized Brief Pulse's capacity to isolate what all true believers of convulsion theory believed in—the grand mal seizure as the sole, authentic corrective (Department

---

[118] Medcraft has been in business making shock devices since about 1945 - first a slightly weaker model, then, since 1950 to the present a more powerful model, the BS-24. Individuals shocked with SW in the U.S. were probably shocked with the Medcraft BS-24 capable of 200 Joules of Energy Output not including Glissando. Medcraft continues to make the same device up to the very date of this publication.

[119] Weiner has continued in this role for some forty-five years. In some respects, Weiner might be looked at as a highly paid lobbyist.

[120] Ottosson (1960) and followers were convinced of the convulsion theory invented by Von Meduna (1938) - the theory that the adequate grand mal seizures evinced contained an unknown curative or therapeutic ameliorative. Ottoson's beliefs were rooted in the erroneous identification of convulsions as the common therapeutic agent in chemically, as well as electrically induced seizures. It is now understood that the agency in those early experiments was chemical inducer itself- just as the electricity has now been identified as the primary agent in "ECT" efficacy (Robin and Tissera, 1982), both of which are harmful. It seems more and more likely that the convulsion in ENR is nothing but a "convenient" side-effect (1982).

of Health and Human Services, 1982c, p.236). Brief Pulse, after all, via greatly reduced electrical energy, seemed capable of isolating the seizure from excessive electricity, eliminating the devastating cognitive impairment reflective of deeply disturbing brain damage. The damage, of course, could be solely attributable to high electrical energy SW devices such as the Medcraft B-24 and the Molac II.

It may be that the potential to actualize such a breakthrough possibility - separation of the therapeutic convulsion from the damaging side-effects of high electrical output seduced Weiner wholeheartedly, that it appealed to him as the kind of opportunity of which every scientist dreams. If it could be shown that the therapeutic agent was an actual isolatable entity - not merely electrical brain damage-- if the convulsion actually did release some esoteric yet unidentified chemical-then perhaps this chemical could be secluded, identified and applied even sans the electrical (or chemical) injury which had always heretofore accompanied it. Or if the adequate convulsion could be induced with the most minimal electrical output possible through Brief Pulse, thereby eliminating the damaging side-effects of electricity to memory - such an achievement might prove comparable to the cure for polio, or even cancer. Separating the therapeutic grand mal convulsion from the suprathreshold electrical dosing present in SW resulting in unnecessary memory and quite possibly brain damage (Liberson 1948; Ottosson 1960; Wilcox 1946) might well prove the long-awaited cure for certain types of "mental illnesses," particularly the longest-standing bane of humankind--depression.

In short, just as Ottosson (1960) had been convinced in 1960 and Liberson in 1940, isolatable grand mal convulsions (through BP) once again appeared to be emerging as a true medicinal agent for depression and other so-called mental illnesses, a tremendous blessing for those miserably languishing in the throes of these "cerebral ailments." Moreover, proving isolatable convulsions as the successful ameliorative would go a long way in proving the existence of mental illness itself as a verifiable and actual medical disease. In fact, the successful separation of the therapeutic effects of convulsion from electrical brain damage and/or memory trauma would prove ECT critics wrong -- critics who had dared to identify the so-called "therapeutic" effect of "ECT" as nothing more than brain damage – the origin, however, of which even the most ardent opponents of the procedure chiefly associated with the excessive electricity utilized in SW (Breggin 1979; Department of Health and Human Services, 1982a, p.21). Weiner would at long last prove these critics wrong, critics like Peter Breggin who had famously proclaimed that separation of the ameliorant and brain damage was impossible in that the damage and the "treatment" were one (Breggin, 1979).

"Infidels" and "disbelievers" such as psychiatrists Peter Breggin and Lee Coleman, neurologists like John Friedberg and neuroscientists like Peter Sterling who for years had flagrantly and blasphemously denied any therapeutic value of convulsion would finally be proven wrong! (Breggin, 1979, 1991; Friedberg, 1976, 1977). Skeptics and heretics such as psychiatrist Thomas Szasz and R. D. Laing who had vociferously endorsed the sacrilegious notion that so-called "mental illness" has no physical basis at all -- but is rather mental, emotional, or even spiritual in nature (Laing, 1967; Szasz, 1974) would once and for all be humbled, even humiliated. [121]

Much then, appeared to be at stake -- perhaps the viability of biological psychiatry itself--the mainstay philosophy of which assumes "mental illness" to be a true physical disease which can, therefore, be cured somatically. To modern psychiatric orthodoxy, the potential demise of ECT must have appeared as if the old Freudians, the repugnant environmentalists of the past, had risen from the dead in an attempt to destroy the neo-mental health fundamentalism of the modern era -- bio-psychiatry. It was a high religious war; Weiner, bio-psychiatry's newest high priest.

That Weiner was probably sincere in his efforts to utilize ECT at threshold, and that he was absolutely convinced that just above threshold seizures administered with Brief Pulse are as effective as suprathreshold administered seizures with SW cannot be doubted if one goes by Weiner's Petition and Weiner's earlier statements up through about 1982. Certainly, Weiner's convictions regarding the safety and efficacy of just above threshold seizures are replete throughout his [122] APA Petition to the FDA, several examples of which we have observed. [123]

---

[121] Szasz maintains that there can be no medical cure for "mental illnesses" in that these "illnesses" are medical non-entities; as physical diseases, they simply do not exist.

[122] Weiner, the Chairman of the APA Task Force on ECT, authored the APA Petition to Reclassify.

[123] While Weiner was aware of the failed BP experiments of the 1940s and 1950s (Weiner, 1988), it is possible that Weiner believed BP had never been given a fair chance (Department of Health and Human Services, 1982a,), first because clinical practitioners were unwilling to give up the habit of SW and secondly because the earlier studies may have been methodologically flawed and therefore "did not make a major impact on clinical practice" (p. E12). On the other hand, Weiner cannot avoid knowledge that the later BP devices are electro-oriented.

The APA/Weiner defense for the continuation of "ECT" at these hearings, in short, is clearly the resurrection of Brief Pulse in conjunction with the basis for "ECT" itself-- "convulsion theory"--which espouses the efficacy of adequate convulsion alone, a proposition, albeit suppressed, seemingly disproved some twenty-five or so years earlier and would be again through the modern history of Brief Pulse, as we shall soon see evidenced in this manuscript.

Certainly, a number of new studies cited in Weiner's 1982 Petition, seemed strongly expressive and reinforcing of Ottosson's (1960) antecedent conviction that a grand mal seizure by itself -- certainly not electricity, much less electrical brain damage -- is the true and only therapeutic agent in "ECT. " The main idea is that through the minimal dosage, just above threshold, Brief Pulse device, the "therapeutic convulsion," as an "authentic therapeutic ameliorative" is isolatable from the suprathreshold electrical damage of the older SW devices. (Department of Health and Human Services, 1982a, 1, A40-A41; Fink, 1979, pp 21-29; Greenblatt, 1977, pp.13-23; Small and Small, 1981; Weiner, 1979). Within the Summary Minutes of Weiner's 1982 *Petition To Reclassify ECT Devices*, Weiner, delineates the following:

> The petition . . included the results of recent studies which were performed to measure the amount of energy required to produce seizures with various types of waveforms. It was found that brief pulses would induce seizures with considerably less energy than sine wave. (Weiner, Department of Health and Human Services, 1982b, p.5)

Weiner next relates to the FDA, his conviction in the efficacy of adequate seizures at minimal stimulus and his familiarity of the early reduced output devices:

> The original choice of stimulus waveform [SW]. . . was based upon convenience rather than upon any scientific rationale (Cerletti and Bini, 1938). Within a few years, Liberson (1945), Offner (1946) and others began to work with waveforms having a shorter phase duration [BP], finding that these were more energy efficient with respect to seizure threshold, and as therapeutically effective. (Department of Health and Human Services, 1982a, p. E12)

That Weiner is an apparent Ottossonian (disciple of Ottosson who believed in the efficacy of the adequate seizure alone) is found in these statements within the same petition:

> The major recognized therapeutic factor with ECT is its ability to produce generalized seizure activity. . . . [P]atients who do not seize . . or who develop abbreviated seizures (e. g. Ottosson, 1960) . . . do not respond well. (Department of Health and Human Services, 1982a, p. E9)

And again:

> That the electricity itself is not a major therapeutic agent is substantiated by the equal therapeutic results of chemically induced seizures. [124] (Department of Health and Human Services, 1982a, p. E12)

Thus, Weiner appears to have been a full-fledged disciple of convulsion theory. In addressing the FDA, he clearly appears inspired by minimal stimulus BP "stolidly grounded" in "convulsion theory" and its' numerous progenitors. While writing on, commenting upon, and submitting the *1982 Petition to Reclassify*, the 108J MECTA "C" BP device and the 140J MECTA "D" were in effect. At this juncture, while these devices were already growing progressively more powerful, the two were yet limited to a 1.1 and 1.4 threshold output respectively and so minimal stimulus (although the "D" had "Impedance Override"). While the "D" did breach the APA guidelines (of a 110J ceiling) it supposedly did so only if Impedance became exceptionally high. In fact, if an actual maximum impedance of about 400 ohms is used to calculate actual maximum Energy Output of these devices, Weiner correctly reports the actual maximum figures of 100-110 Joules to the FDA, at least for the MECTA "C" (Department of Health and Human Services, 1982a, p. A12). In that both the MECTA "C" and "D" [125] appear to conform to the actual Energy Output limit (within the 1982 APA Standard) in most

[124] This line of reasoning is now known to be incorrect. The efficacy of these techniques was almost certainly due to the damage each of these procedures wreaked on their victims (Robin and Tissera, 1982).

[125] In fact, the 134-140J MECTA "D" actually violated the 110J 1982 APA ceiling.

circumstances as we shall see, Weiner, in 1982, appears convinced that BP-BL (Brief Pulse bilateral) placement and BP-UL (Brief Pulse unilateral) placement just above threshold electrical doses are both therapeutically effective so that suprathreshold or at least super suprathreshold doses of electrical energy are unnecessary. [126] [127]

In the 1982 public testimony portion of the hearing, while conversing with FDA panel consultant, Dr. Frances Conley, Weiner clearly takes the position suggested by Utah, that "ECT" should be administered with minimal stimulus Brief Pulse output and that the American standard should reflect this. Conley pointedly asks Weiner:

> Conley - Is the unilateral application of electrodes versus bilateral; sine wave versus pulse wave; really important in terms of the development of the optimal machine that is going to guarantee efficacy and safety? . . [C]an a Standard be written at the present time which can assure "adequacy" of seizure threshold within confines?
>
> Weiner - The adequacy of seizure thresholds - there is no question. I can't imagine people would have an argument on that based on the data that we have collected. . . . [W]e are claiming, based on the data, that both unilateral and bilateral and sine wave or pulse are equally effective. (Department of Health and Human Services, 1982c, p.236)

That both Weiner and MECTA (for whom Weiner spoke) unequivocally hold seizure alone to be the therapy in "ECT," that the purpose and successful goal of the MECTA "C" and "D" BP devices was induction of adequate seizures with minimal or (just above) threshold dosages of electricity, and that both UL and BL ECT at Brief Pulse minimal stimulus are equally effective, are all "confirmed" not only by Weiner's statement above, but by Weiner's petition statement below:[128]

> Regardless of electrode placement, the determinant of successful treatment remains the induction of adequately generalized seizures. (Department of Health and Human Services, 1982a, p.4)

Though cautiously, Weiner's 1982 Petition (to the FDA) contains his confirmation of UL efficacy at (just above) threshold output, citing placement (of the electrodes) alone as the corrective:

> The relative efficacy of unilateral nondominant vs. bilateral ECT has been considered in numerous studies. d'Elia and Raotma (1975) . . . observed that the more precise the methodology, the more equivalent the efficacy. (p. E10). . . [A]ll of the . . . studies which found a significant therapeutic advantage for bilateral ECT utilized . . . frontotemporaparietal electrode placement . . . while those who utilized a more widespread frontotemporaparietal placement . . . have reported a relative therapeutic equivalence between the two types of electrode placement. (Department of Health and Human Services, 1982a, p. E11)

In essence, when electrodes have adequate spacing (one electrode placed on a temple and the other toward the back of the head) or UL electrode placement (requiring half the electrical dosage of BL electro

---

[126] The other possibility is that following FDA approval, Brief Pulse manufacturers planned to substitute their then current machines for the more powerful present day models. Unfortunately for Weiner and the APA, Marilyn Rice, an expert in Washington bureaucracy and an injured shock victim, met Weiner head-on with Committee For Truth In Psychiatry and may have foiled Weiner's plans. While Rice never won her law-suit against the Hospital who had shocked her with a MECTA device and ruined her career as a Washington D.C. coordinator for the National Budget, she was influential in stopping the FDA from re-classifying the machine from Category III (most dangerous for which a standard cannot or has not been written) to Category II. While Rice was the only survivor allowed to speak at the 1979 public hearings, Rice petitioned to question Weiner for two hours in front of the FDA. Her petition was denied.

[127] Tellingly, Weiner petitioned not only for Brief Pulse devices, which he favored, but also for SW device companies, both English and American, allegedly seeking to limit SW output to 1.0Amperes (Department of Health and Human Services, 1982a, p.13), somewhat reducing maximum outputs administered in the ten and twenty year old categories with SW Unfortunately, the APA never petitioned the FDA to adopt 1982 APA Standard, therefore, the SW modifications never took place.

[128] While Weiner now publicly denies affiliation with MECTA, he has early roots there. That Weiner aided in editing their manual, appears on MECTA videos.

placement), Weiner claims the outcome seems about as effective as BL electrode placement (electrodes placed on opposite temples). In his Petition, then, Weiner attempts to convince FDA that BP can be and has been successfully resurrected, that BP as a substantially safer treatment mode would soon replace SW, and that minimal stimulus Brief pulse parameters would be written into the first American Standard for "ECT. " If Weiner knew of the early (1940-1950s) failed attempts at Brief Pulse (which he certainly did) perhaps Weiner reasoned that Brief Pulse at that time hadn't prospered due to its novelty or due to the lack of properly informed clinicians regarding its advantages. Perhaps, he reasoned, if clinicians had just been properly informed, they would certainly have seen the advantage and replaced SW with Brief Pulse.

Did They Know?

On the other hand, Weiner and his Brief Pulse manufacturers may have just been biding their time, that is, simply waiting for the investigation to end before augmenting their Brief Pulse devices to the excessive electrical outputs they knew the devices had to emit in order to achieve efficacy, efficacy with respect to the looked for changes in behavior and mood psychiatrists and family members typically seek. Indeed, there is ample evidence in the 1979 hearings that Weiner and the absentee manufacturers hoped for a Class II categorization without having to submit a standard which would lock the devices into minimal stimulus parameters. For example, while in 1979, Weiner admits that ". . . a briefer, narrower pulse width allows one to induce a generalized seizure with a lower total amount of energy . . . " and that Utah had concluded ". . . performance standards could be written" around minimal stimulus parameters (Food and Drug Administration, 1979, May 29, p.81), Weiner continuously retorts, "I do not have enough data" (Ibid, 83) and "The extent to which we will be able to get specific is hard to tell, since we have not completed our review of the literature" (Ibid, 84).

Indeed, amongst the five voting panelists who in 1979 were to decide whether to put the device into Class II or Class III, the final tally appears to have been three for Class III and two for Class II. Only upon failing, then, did Weiner actually pen a standard confining the Brief Pulse device to minimal stimulus, not for adoption, however, but merely in hopes of influencing the Panel's decision to place the Brief Pulse device into Class II. Why, moreover, didn't Weiner report to the FDA a major power augmentation of Brief Pulse devices implemented by both MECTA and Somatics in 1982, just following the close of the FDA investigation, as we shall soon witness?

Chapter 10

The First American Standard, the 1982 APA Standard for BP and SW Devices

Failing to move up from Class III without an actual standard, Weiner finally writes and presents the looked for standard, presenting it to the FDA within the "1982 Petition to Reclassify" just before the close of the investigation. Though never officially adopted, as Weiner was not yet ready to fully commit, Weiner's now often referred to 1982 APA or American Psychiatric Association Standard for ECT was submitted to the FDA for perusal just prior to the investigation's conclusion. Under this standard, SW devices (specifically the Medcraft B-24) were for a period to be allowed to continue until such time BP manufacturers were in full swing. While potentially capable of 200 maximum Joules (Department of Health and Human Services, 1982a, G3-G4), however, the APA Standard would limit SW devices to 170 maximum Joules.

> 5.1:4.1 Sine Wave Devices
> 2a. A maximum stimulus output energy [for sine wave devices] must not exceed 140 Joules @ 220 Ohms, and must not exceed 170 Joules over the entire load range of 100-600 Ohms . . . (Department of Health and Human Services, 1982a, 12).

Though permitted under the standard for a while, the continuation of Medcraft's B-24 SW was to be but a temporary measure until such time all machines could be replaced by Brief Pulse. But why allow SW at all? Could it be that Medcraft knew full well that Brief Pulse devices would soon have to increase in power, approaching and even equaling that of SW in order to be effective? From his personal testimony before the 1982 FDA Panel, Weiner states:

> Some people hear the panel have come to the conclusion . . . from this data - that sine wave is not justifiable for inclusion in the Standard. The eventual Standard as we see it - as a national Standard - might not have sine wave in it - based on input from engineers from the International Electro Technical Commission. (Department of Health and Human Services" 1982**c**, p.237)

Thus, Weiner suggests that once the standard was finalized for official adoption, SW devices would have to go. In the meantime, however, until the finalized standard, SW could remain.

The new American Brief Pulse device manufacturer MECTA, by now producing the MECTA "C" and "D" and an even newer American company, Somatics Inc. , another up and coming Brief Pulse manufacturer with another new BP device known as the "Thymatron" became the looked to Brief Pulse device manufacturers for the United States, both of which would hopefully insure the safety of the "ECT" procedure via reduced EO compared to SW. Indeed, the essence of the 1982 APA Standard (presented within Weiner's *Petition to Reclassify*), that is, what appeared to be the upcoming, but not yet officially adopted Standard for all "ECT" devices contained the following excerpts referring to Brief Pulse parameters:

> 5.1:4.3 Pulse stimuli
>
> 2a. Maximum stimulus output energy must not exceed 70 Joules @ 220 Ohms, and must not exceed 110 Joules over the entire load range of 100 to 600 Ohms, (the use of pulse stimuli is associated with a lower seizure threshold than with . . sine wave stimuli) (Department of Health and Human Services, 1982a, 13).

Included in the standard itself, that is, from Weiner's 1982 *Petition to Reclassify*, is this passage:

> For pulse stimuli, a range of 3 to 100 Joules was found. In terms of upper values, less than 1% of seizure thresholds were greater than 60 Joules. A less conservative stance with respect to allowable output energy maxima appears to be justifiable for the low energy, pulse stimulus, particularly given concern among clinicians about the ability of the device to produce seizures in all patients. Because of this, limits of 70 Joules @ 220 ohms and 110 Joules over the entire applicable load range (100-600 Ohms) appear reasonable. (Department of Health and Human Services, 1982a, E20)

And again from Weiner's 1982 *Petition to Reclassify* incorporating the would be standard:

> Using a pulse device, the [APA] Task Force [1978] has determined that only 0.6% of seizure thresholds were greater than 70 Joules and that none were greater than 100 Joules. (Department of Health and Human Services, 1982a, p. A53)

Thus, according to Weiner, no seizure administered with Brief Pulse, ever requires more than 100 Joules seemingly under any circumstances. The extra ten joules in the 110 Joule ceiling is allowed by the 1982 APA Standard merely to accommodate just above seizure threshold for the oldest most seizure recalcitrant recipient. Consequently, with adoption of the 1982 APA Standard, the Brief Pulse device would never need to surpass nor be allowed to surpass 110 joules, permanently circumscribing all Brief Pulse devices to circa half the power of SW. Apparently, Brief Pulse was capable of inducing adequate seizures with no more than 100 joules in even the oldest most seizure recalcitrant recipient under any conditions. It is from the above statement, therefore, that confining Brief Pulse outputs to a 110J maximum insures that all outputs for all age recipients are confined to just above minimal stimulus, about which we will go into much more detail in the next section.

In any case, the FDA, prompted by Utah, had what they were looking for with the 1982 APA Standard. Consequently, Weiner representing both the APA and the manufacturers, hoped this would be enough to raise the status of the ECT device from Class III to Class II. Indeed, an official regulatory standard confining all "ECT" devices to 110J, would eliminate SW so that all future devices would be Brief Pulse. In fact, circumscribing all Brief Pulse devices to 110 Joules meant confining all outputs for all age categories to 1.1 fold threshold or just above seizure threshold, as we shall soon see. In short, the APA Standard, if adopted, would insure minimal stimulus for all age categories and so some modicum of safety for consumers. Had the 1982 APA Standard been officially adopted as the U. S. standard for "ECT" then, that is, had the 110J maximum been adopted for all "ECT" devices, Brief Pulse would have eclipsed SW, that is, SW with its excessive brain disabling electrical energy outputs would have been discarded, and minimal stimulus outputs with Brief Pulse, half that of SW would have been guaranteed. Certainly, such a regulatory maxim was exactly what both Utah and FDA had been looking for in an American standard for ECT. In officially adopting the 1982 APA Standard, then, FDA believed some modicum of safety and apparent efficacy (in that Brief Pulse at just above threshold could induce the same adequate seizures as SW) could be assured. Moreover, adopting the 1982 APA Standard would have guaranteed Brief Pulse manufacturers a Class II categorization at the least and perhaps even Class I. So why didn't Weiner and the Brief Pulse manufacturers formally submit the proposed 1982 APA Standard for official FDA adoption? The simple answer is -- devices at minimal stimulus are simply ineffective, information which neither Weiner nor the two Brief Pulse manufacturers knew at the time, or information which neither Weiner nor the two Brief Pulse manufacturers were willing to reveal to the FDA. Indeed, neither Weiner nor the Brief Pulse manufacturers were in a position to ban SW at all, lest Medcraft reveal their secret.

Conclusion

Thus, it was as a result of the resurrection of Liberson's Brief Pulse minimal stimulus device of the past with the concomitant (albeit false) assertion that the device is effective at (just above) threshold with both forms of electrode placement, (as reflected in Weiner's proposed APA Standard) that FDA allowed the ECT industry to cross over into the twenty-first century. The shock industry, then, by promising minimal stimulus, lower output BP, won an enormous victory over the tired, exhausted, and crippled anti-psychiatry movement which, like Rice, could only warn the FDA of the danger of permitting such machines to repeat history, to reiterate what had already been learned during the SW era of the 40s and 50s. It should not surprise anyone, therefore, that Brief Pulse devices surreptitiously increase in power over the next forty-five years as is here revealed in detail within this manuscript.

In any case, by developing the promise of a "new and improved" ECT device in the form of Brief Pulse alone, the demise of “ECT” was fended off and a reprieve gained by the “ECT” industry as a whole. Not surprisingly, moreover, due to Weiner's delay tactics--the 1982 APA Standard was never officially adopted. Yet, it had served its purpose. Through its composition and the promise of its future submission, the "ECT industry" as a whole managed to remain alive. On the other hand, anti-shock advocates did achieve one important goal. So long as the there was no official FDA approved American standard, FDA panelists refused to grant the ECT device a Class II categorization. Indeed, "ECT" has been relegated to Class III where it yet remains today. (Unfortunately, this may no longer be true.)

Over time, the Utah recommendations and the 1982 APA Standard penned by Richard Weiner, guaranteeing minimal stimulus threshold output to induce adequate seizures for all age categories, has slowly faded from memory. Indeed, even Medcraft has never been prohibited from marketing its powerfully destructive ENR device, the B-24 SW, a device with twice the output of the prototypical MECTA “C. ” In fact, the B-24 SW continues to be marketed and applied even today throughout America. In the end, even though the 1982 FDA Panelists granted the Brief Pulse industry another 30 months to submit the final American Standard, Weiner, the APA, and the manufacturers all neglected to do so. Instead, manufacturers (and only because "ECT" was grandfathered in) all submitted pre-market approval submissions. To date, then, no acceptable standard for ECT has ever been submitted for official FDA adoption just as no American standard for ECT has ever been officially adopted. To date--there is no official standard.

PART II

SECTION II: The 1982 APA Standard in Detail

CHAPTER 11

Interpreting the 1982 APA Standard

The essence of the often deemed "1982 APA Standard for ECT" is composed of the three passages below. While Weiner and the APA Task Force on ECT submitted this proposed standard to the FDA for perusal and discussion in 1982 during the 1976-1982 FDA investigation of ECT devices, and while refinements were promised after which these specified machine parameters were to become the first American Standard for ECT, this same 1982 APA Standard for ECT, in fact, was never re-submitted or adopted. Even so, the parameters regulating outputs for minimal stimulus identified within the proposed guidelines are yet referred to as the 1982 APA Standard to which the first generation Brief pulse device, the 108J MECTA “C” presented to the FDA at this time, actually conformed. Moreover, authorized adoption of this standard, if Weiner, the APA, and the device manufacturers had ever officially re-submitted it, was to include removal of the SW portion below and so SW generally, leaving only the Brief Pulse standard and thus the reduced output Brief Pulse device as the sole instrument for applying ECT in the U. S. In short, the 1982 APA Standard was to be the American Standard. This once promising standard known as the “1982 APA Standard” contains the following regarding SW and Brief Pulse devices:

> 5.1:4.1 Sine Wave Devices
>
> 2a. A maximum stimulus output energy [for sine wave devices] must not exceed 140 Joules @ 220 Ohms, and must not exceed 170 Joules over the entire load range of 100-600 Ohms . . . . (Department of Health and Human Services, 1982a, 12)

For Brief Pulse, the 1982 APA Standard reads:

> For pulse stimuli, a range of 3 to 100 Joules was found. In terms of upper values, less than 1% of seizure thresholds were greater than 60 Joules. A less conservative stance with respect to allowable output energy maxima appears to be justifiable for the low energy, pulse stimulus, particularly given concern among clinicians about the ability of the device to produce seizures in all patients. Because of this, limits of 70 Joules @ 220 ohms and 110 Joules over the entire applicable load range (100-600 Ohms) appear reasonable. " (Department of Health and Human Services, 1982a, E20)

The above passage regarding Brief Pulse is the core of Weiner’s 1982 *Petition to Reclassify* “ECT” devices and so the essence of the 1982 APA Standard. However, one very important adjunct included in the APA standard for Brief Pulse is:

> Using a pulse device, the [APA] Task Force [1978] has determined that only 0.6% of seizure thresholds were greater than 70 Joules and that none were greater than 100 Joules (Department of Health and Human Services, 1982a, p. A53).

It is because of this assertion concerning Brief Pulse within the 1982 APA Standard that the high watermark for minimal stimulus Brief Pulse came to be 100 maximum joules so that the maximum output for any Brief Pulse device should not exceed 110J (just above threshold) according to the standard. In short, according to the APA standard, the assertion exists that no recipient ever requires more than 100 joules to adequately seize even the oldest recipient on a Brief Pulse device and thus no Brief Pulse instrument need ever exceed 110 joules.

So what do the figures mean: "140J @ 220Ω" (in the case of SW) and "70J at 220Ω" (in the case of BP) "over the entire applicable load range (100-600 Ohms)" and how do manufacturers interpret these phrases?

The figures 100-600Ω (Ohms) are easily recognizable as a measures of resistance or impedance. In a word, no treatment Impedance should drop below 100Ω or exceed 600Ω for SW or Brief Pulse devices.

A general principle applied to both SW and BP, is that the older the recipient, the higher the resistance. With respect to BP exclusively, however, the greater the bodily resistance (of skull, skin, blood, tissue), the more electrical energy must be emitted to maintain a consistent Amperage in all age categories. While the same principle holds true for SW-- the older the recipient, the higher the resistance, SW cannot increase Voltage to maintain a consistent Amperage as does BP. Indeed, with SW, the greater the resistance, the more diminished the Amperage. Even so, because "pulse stimuli [Brief Pulse] is associated with a lower seizure threshold than . . . sine wave," BP yet requires less energy output (that is, fewer joules) than SW to achieve the same adequate seizure at each Impedance (or age) level.

Generally speaking, then, the phrases "140J at 220Ω" and 70J at 220Ω" are "Equivalent Ratios," both standards of which lean toward insuring the least amount of electricity possible with their respective devices. (SW does not actually apply the least amount in that Brief Pulse requires much less). As we can see, therefore, the standard for Brief Pulse limits output to 70J at 220Ω; whereas, the standard for SW limits output to 140J at 220Ω meaning that SW requires up to 140J to elicit an adequate seizure at 220Ω; whereas, BP requires no more than 70J to elicit an adequate seizure at the same 220Ω of resistance. The BP waveform can thus be deemed "more efficient" than SW. One reason for its greater efficiency is that, in addition to consistent Amperage, the Brief Pulse is broken up or intermittent as opposed to the Sine Wave which is continuous, so that with BP, more precise or smaller outputs can be measured with respect to inducing an adequate seizure in all age categories. Because SW requires at least twice as much EO as BP to induce the same adequate seizure, and because the goal regarding safety is the least amount of electrical energy possible to induce an adequate seizure in every age category, Brief Pulse is considered superior as it can produce much less cognitive dissonance regarding both long and short term memory damage. This superiority is illustrated via Weiner's comparative graphs conspicuously depicted within the 1982 *Petition to Reclassify* and so the 1982 APA standard itself. See below:

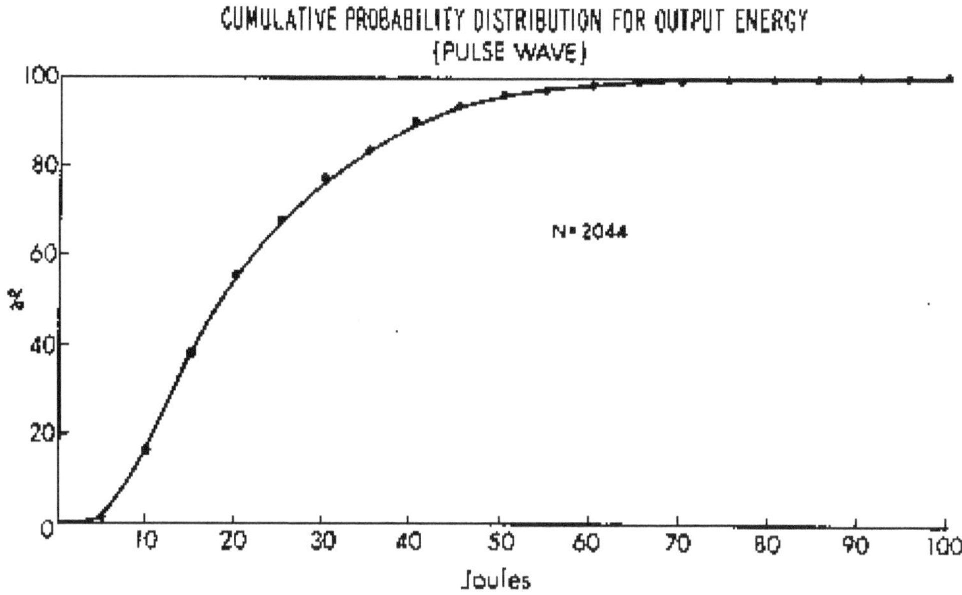

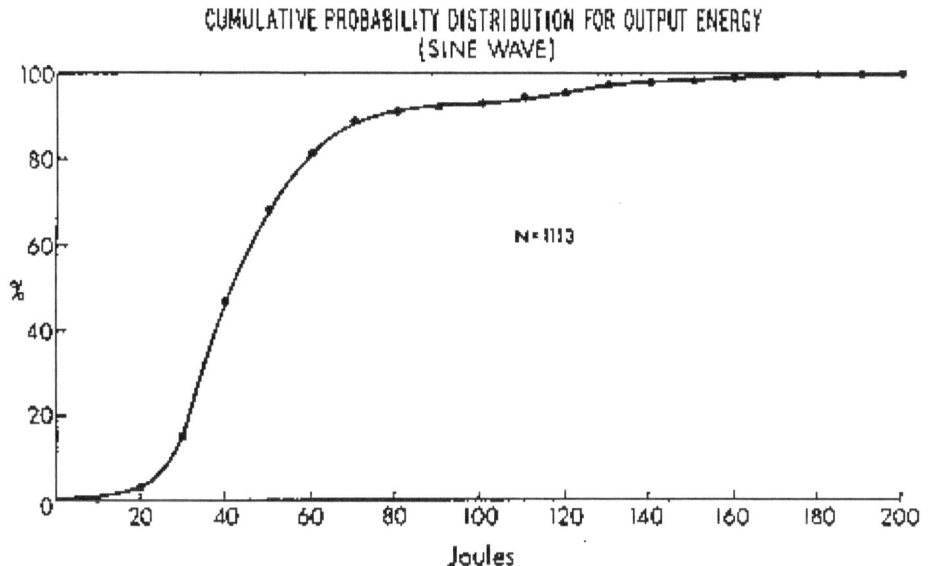

In short, both the 1982 APA Standard together with Weiner's graphs (above) submitted to the FDA plainly illustrate BP's superiority over SW by virtue of requiring half the output (in Joules) of SW to induce an adequate seizure in every age category.

The two graphs together make up a clear comparative analogy of BP to SW, showing BP's ability to induce half the EO of SW over each respective power spectrum. Note the 100 Joule cumulative EO (Energy Output) or 100J maximum of BP compared to the 200 Joule maximum of SW to induce the same adequate seizures. According to the 1982 APA Standard then, Brief Pulse never need exceed just above 100J (specifically, 110J) to achieve adequate seizures in even the oldest most seizure recalcitrant recipient as opposed to SW, which can emit up to 200J, twice that of Brief Pulse. Naturally, FDA as did Utah, wanted the "new and improved" Brief Pulse device to supplant SW for all "ECT" devices subsequent to 1976. Indeed, the proposed standard limiting output to 110 maximum joules (i.e. , the 1982 APA Standard) did just that and so was clearly acceptable to the FDA had Weiner and the manufacturers chosen to submit the standard for adoption. In fact, the FDA would have almost certainly promoted the "ECT" BP device to Class II or even Class I had the standard been adopted. So why did Weiner and the manufacturers hesitate?

ER/RRC and the 110J Ceiling

Logically expanding the SW and BP ER/RRCs (Equivalent Ratio/Rate Rise Ceiling) to other Impedances, we can theoretically derive general output limits for various Impedances (all of which correspond to age). In so doing, we find that in all instances, SW requires twice the output of BP. For example, at 90Ω of Impedance, the maximum EO limit for SW appears to be (140J/220Ω = XJ/90Ω. X =) 57J while the maximum EO for BP at the same 90Ω appears to be (70J/220Ω = XJ/90Ω. X =) 28J, half the output of SW (57 ÷ 2 = circa 28J). Since such phrases--"140J at 220Ω" and "70J at 220Ω"--are generally meant to compel gradient output limits with respect to age, and because rising outputs are generally based on Equivalent Ratios, this manuscript deems such phrases "Equivalent Ratio/Rate Rise Ceilings" (ER/RRC). Thus, through the APA proscribed ER/RRC, we can see that decreasing Impedance corresponds to decreasing age to which lower and lower EO maximums must be adhered. Conversely, with increasing Impedances corresponding to increasing age, increasing EO maximums can be administered so that, in general, ceilings exist for every age level.

Unfortunately, this is not the whole story, that is , age ceilings cannot be accurately deduced with ER/RRCs alone. Importantly, within the APA Standard, both the SW device and the BP device also have proscribed EO ceilings. For SW, the recommended ceiling is 170J while for BP, the proscribed ceiling is 110J. In short, both the "140J at 220Ω" and the "70J at 220Ω" phrases within the 1982 APA Standard are not ER/RRCs merely, but what shall be deemed conditional-ER/RRCs. That is, the ER/RRC is conditioned by the recommended SW ceiling of 170J and the absolute BP ceiling of 110J respectively. Unfortunately, SW decreases in power over Duration, whereas, BP does not so that opposing paradigms must be utilized as we shall eventually see. In any case, under the 1982 APA Standard, both the recommended 170J ceiling for SW devices and the proscribed 110J ceiling for BP devices further limit the overall maximums with respect to various Impedances or ages. Thus, we cannot rely on ER/RRC alone to deduce specific machine ceilings for specific ages either for either SW or BP.

For now, however, let us ignore SW and concentrate on the 1982 APA Standard for BP devices which is a "70J at 220Ω" ER/RRC conditioned by a 110J ceiling. (After all, in time, the inferior SW was to be completely supplanted by the reduced Energy Output BP device). Indeed, what actually determines the maximum EO ceiling at any Impedance is not the ER/RRC alone, but rather the proscribed 110J ceiling and this, in turn determines what this manuscript deems the "Multifold Threshold Titration Level Output Intensity" (MTTLOI), a concept critical in understanding Brief Pulse machines as they become more and more powerful, as we shall see. MTTLOI defines how many times threshold a particular device is designed to emit EO for all age categories, particularly with Brief Pulse. Thus, while the first generation MECTA "C" BP device was limited to a (110J ÷100J =) 1.1 MTTLOI or minimal stimulus, as we shall see, depicting the increasing MTTLOI for later BP devices reveals just how powerful subsequent BP devices become. Basic to this understanding, however, is crucial recognition that according to the APA Standard presented to the FDA in 1982, 100 Joules is the maximum output required to seize the oldest most seizure recalcitrant individual, the 100 year old male. While manufacturers later qualify this assertion as devices become more powerful, the original standard indicates that the 100J maximum includes all special circumstances. Indeed, the APA Standard is based on the premise that 100J is the highest output ever needed to seize any recipient under any conditions. Consequently, a Brief Pulse machine which is limited to just above 100J can be considered a minimal stimulus device.

> Using a pulse device, the [APA] Task Force [1978] has determined that only 0.6% of seizure thresholds were greater than 70 Joules and that none were greater than 100 Joules (Department of Health and Human Services. (1982a, p. A53)

In short, the maximum 110J output depicted in the 1982 APA Standard for BP devices and which can only be applied to the oldest, most seizure recalcitrant age category, the 100 year old male, in that it is the oldest recipient who has the highest possible Impedance, can never exceed (110J ÷ 100J =) 1.1 times threshold according to the 1982 APA Standard, or stated differently, a 1.1 Multifold Threshold Titration Level Output

Intensity (MTTLOI). Moreover, because the MTTLOI of any BP device must be consistent for all age categories, that is, because the electrical dosage over threshold must be consistent for all age groups, and because the 100 year old cannot receive more than a 1.1 MTTLOI, neither can any other age category receive more than a 1.1 MTTLOI. For example, if the 65 year old seizes at about 42.2J and the 70 year old seizes at about 49J, the Brief Pulse device must not administer more than (1.1 x 42.2J =) 46.42J or a 1.1 MTTLOI for the 65 year old recipient and (1.1 x 49J =) 53.9J or a 1.1 MTTLOI for the 70 year old recipient. In short, it is the MTTLOI (which the 1982 APA Standard limits to 1.1 times threshold) which determines the ultimate maximum or default output for each specific age or Impedance.

Thus, all we need to determine the designed power of any BP device is the MTTLOI of that device which can be derived simply by dividing the maximum machine output in joules by 100J. For example, if the machine is limited to 110J, we can simply divide 110J by 100J to obtain the (110J ÷100J =) 1.1 MTTLOI delivered to every recipient and which the APA Standard prescribes. Since, according to the 1982 APA Standard, no BP device can exceed 110J, the standard mandates that no BP device can exceed a (110J ÷ 100J =) 1.1 MTTLOI for any recipient. (Of course, subsequent devices breach this standard, as we shall soon learn). In sum, all we need is the overall maximum output of any device to determine the MTTLOI delivered to all recipients for that particular BP device. This, in turn, reveals the most important BP device dynamic—the power of the device.

The APA Standard and the MTTLOI Continued

100 Joules, then, according to the standard, is the maximum output required to seize even the oldest, most seizure recalcitrant recipient which makes 100J the maximum output required to seize any recipient of any age category under any circumstances. Stated differently, 100J is the minimum amount of power required to seize all 100 year old recipients 100% of the time. Again, from the 1982 APA Standard authored chiefly by Richard Weiner:

> Using a pulse device, the [APA] Task Force [1978] has determined that only 0.6% of seizure thresholds were greater than 70 Joules and that none were greater than 100 Joules. (Department of Health and Human Services, 1982a, p. A53)

Thus, the 110J proscribed in the standard is just above threshold for the most seizure recalcitrant recipient that can be encountered. In short, the 110J maximum of the 1982 APA Standard assures that the device will emit only a 1.1 MTTLOI, that is, minimal stimulus or just above seizure threshold outputs for all Brief Pulse recipients.

Again, the 1982 APA Standard for Brief Pulse states:

> For pulse stimuli, a range of 3 to 100 Joules was found. In terms of upper values, less than 1% of seizure thresholds were greater than 60 Joules. A less conservative stance with respect to allowable output energy maxima appears to be justifiable for the low energy, pulse stimulus, particularly given concern among clinicians about the ability of the device to produce seizures in all patients. Because of this, limits of 70 Joules @ 220 ohms and 110 Joules over the entire applicable load range (100-600 Ohms) appear reasonable. (Department of Health and Human Services, 1982a, E20)

The 1982 APA Standard thus sets maximum output for Brief Pulse devices at 110 Joules which is a critically important parameter in the APA Standard in that it asserts a ceiling for BP devices, generally. In short, "limits of 70 Joules @ 220 ohms and 110 Joules over the entire applicable load range (100-600 Ohms)" means the device is to emit gradient outputs with respect to age never exceeding a 1.1 MTTLOI and that the device is never to emit more than 110J under any circumstances in that no higher output is ever needed to induce an adequate seizure for any recipient no matter the age or circumstance. By implication then, the 1982 APA Standard sets the overall MTTLOI maximum at (110J ÷ 100J =) 1.1. That is, because the oldest recipient must never receive more than a 1.1 MTTLOI and because the MTTLOI must be gradational and uniform, no recipient of any age shall receive electrical energy outputs exceeding 1.1 fold threshold. You will not be surprised to hear, of course, that Brief Pulse manufacturers seriously breach this standard following the close of the FDA investigation in 1982, so that the machines become more and more powerful over time, as we shall witness.

At this point, however, we need to concentrate on the fact that the 100 Joules identified within the 1982 APA Standard as the maximum output required for any recipient under any circumstances reflects the premise and promise that adequate seizures alone comprise the "ECT therapy," that "adequate" means "adequate" and that EO in excess of that necessary to induce adequate seizures increases the danger of memory dysfunction and quite possibly brain damage (Wilcox, 1946). In short, it is well established in the 1982 *Petition to Reclassify . . .* containing the APA Standard (Department of Health and Human Services, 1982a) and upon which the prototypical MECTA "C" parameters are based, that no circumstance exists for which any Brief Pulse device need use an output in excess of 100 Joules to induce an adequate seizure in even the oldest age category. It is for this reason that 110J, or just above seizure threshold for the oldest most seizure recalcitrant recipient in all circumstances, is identified within the 1982 APA Standard as the overall maximum allowed for BP devices generally, the ER/RRC and 110J ceiling together, guaranteeing a 1.1 minimal stimulus output for every age ECT recipient.

The ER/RRC of "70J at 220Ω" in short, establishes generally that recipients must be administered electrical dosages in keeping with their ages or Impedances. That is, Impedance or age must be taken into consideration in electrical dosing, mandating gradational electrical output with respect to age. But it is the 1982 APA overall ceiling Standard of 110J that mandates a specific uniform 1.1 MTTLOI maximum for all recipients, assuring consistency by mandating that recipients of all ages never receive more than the same 1.1 MTTLOI administered to the oldest recipient.

That no recipient at any time requires more than 100J to adequately seize is why the 100 Joule figure is of such great significance even to modern manufacturers, accounting for its' redundant utilization within manufacturer reporting paradigms and formulas, as we shall soon see. Indeed, encompassed within the 110 Joule APA ceiling parameter and the "70J at 220Ω" ER/RRC is the assumption of minimal stimulus efficacy, that is, efficacy of the adequate seizure alone, and thus the assumed viability of convulsion theory as an authentic therapeutic principle. Also encompassed within the 110 Joule APA ceiling parameter and the "70J at 220Ω" ER/RRC is the assurance of a much improved and much safer procedure using Brief Pulse, but Brief Pulse limited to a 1.1 MTTLOI or just above seizure threshold for all age recipients. That Brief Pulse uses half the EO of SW to induce these adequate seizures plainly implies (within the standard) fully supplanting SW with Brief Pulse followed by the eventual elimination of SW altogether. Conversely, the necessity of outputs in excess of 110 Joules with Brief Pulse implies failure of the adequate seizure with respect to efficacy, and so failure of convulsion theory generally. The necessity of suprathreshold dosing to make the procedure work is clearly a concept Brief Pulse manufacturers sought to avoid in front of the FDA. In fact, both Utah and the FDA had concluded that basing machines upon suprathreshold amounts of electricity (in lieu of seizure), results in unavoidable cognitive dysfunction almost certainly reflective of brain damage so that excessive electrical output is precisely the dynamic that Utah, the FDA, and supposedly the APA wished to thwart. Indeed, elimination of excess electricity is the sole rationale for the standard's new utilization of Brief Pulse and possibly the continuation of "ECT" subsequent to 1976. As we shall see, machines deliberately based on adequate amounts of electricity are not "ECT" devices at all, but "ENR" devices, something very different. Moreover, covering up outputs in excess of 110J will soon become the hallmark of manufacturer deception, as we shall also shortly see.

What we should take away from this explanation of the 1982 APA Standard for ECT then, is the difference between "ECT" or adequate convulsion devices with their reduction in cognitive dysfunction or memory impairment through reduced electrical energy and what we shall deem, ENR (Electro Neurotransmission Reduction) or adequate electricity devices with their intentionally suprathreshold dosages of electricity associated with long term memory impairment, and engendering the inextricable relationship of efficacy and damage. Sincere or not, with the introduction of the 1982 APA Standard and the MECTA "C," Weiner and company zealously sought to convince Utah and the FDA that henceforth, the 1982 APA Standard or some facsimile thereof, would regulate the ECT procedure to assure the utilization of Brief Pulse devices alone, all of which would be confined to minimal stimulus outputs much less than that of SW. Brief Pulse devices then, would induce adequate convulsions with much less electricity than SW in full accordance with the main principle of convulsion theory—induction of the adequate convulsion alone with the least amount of electricity possible. Indeed, it was the existence of the MECTA "C" BP device designed in total compliance with the new 1982 APA

Standard for Brief Pulse, that helped convince the FDA that a new and improved, safer device limited to a "70J at 220Ω" ER/RRC and a 110 Joule ceiling would either eliminate or greatly reduce memory dysfunction via reduced output; in short, that a true "ECT" device was indeed possible around which a standard could be written and enforced. Indeed, Weiner's 1982 APA Standard gave the FDA the impression that what we now refer to as ENR or adequate electricity devices would henceforth be eliminated. In fact, neither Weiner, nor the various APA Task Forces for ECT, all of which Weiner chaired, nor the two American Brief Pulse manufacturers to date, have ever given the FDA reason to believe that any American BP device has surpassed the 200 Joule mark identified with SW. As you may have guessed, however, this is a totally false impression.

SW Vs BP

Even though both American and English made SW devices were capable of emitting Energy Outputs far in excess of Brief Pulse, perhaps because there was only one U. S. SW manufacturer (Medcraft) in 1982, and perhaps because a number of SW devices were yet in use (the Molac II, the B-24 and some partial SW devices), APA representative Weiner via his *Petition to Reclassify,* recommended keeping SW for a time, but limiting SW to 170J (in lieu of 200J). In contrast, as noted, Weiner requested 110 joules as the maximum for Brief Pulse devices. In fact, BP maker MECTA was the single BP manufacturer at this time, producing the looked for lower energy output device (the MECTA C) which the 1982 APA standard demanded (Department of Health and Human Services, 1982a, pp.12-14). The continuation of SW, as noted above, was to be temporary until such time all "ECT" machines could be replaced by Brief Pulse.

In addition, Weiner asserts at this time that Energy Output depicted in "Joules" is the best way of "represent[Ing] the major measure of stimulus intensity" for all ECT devices.

> [O]utput Energy [Joules] is perhaps the best single measure for assessing stimulus intensity . . . (Ibid, p.8).

Indeed, MECTA openly paraded before the FDA the <u>actual</u> Energy Output maximum of the 108J MECTA "C," in total compliance with the 110J ceiling stipulated by the 1982 APA Standard. In fact, the MECTA "C" was legitimately much safer than the SW devices of old by virtue of reduced output. There is no question that from about 1978 to 1982, the existence of the 108J MECTA "C," as opposed to the 200J B-24 SW, was exemplary of a minimal stimulus Brief Pulse device emitting roughly half the output of SW (Department of Health and Human Services, 1982a, E20, G3-G4).

Although Weiner included SW in his Petition to obtain FDA approval, in brief, he ultimately sought its total elimination, along with suprathreshold dosing generally or so it seemed.

> Some people hear the panel come to the conclusion . . . from this data - that sine wave is not justifiable for inclusion in the Standard. The eventual Standard as we see it - as a national Standard - might not have sine wave in it - based on input from engineers from the International Electro-Technical Commission. (Department of Health and Human Services, 1982**c**, p.237)

Weiner's 1982 Petition to Reclassify (submitted to the FDA that very year), clearly advised manufacturers to inform practitioners that "ECT" should only be administered at minimal stimulus:

> Document (instruction manual) must include . . . a statement that intensity settings should be selected so as to induce an effective seizure with minimal energy. (Ibid, p.15)

Thus, we see ample proof in the 1982 Petition to Reclassify that the MECTA "C" device, in accordance with the APA Standard, was as close to a true ECT device as possible, a device based upon convulsion, not electricity, with both BL and UL administered (at this time) at (just above) threshold output or an attempt to do so in every instance.

Certainly, there is almost no discussion of suprathreshold output in the 1982 Petition. In fact, the few allusions to "suprathreshold" are decidedly negative. Conversely, both UL and BL ECT are defended as efficacious at just above threshold with Brief Pulse.

We should note that by using the 110J ceiling, the maximum Impedance reachable at a "70J at 220Ω" ER/RRC is 345Ω (70J/220Ω = 110J/345Ω). Indeed, we can determine the ER/RRC used for a Brief Pulse device limited to 110J with any maximum Impedance. For example, if maximum output is 110J and Impedance is 500Ω, the ER/RRC must be reduced to "48J at 220Ω," a figure we derive by maintaining the 110J ceiling with maximum Impedance and cross multiplying (XJ/220Ω = 110J/500Ω; X = "48J at 220Ω"). Thus, we see that to overcome higher Impedances without exceeding the 110J ceiling, we must lower the ER/RRC. This is why the MECTA "C" (and "D)" for example, in order to overcome a higher Impedance, used a "59J at 220Ω" ER/RRC in lieu of a "70J at 220Ω" ER/RRC. MECTA C: 59J/220Ω = 108J/402Ω. (The D also used "59J at 220Ω" although it breached the 110J ceiling as we shall discuss: 59J/220Ω = 134J/500Ω). [129]

A problem yet arises. While we can determine the MTTLOI with maximum output (simply by dividing maximum output by 100J) and, in turn, the default output delivered to the 100 year old recipient, we cannot, with the information provided, discover default outputs at ages other than 100 years in this manner. Too, because manufacturers almost immediately dispense with the 110J ceiling following the 1976-1982 FDA investigation of "ECT," as we shall see, and so begin to circumvent the 1982 APA Standard, it is important to deduce not only the maximum output for a device, but default outputs delivered to all age recipients. Below is a list of Brief Pulse formulas which we will need in understanding how manufacturers actually calibrate their Brief Pulse devices.

Formulas for finding Brief Pulse Parameters:

Charge = Duration x Current x (hz x 2) x WL
Charge = EO/Current x Impedance
EO = Charge x Current x Impedance
Duration = Charge/Current x (hz x 2) x WL
EO = Voltage x Current x (hz x 2) x WL x Duration
EO = (Current squared) x Impedance x (hz x 2) x WL x Duration
Ohm's Law: Current = Voltage/Ω; Ω = Voltage/Current; Voltage = Current x Ω

Until Now

Until now, no one has written of the exact method by which modern Brief Pulse ECT device manufacturers figure and report EO (Energy Output) ceilings (and other maximum parameters) in alleged conformity to APA and IEC standards--and with good reason. Manufacturers wish to keep both the method of determining and the actual power of their devices hidden. Reasons for this secrecy include their need to suppress the following facts: (1) Shock devices do not work at just above threshold thus undermining convulsion theory itself, (2) convulsion is not the agent of efficacy but rather electricity is the agent of efficacy again undermining convulsion theory itself, and (3) modern BP devices deliver excessive electrical dosages surpassing the cumulative EO of the older SW (Sine Wave). This is because (4) modern BP devices must electrically "titrate" individuals at high enough electrical outputs to obtain specific Multifold Suprathreshold Titration Level Output Intensities (MTTLOIs) (5) long known to be injurious to the brain. In brief, manufacturers have fabricated Brief Pulse machines to deliver injurious Multifold Threshold Titration Level Output Intensities of electrical energy as the only means to achieve efficacy. In a nutshell, manufacturers knowingly cover up the true power of modern day ECT devices in order to prevent the public from grasping the true aim of ECT--diminished brain faculty through modification or destruction of neurons without which--no "efficacy" occurs. The inextricable relationship of injury and electrical dosing (far in excess of that required to induce an adequate seizure) has long been understood by early researchers (Friedman, 1942; Liberson, 1945a; 1945b; 1946, 1946, 1949; Ottosson, 1960; Wilcox, 1946). In explaining the "therapeutic" mechanism at work in both the early and modern ECT eras, the cogent elucidation that injury and efficacy are synonymous with respect to the ECT procedure has for many years

[129] The "D," of course, was the first to exceed the 110J ceiling, but confined to a 134J ceiling, yet used a lower ER/RRC to overcome a 500Ω ceiling.

been the criticism of brilliant researcher, lecturer, and author, psychiatrist Peter Breggin (Breggin, 1979; 1991; 1998), as well as neurologist Robert Grimm and neurologist author John Friedberg (Friedberg, 1971; 1976) and, in fact, numerous other contemporary scientists (Johnstone, 1992; Sament, 1983). However, though complaints of long term memory dysfunction following ECT are infamously longstanding and ubiquitous (Cameron, 1997), neither mathematical nor electrical proof, nor any explanation for the apparent lack of substantial MRI evidence depicting what scientists have uniformly held to be the inextricable relationship of injury and efficacy as a result of "ECT," has ever (until now) been convincingly forthcoming. This manuscript seeks to lay bare before the public the very long sought-after missing links connecting injury with efficacy, paying particular attention to so-called modern ECT administered by so-called modern ECT devices known as "Brief Pulse. " It is the perspective of this author that what is often mistaken for "ECT" (Electro Convulsive Therapy) based on adequate seizures is actually ENR (Electro Neurotransmission Reduction) based on adequate dosages of electricity in that manufacturers have gone to great lengths to hide this critical detail.

1982 APA Standard--More Elements

As noted, the 1982 APA Standard for modern day BP (Brief Pulse) devices in the United States can be epitomized via two important ceilings: what this manuscript has deemed a 1) a Rate Rise Ceiling of "70 Joules at 220Ω" and 2) an Absolute EO Ceiling of "110 maximum Joules" (Department of Health and Human Services, 1982a, p. E20).

While the ceiling is 110J, we cannot, as noted, rely on the 110J ceiling without implementing the ER/RRC. To ignore ER/RRC facilitating gradational outputs, would be to allow the maximum 110J ceiling to be emitted in every age category. To do so, would not only result in an inconsistent MTTLOI (Multifold Threshold Titration Level Output Intensity), but except for the 100 year old, far too much EO (Energy Output) at every age level. For example, if we administer 110J to each age category and then divide by the age-related threshold output (the derivatives of which shall be discussed), other than the oldest, we obtain both an unacceptably varied and an unacceptably high MTTLOI for each age category. (Age related threshold outputs used by Brief Pulse manufacturers are identified in this manuscript for the first time.) Threshold outputs of 1.0J, 16J, 42J, 81J, and 100J for recipients 10, 40, 65, 90, and 100 years are identified below. Conversely, administering 110J to each age category results in both inconsistent and dangerously high MTTLOIs.

10 year old: **110J ÷ 1.0J = 110 MTTLOI**

40 year old: **110J ÷ 16J = 6.9 MTTLOI**

65 year old: **110J ÷ 42J = 2.6 MTTLOI**

90 year old: **110J ÷ 81J = 1.35 MTTLOI**

100 year old: **110J ÷ 100J = 1.1 MTTLOI**

Using, in this Instance, the 110J maximum without an ER/RRC could result in the full 110J or a 110 MTTLOI administered to the ten year old (see above), that is, an output 110 times threshold while the 100 year old receives a 1.1 MTTLOI or 1.1 times threshold. In short, absence of an ER/RRC results in both gradational absence and an inconsistent MTTLOI. We can see from the examples above then, that the ER/RRC serves the purpose of reducing outputs relative to diminishing age or Impedance so that the lower the Impedance or age, the less EO administered to maintain, for example, a 1.1 MTTLOI.

On the other hand, neither can we use ER/RRC without considering a consistent MTTLOI, i.e. , the 1.1 MTTLOI inherent in the 110J ceiling. [Again, we derived the APA 1.1 MTTLOI by dividing the maximum 110J by 100J (110J ÷ 100J = 1.1)]. As an experiment, let us attempt to derive age-related Impedances for a 110J maximum BP device, the highest output allowed by the APA Standard, based on the 70J at 220Ω ER/RRC alone, without taking into consideration the 1.1 MTTLOI inherent in the 110J ceiling. Let us first derive maximum Impedance for a 70J at 220Ω ER/RRC with a 110J ceiling: 70J/220Ω = 110J/XΩ; X = 346Ω. Let us then divide 346Ω by 10 (as do manufacturers) to derive Impedances for each age category. For example, 346Ω ÷ 10 =

34.6Ω for the ten year old, (34.6Ω + 34.6Ω =) 69.2Ω for the twenty year old, (34.6Ω + 34.6Ω + 34.6Ω =) 103.8Ω for the thirty year old, etc. so that we derive the chart below.

Age-related Impedances for Theoretical BP Device Limited to 110J

AGE	IMPEDANCE
10	34.6
20	69.2
30	103.8
40	138.4
50	173
60	207.6
65	225
70	242.2
80	276.8
90	311.4
100	346

Using the 70J at 220Ω ER/RRC alone (without the 1.1 MTTLOI) and cross multiplying, using age related Impedances, we derive the following incorrect default outputs for each age category:

10 year old: **70J/220Ω** = ***11.1J***/35Ω

40 year old: **70J/220Ω** = ***44J***/138Ω

65 year old: **70J/220Ω** = ***72J***/225Ω

90 year old: **70J/220Ω** = ***99J***/311Ω

100 year old: **70J/220Ω** = ***110J***/*346Ω*

Without taking into consideration the 1.1 MTTLOI, based on a machine utilizing a "70J at 220Ω ER/RRC" and the speculative Impedances above, a ten year old child who may have a resistance of about 35Ω on this device can yet receive outputs of up to circa 11J, whereas a 40 year old who has a resistance of about 138Ω on this device can receive outputs up to 44J. A 65 year old who has a resistance of about 225Ω can receive outputs up to 72J, a 90 year old who may seize at about 311Ω can receive outputs up to 99J, and a 100 year old who can seize at about 346Ω can receive up to 110J.

Thus while the ER/RRC properly impels graduated output limits relative to age or Impedance, and while the device is limited to 110 maximum joules in accordance with the APA Standard, there is yet a problem with the outputs delivered. Dividing outputs based on ER/RRC alone by the age-related "relative constants" or constant threshold outputs for each age category (never revealed by any manufacturer) of 1.0J, 16J, 42.25J, 81J, and 100J respectively, that is, the minimum output required to seize all recipients of each respective age category under any circumstances, results in inconsistent or non-uniform MTTLOIs.

70J/220Ω = ***11.1J***/35Ω; 11.1 ÷ 1.0J = 11.1 MTTLOI (10 yr. old)

70J/220Ω = ***44J***/138Ω; 44.0J ÷ 16J = 2.75 MTTLOI (40 yr. old)

70J/220Ω = ***72J***/225Ω; 72.0J ÷ 42.25 = 1.7 MTTLOI (65 yr. old)

70J/220Ω = ***99J***/311Ω; 99.0J ÷ 81J = 1.22 MTTLOI (90 yr. old)

70J/220Ω = ***110J***/*346Ω*; 110J ÷ 100J = 1.1 MTTLOI (100 yr. old)

Based only on outputs derived by the ER/RRC of 70J at 220Ω with various age-related Impedances, even honoring the 110J ceiling, therefore, the 10 year old child ends up receiving an 11.1 MTTLOI or 11 times threshold, the 40 year old, a 2.75 MTTLOI or 2.75 times threshold, the 65 year old a 1.7 MTTLOI or 1.7 times threshold, the 90 year old a 1.2 MTTLOI or 1.2 times threshold, and only the 100 year old a correct 1.1 MTTLOI or 1.1 times threshold. Thus, simply deriving output from Impedances derived by the 70J at 220Ω ER/RRC even incorporating the 110J ceiling, while the ER/RRC does provide gradational outputs, it fails to render consistent MTTLOIs.

Because Brief Pulse devices must and do emit a uniform Multifold Threshold Titration Level Output Intensity (MTTLOI) for all age categories, regardless of Impedance or changes in Impedance age-wise, we must force all age categories to conform to the same MTTLOI administered to the oldest recipient, in essence, the lowest common denominator. (Remember, we derived 1.1 by dividing the maximum 110J output by 100J (110J ÷ 100J = 1.1 MTTLOI.) Thus, in lieu of simply using Impedances and the ER/RRC alone to derive age-related outputs, we must use the pre-determined age-related threshold outputs or age-related "relative constants" secretly used by manufacturers, more or less ignoring Impedance altogether. Only then can we hope to attain a uniform MTTLOI. To conform to the 1982 APA Standard based on a conditional "70J at 220Ω" ER/RRC with conditional 110J ceiling then, that is, a conditional ER/RRC of "70J at 220Ω," we must add another element. First, we must (1) base the machine on a maximum "70J at 220" ER/RRC thereby compelling gradational outputs with respect to age and Impedance, (2) adhere to the 110J overall maximum, and finally 3) adhere to a uniform maximum 1.1 MTTLOI.

Attaining a Uniform MTTLOI

What we have failed to consider in basing our default outputs only on ER/RRC and age related Impedances and even a 110J maximum above then, is that all age categories must have the same MTTLOI as the oldest age recipient and this principle pertains to all Brief Pulse devices. We must begin then, by understanding that the maximum output—in this case "110J," can only be administered to recipients in the oldest age category or 100 year old recipient. This is because the oldest recipient has the highest Impedance threshold so that only the oldest age recipient can be administered the highest output. According to Weiner's own 1982 APA Standard, we must remember what Weiner himself implied to the FDA via the 1982 APA Standard--it can take up to 100 Joules to seize all 100 year old recipients, but never more than 100J.

> Using a pulse device, the [APA] Task Force [1978] has determined that . . . of seizure thresholds . . . none were greater than 100 Joules. (Department of Health and Human Services, 1982a, p. A53)

Thus, while 100J is the minimum output required to seize all 100 year old recipients, we must also have the minimum output required to seize each of the other age-related categories? Like the 100J minimum output it takes to seize all 100 year old recipients then, we must also have the knowledge that 1.0 Joule seizes all ten year old recipients, but never more than 1.0J. Indeed, each age category has a minimum default output manufacturers use to induce adequate seizure for all members of that age category, figures never before revealed. (The author discovered these never before seen "relative constants" for all age categories from the default outputs of various BP machines as we shall eventually see.) Thus, under the APA Standard, a 100 year old recipient receiving the full 110J allowed, is receiving a 1.1 fold threshold output or 1.1 MTTLOI (110J ÷ 100J = 1.1) so that the 10 year old must also be administered a 1.1 MTTLOI (1.1J ÷1.0J = 1.1) as well as all other age groups. To determine the 1.1 MTTLOI default output for all age categories then, we must first have the age-related threshold outputs manufacturers use as constants or what we the author has deemed "relative constants" for each age category with respect to BP devices generally. These secret "relative constants" used by all manufacturers of Brief Pulse devices are revealed for the first time, below.

10 year old male = 1.00J
20 year old male = 4.00J
30 year old male = 9.00J
40 year old male = 16.00J
50 year old male = 25.00J

60 year old male = 36.00J
65 year old male = 42.25J
70 year old male = 48.97J
80 year old male = 64.00J
90 year old male = 81.00J
100 year old male = 100.00J

Relative Constants

Because Impedances may increase with increased electricity, some may challenge the idea that the threshold outputs above can be relatively constant. For example, if we administer 200J to a 100 year old recipient (200J ÷ 100J = 2.0 MTTLOI), the Impedance may increase from say 400Ω to 450Ω or even 500Ω so that the MTTLOI is less than 2.0. This, however, in no way negates the fact that the original 100J is enough to seize all 100 year old recipients even at the end of a treatment series. As such, even if the Impedance does increase, because all 100 year old recipients seize at 100J in all circumstances, we can confidently assume in spite of a possible Impedance increase, that the one hundred year old receiving 200J receives at least two fold the electrical energy output required to induce a seizure. That is, at 200J, we can say the recipient receives a (200J ÷ 100J =) 2.0 fold or 2.0 MTTLOI even if Impedance does somewhat rise. It is also true that individual 100 year old recipients inherently have slightly different Impedances. So while some variation in threshold Impedance and threshold output may exist, 100J remains the minimum output required to seize all 100 year old recipients. Manufacturers, therefore, ignore these slight variations in Impedance and use the "relative thresholds" above as constants to calibrate specific default outputs on their Brief Pulse devices. To illustrate, 100J is the minimum output required to induce an adequate seizure in all 100 year old recipients even at the end of a treatment series. Moreover, because 100J is a liberal figure, slight rises in Impedance do not affect this fact. In brief, manufacturers only consider "constant threshold outputs" in setting default outputs in every age category with respect to each individual Brief Pulse device. That is, manufacturers set their devices to default outputs based entirely upon age and the correlating "constant threshold outputs" above--all perfect squares, generally. To illustrate, the "relative constant" seizing all 90 year olds is 81J. If the manufacturer wishes his BP machine to emit a 2.0 MTTLOI for all recipients then, all 90 year old recipients are administered a default output of (2.0 MTTLOI x 81J =) 162J just as the 100 year old is administered a default output of (2.0 MTTLOI x 100J =) 200J. In this way, manufacturers get a gradational output based on the ER/RRC, but a a uniform MTTLOI for all age categories based on "relative constants" even at the end of a "treatment" series. In brief, a "relative output constant" is the minimum output required to seize all members of a respective age group regardless of slight changes in Impedance. Indeed, most recipients seize at less or even much less than the relative constants used by manufacturers. Thus, while Impedances may increase with increasing outputs, the "relative constants" are high enough for manufacturers to simply ignore any Impedance increases. Because all recipients in a particular age category seize at the relative constant output pertaining to their age category in all circumstances then, it is quite correct to conclude that, for example, a 100 year old administered 300J of electrical output receives a 3.0 MTTLOI.

From this experiment, we can conclude that while the ER/RRC (of "70J at 220Ω" under the 1982 APA Standard) compels manufacturers to administer gradational outputs relative to age, it is the conditional 110J ceiling which assures a minimal stimulus 1.1 MTTLOI for all recipients and which can be calibrated with the now known relative constants for each age category. Regardless of whether or not the above threshold outputs are, in fact, real constants, in treating them as such, manufacturers achieve uniform MTTLOIs for each respective Brief Pulse device. The 1982 APA Standard therefore, with its "70J at 220Ω" conditional -ER/RRC and 110J ceiling in conjunction with the relative output constants for each age category, mandates both the use of Brief Pulse devices and minimal stimulus output in all age categories. In fact, it mandates gradational outputs relative to age, and a uniform maximum 1.1 MTTLOI with BL ECT in every age category. As we shall see, moreover, while manufacturers violate the APA Standard almost immediately following the investigations' closure, they continue to use "relative constants."

The Simple Way

It should not surprise the reader that following the FDA investigation, Brief Pulse devices begin to breach the APA 110J ceiling and with it, the 1.1 MTTLOI or minimal stimulus mandate. Neither should it surprise the reader that Brief Pulse manufacturers do not want the power of their devices to be revealed. However, once the Equivalent Ratio/Rate Rise Ceiling (ER/RRC) and maximum output for a particular device are known, along with the previously unrevealed "relative constants", there is a simple way to find the MTTLOI pertaining to all age categories for any particular Brief Pulse device. As already noted elsewhere, to find MTTLOI for any Brief Pulse, we simply derive maximum output in joules and divide by 100J. According to the 1982 APA Standard, 100J, as noted, is the relative constant or most minimum output required to seize all recipients in any and all circumstances in the oldest, most seizure recalcitrant 100 year old category (Department of Health and Human Services, 1982a, p. A53). The MTTLOI for the oldest age category then becomes the MTTLOI required for all age recipients for that respective BP device.

To demonstrate, since no 100 year old ever needs more than 100J to seize, if he or she is administered the maximum 110J output allowed by the 1982 APA Standard, the Multifold Threshold Titration Level Output Intensity (MTTLOI) for the 100 year old on a machine delivering 110 maximum joules is (110J ÷ 100J =) 1.1 not only for the 100 year old, but for all age recipients.1.1 times threshold makes sense in that the 1982 APA Standard circumscribes all outputs for all age categories to just above seizure threshold. A 1.1 MTTLOI for all age categories assures that (1), a seizure is induced, and (2), that the seizure is induced at minimal stimulus or the least amount of electrical energy possible, just as the 1982 APA Standard intends.

Using our 1.1 MTTLOI and our Chart of age related (Relative) Threshold Constants below, we can now determine the default output delivered to each age category on a Brief Pulse device which has a 110J maximum EO, or a 1.1 MTTLOI, the maximum MTTLOI allowed by the 1982 APA Standard for every age category. Once again, the Relative Constants are:

10 year old male = 1.00J
20 year old male = 4.00J
30 year old male = 9.00J
40 year old male = 16.00J
50 year old male = 25.00J
60 year old male = 36.00J
65 year old male = 42.25J
70 year old male = 48.97J
80 year old male = 64.00J
90 year old male = 81.00J
100 year old male = 100.00J

Since the same 1.1 MTTLOI applied to all 100 year old recipients is the same MTTLOI which must be applied to all age recipients, we simply multiply each age-related threshold constant (above) by 1.1 to obtain the default output delivered in that age category on a 110J maximum output BP device. In so doing, we find that the 100 year old who seizes at 100J is delivered a default output of (100J x 1.1 =) 110J, the 90 year old who seizes at 81J a default output of (81J x 1.1 fold =) 89.1J, the 80 year old who seizes at 64J a default output of (64J x 1.1 fold =) 70.4J, the 70 year old who seizes at 49J a default output of (49J x 1.1 fold =) 54J, the 65 year old who seizes at 42.25J a default output of (42.25J x 1.1 fold =) 46.5J, the 60 year old who seizes at 36J a default output of (36J x 1.1 fold =) 39.6J, the 50 year old who seizes at 25J a default output of (25J x 1.1 fold =) 27.5J, the 40 year old who seizes at 16J a default output of (16J x 1.1 fold =) 17.6J, the 30 year old who seizes at 9J a default output of (9J x 1.1 fold = 9.9J, the 20 year old who seizes at 4.004J a default output of (4.004J x 1.1 fold =) 4.4J, and finally, the 10 year old child who seizes at 1.0J a default output of (1.0J x 1.1 fold =) 1.1J. Thus by repeating the simple process of multiplying 1.1 fold or a 1.1 MTTLOI times the known relative threshold constants for all age categories, we are able to derive the default outputs on a BP device delivering 110 maximum joules or a 1.1 MTTLOI maximum. In short, we have formulated a minimal stimulus or just above threshold output chart with BL ECT that complies with the 1982 APA Standard in all age categories.

By multiplying age-related threshold outputs (relative constants) by a factor of 1.1, we can depict the default outputs for a 110J Brief Pulse device in accordance with the 1982 APA Standard

AGE	THRESHOLD OUTPUT	DEFAULT OUTPUT IN JOULES	MTTLOI
10	1.0J	X 1.1 = 1.1	1.1
20	4.0J	X 1.1 = 4.4J	1.1
30	9.0J	X 1.1 = 9.9	1.1
40	16.0J	X 1.1 = 17.6	1.1
50	25.0J	X 1.1 = 27.5	1.1
60	36.0J	X 1.1 = 39.6	1.1
65	42.25J	X 1.1 = 46.5	1.1
70	49J	X 1.1 = 53.8	1.1
80	64J	X 1.1 = 70.4	1.1
90	81J	X 1.1 = 89.1	1.1
100	100J	X 1.1 = 110.0	1.1

Each age category above now emits the consistent maximum 1.1 MTTLOI allowed with BL ECT according to the standard, in brief, just enough output (in joules) to overcome the various age-related Impedances to elicit an adequate grand mal seizure at what can be deemed, minimal stimulus (the least amount of electricity necessary to induce a grand mal seizure). Moreover, all recipients are delivered a consistent 1.1 MTTLOI. In spite of the fact that the great majority of recipients would seize with less than the relative constant used by manufacturers, it is certain that by using these relative constants, all recipients will seize in all age categories in all circumstances. We can now see that the aim of the 1982 APA Standard is to limit output to a consistent 1.1 MTTLOI with BL ECT. In short, the 1982 APA Standard was designed to regulate output to the most minimal stimulus output possible while yet assuring induction of a so-called adequate seizure in each age category.

Deriving Relative Constants

A quick word for the curious regarding how the author derived the relative constants used by BP manufacturers. On the back covers of Somatics manuals, enough information is provided to derive maximum machine outputs. Simply by dividing maximum output by 100J, one can derive the MTTLOI for the oldest recipient and thus all recipients "treated" by that particular Brief Pulse device. Moreover, enough information is provided to derive the default EO (Energy Output) in joules delivered to each age category with that same BP device. All relative constants can be derived simply by dividing the default outputs delivered in each age category by the machine's MTTLOI. In short, once a machine's maximum EO is deduced, one can deduce the MTTLOI for that BP device simply by dividing by 100J. One can then divide the default EO delivered to each age group by the machine's consistent MTTLOI to derive the relative constants used by manufacturers. This works for both MECTA and Somatics devices and the derivations are the same for both companies regardless of the device generation. (This shall be discussed in more detail later.)

Mitigations

So what if manufacturers argue that the 100 year old may occasionally have a higher Impedance than the 345Ω limit above limited to "70J at 220" (70J/220Ω = 110J/345Ω) and so must breach the 110J ceiling? This is improbable in that like 100J for 100 year old recipients, all the age-related relative constants are adequate to induce a seizure for all members of that particular age category under any circumstances.

> Using a pulse device, the [APA] Task Force [1978] has determined that only 0.6% of seizure thresholds were greater than 70 Joules and that none were greater than 100 Joules. (Department of Health and Human Services, 1982a, p. A53)

Higher Impedances such as 410Ω and, in fact, much higher can be overcome in accordance with the 1982 APA Standard simply by lowering the overall ER/RRC as seen earlier. For instance, by lowering the ER/RRC from "70J at 220Ω" (which is the maximum ER/RRC under the 1982 APA Standard) to an allowable "59J at 220Ω," a BP machine based on this lower ER/RRC can now overcome a 400Ω Impedance with very nearly the same 110J ceiling stipulation.

70J/220Ω = 110J/345Ω

59J/220Ω = 108J/400Ω

Practically, an increase in Voltage in spite of a reduction in Duration (in order to remain below the 110J ceiling) will elicit a seizure at a higher Impedance. For example, using Ohm's Law, we can see that the Voltage of a Brief Pulse device based on a "70J at 220Ω" ER/RRC requires only 276V to overcome a 345Ω Impedance.

70J/220Ω = 110J/345Ω
Ohm's Law: Voltage = Current x Ω
.8A x 345Ω = 276V

Such a device would emit a 400mC Charge maximum and a 2.38 Second maximum Duration.

Charge = EO/Current x Impedance:
Charge = 110J ÷ .8A x 345Ω Charge = .400C or 400mC

Duration = Charge/Current x (hz x 2) x WL:
Duration = .400C ÷ .8A x 140 x .0015 = 2.38 sec

On the other hand, a 110J Brief Pulse machine based on a "59J at 220Ω" ER/RRC can overcome a higher 400Ω Impedance, simply by increasing the Voltage from 276V to 320V.

59J/220Ω = 107.5J/400Ω
Ohm's Law: Voltage = Current x Ω
.8 **x 400Ω = 320V**

To avoid surpassing the 110J ceiling, the Charge must be reduced from 400mC to 336mC and the Duration from 2.38 Sec. to 2.0 Sec. This is borne out by the formula: Charge = EO/Current x Impedance:

Charge = EO/Current x Impedance
Charge = 107.8J ÷ .8A x 400**Ω** = .336 or 336mC

And from the formula: Duration = Charge/Current x (hz x 2) x WL, we get:
Duration = .336 ÷ .8A x 140 x .0015 = 2.0 sec.

"70J at 220Ω" ER/RRC

VOLTAGE	POWER % @ Age	AGE Yrs	Ω Ohms	FREQUENCY (Hz)	DURATION (SECs)	CURRENT mAmps	ENERGY Joules	CHARGE mC
276	100	100	345	70	2.38	800	110J	400

"59J at 220Ω" ER/RRC

VOLTAGE	POWER % @ Age	AGE Yrs	Ω Ohms	FREQUENCY (Hz)	DURATION (SECs)	CURRENT mAmps	ENERGY Joules	CHARGE mC
320	100	100	400	70	2.0	800	107.5J	336

Thus, lowering the ER/RRC under the APA Standard by increasing Voltage and modifying Charge and Duration results in the machine's capacity to overcome a higher maximum Impedance while yet adhering to the conditional 110J APA ceiling. In short, lowering the ER/RRC from "70J at 220Ω" to "59J at 220Ω" enables a Brief Pulse device to overcome a 400Ω recipient Impedance at just under 110J, acceptable under the 1982 APA Standard in that "59J at 220Ω" is below the "70J at 220Ω" ER/RRC maximum identified in the APA Standard. This point addresses the call for more powerful devices in order to overcome higher Impedances.

Experimentally, we can see that so long as maximum Impedance remains unchanged, lowering the ER/RRC actually reduces the maximum output allowed in keeping with the APA Standard.

70J**/220Ω* = <u>110J**/346Ω*</u> (100 years)

vs

59J**/220Ω* = <u>93J**/346Ω*</u> (100 years)

In contrast, if we violate the APA Standard and increase the ER/RRC, for instance, from 70J at 220Ω to 80J at 220Ω, even if we maintain the overall ceiling cap of 110 Joules, maximum Impedance falls dramatically:

80J/220Ω = *110J/<u>**302.5Ω**</u>*

Importantly, remaining true to the 110J ceiling, we can increase the Brief Pulse machine's capacity to overcome a higher Impedance, simply by lowering the ER/RRC. That maximum EO is reduced somewhat is of no import.

59J**/220Ω* = <u>108J**/400Ω*</u> (100 years)

In sum, the main function of ER/RRC, i.e. the "70J at 220Ω," as noted, is simply to assure that maximum outputs relative to age are administered on a gradational scale but also to maintain a reasonable output through comparison to other devices. (Manufacturers stop reporting ER/RRC for their later more powerful BP devices as we shall see.) The 110J ceiling, on the other hand, mandates the 1.1 MTTLOI for all age levels so that the only means of increasing Impedance in accordance with the APA Standard is by lowering the ER/RRC. In short, the dual elements of the APA Standard, ER/RRC and a stipulated ceiling in joules assure that output must be delivered both gradationally, in a consistent manner, and at minimal stimulus. Specifically then, the "70J at 220Ω" ER/RRC maximum assures gradational output relative to age), while the 110J ceiling assures adequate seizure with output that never exceeds a 1.1 MTTLOI in any age category. The 1982 APA Standard thus compels both MTTLOI consistency, adequate seizure and minimal stimulus output for all age categories. Of course, to determine actual maximum output per Impedance or each age level, we must bring in that never mentioned or revealed even in the APA Standard, the never before presented relative threshold constants used by manufacturers for each particular age category. Once known, we simply multiply the relative constant for a specific age category by the consistent MTTLOI to determine specific default outputs for each age category on any specific Brief Pulse device.

So, remaining true to the APA Standard with its regulatory 110J ceiling, a 1.1 MTTLOI, and a "70J at 220Ω" conditional-ER/RRC maximum, a legal Brief Pulse device, that is, a device which conforms to the APA Standard, can be made to overcome Impedances greater than (70J/220Ω = 110J/<u>345Ω</u>) 346Ω simply by reducing the ER/RRC. While some rise in Impedance may occur due to increased electrical output intensity over threshold (i.e. 2.0 fold threshold--illegal under the APA Standard), such increases are not necessary to induce adequate seizure. Moreover, while manufacturers eventually make the argument that Impedances may double at the end of a "treatment series," as we shall see, such claims are exaggerated. In fact, the liberal threshold output or relative constant for each age category is almost certainly adequate to overcome seizure threshold for all age recipients under any circumstances, including the end of a "treatment" series.

> Using a pulse device, the [APA] Task Force [1978] has determined that only 0.6% of seizure thresholds were greater than 70 Joules and that none were greater than 100 Joules. (Department of Health and Human Services, 1982a, p. A53)

In short, overcoming very enhanced Impedances is perfectly possible with the "70J at 220Ω" ER/RRC, still conditionally limited to a 110J ceiling and thus a maximum 1.1 MTTLOI for all age categories, all in accordance with the 1982 APA Standard simply by reducing the ER/RRC. The point here is that devices do not have to become more powerful to overcome higher Impedances. Such arguments are simply manufacturer justifications for increasing the power of their Brief Pulse devices as we shall soon observe.

First Generation BP Devices

Indeed, the original MECTA "C" emitting a maximum 108 Joules, as noted, is based on just such a "59.4J at 220Ω" ER/RRC and could probably overcome a circa 400Ω maximum Impedance: **59.4J/220 = 108J/400Ω**. Indeed, Impedances for the minimal stimulus MECTA "C" based on a uniform MTTLOI of 1.08 most likely resembles the profile below. Note that regardless of increased Impedance, because the threshold outputs remain "constant," the relationship between default outputs and MTTLOI remains constant. In short, a 108J maximum results in a 1.08 MTTLOI just as a 110J maximum results in a 1.1 MTTLOI for all age recipients.

AGE	IMPEDANCE	OUTPUT IN JOULES
10	40	1.08
20	80	4.32
30	120	9.72
40	160	17.28
50	200	27.0
60	240	38.88
70	280	52.88
80	320	69.12
90	360	87.48
100	400	107.5

Below, in much more detail, is the probable actual MECTA "C" presented to the FDA based on a "59.4J at 220Ω" conditional-ER/RRC and a uniform 1.08 MTTLOI in every age category. The machine entirely adheres to the 1982 APA Standard. Note the increase from a 346Ω Impedance to a 400Ω Impedance and the corresponding reduction in MTTLOI from 1.1 to 1.08 due to reducing the ER/RRC.

Possible Actual CONSTANT CURRENT **MECTA "C"** BP DEVICE
(1st GENERATION) by MECTA Corp.1976
BASED ON A ***CONDITIONAL*** 70J at 220Ω ER/RRC (that is, limited to a 110J ceiling) or
a Pure **"59J at 220"** ER/RRC **(59.4J/220Ω = 108J/400Ω)**

VOLTAGE	POWER % @ Age	AGE Yrs	Ω Ohms	FREQUENCY (Hz)	DURATION (SECs)	CURRENT mAmps	ENERGY Joules	CHARGE mC
32	10	10	40	20	.703	800	1.08	33.75
64	20	20	80	40	.703	800	4.32	67.5
96	30	30	120	60	.703	800	9.72	101.25
128	40	40	160	60	.938	800	17.28	135
160	50	50	200	60	1.17	800	27	168.75
192	60	60	240	70	1.21	800	38.88	202.5
208	65	65	260	70	1.31	800	45.63	219.38
224	70	70	280	70	1.41	800	52.88	236.1
256	80	80	320	70	1.61	800	69.12	270
288	90	90	360	70	1.81	800	87.48	303.75
320	100	100	400	70	2.0	800	107.5J	336

.0015 Second Pulse Width

The MECTA "C" above was known to have a .0015 Sec. Wave Length, a .8A Constant Current, a 2.0 Second maximum Duration, an approximate 108 Joule maximum output, and a variable 20 to 70 Hertz Frequency. The 320V maximum is speculative but probable for this early Brief Pulse model. In that 100 Joules is known to seize all 100 year old recipients, 108 Joules is a 1.08 fold threshold output, that is, just above threshold (or 100J). In that the Multifold Threshold Titration Level Output Intensity must be uniform, the remaining default outputs per specific age groups can be derived by multiplying 1.08 times the "constant" seizure thresholds for each age category. Although Impedances may rise with increased output, seizure thresholds remain relatively constant in that they are liberally construed. In short, if 100J is the maximum amount needed to induce seizures in all recipients in all circumstances, the MECTA "C," in accordance with the APA Standard, was a just above threshold output device designed for minimal stimulus outputs with BL ECT in all age categories. Indeed, based on relative constants which includes 100J for the 100 year old category, the 1.08 x threshold outputs just surpass the "electrical dosages" required to induce a grand mal seizure in each age category. While this impressed the FDA, such machines, as we shall see, were not to endure.

A 108J maximum at 400Ω is indeed allowed based on an acceptable "59.4J at 220Ω" ER/RRC (in that this ER/RRC does not exceed the "70J at 220Ω" maximum specified in the APA Standard) just as the 108J maximum output is below the overall APA maximum of 110J. In short, the APA Standard can easily accommodate a 100 year old with a 400Ω Impedance (and this can be facilitated simply by increasing Voltage or some other parameter as we have seen) while yet remaining at or under the 110J maximum or (110J ÷ 100J =) 1.1 MTTLOI. In this case the threshold output is a (108J ÷100J =) 1.08 MTTLOI in all age categories, still minimal stimulus and still below the 1.1 MTTLOI maximum indirectly specified in the 1982 APA Standard.

All Ages

But can the APA Standard accommodate increased Impedances while still adhering to minimal stimulus or a 1.1 MTTLOI (or below) in all age categories? For example, does the machine conform to the same 1.1 MTTLOI (or under) for the 90 year old with a correspondingly increased Impedance? Just as a higher Impedance is found for the 100 year old (from 346Ω to 400Ω), we must assume Impedance has correspondingly risen for the 90 year old, in this case, from 311Ω to a relative 360Ω (346Ω/400Ω = 311Ω/360Ω); see Impedances for "70J at 220Ω" above as opposed to Impedances for "59J at 220Ω" above). Based solely on the ER/RRC, going from an allowable 70J at 220Ω to an allowable 59.4J at 220Ω ER/RRC (to accommodate the increased Impedance), appears to allow a maximum output for the 90 year old of ***97.2J*** (**59.4J/220 = *97.2J*/360Ω**). However, we need the 90 year old to be administered the same 1.08 MTTLOI as the 100 year old who receives 108 maximum joules. For this to occur, we must further modify, multiplying threshold output for the ninety year old which is (81J) by 1.08 to obtain not 97.2J, but an (81J x 1.08 =) ***87.48J*** default output, well below the 97.2J maximum "allowed by the 59.4J at 220Ω ER/RRC alone. Indeed, at 87.48J, the 90 year old recipient is administered the same 1.08 MTTLOI as the 100 year old at 108J. That is, both the 90 year old and the 100 year old are administered the same (87.48J ÷ 81J =; 108J ÷ 100J =) 1.08 MTTLOI. What we have confirmed then, is that the ER/RRC, besides insuring gradational outputs, is chiefly useful for discovering overall maximum output and the uniform MTTLOI for a particular device. All other default outputs must be determined by multiplying the "relative constant" for a particular age category by the default MTTLOI (1.08) for that particular BP device.

To obtain all other default outputs with respect to age then, we simply take the MTTLOI obtained for the 100 year old (108J ÷100J = 1.08 MTTLOI) and multiply by the relative output constant for any particular age category. For example, for the ten year old , we must multiply the threshold output or relative constant for the ten year old child (1.0J) by the 1.08 MTTLOI to derive a (1.08 x 1.0J =) ***1.08J*** default output for the ten year old child on this particular BP device. Thus, at 1.08J, the 10 year old child is administered the same (1.08J x 1.0J =) 1.08 MTTLOI as the 90 year old and the 100 year old adult.

Applying the APA Standard at the Highest Impedances

But can the APA Standard consisting of a "70J at 220Ω" conditional-ER/RRC with 110J overall ceiling, thereby mandating minimal stimulus outputs of 1.1 fold or less for all age groups, accommodate extraordinarily high

Impedances up to the highest allowable APA Impedance of 600Ω? Let us use 562Ω as the experiment in that this Impedance figure is significant as we shall later see.

To overcome an Impedance of 562Ω while remaining in compliance with the 1982 APA Standard, we must reduce the ER/RRC even further, using an allowable "43J at 220Ω" conditional-ER/RRC still limited, of course, to a 110J overall ceiling.

XJ/220Ω = 110J/562.5Ω = *43J/220Ω*
***43J/220Ω* = 110J/562.5Ω**

We can see above that in using a "43J at 220Ω" conditional-ER/RRC, 110J remains the maximum output in accordance with the APA Standard and this 110J maximum output applies only to a 100 year old recipient with an inordinately and, in fact, unrealistically (at a 110J maximum output) high Impedance of 562Ω. In any case, at 110 joules, the 100 year old yet receives a (110J ÷100J =) 1.1 MTTLOI or just above threshold output in accordance with the APA standard. (Here we also see that reducing ER/RRC does not necessarily reduce the 110J APA ceiling.)

Using Ohm's Law, we find that the Voltage of a Brief Pulse device based on a "43J at 220Ω" conditional-ER/RRC requires 450V to reach a maximum 562Ω Impedance.

43J*/220Ω = *110/562Ω
Ohm's Law: Voltage = Current x Ω
.8 **x 562Ω = 450V**

To avoid surpassing the 110J ceiling, the maximum Charge and maximum Duration must be reduced from the 336mC of the MECTA "C" to 245mC and from the 2.0 Second Duration of the MECTA "C" to 1.45 Sec. Using the formula: Charge = EO/Current x Impedance, we get:

Charge = EO/Current x Impedance
Charge = 110J ÷ .8A x 562Ω = **.245 or 245mC**

And from another formula: Duration = Charge/Current x (hz x 2) x WL, we get:
Duration = .245 ÷ .8A x 140 x .0015 = **1.45 sec.**

"70J at 220Ω" ER/RRC

VOLTAGE	POWER % @ Age	AGE Yrs	Ω Ohms	FREQUENCY (Hz)	DURATION (SECs)	CURRENT mAmps	ENERGY Joules	CHARGE mC
276	100	100	345	70	2.38	800	110J	400

"59J at 220Ω" ER/RRC

320	100	100	400	70	2.0	800	107.5J	336

"43J at 220Ω" ER/RRC

450	100	100	562	70	1.45	800	110J	245

Thus, by increasing the Voltage and reducing both Duration and Charge, 110J can be made to overcome even a 562Ω Impedance with a legal 1.1 MTTLOI. Moreover, rises in Impedance for all other age categories can be overcome in exactly the same manner, simply by increasing Voltage, and decreasing Charge and Duration and so maintaining a 1.1 MTTLOI or below. In sum, there appears to be no need to increase electrical output (in joules) even in the unlikely event that Impedance reaches as high as 562Ω with a 110J maximum output BP device. In turn, there appears to be no need to breach the 1982 APA 110J ceiling Standard simply to overcome improbably high Impedances. So long as all the age-related (relative) output constants are reached for every age level, adequate seizure can be induced in every age category, regardless of Impedance. Indeed, BP devices, unlike SW devices, are inherently made to automatically increase in Voltage to maintain Amperage when higher Impedances must be overcome. If true, moreover, the first generation MECTA "D," unnecessarily breached the 110J APA ceiling in order to accommodate atypically high Impedances. In addition, second and third generation BP devices, as we shall see, need not have increased electrical output simply to accommodate atypically high Impedances, but were almost certainly manufactured, as we shall discover, simply because manufacturers began to realize or already knew that adequate seizure alone is ineffective.

In short, the 1982 APA Standard, that is, the ER/RRC of "70J at 220" with its conditional 110J overall ceiling can accommodate even extremely high Impedances while yet confining all outputs in all age categories to a consistent 1.1 fold or Multifold Threshold Titration Level Output Intensity, in short, minimal stimulus output for all recipients with a "70J at 220Ω" ER/RRC or below.

Applying the 1982 APA Standard

Importantly then, ER/RRC by and of itself, though mandating gradational age-related outputs, does not identify specific age-related machine outputs. Rather, it is the second aspect, the Standard's critical 110J ceiling that stipulates the uniform 1.1 MTTLOI (110J ÷ 100J = 1.1 fold) for all recipients. (This principle holds true for both conditional-ER/RRCs and pure-ER-RRCs as we shall later see.) The uniformly applied MTTLOI or 1.1 fold threshold output maximum, the highest titration level intensity above that required to induce an adequate seizure allowed by the APA Standard in every age category, is derived from the APA 110J ceiling stipulation. Thus, it is neither the "70J at 220Ω" conditional-ER/RRC nor the 110J overall ceiling, but "70J at 220Ω" ER/RRC and 110J overall ceiling combined that stipulates output. Without the ER/RRC, the 110J ceiling could be administered in every age category. Without the 110J ceiling stipulation, though gradationally administered, maximum output could surpass the 1.1 MTTLOI stipulation. For example, maximum output could be based on maximum machine Impedance allowing up to, with a 70J at 220Ω ER/RRC, (70J/220Ω = XJ/600Ω =) 190J maximum, or a 1.9 MTTLOI, nearly twice threshold in every age category. Thus, it is the APA Standard's 110J ceiling together with the ER/RRC which mandates gradational output conforming to a uniform 1.1 MTTLOI maximum or minimal stimulus output for all age categories. Critically then, the 1982 APA Standard mandates a maximum 1.1 MTTLOI for all made-in-America Brief Pulse (BP) machines regardless of Impedance. Plainly, the 1982 APA Standard was designed to prohibit any individual from being administered more than 1.1 times the amount of electrical energy required to induce a so-called adequate seizure in any age category. Moreover, because this 1.1 (or less) MTTLOI must be uniformly applied to all age recipients, knowledge of "relative threshold constants" are required. With all aspects of the standard working together then, the APA Standard guarantees minimal stimulus outputs (of 1.1 fold threshold or less) in all age categories regardless of Impedance. With a knowledge of the relative output constants, moreover, specific default outputs guaranteeing both efficacy and minimal stimulus per age category can be identified. Indeed, this is the very promise of its design. Why then, has no Brief Pulse manufacturer provided regulators or the general public with the "relative threshold constants" ?

The APA Standard continued

The ER/RRC concomitant with the all-important 110J ceiling, mandates a uniform Multifold Threshold Titration Level Output Intensity of no more than 1.1 fold threshold in all age categories, critical in that the higher the "dosages" of electricity above threshold, the more potentially damaging the procedure. Thus the APA Standard is designed to guarantee seizure without excessive outputs. Both Utah, the FDA, and even the APA all agreed during the 1976-1982 FDA hearings that excessive or unnecessarily high electrical dosing has long been linked to cognitive dysfunction and brain injury (Proctor and Goodwin, 1943; Alexander and Lowenbach, 1944; Cronholm and Ottosson, 1963; Dunn, Giuditta, Wilson, and Glassman, 1974; Echlin, 1942; Essman, 1968; Friedman, 1942; Friedman, Wilcox, and Reiter, 1942; Gordon, 1982; Liberson, 1945a; Liberson, 1949; Malitz, Sackheim, and Decina, 1979; McGaugh and Alpern, 1966; Ottosson, 1960; Proctor and Goodwin, 1943; Reed, 1988; Squire and Zouzounis, 1986; Wilcox, 1946). Conversely, limiting electrical energy only to that guaranteed to elicit an adequate seizure is essentially associated with increased safety. The original idea of the Brief Pulse device as supported by the 1982 APA Standard and as supported by the Utah Report condoned by FDA then, was quite obviously to limit the amount of electricity to only that necessary to elicit adequate seizures, in short, the least amount of electricity possible to induce a grand mal seizure. Within Richard Weiner's "1982 Petition to Reclassify" wherein the 1982 APA standard is located, even Weiner informs:

> The function of an ECT device is to deliver an electrical stimulus intensity to produce a generalized seizure. [130] Stimuli of lesser intensity result in ineffective treatments, while stimuli of greater intensity may result in adverse effects upon central nervous system functioning and/or structure . . . . (Department of Health and Human Services, 1982a, p. A41)

Thus, the "70J at 220Ω" ER/RRC in conjunction with the overall 110 Joule ceiling comprising the 1982 APA Standard for Brief Pulse Devices, limits output (for BL ECT) to effective minimal stimulus or just above threshold outputs, that is, just above the amount of electrical energy necessary to elicit an adequate (grand mal) seizure for all age categories. Because the Brief Pulse device could elicit these seizures at half the output (or less) than the maximum output elicited by SW--100 maximum Joules as opposed to 200 maximum Joules (affirmed by the APA Standard and Weiner himself)--the Brief Pulse device, in accordance with the 1982 APA Standard, was touted to be a great advancement over SW which was to be ultimately discarded.

The overall Absolute EO Ceiling of "110 Joules" together with the "70J at 220Ω" ER/RRC assuring gradational outputs relative to age, both of which are clearly specified within the 1982 APA Standard--assured minimal stimulus output for all age categories. Significantly, the clearly delineated 110J ceiling within the APA Standard is based on the assertion (within the same document) that adequate seizures can be induced with Brief Pulse in even the oldest, most seizure-recalcitrant recipient with never more than 100 Joules. Within the 1982 document itself, as noted, the central author of the 1982 APA standard-- psychiatrist and electrical engineer Richard Weiner--reassuringly states to the FDA in absolute terms (as already noted above):

> Using a pulse device, the [APA] Task Force [1978] has determined that only 0.6% of seizure thresholds were greater than 70 Joules and that none were greater than 100 Joules. (Department of Health and Human Services, 1982a, p. A53)

Thus, using Bilateral ECT (by far the most common form), the 110 Joule ceiling of the 1982 APA Standard is ten joules higher than the least amount of electrical energy necessary (100J) to induce an adequate seizure in even the most seizure-resistant recipient--and thus all 100 year old males in all scenarios. Concisely, according to the APA Standard, no 100 year old, a few of whom may have a seizure threshold up to 100 joules, can be administered more than a 1.1 MTTLOI or 110J maximum joules (110J ÷ 100J = 1.1 fold) which is thus minimal stimulus for BL ECT. Moreover, in that all age categories must be uniformly titrated, by extrapolation, the APA Standard guarantees that no age category can be administered more than a 1.1 MTTLOI, a guarantee of effective, but just above threshold output, assuring that output in every age group can induce the "required" adequate seizure, but with the least amount of electricity possible. The 1982 APA Standard's "70J at 220Ω" ER/RRC in conjunction with the overall 110 Joule ceiling then, plainly guarantees, as noted, a 1.1 MTTLOI maximum for all age categories. In that the theory behind ECT--convulsion theory-- is plainly based on the induction of the "adequate seizure alone" and not electricity--the aim of the new reduced energy Brief Pulse device encouraged by both Utah and the FDA, strictly regulated by the 1982 APA Standard--is utilization of the least amount of electricity to induce the adequate seizure, thereby insuring recipients the most effective, safest procedure possible. To reiterate, the 100 Joule maximum threshold constant for the 100 year old male, clearly the significant factor in the determination of the 110J APA ceiling, together with a "70J at 220Ω ER/RRC guarantees gradational outputs relative to age based on a uniform 1.1 MTTLOI maximum for each and every recipient. That is, the APA Standard comprised of the 110J ceiling together with a "70J at 220Ω" ER/RRC guarantees effective (by virtue of enough electrical energy to induce an adequate seizure) uniform, minimal stimulus outputs (by virtue of the maximum 1.1 MTTLOI) for all age categories, a goal manifestly illustrated by the newly resurrected prototypical MECTA "C" presented to the FDA within the 1976-1982 hearings on ECT.

[130] A device with a totally disparate function then, i.e., a machine designed to deliver adequate dosages of electricity to be effective, cannot be an "ECT" device.

FDA Approval

Representing all American manufacturers, Weiner, in effect, avowed to the FDA via the 1982 APA Standard (and in person) that in using the new BP device (in lieu of the older SW devices) to administer the most common form of ECT--BL ECT, no recipient would ever need receive more than 110 maximum Joules (guaranteed by the 110J ceiling) and that no recipient would ever be administered more than a 1.1 MTTLOI (based on the "70J at 220Ω" ER/RRC in conjunction with the 110J ceiling)--that is, that via the new Brief Pulse device, adequate seizures could be induced with never more than just above seizure threshold or minimal stimulus output.

Much touted both by the APA and BP manufacturers as having the advantage of inducing adequate seizures in all instances at circa 110J or less, one-quarter to one-half the energy output of the SW device which allegedly emitted up to 200J (Department of Health and Human Services, 1982a, G3-G4), the BP device, presented by way of the1982 APA Standard, convinced the FDA of the much improved safety of ECT over SW, a precept wholly accepted and much underpinned by the general media.

It was the 108 Joule MECTA "C" BP device presented to the FDA (and thus the public) during the pivotal FDA hearings on ECT from 1976 to 1982, together with the then new 1982 APA Standard, therefore, which epitomized and convinced the FDA that the "new and improved" Brief Pulse apparatus specifically limited to 110J and a "70J at 220Ω" ER/RRC, would now emit minimal stimulus outputs in all age classes. The APA Standard, manifested by the MECTA "C," therefore, was the assurance both the public and the FDA required that the new and improved Brief Pulse device, limited to 110J, circa half the output of the much more dangerous 200J SW device would be safely administered from that point forward. Indeed, the APA standard newly substantiated the overall superiority of Brief Pulse safety over SW. It was thus the MECTA "C" and the 1982 APA Standard which launched the new Brief Pulse era of "ECT. " It was upon this assurance moreover, that manufacturers of the new BP device via spokesperson Richard Weiner convinced the FDA that a standard could indeed be written and machines built in accordance with such a standard, guaranteeing the improved safety and equal efficacy of ECT thereby propelling ECT into the next century as a perfectly legitimate medical procedure wherein for the first time in many years, safety outweighed risk. A true "ECT" device based on "true ECT" finally seemed possible wherein memory dysfunction could be mitigated or even eliminated, indeed guaranteed by a new legitimate standard. Thus, it was the 1982 APA Standard together with the MECTA "C" which propelled the promise of an equally effective, much safer reduced EO device into the post FDA era thereby attaining FDA approval which, in turn, pledged both the safety and efficacy of ECT to the public general.

Conditional ER/RRC

A little more discussion regarding the word "conditional" may be warranted. The ER/RRC of "<u>70J at 220Ω</u>" with 110J ceiling is Conditional in that maximum output is not based purely on the APA Impedance maximum of 600Ω, but on the stipulated 110J ceiling. This can be confirmed from the fact that a Pure-ER/RRC interpretation of "70J at 220Ω" relative to the maximum APA Impedance of <u>600Ω</u>--results in an illegal output under the 1982 APA Standard--of <u>191 Joules</u>, an EO well in excess of the clearly specified 110J ceiling.

70J/220Ω = XJ/600Ω. <u>X = 191J</u>

Plainly then, the "<u>70J at 220Ω</u>" phrase within the APA Standard is not a pure-ER/RRC. Rather, it is a Conditional-ER/RRC and this is due to the 110J ceiling manifestly identified within the APA Standard which, in conjunction with the ER/RRC, serves to implement a maximum 1.1 MTTLOI in every age category. The importance of the conditional-ER/RRC within the APA Standard; therefore, is not to identify a maximum overall ceiling or even maximum output for specific age groups (both of which are accomplished by the clearly specified 110J ceiling in conjunction with relative constants), but rather to insure gradationally decreasing output ceilings in accordance with decreasing age or Impedances. In any case, it is important to understand the concept of a "conditional-ER/RRC" in that following the FDA investigation, conditional-ER/RRC transmutes into pure-ER/RRC no longer based on the 110J ceiling, but based on maximum Impedance alone, as we shall soon see.

An Easy but Important Mechanism

So long as both elements are known, that is, ER/RRC and the overall maximum output, the easiest mechanism for determining the power and purpose of a Brief Pulse device is simply to divide maximum overall power in Joules (once it is determined) by 100J (the minimum output required to seize even the oldest most seizure-recalcitrant 100 year old male in all circumstances; see Weiner's assertion above). In short, the MTTLOI for any BP device is derived from the machine's maximum EO divided by 100J. It is because the MTTLOI derived for the oldest age category acts as a common denominator, that this common denominator acts as the MTTLOI for all other age categories and so must be uniformly applied. For example, if maximum power on a Brief Pulse device is 110J and an ER/RRC is in place to guarantee gradational outputs, we need merely divide the 110J overall maximum output by 100J to obtain the uniform MTTLOI for the BP device in general. Indeed (110J ÷ 100J =) 1.1 is the maximum MTTLOI allowed by the APA Standard. If, on the other hand, maximum output is 108 joules as is the case with the MECTA "C," simply by dividing 108J by 100J, we can determine that the power and purpose of the MECTA "C" is to deliver a 1.08 MTTLOI or just above threshold output to every age recipient. Later Brief Pulse devices, as we shall see, breach the 1982 APA Standard, emitting much more than 110 joules and so have much higher MTTLOIs. Even so, once we deduce maximum output for these devices, whether this be from a conditional-ER/RRC (i.e.70J at 220Ω with 110J ceiling) or pure-ER/RRC (i.e. "100J at 220Ω" with no stipulated ceiling and so (100J/220Ω = XJ/562Ω; X =) 256J , we simply divide the maximum overall machine output (once we have it) by 100J (i.e.110J ÷ 100J = **1.1 MTTLOI**; 256J ÷ 100J = **2.56 MTTLOI**) to determine the MTTLOI for that particular BP device.

PART III

Section III: First Generation Brief Pulse Devices

CHAPTER 12

1st Generation BP Devices Based on Conditional-ER/RRC within the 1982 APA Standard

Between 1976-1982, Brief Pulse was portrayed as a device which could effectively induce adequate seizures and efficacious treatment at between one quarter (Grahn, 1976, October 15, p.10; Grahn, Jerhrich, Couvillon, and Moench,1977, p.52) and then one half the output of SW (Department of Health and Human Services, 1982a, G3-G4). It is difficult to trace the exact devolution[131] of MECTA devices--the first modern-day resurrections of Brief Pulse devices--in that Voltage increases are either not reported or not reliably reported by MECTA. A further complication is MECTA's practice of name overlap regarding devolving apparatuses. Thus, even when power increases are identified from one generation to the next, the machine name, which often remains the same, cannot be depended upon to distinguish between the two. We can be certain, however, that from 1976-1982 (the span of time FDA publicly investigated the "ECT" device), although the cumulative output of Brief Pulse remained well below the cumulative power of SW, MECTA BP devices began increasing in power and that post 1982 (following the FDA investigation), BP devices began to intensify in power. For instance, in 1976 and 1977, Grahn (author of the Utah Report) described the MECTA BP device as capable of 81 maximum Joules, utilizing one-quarter the power of SW (Grahn, 1976, October 15, p.10; Grahn, Jerhrich, Couvillon, and Moench,1977, p.52). The 81J MECTA BP device depicted by Grahn (below) may have been an early "A" or "B" device or possibly an earlier version of the later MECTA "C" device. For that reason, we shall refer to this 81J apparatus as the early MECTA "C" device. Using a few simple calculations and parameters provided by Utah (Grahn, 1976, October 15, p.10; Grahn, Jerhrich, Couvillon, and Moench,1977, p.52), we can determine that the early 81J MECTA BP device described by Grahn between 1976-1977, utilized approximately 240V, and could overcome at least 300Ω of Impedance.

Early MECTA "C" (circa 1976)

Impedance-Based Formula for Finding Output:
.8A. x .8A. x 301Ω x 140 Pulses x .0015 PW x 2.0 Sec. = **81J**.

Amperage x Impedance = Voltage
.8A x 301Ω = circa **240V**

Voltage-Based Formula for Finding Output:
240V x .8A. x 140 Pulses x .0015 PW x 2.0 Sec. = **81J**.

---

[131] "Devolution" refers to the increase in power in lieu of the sought after decrease in power of the Brief Pulse device, particularly compared to SW.

Formulaically, we can speculatively deduce the early "C"s parameters. The Early MECTA "C" described above was known to have a .0015 Sec. Wave Length, a .8A Constant Current, a 2.0 Second maximum Duration, an approximate 81 Joule maximum output, and a variable 20 to 70 Hertz Frequency. Both the 300Ω maximum Impedance and 240V maximum Voltage can be derived (see above). Voltage for remaining age categories is speculatively derived by dividing 240V by 10 (240V ÷ 10 = 24) and then subtracting 24V from each descending age category. For example, Voltage for the 90 and 80 year old categories are speculatively derived as 216V and 192V (240V - 24 = 216V; 216V - 24 = 192V). ER/RRC is known. Maximum Impedance is derived from ER/RRC or Ohm's Law. (59/220Ω = 81J/301Ω; 240V ÷ .8A = circa 301Ω). Remaining Impedances are speculatively derived by dividing 300Ω by 10 and subtracting that figure for each descending age category (300Ω ÷ 10 = 30; 300Ω - 30Ω = 270Ω for the 90 year old). Remaining EOs are derived by multiplying .81 x relative constant Threshold outputs for each age category (used by manufacturers). Charges are derived through the formula: Charge = EO ÷ Current x Impedance.

In that Weiner depicts 100 Joules to seize even the oldest (100 years) most seizure recalcitrant recipient under any circumstance and which becomes the seizure threshold minimum (for BL ECT) around which all American BP devices are eventually calibrated, the fact that the early MECTA "C" emitted a maximum of only 81 joules, a (81J ÷ 100J =) .81 MTTLOI, allegedly not enough to elicit adequate seizures with BL ECT for all recipients all the time, is perplexing. Indeed, the MTTLOI must be uniform, so that if we utilize 81J for the 100 year old, which is a .81 MTTLOI, the remaining default outputs must also be derived by multiplying .81 times the seeming "constant" seizure thresholds manufacturers use for each age category.

The Early MECTA "C" (CONDITIONAL ER/RRC) limited to 81 maximum Joules and thus .81 fold in every age category with BL ECT

AGE	Impedance Threshold (Ω)	Threshold Output in Joules	MECTA "C" EO (Joules)	Multifold Thresh. Titration Level
10	30	1.0	.81	.81
20	60	4.0	3.24	.81
30	90	9.0	7.29	.81
40	120	16.0	12.96	.81
50	150	25.0	20.25	.81
60	180	36.0	29.16	.81
65	195	42.6	34.50	.81
70	210	49.0	39.69	.81
80	240	64.0	51.84	.81
90	270	81.0	65.61	.81
100	301	100	81	.81

The Early MECTA "C" (CONDITIONAL ER/RRC) limited to 81 maximum Joules and thus .81 fold threshold in every age category with BL ECT

This suggests that either 1) most 100 year old recipients do seize at 81J or less from which we must conclude that either the 100J threshold maximum figured for the 100 year old category is well above threshold for most 100 year old recipients:

> Using a pulse device, the [APA] Task Force [1978] has determined that only 0.6% of seizure thresholds were greater than 70 Joules . . . . (Department of Health and Human Services, 1982a, p. A53)

or 2) that the early MECTA "C" was designed for UL ECT. Indeed, according to Grahn, what we have deemed the early "MECTA 'C'" could elicit seizures at one quarter the output of SW. In that Weiner depicts BP as using half the output required for SW to elicit the same adequate seizure with BL ECT, and in that UL (Brief Pulse) ECT requires one half the output of BL (Brief Pulse) ECT or 50J maximum to induce the same adequate seizure, and finally, in that Weiner depicts SW as requiring 200J to elicit adequate seizures inclusive of all age recipients, then the 50 maximum joules required for UL ECT with BP indeed equals one quarter the 200J output required for SW (200J ÷ 50J = 4). In short, the early MECTA "C" may have been exclusively designed to utilize UL ECT.

The Early MECTA "C" (CONDITIONAL ER/RRC) limited to 81 maximum Joules and thus an 1.62 fold in every age category with UL ECT

AGE	Impedance Threshold (Ω)	Threshold Output in Joules	MECTA "C" EO (Joules)	Multifold Thresh. Tit. Lev, UL ECT
10	30	.5	.81	1.62
20	60	2.0	3.24	1.62
30	90	4.5	7.29	1.62
40	120	8.0	12.96	1.62
50	150	12.5	20.25	1.62
60	180	18.0	29.16	1.62
65	195	21.3	34.50	1.62
70	210	24.5	39.69	1.62
80	240	32.0	51.84	1.62
90	270	40.5	65.61	1.62
100	301	50.0	81	1.62

The Early MECTA "C" (CONDITIONAL ER/RRC) limited to 81 maximum Joules and thus 1.62 fold threshold in every age category with UL ECT

In any case, the early 81J MECTA "C" below complies with Weiner's 1982 APA Standard, and so was designed for minimal stimulus outputs in all age categories probably with UL ECT. Such machines, as has been noted, were not to endure.

Formulas for finding Brief Pulse Parameters:

Charge = Duration x Current x (hz x 2) x WL
Charge = EO/Current x Impedance
EO = Charge x Current x Impedance
Duration = Charge/Current x (hz x 2) x WL
EO = Voltage x Current x (hz x 2) x WL x Duration
EO = (Current squared) x Impedance x (hz x 2) x WL x Duration
Ohm's Law: Current = Voltage/Ω; Ω = Voltage/Current; Voltage = Current x Ω

Possible Actual CONSTANT CURRENT Early **MECTA "C"** BP DEVICE
(1st GENERATION) by MECTA Corp.1976.
Conformed to the ***CONDITIONAL*** 70J at 220Ω ER/RRC with 110J ceiling 1982 APA Standard
This early "C" was based on a **"59J at 220"** ER/RRC **with 81J Ceiling**

VOLTAGE	POWER % @ Age	AGE Yrs	Ω Ohms	FREQUENCY (Hz)	DURATION (SECs)	CURRENT mAmps	ENERGY Joules	CHARGE mC
24	10	10	30	20	.703	800	.81	33.75
48	20	20	60	40	.703	800	3.24	67.5
72	30	30	90	60	.703	800	7.3	101.25
96	40	40	120	60	.938	800	13	135
120	50	50	150	60	1.17	800	20.3	168.75
144	60	60	180	70	1.21	800	29.2	202.5
156	65	65	195	70	1.31	800	34.5	219.38
168	70	70	210	70	1.41	800	39.7	236.1
192	80	80	240	70	1.61	800	51.8	270
216	90	90	270	70	1.81	800	65.6	303.75
240	100	100	301	70	2.0	800	81J	336

.0015 Second Pulse Width

The early MECTA "C" above based on an ER/RRC of "59J at 220Ω" and an "81J" maximum output complied with the "70J at 220Ω" ER/RRC and "110J" ceiling maximum depicted within the 1982 APA Standard.

It was a true "ECT" device in that it could induce adequate seizures at just above threshold outputs with UL ECT at about one-quarter the emissions needed with SW (which appears to be used exclusively with BL ECT).

The Slightly Later MECTA "C" (circa 1979)

Next comes the slightly later, slightly more powerful MECTA "C. " Formulaically, we can speculatively deduce the latter "C"s parameters with a few known ones such as Amperage (.8A), the ER/RRC (59J at 220Ω), maximum output (108J), Hertz (70), maximum Pulse Width (.0015Sec.), and maximum Duration (2.0 Seconds). For example, from the ER/RRC and maximum output, we can derive maximum Impedance and maximum Voltage. Note, the Voltage increase from 240V for the earlier MECTA "C" to 320V for the later MECTA "C. "

Later (1979) MECTA C: ER/RRC and maximum output/Impedance:
59/220Ω = **108J/402Ω**.

Voltage = Current x Impedance
.8A x 402Ω = circa **321V**

Impedance-Based Formula for Finding Maximum Output:
.8A. x .8A. x **402Ω** x 140 Pulses x .0015 PW x 2.0 Sec. = **108J**.

Voltage-Based Formula for Finding Maximum Output:
320V x .8A. x 140 Pulses x .0015 PW x 2.0 Sec. = **108J**.

Right away, we can see that the later, slightly more powerful MECTA "C" device below contains many of the same basic parameters as Grahn's (1976-77) earlier MECTA "C," except that it now emits an approximate 108J maximum in lieu of the earlier 81J, and can now overcome a 402Ω ceiling as opposed to a 301Ω ceiling, all of which yet conformed to Weiner's 1982 APA Standard. Significantly, the more powerful MECTA "C" is presented in Weiner's *1982 Petition to Reclassify* as emitting one-half (in lieu of one-fourth) the total emission of SW (Department of Health and Human Services, 1982a, G3-G4), a change from the earlier model described in the Utah Report. The slightly later MECTA "C," as noted, in lieu of the earlier "C's" 240V maximum apparently increases to a probable 320V maximum (Food and Drug Administration, 1984, attachment I) responsible for enhancing maximum output, as noted, from 81 Joules to 108 Joules (Ibid). With the exception of increased Voltage, then, the later "C" utilizes the same .8 Ampere Current, the same .0015 Second Pulse Width, the same 140 Pulses, the same 2.0 second maximum Duration and the same "59J at 220Ω" ER/RRC as the earlier MECTA "C," (Food and Drug Administration, 1984, attachment I; Grahn, 1976, October 15, p.10; Grahn, Jerhrich, Couvillon, and Moench,1977, p.52). Indeed, an unidentified 320V MECTA device is depicted within MECTA's 1984, 510K (pre-market application) files (Food and Drug Administration, 1984, attachment I) almost certainly the one described here. This later model "C" (320V, 108J) with its 108J maximum appears to be able to overcome a maximum Impedance of circa 402Ω in order to emit adequate seizures with BL ECT in all age categories and in all instances (Department of Health and Human Services, 1982a, A53, E20; Food and Drug Administration, 1984, Attachment I).

> Using a pulse device, the [APA] Task Force [1978] has determined that [of] . . . seizure thresholds . . . none were greater than 100 Joules (Department of Health and Human Services, 1982a, p. A53).

In fact, age-related dosing in general, and thus the titration level intensity (MTTLOI) appears to increase from a (81J ÷ 100J =) .81 MTTLOI to a (108J ÷ 100J =) 1.08 MTTLOI for all age categories with BL ECT. If 100J is the maximum required for the 100 year old recipient in all circumstances using BL ECT, then 108J makes the device "just above threshold" or minimal stimulus for all age categories with BL ECT.

The later MECTA "C" (CONDITIONAL ER/RRC) limited to 108 maximum Joules and thus 1.08 fold in every age category

AGE	Impedance Threshold (Ω)	Threshold Output in Joules	MECTA "C" EO (Joules)	Multifold Thresh. Titration Level
10	40	1.0	1.08	1.08
20	80	4.0	4.32	1.08
30	120	9.0	9.72	1.08
40	160	16.0	17.28	1.08
50	200	25.0	27	1.08
60	240	36.0	38.88	1.08
65	260	42.6	46	1.08
70	280	49.0	52.95	1.08
80	320	64.0	69.12	1.08
90	360	81.0	87.48	1.08
100	400	100	108	1.08

The later MECTA "C" (CONDITIONAL ER/RRC) limited to 108 maximum Joules and thus 1.08 fold in every age category with BL ECT

For whatever reason, this more powerful MECTA "C," is depicted in 510K files as emitting 53.7J at 200Ω tantamount to (53.7J/200Ω = XJ/220Ω =) 59J at 220Ω, (Food and Drug Administration, 1986B), once again epitomizing the Brief Pulse device to the FDA as conforming to the 1982 APA Equivalent Ratio/Rate Rise Ceiling (ER/RRC) of "70J at 220Ω" and 110J ceiling output (Department of Health and Human Services, 1982a, E20). Of equal importance then, not only did these devices conform to the ER/RRC, but both the earlier 81J "C" and later 108J MECTA "C" conformed to the 1982 APA Standard's 110J ceiling for modern day Brief Pulse devices. In short, these initial Brief Pulse machines presented to the FDA between 1976 and 1982, conformed to the 1982 APA Standard looked for by the FDA (Ibid). Of interest is the fact that at 81 Joules maximum, the early MECTA "C" emitted a .81 MTTLOI with BL ECT, quite possibly not enough to induce adequate seizures with BL ECT in all age categories, all of the time. On the other hand, as noted above, this same early "C" emitted a (81J ÷ 50J =) 1.62 MTTLOI for UL (unilateral) ECT at all age levels, more than enough to seize all recipients with UL ECT all of the time. For this reason, the earlier MECTA "C," as noted above, may have been predominantly designed for UL ECT and may even have represented an increase in power compared to what may have been even earlier "A" and "B" models emitting outputs even closer to threshold with UL ECT. The final, more powerful MECTA "C" at 108 Joules maximum on the other hand, appears to have been designed for just over threshold output with BL ECT for all ages all of the time, suggesting that manufacturers were already coming to the conclusion that UL ECT, although eliciting the same adequate seizures, was simply not as effective as BL ECT. In any case, all MECTA machines up to this point were clearly designed to emit minimal stimulus outputs (just over threshold), the first several devices predominantly with UL ECT and the final, most powerful "C" with BL ECT, all of which could yet successfully induce adequate seizures at far less output than SW. By the time the 108J MECTA "C" was presented to the FDA circa 1979, therefore, BP machines had already begun advancing in power, despite the successful induction of adequate seizures in all age categories.

Possible Actual CONSTANT CURRENT Later **MECTA "C"** BP DEVICE
(1st GENERATION) by MECTA Corp.1979
Conforming to the ***CONDITIONAL*** 70J at 220Ω ER/RRC with 110J ceiling of 1982 APA Standard.
This later "C" is based on a **"59J at 220"** ER/RRC **with 108J Ceiling**

VOLTAGE	POWER % @ Age	AGE Yrs	Ω Ohms	FREQUENCY (Hz)	DURATION (SECs)	CURRENT mAmps	ENERGY Joules	CHARGE mC
32	10	10	40	20	.703	800	1.08	33.75
64	20	20	80	40	.703	800	4.32	67.5
96	30	30	120	60	.703	800	9.72	101.25
128	40	40	160	60	.938	800	17.28	135
160	50	50	200	60	1.17	800	27	168.75
192	60	60	240	70	1.21	800	38.88	202.5
208	65	65	260	70	1.31	800	45.63	219.38
224	70	70	280	70	1.41	800	52.88	236.1
256	80	80	320	70	1.61	800	69.12	270
288	90	90	360	70	1.81	800	87.48	303.75
320	100	100	400	70	2.0	800	107.5J	336

.0015 Second Pulse Width

Above, is the probable actual later MECTA "C" based on a 59.4J at 220Ω conditional-ER/RRC utilizing a uniform 1.08 MTTLOI in every age category. The later "C" was presented to the FDA as entirely adhering to the 1982 APA Standard guaranteeing minimal stimulus outputs with a Brief Pulse device (but with BL ECT). Note the increase from a circa 300Ω Impedance to a circa 400Ω Impedance, the corresponding increase in Voltage from 240V to 320V, and the increase in MTTLOI from .81 to 1.08 for BL ECT in all age categories.

To reiterate: The MECTA "C" above was known to have a .0015 Sec. Wave Length, a .8A Constant Current, a 2.0 Second maximum Duration, an approximate 108 Joule maximum output, and a variable 20 to 70 Hertz Frequency. In that 100 Joules is known to seize all 100 year old recipients in all circumstances, 108 Joules is a 1.08 MTTLOI, that is, just above threshold. In that the MTTLOI must be uniform, the remaining default outputs per specific age groups can be derived by multiplying 1.08 times the relative constant seizure thresholds used for each age category. Although Impedances may rise with increased output, seizure thresholds either remain relatively constant, or BP manufacturers simply use them as constants to calibrate their devices. In short, in accordance with the APA Standard, the MECTA "C" is a just above threshold output device designed for minimal stimulus outputs with BL ECT in all age categories. At a 1.08 MTTLOI, outputs just surpass the electrical energy output required to induce a grand mal seizure in each age category. Such minimal stimulus machines, as has been noted, just as the BP devices of the 40s and 50s, were not to persist.

MECTA "C" Conforms to the 1982 APA Standard

Enthusiastically sanctioned by the FDA, this later, more powerful "C" conformed to the 1982 APA Standard, as noted, which stipulates a maximum 70J at 220Ω ER/RRC,[132] 110J maximum ceiling, and 600Ω maximum Impedance, conditions which could only be met by the more efficient Brief Pulse device as opposed to SW. Thus, the APA Standard licitly sanctioned the later MECTA "C" BP device, a device based on a "59J at 220Ω" ER/RRC, an overall maximum output of 108J, and which could licitly overcome a maximum Impedance of circa 402Ω. In short, what appears to be the quintessential Brief Pulse device looked for by the FDA, the later more powerful MECTA "C," clearly conformed to the "safety" parameters promulgated by Weiner's 1982 APA Standard, which by comparison, implicated SW as unsafe at allegedly twice (200J) the output (Department of Health and Human Services, 1982a, G3-G4). (The "C" as we shall see, could legitimately emit half the output of SW even when SW is set at minimal stimulus in all age categories.) While increasing in power, therefore, and in spite of the fact that the 108J MECTA "C" with BL ECT emitted twice the output necessary to induce adequate seizures compared to UL ECT, the 108J MECTA "C" was legitimately designed to induce minimal stimulus or just over threshold with BL ECT, and so perfectly reflected the stipulations depicted within the 1982 APA Standard. Still, however, neither Weiner nor the manufacturers would endorse the 1982 APA Standard

[132] ER/RRC, Equivalent Ratio-Rate Rise Ceiling, a term invented by the author, is a phrase we find in the 1982 APA Standard which limits the device generally to an output and Impedance based upon the equivalent ratio of "70J at 220Ω" except that the device cannot surpass 110J. This concept shall be discussed in detail in the next section.

for official adoption as the American Standard. Consequently, having been "grandfathered in" by the FDA[133] and so permitted to continue into the next decade and beyond, the ECT device remained in the most dangerous, standardless, FDA Class III category for medical devices, generally

MECTA (1981) D and D-1

Toward the end of the investigation, about 1982 or so, close on the heels of the 108J MECTA "C," MECTA suddenly began creating even more powerful BP devices. For example, the circa 1982 MECTA "D" (or D-1) was described by Glen and Weiner (1983) as the same device as the (108J) MECTA "C" with the exception of incorporating an Impedance Override enabling not 108J, but between 134 and 141 maximum Joules for "difficult cases. " That is, the Impedance Override was supposedly used in instances wherein greater power was needed to overcome exceptionally high Impedance (Ibid). Significantly, and indicative of the fact that "electroconvulsive therapy" is not (even with the production of so-called "adequate seizures") effective at minimal stimulus (as we shall see), it was the MECTA D which first surpassed the circa 110J ceiling established by the 1982 APA Standard. Since the output over 110J was supposed to be an exception, and because the maximum output still did not exceed the alleged 200J maximum of SW, we shall continue to categorize the D/D-1 amongst first generation BP devices in approximate conformity with the 1982 APA Standard (though, in fact, surpassing the 110J ceiling). In that we are provided a number of MECTA "D" parameters--Frequency, Duration, Pulse Width, and Current--and which are the precise parameters of both early and late MECTA "C"s--it is once again Voltage (by this time no longer provided by MECTA) which must have increased in order to occasion the circa 134-141 Joules of power. The 320V, 108J MECTA "C," then, now became (in all probability), either the 400V, 135J or the 420V, 140J MECTA "D/D-1. " We shall, for clarity's sake, treat them as two devices, the "D" and the "D-1. " Tellingly, both the D's maximum machine Impedances and, as already noted, maximum Voltages were suddenly withheld by MECTA. For all subsequent MECTA devices, in fact, MECTA fails to report maximum Voltage, maximum Impedance, and maximum EO. Sometimes reported as 53.7J at 200Ω and at other times as 59.14J at 220Ω (equivalent ratios), the MECTA "D" was allegedly designed to honor the "110J APA ceiling" of the APA Standard, with the "exclusion" of "conditional Override" for "exceptional cases. " "Impedance Override" more than likely entailed increased Voltage from 320 to 400 or 420V. More powerful than the latter "C," the "D/D-1," based on an approximate 134-141J maximum energy output, was probably capable of overcoming Impedances of between 500 and 525Ω. The following contains detailed information regarding possible MECTA D/D1 parameters.

MECTA (1982) D/D-1 *(Probable)*

53.76/200Ω = 59.14J/220Ω

MECTA D/D-1: Conforms to *"70J at 220Ω" Conditional-ER/RRC, but now contains the "exceptional" 134 or 141J ceiling (as opposed to the APA 110J ceiling).*

70J/220Ω = **134J/421Ω** *or*
70J/220Ω = **141J/443Ω**

However, Impedance increases by lowering the ER/RRC. Thus:

53.76J/200Ω = **134J/500Ω** *or*
59.10J/220Ω = **134J/500Ω**

---

[133] "Grandfathered" refers to devices allowed to continue being manufactured without adherence to FDA criteria for new medical devices simply because the older devices had been utilized up to the moment of FDA's new Congressional appointment. As a result, the B-24 SW, though highly criticized, still remains in use. FDA appears to have allowed the grandfathering based on the promise of Weiner's 1982 APA Standard becoming effective through manufacturer application, an application which Weiner and the manufacturers put off indefinitely.

or

53.76J/200Ω = **141.12J/525Ω** *or*
59.10J/220Ω = **141.12J/525Ω**

Conformation:

Voltage-Based Formula for Finding Maximum Output:
400V x .8A. x 140 Pulses x .0015 PW x 2.0Sec. = **134.4J**.

Impedance-Based Formula for Finding Maximum Output:
.8A. x .8A. x **500Ω** x 140 Pulses x .0015PW x 2.0Sec. = **134.4J**.

or

Voltage-Based Formula for Finding Maximum Output:
420V x .8A. x 140 Pulses x .0015 PW x 2.0Sec. = **141.12J**.

Impedance-Based Formula for Finding Maximum Output:
.8A. x .8A. x **525Ω** x 140 Pulses x .0015PW x 2.0Sec. = **141J**.

MECTA does not camouflage the maximum outputs for the two MECTA Cs; in fact, the outputs were much publicized. While neither Weiner nor MECTA, in 1982, reported to the FDA the potential 134-141J output of the "D" or "D-1," it more or less did so about 1984, two years following FDA's formal investigation. Revealingly, however, as already noted, MECTA fails to provide Voltage for the D/D-1 and this begins a precedent for all future MECTA BP devices. As MECTA, quite possibly in attempts to achieve "efficacy," had begun to steadily increase the power of its BP devices, the D/D-1, though still based on a conditional-ER/RRC (that is, limited to a specific EO ceiling though not 110J), was the first BP machine to breach the 110J APA apex.

MECTA Corporation needed both an explicable and uniform method of justifying the surpassing of the APA 110J ceiling, a difficult proposition in that by APA's own contention, "adequate seizures" could be elicited in all cases with never more than 100 joules--the basis of the 1982 APA Standard's 110J ceiling (Department of Health and Human Services, 1982a, A53; E20; G3-G4). While the D and D-1's 134-141J maximums were purportedly used for unusual circumstances only, in which an alleged Impedance was abnormally high, the D-1's probable "141J" maximum either coincidentally or deliberately doubled the "70J" figure contained within the APA ER/RRC phrase of "70J at 220Ω," opening up a new possible interpretation of the "70J at 220Ω" phrase not limited to 110J, but as a mean or average, as we shall soon see. Thus, this exact doubling dynamic may have acted as a segue for what would soon devolve into an "average" or "mean" interpretation of "70J at 220Ω" (70J/220Ω = 140J/440Ω) raising the ceiling from 110 to 140J for all BP devices. In short, the 53J at 200Ω (or equivalent 59J at 220Ω) phrase reported for the quintessential MECTA "C" (59J/220Ω = 108J/402Ω) and again for the MECTA D/D-1 (59J/220Ω = 134J/500Ω; 59J/220Ω = 140J/525Ω), was beginning to transition from a 70J at 220Ω conditional-ER/RRC with 110J ceiling to a quasi or mean-like ER/RRC interpretation creating a new maximum ceiling of (70J/220Ω = <u>XJ</u>/440Ω; X =) 140J. In fact, with an upcoming change in the ER/RRC from "70J at 220Ω" to "100J at 220Ω," an even newer "average" ceiling would emerge of (100J/220Ω = <u>XJ</u>/440Ω; X =) 200J as we shall soon observe. Finally, manufacturers would resort to what this author has deemed the "Mectan Transmutation" (to be discussed later), once again reinterpreting the newer "100J at 220Ω" not even as an average, but as a pure-ER/RRC limited only by maximum machine Impedance, justifying an even higher ceiling of (100J/220Ω = <u>XJ</u>/600Ω; X =) 272J. In any case, the clear energy output ceiling of 110J within the original 1982 APA Standard had now been breached both permanently and surreptitiously.

MECTA D/D1 continued

For now, however, mathematically justifying the surpassing of the 110J apogee of the 1982 APA Standard through the *exceptional* or *difficult case* rationale, MECTA increased Voltage from 325 to between 400V-420V to create the MECTA D and/or D-1 with "Impedance Override. " This increase enabled manufacturers to surpass the 110J APA maximum for the first time since the introduction of the tentatively proposed 1982 APA Standard. Indeed, the "difficult case" rationale would soon "blossom" into an incipient re-interpretation and then total alteration of the 1982 APA Standard generally, eventually "justifying" even grosser breachings of the APA standard as the history of the modern day Brief Pulse device unfolds. It was this MECTA "D" "exception" then, that began quietly unlocking the "sealed door" of the minimal stimulus regulatory mechanism that the 1982 APA Standard attempted to provide, a standard which, no doubt, the FDA had wanted to approve.

In brief then, the D and/or D-1 appears to have been the first modern day BP device to surpass the APA 110 Joule ceiling. By rationalizing its 134-141J output as "exceptional," Brief Pulse manufacturers for the first time since the onset of the FDA hearings, had discovered an initial justification allowing their BP devices to surpass the APA ceiling stipulation of 110 maximum Joules. Few understood that what appeared to be a very subtle change occurring almost invisibly, was for manufacturers, a quiet victory. No public entity thought to object; indeed, none discerned its portentous significance.

The MECTA "D/D-1" (CONDITIONAL ER/RRC) limited to 134 maximum Joules and thus 1.34 fold threshold in every age category

AGE	Impedance Threshold (Ω)	Threshold Output in Joules	MECTA "D" EO (Joules)	Multifold Thresh. Titration Level
10	50	1.0	1.34	1.34
20	100	4.0	4.32	1.34
30	150	9.0	9.72	1.34
40	200	16.0	17.28	1.34
50	250	25.0	27	1.34
60	300	36.0	38.88	1.34
65	325	42.6	46	1.34
70	350	49.0	52.95	1.34
80	400	64.0	69.12	1.34
90	450	81.0	87.48	1.34
100	500	100	134	1.34

Note on the table above how the slight increases in Impedance have no effect on threshold outputs. This is because these outputs are used by manufacturers as relative constants in spite of slight Impedance increases. Manufacturers calibrate their devices with these relative constants for all BP device generations.

<u>Probable Actual</u> CONSTANT CURRENT **MECTA "D"** BP DEVICE
(1st GENERATION) by MECTA Corp.1980
BASED ON A ***<u>Conditional</u>***-ER/RRC (but now limited to 134.4J)
ER/RRC = **"59J at 220Ω" or "80J at 300Ω"**

VOLTAGE	POWER % @ Age	AGE Yrs	Ω Ohms	FREQUENCY (Hz)	DURATION (SECs)	CURRENT mAmps	ENERGY Joules	CHARGE mC
40	10	10	50	20	.448	800	1.344	33.6
80	20	20	100	40	.563	800	4.32	54
120	30	30	150	60	.563	800	9.72	81
160	40	40	200	60	.750	800	17.28	108
200	50	50	250	60	.937	800	27	135
240	60	60	300	70	.964	800	38.88	162
260	65	65	325	70	1.05	800	46	177
280	70	70	350	70	1.125	800	52.95	189
320	80	80	400	70	1.286	800	69.12	216
360	90	90	450	70	1.45	800	87.48	243
400	100	100	500	70	2.0	800	134.4J	336

.0015 Second Pulse Width

The MECTA "D-1" (CONDITIONAL ER/RRC) limited to 141 maximum Joules and thus 1.41 fold in every age category

AGE	Impedance Threshold (Ω)	Threshold Output in Joules	MECTA "D" EO (Joules)	Multifold Thresh. Titration Level
10	52.5	1.0	1.41	1.41
20	105	4.0	5.64	1.41
30	157.5	9.0	12.69	1.41
40	210	16.0	22.56	1.41
50	262.5	25.0	35.25	1.41
60	315	36.0	50.76	1.41
65	341.25	42.6	60.06	1.41
70	367.5	49.0	69.09	1.41
80	420	64.0	90.24	1.41
90	472.5	81.0	114.21	1.41
100	525	100	141	1.41

The MECTA "D/D-1" (CONDITIONAL ER/RRC) limited to 141 maximum Joules and thus 1.41 fold threshold in every age category

Note again on the table above how the slight increases in Impedance have no effect on threshold outputs. This is because manufacturers use these relative constants to calibrate all BP device generations.

Probable Actual CONSTANT CURRENT **MECTA "D-1"** BP DEVICE
(1st GENERATION) by MECTA Corp.1980
BASED ON A ***Conditional***-ER/RRC (but now limited to 141.1)
ER/RRC = **"59J at 220Ω" or "80J at 300Ω"**

VOLTAGE	POWER % @ Age	AGE Yrs	Ω Ohms	FREQUENCY (Hz)	DURATION (SECs)	CURRENT mAmps	ENERGY Joules	CHARGE mC
42.5	10	10	52.5	20	.70	800	1.41	33.6
85	20	20	105	40	.70	800	5.64	67.1
127.5	30	30	157.5	60	.70	800	12.69	101
170	40	40	210	60	.93	800	22.56	134
212.5	50	50	262.5	60	1.17	800	35.25	168
255	60	60	315	70	1.2	800	50.76	201
276.25	65	65	341.25	70	1.31	800	60.06	220
297.5	70	70	367.5	70	1.4	800	69.09	235
340	80	80	420	70	1.6	800	90.24	268.6
382.5	90	90	472.5	70	1.8	800	114.21	302
425	100	100	525	70	2.0	800	141.12	336

.0015 Second Pulse Width

The MECTA "D/D-1" (CONDITIONAL ER/RRC) above is limited to 141 maximum Joules and thus a 1.41 fold threshold or MTTLOI in every age category, breaching the 1982 APA Standard.

Not surprisingly, the exception soon became the rule. Thenceforward, the 1982 APA ceiling Standard of 110 Joules was routinely ignored not only by MECTA but by two subsequent BP manufacturers, Somatics and Elcot. The MECTA D/D-1's precedential violation of the 110 Joule APA ceiling standard was critically undermining of the standard in that once BP devices surpassed the 110J mark, it was only a matter of time before BP machines would once again begin approaching the 200J power maximum of SW devices compared to which BP was supposed to be greatly reduced and, therefore, superior. In turn, future BP devices would quickly lose their minimal stimulus character, no longer electroconvulsive therapy devices at all, but adequate electrical dosage devices, devices wholly based on multiple threshold outputs of electricity, in short, ENR or "Electro Neurotransmission Reduction" devices, as we shall see. In that both the FDA sponsored Grahn Report and the APA Standard itself stipulate minimal stimulus and reduced energy output (allegedly the hallmark of BP ECT devices) as the inherent safeguard against the risk of memory morbidity, and so the high possibility of brain damage, outputs approaching that of SW should have been by definition dangerously unacceptable, indeed, seen as potentially brain-injurious. In fact, this almost certainly would have been the case had the enhancements been at all conspicuous. Plainly, as the waxing power of BP began approaching that of SW, the advantage of BP over SW, that is, the enhanced safety of "ECT" via reduced EO Brief Pulse began to be compromised. With manufacturers' need for increasing power to make the Brief Pulse device more effective, the very premise upon which convulsive theory rests, seemed more and more fallible--in fact, debunkable and discardable just as it had in the 40s and 50s. As implied through the 1976-77 FDA sponsored Grahn investigation, the risk accompanying higher and higher electrical dosages and thus higher and higher MTTLOIs which subsequent BP devices were gradually beginning to deliver, the same problem began to present itself for modern day Brief Pulse manufacturers it had for early BP device manufacturers, the dire predicament of plainly compromising the "improvement" gained and thus the benefit Brief Pulse machines were touted to provide for that of "efficacy." Conversely, leaving machines minimal stimulus presented the real possibility of their becoming unmarketable just as the Brief Pulse devices of the 40s and 50s had become unmarketable.

Despite manufacturers' boasts, indeed, the fact that no more than 100 Joules was ever required to seize any recipient of any age in any circumstance, and despite the MECTA "C" emission of 108 maximum Joules, more than enough to seize all 100 year old recipients under any reasonable circumstance, the machine did not produce the results for which administrators were looking. It was the inability to achieve results then--not seizure recalcitrant recipients--which appears to have initiated the more powerful MECTA "D" most probably resembling the charts above.

Note how both the "C," the "D" and the "D-1" all have a "59J at 220Ω" or "80J at 300Ω" ***<u>Conditional</u>***-ER/RRC. But notice also the conditional ceiling increase for the "D" and "D-1" from the 110 Joule APA maximum to new overall maximums of circa 134 and 141 Joules respectively, an escalation almost certainly achieved through increased Voltage. MECTA openly reported an approximate 140 Joules for the MECTA "D" (Glen and Weiner 1983) but only following the 1976-1982 FDA investigation and allegedly, only as an exceptional means to overcome particularly recalcitrant cases (regarding seizure). Purportedly for recipients with particularly high seizure thresholds then, the MECTA "D" and "D-1" with "Impedance Override" then, became the first BP devices to surpass the APA's 110 Joule ceiling standard. Moreover, "Impedance Override" may not have been simple additional output utilized for so-called seizure recalcitrant recipients, but rather, additional power added to each age category as illustrated in the charts above.

Easy Solution

In fact, MECTA could have had the MECTA "D-1" overcome a resistance of up to 525Ω more simply by increasing Voltage, and reducing Duration, thereby remaining within the 110 Joule ceiling and even the 1.1 MTTLOI in all age categories. For example, instead of 90 and 100 year old recipients receiving 1.9 and 2.0 seconds respectively on the D-1, they could have received 1.4 and 1.55 seconds respectively allowing the machine to overcome the same 525Ω in accordance with the APA Standard. In sum, the "D-1" could easily have been made to overcome the same higher resistances while yet respecting the 110J minimal stimulus integrity and the 1.1 MTTLOI of the 1982 APA ceiling by using a "46J at 220Ω" ER/RRC. See below.

The MECTA "D-1" (CONDITIONAL ER/RRC) could have reached 525Ω limited to 110 maximum Joules and thus 1.1 fold in every age category simply by increasing Voltage and reducing Duration

AGE	Impedance Threshold (Ω)	Threshold Output in Joules	MECTA "D" EO (Joules)	Multifold Thresh. Titration Level
10	52.5	1.0	1.1	1.1
20	105	4.0	4.4	1.1
30	157.5	9.0	9.9	1.1
40	210	16.0	17.6	1.1
50	262.5	25.0	27.5	1.1
60	315	36.0	39.6	1.1
65	341.25	42.6	46.86	1.1
70	367.5	49.0	53.9	1.1
80	420	64.0	70.4	1.1
90	472.5	81.0	89.1	1.1
100	525	100	110	1.11

HYPOTHETICAL NON-EXISTENT CONSTANT CURRENT **MECTA "D-1"** BP DEVICE
(1st GENERATION) by MECTA Corp.1980 Limited to 110J
BASED ON A ***CONDITIONAL*** ER/RRC in Conformity with the 1982 APA Standard
With a Legal **"46J at 220Ω"** ER/RRC

VOLTAGE	POWER % @ Age	AGE Yrs	Ω Ohms	FREQUENCY (Hz)	DURATION (SECs)	CURRENT mAmps	ENERGY Joules	CHARGE mC
42.5	10	10	52.5	20	.53	800	1.1	25.2
85	20	20	105	40	.55	800	4.4	52.3
127.5	30	30	157.5	60	.55	800	9.9	78.5
170	40	40	210	60	.73	800	17.6	105
212.5	50	50	262.5	60	.91	800	27.5	131
255	60	60	315	70	.93	800	39.6	157
276.25	65	65	341.25	70	1.07	800	48.86	179
297.5	70	70	367.5	70	1.09	800	53.9	183
340	80	80	420	70	1.25	800	70.4	210
382.5	90	90	472.5	70	1.41	800	89.1	236
425	100	100	525	70	1.55	800	110	261

.0015 Second Pulse Width

XJ/220 = 110J/525Ω = 46J at 220Ω ER/RRC

Charge = Duration x Current x (hz x 2) x WL
Charge = EO/Current x Impedance
EO = Charge x Current x Impedance
Duration = Charge/Current x (hz x 2) x WL
EO = Voltage x Current x (hz x 2) x WL x Duration
EO = (Current squared) x Impedance x (hz x 2) x WL x Duration
Ohm's Law: Current = Voltage/Ω; Ω = Voltage/Current; Voltage = Current x Ω

Conclusion:

Simply by limiting Duration, therefore, the D devices need not have breached the APA 110J ceiling, the 1.1 MTTLOI, or even the "70J at 220Ω" ER/RRC decreed by the 1982 APA Standard. By reducing Duration, MTTLOI would have dropped from a uniform 1.41 MTTLOI for all age categories to a uniform and legal 1.1 MTTLOI for all age categories. Such a device could have overcome the same 525Ω Impedance in keeping with minimal stimulus and the 1982 APA Standard. This option suggests that MECTA was increasing the power of its Brief Pulse devices not because they failed to induce adequate seizures in all age categories, nor because of seizure recalcitrant recipients, but because they know that so-called "ECT" simply does not work by inducing adequate convulsions alone. Rather its efficacy depends upon adequate, damaging doses of electricity, as we shall witness.

Note from the chart above that simply by increasing Voltage and reducing Duration, MECTA "D" devices could have readily overcome a 525Ω Impedance while yet adhering to the APA 110 Joule ceiling. Increased output is not actually needed to overcome higher Impedances, but only increased Voltages. Unfortunately, the necessity of increasing the procedure's effectiveness by increasing the electrical energy formed a dangerous and insidious precedent which, as we shall soon discover, continues throughout the modern history of Brief Pulse just as it did during the SW era via using SW devices in lieu of Brief Pulse. Indeed, by breaching the 110J ceiling, the actual 1980 MECTA "D" devices became precedential in surpassing the integrity of minimal stimulus prescribed by the 1982 APA Standard. This breaching of the 1982 APA Standard violated the promise made by manufacturers via Weiner to the FDA (through the APA Standard) of a "new and improved" Brief Pulse device utilizing reduced output. In short, by 1980, all age recipients began receiving between a 1.34 and 1.41 MTTLOI in lieu of the 1.1 MTTLOI prescribed by the 1982 APA Standard. The MECTA "D" devices thus appear to have been the first indication in the modern BP era that an electro-oriented in lieu of convulsion-oriented device is necessary to make the procedure work—no longer an ECT devices at all. Once the ceiling and thus the just above threshold titration level paradigm was broken, moreover, both output and titration level steadily rises with each new machine generation, information which manufacturers have ardently suppressed, as we shall momentarily observe.

PART IV

SECTION IV: Second Generation BP Devices

Chapter 13

Early 2nd Generation BP Devices--MECTA D-2, Early MECTA SR1, 2; Early Somatics' Thymatron

The maximum output of the late first generation MECTA D/D-1, as noted above, was eventually reported (more or less), but only following the hearings. The machine was, after all, still well below the 200J maximum of SW. As BP machines grew even more powerful, however, MECTA newly began limiting what it reported. Subsequent to the D/D-1, MECTA suddenly began subjecting all models to a new encrypted reporting policy. Beginning with the D-2 and/or early MECTA SR-1 and 2, MECTA's underreporting and/or total failure to report, made actual Outputs, actual Voltages, and actual Impedances (most critically--maximums of all three) impossible to determine. What can be determined is that MECTA BP devices continually increased in power; that the MECTA D-2, and/or early MECTA SR1 (and 2) dramatically evolved in potency compared to the earlier 81J and 108J MECTA "Cs" and even compared to the 140J MECTA D/D-1. By 1984, the MECTA D-2, and/or early MECTA SR1 and 2 had circa doubled the power of the circa 100J MECTA "C" Brief Pulse prototype presented to the FDA between 1976 and 1982 (Department of Health and Human Services, 1982a, G3-G4). But how, with MECTA's withholding of vital parameters, can this augmentation be determined? While actual Voltage, maximum Impedance, and maximum EO became unavailable for the MECTA D-2/early SR1 and 2 (just as these parameters were to become unavailable for all subsequent MECTA devices),[134] cogent speculation is possible. Viable conjecture is achievable due to Somatics Incorporated, MECTA's twin sister, providing enough parameters to determine a 200J maximum output and a circa 440Ω maximum Impedance for its very similar, early Thymatron apparatus.[135] This is significant in that Somatics' devices have a long history of immediately emulating Mectan precedents regarding power and that the early Thymatron device immanently followed the production of the precedent setting MECTA D-2/early SR-1 and SR 2. Based upon the historical similitude of Somatics and MECTA machine evolution, therefore, it is highly probable that both the D-2/early SR-1 and early SR 2, emitted the same approximate 200J output and 440Ω maximum Impedance as the early 200J Thymatron device by Somatics (Cameron, 1994). Plausibly surmising that the MECTA D-2/early SR-1 and SR-2 emitted the same approximate 200J/440Ω maximum as the Thymatron then, we can determine (via mathematical formulas) that early second generation MECTA BP devices (the D-2/MECTA SR-1 and 2) utilized a maximum 350 Volts, a reduction from the probable 400-420V D-1 maximum above, but over-compensated by an increased pulse width of .002ms up from the .0015ms pulse width of the D/D-1. (Both pulse width parameters are provided by MECTA). Plugging into known formulas for Brief Pulse, a 350V maximum along with the remaining available electrical parameters which are provided by MECTA for the D-2/MECTA

[134] The very existence of the D-2 is difficult to trace. Parameters and other information for the MECTA D-2 are almost non-existent. Only two, rather obscure allusions to the D-2 along with some of its' parameters could be located by the author--both within 510K files submitted to the FDA by Manufacturers other than MECTA--both of which had to be obtained via Freedom of Information (Food and Drug Administration, 1986B, p.4).

[135] Enough parameters to deduce actual output are provided for the early Thymatron, as we shall see.

SR-1 and 2 (Food and Drug Administration, 1986B, p.4; see Food and Drug Administration, 1984 [136]), [137] these MECTA devices, as already noted, then, can be projected by extrapolation to have emitted the same approximate 200J at 440Ω maximums as the early Thymatron device by Somatics. The reporting "coincidence" of the new "100J at 220Ω" phrase first reported by MECTA and then Somatics for all MECTA and Somatics BP devices at this juncture, the D-2/early SR-1 and early SR-2, and immediately following, Somatics' early Thymatron device, bolsters the hypothesis that the new circa "100J at 220Ω" phrase was re-interpreted by both companies no longer as a conditional-ER/RRC with 110J ceiling, but an ER/RRC-mean. [138] In short, all these early enhanced second generation BP devices reported via the new circa "100J at 220Ω" phrase first reported by MECTA between 1982-83 for its MECTA D-2/early SR-1 and SR-2 followed by Somatics which reported the same circa "100J at 220Ω" phrase for its early Thymatron in 1983, appear to represent unreported 200J maximums (more or less) at unreported 440Ω maximum Impedances. In short, both early second generation MECTA and Somatics BP devices appear to have emitted 200J at about 440Ω (100J/220Ω = 200J/440Ω). At this point in time then, we can conclude that the newly reported "100J at 220Ω" phrase reported by all four American BP manufacturers was interpreted by MECTA and Somatics (and probably Elcot--now defunct) as a simple (but radically altered) ER/RRC-mean.

Somatics' Thymatron (Early Second Generation Brief Pulse)

The later first generation D/D-1 at a probable 140J, as noted, was the first modern day BP device to surpass the 110J mark, the APA maximum and the maximum output by which Brief Pulse could be denoted as "minimal stimulus" (just above threshold) with BL-ECT, allegedly twice as safe as the supposed 200J maximum emitted by SW (Department of Health and Human Services, 1982a, G3-G4). Because the new 140J maximum was supposedly an anomaly for exceptionally stubborn cases and the normal maximum Brief Pulse output was still accepted as the 110J ceiling identified by the 1982 APA Standard, the 140J D/D-1 can still be deemed a first generation BP device. However, the more powerful 1983 MECTA D-2/early SR 1 and 2 reported by MECTA with a circa "100J at 220Ω" or sometimes "100J at a typical 220Ω" phrase were the first Brief Pulse devices to deliberately ignore the 1982 APA 110J ceiling Standard and so actually equal SW in cumulative power. Breaking both the "70J at 220Ω" ER/RRC and the 110J ceiling of the 1982 APA Standard, these early second generation BP machines based on a "100J at 220Ω" Mean-ER/RRC reaching a 200J ceiling, therefore, are the beginning of what this manuscript has deemed "second generation" BP devices. The circa "100J at 220Ω" ER/RRC newly reported for the D-2/early SR-1 and 2, in short, appears to have been clandestinely interpreted by MECTA as a Mean-ER/RRC, that is, 100J is half the actual 200J Output maximum the machines actually emitted and 220Ω half the actual 440Ω maximum Impedance the D-2/early SR-1 and 2 actually reached. [139] Not surprisingly then, it was with the production of the D-2/early SR-1 and 2 that actual maximum output reporting (in Joules) was peremptorily dropped for MECTA BP devices generally. In brief, what was assumed to be a "100J at 220Ω" conditional-ER/RRC with 110J ceiling, was in fact, newly, but surreptitiously interpreted (by MECTA) as a Mean-ER/RRC enabling the D-2/early SR-1 and 2 to emit a 200J maximum output, furtively and calculatingly surpassing the 1982 APA ceiling for the first time since the standard's inception. Thus, it was with the introduction of the probable 200J MECTA D-2/early SR-1 and 2 closely followed by several other U.S. BP manufacturers, that MECTA introduced and implemented an adroit method both of surpassing and concealing actual maximum EO. It was with the introduction of these specific devices then, that MECTA (closely

---

[136] See letter to Bureau of Medical Devices, Sept 27, 1984, see Attachment I - Comparison of electrical parameters of the MECTA, Medcraft, and Thymatron machines.

[137] The D-2 utilized 800mA current, 90Hz maximum Frequency (180 Pulses), and 2.0 Seconds maximum Duration (Food and Drug Administration, 1986B, p.4). The D-2 appears to have increased in Frequency and Duration compared to the D-1, and appears to be the BP device first equaling SW in power.

[138] Unconditional ER-mean is an ER Output/Impedance which is also the mean Output/Impedance.100J/220Ω (mean) = 200J/440Ω (maximum). The absolute 100-110J ceiling has been dropped.

[139] It is possible the D-2 retained the same Voltage as the D-1 (420V), emitting circa 240 maximum Joules at 525Ω, the first Pure-ER/RRC: [Volt.-oriented formula--420V x .8A. x 180 Pulses x .002PW x 2.0 Sec. = 241.92J or Imp.-oriented formula--.8A. x .8A. x 525Ω x 180Pulses x .002PW x 2.0Sec. = 241.92J (Pure ER/RRC: 100J/220Ω = 240J/525Ω.) However, due to the D-2's increase in Pulse Width, it is more probable the D-2's Voltage was instead reduced to 350, emitting a maximum 200J. In short, the D-2 was in all probability equal to or similar to the early SR1 and even SR2, based on Mean-ER/RRC.

followed by Somatics) graduated from breaching the 110J mark as an exception (i.e. the D-1) to breaching the 110J APA ceiling as the invisible, but general rule.

MECTA's inventive interpretation of its newly devised phrase: "100J at 220Ω" as an unexplained "mean" or "typical output" at an unexplained "mean," or "typical Impedance," now wholly supplanted the APA's Conditional-ER/RRC Standard of "70J at 220Ω" with "110J ceiling. " It was the new interpretation of the newly reported "100J at 220Ω" phrase, moreover, which now "justified" (albeit unexplicated and unreported by MECTA) MECTA's new unreported ceiling of approximately 200 maximum Joules. The innocuous sounding "100J at 220Ω" phrase reported for the D-2/early SR-1 and 2 in pre-market applications then, insidiously included a total disregard for the APA "110J" ceiling. In fact, the Mean-ER/RRC interpretation of the new mild sounding "100J at 220Ω" phrase now provided manufacturers with the mathematical basis for producing 200J BP devices equal to that of SW in cumulative power without actually reporting any increase at all (Department of Health and Human Services, 1982a, G3-G4). The APA minimal stimulus safeguard--the APA "70J at 220Ω" ER/RRC with conditional 110J maximum--was now fully corrupted. In short, increased electrical dosing from a 1.1 MTTLOI to a 2.0 MTTLOI for all age categories, the aim behind the warping of the standard, imperceptibly accompanied the new "100J at 220Ω" reporting phrase.

In brief, the D-2/early SR 1 and 2, with its newly accompanying phraseology--"100J at 220Ω"--inventively albeit secretly re-interpreted by MECTA as a Mean-ER/RRC, had wholly supplanted the 1982 APA Standard (Food and Drug Administration, 1984, Attachment II). Invisible to all but the manufacturers, the critical 110J APA ceiling had been shrewdly supplanted with what was actually a 100J mean (interpretation of the new "100J at 220Ω" phrase)--while the 110J ceiling had now been wholly (albeit secretly) discarded. Moreover, to complete the curtain of invisibility, MECTA had not only curtailed the reporting of their machines' actual maximum outputs with the introduction of the D-2/early Sr-1 and 2, but had also abandoned the reporting of maximum Voltage and maximum Machine Impedance, two parameters necessary to at least formulaically deduce maximum output for the D-1/early SR 1 and 2. Finally, along with the new "100J at 220Ω" phrase immediately emulated by the three remaining American BP manufacturers (MECTA, Somatics, and Medcraft), Machine Readout displays on these new early second generation Brief Pulse devices manufactured by MECTA and Somatics, failed to depict the actual 200 Joule maximums the devices actually administered. Instead the devices depicted deceptive 100J Readout maximums read by administering physicians. [140] (This incredible deception shall be painstakingly scrutinized a little later in the manuscript.)

It was at this point, the point during which MECTA and Somatics Brief Pulse devices first began equaling the cumulative power of the SW devices of old, that a conspiratorial stratagem to actively create the ongoing impression of circa 100J, minimal stimulus Brief Pulse machines, may have been initiated and agreed upon by all four BP manufacturers (MECTA, Somatics, Medcraft, and Elcot). MECTA and Somatics in particular seemed to have agreed upon a ploy to uniformly underreport actual machine power in order to mimic conformity to the "110J" ceiling clearly depicted within the 1982 APA Standard! Medcraft and Elcot also reported "100J at 220Ω," for their second generation BP devices, but Elcot soon folded while Medcraft actually limited its Brief Pulse device to 99 maximum Joules, albeit corrupting the APA Standard in an entirely different way--as we shall soon see.)

The subsequent formulas depict the mathematical specifics for calculating what was most probably maximum output for the D-2/early SR1 and 2s, exposing for the first time, MECTA's newly reported phrase "100J at 220Ω" as an ER/RRC-Mean, totally bypassing the (110J) APA ceiling. (The MECTA D-2 and early SR-1 as noted previously, were either the same or almost the same devices, while the early MECTA SR-2 was but a slight variation of the early D-2/SR-1). Immediately following MECTA's introduction of what in this manuscript is referred to as the early second generation Brief Pulse devices depicted below (D-2/early SR-1 and SR-2), Somatics too, introduced its early second generation Brief Pulse device, the Thymatron, the overall output of which was almost certainly emulative of the early second generation MECTA BP devices below (the D-2/early SR-1 and early SR-2) as we shall soon grasp.

---

[140] There is every reason to believe that as a result of machine readouts depicting half the maximum output these devices actually educed, administering physicians themselves were deluded into believing they were delivering minimal stimulus when in fact second generation BP devices delivered 2.0-2.5 fold minimal stimulus outputs for BL ECT in every age category.

(1983-1985) MECTA D-2/Earliest MECTA SR-1 [141] *(probable 200J outputs)*

MECTA D-2/Early SR-1: Voltage-Based Formula for Finding Actual Output: (Speculative 350V)
350V x .8A. x 180 Pulses x .002PW x 2.0 Sec. = **201.6J**.

MECTA D-2/Early SR-1: Impedance-Based Formula for Finding Actual Output: [142] *(Parameters result in a circa 440Ω maximum Impedance)*
.8A. x .8A. x **437.5Ω** x 180Pul x .002PW x 2.0Sec. = **201.6J**.

MECTA D-2/Earliest MECTA SR-1: (Probable) Mean-ER/RRC
(Reported) **100J/220Ω =** (Actual maximums) **201.6J/437.5Ω**

The early SR-2 (below) achieved the same maximum Output and Impedance as the early SR-1 above, but with the variation of a reduced PW (Pulse Width) compensated by increased Duration (of up to 3.0 Seconds).

(1983-1985) *Earliest* ***MECTA SR-2*** *(most probable)*

Earliest MECTA JR/SR-2: Volt. -Based Formula for Finding Output:
350V x .8A. x 150 Pulses x *.0016PW* x 3.0 Sec. = **201.6J**.

Earliest MECTA SR-2: Imped-Based Formula for Finding Actual Output:
.8A. x .8A. x **437.5Ω** x 150Pul. x .*0016* PW x 3.0Sec. = **201.6J**.

Earliest MECTA SR-2: Probable Mean-ER/RRC
(Reported) **100J/220Ω =** (Actual maximums) **201.6J/437.5Ω**.

(1983-1985) *Actual output of the earliest* ***Thymatron*** *by* ***Somatics*** = 201 Joules. [143] *(Non-speculative)*

Earliest Thymatron - Volt. -Based Formula for Output:
400V x .9Amps x 140 Pulses x .001 PW x 4.0 Sec. = **201J**. [144]

---

[141] Within an Elcot 510K file, in a rare allusion to the MECTA D-2, the D-2 is comparatively described as being almost identical to the early MECTA SR1 (Food and Drug Administration, 1986B, p.4). D-2: 800mA Current, 40-90 Hz (up to 180 Pulses), adjustable 1.0-2.0 milliseconds Pulse Width, adjustable .5-2.0 Seconds Duration, and reported as "100J at 220Ω" (what would be, at 350V maximum, an unexplained Mean-Output/Impedance or Mean-ER/RRC). Early SR1: 550-800mA Current, 40-90 Hz (up to 180 Pulses), adjustable 1.0-2.0 milliseconds Pulse Width, adjustable .5-2.0 Seconds Duration, and at 350V, an unexplained Mean-ER/RRC of "101.4J at 220Ω." For all practical purposes, the D-2 and early SR-1 were synonymous.

[142] D-2 and early SR 1@2: From the 350V assumption, maximum output can be derived. From the maximum Output, maximum Impedance can be derived. Remaining parameters are provided. From maximums, mean-ER/RRC can be derived.

[143] Somatics claimed for its' earliest Thymatron, a maximum of 182 Joules. (Food and Drug Administration, 1984, see letter to Bureau of Medical Devices, Sept 27, 1984, see Attachment I - Comparison of electrical parameters of the MECTA, Medcraft, and Thymatron machines). In fact, utilizing Somatics own provided parameters, the earliest reported Thymatron can mathematically be shown (above) to have emitted approximately 201 Joules.

[144] Some parameters for the earliest Thymatron, including 400 maximum Volts (but which may be closer to 399V) are found in FDA 510K files submitted by Somatics and obtained under (FOI) Freedom of Information (Food and Drug Administration, 1984, see attachment I - Comparison of electrical parameters of the MECTA, Medcraft and Thymatron machines). Maximum Impedance of early Thymatron output can be obtained as a derivative of parameters provided.400V x .9Amps x 140Pulses x .001 PW x 4.0 Seconds = 201Joules. .9 x .9 x XΩ x 140 Pulses x .001 PW x 4.0 Seconds = 201Joules. .4536X = 201J. X = 443.12Ω. Voltage for each age is based on Percent Energy provided by Somatics. For instance, a 40 year old recipient receives 40% of the 399V maximum. .4 x 399 = 159.6V. All other parameters can be deduced from various known formulas. Note the reported "100J at 220Ω" here was actually an approximate 200J at 440Ω. This makes the "100J at 220Ω phrase a mean-ER/RRC.

Earliest Thymatron - Imped-Based Formula for Finding Actual Output:
.9 x .9 x **443Ω** x 140 Pulses x .001 PW x 4.0 Sec. = **201J**.

Earliest Thymatron: Mean-ER/RRC
(Reported) **100J/220Ω =** (Actual maximums) **201J/443Ω**

Only the MECTA devices above are "probable" in that Somatics actually provides Percent Energy, Frequency (Hertz), Duration, Number of Pulses, and Charge parameters for its early Thymatron. [Maximum Voltage was discovered from FDA pre-market 510K files submitted by Somatics in 1984 (Food and Drug Administration, 1984, see attachment)]. Percentages of maximum Energy delivered (provided by Somatics) correlate to age. Voltages per age category can be derived from (reported) Percentage of Energy applied multiplied by maximum Voltage. For example, a thirty year old receives 30% of the 400V maximum or (.3 x 400V =) 120V; a fifty year old receives 50% of the 400V maximum or (.5 x 400V) = 200V. All other parameters are derivable though one or more of the following formulas utilized for Brief Pulse Devices (see above footnote):

Charge = Duration x Current x (hz x 2) x WL
Charge = EO/Current x Impedance
EO = Charge x Current x Impedance
Duration = Charge/Current x (hz x 2) x WL
EO = Voltage x Current x (hz x 2) x WL x Duration
EO = (Current squared) x Impedance x (hz x 2) x WL x Duration
Ohm's Law: Current = Voltage/Ω; Ω = Voltage/Current; Voltage = Current x Ω

Thus, while Somatics, like MECTA no longer provided EO in Joules and no longer provided maximum EO, the various EOs administered per age category for the Thymatron are formulaically derivable. An accurate representation of the early second generation Thymatron BP device appears below. Note the Mean ER-RRC interpretation of the reported "100J at 220Ω" phrase. Note too, the 2.0 MTTLOI delivered to every age group.

ACCURATE EARLY CONSTANT CURRENT THYMATRON BRIEF PULSE DEVICE
BASED ON ***MEAN***-ER/RRC INTERPRETATION OF 100J at 220Ω
by Somatics Inc.1982-3 (.001 Second Pulse Width Maximum)

VOLTAGE	POWER % @ Age	AGE Yrs	Ω Ohms	FREQUENCY (Hz)	DURATION (SECs)	CURRENT mAmps	ENERGY Joules	CHARGE mC
39.9	10	10	44.18	30	.93	900	2.004	50.4
79.8	20	20	88.84	30	1.87	900	8.06	100.8
119.7	30	30	133.19	50	1.68	900	18.10	151
159.6	40	40	177.36	50	2.24	900	32.18	201.6
199.5	50	50	221.7	50	2.8	900	50.27	252
239.4	60	60	266	70	2.4	900	72.39	302.4
259.35	65	65	288.15	70	2.6	900	84.96	327.6
279.3	70	70	310.3	70	2.8	900	98.537	352.8
319.2	80	80	354.7	70	3.2	900	128.7	403.20
359.1	90	90	398.8	70	3.6	900	162.8	453.6
399	100	100	**443**	70	4.0	900	**201**	**504**

.001Sec. Pulse Width

Note that EO for both MECTA and Somatics devices, appear to be based upon the same "relative threshold constants" (discussed earlier).

Default Outputs Allowed per age Category Based on a Uniform 2.0 fold Threshold Maximum in Defiance of the 1982 APA Standard--the Thymatron

AGE	Relative Threshold Constants	Maximum Multifold Threshold Output	Max. Output Allowed per Age Category
10	1.0	x 2.0	2.0 Joules
20	4.0	x 2.0	8.0 Joules
30	9.0	x 2.0	18.0 Joules
40	16.0	x 2.0	32.0 Joules
50	25.0	x 2.0	50.0 Joules
60	36.0	x 2.0	72.0 Joules
65	42.25	x 2.0	84.5 Joules
70	48.97	x 2.0	98.0 Joules
80	64.0	x 2.0	128.0 Joules
90	81.0	x 2.0	162.0 Joules
100	100.0	x 2.0	200.0 Joules

Based on the early Thymatron device above, which is almost certainly a facsimile of MECTA's early second generation D-2/*early* SR1 and *early* second generation SR2 BP devices, we can conclude that the early second generation MECTA devices emit the same circa 200 Joule outputs as the early second generation Somatics device above--the Thymatron. Moreover, like the Thymatron in relation to the Thymatron's later more powerful second generation device (the Thymatron DG), the Charge and pulses delivered per age category for the early second generation MECTA D-2/early SR 1 and early SR2 devices are most likely the same Charge and number of pulses delivered per age category for MECTA's later, more powerful second generation BP devices, the later JR/SR 1 and 2, as we shall observe. In that Pulse Widths, maximum Durations, and constant currents are known for early second generation MECTA BP devices, and because we can be reasonably certain that maximum output for these earlier devices are the same approximate 200 joules emitted by the early Thymatron (which almost certainly emulated MECTA), we can deduce (using a round figure), a 350V maximum, from which we can then formulaically deduce maximum EO for early second generation MECTA devices. Thus, maximum output for the early JR/SR 1 or what may have been deemed the D-2 emitted a (**350V** x .8A. x 180 Pulses x .002PW x 2.0 Sec) = **201.6J** maximum output. Using its slightly different parameters, we can deduce the same (**350V** x .8A. x 150 Pulses x .0016PW x 3.0 Sec.) = **201.6J** maximum output for the early JR/SR 2. Like Somatics' Thymatron device, age-related Voltage outputs for the early MECTA devices can be found simply by multiplying percentage of power (tantamount to age) by maximum Voltage (the method used by manufacturers). For example, a thirty year old receives 30% of the 350V maximum or 105V, a fifty year old 50% of the 350V maximum or 175V. With this information, Durations and Impedances for each age category can be determined (formulaically), resulting in the following charts for these early second generation MECTA Brief Pulse devices.

Early (Approximate) 2nd GENERATION CONSTANT CURRENT **D-2/JR/SR 1** BRIEF PULSE "ECT" DEVICE BASED ON ***MEAN***-ER/RRC OF "101.4J at 220Ω" by MECTA Corp.1985 (.002 Second Pulse Width Maximum) Made for U. S. A.

VOLTAGE	POWER % @ Age	AGE Yrs	Ω Ohms	FREQUENCY (Hz)	DURATION (SECs)	CURRENT mAmps	ENERGY Joules	CHARGE mC
35	10	10	44	40	.5	800	2.25	64
70	20	20	87.5	40	.9	800	8.06	115.2
105	30	30	131	60	.9	800	18.1	172.8
140	40	40	175	60	1.2	800	32.3	230.4
175	50	50	219	60	1.5	800	50.5	288
210	60	60	262.5	90	1.2	800	72.6	345.6
227.5	65	65	284	90	1.3	800	85	374.4
245	70	70	306	90	1.4	800	98.7	403.2
280	80	80	350	90	1.6	800	129	460.8
315	90	90	394	90	1.8	800	163.4	518.4
350	100	100	437.5	90	2.0	800	201	576

.002Sec. Pulse Width

Early (Approximate) 2nd GENERATION CONSTANT CURRENT **JR/SR 2** BRIEF PULSE
"ECT: DEVICE BASED ON ***MEAN***-ER/RRC OF "101.3J AT 220Ω"
by MECTA Corp.1985 (.001 Second Pulse Width Maximum) Made for U. S. A.

VOLTAGE	POWER % @ Age	AGE Yrs	Ω Ohms	FREQUENCY (Hz)	DURATION (SECs)	CURRENT mAmps	ENERGY Joules	CHARGE mC
45	10	10	44	75	.375	800	2.53	72
90	20	20	87.5	75	0.6	800	8.06	115.2
135	30	30	131	75	0.9	800	18.12	172.8
180	40	40	175	75	1.2	800	32.26	230.4
225	50	50	219	75	1.5	800	50.46	288
270	60	60	262.5	75	1.8	800	72.58	345.6
292.5	65	65	284	75	1.95	800	85.06	374.4
315	70	70	306	75	2.1	800	98.7	403.2
360	80	80	350	75	2.4	800	129	460.8
405	90	90	394	75	2.7	800	163.4	518.4
350	100	100	437.5	75	3.0	800	201.6	576

.0016Sec. Pulse Width

Again, note that EO for both MECTA and Somatics devices appear to be based on the same "relative threshold constants."

Circa Maximum Outputs Allowed per age Category by a Uniform 2.0 fold Threshold Maximum in Defiance of the 1982 APA Standard
MECTA D-2/Early JR/SR 1 and Early JR/SR 2

AGE	Threshold Constants	Maximum Multifold Threshold Output	Max. Output Allowed per Age Category
10	**1.0**	**x 2.0**	**2.0 Joules**
20	**4.0**	**x 2.0**	**8.0 Joules**
30	**9.0**	**x 2.0**	**18.0 Joules**
40	**16.0**	**x 2.0**	**32.0 Joules**
50	**25.0**	**x 2.0**	**50.0 Joules**
60	**36.0**	**x 2.0**	**72.0 Joules**
65	**42.25**	**x 2.0**	**84.5 Joules**
70	**48.97**	**x 2.0**	**98.0 Joules**
80	**64.0**	**x 2.0**	**128.0 Joules**
90	**81.0**	**x 2.0**	**162.0 Joules**
100	**100.0**	**x 2.0**	**200.0 Joules**

Again, note the Mean-ER/RRC interpretation of MECTA's reported phrase, circa "101.3J at 220Ω. " Note that MECTA's D-2/early second generation SR-1 and early second generation SR-2, (immediately followed by Somatics' early second generation Thymatron above), are all reported with the new circa "100J at 220Ω" phrase, emitting (albeit unreported) approximate 200J maximums at approximate 440Ω maximum Impedances for both MECTA and Somatics BP devices. [145] In spite of the successful induction of adequate seizures in all age categories at half the output (100J) of SW (200J), Brief Pulse manufacturers MECTA and Somatics, impelled by what appears to have been inefficacy of the adequate convulsion, now produce unreported 200J Brief Pulse devices. Moreover, reluctance to report outputs equaling that of SW appear to have prompted a new and invisible reporting interpretation of the innocuous sounding "100J at 220Ω" phrase, simultaneously accompanied (on the part of both companies) by the discontinuation of actual maximum output reporting in Joules. In fact, the introduction of the "100J at 220Ω" phrase, newly and secretly interpreted by MECTA and Somatics at this juncture as an unexplicated mean-ER/RRC, had actually generated a new unreported maximum ceiling for Brief Pulse devices, as observed above, of circa 200 maximum Joules, the same maximum

[145] Somatics did not report the 201J maximum, but--typical of Somatics--revealed enough information to be able to calculate maximum output indirectly.

output as SW devices (though in disparate age categories) which the "reduced output" Brief Pulse devices had supposedly been resurrected to replace. What seemed to be based on the APA Standard, therefore, that is, a slightly higher conditional-ER/RRC (100J at 220Ω), but with seemingly the same 110J ceiling, had actually transmuted into a 100J at 220Ω Mean-ER/RRC permitting a new 200J ceiling. This, of course, meant a new two-fold MTTLOI for all age categories in lieu of the 1.1 MTTLOI mandated by the APA Standard. Along with this secret transmutation, as noted, came the precedential elimination of maximum output reporting in joules.

The new "100J at 220Ω" phrase then, had created the subtle, but colossal misimpression that the phrase was simply a new, slightly increased conditional-ER/RRC, with the same circa 110J ceiling. Indeed, based on communication between FDA regulators and manufacturer representatives, FDA regulators appear to have interpreted the new phrase in just this manner. In short, the phrase appeared to replace the previous APA conditional-ER/RRC of "70J at 220Ω. " In actuality, of course, with the new "100J at 220Ω" phrase, MECTA, by 1984, immediately followed by Somatics, had actually supplanted both the "70J at 220Ω" conditional-ER/RRC and the critical 110J output ceiling mandated within the 1982 APA Standard with a new 200J ceiling. In sum, the new phrase was secretly interpreted by manufacturers, MECTA and Somatics, as an unexplicated "100J at 220Ω" ER/RRC-mean (100J/220Ω = 200J/440Ω). As noted too, MECTA first applied this new reporting mechanism to its new MECTA D-2/early MECTA SR1 and early SR2, soon followed by Somatics' similar application of an almost identical "100J at 220Ω" reporting phrase for its new "Thymatron" device. [146] This new reporting of circa 100J at 220Ω, easily mistaken for a slightly modified conditional-ER/RRC with the same 110J APA ceiling intact, successfully covered up not only the sudden dropping of the 110J ceiling regulating modern day Brief Pulse devices to a 1.1 MTTLOI minimal stimulus output for all age recipients, but covered up the new 200J output of these same early enhanced second generation BP devices. The enhancement was further suppressed, as noted, by the discarding of actual output reporting (in joules) and any means of deducing it. In fact, by 1984, compared to the first generation 108J MECTA "C" which had, in fact, conformed to the 110J maximum set by the 1982 APA Standard, early second generation BP devices manufactured by both MECTA and Somatics had approximately doubled in maximum output. Indeed, at 200 Joules, early MECTA and Somatics second generation BP devices, had actually re-equaled SW in cumulative power (Department of Health and Human Services, 1982a, G3-G4).

Somatics' similarly unexplicated ER/RRC-Mean interpretation of the same circa "100J at 220Ω" phraseology, as well as Somatics' similar omission of all actual output reporting for all subsequent Somatics Brief Pulse devices, not only seems to have been prompted by the same concerns (as MECTA), namely, nullification of Brief Pulse's safety over SW, suggests early conspiracy between MECTA and Somatics. The uniform reporting of the circa "100J at 220Ω" phrase soon imitated by U. S. manufacturers Medcraft and Elcot, along with an identical omission of maximum output reporting (with the exception of the Medcraft B-25 which actually limited its B-25 BP device to 100 Joules), in fact, suggests a high degree of co-operation amongst all four BP manufacturers.

In summary, beginning with the end of the 1976-82 FDA investigation of "ECT," it was the MECTA D-2/early SR-1 which first appears to have equaled SW in cumulative output, and for which the precedential transition from actual output reporting to an unexplicated "100J" mean[147] was initially generated and put into practice. Moreover, (excepting Medcraft) it was with the inception of the MECTA D-2/early SR-1 and its accompanying "100J at 220Ω" mean-ER/RRC interpretation, that manufacturers' adherence to the 110J APA ceiling was first permanently and deliberately circumvented and with which reporting of actual output in joules ceased. Certainly, if the sudden equivalency of Brief Pulse with Sine Wave output had been understood---that is, had it been revealed that both the early second generation Brief Pulse device and Sine Wave device emitted the same 200J maximums--serious concerns over Brief Pulse safety, in fact, misgivings regarding convulsion theory generally, might have been raised, most probably with the FDA. Indeed, the equaling of Brief Pulse

---

[146] Somatics initially reported for the Thymatron device an actual emission of 182J maximum, an under-report. But Somatics, like MECTA, quickly dropped the reporting of actual output (in joules). In fact, the early Thymatron had an actual 200J potential. In the brief period of time Somatics reported a semblance of actual output (for the early Thymatron), the slight underreporting of 182J as opposed to 200J may have been due to the fear that reporting of the actual 200Jmaximum would clearly equal SW in power (Department of Health and Human Services, 1982a, G3-G4).

[147] That "100J at 220Ω" as a mean-ER/RRC resulting in a 200J at 440Ω annihilated the 110J APA ceiling. In short, in switching from conditional-ER/RRC to Mean-ER/RRC with Impedance limited to 440Ω, manufacturers had almost doubled the output, in fact, doubling titration outputs in every age category. When no objection was made to this invisible transition, manufacturers soon increased Impedance, transitioning to Pure-ER/RRC alone as we shall see, enhancing power even more.

power to Sine Wave, seriously upsetting the so-called "benefit to risk" advantage of the new Brief Pulse apparatus and thus "ECT" in general, may also have invited protests from anti-shock groups world-wide, possibly re-prompting an FDA and even ERA (European Regulatory Agency) inquiry. Beginning with the 200J D-2/early SR-1, early SR-2 then, the subsequent reporting by all four American BP manufacturers of the same circa "100J at 220Ω" phrase to the FDA for all made-for-America Brief Pulse devices manufactured from about 1983 to about 1995, in conjunction with three of the four American manufacturers' furtive and uniform discarding of both the 110J APA ceiling and actual output reporting in joules,[148] strongly suggests a conspiratorial cover-up of the equaling (and eventual surpassing, as we shall see) of Brief Pulse power compared to Sine Wave and thus the doubling of Brief Pulse default outputs administered in all age categories. This, of course, meant the permanent eradication of minimal stimulus outputs. Moreover, even as these early second generation BP devices began emitting 200 actual Joules, these same second generation BP devices began displaying false Machine Readouts depicting 100 maximum Joules, as we shall see in more detail, more than suggestive of an illusory adherence to the 1982 APA Standard and thus what appeared to be the continuation of improved Brief Pulse safety over Sine Wave via greatly reduced energy output. The "100 Joule" depiction, of course, continued to (falsely) suggest minimal stimulus output for all age categories.

[148] Medcraft alone maintained the APA 110J ceiling for their BP device, the B-25, although Medcraft alone, breached ER/RRC, as we shall. Moreover, Medcraft continued to produce the much criticized B-24 SW device.

Chapter 14

The Mectan Transmutation

The Mectan Transmutation is the manufacturer conversion of the conditional ER/RRC with a maximum ceiling of 110J stipulated in the 1982 APA Standard, to a pure-ER/RRC with a new ceiling based only on maximum machine Impedance. The Mectan Transmutation begins, as noted above, about 1982 with second generation Brief Pulse devices. All second generation BP devices violate the 1982 APA Standard and all second generation BP devices emit at least as much electrical energy output as SW at maximum settings though in opposing age categories.

The original APA Standard presented to the FDA in 1982 contains the following three principles, the first two explicitly and the third implicitly:

Original 1982 APA Standard for BP devices:
(1) A conditional-ER/RRC maximum of 70 Joules at 220Ω
(2) A conditional maximum EO ceiling of 110 Joules
(3) A MTTLOI maximum of 1.1 (110J ÷ 100J = 1.1) for all age categories

Toward the end of 1982, almost immediately following the close of the FDA investigation on ECT, MECTA, Somatics, and even Medcraft newly began reporting all existing BP devices as circa "100 Joules at 220Ω. " No new EO ceiling was reported.

The evident FDA assumption of this reporting was that "100J at 220Ω" was but a newer, slightly higher conditional-ER/RRC with the same 110J ceiling yet intact or even the assumption that the newer BP devices were newly limited not to 110J, but to circa 100 joules. Thus, even with a slightly higher ER/RRC, the maximum 1.1 MTTLOI appeared to remain intact, continuing to assure minimal stimulus or just above threshold outputs for all age groups as directed by the 1982 APA Standard. In short, no significant change seemed to have occurred with the reporting of circa "100J at 220Ω" by MECTA, Somatics Incorporated (a new Brief Pulse company), and Medcraft for their newer Brief Pulse devices.

In fact, with the reporting of "100J at 220Ω" by all three American Brief Pulse manufacturers, unbeknownst to the FDA or any advocacy or regulatory agency, two of the three manufacturers--MECTA and Somatics had surreptitiously dropped the 110J APA ceiling, while Medcraft had altogether dropped ER/RRC (which shall be discussed later). Indeed, by about 1983, both MECTA and Somatics had begun secretly interpreting the new "100J at 220Ω" phraseology as a Pure-ER/RRC sans the conditional 110J APA ceiling stipulation. By a "Pure-ER/RRC," we mean that the "100J at 220Ω" phrase was no longer being limited to the 110J ceiling. Indeed, MECTA and Somatics now figured a new unreported ceiling based now on maximum machine Impedance in turn limited only by the 600Ω maximum APA stipulation. Because MECTA appears to have initiated the conversion, the author has deemed the change, "the Mectan Transmutation. " Astoundingly, the Mectan Transmutation changed the ceiling for Brief Pulse devices from 110 maximum joules and thus a 1.1 MTTLOI to a new never before reported ceiling of 273 Joules or a 2.73 MTTLOI for all age categories as we shall see.

In short the 1982 APA Standard was transmuted from:

1) a Conditional-ER/RRC of "70J at 220Ω" to a Pure-ER/RRC of "100J at 220Ω. "
2) a conditional ceiling of 110J to a pure or Impedance based ceiling of 273J.
(100 Joules/220Ω = X Joules/600Ω. [149] X = 273 Joules).
3) a MTTLOI maximum of 1.1 (110J ÷ 100J = 1.1) to a MTTLOI maximum of 2.73 for all age categories.

In brief, the Mectan Transmutation clearly and seriously breached the 1982 APA Standard. As a result, Brief Pulse was no longer confined to just above threshold output, but to a 2.73 fold output or 2.73 MTTLOI. Unbeknownst to any but MECTA and Somatics, maximum output had now soared beyond that of SW, albeit, as noted, in opposing age categories, as we shall observe.

Not only did both the dropping of the 110J APA ceiling and the new 273J ceiling go unreported by MECTA and Somatics, but the misleading method of surpassing the 110J APA ceiling appears to have been calculated. That is, the supplanted reporting of a 100J unexplained pure-ER (Equivalent Ratio) in lieu of the previous 110J ceiling reflective of just above minimal stimulus, appears to have been designed. In short, the deliberate use of the "100J" figure associated with the minimum output needed to induce a grand mal seizure in the most seizure recalcitrant recipient, together with the abrupt and now total omission of actual Energy Output reporting (in joules), created a serious misimpression, constituting what can only be described as a deceptive "double standard. " [150] In brief, what is actually a dramatic ceiling augmentation instead appears to simulate the original 100J maximum alluded to within the 1982 APA Standard. 100J, remember, is highly suggestive of the minimum threshold output required to seize all 100 year old recipients which both Weiner and Utah Biomedical Test Laboratory had suggested to the FDA. Indeed, 100J is identified within the 1982 APA Standard as minimal stimulus, to which FDA agreed. This new impression, of course, was illusory. In fact, the transition created a new unreported ceiling of grossly higher dimensions. The 110J ceiling, while appearing intact then or even lowered to 100J, had actually been dropped by manufacturers so that by 1983, the Mectan Transmutation had generated a new never before reported 273J ceiling for American Brief Pulse devices. Certainly, by 1985 the single phrase "100J at 220Ω" was being reported by all four American BP Manufacturers (MECTA, Somatics, Medcraft, and Elcot) for what were actually second generation BP devices, followed in 1989 by a similarly deceptive phrase "100J at 300Ω" utilized for all European BP manufacturers, as we shall eventually examine. Indeed, by 1985, MECTA's and Somatics' reporting of actual maximum output had been ubiquitously discarded and, though all later second generation BP machines easily surpassed 200J at this point, these very devices brazenly displayed false machine Readouts of circa 100 maximum Joules. (Elcot had become defunct by this time while Medcraft retained an actual 100J maximum for its B-25 Brief Pulse device, but violated the APA Standard in yet another way, as we shall observe later.)

In brief, under the newly contrived Pure-ER/RRC method invented by MECTA (most likely by electrical engineer-psychiatrist Richard Weiner), in spite of deceptive and misleading output reporting of second generation BP devices, the new maximum ceiling in fact, and skyrocketed from an Absolute 110 Joules to a never before reported and unprecedented 273 Joules,[151] surpassing the 1982 APA ceiling Standard by some 163 Joules. Critically, in spite of appearances, therefore, what were actually second generation BP devices were no longer minimal stimulus instruments at all, but adequate electricity devices, devices which could now emit a MTTLOI of up to 2.73 fold threshold to all recipients in all age categories. Unbeknownst consumers, physicians themselves, and even the FDA, the 1982 APA Standard no longer served to limit output to just above threshold, to just enough electrical energy to induce adequate seizures. Indeed, at this juncture, the

---

[149] 600Ω is the maximum Impedance ceiling permitted under the original FDA/APA Standard.

[150] By "double standard," the author is referring to what looks like the continuous emphasis of the 100 Joule maximum to induce a seizure in any recipient, but which is actually an unexplained unauthorized pure-ER/RRC of 100J at 220Ω against the 600Ω maximum Impedance, permitting up to 273 Joules. This is significant in that the original standard touts the 100J maximum to induce seizures for BP devices compared to the 200J maximum utilized for the older SW models, as a significant improvement over SW by virtue of half the required electricity.

[151] Only in the sense that Somatics and MECTA appear to limit their devices to 273 maximum Joules derived from an equivalent ratio of 100 Joules at 220Ω to Maximum EO at Maximum Impedance (600Ω) does 100 Joules at 220Ω appear to be (albeit manufacturer contrived) a Standard. Such a "Standard," however, surpasses the output of the older SW devices, defeating the purpose of the "Standard" itself. Moreover, the "standard" is surreptitious).

unadopted standard no longer protected recipients from excessive, unnecessary dosages of electricity with respect to the induction of a grand mal seizure.

The Newer Brief Pulse Machines-The Mectan Transmutation Continued

As noted, from 1976-1982, the period of FDA scrutiny regarding "ECT" devices, the archetypal MECTA "C" MECTA submitted to the FDA emitted a maximum 108 Joules, and thus a 1.08 MTTLOI for all age groups. By about 1983 or 84, MECTA's second generation JR/SR 1 and 2, while appearing to emit the same circa 100 Joules and thus the same circa 1.1 MTTLOI emitted by the MECTA "C" for all age categories, now emitted an actual unreported 259J maximum for its later second generation BP devices or an unreported 2.59 MTTLOI for all age categories. Immediately following MECTA's enhancements, BP manufacturer Somatics Incorporated, reported the same (circa) "100J at 220Ω" phrase for its new later second generation BP device, the Thymatron DG, while surreptitiously boosting its power to 252 Joules and thus an unreported 2.52 MTTLOI for all age categories. Thus, while appearing to emphasize the "100 Joules" reported by all four American BP manufacturers (MECTA, Somatics, Elcot, and Medcraft), in fact, three of these manufacturers had at this juncture switched to an unreported "100J at 220Ω" pure-ER/RRC interpretation, no longer limiting output to the 110J APA ceiling and thus the 1.1 MTTLOI ceiling for all age categories. Rather, MECTA, Somatics, and Elcot based the new unreported ceiling on maximum machine Impedance which could potentially rise to 600Ω or a 273J ceiling (100J/220Ω = 273J/600Ω). [152] As a result, electrical titration levels for these later second generation BP devices soared from 1.1 fold or minimal stimulus output (1.1 MTTLOI) to a default of more than 2.5 fold minimal stimulus (2.5 MTTLOI) for all age recipients, a fact which would not be discovered (and then only indirectly) until 1996 by Beale and Cameron (Beale et al.; Cameron, 1996).

From about 1983 to approximately 1995 then, with the exception of Medcraft's B-25 (which grossly violates the APA standard in a very different manner as we shall learn), the circa 100 Joule ceiling intimated by three of the four American BP manufacturers for what were actually later second generation BP devices (including the now defunct, Elcot), was actually at least 2.5 fold 100 Joules, that is, at least 2.5 fold minimal stimulus output for all age categories. Succinctly then, as early as 1982 or 1984, the 110J APA ceiling stipulation had been dropped by three of the four then extant American BP manufacturers (MECTA, Somatics, and Elcot), the latter of which is now defunct, two of which (MECTA and Somatics) continue to produce mega powerful Brief Pulse devices even today. Moreover, it is at this same juncture, late 1982, early 1983, that both MECTA and Somatics unilaterally discard actual output reporting (in joules).

From a Conditional to a Mean to a Pure ER/RRC--The Mectan Transmutation Continued

As has been discussed, the ceiling for Brief Pulse devices formally submitted by Weiner and manufacturers to the FDA via the 1982 APA Standard was a "70J at 220Ω" ER/RRC and a "110J" ceiling. The MECTA "C," representing the Brief Pulse device for the entirety of the FDA investigation between 1976 and 1982 was based on and correctly reported to the FDA,[153] as having a "59J at 220Ω" ER/RRC well within the "70J at 220Ω" ER/RRC APA specification. Moreover, the "C" was correctly reported as having a 108 Joule maximum output, also in conformity with the 1982 APA 110J ceiling requirement (Department of Health and Human Services, 1982a, A53; E20; G3-G4). Eliciting a uniform (108J ÷ 100J =) 1.08 MTTLOI for all age categories and authentically minimal stimulus, the "C" exhibited to the FDA became the prototypical exemplar for the 1982 APA Standard. Conversely, by late 1982 or 1983, immediately following the close of FDA's formal investigation of "electroconvulsive therapy devices," MECTA, on its' own (straightway followed by Somatics) devised and introduced the aforementioned new phraseology, "100J at 220Ω" (in lieu of "70J at 220Ω") but with an unpublicized interpretation, precipitously giving all U. S. Brief Pulse manufacturers the secret go-ahead to set their Brief Pulse EO ceilings at much higher levels than that allowed under the 1982 APA Standard. Incredibly, as has been noted, this same stratagem enabled manufacturers to hide this latter fact. Specifically, directly following the FDA's public investigation of "ECT," MECTA Corporation, sometime between late 1982 and early

---

[152] We shall go into specific details a little later.

[153] Parameters for the MECTA "C" as reported by MECTA were clearly in accord with the 1982 APA Standard.

1983, began newly reporting "100J at 220Ω" for its new MECTA "D-2"/early JR/SR 1 BP device or what appeared to be a simple new, very modest rise in the ER/RRC with no ceiling change whatsoever. [154] Almost simultaneously, new manufacturer, Somatics Incorporated, also began reporting what appeared to be the same new unauthorized, but only modestly higher Equivalent Ratio/Rate Rise Ceiling of "100J at 220Ω" for its' new "Thymatron" device (Food and Drug Administration, 1984). From comments made by FDA investigators who received 510K submissions from these manufacturers newly describing their latest Brief Pulse devices with the phrase "100J at 220Ω," we can see that FDA personnel clearly assumed the APA 110J ceiling, intact. Indeed, presuming the 110 Joule ceiling intact as FDA monitors certainly did, the increased ER/RRC did not seem nor would it have been of any great significance.

By approximately 1984 then, while all four manufacturers (Somatics, MECTA, Elcot, and Medcraft) reported their BP machines via the new circa "100J at 220Ω" phrase in "510K pre-market" applications submitted to the FDA, neither MECTA nor Somatics nor any other manufacturer remembered to mention any change in the 110J APA ceiling. Succinctly, none of the manufacturer submitted "pre-market" applications mentions any increase in the APA 110J ceiling. (Note that manufacturers, at this point, submitted pre-market applications in lieu of the expected updated 1982 standard, one or the other of which was required).

With no reason to doubt the 110J ceiling unmistakably depicted in the 1982 APA Standard then, the new "100J at 220Ω" phrase reported by all four manufacturers, seemed but an innocuous ER/RRC increase in that it appeared to have no actual effect on the uniform 1.1 MTTLOI maximum still ostensibly guaranteed by the APA standard's 110J ceiling. Thus, while technically, the ER/RRC had increased, there appeared to be no change in the minimal stimulus output still seemingly assured by the 1982 APA Standard. Seen as but a modest, insignificant increase in what was still held to be a conditional-ER/RRC then, [155] FDA officials had no idea that a radical re-interpretation affecting the overall ceiling and thus the MTTLOI had actually taken place. To FDA investigators, as noted above, the new phrase appeared to be but a newer, slightly higher conditional-ER/RRC, leaving the original APA maximum ceiling of "110 Joules" unchanged and thus the 1.1 MTTLOI unaffected. Minimal stimulus titration outputs and thus the increase in safety which Brief Pulse devices seemed to offer over SW for all age categories seemed secure.

By manufacturers subtly referring to the "220Ω" aspect of the "100J at 220Ω" ER/RRC phrase as "typical Impedance," [156] gradational outputs in accordance with what appeared to remain a 1.1 MTTLOI appeared unaltered. Consequently, the natural assumption of a slightly enhanced conditional-ER/RRC within newly submitted pre-market applications failed to arouse concern amongst FDA officials. In fact, unbeknownst to the FDA or any public advocacy group, manufacturers had at this point begun interpreting the newly reported "100J at 220Ω" phrase, as has been discussed, as a Mean-ER/RRC permitting a 200J ceiling at 440Ω (100J/220Ω = 200J/440Ω) which soon devolved into to a Pure-ER/RRC interpretation permitting up to 273J relative to the maximum APA Impedance of 600Ω (100J/220 = 273J/600Ω). This change, of course, grossly enhanced the MTTLOI delivered to all age categories. In truth, this was an invisible change radically violating the APA Standard. The covert interpretation of the new "100J at 220Ω" phrase first as a Mean-ER/RRC, and then as a Pure-ER/RRC no longer based upon a 110J ceiling, but upon the maximum allowable Impedance of 600Ω, dramatically affected "electrical dosing" or MTTLOI at every age level. Not understood was the fact that MECTA and Somatics were not simply reporting a new conditional-ER/RRC of "100J at 220Ω" supplanting the previous conditional-ER/RRC of "70 Joules at 220Ω," [157] but that the change had included the unreported dropping of the 110 Joule ceiling, first doubling and then more than doubling the maximum allowable energy output and thus the maximum electrical "titration" level outputs allowed at every age level.

---

[154] The original 1982 APA ceiling Weiner submitted to the FDA, was a "70J at 220Ω" ER/RRC with 110J ceiling.

[155] Conditional meaning limited to a 110J ceiling.

[156] In that maximum EO is not consistently predictable with SW, reporting a "typical" output at a "typical" Impedance might be acceptable with SW devices such as the B-24. Reporting "typical" output with BP devices is inexcusable in that maximum output is consistent, specific, and predictable and thus can be specifically reported. In fact, "typical" 220Ω Impedance for BP devices was actually being interpreted as a mean.

[157] Charge increased along with EO. The previous Charge ceiling appears to have been based upon ER/RRC of 70 Joules at 220Ω. A new Charge ceiling (as well as EO ceiling) became based upon the new ER. The Thymatron DG device utilizes .9 Amperes Constant Current. Charge = EO/Current x Impedance. Charge = 70 Joules/.9 Amperes x 220Ω = .354 Coulombs.100 Joules/.9 Amperes x 220Ω = .504 Coulombs. Thus, the Charge ceiling for the Thymatron DG using the ER/RRC of 70 Joules at 220Ω is .354 Coulombs, about the maximum Charge of the MECTA "C." Charge ceiling for Thymatron DG using the new ER of 100 Joules at 220Ω is .504 Coulombs.

What were actually second generation Brief Pulse devices had clandestinely jumped from first generation devices limited to a uniform 1.1 MTTLOI, to second generation machines emitting first a 2.0 and then a circa 2.5 MTTLOI in every age category. No longer were second generation BP devices the minimal stimulus devices presented to the FDA during the official investigation period; no longer were Brief Pulse devices convulsive therapy devices at all. Overnight, they had become adequate electrical dosage (or ENR) devices designed to deliver consistent MTTLOIs first of 2.0 and then circa 2.5 fold threshold to every age category.

In sum, the 100 joules at a so-called "typical" 220Ω first introduced by MECTA in late 1982, had actually been interpreted by MECTA (and then Somatics) first as an ER/RRC-Mean,[158] and then as a Pure-ER/RRC.[159] In fact, clandestinely interpreting the newly reported "100J at a 'typical' 220Ω" phrase as a mean output at a mean Impedance created the first major mathematical rationale for the manufacturing of the much more powerful devices manufacturers actually sought, now that they had "gotten by" the FDA. "Mean" interpretation, in short, first enabled manufacturers to create machines capable of unreported and unauthorized 200J maximums at 440Ω maximum Impedances (100J/220Ω = 200J/440Ω), virtually twice the power of the MECTA "C" with twice the MTTLOI output, and thus twice the electrical energy output of first generation BP devices. Such machines delivered default outputs not of 1.1, as noted, but 2.0 fold minimal stimulus to every age recipient. Following manufacturers secret interpretation of "100J at 220Ω" as a "mean," manufacturers soon morphed the same "100J at 220Ω" phrase into an even cleverer, even more powerful transmutation, no longer as a simple mean, but as a Pure-ER/RRC. In brief, MECTA and Somatics began interpreting "100J at 220Ω" as a pure Equivalent Ratio to maximum machine Impedances which could theoretically reach up to 600Ω. Thus, this slightly later transmutation of the same "100J at 220Ω" phrase justified even more powerful second generation BP devices with potential emissions up to 273 maximum Joules (100J/220Ω = 273J/600Ω), in short, up to a potential 2.73 MTTLOI in all age categories. Accordingly, but known only to manufacturers, the new "100J at 220Ω" phrase first accompanied the advent of the 1982-3 MECTA D-2/early SR 1 and Somatics' new "Thymatron," based on mean-ER/RRC, and then the later second generation MECTA JR/SR1@2 and the later second generation Thymatron DG based on a pure-ER/RRC. Both manufacturers practiced the wholesale dropping of the 110J ceiling within the 1982 APA Standard. Moreover, both major American Brief Pulse manufacturers (MECTA and Somatics) implemented the final transmutation (to Pure-ER/RRC) in conjunction with the total abandonment of both actual and maximum EO reporting. Never reported to the FDA, therefore, the new undisclosed interpretations (Mean and Pure) went unnoticed by FDA officials and thus the public at large. Manufacturers' secret interpretation of the "100J at 220Ω" phrase first as an ER/RRC-mean, then as a Pure-ER/RRC, secretly doubling and then more than doubling the power of all second generation BP devices, changed the very nature of the BP device from a minimal stimulus instrument to machines now emitting 2.5 and 5.0 fold threshold default outputs with the administering of BL and UL "ECT" respectively, not only breaching the 1982 APA standard, but ultimately surpassing the overall maximum output of even the SW devices of old.

Mectan Transmutation Concluded

As noted above then, in lieu of the FDA approved 1982 APA 110J maximum EO ceiling, manufacturers, beginning with the MECTA D-2/early SR 1, directly followed by Somatics early Thymatron device, began reporting--not a conditional "100J at 220Ω" ER/RRC with 110J ceiling--but what was actually a 100J average or mean,[160] only to eventually transmute the same "100J at 220Ω" phrase into a Pure-ER/RRC no longer limited by a 110J ceiling, but by maximum machine Impedance. In short, the Mectan Transmutation permitted not 110 maximum joules, but potential maximum outputs up to 273 Joules. These transmuted interpretations were never (and have never been) explained or reported in any journal or by any agency (until now). The end result

---

[158] This simply means a Pure mean.100J at 220Ω allows 200J at 440Ω.

[159] Pure ER/RRC means the "100J at 220Ω" is based only as an ER to maximum output and maximum machine Impedance (100J/220Ω = XJ/600Ω; X = 273J), no longer the 110J APA ceiling.

[160] The interpretation of the reported 100J at 220Ω phrase first as a mean Output and mean Impedance, followed by the unexplained and unauthorized transmutation of 100J at 220Ω as a Pure-ER/RRC in lieu of actual EO--is a twist on the well-known reporting of averages to create false statistical impressions. By 1985, "100 Joules at 220Ω" had become the unexplained equivalent of 273 Joules at 600Ω, the actual new and unreported maximums for second generation BP devices.

of this "Mectan Transmutation" was the apparition of 100J BP devices or devices appearing to be limited to 110 Joules, even as the transmutation opened up a hidden door allowing powerful Brief Pulse energy emissions first equaling the 200J maximum power of SW (through *Mean*-ER/RRC), and then surpassing the maximum power of SW (through *Pure*-ER/RRC). Incredibly deceptive then, by 1985 what appeared to be virtually the same ER/RRC principle with the circa 110J ceiling depicted within the 1982 APA Standard, limiting Brief Pulse devices to the same approximate maximum output emission as the archetypal MECTA "C," the Mectan Transmutation had actually transmogrified the "100J at 220Ω" phrase into a means of obtaining outputs up to 273 potential Joules (Cameron, 1994). In short, the pure-ER/RRC interpretation of the seemingly innocuous circa "100J at 220Ω" phrase reported in 1985 by all four U. S. BP device manufacturers, had devolved for three of the four American manufacturers (MECTA, Somatics, Elcot), into a mechanism both sanctioning and camouflaging grossly enhanced outputs. (While Elcot dissolved, Medcraft, the fourth American manufacturer used the same reporting phrase--"100J at 220Ω"-- for a different purpose, to justify bypassing ER/RRC, thereby permitting emissions of up to 100 Joules not merely in the oldest age category, but the youngest, grossly surpassing minimal stimulus in almost every age class, as we shall ultimately observe. [161])

Using "100J at 220Ω" to Camouflage Maximum EO--Mectan Transmutation Continued

Because "100J at 220Ω," is actually a Pure-ER/RRC to maximum EO at maximum machine Impedance, manufacturers could combine these two Equivalent Ratio figures (100J and 220Ω) with all other maximum machine parameters (Duration, Frequency, and Pulse Width, Amperage) to suggest their second generation BP devices were limited to circa 100 maximum Joules. By inserting a false constant of "220Ω" (which is not an actual, but an ER Impedance) into the Energy Output formula: Amp. x Amp. x **220Ω** x maximum Pulses x maximum PW x maximum Duration = Equivalent Ratio-Energy Output, containing all true maximum parameters of a device with the exception of Impedance, manufacturers were able to derive an ER-EO (Equivalent Ratio Energy Output) in joules in lieu of the actual output in joules. To rephrase, using "220Ω" in lieu of actual machine Impedance, the EO derived was not actual, but an ER-EO (Equivalent Ratio-Energy Output). It was by using the product of all actual maximum parameters with a non-actual average "220Ω" Impedance, that manufacturers were able create the false impression that maximum EO (in joules) never exceeded circa 100 Joules. Actual EO was not only suppressed in this way, but because the math product never significantly exceeded circa 100 maximum Joules, a totally false impression was created that the machine adhered to the 1982 APA Standard. Understood by only a few, this false circa 100 Joules (which came to be depicted on machine readouts for all American-made second generation BP devices as we shall see) suggested that second generation BP devices continued to be limited to circa 100 maximum joules and so were really first generation BP devices. The circa 100 joules, of course, was but an ER-EO (Equivalent Ratio-Energy Output) in lieu of the actual output which was never reported.

To illustrate, Somatics' second generation Thymatron DG (which we will examine in detail later) uses actual maximum parameters of .9A current, 140 maximum pulses, a .001 second pulse width, a 4.0 second maximum Duration, and a never before reported 555Ω machine maximum. Using all actual maximum parameters with the exception of actual maximum Impedance (supplanted by 220Ω), we obtain what appears to be 100 maximum Joules: EO = .9A x .9A x 220Ω x 140 Pulses x .001PW x 4.0 Sec Duration = 100J. The derivation, of course, is deceptive in that although true maximum parameters for Duration, Frequency, Amperage, and Pulse Width are utilized, simply by using the one ER-Impedance of 220Ω, actual EO becomes radically misrepresented. In short, the 100J EO derived here is not the maximum machine output at all, but an ER (Equivalent Ratio) output. To find actual EO, we must use actual maximum machine Impedance (up to 600Ω) which for the DG is 555Ω (not provided by Somatics). Thus, only by supplanting the misleading "220Ω" ER with the actual maximum machine Impedance of "555.5Ω" can we find the actual maximum EO for the DG of 252J. Using the same maximum figures for all parameters; therefore, but this time supplanting the misleading "220Ω"

---

[161] One of the manufacturers, Medcraft as noted, actually limited its new BP device, the B-25, to approximately 100 Joules maximum (while seriously breaching the Standard in yet another manner as we shall see). The fact that all four BP manufacturers reported the same circa "100J at 220Ω" phrase with misleading circa 100J machine readouts on MECTA and Somatics' devices together with an actual 100J Medcraft device enhanced the illusion that all American BP manufacturers adhered to a uniform maximum output of circa 100 maximum Joules.

ER Impedance with the actual 555Ω maximum machine Impedance, we find that the Thymatron DG has an actual maximum output of (EO = .9A x .9A x 555.5Ω x 140 Pulses x .001PW x 4.0 Sec. Duration =) 252J. Conversely, while the reported "100J at 220Ω" phrase can be used to derive all other maximum parameters accurately, both the circa "100J" (actually 99.7J) figure and the "220Ω" figure are but ERs (Equivalent Ratios) to the DG's actual unreported maximum EO and unreported maximum Impedance of 252 Joules and 555.5Ω respectively (99.7J/220Ω = **252J**/555.5Ω). True maximum EO, in brief, is never reported by Somatics. Consequently, the illusion of the 100J minimal stimulus BP device continued to remain intact until around 1990, as we shall see.

So clever is the Mectan Transmutation, so shrewd is this method of reporting, that, from 1976 to 2023, a span of almost fifty years--the entire breadth of the modern day Brief Pulse Era which began with the re-introduction of modern-day BP devices in 1976--no regulatory body ever realized that the ubiquitous "100J at 220Ω" phrase reported by every U. S. BP manufacturer since about 1983, was actually used to cover up new unreported BP maximums, first up to 200J at 440Ω, and, by 1985, up to 273 Joules at 600Ω. In short, no regulatory body ever apprehended that the newly reported "100J at 220Ω" phrase no longer incorporated the 110J ceiling aspect promised to the FDA via the 1982 APA Standard which had guaranteed minimal stimulus output in all age categories. [162] Nor did any regulatory body ever understand that in lieu of the 1982 APA Standard depicting a conditional-ER/RRC of "70J at 220Ω" with an absolute EO ceiling of 110J, what appeared to be a simple new conditional-ER/RRC of "100J at 220Ω" with the same 110J ceiling intact, had, in fact, transmogrified into a Pure-ER/RRC permitting circa (273J ÷ 110 =) 2.5 times the EO stipulated in the 1982 APA Standard. Designed to insure minimal stimulus safety via the new much more efficient BP apparatus allegedly half as powerful as SW, the minimal stimulus output mandated by the APA Standard appeared to regulatory bodies such as the FDA, to persist unaltered. In fact (as we shall see), bolstering the illusion of 100J BP devices in lieu of what were actually much more powerful second generation BP devices, misleading manufacturer-devised Machine Readouts appeared, falsely displaying (for administering psychiatrists) false maximum outputs of circa 100 maximum Joules! On the other hand, if we follow the true history of MECTA and Somatics BP devices from first to second generation (and later to third generation) BP devices, we can trace the devastating devolution of the modern Brief Pulse apparatus itself.

First generation includes the 1976-1981---81J-110J MECTA "C;" followed by the 1982---140J MECTA D-1, still allegedly based on the APA's conditional-ER/RRC of 110 Joules but which supposedly allowed up to 140 Joules for "exceptional cases. "

Second generation BP devices begin with the 1983, 200J MECTA D-2, early MECTA JR/SR-1 and JR/SR-2 BP devices as well as the early 1983, 200J Thymatron by Somatics all of which were based on an unreported Mean-ER/RRC interpretation of the newly introduced "100J at 220Ω" phraseology. Next, comes the later second generation BP devices which include the 1985 MECTA SR-1 and SR2 (of the same name), and Thymatron DG capable of unreported 259 and 252J maximums respectively, all based on the newer surreptitious Pure-ER/RRC interpretation of the same "100J at 220Ω" phrase. No longer limited to 110 Joules or even 200 Joules, these later model second generation BP devices, as noted, were actually only limited by a Pure-ER/RRC interpretation of the now familiar "100J at 220Ω" phrase, but this time relative to maximum machine Impedance up to the maximum allowable APA Impedance of 600Ω (100J/220 = 273J/600Ω). No longer were Brief Pulse machines confined to 110 maximum Joules or "minimal stimulus" outputs. Moreover, it was with the 1983 introduction of the MECTA D-2/MECTA JR/SR 1@2 and the early Thymatron, both capable of 200 unreported Joules, that all four BP manufacturers began simultaneously eliminating (with the exception of Medcraft), the reporting of *actual* output in Joules, and most conspicuously, *maximum* output in Joules.

If Weiner's original assertion is accurate (and I believe it is) that, "Using a pulse device, . . . only 0.6% of seizure thresholds . . . [are] greater than 70 Joules and that none . . . [are] greater than 100 Joules" (Department of Health and Human Services, 1982a, p. A53) and this holds true with BL "ECT" and if adequate convulsions are actually effective, then there is no justifiable rationale for allowing these outputs to exceed the 110J APA ceiling, circumscribing all outputs to that needed to induce adequate seizures at a 1.1 MTTLOI maximum. If Weiner's original 100J assertion is true, that no recipient ever requires more than 100J to seize and if convulsion is the sole ameliorative dynamic in ECT, then there can be no justification for permitting a never before explained 100J Pure-ER/RRC to emit up to 273 Joules or a 2.73 MTTLOI for all age categories unless, of course, adequate seizure is not effective. Certainly, the concomitant elimination of actual output reporting itself

---

[162] 600Ω is maximum FDA Impedance.100J/220Ω = XJ/600Ω. XJ = 273J.

by both major Brief Pulse manufacturers cannot be sufficiently explained other than to cover up the dramatic new increases in Brief Pulse power and MTTLOI administered to all age categories. Additionally, the supplanting of this dramatic new ceiling with an unexplained "100J" ER, thereby creating illusory 100J Machine Readout maximums accepted in good faith by practicing physicians, cannot be comprehended but as a calculated manufacturer ploy to suggest the same 110J maximum promised to the FDA in 1976, and seemingly secured under the 1982 APA Standard. Engendering the deliberately specious impression that a 110J ceiling for BP devices continued to remain in effect, [163] an impression which has continuously sustained BP's reputation as a reduced EO device for over fifty years, can only be understood as fraud. In short, there can be no rationale except a cover-up in manufacturers' uniformly reporting "100J at 220Ω" and concomitantly failing to explain the phrase's function as a Pure-ER/RRC effectuating a dramatic new ceiling, even as Machine Readouts depicting false 100J maximums were used to suppress this very augmentation. In short, from 1982 to 1985 via the application of MECTA's new "100J at 220Ω" Pure-ER/RRC methodology deemed here "the Mectan Transmutation"-- Brief Pulse manufacturers managed to camouflage the new maximum EO [164] of 273J and thus a 2.73 MTTLOI for all age categories by depicting the "100J" figure via machine readouts. In sum, manufacturers clearly failed to report the dramatic new ceiling enhancement, indeed hiding this information by using a false "220Ω" average to depict circa 100J ceiling readouts for both earlier and later second generation BP devices. To be certain, the Mectan Transmutation allowed dramatic new power and electrical titration enhancements without revealing this to either the public or the FDA even as spurious machine readouts continued to create the false impression of minimal stimulus or just above threshold output devices in conformity with the 1982 APA Standard.

---

[163] The notion of deliberately creating the false impression that BP machines are limited to approximately 100 Joules is buttressed by the fact that in 1989, Weiner spearheaded the continuous and unexplained utilization of the "100 Joule" ER methodology within the 1989 IEC (international) Standard, but at an unexplained ER Impedance of 300Ω (in lieu of 220Ω), creating a similar misimpression in Eurasia of reduced energy BP devices compared to SW - as we shall see.

[164] The cover-up entails calculating machine readouts by substituting "typical Impedance" ("220Ω) for all actual Impedances so that maximum output appears to be about 100 maximum joules. Actual EO is never reported. Moreover, there is no attempt to reduce parameters such as Duration to maintain an actual 110J ceiling.

Chapter 15

Later Second Generation Brief Pulse Devices: Transition from Mean to Pure-ER/RRC

Not surprisingly, following FDA's public investigation of "ECT" devices from 1976 to 1982, Brief Pulse machines continued to increase in power. By 1985, the early enhanced second generation MECTA BP devices had devolved from probable unreported 200J maximums to even newer SR1 and 2s (of the same name) emitting unreported 259J maximums, while Somatics' early Thymatron, also capable of an unreported 200J output, similarly devolved into an unreported 252J device known as the "Thymatron DG" (Cameron, 1994). Thus, by 1985, MECTA, Somatics, and even Elcot BP devices, not only equaled, but had begun to surpass SW in cumulative output or power (Cameron, 1994; Department of Health and Human Services, 1982a, G3-G4). In spite of escalating power, moreover, all four U. S. BP manufacturers--including the now defunct Elcot--uniformly continued reporting the same circa "100J at 220Ω" phraseology they had reported for the slightly earlier 200J second generation MECTA and Somatics BP devices. Of course, the reported "100J at 220Ω" phrase was suggestive of but a slightly higher conditional-ER/RRC yet adhering to the APA 110J ceiling. On the surface, therefore, nothing seemed to change with the transition from a "70J at 220Ω" conditional-ER/RRC with 110J ceiling to a circa "100J at 220Ω" conditional-ER/RRC with 110J ceiling. In fact, based on machine readouts, manufacturers appeared to be producing almost the same circa 110J minimal stimulus Brief Pulse device presented to the FDA between 1976 and 1982.

As usual, Somatics' power increase from an unreported 200J Brief Pulse device to an unreported 252J Brief Pulse device, immediately followed MECTA's precedential device enhancement from MECTA's (unreported) 200J devices to its even newer unreported 259J devices. The increases moreover, altered neither the uniform reporting by all three extant manufacturers of "100J at 220Ω" nor their uniform Machine Readouts depicting circa 100J maximums. MECTA's and Somatics transition from 2.0 fold threshold outputs to circa 2.5 fold threshold outputs was achieved by a simple trick. The two manufacturers simply re-interpreted circa "100J at 220Ω" from what they had secretly rendered as a Mean-ER/RRC (doubling the power of BP) to a newer rendering of the same "100J at 220Ω" phrase as a Pure-ER/RRC newly based on maximum machine Impedance, increasing power even further. Instead of interpreting "100J at 220Ω" as a mean-ER-Output at a mean-ER--Impedance, enabling up to 200J at 440Ω, the innovative Pure-ER/RRC interpretation of the same "100J at 220Ω" phrase became newly based on the APA Impedance maximum of 600Ω, enabling these same two manufacturers to creep from an unreported 200J Brief Pulse maximum to an unreported 273J Brief Pulse maximum. [165]

Mean-ER/RRC Interpretation: **100J/220Ω = *200J*/440Ω**.

[165] In that MECTA seems always to set the precedent in such matters, and in that Weiner is most closely affiliated with MECTA, it is the author's opinion that APA representative and electrical engineer-psychiatrist Richard Weiner is the primary author of said innovations.

Pure-ER/RRC Interpretation: **100J/220Ω = <u>273J</u>/<u>600Ω</u>**. [166]

BP machines had now transitioned from a <u>Conditional-ER/RRC</u> with 110J ceiling, to a <u>Conditional-ER/RRC</u> with <u>Impedance Override</u> (enabling up to a 140J maximum), to a <u>Mean-ER/RRC</u> interpretation virtually doubling output to 200 maximum Joules, to a <u>Pure-ER/RRC</u> interpretation based on maximum (machine) Impedance, allowing an even newer unreported ceiling of up to 273 maximum Joules. In brief, machines had devolved from 1.1 fold threshold outputs for all age recipients, to 1.4 fold threshold outputs, to 2.0 fold threshold outputs, to potential 2.73 fold threshold outputs for all age recipients. Incredibly, all power increases surpassing 140 Joules were suddenly rendered invisible (by manufacturers) and so went unreported. The MECTA and Somatics transition from "70J at 220Ω" with 110J maximum to a "100J at 220Ω" <u>Mean-ER/RRC</u> (discarding the 110J ceiling) and finally to the "100J at 220Ω" <u>Pure-ER/RRC</u> (also discarding the 110J ceiling) occurred with almost no reporting changes whatsoever, and thus no manifest increases in power. The term "typical" within the bandied phrase, "100J at a 'typical' 220Ω Impedance" newly interpreted as a Mean-ER/RRC, and then re-interpreted as a Pure-ER/RRC together with spurious machine readouts totally camouflaged actual output. [167] In short, it was not the reported transition from "70J at 220Ω" to "100J at 220Ω" which so altered the outcome, but the unreported transmutation from the "70J at 220Ω" conditional-ER/RRC with 110J ceiling depicted within the APA Standard to a "100J at 220Ω" Pure-ER/RRC sans 110J ceiling newly based on maximum Impedance that so dramatically corrupted the Standard. In brief, it was the dropping of the 110J ceiling stipulation. Even so, conspicuous Machine Readouts depicting circa 100 Joule maximums utilized by all four Brief Pulse manufacturers, all of which now used the uniform circa "100J at 220Ω" phrase to depict the power of their newer Brief Pulse devices, continued to reassure physicians, officials, and consumers alike that Brief Pulse devices remained unaltered in both power and minimal stimulus titration. Indeed, Brief Pulse devices seemingly continued to emit a maximum 100 Joules in most cases and thus a 1.0 fold or at most a 1.1 MTTLOI for all age categories in accordance with the 1982 APA Standard minimal stimulus regulations. Not only did later second generation MECTA SR-1 and 2 models and Somatics' later second generation Thymatron DG appear relatively unaltered with respect to the earlier second generation D-2/SR1 and SR 2, and Somatics' earlier second generation Thymatron, therefore, but the uniform reporting of "100J at 220Ω" together with uniform machine Readouts of circa 100 maximum Joules (by all four manufacturers) continued to suggest that all Brief Pulse devices continued to adhere to the 1982 APA Standard guaranteeing minimal stimulus output. Machines not only appeared substantially unaltered in power from early second generation to later second generation BP devices then, but appeared virtually unaltered in power from the first generation MECTA "C" which had clearly been limited to 108 maximum Joules or a 1.08 MTTLOI for all age categories. In sum, Brief Pulse machines appeared not only unaltered from the first generation minimal stimulus devices to what were actually later second generation BP devices, but appeared improved by reducing maximum output even further from 110J to circa 100J. The redundancy and emphasis of the same circa "100J" figure from first generation to early and then later second generation Brief Pulse devices, all of which actually emitted (i.e. Medcraft) or falsely depicted "100J" machine readout maximums (MECTA and Somatics), appeared to assertively "confirm" ongoing, even improved minimal stimulus outputs for every Brief Pulse device manufactured from about 1979 onward. [168]

In addition, under the International Standard (IEC--International Electro-Technical Commission standard) as we shall later observe, based on an emulative Pure-ER/RRC interpretation of a remarkably similar phraseology, "100J at 300Ω," the same method would eventually provide made-for-Europe BP manufacturers, with a similar hidden capacity to utilize up to 226 unreported Joules (and more), all while similarly seeming to emit the same approximate 100J maximums as their made-for-America counterparts. No longer minimal

---

[166] Methodological permutations of this sort permitting higher and higher output while intimating or enabling the reporting of the same 110J maximum, appear to consistently emanate from MECTA Corporation, implicating psychiatrist-electrical engineer and APA/manufacturer-spokesperson, Richard Weiner.

[167] Instead of a 220Ω mean to an actual 440Ω, the new interpretation allowed a 220Ω ER to an actual 600Ω.100J/220Ω = <u>**200J**</u>/440Ω **vs** 100J/220Ω = <u>**273J**</u>/600Ω.

[168] As outputs increased from 108 to 200 to circa 250 maximum Joules, and thus increased in multifold threshold titration levels, maximum Impedances also increased, a fact which should have been a tip-off to increasing power. While MECTA ceased reporting maximum Impedance, Somatics fortunately did and so increases in power can be confirmed from this fact alone. The Thymatron DG was reported to have the capacity of overcoming a 555Ω maximum Impedance. Impedances, in fact, had increased from about 400Ω (MECTA C), to about 440Ω (early D-1, SR-1 and 2; Thymatron) to circa 555Ω and 562Ω respectively (later SR-1-2, and Thymatron DG).

stimulus devices at all, international BP devices too, like their American counterparts, would soon surreptitiously and imperceptibly surpass SW in power, emitting and surpassing a 2.26 MTTLOI in all age categories. [169]

Specific Parameters of Later Second Generation Made-for America BP Devices: The MECTA SR 1 and 2 and Somatics' Thymatron DG Based on Pure-ER/RRC

As MECTA devices escalated in power, the 200J D-2/early SR-1 and early SR-2 soon evolved into the later SR-1 and SR-2 models (having the same name) now capable of emitting up to 259 maximum joules. Like the earlier second generation BP devices, both later second generation MECTA SR-1 and SR-2 BP devices were based on the same circa "100J at 220Ω" phrase, but in lieu of a Mean-ER/RRC, as noted, manufacturers newly interpreted the phrase as a Pure-ER/RRC to maximum machine Impedance. The Pure-ER/RRC interpretation now relative to maximum machine Impedance which facilitated these new (unreported) maximum emissions of up to 259J for MECTA devices, meant a new 2.59 MTTLOI with MECTA devices for all age categories. To accommodate the greater power facilitated by the newest Pure-ER/RRC interpretation of circa "100J at 220Ω," the later MECTA SR-1 and SR-2 devices increased in Voltage from a probable 350V maximum to a probable 450V maximum, and could now overcome a maximum Impedance of approximately 562.5Ω (without reducing the ER/RRC [170]). In reality, the APA absolute ceiling of 110 Joules had by this time, of course (and in spite of all appearances to the contrary) entirely disappeared. Assuming a maximum 450V and maximum 562Ω machine Impedance, maximum output for these machines can be deduced formulaically as seen below.

(1985-2000) **Later Second Generation MECTA SR-1** (probable):

Later 2nd generation SR-1: Voltage-Based Formula for Finding Maximum Output: (based on speculative 450V maximum [171]).
450V x .8A. x 180 Pulses x .002 PW x 2.0 Sec. = **259.2J**.

Later 2nd generation SR-1: Impedance-Based Formula for Finding Maximum Output:
.8A. x .8A. x 562.5Ω x 180 Pulses x .002PW x 2.0 Sec. = **259.2J**.

Later 2nd generation MECTA SR-1: Based on Pure-ER/RRC
(Reported) "101.4J/220Ω" = (Actual Unreported) 259J/562.5Ω.

(1985-2000) **Later Second Generation MECTA SR-2** (probable):

Later 2nd generation SR-2: Voltage-Based Formula for Finding Maximum Output: (Based on speculative 450V maximum)
450V x .8A. x 180 Pulses x .001PW x 4.0 Sec. = **259J**.

Later 2nd generation SR-2: Impedance-Based Formula for Finding Maximum Output:
.8A. x .8A. x 562.5Ω x 180Pul. x .001 PW x 4.0Sec. = **259.2J**.

---

[169] IEC Standard (European) is based upon a 500Ω maximum Impedance in lieu of 600Ω maximum (American), thus the slightly lower maximum output.

[170] No reduction was necessary in that there was no longer a 110J ceiling.

[171] While actual maximum Voltage and actual maximum Impedance are no longer provided by MECTA at this point, Somatics' later second generation Thymatron DG, the complement of MECTA's later SR1 and SR2 devices, increased in Voltage from the earlier Thymatron version by 100V (300V to 400V), parameters provided by Somatics. As a result, the Thymatron DG can be accurately calculated to emit a maximum 252J at 555.5Ω. The DG immediately followed MECTA's later SR1and SR2 models, the power of which the Somatics' DG almost certainly emulated. By speculating on a similar increase of 100V for MECTA's later SR1 and 2 models (350V to 450V), we obtain new parameters almost identical to that of Somatics' DG. In short, MECTA's later SR1 and 2 appear to have precedentially emitted a circa maximum 259J at circa 562.5Ω. Based on the reported circa "100J at 220Ω" reported for the later second generation BP devices of both MECTA and Somatics, the utilization of Pure ER/RRC becomes apparent (see above).

***Later 2nd generation SR-2**: Based on Pure-ER/RRC* (probable):
(Reported) "101.3J/220Ω" = (Actual Unreported) 259J/562.5Ω.

As the second generation Somatics device, like the MECTA devices similarly escalated in power, the 200J Thymatron soon evolved into the later Thymatron DG. As noted, the later Thymatron DG, like the later MECTA devices, incorporated the newly contrived Pure-ER/RRC interpretation of the same circa "100J at 220Ω" phrase (previously interpreted as a Mean-ER/RRC) "permitting" a new unreported maximum emission of approximately 252J, in essence, a new 2.52 MTTLOI for all age categories. To accommodate the greater power facilitated by the newest Pure-ER/RRC interpretation of circa "100J at 220Ω," the Thymatron DG device increased its Voltage from a 400V to a 500V maximum, and could now overcome a maximum Impedance of approximately 555.5Ω (without reducing the ER/RRC). The APA absolute ceiling of 110 Joules had by this time, as noted above (and in spite of appearances to the contrary) entirely disappeared. In that Somatics provides the DG's 555.5Ω Impedance maximum, the Voltage can be determined accordingly (Ohm's law:.9A x 555.5Ω = 500V), so that the DG's formulaically derived maximum output below is not speculative, but factual. See proofs below:

(1985-2000) Evolved **Thymatron DG** by Somatics [172]

***Thymatron DG** – Voltage-Based Formula for Finding Maximum Output:*
500V x .9 Amps x 140 Pulses x .001 PW x 4.0 Sec. = **252J**.

***Thymatron DG** - Impedance-Based Formula for Finding Maximum Output:*
.9 x .9 x 555.5Ω x 140 Pulses x .001 PW x 4.0 Sec. = **252J**.

***Thymatron DG**: Based on Pure-ER/RRC*
(Reported) "99.4 Joules/220Ω" = (Actual Unreported) 252J/555.5Ω

The end effect of the *Mectan Transmutation* is that while both early and later second generation BP devices equaled and then surpassed SW in power, these BP devices continue to conform in appearance to the 110J ceiling Standard guaranteed under the 1982 APA Standard, a regulation meant to insure the maintenance of BP devices at half the power of SW. In actuality, of course, second generation BP devices--no longer minimal stimulus mechanisms at all--now surpassed SW in cumulative power.

More on Later Second Generation BP Devices--U.S. BP Devices between 1983-1995. Why the Power Increase and Why the Cover-Up?

The phrase, second generation BP devices, as used in this manuscript refers to the earlier, but more emphatically, to the later second generation Brief Pulse devices mentioned above. Most second generation Brief Pulse devices were manufactured after 1985, and are generally 2.5 fold the power stipulated by the APA ceiling Standard of 110 Joules, in essence, machines circa 2.5 times as powerful as the first generation MECTA "C" represented to the FDA as conforming to the 1982 APA Standard. This, of course, directly translates into a 2.5 MTTLOI administered to every individual recipient (as opposed to the 1.1 MTTLOI prescribed by the APA Standard). The power of made-for-America second generation BP devices, as noted above, was facilitated by the manufacturer devolved Pure-ER/RRC interpretation of the invented "100J at 220Ω" phrase for U. S. Brief Pulse devices and a similar interpretation of the "100J at 300Ω" phrase used for international Brief Pulse devices, as we shall eventually see. While there were a series of BP devices from 1976 to 1985, therefore, the

[172] The earlier Thymatron was based on a mean-ER/RRC of "100J at 220Ω" to actual output at actual maximum Impedance (approximately 100J/220Ω = 200J/440Ω). The same approximate "100J at 220Ω" for the later Thymatron DG, capable of up to 252 Joules, is based on a Pure-ER/RRC interpretation of the same circa "100J at 220Ω" "permitting" the surpassing of the earlier 200J Thymatron by 52J (100J/220Ω = 252J/555Ω).

phrase "second generation BP devices" contrasts with "first generation BP devices" [173] emerging around 1976, all of which generally conformed to the 1982 APA ceiling Standard of 110 Absolute Joules as well as the conditional-ER/RRC of "70J at 220." MECTA and Somatics "second generation BP devices," on the other hand, are all based on what the author of this manuscript has deemed "the Mectan Transmutation," the beginning of which was the introduction of the new phrase "100J at 220Ω" interpreted as a Mean-ER/RRC, and later Interpreted as a Pure-ER/RRC to maximum machine Impedance. Thus, while early second generation BP devices generally doubled the output of first generation BP devices, later second generation BP devices emitted about 2.5 fold first generation BP devices, first equaling, therefore, and then surpassing SW in power. In short, the early and later MECTA "C" and even the 140J MECTA D-1" are categorized here as "first generation BP devices" all more or less conforming to the 1982 APA Standard, whereas Somatics' early 200J Thymatron, MECTA's 200J D-2/early SR-1 and 2, Somatics' later 252J Thymatron DG and MECTA's later 259J SR 1 and 2s, are all deemed "second generation BP devices" in that all generally double in power, deliberately breaching the 1982 APA Standard. Second generation BP devices also include American made, made-for-Europe Brief Pulse devices emitting about 226 Joules and more as we shall ultimately investigate. [174] In any case, it is the later made-for-America second generation BP devices, which emit circa 2.5 fold threshold outputs to all age categories. In sum, all second generation BP devices have in common the first serious and intentional breaching of the 1982 APA Standard and thus the first serious breaching of the minimal stimulus outputs guaranteed under the APA standard, surpassing most first generation BP devices 2.0 to 2.5 fold. They are also the first devices to employ clever mechanisms to cover up this breach.

Why Do Second Generation BP Devices Breach the 1982 APA Standard when all first generation BP devices have the Capacity to Induce Adequate Grand Mal Seizures in all Circumstances?

It was for a very specific reason that in 1983, beginning with the second generation MECTA D-2/early SR1 and SR-2, closely followed by Somatics' second generation Thymatron near that same year, that manufacturers secretly began increasing the power of their Brief Pulse devices, first to circa 2.0 fold the APA 110J ceiling Standard, and then, by 1985, circa 2.5 fold. But why, in spite of the fact that first generation BP devices like the MECTA "C" could induce adequate seizures in all circumstances at half the output of SW with a 1.1 MTTLOI, did the new default settings for the early and then later second generation BP machines rise first to a 2.0 fold threshold and finally to a circa 2.5 fold threshold output in all age categories? In examining the devolution of BP devices generally, that is, their increases in power from generation to generation, one manufacturer assumption becomes apparent; unless the electrical dosing of these devices is set to equal or surpass that of SW, the so-called "adequate seizure" by itself is, in fact, inadequate (Cameron, 1994; Robin and De Tissera, 1982; Sackeim, 1991, p.233-234). In short, adequate seizures alone simply do not nor ever have worked! Put more scientifically, manufacturers soon came to realize that although so-called "adequate seizures" (of twenty-five or more seconds in length) can be successfully induced with minimal stimulus (or just above threshold) electrical output, with half or even less than half the EO of SW, adequate seizures by and unto themselves are, in fact, "therapeutically" ineffective. In brief, minimal stimulus induced adequate seizures produce neither the looked-for anti-depressant effect nor the changes in behavior which constitute a "successful result" for practicing physicians and thus manufacturers. Consequently, in spite of the prototypical earlier 81J MECTA "C" and the 108J MECTA "C" presented to the FDA between 1976 and 1982 inducing adequate seizures at one-quarter to one-half the EO of SW, by 1985, U. S. BP manufacturers felt compelled to produce devices about 2.5 fold what Bi-Lateral (BL) "ECT" actually required to induce adequate seizures in each individual age category. Indeed, in 1994, though these devices had already been on the market for almost ten years, researchers Beale et al. (1994) tested for the so-called "titration level" of what were actually second generation MECTA BP devices. Beale and his team measured the *pre-set* cumulative electricity utilized, that is, the individual doses of Charge emitted with respect to age only to discover electrical emissions generally pre-set

[173] "First generation devices" here refers to those BP devices introduced starting about 1976 (the beginning of the modern "BP Era") and which conformed to the 1982 APA Standard. They are not to be confused with the initial introduction of BP in the 1940s-50s.

[174] BP devices, as a result of early experimentation with new wave forms in the 1940s and 1950s (Cameron, 1994), made a brief appearance during *the SW Era* (1939-1976). In that BP devices were quickly discarded during this period, SW dominated, thus the era from 1939 to 1976, is rightfully deemed *the SW Era.*

at 2.5 times threshold for BL (Bilateral) electrode placement (one electrode on each temple) and so by implication, pre-set at 5.0 times threshold for UL (Unilateral) electrode placement (one electrode on one temple and the other closely spaced) in every age category. [175] As previously noted, because the most powerful MECTA "C" device, a device manufactured to conform to the 1982 APA Standard, delivered an absolute maximum EO of 108 Joules (Department of Health and Human Services, 1982a, pp. A53, E20, G3-G4), the "C" can be considered a true "minimal stimulus" apparatus limited in terms of Charge (and EO in joules as we have seen [176]) to a 1.08 MTTLOI (just above threshold) for each individual recipient (via BL ECT). [177] By comparison, MECTA and Somatics set their later second generation BP devices at circa 2.3 to 2.5 fold that of first generation devices--an event clearly compromising the reduced output advantage of BP over SW. Once again then, if the just above threshold outputs used by manufacturers could induce adequate grand mal seizures in all circumstances, why did MECTA and Somatics feel compelled to more than double the output and MTTLOI of the MECTA "C"? There can be but one answer. MECTA and Somatics felt constrained to double the Energy Output necessary to induce adequate seizures in an attempt to achieve efficacy. Manufacturers MECTA and Somatics enhanced the power of their BP devices from circa 100J first generation BP devices to circa 250J second generation BP devices, not for exceptionally seizure recalcitrant recipients (as had been alleged with the 140J MECTA D-1), nor because UL ECT "takes twice the output to be effective," nor because Impedance increases over a series of "treatments" (as shall be claimed), but simply to make the procedure "work," in short, to attain the results psychiatrists looked for. So why didn't either MECTA or Somatics simply report the increased outputs; why did they conceal the enhancement? This answer is also simple. Factually, BP devices are able to induce adequate seizures at half (or less than half) the output of SW and are thus twice as safe cognitively. Reduced electrical output, as FDA, Utah, and even APA had acknowledged between 1976 and 1982, is the main advantage of Brief Pulse over SW in that all three noted that it is excessive dosages of electricity which cause the majority of the cognitive dissonance of which so many recipients complain. Consequently, had regulatory agencies been informed of the dramatically increased power of the later second generation MECTA and Somatics BP devices, that is, had they known that modern day BP devices had actually begun surpassing SW in overall power, and had they known that default outputs were no longer limited to a 1.1 MTTLOI or minimal stimulus in accordance with the APA Standard, but rather 2.5 fold threshold for all age recipients, not only would the euphemistic rationale behind the need for excess power only for "exceptional" or "difficult" cases have been debunked (Food and Drug Administration, 1985, see "Conference and Call Records" 8/05/85) in that that 2.5 fold threshold outputs were now being administered to all recipients in order to get the procedure to "work," but the necessity of increased electricity might have called into question the validity "convulsion theory" itself.

In short, manufacturers had deliberately calibrated second generation BP machines to deliver excessive 2.5 fold threshold outputs not merely for a few individually difficult cases, but for every individual recipient routinely--otherwise--as all manufacturers secretly knew, the devices were simply ineffective. This was obviously problematic as the main advantage, the main selling point of Brief Pulse, as we have already seen, was its capacity to induce grand mal seizures at greatly reduced outputs compared to SW, resulting in much less cognitive dissonance. Moreover, "ECT" is based on convulsion theory which maintains that a "therapeutic effect" is derived from adequate convulsion alone. According to this theory, electrical energy in excess of that required to induce an adequate seizure should not be necessary. Indeed, this had been the findings of Utah with which FDA agreed as well as APA's entire argument for continuing the procedure into the next decade with the newer, much safer Brief Pulse device. Plainly, cognitive dissonance is specifically identified with more electricity than needed to induce the adequate seizure, the antidote to which was the least amount of electricity possible to induce the same adequate seizure. In short, manufacturers found themselves between a rock and a hard place. They knew they had to increase the power of their devices to make the procedure work, but they

---

[175] Using UL electrode placement, a grand mal seizure can be elicited with half the output required for BL ECT. The same amount of electricity used for BL ECT on the MECTA "C," therefore, elicits a 2.16 fold threshold dosage of electricity with UL ECT.

[176] Beale measured in terms of Charge. Here, MTTLOI measured via Charge equals MTTLOI measured in EO (Joules) as we shall eventually see, although Charge can be deceiving as we shall also see.

[177] With the same electrical output inducing a 1.08 fold threshold output using BL ECT, the MECTA "C" could emit a 2.16 fold threshold (1.08 x 2 = 2.16) using UL ECT. As a result, about 1987, UL ECT was quickly declared "dose sensitive" meaning efficacy could not be achieved with just above threshold output dosing for UL ECT, that UL as opposed to BL "ECT" required a 2.0 MTTLOI to be effective. In truth, neither UL nor BL ECT is effective at threshold, as we shall discover.

could not reveal this fact to the FDA, the general public, or administering physicians for fear of losing the chief selling point of Brief Pulse--increased safety though reduced output.

It was in order to simultaneously permit and camouflage the sudden, dramatic power enhancements which occurred in Brief Pulse devices from first to second generation, therefore, that manufacturers, in 1983, began radically transitioning the standard from its straightforward method of applying a conditional-ER/RRC of "70J at 220Ω" with a clearly quantified 110J ceiling to a newer "100J at 220Ω" phrase with a much higher ceiling based on maximum machine Impedance. In short, manufacturers quietly dispelled the minimal stimulus stipulation guaranteed by the 110J APA ceiling, and not only failed to report it, but actively suppressed the information. Succinctly, manufacturers could not afford to reveal that they were secretly interpreting the newly reported "100J at 220Ω," first as an unexplained "mean-ER/RRC," and then as an unexplicated Pure-ER/RRC, allowing much higher outputs. How could they? Increased output meant that the "new and improved" reduced output Brief Pulse device encouraged by Utah in 1978, and around which Weiner and the APA had strongly suggested a standard could be written, was not actually an improvement. In fact, in that the machines were more powerful, the machines might actually be worse. Amazingly, then, manufacturers--on their own volition, while totally discarding the 110J cap, did so in complete secrecy. As a result, the routine circa 2.5 fold threshold outputs delivered by default with second generation BP machines to each individual recipient using BL-ECT, and default circa 5.0 fold threshold outputs delivered to each individual with UL ECT were not discovered for another ten years. Not until 1994, did the researcher Beale finally identify the 2.5 MTTLOI emissions of what were actually the later second generation MECTA and Somatics Brief Pulse devices. In short, Beale's discovery only occurred following ten years of marketing and PR depicting these same second generation BP devices as minimal stimulus, as "kinder and gentler" than SW, as "new and improved" machines vastly improving the old "ECT" by virtue of reduced electrical output. In sum, the clever Mectan Transmutation facilitating first the 200J maximum of the MECTA D-2/early SR-1 and 2 and early Somatics' Thymatron, and finally the 259J maximum of the later SR1 and 2 and the 252J maximum of the Thymatron DG, had not only successfully implemented these outputs, but had camouflaged them as well. Overall, the Mectan Transmutation had successfully hidden the administering of increased default outputs two and a half times minimal stimulus to perhaps a million "ECT" recipients (over ten years) in America alone, all without informing FDA, all without informing physicians and all without informing recipients, indeed, all to achieve a short term anti-depressant effect and all to achieve the behavioral changes third parties wanted to see.

Chapter 16

Seamless Illusion

As previously noted, the first use of the Mectan Transmutation invented by MECTA was Mean-ER/RRC, furtively "justifying" the building and marketing of the 200J D-2/early MECTA SR 1 and 2, closely followed by the early 200J Thymatron by Somatics, just as the second use of the Mectan Transmutation was Pure-ER/RRC "justifying" the production and marketing of the slightly later 259J MECTA SR1 and 2 closely followed by Somatics' 252J Thymatron DG. As noted, while the D-2/early SR 1 and 2 and the early Thymatron doubled the circa 100J ceiling stipulated within the 1982 APA Standard, thereby equaling SW in power, the later JR/SR 1 and 2 and Thymatron DG emitted two and a half times the circa 100J APA ceiling, surpassing SW in power. Even so, manufacturers reported all MECTA and Somatics second generation BP devices with the same unexplained "100J at 220Ω" phrase with no additional elaboration. In short, no mention was made of manufacturers having dropped the 110J ceiling, nor did manufacturers report the newly enhanced ceilings. Due to the Mectan Transmutation, therefore, all Brief Pulse machines beginning with the reduced output 108J MECTA "C" device presented both to the FDA and the general public about 1978 through to second generation made-for-America BP devices marketed up through about 1995, appeared to be restricted to circa 100J maximums or minimal stimulus outputs. What was actually a series of Brief Pulse devices incorporating higher and higher outputs in both power and titration then, appeared to be a seamless series of circa 100J BP devices. In addition, MECTA reported the same circa "100J at 220Ω" phrase for both earlier and later second generation BP devices of the same name just as Somatics did for its Thymatron and DGx, though the later devices consisted of increased ceilings and titration intensities. In fact, all three companies (MECTA, Somatics and Medcraft) depicted circa 100 maximum Joules on Machine Readouts in seeming accordance with the APA Standard. While appearing to be an unbroken production of 100J BP devices from about 1976-1995, then, MECTA and Somatics BP devices, as noted, had actually incorporated enhancements peaking at about 259 maximum Joules--circa 2.5 fold the APA Standard, ipso facto, accommodating a hidden 2.5 MTTLOI applied to each individual recipient (Beale et al, 1994). In short, the uniform reporting of "100J at 220Ω" reminiscent of the circa "100J" minimal stimulus output guaranteeing adequate seizures with minimal output for all age recipients, along with MECTA's and Somatics' simultaneous and permanent discarding of maximum output reporting in joules, indeed, their discarding of all output reporting in joules, and finally the appearance of what appeared to be uniform Machine Readouts of circa 100 maximum Joules (read by administering physicians) for all MECTA, Somatics, and Medcraft BP devices, acted collectively and collaboratively to create the appearance of consistent and continuous 100J minimal stimulus devices for all three extant U. S. BP manufacturers. [178] As such, the power enhancements which took place from 1976 to 1995 culminating in MECTA's 259J SR1@2 devices, Somatics' 252J Thymatron DG, and even Elcot's (now defunct) equally powerful MF-1000, were never reported or acknowledged. [179]

---

[178] Never fully understood by regulators was the fact that Machine Readouts limited to 100 maximum Joules for these powerful second generation BP devices, were based --as we shall see—upon a false constant Impedance of "220Ω" resulting in gross under-reporting.
[179] Medcraft breached the APA Standard in a completely different way as shall be discussed later.

But did the subtle and confusing new role of the familiar "100J" figure newly juxtaposed with the "220Ω" [180] phrase together with 100J Machine Readout maximums really result in gross misinterpretation by FDA overseers? Did the new "100J at 220Ω" reports and machine readout maximums in conjunction with manufacturer brochures still suggestive of reduced output Brief Pulse machines actually deceive FDA officials? In a memo placed within an August 5, 1985 FDA 510K pre-market application filed by MECTA FDA overseer Harold Walder, Walder makes the following comment with respect to MECTA's new "100J at 220Ω" description of what were actually second generation BP devices. Inquiring about MECTA's latest "100J at 220Ω" reports as opposed to the previous "'70J at 220Ω" phrase with conditional 110 Joule ceiling depicted within the 1982 APA Standard, Walder comments:

> *I asked Dr. Weiner what the latest revision of the APA standard for ECT devices identified for energy output [meant], and how that compared to devices presently marketed and in use. Dr. Weiner replied that 70 Joules is presently the recommended maximum energy output; however, it probably would be changed at the next standard update to 100J, to reflect the IEC Standard and presently marketed devices.*
>
> *Dr. Weiner informed me that a 100J output is not a dangerous level of output, and is sometimes required to induce a generalized convulsion.*
>
> (Food and Drug Administration, 1985, Conference Call Record, Time 1415, August 5, 1985)

Based on Weiner's explanation, Walder is clearly under the impression that the original 1982 APA "70J at 220Ω" phrase limited BP devices to 70 Absolute Joules, and that the newer BP devices reported as "100J at 220Ω," expanded this 70J ceiling to a 100 Joule ceiling. In fact, the Standard's original "70J at 220Ω" phrase does not depict a maximum ceiling of "70J," but rather a conditional-ER/RRC. Indeed, the second part of the APA Standard depicts--not a 70J, but--a 110J ceiling. Clearly confused by Weiner's explanation, Walder misguidedly assumes both the "70J" term within the original "70J at 220Ω" phrase and thus the "100J" term within the newer "100J at 220Ω" phrase, delineations of maximum output. Failing to comprehend that with the adoption of the new "100J at 220Ω" phrase, manufacturers had actually dropped the 110J APA ceiling, Walder makes the incorrect supposition that the "100J" term within the "100J at 220Ω" phrase represents a new maximum output ceiling of 100 Joules, thus newly limiting BP devices (in Walder's mind) to a "slightly higher" maximum output. Weiner, moreover, appears to reinforce Walder's spurious assumptions. In fact, by 1985, no longer minimal stimulus machines at all and thus no longer "ECT" devices, MECTA Brief Pulse devices, as noted, were emitting circa 259J maximums and thus a 2.59 MTTLOI for each individual recipient, 2.6 times minimal stimulus and 2.6 times 100J.

Distinctly then, Walder's statements (above) suppose the "100J at 220Ω" phrase depictive of a 100J ceiling. Following the official 1976-1982 FDA investigation, therefore, FDA overseers, appear to have understood neither the original APA Standard (as having a 110J ceiling) nor the manufacturer-interpretation of the later "100J at 220Ω" phraseology as a Pure-ER/RRC interpretation facilitating an unconscionable 273J ceiling. Weiner-led FDA overseers such as Walder, clearly assume either an original 70J ceiling, that the APA 110J ceiling remained intact, or that the newer "100J at 220Ω" phraseology incorporated but a slightly more restrictive 100J ceiling as opposed to the original 110J ceiling within the 1982 APA Standard. FDA overseers then, or at least Walder at this juncture, appear to have had no idea that manufacturers had totally eliminated the 110J APA ceiling. Not understood was the detail that of the four then extant American Brief Pulse manufacturers, all of which had submitted 510Ks uniformly reporting the same circa "100J at 220Ω" phrase, three had altogether dropped the APA ceiling, transitioning to Pure-ER/RRC interpretation, allowing unconscionably higher outputs, while the fourth violated the APA minimal stimulus restriction in an entirely different manner (as we shall see). Influenced by Weiner, who in turn represented all four manufacturers, FDA officials, the public, and the media all seem to have misconstrued the "100J" delineation within the new uniform phrase, "100J at 220Ω" as a "100J" maximum output. In short, none but the manufacturers themselves

---

[180] Medcraft does not bother with the contingency--"at 220Ω" (Medcraft Corporation, 1986a). This is due to the fact that the Medcraft-25 is the only modern day BP device which actually delivers a maximum "99 Joules." On the other hand, Medcraft seriously and dangerously breaches the APA Standard in another manner, as we shall see.

understood that the new "100J at 220Ω" phrase reported by all four manufacturers had quickly devolved first into a 100J "mean" thereby doubling output from circa 100 maximum Joules to circa 200 maximum Joules, and second into a Pure-ER/RRC facilitating an even higher ceiling of up to 273 maximum Joules. [181] (At this point, Elcot quickly dissolved its company, while Medcraft starkly deviated from the other manufacturers but in an equally illicit manner, as we shall see.) Remarkably, the actual 200J outputs emitted by the MECTA D-2/early MECTA SR1 and SR2, and Thymatron, went totally unnoticed by the FDA--as did the respective 259 and 252 joule maximums of the slightly later even more enhanced MECTA SR-1 and SR-2 and Somatics Thymatron DG models. [182] Indeed, the MTTLOI had skyrocketed from a 1.1 and 2.2 MTTLOI with BL and UL ECT respectively, to a 2.5 and 5.0 MTTLOI with BL and UL ECT respectively (Abrams and Swartz, 1988, p.28; Beale et al. ; 1994; Somatics Incorporated, 1993a). [183] All the while, misleading machine readouts continued to depict just above threshold outputs with BL ECT. Not only had the gross enhancement in maximum power gone unreported and unnoticed, therefore, but so had the gross Multifold Threshold Titration Level Output Intensity enhancement (reflected in both Charge and EO) for each individual recipient (Beale et al. , 1994). Overburdened, FDA had made the classic mistake of trusting manufacturers to regulate themselves.

A Closer Look at Supplanting "70 Joules at 220Ω" with "100 Joules at 220Ω"

The 1982-3 transmutation to a "100J at 220Ω" unreported Mean and then Pure-ER/RRC, first by MECTA and then Somatics, as noted, went unnoticed by both the FDA and the general public. The reasons are natural. Firstly, the transformation did not occur in the public eye; the first mathematical transmutation to enhance BP devices occurred early in late 1982 or early 1983, mere months following the FDA's final public hearing for "ECT" devices. The FDA investigation of "ECT devices" which had begun in 1976, had included major public hearings both in 1979 and 1982, and then concluded. Secondly, the "100J at 220Ω" phraseology, newly reported to the FDA first by MECTA (Food and Drug Administration, 1985, MECTA Instruction Manual, pp.4, 4a) [184] and then Somatics (Food and Drug Administration, 1985, Attachment I--Comparison of electrical parameters of the MECTA, Medcraft, and Thymatron Machine) contained the same juxtaposition of output to Impedance as the *"70J at 220Ω"* phrase contained within the 1982 APA Standard, although the original standard had included a specific 110J cap (Department of Health and Human Services, 1982a, p. E20). The juxtaposing of the same "220Ω" term with "100J," however, a figure almost identical to the 1982 APA absolute ceiling of "110 Joules" (Ibid, 1982a, A53; E20), and the specific 100J figure previously identified by Weiner as the maximum output required to induce an adequate seizure in any recipient in what appeared to be any circumstance, effectively created both confusion and camouflage. [185]

> Using a pulse device, the [APA] Task Force [1978] has determined that only 0.6% of seizure thresholds were greater than 70 Joules and that none were greater than 100 Joules. (Weiner--Department of Health and Human Services, 1982a, p. A53)

---

[181] 100J/220Ω = XJ/600Ω. X = 273J. (600Ω is maximum Impedance permitted under the 1982 APA Standard [Department of Health and Human Services, 1982a, E20]).

[182] Somatics' Inc. reported the same "100J at 220Ω" for both the 1983 Thymatron and 1985 Thymatron DG, but which emitted unreported maximum outputs of 200J and 252J respectively.1983 Thymatron: Mean-ER = 100J/220Ω = 200J/440Ω.1985 Thymatron DG: Pure-ER/RRC = 100J/220Ω = 252J/555Ω. (Maximum machine Impedance for Thymatron DG = 555.5Ω).

[183] The APA Standard does not actually allow a 2.2 MTTLOI for UL ECT. Manufacturers merely claimed ECT "dose-sensitive" requiring twice the MTTLOI as BL ECT.

[184] While the reporting to the FDA of "100J at 220Ω" within 510K files featured Somatics followed by MECTA, in fact, the earlier introduction of the D-2 suggests it was MECTA which initiated and invented both the phraseology and the transmutational method (Food and Drug Administration, 1985, Comparison of MECTA D, JR, SR and Somatics Thymatron Devices; Conference and Call Record, Time 1415, 8/15/85). Nevertheless, manufacturers--particularly MECTA and Somatics, but also Medcraft and the defunct Elcot, appear complicit in this cover-up, applying the phraseology and the method, simultaneously.

[185] While the ceiling standard for BP devices is actually 110J, it is acknowledged in the same paragraph that actual range in threshold (for all recipients) is 3-100J. The same paragraph explains that only "1% of seizure thresholds are greater than 60 Joules" (Department of Health and Human Services, 1982a, E20). It is actually the 100J mark which is the minimum output needed to seize all recipients.

While both an FDA conditional ER/RRC of "70J at 220Ω" and a separate, but related absolute EO ceiling of "110J" is clearly delineated within the 1982 APA Standard, manufacturers never mention a separate overall ceiling in their newly reported "100J at 220Ω" phraseology, an omission which suggests either a simple increase from a conditional "70J at 220Ω" ER/RRC with 110J ceiling to a conditional "100J at 220Ω" ER/RRC with 110J ceiling, or a combination conditional "100J at 220Ω" ER-RRC incorporative of an even more stringent 100J ceiling. In either case, with what appeared to be a 100 or 110J cap in place, the ER/RRC change seemed moot in that the caps yet appeared to limit electrical titrations to between 1.0 and 1.1 fold threshold--seemingly minimal stimulus--for all age categories. [186] Thirdly, except for Medcraft, manufacturers at this time simultaneously and precipitously stopped reporting actual EO. Instead, misleading maximum Machine Readouts confined to circa 100 Joules on virtually all second generation BP devices, plainly promoted the notion that a circa 100J ceiling had been steadfastly maintained. Thus, while all four BP manufacturers fully acknowledged--in 510K files--an increase in the ER/RRC (from "70J at 220Ω" to "100J at 220Ω"), nothing on the part of any manufacturer indicated that the 110J APA ceiling had been seriously altered, much less enhanced. From the standpoint of the FDA and the public then, no significant change appeared; certainly none apparent in the overall power of BP devices and thus none apparent in overall titration. Indeed, based on manufacturers' reports, a circa 100J ceiling appears to remain consistent from BP's incipience in 1976 through to the year 1995 and even beyond.

By blending the central configurations within the APA Standard, that is, what appeared to be a close approximation of the APA 110J ceiling with the same "220Ω" phrase found within the "70J at 220Ω" conditional-ER/RRC aspect of the APA standard, FDA and even practicing physicians, as noted, assumed the new "100J at 220Ω" phrase either a simple new conditional-ER/RRC with 110J ceiling yet intact or a new conditional-ER-RRC incorporative of an even more stringent 100J ceiling. What appeared to be a subtle blending of elements already within the APA Standard, therefore, effectively rendered the dropping of the 110J ceiling and thus the new unexplained Pure-ER/RRC interpretation of the same "100J at 220Ω" phrase invisible. In short, inconspicuousness was achieved by the juxtaposing of the familiar "100J" term initially subsumed within the 110J APA ceiling, with the same "220Ω" initially used to express a conditional-ER/RRC.

Totally undiscovered then, manufacturers continued interpreting the seemingly familiar phrase, "100J at 220Ω," as an entirely new Pure-ER/RRC, that is, with no conditional output ceiling whatsoever. Utilizing Pure-ER/RRC interpretation, MECTA, Somatics, and Elcot, as we have seen, had actually discarded the 110J ceiling at least ten years before Beale discovered the increase. Indeed, the transmutation had occurred in consonance with the total, precipitous, and unprecedented omission of all actual output reporting by these same three U.S. BP manufacturers. Certainly, all MECTA, Somatics, and Elcot second generation BP devices grossly exceeded the 110J ceiling. [187] In fact, the omission of actual output reporting by three of the four BP manufacturers had simultaneously commenced with the reporting of "100J at 220Ω" by all four BP manufacturers. (The fourth manufacturer, Medcraft, as noted, maintained the 100J ceiling.) Remarkably then, all four BP manufacturers within all four 510K files uniformly failed to communicate the 173J increase in cumulative output exploited by three of the four manufacturers, MECTA, Somatics, and Elcot.

What looked to have been a simple, singular, and even modest transition from "70J at 220Ω" to "100J at 220Ω," then, did not, as noted, appear critical to regulatory agents. Comments by FDA investigators patently indicate the assumption that either the "100J" figure within the new phraseology, or at most the 110J ceiling within the original APA Standard, continued to regulate maximum output to minimal stimulus titration levels in all age categories. Even if the enhanced power of these machines had been suspected; moreover, due to false Machine Readouts depicting only 100 maximum Joules, the ubiquitous and dramatic titration increases which had actually occurred in conjunction with the new power enhancements may yet been disregarded. [188] Not until 1994, in any case, did Beale et al. (1994) discover that a default 2.5 MTTLOI with BL "ECT" and a 5.0 MTTLOI

---

[186] The implication according to Weiner's statement is that the 100 year old male, the most seizure recalcitrant recipient, never requires more than 100 Joules to adequately seize.

[187] Medcraft's BP device remained confined to an actual 100 Joule ceiling. Medcraft's device, however, defied the APA Standard in a different manner, as we shall see.

[188] A machine which emits 252 Joules, but only utilizes 100 Joules would yet comply with the standard. This, however, was not the case. All the power was, in fact, utilized so that the devices had evolved from just over threshold to circa 2.5 fold threshold in all age categories.

with UL "ECT" was being administered to every individual recipient with MECTA (and Somatics) BP devices. [189] [190]

It is apparent from all four 510K files that with the reporting of circa "100 Joules at 220Ω" by all four U. S. manufacturers, FDA officials assumed the APA 110J ceiling preserved. This was a notion encouraged both by manufacturer brochures, and as noted, by uniform Machine Readout depictions of circa 100 maximum Joules on second generation BP devices produced by all four U. S. BP manufacturers (Cameron, 1994; Food and Drug Administration, 1986B; Medcraft Corporation, 1986a; Sackeim and Weiner, 1993, pp 13-14; Somatics Incorporated, 1993b). Before the Beale study, no significant increase in output (starting from the MECTA "C" forward) had ever been noted or reported. In fact, titration was actively reported to be the same as that of first generation BP devices, minimal stimulus or just above threshold output for all age categories. [191]

To sum up then, in spite of dramatic power and titration increases occurring in all U. S. BP devices from approximately late 1983 to 1985--virtually no notification of cumulative power or titration increases, nor any explanation of the entirely new, unauthorized methodology by which actual EO was secretly enhanced--was ever announced or reported by any U. S. BP manufacturer. Indeed, within a year following the six year public, federal investigation of "ECT" from 1976 to 1982, including a two year investigation by the Utah independent Biomedical Test Laboratory (employed by the FDA itself) recommending reduced energy output Brief Pulse (Grahn et al. , 1977) resulting in the creation of the 1982 APA Standard limiting output to 110 maximum Joules, manufacturers had inconspicuously and illicitly fabricated a deceptively similar-sounding "standard," seemingly conforming to the 110J ceiling depicted within the 1982 APA Standard. In fact, this seeming similar standard, the Mectan Transmutation, breached the 1982 APA Standard in a gross and secretive manner. Certainly, the new methodology, which the author has deemed "The Mectan Transmutation," enabled the gross and surreptitious surpassing not only of the 110J ceiling, but, as noted, the surpassing of the recognizably insidious 200J SW devices of the past. [192] In transitioning from "70J at 220Ω" with a 110J ceiling, to the singly reported phrase, "100J at 220Ω," inconceivably, MECTA's new 1983-85 imitation standard--the "Mectan Transmutation," first through Mean and then through Pure-ER/RRC, had precipitously provided BP manufacturers with a new unreported ceiling of up to 273 Joules. In addition, it had increased the titration ceiling from the APA 1.1 MTTLOI to a 2.73 MTTLOI for all BL recipients of every age category. In short, as early as 1983, apparently led by spokesperson Richard Weiner,[193] manufacturers had begun applying this nefariously clever reporting facsimile of "100J at 220Ω," the new interpretation of which enabled a new ubiquitous delivery of suprathreshold dosages of electricity, while at the same time revealing no perceptible or substantial change in power or titration whatsoever. [194] It is worth noting that APA and manufacturer spokesperson Richard Weiner created both the

---

[189] It was Cameron who in 1994 discovered the enhanced power (Cameron 1994).

[190] For a brief period, just before peremptory dropping of maximum output reporting entirely, Somatics, in conjunction with reporting "100J at 220Ω" for its early Thymatron, reported a 187J maximum for this device, still an underreport, however, as the actual output was circa 200 maximum Joules. Due to Machine Readouts of circa 100 maximum joules on this and later devices, moreover, agencies may have likened the increased output to an automobile capable of reaching 187 mph, but governed by a 100 mph speed limit. Regulatory agencies had no way of knowing that manufacturers themselves had secretly increased the speed limit to 200, then 273 mph, and that the increased power of second generation BP devices, would ultimately utilize up to 259 maximum Joules. Power and thus titration was enhanced at each age level for each individual recipient up to 2.59 fold threshold (Beale et al., 1994).

[191] The false reporting for second generation BP devices of threshold efficacy for BL-ECT as well as the false reporting of 2.0 to 2.5 times threshold application for UL-ECT (when it was double that) is inexcusable, and has continued to persist in various forms from 1983 to the relative present (Abrams, 1996, p.703; Abrams and Swartz, 1988; Beale et al., 1994). The increase in power from the later MECTA "C"--108J, to second generation BP devices such as the Thymatron DG--252J, only became apparent in 1994 through Beale's discovery of previously unreported 2.5 and 5.0 fold threshold minimal stimulus titration levels with BL and UL-ECT respectively (Beale et al., 1994; Cameron 1994). Due to the length of time which had elapsed from utilization to discovery, however, as well as numerous other publications smothering Beale's single publication, the significance of this fact was paid little or no attention.

[192] Invidiously, the methodological transmutation which made this double standard possible, appears to have been engineered, orchestrated, and perfected by APA Representative, Chairman of the ECT Task Force, and Manufacturer spokesperson Richard Weiner, all without Federal approbation or public knowledge.

[193] Weiner represented all manufacturers at the APA hearings.

[194] To be discussed later, manufacturers had been forced to administer suprathreshold dosages in that convulsion theory is false (Cameron, 1994). Thus, by hiding ubiquitous suprathreshold dosing, manufacturers also hid the fact that convulsion theory is a non-viable hypothesis, and that the machine and the procedure only achieves "efficacy" as a result of excessive, dangerous, and damaging dosages of electricity, necessarily equaling or surpassing SW in power.

1982 APA Standard and most probably, the deceptive 1983 Mectan Transmutation consisting of "100J at 220Ω" being secretly interpreted as a Pure-ER/RRC.

Never elucidated by any manufacturer, then, is the fact that not only was the "100 Joules" contained within the new ER/RRC, "100J at 220Ω" unrelated to the circa "110J" EO ceiling specified within the 1982 APA Standard or the 100J figure used to mark minimum stimulus for all recipients, but that, in fact, manufacturers had entirely dropped the APA "110J" absolute EO ceiling. Hidden was the detail that the new ER/RRC of "100J at 220Ω" was being applied in a way that no longer limited outputs to 100 or even 110J, but allowed up to a never reported 273J. By dropping the 1982 "110J" ceiling and employing "100J at 220Ω" as a Pure-ER/RRC, that is, an ER/RRC no longer limited by the 110J ceiling, but only by the APA maximum Impedance of 600Ω, manufacturers had implemented a totally new, unauthorized and unreported maximum output and MTTLOI. Thus, while manufacturers reported the visible transition from "70J at 220Ω" to "100J at 220Ω," the dropping of the "110J ceiling" and the subsequent application of Pure-ER/RRC in lieu of a conditional-ER/RRC went unobserved. Paradoxically moreover, the inclusion of the familiar "100J" term within the new "100J at 220Ω" ER/RRC phrase actually appeared to be an improvement over the original standard, requiring an even lower EO ceiling than the 110J ceiling within the initial APA Standard.

Remarkably then, manufacturers' new method of reporting--the Mectan Transmutation--permitted dramatically higher cumulative output and titration, while yet seeming to conform to the 110J APA ceiling. In reporting what was actually an unexplained Pure-ER/RRC of "100J at 220Ω," and in simultaneously failing to report actual output in joules, manufacturers had not only discovered a means of breaking through the prohibitive 110J APA ceiling, first equaling and then surpassing in power the insidious SW devices of old, but did so devoid of visibility. This manuscript marks the first time the Pure-ER/RRC methodology deemed here "The Mectan Transmutation," collaboratively utilized by BP manufacturers MECTA and Somatics for simultaneously obtaining and camouflaging their new maximum 273J ceiling for second generation BP devices, has ever been reported (Cameron, 1994 [195]).

[195] In 1994, Cameron reported for the first time, true outputs of second generation BP devices (Cameron 1994). Here, explained for the first time, is "The Mectan Transmutation" of the APA Standard entailing the dropping of the 110J APA ceiling for the purpose of secretly increasing the multifold threshold titration level outputs for all age recipients.

Chapter 17

Unnoticed---Richard Weiner and the APA

By supplanting the 70J figure specified in the 1982 APA conditional-ER/RRC as "70J at 220Ω" with the output specified in Weiner's declaration that no Brief Pulse output over 100 Joules is ever required to induce an adequate grand mal seizure in any recipient, manufacturers may have counted on the assumption that the "100 Joules" alluded to within the new "100J at 220Ω" phraseology would be mistaken for an absolute ceiling. For one, the new "100J" figure appears to be entirely related to the 110J ceiling (just above threshold) promised to the FDA in the 1982 APA Standard, a ploy which--deliberate or not--succeeded in extraordinary fashion. The uniform utilization of the "100J" output figure by all four U. S. BP manufacturers in conjunction with the sudden failure to report actual EO first by MECTA followed by Somatics and Elcot, strongly intimated a "100J" ceiling stasis regarding maximum output. Given the circa 100J maximum Readouts displayed on machines made by all four manufacturers, it is not difficult to understand how the actual transmutation to Pure-ER/RRC, and thus the gross power and MTTLOI enhancements actually emitted by second generation BP devices, went unregarded. In fact, as a result of the Mectan Transmutation, beginning with MECTA, followed by Somatics Incorporated, and then Elcot, dramatic new power and MTTLOI increases went virtually unobserved for over twenty years (1983-1995), and in some respects, right up to the present.

On the other hand, while regulatory agencies, the public, the media, and even practicing physicians were unaware of the 1983 Mectan Transmutation, U. S. BP manufacturers, as well as Weiner's APA Task Force on ECT, appear to have been acutely aware of it. [196] For instance, Somatics Incorporated almost immediately began utilizing the same new transmuted phraseology (Food and Drug Administration, 1986B, pp 85-86; Sackeim, and Weiner 1993) to create and justify the unreported 252 Joule output of its Thymatron DG (Cameron, 1994), while Elcot reported the same "100J at 220Ω" phrase for its even more powerful BP device--the MF-1000 (Elcot Incorporated, 1993; Medcraft Corporation, 1986a). Confusingly, Medcraft, which also reported the same circa "100J at 220Ω" phrase for its' B-25 BP device actually did limit its BP device to circa 100 Joules as mentioned (although dangerously ignoring ER/RRC limitations as we shall later observe). By all four BP manufacturers concurrently reporting the same unexplicated "100J at 220Ω" phrase, by concomitant uniform Machine Readouts of circa 100 maximum Joules, by three of the four manufacturers precipitously omitting actual and maximum EO in their reporting of machine parameters,[197] and finally by one of the BP manufacturers, Medcraft, actually limiting its BP device to circa 100 maximum Joules, regulatory agencies, the general public, and the media proper acquiesced to the same dangerous illusion--that all Brief Pulse devices remained regulated by the 1982 APA Standard's 110J APA ceiling. From about 1978 to at least the year 1995,

---

[196] The APA Task Force on ECT, under the auspices of Standard Keeper and Chairman Richard Weiner, was entrusted with creating, maintaining, and in a manner, enforcing of the 1982 APA Standard. Weiner, who must certainly have been aware of the later transmutation, and most probably invented it, never reported the increase in EO to the FDA, but rather appears to have aided MECTA, Richard Abrams of Somatics Inc., and then Eurasian manufacturers (as we shall see) in devising and applying the same hidden transmutation to the newer much more powerful BP devices.

[197] Medcraft could afford to report 100J in that their BP device was actually limited to that output.

with respect to power and titration then, the BP apparatus as a minimal stimulus instrument seemed to persist virtually unchanged! [198]

No manufacturer nor any proponent-expert, including electrical engineer Richard Weiner, Chairman of the APA Task Forces on ECT, acting APA Standard Coordinator between the FDA, APA, and manufacturers, as well as chief designer of the new reporting methodology itself, has ever publicly explained, published, or clarified these hidden enhancements of power and titration, much less the manner used to obtain them. In short, no explanation of what the author has deemed the "Mectan Transmutation" initiated circa 1983 both for publicly underreporting and secretly facilitating greatly augmented outputs, has ever been published, much less examined. Notably, neither Weiner nor any machine manufacturer ever reported to the FDA (or the public) the dropping of the APA ceiling (by three of the four American BP companies), the critical component in facilitating what are actually major transgressions of the APA Standard itself. Significantly, it was the never reported abandonment of the standard's main safeguard--the 110J APA ceiling--as a result which the reinterpretation of the "100J at 220Ω" phrase as a Pure-ER/RRC enabled grossly serious breaches of the 1982 APA Standard, that utterly compromised the so-called "new and improved" Brief Pulse device and its promissory usage of half the EO of SW (Department of Health and Human Services, 1982a, G3-G4). Brief Pulses devices, ostensibly, were never to surpass 110 Absolute Joules (Ibid, A53; E20).

But while a number of key individuals had to have been involved in the power and titration cover-up of BP devices immediately following the 1976-1982 FDA investigation, the transmutation itself was in main conceived and led, as has been pointed out, by just one individual--electrical engineer-psychiatrist Richard Weiner. It was in main Richard Weiner, in short, who appears to have devised and effectuated the unauthorized and deceptive methodology known (in this manuscript) as the Mectan Transmutation, both enabling and cloaking new major enhancements in power and MTTLOI in abject violation of the 1982 APA Standard, totally undermining its purpose. Indeed, it was Weiner who edited MECTA's manual, first describing the early D-2/early MECTA SR 1@2 devices with the "100J at 220Ω" phrase intimating maximum outputs of 100 Joules, thereby disguising the power of the early second generation 200J BP devices (Sackeim and Weiner, 1993, p. ii). Moreover, Weiner himself may have participated in the actual designing of these early second generation BP devices, predecessors to the slightly later, even more enhanced 259J second generation MECTA BP devices (which he may also have helped design), devices yoked to Weiner's transmutational "100J at 220Ω" reporting methodology here deemed the Mectan Transmutation (Sackeim and Weiner, 1993, p. ii). Astonishingly, moreover, it was this very same Richard Weiner who represented every extant American ECT manufacturer to the FDA during FDA's formal investigation of the machine and the procedure between 1976 and 1982. Indeed, Weiner was not only the single public spokesperson on behalf of all U. S. manufacturers at the time, but it was Weiner who wrote the 1982 APA Standard tendering the promise of future minimal stimulus output, half the power of SW, convincing FDA of a new and improved, safer "ECT," securing its ongoing use for another half century in the United States and, as it turns out, the world.

In League with Representatives of the APA

Weiner has been the Chairman of all the APA Task Forces on ECT from about 1982 through to about 1995 and perhaps beyond. In light of Weiner's having represented all four U. S. manufacturers of ECT devices to the FDA, and the fact that several manufacturer-affiliated experts have been members of these APA Task Forces on "ECT," responsible for submitting reports both to the FDA and the public, one might argue that U. S. manufacturers of ECT devices conspired with APA Task Forces on ECT to cover-up the surreptitious supplanting of the 1982 APA Standard via the Mectan Transmutation. Indeed, it was the invisible metamorphosis within the Mectan Transmutation that facilitated the dropping of the 110J APA ceiling without notification to or authorization of the FDA or any other regulatory body. In brief, the illegitimate and unreported dropping of the 110J Brief Pulse maximum by three of the four manufacturers through the new utilization of Pure-ER/RRC, appears to have occurred with full Task Force approbation. [199] Aware that what appeared to be a simple transition from a "70J at 220Ω" to a "100J at 220Ω" conditional ER-RRC with 110J Energy Output

---

[198] While manufacturer-affiliated proponents since about 1994 (Beale, 1994) have obliquely conceded to the necessity of suprathreshold dosing, only one paper--the author's--has ever depicted true output (Cameron, 1994).

[199] 100J/220Ω = XJ/600Ω. X = 273J, approximately 2.73 fold the APA Standard. The new actual maximum was never reported.

ceiling intact was actually a dramatic increase in power, the Task Force appears to have totally abrogated its duty to protect the 1982 APA Standard as a minimal stimulus safeguard for BP devices generally. In fact, the APA Task Forces with Weiner at their helm, appear to have wholly suppressed this transformation. [200] Moreover, with the exception of Medcraft's reporting, three of the U. S. manufacturers, in seeming collaboration with the APA Task Forces on ECT, appear to have resolved from 1983 forward, never again to report actual EO. [201] Indeed, all four American manufacturers of second generation BP devices (including Medcraft), as noted, began reporting the same circa "100J at 220Ω" phrase for their devices, uniformly suppressing the elimination of the 110J ceiling for three of the four manufacturers. It is not surprising then, that until the author more than a decade later, in 1994 (Cameron, 1994) pointed out that the actual EO of Brief Pulse devices had surpassed that of SW, no Task Force member appears to have taken note (Cameron, 1994). [202] In fact, numerous journal articles implicitly or overtly lauding the "reduced output" of Brief Pulse, ignoring Cameron's and Beale's findings, continued and continue to flood the academic literature. [203] It is not surprising, therefore, that media (and even administering physicians) naïvely continue to engender the notion of Brief Pulse as "new and improved" by virtue of reduced output. As a result of this cover-up, and perhaps FDA's over-dependence upon Richard Weiner and the APA Task Forces on ECT, that is, dependence upon manufacturers to honestly self-report, the idea of Brief Pulse as a reduced output device continues even today. Even following Cameron's 1994 publication exposing Brief Pulse as a higher energy output device compared to SW and Beale's 1994 publication showing default outputs 2.5 fold threshold for all recipients, the idea that Brief Pulse remains a reduced output apparatus remains so entrenched in the so-called "professional literature," (much of which is written by manufacturer-affiliated "experts") that medical facilities, practitioners, the public, and even the media, continue to cling to the totally false impression that Brief Pulse, by virtue of reduced output, is now much less dangerous than the SW devices of old (Satcher, David, August 16,1999).

---

[200] Manufacturers, culpable of dropping the FDA 110J EO ceiling, were by 1985, producing unreported, unauthorized machines capable of between 252J--259J. Such outputs not only violated the APA ceiling, but violated principles of (1) minimal stimulus, (2) BP as a reduced output device, and (3) convulsion theory itself--all three of which were presented to the FDA between 1976-1982 as the basis for the APA Standard designed to improve safety over SW (Department of Health and Human Services, 1982a; 1982b; 1982c; Grahn, 1976, October 15; Grahn et al., 1977). It was predominantly the promised implementation of reduced output using BP, in fact, which influenced the FDA to permit the continued use of ECT generally. Indeed the Utah Report (Grahn, 1976, October 15; Grahn et al., 1977) implicitly confirmed that a Standard for ECT could be written [only] if based upon the three principles above, principles manifested in the 110J ceiling for BP devices prominently stipulated in the 1982 APA Standard (Department of Health and Human Services, 1982a, A53, E20, G3-G4).

[201] Since 1983, neither MECTA nor Somatics has reported actual EO figures. Elcot dissolved.

[202] Even though the author revealed true EO of devices in 1994, and alluded to the misleading reporting of EO based upon a false constant Impedance of "220 Ohms," the explanation of how manufacturers created a double standard--one for reporting, and one for determining actual machine output--is explained here for the first time. How manufacturers transitioned from reporting actual EO (in Joules) to utilizing a new unexplained, unauthorized Pure-ER/RRC interpretation of "100J at 220Ω" while failing to report the resultant new unauthorized maximum grossly breaching the 1982 APA ceiling, is seen here for the first time.

[203] Manufacturer affiliated proponents of ECT are responsible for most of these articles. Articles by Weiner, Sackeim, and Abrams, all affiliated with U.S. manufacturers, constitute several hundred treatises.

CHAPTER 18

"Dose Sensitive"

Critically then, the new secret 1983-85 increase in power became veiled by the subtle and unauthorized transition from the original interdependent ER/RRC of "70 Joules at 220Ω" with 110 Joule EO ceiling, to what appeared to be either a simple new conditional-ER/RRC of "100 Joules at 220Ω" having no effect on the 110J ceiling, or a new combination "100 Joules at 220Ω" conditional-ER-RRC incorporating an even more stringent 100 Joule ceiling. " [204] Of equal importance to the new hidden power increases, moreover, was the manufacturers' use of relative constants showing knowledge of the minimal outputs at which all recipients of a particular age category seize. Awareness of these threshold constants are critical in figuring the MTTLOI specific to each age category with respect to each new increasingly powerful Brief Pulse generation, as increased MTTLOI was and is the very purpose of the overall enhancements. [205] In short, neither the new 1983-85 MTTLOI enhancements nor the method for uniformly attaining them on a particular BP device, have ever been revealed or explained by manufacturers or manufacturer-affiliated experts--including the APA Task Forces on ECT (Beale et al. , 1994; Abrams and Swartz, 1988; Somatics Incorporated, 1993a). Not only did manufacturers and the APA Task Forces continue to suggest that what were actually second generation BP devices continue to emit the same (approximate) 100J ceiling as that emitted by the quintessential (first generation) 108J MECTA "C," but as noted above, manufacturers of these augmented devices continued to report or imply the same circa 1.1 MTTLOI as that of the 108J MECTA "C." Indeed, manufacturers claimed just above threshold efficacy for BL "ECT" and approximately 2.0 fold threshold efficacy for UL "ECT" (Abrams and Swartz, 1988, p.28; Somatics Incorporated, 1993a)]. In fact, as noted, the default MTTLOI on second generation BP devices, had first doubled and then risen to circa 2.5 fold threshold for every individual recipient receiving BL "ECT" and thus circa 5.0 fold threshold for UL "ECT" (Beale et al. , 1994). Still intimating just above threshold outputs for BL "ECT," however, manufacturers continued to describe BL "ECT" as "non-dose sensitive," that is, effective and thus administered at just above threshold [206] with what were assumed to be first generation BP devices, now depicting UL "ECT" as anomalously "dose-sensitive." Newly asserting that UL "ECT" required anomalous outputs of twice fold minimal stimulus to be effective then, manufacturers enabled their devices to administer to UL "ECT" recipients the same output administered to BL "ECT" recipients. What was not revealed was that the later second generation BP machines were actually administering 2.5 fold threshold outputs to BL recipients and so, with the declaration of anomaly, 5.0 fold threshold outputs to UL recipients. In short, then, what were actually second generation devices were actually administering a default circa 5.0 MTTLOI to all UL "ECT" recipients. Moreover, this hidden fact did not prevent manufacturer demands for even more enhanced machines purportedly required for the so-called "dose-sensitivity" of UL-"ECT," leaving the FDA to falsely assume so-called "non dose-sensitive" BL-"ECT" continued to be administered at just above

[204] A third interpretation might be the reporting of a "typical" 100 Joules at a "typical" 220Ω," again indicating the utilization of circa 100 Joules most of the time. All three interpretations are spurious.

[205] It is vital to understand that the purpose of power increases was not to make UL "ECT" effective, overcome anomalous thresholds for a "few" seizure recalcitrant individuals, or even to overcome increasing thresholds over a series, but solely to increase the MTTLOI of all recipients for each new increasingly powerful BP device.

[206] Threshold or rather just above threshold means just enough electricity to induce a so-called "adequate seizure."

threshold output with what were assumed to be first generation BP devices. (BL "ECT" was actually being administered at 2.5 fold threshold with second generation devices.) So redundantly and relentlessly did manufacturer-affiliated APA Task Force reports, brochures, and journal publications churn out false descriptions of BL and UL "ECT" as inherently antithetical in their alleged "non-dose sensitive" versus "dose sensitive" efficacy roles,[207] so eschewed and concealed were the radical new power and MTTLOI enhancements of second generation BP devices for both BL and UL ECT,[208] that neither the true power of these second generation BP devices nor the resultant MTTLOI for each form of ECT administered by these machines, much less the inextricable relationship between power and MTTLOI, has ever been explained or examined even to administering physicians--until now. [209]

"Dose Sensitive" Unilateral (UL) "ECT"

In short, deeming "UL ECT dose-sensitivity" an "ECT" anomaly, helped maintain the illusion that BL "ECT" continued to be administered at (just above) threshold on what were actually second generation Brief Pulse devices even as late as 1994 and beyond. It has long been freely admitted and indeed widely known (including the period between 1976 and 1982 during which FDA inquired into "ECT") that adequate UL "ECT" seizures can be induced at half the electrical energy required for BL "ECT." Because UL "ECT" was suddenly deemed "dose sensitive," however, UL ECT (as opposed to BL ECT) allegedly required a 2.0 fold threshold output (as opposed to "just above threshold" or minimal stimulus) to be effective, conveniently eliminating UL ECT as a means of administering half the output required for BL "ECT. " In any case, this "discovery" should have meant that first generation Brief Pulse machines pre-set for just above threshold output with BL-ECT, required no output accommodation whatsoever for so-called "dose-sensitive" UL ECT, in that, if true, the electrical energy required for just above seizure threshold with BL ECT was already twice that required for UL ECT. In brief, the same output could be used for both on first generation devices. Thus, the MECTA "C" set for minimal stimulus or just above threshold output with BL ECT should have required no output enhancement to attain a 2.0 fold threshold output with UL "ECT. " [210] In other words, the 108 joules set for inducing an adequate seizure with BL ECT for a 100 year old male meant that, although an adequate seizure could be induced with 50 or 54 Joules with UL ECT for the same 100 year old recipient, the same 108J could be used for "dose-sensitive" UL ECT allegedly requiring "twice" threshold to be "effective. " Due to "dose-sensitivity," in other words, the same 108J used for "non-dose sensitive" BL ECT could be administered to the same 100 year old for "dose-sensitive" UL "ECT. " In short, if UL was truly "dose sensitive" and BL was truly "non-dose sensitive" both BL ECT and UL ECT could be administered to the same 100 year old recipient with the very same circa 100J output with the exact same efficacy. Indeed, the same minimal stimulus "electrical output" administered to any particular age group using BL ECT, could be administered to the very same age category "effectively" using UL ECT with a first generation BP device such as the MECTA "C." Even so, manufacturers had invented a method of doubling the output for UL "ECT" expanding the notion of "minimal stimulus" at least with UL ECT. Indeed, manufacturers had not only invented at least one new rationale for enhancing the power of their BP devices, as we shall see, but due to "dose-sensitivity," "UL ECT" had been effectively removed as a means of reducing electrical output any further. On the other hand, this yet meant there was no need to increase the power of first generation BP devices such as the MECTA "C," as the MECTA "C" was already capable of accommodating

---

[207] Richard Weiner, Harold Sackeim, Richard Abrams, and Max Fink, all of whom have ties to manufacturers, have produced and, in fact, flooded the academic journals with a myriad of professional papers to this effect.

[208] Enhanced power and enhanced titration levels dawned simultaneously with the invisible dissolution of the APA ceiling.

[209] The need for power enhancement discussed in many so-called "professional papers" suppressed the fact that a major power enhancement in BP devices had already occurred between 1983 and 1985 with what were actually second generation BP devices. Indeed, such publications continued to emphasize UL alone as "dose-sensitive," squelching the fact that MECTA and Somatics devices had been set to administer BL ECT at 2.5 times minimal stimulus since at least 1985 (Beale et al., 1994). These publications underreporting the power of BP devices then, "justified" the call for "new" power enhancements based on "dose-sensitive UL-ECT alone" as opposed to "non-dose sensitive BL ECT" as well as supposed exceptional cases of extraordinarily high Impedance. That manufacturers had augmented titration to 2.5 fold threshold in 1985 for all BL recipients and 5.0 fold threshold for all UL recipients and were actually striving for a second doubling of titration with third generation BP devices as we shall eventually see, an action actually implemented about 1994, has never been disclosed.

[210] In short, the same dosage could be administered for both BL and "dose-sensitive" UL ECT.

so-called "dose-sensitive "UL ECT." In fact, unbeknownst to administering physicians, indeed, unbeknownst to any but manufacturers themselves and their academic affiliates, unreported second generation Brief Pulse machines (via the Mectan Transmutation) were already administering BL ECT--not at just above threshold--but at 2.5 fold threshold in every age category and had been doing so since at least 1984. Equally unbeknownst to administering physicians, was that what were actually second generation Brief Pulse devices were already administering UL ECT--not at a 2.0 fold threshold output, but using the same output emitted for BL "ECT"-- at a 5.0 fold threshold output for every age category (Beale et al. , 1994). Succinctly, then, the 100 year old recipient was actually being administered BL ECT not at 108 Joules or just above threshold, but at a default circa 250 Joules or a 2.5 MTTLOI, while the same 100 year old, with the same circa 250 Joules, was being administered a default output with UL ECT of a circa 5.0 MTTLOI. In brief then, even as manufacturers began calling for more powerful BP devices in order to administer UL ECT effectively, a consistent MTTLOI default of 2.5 and 5.0 for BL and UL "ECT" respectively was already being administered to each individual recipient in all age categories with what were actually MECTA and Somatics second generation BP devices. Unfortunately, the 2.5, 5.0 MTTLOI administered via MECTA and Somatics second generation BP devices with BL and UL "ECT" respectively remained unknown and unreported even to practicing physicians for at least ten years until Beale published his study in 1994 (Beale et al.1994), and even then, only through Beale's single publication and perhaps a single other corroborative periodical (Cameron 1994).

In spite of the secretly enhanced outputs already delivered by the later second generation BP devices then, both before and after Beale's findings, manufacturer-affiliated "experts" continued to demand more powerful Brief Pulse devices with the same spurious rationale. Indeed, while BL ECT was touted as non-dose sensitive and, therefore, supposedly administered at just above threshold, a suggestion which served to maintain the illusion that what were actually second generation BP devices remained first generation reduced output devices compared to SW, power enhancement appeals continued. In sum, manufacturers wanted even more powerful Brief Pulse devices.

"Dose Sensitive" Unilateral (UL) "ECT" and "Doubling of Impedance over a Series"

Because BL ECT was allegedly "effective" at just above threshold, the demand for even more powerful BP devices had to be justified by so-called "dose sensitive" UL ECT alone. In short, the "new" power enhancements which seemed to apply only to "dose-sensitive" UL ECT, appeared to have no applicability to the much more commonly utilized BL ECT. Thus, from as early as 1978 to at least 1994, the call for suprathreshold dosing and thus more powerful devices was almost entirely attributed to so-called "dose sensitive" UL ECT alone. Meanwhile, the spurious suggestion of BL ECT as effective at just above threshold, not only aided manufacturers in concealing what had already been ubiquitous new power distensions for all forms of ECT since about 1983 (Abrams, 1996, p.703; Abrams and Swartz, 1988, p.28; Beale et al. , 1994), but aided in concealing the real significance of the call for more powerful Brief Pulse devices. It was only by virtue of the more rarely utilized, but allegedly more desirable "dose-sensitive" UL ECT, then, that manufacturer affiliated experts were able to openly discuss the need for "new" more powerful Brief Pulse devices,[211] even as the reporting of just above threshold efficacy for conventional BL "ECT" continued to succor the long-standing and persistent notion of convulsion (not electricity) as the sole agent of "efficacy. " [212] [213] The claim of BL ECT at just above threshold efficacy accompanied by the contiguous reporting of what appeared to be the same circa 100J ceiling emitted by the 1979 MECTA "C" then, effectively covered up second generation power enhancements created for the express purpose of dramatically increasing MTTLOIs for both BL and UL "ECT" in every age category (Beale et al, 1994). None but manufacturers knew, of course, that Brief Pulse devices had already more than doubled in output since the days of the MECTA "C. " It was the assertion of dose-

[211] The first major power enhancement, unbeknownst to either administering physicians or FDA, had taken place late 1982 or early 1983.

[212] Convulsion theory is the notion that it is the adequate convulsion alone (not electricity or the inducing agent) which is therapeutically "beneficial." The illusion of just above threshold efficacy for BL ECT was necessary to maintain the theory's viability.

[213] Evidence suggests that manufacturers have known of the invalidity of convulsion theory since at least 1950 (Cameron, 1994). Nevertheless, BP era manufacturers, like SW manufacturers of the past, continue to maintain convulsion theory as the medical hypothesis behind "ECT."

sensitivity for UL ECT alone, therefore, which allowed manufacturers to call for even more powerful devices, in fact, unbeknownst to any but manufacturers, what were actually to be third generation Brief Pulse devices.

There was, however, the one logical flaw in the call for more powerful BP devices based on UL "dose-sensitivity " alone. First generation BP devices capping at 110J should have been able to accommodate both BL just above threshold outputs and twice threshold UL "ECT. " To overcome this objection, manufacturers now introduced the concept of "doubling of Impedance over a treatment series. " As such, BL "ECT" needed to begin with twice threshold outputs and UL ECT quadruple threshold outputs in order for BL to remain above threshold and UL twice threshold at the end of a treatment series.

The routinely administered, clinically automated application of unidentified and unreported suprathreshold dosages of electricity for BL ECT, for which second generation BP machines had already been created and surreptitiously pre-set, had, of course, already ubiquitously and dramatically enhanced MTTLOIs for all MECTA and Somatics Brief Pulse recipients for all forms of "ECT."[214] Indeed, second generation BP devices had been emitting more than twice threshold with BL "ECT" and more than quadruple threshold with UL "ECT" since at least 1985. The call for more powerful machines for UL ECT only, therefore, not only veiled the power and MTTLOI enhancements which had taken place between 1983 and 1985, but abetted the ongoing sixty year old hoax maintaining the pseudo-viability of convulsion theory itself.[215] [216] The failure to report power enhancements and actual output (particularly in Joules), the false attribution of so-called "dose-sensitivity" to UL ECT alone,[217] [218] the dereliction of manufacturers in reporting pre-set 2.5 MTTLOIs with BL ECT while falsely maintaining BL threshold efficacy, the deceptive uniform reporting of "100J at 220Ω" invisibly interpreted as a Pure-ER/RRC, the failure to reveal manufacturer utilization of "relative constants," and finally, the artfully uniform reporting of 100J Machine Readout maximums by all four Brief Pulse manufacturers [219] more than effectively covered up the first enhancements of what were, as noted above, actually second generation BP devices. Certainly, the willful neglect of manufacturers to report the failure of just above threshold efficacy in spite of the induction of adequate seizures not simply with UL ECT but with both BL and UL ECT (Beale et al, 1994; Cameron, 1994) not only served to cover up the need for and utilization of souped up second generation BP devices emitting Multifold Threshold Titration Level Output Intensities for both forms of "ECT" for all age levels, but continued to serve the then sixty year old "ECT" industry myth of "convulsion" as the viable scientific principle upon which "ECT" allegedly works. Indeed, the supposed "newest, most modern, most vastly improved gadgets"--Brief Pulse devices--were purportedly based on the most reduced outputs possible for inducing "adequate seizures. " Given the extent and audacity of the cover-up, it is little wonder why such market-hype--such wholly fraudulent claims--were and have been altogether consumed both by the public and the medical community in general. Not only were all four U. S. BP manufacturers culpable in this ongoing deception, but so too were manufacturer affiliated experts, a number of whom comprised (and continue to comprise) the ongoing APA Task Forces on ECT.

---

[214] Medcraft was breaching the APA Standard in another manner while Elcot was now defunct.

[215] The inefficacy of adequate seizures alone--that is--adequate seizures induced by minimal stimulus—confirmed by both the need and the existence of suprathreshold Brief Pulse devices, in turn confirms the non-viability of convulsion theory itself (Cameron, 1994).

[216] Both BL and UL are "dose-sensitive"--that is--ineffective at just above threshold even with the induction of "adequate seizures" thereby requiring multifold threshold dosages of electricity. This has been known but unacknowledged by manufacturers since the initial introduction of BP in the late 1940s (Cameron, 1994). The fact that both BL and UL require suprathreshold dosages of electricity to be effective, suggests a direct relationship between efficacy and electrically induced cognitive dysfunction indicative of brain damage (Cameron, 1994).

[217] Only in 1994, ten years after the fact, when Beale published findings of BP machines typically administering 2.5 times threshold for BL and 5.0 times threshold for UL, was the academic community apprised of the practice of ubiquitous suprathresholding (Beale at el., 1994). Moreover, it was only with the publication of Cameron's article that the academic community was first apprised of the enhanced power of what were actually second generation BP machines (Cameron, 1994).

[218] The notion that UL alone is "dose-sensitive" indirectly implied that BL was being administered at just above threshold, a complete falsehood (Beale et al., 1994).

[219] Additional misleading reporting methods will be described later.

Anomaly

Thus, the ironic presentation of UL ECT "dose-sensitivity" and the need for suprathreshold dosing as a UL ECT *anomaly* [220] (Abrams, 1996, p.703; Abrams and Swartz, 1988, p.28) juxtaposed with the protracted false reporting of BL ECT threshold efficacy (Abrams, 1996, p.703; Department of Health and Human Services, 1982a, pp. A18, A20, A41, A44-A45; Beale et al. , 1994) convincingly suggested continuous utilization of minimal stimulus or just above threshold output generally. Additionally, several other seemingly corroborative factors (such as the depicting of the 100J machine maximums mentioned above), effectively maintained the crucial illusion that "ECT" devices--via the 1976 resurgence of the "new and improved" Brief Pulse device--continued to remain a dramatic improvement over SW by virtue of reduced output. [221] In a kind of Orwellian "doublethink," then, the need for suprathreshold dosing with Brief Pulse for UL "ECT" alone along with the concept of doubling Impedance over a series, "justified" the demands for higher output Brief Pulse devices, even as the suggestion of BL minimal stimulus efficacy continued to reinforce the notion of BP as a reduced output device compared to SW. Maintaining the notion that adequate convulsions alone are therapeutic via the illusion of BL just above threshold efficacy, what were now "ENR" (adequate electricity or Electro Neurotransmission Reduction) devices continued to pass as convulsive therapy or "ECT" devices (Cameron, 1994 [222]) purportedly emitting reduced output, minimal stimulus dosages of electricity. This illusion, in fact, managed to entirely suppress the detail that what were actually MECTA and Somatics second generation BP machines had by 1994, long since surpassed SW in cumulative output, and had been emitting routine suprathreshold dosages of electricity for both UL and BL "ECT" (in the United States [223]) since at least 1985. The surpassing of SW both in maximum output and cumulative output in most age categories, was and is a knowing violation of the central conclusions made by the Utah Biomedical Test Laboratory (Grahn, 1976; Grahn et al. , 1977) and around which the 1982 APA Standard had been created to protect consumers (Department of Health and Human Services, 1982a, A53; E20). Indeed, the primary FDA requisite for the ongoing utilization of "ECT" (see the Utah investigation) appeared to be wholly contingent upon the efficacy of BP minimal stimulus induced "adequate convulsions," generally half the output of SW. Moreover, based on the Utah Biomedical Test Laboratory Report, reduced output, minimal stimulus induced adequate seizures with Brief Pulse, circa half the output of SW, appears to have been the single criterion and circumstance wherein Utah had agreed "benefit could outweigh risk" (Grahn, 1976; Grahn et al. , 1977; Read and Bentall 2010). Certainly it was the reassurance of Brief Pulse's greatly reduced output compared to SW and the assurance of minimal stimulus induced seizures with Brief Pulse alone in accordance with the 1982 APA Standard, which assuaged lay and professional activists enough (as well as consumer organizations such as *Public Citizen*) to walk away from the final FDA hearings in 1982, believing greatly reduced output to be the future of a new and improved, much less harmful procedure with much less or no cognitive dissonance whatsoever (Food and Drug Administration, 1979, May 29, pp.51-52).

---

[220] From about 1976 to 1983, both UL and BL minimal stimulus induced adequate seizures with BP were presented as effective. About 1983, UL alone began to be described as "dose-sensitive." Currently, by the year 2000, manufacturers had begun to acknowledge the "dose-sensitivity" of both UL and BL "ECT," a process so protracted and extended, however, that regulatory bodies appear to have lost sight of the overall fact that by this admission, convulsion theory had been proven fallacious. Moreover, in that the procedure cannot be administered with reduced or minimal stimulus output, the procedure cannot be administered safely. Finally, these facts underpin the conclusion that "ECT" administered with BP no longer has any significance, and that such a procedure is no longer "ECT," but ENR based on adequate dosages of electricity.

[221] FDA approval criteria for medical devices is, in essence, simultaneous safety and efficacy wherein benefit outweighs risk. BP can induce seizures at greatly reduced dosages compared to SW. That adequate seizures are ineffective, and that BP requires suprathreshold dosing for both BL and UL placement, undermines not only convulsion theory itself, but BP's advantage in eliciting adequate seizures at greatly reduced dosages.

[222] Only minimal stimulus devices can be deemed "ECT" ("electroconvulsive therapy") devices in that suprathreshold devices are actually "ENR" (Electro Neurotransmission Reduction) devices, the latter based not upon adequate convulsion, but upon adequate doses of electricity. Indeed, effective "ECT" devices are non-existent.

[223] Eurasian BP devices also began to surpass SW. The Eurasian transition to more powerful BP devices, though also influenced by the Americans, came slightly later, as we shall see (see English and Canadian Devices in this manuscript).

In Conclusion

The false engendering of minimal stimulus efficacy via the protracted, but fallacious reporting of BL threshold output and efficacy (Abrams, 1996, p.703) implying greatly reduced dosages of electricity with Brief Pulse, in conjunction with manufacturers' failure to report dramatic EO and MTTLOI increases implemented between 1983-1985, not only enabled manufacturers to present a false public image of reduced output Brief Pulse for the purpose of circumventing FDA scrutiny, but created an illusory bridge from SW to the "modern" BP Era, for the purpose of transporting the "ECT" procedure generally from the twentieth to the twenty-first century. In short, the illusion of minimal stimulus efficacy with the "new and improved" BP device along with the 1982 APA Standard allowed the practice of "ECT" to survive the FDA investigation between 1976 and 1982, keeping the procedure alive as an advancement of twenty-first century techno-medicine. Thus, it was convulsion theory or the efficacy of the "adequate seizure" as a viable medical hypothesis along with a new means of greatly reducing the electrical energy required to induce them which kept the procedure afloat following the entrance of the FDA. In short, it was the engendering of minimal stimulus efficacy, that is, efficacy of the adequate convulsion alone via the greatly reduced electrical output of Brief Pulse that had lighted the promise of a much safer much more improved procedure for future recipients. Manufacturers themselves realized that convulsion theory could be true if and only the induction of the "adequate" seizure alone makes the procedure effective and so seizures were induced at the most minimally needed electrical stimulus possible. It is, in fact, the enduring myth of convulsion theory or the induction of the adequate seizure alone as the procedure's basic premise which has perennially and perdurably maintained the procedure's viability, obscuring the underlying fact that neither minimal stimulus UL nor minimal stimulus BL ECT invokes any meaningful therapeutic or ameliorative response (Cameron, 1994). It is for this reason that manufacturers had to secretly increase the power and MTTLOI of their Brief Pulse devices. Naturally, Brief Pulse manufacturers could not afford to reveal the plain fact that "adequate convulsion" alone is, in fact, inadequate. This simple fact--that both BL and UL ECT require suprathreshold dosages of electricity in order to be effective--clearly and definitively countermines "adequate convulsion" as the sole or even contributing agent of efficacy, in turn countermanding adequate convulsion theory itself. That both BL and UL ECT are ineffective when administered at minimal electrical Brief Pulse dosages powerful enough to produce fully adequate seizures (Sackeim, 1991, p.233-234 [224]), and that the procedure is only effective at suprathreshold dosages of electricity--facts corroborated by the simple power and MTTLOI levels manufacturers themselves have required of both SW and modern day BP devices in order to make the procedure "work"--entirely controverts the premise that adequate seizure is the agent of efficacy in "ECT. " Indeed, the necessity of suprathreshold dosages of electricity for both UL and BL "ECT" entirely invalidates the notion of electricity as but the catalyst for inducing adequate seizures. Indeed, adequate *seizure* inefficacy, and the need of suprathreshold *dosing* for both BL and UL ECT, points to electricity itself (and its effect on the brain) as the sole agent of "efficacy. " This revelation was and continues to be problematic for "ECT" device manufacturers in that, electrical dosing surpassing that required for adequate minimal stimulus induced seizures, has long been associated with long-term cognitive dysfunction, suggestive of brain injury, a fact which Utah itself all too clearly pointed out (Alexander and Lowenbach, 1944; Breggin, 1979; Cronholm and Ottosson, 1963; Department of Health and Human Services, 1982a, p. A41; Dunn, Giuditta, Wilson, and Glassman, 1974; Echlin, 1942, 1942; Essman, 1968; Friedman, 1942; Friedman, Wilcox, and Reiter, 1942; Gordon, 1982; Liberson, 1945a; Liberson, 1949; Malitz, Sackheim, and Decina, 1979; McGaugh and Alpern, 1966; Ottosson, 1960; Proctor and Goodwin, 1943; Reed, 1988; Squire and Zouzounis, 1986; Wilcox, 1946). Certainly, the inextricable relationship of suprathreshold dosing and brain damage was the very impetus suggesting the need for reduced output devices such as Brief Pulse in Utah's conclusions, conclusions wholly condoned by the FDA. Quite simply, the single plausible explanation for the manufacturer cover-up of enhanced power and titration in both SW and BP devices is suppression of the requisite need for brain damaging dosages of electricity, specifically, as is now known, to effectuate widespread diminution of neurotransmitters,

[224] While acknowledgements of threshold inefficacy such as the one alluded to in the Sackeim reference above are extant, manufacturers generally, i.e. Somatics Inc., never make it entirely clear that this refers to both UL and BL placement. Moreover, such acknowledgements contradict other later statements of BL threshold efficacy (Abrams, 1996, p.703). The fact that it was not revealed until 1994 that U.S. BP manufacturers had been routinely administering suprathreshold dosages of electricity for both UL and BL "ECT" since approximately 1983 (Beale at al., 1994), a fact even now little understood or appreciated, bespeaks of manufacturer cover-up.

particularly within the left pre-frontal lobe (Perrin, 2012). In brief, the later BP devices, just as the older SW devices no longer remain "ECT" devices at all, but rather ENR devices. Adequate convulsion with respect to ENR devices, as we shall see, is neither the goal of the ENR apparatus nor the treatment, but, only an unavoidable and somewhat "convenient" side-effect.

In sum, for at least ten years following the FDA investigation, American manufacturers, in league with Richard Weiner, APA Task Force members, and manufacturer-affiliated "experts," covered up the dramatic power and titration level increases inherent in American BP machines manufactured after 1982, deceiving both the FDA and the public at large (including both the media and administering physicians themselves). The purpose of this cover-up was and is to secret the requisite reduction of neurotransmitters and thus requisite reduction of transmissions necessary to achieve "efficacy" via adequate amounts of electricity while at the same time avoiding the debunking of convulsion theory itself. This new Brief Pulse Era power enhancement and cover-up, as we shall see, would soon extend world-wide by way of a similarly deceptive stratagem suggestive of the same 100 Joule maximums with respect to made-for-Europe devices under the 1989 International Electro Technical Commission (IEC) Standard. In America, the 2.5 fold power amplification (in terms of EO and Charge) emitted by second generation Brief Pulse devices--going from 110 Joules up to 259 Joules, surpassing the 200J maximum of SW against which Brief Pulse had been presented to the public and the FDA as a reduced output device half the power of SW (Department of Health and Human Services, 1982a, A53, E20, G3-G4), remained hidden both to the public general and the academic community at large. The first hint of this increase came in 1994, as noted, with Beale's study (Beale et al. , 1994) but which failed to emphasize the significance of the find due to Beale's reporting in terms of Charge instead of Joules. Equally unreported were increases in MTTLOI from a 1.1 and 2.2 MTTLOI with BL and UL "ECT" respectively with first generation BP devices to a 2.5 and 5.0 MTTLOI with BL and UL "ECT" respectively with second generation BP devices for every age recipient (Ibid). Thus, due to the manufacturer-devised Pure-ER/RRC methodology known as the Mectan Transmutation in addition to numerous other reporting aberrations and improprieties, including spurious machine readouts suggesting 100 maximum Joules and manufacturers' decision to no longer report actual output in Joules, Brief Pulse devices from 1976 to 1994 appeared to the FDA, physicians at large, the media, and most importantly the general public, largely unchanged and unamplified. Rather, manufacturers gave the modern day second generation Brief Pulse device, purportedly based on convulsion theory or induction of the adequate seizure alone, the totally false persona of a minimal stimulus apparatus, limited, as noted, to a circa 100J ceiling in direct accordance with the APA Standard. In short, the Brief Pulse device yet appeared vastly improved over SW by virtue of radically reduced output. The falsely purported 2.0 fold threshold output for so-called "dose-sensitive" UL "ECT" (which was actually 5.0 fold threshold at this time) was misleadingly presented as an "anomaly. "

A Word on Medcraft's BP Device Compared to MECTA and Somatics

As has been mentioned, while all American Brief Pulse manufacturers reported approximately “100J at 220Ω” for what were actually much more powerful second generation made-for-America BP devices, two of the three currently existing manufacturers--MECTA and Somatics--[225] surreptitiously interpreted the “100J at 220Ω” phrase first as a Mean-ER/RRC and then as a Pure-ER/RRC, dropping the 110J ceiling and creating a new theoretical ceiling of up to 273 unreported Joules. Medcraft alone (of the remaining three extant manufacturers) although reporting the same approximate “100J at 220Ω” phrase appears to have interpreted the phrase in a variant, almost antithetical manner. According to early 510K (pre-market) submissions, though describing its "new" Brief Pulse device, the B-25, by the same circa "100 Joules at 220Ω" expression, Medcraft, unlike MECTA and Somatics, actually did confine the overall maximum output of its "new" Brief Pulse device to 99 absolute Joules in accordance with the APA Standard (Food and Drug Administration, 1986B, pp.56, 78). On the other hand, and rather bizarrely, the Medcraft B-25 Brief Pulse, unlike MECTA and Somatics BP devices,

[225] Elcot dissolved around 1986.

apparently has the capacity to emit 99J maximums not only at the oldest age level, but at all Impedances, that is, at any age level, including the youngest! (Food and Drug Administration, 1986B). [226]

If Medcraft's 510K report can be taken at face value, (as it no doubt can) Medcraft appears to have interpreted its "99J at 220Ω" phrase not as a Pure-ER/RRC (or any kind of ER/RRC) as do MECTA and Somatics, but rather as a maximum 99J ceiling at all Impedances. In light of the 1982 APA Standard depicting a 110J ceiling and in light of readouts depicting circa 100 maximum Joules for machines produced by all three extant manufacturers of second generation made-for-America BP devices (MECTA, Somatics, and Medcraft), indeed a circa "100J" ceiling was and should have been anticipated for all three, but certainly not administered at all Impedances.

It is true that in contrast to both MECTA and Somatics, whose devices grossly and unexpectedly surpass the 110J ceiling, Medcraft alone appears to have to have remained under the 110J ceiling stipulation for its own B-25 Brief Pulse device. Unfortunately, Medcraft fails to interpret its "99J at 220Ω" phrase as a *Conditional*-ER/RRC or ER/RRC of any sort, as mentioned. Indeed, while Medcraft does adhere to the 110J ceiling of the APA Standard then, it totally drops the ER/RRC aspect of the standard. Thus, while the output on MECTA and Somatics made-for-America second generation BP devices grossly surpass 110 Joules (in that they are based on a 600Ω maximum Impedance potential in lieu of the conditional output ceiling of 110 Joules), MECTA and Somatics second generation BP device outputs at least adhere to the ER/RRC precept of the APA standard, that is, the machines have gradational outputs relative to age. In short, based on the ER/RRC or gradational output precept, MECTA and Somatics devices accommodate Impedances below 220Ω with proportionately lower outputs. For example, in accordance with a "100J at 220Ω" Pure-ER/RRC, because MECTA and Somatics maintain the ER/RRC principle, maximum output for a second generation machine recipient never rises above a 2.59 and 2.52 MTTLOI respectively. This means that while a 100 year old receives a 252J output on the Thymatron DG, the ten year old receives a 2.52J output and this is due to the administering of a uniform MTTLOI in conjunction with the ER/RRC precept. Therefore, whereas MECTA and Somatics violate the 110J ceiling, they yet conform to an ER/RRC which incorporates a uniform MTTLOI for all age recipients. Medcraft, conversely, while adhering to the 110J ceiling, allows its B-25 Brief Pulse device to reach 99 Joules at even the lowest of Impedances (or age categories), Impedances well below 220Ω. Succinctly, MECTA and Somatics violate the 110J Absolute ceiling, but adhere to a "100J at 220Ω" (albeit pure) ER/RRC, limiting the rate at which output rises in accordance with age and Impedance; whereas, Medcraft adheres to the 110J Absolute ceiling but fails to interpret its "99J at 220Ω" as an ER/RRC. In a word, while adhering to a 99J ceiling, Medcraft fails to mandatorily reduce its maximum output of 99 Joules in even the youngest age categories. These revealing antithetical interpretations regarding the commonly reported phrase circa "100J at 220Ω" shall be discussed in more detail in later sections. In addition and perhaps just as telling, Medcraft continues to market its' much more popular B-24 SW device, the same instrument it manufactured in 1950, a device which was allegedly to be supplanted via the re-introduction of Brief Pulse as early as 1976.

[226] Remember, even Brief Pulse devices limited to 110 Joules only administered this maximum to 100 year old recipients with a circa 100J threshold thereby administering one times threshold, not ten year olds with a 1.0J threshold, thereby administering 100 times threshold.

CHAPTER 19

Weiner and the Promise of a Safer ECT

Regardless of the anomalous Medcraft B-25 (to be discussed again later), therefore, the two main (extant) American BP manufacturers, MECTA and Somatics on their own initiative, precipitously dropped and so violated the 1982 APA 110J EO ceiling, instead utilizing unreported and unauthorized maximum outputs of up to circa 260 Joules for their made-for-America second generation BP devices. The purpose behind the amplification was in order to deliver unreported suprathreshold dosages of electricity for both BL and UL electrode placement of respectively 2.5 and 5.0 fold threshold in every age category--titration levels unbeknownst either to administering physicians or recipients themselves and thus administered without informed consent. Such (unreported) Multifold Threshold Titration Level Output Intensities (Cameron, 1994) routinely utilized in the application of BL and UL ECT respectively with second generation BP devices (Beale et al. , 1994), violate three important principles (1) minimal stimulus induced seizures, (2) the notion of BP as a reduced EO device, and (3) efficacy of the adequate seizure--all three assumptions of which Utah Biomedical Test Laboratory presented to the FDA as necessary stipulations to be incorporated into an acceptable written standard for ECT devices. Only a standard based on and incorporating these three principles--(1) minimal stimulus, (2) reduced EO compared to SW (which only BP can deliver), and (3) efficacy of the "adequate seizure" conforms to the FDA/Utah call for simultaneous safety and efficacy reflected in Weiner's 1982 APA Standard. In short, according to Utah, the single set of circumstances in which benefit of the ECT procedure surpasses risk is the one in which all three principles are present. These principles, in accordance with the 1982 APA Standard, in brief, were Utah's stipulations for increased safety with Brief Pulse over the previous and objectionable SW devices of the past (Department of Health and Human Services, 1982a, A18, A20, A41, A44-A45, A53, E20, G3-G4; Ibid 1982b; Ibid 1982c; Grahn, 1976, October 15; Grahn et al. , 1977). Succinctly then, the conclusion and assumption of the Utah test laboratory that a standard for ECT could indeed be written, was clearly based on the three maxims reflected within the 1982 APA Standard--(1) assurance of minimal stimulus, that is, the least amount of electricity possible to induce the adequate convulsion, (2) that this could and so would be achieved with half the electrical energy output of SW by virtue of BP (3) and that "ECT" is based on the electrically catalyzed induction of the adequate convulsion alone, that is, that adequate convulsion is the lone ameliorative in ECT and thus the single aim of the procedure. The 1982 APA Standard presented to the FDA (by APA Task Force Chairman Weiner and colleagues) at the conclusion of the FDA hearings in 1982 clearly incorporated all three stipulations, all three of which were clearly understood and seemingly promised by Weiner for any future standard and so for all future "ECT. " Indeed, it was these three principles unmistakably incorporated into the 1982 APA Standard which formed the basis of FDA's approbation for the ongoing utilization of ECT in America.

In sum, it was the Utah recommendation that only the presence of the first two principles could assure a reasonable degree of both safety and efficacy with respect to the new and Improved ECT, and that both were based on the assumptive bedrock of the third principle that induction of the adequate seizure alone is the single therapeutic agent and thus the single goal of that which constitutes ECT. Indeed, it was Utah's opinion and recommendation that these three principles could be written into a standard which persuaded FDA that future ECT devices could be both safe and effective and should, therefore, continue into the future. The manifest condition, however, was that these three assurances become mandatory through a soon to be submitted written standard (Grahn, 1976, October 15; Grahn et al. , 1977). It was, then, these three principles which formed the heart of the 1982 APA Standard clearly stipulating the use of the reduced output BP device explicitly limited to a “70J at 220Ω” ER/RRC and a conditional 110J ceiling, slightly more than the minimum amount of energy required to induce adequate seizures with BL ECT for all recipients in all circumstances written into regulatory jargon by Richard Weiner. It is adherence to these three defining principles alone, therefore, which according to Utah and the FDA, constitute the meaning of "Electro Convulsive Therapy" alone which is safe enough to administer to human beings. Without these three principles, Weiner knew full well that neither Utah nor the FDA would readily acquiesce to the ongoing use of the “ECT” into the future.

Based on sound engineering principles then, the APA Standard was comprised of the clearly safer 110J maximum Brief Pulse device based on a uniform 1.1 MTTLOI ceiling, just above the minimal dosage (100J) required to induce adequate seizures in all age recipients in all circumstances with BL ECT, and which, due to the "70J at 220Ω" ER/RRC included gradational outputs relative to age. Thanks to the unofficially adopted, but FDA approved 1982 APA Standard, the wave of all future ECT devices would thenceforward be based on a 110J maximum Brief Pulse apparatus soon to supplant the archaic 200J SW devices of the past. It was these three maxims, manifested in the conjoined regulatory dynamic of a “70J at 220Ω” conditional-ER/RRC with 110J ceiling in turn based upon the substratum--efficacy of the adequate seizure--which formed the stipulation of a greatly reduced output much safer procedure that ultimately convinced FDA officials to permit the ongoing utilization of the ECT practice within the United States s noted (and ultimately the world). Hence, in spite of the fact that the 1982 APA Standard was never formally adopted,[227] the 1982 APA Standard submitted to the FDA by Weiner stood as the manifest promise of adherence to the Utah-FDA criteria newly guaranteeing the preponderance of benefit over risk. In short, FDA expected a finalized standard without which FDA would refuse to remove the machine from the lowest medical device category. [228] Engendering hope for the simultaneity of safety and efficacy for the modern age then, the prototypical APA Standard was to be based upon the application of the three Utah recommended determinants 1) the least amount of electricity possible to induce the adequate convulsion, 2) radically reduced Brief Pulse output compared to SW, and 3) efficacy of the adequate seizure. A standard enforcing these three maxims, i.e. the 1982 APA Standard, could for the first time ever, impose a regulatory formula upon the ECT industry guaranteeing consumers at least a modicum of safety, some degree of assurance that along with effective treatment, benefit would at long last outweigh risk. Certainly, it was this formula endorsed by Utah and so the FDA, backed by specific promises guaranteed by Weiner's FDA approved standard that allowed "ECT" to continue on into the modern age. Alas, the APA Standard was the modern era's assurance that the controversial ECT procedure of the past remained past and that recipient complaints would at last be addressed with the safety of new regulatory parameters describing a true ECT apparatus with the capacity to induce adequate seizures with minimal stimulus output (Department of Health and Human Services, 1982a, A53, E20, G3-G4). [229] Indeed, the ground-breaking 108 Joule MECTA "C" Brief Pulse device in complete adherence with the 1982 APA Standard served as manifest proof of this guarantee.

Breaching of the 1982 APA Standard

As we shall continue to observe, MECTA's, and Somatics' [230] surreptitious violations of the 1982 APA Standard, in short, gross violations of the 1.1 MTTLOI for BP devices,[231] undermines all three principles of what was

[227] Weiner convinced officials that the standard needed more refining and that more input was needed from other interested parties.

[228] In fact, the standard never was submitted for official adoption and so the device remains in the lowest class—those devices for which a standard cannot or has not been written—to this day.

[229] The circa 100 Joule ceiling was, in essence, the assurance of minimal stimulus dosing in that according to Weiner, adequate seizures can be induced in virtually every person with never more than 100 Joules.

[230] Medcraft’s violations will be discussed separately.

[231] Manufacturers have more recently begun to acknowledge that threshold convulsions are ineffective and therefore that suprathreshold dosages are necessary with both BL and UL (Sackeim, 1991, p.233-234). This fact does not relieve manufacturers of the congressional mandate to produce a reasonably safe product in accordance with the 1976 Medical Devices Act calling for both safety and efficacy. The fraudulent double standards created by manufacturers support the conclusion that the procedure can never be administered both safely and efficaciously. In short, the procedure is incapable of being administered “effectively” wherein benefit

supposed to be the improved safety of future "ECT" devices. Determined by the Utah-FDA investigation conducted between 1976-1982, these criteria seemed to be guaranteed by the 1982 APA Standard incorporating these very principles. In contrast, the gross breaching of the 110J ceiling and thus the breaching of titration regulations via the supplanting of the 110J ceiling with a never before explained 100J Pure-ER/RRC, an indefensibly deceptive transmutation, spread cancer-like across the globe (as we shall see), failing to eliminate or reduce the ubiquitous memory dysfunction closely associated with SW devices of the past (Janis, 1950; Squire, 1986; Squire, and Chace, 1975; Squire, and Slater, 1983; Squire, Slater, and Miller, 1981). Instead, the unprecedented, moreover, furtive amplification of modern day Brief Pulse devices may actually have exacerbated these complications (Cameron, 1997; Squire and Zouzounis, 1986; Andre 2009). Ironically, continued or even enhanced memory dysfunction (the continual prevalence of which is ignored or neglected) is almost certainly due to enhanced neurotransmitter damage as a direct result of increased electricity (see MRI Studies in this manuscript; Perrin, 2012). [232] [233] The grave transgressions of U. S. manufacturers MECTA and Somatics,[234] followed by the participatory emulation of English, Canadian (and other Eurasian) BP manufacturers (as we shall see), utilizing the same Weiner invented Mectan Transmutation, that is, the same misleading 100J Pure-ER/RRC transmogrification, a hoax camouflaged by false Machine Readouts spuriously limited to 100 maximum Joules producing the uniform illusion of 100J ceilings for second generation BP devices throughout the world, indeed appears to be a world-wide manufacturer conspiracy. Certainly, this international manufacturer complicity to hide the true power of "ECT" devices, may be one of the most wide-spread and perfidious instances of consumer fraud ever perpetrated. The ultimate price of this fraud is yet another era of increased output devices resulting in tens of thousands of instances of unreported morbidity attributable to brain damage and though not the subject of this manuscript increased, hidden, and unreported mortality (Cameron, 1994; Read and Bentall 2010).

While we have now examined the devolution and transmutation of the reporting process itself and its relationship to the 1982 APA Standard, as well as deception in general, regarding made-for-America second generation BP devices, we have taken but a cursory look at the specific, unreported enhancements inherent in the second generation Brief Pulse machinery itself. Let us now examine in specific detail the later second generation Somatics and MECTA made-for-America Brief Pulse devices manufactured from approximately 1985 to about 1995, devices capable emitting outputs not of 110 Joules, but of never before reported outputs of 252 and 259 Joules respectively.

---

outweighs risk, a conclusion warranting the banning of the procedure under the Medical Devices Act and other statutes regarding fraud. Every important piece of evidence points to "efficacy" as a result of electrical closed head injury (Breggin, 1998).

[232] See Cameron's (1994) article "Sham Statistics, the Myth of Convulsive Therapy, and the Case for Consumer Misinformation."

[233] It is noteworthy that The Texas Reporting System reveals a much higher death rate than is reported by manufacturers and manufacturer-affiliated proponents of "ECT." Proponents often either deny or rationalize away death statistics as "death due to causes other than ECT." "Other" causes typically include heart attack, pulmonary edema, and stroke, often immediately following the procedure. Statistics on memory dysfunction for The Texas Reporting System are unscientifically reported by administering physicians in lieu of recipients themselves. No TRS provision exists for follow-up interviews to investigate continuing or long-term memory complaints. MRI evidence of brain damage has been repressed (see sections on Texas Reporting System and MRI). Damage, moreover, occurs on a synaptic level, imperceivable even by MRI but can be proven through reduced connectivity (Perrin 2012).

[234] American manufacturer Medcraft is also culpable of violating titration regulations but does so in an entirely different manner. Manufacturer Elcot is defunct.

SECTION V: LATER 2ND GENERATION BP DEVICES: DETAILS

CHAPTER 20

1982 APA Standard Vs Second Generation Made-For-America BP Devices

In observing the transmuted, deceptive, and somewhat complex method by which manufacturers report and derive conflicting [235] machine ceilings for second generation BP devices, it is again helpful to remind ourselves that the 1982 APA Standard calls for an absolute ceiling of 110 maximum Joules and a conditional Equivalent Ratio-Rate Rise Ceiling (ER/RRC) of "70 Joules at 220Ω. " The APA Standard's conditional-ER/RRC of "70J at 220Ω"--the output/Impedance ratio mandating gradational outputs up to the conditional APA ceiling of 110 maximum Joules, limits the MTTLOI (electrical dosing) for BL (bilateral) ECT to a 1.1 MTTLOI or just above threshold output and a 2.2 MTTLOI for "dose sensitive" UL (unilateral) "ECT" (in terms of Charge and Joules). [236] No figuring or calculating is necessary to derive the APA Absolute ceiling in that the ceiling is clearly stipulated in the standard as 110 Joules (Department of Health and Human Services, 1982a, p. A53; E20), and thus a 1.1 MTTLOI for all other age categories. In that MECTA and Somatics Brief Pulse devices emit a consistent MTTLOI for all age recipients, the APA standard implicitly stipulates that no age category administered BL ECT can receive more than a 1.1 MTTLOI or a just above threshold output. The same dosage emitted for "dose-sensitive" UL ECT, moreover (110 Joules for the same 100 year old male) evinces a maximum 2.2 fold threshold output in quasi-adherence to the APA Standard for every age category. [237] As we have seen, however, beginning about 1985, manufacturers surreptitiously dropped the 110J ceiling. Beginning with Somatics' Thymatron DG discussed in the following chapters, manufacturers created a paradigm with respect to reporting apparent 100J ceilings to the public, while secretly configuring, through the unreported Mectan Transmutation, much higher actual outputs for their second generation BP devices.

---

[235] The Medcraft BP device emits 99 maximum joules but fails to adhere to the APA ER/RRC precept, while MECTA and Somatics BP devices adhere to the ER/RRC precept, but fail to adhere to the 110J ceiling precept, emitting 259 and 252 Joules respectively.

[236] The same output required for BL threshold outputs, is twice that needed to induce an adequate seizure with UL ECT. The original APA Standard limits devices to about 1.1 times threshold for BL ECT, which should apply to UL ECT as well. Instead, the same default outputs with respect to age used for BL ECT are commonly utilized for UL ECT as well which means that recipients can receive a 2.2 MTTLOI even under the 1982 APA Standard. Initially, manufacturers did not reveal that UL ECT was applied at the same output as BL ECT. Once revealed, however, manufacturers quickly developed the spurious notion of "dose-sensitivity" for UL ECT--that is-- that UL ECT alone requires a two-fold threshold output to be effective.

[237] If 100J is the minimum required to emit an adequate seizure for all 100 year old recipients in all circumstances with BL ECT, 50J is the minimum required to emit an adequate seizure for all 100 year old recipients in all circumstances with UL ECT.

CHAPTER 21

SOMATICS MADE-FOR-AMERICA SECOND GENERATION BP DEVICE--THE THYMATRON DG

Somatics Figures EO for the Thymatron DG

Specific known maximum parameters for the Thymatron DG, the second generation BP device manufactured about 1985 by the American company, Somatics Incorporated, are as follows: maximum constant current - .9 Amperes; maximum number of Pulses - 140; maximum Pulse Width - .001 Seconds; maximum Duration - 4.0 Seconds; and maximum Machine Impedance 555.5Ω (Abrams and Swartz, 1988; Swartz and Abrams, 1996). Somatics specifically reports "99.4J at 220Ω," privately interpreting the phrase as a Pure-ER/RRC [238] permitting up to 252 unreported joules (99.4J/220Ω = XJ/555.5Ω. **X = 252J**). Maximum output on the machine readouts, read by administering physicians, on the other hand, depicts 99.4J [239] (a reverse-ER, as has been mentioned) in lieu of actual maximum output. This discrepancy between the reported 99.4J maximum output and the actual 252J maximum output is inherent in the DG's programming. The machine automatically plugs in a misleading but ubiquitous 220Ω Impedance in lieu of all actual Impedances up to 555.5Ω to calculate displayed readouts. In lieu of the actual maximum Impedance of 555.5Ω, therefore, the machine plugs in a misleading "220Ω," to achieve a false derivative Readout maximum of 99.4 Joules (99.4J/555.5Ω = XJ/220Ω. **X = 99.4J**). The DG's actual output at the actual maximum 555.5Ω as noted, is a never before reported 252 Joules. Interestingly, with the exception of Impedances, all other maximum machine parameters used for calculating readouts, as noted, are accurate. In short, the 220Ω substitution directly affects machine readouts only in Joules. Even though all other parameters are accurate, by plugging 220Ω (in lieu of actual Impedance) into any of several possible formulas for determining output, [240] the DG calculates, obtains, and reports to physicians misleading Energy Output readouts for every age group, including, as noted, the Maximum Machine Readout, instead depicting between 99.4 and 99.7Joules (for the Thymatron DG). The machine actually emits, as noted above, 252 maximum joules, and thus a 2.52 MTTLOI for all age categories.

False Maximum Machine Readout:
.9 x .9 x **220Ω** x 140 Pulses x .001 x 4 Seconds = **99.79J.** [241]

Actual Maximum Machine Output:
.9 x .9 x **555.5Ω** x 140 Pulses x .001 x 4 Seconds = **252J**

---

[238] By Pure-ER/RRC, the author means sans prescribed ceiling of 110J, leaving actual maximum output based purely on the ER/RRC of 99.4J/220Ω to maximum output at 555.5Ω (99.4/220Ω = **252J**/.555.5Ω). Though not apparent, therefore, the conditional 110J ceiling had been dropped.

[239] The Thymatron DG depicts a maximum machine readout of 99.4J.

[240] i.e., EO = current squared x Impedance x Frequency x Pulse Width x Duration

[241] Somatics actually reports 99.4J at 220Ω--not 99.79J at 220Ω.

Thus, the circa (252 ÷ 108 =) 2.3 fold power enhancement (from the 1982, 108J MECTA "C") to the 1985, 252J Thymatron DG, more than doubling the MTTLOI from approximately just above threshold with BL ECT and just over 2.0 fold with UL ECT, to an unreported 2.52 MTTLOI with BL ECT and a circa 5.0 MTTLOI with UL ECT (Beale et al. , 1994). In fact, the DG's actual maximum output has never been reported until now and indeed, has been deliberately hidden from view. Moreover, by supplanting the actual maximum machine Impedance of 555.5Ω with a false "220Ω constant" in the machine's computer, Somatics continues to report to the public, to regulatory agencies, and even to practicing physicians (Abrams and Swartz, 1988) the same approximate 100J Maximum Readout (99.4J) for its powerful Thymatron DG as that stipulated by the 1982 APA Standard (110J), and the same approximate maximum output (99.4J) as that emitted by the MECTA "C" (108J), the device used to represent conformity with the 1982 APA Standard to the FDA between 1976 and 1982. [242]

Certainly, the circa 100J redundancy via Somatics' depiction of a 99.4J maximum readout,[243] the reporting of "99.4 at 220Ω" within brochures and manuals and to the FDA, and finally the total omission of actual maximum output reporting (in terms of joules), has actively misled regulatory agencies and practicing physicians into interpreting the "99.4J at 220Ω" phrase reported by Somatics as a conditional-ER/RRC with circa 100J ceiling. In short, the Thymatron DG appears to be based on a "99.4J at 220Ω" conditional-ER/RRC, with a maximum output potential of approximately 100J in conformity with the 110J APA ceiling. [244]

Of course, to figure true maximum output from the "99.4J at 220Ω" Somatics reports for its second generation Thymatron DG, we must utilize--not the false 220Ω constant employed for the machine's readouts, resulting in a maximum readout of 99.4J--but the actual maximum Machine Impedance of 555.5Ω. Fortunately, unlike MECTA, Somatics provides the 555.5Ω maximum Impedance figure making manual calculation possible. Manual calculation is necessary, moreover, in that Somatics interprets its reported "99.4J at 220Ω" phrase, as noted, not as the expected conditional-ER/RRC with 99.4J ceiling (conforming to the APA 110J ceiling), but as a Pure-ER/RRC to maximum machine Impedance (555.5Ω) absent the 110J APA ceiling stipulation. As such, Somatics (and other BP manufacturers) wholly and surreptitiously surpass the 110J FDA safety ceiling, grossly surpassing minimal stimulus output.

Plugging in the maximum APA Impedance ceiling of 600Ω and the remaining maximum DG parameters into the Impedance formula for calculating EO for BP devices generally, we can (by applying Pure-ER/RRC interpretation) ascertain the potential ceiling for the DG BP device as well as second generation BP devices generally.

Expressed in an Impedance-oriented formula for deriving EO:

EO = .9 x .9 x 600Ω x 140 Pulses x .001 x 4.0 Seconds = 272J.

Expressed in a Voltage-oriented formula for deriving EO:

EO = .9 x 540 Volts x 140 Pulses x .001 x 4.0 Seconds = 272J.

Based on the Mectan Transmutation then, the new maximum potential for the DG (and other second generation BP devices) corresponds to a Pure-ER/RRC derivation of "100J at 220Ω. "

100J/220Ω = XJ/600Ω. X = 272J.

Perhaps because the IEC (international) Standard, in effect since about 1987 (and which we shall examine later) appears to have limited "ECT" devices to about 500 Volts, Somatics may have supplanted the 540 Volts (necessary to emit the full 272J potential) with a 500 Volt maximum, in turn corresponding to the 555.5Ω

---

[242] Readouts are not depicted only for the eldest, but are misrepresented for all age categories.

[243] Reverse-ER: 252J/555.5Ω = 99.4J/220Ω

[244] Machine Readouts are based on a ubiquitous false constant--220Ω Impedance; whereas Somatics actually interprets "99.4J at 220Ω" as a pure-ER/RRC to create a maximum output based on (in the case of the Thymatron DG) 555.5Ω (99.4J/220Ω = XJ/555.5Ω. X = 252J). The 110J ceiling dropped, actual maximum output has never been reported.

Impedance maximum it reports, slightly reducing maximum DG output potential from 272 to 252 maximum Joules. Thus the Thymatron DG's actual maximum output is 252 Joules:

Expressed via the Voltage-oriented formula for deriving EO on a Brief Pulse device:

EO = .9 x 500 Volts x 140 Pulses x .001 x 4 Seconds = 252J.

Expressed via the Impedance-oriented formula for deriving EO on a Brief Pulse device:

EO = .9 x .9 x 555.5Ω x 140 Pulses x .001 x 4 Seconds = 252J.

In summary then, a false constant of 220Ω is used to depict DG Machine Readouts, resulting in a maximum DG Machine Readout of 99.4J. Re-substituting the DG's actual 555.5Ω maximum Impedance in place of the misleading 220Ω constant, gives us the DG's true ceiling of 252 joules. In lieu of the apparent 1.1 MTTLOI for all age categories, the DG actually emits a 2.52 MTTLOI for all age categories. Clearly, one method is used for public reporting (as well as machine outputs reported to physicians), the other, the actual but unreported one, known only to manufacturers. It is through Pure-ER/RRC interpretation or Mectan Transmutation then, that manufacturers actually determine and enable a newer, higher, and completely unrecorded ceiling and thus a newer, higher, and completely unrecorded Multifold Threshold Titration Level Output Intensity (2.52 fold threshold) administered to all age categories.

THE THYMATRON DG continued

In conclusion, unbeknownst to any but manufacturers, the reported "99.4J at 220Ω" is actually interpreted by Somatics as a Pure-ER/RRC. Application of Pure ER/RRC is the manufacturer method used for determining actual maximum output relative to actual maximum machine Impedance of 555.5Ω resulting in an actual maximum output of 252J or a default 2.52 MTTLOI for all age levels. Machine Readouts, on the other hand, as seen above, are determined by using a false 220Ω constant for a false maximum Machine Readout of 99.4J (as well as false readouts for all other age categories).

As noted, this false constant substitution method, gives regulatory agencies, administering physicians, the public, and the media, the untrue notion that the "99.4J at 220Ω" phrase reported publicly and to the FDA for the Thymatron DG has a maximum ceiling of 99.4 absolute joules, conforming to the APA Standard of 110 maximum joules and, therefore, minimal stimulus output with BL ECT. Camouflaged, of course, is that the original APA ceiling of 110J has been entirely dropped by Somatics. Camouflaged too, the "99.4J at 220Ω" phrase reported for the DG is no longer a conditional-ER/RRC with a maximum ceiling of 110 Joules, but a Pure-ER/RRC relative to maximum machine Impedance sans the APA 110J ceiling, enabling Somatics' Thymatron DG an unreported maximum output of up to 252 maximum joules, while reporting a circa 100J maximum. In turn, the device administers an unreported 2.52 MTTLOI default with BL ECT, as noted, for all age recipients and thus a 5.04 MTTLOI default for every age recipient administered "dose-sensitive" UL ECT.

Once aware of the Pure-ER/RRC interpretation, therefore, and in spite of machine readouts, simply by setting up a Pure-ER of "99.4 Joules at 220Ω" to Somatics maximum machine Impedance of 555.5Ω, one can easily determine the DG's actual, unreported maximum output of 252 Joules.

99.4J/220Ω = XJoules/555.5Ω. X = 252J.

Incredibly, by substituting within the machine's computerized readout calculations a false constant Impedance of 220Ω for all actual Impedances, the derived Machine Readouts read by physicians and regulatory agencies fail to depict actual outputs, but rather what might be deemed "reverse-ERs" (Equivalent Ratios).

251J/555.5Ω = XJ/220Ω. X = 99.4J.

The misleading maximum Machine Readout for the Thymatron DG of "99.4J", then (as well as all other misleading readouts), as has been noted, is the direct result of supplanting the DG's actual 555.5Ω maximum Impedance (as well as all other actual Impedances) with a pseudo 220Ω constant Impedance. Thus, as has been mentioned, the DG depicts a maximum Readout of 99.4J in lieu of its actual 252J maximum.

All output readouts on the Thymatron DG, in fact, are reverse-ER outputs derived from a substituted false constant Impedance of 220Ω. These readouts, together with the 99.4J maximum readout, falsely suggest the continuation of minimal stimulus outputs in conformity with the 1982 APA Standard. Spurious machine readouts in juxtaposition to actual outputs (known only to manufacturers), is quite literally, the proverbial "double standard."

Possible Arguments

Manufacturers might argue that the allowable APA Impedance ceiling of 600Ω implies and is thus approbative of a Pure-ER/RRC and thus the utilization of outputs surpassing 100 Joules. Such, however, is not the case. While the 1982 APA Standard does indeed permit a maximum Impedance of 600Ω, overcoming Impedances even up to 600Ω need not conflict with the express 110J ceiling Standard clearly stipulated within the 1982 APA Standard (as seen earlier). Firstly, the age-related "relative constants" manufacturers use to configure their Brief Pulse devices, do not require any increase in output to induce adequate seizures regardless of circumstances. Secondly, while Impedance can increase over a series of treatments (all of which relative constant thresholds can accommodate), Impedances chiefly increase due to increases in EO. The simple solution--maintain the 110J ceiling. Thirdly, by mere reduction of ER/RRC so that Voltage can be increased, high Impedances can be overcome, as we saw earlier, without surpassing the circa 100J (or 110J) ceiling. For example, by confining the 320V MECTA "C" to a permissible "59J at 220Ω" (Food and Drug Administration, 1984, Attachment I [245]) in lieu of the APA Standard's maximum "70J at 220Ω" (Department of Health and Human Services, 1982a, A53, E20), the "C" could legally overcome Impedances up to 400Ω (in lieu of its normal 345Ω) without surpassing the 110J ceiling. [246] [247] In fact, even the much more powerful second generation BP devices, i.e. MECTA's 450V SR1 and 2 and the 500V Thymatron DG, could have overcome even very high Impedances, certainly up to 600Ω, while yet remaining within a circa 100J ceiling simply by reducing any of a number of electrical variables such as Duration and Charge. Certainly, the circa 100J ceiling could be maintained by reducing Amperage (Current), Duration, Frequency, Charge or a combination of all four. [248] Quite logically then, the APA Standard, while permitting Impedances up to 600Ω, implicitly calls for modification of electrical parameters in order to maintain its stipulated 110J ceiling insuring minimal stimulus output in all age categories.

To illustrate, the Thymatron DG could be made to overcome its maximum machine Impedance of <u>555.5Ω</u> while yet confining maximum output to 100J or less, simply by reducing Current from a constant .9 Amperes to a constant .567 Amperes. Plugging this reduced constant Amperage into the Impedance based formula below affirms the DG's capacity to simultaneously overcome a 555.5Ω Impedance while yet maintaining a 100J ceiling:

---

[245] The MECTA "C" is not actually named here. It is possible this is the MECTA "D" and that a MECTA "D-1" and "D-2" followed. Whether or not this is the later model MECTA "C" or early MECTA "D," however, is of no consequence.

[246] 70J/220Ω = 110J/XΩ; X = 345Ω.59J/220Ω = 108J/XΩ. X = 403Ω. By using a conditional ER/RRC of 59J at 220Ω, Voltage can be increased which results in overcoming higher Impedances.

[247] In fact, due the maximum parameters of the MECTA "C", the machine was forced to remain at "59J at 220Ω"in order to remain within the 110 Joule APA ceiling. .8 x .8 x <u>220Ω</u> x 140 Pulses x .0015 PW x 2.0 Seconds = <u>59.136J</u>. .8 x .8 x <u>403Ω</u> x 140 Pulses x .0015 PW x 2 Seconds = <u>108J</u>. ER = <u>59J/220Ω = 108J/403Ω</u>. In short, MECTA modified the "C" for the FDA in order overcome higher Impedances and remain in conformity to the APA Standard. See section on the 1982 APA Standard.

[248] Of course, while the potential exists, MECTA second generation BP devices do not actually incorporate incrementally reduced Duration or Frequency (or Amperage) to compensate for increasing Voltages and thus, do not maintain a 100 or 110 Joule ceiling. However, in that Machine Readouts are misleadingly limited to circa 100J maximums on second generation BP devices, there is reason to suspect, particularly in light of FDA commentary within 510K pre-market applications, that FDA officials (and other regulatory bodies) assumed such devices were indeed limited to 100 or 110J and consequently, that the reported "100J at 220Ω" phrase was somehow incorporative of the 1982 APA ceiling standard of 110 maximum Joules. In short, "100J at 220Ω" was assumed to be a conditional-ER/RRC with 110J ceiling yet intact.

EO = **.567 Amperes** x .567 Amperes x 555.5Ω x 140 Pulses x .001 Pulse Width x 4 Seconds = 100 Joules.

Note that with this Amperage, Voltage is also modified, neither of which mathematically affects overcoming the DG's 555.5Ω maximum Impedance.

EO = **315V** x **.567A** x 140 Pulses x .001 PW x 4.0 Secs = **100J**.

In short, simply by reducing the DG's Constant Current from .9 Amperes to .567 Amperes, both a 100J ceiling and the DG's capacity to overcome a 555.5Ω Impedance can be maintained.

Another, perhaps more practical example in which neither Voltage nor Current need be decreased, is the simple reduction of Duration. For instance, maximum **Duration** (in lieu of Amperage) could be reduced from the DG's current 4.0 Second maximum (for one hundred year old recipients) to 1.587 Seconds. In this case too, (and without reducing the DG's .9 Ampere constant current) the DG's maximum Impedance of 555.5Ω can be mathematically overcome without surpassing 100 Joules:

EO = .9 Amperes x .9 Amperes x 555.5Ω x 140 Pulses x .001 Pulse Width x **1.587 Secs Duration** = **100 Joules**.

Note then, that neither Voltage nor Amperage need be reduced.

EO = **500V** x **.9 Amperes** x 140 Pulses x .001 Pulse Width x **1.587 Secs Duration** = **100 Joules**.

Perhaps even more practically, **Frequency** (number of pulses) might be reduced. Here again, even at maximum DG Voltage (for the 100 year old recipient), simply by reducing the number of pulses from **140** to **56**, the maximum Impedance of 555.5Ω can again be overcome without surpassing the circa 100J ceiling:

EO = .9 Amperes x .9 Amperes x 555.5Ω x **56 Pulses** x .001 Pulse Width x 4.0 Seconds = **100 Joules**.

Note in this instance, how Amperage, Voltage, and even Duration all remain unaltered:

EO = **500V** x **.9 Amperes** x **56 Pulses** x .001 Pulse Width x 4.0 Seconds = **100 Joules**.

In conclusion, all current age-relevant Impedances could be overcome to induce adequate convulsions with the DG in every age category without violating the APA ceiling Standard of 110 maximum Joules (Department of Health and Human Services, 1982a, p. A53) or minimal stimulus in any age category. Succinctly, the 600Ω maximum Impedance allowed under the 1982 APA Standard in no way countermands the mandatory 110J ceiling found within the same Standard. Reducing any number of electrical parameters in order to maintain the 110J ceiling is thus clearly implicit within the 1982 APA Standard. Plainly, no conflict need arise in terms of the (APA) Standard's maximum allowable 600Ω Impedance and its stipulated EO ceiling (for BP devices) of 110 maximum Joules. In spite of such obvious measures to assure minimal stimulus as promised by the APA Standard, however, extant American manufacturers of second generation BP devices--MECTA and Somatics--failing to modify their devices in any of the above manners, grossly enhance EO in order to increase MTTLOI.

But even more unforgivable is the simple fact that Impedances rise directly due to increased electrical output. By simply maintaining the EO ceiling of 110J along with uniform, gradationally reduced outputs for younger and younger recipients, maximum Impedances rarely, if ever, surpass 450Ω. In Weiner's own words, within the 1982 ECT Task Force Report containing the 1982 APA Standard itself:

> Using a pulse device, the [APA] Task Force [1978] has determined that only 0.6% of seizure thresholds were greater than 70 Joules and that none were greater than 100 Joules. (Department of Health and Human Services, 1982a, p. A53)

Thus, while manufacturers rationalize the need for higher and higher electrical outputs, the simple truth is, while higher electrical outputs are needed to make the device "work," higher electrical outputs are not needed to induce adequate convulsions. Plainly then, and the thesis of this manuscript, second generation Brief Pulse devices are not "ECT" devices at all, but ENR (Electro Neuro-transmission Reduction) devices, machines dependent upon high electrical dosages of electricity most likely to deliberately short circuit or disable a certain percentage neurotransmitters in order to reduce the number of transmissions in the recipient's left prefrontal lobe as permanently as or for as long a period as possible. Indeed it is only from the destruction of tens of thousands of neural transmitters that an effect is observed.

Unforgivably then, not only do MECTA and Somatics ignore the APA Standard's 110J ceiling constraint, but both MECTA and Somatics continue to depict maximum output readouts of circa 100 maximum Joules for their second generation BP devices. This spurious feat, achieved through the utilization of a false 220Ω constant (resulting in reverse-ER depictions), is blatantly deceptive. As previously noted, by employing (within the device's computer) "220Ω" as a false constant, and thus as an unchanging multiplier in lieu of actual Impedances, the Somatics DG machine, even while using all other actual machine parameters as multiplicands, manifestly depicts a false 99.4J maximum output while actually surpassing the 100J mark some 2.5 fold (252J). [249] Somatics' practice of reporting an unexplicated "99.4J at 220Ω" phrase along with the machine's maximum output readout of 99.4J for its Thymatron DG plainly connotes a false adherence to the APA Standard, and thus a false adherence to minimal stimulus output. To be clear, even as the Thymatron DG portrays a maximum 99.4J readout, the machine is actually emitting an unreported 252J maximum at an actual 555.5Ω maximum Impedance. There are no actual reductions of electrical parameters to maintain an actual 99.4J or even 110J ceiling to avoid cognitive dissonance. In short, a 99.4J Readout appears in place of the 252 Joules actually being emitted for the 100 year old recipient in order to cover up actual output. Moreover, similarly false EO readouts (in joules) appear in all other age categories. Via the unexplained transmutation from conditional-ER/RRC to Pure-ER/RRC, that is, from a 110J APA ceiling seemingly corroborated by circa 100J readout maximums supplanting hidden outputs up to 252 and 259 joules respectively, Somatics and MECTA utilize a Double Standard of reporting, similar to keeping two sets of books. Briefly then, the Somatics DG renders the impression of adherence to the APA ceiling Standard, even while grossly violating it. [250]

Somatics Creates New Parameter Ceilings

As noted, by transitioning to a circa "100J at 220Ω" Pure-ER/RRC [251] and thus ironically ignoring the APA 110J ceiling, Somatics was able to increase the DG's electrical energy output from a 1.1 MTTLOI (see the MECTA C) to an unreported 2.52 MTTLOI (via the utilization of 252 maximum Joules). [252] The enhancement occurred even while simultaneously reporting (via Reverse ER) what appears to be the same circa 100J ceiling utilized by the DG's predecessor, the 108J MECTA "C. " The MECTA "C," of course, actually did remain within the 110J ceiling specified within the 1982 APA Standard and as such was the last true minimal stimulus output Brief Pulse device, in essence, the last of the "ECT" devices (Department of Health and Human Services,

---

[249] Reverse-ER = **251J/555.5Ω** = **99.4J/220Ω**. A 99.4J maximum is reported by Somatics for the DG and DGx via maximum machine readouts.

[250] While 252J is not utilized in every instance, of course, the overall power increase is distributed amongst all ages in order to increase the uniform titration level to 2.52 fold threshold at every age level. Outputs at every age level, moreover, are misreported via machine readouts.

[251] Reporting what was actually a circa 100 Joule ER (via machine readouts) in lieu of 100 or 110 absolute Joules meant manufacturers no longer reduced electrical parameters in order to maintain the 110 Joule ceiling. The unauthorized change was never reported.

[252] While the DG can emit 252 maximum Joules, the new potential ceiling, based on the unexplained pure-ER of 100 Joules at 220 to an unreported 600Ω maximum Impedance is actually 273 Joules (100J/220Ω = XJ/600Ω. X = **273J**). Thus 273 Joules became the new unreported and unauthorized maximum ceiling. American manufacturers of second generation BP devices, MECTA and Somatics, had covertly transmuted the 110J ceiling depicted in the 1982 APA Standard assuring minimal stimulus to all age recipients to a newer unreported ceiling of 273 Joules or a 2.73 MTTLOI for every age category.

1982a, p. A53; G3-G4). The invisible transmutation from a "70J at 220Ω" conditional-ER/RRC with 110J ceiling to a circa "100J at 220Ω" unexplicated Pure-ER/RRC, newly limiting MECTA and Somatics second generation BP devices only to maximum machine Impedance or the maximum APA Impedance of 600Ω (in lieu of the 110J ceiling), meant BP devices were no longer confined to minimal stimulus (1.1 MTTLOI) or 110 Absolute Joules. Conversely, as noted, the transmutation actually raised the ceiling to a never before reported 273J maximum. From about the year 1984 to about the year 1995, therefore, the math product of the maximum electrical parameters used for made-for-America second generation BP devices was no longer limited to 110 Joules, but to a new, invisible, and unreported maximum output of 273 Joules. [253] [254]

It is by utilizing a false constant Impedance of "220Ω" to derive and depict machine readouts then,[255] that the reported maximum on the Thymatron DG [256] seems to be 99.4 joules. It is through the false and invisible utilization of the "220Ω" Impedance "constant" for all age categories, moreover, that the DG's false 99.4 Joule product is depicted as the DG's "maximum Machine Readout. " To derive the DG's actual unreported maximum output of 252 Joules, as previously stated, one must manually re-multiply the machine's actual parameters not by the 220Ω false constant Impedance invisibly programmed into Somatics' computer, but, by its actual maximum Impedance of 555.5Ω. Only in this manner is the DG's actual 252J ceiling revealed. The same principle applies to all other age categories, that is, to discover actual age-related outputs, one must manually plug in actual age-related Impedances in lieu of the uniformly false 220Ω "constant" used for deriving all machine readouts on the DG. Utilizing the Impedance formula for obtaining output, then, we can see how Somatics uses a double standard, one based on the misleading 220Ω constant for deriving pseudo outputs up to 99.4J for reporting and readout purposes, and a second based on actual Impedances up to 555.5Ω for deriving the DG's actual maximum outputs with respect to age of up to 252 joules:

1) Reported (ER) EO = *.9 Amperes* x *.9 Amperes* x **220Ω** x *140 Pulses* x *.001 Pulse Width* x 4.0 *Seconds* = **99.4/7J**.

2) Unreported (Actual) EO = *.9 Amperes* x *.9 Amperes* x **555.5Ω** x *140 Pulses* x *.001 Pulse Width* x 4.0 *Seconds* = **252J**.

All machine readouts up to the "99.4J maximum" output (rounded down from "99.7J" [257]) reported by Somatics to administering physicians via machine readouts are but reverse-ERs or "paper outputs" (based upon a uniformly false 220Ω Impedance) as opposed to actual outputs based on actual Impedances. In lieu of an actual 252 Joules at the actual maximum machine Impedance of 555.5Ω seen below, the machine reads out 99.4 Joules. 99.4J of course, is but a reverse-ER "maximum. "

252/555.5Ω = **XJ**/220Ω = **X = 99.4/7J**.

In summary then, via an unexplicated Pure-ER/RRC interpretation of Somatics' reported "99.4J at 220Ω" for its second generation Thymatron DG in conjunction with a multitude of machine readouts which are actually

---

[253] Based on a false 220Ω maximum, maximum Energy Output appears to equal 100 Joules (EO = .9 Amperes x .9 Amperes x 220Ω x 140 Pulses x .001 Pulse Width x 4.0 = ***100 Joules***). Based on actual Impedance, EO could soar as high as 273 Joules. (EO = .9 Amperes x .9 Amperes x 600Ω x 140 Pulses x .001 Pulse Width x 4.0 = ***273 Joules***). What was actually reported as maximum then, was not actual output but a reverse-ER: 273J/600Ω = ***100J***/220Ω.

[254] In the case of the actual Thymatron DG, the output product of the misleading 220Ω constant multiplied by all other maximum parameters = ***99.7J.*** Substituting in the actual maximum Machine DG Impedance of 555.5Ω (in place of 220Ω), the device emits an actual 252J. EO = .9 Amperes x .9 Amperes x 220Ω x 140 Pulses x .001 Pulse Width x 4.0 = 99.7 Joules. EO = .9 Amperes x .9 Amperes x 555.5Ω x 140 Pulses x .001 Pulse Width x 4.0 = 252 Joules. We see that the EO reported for the 100 year old recipient is but the reverse-ER of actual maximum output at actual maximum Impedance: ***252J***/555.5Ω = ***99.7J***/220Ω.

[255] All the output readouts (in Joules) are misleading.

[256] Reported maximum parameters are actual with the exception of EO in Joules and the "220Ω from which the false maximum output is derived. Through readouts then, manufacturers falsely report a maximum of approximately 100J. In short, while a true maximum Impedance of 555.5Ω is reported, an invisible 220Ω is utilized to derive the reported maximum output of circa 100J. All other reported outputs for remaining age categories are similarly derived.

[257] Somatics actually reports "99.4J at 220Ω." The more accurate figure appears to be "99.7J at 220Ω." In that the difference is negligible, the author uses the two phrases interchangeably.

Reverse-ERs, that is, outputs based on a false 220Ω Impedance, makers of the Thymatron DG device intimate a maximum output of 99.4J while, in fact, the machine emits an unreported maximum of 252 Joules. [258] Additionally misleading, is that although "99.4/7J at 220Ω" is the Reverse-ER (Reverse-Equivalent Ratio) of "252J at 555.5Ω" (252J at 555.5Ω = 99.7J at 220Ω) and that the hidden 220Ω "constant" is used to calculate the 99.4/7J readout maximum, all other DG parameters--Amperage, Frequency, Pulse Width, Duration, and even maximum Impedance (though not used to calculate the machine's readouts)--are reported factually. The result, as we have witnessed, is that the 99.4/7 Joule readout maximum appears accurate. This deceptive method of reporting which, once again, the author has deemed, "the Mectan Transmutation," facilitates the appearance, as has been noted, of a circa 100J maximum output in accordance with the APA Standard, while simultaneously enabling the device to emit an unreported 252 Joule maximum or a 2.52 MTTLOI default in all age categories. As such, second generation BP devices appear first generation BP devices.

Actual maximum parameters for the Somatics' Thymatron DG, the .9 Ampere constant current, the maximum 140 Pulses (70 hertz), the maximum .001 Second PW (Pulse Width), the maximum 4.0 Seconds Duration, and the maximum Impedance of 555.5Ω, all factual DG calibrations, are provided (though not utilized by Somatics to calculate machine readout depictions). The 252J maximum, of course, has never been reported; in fact, it has been supplanted by the 99.4/7J Readout maximum. In conclusion, the unexplained pure-ER/RRC interpretation of the reported "99.4/7J at 220Ω" phrase[259] for the second generation Thymatron DG, allows a maximum output--not of the 99.4/7 maximum DG Readout derived from a false 220Ω Impedance)--but of 252 unreported Joules.

(ER) 99.4/7J/220Ω = **XJ/555.5Ω. X = 252J (Actual)**.

The Average Deception

If put to it, manufacturers might attempt to explain the Mectan Transmutation in terms of the APA Standard the following way. "All maximum machine parameters multiplied by an average 220Ω must not surpass 100 Joules." [260] But declaring that machines must not surpass 100J based on a "220Ω average" (in lieu of actual maximum Impedance) is simply a clever way of saying the devices must no longer remain limited to the 110J APA ceiling the Standard clearly specifies, but to a 100J ***mean***. A 100J "average can in no way be likened to a 110J ceiling. Indeed, the Pure-ER/RRC interpretation of "100J at 220Ω" comprising the Mectan Transmutation entirely suppresses maximum output which manufacturers then fail to report. Clearly, it is only by multiplying actual maximum parameters by actual maximum Impedances (i.e.555.5Ω) that we obtain factual maximum outputs--no longer of 110 Joules, for example, but of the DG's 252J maximum (99.7J/220Ω = 252J/555.5Ω).

Moreover, by using manufacturers' creative method of limiting maximum parameters to a (math) product of circa 100 Joules by using a 220Ω average, all parameters (i.e. Frequency, Pulse Width and Duration) dramatically increase compared to the MECTA C. This is clearly because maximum EO is allowed to grossly surpass the 110J ceiling specified in the APA Standard. In fact, age related outputs are no longer proscribed to a just above threshold 1.1 MTTLOI, but a 2.52 MTTLOI in all age categories, circa 2.5 times threshold in all age categories.

Once again then, circa "100J at 220Ω" is but an ER output at an ER Impedance, in short, a reverse ER/RRC (252J/555.5Ω = 99.7J/220Ω). Multiplying a 220Ω Impedance average with multiplicands, i.e. the DG's .9 **actual** Amperes, 140 **actual** Pulses, its .001 **actual** Pulse Width, and 4.0 Second maximum **actual** Duration misleadingly results in a "maximum" output of 99.4/7J. But 99.4/7J, of course, is but an ER. Actual maximum

---

[258] In a few age categories, those utilizing less than 220Ω, outputs are slightly over-reported. In any case, the overall effect is that the machine appears to remain under 100 maximum Joules maintaining the ongoing illusion of minimal stimulus.

[259] The Thymatron DG in Somatics 1988 *ECT Instruction Manual* is misleadingly reported thusly: "Energy: at 220 ohm impedance: 4.97J to 99.4J" (Abrams and Swartz 1988). The misleading 99.4J at 220Ω phrase reported by Somatics is in actuality, a Reverse-ER. The device actually emits a 252J maximum output at 555.5Ω.

[260] Several formulas are workable; for instance, EO = Current Squared x Impedance (220Ω) x PW x Duration = 100 Joules maximum. EO = Current x Voltage x Impedance (220Ω) x PW x Duration = 100 Joules maximum. EO = Charge x Current x Impedance (220Ω) = 100 Joules maximum.

output--252 Joules--can only be determined, once again, by using the DG's actual maximum Impedance of 555.5Ω which in turn determines the actual MTTLOI delivered by any particular BP device. [261]

Reported EO Maximum = *.9 Amperes* x *.9 Amperes* x **220Ω** x *140 Pulses* x *.001 Pulse Width* x 4.0 *Seconds* = **99.7 Joules**. [262]

Actual EO Maximum = *.9* x *.9* x **555.5Ω** x *140 Pulses* x *.001* x 4.0 *Seconds* = **252 Joules.**

252J ÷ 100J = **2.52 MTTLOI**.

In short, while none of the above actual maximum parameters used in conjunction with the misleading 220Ω "average" can exceed a circa 100J product,[263] it is only by utilizing the actual maximum machine Impedance (for the DG) of 555.5Ω that the actual maximum output of 252 Joules can be derived and so the all-important MTTLOI.

Finally, in that 220Ω is but a Pure ER-Impedance, the 99.4/7J maximum Somatics reports via Machine Readouts, is but an ER-output or what might be described as a Reverse-ER (to actual maximum output at actual maximum Impedance). Thus, in reporting "99.4J at 220Ω" as well as depicting a maximum machine Readout of 99.4J, Somatics is reporting not an actual maximum output of 99.4 Joules, but a Pure-99.4J Reverse-ER maximum, in essence, what might loosely amount ot all outputs averaged.

252 Joules/555.5Ω = **X Joules**/220Ω. **X = 99.4/7 Joules**

Only by juxtaposing the Pure-ER phrase ("**99.4J** at 220Ω") with the actual maximum output at the actual maximum Impedance (of 555.5Ω"), can we see both the Reverse-ER nature of Somatics' reporting system and derive the DG's actual maximum output. Indeed, it is only by flipping the Reverse ER that we can manually derive and see the true unreported maximum output of 252 actual Joules for the Thymatron DG.

99.4/7 Joules/220Ω = **X Joules**/555.5Ω. **X = 252 Joules**

Thus, the Mectan Transmutation transmutes what was an actual circa "100 Joule" APA ceiling (110J) into a circa "100J" ER output (or "average") enabling not only a dramatic increase in ancillary parameters for second generation BP devices (such as Pulse Width, Duration, Hertz, Charge etc.) but a grossly enhanced and unreported energy output ceiling. [264] The purpose of this method is obvious--1) to escalate the 1.1 MTTLOI of the APA Standard to a circa 2.5 MTTLOI for each individual recipient, and 2) to do so secretly. Amazingly, like the power of Bilbo Baggins' ring in *Lord of the Rings*, the transmutation from an actual circa 100J ceiling (under the 1982 APA Standard) into an unexplained 100J ER, renders actual power invisible.

Thc "100J" ER

More simply, the new and furtive Pure-ER/RRC interpretation of the circa phrase "100J at 220Ω" along with the dropping of the 110J ceiling meant that output for each age group could be newly increased via new default

[261] Variations of the alternative parameters are of course permitted--so long as the multiplication of these parameters with 220Ω does not supersede 100 maximum Joules (but which is actually but an unreported ER to the actual output). In any case, finding an average maximum output is wholly deceptive.

[262] 99.7 Joules is--perhaps due to rounding--depicted as 99.4 Joules by Somatics. The difference is negligible.

[263] While some other manipulation of the actual parameters could occur, that is, varying combinations of Pulse Width, Duration , etc., the total EO cannot exceed 100J. Even so, it is but the pure-ER of "100 Joules at 220Ω" against the actual machine Impedance maximum that true maximum EO can be derived.

[264] While Somatics Thymatron DG device emits a maximum of 252 Joules, the actual general maximum "allowed" under the Mectan Transmutation of the APA Standard, is 273J.100J/220Ω = XJ/600Ω. X = 273J. Compared to the APA's 110J ceiling, 273J represents an enormous increase in output. The invisible purpose of this enhanced output is to accommodate enhanced suprathreshold dosing for all age categories (Beale et al., 1994).

outputs. In the case of the Thymatron DG, this meant a 2.52 MTTLOI as opposed to a 1.1 MTTLOI for every age category. For instance, a 40 year old person with an Impedance of about 160Ω, who seizes at about 16J can be administered about 17.6 Joules (16J x 1.1 = 17.6J) under the 1.1 MTTLOI allowed by the 1982 APA Standard. Under manufacturers new Pure-ER/RRC interpretation, the same 40 year old under the Mectan Transmutation could now be administered 2.52 fold 16.0 Joules (16 x 2.52) or about 40 maximum Joules. In short, under a Pure-ER/RRC interpretation of circa "99.4/7J at 220Ω," the 40 year old now receives a default output of about 40 Joules on the Thymatron DG as opposed to the previous APA maximum of about 17.6J, about (40J ÷ 17.6J = 2.27) 2.3 fold that allowed under the APA Standard.

Thus, under a conditional-ER/RRC of circa "100J at 220Ω," that is, with the 110J ceiling intact, the default output for the 40 year old is about that of the MECTA "C." Moreover, this 2.3 fold increase, this holds true for every other age recipient as well. It should again be pointed out that, except for the oldest recipient, simply finding an ER output based on "100J at 220Ω" at varying age Impedances is insufficient to determine specific default outputs. Instead, we must first determine actual maximum machine output which for the DG is circa (99.4J/220Ω = XJ/555.5Ω =) 252J and so a (252J ÷ 100J =) 2.52 MTTLOI for every age category which we discover by multiplying 2.52 by threshold constants.

In short, the default output depends entirely upon maximum machine output from which we can then determine the critically important uniform MTTLOI administered to every recipient for each particular device. "Pure" then, under the Mectan Transmutation, refers only to the derivation of maximum output, no longer a set or conditional ceiling of 110J, but now derived from maximum machine Impedance alone (i.e. 99.4/7J/220Ω = ***252J***/555.5Ω) in turn from which we can determine the new uniform MTTLOI (i.e. 2.52 fold) for all age recipients by dividing by 100J. This contrasts with the "Conditional-ER/RRC" or clear 110J ceiling stipulation mandated within the 1982 APA Standard, limiting all recipient outputs to a 1.1 MTTLOI ceiling.

The most important change from Conditional to Pure-ER/RRC, therefore, is the increase in maximum output (in joules) in that it is maximum output which determines the uniform MTTLOI applied to all age categories. In short, it is the uniform MTTLOI multiplied by age-related relative threshold constants which gives the Brief Pulse machine its degree of power or output. Specifically, a Brief Pulse machine based on a 1.1 MTTLOI wherein the ten year old receives 1.1 Joules and the 100 year old receives 110 Joules is far less powerful than a Brief Pulse device based on a 2.52 MTTLOI wherein the ten year old receives 2.52 joules and the 100 year old 252 joules. In effect, the maximum 110J maximum output for the 100 year old based on the APA Standard's conditional-ER/RRC of "70J at 220Ω" with 110J ceiling and thus a 1.1 MTTLOI administered to all age categories uses far less output and is thus far less dangerous than the 252J maximum output administered to the same the 100 year old recipient. The latter, of course, is based on a Pure-ER/RRC of 99.4/7J at 220Ω with a 555.5Ω maximum Impedance and thus a (99.4J/220Ω = 252J/555Ω; 252J ÷ 100J =) 2.52 MTTLOI administered to all age recipients. The former is based on a Conditional ER/RRC with a 110J ceiling. In both cases, the uniform MTTLOI for all age categories means that outputs rise relative to increasing age and fall relative to decreasing age. However, under the new Mectan Transmutation as opposed to the APA Standard,[265] all outputs educed by the DG are based upon a much higher 2.52 MTTLOI as opposed to the 1.1 MTTLOI indirectly identified by the APA Standard. In sum, the DG is about 2.3 times more powerful and emits about 2.3 times the electrical energy in all age categories as that allowed by the 1982 APA Standard (2.52 ÷ 1.1 = 2.3). Critically then, the APA Standard limits output to ECT or just above seizure threshold, whereas, the Mectan Transmutation allows ENR, output well above seizure threshold. ECT is based on adequate convulsion; ENR is based on adequate amounts of electricity well above seizure threshold.

Figuring the MTTLOI

Default outputs for a particular BP device cannot be figured by either Conditional or Pure-ER/RRC alone,[266] but by the machine's maximum output from which we obtain the uniform MTTLOI for each particular Brief Pulse

---

[265] The APA Conditional-ER/RRC is actually "70J at 220Ω."

[266] "Pure" refers to the derivation of maximum output, i.e.99.4J/220Ω = 252J/555/5Ω, as opposed to "Conditional" referring to the clear 110J ceiling stipulation found in the APA Standard regardless of ER/RRC. In brief, the latter implicitly stipulates a 1.1 fold

device by dividing maximum output by 100J. To further determine specific default outputs for every age category on any particular BP device, we must have access to the relative threshold constants manufacturers use for each specific age category. Indeed, it is the MTTLOI which acts as the multiplier for each age-related relative constant. Thus, to determine a 1.08 MTTLOI for the ten year old child and the 100 year old man (for the MECTA "C" ECT device), we must multiply 1.08 x 1.0J (relative constant) for the ten year old child and 1.08 x 100J (relative constant) for the 100 year old adult. To determine a 2.52 MTTLOI for the ten year old child and the 100 year old adult (for the Thymatron DG ENR device), we must multiply 2.52 x 1.0J for the ten year old child and 2.52 x 100J for the 100 year old adult. Importantly, in that the thresholds or relative constants are already designed to emit far greater outputs than that needed to induce an adequate seizure for any age category under any circumstance, outputs exceeding these threshold constants relative to age are simply not necessary to induce adequate convulsion. While 1.1 fold the threshold output makes sense with respect to just above threshold stimulus for an ECT device, therefore, 2.52 fold threshold does not, at least if ECT is being administered. Because outputs exceeding just above threshold are known to result in increased cognitive dissonance almost certainly reflective of brain damage, we can expect manufacturers to both hide, but also to justify greater outputs than those necessary to emit adequate seizures in every age category. It should not be surprising, then, that Somatics refuses to report either the default energy outputs (joules) applied to every age category or the overall maximum energy output (joules) for its second generation Thymatron DG. In anticipating both subterfuge and justifications, we are not disappointed. In any case, it is not the pure-ER/RRC of circa "100J at 220Ω" with regard to various age-related Impedances which determines the various default outputs with respect to age, but upon the MTTLOI and unreported "relative (threshold) constants" secretly used by Brief Pulse manufacturers. Attempting to derive meaning from the Mectan Transmutation based on the circa "100J at 220Ω" Pure-ER/RRC provided, but not explained by manufacturers is not really possible. Instead, we must derive the highest machine Impedance (i.e.555Ω) in order to derive the highest machine output (i.e. 252J) divided by 100J to determine the uniform MTTLOI for that particular BP device. The MTTLOI must then be multiplied by age-related relative constants to determine the various age related default outputs for that particular Brief Pulse device. As we have discovered then, the highest output the DG delivers, 252 Joules, emitted by default to the DG's oldest recipient, the 100 year old male, must be divided by 100J to determine the DG's (252J ÷ 100J =) 2.52 MTTLOI not only for the 100 year old male, but for all other age recipients.

99.4/7J/220Ω = <u>252J</u>/555.5Ω [267]
252J ÷ 100J = 2.52 MTTLOI

Of course, the 252J emitted by default to the 100 year old male results in the 2.52 Multifold Threshold Titration Level Output Intensity (252J ÷ 100J = 2.52) which must be multiplied by each relative output constant to determine the default output at every age level. Succinctly, the default output for each age recipient is determined first by the overall maximum machine output (i.e. 252J) divided by 100J (252J ÷ 100J =) 2.52 to determine the MTTLOI which then must be multiplied by each age-related relative constant to determine default outputs in every age category for any particular device. Thus, 2.52 x 100J = default output of 252J administered to the 100 year old recipient; thus, 2.52 x 1.0J = default output of 2.52J administered the ten year old child on the Thymatron DG.

The new unexplicated Pure-ER/RRC interpretation of the DG's reported "99.4/7J at 220Ω" relative to the DG's maximum machine Impedance, 555.5Ω, newly allows (but also limits) output to 252 maximum Joules for the DG. But more importantly, the 252J maximum determines the uniform Multifold Threshold Titration Level Output Intensity (MTTLOI) of 2.52 for every age category for this particular Brief Pulse device. The MTTLOI then becomes the multiplier (with respect to relative threshold output constants) to determine the default output administered to every age category for any particular BP device.

---

threshold output in all age categories or minimum stimulus, whereas the latter, in the instance of the DG based on a 99.4/7J at 220Ω "Pure ER/RRC" and a 555.5Ω maximum Impedance permits a multifold threshold output of 2.52 fold in every age category.

[267] Theoretically, a Pure-ER/RRC of circa "100J at 220Ω" based upon 600Ω (maximum allowable APA Impedance) for the 100 year old male is 2.73.100J/220Ω = 273J/600Ω.273J ÷ 100J = 2.73 or a maximum 2.73 MTTLOI for all age categories.

Default Outputs Derived from the 1982 APA Standard vs Default Outputs for the Second Generation Thymatron DG

As we can see from the two tables below, MTTLOIs newly jumped from the APA's 1.1 fold threshold output limit for all age categories (to which the MECTA "C" ECT device adhered) to an unreported 2.52 fold threshold delivered to all age categories by the "new and improved" second generation Thymatron DG ENR device.

1982 APA Standard

AGE	Threshold Constants		Maximum MTTLOI Allowed	Max. Output Allowed per Age Category
10	1.0		x 1.1	1.1 Joules
20	4.0		x 1.1	4.4 Joules
30	9.0		x 1.1	9.9 Joules
40	16.0		x 1.1	17.6 Joules
50	25.0		x 1.1	27.5 Joules
60	36.0		x 1.1	39.6 Joules
65	42.25		x 1.1	46.5 Joules
70	48.97		x 1.1	53.9 Joules
80	64.0		x 1.1	70.4 Joules
90	81.0		x 1.1	89.1 Joules
100	100.0		x 1.1	110.0 Joules

ECT Device (adequate convulsion)

Second Generation Thymatron DG--Mectan Transmutation

AGE	Threshold Constants		MTTLOI	Default Output Emitted per Age Category
10	1.0		x 2.52	2.52 Joules
20	4.0		x 2.52	10.08 Joules
30	9.0		x 2.52	22.68 Joules
40	16.0		x 2.52	40.32 Joules
50	25.0		x 2.52	63.00 Joules
60	36.0		x 2.52	90.72 Joules
65	42.25		x 2.52	106.50 Joules
70	48.97		x 2.52	123.40 Joules
80	64.0		x 2.52	161.28 Joules
90	81.0		x 2.52	204.12 Joules
100	100.0		x 2.52	252.00 Joules

ENR Device (adequate electricity)

Why Indirectly Report Maximum Output in Terms of Equivalent Ratio (ER) Only?

As noted above, with the exception of EO and Voltage, Somatics openly reports maximum electrical parameters for its Thymatron DG. For example, Somatics reports the DG's maximum parameters as .9 Amperes, 140 Pulses, a .001 Second Pulse Width, and 4.0 Seconds Duration. Somatics even reports the maximum Impedance the machine is capable of overcoming at 555.5Ω. Only maximum EO and Voltage are not reported. On the other hand, we can now understand that it is maximum EO from which we can obtain the never reported, but uniform and little understood MTTLOI--the most critically important measure of a Brief Pulse device. In fact, no "ECT" device company reports MTTLOI or "relative threshold constants. " What Somatics (as well as other American BP manufacturers) emphasizes in the reporting of its second generation BP device is the circa "100J at 220Ω" phrase, specifically "99.4 Joules at 220Ω" for the Thymatron DG. While the reporting of this phrase might be useful should purveyors understand it to be a Pure-ER/RRC (allowing 252 Joules) rather than a Conditional-ER/RRC (limited by 100 or 110 maximum Joules), there is no logical reason for Somatics' withholding of either simple maximum output (or simple maximum Voltage). Moreover, by not clarifying its reported "99.4J at 220" phrase as a Pure-ER/RRC from which we can derive the new (unreported) maximum output of 252 Joules newly based on maximum machine Impedance, machine readouts limited to 99.4J leaves purveyors with the distinct impression (via Conditional-ER/RRC interpretation) that the APA maximum output of 110 Joules continues to remain intact. In fact, the strong suggestion is that the machine's maximum output is 99.4 Joules (seemingly corroborated by the machine read-outs) and thus the looked for minimum stimulus output in all age categories of about 1.0 MTTLOI. The impression, as already noted, is clearly strengthened by Machine Readouts depicting 99.4 Joules as maximum output, depictions observed by physicians, depictions seemingly corroborative of a circa 100J ceiling. To highlight the absurdity of Somatics' reporting what appears to be a Conditional-ER/RRC of "99.4J at 220Ω" with a 100 or 110J ceiling, let us portray the only other unreported maximum parameter—Voltage--in like manner.

Using Ohm's Law to express the ER/RRC phrase "99.7J at 220Ω" [268] in terms of Voltage, we can first determine that at 220Ω, the Thymatron DG seems to utilize approximately 198 Volts.

Ohm's Law: <u>Voltage = Current x Impedance</u>. .9A x 220Ω = <u>198 Volts</u>.

In fact, the actual Voltage emitted at an actual 220Ω by the Thymatron DG, is <u>198V</u> - or - literally, <u>198 Volts at 220Ω</u>. The actual correlation of <u>198V at 220Ω</u> can be confirmed by referring to the Detailed Chart of the Thymatron DG in this manuscript. [269] "198V" is thus the equivalent of "220Ω. " Not surprisingly, therefore, just as 99.7J is not emitted at 220Ω, neither is 99.7J emitted at 198V. Rather, it is 40J which is emitted at 220Ω, just as it is 40J which is emitted at 198V.

Neither is it surprising that using all maximum parameters, we can plug in the spurious 198V figure (in lieu of the spurious 220Ω figure), but this time into the Voltage-oriented formula: (<u>EO = Current x Voltage x Pulses x Pulse Width x Duration</u>) to obtain the same spurious <u>99.7J</u> figure as that obtained with the spurious 220Ω figure when using the Impedance-oriented formula: <u>EO = Amperage x Voltage x Pulses x PW x Duration</u>.

Voltage-oriented formula:
EO = .9 Amperes x <u>**198 Volts**</u> x 140 Pulses x .001 PW x 4.0 Seconds =
<u>**99.7 Joules**</u>. [270]

Impedance-oriented formula:
EO = .9 Amperes x .9 x <u>**220Ω**</u> x 140 Pulses x .001 PW x 4.0 Seconds =
<u>**99.7 Joules**</u>.

By supplanting 220Ω with 198V, in short, we can newly express the DG's misleadingly reported ER/RRC of "<u>99.7J at **220Ω**</u>" as "<u>99.7J at **198 Volts**</u>. "

Like the "99.7J at 220Ω" Pure-ER/RRC phrase then, we can similarly see (from consulting the chart below) that only 40J is emitted at 198V (just as only 40J is emitted at 220Ω). Once again, this is because at this age level (about 40 years of age with a threshold of about 16J) it is 40 Joules--not 99.7 Joules--which conforms to the DG's 2.52 MTTLOI (2.52 x 16J = 40J). In either case, however, that is, using either a 220Ω or 198V ER as the multiplier in conjunction with all other parameters but at actual maximums, a spurious 99.7 Joules is derived (See formulas above). Thus, either 198 Volts or 220 Ohms can be used as a false constant (or "average") for deriving the circa 100J maximum (which as before, is actually only an ER or "average").

---

[268] 99.7 Joules is more accurate than Somatics' reported 99.4 Joules.

[269] From the Detailed Chart, we can see the Thymatron DG utilizes <u>200V at 222.2Ω</u>. Setting up an ER, 222.2Ω/200V = 220Ω/XV. X = <u>198 Volts</u> (at 220Ω).

[270] <u>99.8 Joules</u> ÷ .9 Amperes x 140 Pulses x .001 Pulse Width x 4 Seconds = <u>198 Volts</u>.

In brief, a 198V false constant just like the 220Ω false constant can be plugged into the machine's computer at every age level to similarly derive false readout maximums (in all age categories) of up to 99.4J for the 100 year old recipient. Using such a false "constant," of 220Ω or 198V, therefore, results in spurious readouts for all age recipients, none greater than 99.4 Joules.

On the other hand, just as we used the DG's actual maximum Impedance of 555.5Ω to derive the actual unreported maximum output of (99.7J/220Ω = X/**555.5Ω**. X =) ***252J*** from the Pure-ER/RRC phraseology 99.7J at 220Ω we can derive the same 252J maximum from the actual maximum Voltage of 500V (**not provided by Somatics**).

99.7J/198V = **252J**/500V [271]

Critically, and in spite of machine readouts then, "99.7J at 198V" is a Pure-ER/RRC phrase as opposed to a Conditional-ER/RRC actually limiting output to 99.7J (or 99.4J). Just as the Pure-ER/RRC phrase "99.7J at 220Ω" is not a Conditional-ER/RRC actually limiting output to 99.7J (or 99.4J), neither is "99.7J at 198V" a Conditional-ER/RRC limiting output to 99.7J. Rather, "99.7J at 198V" is a Pure-ER/RRC allowing up to (99.7J/198V = XJ/500V =) 252 maximum Joules for the DG. Using the actual maximum unreported 500V then, just like actual maximum Impedance, we can derive the DG's true maximum output of (99.7J/198V = XJ/500V; X =) 252J. Similarly, of course, "198V at 220Ω" is but a Pure-ER/RRC based on a 500V maximum, just as "99.7J at 220Ω" is but a Pure-ER/RRC based on a 555.5Ω maximum, allowing a never before reported 252J DG ceiling or a 2.52 MTTLOI in all age categories. Thus, just as we must use actual maximum Impedance to derive the actual unreported maximum EO, we must use the unreported actual maximum Voltage to derive the actual unreported maximum EO.

99.7J/198V = XJ/**500V**: X = ***252J***.

99.7J/220Ω = XJ/**555.5Ω**: X = ***252J***.

Had we not understood "99.7J at 198V" to be the Pure-ER/RRC it actually is, and had the APA ER/RRC remained a Conditional ER/RRC of "70J at 220Ω" or "70J at 198V" with a 110J ceiling or even a circa 100J ceiling, we logically would have assumed "99.7J at 220" or "99.7J at 198V" a Conditional-ER/RRC with a 99.7J ceiling. Certainly, with maximum readouts depicting a 99.7J (or 99.4J) maximum we would not suspect that the 110J ceiling had, in fact, been discarded. In short, because of the 99.4J maximum machine readout, we logically assume "99.4/7J at 198V" or "99.4/7J at 220Ω" a Conditional-ER/RRC (with 110J ceiling intact) just as the APA Standard prescribes. Who could imagine the machine's computer incorporating a 198V or 220Ω false constant for all age groups to depict readouts falsely limited to 99.4 maximum Joules when, in fact, the machine emits a never before reported 252 maximum Joules? Actually limited to a circa 100 or even 110 maximum Joules, what appears to be a Conditional ER/RRC transition from "70J at 198V" to "99.4J at 198V," or "70J at 220Ω" to "99.4J at 220Ω" is inconsequential. With the DG's machine readouts depicting a 99.4 maximum, read by the administering physician, there is simply no reason to suspect that the 1982 APA ceiling of 110J had been dropped. With no mention of the new actual maximum output of 252J, and with readouts limited to 99.4 maximum Joules, who could have imagined that the implied 1.1 MTTLOI inherent in the 1982 APA Standard had been newly transmuted to a circa 2.52 MTTLOI in every age category for what were actually second generation BP devices?

To the point then--how could physicians or regulators have identified the new maximum outputs of what were actually second generation Brief Pulse devices with readouts based on totally spurious "constants" or "averages" still suggesting minimal stimulus outputs? Are physicians and regulators really supposed to have derived actual maximum outputs having no idea that an invisible stratagem had transmuted the "100J at 220Ω" ER/RRC from conditional to pure? What clue is provided for physician or regulator that the machine readouts on what were actually second generation Brief Pulse devices were being underreported 2.5 fold? With misleading readouts absurdly derived from a hidden, moreover, false constant or "average" 220Ω for every age

---

[271] Though neither maximum Voltage nor maximum Output is provided by Somatics, fortunately, Somatics provides maximum Impedance from which we can derive actual maximum Voltage from Ohm's Law: Voltage = Current x Impedance: .9A x 555.5Ω = 500V.

group, what official could have suspected the grossly higher outputs emitted? Why indeed would physician or regulator have reason to doubt machine readouts depicting circa 100 maximum joules in accordance with the APA Standard? On the other hand, why didn't manufacturers simply provide physicians and regulators with actual machine maximums, or the 2.52 MTTLOI emitted and configured via the requisite relative constants used to build machines of specific multifold threshold characters? In fact, only with the reporting of actual maximum output (published for the first time in this manuscript) does the "99.4J at 220Ω" phrase reveal itself for what it actually is--no longer a Conditional-ER-RRC with 110J ceiling at all, but a Pure-ER/RRC relative to maximum machine Impedance grossly enhancing the Brief Pulse ceiling to 252 joules (for the DG) in order to grossly enhance the MTTLOI from 1.1 to 2.52 for every individual recipient of this device.

Why Indirectly Report Maximum Output in Terms of Equivalent Ratio (ER) Only?. . . continued

Just as the maximum output of 252J actually correlates with the actual maximum Impedance of **555.5Ω** on the DG then, so too does 252J actually correlate with **500V** (See the DG chart). Contrarily, just as 220Ω fails to actually correlate with 99.4J on the DG chart, so too does 198V fail to correlate with 99.4J on the machine (instead correlating with 40J). Consulting the Thymatron DG Detailed Chart below for actual correlations, we observe, as noted, that at 198 Volts and 220Ω, 40J--not 99.7J--is emitted. [272] Thus, except as an ER to actual maximum output at either actual maximum machine Impedance or actual maximum machine Voltage ("252J at 555Ω" and "252J at 500V"), neither the 220Ω figure nor the 198V figure (in "99.4J at 220Ω" or "99.4J at 198V" respectively) has any actual relevance to 99.4J. [273] This, as already noted, is because both 99.4J at 220Ω and 99.4J at 198V are actually Pure-ER/RRCs (Pure-Equivalent Ratios) to maximum Impedance and maximum Voltage respectively. Critically importantly to comprehend then, is that the 40J which is emitted at 220Ω and 198V--is the output needed to reach the DG's consistent 2.52 MTTLOI administered at all age levels (in this instance, for a 40 year old recipient seizing at a base 16J).

Essentially, the 2.52 MTTLOI figure administered to all age groups on the DG is derived from true maximum output as noted (administered to the 100 year old recipient) in turn derived from the circa "99.4J at 220Ω" unexplicated Pure ER/RRC relative to the actual 555.5Ω maximum Impedance (99.7J/220Ω = **252J**/555.5Ω). This maximum output is then divided as has been explained, by the constant threshold output (100 Joules) for this same 100 year old adult (252J ÷ 100J = 2.52). The derived 2.52 figure for the Thymatron DG, the MTTLOI for the 100 year old adult, thus becomes the default MTTLOI administered to all age categories.

$$99.7J/220\Omega = XJ/555.5\Omega \quad \text{Ceiling} = 252 \text{ Joules}$$

Relative Threshold Output Constant (RTOC) for a 100 year old male = 100 Joules.

$$252 \text{ Joules} \div 100J = \underline{2.52 \text{ MTTLOI}}$$

In short, it is the Pure-ER/RRC to the maximum machine ceiling at the machine's maximum Impedance capacity (of 252J at 555Ω) administered to the 100 year old adult which determines the uniform MTTLOI (i.e. 2.52 fold) and thus all default outputs for all age categories (based on relative output constants). In that it is the maximum ceiling alone which determines not only the MTTLOI for all age categories in turn determining maximum outputs for each age group (i.e. 2.52 x threshold output), knowledge of the overall maximum machine output in Joules is imperative. A ceiling of 252 Joules, as noted, permitting a 2.52 MTTLOI for the 100 year old male with a circa 100J threshold output, determines the machine's default settings based on 2.52 fold threshold constants in every age category. We must, of course, multiply 2.52 times respective threshold outputs to derive default outputs for all age recipients. But is this what physicians or regulators are expected to do in order to see just how much output is delivered to each age recipient? Why, in short, do manufacturers leave out the three most vital pieces of information--maximum output in Joules, uniform MTTLOI, and relative threshold

---

[272] Conversely, at 100J, approximately 330V (or 367Ω)--not 198V (or 220Ω)--is emitted.

[273] Consulting the Detailed Thymatron DG Chart, the DG emits 90.72 Joules at 333.3Ω and 300V. Setting up ERs, 90.72J/333.3Ω = 100J/XΩ. X = 367Ω.90.72J/300V = 100J/XV. X = 330V. Thus, the DG actually emits 100 Joules at 367Ω and 330V.

output constants--instead reporting what appears to be a conditional-ER/RRC phrase such as "99.4J at 220Ω" with skewed machine readouts based on an "average" Impedance culminating in spurious circa 100J device maximums?

The answer is painfully obvious: Not only is the unreported interpretation of the circa "100J at 220Ω" phrase as a pure-ER/RRC a clever mechanism both for secretly enhancing and furtively facilitating default outputs based on the single unreported MTTLOI for every age category, but the circa "100J at 220Ω" phrase contains the "100J" figure strongly associated with minimal stimulus output. In short, as we continuously see, the circa 100J figure is deceptively reminiscent of the proclaimed 100J minimum allegedly needed to induce adequate seizures in even the most seizure recalcitrant individuals for all age categories (Department of Health and Human Services, 1982a, p. A53). Absence of actual output reporting in Joules, the failure to report Pure-ER/RRC interpretation of circa "100J at 220Ω, the failure to report default MTTLOIs, the failure to report relative constants, the redundant use of the familiar "100J" figure within the generally reported "100J at 220Ω" phrases utilized by every American manufacturer of second generation BP devices, and finally, the false reporting of maximum output readouts culminating in a 100J maximum for every made-for-America second generation BP device, all serve as mechanisms to grossly enhance maximum output on MECTA and Somatics BP devices in order to enhance the machine's MTTLOI, even as these same mechanisms are misleadingly suggestive of the continuation of minimal stimulus in all age categories in adherence to the 1982 APA Standard.

"100J" ER Camouflage

The fact that there is no actual correlation of 99.4J and 220Ω on the Thymatron DG, and that with the appearance of the second generation BP device, Somatics and MECTA dropped the 110J ceiling, makes Somatics' (and similarly MECTA's) reporting of "99.4J at 220Ω" (in lieu of actual maximum output at actual maximum Impedance) not only confusing, but extremely misleading. Both the somewhat abstract "99.4J at 220Ω" ER/RRC reported by Somatics and Somatics' new unexplained Pure-ER/RRC interpretation seemingly patterned after the "70J at 220Ω" Conditional-ER/RRC depicted within the 1982 APA Standard, successfully camouflages the transmutational mechanism grossly enhancing maximum output and so MTTLOI in every age category. [274] Unlike the "70J at 220Ω" APA standard governed by a 110 Joule ceiling guaranteeing minimal stimulus outputs of 1.1 fold threshold (with BL ECT) in every age category, second generation BP devices based on the new circa "100J at 220Ω" Pure-ER/RRC interpretation, as we can see, are no longer circumscribed by the 110J output ceiling. Ironically, by enabling manufacturers to grossly surpass the 110J mark, the Pure-ER/RRC interpretation upon which Somatics and MECTA second generation BP devices are based, enables manufacturers to grossly surpass minimal stimulus output. In short, while the APA Standard limits output to 110 Joules and thus a 1.1 MTTLOI, second generation BP devices emit up to 272 Joules and thus a potential 2.73 MTTLOI for every age recipient. Typically, as we have observed, the second generation Somatics and MECTA machines educe a never before reported circa 2.5 MTTLOI.

The circa 100J at 220Ω phrase reported by both Somatics and MECTA, in brief, is no longer interpreted as a conditional-ER/RRC with a 100J or 110J ceiling[275] Rather the circa "100J at 220Ω" phrase, as has already been noted, is a newly engendered Pure-ER/RRC based upon maximum allowable machine Impedance up to 600Ω newly "permitting" up to 272 maximum Joules. [276] Ironically, then, the seemingly familiar "100J" figure

---

[274] The new circa "100J at 220Ω" phrase is only relevant with respect to the new manner of deducing maximum output via maximum machine Impedance. To discover outputs at any other age group, the new MTTLOI as well as the unreported threshold output constants for particular age categories must be known, figures never explained or released by any Brief Pulse manufacturer. On the other hand, simply by being informed of maximum machine output in Joules and dividing this figure by 100, one could immediately know the MTTLOI for all age categories. Instead of reporting the new ceiling both MECTA and Somatics dropped maximum output reporting altogether in lieu of the new circa "100J at 220Ω" unexplained Pure-ER/RRC phrase. Neither reported or explained MTTLOI nor did they report the dropping of the 110J ceiling.

[275] The implication that "100 Joules" is a "typical output" in that it is derived from a "typical 220Ω" is misleading. While the term "typical 220Ω" may have once depicted "mean," even this is misleading. Indeed, the equivalent 198 Volts of the DG's 500 Volt capacity, and the 220Ω of the DG's 555.5Ω capacity, make it clear that these figures no longer represent "mean" or median. They are, as has been noted, ERs to unreported maximums. Finally, on the DG machine itself, "99.4J has no actual equivalency to 220Ω.

[276] The phrase "100J at 220Ω," like "70J at 220Ω," may be an ER/RRC; however, instead of a Conditional-ER/RRC based on a 110J ceiling, "100J at 220Ω is a Pure-ER/RRC based on maximum machine Impedance. There appears to be no plausible rationale for

within the new "100J at 220Ω" phrase serves to cover up the annihilation of the familiar 110J ceiling within the APA Standard. The purpose of the APA 110J ceiling was to circumscribe maximum output to just over 100J or just over threshold for the oldest recipient and so all other age categories as well. The Thymatron DG, for example, reporting "99.4J at 220Ω," and displaying a 99.4J maximum machine readout, emits a maximum output not of 99.4J as has been noted, but of an unreported 252J while MECTA second generation BP devices, utilizing the same reporting mechanism, also display a circa 100J maximum while emitting approximately 259J as we shall momentarily examine. With the reported transition of "70J at 220Ω" to circa "100J at 220Ω" then, both companies through the invisible transition from Conditional to Pure-ER/RRC, abandon the 1.1 MTTLOI ceiling or minimal stimulus, instead implementing new unreported circa 2.5 MTTLOIs for all age recipients, 2.3 fold minimal stimulus (see Beale et al.1994).

To recap then, the interpretation of the circa "100J at 220Ω" phrase reported first by MECTA and subsequently by Somatics may best be described as the transition from a Conditional-ER/RRC with a 110J ceiling to a Pure-ER/RRC with a new ceiling based on the machine's actual maximum Impedance up to (in the case of made-for-America BP devices) 600Ω, i.e. the Thymatron DG (99.4J/220Ω = **252J**/555.5Ω). In short, the new circa "100J at 220Ω" phrase invented by MECTA in 1983 (and then adopted by other American manufacturers such as Somatics) was, unlike the previous "70J at 220Ω" conditional-ER/RRC, newly interpreted by manufacturers as a Pure-ER/RRC to a new maximum output at maximum machine Impedance. Thus, unlike the conditional "70J at 220Ω" phrase within the 1982 APA Standard, both MECTA and Somatics interpret the newer "100J at 220Ω" phrase sans any deference to the APA 110J ceiling. That is, the circa "100J at 220Ω"-ER/RRC becomes "pure"--devoid of the critically conditional 110J ceiling. In sum, the new circa "100J at 220Ω" phrase misleadingly eliminates the APA 110J upper limit and thus the original guarantee of minimal stimulus. Unlike the APA Standard, therefore, the new circa "100J at 220Ω" phrase is newly dependent for its ceiling not upon the previous 110J APA ceiling stipulation, but upon the maximum Impedance the machine is capable of overcoming (i.e. 99.4J/220Ω = ***252J***/555.5Ω). The unforgiveable failure to report the new maximum output can only be appreciated in light of the degree to which it rises to 273J along with a new maximum MTTLOI of 2.73.

As a result, the Thymatron DG, like the precedential made-for-America MECTA second generation BP devices, emits 40 Joules for the 40 year old recipient, 2.3 times higher than the first generation MECTA "C" BP device which emitted circa 17 Joules for the same 40 year old recipient (40J ÷ 17J = 2.35). Indeed, the new 40J output represents a new 2.5 MTTLOI per age recipient on second generation Somatics and MECTA BP devices as opposed to the 1.08 MTTLOI delivered by the made-for-America first generation BP devices. To be clear, then, the outputs under the new circa "100J at 220Ω" Pure-ER/RRC interpretation emit a new 2.5 MTTLOI in all age categories compared to the 1.1 MTTLOI allowed under the APA Standard. But it is only at the highest Impedance, that is, the oldest age category (on MECTA and Somatics second generation BP devices) that significance of the Pure-ER/RRC interpretation of the new circa "100J at 220Ω" is revealed, in spite of the fact that the new ceilings and consequently, new MTTLOIs are not only never reported or explained, but hidden from view via spurious machine readouts. For instance, in the case of Somatics' Thymatron DG, the output has risen from a maximum 110J ceiling to a fully unreported 252 Joule ceiling (100J/220Ω = 252J/555.5Ω) for the 100 year old recipient. In that minimum threshold to induce an adequate seizure for all 100 year old recipients is allegedly 100 Joules, it is the never reported 252J overall maximum output reflecting the new 2.52 MTTLOI applied to every age category that is the most illuminating in terms of power. It is thus remarkable that MTTLOI, the most critically important profile aspect of any Brief Pulse device, is neither discussed, nor reported, nor explained by any "ECT" device manufacturer. Indeed, as already noted, maximum output in Joules and thus MTTLOI is suppressed by manufacturers and in fact, deliberately camouflaged. In spite of its being hidden to both professionals and the public alike, however, we shall now examine in even more detail how companies such as Somatics and MECTA determine the Energy Outputs needed to evince the new circa 2.5 MTTLOI for each individual age category on their second generation BP devices.

MECTA and Somatics' using the circa phrase "100J at 220Ω," other than (1) the confusing use of the "100J" figure to create the false impression of a 100J ceiling (2) in order to cover up a new EO circa 2.5 times 100J (3) for the purpose of increasing MTTLOI for every age recipient.

CHAPTER 22

Determining EO (Joules) and MTTLOIs for Various Age Groups on Various BP Machines

Numerous new, never-before-seen tables and charts are presented in this manuscript. Specific parameters for these charts have been derived in a number of different, sometimes complicated manners. However, one simple means of deriving and confirming the numbers depicted on these charts can be found via the following method. Beale, in a 1994 study, determined that MECTA and Somatics second generation BP devices utilized circa 2.5 Multifold Threshold outputs in Charge for every age category (Beale et al.1994). Because EO thresholds per age (in Joules) are relatively constant and Charge thresholds vary (as we shall later see), in order to meaningfully contrast devices , we need to convert to Joules (as opposed to Charge) for every machine generation. Fortunately, based upon parameters provided by Somatics for its Thymatron DG---<u>Frequency</u> (Number of Pulses or Hertz x 2), Stimulus <u>Duration</u>, <u>Wave Length</u>, constant Current or <u>Amperage</u>, <u>maximum Impedance</u>, indirectly derived <u>maximum Voltage</u>, and finally <u>Charge</u> delivered, maximum EO in Joules can be accurately determined for the Thymatron DG. [277] As noted, if the second generation made-for-America Thymatron DG emits about 252 Joules maximum, and MECTA's second generation made-for-America BP devices emit about 259 Joules maximum, and if, as Beale claimed, these made-for-America second generation BP devices use circa 2.5 multifold threshold outputs for all age categories, simply by dividing 252 and 259 Joules respectively by 2.5, we should and do derive the circa 100 Joule threshold output for the 100 year old adult identified in this manuscript. (Although Beale worked in Charge, titration level via Charge here (though not always) is tantamount to titration level via EO in joules--proof of which is provided both in the footnote below and in ensuing pages [278].) This corresponds with Weiner's implied assertion within the 1982 APA Standard that no more than 100 Joules is ever needed to induce an adequate seizure in any recipient in what appears to be any treatment setting (Department of Health and Human Services, 1982a, p. A53).

Let us begin, therefore, with the simple, but paramount premise that (using BL ECT), circa 100 Joules is used as the consistent relative threshold output constant for the 100 year old adult on all modern-day BP devices. [This is conservative in that even Weiner's assertion indicates that threshold outputs for the 100 year old are almost always much less than 100 Joules (ibid).] Since maximum output is always reserved for the 100 year old adult, and in that maximum machine output can be determined by any of several formulas (provided earlier--see footnote below), we can, as noted previously, easily derive the MTTLOI administered to the 100 year old adult, as heretofore explained, simply by dividing maximum output in Joules (of any particular

---

[277] EO = Charge x Current x Impedance. EO = .504C x .9A x 555.5Ω = 252 Joules. EO = (Current squared) x Impedance x (hz x 2) x WL x Duration. EO = .9 x .9 x 555.5Ω x 140 x .001Sec. x 4.0 Seconds = 252 Joules.

[278] We know both maximum Charge and maximum EO for the 100 year old male on the Thymatron DG-- 252 Joules and 504mC respectively.504 ÷ 2.52 = 200mC.252J ÷ 2.52 = 100J. EO = Charge x Current x Impedance: 200C x .9A x 555.55Ω = 100 J. Charge = EO/Current x Impedance: 100J ÷ .9A x 555.5Ω = 200mC.252/.504C = X/.200C = 100 J.252/.504C =100J/XC = .200C.100J x 2.52 = <u>252J</u>.200mC x 2.52 = <u>504mC</u>. The same Charge/EO/Titration level relationship can be shown at any age level with any modern day BP device.

machine) by 100J. For example, for the Thymatron DG, a (252 Joules ÷ 100 Joules =) 2.52 MTTLOI is administered to the 100 year old adult. In short, the Thymatron DG delivers to the 100 year old male, 2.52 fold the amount of energy (or electricity) required to induce an adequate grand mal seizure (even at the end of a series[279]). Simply by taking 1/100th the maximum output that a machine can deliver then, for example, simply by dividing the DG's 252 Joule maximum or the MECTA SR 1 and 2 259 Joule maximums by the 100 Joule relative threshold output constant for 100 year old recipients, we can ascertain default titration levels of a 2.52 MTTLOI and 2.59 MTTLOI respectively administered by default to 100 year old adults by these specific second generation Brief Pulse devices.

Moreover, in that MECTA and Somatics BP devices are engineered to administer a consistent MTTLOI to every age recipient, we can confidently assert that the Somatics Thymatron DG machine utilizes a 2.52 MTTLOI for every individual recipient just as second generation made-for-America MECTA BP devices utilize a 2.59 MTTLOI for every age recipient. Given uniform MTTLOI consistency in all age categories, we can confirm the specific relative threshold output constants manufacturers use in each age category simply by dividing the various default outputs delivered to each age group on a particular BP device (once we have figured them), by the uniform MTTLOI utilized on that device (i.e. by 2.52 in the case of the DG). [280] Relative threshold output constants[281] (in Joules relative to age) discovered in this manner (although never before reported by any manufacturer) turn out, as implied in their namesake, to be constants,[282] or are at least treated as such by manufacturers. Relative threshold constants, as noted, are mathematically utilizable for any generation MECTA or Somatics BP device, as we shall see. Of critical importance, therefore, we must understand that manufacturers determine the output administered at each age level by multiplying these age-related relative threshold output constants by the MTTLOI determined (by manufacturers) for any particular BP device.

In sum, the maximum machine output in Joules becomes the critical parameter in that once we know the maximum EO in Joules for a given BP device, we can easily determine the uniform MTTLOI for that same device simply by dividing maximum output by 100J. From this, virtually all other electrical parameters delivered by that machine can be determined, including relative threshold output constants in Joules and default outputs actually delivered, and without which, the power and purpose of a specific Brief Pulse device becomes indiscernible.

Converting Charge in Millicoulombs to EO in Joules and Vice-Versa

As noted, maximum output for the DG is 252 Joules or a (252J ÷ 100J =) <u>2.52</u> **M**ultifold **T**hreshold **T**itration **L**evel **O**utput **I**ntensity (MTTLOI) for all age recipients. But this can also be confirmed Charge-wise. For example, the Charge output administered by the Thymatron DG (as reported by Somatics) to a 70 year old recipient is 352.8mC. Thus, threshold output in terms of Charge for the 70 year old is (352.8mC ÷ 2.52 =) 140mC. To find this in terms of Joules, we first find 70% of the maximum Voltage. .70 x 500V (maximum Voltage provided by Somatics and also determinable via Ohm's Law) = 350V used to seize the 70 year old male. EO (delivered) = Voltage x Current x (hz x 2) x WL x Duration. EO = <u>350V</u> x .9A x 140Pulses x .001Sec. x 2.8Sec = <u>123.48J</u> (delivered to the 70 year old—see chart below). Thus, 123.48J and 352.8mC is delivered to the 70 year old on the Thymatron DG. We can now determine Impedance through the formula: EO = (Current squared) x Impedance x (hz x 2) x WL x Duration. Thus, 123.48J = .9 x .9 = <u>XΩ</u> x 140 Pulses x .001 Sec. x 2.8 Sec. Impedance = <u>388.8Ω</u>. (This is also 70% of maximum Impedance: .7 x 555.5Ω = 388.8Ω.) To confirm: EO = Charge x Current x Impedance. EO = .3528C x .9A x <u>388.8Ω</u> = <u>123.45J</u>.

---

[279] This assumes 100J will seize the 100 year old in any treatment setting, i.e. the end of a treatment series. While Weiner later denies this claiming output must be increase due to rise in Impedance over a "treatment course," his initial assertion within the APA Standard contradicts his later claim. Indeed, the author's definition of a relative threshold output constant(used by BP manufacturers) is the minimum amount of electricity needed to generate an adequate seizure in a specific age category in any treatment setting. Relative threshold constants, therefore, provide much more than enough electrical output to induce adequate convulsions in typical "treatment" settings.

[280] Manufacturers may have determined these threshold outputs through trial and error.

[281] "Relative threshold output constant" is the author's nomenclature as manufacturers have never identified, revealed, or discussed their existence.

[282] Charge, now used by all BP manufacturers, the threshold outputs of which vary from machine to machine, are not suitable for comparative purposes.

Threshold output or the relative constant used for the 70 year old can be determined (in Joules) simply by dividing the 123.45J delivered to this age category by the 2.52 uniform MTTLOI. Thus, threshold output in joules for the 70 year old is (123.45J ÷ 2.52 = 48.98J =) 49J. (To confirm): 123.45J/.3528C = XJ/.140C = 49 Joules. In sum, the relative threshold output constant for a 70 year old is 49 Joules or 140mC. The Thymatron DG thus delivers a 2.52 default MTTLOI or default 123.45 Joules in EO and 352.8mC in Charge to the 70 year old recipient.

We have thus found the EO default delivered in joules and the Charge default delivered in mC to the 70 year old recipient on the DG. We can complete detailed age-related charts in this manner, for any MECTA or Somatics BP machine. Most importantly, moreover, we can comprehend the comparative power and consequently, the specific aim of any particular BP device. In short, by identifying the threshold output, that is, the relative constant in joules per age category and the actual age-related outputs delivered, we can not only determine output delivered to each age category, but the uniform MTTLOI delivered to all age categories for any specific device, and thus the power and aim of the apparatus. In sum, by discovering the specific MTTLOI the device delivers, we can understand what any specific Brief Pulse device is designed to deliver to each individual recipient. For example, the MECTA "C" is designed to deliver a 1.08 MTTLOI to all age categories while the DG is designed to deliver a 2.52 MTTLOI to all age recipients.

Converting Charge in Millicoulombs to EO in Joules Continued

Let us determine threshold output by an even simpler method from which we can easily determine Energy Output delivered in Joules or Millicoulombs in Charge for (for example) a 90 year old. [283] Charge delivered to the 90 year old--453.6mC--is provided by Somatics:

1) 453.6mC ÷ 2.52 = 180mC (Charge threshold for 90 yr. old recipients)
2) EO = Charge x Amp x Impedance:
.180C x .9A x 500Ω = 81 Joules (EO threshold for 90 yr. old recipients).
3) 81J x 2.52 = 204.12J (default DG EO delivered to 90 yr. old recipients).
4) Confirmation by ER: 204.12J/.4536C = XJ/.180C = 81J RC (Relative Constant) for the 90 year old.

Thus, given maximum machine output in Joules and then dividing by 100J, we can obtain the uniform MTTLOI used for any particular device. Given Charge delivered relative to age, Impedance to overcome relative to age, and Amperage (a constant), we can also obtain threshold outputs in Joules for every age level (see above example). These threshold outputs in Joules, as noted, turn out to be important relative constants utilized in all modern BP devices.

100 year old male = 252.00J ÷ 2.52 = ***100.00J***
90 year old male = 204.10J ÷ 2.52 = ***81.00J***
80 year old male = 161.28J ÷ 2.52 = ***64.00J***
70 year old male = 123.40J ÷ 2.52 = ***48.97J***
65 year old male = 106.47J ÷ 2.52 = ***42.25J***
60 year old male = 90.72J ÷ 2.52 = ***36.00J***
50 year old male = 63.00J ÷ 2.52 = ***25.00J***
40 year old male = 40.32J ÷ 2.52 = ***16.00J***
30 year old male = 22.68J ÷ 2.52 = ***9.00J***
20 year old male = 10.09J ÷ 2.52 = ***4.004J***
10 year old male = 2.52J ÷ 2.52 = ***1.00J***

[283] Discrimination in outputs between men and women can be hazy and in fact, is often times ignored.

Critically important therefore, provided a Brief Pulse machine's constant Amperage, maximum overall output, Charge administered for each age category,[284] and the Impedance for each age category,[285] threshold constants in Joules can be determined for every age group. In short, the "relative threshold constants" depicted in joules used by American Brief Pulse manufacturers for every age category on every BP device is not speculative but factual, in that they are mathematically deducible given specific electrical parameters. That manufacturers actually use these "relative constants" to determine age related default outputs with respect to their Brief Pulse devices is not hypothetical, but elemental. This is certainly the case with Somatics Incorporated. Moreover, these relative constants (which have been revealed for the first time here) become crucial for both manufacturers and purveyors of these devices in readily determining default outputs (in joules) with respect to each age category and so in determining the comparative power of any specific Brief Pulse device.

Crucially, once the default MTTLOI with BL ECT (i.e. 2.52) has been determined for a machine by dividing maximum machine output (i.e. 252J) by 100 Joules, the Charge and EO (in Joules) delivered in any age category can then be divided by this same MTTLOI (i.e. 2.52) to determine threshold Charges and threshold EOs (in Joules) for any specific age group. [286] In brief, once threshold outputs and actual outputs delivered in Joules (or Charge) are determined, both the power and purpose of a device becomes manifest. For instance, on the second generation made-for-America Thymatron DG as noted, in terms of Charge and EO, the machine is set to deliver a uniform 2.52 MTTLOI with BL ECT to all age recipients. While threshold output for the forty year old in general is 16 Joules or 80mC, then, the machine actually delivers 40.3 Joules or 201.6mC. From this information, we can plainly see that the machine is not minimal stimulus and that the goal of the DG machine with BL placement, is to deliver a 2.52 MTTLOI to the forty year old (40.3J ÷ 16J = <u>2.52</u>; 201.6mC ÷ 80mC = <u>2.52</u>) and indeed to all other age recipients. In short, once age related thresholds and delivered outputs are known, we can see the uniform MTTLOI delivered by any particular BP device to all age recipients. Moreover, we can understand the comparative power and thus the nature and goal of the specific BP device.

Recap for Determining Relative Threshold Output Constants

To recap then:
Beale tells us, in essence, that maximum Charge for second generation MECTA and Somatics BP devices represents a 2.5 fold threshold output for the oldest and thus for all recipients. For example, if we divide the maximum Charge for the DG of 504mC (provided by Somatics) by 2.5, we obtain a 201.6mC threshold Charge for the 100 year old male. However, if we take this same 504mC Charge and divide by the more accurate 2.52 figure (exactly one hundredth of the maximum EO on the DG), we derive a perfect (504mC ÷ 2.52 =) <u>200mC</u> threshold Charge for the 100 year old male, a slightly more accurate figure. Through the formula EO = Charge x Current x Impedance, we can then convert the 200mC figure into Joules.

$$.200C \times .9A \times 555.55\Omega = 100 \text{ Joules.}$$ [287]

The 100J relative threshold constant for the 100 year old adult can again be confirmed through the default EO and default Charge delivered, relative to threshold EO and relative threshold Charge of the same 100 year old recipient (Equivalent Ratio):

$$252/.504 = X/.200 = 100 \text{ Joules}$$ [288]

---

[284] We can simply multiply age as a percentage times maximum Charge to deduce this figure. i.e. .70 x .504C = .3526C for the 70 year old recipient.

[285] We can simply multiply age as a percentage times maximum Impedance to deduce this figure. i.e. .70 x 555.5Ω = 388.85Ω for the 70 year old recipient.

[286] While we can obtain threshold Charges, only threshold outputs in terms of Joules are constant, that is, threshold charges vary with varying machines, whereas, threshold outputs in terms of Joules remain constant, as we shall see.

[287] Even using the 201.6mC figure, we obtain a circa 100 Joules. .201.6 x .9A x 555.5Ω = 100.79J.

[288] Here, of course, 252 Joules and .504mC and 100 Joules and .200mC directly correlate on the DG.

If we now take the maximum (.504C x .9A x 555.5Ω =) 252 Joule output obtained by the formula: EO = Charge x Amperage x Impedance and divide this maximum output by exactly 100 Joules, we confirm Beale's 2.5 MTTLOI findings found in terms of Charge for every age level on the DG, but converted into Joules: 252J ÷ 100J = 2.52 fold. Dividing maximum EO in Joules by 100J to discover the MTTLOI for a particular BP device is a precept which works for any BP device.100 Joules therefore, appears to be the "threshold constant" manufacturers use for a 100 year old adult utilized not only to calculate the Thymatron DG and MECTA BP devices with BL "ECT," but is the threshold constant used for the 100 year old adult in modern day BP devices, generally. Simply by dividing maximum EO (of any BP machine) by 100J, therefore, allows us to identify the default MTTLOI (with BL "ECT") administered by that specific BP device. Moreover, we can convert the Charge (in mC) delivered in any age category to the EO (in Joules) delivered in any age category (Charge x Amperage x Impedance = EO), revealing the default output in millicoulombs and joules delivered by a specific BP device. Dividing this figure by the MTTLOI determined from maximum machine Output divided by 100J reveals the secret relative threshold output constant for that particular age category utilized by all American (and probably European) Brief Pulse manufacturers (with the exception of Medcraft as we shall see).

The importance of converting Charge to Joules is important for the following reason. Although we can always determine the amount of Charge (mC) required to reach a specific MTTLOI on a particular machine, and although we can always accurately convert the Charge figure to EO or Joules, and although the MTTLOI derived from Charge will always match the MTTLOI derived from EO (in Joules), threshold outputs in terms of Charge can change from machine to machine, whereas, threshold outputs in terms of EO (Joules) remains constant. The importance of this consistency becomes apparent in accurately contrasting various generations of BP devices as we shall observe. In brief, only by expressing MTTLOIs in terms of Joules can we consistently and meaningful contrast various generations and even various kinds of Brief Pulse devices.

Given Charge, Amperage, and Impedance for a particular age level then, and the maximum machine output from which we can obtain the MTTLOI for that particular Brief Pulse device, we can obtain the accurate relative threshold output in Joules for that particular age level which manufacturers (MECTA and Somatics) treat as unchanging constants in calculating the default outputs of more and more powerful Brief Pulse devices.

Converting Charge in Millicoulombs to EO in Joules Continued

Let us illustrate the Charge/Joules relationship for a different age group delivered output on the DG, i.e. the 90 year old as opposed to the 100 year old. The DG delivers a 453.6mC Charge to all 90 year old recipients (provided by Somatics). Thus:

453.6mC ÷ 2.52 = 180mC. (Threshold Charge for 90 yrs.)

.180C x .9A x 500Ω = 81 Joules. (Threshold Constant in Joules derived from Charge for 90 yrs.)

81J x 2.52 = 204.12J (Joules the DG actually delivers to all 90 yr. olds)

180mC x 2.52 = 453.6mC (Charge the DG actually delivers to all 90 yr. olds)

<u>ER: 204.12J/.4536C = XJ/.180C = *81* Joules</u> (Thus, the threshold output constant in Joules for a 90 year old is derived through ER of <u>delivered-Joules/delivered-Charge</u> to <u>threshold-Joules/threshold-Charge</u>).

Once the threshold output constant and the actual EO delivered is known (preferably in Joules), the relative power and purpose of the device becomes manifest. For example, as noted, the DG is a device designed with enough power to deliver a 2.52 MTTLOI to every age category.

<u>Delivered EO for 90 yrs. ÷ Relative constant for 90 yrs. = MTTLOI</u>.
<u>204.12J ÷ 81J = 2.52 MTTLOI</u>

Importantly then, not only is 100 Joules the EO threshold constant used for a 100 year old adult in all modern day BP devices, but manufacturers similarly use all the other age-related threshold constants (depicted in Joules above) to calculate the default outputs for their BP devices. Since Charge thresholds vary from machine to machine, and EO thresholds remain constant, as we shall see, ubiquitous conversion to EO delivered (in Joules) is critical in order to meaningfully contrast devices. Moreover, as already noted, simply by knowing overall maximum EO in Joules, simply by dividing that overall maximum by 100J, we can identify the MTTLOI of any Somatics or MECTA BP device, thereby identifying the machine's power objective. In fact, armed with this information, by plugging in Voltage, Impedance,[289] and a few other basic parameters, we can now create accurate tables and charts denoting not only actual EOs delivered (in Joules) for every age recipient for any modern-day BP device, but all other parameters as well.

No manufacturer provides these threshold outputs (particularly in Joules) and none provide the consistent default MTTLOI of which each modern day BP device is capable and with which the machine's objective is clearly identifiable. Even so, Somatics does provide us with an initial chart containing enough information to formulaically deduce maximum output and thus the consistent MTTLOI default applicable to every age level assuming we know the "code" (that is, assuming we know to divide the machine's maximum Output by 100J and assuming we know that the 1982 APA ceiling has been discarded). Assuming we are informed then, from this information, we can formulaically deduce delivered outputs and the threshold output constants for every age level. Based on these derivatives of various provided parameters, then, it is possible to construct an accurate overall picture (chart-wise) of the second generation Thymatron DG, including, as noted, Energy Outputs (in Joules) delivered at every age level. Based on threshold outputs per age category together with the default MTTLOI utilized (neither of which any manufacturer provides), we can easily determine the DG's character.

Beale's Study and the Thymatron DG

As noted above, Beale's study identified what this manuscript deems a circa 2.5 MTTLOI in terms of Charge delivered with BL electrode placement on second generation MECTA and Somatics BP devices for all recipients. As also noted above, in that Somatics provides the maximum DG Charge of 504mC, simply by dividing 504mC by 2.5, we can determine the approximate threshold output in Charge (not the actual Charge delivered) of 201.6mC for the 100 year old male. Translating this into Joules through the formula EO = Charge x Current x Impedance (.2016C x .9A x 555.5Ω = 100.79 Joules), we derive a circa 100 Joule threshold output for the 100 year old adult (which, as already noted, turns out to be a relative constant). Multiplying this figure by 2.5 we can now confirm that the Thymatron DG emits a maximum EO of about 252J (100.79 x 2.5 = 251.9).

We can, however, as also noted above, more accurately divide 504mC by the truer MTTLOI of 2.52 (based on an exact 100J threshold output constant for the 100 year old adult) from which we get an exact 200mC Charge (504mC ÷ 2.52 = 200mC). Translating 200mC back into Joules through the formula EO = Charge x Current x Impedance, we again obtain 100 Joules for the threshold output of the 100 year old male: .200C x .9A x 555.5 = <u>100 Joules</u>. Conversely, 100 Joules x 2.52 = **252 Joules**, the maximum machine output as well as the output delivered to the 100 year old adult in order to evince a 2.52 MTTLOI on the Thymatron DG. In that Voltage, Hertz, Duration, and Charge for the Thymatron DG for each age group is known, and in that Current and Wave Length are constants on this device (.9A and .001Sec.), we can use the formula <u>EO = Voltage x Current x (Hz x 2) x WL x Duration</u>, to determine the default EO delivered in each age category on the Thymatron DG. Too, we can confirm Charge delivered to varying age groups through the formula <u>Charge = Duration x Current x (Hz x 2) x WL</u>. By dividing Charge outputs and EOs (Joules) by 2.52, moreover, we can, as noted, determine and confirm circa threshold outputs for every age level.

In that threshold outputs in Joules are constants, or are at least used as constants by manufacturers Somatics and MECTA, once these threshold output constants are known, they can, as we have seen, be applied to all modern BP devices, including MECTA devices. (Although we can also determine or confirm varying Charge thresholds for the DG, unlike EO, Charge thresholds, as noted, can vary from machine to machine. For example, whereas 100J remains the threshold output constant for the 100 year old on all BP

---

289 Voltages and Impedances can be found for each age group simply by dividing maximum Voltage and maximum Impedance by age related percentages, i.e.70 years = 70%.

devices generally, Charge threshold for this same 100 year old may vary from 200mC on one machine to 250mC on another, which shall be discussed in more detail a little later on. [290]

Let us now take the original made-for-America Thymatron DG for which all parameters are either known or can be remotely derived and from which we can discover the "constant" EO thresholds for all age levels and thus (via the MTTLOI) default outputs emitted to every age category.

Creating Tables and Charts for the Brief Pulse Devices

ACTUAL CONSTANT CURRENT THYMATRON DG BRIEF PULSE ECT DEVICE [291]
by Somatics Inc.1983
BASED ON PURE-ER/RRC INTERPRETATION OF 99.4/7J At 220Ω.

VOLTAGE	POWER % @ Age	AGE Yrs	Ω Ohms	FREQUENCY (Hz)	DURATION (SECs)	CURRENT mAmps	ENERGY Joules	CHARGE mC
50	10	10	55.5	30	.93	900	2.51	50.4
100	20	20	111	30	1.87	900	10.09	100.8
150	30	30	166.6	50	1.68	900	22.68	151
200	40	40	222.2	50	2.24	900	40.32	201.6
250	50	50	277.7	50	2.8	900	63	252
300	60	60	333.3	70	2.4	900	90.72	302.4
315	63	63	350	70	2.512	900	99.7	316.5
325	65	65	361.1	70	2.6	900	106.47	327.6
350	70	70	388.8	70	2.8	900	123.4	352.8
400	80	80	444.4	70	3.2	900	161.28	403.20
450	90	90	500	70	3.6	900	204.1	453.6
500	100	100	**555.5**	70	4.0	900	**252**	**504**

.001 Sec. PW

If 504mC represents 2.5 fold threshold for the 100 year old recipient, then (504mC ÷ 2.5 =) 201.6mC is the threshold output in Charge for this same 100 year old recipient for the same Brief Pulse device. Similarly, if 504mC represents 2.52 fold threshold, then (504 ÷ 2.52 =) 200mC is probably the more accurate threshold figure for the DG. We can then, as previously noted, convert the 200mC figure into Joules by the formula EO = Charge x Current x Impedance. [292]

.200C x .9A x 555.55Ω = 100 Joules.

The 100J figure, as noted previously, can be confirmed through ER, that is, Joules delivered/Charge delivered to threshold in Joules/threshold in mC.

252/.504 = X/.200 = 100 Joules

Dividing the DG's 252 Joule output maximum by 100J, of course, gives us the DG's MTTLOI of 2.52 (252J ÷ 100J = 2.52 fold threshold), serving as the uniform MTTLOI for every age category for the Thymatron DG. As a relative constant, 100 Joules can now be presumed the EO threshold for a 100 year old adult not only for the

---

[290] MECTA does not provide maximum EO in Joules; nor does it provide accurate maximum Impedance. Consequently, slight speculation is needed with respect to MECTA BP devices in order to create complete tables and charts. Fortunately, MECTA and Somatics produce inveterately comparable devices. While "speculative" therefore, accuracy of figures used for MECTA tables in this manuscript are done so with a high degree of probability.

[291] It should be pointed out that not only does the 1982 APA Standard implicitly limit all outputs to a 1.1 MTTLOI for all age categories which the DG breaches by emitting a 2.52 MTTLOI in all age categories, but "the APA Standard also prohibits "treatment" to recipients evincing below 100Ω Impedance. In short, "ECT" for individuals under about sixteen years of age should be prohibited. (See the DG chart).

[292] Even using the 201.6mC figure, we obtain a circa 100 Joules. .201.6 x .9A x 555.5Ω = 100.79J.

Thymatron DG, but, as noted, for MECTA BP devices as well. [293] Given Charge and Impedance, as noted above, we can obtain these threshold output constants in Joules for every age level, which, of course, as constants can then be utilized for all modern BP devices (again, with the exception of Medcraft as we shall observe).

As we have seen, Somatics informs us that the 90 year old receives 453.6mC Charge on the DG (Abrams and Swartz, 1988, back cover). Dividing by 2.52, we obtain a threshold Charge of 180mC. We then, as noted, convert this figure to the threshold output constant in Joules (81J). Multiplying by 2.52, we can confirm that the 90 year old male receives 204.12 Joules or a 2.52 MTTLOI. Finally, as also noted above, we can again confirm these figures through ER: Output delivered in Joules/Output delivered in Charge = Threshold output In Joules/Threshold output in Charge for the 90 year old male.

453.6mC ÷ 2.52 = 180mC.
.180C x .9A x 500Ω = 81 Joules.
81J x 2.52 = 204.12J
204.12J/.4536C = XJ/.180C = 81 Joules

All other **relative threshold output constants** in Joules can be similarly obtained from which we get the following table:

100 year old male = 252.00J ÷ 2.52 = **100.00J**
90 year old male = 204.10J ÷ 2.52 = **81.00J**
80 year old male = 161.28J ÷ 2.52 = **64.00J**
70 year old male = 123.40J ÷ 2.52 = **48.97J**
65 year old male = 106.47J ÷ 2.52 = **42.25J**
60 year old male = 90.72J ÷ 2.52 = **36.00J**
50 year old male = 63.00J ÷ 2.52 = **25.00J**
40 year old male = 40.32J ÷ 2.52 = **16.00J**
30 year old male = 22.68J ÷ 2.52 = **9.00J**
20 year old male = 10.09J ÷ 2.52 = **4.004J**
10 year old male = 2.52J ÷ 2.52 = **1.00J**

Since thresholds in Joules remain as or are treated as constants, not only is 100 Joules used as a constant EO threshold for a 100 year old for most modern day BP devices, but all the remaining EO age-related EO thresholds above, all of which were determined in the exact same manner, are similarly treated as constants. In that Charge thresholds vary and so can be misleading, it is EO thresholds alone (in joules) which must be utilized in order to unveil a consistent character profile of the Brief Pulse device, particularly, as has been noted, compared to BP devices of differing generations as we shall see. (Manufacturers eventually shy away from reporting in Joules for this very reason.)

Character Profile of Somatics Second Generation Thymatron DG

AGE	MULTIFOLD THRESHOLD TITRATION LEVEL OUTPUT INTENSITIES	ENERGY DELIVERED Joules	Threshold Constants Joules
10	2.52	2.52	1.00
20	2.52	10.09	4.00
30	2.52	22.68	9.00
40	2.52	40.32	16.00
50	2.52	63	25.00
60	2.52	90.72	36.00
65	2.52	106.47	42.25
70	2.52	123.4	49.00
80	2.52	161.28	64.00
90	2.52	204.1	81.00

[293] According to an earlier Weiner assertion, Weiner implies that 99% of 100 year old recipients seize with much less power, but 100% will seize with 100J.

100	2.52	**252**	**100.00**

In juxtaposing actual EOs delivered by the DG (in Joules) with threshold constants for every age category, the character of the device is revealed. The clear purpose of the Thymatron DG device above is to deliver a 2.52 MTTLOI to every age category.

Simply by knowing the actual maximum EO of a device (in joules), then, along with a few other basic parameters, i.e. maximum Voltage and maximum Impedance which can be plugged into the formulas below, we can, as noted, create accurate detailed tables and charts including the MTTLOI and specific outputs delivered in both EO and Charge to every age level with any MECTA or Somatics BP device. [294]

Charge = Duration x Current x (hz x 2) x WL
Charge = EO/Current x Impedance
EO = Charge x Current x Impedance
Duration = Charge/Current x (hz x 2) x WL
EO = Voltage x Current x (hz x 2) x WL x Duration
EO = (Current squared) x Impedance x (hz x 2) x WL x Duration
Ohm's Law: Current = Voltage/Ω; Ω = Voltage/Current; Voltage = Current x Ω

[294] The charts provided in this manuscript, particularly MECTA charts, were not necessarily constructed with the benefit of the above EO thresholds in that the understanding that manufacturers use EO thresholds as constants only occurred (to the author) after fifteen years or so of research. Instead, much more circuitous methods were utilized. Nevertheless, charts in this manuscript very closely approximate parameters based on the constant EO thresholds above. Differences are negligible. MECTA refuses to provide maximum EO and maximum Voltage and as a result, all MECTA charts are represented as "speculative." Should MECTA ever be forced to disclose complete and accurate information, the author would be only too happy to "correct" what are almost certainly slight inaccuracies.

CHAPTER 23

Early 2nd Generation Somatics BP Devices vs *Later* 2nd Generation Somatics BP Devices.

To understand how important the reporting of Joules or Energy Output (EO) is for comparing machines, let us compare the information Somatics provides physicians for its early Thymatron (Abrams and Swartz 1985) to the later more powerful Thymatron DG above (Abrams and Swartz 1988). Somatics readily imparts the information for its early and later Thymatron and Thymatron DG below. [295]

EARLY CONSTANT CURRENT **THYMATRON** BRIEF PULSE DEVICE
by Somatics Inc.1982-3
BASED ON PURE-ER/RRC <u>INTERPRETATION</u> OF <u>100J At 220Ω</u>

POWER % @ Age	AGE Yrs	FREQUENCY (Hz)	DURATION (SECs)	CURRENT mAmps	CHARGE mC
10	10	30	.93	900	50.4
20	20	30	1.87	900	100.8
30	30	50	1.68	900	151
40	40	50	2.24	900	201.6
50	50	50	2.8	900	252
60	60	70	2.4	900	302.4
65	65	70	2.6	900	327.6
70	70	70	2.8	900	352.8
80	80	70	3.2	900	403.20
90	90	70	3.6	900	453.6
100	100	70	4.0	900	**504**

Pulse Wave = .001Sec.

LATER CONSTANT CURRENT **THYMATRON <u>DG</u>** BRIEF PULSE DEVICE
by Somatics Inc.1985
BASED ON PURE-ER/RRC <u>INTERPRETATION</u> OF <u>99.4/7J At 220Ω</u>

POWER % @ Age	AGE Yrs	FREQUENCY (Hz)	DURATION (SECs)	CURRENT mAmps	CHARGE mC
10	10	30	.93	900	50.4
20	20	30	1.87	900	100.8
30	30	50	1.68	900	151
40	40	50	2.24	900	201.6
50	50	50	2.8	900	252
60	60	70	2.4	900	302.4
65	65	70	2.6	900	327.6
70	70	70	2.8	900	352.8
80	80	70	3.2	900	403.20
90	90	70	3.6	900	453.6
100	100	70	4.0	900	**504**

Pulse Wave = .001Sec.

---

[295] In addition, Somatics does provide the DG's maximum Impedance (555.5Ω) and maximum Voltage (500V).

By reporting Charge (in lieu of EO) for each age category, the above two machines--Somatics' early and later second generation BP devices--appear identical in power. Now let us add Voltages, Impedances, and most importantly, manually derived age-related EO in Joules.

EARLY CONSTANT CURRENT **THYMATRON** BRIEF PULSE DEVICE
by Somatics Inc.1982-3
BASED ON PURE-ER/RRC INTERPRETATION OF 100J At 220Ω

VOLTAGE	POWER % @ Age	AGE Yrs	Ω Ohms	FREQUENCY (Hz)	DURATION (SECs)	CURRENT mAmps	ENERGY Joules	CHARGE mC
39.9	10	10	44.18	30	.93	900	2.004	50.4
79.8	20	20	88.84	30	1.87	900	8.06	100.8
119.7	30	30	133.19	50	1.68	900	18.10	151
159.6	40	40	177.36	50	2.24	900	32.18	201.6
199.5	50	50	221.7	50	2.8	900	50.27	252
239.4	60	60	266	70	2.4	900	72.39	302.4
259.35	65	65	288.15	70	2.6	900	84.96	327.6
279.3	70	70	310.3	70	2.8	900	98.537	352.8
319.2	80	80	354.7	70	3.2	900	128.7	403.20
359.1	90	90	398.8	70	3.6	900	162.8	453.6
399	100	100	**443**	70	4.0	900	**201**	**504**

Pulse Wave = .001Sec.

ACTUAL CONSTANT CURRENT THYMATRON DG BRIEF PULSE EST DEVICE
by Somatics Inc.1985
BASED ON PURE-ER/RRC INTERPRETATION OF 99.4/7J At 220Ω

VOLTAGE	POWER % @ Age	AGE Yrs	Ω Ohms	FREQUENCY (Hz)	DURATION (SECs)	CURRENT mAmps	ENERGY Joules	CHARGE mC
50	10	10	55.5	30	.93	900	2.52	50.4
100	20	20	111	30	1.87	900	10.09	100.8
150	30	30	166.6	50	1.68	900	22.68	151
200	40	40	222.2	50	2.24	900	40.32	201.6
250	50	50	277.7	50	2.8	900	63	252
300	60	60	333.3	70	2.4	900	90.72	302.4
325	65	65	361.1	70	2.6	900	106.47	327.6
350	70	70	388.8	70	2.8	900	123.4	352.8
400	80	80	444.4	70	3.2	900	161.28	403.20
450	90	90	500	70	3.6	900	204.1	453.6
500	100	100	**555.5**	70	4.0	900	**252**	**504**

Pulse Wave = .001Sec.

By viewing the EO columns below in Joules, we can now see that in spite of perfectly equal Charge outputs in every age category, the later machine--due to increased Voltages--has increased in overall power by about 50 Joules. [296]

ENERGY in Joules for the earlier Thymatron	ENERGY in Joules for the later Thymatron DG
2.004	2.52
8.06	10.09
18.10	22.68
32.18	40.32
50.27	63
72.39	90.72
84.96	106.47
98.537	123.4
128.7	161.28
162.8	204.1
201	**252**

[296] While Impedance appears to increase from about 443Ω to about 555.5Ω with the increase in Voltage (from 400V to 500V) and EO (from about 200J to about 250J) from earlier to the later device, we must remember that in spite of Impedance increases with increasing power, an adequate grand mal seizure can almost certainly be induced in the 100 year old recipient with never more than 100 Joules. Thus, in spite of increasing Impedance, we can accurately say that the early Thymatron applies 2.0 fold threshold outputs at all age levels while the Thymatron DG applies 2.5 fold threshold outputs at all age levels.

Critically, the now apparent increase in power affects the MTTLOI applied to every age category. By identifying maximum EO (which all manufacturers failed to report by about 1983), we can quickly see that while the ***Thymatron*** utilizes a circa 2.0 MTTLOI, the ***Thymatron DG*** utilizes a circa 2.5 MTTLOI in all age categories. This can be confirmed simply by consulting the constant threshold output table for each age category (above) and multiplying these relative constants by 2.01 for the Thymatron and 2.52 for the Thymatron DG to obtain default outputs delivered in each age class. For instance, the threshold output for the ten year old is 1.0 Joule while the threshold output for the 100 year old is 100 Joules. In that the ***Thymatron*** delivers circa 2.01 Joules to the ten year old child (1.0 x 2.01 = 2.01 Joules) and 201 Joules to the 100 year old adult (100J x 2.01 = 201 Joules), the ***Thymatron*** delivers a 2.01 MTTLOI in each age category. Working in reverse, of course, a (201 Joules ÷ 100 Joules =) 2.01 MTTLOI is delivered to the 100 year old while the same (2.01 Joules ÷ 1.0 Joule =) 2.01 MTTLOI is delivered to the ten year old child. In brief, in that the ***Thymatron DG*** delivers circa (1.0 x 2.52 =) 2.52 Joules to the ten year old child and (100J x 2.52 =) 252 Joules to the 100 year old adult, the ***Thymatron DG*** delivers a 2.52 MTTLOI in each age category. Again working in reverse, we get the same result: a (252 Joules ÷ 100 Joules; 2.52 Joules ÷ 1.0 Joule =) 2.52 MTTLOI for both the 100 year old adult and ten year old child. Using the relative output constants in joules, all age-related outputs are similarly revealed, exposing the power disparity between the two devices. Charge reporting without EO reporting as we can see from the charts above, therefore, is not only inadequate, it is highly misleading. Without EO reporting, the increase in both power and MTTLOI from the earlier to the later BP device remains invisible.

Determining EO (Joules) and MTTLOIs for Various Machines Continued

While MECTA's and Somatics' use of circa "100J at 220Ω" emphasize the "100J" figure suggestive of the 1982 APA ceiling, in fact, the "100J at 220Ω" phrase is arbitrary. Numerous other pure-ER/RRC phrases could have accomplished the same manufacturer goal of enhancing overall output and titration (albeit none so misleadingly). For instance, altering the original conditional-ER/RRC phrase from "70J at 220Ω" to a Pure-ER/RRC of "70J at 150Ω" (in lieu of 100J at 220Ω") enhances overall output to the same extent. [297] A Pure-ER/RRC interpretation of "70J at 150Ω" mathematically "permits" virtually the same potential output increases ("70J/150Ω" = "**102.6J**/220Ω" = "**259J**/555.5Ω"[298]) as a Pure-ER/RRC interpretation of "100J at 220Ω" (i.e. "100J at 220Ω" = "**68J**/150Ω" = "**253**J/555.5Ω"). It is the circa "100J at 220Ω" phrase, however, which facilitates manufacturers' goals of (1) enhancing potential cumulative output up to 273J in order to (2) grossly and ubiquitously enhance the overall MTTLOI for all age categories, while simultaneously (3) suggesting the same circa 100J ceiling as the 1982 APA Standard indicative of minimal stimulus output (with BL ECT) which Brief Pulse manufacturers promised the FDA. The intentional use of "100J" as a deceptive strategy is incontrovertibly supported by circa 100J maximum machine readouts created for and read by administering physicians. Amazingly, then, specifically modifying the APA phrase "70J at 220Ω" to "100J at 220Ω," that is, specifically utilizing the "100J" figure for a completely novel Pure-ER/RRC interpretation, sustained the false impression that the circa 110 Joule ceiling stipulation within the 1982 APA Standard (just over the 100J minimum guaranteeing minimal stimulus), continued to apply. In fact, a similar phrase constructed for the 1989 IEC (international) Standard--"100J at 300Ω"--(apparently formulated by the same American psychiatrist-engineer Richard Weiner) as we shall see, also furtively interpreted as a Pure-ER/RRC (and which could have been depicted as, for instance, "73J at 220Ω" (= 100J/300Ω), [299] similarly exploits the same "100J" figure. In point of fact, utilization of the "100J" term within the circa "100J at 220Ω" (and "100J at 300Ω") phrases veil MECTA's

---

[297] A "70J at 150Ω" ER/RRC in lieu of "70J at 220Ω" lowers the ER-Impedance relative to 70J, thus increasing power permitted at lower Impedances (70J/220Ω = 190J/600Ω; 70J/150Ω = 280J/600Ω). This has the same effect as raising the ER-Output to 100J relative to "220Ω" (100J/220Ω = 273J/600Ω) In both cases, power is almost equally enhanced.

[298] 100J at 220Ω enables devices to reach up to 273J (at 600Ω); whereas, 70J at 150Ω enables approximately the same output (circa 280J).99.4J at 220Ω (reported by Somatics) enables the DG at 555.5Ω to reach approximately 252J whereas 70J at 150Ω (interpreted as a Pure-ER/RRC) permits the same circa 260J maximum (70J/150Ω = 259J/555.5Ω).

[299] While "73J at 220Ω" (=100J/300Ω) appears similar to the APA Standard's "70J at 220Ω," the "73J at 220Ω" variation of "100J at 300Ω"is actually a Pure-ER/RRC (allowing around 226 Joules), as opposed to the APA conditional ER/RRC of "70J at 220Ω" (stipulating a 110J ceiling). In any case, manufacturers deliberately chose to report the "100J at 300Ω" phrase containing the "100J" figure for the international standard (as we shall see later).

(and Somatics') new Pure-ER/RRC interpretation by neatly filling in what would otherwise have been an extremely conspicuous void--the total elimination of the 110J ceiling based on the "100J" minimum guaranteeing just above seizure thresholds for all age recipients. [300] In short, because MECTA's (and Somatics') pure-ER/RRC interpretation of the "100J at 220Ω" phrase altogether eliminates the 110J APA ceiling, the new "100J" construction, intentional or not, served to cover up an otherwise extremely stark discrepancy between the APA Standard and the power of modern BP devices.

Together, however, the arbitrary nature of the circa "100J at 220Ω" and "100J at 300Ω" phrases reported by both MECTA and Somatics, or rather, the use of the circa "100J figure" in both the "new "100J at 220Ω" and "100J at 300Ω" phrases (as we shall see) and spurious readouts of circa 100 maximum joules on both devices, is more than suggestive of deliberate deception. Clearly, the conspicuous use of "100J" helped to successfully cover up the circa 2.5 MTTLOI transitional increase in every age category from first to later second generation made-for-America BP devices. Moreover, while Somatics' and MECTA's use of the "100J at 220Ω" phrase interpreted as a Pure-ER/RRC by transmutes the APA 110J ceiling into a 100J pure-ER covering up never before reported machine outputs of 252 and 259 Joules respectively, Medcraft Incorporated, the third extant American BP manufacturer, interprets the same "100J at 220Ω" phrase in an entirely antithetical manner (as we shall later examine--see "Medcraft" below).

---

300 Both "100J at 220Ω" and "100J at 300Ω" phrases are suggestive of the Conditional-ER/RRC interpretation of the 1982 APA Standard's "70J at 220Ω" with 110J ceiling, which they are not.

CHAPTER 24

Somatics' Prompts False Equivalence of DG's .504C Max. Charge to Spurious 99.4J Max. Output

Charge is cumulative electricity measured in Coulombs or millicoulombs (bundles of electrons). From the Charge-oriented formula for finding EO in Joules (EO = **Charge** x Current x Impedance), maximum Charge, as we have seen, acts as yet another reportable electrical parameter for obtaining what appears to be Somatics' circa 100J maximum EO. Thus, like other maximum DG parameters (maximum Impedance, maximum Voltage, maximum Current, maximum Duration), Somatics can use actual maximum Charge as yet another convincing multiplicand to create the circa misleading "100J" product depicted as maximum output on made-for-America second generation BP devices. Because Somatics (and MECTA) program a false 220Ω Impedance "constant" (or, if you will "average") into the machines' computers, Somatics can claim its maximum Charge of .504C limits output to a circa 100 Joules (but which is actually, as we have seen, an ER). Misleadingly then, we can use the "99.4/7J at 220Ω" phrase reported by Somatics[301] with actual Maximum Current (.9A) to determine the true maximum Charge of .504C for the DG just as we can use the true maximum Charge of .504C to deduce the misleading circa 100J figure. [302]

> .504 Coulombs x .9 Amperes x 220Ω Impedance = ***99.7J*** (Reported EO for DG or actually 99.4J).

A derivative of the Charge-oriented formula for deriving output above, of course, yields the same actual maximum DG Charge:

> 99.7J ÷ .9 Amps x 220Ω = ***.504C*** (Maximum Charge).

In brief, the unexplained ER/RRC phrase reported by Somatics of 99.4J at 220Ω, can be (misleadingly) used to derive and report a true Charge ceiling of .504 Coulombs for the Thymatron DG (and vice-versa). This is because 99.4J at 220Ω is a misleading Pure-ER/RRC to actual maximum output at actual maximum Impedance (252J at 555.5Ω).

Because "99.4/7J at 220Ω" is but a pure-ER/RRC to actual unreported maximum output at actual maximum machine Impedance (252J at 555.5Ω), manufacturers could use actual EO and actual maximum Impedance to derive the same actual maximum Charge of 504mC (and vice-versa).

> **.504 Coulombs** x .9 Amperes x *555.5Ω Impedance* = ***252J*** (Unreported EO for DG).

---

[301] Somatics reports "99.4J at 220Ω." The author will utilize "99.7J at 220Ω" in that it appears more accurate. The negligible difference may be due to rounding.

[302] The derivative formula for determining maximum DG Charge is actually: 99.7J ÷ 9 Amps (Constant Current) x 220Ω = Maximum Charge. Maximum Charge = .504 Coulombs.

Using a derivative of the same formula:

252J ÷ .9 Amps x *555.5Ω*. = ***.504C*** (Maximum Charge).

In that "99.4/7J at 220Ω" is the Pure-ER/RRC of actual maximum Output (252J) at actual maximum Impedance (555.5Ω), the application of either set of numbers using the formula EO ÷ Amperage x Impedance results in the same actual maximum Charge (see above). Somatics' neglect to explain the phrase "99.4/7J at 220Ω" as a Pure-ER/RRC together with the avoidance of actual maximum output reporting (252J), leads to a deceptive correlation between the DG's actual maximum Charge of .504C and what only appears to be an actual maximum output of 99.4/7J as we shall see in more detail directly below.

Somatics' Engenders a False Equivalence of the DG's .504C Maximum Charge to a Spurious 99.4J maximum Output Continued

Observe a Somatics' statement excerpted from several of its' advertising fliers--one for its DG; another for its DGx (an overseas variation of the DG).

> Maximum output across 220 ohms Impedance: 504 millicoulombs, 99.4 joules. (Somatics Incorporated, 1993b, p.3; Somatics Incorporated, 1998, p. 3)

By reporting actual maximum Charge (.504C) with the unexplained ER Output of 99.4J, the statement suggests that 99.4J occurs at the maximum .504 Coulombs and that both figures are maximums. The correlation is a false one.

While .504 Coulombs is the accurately reported maximum Charge (cumulative electricity) provided by Somatics for the Thymatron DG, the parameter only proves meaningful in conjunction with actual maximum output (252J). Unfortunately, Somatics only reports the maximum Charge ceiling for the DG in conjunction with the unexplained ER phraseology: "99.4 Joules at 220Ω. " Additionally, Somatics juxtaposes its .504C report with a 99.4J Machine Readout maximum (or what is actually an unexplained ER-output or Reverse-ER). In brief, the reporting of the actual maximum .504 Coulomb Charge for the DG (along with other actual maximum parameters) in tandem with an unexplicated ER output of 99.4 Joules (in lieu of actual maximum output in Joules) as well as a 99.4J machine readout maximum (based on a false or misleading 220Ω constant in lieu of actual maximum Impedance)--creates a false equivalency between the .504C maximum Charge and the reported 99.4J output. This false equivalency, misleadingly suggesting 99.4J as the maximum output for the Thymatron DG (see Abrams, 1996, p.703; Sackeim, 1991, p.234), is in seeming compliance with the APA Standard.

Expressed slightly differently, in that the reported actual Charge ceiling for the Thymatron DG can be obtained by utilizing the reported 99.4J derived from a 220Ω "typical" Impedance (or what is actually an ER-Impedance) all in conjunction with the DG's actual Constant Current of .9 Amperes, the false 99.4/7J appears to correspond to the actual DG Charge maximum of .504C.

Charge = 99.7 Joules/220 x .9 Amperes = .504 Coulombs.

Succinctly, in that .504C is the DG's actual reported maximum Charge and because maximum Charge (through both derivation and reporting) appears to correspond to 99.4/7J, 99.4/7J appears to be the Thymatron DG's actual maximum output. In fact, as thoroughly noted, while the .504C maximum Charge is actual, 99.4J (EO) is but an unexplained reverse-ER. Due to the false correspondence suggesting parity between maximum Charge and what appears to be a maximum output of 99.4J, however, both Charge and EO, as noted, appear to conform to the APA Standard, and thus minimal stimulus. Indeed, neither Charge nor EO, actually conform. Not readily comprehensible is the relationship between ER-output at ER-Impedance and actual maximum output at actual maximum Impedance, or that actual maximum Charge is derivable from both the reported, but unexplained "99.4J at 220Ω" Pure ER-RRC as well as the actual unreported maximum EO of 252J at 555.5Ω.[303]

Charge = **99.7 Joules/220Ω** x .9 Amperes = **.504 C**.[304]
Charge = **252 Joules/555.5Ω** x .9 Amperes = **.504 C**.

Finally, as we have now observed, the apparent correspondence between what appears to be an actual 99.4J and an actual .504C Charge is reinforced by the machines' depiction of "99.4J" as maximum output.

Somatics' reporting of its .504 Coulomb Charge ceiling has by itself, little or no meaning; moreover, its juxtaposition with 99.4J is deceptive. The maximum Charge ceiling of .504C becomes significant only when juxtaposed with actual maximum output--the maximum 252J actual equivalent of the .504C maximum Charge, but which goes unreported by Somatics (and other BP manufacturers such as MECTA).

In conclusion, the reporting of the maximum .504C Charge in conjunction with an unexplained ER of 99.4J (sans the reporting of actual maximum EO) is mendacious. False equivalency between actual maximum Charge and what is actually an ER output (in lieu of actual output), reinforces the suggestion that the Thymatron DG is limited to approximately 100 absolute Joules and thus virtually unchanged with respect to both the APA Standard and the 108J MECTA C. Plainly, the machine, which is, in fact, an "ENR" apparatus (one depending upon adequate electricity to be effective), is misleadingly depicted as a minimal stimulus or "ECT" device.

Theoretical Examination of Actual Correspondence of the .504C maximum Charge With an Actual 100J Maximum Ceiling

The following reiteration of Threshold Output Constants and Formulas for determining Brief Pulse parameters may act as helpful resources for the explanation following relative constants:

Threshold Outputs

100 year old male = 252.00J ÷ 2.52 = **100.00J**
90 year old male = 204.10J ÷ 2.52 = **81.00J**
80 year old male = 161.28J ÷ 2.52 = **64.00J**
70 year old male = 123.40J ÷ 2.52 = **48.97J**
65 year old male = 106.47J ÷ 2.52 = **42.25J**
60 year old male = 90.72J ÷ 2.52 = **36.00J**
50 year old male = 63.00J ÷ 2.52 = **25.00J**
40 year old male = 40.32J ÷ 2.52 = **16.00J**
30 year old male = 22.68J ÷ 2.52 = **9.00J**
20 year old male = 10.09J ÷ 2.52 = **4.004J**
10 year old male = 2.52J ÷ 2.52 = **1.00J**

Brief Pulse Formulas

Charge = Duration x Current x (hz x 2) x WL
Charge = EO/Current x Impedance
EO = Charge x Current x Impedance
Duration = Charge/Current x (hz x 2) x WL
EO = Voltage x Current x (hz x 2) x WL x Duration
EO = (Current squared) x Impedance x (hz x 2) x WL x Duration
Ohm's Law: Current = Voltage/Ω; Ω = Voltage/Current; Voltage = Current x Ω

The reporting of actual maximum Charge (.504C) in conjunction with an alleged 99.4/7J maximum which is really an ER-output falsely suggests the maintaining of a circa 100J ceiling (in accordance with the 110J

[303] The 555.5Ω maximum is reported by Somatics.

[304] This same practice enabling a double standard is followed by MECTA. Charge = 101.3 Joules ÷ 220Ω x .8 Amperes = .576 Coulombs. Charge = 276.48 Joules ÷ 600Ω x .8 Amperes = .576 Coulombs.

ceiling depicted in the 1982 APA Standard [305]). In fact, there is no literal correlation of 99.7J, 220Ω, or .504C. on the actual DG. See the Thymatron DG below:

ACTUAL CONSTANT CURRENT THYMATRON DG BRIEF PULSE ECT DEVICE
by Somatics Inc. 1983
Based on Constant Current of **.9A** and a Pure-ER/RRC of 99.4/7J at 220Ω

VOLTAGE	POWER % @ Age	AGE Yrs	Ω Ohms	FREQUENCY (Hz)	DURATION (SECs)	CURRENT mAmps	ENERGY Joules	CHARGE mC
50	10	10	55.5	30	.93	900	2.51	50.4
100	20	20	111	30	1.87	900	10.09	100.8
150	30	30	166.6	50	1.68	900	22.68	151
200	40	40	222.2	50	2.24	900	40.32	201.6
250	50	50	277.7	50	2.8	900	63	252
300	60	60	333.3	70	2.4	900	90.72	302.4
315	63	63	350	70	2.512	900	99.7	316.5
325	65	65	361.1	70	2.6	900	106.47	327.6
350	70	70	388.8	70	2.8	900	123.4	352.8
400	80	80	444.4	70	3.2	900	161.28	403.20
450	90	90	500	70	3.6	900	204.1	453.6
500	100	100	**555.5**	70	4.0	900	**251**	**504**

WL = .001

Note that increasing Charges and Durations result in increasing EOs up to circa 252J. Newly based on a Pure-ER/RRC of 99.4J (or 99.7J) at 220Ω,[306] this device is in no way limited to minimal stimulus or just above threshold output as the manufacturer implies, but upon an unreported 2.52 MTTLOI default output in every age category. In short, the 110J APA ceiling standard is breached. Note moreover, not only the lack of any literal 99.4/7J, 220Ω, and .504C correspondence. Note the actual correspondences of the actual 252J EO maximum with the actual 555.5Ω maximum Impedance, with the actual maximum .504C maximum Charge.

Note how there is no one-to-one or literal correspondence of 99.4/7J, 220Ω, and .504C. The correlation exists only in the "99.4/7J at 220" ER relationship to actual (unreported) maximum output and actual maximum Impedance. Thus the "99.4/7J at 220Ω" relationship to the maximum Charge of .504C is comprised of ER only. The literal correspondence amongst the true maximums, as can be seen in the last row above, is 252J, 555.5Ω, and .504C.

To further demonstrate the misleading nature of Somatics' (and MECTA's) reporting system, it is noteworthy that an actual 99.4/7J overall maximum (or minimal stimulus output) could, in fact, be made to correspond to the reported .504C Charge maximum on the DG through any a number of methods, all entailing the incremental reduction of various electrical parameters.

For instance, without altering any other electrical parameter, simply by reducing Constant Current from *.9 Amperes* to *.357 Amperes*, a maintainable 99.4/7J ceiling could be made to correspond to the machine's actual .504C maximum Charge. [307] Thus, if constant current alone were reduced from *.9 Amperes* to *.357 Amperes* , an actual 99.7J ceiling could be maintained both at the actual .504C maximum Charge and the actual 555.5Ω maximum Impedance. We can confirm this through the Charge oriented formula for finding EO (EO = Charge x Impedance x Current):

EO = .504C. x 555.5Ω x **.356A** = **99.7J**.

Or

Charge = **99.7J**/555.5Ω x **.356Amperes** = .504C. [308]

---

[305] While the standard maximum is actually 110 Joules, the 10 Joules above 100 Joules allows for the just above threshold minimum assuring adequate seizure in even the most seizure recalcitrant recipient in all treatment.

[306] Note how minimal stimulus or the 1.1 fold threshold titration level implied under the 1982 APA Standard is violated as the machine emits 2.52 fold threshold outputs in all age categories.

[307] (Actual): Charge = 252 Joules ÷ 555.5Ω x .9 Amperes = .504 Coulombs. (Theoretical): Charge = 100 Joules ÷ 555.5Ω x .357 Amperes = .504 Coulombs.

[308] This formula is a derivative of the Charge-oriented formula: EO = Charge x Impedance x Amperage

The non-existent, theoretical DG limited to the .356A constant current described above would then evince minimal stimulus or seizure threshold output at every age level (see theoretical chart below)

Theoretical CONSTANT CURRENT THYMATRON DG BRIEF PULSE ECT DEVICE BASED ON REDUCED CONSTANT CURRENT OF **.356A**
Conditional-ER/RRC is now 39.5J at 220Ω [309]

VOLTAGE	POWER % @ Age	AGE Yrs	Ω Ohms	FREQUENCY (Hz)	DURATION (SECs)	CURRENT mAmps	ENERGY Joules	CHARGE mC
50	10	10	55.5	30	.93	900	1.0	50.4
100	20	20	111	30	1.87	900	4.0	100.8
150	30	30	166.6	50	1.68	900	9.0	151
200	40	40	222.2	50	2.24	900	16	201.6
250	50	50	277.7	50	2.8	900	25	252
300	60	60	333.3	70	2.4	900	36	302.4
315	63	63	350	70	2.512	900	39	316.5
325	65	65	361.1	70	2.6	900	43	327.6
350	70	70	388.8	70	2.8	900	49	352.8
400	80	80	444.4	70	3.2	900	64	403.20
450	90	90	500	70	3.6	900	81	453.6
500	100	100	**555.5**	70	4.0	900	**99.7**	**504**

WL = .001

Instead of being the 2.52 MTTLOI ENR device that the Thymatron DG actually is, the theoretical machine above, like the MECTA "C," once again becomes an ECT or adequate convulsion device in lieu of an ENR or adequate electricity device so that all outputs are limited to minimal stimulus in every age category. Ironically, just such a non-existent device is implied via Somatics' reporting of what appears to be a Conditional-ER/RRC of "99.4J at 220Ω" (with 99.4J within the 110J ceiling stipulation) illusorily corresponding to the .504C ceiling. Note the theoretical .504 with circa 99.4/7J correspondence on the theoretical machine above. Slight increases in EO, moreover, (for just above threshold outputs in all age categories) need only a slight increase in constant current. Compare the non-existent device directly above to the actual Thymatron DG (above that).

Indeed, numerous other methods are possible for modifying the actual Thymatron DG to induce minimal stimulus outputs, modifications which do not require altering the constant .9A current. For instance, to engineer a true (BL ECT) minimal stimulus Thymatron DG device and still overcome the same high Impedances of up to 555.5Ω (due to high Voltages), we could simply reduce Durations. Just by reducing Durations then, the current DG could be modified to conform to the 1982 APA prescribed ceiling of 110 Joules. Such a non-existent or hypothetical machine (with reduced Durations) appears below:

HYPOTHETICAL **Minimal Stimulus** THYMATRON DG CONSTANT CURRENT BP Device BASED ON Conditional-ER/RRC of 42.77J at 220Ω
thus conforming to the 1982 APA CONDITIONAL-ER/RRC of "70J at 220" with 110J ceiling

VOLTAGE	POWER % @ Age	AGE Yrs	Ω Ohms	FREQUENCY (Hz)	DURATION (SECs)	CURRENT mAmps	ENERGY Joules	CHARGE mC
50	10	10	55.5	70	.16	900	1.08	21.6
100	20	20	111	70	4.0	900	4.3	43
150	30	30	166.6	70	4.0	900	9.7	64.7
198	40	40	220	70	4.0	900	17.3	87.4
250	50	50	277.7	70	3.166	900	27	108
300	60	60	333.3	70	2.63	900	42	140
315	63	63	350	70	2.512	900	45.6	144.8
325	65	65	361.1	70	2.435	900	46.5	143.1
350	70	70	388.8	70	2.261	900	53	151.5
400	80	80	444.4	70	1.978	900	69	172.5
450	90	90	500	70	1.758	900	87.5	194
500	100	100	555.5	70	1.583	900	108	216

WL = .001

[309] 99.7/555.5Ω = XJ/220Ω. = 39.5J/220Ω

Here, because Duration drops dramatically, Charge is correspondingly reduced. Thus we no longer have a circa 100J, .504C correspondence as in the hypothetical machine above this one and this is because we no longer need a .504C maximum Charge, but only the .216C maximum Charge necessary to reach the 108J ceiling. Moreover, we have a facsimile of the original 108J MECTA "C," except that the above theoretical device (with its higher Voltages) is able to overcome much higher Impedances (than the original "C"). The conditional-ER/RRC with a 108J ceiling (the same ceiling as the MECTA C) upon which the hypothetical machine above is based is "42.77J at 220Ω," [310] similar to the "C," moreover, conforming to the 1982 APA Standard in all respects. This conformity includes the original APA "70J at 220Ω" conditional-ER/RRC (and 110J ceiling). [311] Note that just above threshold output is emitted at every age level on the non-existent device above. Needless to say, no such modern-day BP machine exists.

Finally, note that while the actual Thymatron DG and the theoretically reduced Durations conforming to minimal stimulus have no corresponding parameters with respect to the three reported ones -100J, 220Ω, and .504C, and while the theoretically reduced Amperage device contains only two (of three) corresponding parameters (99.7J and .504C), none of the machines correspond with respect to all three parameters--99.7J, 220Ω, and .504C. At most then, a maximum of two of the three reported parameters (circa 99.7J and .504C) correspond one to another, but only on the non-existent reduced Amperage device. It is this non-existent correspondence of a 99.4J output maximum with an actual .504C maximum Charge, which Somatics falsely suggests in its misleading reporting scheme, a correspondence which in no way exists via the actual Thymatron DG. Indeed, a BP device limited to 99.4J requires far less Charge. Indeed, the .504C Charge is only necessary due to DG's actual, but unreported 252J maximum. [312]

Experiment

Just as an experiment, however, let us build a device limited to a circa 99.7J maximum wherein all three parameters--99.7J, 220Ω, and .504C--literally correspond. Maintaining a Constant Current of .9 Amperes, we can reach the 99.7J ceiling at 220 by increasing Duration at this early juncture with a maximum 4.0 second Duration. We can then maintain the 99.7J ceiling via incrementally decreasing Duration wherein Charge correspondingly decreases.

---

[310] XJ/220Ω = <u>108J/555.5Ω</u>; X = 42.77J. While the APA Standard was based on a Conditional 70J at 220Ω ER/RRC with 110J ceiling, the MECTA "C" was based on a "59J at 220Ω" Conditional-ER/RRC still in accordance with the APA Standard (59J/220Ω = <u>108J/403Ω</u>). This is because limited to a 110J ceiling, the lower the Conditional-ER/RRC (i.e. "59J at 220Ω" or "42J at 220Ω" as opposed the APA "70J at 220Ω") the higher the maximum Impedance allowed. This safeguard fails upon the transmutation of Conditional-ER/RRC with 110J ceiling to Pure-ER/RRC with ceiling based only upon the maximum Impedance of 600Ω: 70J/220Ω = <u>190J/600Ω</u>; 100J/220Ω = <u>272J/600Ω</u>. In short, the ceiling is augmented from 110J to 272J, grossly altering the standard from one assuring minimal stimulus or a 1.1 MTTLOI to a possible 2.72 MTTLOI for all age groups making the actual device an ENR apparatus.

[311] All outputs on the hypothetical machine above are well below a "70J at 220Ω" ER/RRC, and since the ceiling is 108 Joules, all outputs are also confined to a 1.08 MTTLOI in adherence with the APA Standard.

[312] Though we are looking at experimental BP devices capable of reaching 555.5Ω without transgressing the 1982 APA Standard, in fact, such high Impedances only arise from the unnecessarily high 2.52 MTTLOI outputs.

Experimental Somatics THYMATRON DG 2nd GENERATION CONSTANT CURRENT BP Device BASED ON CONDITIONAL-ER/RRC INTERPRETATION[313] AND ACTUAL PHYSICAL CORRELATION OF 99.7J at 220Ω PEAKING AT CORRESPONDING ACTUAL 504C. CHARGE

VOLTAGE	POWER % @ Age	AGE Yrs	Ω Ohms	FREQUENCY (Hz)	DURATION (SECs)	CURRENT mAmps	ENERGY Joules	CHARGE mC
50	10	10	55.5	70	4.0	900	25.15	504
100	20	20	111	70	4.0	900	50.3	504
150	30	30	166.6	70	4.0	900	75.5	504
198	40	40	220	70	4.0	900	99.7	504
250	50	50	277.7	70	3.166	900	99.7	399
300	60	60	333.3	70	2.63	900	99.7	332.3
315	63	63	350	70	2.512	900	99.7	316.5
325	65	65	361.1	70	2.435	900	99.7	306.8
350	70	70	388.8	70	2.261	900	99.7	284.9
400	80	80	444.4	70	1.978	900	99.7	249.3
450	90	90	500	70	1.758	900	99.7	221.6
500	100	100	555.5	70	1.583	900	99.7	199.4

The above non-existent machine depicts maximum output allowed at each Impedance level and with a conditional overall ceiling of 99.7J. Note the physically corresponding 99.7J at 220Ω with corresponding peak Charge of .504C. As Impedances surpass 220Ω (at which point 99.7J initially occurs here), maximum allowable Charge must decrease via decreasing Durations in order to maintain the 99.7J ceiling. Such a machine would grossly violate the principle of ER/RRC which compels uniformly reduced outputs with respect to descending age or Impedance. Such a hypothetical device, moreover, is not a minimal stimulus apparatus.

While it is possible to engineer a device which peaks at 99.7J, 220Ω, and a .504C maximum Charge as the reported phrase "99.4J at 220Ω" and the reported maximum .504C Charge seem to imply, such a machine, while adhering to a circa 100J ceiling, is immediately problematic. Permitting a circa 100J output at almost every Impedance level not only undermines minimal stimulus outputs at all age levels, but destroys any semblance of a uniform MTTLOI and thus any semblance of uniformly reduced outputs with respect to descending age or Impedance. For instance, while minimal stimulus can be maintained for the 100 year old male at a circa 100J maximum and thus a 1.0 fold or minimal stimulus threshold output, this same 100J output at other age levels creates not only unacceptably high MTTLOIs (grossly above minimal stimulus) but a hodge-podge of MTTLOIs. For example, the 40 year old recipient, wherein the corresponding 100J, 220Ω, and .504C parameters occur, receives a circa a 6.0 MTTLOI (100J ÷ 16J = 6.25 fold threshold) while the ten year old receives a 25 MTTLOI. Thus, not only does a machine with corresponding coordinates of 100J, 220Ω, and .504C fail to remain a minimal stimulus device, but any semblance of a uniform MTTLOI is necessarily destroyed. In short, such a machine violates the ER/RRC portion of the APA Standard. Amazingly, the Medcraft B-25 BP device, as we shall later see, is patterned after just such an interpretation.

The primary purpose of the 1982 APA Standard is to mandatorily reduce emissions to uniform minimal stimulus outputs in all age categories--which only a Brief Pulse device can do. The Somatics manner of reporting what appears to be a conditional-ER/RRC of 99.4J at 220Ω incorporative of a 99.4J overall ceiling, seemingly confirmed by the DG's maximum Machine Readout of precisely 99.4 Joules superficially corresponding to the .504C maximum Charge, bolsters the suggestion of a circa 100J ceiling similar to that reflected in the hypothetically reduced Amperage machine several charts above. Indeed, based on the expectation, implication, assumption, and reporting suggesting that all modern day BP devices emit minimal stimulus outputs in all age categories, regulatory bodies appear to have interpreted the DG's reported "99.4J" and maximum Charge of .504C as correspondent, a feat only possible through reduced Amperage (from .9A to .356A). All other attempts at correspondence (of a 99J ceiling and a .504C maximum Charge) grossly violate the ER/RRC precept in the APA Standard, that is, the notion of a uniform MTTLOI in all age categories and

[313] Except for Duration and thus EO and thus Charge, figures for the theoretical DG above interpreted conditionally, that is up to a 99.7J ceiling, are the same as those depicted on the actual DG Chart interpreting 99.7J at 220Ω as a Pure-ER/RRC. Voltage at initial 99.7J above is estimated at 63% of 500V (Maximum) = 315V. Ohm's Law: Impedance = Voltage/Current. Impedance (at initial 99.7J) = 315V ÷ .9A = 350Ω. Peak Charge (at 99.7J) = EO ÷ Current x Impedance. Peak Charge = 99.7J ÷ .9A x 350Ω = 316.5mC. Duration (at 99.7J) = 99.7J ÷ 315V x .9A x 140 Pulses x .001PW = 2.512 Seconds. Increasing Impedances remain unchanged (from actual DG). Decreasing Durations at increasing Impedances are derived from the formula above using corresponding increasing Voltages (unchanged from DG) and 99.7J as the conditional ceiling. Decreasing Charges are derived using 99.7 Joules maximum EO with corresponding increasing Impedances and Constant .9Amperes: Decreasing Charges = 99.7J ÷ .9A x Corresponding Increasing Impedances depicted above.

thus descending outputs with respect to descending age. In brief, a true minimal stimulus device emitting .9A limited to 99.4 Joules requires much less than the .504C Charge actually utilized by the DG. (See the ***HYPOTHETICAL*** **Minimal Stimulus** THYMATRON DG culminating at .215C above.) Thus, the DG's reported readout maximum of 99.4J together with descending outputs below 99.4J connoting minimal stimulus outputs in all age categories is not only illusory, but deceptive. The DG only appears to conform to the 1982 APA Standard designed to limit BP devices to minimal stimulus or a 1.1 MTTLOI maximum in all age categories expected of all modern day BP manufacturers. In brief, Somatics' implications that the DG is a minimal stimulus device is duplicitous. Not surprisingly then, the Thymatron DG's gross surpassing of minimal stimulus output via its 2.52 MTTLOI for all age categories has totally escaped the attention of FDA officials, physicians, advocacy organizations, and the public alike.

In sum, the circa “100J at 220Ω” phrase reported by Somatics containing the circa "100J" figure is both arbitrary and misleading. Moreover, any actual correspondence of circa 100J and .504C is both illusory and highly deceptive. Literal correspondence of even two of the three reported "100J, 220Ω, and .504C figures is patently non-existent and as such, the DG is not the minimal stimulus device it purports to be. While Somatics (and MECTA) could easily have engineered their second generation BP devices to induce minimal stimulus outputs based on a conditional-ER/RRC of circa "100J at 220Ω" limited to a maximum of 100 or even 110 Joules and thus minimal stimulus in all age categories with BL-ECT as both implied and expected, the strong implication created by these manufacturers that their second generation BP devices do so, is only apparition. Quite contrarily, all modern day MECTA and Somatics BP machines are electro oriented rather than minimal stimulus driven and thus ENR or adequate electricity devices in lieu of ECT or adequate seizure devices. Plainly, manufacturers have striven to cover up this datum.

Concluding Charge Reporting

Plainly, manufacturers' reporting of their machines' actual maximum Charge in no way dispels manufacturers' deliberately engendered implication that their BP devices are limited to about 100 maximum Joules--the hallmark of minimal stimulus. The reporting of actual Charge fails to reveal that Machine Readouts depicting circa 100 maximum Joules on second generation BP devices are, in fact, reverse-ERs[314] and that all readouts are based on a 220Ω false constant (or "average") in lieu of actual Impedance. Nor does the reporting of actual maximum Charge reveal that the circa “100J at 220Ω” phrase reported by MECTA and Somatics for their second generation BP devices is no longer conditional, but a pure-ER/RRC, expulsive of the 110J ceiling. Indeed, the reporting of actual maximum Charge not only fails to reveal actual maximum output (in joules) and thus a major enhancement in power over first generation BP devices, but in conjunction with the circa 100J readout maximum, the .504C maximum Charge report actually engenders the notion of a .504C, circa 100J equivalency and thus the illusion of a circa "100J at 220Ω" conditional--ER/RRC incorporative of a 100 or 110J ceiling.

This false notion of a circa 100J output maximum is further bolstered by the confusing fact that the .504C Charge maximum can be derived from either the DG's reported "99.4J at 220Ω" or the DG's unreported "252J at 555.5Ω" phrases. In fact, the misleading machine readout maximum of 99.4J intimates that Somatics reduces alternative parameters such as Duration in order to conform to the 110J ceiling stipulated within the 1982 APA Standard. In short, second generation MECTA and Somatics BP devices remain in appearance, minimal stimulus devices. Indeed, by supplanting the DG's actual but never reported 252J maximum with a reported but misleading 99.4J maximum, that is, in light of the DG's Maximum Machine Readout of 99.4J and thus what appears to be a “99.4J at 220Ω” conditional--ER/RRC with 99.4J ceiling, the additional reporting of the actual .504C maximum Charge does nothing to dispel the overall impression that second generation BP devices remain limited to 110 maximum Joules. Specifically, Somatics’ accurate reporting of . a 504C Charge maximum in no way compensates for the failure to report actual maximum output in terms of Joules and thus the true 2.52 MTTLOI for the device. Indeed, the reporting of actual Charge, with the concomitant reporting of an unexplained 99.4J reverse-ER is designedly deceptive.

---

[314] For example: 252J/555.5Ω = 100J/220Ω.

Broader Implications of Failure to Report Actual Maximum Output in Joules in Conjunction with Misleading Readouts of circa 100 Maximum Joules

Reporting of maximum Charge in lieu of maximum EO (in Joules), from about 1983 to the present, looks to have been a manufacturer trend world-wide (International Electrotechnical Commission, 1997, Dec 26). There are, moreover, serious repercussions in doing so. For example, the reporting of maximum Charge to depict second generation BP devices appears to have become a mechanism not only for avoiding the reporting of actual maximum output in Joules, but for reporting actual maximum Charge in tandem with unexplained Reverse-ERs comprising a Machine Readout maximum of circa 100 Joules. Such a practice is deliberately suggestive of a circa 100J ceiling for second generation BP devices generally. In fact, it is this ploy which actively engenders the false appearance of an unbroken minimal stimulus continuum from about 1976 onward. Indeed, the tangential repercussions of reporting actual maximum Charge while neglecting and, in fact, misrepresenting maximum Output (in Joules) are manifold. This is because SW and first generation BP devices, i.e. the Medcraft B-24 SW, the first generation MECTA “C” BP devices, and even the 1982 APA Standard itself, all depict actual maximum outputs in terms of Joules. By no longer reporting actual maximum outputs in Joules (except through misleading machine readouts and the circa phrase "100J at 220Ω") for second generation BP devices, comparison to SW and first generation Brief Pulse devices as well as testing for compliance with the 1982 APA 110J ceiling Standard, become impracticable. Clearly, the practice of reporting an unexplained "100J" Reverse-ER output in tandem with actual maximum Charge is both disingenuous and devious. As a result, regulatory agencies, practitioners, the media, and the public at large have been left with the mistaken notion that modern day BP machines continue to remain limited to a uniformly reported (circa) 100 maximum joules with age related descending outputs, ubiquitously conforming to the 1982 APA Standard and are thus minimal stimulus devices.

Specifically, Somatics’ supplanting of actual maximum output (in joules) with an actual maximum .504C Charge ceiling fails to reveal that the second generation Thymatron DG (at 252 maximum Joules) surpasses by 2.3 fold, as noted, the circa 110J ceiling of the 1982 APA Standard (Cameron, 1994; Department of Health and Human Services, 1982a, A53; E20), a gross MTTLOI enhancement affecting all age recipients. Neither does the substitute reporting of .504 Coulombs maximum Charge in lieu of maximum EO (in joules) reveal that the 200J maximum generally depicted for SW devices (Department of Health and Human Services, 1982a, G3-G4) has been eclipsed by the Thymatron DG (and other second generation BP devices). In addition, the reporting of a .504C maximum Charge for the DG in conjunction with the DG’s 99.4J maximum Machine Readout (as well as the unexplained Pure-ER/RRC phrase of “99.4J at 220Ω”), fails to reveal, as we have seen, that 504C. and 99.4J are not equivalent "maximums. " Plainly, maximum Charge reporting alone (sans actual maximum output in joules), much less in tandem with what appears to be a circa 100J readout maximum, fails to disclose, as we have seen, that the DG (and other modern day BP devices) no longer utilize minimal stimulus dosing, but rather multifold threshold dosages of electricity 2.5 and 5.0 fold minimal stimulus for both BL and UL ECT respectively. Indeed, these MLTLOIs are ubiquitously applied via Somatics and MECTA second generation BP devices (Beale et al. , 1994).

Reporting Charge ceilings in lieu of, rather than, in addition to actual output in joules, as well as reporting actual Charge in conjunction with an unexplained circa 100 Joule ER-output, suggesting that Somatics' "99.4J at 220Ω” phrase is a Conditional-ER/RRC with a 100 or 110J ceiling in lieu of a Pure--ER/RRC with a 252J ceiling, engenders the misleading impression that what are actually second generation Brief Pulse devices maintain their markedly increased safety advantage over SW via reduced output. The same reporting mechanism indicates that even later, more powerful model BP devices continue to remain much safer than SW via reduced output, a totally false, albeit extremely beneficial image for manufacturers in the marketing of their so-called "new and improved" modern day Brief Pulse apparatuses.

Unlike Charge, output in Joules per Second directly converts to the familiar "watts" measurement (as in the everyday light bulb), a much more significant and far less cryptic measure of electricity (particularly to the lay public) than the reporting of Charge (or cumulative electricity) alone, measured in Coulombs or Millicoulombs. [315] Even the accurate reporting of actual Charge, in short, does not and cannot replace the reporting of actual EO (in Joules). Certainly, actual EO remains concealed with the reporting of actual maximum Charge alone. To avoid specious assumptions and out and out chicanery, both true Charge

[315] See light bulb analogies under “Third Generation BP Devices.”

maximums and true EO maximums need be reported in tandem. The odious practice of maximum Charge reporting in conjunction with an ER-output in joules, particularly via a false maximum machine readout of circa 100 Joules suggesting a deceptively lower maximum output (in Joules) than actually occurs, facilitates the double standard of reporting what appears to be just above threshold or minimal stimulus, while furtively enabling much higher, wholly unreported outputs reflective of much higher MTTLOIs. The harm that comes from both Somatics' and MECTA's failure to report actual output in joules, indeed, supplanting the reporting of actual output in joules with machine readouts depicting unexplicated Reverse-ERs of what appear to be circa 100J maximums indicative of a circa "100J at 220Ω" Conditional-ER/RRC limiting output to circa 100 or 110J, cannot but be calculated. Reporting a misleading 100J readout maximum in conjunction with actual maximum Charge, the indefensible failure to explain or report the MTTLOI for each specific Brief Pulse device, and finally, the total neglect to report the relative output constants used by the two major BP manufacturers in the United States, is not only devious, but inexcusable. Certainly, Brief Pulse constant current devices, unlike SW devices, have specific, consistent, predictable, and, therefore, highly reportable outputs, particularly in terms of joules. In short, Somatics could easily report a specific maximum EO of 252J in conjunction with its actual maximum Charge of .504C for the Thymatron DG, yet fails in this endeavor. This failure comes in spite of the 1982 APA Standard (as well as the 1989 IEC Standard) clearly calling for manufacturers to do so (Food and Drug Administration, 1986A, p.160; International Electrotechnical Commission, 1989, p.21). Certainly, for even a modicum of truth with respect to informed consent, it should be incumbent upon manufacturers to identify and explain the MTTLOI that each Brief Pulse machine delivers, a precept entirely ignored by every BP manufacturer.

Indeed, the opposite has occurred. The practice of suggesting equivalency between actual Charge and what only appears to be maximum output in joules (but which is actually an ER-output) has been ongoing in America since approximately 1982, the time period during which three of the four American BP Manufacturers MECTA, Somatics, and Elcot began marketing souped-up second generation BP devices capable of at least 250 unreported Joules. This means that since at least 1985, MECTA and Somatics Brief Pulse machines (Elcot soon became defunct) have been emitting a circa 2.5 and 5.0 fold minimal stimulus output with BL and UL "ECT" respectively to every age category for years, even as these same manufacturers have deliberately engendered the Illusion of minimal stimulus devices throughout the same period. (The fourth manufacturer of Brief Pulse devices, Medcraft, deviates in an entirely different manner, as we shall soon see).

Summation

The fact that (1) Somatics' maximum Charge ceiling of .504 Coulombs for the Thymatron DG can be derived both from the reported "99.4J at 220Ω" (ERs) as well as the actual maximums of <u>252J at 555.5Ω</u>, (2) that true maximum Charge is reported in tandem with "99.4J at 220Ω," readily misinterpretable as a conditional-ER/RRC limiting devices to circa 100 maximum Joules, (3) that two of the three extant made-for-America manufacturers of second generation BP devices use false Machine Readout maximums of circa 100 maximum Joules, (4) that the exploitation of the "100J" figure" within the "100J at 220Ω" phrase is arbitrarily contrived, (5) that "110 Joules" is the specific maximum output ceiling identified within the 1982 APA Standard as just above threshold, (6) that a 100 Joule ceiling is highly suggestive of minimal stimulus, (7) that the circa "100J at 220Ω"phrase reported by all four BP manufacturers is actually an unexplained Pure-ER/RRC relative to maximum Impedance grossly enhancing the previous EO ceiling (8) that one of the three extant BP manufacturers (Medcraft) uses and reports an actual 100J maximum (as we shall see) as opposed to a 100J reverse-ER, (9) that Multifold Threshold Titration Level Output Intensities cannot be consistently identified using Charge alone in that Charge thresholds vary, whereas EO thresholds in Joules do not, (9) that manufacturers fail to explain or report their use of threshold output "constants" (in joules) at every age level used to configure all default outputs on moder day Brief Pulse devices, and finally (10) that the inclusions and exclusions of this reporting system result in the false, but powerful suggestion of machine uniformity by all four U.S. BP manufacturers (MECTA, Somatics, Medcraft, and originally Elcot) not only with each other but with the 1982 APA Standard falsely connoting minimal stimulus titration level outputs for all age categories on all modern day BP devices, intimate a deliberate and conspiratorial intent to deceive. Such multi-level tactics by all four manufacturers are quite simply concrete multifarious manifestations of conspiracy to defraud the public general. [316] In short, these various stratagems covertly cover up that by 1983, the APA 110J ceiling had been dropped by virtually every major manufacturer of BP machines, all of which (including Medcraft) had by that same time become adequate electricity or ENR devices in lieu of adequate seizure or ECT devices, surpassing SW generally in both cumulative output and titration.

Since approximately 1985, Somatics had so consistently and prolifically reported the actual .504 Coulomb maximum Charge ceiling for the DG in lieu of maximum EO in Joules, that Great Britain's Royal College of Psychiatry, in its' 1995 *The ECT Handbook: . . .* , mistakenly believed the figure to be an international standard, alluding to five non-existent .504 Coulomb Charge ceiling references ostensibly discoverable within the general IEC Standard for Electrical Medical Devices (International Electrotechnical Commission, 1977, 1988; Royal College of Psychiatry, 1995, pp.126, 134, 140 footnotes, 7,9,11). [317] [318] [319] In contrast, the maximum EO of 252 Joules (to which the .504C Charge ceiling actually corresponds, and from which the .504C Charge ceiling can be derived), has never been reported by Somatics, in any psychiatric journal, or by any regulatory entity to date.

This manuscript represents the first time actual outputs in joules for MECTA, Somatics, Medcraft, and now one Canadian and several English Brief Pulse devices have ever been published. Moreover, this manuscript represents the first time MTTLOI profiles of modern-day BP devices have ever been identified, explained, or reported, the significance of which becomes especially transparent through comparative EO reporting in joules as we shall see. The reporting of maximum Charge outputs sans energy outputs (in joules) is, in effect, valueless; while the prolific reporting of actual maximum Charge in conjunction with an unexplicated circa 100J Reverse-ER readout and thus what appears to be a conditional-ER/RRC of circa "100J at 220Ω" engenders a false equivalency between actual maximum Charge and what only seems to be a circa 100J maximum output. To be plain, the conspicuous absence of actual output reporting (in joules) for MECTA and Somatics second generation BP devices, all of which either grossly surpass the APA 110J ceiling, falsely facilitates the ongoing illusion of minimal stimulus devices even as these same second generation BP devices have been delivering unreported MTTLOIs of at least 2.5 fold with BL ECT in all age categories since at least 1985 (e. g. Abrams, 1996, p.703; Sackeim, 1991, p.234). [320]

---

[316] While all four report approximately 100J Maximum Machine Readouts, only one, Medcraft's B-25, is accurate.

[317] In personal communications with the Chairman of the Committee for General Medical Devices, a Mr. Sidebottom was unable to find .504 Coulombs on a version of the general Standard he had on CD disc. A later personal communication from AAMI (Association for the Advancement of Medical Instrumentation), again confirmed that the .504C Charge ceiling nowhere exists within the general Standard for medical devices. Moreover, the author himself, searching a hard copy of the written Standard, was similarly unable to locate the existence of such a Standard.

[318] Although unlikely, perhaps the mistaken references are to an IEC 500V maximum (International Electrotechnical Commission, 1988, 10.2.2, p.67), indirectly leading to a .504 Coulomb ceiling, at least for the Thymatron DG. Impedance = Voltage/Current. Impedance = 500V/.9 Amperes = 555.5Ω. EO = Current squared x Impedance x Pulses x Pulse Width x Duration. EO = .9 Amperes .9 Amperes x 555.5Ω x 140 Pulses x .001 Pulse width x 4 Seconds Duration = 252 Joules. Charge = EO/Current x Impedance. Charge = 252 Joules/.9 Amperes x 555.5Ω = .504 Coulombs.

[319] The above footnote reference (International Electrotechnical Commission, 1988, 10.2.2, p.67) refers to a Section in IEC 60601-1 on general electrical medical devices which, in 1988, replaced an earlier section, perhaps in effect since 1977. In that the author was unable to procure the earlier section, it must be assumed the 500 Volt limit was in effect in the earlier version as well. It is possible, however, that influenced by ECT manufacturer affiliated experts sitting on both the International ECT Committee (62D Committee) and International General Committee (62A Committee) for medical electrical devices, Voltage within the 1988 section was increased (from the earlier version) to accommodate much higher output. For instance, a limit of 220 Volts would limit the Thymatron DG to approximately 110J (EO = .9 x 220 Volts x 140 Pulses x .001 Pulse Width x 4 Seconds = 110.88J); whereas 500 Volts facilitates 252J for the Thymatron DG parameters (EO = .9 x 500 Volts x 140 Pulses x .001 Pulse Width x 4 Seconds = 252J).

[320] Adding to the confusion, as we shall investigate, is BP manufacturer Medcraft's reporting of an actual 99J ceiling for its' sole BP device, the B-25, even while it continues to manufacture and market the allegedly outdated (and generally unreported, 200J) B-24 SW device. Moreover, Medcraft's B-25 violates the APA Standard (as we shall see) in an altogether different manner than MECTA and Somatics' second generation BP devices.

CHAPTER 25

MECTA MADE-FOR-AMERICA 2ND GEN. BP DEVICE Details: MECTA Figures Ceilings for FDA

MECTA secretly figures output ceilings for its' second generation made-for America BP machines, the later MECTA JR/SR 1 and later MECTA JR/SR 2, in the same manner Somatics figures output ceilings for its Thymatron DG. In fact, MECTA appears to have devised the methodology first. Certainly by 1985, MECTA had replaced the reporting of maximum EO in joules and dropped the 110J ceiling mandated by the 1982 APA Standard in reporting the unexplained phrase, "101 Joules at 220Ω" for its second generation BP devices (the MECTA JR/SR 1 and MECTA JR/SR 2). Like Somatics, the phraseology appears to be a new conditional-ER/RRC with the original APA 110J (or an even lower 101J) ceiling intact, similar to the original 1982 APA conditional-ER/RRC of "70J at 220Ω" circumscribed by a 110J ceiling. In short, MECTA's reported circa "101J" is falsely implicit of maximum EO on these second generation MECTA BP devices in that like the Somatics DG and DGx, both MECTA second generation BP devices the (JR/SR 1 and 2) depict Maximum Machine Readouts of circa 101J, reinforcing the ongoing illusion of the circa 110J ceiling for what are actually second generation BP devices. In short, these machines, in spite of the increase in ER/RRC from 70J at 220Ω" to "101J at 220Ω" yet appear to maintain the minimal stimulus output guaranteed by the 1982, 110J APA ceiling (making the APA's "70J at 220Ω" phrase a conditional-ER/RRC). MECTA's new "101J at 220Ω" report depicting what are actually second generation BP devices, as noted above, appears to have occurred just prior to Somatics similar sounding "99.4J at 220Ω" phrase newly depicting its second generation DG and DGx devices. In short, MECTA's approach was precedential and so followed by Somatics. [321] Based upon MECTA's reports to the FDA as well as its 101J maximum machine readouts, MECTA's second generation made-for-America BP devices, just as Somatics' made-for-America second generation DG device which followed, appear to utilize what appears to be a slightly higher conditional-ER/RRC (from "70J at 220Ω" to circa "100J at 220Ω"), nevertheless continuing to conform to the 1982 APA ceiling Standard of 110 maximum Joules, that is, the same minimal stimulus 1.1 MTTLOI in all age categories.

In fact, by 1985, MECTA (like Somatics which followed) had transitioned from using and reporting the APA conditional-ER/RRC of "70J at 220Ω" with a clear, separate, and straight-forward APA ceiling of 110 maximum Joules, to a "101.4J at 220Ω" Pure-ER/RRC permitting up to 259 unreported joules. "Pure" once again, here means the 110J APA ceiling has been dropped, the newly reported "101J at 220Ω" ER/RRC no longer conditioned by any specific ceiling whatsoever. Quite unlike the 1982 APA standard then, the new unreported EO ceiling, like Somatics' device which followed, was limited only by maximum machine Impedance up to the maximum allowable APA Impedance of 600Ω (101J/220Ω = 275J/600Ω). Like Somatics above, MECTA's new unreported ceiling had become limited--no longer by the 110J ceiling--but only by the pure-ER relationship of

---

[321] Somatics began reporting 99.4 Joules at 220Ω in 1983, furtively interpreting the phrase first as a mean, then as a Pure-ER/RRC. The unauthorized transition was made with the knowing approval of psychiatrist Richard Weiner, both an electrical engineer and the APA ECT Task Force Chairman during this period. Weiner has not only continually represented the APA and all American ECT device companies to the FDA since about 1976, but has a long-standing association with MECTA as a consultant (Cameron, 1994; Sackeim and Weiner, 1993; Glen and Weiner, 1983) in what should have been seen as an obvious conflict of interests.

"101.4J at 220Ω" to maximum machine Impedance up to the maximum FDA Impedance of 600Ω, in short, by what for MECTA was actually a new 275 joule ceiling (101J/220Ω = 275J/600Ω). Succinctly, the 110J ceiling no longer applied, resulting in greatly increased output (and thus a greatly increased MTTLOI) from 110J (or a 1.1 MTTLOI) up to a potential 275 Joule maximum or a 2.75 MTTLOI. In that the APA 110J ceiling had actually been dropped under (what the author has deemed) the "Mectan Transmutation," Duration parameters (for example) no longer correspondingly decreased to maintain the anticipated 110J (or 101J) ceiling as did the MECTA "C" presented to the FDA between 1976-1982. Instead, like Somatics which followed, MECTA's second generation BP machines reached new unreported outputs at unreported machine Impedances of about 259.2J at 562.5Ω. [322] (Pure--ER/RRC: 101.4J/220Ω = 259.2J/562.5Ω). Amazingly, then, by 1982, in spite of MECTA's no longer making any attempt to maintain the 110J APA ceiling, MECTA's reporting of "101.4/3J at 220Ω" in tandem with misleading Machine Readout maximums of approximately 101 maximum Joules for both its new MECTA SR1 and MECTA SR2 second generation BP devices, continued and yet continues to suggest conformity to the 110J ceiling prescribed under the 1982 APA Standard. This, of course, maintained the illusion of continuous just above threshold output, that is, minimal stimulus outputs for all age categories. [323] In fact, based on the machine's readouts, MECTA's second generation SR1 and 2 BP devices appeared to emit even lower maximum outputs than the prototypical 108J MECTA "C" presented to the FDA during the original FDA hearings (from 1976-1982). In truth, by 1985, MECTA had secretly, and sans FDA authority, raised its' machine ceilings from 108 maximum joules to approximately 260 maximum Joules, circa 2.5 fold the original APA ceiling (Cameron, 1994). Indeed, by default, second generation made-for-America MECTA BP devices deliver an unreported 2.59 MTTLOI to every age category.

In summation, then, secretly transmuting the APA conditional-ER/RRC of "70J at 220Ω" with a clear 110J ceiling into a "101J at 220Ω" pure-ER/RRC (sans 110J ceiling), thereby circumventing the mandate for minimal stimulus outputs at all age levels, MECTA was able to market what were actually new, second-generation MECTA JR/SR 1 and 2 BP devices capable of unreported emissions 2.5 fold the APA ceiling, surpassing even SW in cumulative power (Cameron, 1994). The new second generation MECTA machines now elicited not 1.1, but more than 2.5 times threshold in every age category, all while MECTA reported (via misleading machine readouts) false 101J maximums for these same devices in seeming conformity to the 1982 APA Standard.

2nd Generation JR/SR 1

Below are the two expected, but non-existent JR/SR 1 BP devices representing 101J maximums followed by the actual JR/SR 1 BP device marketed by MECTA.

[322] MECTA reveals neither maximum energy output (joules) nor maximum Impedance. As previously explained and will again be explained below, the maximum Output and maximum Impedance for the MECTA second generation SR2 and SR1 BP devices are based upon a speculative 450 Volts. It is, however, possible that MECTA's Output/Impedance ER is based not upon a 562.5Ω (and 450V) maximum as speculated, but (like Somatics) upon a 555.5Ω (and thus 444.4 Volt) maximum, in which case actual maximum output is not 259J but 256J. (101.4J/220Ω is **256J**/555.5Ω). The difference, however, is negligible.

[323] For example, what was actually a second generation MECTA model JR/SR 1 was reported in MECTA's 1993 *MECTA Instruction Manual* as having a "minimum power [of] 2.66 Joules for a 220Ω patient Impedance" and a "maximum power [of] 101.4 Joules for a 220Ω patient Impedance" (Sackeim and Weiner 1993 p 13). The MECTA JR/SR 2 was similarly described as having a "minimum power [of] 12.67 Joules for 220Ω patient Impedance" and a "maximum power [of] 101.4 Joules for a 220Ω patient Impedance" (Sackeim and Weiner 1993 p 14). This confusing manner of reporting what was actually a 259 Joule maximum (at a 562Ω maximum Impedance or 2.59 fold threshold) creates the illusion of continuous minimal stimulus devices similar to the 108J MECTA "C."

Expected SR1 Devices Limited to 101 maximum Joules

Expected 2nd GENERATION CONSTANT CURRENT **JR/SR 1** ***TRUE MINIMAL STIMULUS*** BRIEF PULSE **ECT** DEVICE BASED ON **Conditional-ER/RRC OF "101.4J AT 220Ω"** via ***Reduced Durations***.

VOLTAGE	POWER % @ Age	AGE Yrs	Ω Ohms	FREQUENCY (Hz)	DURATION (SECs)	CURRENT mAmps	ENERGY Joules	CHARGE mC
45	10	10	56.25	40	.087	800	1.13	25
90	20	20	112.5	40	.165	800	4.3	48
135	30	30	168.75	60	.232	800	9	67
180	40	40	225	60	.309	800	16	89
225	50	50	281.25	60	.386	800	25	111
270	60	60	337.5	90	.502	800	39	145
292.5	65	65	365.63	90	.510	800	43	147
315	70	70	393.75	90	.551	800	50	159
360	80	80	450	90	.627	800	65	181
405	90	90	506.25	90	.703	800	82	203
450	100	100	562.5	90	.782	800	101.4	225

.002 Second Pulse Width

The theoretical device above is the kind of minimal stimulus device expected of the reported "101.4J at 220Ω" ER/RRC wherein maximum output is limited to 101.4 Joules or a 1.01 fold threshold output at every age level similar to the MECTA "C. " The "improvement" seems to be that the newer machine, though yet minimal stimulus with BL ECT, could overcome higher Impedances than the MECTA "C. " The expected 101.4J maximum and 1.01 fold just above threshold outputs in all age categories is theoretically maintained here by reduced Duration and Charge. ***In fact, the above device is purely imaginary.***

A variation of the expected device via reduced constant Amperage can be seen below:

Expected 2nd GENERATION CONSTANT CURRENT **JR/SR 1** ***TRUE MINIMAL STIMULUS*** BRIEF PULSE **ECT** DEVICE BASED ON **Conditional-ER/RRC OF "101.4J AT 220Ω"** via ***Reduced Constant Amperage of .313A***

VOLTAGE	POWER % @ Age	AGE Yrs	Ω Ohms	FREQUENCY (Hz)	DURATION (SECs)	CURRENT mAmps	ENERGY Joules	CHARGE mC
45	10	10	56.25	40	.5	313	1.13	64
90	20	20	112.5	40	.9	313	4.3	115.2
135	30	30	168.75	60	.9	313	9	172.8
180	40	40	225	60	1.2	313	16	230.4
225	50	50	281.25	60	1.5	313	25	288
270	60	60	337.5	90	1.2	313	39	345.6
292.5	65	65	365.63	90	1.3	313	43	374.4
315	70	70	393.75	90	1.4	313	50	403.2
360	80	80	450	90	1.6	313	65	460.8
405	90	90	506.25	90	1.8	313	82	518.4
450	100	100	562.5	90	2.0	313	101.4	576

.002 Second Pulse Width

The theoretical device above is also the kind of minimal stimulus device expected of the reported "101.4J at 220Ω" wherein maximum output is again limited to 101.4 Joules (in accordance with the machine readouts) as all outputs are just above threshold at every age level, similar to the MECTA "C. " Again, the "improvement" might have been that this machine, though yet minimal stimulus with BL ECT, could overcome higher Impedances than the MECTA "C. " The expected 101.4J maximum and 1.01 just above threshold outputs in all age categories is maintained here by reduced constant Amperage. Charge and Duration are unchanged from that of the actual JR/SR 1. ***The device here, just as the one above, is also purely imaginary.***

Below is the actual second generation JR/SR 1 figured from the following formulas:

Charge = Duration x I x (hz x 2) x WL; Charge = EO/I x Impedance; EO = Charge x I x Ω
Duration = Charge/I x (hz x 2) x WL; EO = V x I x (hz x 2) x WL x Duration
EO = (Current squared) x Ω x (hz x 2) x WL x Duration; Ohm's Law: I = Voltage/Ω; Ω = V/I; V = I x Ω

PROABLE ACTUAL[324] 2nd GENERATION CONSTANT CURRENT **JR/SR 1** BRIEF PULSE BRIEF PULSE **ENR** DEVICE [325] BASED ON **PURE-ER/RRC** OF "101.4J AT 220Ω" by MECTA Corp.1985 Made for U. S. A.

VOLTAGE	POWER % @ Age	AGE Yrs	Ω Ohms	FREQUENCY (Hz)	DURATION (SECs)	CURRENT mAmps	ENERGY Joules	CHARGE mC
45	10	10	56.25	40	.5	800	2.88	64
90	20	20	112.5	40	.9	800	10.37	115.2
135	30	30	168.75	60	.9	800	23.33	172.8
180	40	40	225	60	1.2	800	41.47	230.4
225	50	50	281.25	60	1.5	800	64.8	288
270	60	60	337.5	90	1.2	800	93.31	345.6
292.5	65	65	365.63	90	1.3	800	109.51	374.4
315	70	70	393.75	90	1.4	800	127	403.2
360	80	80	450	90	1.6	800	165.89	460.8
405	90	90	506.25	90	1.8	800	209.95	518.4
450	100	100	562.5	90	2.0	800	259.2	576

.002 Second Pulse Width

The above profile of the actual made-for America second generation JR/SR 1 is speculative, but probable. Unreported EOs depicted on the above chart are based upon known variables - Constant Current (.8A); Maximum Duration (2.0 Seconds but variable from .5 Seconds); Maximum Pulse Width (.002 but variable from .001); Maximum Frequency (180 Pulses but variable from 80); and Maximum Charge[326] (Sackeim and Weiner, 1993). Speculative variables include Impedance, Voltage, EO, and Corresponding Age. [327] Note the 65 and older Age Category surpassing 100 Joules. Note to that maximum output surpasses the 1982 ceiling Standard of 110J by approximately 150 Joules. Though the actual JR/SR 1 can be adjusted from a .001-.002 second Wave Length, all calculations above are based on a .002 second PW. Frequency, which can be adjusted from 40 to 90 Hz (80-180 waves) must be reduced to accommodate the actual lower outputs for younger age populations reflected at the top of the chart. The actual JR/SR 1 has manually controlled variable dials according to an age/output chart provided to administering physicians (but unavailable to the author). Outputs suggested by charts turn out (upon mathematical derivations) to be circa 2.6 and 5.2 times threshold with BL and UL ECT respectively. Machine Readouts (on actual machines) depict incremental output increases up to a misleading 101.4J, about 158J less than the actual output, thereby misleading administering physicians. Outputs reflected on the above chart are actual.

2nd Generation JR/SR 2

Below are two hypothetical, non-existent JR/SR 2 BP devices representing 101J maximums followed by the actual JR/SR 2 BP device marketed by MECTA.

Expected 2nd GENERATION CONSTANT CURRENT **JR/SR 2** ***TRUE MINIMAL STIMULUS*** BRIEF PULSE **ECT** DEVICE BASED ON Conditional-ER/RRC OF "101.3J AT 220Ω" via **Reduced Durations**.

VOLTAGE	POWER % @ Age	AGE Yrs	Ω Ohms	FREQUENCY (Hz)	DURATION (SECs)	CURRENT mAmps	ENERGY Joules	CHARGE mC
45	10	10	56.25	90	.174	800	1.13	25
90	20	20	112.5	90	.330	800	4.3	48
135	30	30	168.75	90	.464	800	9	67
180	40	40	225	90	.618	800	16	89

[324] Unlike Somatics, MECTA refuses to reveal actual maximum Impedance or Voltage. Consequently, maximum EO is "speculative." Nevertheless, in that we can be certain Somatics second generation BP devices closely resemble MECTA's second generation BP devices, the speculations are generally reliable.

[325] It should be pointed out that not only does the 1982 APA Standard implicitly limit all outputs to a 1.1 MTTLOI for all age categories which both the SR 1 and 2 breach by emitting a 2.59 MTTLOI in all age categories, but "the APA Standard also prohibits "treatment" to recipients evincing below 100Ω Impedance. In short, "ECT" for individuals under about sixteen years of age should be prohibited. (See the JR/SR 1 and 2 charts).

[326] SR 1--Charge in millicoulombs is calculated from known variables: Current (.8A) x [hz x 2 (=180)] x Wave length (.002) x Duration (2.0 Seconds) = .576C Maximum Charge.

[327] Approximate Voltage for SR1 is based upon the SR 2's probable 256 maximum Joules derived from its 256 step setting dial apportioned equally over Duration. Impedance for SR1@ 2 is calculated from Ohm's law: Impedance = Voltage/Current. EO is calculated from formulas, utilizing specific Resistances or specific Voltages. EO = Volts x Current x [Hz x 2] x Wave length (SR 1-.001 or SR 2-.002) x Duration--or--EO = (Current squared) x Impedance (Ω) x [Hz x 2] x Wave length (SR 1-.001 or SR 2-.002) x Duration.

225	50	50	281.25	90	.772	800	25	111
270	60	60	337.5	90	1.00	800	39	145
292.5	65	65	365.63	90	1.02	800	43	147
315	70	70	393.75	90	1.10	800	50	159
360	80	80	450	90	1.25	800	65	181
405	90	90	506.25	90	1.41	800	82	203
450	100	100	562.5	90	1.56	800	101.3	225

.001 Second Pulse Width

This theoretical device above is the kind of minimal stimulus device expected of MECTA's reported "101.3J at 220Ω" (a seeming conditional-ER/RRC) wherein maximum output is limited to 101.3 Joules (in accordance with machine readouts). Here, all outputs are just above threshold at every age level, similar to the MECTA "C. " The "improvement" over the "C" is that such a machine, though yet minimal stimulus (for BL ECT), would be able to overcome higher Impedances. The expected 101.3J maximum here is maintained by reduced Duration and Charge. ***Unfortunately, the above device is purely imaginary*.**

Expected 2nd GENERATION CONSTANT CURRENT **JR/SR 2** ***TRUE MINIMAL STIMULUS***
BRIEF PULSE **ECT** DEVICE BASED ON Conditional-ER/RRC OF "101.3J AT 220Ω"
via **Reduced Constant Amperage** of .313A

VOLTAGE	POWER % @ Age	AGE Yrs	Ω Ohms	FREQUENCY (Hz)	DURATION (SECs)	CURRENT mAmps	ENERGY Joules	CHARGE mC
45	10	10	56.25	90	0.5	313	1.13	72
90	20	20	112.5	90	0.8	313	4.3	115.2
135	30	30	168.75	90	1.2	313	9	172.8
180	40	40	225	90	1.6	313	16	230.4
225	50	50	281.25	90	2.0	313	25	288
270	60	60	337.5	90	2.4	313	39	345.6
292.5	65	65	365.63	90	2.6	313	43	374.4
315	70	70	393.75	90	2.8	313	50	403.2
360	80	80	450	90	3.2	313	65	460.8
405	90	90	506.25	90	3.6	313	82	518.4
450	100	100	562.5	90	4.0	313	101.3	576

001 Second Pulse Width

The theoretical device above is the kind of minimal stimulus device expected of the reported "101.3J at 220Ω" (conditional-ER/RRC) reported by MECTA wherein maximum output is limited to 101.3 Joules (in accordance with machine readouts) and wherein all outputs are just above threshold at every age level similar to the MECTA "C. " Again, the "improvement" over the "C" is that this machine, though maintaining minimal stimulus with BL ECT, would be able to overcome higher Impedances. The expected 101.3J maximum here is maintained by reduced Constant Amperage. Charge is unchanged from that reported for the actual JR/SR 2. ***Again, the above device is purely imaginary*.**

Below is the **actual** second generation JR/SR 2:

PROBABLE ACTUAL 2nd GENERATION CONSTANT CURRENT **JR/SR 2** BRIEF PULSE
ENR DEVICE BASED ON PURE-ER/RRC OF "101.3J AT 220Ω"
by MECTA Corp.1985 (.001 Second Pulse Width Maximum) made for U. S. A.

VOLTAGE	POWER % @ Age	AGE Yrs	Ω Ohms	FREQUENCY (Hz)	DURATION (SECs)	CURRENT mAmps	ENERGY Joules	CHARGE mC
45	10	10	56.25	90	0.5	800	3.24	72
90	20	20	112.5	90	0.8	800	10.37	115.2
135	30	30	168.75	90	1.2	800	23.33	172.8
180	40	40	225	90	1.6	800	41.47	230.4
225	50	50	281.25	90	2.0	800	64.8	288
270	60	60	337.5	90	2.4	800	93.31	345.6
292.5	65	65	365.63	90	2.6	800	109.51	374.4
315	70	70	393.75	90	2.8	800	127	403.2
360	80	80	450	90	3.2	800	165.89	460.8
405	90	90	506.25	90	3.6	800	209.95	518.4
450	100	100	562.5	90	4.0	800	259.2	576

.001 Second Pulse Width

The chart above is speculative, but probable. Unreported EO depicted in the above chart is based upon known variables--Constant Current (.8A); Maximum Duration (4.0 Seconds but variable from .1); Maximum Pulse Width (.001); Maximum Frequency (180 Pulses);

and Maximum Charge [328] (Sackeim and Weiner, 1993). Speculative variables include Impedance, Voltage, EO, and Corresponding Age. [329] Note the 65 and older Age Category surpassing 100 Joules. Note too that maximum output surpasses the 1982 APA ceiling Standard by approximately 160 Joules. Duration = Charge/Current x (hz x 2) x WL. WL or PW for the JR/SR-2 is .001 seconds and cannot be adjusted. Frequency at 90 Hz (180 pulses) cannot be adjusted, but descending outputs compelled (by the ER/RRC principle) for descending age levels are accommodated by the uniform 2.59 MTTLOI. Dials, i.e. Duration, are adjusted manually according to an age/output chart (unavailable to author). MECTA's suggested outputs (upon mathematical derivation) turn out to be circa 2.6 and 5.2 times threshold with all BL and UL recipients respectively. Machine Readouts (on the actual machine) depicting incremental increases in output up to a 101.3J maximum, are highly misleading. [See actual (speculative) outputs on the above chart.]

Note relative constants in Joules regarding threshold outputs:

10 year old male = 3.24J ÷ 2.59 = **1.25J (Exceptional; usually 1.0J)** [330]
20 year old male = 10.37J ÷ 2.59 = **4.004J**
30 year old male = 23.33J ÷ 2.59 = **9.00J**
40 year old male = 41.47J ÷ 2.59 = **16.00J**
50 year old male = 64.80J ÷ 2.59 = **25.00J**
60 year old male = 93.31J ÷ 2.59 = **36.00J**
65 year old male = 109.51J ÷ 2.59 = **42.25J**
70 year old male = 127.00J ÷ 2.59 = **49.00J**
80 year old male = 165.89J ÷ 2.59 = **64.00J**
90 year old male = 210.00J ÷ 2.59 = **81.00J**
100 year old male = 259.00J ÷ 2.59 = **100.00J**

We should note that, in spite of minor differences in overall output, the MECTA devices are based on the same relative constants upon which the Somatics' devices are based. For example, the MECTA devices emit a known .576C maximum Charge. We can also be fairly certain, the machines emit a maximum EO of 259.2J. Simply by dividing .576C by 2.592 then, we obtain .222C, the threshold output in Charge for the 100 year old category on this device. We can then convert this to EO to obtain the consistent 100J relative constant for the 100 year old category, then multiply by the 2.59 MTTLOI to obtain the default output administered to the 100 year old recipient of 259J. To confirm, we can use the ER of maximum output in joules and maximum output in Charge to relative threshold constant in joules to relative threshold constant in Charge from which we again obtain the 100J relative threshold constant for the 100 year old recipient.

1) 576mC ÷ 2.59 = **222.2mC** (threshold Charge for 100 yr. old)
2) Threshold EO = Threshold Charge x Amp x Impedance:
.222C x .8A x 562.5Ω = **100 Joules** (thresh. EO constant for 100 yr. old).
3) 100J x 2.59 = 259J (default MECTA JR 1 and 2 EO delivered to 100 yr).
4) Confirmation by ER: 259J/.576C = XJ/**.222C** = **100 Joules**

We can obtain the relative constants and default outputs delivered by this machine to all other age categories in almost the exact same manner. For example, maximum Voltage for these devices is 450V. Taking 50% of this power delivered to the 50 year old recipient, we obtain (.5 x 450V =) 225V. Using Ohm's Law, Ω = Voltage/Current, we derive an Impedance of (225V ÷ .8A =) 281.25Ω. We can also determine Charge delivered

---

[328] SR 1--Charge in millicoulombs is calculated from known variables: SR 2--Current (.8A) x [hz x 2 (180)] x Wave length (.001) x Duration (4.0 Seconds) = .576C Maximum Charge

[329] Approximate Voltage is based upon the SR 2's probable 256 maximum Joules derived from its 256 step setting dial apportioned equally over Duration (.5--4.0 Seconds). Impedance is calculated from Ohm's law: Impedance = Voltage/Current. EO is calculated from formulas, utilizing specific Resistances or specific Voltages. EO = Volts x Current x [Hz x 2] x Wave length (SR 1-.001 or SR 2-.002) x Duration--or--EO = (Current squared) x Impedance (Ω) x [Hz x 2] x Wave length (SR 1-.001 or SR 2-.002) x Duration.

[330] The 1.25J relative constant for the 10 year old in lieu of the usual 1.0J may be to avoid the more conspicuous 1.0J connective pattern with a 100J relative constant for the 100 year old and so avoid detection.

to the 50 year old by taking 50% of the maximum Charge or (.5 x .576C =) .288C.[331] We then obtain threshold Charge for the 50 year old on this device by dividing the Charge delivered, by the machine's 2.59 MTTLOI (.288C ÷ 2.59 =) .111C. To obtain the relative threshold constant in joules for the 50 year old recipient, we convert threshold Charge to threshold joules (Threshold EO = Threshold Charge x Amp x Impedance), thus (.111C x .8A x 281.25Ω =) 25J. To obtain the output in joules actually delivered to the 50 Year old, we multiply threshold in joules by the machine's MTTLOI for (25J x 2.59 =) 65J. To confirm of these figures, we use the ER of the default EO (65J) and default Charge delivered to the fifty year old (.111C) to the threshold constant (XJ) and threshold Charge (.111C) for the 50 year old, once again obtaining the consistent relevant output constant in joules for the 50 year old age category of 25J.

1) 288mC ÷ 2.59 = 111mC (threshold Charge for 50 yr. old)
2) Threshold EO = Threshold Charge x Amp x Impedance:
.111C x .8A x 281.25Ω = 25 Joules (thresh. EO constant for 50 yr. old).
3) 25J x 2.59 = 65J (default MECTA JR 1 and 2 EO delivered to 50 year).
4) Confirmation by ER: 65J/.288C = XJ/.111C = 25 Joules

[331] Somatics provides Charge emissions relative to age for the Thymatron DG (Abrams and Swartz, 1988, back cover). It is this method of multiplying power percentage by maximum Charge by which Somatics derives its various Charge emissions relative to age. For example, the Thymatron DG delivers 252mC to 50 year old recipients (Ibid). Maximum Charge is 504mC. .5 x 504mC = 252mC or .252C (Ibid). It is only logical that MECTA, emulated by Somatics, derives its Charge emissions in the exact same fashion.

CHAPTER 26

Later 2ND Generation MECTA 1 & 2 BP Devices Based on Pre-determined "Relative Constants"

We should probably take a moment to prove that MECTA second generation BP devices are based on the same relative constants Somatics BP devices are based, that is, that these relative threshold constants in joules are indeed "constant" or at least that both manufacturers treat them as such.

BP FORMULAS:
Charge = Duration x Current x (hz x 2) x WL
Charge = EO/Current x Impedance
EO = Charge x Current x Impedance
Duration = Charge/Current x (hz x 2) x WL
EO = Voltage x Current x (hz x 2) x WL x Duration
EO = (Current squared) x Impedance x (hz x 2) x WL x Duration
Ohm's Law: Current = Voltage/Ω; Ω = Voltage/Current; Voltage = Current x Ω

Based on Somatics calculations, we simply take maximum Voltage for any BP device, which we speculated at 450V for the MECTA 2 and multiply a power percentage regarding age to determine Voltage for every age category. For example, the fifty year old receives 50% power or .5 x 450V = 225V. We can determine all Voltages for all age categories in this manner. From this, through Ohm's Law, we can then determine all Impedances with respect to age. For example, for the fifty year old, Impedance = (225V ÷ .8A =) 281.25Ω. We can determine all Impedances for all age categories in this manner.

We have also speculated that maximum Charge is .576C. Based upon the Somatics methodology, we can again multiply power with respect to age to determine all Charges delivered at each specific age category. For example, for the fifty year old, .5 x .576C = .288C. We now have enough information to determine EO for each age category. For example, using the formula: EO = Charge x Current x Impedance, we can determine the EO delivered to the fifty year old is (EO = .288C x .8A x 281.25Ω =) 64.8J. We can now take the default output delivered to the fifty year old and divide by the machine's MTTLOI (determined by taking maximum output divided by 100J or (259.2J ÷ 100J =) 2.59 to obtain the relative threshold constant for the fifty year old recipient which is (64.8J ÷ 2.59 =) 25J. In this manner, we can prove that both later second generation MECTA BP devices are based on the below identified relative threshold constants so that both later MECTA BP devices are designed to deliver a 2.59 MTTLOI to each age recipient. All relative threshold constants (see below) and all default outputs with respect to age can be deduced in this manner. In that we have derived these relative threshold constants for both MECTA and Somatics BP devices, we can conclude that both manufacturers utilize them.

Pre-Determined Relative Constants

10 year old male =	3.24J ÷ 2.59 =	**1.25J (exception)**
20 year old male =	10.37J ÷ 2.59 =	**4.004J**

30 year old male = 23.33J ÷ 2.59 = **9.00J**
40 year old male = 41.47J ÷ 2.59 = **16.00J**
50 year old male = 64.80J ÷ 2.59 = **25.00J**
60 year old male = 93.31J ÷ 2.59 = **36.00J**
65 year old male = 109.51J ÷ 2.59 = **42.25J**
70 year old male = 127.00J ÷ 2.59 = **49.00J**
80 year old male = 165.89J ÷ 2.59 = **64.00J**
90 year old male = 210.00J ÷ 2.59 = **81.00J**
100 year old male = 259.00J ÷ 2.59 = **100.00J**

Below is the probable actual 2nd generation JR/SR 2 BP ENR device.

PROBABLE ACTUAL [332] 2nd GENERATION CONSTANT CURRENT **JR/SR 2** BRIEF PULSE **ENR** DEVICE BASED ON PURE-ER/RRC OF "101.3J AT 220Ω" by MECTA Corp.1985 (.001 Second Pulse Width Maximum) made for U. S. A.

VOLTAGE	POWER % @ Age	AGE Yrs	Ω Ohms	FREQUENCY (Hz)	DURATION (SECs)	CURRENT mAmps	ENERGY Joules	CHARGE mC
45	10	10	56.25	90	0.5	800	3.24	72
90	20	20	112.5	90	0.8	800	10.37	115.2
135	30	30	168.75	90	1.2	800	23.33	172.8
180	40	40	225	90	1.6	800	41.47	230.4
225	50	50	281.25	90	2.0	800	64.8	288
270	60	60	337.5	90	2.4	800	93.31	345.6
292.5	65	65	365.63	90	2.6	800	109.51	374.4
315	70	70	393.75	90	2.8	800	127	403.2
360	80	80	450	90	3.2	800	165.89	460.8
405	90	90	506.25	90	3.6	800	209.95	518.4
450	100	100	562.5	90	4.0	800	259.2	576

.001 Second Pulse Width

332 Unlike Somatics, MECTA refuses to reveal actual maximum Impedance or Voltage. Consequently, maximum EO is "speculative." Nevertheless, in that we can be certain Somatics second generation BP devices closely resemble MECTA's second generation BP devices, the speculations are reliable.

CHAPTER 27

Comparing Early 2nd Generation MECTA BP Devices to Later 2nd Generation MECTA BP Devices

To again appreciate the importance of transparency regarding the accurate reporting of Energy Output in Joules, like the Somatics' devices, let us compare the information MECTA provides for its early second generation BP devices to its later more powerful second generation BP devices. MECTA provides the general information below for the ***early*** 2nd generation D-2/JR/SR 1, emphasizing Charge.

Early (Approximate) 2nd GENERATION CONSTANT CURRENT **D-2/JR/SR 1** BRIEF PULSE "ECT" DEVICE BASED ON ***MEAN***-ER/RRC OF "101.4J AT 220Ω" by MECTA Corp.1982-3 (.002 Second Pulse Width Maximum) made for U. S. A.

POWER % @ Age	AGE Yrs	FREQUENCY (Hz)	DURATION (SECs)	CURRENT mAmps	CHARGE mC
10	10	40	.5	800	64
20	20	40	.9	800	115.2
30	30	60	.9	800	172.8
40	40	60	1.2	800	230.4
50	50	60	1.5	800	288
60	60	90	1.2	800	345.6
65	65	90	1.3	800	374.4
70	70	90	1.4	800	403.2
80	80	90	1.6	800	460.8
90	90	90	1.8	800	518.4
100	100	90	2.0	800	576

.002Sec. Pulse Width

MECTA also provides the information below for the ***later*** 2nd generation JR/SR 1 also emphasizing Charge.

Later (Approximate) 2nd GENERATION CONSTANT CURRENT **JR/SR 1** BRIEF PULSE ECT DEVICE BASED ON ***PURE***-ER/RRC OF "101.4J AT 220Ω" by MECTA Corp.1985 (.002 Second Pulse Width Maximum) Made for U. S. A.

POWER % @ Age	AGE Yrs	FREQUENCY (Hz)	DURATION (SECs)	CURRENT mAmps	CHARGE mC
10	10	40	.5	800	64
20	20	40	.9	800	115.2
30	30	60	.9	800	172.8
40	40	60	1.2	800	230.4
50	50	60	1.5	800	288
60	60	90	1.2	800	345.6
65	65	90	1.3	800	374.4
70	70	90	1.4	800	403.2
80	80	90	1.6	800	460.8
90	90	90	1.8	800	518.4
100	100	90	2.0	800	576

.002Sec. Pulse Width

By emphasizing Charge for each age category, like the Somatics devices, the above two machines appear identical. No increase in power appears to have taken place. Now let us add Voltages, Impedances, and most importantly, EO in Joules derived by the author for the same machines.

Early (Approximate) 2nd GENERATION CONSTANT CURRENT **JR/SR 1**
BRIEF PULSE ENR DEVICE BASED ON ***MEAN***-ER/RRC OF "101.4J AT 220Ω"
by MECTA Corp.1985 (.002 Second Pulse Width Maximum) made for U. S. A.

VOLTAGE	POWER % @ Age	AGE Yrs	Ω Ohms	FREQUENCY (Hz)	DURATION (SECs)	CURRENT mAmps	ENERGY Joules	CHARGE mC
35	10	10	44	40	.5	800	2.25	64
70	20	20	87.5	40	.9	800	8.06	115.2
105	30	30	131	60	.9	800	18.1	172.8
140	40	40	175	60	1.2	800	32.3	230.4
175	50	50	219	60	1.5	800	50.5	288
210	60	60	262.5	90	1.2	800	72.6	345.6
227.5	65	65	284	90	1.3	800	85	374.4
245	70	70	306	90	1.4	800	98.7	403.2
280	80	80	350	90	1.6	800	129	460.8
315	90	90	394	90	1.8	800	163.4	518.4
350	100	100	437.5	90	2.0	800	201	576

.002Sec. Pulse Width

Unlike Somatics, MECTA provides ***neither*** maximum Impedance (which is probably 562.5Ω) ***nor*** maximum Voltage (which is probably 450V) and certainly not EO in joules for the later 2nd generation JR/SR 1.

Later (Approximate) 2nd GENERATION CONSTANT CURRENT **JR/SR 1**
BRIEF PULSE ENR DEVICE BASED ON ***PURE***-ER/RRC OF "101.4J AT 220Ω"
by MECTA Corp.1985 (.002 Second Pulse Width Maximum) made for U. S. A.

VOLTAGE	POWER % @ Age	AGE Yrs	Ω Ohms	FREQUENCY (Hz)	DURATION (SECs)	CURRENT mAmps	ENERGY Joules	CHARGE mC
45	10	10	56.25	40	.5	800	2.88	64
90	20	20	112.5	40	.9	800	10.37	115.2
135	30	30	168.75	60	.9	800	23.33	172.8
180	40	40	225	60	1.2	800	41.47	230.4
225	50	50	281.25	60	1.5	800	64.8	288
270	60	60	337.5	90	1.2	800	93.31	345.6
292.5	65	65	365.63	90	1.3	800	109.51	374.4
315	70	70	393.75	90	1.4	800	127	403.2
360	80	80	450	90	1.6	800	165.89	460.8
405	90	90	506.25	90	1.8	800	209.95	518.4
450	100	100	562.5	90	2.0	800	259.2	576

.002Sec. Pulse Width

By viewing the EO columns alone (joules), we can now see that, in spite of perfectly equal Charge outputs in every age category, due to increased Voltages, the later 2nd generation BP machine has increased in overall power from 200 to circa 260 joules.

ENERGY in Joules for the Early 2nd Generation JR/SR 1	ENERGY in Joules for the Later 2nd Generation JR/SR 1
2.25	2.88
8.06	10.37
18.1	23.33
32.3	41.47
50.5	64.8
72.6	93.31
85	109.51
98.7	127
129	165.89
163.4	209.95
201	259.2

Critically, this increase in power affects the uniform MTTLOI applied to every age category and thus the character and aim of the Brief Pulse machine. By identifying maximum EO in joules (which MECTA and Somatics neglect to report), we can quickly see that while the early second generation D-2/JR/SR 1 emits a circa 2.0 MTTLOI in every age category, the later second generation JR/SR 1, emits a 2.59 MTTLOI in every age category, neither of which is visible through Charge reporting alone. The MTTLOI in Joules can be confirmed for each device simply by consulting threshold output constants in each age category (see above) and multiplying each by 2.01 or 2.59 respectively to obtain the default outputs delivered (in each age class) for each respective device (2.01 x 100J = 201J; 2.59 x 100J = 259J). [333] Conversely, the default EO in joules emitted can be divided by 2.01 or 2.59 respectively to derive the same constant threshold outputs (i.e. 201J ÷ 2.01 = 100J; 259J ÷ 2.59 = 100J). Charge reporting without EO reporting, in short, is not only inadequate, but dishonest. Without EO reporting, both the increase in power and increase in MTTLOI from MECTA's earlier to MECTA's later second generation JR/SR 1 BP device is invisible.

Now let us compare the information MECTA provides for its earlier second generation JR/SR 2 BP device to the information it provides for its later second generation JR/SR 2 BP device. MECTA provides the general information on both tables below for its earlier and later JR/SR 2 emphasizing Charge.

Earlier (Approximate) 2nd GENERATION CONSTANT CURRENT **JR/SR 2** BRIEF PULSE ENR DEVICE BASED ON ***MEAN***-ER/RRC OF “101.3J AT 220Ω” by MECTA Corp.1982-3 (.0016 Second Pulse Width Maximum) made for U. S. A.

POWER % @ Age	AGE Yrs	FREQUENCY (Hz)	DURATION (SECs)	CURRENT mAmps	CHARGE mC
10	10	75	.375	800	72
20	20	75	0.6	800	115.2
30	30	75	0.9	800	172.8
40	40	75	1.2	800	230.4
50	50	75	1.5	800	288
60	60	75	1.8	800	345.6
65	65	75	1.95	800	374.4
70	70	75	2.1	800	403.2
80	80	75	2.4	800	460.8
90	90	75	2.7	800	518.4
100	100	75	3.0	800	576

.0016 Sec. Pulse Width

PROBABLE ACTUAL Later 2nd GENERATION CONSTANT CURRENT **JR/SR 2** BRIEF PULSE ENR DEVICE BASED ON ***PURE***-ER/RRC OF “101.3J AT 220Ω” by MECTA Corp.1985 (.001 Second Pulse Width Maximum) made for U. S. A.

POWER % @ Age	AGE Yrs	FREQUENCY (Hz)	DURATION (SECs)	CURRENT mAmps	CHARGE mC
10	10	90	0.5	800	72
20	20	90	0.8	800	115.2
30	30	90	1.2	800	172.8
40	40	90	1.6	800	230.4
50	50	90	2.0	800	288
60	60	90	2.4	800	345.6
65	65	90	2.6	800	374.4
70	70	90	2.8	800	403.2
80	80	90	3.2	800	460.8
90	90	90	3.6	800	518.4
100	100	90	4.0	800	576

.001 Sec. Pulse Width

[333] Oddly, the mechanism of multiplying 2.01 and 2.59 by threshold outputs to determine titration level outputs, works in every category with one exception--that of the ten year old child. Either the author is slightly off in that particular calculation or MECTA is inconsistent in this one age class. Could it be that for instance, 2.59 Joules and 259 Joules in the ten and 100 year old age categories respectively might too readily reveal this easy method of discovering titration levels used per respective BP device? Is it possible that this slight but extremely misleading inconsistency is deliberate?

Once again, by reporting Charge sans EO for each age category, the above two machines appear identical in power. Now once again, let us add Voltages, Impedances, and most importantly, EO in Joules (none of which are provided by MECTA) newly derived by the author and reported below.

Earlier (Approximate) 2nd GENERATION CONSTANT CURRENT **JR/SR 2** BRIEF PULSE ENR DEVICE BASED ON ***MEAN***-ER/RRC OF "101.3J AT 220Ω" by MECTA Corp.1985 (.0016 Second Pulse Width Maximum) made for U. S. A.

VOLTAGE	POWER % @ Age	AGE Yrs	Ω Ohms	FREQUENCY (Hz)	DURATION (SECs)	CURRENT mAmps	ENERGY Joules	CHARGE mC
45	10	10	44	75	.375	800	2.53	72
90	20	20	87.5	75	0.6	800	8.06	115.2
135	30	30	131	75	0.9	800	18.12	172.8
180	40	40	175	75	1.2	800	32.26	230.4
225	50	50	219	75	1.5	800	50.46	288
270	60	60	262.5	75	1.8	800	72.58	345.6
292.5	65	65	284	75	1.95	800	85.06	374.4
315	70	70	306	75	2.1	800	98.7	403.2
360	80	80	350	75	2.4	800	129	460.8
405	90	90	394	75	2.7	800	163.4	518.4
350	100	100	437.5	75	3.0	800	201.6	576

.0016 Sec. Pulse Width

Unlike Somatics, MECTA provides ***neither*** maximum Impedance (but which is most probably 562.5Ω) ***nor*** maximum Voltage (but which is most probably 450V) ***nor***, of course, EO in joules for its later second generation JR/SR 2.

PROBABLE ACTUAL Later 2nd GENERATION CONSTANT CURRENT **JR/SR 2** BRIEF PULSE ENR DEVICE BASED ON ***PURE***-ER/RRC OF "101.3J AT 220Ω" by MECTA Corp.1985 (.001 Second Pulse Width Maximum) Made for U. S. A.

VOLTAGE	POWER % @ Age	AGE Yrs	Ω Ohms	FREQUENCY (Hz)	DURATION (SECs)	CURRENT mAmps	ENERGY Joules	CHARGE mC
45	10	10	56.25	90	0.5	800	3.24	72
90	20	20	112.5	90	0.8	800	10.37	115.2
135	30	30	168.75	90	1.2	800	23.33	172.8
180	40	40	225	90	1.6	800	41.47	230.4
225	50	50	281.25	90	2.0	800	64.8	288
270	60	60	337.5	90	2.4	800	93.31	345.6
292.5	65	65	365.63	90	2.6	800	109.51	374.4
315	70	70	393.75	90	2.8	800	127	403.2
360	80	80	450	90	3.2	800	165.89	460.8
405	90	90	506.25	90	3.6	800	209.95	518.4
450	100	100	562.5	90	4.0	800	259.2	576

.001 Sec. Pulse Width

Again, by viewing the EO columns alone, we can now see that in spite of perfectly equal Charge outputs in every age category, due to increased Voltages, the later second generation BP machine has increased in overall power by about 60 Joules going from a 2.01 MTTLOI to a 2.59 MTTLOI in every age category.

ENERGY in Joules for the Early 2nd Generation JR/SR 2	ENERGY in Joules for the later 2nd Generation JR/SR 2
2.53	3.24
8.06	10.37
18.12	23.33
32.26	41.47
50.46	64.8
72.58	93.31
85.06	109.51
98.7	127
129	165.89
163.4	209.95
201.6	259.2

As noted above, this critical increase in power affects the uniform MTTLOI applied to each age category and thus the aim and profile of the device. By identifying maximum EO (which both MECTA and Somatics have dropped), we can quickly see that while the earlier second generation JR/SR 2 emits a circa 2.0 MTTLOI, the later second generation JR/SR 2 increases the MTTLOI to a circa 2.59 for all age categories. Once again, this can be confirmed by consulting threshold output constants in each age category and multiplying either by 2.01 or 2.59 respectively to obtain Joules emitted in each age class. [334]

So what happened with respect to Charge? Why wasn't the disparity in power apparent in the Charge reporting alone? Quite simply, Charge thresholds decrease from the early second generation MECTA devices to the later second generation MECTA devices. To Illustrate, while both emit the same 288mC Charge for the fifty year old recipient, we divide 288mC by 2.0 (the MTTLOI) to obtain the Charge threshold for the fifty year old of 144mC for the earlier MECTA device, while we divide the same 288mC by 2.59 (the MTTLOI) to obtain the Charge threshold for the same 50 year old of 111mC for the later MECTA device. In contrast, the threshold output in joules for the same fifty year old remains the same for both devices. In brief, Charge thresholds can change from device to device; whereas, EO thresholds (joules) remain constant.

Early JR/SR 1 and 2

1) 288mC ÷ 2.01 = **144mC** (threshold in Charge for 50 yr. old)
2) Threshold EO = Threshold Charge x Amp x Impedance:
.144C x .8A x 219Ω = 25 Joules (threshold EO constant for the 50 yr. old).
3) 25J x 2.01 = 50.25J (default EO delivered by early second generation MECTA JR 1 and 2 to 50 year old).
4) Confirmation by ER: 50.25J/.288C = XJ/.144C = **25 Joules**

Later JR/SR 1 and 2

1) 288mC ÷ 2.59 = **111mC** (threshold in Charge for 50 yr. old)
2) Threshold EO = Threshold Charge x Amp x Impedance:
.111C x .8A x 281.25Ω = 25 Joules (threshold EO constant for the 50 yr. old).
3) 25J x 2.59 = 65J (default output in joules delivered by later second generation MECTA JR 1 and 2 EO to 50 year old).
4) Confirmation by ER: 65J/.288C = XJ/.111C = **25 Joules**

We shall discuss this phenomenon later. But as the reader can now see, Charge reporting without EO reporting, is not only inadequate, but can be and often is highly misleading. In any case, without EO reporting, critical increases in power and titration can and often do remain invisible.

---

[334] As noted in the above footnote, the mechanism of multiplying 2.01 and 2.59 by threshold outputs to determine titration level, works in every category with one exception- that of the ten year old child. Once again, the author is either slightly off in this particular calculation or MECTA is inconsistent in this one age class. Could such a slight, but extremely misleading inconsistency be deliberate?

CHAPTER 28

Determining Maximum Electrical Parameters (other than EO) for MECTA 2nd Gen. BP Devices

Like the later Somatics device, maximum parameters of MECTA's later JR/SR 1 @ 2 second generation BP device (Amperage, Frequency, Pulse Width, Duration[335]) are limited to an artificial "220Ω" multiplier (of various multiplicands) which when combined must not exceed a product of approximately 101 Joules. As previously noted, however, this 101 Joules is but an unexplained ER (or Reverse-ER) output, the result of a false or "average" "220Ω" constant artificially replacing the actual maximum Impedance. In turn, it is this unexplained ER (or Reverse-ER) of 101 Joules in lieu of actual maximum output in Joules which is reported to physicians in the form of Machine Readouts for both of MECTA's later (and earlier) SR 1 and SR 2 second generation BP devices. Unexplained is the fact that rather than multiplying maximum parameters by the 220Ω false constant (or average) to derive the 101J ER maximum, maximum parameters should be multiplied by the actual though unreported maximum Impedance of 562.5Ω. [336] Only then can we derive the machine's actual unreported maximum output of approximately 260J and only then can we see the machine's true character of delivering a 2.59 MTTLOI to all age recipients. Multiplying maximum electrical parameters with the artificial constant or "average" of "220Ω" gives us a false maximum readout of 101J while multiplying maximum electrical parameters with the actual (unreported) maximum Impedance of 562.5Ω, gives us the actual maximum output of 259J for both of MECTA's later second generation BP devices.

SR 1: Reported Output = .8 Amperes x .8 Amperes x **220Ω** x
180 Pulses x *.002 Pulse Width* x 2.0 *Seconds* = ***101.376J***.

SR 1: Unreported Output = .8 Amperes x .8 Amperes x **562.5Ω** x
180 Pulses x *.002 Pulse Width* x 2.0 *Seconds* = ***259.2J***.

SR 2: Reported Output = .8 Amperes x .8 Amperes x **220Ω** x
180 Pulses x *.001 Pulse Width* x 4.0 *Seconds* = ***101.376J***.

SR 2: Unreported Output = .8 Amperes x .8 Amperes x **562.5Ω** x
180 Pulses x *.001 Pulse Width* x 4.0 *Seconds* = ***259.2J***.

Clearly, the reported 101J maximum machine Readout is but an ER (or Reverse-ER) based on an artificial 220Ω Impedance "average," as opposed to the actual maximum output of 259.2J at the actual maximum Impedance of 562.5Ω, both of which go unreported. We can now see that the 110J APA ceiling, while appearing

---

[335] Alternative parameters are defined here as electrical measurements other than EO (Joules).

[336] "Maximum Machine Impedance" is the unreported maximum Impedance (in human recipients) reached by a MECTA BP device.

to remain intact, has, in fact, been dropped by MECTA and that circa 101J is only the Reverse-ER of the actual maximum output (259.2J) which, as noted above, goes completely unreported.

ER: ***101.4/.3J/220Ω*** = ***259.2J/562.5Ω***

MECTA does not provide Voltage. But by indicating 101J as maximum output, MECTA is indirectly reporting a misleading 176V maximum. [337] Because 101J is but an ER output maximum, 176V is but an ER-Voltage maximum equivalent to a 220Ω ER-Impedance maximum. [338] As such, in lieu of the reported "101J at 220Ω" ER/RRC, the ER/RRC could be expressed as: **176V at 220Ω or 176V at 101.3J**. [339] Below, we see how ER-Voltage or ER-Impedance, can be used to derive the reported, but entirely misleading ER-Output maximum.

SR 1: Reported EO = .8 x .8 Amperes x **220Ω** x 180 Pulses x .002 Pulse Width x 2.0 Seconds = **101.376 Joules**.

SR 1: Reported EO = **176V** x .8 Amperes x 180 Pulses x .002 Pulse Width x 2.0 Seconds = **101.376 Joules**.

SR 2: Reported EO = .8 x .8 Amperes x **220Ω** x 180 Pulses x .001 Pulse Width x 4.0 Seconds = **101.376 Joules**.

SR 2: Reported EO = **176V** x .8 Amperes x 180 Pulses x .001 Pulse Width x 4.0 Seconds = **101.376 Joules**.

Compare the ER-Voltage (176V), ER-Impedance (220Ω), and ER-Output (101.3J) above to actual maximum Voltage (450V) [340] utilized at actual maximum Impedance (562.5Ω) at actual maximum output (259.2J), none of which MECTA reports.

SR 1: Actual EO = .8 Amperes .8 Amperes x **562.5Ω** x 180 Pulses x .002 Pulse Width x 2.0 Seconds = **259.2J**.

SR 1: Actual EO = **450V** x .8 Amperes x 180 Pulses x .002 Pulse Width x 2.0 Seconds = **259.2J**.

SR 2: Actual EO = .8 Amperes .8 Amperes x **562.5Ω** x 180 Pulses x .001 Pulse Width x 4.0 Seconds = **259.2J**.

---

[337] By using a derivation of the Voltage oriented formula for discovering EO and the depicted 101J maximum EO, we obtain the indirectly reported 176V figure. Voltage = EO/Current x Pulses x Pulse width x Duration. (SR 2: Voltage = 101J/.8A x 180 Pulses x .001PW x 4.0Sec = 176V; SR 1: 101J/.8A x 180 Pulses x .002 PW x 2.0 Sec. = 176V).

[338] Using a reverse-ER of 176V/220Ω to maximum Impedance, we can determine actual maximum Voltage: 176V/220Ω = XV/562.5Ω. **X = 450V.** We can also find maximum Voltage using a reverse ER of 101.4J/176V to true maximum Output 101.4J/176V = 259.25J/XV. **X = 450V.**

[339] A second method of deriving the ER-Voltage is through the formula: Voltage = Current x Resistance. Voltage = .8 Amperes x 220Ω = 176 Volts.

[340] As noted, from the 176V-ER, using speculative actual Impedance or speculative actual EO, we can derive actual Voltage.**176V/220Ω = XV/562.5Ω.** ***X = 450V***.**101.4/176V = 259.25J/XV** = ***450V***. Actual Voltage on second generation MECTA BP devices (not provided by MECTA) is between 444.4 - 480 Volts. Possibilities: (1) Voltage = **256 Joules**/.8 Amperes x 180 x .001 x 4.0 = **444.4 Volts**. (2) Voltage = **276 Joules**/.8 Amperes x 180 x .001 x 4.0 = **480 Volts**. In that maximum possible Impedance of 600Ω is probably not used and in that manufacturers favor round numbers for Voltage, the author speculates **450V** as the correct maximum for second generation MECTA BP devices, emitting **259.2J** maximums. Voltage = **259.2 Joules**/.8 Amperes x 180 x .001 x 4.0 = **450 Volts**.

SR 2: Actual EO = **450V** x .8 Amperes x 180 Pulses x .001 Pulse Width x 4.0 Seconds = **259.2J**. [341]

Actual maximum Voltage (450V), then, is at least 2.56 fold [342] the required Voltage (176V) needed to emit the misleading 101.4/3J maximum Output reported via readout displays on all later second generation MECTA BP devices. This is because actual maximum output is not the reported 101.4/3J, but a much more probable albeit unreported 259.2J.

Deliberate "101J" Figure Arbitrary

That MECTA's reported "101.376J at 220Ω," like Somatics' "99.4J at 220Ω," has no literal correlation and is but an arbitrary (unexplained) Pure-ER/RRC phrase which can be seen by checking the detailed charts above, [343] and from the fact that numerous EO/Impedance combinations could be used to express the same Pure-ER/RRC to derive the same actual maximum output. Thus, while "101J at 220Ω" is but one possibility, numerous other equivalent Pure-ER/RRC phrases could be used. For example:

*101.376J/220Ω = 150J/327Ω = **259.2J**/562.5Ω*

In short, the arbitrary utilization of a circa 100J figure to express an unexplained Pure-ER/RRC (i.e. , 101.3J at 220Ω) suggestive of a circa 100J ceiling (or even circa 110J ceiling) seemingly corroborated by a spurious machine readout maximum of 101J appears deliberately suggestive of conformity to the APA 110J ceiling guaranteeing minimal stimulus, which by this time, both MECTA (and Somatics) had entirely discarded.

False Implications

MECTA's new reporting of "101J at 220," the "220Ω" figure of which is sometimes described as "typical," seemingly suggestive of average Impedance, does nothing to dispel the assumption of a 101J or 110J ceiling. In brief, no aspect of MECTA's reporting mechanism allays the natural assumption of "101J at 220Ω" as a conditional-ER-RRC (in lieu of a Pure-ER/RRC) with either 101J or 110J as maximum output in accordance with the APA Standard. What regulators had no way of realizing is that MECTA had mutated the so-called "typical 220Ω" into a false constant supplanting all actual Impedances for the sole purpose of calculating misleading readout displays suggestive of minimal stimulus. The result is EO readouts (in Joules) grossly lower than the actual EOs administered to recipients with Impedances higher than "220Ω. " In short, EO displays are misleadingly limited to 101 Joules maximum. To be plain, EO displays based on actual Impedances result in the much higher actual Energy Outputs truly emitted by second generation MECTA BP devices. Based on

---

[341] Through the probable maximum Voltage, Impedance and Energy Output figures here are extremely probable and yet we must call them approximate in that given only the parameters MECTA provides, actual maximum Voltage, actual maximum Impedance, and actual maximum Output are impossible to derive.

[342] 450V ÷ 176V = 2.56 fold

[343] It is only due to an ER abstraction that the maximum 2.0 Second Duration for the SR1 (4.0 Seconds for the SR 2), 180 Pulses, and the 220Ω ER are utilized to derive the seemingly significant **101.4J** figure. The actual JR/SR 1 machine at an actual 220Ω, utilizes 60 pulses at approximately 1.2 Seconds, emitting 40J; whereas, the JR/SR 2 at an actual 220Ω, utilizes 180 pulses at approximately 1.6 Seconds to emit 40J—not 100J. Thus there is no literal correlation. Too, the "101J at 220Ω" phrase is arbitrary in that numerous other combinations could have been utilized to express the same pure-ER/RRC from which the actual 259J ceiling can be derived, i.e. "150J at 327Ω" (101J/220Ω = 150J/327Ω; .8 Amperes .8 Amperes x **327Ω** x 180 Pulses x .001 Pulse Width x 4.0 Seconds = **150J**; 150J/327Ω = **259J**/562.5Ω). Both the "101J at 220Ω" Pure-ER/RRC suggestive of a conditional-ER/RRC with 101J ceiling bolstered by the false machine readout maximum of 101.4J, and the fact that the "101J at 220Ω" phrase is but an arbitrary Pure-ER phrase all indicate deliberate deception with respect to emphasis of the circa 100J figure indicating minimal stimulus; actual maximum output is a probable unreported 259.2J (see Charts).

Machine Readouts limited to 101Joules, however, administering physicians naturally assume maximum output for second generation MECTA BP devices limited to 101 maximum Joules, i.e. just above threshold for all age recipients.

In sum, the second generation SR1 @ 2 BP machines depict (for physicians) incrementally increasing output readings peaking at 101.4/3J. Maximum Machine Readouts of approximately 101J for both MECTA second generation BP devices bolster the natural interpretation of "101J at 220Ω" as a conditional-ER/RRC wherein 101J is the absolute ceiling. In turn, the 101J maximum output depiction suggests conformity to the APA 110J ceiling, the ceiling Richard Weiner, representing both American BP manufacturers and the American Psychiatric Association, suggested to the FDA as the Brief Pulse ceiling in 1982 (Department of Health and Human Services, 1982a, A53; E20). Succinctly, the freshly devised unreported Mectan transmutation utilizing a new unreported ceiling based on a Pure-ER/RRC interpretation (that is--sans the 110J ceiling) of the seemingly innocuous "101J at 220Ω" phrase newly contingent upon maximum machine Impedance not only failed to indicate the dropping of the circa 110J ceiling, but in fact, suggested its conservation. [344]

Beginning with MECTA (and perhaps Somatics almost simultaneously), all four American manufacturers between 1983 and 1985 began reporting the circa "100J at 220Ω" phrase for their then new second generation BP devices. Machines by all four BP manufacturers (MECTA, Somatics, Medcraft, and Elcot) ubiquitously exhibited maximum Machine Readouts of circa 100 Joules. Furtively applying this novel means of reporting what appeared to adhere to the 1982 APA ceiling standard of 110J, three of the manufacturers (MECTA, Somatics, and Elcot), as noted, actually began interpreting the new "100J at 220Ω" phraseology in a manner no longer based on a 110J ceiling, but on maximum machine Impedance allowing much higher unreported outputs and thus much higher MTTLOIs (circa 2.5 fold) than the "just above threshold" 1.1 MTTLOI outputs mandated by the APA 110J ceiling. Simply put, MECTA immediately followed by Somatics,[345] transmuted the APA "70J at 220Ω" *conditional-ER/RRC* (with 110J ceiling) to a "100J at 220Ω" *Pure-ER/RRC* based on maximum machine Impedance, thereby, secretly dropping the 110J ceiling and obtaining a new invisible output potential (newly based on the APA 600Ω maximum) of 273J for second generation BP devices, generally. [346] Neither the transmutation nor the new ceiling has ever been reported--until now.

Pure-ER/RRC: 100J/220Ω = XJ/600Ω. **X = 273J**.

Figuring MECTA Machine Parameters

In that MECTA (since about 1983) has refused to divulge actual Voltage, actual maximum Output (in Joules), and actual maximum Impedance, the electrical parameters cannot be determined except through speculation. In fact, it is theoretically possible that MECTA via the un-condoned Pure-ER/RRC interpretation deemed the Mectan Transmutation, utilizes the full 600Ω Impedance maximum (permitted by the APA Standard) and thus the new potential 276J maximum for its later MECTA second generation SR 1 and 2 BP devices. To determine this figure, we merely need supplant the artificial 220Ω false constant (MECTA uses for its machine readout calculations) with the potential 600Ω maximum Impedance (permitted by the APA). In short, by first using 220Ω and then supplanting that with 600Ω, we can derive first MECTA's 101J reported output maximum and then MECTA's possible 276J maximum output:

[344] The APA ER/RRC of "70J at 220Ω," was like the later circa "100J at 220Ω" an obvious ER/RRC mandating descending outputs relative to descending age), but, unlike "100J at 220Ω," "70J at 220Ω," was a conditional (--not pure--) ER/RRC, limiting all outputs to a clear 110 absolute ceiling (70J/220Ω = 110J/345Ω). This is why, in order to increase Impedance, one had to decrease the ER/RRC, i.e.59J/220Ω = 110J/410Ω. The 108J MECTA "C" presented to the FDA based on "59J at 220Ω" was clearly designed to conform to both aspects of the 1982 APA Standard —the "70J at 220Ω" ER/RRC compelling gradient outputs relative to age and the 110J ceiling compelling minimal stimulus output for all age categories.

[345] Elcot dropped out, becoming defunct while Medcraft violated the APA Standard in an entirely different manner as we shall observe in detail a little later on.

[346] Although the APA Standard permitted 600Ω, the same Standard clearly limited EO to 110 maximum Joules. Thus if overcoming 600Ω was actually needed, manufacturers should have reduced other electrical parameters in order to maintain the 110 Joule ceiling. The Mectan Transmutation resulting in EO grossly surpassing 110 Joules is a clear a violation of the 1982 APA Standard.

SR 1: **Reported (ER) EO** = .8 Amperes x .8 Amperes x **220Ω** x 180 Pulses x .002 Pulse Width x 2.0 Seconds = **101.376J**.

SR 2: **Reported (ER) EO** = .8 Amperes x .8 Amperes x **220Ω** x 180 Pulses x .001 Pulse Width x 4.0 Seconds = **101.376J**.

SR 1: **Unreported Actual EO** = .8 Amperes x .8 Amperes x **600Ω** x 180 Pulses x .002 Pulse Width x 2.0 Seconds = **276.48 Joules**.

SR 2: **Unreported Actual EO** = .8 Amperes x .8 Amperes x **600Ω** x 180 Pulses x .001 Pulse Width x 4.0 Seconds = **276.48 Joules**.

If the 276J figures are correct, the second generation MECTA (SR 1 @ 2) devices utilizes a maximum 480V and emits a maximum 276J output. [347]

SR 1: EO = **480V** x .8Amps x 180 Pulses x .002 Pulse Width x 2.0 Seconds = **276.48 Joules**.

SR 2: EO = **480V** x .8Amps x 180 Pulses x .001 Pulse Width x 4.0 Seconds = **276.48 Joules**.

We can, however, in spite of MECTA's neglect to report maximum output in joules, get a hint from MECTA's machine dials. In that the second generation MECTA BP JR/SR 2 machine dial for varying the Duration (from 0.5 to 4.0 seconds) is cryptically subdivided into precisely 256 unexplained increments (Sackeim and Weiner, 1993, p.3), both MECTA SR 1 and 2 devices may emit circa 256J maximums, a theory which seems to bear out in that the resulting maximum Impedance is a derivable 555.5Ω, the exact maximum Impedance utilized and reported by Somatics for its Thymatron DG.

(.8A x .8A x **XΩ** x 180 Pulses x .002 Pulse Width x 2.0 Sec. = 256J; .4608X = 256J; **X = 555.5Ω**).

The similar increase in power from first to second generation MECTA devices followed by a similar increase in power from first to second generation Somatics' devices, suggests that the Somatics second generation Thymatron DG BP device [348] (for which we can derive exact parameters) is highly emulative of second generation MECTA SR1 and 2 BP devices. In fact, the two manufacturers appear to have used uniform reporting mechanisms to strengthen the impression of conformity both to each other and to the 1982, 110J APA ceiling Standard. Based on a more likely 555.5Ω maximum Impedance (in lieu of 600Ω), then, second generation MECTA BP devices appear to have circa **256J** output ceilings (in lieu of 276J ceilings based on maximum allowable APA Impedance):

SR 1: EO = .8 Amperes x .8 Amperes x **555.5Ω** x 180 Pulses x .002 Pulse Width x 2.0 Seconds = **256 Joules**.

SR 2: EO = .8 Amperes x .8 Amperes x **555.5Ω** x 180 Pulses x .001 Pulse Width x 4.0 Seconds = **256 Joules**.

---

[347] (Ohm's Law): Voltage = Impedance x Current. Voltage = 600Ω x .8 = 480 Volts. Both SR 1 and 2, regardless of varying parameters, are equally powerful.

[348] Somatics, unlike MECTA, reveals for its Thymatron DG a maximum Impedance of **555.5Ω**.

On the other hand, at a **555.5Ω** and **256J**, maximum Voltage for the MECTA devices is **444.4 Volts**. We can determine the 444.4V maximum by using the Voltage-oriented formula for determining output for BP devices in conjunction with the possible 256J maximum output:

SR 1: EO = **444.4 Volts** x .8 Amperes x 180 Pulses x .002 Pulse Width x 2.0 Seconds = **256 Joules**.

SR 2: EO = **444.4 Volts** x .8 Amperes x 180 Pulses x .001 Pulse Width x 4.0 Seconds = **256 Joules**. [349]

256J maximums for second generation MECTA BP devices, then, are probable. However, in that most manufacturers seem to prefer round numbers for Voltage, the author speculates that an actual 450V maximum (in lieu of a 444.4V maximum) is used for MECTA second generation BP devices, resulting in a slightly higher maximum output of 259.2J [350] and from which we can derive an actual maximum Impedance not of 555.5Ω, but 562.5Ω. (Odd figures for Impedance rather than Voltage are the norm.) The author thus speculates that second generation made-for-America SR 1 and SR 2 MECTA BP devices emit a maximum energy output of **259.2J**, a maximum Impedance of **562.5Ω**, and a maximum Voltage of **450V**. (Remaining electrical parameters are provided by MECTA.) Thus:

SR1: (Voltage-Oriented Formula For Finding Output):
EO = **450 Volts** x .8 Amperes x 180 Pulses x .002 Pulse Width x 2.0 Seconds = **259.2 Joules**.

SR 1: (Impedance-Oriented Formula For Finding Output):
EO = .8 Amperes x .8 Amperes x **562.5Ω** x 180 Pulses x .002 Pulse Width x 2.0 Seconds = **259.2 Joules**. [351]

SR 2: (Voltage-Oriented Formula For Finding Output):
EO = **450 Volts** x .8 Amperes x 180 Pulses x .001 Pulse Width x 4.0 Seconds = **259.2 Joules**.

SR 2: (Impedance-Oriented Formula For Finding Output):
EO = .8 Amperes x .8 Amperes x **562.5Ω** x 180 Pulses x .001 Pulse Width x 4.0 Seconds = **259.2 Joules**.

In short, beginning about 1985, (just before Somatics Incorporated followed suit), MECTA began reporting what appeared to be a new Conditional-ER/RRC of circa "101J at 220Ω" while, in fact, furtively interpreting the phrase as a "Pure-ER/RRC" to maximum machine Impedance in order to increase the power of its BP devices. This surreptitious interpretation transmuted the potential EO ceiling for second generation BP devices from what appeared to be a reported 101J maximum (seemingly corroborated by machine readouts) to an unreported 273J potential maximum (101J/220Ω = 273J/600Ω). Grossly surpassing the 110J APA maximum, then, both Somatics and MECTA second generation BP device machines electronically depicted artificially reduced readout maximums of circa 100 Joules perhaps alongside actual Impedances read by physicians. Marketed in the U. S., newly enhanced (second generation) MECTA BP devices based upon probable unreported 450V maximums were, in fact, capable of unreported outputs up to about 260 Joules--2.5 fold the

[349] SR1 Voltage = .8 Amp x 180 Pulses x .002 PW x 2.0 Sec ÷ 256J = 444.4V; SR2 Voltage = .8 Amp x 180 Pulses x .001 PW x 4.0 Sec ÷ 256J = 444.4V.

[350] The 256 increments on the Duration dial which probably represents Joules may be an attempt at rounded uniformity with second generation Somatics devices or vice-versa.

[351] Maximum Impedance SR 1 = 259.2J ÷ .8 Amps x .8 Amps x 180 Pulses x .002 PW x 2.0 Secs. = 562.5Ω; SR 2 = 259.2J ÷ .8 Amps x .8 Amps x 180 Pulses x .001 PW x 4.0 Secs. = 562.5Ω.

110J APA ceiling which by this time, both MECTA and Somatics had almost simultaneously discarded. Neglecting to maintain a circa 100J (or even 110J) ceiling via the expected reduction of various electrical parameters (i.e. reduced Duration) as the APA Standard implicitly compelled, MECTA's second generation BP devices began secretly surpassing even the 200J SW maximum depicted in the 1982 APA Standard (compared to which Brief Pulse devices were touted to be reduced by half). [352] Even as Brief Pulse machines secretly increased in power, therefore, MECTA continued to report 101J maximums for its second generation JR/SR 1 and 2 BP devices via what appeared to be "101.4J at 220Ω" and "101.3J at 220Ω" conditional-ER/RRCs, seemingly corroborated by misleading Machine Readouts of 101 maximum Joules. The illusion of circa 100J maximums, as has been noted, continued to suggest just above threshold outputs for all age categories. In short, MECTA, followed by Somatics, had cleverly transmuted the APA "70J at 220Ω" conditional-ER/RRC (with 110J ceiling) into a "101J at 220Ω" Pure-ER/RRC (sans 110J ceiling) newly based on maximum machine Impedances, resulting in MTTLOIs no longer just above threshold at 1.1 fold, but circa 2.6 fold threshold in every age category. In essence, MECTA (and Somatics) had turned the 110J APA ceiling into a 101J ER--without ever explaining or disclosing the transition! The actual machine ceiling for MECTA second generation BP devices--a probable 259.2 maximum Joules--remains unreported (by MECTA) even to this day (Cameron, 1994). [353]

[352] The 200J SW potential was depicted by Weiner in the 1982 APA Standard as twice the output evinced by the purported 100J maximum elicited by BP devices, therefore greatly "improved over SW" by virtue of greatly reduced output.

[353] MECTA refuses to divulge Voltage. Based upon the 555.5 Ω used by Somatics and 256 increments on the MECTA Duration dial assumed to represent Joules, the author in a previous paper conservatively estimated 256 Joules and 444.4 Volts for second generation MECTA BP devices (Cameron, 1994). More likely, second generation MECTA devices use 450 Volt maximums and thus a 259J maximum EO. Theoretically, however, based upon the 600Ω APA ceiling, it is possible MECTA devices could use circa 480 Volts emitting up to 276 Joules. [EO = Current squared x Impedance x Pulses x Wave Length x Duration. SR 2: EO = .8 x .8 Amps x 600Ω x 180 Pulses x .001 Pulse Width x 4 Seconds Duration = 276 Joules. Voltage = Joules/Current x Pulses x Pulse Width x Duration. Voltage = 276 Joules/.8 Amps x 180 Pulses x .001 Pulse Width x 4 Seconds Duration = 479 Volts. (SR 1: Use 2.0 Sec Duration and .002 WL to obtain same outcome.) Also Voltage = Current x Resistance. Voltage = .8 x 600Ω = 480Volts.]

CHAPTER 29

Correlation of Max. Charge to Spurious EO Max. of 2nd Gen. MECTA BP Devices

MECTA, like Somatics, similarly creates a false correlation between maximum Charge and what appears to be a circa 101J ceiling. Indeed, for MECTA's second generation JR/SR 1 and 2 BP devices, MECTA reported the "101J at 220Ω" phrase along with true maximum Charge (cumulative electricity) of .576C. In short, using the Charge-oriented formula: EO = Charge x Impedance x Constant Current, but plugging in the false constant 220Ω Impedance with the maximum Charge of .576C, maximum EO for both the SR 1@2 seems to be 101J.

.576C (Charge) x 220Ω x .8A = 101.4/3J (EO)

Conversely, by plugging in MECTA's reported phrase "101.4/3J at 220Ω" into a derivative of the above Charge-oriented formula, we can obtain true maximum Charge for MECTA's second generation JR/SR 1 and 2 BP devices.

101.4/3J ÷ 220Ω x .8 Amperes = **.576C (Charge)**

In short, the 101.4/3J figures depicted as maximum output on second generation MECTA SR1@2 machine Readouts can be derived by multiplying actual maximum Charge by the reported 220Ω Impedance figure in conjunction with constant current. Conversely, the actual maximum .576C Charge for MECTA's made-for-America second generation SR 1 @ 2 BP devices (Royal College of Psychiatry, 1995, p.125) can be derived from MECTA's reported phrase: "101.4/3J at 220Ω" in conjunction with constant current. Thus, the .576C actual maximum Charge for the devices appears to correlate with what seems to be a 101.4/3J maximum EO on both devices. Consequently, the reported 101J EO and .576C Charge appear to be corresponding maximums once again creating the spurious impression of minimal stimulus devices adhering to the 110J APA ceiling. In fact, such a device could only exist by reducing one or more electrical parameters, such as reducing the .8A constant current of the MECTA SR1 and 2 to a .313A constant current as depicted below.

Expected 2nd GENERATION CONSTANT CURRENT **JR/SR 1** BRIEF PULSE ECT DEVICE with Reduced .313A Reduced Amperage based on Conditional-ER/RRC of "101.4J at 220Ω" with Maximum 101.4J

VOLTAGE	POWER % @ Age	AGE Yrs	Ω Ohms	FREQUENCY (Hz)	DURATION (SECs)	CURRENT mAmps	ENERGY Joules	CHARGE mC
45	10	10	56.25	40	.5	313	1.13	64
90	20	20	112.5	40	.9	313	4.3	115.2
135	30	30	168.75	60	.9	313	9	172.8
180	40	40	225	60	1.2	313	16	230.4
225	50	50	281.25	60	1.5	313	25	288
270	60	60	337.5	90	1.2	313	39	345.6
292.5	65	65	365.63	90	1.3	313	43	374.4
315	70	70	393.75	90	1.4	313	50	403.2
360	80	80	450	90	1.6	313	65	460.8
405	90	90	506.25	90	1.8	313	82	518.4
450	100	100	562.5	90	2.0	313	101.4	576

.002 Second Pulse Width

Expected 2nd GENERATION CONSTANT CURRENT **JR/SR 2** BRIEF PULSE ECT DEVICE With Reduced.313A Amperage based on Conditional-ER/RRC OF "101.3J AT 220Ω" with 101.3J Ceiling

VOLTAGE	POWER % @ Age	AGE Yrs	Ω Ohms	FREQUENCY (Hz)	DURATION (SECs)	CURRENT mAmps	ENERGY Joules	CHARGE mC
45	10	10	56.25	90	0.5	313	1.13	72
90	20	20	112.5	90	0.8	313	4.3	115.2
135	30	30	168.75	90	1.2	313	9	172.8
180	40	40	225	90	1.6	313	16	230.4
225	50	50	281.25	90	2.0	313	25	288
270	60	60	337.5	90	2.4	313	39	345.6
292.5	65	65	365.63	90	2.6	313	43	374.4
315	70	70	393.75	90	2.8	313	50	403.2
360	80	80	450	90	3.2	313	65	460.8
405	90	90	506.25	90	3.6	313	82	518.4
450	100	100	562.5	90	4.0	313	101.3	576

.001 Second Pulse Width

Note the corresponding 101.4J maximum with the .576C Charge maximum on the hypothetical devices above. *In fact, the two devices above are non-existent* .

Even so, like Somatics, the misleading 101.3/4J EO "maximum" reported for both MECTA second generation BP devices seems to be corroborated by an actual .576C Charge maximum. In fact, in light of the APA conditional-ER/RRC of "70J at 220Ω" with 110J ceiling depicted in the 1982 APA Standard, a similar conditional-ER/RRC interpretation of "101J at 220Ω" with 110J ceiling is anticipated, an assumption plainly advanced by the depiction of a 101J maximum Machine Readout on both MECTA BP devices. Indeed, MECTA never reports the actual maximum output of these devices (in joules). Moreover, while maximum Charge is accurately reported, regulatory agencies, physicians, or consumers, never adequately informed that MECTA's newly reported 101.4/3J at 220Ω is ***not*** a conditional-ER/RRC incorporative of a 101J (or even 110J) ceiling in similar to the APA Standard, but is a Pure-ER/RRC (sans either 101 or 110J ceiling). Indeed, though unreported, both machines more than double the 110J APA maximum. [354] Never clarified is that the circa 100J figures reported by both MECTA and Somatics for their second generation BP devices have absolutely no relevance to the APA 110J ceiling, or that both companies have transmuted the "70J at 220Ω" conditional-ER/RRC with 110J APA ceiling to a circa 100J at 220Ω Pure-ER/RRC with a new maximum output based only on maximum machine Impedance. Never reported to any agency, on their own volition, both MECTA and Somatics transmuted the "70J at 220Ω" conditional-ER/RRC with 110J ceiling, to a circa "100J at 220Ω" Pure-ER/RRC limited only by maximum machine Impedance up to 600Ω (100J/220Ω = 273J/600Ω). Neither report that Machine Readouts on MECTA (and Somatics) second generation BP devices are not actual outputs at all, but Reverse-ERs (more or less, an "average") misleadingly suggestive of the circa 100J maximum depicted in the 1982 APA Standard. Certainly, regulatory agencies had no notion that accompanying MECTA's and Somatics' secret transmutation methodology was the total dropping of the 110J APA ceiling.

Left to Assume

Regulatory overseers were thus left to assume the original 110J APA ceiling intact within the neoteric "101.4/3J at 220Ω" phrases MECTA began reporting for its second generation BP devices. Certainly, as noted previously, the circa "100J at 220Ω" phrases (reported by both MECTA and Somatics) may even have appeared to represent a more compact version of the APA Standard itself, that is, a combination conditional-ER/RRC of "100J at 220Ω" with circa 100J ceiling suggesting a slight augmentation of RRC (Rate Rise Ceiling) but with an even stricter overall ceiling. With the ceiling intact or even reduced, the RRC increase as we have seen, would have no impact on the APA Standard and thus seemingly no impact on the devices which appeared to remain at a 1.1 or even 1.0 MTTLOI retaining minimal stimulus output status. The fact that a circa 100J reverse-ER had precipitously and without elaboration, supplanted the 110J APA ceiling masking the ER nature of the

---

[354] The phrase "101J at 220Ω" is similar in construction to the original APA conditional-ER/RRC of "70J at 220Ω." As such, the new ER/RRC of "101J at 220Ω"doesn't seem to affect the APA ceiling of 110J. Maximum Machine Readouts depicting 101 Joules in tandem with true maximum Charge engender the assumption that BP machines continue to be limited to approximately 100 maximum Joules and thus minimal stimulus output at all age levels. MECTA's actual maximum output of 259.2 Joules has never been reported.

new circa 100J figure, that is, that a Pure-ER/RRC interpretation of the new circa "100J at 220Ω" phrase had replaced the APA's conditional-ER/RRC of "70J at 220Ω" with 110J ceiling could not have been known by any but the manufacturers themselves. Instead, as noted previously, overseers such as the FDA were left to assume the new circa "100J at 220Ω" phrase but a new conditional-ER/RRC with a newer, stricter circa 100J ceiling for BP devices generally, leaving the 110J APA ceiling unaltered. The facts that false maximum Machine Readouts for MECTA devices of 101.4/3J are depicted in tandem with the actual maximum charge of .576C, that the .576C actual maximum Charge can be mathematically derived from the reported, but unexplained "101J at 220Ω" ER-phrases and vice-versa, suggesting a maximum output of "101" maximum Joules, the fact that readout maximums on the machines themselves depicted 101 maximum Joules, and finally that actual maximum outputs for the second generation SR1 @ 2s were never and have never been reported in any academic journal or MECTA manual to date, all acted in unison to create a seeming parity between an actual .576C maximum Charge and what appeared to be an actual 101J maximum output for both of MECTA's second generation BP devices. Both figures (actual Charge and the Reverse-ER-output of 101 Joules) appear to be actual maximum parameters, seemingly corroborative of 101J maximum outputs. In sum, the machines appear to be but minimal stimulus extensions of the MECTA "C," whereas, in fact, the new ceiling (allowed by manufacturers) had actually risen from 110 to 273 Joules.

Correlation of Maximum Charge to Spurious EO Maximum of Second Generation MECTA BP Device continued:

Exacerbating the deception as has been noted and unbeknownst to regulatory agencies, the same reported **.576C** maximum Charge derivable from the unexplained **"101J at 220Ω"** Pure-ER/RRC phrase is also derivable from the true but unreported maximum Output/maximum Impedance phrase: **259.2J at 562.5Ω**.

101.4/3J/*220Ω* x .8 Amperes **= .576C (Charge)**

or

259.2J/*562.5Ω* x .8 Amperes **= .576C (Charge)**

Conversely, while the Reverse-ER Impedance of **220Ω** can be used with the actual maximum Charge of **.576C** to derive the reverse-ER Output of **101J**, the actual maximum Impedance of **562.5Ω** can also be used with the actual maximum Charge of **.576C** to derive the actual maximum output of **259.2J**. [355]

.576C x 220Ω x .8A = 101.3J (EO)

or

.576C x 562.5Ω x .8A = 259.2J (EO) [356]

In brief, the same .576C Charge ceiling used to derive what appears to be a conditional--ER/RRC of 101.4/3 Joules at 220Ω with an implicit 101 ceiling can be similarly used to derive the true unreported maximum output of circa **259.2J** at a true unreported maximum Impedance of **562.5Ω**, neither of which

[355] In fact, .576C can be derived from an infinite number of ERs. For example, 259.1J/562.5Ω = 184.2J/400Ω.184.2J/400Ω x .8A = .576C.

[356] Derivative EOs from a possible 600Ω and 555.5Ω are as follows: EO = .576 Coulombs x *600Ω* x .8 Amperes = **276.48J**; Charge = **276.48J**/600Ω x .8 Amperes = .576 Coulombs. EO = .576 Coulombs x *555.5Ω* x .8 Amperes = **256J**; Charge = **256J**/*555.5Ω* x .8 Amperes = .576 Coulombs. Note how all the phrases are ERs to one another: 101.4J/220Ω = 276.48J/600Ω = 259.1J/562.5Ω = 256J/555.5Ω.

MECTA has ever reported. [357] [358] Indeed, as has been noted, manufacturers, at this point, no longer confined maximum output to the conditional 110J APA ceiling (guaranteeing minimal stimulus), but rather to the pure-ER (in MECTA's case) of "101J at 220Ω" to (in MECTA's case again) the unreported maximum machine Impedance of 562.5Ω to achieve a never before reported 259.2J maximum output. This transmutation, however, is by no means apparent in that, as noted above, the same reported .576 Coulomb Charge ceiling which can be derived from the actual but unreported maximum output of 259.2J at the actual but unreported maximum Impedance of 562.5Ω, can also be derived from the unexplained "101.4J at 220Ω" Pure-ER/RRC phrase reported for both SR1@2 BP devices.

The phenomenon of the actual .576C Charge maximum derived from two different output/Impedance relationships as well as the same .576C Charge maximum used to derive both a true maximum EO of 259.2J and a false maximum output of 101J is due to the "101J at 220Ω" Pure-ER relationship to the actual but unreported maximum 259.1J Output at maximum 562.5Ω Impedance.

Pure-ER/RRC: **101.4/3J/220Ω = 259.1J/562.5Ω**

The secret of this magic trick then, is the pure-ER relationship of the two phrases. No longer limited by the APA 110J ceiling, this Pure-ER relationship between the two phrases (one visible and one invisible) permits MECTA to derive the same .576C maximum Charge from both the reported "101J at 220Ω" and the unreported "259.1J at 562.5Ω" phrases. Even more importantly, however, the same actual .576C Charge maximum can be used with a false 220Ω "constant" to derive an apparent maximum EO of "101.4/3J. " Of course, the same actual .576C Charge maximum can be used with the actual unreported 562.5Ω to derive the actual but never reported maximum EO of 259.1J. [359] It is through this (Reverse ER) phenomenon, therefore, that MECTA depicts 101.3 and 101.4 maximum Joules respectively for its second generation BP devices, via machine readouts.

A true 101J at 220Ω conditional-ER/RRC limited by a 101 or even 110J overall ceiling would, like the APA standard, would limit these machines to a consistent just above threshold output for all age categories with BL ECT. Certainly, the 110J original maximum output depicted within the 1982 APA Standard represents the litmus of just over threshold safety and thus true superiority over SW. In that the .576 Coulomb maximum Charge can be derived both from the unexplained pure-ER phrase, "101J at 220Ω" and the actual unreported maximums of "259.1J at 562.5Ω," [360] like Somatics' reporting of "99.4J at 220Ω," MECTA's omission of true maximum output (and in MECTA's case, omission of true Impedance) renders the reporting of even true maximum Charge alone not only insufficient, but compellingly misleading. Moreover, reporting maximum Charge (.576 Coulombs) in tandem with an unexplained ER Energy Output or what only appears to be a maximum output of 101.4/3J (or even 110J) while neglecting to report actual maximum output itself, is actively deceptive. This practice effectively enables a double standard of reporting what appears to be a 101.4/3J maximum output (superficially substantiated via maximum Machine Readouts) while secretly permitting 259.1 Joules for MECTA second generation BP devices. Certainly, the reported 101J phrase in the absence of actual maximum output (as well as actual maximum Impedance) misleadingly suggests "conformity" to the 1982 APA ceiling Standard of 110 maximum Joules.

Fully cognizant of the new actual maximum outputs (of a probable 259.1 Joules) for their second generation made-for America JR/SR 1 and 2 devices marketed throughout the Western hemisphere, from about 1983 forward, MECTA Corporation and Somatics began simultaneously omitting the reporting of actual maximum

---

[357] The author speculates maximum Impedance at 562.5Ω derived from a speculative 450V maximum emitting a speculative 259.1J maximum. However, it is possible the maximum Impedance for MECTA's second generation BP devices could be either 600Ω or 555.5Ω derived from possible maximums of 480V and 444.4V respectively, emitting respective maximums of 276.48J or 256J. These probable outputs used for MECTA's second generation BP devices within the U.S. and other non-IEC mandated countries have never been reported to the public, any Regulatory Agency, or published in any major journal (Cameron, 1994).

[358] 562.5Ω is derived from unreported maximum machine Voltage of 450V derived circuitously by the author. MECTA neglects to report actual maximum output, actual maximum Impedance, and actual maximum Voltage.

[359] Other possible actual maximums include: 276.48J at 600Ω and 256J at 555.5Ω.

[360] MECTA refuses to divulge maximum Voltage or maximum Impedance and thus the following actual maximums are, as noted, possible for the JR/SR 1 @ 2; a 600Ω ceiling based upon 480V emitting 276J; a 562.5Ω ceiling based on 450 Volts emitting 259.1J, or a 555.5Ω ceiling based on 444.4 Volts emitting 256J. Of the three, the author speculates 259.1J as the most probable and it is this figure the author assumes as maximum output for the made-for America MECTA JR/SR 1@ 2.

output (in joules), instead, reporting actual maximum Charge (i.e. .576 Coulombs for MECTA devices) in tandem with an unexplained pure-ER-EO of circa 100 Joules. [361] Significantly, MECTA and Somatics (and even the now defunct Elcot), began excluding the reporting of actual maximum output (in joules) just as their BP devices began equaling and then surpassing SW in power. Instead, these same manufacturers implemented (in unison) the misleading practice of reporting an unexplained circa 100J pure-ER output in conjunction with actual maximum Charge. In addition to the elimination of actual output reporting, moreover, MECTA is unique amongst American manufacturers, as noted, in also omitting not only maximum Impedance, but actual maximum Voltage,[362] making a false correlation between the actual .576C Charge maximum and a reported (but false) 101J output maximum, inevitable. [363]

Critically then, in the absence of actual Output and actual Impedance reporting, the derivation and reporting of what appears to be a 101J maximum output using actual maximum Charge, actively suggests an actual 101J ceiling for MECTA's second generation SR1 and 2 devices. This false conclusion, as noted, is heavily bolstered by machine readout maximums of 101 Joules depicted on both SR1 and SR2 second generation MECTA BP devices. (Both machines depict false 101 Joule maximums, as noted, as a result of a specious calculation based on a misleading maximum Impedance of 220Ω.) Not only is the discarding of actual maximum Output reporting in no way compensated by the reporting of actual maximum Charge alone then, but manufacturers' supplanting of actual maximum Output (259.1J) with the arbitrary utilization of an unexplicated "101J" ER-EO depicted as actual maximum Output on the devices themselves, is blatantly deceptive.

Thus, APA Task Force Chairman Richard Weiner, the probable inventor of the illusory Mectan transmutation from a "70J at 220Ω" conditional-ER/RRC with 110J ceiling, to a new unreported ceiling (for MECTA devices) of 259.1J based on what is actually a "101J at 220Ω" Pure-ER/RRC relative to the machines' unreported maximum Impedance of 562.5Ω (for MECTA devices), drastically augmented the power outputs not only of second generation made-for-America BP devices such as MECTA and Somatics, but Canadian and European BP devices as well, the manufacturers of which soon followed suit, as we shall see. [364] [365]

Correlation of Maximum Charge to Spurious EO Maximum of Second Generation MECTA BP Devices Continued

Like the Somatics second generation BP device, then, MECTA's reported 101J at 220Ω phrase can be used to derive MECTA's reported .576 Coulomb Charge maximum for both of MECTA's later SR 1 and SR 2 second generation BP devices. Consulting the speculative but highly probable detailed MECTA Charts below (created by the author); however, we can observe that at 101.4J, it is not 576mC (.576C) which is emitted, but approximately .347C (of Charge). Certainly, at 220Ω, it is not .576C of Charge which is emitted, but .225C. Thus, the phrase "101J at 220Ω" has no literal correspondence to .576C at either 220Ω or 101.4/3J for the actual SR1 @ 2 BP devices. Nor does 101J literally correspond to 220Ω. This is because the reported "101J at 220Ω" phrase is, as already noted, but a pure-ER/RRC to the machines' actual maximum output at the machines' actual maximum Impedance. On the other hand, the maximum .576C Charge does literally correspond to the unreported actual maximum machine output of 259.2J and the unreported actual maximum

---

[361] While ER reporting is precedential within the APA Standard (of "70J at 220Ω"), never before had the 100J ceiling been surpassed. Neither had actual output reporting for BP devices been eliminated or suppressed, a phenomenon which occurred with the production of the second generation BP devices.

[362] Actual EO cannot be calculated without Voltage or Impedance. The author, via a number of mathematical inferences, speculates MECTA SR 1 and 2 devices utilize between 444.4 and 480 Volts to emit a maximum Impedance of between 555.5Ω and 600Ω. The author speculates that utilization of 450 Volts to emit 259.2 Joules at 562.5Ω maximums are the most probable. These derivations are discussed elsewhere.

[363] MECTA reports 101.4/3J at 220Ω in conjunction with a maximum Machine Readout of 101.4/3 Joules suggesting a peak maximum output of approximately 100J.

[364] European BP manufacturers report Charge in the same manner. Actual EO is never reported (Royal College of Psychiatry, 1995, pp 124-125).

[365] The 1989 IEC Standard, heavily influenced by Weiner, is based on a published "100J at 300Ω" phrase, similar to the American"100J at 220Ω" phraseology. In effect, the illusion depicting a 100J maximum EO for BP devices extends, via imitation of the American methodology, into Canadian, European and possibly Asian device makers.

machine Impedance of 562.5Ω as all three are actual maximum parameters for MECTA second generation Brief Pulse devices.

PROBABLE ACTUAL 2nd GENERATION CONSTANT CURRENT **JR/SR 1** BRIEF PULSE "ECT" DEVICE BASED ON ***PURE***-ER/RRC OF "101.4J AT 220Ω"
by MECTA Corp.1985 (.002 Second Pulse Width Maximum) Made for U. S. A.

VOLTAGE	POWER % @ Age	AGE Yrs	Ω Ohms	FREQUENCY (Hz)	DURATION (SECs)	CURRENT mAmps	ENERGY Joules	CHARGE mC
45	10	10	56.25	40	.5	800	2.88	64
90	20	20	112.5	40	.9	800	10.37	115.2
135	30	30	168.75	60	.9	800	23.33	172.8
180	40	40	225	60	1.2	800	41.47	230.4
225	50	50	281.25	60	1.5	800	64.8	288
270	60	60	337.5	90	1.2	800	93.31	345.6
292.5	65	65	365.63	90	1.3	800	109.51	374.4
315	70	70	393.75	90	1.4	800	127	403.2
360	80	80	450	90	1.6	800	165.89	460.8
405	90	90	506.25	90	1.8	800	209.95	518.4
450	100	100	562.5	90	2.0	800	259.2	576

.002Sec. Pulse Width

PROBABLE ACTUAL 2nd GENERATION CONSTANT CURRENT **JR/SR 2** BRIEF PULSE "ECT" DEVICE BASED ON ***PURE***-ER/RRC OF "101.3J AT 220Ω"
by MECTA Corp.1985 (.001 Second Pulse Width Maximum) Made for U. S. A.

VOLTAGE	POWER % @ Age	AGE Yrs	Ω Ohms	FREQUENCY (Hz)	DURATION (SECs)	CURRENT mAmps	ENERGY Joules	CHARGE mC
45	10	10	56.25	90	0.5	800	3.24	72
90	20	20	112.5	90	0.8	800	10.37	115.2
135	30	30	168.75	90	1.2	800	23.33	172.8
180	40	40	225	90	1.6	800	41.47	230.4
225	50	50	281.25	90	2.0	800	64.8	288
270	60	60	337.5	90	2.4	800	93.31	345.6
292.5	65	65	365.63	90	2.6	800	109.51	374.4
315	70	70	393.75	90	2.8	800	127	403.2
360	80	80	450	90	3.2	800	165.89	460.8
405	90	90	506.25	90	3.6	800	209.95	518.4
450	100	100	562.5	90	4.0	800	259.2	576

.001 Sec. Pulse Width

Note the true correlation of .576C, 562.5Ω, and 259.2J on the MECTA devices above. The .576C Charge maximum is derivable via the "101J at 220Ω" phrase solely due to the phrase's pure-ER relationship with the true maximums of 259.1J at 562.5Ω. "101J at 220Ω" then, is not, as might be expected, either a literal or Conditional-ER/RRC peaking at a maximum output of 101 Joules and thus .576C. The relationship between the maximum Charge of .576C with 101 Joules and 220Ω exists only as a pure-ER to actual maximum Output at actual maximum Impedance so that 220Ω is used in place of actual maximum Impedance to derive a reverse-ER output in lieu of actual maximum Output. Moreover, the relationship between .576C and "101J at 220Ω" is arbitrary. With respect to the "101J at 220Ω" phrase as a Pure-ER/RRC to actual maximum Impedance at actual maximum Output, an infinite number of Output/Impedance phrases also equivalent to the unreported true maximums of "259.1J at 562.5Ω" could have equally sufficed, all of which could have been used to deduce the same .576C Charge maximum. For example, in lieu of 101J at 220Ω, MECTA could have used the Pure-ER/RRC phrase "46J at 100Ω. " [366]

101.3J/220Ω = **46J/100Ω** = 259J/562Ω; **101.3J ÷ (220Ω** x .8A) = **.576C**; **46J ÷ (100Ω** x .8 Amperes) = **.576C (Charge)**
EO = Charge x Current x Impedance; Charge = EO/Current x Impedance.

[366] 101J/220Ω = XJ/100Ω. XJ = 46J.

In short, the use of circa "100J" (as well as "220Ω") is capricious, as numerous other Pure ER/RRC expressions could apply. Indeed, and as noted above, the .576C maximum Charge is achieved neither at 101J nor at 220Ω. The .576C maximum Charge is reached only at the SR 1 and 2 actual unreported maximum output of 259.1J as well as at the unreported actual maximum Impedance of 562.5Ω (see detailed Charts above). Only the 259J maximum output and the 562Ω maximum Impedance literally correspond to the actual .576C maximum Charge. To be clear then, the maximum .576C Charge has no literal correspondence to either 101J or 220Ω. In that MECTA does not provide Charts containing actual output (in Joules) and in that actual output reporting in Joules had, in fact, been discarded by MECTA at this juncture, the want of any literal correspondence between .576C, 101J, and 220Ω and particularly of .576C and 101J, has never been revealed. Indeed, the use of circa 100 Joules in conjunction with actual Charge maximum is highly suggestive of a .576C Charge, 101J output equivalence in turn suggestive of a 101J output maximum indicative of minimal stimulus.

In conclusion, the reported maximum Charge of .576 Coulombs for MECTA BP devices derivable from an unexplained pure-ER interpretation of "101.4/3J at 220Ω," has no literal equivalence. The .576C maximum is only literally equivalent to the unreported maximum EO of 259.1 Joules and maximum Charge of 562.5Ω. Actual maximum Charge, of course, should be reported in direct correlation with actual maximum output, the equivalence of which is impossible to discern in the absence of maximum output reporting (in joules). Because an unexplained circa 100J pure-ER or what might be termed a Reverse-ER is reported in place of actual maximum output by two of the three extant U. S. BP manufacturers of second generation BP devices (MECTA and Somatics) [367] while the third American manufacturer, Medcraft, reports an actual circa 100J maximum output at an actual 220Ω (though misleading in an entirely different way as we shall see), all three manufacturers appear to be in agreement. In short, all three report the same circa "100J at 220Ω" phrase for their BP devices. In addition, this agreement suggests a conditional-ER/RRC interpretation of the reported "100J at 220Ω" phrase, that is, a circa 100J ceiling in conjunction with maximum machine Charge on all three Brief Pulse devices. It is an illusion highly and deliberately suggestive of minimal stimulus output for all three American manufacturers in accordance with the 1982 APA Standard, untrue for even one of these Brief Pulse manufacturers-as we are observing.

---

[367] The exception appears to be Medcraft which reports an actual circa 100J maximum for its B-25 BP device, but which adds to the illusion of uniformity amongst manufacturers. The Medcraft device, moreover, contains its own serious breachings of the APA Standard.

CHAPTER 30

Beale's Discovery--MECTA Surpasses Necessary Charge for Minimal Stimulus

The reporting of what is actually a 101J ***ER*** depicted (on second generation MECTA machines) as maximum output (in lieu of ***actual*** maximum output) is entirely misleading, particularly given that BP machines surpassing 110 maximum Joules clearly violate the 1982 APA Standard. In fact, second generation MECTA machines are no longer minimal stimulus or adequate seizure devices at all, but rather multi-fold threshold or adequate electricity devices this manuscript deems ENR devices. Unknown is that MECTA's unexplained Pure-ER/RRC report of "101.4/3J at 220Ω" impelling a surreptitious and illegal maximum output of 259.1J (and thus a 2.59 MTTLOI for all age levels) at an unreported maximum machine Impedance of 562.5Ω requires much more Charge than that necessary for a BP device confined to the 110J ceiling prescribed by the 1982 APA Standard. As clearly delineated above, moreover, the actual .576C Charge maximum used and reported by MECTA for both its second generation BP devices can misleadingly be derived from the reported, but unexplained Pure-ER/RRC "101 at 220Ω" phrase.

EO ÷ (Impedance x Current) = Charge

101J ÷ (220Ω x .8 Amperes) = .576 Coulombs

As we have seen, however, the reported Charge ceiling of .576C directly corresponds--not to 101.4/3J--but to an actual unreported maximum output of 259.1J, and not to 220Ω, but to an actual maximum Impedance of 562.5Ω (see actual MECTA machine charts above). Actual maximum Charge is derivable from the phrase 101J at 220Ω only because the 101J at 220Ω phrase is a Pure-ER/RRC to actual unreported Output/Impedance maximums of 259.1J at 562.5Ω.

Pure-ER/RRC: **101.3J/220Ω = 259.1J/562.5Ω**

101.3J ÷ (220Ω x .8 Amperes) = .576 Coulombs

259.1 Joules ÷ (562.5Ω x .8 Amperes) = .576 Coulombs

Additionally, as also noted above, numerous ER expressions could suffice to express the same Pure-ER/RRC, all from which the same true maximum Charge of .576C can be derived. [368] The use of the circa 100J figure then, a figure suggestive of minimal stimulus output, appears deliberately misleading.

So why did Beale's 1994 publication exposing that what are actually second generation BP devices emitting circa 2.5 fold threshold outputs (Beale et al.1994) go relatively unnoticed while the discovery should

[368] An infinite number of ERs (to actual maximums, 259.1J at 562.5Ω) can be used to derive the same .576 Coulomb Charge. For example, in lieu of "101.4J at 220Ω," a "75J at 162.72Ω" pure-ER/RRC can be used.259.1J/562.5Ω = **75J**/XΩ. X = **162.72Ω**.7**5J at 162.72Ω** = **259.1J at 562.5Ω**. We can now derive maximum Charge from new Pure-ER/RRC expression: **75J/162.82Ω** x .8 Amperes = **.576 Coulombs**.

have been startling? The chief reason for its neglect is that Beale reported in terms of Charge. If the reported .576C Charge emitted by second generation MECTA BP devices, for example, is 2.5 fold minimal stimulus (using BL ECT) as Beale suggests, minimal stimulus for the 100 year old male on MECTA devices should be about .230C (.576 ÷ 2.5 = .230C). In short, according to Beale, the machines emit a 2.5 fold minimal stimulus output or 2.5 times the threshold Charge of .230C for the 100 year old recipient. Because Beale reports his findings in terms of Charge rather than Joules, however, and because both the reported (but unexplained) ER phrase (i.e. 101.3J at 220Ω) and the machine readouts (i.e. 101J maximum joules) employ Joules, both of which are suggestive of circa 100 Joule maximums,[369] Beale's Charge findings appear irrelevant. In brief, if the devices (seem to) emit a 101J overall maximum output which is minimal stimulus or just above threshold for all recipients, what significant difference does a .576C maximum Charge make even if it is 2.5 fold the .230C threshold required? In short, the 101J readout maximum appears to contradict Beale's findings. Conversely, Beale failed to expose the 101J readout maximum as misleading or fraudulent. Because of the 101J machine readout maximum then, regulatory agencies as well as most lay readers, including physicians who used the machines, continued to assume second generation BP machines reflected profiles similar to the expected (albeit fictitious) charts below.

Illusory Minimal Stimulus 2nd GENERATION CONSTANT CURRENT **JR/SR 1** DEVICE BASED ON ILLUSORY ***CONDITIONAL***-ER/RRC OF "101.4J AT 220Ω" with FALSE CORRELATION BETWEEN Minimal Stimulus EO in JOULES and ACTUAL CHARGE

VOLTAGE	POWER % @ Age	AGE Yrs	Ω Ohms	FREQUENCY (Hz)	DURATION (SECs)	CURRENT mAmps	ENERGY Joules	CHARGE mC
45	10	10	56.25	40	.5	800	1.13	64
90	20	20	112.5	40	.9	800	4.3	115.2
135	30	30	168.75	60	.9	800	9	172.8
180	40	40	225	60	1.2	800	16	230.4
225	50	50	281.25	60	1.5	800	25	288
270	60	60	337.5	90	1.2	800	39	345.6
292.5	65	65	365.63	90	1.3	800	43	374.4
315	70	70	393.75	90	1.4	800	50	403.2
360	80	80	450	90	1.6	800	65	460.8
405	90	90	506.25	90	1.8	800	82	518.4
450	100	100	562.5	90	2.0	800	101.4	576

.002Sec. Pulse Width

Illusory Minimal Stimulus 2nd GENERATION CONSTANT CURRENT **JR/SR 2** DEVICE BASED ON ILLUSORY ***CONDITIONAL***-ER/RRC OF "101.3J AT 220Ω" with FALSE CORRELATION BETWEEN Minimal Stimulus EO in JOULES and ACTUAL CHARGE

VOLTAGE	POWER % @ Age	AGE Yrs	Ω Ohms	FREQUENCY (Hz)	DURATION (SECs)	CURRENT mAmps	ENERGY Joules	CHARGE mC
45	10	10	56.25	90	0.5	800	1.13	72
90	20	20	112.5	90	0.8	800	4.3	115.2
135	30	30	168.75	90	1.2	800	9	172.8
180	40	40	225	90	1.6	800	16	230.4
225	50	50	281.25	90	2.0	800	25	288
270	60	60	337.5	90	2.4	800	39	345.6
292.5	65	65	365.63	90	2.6	800	43	374.4
315	70	70	393.75	90	2.8	800	50	403.2
360	80	80	450	90	3.2	800	65	460.8
405	90	90	506.25	90	3.6	800	82	518.4
450	100	100	562.5	90	4.0	800	101.4	576

.001 Sec. Pulse Width

As machine readouts seem to corroborate the correlation of a 101.3/4J maximum output (which is minimal stimulus) and a .576C maximum Charge (even though .576C is a circa 2.5 fold minimal stimulus in terms of Charge), it is easy to see why the significance of Beale's findings went unrecognized.

---

369 The 101J at 220Ω phrase falsely appears to be Conditional-ER/RRC with circa 101J ceiling corroborated by machine readouts depicting 101 maximum Joules.

In fact, while the output in Joules on the above charts is minimal stimulus, there is something wrong with the math in the above charts and we can identify the error by using both formulas for finding Charge for Brief Pulse devices. The two main formulas for finding Brief Pulse Charge which must substantiate each other are: (A) *Charge = Duration x Current x (hz x 2) x WL* and (B) *Charge = EO/Current x Impedance*.

If we plug maximum parameters into the first Charge formula (which excludes EO in Joules)--*Duration x Current x (hz x 2) x WL = Charge*--everything appears in order. We indeed get a Maximum Charge of .576C which appears to correlate with the 101.3J readout maximum in Joules (minimal stimulus for the 100 year old) for both devices.

JR/SR 1
2.0 Seconds x .8A x 180pulses x .002(WL) = ***.576C***.
JR/SR 2
4.0 Seconds x .8A x 180pulses x .001(WL) = ***.576C***.

However, if we plug maximum parameters into the second Charge formula-- *EO/Current x Impedance = Charge* (which includes the alleged maximum EO in Joules, that is, the 101.3J and 101.4J maximum machine readouts respectively--everything goes awry. Using the 101.3J or 101.4J maximum machine readouts, we derive a totally different maximum Charge ***not of .576C, but of 225mC,*** a Charge approximating Beale's expected minimal stimulus or threshold Charge output of about .230C.

JR/SR 1
101.4J ÷ (.8A x 562.5Ω) = ***.225mC***.

JR/SR 2
101.3J ÷ (.8A x 562.5Ω) = ***.225mC***.

Because we no longer obtain the reported ***576mC,*** but the circa ***225mC*** which Beale implies is just above threshold for the 100 year old, we must assume that it is 225mC--not 576mC which corresponds to the minimal stimulus output of 101.3 maximum Joules. But this means that the minimal stimulus output in Joules of 101.3J (for the 100 year old) does not correspond to the .576C maximum Charge on the charts above, but to a minimal stimulus Charge maximum of 225mC (for the 100 year old) as expected. So why the Charge maximum of 576mC which Beale correctly reports as 2.5 fold minimal stimulus?

In fact, the .576C maximum Charge (which is accurate for these devices) correlates not to the machine's reported 101.3J maximum output, but to the invisible, never before reported 259.1J actual maximum output on these devices. Indeed, like the .576C Charge maximum, the true 259.1J EO maximum is predictably 2.5 fold minimal stimulus output (for the 100 year old). In short, the 101.3J minimal stimulus output depicted on machine readouts allegedly correlating to the reported (and actual) .576mC maximum Charge is illusory. No such correlation exists. The actual correlation as we have seen, is between the actual .576C Charge emitted and the actual (but never reported and never seen) 259.1 Joules actually emitted (for the 100 year old recipient), both of which are circa 2.5 fold threshold.

So how does MECTA impel the devices to speciously read out false 101.3J and 101.4J maximum outputs using the correctly reported Charges, correctly reported Duration, correctly reported Amperage, and correctly reported Pulse Width? MECTA accomplishes this illusion, as we have seen, in the same way Somatics does, by supplanting all actual (but never reported) Impedances with a single false 220Ω "typical" Impedance "constant" into the machines' computers.

Blatant Deception

Thus, while the above illusory devices seem to be based upon the 1982 APA Standard incorporative of the FDA sponsored Utah Biomedical Test Laboratory recommendations (Grahn, 1976; Grahn et al, 1977), in fact, the maximum output of 101J both implied and directly reported by MECTA for their second generation SR1@2 BP devices seemingly based on a conditional-ER/RRC limiting output to 101.4/3 actual Joules and thus a 1.01

MTTLOI for all age categories--is illusory. Indeed, based on MECTA 510K submissions to the FDA (Food and Drug Administration, 1985), FDA appears to have interpreted MECTA's reported phrases "101.4/3J at 220Ω" in just this illusory manner. As noted then, to project the illusion of what appear to be the minimal stimulus BP devices depicted above, MECTA covertly substitutes all actual Impedances with a single false "constant" (deemed "typical" Impedance) of "220Ω" resulting in misleading Machine Readouts, including the highly suggestive but false 101J maximum, all a result of the "220Ω" substitution. This tactic, directly affecting machine readouts read by physicians, creates the illusion of a minimal stimulus device similar to the illusory and mathematically incorrect minimal stimulus devices seen above. The actual false readouts as a result of the 220Ω substitution for all age categories can be seen below. Pure-ER/RRC relationships exist with respect to Charge for all age categories so that while all EO readouts are false, Charge outputs are correct.

Deceptive 2nd GENERATION MINIMAL STIMULUS CONSTANT CURRENT **JR/SR 1** BP ECT DEVICE **with Misleading Actual Machine Readouts Derived from False 220Ω Impedances in all Age Categories**

VOLTAGE	POWER % @ Age	AGE Yrs	Ω Ohms	FREQUENCY (Hz)	DURATION (SECs)	CURRENT mAmps	ENERGY Joules	CHARGE mC
45	10	10	220	40	.5	800	11.26	64
90	20	20	220	40	.9	800	20.28	115.2
135	30	30	220	60	.9	800	30.41	172.8
180	40	40	220	60	1.2	800	40.55	230.4
225	50	50	220	60	1.5	800	50.69	288
270	60	60	220	90	1.2	800	60.83	345.6
292.5	65	65	220	90	1.3	800	65.89	374.4
315	70	70	220	90	1.4	800	70.96	403.2
360	80	80	220	90	1.6	800	81.1	460.8
405	90	90	220	90	1.8	800	91.24	518.4
450	100	100	220	90	2.0	800	101.4	576

(.002 PW)

All the above readouts in Joules are obtained through the following formula using a false "constant 220Ω. " <u>(Current squared) x 220Ω x (hz x 2) x WL x Duration = EO</u>. For example, the maximum output readout (and readout for the 100 year old) is obtained thusly: <u>.8 x .8 x 220Ω x 180 x .002 x 2.0 = **101.3J**</u>.

Insidiously, as already explained, because "101J at 220Ω" is the perfect ER of the unreported but actual maximums of "562.5Ω at 259.1J," the actual maximum Charge of .576C can be accurately, but misleadingly derived using either the ER maximum output/Impedance or actual maximum output/Impedance. For instance:

(A) <u>*Duration x Current x (hz x 2) x WL*</u> = <u>*Charge*</u>

1) (JR/SR 1) 2.0 Sec x .8A x 180Pulses x .002WL = <u>**.576C**</u>

(B) <u>*EO ÷ Current x Impedance*</u> = <u>*Charge*</u>

2) (JR/SR 1: <u>Machine **Readout**</u> maximum in Joules) <u>***101.3J***</u> ÷ (.8A x <u>**220Ω**</u>**)** = <u>**.576C**</u>

3) (JR/SR 1: <u>**Actual** Unreported</u> maximum in Joules) <u>**259.1J**</u> ÷ (.8A x <u>**562Ω**</u>**)** =<u>**.576C**</u>

Thus, by using a "220Ω" Impedance for all age categories, all age related EO is spurious while the Charge reported for all age categories is accurate as reflected in the charts above. In fact, this is exactly what second generation MECTA BP devices do.

Of course, if we plug in the actual, but unreported <u>maximum Impedances of, for example, of 562.5Ω</u> for the 100 year old recipient along with the <u>false 101.3J EO maximum</u> displayed, we obtain Beale's circa .225C threshold Charge maximum revealing that, as Beale asserted, the actual .576C emitted is circa 2.5 fold minimal stimulus in terms of Charge:

101.3J ÷ (.8A x 562.5Ω} = **.225C** (**.576C** ÷ **.225C** = **2.56**).

Conversely, since 259.1J is also circa 2.5 fold minimal stimulus in joules (**259.1J** ÷ 2.5**6** = **101J**), we can see that the actual Charge of .576C for the 100 year old recipient is as Beale asserted, circa 2.5 fold the minimal stimulus Charge of 225C. Thus, we can see that the correlation of 101.4 Joules with .576C falsely suggestive of minimal stimulus output at 576C on the JR/SR1 is totally deceptive.

259.1 ÷ (8A x 562.5Ω) = **.576C** (**.576C** ÷ **.225C** = **2.56**).

Finally, we can see that a spurious 101J "maximum" output readout indicative of a 1.01 MTTLOI or minimal stimulus output for all age levels, is bolstered by the false correlation readouts of 101J and .576C. This false and misleading correlation, as noted, suggests the false correspondence is deliberate.

All Charge Depictions (mC) Accurate; all Energy Output Depictions (joules) Inaccurate

Ingeniously, with Weiner's misleading Pure-ER/RRC system in place, all Charge outputs can be accurately derived and reported in tandem with all the above false EO readouts in Joules (see Chart above), despite all SR1 Energy Output readouts being grossly incorrect. This is because each and every EO readout along with the false 220Ω constant from which it is derived has a perfect ER output/Impedance relationship with the (albeit unreported) output/Impedance actually emitted in each age category. For example, the false 30.41J readout at the false 220Ω constant for the 30 year old is the perfect ER of the actual unreported 23.33J maximum administered at the actual unreported 168.75Ω Impedance maximum actually administered to the 30 year old recipient on the actual MECTA device (Compare actual SR 1 and 2 BP devices to the Deceptive Chart directly above).

(Readout) 30.41J/220Ω = (Actual but unreported) 23.33J/168.75Ω. In short:
(Readout) 30.41J/220Ω = (Actual) 23.33J/168.75Ω.

For the ten year old: the false 11.26J readout at the false 220Ω constant is the perfect ER of the actual 2.88J actually administered at an actual 56.25Ω.

(Readout) 11.26J/220Ω = (Actual but unreported) 2.88J/56.25Ω. In short:
(Readout) 11.26J/220Ω = (Actual) 2.88J/56.25Ω.

You may have noted that the two readouts above actually displayed on the MECTA devices are higher than outputs actually emitted. This is because the false "constant 220Ω" is higher than the actual Impedances used in the lower age categories. But while EO readouts in the lower age groups are slightly greater than those actually administered, all remaining readouts are lower than those actually emitted, indeed, in the oldest categories, grossly lower until readout displays maximize at 101 Joules (in lieu of the actual 259J emitted). The benefit to manufacturers of basing all readouts on a single false (often deemed "typical") 220Ω Impedance is in grossly lower readouts overall compared to those actually administered. Of particular importance is the fact that maximum output appears to be circa 100 maximum joules. Specifically, the 100 year old recipient, as noted, is administered an actual 259 Joules as opposed to the false and misleading 101J maximum readout (based on the false 220Ω "constant"). In brief, the readouts provide the overall impression of minimal stimulus output for all recipients generally, due to the appearance of the circa 100J ceiling in accordance with the 1982 APA Standard. Note all misleading readouts, all based on a "typical" 220Ω Impedance, are falsely calculated into the SR2 machine below.

Deceptive 2nd GENERATION MINIMAL STIMULUS CONSTANT CURRENT **JR/SR 2** BP ECT DEVICE **with Misleading Actual Machine Readouts Derived from a False 220Ω Impedance in all Age Categories**

VOLTAGE	POWER % @ Age	AGE Yrs	Ω Ohms	FREQUENCY (Hz)	DURATION (SECs)	CURRENT mAmps	ENERGY Joules	CHARGE mC
45	10	10	220	90	0.5	800	12.60	72
90	20	20	220	90	0.8	800	20.28	115.2
135	30	30	220	90	1.2	800	30.41	172.8
180	40	40	220	90	1.6	800	40.55	230.4
225	50	50	220	90	2.0	800	50.69	288
270	60	60	220	90	2.4	800	60.83	345.6
292.5	65	65	220	90	2.6	800	65.89	374.4
315	70	70	220	90	2.8	800	70.96	403.2
360	80	80	220	90	3.2	800	81.10	460.8
405	90	90	220	90	3.6	800	91.24	518.4
450	100	100	220	90	4.0	800	101.4	576

(.001 PW)

Note that the illusory readouts based on the false 220Ω substitution of actual Impedances affects only EO readouts in Joules; all other parameters (with the exception of Impedance) remain true and actual. In short, Charge is accurate, Duration is accurate, Frequency is accurate, Wave Length is accurate, and Current is accurate. Only EO depictions (and the invisible false constant Impedances of 220Ω) are specious, creating via machine readouts, the overall illusion of minimal stimulus outputs in accordance with the APA Standard. Compare the spurious, but actual output readout in the above two charts to what would be actual minimal stimulus in the two illusory charts above those. Compare all four actual MECTA outputs. [370] In sum, the false readouts above imitate minimal stimulus while suppressing actual outputs.

Thus, by supplanting all actual Impedances with a false 220Ω constant, the machines seem to be delivering a maximum output of 101.3J or 101.4J (seemingly minimal stimulus) while simultaneously delivering the reported .576C maximum Charge. As a result, what is mistaken for an actual 100J maximum seems to correlate to the actual .576C Charge ceiling so that Beale's findings of 2.5 fold threshold Charge are largely ignored.

In fact, Beale was correct. As noted earlier, outputs on these second generation BP devices Charge-wise (as well as EO-wise in Joules, but which Beale never reports) are approximately 2.5 fold threshold for what are actually second generation BP devices. If these second generation .8A constant current MECTA BP devices had actually reduced maximum output to the 101 Joule maximum depicted via readouts and if all outputs consistently emitted the same 1.01 MTTLOI implied by these MECTA readouts, maximum Charge would necessarily have been reduced circa 2.5 fold, as already noted, to a circa (.576C ÷ 2.5 =) .230C maximum. Compare the deceptive machine readout charts above to the outputs actually emitted by second generation SR1 and SR2 BP devices below:

[370] Administering psychiatrists have no way of knowing that the readout of 12.6 joules for the ten year old child is actually 12.6 fold threshold in that threshold outputs are never provided. They simply assume this is minimal stimulus, particularly in that readouts never surpass 101 joules. Administering physicians have no idea that the machine actually emits 259 joules or a 2.59 MTTLOI in all age categories.

PROBABLE **ACTUAL** 2nd GENERATION CONSTANT CURRENT **JR/SR 1** BRIEF PULSE "ECT" DEVICE BASED ON ***PURE***-ER/RRC OF "101.4J AT 220Ω" by MECTA Corp.1985 (.002 Second Pulse Width Maximum) Made for U. S. A.

VOLTAGE	POWER % @ Age	AGE Yrs	Ω Ohms	FREQUENCY (Hz)	DURATION (SECs)	CURRENT mAmps	ENERGY Joules	CHARGE mC
45	10	10	56.25	40	.5	800	2.88	64
90	20	20	112.5	40	.9	800	10.37	115.2
135	30	30	168.75	60	.9	800	23.33	172.8
180	40	40	225	60	1.2	800	41.47	230.4
225	50	50	281.25	60	1.5	800	64.8	288
270	60	60	337.5	90	1.2	800	93.31	345.6
292.5	65	65	365.63	90	1.3	800	109.51	374.4
315	70	70	393.75	90	1.4	800	127	403.2
360	80	80	450	90	1.6	800	165.89	460.8
405	90	90	506.25	90	1.8	800	209.95	518.4
450	100	100	562.5	90	2.0	800	259.2	576

.002Sec. Pulse Width

PROBABLE **ACTUAL** 2nd GENERATION CONSTANT CURRENT **JR/SR 2** BRIEF PULSE "ECT" DEVICE BASED ON ***PURE***-ER/RRC OF "101.3J AT 220Ω" by MECTA Corp.1985 (.001 Second Pulse Width Maximum) Made for U. S. A.

VOLTAGE	POWER % @ Age	AGE Yrs	Ω Ohms	FREQUENCY (Hz)	DURATION (SECs)	CURRENT mAmps	ENERGY Joules	CHARGE mC
45	10	10	56.25	90	0.5	800	3.24	72
90	20	20	112.5	90	0.8	800	10.37	115.2
135	30	30	168.75	90	1.2	800	23.33	172.8
180	40	40	225	90	1.6	800	41.47	230.4
225	50	50	281.25	90	2.0	800	64.8	288
270	60	60	337.5	90	2.4	800	93.31	345.6
292.5	65	65	365.63	90	2.6	800	109.51	374.4
315	70	70	393.75	90	2.8	800	127	403.2
360	80	80	450	90	3.2	800	165.89	460.8
405	90	90	506.25	90	3.6	800	209.95	518.4
450	100	100	562.5	90	4.0	800	259.2	576

.001 Sec. Pulse Width

Here again, as in the deceptive readout charts above, both Charge formulas substantiate the above profiles:

1) Duration x Amperage x (hz x 2) x WL = Charge:
   4.0 Seconds x .8A x 180pulses x .001(WL) = ***.576C***.

2) EO ÷ (Current x Impedance) = Charge:
   101.3J ÷ (.8A x **220Ω**) = ***.576C***
   259.2J ÷ (.8A x **562.5Ω**) = ***.576C***.

Without true EO reporting in joules, the deceptive 101J readout maximum is almost impossible to detect as specious. [371]

In brief, it was Beale's reporting in terms of Charge alone unaccompanied by actual Energy Output in Joules which failed to inform readers, physicians, and regulators alike of its importance, detracting from the significance of Beale's findings, ultimately resulting in the virtual ignoring of Beale's study altogether. In spite of Beale's findings, therefore, because of the second generation machine readouts of 101 maximum Joules, media, physicians, and regulatory agencies alike continue to believe second generation BP devices are limited

[371] There are identifiable inconsistencies regarding the deceptive readout charts above. For example, 101 Joules for the 100 year old is a 1.1 fold threshold output while the 11.2 and 12.6 readout outputs depicted for the ten year old are eleven and twelve fold threshold respectively. This is because the outputs create the mere illusion of minimal stimulus output. Such a disparity would mean no multifold threshold titration level consistency which is untrue both for MECTA and Somatics BP devices. Too, we find disparities for EO using the Voltage oriented formula (EO = Voltage x Current x (hz x 2) x WL x Duration) as seen below.

to circa 100 maximum Joules, maintaining the illusion of the minimal stimulus BP device Brief Pulse was originally touted to be.

Had Beale reported in Joules in lieu of Charge, that is, had he reported that MECTA devices were emitting circa 259 Joule maximums in lieu of 101J maximums and that 259 Joules represents a circa 2.5 fold minimal stimulus threshold output (101J x 2.56 = 259J) in every age category, his publication might have alarmed both regulatory agencies and physicians alike, particularly in that machine readouts might have been recognized as the specious outputs they are.

CHAPTER 31

Exact False Machine Readout Depictions

Exact false or misleading EO readouts in joules depicted on both second generation MECTA BP devices for all ages as shown above are attained by using a false 220Ω constant in lieu of actual age-related Impedances within the following Impedance oriented formula:

1) **EO** = (Current squared) x ***220Ω*** x (hz x 2) x WL x Duration.

JR/SR 2 Machine Readouts

EO **(for 100 year old)** = .8A x .8A x ***220Ω*** x 180 x .001 x 4.0 Seconds = ***101.3J***

EO = **(for 60 year old)** .8A x .8A x ***220Ω*** x 180 x .001 x 2.4 Seconds = ***60.8J***

If, however, we attempt to derive these same readouts using the ***Voltage*** **oriented formula** for finding EO which does not contain the Impedance parameter, the EOs derived are actual, radically differing from the readout depictions attained with 220Ω; true EO figures attained in this way are never revealed or reported by MECTA.

2) **EO** = ***Voltage*** x Current x (hz x 2) x WL x Duration

For example,

JR/SR 2

EO = (for 100 year old) Voltage x Current x (hz x 2) x WL x Duration; ***450V*** x .8A x 180 x .001 x 4.0 Seconds = ***259.2J***.

EO = (for 60 year old) Voltage x Current x (hz x 2) x WL x Duration; ***270V*** x .8A x 180 x .001 x 2.4 Seconds = ***93.3J***.

It is for this reason that MECTA divulges neither Voltages nor Impedances.

On the other hand, we can derive accurate Charges from any Charge formula 1) (*Charge = Duration x Current x (hz x 2) x WL*, or 2) *Charge = EO/Current x Impedance*) using either the false EO readout with false 220Ω constant or actual EO with actual Impedance. This is due, as noted, to each misleading EO readout, although false, being based upon a perfect ER of EO Readouts at 220Ω to actual (but unreported) outputs at actual (unreported) Impedances.

For instance, using the Charge formula: Charge = _Duration x Current x (hz x 2) x WL_, plugging in accurate Duration, we can derive accurate Charges delivered to both 100 and 60 Year old (and any other) recipient.

Charge = _Duration x Current x (hz x 2) x WL_: 4.0 x .8A x 180 x .001 = ***.576C***
Charge = _Duration x Current x (hz x 2) x WL_: 2.4 x .8A x 180 x .001 = ***.345C***

Using the second Charge formula: Charge = _EO ÷ Current x Impedance_, we can also derive the actual Charge delivered to both the 100 and 60 Year old (and any other) recipient by using either the false readout and false 220Ω constant (ER) or the actual EO delivered and actual Impedance overcome. For example,

Charge (**100** YR. OLD) = _EO ÷ Current x Impedance:_
(EO _Readout_) ***101.4J*** ÷ (.8A x ***220Ω)*** (False Impedance) = **.576C (Actual Charge)**.
(_Actual EO_) ***259.2J*** ÷ (.8A x **562.5Ω)** (Actual Impedance) = **.576C (Actual Charge)**.

Charge (**60** YR. OLD) = _EO ÷ Current x Impedance:_
(EO _Readout_) ***60.83J*** ÷ (.8A x ***220Ω)*** (False Impedance) = **.345C (Actual Charge)**.
(_Actual EO_) ***93.31J*** ÷ (.8A x ***337.5Ω)*** (Actual Impedance) = **.345C (Actual Charge)**.

In all age categories, the False EO Readouts at a false 220Ω are Perfect Equivalent Ratios to actual (unreported) EOs at actual (unreported) Impedances.

(***100 Yrs: False EO Readout/False 220Ω = Actual EO/Actual Impedance***):
101.4J/220Ω = 259.2J/562.5Ω;

(***60 Yrs: False Readout/False 220Ω = Actual EO/Actual Impedance***):
60.83J/220Ω = 93.31J/337.5Ω;

The pseudo equivalence of ER-EO readouts to actual Charges is, as we have seen, insidiously misleading. By using all actual parameters except EO and Impedance, both regulatory agencies and physicians assume false Readout depictions actual. The readouts depicting spurious outputs up to 101 maximum Joules, are meant to create the illusion of minimal stimulus outputs in all age categories. In fact, through careful observation, we can detect something irregular in these readouts. Careful analysis reveals that MTTLOIs based on such readouts are grossly inconsistent. Based on the readouts, while the 100 year old appears to receive a 1.01 MTTLOI and thus minimal stimulus, the ten year old could not actually receive the 12.6 joules the readout depicts, which would be an eleven or twelve MTTLOI. None but manufacturers ever notice this, however, in that Relative Threshold EO constants have never (until now) been revealed. While the readouts are designed to give the overall impression of minimal stimulus, therefore, close scrutiny reveals that the readouts lack a consistent MTTLOI, unnoticeable without knowledge of the relative age-related threshold constants in joules. Because MECTA and Somatics devices actually do deliver a consistent MTTLOI for all age categories (though much greater than the false 101J maximum implies), the readout depictions are obviously spurious, designed simply to create the impression of minimal stimulus in compliance with the 1982 APA Standard.

Let us, in fact, compare a true minimal stimulus output of 1.01 MTTLOI in all age categories (using BL ECT) to the MECTA Readouts and finally to the actual unreported Second Generation JR/SR 2 ENR outputs.

Comparative of true 1.01 Fold, Minimal Stimulus Outputs, in ALL AGE GROUPS to MECTA'S Illusory Readouts, to Actual Outputs Emitted in Joules by the 2nd Generation JR/SR 2

Age Yrs	1.01 Fold Threshold--True Minimal Stimulus Outputs in Joules	Illusory Readouts Based on 220Ω Constant	Actual Unreported Output in Joules of 2nd Gen. JR/SR 2
10	1.01	12.60	3.24
20	4.04	20.28	10.37
30	9.09	30.41	23.33
40	16.16	40.55	41.47
50	25.25	50.69	64.8
60	36.36	60.83	93.31
65	42.67	65.89	109.51
70	49.46	70.96	127
80	64.64	81.10	165.89
90	81.8	91.24	209.95
100	101.4	101.4	259.2

While the illusory machine readouts based on 220Ω do not precisely match true minimal stimulus output, and, in fact, exceed the output actually delivered in a few of the younger age categories, the overall impression, particularly from age 65 and older is that of minimal stimulus. This false impression is chiefly due to the maximum output reading of 101.4 Joules. Now compare the misleading readouts to MECTA's actual outputs (never revealed) which, for the second generation JR/SR 2 above, are a consistent albeit never before reported 2.59 MTTLOI in every age category.

Expected Minimal Stimulus Devices

While MECTA never did so, had they wanted, as already seen, MECTA could have created JR1@ 2 devices actually limiting output in Joules to 101 Joules or true minimal stimulus. In fact, true minimal stimulus devices could have been accomplished by one simple means--reducing Duration. This, of course, as Beale predicted, would also have reduced Charge. As such, and just as Beale implied, true minimal stimulus or "ECT" devices need only have emitted a maximum of about .230C of Charge. No other parameters need have changed. Again, note below the never before reported relative threshold constants in joules used by manufacturers.

Threshold Output "Constants"

10 year old male = 3.24J ÷ 2.59 = ***1.25J*** (Exception)
20 year old male = 10.37J ÷ 2.59 = ***4.00J***
30 year old male = 23.33J ÷ 2.59 = ***9.00J***
40 year old male = 41.47J ÷ 2.59 = ***16.00J***
50 year old male = 64.80J ÷ 2.59 = ***25.00J***
60 year old male = 93.31J ÷ 2.59 = ***36.00J***
65 year old male = 109.51J ÷ 2.59 = ***42.25J***
70 year old male = 127.00J ÷ 2.59 = ***49.0J***
80 year old male = 165.89J ÷ 2.59 = ***64.00J***
90 year old male = 209.95J ÷ 2.59 = ***81.00J***
100 year old male = 259.20J ÷ 2.59 = ***100.00J***

To create a theoretical JR/SR 1 minimal stimulus device actually limited to 101J, we simply multiply 1.01 times minimal stimulus or threshold output for each age category to determine deliverable minimal stimulus EO in Joules (with BL ECT), then derive Duration through the following formula: Duration = EO ÷ Voltage x Amperage x (Hz x 2) x WL. Duration, in turn, affects Charge derived by the following: Charge = Duration x Current x (hz x 2) x WL. Simply by modifying Duration then, we can create the actual minimal stimulus BP ECT device below for which MECTA has simply created the illusion. Amazingly, as already noted, no such machine exists.

Theoretical but Expected 2nd GENERATION **TRUE MINIMAL STIMULUS** CONSTANT CURRENT **JR/SR 1** with Incrementally Reduced Durations Limiting Output to 101 MAXIMUM JOULES and a Consistent 1.01 Multifold Threshold Titration Level Output in Every Age Category BASED ON Actual Conditional-ER/RRC OF "101.4J AT 220Ω" with 101J Ceiling

Incrementally Reduced Durations

VOLTAGE	POWER % @ Age	AGE Yrs	Ω Ohms	FREQUENCY (Hz)	DURATION (SECs)	CURRENT mAmps	ENERGY Joules	CHARGE mC
45	10	10	56.25	40	.175	800	1.01	22.4
90	20	20	112.5	40	.351	800	4.04	44.89
135	30	30	168.75	60	.351	800	9.09	67.33
180	40	40	225	60	.468	800	16.16	89.78
225	50	50	281.25	60	.585	800	25.25	112.22
270	60	60	337.5	90	.468	800	36.36	134.66
292.5	65	65	365.63	90	.507	800	42.67	145.88
315	70	70	393.75	90	.545	800	49.46	157.02
360	80	80	450	90	.624	800	64.64	179.55
405	90	90	506.25	90	.701	800	81.8	202
450	100	100	562.5	90	.782	800	101.4	225.3

(.002 PW)

With the exception of Duration, and thus EO and Charge, the true minimal stimulus chart above depicts all probable actual second generation JR/SR 1 BP parameters. In short, Duration, Charge, and EO parameters have been modified here in accordance with a true "101.4J at 220Ω" Conditional--ER/RRC with 101J ceiling in lieu of MECTA's "101.4J at 220Ω pure"--ER/RRC with 259J ceiling. Note that Voltage, Impedance, Frequency, and Amperage remain unchanged. The above machine is *fictional,* but both feasible and anticipated in that Machine Readouts on the actual JR/SR1 device (misleadingly) depict a 101.4 Joule maximum output suggestive of the device above. Note the peak .225C Charge on the fictional device above as opposed to the JR/SR 1's actual maximum Charge of .576C. Regulatory agencies appear to have interpreted MECTA's reported "101J at 220Ω" ER/RRC (for the SR1) in just the above manner. [Main formula: Duration = Charge ÷ [Current x (hz x 2) x WL].

We can now do the same for the JR/SR 2. To create the theoretical JR/SR 2 minimal stimulus ECT device for which MECTA creates but the impression, we simply multiply the never before reported threshold constants used by manufacturers by an actual 1.01 MTTLOI for each age category to obtain a minimal stimulus EO (with BL ECT) for every age category. We then derive Duration through the following formula: Duration = EO ÷ [Voltage x Amperage x (Hz x 2) x WL]. Reduced Duration affects not only EO, but Charge which is then derived by the following formula: Charge = Duration x Current x (hz x 2) x WL. In short, simply by reducing Duration, we can create the expected minimal stimulus BP ECT device (with BL ECT) below. Remarkably, no such machine exists.

Theoretical but Expected 2nd GENERATION **TRUE MINIMAL STIMULUS** CONSTANT CURRENT **JR/SR 2** with Incrementally Reduced Durations Limiting Output to 101 MAXIMUM JOULES and a Consistent 1.01 Multifold Threshold Titration Level Output in Every Age Category BASED ON Actual Conditional-ER/RRC OF "101.3J AT 220Ω" with 101J Ceiling

Incrementally Reduced Durations

VOLTAGE	POWER % @ Age	AGE Yrs	Ω Ohms	FREQUENCY (Hz)	DURATION (SECs)	CURRENT mAmps	ENERGY Joules	CHARGE mC
45	10	10	56.25	90	.1556	800	1.01	22.4
90	20	20	112.5	90	0.312	800	4.04	44.89
135	30	30	168.75	90	.468	800	9.09	67.33
180	40	40	225	90	.647	800	16.16	89.78
225	50	50	281.25	90	.779	800	25.25	112.22
270	60	60	337.5	90	.935	800	36.36	134.66
292.5	65	65	365.63	90	1.01	800	42.67	145.88
315	70	70	393.75	90	1.09	800	49.46	157.02
360	80	80	450	90	1.25	800	64.64	179.55
405	90	90	506.25	90	1.40	800	81.8	202
450	100	100	562.5	90	1.565	800	101.3	225.3

(.001 PW)

With the exception of Duration, EO, and Charge, the Chart above depicts the same electrical parameters as the actual second generation JR/SR 2 BP ENR device. In short, Duration, Charge, and EO parameters have been modified in accordance with a true "101.3J at 220Ω" Conditional--ER/RRC with 101J ceiling in lieu of MECTA's "101.3J at 220Ω" Pure"--ER/RRC with 259J ceiling. Note that Voltage, Impedance, Frequency, and Amperage remain unchanged. The above machine is *fictional,* but both feasible and anticipated in that Machine Readouts on the actual JR/SR2 device spuriously depict a 101.3 Joule maximum output merely suggestive of minimal stimulus. Note the peak .225C Charge on the fictional device above as opposed to the JR/SR 2's actual maximum Charge of .576C. Regulatory agencies appear to have interpreted MECTA's reported "101J at 220Ω" ER/RRC (for the SR2) in the above manner. [Main formula: Duration = Charge ÷ [Current x (hz x 2) x WL].

MEDCRAFT MADE-FOR-AMERICA SECOND GENERATION BP DEVICE--A WORD

Although the Medcraft second generation BP device, the B-25, is similarly reported as circa **"100J at 220Ω,"** (specifically "99J at 220Ω"), Medcraft interprets the phrase so divergently and the device is so inherently different from the actual second generation Somatics and MECTA BP devices depicted a few paragraphs above, that discussion of Medcraft's BP device will be deferred to a slightly later section. It should be mentioned, however, that although Medcraft does, in fact, limit its BP device, the Medcraft B-25, to an actual (circa) 100J maximum in conformity with the APA Standard, the Medcraft B-25 BP device seriously breaches the ER/RRC aspect of the same 1982 APA Standard as we shall soon see in detail. Before doing so, however, it is first necessary to examine MECTA and Somatics BP devices under the purview not of the APA Standard, but the IEC or international standard for ECT.

SECTION VI: INTERNATIONAL STANDARD (vs Devolved Made-For-America BP Devices)

CHAPTER 32

1989 International Standard Uses Same Double Standard Employed by U.S. BP Manufacturers

General Overview of IEC Standard

The IEC or International Electrotechnical Commission Standard contains information and regulations for various types of electrical equipment, including medical electrical equipment. This includes "ECT. " Europe in general, then, adheres or did adhere to the international standard for ECT devices published by International Electrotechnical Commission in Switzerland, specifically in 1989. The heart of the Swiss 1989 International Electrotechnical Commission (IEC) Standard for ECT devices can be found in Section 51.2 (of the IEC standard) which reads:

> 51.2 Limitation of Output Values:
> The output energy shall be limited to a maximum of 100J at 300Ω for each treatment initiation. (International Electrotechnical Commission, 1989, p.23)

It is important to understand that American Richard Weiner, chairman of the APA Task Forces in the U. S. and main spokesperson to the FDA for all extant U. S. manufacturers (Medcraft, Somatics, and MECTA), chaired not only the committee to create the 1982 APA Standard for U. S. devices, but also served as the chief administrator on the International Committee which created the 1989 International Standard for ECT Devices (Association for the Advancement of Medical Instrumentation, 1998, February 4; International Electrotechnical Commission, 1997, Dec 26; Department of Health and Human Services, 1982a). Several problems may have confronted Weiner in the creation of the 1989 International Standard adhered to in Europe. All American BP manufacturers were by 1989 misleadingly reporting circa 100J ceilings for their second generation BP devices made in and for America. Moreover, all four U. S. manufacturers, MECTA, Somatics, Elcot (now defunct), and Medcraft were newly reporting these made-for-America BP devices with the same circa "100J at 220Ω" phrase. In three of the four instances, this was a contrived phraseology for what appeared to be a conditional-ER/RRC in seeming conformity with the 1982 APA (American Psychiatric Association) Standard, that is, seemingly based on a circa 100J or 110J ceiling output. [372] Indeed, only one American BP manufacturer, Medcraft, though breaching the APA Standard in another way to be discussed later, accurately reported and actually limited

[372] As previously noted, the phraseology without accompanying explanation, appears to be either a combination ER/RRC/Absolute EO ceiling of circa 100 Joules, or a new conditional-ER/RRC with the original 110J ceiling intact. In actuality, the phrase is an unexplained Pure-ER/RRC, that is, a pure-ER phrase to a new unreported maximum EO at maximum machine Impedances.

output of its made-for-America BP device, the B-25, to a circa 100J ceiling (Food and Drug Administration, 1986A). Medcraft, then, while violating the APA Standard in another important way, was, in fact, the only American BP manufacturer to actually limit its' second generation made-for-America BP device, the B-25, to a circa 100J ceiling in accordance with the 1982 APA 110J maximum output Standard for Brief Pulse (Food and Drug Administration, 1986B).

For MECTA and Somatics (and Elcot), as we have noted, the contrived and reported manufacturer-created phrase, circa "100J at 220Ω," [373] ironically, neglected to incorporate the APA "110J" ceiling into their misleading reporting paradigm, in spite of circa 100J ceiling readouts on their devices. Moreover, both MECTA and Somatics (and Elcot) failed to report actual maximum outputs (in joules). In short, the "100J at 220Ω" phrase was not, as it appeared, a new conditional-ER/RRC with circa 100J or even 110J ceiling intact (like the original APA Standard's "70J at 220Ω" with a clear 110J ceiling). Rather, as we have seen, it had become an unexplained 100J at 220Ω Pure-ER/RRC sans the circa 110J ceiling. That is, the "100J at 220Ω" phrase no longer limited made-for-America BP devices to a circa 100 ceiling, but newly based on maximum machine Impedances (up to 600Ω), actually allowed a new unreported American ceiling up to 273 Joules, greatly enhancing the MTTLOI. The "100J at 220Ω" pure-ER/RRC (in what the author has deemed "The Mectan Transmutation") as opposed to the expected conditional-ER/RRC (limited by 110J), had, of course, secretly supplanted the APA 110J ceiling with a much higher one, thereby surreptitiously augmenting both output and MTTLOI (Department of Health and Human Services, 1982a, A53, E20).

In effect, while all four U. S. BP manufacturers newly reported circa "100J at 220Ω" for their made-for-America second generation BP devices, three of the American BP manufacturers (MECTA, Somatics, and Elcot), in stark violation of the 1982 APA Standard, had begun utilizing a new unexplained Pure/ER/RRC interpretation in order to bypass the original 110J ceiling, increasing, as noted, the MTTLOI for all age categories. In spite of this gross augmentation; however, both MECTA and Somatics [374] (by apparent agreement) not only desisted in reporting their newer higher EO ceilings (of 259 and 252 joules respectively) to either American regulatory agencies or the American public, but via Machine Readouts (and other inferential strategies), actually appeared to "substantiate" adherence to the 110J ceiling specified within the 1982 APA Standard. While all American made-for-America second generation BP manufacturers reported approximately 100 maximum joules for their second generation BP devices, therefore, three of the four BP manufacturers (Elcot, MECTA, and Somatics) had by this juncture uniformly dropped the 110J ceiling, producing second generation BP devices emitting unreported outputs of up to 260 maximum Joules. [375] In what appears to have been a deliberate cover-up; therefore, manufacturers MECTA and Somatics--(Elcot, as noted below, was by this time defunct)--continued using the same circa "100J" figure with its association of minimum stimulus in reporting their BP devices to the FDA, physicians, and the American public, while unbeknownst to anyone but themselves, as we have seen, were newly treating the "100J" figure as an unexplained Pure-ER. [376] This unexplained circa 100J figure via machine readouts depicting what appeared to be circa 100J maximum outputs, falsely suggested minimal stimulus devices as we have observed. Medcraft on the other hand, reported the same 100J ceiling, but as already noted, actually limited its device to circa 100 maximum joules. Consequently, all four U. S. BP manufacturers reporting the same circa "100J at 220Ω" phrase for their second generation made-for-America BP devices actively engendered the illusion that all four U. S. BP manufacturers uniformly maintained and adhered to the 1982 APA Standard and thus the least amount of electricity precept. This uniform illusion of a circa 100J ceiling engendering the false notion that all made-for-America BP devices continued to maintain minimal stimulus outputs, sustained the image of Brief Pulse machines emitting half the electrical output of SW, seemingly enhancing safety compared to the older SW devices. Succinctly then, by 1985, with the secret introduction of newer more powerful second generation BP devices in the U. S. , three of the four American manufacturers (Elcot, MECTA, and Somatics), had by apparent agreement with each other, gone so far as to drop the reporting of actual maximum output (in joules), while supplanting the 110J ceiling with the unexplained reporting of a "100J" Pure-ER. Of great import then, all four American manufacturers MECTA, Somatics, and Elcot together with the fourth American BP manufacturer, Medcraft, in spite of

---

[373] By MECTA, Somatics, and Medcraft all reporting circa "100J at 220Ω" for their second generation BP devices, not only was an illusion of consistency created, but of devices limited to circa 100 maximum joules.

[374] Elcot, the third manufacturer, dissolved.

[375] The MF-1000 produced by the defunct Manufacturer, Elcot, may have emitted even higher output.

[376] All U.S. BP manufacturers of second generation made-for-America BP devices calculated their devices to read out a maximum of approximately 100 Joules when in actuality, this readout in Somatics and MECTA machines, was but an unexplained ER.

antithetical interpretations of the APA Standard, reported the same circa "100J at 220Ω" phrase for their made-for-America Brief Pulse devices while simultaneously depicting the same maximum machine readout of approximately 100 maximum Joules for their second generation BP devices.

In order for American manufacturers to market their powerful machines internationally, and to sustain the mirage that all second generation BP devices (including those produced overseas) maintained the same 100J ceiling implied by all four American BP manufacturers, a similar reporting mechanism containing a similar misleading phraseology specifying the same misleading 100J figure, became necessary abroad. By 1989, this ploy emerged via the International Electro Technical Commission (IEC) standard for ECT. Just as all three extant American BP manufacturers (MECTA, Somatics, Medcraft)--two via Pure-ER/RRC methodology and one via Pure-Ceiling methodology (as we shall soon see)--indicated 100J maximums in FDA 510K files, marketing brochures, and Machine Readouts, a similar transmutational reporting mechanism emerged by way of the new 1989 international standard seemingly limiting European BP devices to the same circa 100 Joule maximum.

Not surprisingly then, the new 1989 international standard suddenly depicted the same seeming 100J ceiling and thus the same seemingly reduced output (of 100 maximum Joules) engendering the same illusion of Brief Pulse safety compared to SW. The ploy emulated the illusory reporting systems generated by American manufacturers in America, once again seemingly corroborated via machine readouts. In fact, just as in America, the international standard similarly permitted much higher outputs than the reported 100 Joules then similarly depicted for international devices. Peculiarly emulative of the Mectan Transmutation then, the new 1989 IEC Standard--through the same featured "100J" figure--continued to enhance the illusion of minimal stimulus uniformity, internationally, enhancing the marketability of BP machines on the world-wide emporium. In short, a new world-wide standard enabling the reporting of the same 100J figure for Eurasian devices had now been constructed via the then new 1989 International Electro-technical Commission Standard for ECT, but a standard similarly enabling made-for-Eurasian devices, as noted above, much higher, hidden energy outputs than the apparent 100 Joules the standard seemed to purport. [377] In brief, the creation of a similar transmutational mechanism for BP devices via the 1989 IEC standard, newly created the illusion of a hemispheric continuum, suggestive of the same circa 100J maximum reported in the U. S. , but on a world-wide basis, preserving the artifice of Brief Pulse as a reduced output, minimal stimulus device internationally.

But how could such a corrupted international standard have been achieved? In order to actualize and extend the Mectan double standard world-wide, providing BP manufacturers internationally, with the same ability to report a consistent circa 100Js on both continents while furtively producing much more powerful machines, American manufacturers appear to have attained the co-operation of the handful of European, one Canadian, (and some Asian) ECT device manufacturers necessary to do so. In short, uniform application of the same methodology creating the same "100J" illusion for BP devices that had been achieved in America, required international collaboration via various Eurasian manufacturers. Indeed, this is the case, but while a number of "foreign" manufacturers, i.e. German, French, and Japanese which also produce "ECT" devices, were influenced and affected by what actually became the international application of the Mectan Transmutation, the present manuscript chiefly examines the cooperative role of Canadian and English with American manufacturers in expanding and applying the Mectan Transmutation via the IEC Standard. The dominant influence of the American methodology, with resultant corruption of manufacturer reporting in Canada and Great Britain, as well as the U. S. in direct connection with the 1989 International Standard for ECT, becomes transparent with just a little examination.

Corruption Spreads Abroad

Not surprisingly, as noted above, manufacturers chose phraseology for an international standard suggestive of the same "100J" ceiling discoverable within the 1982 APA Standard, and, in fact, very like the Mectan Transmutation (of the APA Standard) which had been so successfully exploited by American manufacturers. In short, what appeared to be a 100J maximum based on a "100J at 300Ω" conditional-ER/RRC under the

---

[377] By all American BP manufacturers reporting approximately 100 Joules for their devices, American manufacturers not only appeared to be in conformity with the 1982 APA Standard, but also with each other. Now, due to a similar transmutational mechanism contained within the IEC Standard for ECT devices along with similarly dubious reporting strategies, the ploy became internationalized.

international standard became, in fact, a 130J Pure-ER/RRC as we shall see. That is, upon close scrutiny of the IEC Standard, the similar seeming 100J ceiling is, in fact, superimposed upon an unexplicated 130J Pure-ER/RRC mechanism within the IEC standard itself, enabling BP manufacturers internationally the same capacity to infer the same circa 100J ceiling even while delivering dangerously multifold, suprathreshold dosages of electricity manufacturers understood world-wide to be absolutely requisite for "efficacy." Indeed, the same implicit understanding exists amongst device manufacturers globally that suprathreshold electrical dosages are essential to make the procedure "work. " [378] Like the Mectan Transmutation then, the new international methodology began to exploit the global reputation of Brief Pulse as a reduced output apparatus compared to SW even as these same BP devices surreptitiously delivered unreported cumulative outputs surpassing that of Sine Wave.

Manufacturers "Improve" the IEC Standard Over the APA Standard

In spite of U. S. BP manufacturers having created a methodology to report or suggest 100 maximum Joules while secretly utilizing excessive multifold threshold dosages of electricity, U. S. manufacturers have had to continuously contend with the clear 1982 APA Standard absolute ceiling mandate of 110 Joules (Department of Health and Human Services, 1982a, A53, E20). [379] In devising the 1989 International (IEC) Standard, therefore, Richard Weiner and other composers of the International Standard, in contrast to the 1982 APA Standard, calculatedly excluded any clear depiction of the "100" or "110 Joule" figure as an absolute ceiling, the clear delineation of which had forced American BP manufacturers not only to concoct, reinterpret, disguise, and apply Weiner's unauthorized transmutation, but to blatantly violate the American Standard in delivering Brief Pulse dosages surpassing that of SW. Imitating the Americans' Pure-ER/RRC contrivance of their reported "100J at 220Ω" phrase which via covert agreement between MECTA and Somatics, had transmuted the APA 110J absolute ceiling into a 100J Pure-ER, international representatives led by none other than American APA Task Force Chairman Richard Weiner, invoked a similar sounding phraseology--"100 Joules at 300Ω"--for the International "ECT" Standard (Department of Health and Human Services, 1982c, p.15; International Electrotechnical Commission, 1989, p.23). Not too surprisingly then, under Weiner's auspices, the international standard came to be based upon the same unexplicated Pure-ER/RRC methodology secretly utilized by MECTA and Somatics in America. So well did the methodology of misleadingly reporting approximately "100 maximum Joules" work for U. S. BP manufacturers, that by the time the International Standard was devised circa 1981 (Department of Health and Human Services, 1982c, p.15) to be eventually adopted in 1989, no U. S. or international regulatory agency had so much as suspected U. S. BP manufacturers of utilizing more than 110 absolute Joules, much less surpassing SW which could allegedly emit an unwanted 200J of cumulative power (Cameron, 1994).

Similar to the American manufacturer-created phraseology of "100J at 220Ω," then, Weiner (the likely chief inventor of the Mectan transmutation) and colleagues introduced the similar sounding phrase, "100J at 300Ω" for international device reporting (International Electrotechnical Commission, 1989, p.23). Headed by Richard Weiner himself, Weiner's self-deemed "International Working Group" for ECT, promulgated and ultimately facilitated IEC adoption of the remarkably familiar sounding phrase "100J at 300Ω." Under Weiner's care, this "100J at 300Ω" phrase soon became featured as the 1989 International Electrotechnical Commission Standard for "ECT"-- the Standard for virtually all BP devices marketed abroad (Department of Health and Human Services, 1982c, p.15). By juxtaposing the term "100 Joules" with the term "300 Ohms," by neglecting to elaborate on the interpretation of this phrase, and finally (unlike the APA Standard), by omitting any clear delineation of the "100" or "110J" figure as a maximum ceiling, European (and American) BP manufacturers were not only able to avoid the possibility of having to explain the transmutation of the phrase into a Pure-ER/RRC which might well have been perceived as starkly illicit, but were able to extirpate (within the standard itself) any legal mandate to interpret the International Standard as a Conditional--ER/RRC. In short, in the

[378] The author is in agreement with psychiatrist Peter Breggin and numerous other responsible professionals who maintain that the procedure must produce damage in order to "work." It is due to this unsavory fact that manufacturers world-wide have gone to such great extremes to cover up.

[379] Until now, the 1982 mandate putting American BP manufactures in clear violation of the 1982 APA Standard, has never been brought to the attention of the FDA or the American public.

absence of an actual circa 100 or 110J cap, manufacturers of overseas devices, unlike manufacturers of made-for-America devices, no longer had to illegally circumvent what otherwise would have been a clearly requisite conditional-ER/RRC interpretation of "100J at 300Ω" with circa 100 or 110J ceiling similar to the APA Standard. Conveniently therefore, in lieu of what appears to be a circa 100J ceiling based on a conditional-ER/RRC interpretation of "100J at 300Ω" for the new international standard, Eurasian (and American) manufacturers immediately, but discreetly interpreted the "100J at 300Ω" phrase in the same manner as the Mectan Transmutation--that is--as an unexplicated 100J (at 300Ω) Pure-ER/RRC to output at maximum machine Impedance. Based on a maximum IEC Impedance of 500Ω instead of the American Impedance ceiling of 600Ω, therefore, the IEC Standard initially allowed for a never reported 166.6 Joule ceiling (100J/300Ω = ***166.6J***/500Ω). Instead of what appears to be a "100J" ceiling within the IEC Standard itself, then, like the Mectan Transmutation of the American APA Standard, manufacturers of overseas BP devices based unreported maximum outputs for their IEC BP devices not upon a "100J at 300Ω" conditional-ER/RRC (with 100J ceiling), but upon a 100J at 300Ω Pure-ER/RRC to maximum IEC machine Impedance of 500Ω.

But this is not the end of the story. Based on an inconspicuous adjunct principle within the same IEC standard, the standard inconspicuously allowed BP device manufacturers to increase this unreported output by 30%. This meant that instead of "100J at 300Ω," manufacturers could actually base maximum output on a 130J at 300Ω" Pure-ER/RRC and so attain a ceiling for their devices not of 166.6J, but of (130J/300Ω = X/500Ω; X =) **216.6J**. In a word, like the Mectan Transmutation, the furtively unexplained interpretation of what appeared to be a "100J at 300Ω" conditional-ER/RRC was actually being interpreted by manufacturers as a "130J at 300" Pure-ER/RRC, opening wide the door for Brief Pulse output far in excess of the expected "100J" or even "110J" maximum used to guarantee minimal stimulus output. At the same time, of course, and like their American predecessors, manufacturers of BP devices for the Eurasian market (under IEC auspices) continued to give every impression that their BP devices conformed to a circa 100J ceiling. [380] Not only was the "100J" figure the single Energy Output figure (in joules) inferred, alluded to, or even mentioned within the 1989 IEC Standard, but--by international agreement--European BP manufacturers, again like their American counterparts, quite abruptly at this juncture, dispensed with the reporting of actual maximum output in joules on a world-wide basis. [381]

[380] Interestingly "100J at 300Ω" is the ER of "70J at 220Ω," the original APA conditional-ER/RRC with 110J ceiling (100J/300Ω = 70J/220Ω). Weiner may have submitted the "100J at 300Ω" phrase as an international standard early on, with the intention of transmuting the phrase to a pure-ER/RRC which by 1989, manufacturers indeed did, an indication that as early as 1981,Weiner and associates knew full well that minimal stimulus or adequate convulsion "therapy" did not work.

[381] The "100J" illusion created by the International Standard was a tactical "improvement" on the U.S. manufacturer scheme of publicly inferring while secretly surpassing the mandatory 110 joule mark. The superior tactic consisted in excluding any absolute ceiling statement like that found within the 1982 APA Standard concretely limiting BP devices to 110 maximum joules. This exclusion "legally freed" manufacturers to interpret (albeit still surreptitiously) the IEC phrase of "100J at 300Ω" and more specifically the "130J at 300Ω" derivative phrase as a Pure-ER/RRC. Like American manufacturers of made-for-America BP devices, however, manufacturers of IEC BP devices yet continued to suggest a conditional--ER/RRC via machine readouts of circa 100 maximum joules. This maneuver helped maintain the false impression of a circa 100J ceiling continuum for BP devices world-wide and thus the illusion of minimal stimulus outputs with Brief Pulse on a global level.

CHAPTER 33

Great Britain's and Canada's "Ectron Incorporated" follows U.S. Precedent

Under pressure from Canadian and British consumer advocacy groups to create a safer electroshock device, and fully familiar with the reputation of the seemingly circa 100J maximum Brief Pulse device in the U. S. for inducing adequate seizures in all ECT recipients at allegedly half the output of the 200J SW device (Department of Health and Human Services, 1982a, G3-G4)--beginning in 1981, Canadian and European manufacturers such as Canada's and Great Britain's "Ectron Incorporated," Canada's and UK's chief manufacturer of "ECT" devices, began following the American lead in transitioning from Sine Wave to Brief Pulse (Royal College of Psychiatry, 1995, p.129). [382] Like MECTA Corporation's "MECTA C" device, Ectron Incorporated began by manufacturing and reporting a similar prototypical BP device for the UK--the 98J BP Series 2/3--emitting, like the 108J "MECTA C," approximately 100 absolute Joules (Royal College of Psychiatry, p.124). [383] The circa 100J BP device no doubt impressed the ERA (European Regulatory Agency) and then the IEC (International Electro Technical Commission) with its greatly reduced maximum output (compared to SW) just as American manufacturers had impressed the FDA with the greatly reduced output [384] of the "MECTA C. " In Europe (and Canada), just as in the U. S. , then, Brief Pulse made its comeback (from the aborted models manufactured in the 1950s) as a "newer and safer" ECT device for modern times, one vastly improved over SW by virtue of greatly diminished output. Like American manufacturers, moreover, Canada's and UK's _Ectron Incorporated_ quickly discovered adequate seizure alone to be ineffective (Ibid), thus, experiencing the same safety versus efficacy dilemma, the same risk surpassing benefit issue, as had American manufacturers. In order to publicly exploit BP's reputation of inducing adequate seizures at half the output of SW, therefore, just as American manufacturers, Ectron was forced to look for a means of publicizing the circa 100J maximum associated with the reduced output of BP, while at the same time, secretly boosting the power of these devices in order to make the devices "work. "

Meeting internationally, "experts" from Europe, Asia, and the U. S. (some of whom were manufacturer-affiliated), maneuvered themselves onto an International Work Group Committee to produce the first International Standard for ECT devices (Association for the Advancement of Medical Instrumentation, 1998, February 4; International Electrotechnical Commission, 1997, Dec 26; Department of Health and Human Services, 1982a). With Weiner at the helm, the Workgroup quickly voted to adopt the phraseology--"100J at 300Ω"—one remarkably similar to the "100J at 220Ω" phraseology of the Mectan transmutation. Finally, the group successfully pushed for featuring the critical "100J at 300Ω" phrase as the conspicuous heart of the 1989 International Standard for ECT Devices generally (International Electrotechnical Commission, 1989, p.23).

---

[382] Canadian and European manufacturers, like their U.S. counterparts, were meeting public protest against the long term cognitive dysfunction produced by Sine Wave (Freeman and Kendell, 1980). Protests included world-wide "survivor" movements in the form of groups such as "ECT Anonymous." As a result, Canadian and European manufacturers, just as American manufacturers, needed a "new and improved" device.

[383] The 98J maximum EO of Ectron's Series 2/3 can be derived by parameters provided by Ectron to RCP (Royal College of Psychiatry, p.124). EO = .850 Amperes x .850 Amperes x 450Ω x .00125PW x 40 Pulses x 6.0 Seconds = 98 Joules.

[384] Weiner and others, in 1982, had reported (to the FDA) that SW reached a maximum 200 Joules, compared to the BP device which can induce adequate seizures in all age recipients with never more than 100J (Department of Health and Human Services, 1982a, G3-G4).

We should note here that American manufacturers of IEC BP devices (that is, American devices manufactured for the European market) were, in fact, anxious to create their (made-for-Europe) IEC BP devices with power equal to or at least approaching that of their made-for-America second generation BP devices (already secretly capable of up to 260 Joules). Unfortunately for U. S. manufacturers, 500Ω (as opposed to 600Ω) is the maximum Impedance allowed by the IEC. Based on a 500Ω maximum Impedance, then, the modified "100J at 220Ω" pure-ER/RRC used in the U. S. would no longer facilitate up to (100J/220Ω = XJ/600Ω: X =) 272 Joules, but a somewhat reduced (100J/220Ω = **XJ**/500Ω; X =) 227J maximum. Nevertheless, while reduced compared to made-for-America BP devices, American manufacturers were anxious to at least achieve the 227J maximum for their American-made, made-for-Europe BP devices in order to elicit no less than a 2.27 MTTLOI for all age categories. So why didn't Weiner simply suggest the same "100J at 220Ω" phrase for the IEC Standard?

First, use of the made-for-America "100J at 220Ω" phrase as a new international standard would have invited very close IEC scrutiny and thus the genuine potential for exposure as a Pure-ER/RRC. Second, it is possible that while 220Ω is "typical" for American devices, 300Ω may be more "typical" for European devices. In any case, Weiner and committee seemed compelled to stick with an international standard containing "300Ω." So why didn't Weiner simply choose a "136J at 300" Pure-ER/RRC from which can be derived the (136J/300Ω = **XJ**/500Ω X =) 227Joules American manufacturers sought as a minimum for their made-for-Europe BP devices? Why instead did Weiner and company choose a "100J at 300Ω" Pure-ER/RRC which, based on the 500Ω maximum Impedance would only allow a (100J/300Ω = XJ/500Ω; X =) 167 Joule maximum EO?

The "100J at 300Ω" phrase (as opposed to "136J at 300Ω") was chosen as the IEC Standard for several reasons. While anxious to create devices equal to or at least approaching the power of made-for-America second generation BP devices (capable of up to 260 Joules), American manufacturers of made-for-Europe BP devices were equally anxious to at least maintain the impression of a circa 100J ceiling standard seemingly limiting their Brief Pulse devices to minimal stimulus outputs. Critically, then, the "100J at 300Ω" phrase (as opposed, for instance, to "136J at 300Ω"), just like the "100J at 220Ω" phrase used in America, continued to accentuate the important 100J metric, strongly identified with Brief Pulse minimal stimulus output. The 100J figure, after all, was well within the purview of the 110J 1982 APA ceiling Standard, as well as a figure in seeming conformity with the circa 100J readout maximums depicted on the machines of all three extant manufacturers of second generation made-for-America BP devices. In brief, "100J at 300," like "100J at 220Ω" in conjunction with circa 100J readout maximums, seemed once again to substantiate a conditional-ER/RRC limiting output to an apparent 100 maximum Joules in conformity with the APA Standard. [385]

Perhaps not incidentally, moreover, "100J at 300Ω," as has been noted, is the approximate equivalent of the "70J at 220Ω" conditional-ER/RRC depicted within the 1982 APA Standard (70J/220Ω = 95.45J/300Ω). As such, "100J at 300Ω" is also strongly suggestive of the "70J at 220Ω" conditional-ER/RRC limited to the 110J ceiling clearly depicted within the 1982 APA Standard. Amazingly, as shall be examined, American made IEC BP devices, like their made-for-America BP counterparts, incorporate the same false 220Ω "constant" to depict the same false machine readouts culminating in the same false circa 100J maximums. Finally, even if regulators succeeded in decoding the "100J at 300Ω" phrase as a Pure-ER/RRC, the resultant (100J/300Ω = **XJ**/500Ω; X =) 167J ceiling yet appears less than the 200J maximum so strongly associated with SW.

In main then, the conspicuous use of "100 Joules" together with the same circa "100J" maximum machine readouts as those depicted for made-for-America devices, strongly suggested minimal stimulus output machines both to FDA and IEC regulators. In short, the adoption of the "100J at 300Ω" phrase by all IEC Brief Pulse manufacturers similarly encouraged regulators to interpret the "100J at 300Ω" IEC standard as a conditional-ER/RRC with circa 100J ceiling. [386]

Like the Mectan Transmutation in the U. S. , the ploy proved successful. Like the FDA, the IEC appears to have interpreted the "100J at 300Ω" phrase eventually featured in the IEC Standard as a conditional--ER/RRC limiting IEC BP devices to circa 100 Joules. This interpretation, like the APA Standard, calls for the incremental

---

[385] Fabricators of the IEC Standard for ECT needed to use the "100J" figure to suggest minimal stimulus, but actually used a 130J at 300Ω Pure-ER/RRC with the IEC's 500Ω maximum Impedance to attain a secret 217J maximum. Manufacturers then enhanced this 217J maximum though other means in order to reach circa 230J maximum and to attain a Pure-ER/RRC equivalent to "100J at 220Ω" as we shall soon see.

[386] As noted, machine Readouts on second generation IEC BP devices, like made-for-America second generation BP devices, misleadingly seem to be limited to circa 100 maximum joules.

reduction of (most practically) Duration to maintain the circa 100J ceiling thus guaranteeing minimal stimulus outputs in all age categories. In that BP devices generally adhere both to the ER/RRC principle (mandating reduced outputs relative to diminishing age) and a uniform MTTLOI applicable to all age categories, a maximum 100J output--the minimum output necessary to induce an adequate seizure in even the most seizure recalcitrant recipient in all circumstances--appeared to guarantee a uniform 1.0 MTTLOI or the least amount of electricity possible in every age category. In sum, the IEC Standard of "100J at 300Ω," with its conspicuous "100J" figure was entirely reminiscent, 1) of the 100J hallmark associated with minimal stimulus output for BP devices generally, 2) the "100J" figure incorporated within the "100J at 220Ω" Mectan fabrication, and, 3) the circa 100J maximum readout depicted on all American-made second generation BP devices both in the U.S. and abroad. All three, in turn, suggested a conditional-ER/RRC with 100J ceiling further reminiscent of the clear 110J ceiling cap within the 1982 APA Standard. In other words, what would become the 1989 IEC Standard appeared to call for maintenance of the hallmark "100J" ceiling ubiquitously associated with Brief Pulse minimal stimulus in every age category. [387] No other ER/RRC phrase (other than the "100J at 300Ω" phrase) and no other energy output figure (other than the prevalent "100J" figure) is mentioned anywhere within the 1989 IEC Standard. Just as the APA Standard's "70J at 220Ω" with 110J ceiling is indeed a conditional ER/RRC guaranteeing minimal stimulus output, and just as MECTA's and Somatics' circa "100J at 220Ω" phrases only seem to be conditional-ER/RRCs with circa 100J ceilings, so the "100J at 300Ω" IEC Standard with what appears to be the same much publicized 100J ceiling only appears to be a conditional-ER/RRC, guaranteeing minimal stimulus output for all age recipients. Illusorily regulated by a 100J ceiling then, the 1989 IEC Standard via the much touted "new and improved" minimal stimulus Brief Pulse device seemed to guarantee recipients and physicians alike, consistent minimal stimulus outputs, that is, the least amount of electricity possible to induce an adequate seizure in all age recipients.

In Fact

In fact, the "100J at 300Ω" IEC standard, suggestive of a conditional ER/RRC with familiar 100J ceiling positively associated with BP, like the Mectan Transmutation, freshly exploits the reduced Brief Pulse "100 Joule" maximum output reputation internationally. Indeed, the similarity of the IEC phrase to the Mectan Transmutation is extensive. In fact, the IEC "100J at 300Ω" phrase seemingly reflective of the 1982 APA conditional-ER/RRC of "70J at 220Ω with circa 110J ceiling" indicative of a continuous and uniform international conformity to the 1982 APA Standard, also accommodates (like the Mectan Transmutation), secret enhancements for BP devices generally (as we will soon see). Hidden components within the 1989 IEC Standard in tandem with minor additional breaches of the IEC Standard itself, actually facilitate the production of very powerful IEC (made-for-Europe) devices, which are but slight modifications of second generation made-for-America MECTA and Somatics BP devices. Indeed, the power of made-for-Europe second generation MECTA and Somatics BP devices, based on hidden enhancements and slight breaches of the IEC Standard itself, dovetail quite accommodatingly, as we shall witness, into the Mectan Transmutation. Amazingly then, the same hidden and unexplicated Pure-ER/RRC interpretation of the IEC Standard together with hidden components and slight breaches of the IEC Standard itself to be discussed below, served ***not*** to "bridge" the original 1982 APA Standard with the 1989 IEC Standard as was the appearance, but rather to bridge the IEC Standard with the illicit Mectan Transmutation. As we shall observe then, the new 1989 IEC Standard, strongly influenced by Weiner, served to bridge souped-up made-for-Europe IEC BP devices with souped-up made-for-America BP devices.

The APA Standard, the Mectan Transmutation of the APA Standard, and the IEC standard all emphasize a circa 100J ceiling, the first, a mandate, the latter two only seeming mandates of the circa 100J perimeter. In fact, unlike the 1982 APA Standard, the Pure-ER/RRC interpretation of the IEC Standard, like the Mectan Transmutation, both "licenses" and camouflages super-powerful BP devices internationally. In a nutshell, American and Eurasian manufacturers, through undisclosed agreement, interpret the "100J at 300Ω" IEC Standard, as we will explore, as a Pure-ER/RRC similar to the Mectan Transmutation. In lieu of the seeming 100J ceiling expected for an international regulation, then, like the illicit Mectan transmutation of the APA

[387] A true international 100J ceiling would have eliminated SW devices, compelling the use of BP internationally, just as the 1982 APA Standard was meant to insure minimal stimulus BP devices in lieu of SW for all American recipients.

Standard, the unreported ceiling of the IEC Standard is based not on a circa 100J ceiling, but upon a 130J at 300Ω Pure-ER/RRC to a maximum 500Ω Impedance. In effect, the IEC Standard, as has been noted, is a "licensing" of the American Mectan Transmutation, a feat primarily achieved through the deliberate omission of the clearly delineated circa 100J ceiling stipulation visibly discoverable within the 1982 APA Standard.

Though never explained as such, therefore, manufacturers internationally interpreted the IEC "100J at 300Ω" Standard for ECT devices as a "130J at 300Ω" Pure-ER/RRC based not on a 100J (or 110J) ceiling, but on maximum allowable IEC Impedance. Just as the Mectan Transmutation eradicated the 100 or 110J ceiling for American manufacturers, the IEC Standard effectively eradicated the 100J ceiling for Eurasian manufacturers. [388] The interpretation of what is actually a Pure-130J ER (to maximum IEC Impedance) ironically eliminating the 100J ceiling seemingly emphasized within the IEC Standard, wholly enabled Eurasian manufacturers to create devices with nearly the same excessive surpassing of the 100J mark as their American predecessors (as we shall now see). The failure of overseas manufacturers to report actual maximum output and thus actual MTTLOI, left Eurasian regulatory agencies, Eurasian clinicians, and finally, the Eurasian public general, wholly ignorant of the power and thus true aim of all modern-day BP devices just as it had the FDA, American clinicians, and the American public general. [389] In sum, due to manufacturers' interpretation of the 1989 IEC Standard not as the expected "100J at 300Ω" conditional-ER/RRC with 100J ceiling, but as a "130J at 300Ω" Pure-ER/RRC based on maximum IEC Impedance of 500Ω, that is, not as a mandatory 100J ceiling, but as a 130J pure-ER/RRC to maximum IEC Impedance--the Mectan Transmutation came to be utilized internationally. [390]

IEC Standard - A More Perfect Illusion

Manufacturers, as noted above, interpreted both the "100J at 220Ω" Mectan Transmutation (of the APA Standard) and the hidden "130J at 300Ω" IEC Standard (as we shall see) as unexplained Pure-ER/RRCs (limited only to maximum IEC Impedance); whereas, regulators interpreted the manifest "100J at 220Ω" and manifest "100J at 300Ω" depictions as conditional-ER/RRCs with circa 100J ceilings just as the 1982 APA Standard was meant to be interpreted. No doubt, the "100J" figure was featured in the IEC Standard for its' 1) synonymy with the "100J" indicated by Weiner as the minimum output required to induce seizures in all recipients in all circumstances, 2) its proximity to the 110J ceiling depicted within the 1982 APA Standard, 3) the "100J" figure contained within the "100J at 220Ω" Mectan phrase, 4) the 100J BP Machine Readout maximums, 5) the fact that 100J is specifically associated with BP's greatly reduced output, half that of SW, and finally 6) that a 100 Joule ceiling seems to have meant the IEC standard regulated all machines to minimal

---

[388] Unlike Somatics and MECTA's occasional description of "100J at a 'typical' 220Ω," the 1989 IEC Standard never even uses the word, "typical." Regulatory agencies are thus left to assume that the IEC "100J at 300Ω" phrase a conditional-ER/RRC, incorporative of a 100J ceiling. That outside observers are not only supposed to deduce a 130J at 300Ω Pure-ER/RRC interpretation based on maximum Impedance and then derive the Standard's actual maximum output and maximum MTTLOI for themselves, seems ridiculous, particularly given hidden contingencies overtly suggestive of a 100J ceiling such as circa 100J machine readouts. Given the APA ceiling precedent of 110J, bolstered by illusory 100J maximum Machine Readouts not only on American but IEC devices, and finally the reputation of BP as a reduced output device, the tendency for regulatory agencies and professionals to interpret the "100 Joules" referred to in IEC Standard as a maximum ceiling within a conditional-ER/RRC, seems inevitable.

[389] England's Royal College of Psychiatry's *The ECT Handbook* does make several references to the inefficacy of the earlier less powerful English BP devices (Royal College of Psychiatry, 1995, p.129, 132) such as the Ectron 2/3 Series (emitting an actual circa 100 maximum joules), thereby "justifying" the need for more powerful BP devices. Nevertheless, due to under-reporting of English and Canadian BP manufacturers such as Ectron *(which reports 225 Volts in lieu of the actual 375 Volts for the Ectron 2/3, Ibid, p.124)*, original machines such as the Ectron 2/3 Series appear to have emitted only 57 maximum joules in lieu of their actual 98 Joules, resulting in the gross underreporting of Ectron's later more powerful BP devices. In spite of an RCP acknowledgement that later English BP devices have indeed increased in power, therefore, the actual extent of that power, and the fact that the later BP devices surpass that of SW in cumulative power, goes unrecognized.

[390] Framers of the 1989 IEC Standard were careful to remove a circa 100J ceiling stipulation like the one delineated within the 1982 APA Standard (regarding 110 Joules). Thus, unlike American manufacturers' illegal re-interpretation of the 1982 APA Standard, the interpretation of "130 Joules at 300Ω" as a pure-ER/RRC, enabling the gross surpassing of 100 absolute Joules, though yet unreported, no longer becomes technically illegal under the 1989 IEC Standard. In short, a Pure-ER/RRC interpretation, though not the expected interpretation, is not technically ruled out of the IEC Standard by the standard itself. Even so, the "100J at 300Ω" IEC Standard is highly misleading.

stimulus outputs as did the APA Standard. In short, naturally interpreted as a conditional-ER/RRC with circa 100J ceiling similar to the precedential 1982 APA Standard, the 100J figures within both the Mectan Transmutation ("100J at 220Ω") and IEC Standard ("100J at 300Ω") created but the impression of a 100J ceiling internationally. [391]

Thus, from manufacturers' perspective, the IEC "100J at 300Ω" Standard (which was really a "130J at 300Ω perfected Pure-ER/RRC" (overriding the 100J ceiling), supplanted both the APA conditional-ER/RRC (of "70J at 220Ω" with 110J ceiling) and "less perfected "100J at 220Ω" Mectan Transmutation. Unlike the shadow cast (by the APA Standard) over the Pure-ER/RRC interpretation of "100J at 220Ω" then, the IEC Standard contained an implied, but no clearly delineated circa 100 or 110J ceiling. Consequently, from the manufacturers' perspective, the IEC Standard was the Mectan Transmutation "improved," that is, the IEC Standard was the transmuted APA Standard without the 110J ceiling stipulation. [392] While both FDA and IEC, as well as practicing physicians appear to have interpreted both the American "100J at 220Ω" phrase and the "100J at 300Ω" IEC phrase as conditional-ER/RRCs with circa 100J EO ceilings, manufacturers themselves, as noted, furtively interpreted the American "100J at 220Ω" phrase and what was actually an IEC "130J at 300Ω" phrase as Pure-ER/RRCs (wholly overriding the 100 and 110J ceilings). [393] As noted above, the singular allusion to EO via the "100 Joule" phrase featured within the 1989 IEC Standard itself (the composition of which was heavily influenced by Richard Weiner and his American counterparts) together with probable maximum Readouts of the same circa 100 joules depicted on all second generation American made-for-IEC BP devices, naturally suggested a 100J IEC ceiling similar to the 1982 APA 110J maximum.

In sum, both American and Eurasian manufacturers interpreted the IEC Standard of what was actually "130J at 300Ω," like manufacturers had interpreted the "100J at 220Ω" phrase in America, not as the expected conditional-ER/RRC with 100J ceiling--but as a "130J at 300Ω" Pure-ER/RRC relative to maximum Impedance, "justifying" the same ironic and covert gross surpassing of 100 Joules practiced by American manufacturers for their second generation made-for-America BP devices. [394] Pointedly, use of the "100J" figure appeared deliberate, rendering invisible, in effect, the eradication of the "100J" ceiling. As a result, manufacturers' interpretation of the 1989 "100J at 300Ω" IEC Standard as a "130J at 300Ω" Pure-ER/RRC in lieu of a conditional-ER/RRC with 100J ceiling, was impossible for regulators to discern. [395] In essence, the 1989 IEC Standard, like the Mectan Transmutation, permitted Brief Pulse devices to surpass the cumulative output of SW without being noticed. Indeed, compared to the Mectan Transmutation, the 1989 IEC Standard was simply a more perfect illusion.

Conclusion

In conclusion, neither the Mectan Transmutation nor the 1989 IEC Standard for ECT devices identifies actual maximum output, nor does either explain the standards' ER-output/Impedance relationship to actual maximum

---

[391] Creators of the 1989 IEC Standard (presided over by manufacturer-affiliated expert Richard Weiner) may have originally chosen the "at 300Ω" IEC appendage ("100J at 300Ω") in lieu of the Mectan adjunct "at 220Ω," in that both a Mean and a Pure-ER/RRC interpretation of the "100J at 300Ω" IEC Standard (with 30% IEC cushion adjunct to be discussed below) would have accommodated the early second generation 200J D-2, early JR-1@2s and 200J Thymatron. (Mean made-for-America interpretation: 100J/300Ω = ***200J***/600Ω; Pure-ER/RRC made-for-Europe interpretation: 130J/300Ω = ***216J***/500Ω). In brief, perhaps the "100J at 300Ω" phrase was initially proposed (about 1981) to accommodate the earliest second generation American-made BP devices. Weiner may not have predicted that by 1989, the year the IEC Standard was finally adopted for all medical devices, American manufacturers of second generation BP devices would have been so successful in evading detection, that they would feel safe in appending an additional 50-60 Joules to their BP devices through the Pure-ER/RRC variation of the Mectan Transmutation.

[392] 70J at 220Ω = (circa) 100J at 300Ω.

[393] A so-called IEC 62D Committee for ECT devices, in all likelihood composed of manufacturer-affiliated experts, including Richard Weiner, attempted at one point to create a new IEC Standard which included dramatically enhanced EO (for third generation BP devices). The General IEC (62A) Committee for electrical medical devices in general, however, refused to adopt the recommendations of the 62D Committee. In July of 1998 (via a personal communication from IEC in Geneva), the author learned that the two committees had compromised by not passing the new proposed Standard, but, agreeing to the withdrawal of the 1989 IEC Standard for ECT altogether (60601-2-14). The result of this decision was dramatic, as we shall eventually see.

[394] The APA Standard contains a maximum 600Ω Impedance as opposed to the IEC Standard's 500Ω; Differing maximum Impedance limits have some effect on actual unreported maximum outputs between the U.S. and Europe, as we have seen.

[395] In fact, as we shall see, the IEC Standard actually uses an unreported and hidden "130J at 300Ω" Pure-ER/RRC derivation for deriving actual maximum output for IEC BP machines.

output/Impedance. Conversely, both the "100J at 220Ω" and "100J at 300Ω" phrases suggest the same 100J ceiling, seemingly corroborative of ubiquitous machine readouts specifying circa 100J maximums. But while the 1982 APA Standard, written under the auspices of the FDA, specifically identifies a 110J ceiling, thereby forcing American manufacturers to hide the transmutation of machine outputs well in excess of the 110J ceiling, the IEC Standard, though highly deceptive in its single suggestive allusion to a 100J maximum EO, unlike the APA Standard, eliminates any specific stipulation for an actual circa 100J (or 110J) ceiling. In essence, the 1989 IEC Standard appears to be a more devolved Mectan transmutation, both of which suggest 100J ceilings while, in fact, facilitating much higher outputs. Put another way, the IEC Standard is the APA Standard sans the specific 110J ceiling stipulation. Weiner (and team) appear simply to have changed "70J at 220Ω" to "100J at 300Ω" (circa "70J at 220Ω" = "100J at 300Ω") while, in the spirit of the Mectan Transmutation, eradicating the 110J ceiling altogether. At the same time, both the Mectan Transmutation and the 1989 IEC Standard retain and prominently feature the 100J figure. Ironically then, like the Mectan Transmutation, the "100J" feature emphasized by the IEC Standard serves to conceal the dropping of the "100" to "110J" ceiling. Paradoxically, by using and featuring the "100J" term within the IEC Standard, the illusion was created that the circa 100J BP ceiling remained intact, indeed corroborated by circa "100J" maximum IEC machine readouts. Specifically, the 1989 IEC Standard for "ECT" states:

> 51.2 Limitation of Output Values
> The output energy shall be limited to a maximum of 100J at 300Ω for each treatment initiation. (International Electrotechnical Commission, 1989, p.23)

Due to the ambiguity of the above statement, the question is begged: "Does the above declaration suggest a "100J at 300Ω" conditional-ER/RRC with 100J ceiling like the 1982 APA Standard or does it suggest a never before explained Pure-ER/RRC creating an unreported maximum output based on actual maximum Impedance? If so, what is the maximum output allowed. Moreover, If the latter is true, does the unreported ceiling grossly surpass 100 joules, perhaps even permitting a higher EO than SW? Reassuringly, circa 100J readout maximums depicted on the machines themselves appeared to substantiate the former. [396]

Highly Suggestive

Technically designed to surpass 100J or not, the 1989 IEC Standard, just as the Mectan Transmutation upon which the IEC Standard is based, remains ambiguous and so deceptive. Indeed, the IEC Standard's direct allusion to 100J together with the deliberate exclusion of the 110J ceiling (contained within the 1982 APA Standard) is duplicitous. In fact, the conspicuous, coincidental, and singular assertion of "100J" as the featured figure within the 1989 IEC Standard; the exclusion within the IEC Standard of any output other than "100J"; the totally arbitrary nature (and thus the unnecessary featuring) of the "100J" figure; [397] the "coincidental" equivalency (of "100J at 300Ω") with the 1982 APA Standard's "70J at 220Ω" (70J/220Ω = circa 100J/300Ω) phrase; spurious circa 100J machine readout maximums; the conspiratorial omission of maximum output reporting (in joules) by all American and Eurasian BP manufacturers for what were actually second generation BP devices; manufacturers' failure to explain the Pure-ER/RRC interpretation of "100J at 300Ω" both nationally and internationally; and finally misleading equivalencies between Actual Charge and ER-Outputs in joules on both continents, seem deliberately designed to obfuscate. Without question, manufacturers on both continents wished to take full advantage of Brief Pulse's universal status as reduced output, minimal stimulus apparatuses via the ubiquitous suggestion of a circa 100J maximum. Clearly, the reputation of the Brief Pulse device

[396] It should be noted that "100J" actually does occur on some IEC devices at about 300Ω which confusingly seems to validate of the phrase "100J at 300Ω." In fact, a minimal stimulus device limited to 100 or 110J should only reach 100 or 110J at maximum Impedance. In that a 100 year old never needs more than 100J to seize, the literal existence of 100J at 300Ω reveals that 100J is emitted in a much younger age category, in fact, corroborating the application of an excessive MTTLOI at all age levels as opposed to minimal stimulus or just above threshold outputs.

[397] Fabricators of the IEC Standard for ECT wanted to attain a Pure-ER relationship of "100J at 300Ω" to a 166J maximum at the IEC maximum Impedance of 500Ω (100J/300Ω = 166J/500Ω). Had the IEC Standard used the same "220Ω" as the APA Standard, the standard would have had to have been "73J at 220Ω" (73J/220Ω = 166J/500Ω), deviating from the 100J figure.

internationally as one capable of inducing adequate seizures in all recipients with no more than 100 joules, half the output of SW was exploited by the featured 100J phrases in both the Mectan Transmutation and the 1989 IEC Standard.

Thus, just as the Mectan phrase "100J at 220Ω" in conjunction with 100J Machine Readouts, is strongly suggestive of the 110J absolute ceiling denoted within the 1982 APA Standard in turn based on the 100J minimum required to induce adequate seizures in all recipients in all circumstances, so the "100 Joules" described within the 1989 IEC Standard is suggestive of the same circa 110J ceiling and the same 100J minimum, well known by manufacturers and regulatory agencies alike as requiring half the output emitted by SW to accomplish the same task--induction of the adequate seizure. In short, the importance of the 100J figure is that it is the minimum amount of electricity necessary to induce adequate seizures with Brief Pulse in all recipients. 100J, in brief, is emblematic of the least amount of electricity necessary to induce the same grand mal seizure previously induced by the 200J SW device (Department of Health and Human Services, 1982a, A53; E20; G3-G4). European and Canadian BP manufacturers such as Ectron, just as U. S. BP manufacturers, were unquestionably familiar with BP's much touted advantage over SW, that is, BP's singular capacity to induce adequate seizures at a 100J minimum for even the most seizure recalcitrant recipient. In sum, the 100J mark had come to stand for the least amount of power necessary to induce "just above threshold dosing" for every "ECT" recipient under any conditions, a task only Brief Pulse could claim. Certainly, by 1989, both in the U. S. , Canada, and Eurasia, the 100J mark came to symbolize the archetypal new and improved output ceiling, half that of SW (Department of Health and Human Services, 1982a, A53; E20). The 100J ceiling, in short, was and is readily associated with BP's vastly increased margin of safety over SW (Department of Health and Human Services, 1982a, G3-G4). With ECT under assault via the now world-wide anti-psychiatry movement, the 100J ceiling was now highly recognizable as the minimum output needed with Brief Pulse to induce seizures in all recipients and thus minimal stimulus dosing generally, very appealing to regulatory entities globally, including the FDA, the ERA, and the IEC, an achievement of which only the resurrected Brief Pulse device was capable. Based on the premise of "adequate seizure efficacy" (Department of Health and Human Services, 1982a, pp. A-41, A44-A45), the basic premise of convulsion theory itself, the Brief Pulse device, with its capacity to invoke adequate seizures at half the output of SW, had earned the reputation of a "kinder, gentler, newer, exceedingly improved" ECT device world-wide. Indeed, as all manufacturers realized, only the 100J Brief Pulse device alone could rescue ECT from total annihilation.

Unfortunately for proponents of convulsive therapy theory, however, but well understood by manufacturers, "*efficacy* of the adequate seizure" in conjunction with the least amount of electricity necessary to induce them, though an incredibly appealing answer to the cognitive dissonance problem long associated with so-called "ECT," the theory's therapeutic precepts had been thoroughly debunked (Cameron 1994; see Marilyn Rice's comments during the FDA hearings). That is, while the Brief Pulse device can induce adequate seizures at greatly reduced outputs, induction of the seizure is not what makes ECT "work." What makes ECT "effective," unfortunately, and as all manufacturers well know, is adequate amounts of electricity, the one great detail manufacturers have ardently attempted to suppress. Indeed, the fact that "ECT" efficacy is actually based on adequate amounts of electricity (as opposed to adequate seizure) means that minimal stimulus outputs with Brief Pulse, that is, outputs based on the 100J minimum required to adequately seize all recipients, is simply ineffective. That is, adequate seizures simply do not work regardless of Brief Pulse's capacity to induce them at half the output of SW. Put still another way, psychiatrists do not get the looked for effect they seek with adequate seizures alone, even though the minimal stimulus Brief Pulse device is fully capable of inducing them. What is needed, inopportunely, is adequate doses of electricity which all manufacturers know damages the brain, unavoidably resulting in long term memory annihilation. Thus, the same deceptive, all but invisible (and illicit) transmutation that had occurred in America from an actual 110J maximum to an unexplicated 100J Pure-ER, from a conditional-ER/RRC (with 110J ceiling) to a Pure-ER/RRC (grossly surpassing the 110J ceiling), from just above threshold outputs to the multifold threshold outputs of the present, became the single ongoing solution for manufacturers internationally. In sum, in order to survive, manufacturers were forced to apply carefully hidden, tightly suppressed multifold threshold outputs of electricity on the world-wide stage via the same slick employment of American manufacturer chicanery, applied internationally.

Unquestionably, by 1989, no one had yet understood the undisclosed transmutation of the APA Standard which had taken place in America with its resultant draconian enhancement of Brief Pulse electroshock devices, a "necessary" transformation enabling BP manufacturers to furtively create devices roughly 2.5 times as powerful as the 108J MECTA "C," circa 2.5 times the ceiling allowed by the initial 1982 APA Standard, and 2.5

times the touted 100J ceiling manufacturers presented to recipients and psychiatrists alike through the utilization of so-called "new and improved" Brief Pulse devices. Tellingly, no regulatory agency was provided any information which would have led them to understand that by 1989, all BP devices world-wide had grossly surpassed 100 absolute joules--surpassing SW in power. In fact, regulatory agencies were given every indication that what were actually second generation made-for-America BP devices continued to maintain circa 100 maximum joules, perfectly conforming to the 1982 APA Standard (Food and Drug Administration, 1984; Food and Drug Administration, 1985; Food and Drug Administration, 1986A; Food and Drug Administration, 1986B). Who could have conceived in 1989, that this same deceptive method--revealed for the first time here in full—had now been guilefully applied overseas to create the appearance of the same circa 100J ceiling specified within the 1982 APA Standard while actually facilitating circa 2.5 times that output. Who could have fathomed that this same deceitful method had now been incorporated into the 1989 International Standard to create the same ongoing illusion of improved safety (over SW) in Canada and Europe and perhaps even various parts of Asia. [398] So strong was the propaganda hyping reduced output BP devices world-wide, that the 100J output denoted in the 1989 IEC Standard as "100J at 300Ω," continued to suggest the same false 100J maximum, the same false appearance of increased safety over SW, the same false suggestion of BP minimal stimulus, and the same false validation of convulsion theory created by U. S. BP manufacturers via the Mectan transmutation five to seven years earlier. [399] Deceptively, therefore, manufacturers' hidden interpretation of the featured "100J at 300Ω" phrase within the 1989 IEC Standard as a Pure-ER/RRC to maximum machine Impedance, like the Mectan Transmutation before it, in lieu of maintaining the 100J ceiling, had actually, albeit invisibly, altogether eliminated it. [400]

Details: How Manufacturers Manipulated the 1989 IEC Standard of "100J at 300Ω"

As discussed, international manufacturers interpret the 1989 IEC Standard: "<u>100 Joules at 300Ω</u>" (International Electrotechnical Commission, 1989, p.23) as the same unexplicated Pure-ER/RRC to maximum EO at maximum machine Impedance as American manufacturers did via the Mectan Transmutation. Unfortunately for international manufacturers, as previously noted, whereas the APA Standard permits a maximum Impedance of up to 600Ω in the U. S. , the IEC Standard limits Impedance to 500Ω maximum (International Electrotechnical Commission, 1989, p.11). Since the actual maximum EO derivable from the featured IEC Standard of "<u>100 Joules at 300Ω</u>" interpreted as a Pure-ER/RRC is but an unreported <u>166.6 Joules</u>, (<u>100J</u>/300Ω = <u>XJ</u>/500Ω. **X = <u>166.66 Joules</u>**), manufacturers circumvent this limitation by secretly enhancing the "100J at 300Ω" phrase. [401]

Additional 30%

Buried within the IEC Standard, an inconspicuous adjunct subsists permitting an additional 30% Energy Output (joules) to be added to the featured "100J at 300Ω" phrase which manufacturers interpret as a Pure-ER/RRC (to true maximum output at true maximum Impedance), that is, an additional 30% can be added to the featured "100J at 300Ω" phrase. Put differently, the adjunct permits a 30% enhancement of the actual unreported 166.66J EO maximum (International Electrotechnical Commission, 1989, p.21). The exact passage from within the IEC Standard reads:

---

[398] Not until 1994, was it pointed out through a little known study that BP had in fact surpassed SW in power (Cameron, 1994).

[399] In fact, the IEC Standard of "100J at 300Ω" may have been submitted by Weiner and associates before developing the Mectan Transmutation of "100J at 220Ω," which permitted even higher output.

[400] Unlike the 1982 APA Standard, the 100J figure within the IEC Standard, as noted, though indicated as such, was no longer specifically defined as a ceiling.

[401] Note that "100J at 300Ω," the circa equivalent of "70J at 220Ω" permits 200J at the American maximum Impedance of 600Ω (100J/300Ω = <u>200J</u>/600Ω), maximum energy outputs (in joules) for the MECTA D-2, early MECTA JR/SR 1@2 and Somatics' early Thymatron. The 30% IEC adjunct permitting "130J at 300Ω" accommodated 200J outputs under the IEC Standard (130J/300Ω = <u>216J</u>/500Ω). This suggests that the Mectan Transmutation of "100J at 220Ω" permitting up to 273J at 600Ω was developed following the initial 1981 submission of "100J at 300Ω"(i.e.130J at 300Ω) for the IEC Standard, eventually adopted in 1989.

> The measured maximum output energy shall not deviate from the figures given in the accompanying documents by more than +/-30% for the load resistances specified in Sub-Section 6.8.3 [402] (International Electrotechnical Commission, 601-2-14, Section 8, 50.2, p.21).

Thus, in lieu of a "100J at 300Ω" Pure-ER/RRC, the IEC standard actually accommodates an even more invisible "130J at 300Ω" Pure-ER/RRC (.3 x 100J = 30J + 100J = 130J) resulting in an actual unreported maximum output ceiling of 216.66J (using the IEC 500Ω maximum).

130J/300Ω = XJ/500Ω. [403] **X = 216.66 Joules**.

The IEC Standard, in brief, actually "permits" an unreported invisible maximum output of 216.66J, a figure which can be mathematically confirmed simply by adding 30% of 166.66J to 166.66 Joules.

.3 x 166.66J = 50J; 166.66J + 50J = **216.66 Joules**.

Even with this hidden ceiling, however, manufacturers such as Somatics Incorporated and MECTA Corporation, as we shall see, take slight additional liberties, for a very important reason. In lieu of the inconspicuously derived "130J at 300Ω" Pure-ER/RRC phrase, for example, MECTA utilizes an illegal "138J at 300Ω" Pure-ER/RRC to derive an approximate **230J** maximum output for their American made, made-for-Europe IEC BP devices while Somatics utilizes an illegal "136J at 300Ω" Pure-ER/RRC to derive a **227J** maximum output as we shall soon understand. Both MECTA and Somatics were thus able to fabricate slightly modified renditions of their made-for-America BP devices for utilization in countries under the IEC Standard.

MECTA: 138J/300Ω = XJ/500Ω. **X = 230 Joules**

Somatics: 136J/300Ω = XJ/500Ω. **X = 227 Joules**

Other manufacturers, as we shall examine, i.e. the Canadian and English Company, Ectron, grossly breach the already misleading IEC Standard with an approximate 156J at 300Ω Pure-ER/RRC to derive approximately 260 (unreported) joules for its second generation BP devices (i.e. , Ectron Series 5A), in effect, equaling second generation made-for-America BP devices in power and Multifold Threshold Titration Level Output Intensity (MTTLOI).

156J/300Ω = XJ/500Ω. **X = 260 Joules**

Finally, at least one English manufacturer, (perhaps similar to the defunct U. S. manufacturer, Elcot) appears to have ignored the IEC Standard altogether, manufacturing an "experimental" device emitting an even higher EO, as we shall ultimately observe.

In conclusion, manufacturers of IEC BP devices, (for example, American devices manufactured for use in the UK), through application of the same Pure-ER/RRC mechanism utilized in America for made-for America BP devices (deemed the Mectan transmutation), in conjunction with the 30% cushion adjunct together with a few minor breaches of the IEC standard itself, managed to construct "second generation" BP devices with the capacity to emit between 226 and 260 unreported joules. Not surprisingly, these IEC BP devices approached the output power and MTTLOI of second generation made-for-America BP devices. At the same time, equally similar reporting strategies (to those used in America) suggest the same circa 100J maximum engendered for made-for America BP devices. Thus, like American manufacturers, manufacturers of IEC BP ENR devices (including American manufacturers) through exploitation of the IEC Standard itself, appear to have emulated

---

[402] Load Resistances specified in subsection 6.8.3 are 100Ω, 200Ω, 300Ω, and 500Ω (International Electrotechnical Commission, 1989, p.11).

[403] Note that the same "130J/300Ω" Pure-ER with respect to the APA maximum Impedance of 600Ω, permits 260J, coincidentally accommodating unreported second generation BP devices in America.130J/300Ω = 260J/600Ω.

both the Mectan Transmutation and various American reporting strategies, to cover up the true power of their second generation made-for-Europe BP devices. Similar to the history of American manufacturers within the modern American BP Era, then, European and Canadian manufacturers of enhanced IEC-oriented BP devices (including American manufacturers of international BP devices), seem to have followed the American precedent of manufacturing much more powerful second generation BP devices even as both the IEC standard and the reporting of these IEC devices continued to indicate circa 100J ceilings. Too, like their American counterparts, European, Canadian, and American BP manufacturers marketing devices for Europe, abruptly dropped the reporting of actual EO in joules.

CHAPTER 34

MECTA IEC BP Devices

The mathematical logic to determine output for MECTA IEC BP devices remains speculative throughout, in that MECTA consistently abstains from providing enough information to obtain numerous vital parameters and, in fact, appears to have provided some false and/or misleading information. Speculative or not, however, the specs provided in this manuscript for MECTA IEC BP devices, like the MECTA made-for America BP devices, are extremely probable. Though similarly negligent both in providing actual output and elaborating on the nature of provided figures, more often than not, Somatics, unlike MECTA, provides enough accurate information to categorically determine final parameters. In light of the accurate IEC derivations for Somatics devices, and Somatics' historical emulation of MECTA devices (and vice-versa); therefore, unprovided MECTA parameters can be construed through extrapolation.

Both MECTA and Somatics make modified versions of their made-for-America second generation BP devices for use in IEC regulated countries--that is countries under the IEC Standard. Just as MECTA and Somatics' second generation *made-for America* BP devices secretly surpass SW in cumulative EO (Cameron, 1994), so MECTA and Somatics' second generation *IEC* BP instruments also secretly surpass SW in cumulative EO. Nevertheless, irrespective of the 1989 IEC Standard containing a moderately altered phrase ("100J at 300Ω") compared to that used by manufacturers of made-for-America BP devices (circa "100J at 220Ω"), it is mainly due to the IEC maximum Impedance ceiling of <u>500Ω</u> as opposed to the APA sanctioned <u>600Ω</u> maximum Impedance, that both MECTA and Somatics have been forced to reduce the power of second generation made-for-America BP devices marketed under IEC auspices---but only slightly--as has been alluded to above (Royal College of Psychiatry, 1995, pp.124-125).

Underreporting of MECTA IEC BP Devices to Derive a Pseudo 100 Joule Maximum

But have American manufacturers really attempted to give the impression that their IEC BP devices are limited to 100 joules? The Royal College of Psychiatry (RCP) in England informs us that the MECTA JR/SR 2 <u>IEC</u> BP device used in the U. K. (a slightly modified version of the second generation made-for-America JR/SR 2), emits a maximum **<u>.001</u>** second Pulse Width [the same PW used for the second generation made-for-America JR/SR 2 (Royal College of Psychiatry, 1995, p.125)] and a 2.8 second maximum Duration (Ibid)--1.2 seconds less than the made-for-America JR/SR 2 maximum Duration of 4.0 seconds (Royal College of Psychiatry, 1995, p.125). The RCP goes on to inform us at least five different times, that maximum Voltage for all MECTA IEC BP devices is **<u>240V</u>** [404] [405] (Ibid, p.124-125), information MECTA no doubt provided to RCP. Additionally, the RCP informs us that maximum Charge for both the JR/SR 1 and 2 IEC BP devices is **.403C** (Royal College of

[404] A spurious maximum Voltage of 240 is reported at least five times by the RCP for MECTA IEC devices, information the author assumes to have been reported by MECTA (Royal College of Psychiatry, 1995, p.124-125).

[405] MECTA reports a false maximum Voltage of 240 and thus a false maximum Impedance of 300Ω, as well as what may be a false maximum Duration to give the overall impression MECTA has limited MECTA devices marketed under IEC auspices, to 100 absolute Joules.

Psychiatry, 1995, p.125). By simply plugging in these figures into the Voltage-oriented formula for finding EO (EO = Current x Voltage x Pulses x Wave Length (Pulse Width) x Duration), figures provided by MECTA to RCP (Ibid) for MECTA's second generation **IEC** JR/SR **2** marketed in UK, which include maximum Duration of 2.8 **Sec.** and maximum Voltage of **240V** (Ibid), we obtain for the MECTA-made JR/SR **2** IEC BP device a **96.7J** maximum output, very similar to the maximum output MECTA spuriously asserts (via machine readouts) is emitted by its second generation made-for America BP devices.

EO = .8 x 240 Volts x 180 Pulses x .001 Seconds x 2.8 Seconds = **96.768 Joules**.

MECTA also reports to the RCP the same maximum **240V** for MECTA's IEC version of the **JR/SR 1**, but which unlike the **JR/SR 2**, uses a maximum **.0014** Pulse Width and a 2.0 Second maximum Duration. Plugging the reported **240 Volt**, **2.0 Second** maximum Duration, and **.0014 Sec. Pulse Width** (Ibid) into the same formula along with other parameters MECTA provides to the RCP, we once more obtain the same approximate **100J EO** maximum:

EO = .8 x 240 Volts [406] x 180 pulses x .0014 Seconds x 2.0 seconds = **96.768 Joules**.

Thus, MECTA reports for its' second generation **JR/SR 1 and 2 IEC BP devices** (marketed in the U. K. and other IEC-regulated countries) to the Royal College of Psychiatry and thus the European Regulatory Agency (ERA) and IEC, the same circa **100J ceiling** MECTA infers (to the FDA) for its second generation made-for-America JR/SR 1 and 2 BP devices (via machine readouts). [407]

Deductively, therefore, in reporting 240V maximums to RCP, MECTA reports a maximum EO of approximately **96.8J** for its MECTA IEC BP devices. In so doing, MECTA appears to be suggesting that the "100J at 300Ω" phrase featured in the 1989 IEC Standard is a conditional ER/RRC limiting devices to a maximum EO of 100J [408] and that MECTA IEC BP devices conform to this 100J ceiling. As such, "100J at 300Ω" looks to be, like the APA Standard, the anticipated conditional-ER/RRC with circa 100J ceiling; in brief, a standard which circumscribes machines to minimal stimulus outputs for all age categories.

To be sure, because MECTA has specified **240** as maximum Voltage and thus **96.8J** as maximum EO for both its second generation IEC BP devices, maximum machine Impedance in each case is assumed to be 300Ω, this, in spite of the maximum allowable IEC Impedance of 500Ω. Using the Impedance oriented formula to derive the indirectly reported **96.8J** maximum output, then, we can see that maximum Impedance must be **300Ω**:

EO = (Current squared) x Impedance x (hz x 2) x WL x Duration

EO = .8A x .8A x **300Ω** x 180 Pulses x .001 Seconds x 2.8 Seconds = 96.768J
EO = .8A x .8A x **300Ω** x 180 Pulses x .0014 Seconds x 2.0 Seconds = 96.768J

Based on the 96.7J maximum output indirectly reported by MECTA, therefore, the reported .403C Charge maximum, and the two reported maximum Durations of 2.0 and 2.8 Seconds can seemingly be corroborated via the following two Charge formulas:

EO ÷ Current x Impedance = Charge
96.7J ÷ .8A x 300Ω = .403C

---

406 Coincidentally, the early MECTA "C" presented by MECTA to the FDA and Utah as representative of BP is described by Grahn (the private Utah investigative lab contracted by the FDA) as emitting 81 maximum Joules and utilizing 240 maximum Volts, the same Voltage reported by MECTA for its' second generation MECTA IEC devices.

407 MECTA reports 101.4J and 101.3J at 220Ω respectively for made-for-America (second generation) SR1 and 2 devices, implying a conditional ER/RRC with circa 100J ceiling. Moreover, MECTA's made-for America devices display misleading maximum Machine Readouts of 101.4J and 101.3J respectively.

408 As we shall see, 240 Volts is also equivalent to a false 300Ω maximum.

<u>Duration x Current x (hz x 2) x WL = Charge</u>
<u>2.0 Sec.</u> x .8A x 180 Pulses x .0014 = <u>.403C</u>
<u>2.8 Sec.</u> x .8A x 180 Pulses x .001 = <u>.403C</u>

In short, just as MECTA indicates approximate <u>100J</u> ceilings to the FDA for second generation made-for America MECTA BP devices,[409] MECTA indirectly reports to Royal College of Psychiatry in U. K. and thus to the ERA and IEC a similar maximum EO of approximately 100 joules for MECTA made-for-Europe BP devices. Just as MECTA made-for-America devices appear to conform to the 1982 APA Standard with its <u>110J</u> ceiling, MECTA IEC BP devices appear to conform to a similar (100J) maximum output seemingly mandated by the 1989 IEC Standard. Superficially then, MECTA second generation IEC BP machines in apparent conformity to the IEC Standard appear emulative of second generation made-for America BP machines in apparent conformity to the APA Standard, both seeming to limit BP machines on both continents to approximately 100 absolute joules. Both (American and IEC) Standards and so BP manufacturers on a world-wide basis, consequently, <u>appear</u> to limit their BP devices to minimal stimulus output, half the electrical energy output of SW. Based on MECTA's reported parameters to the RCP, then, we fully expect the profile of MECTA Brief Pulse IEC devices to appear thusly:

<u>APPARENT</u> **<u>CIRCA 100J</u>** MECTA 2nd GENERATION CONSTANT CURRENT **<u>JR/SR 1</u> <u>IEC</u>** BRIEF PULSE "ECT" DEVICE BASED ON CONDITIONAL-ER/RRC OF "96.8J AT 300Ω" and thus a 96.8J Ceiling with a 300Ω Maximum Impedance

VOLTAGE	POWER % @ Age	AGE Yrs	Ω Ohms	FREQUENCY (Hz)	DURATION (SECs)	CURRENT mAmps	ENERGY Joules	CHARGE mC
24	10	10	30	40	.465	800	1.0	41.7
48	20	20	60	40	.93	800	4.0	83.3
72	30	30	90	60	.93	800	9.0	125.0
96	40	40	120	60	1.24	800	16	166.6
120	50	50	150	60	1.55	800	25	208.3
144	60	60	180	90	1.24	800	36	250.0
156	65	65	195	90	1.37	800	43	275.6
168	70	70	210	90	1.42	800	48	285.7
192	80	80	240	90	1.65	800	64	333.3
216	90	90	270	90	1.86	800	81	375.0
240	100	100	300	90	2.0	800	96.8J	403.2

(.001--.0014msec Pulse Width; only 0014 used in chart below)

<u>APPARENT</u> **<u>CIRCA 100J</u>** MECTA 2nd GENERATION CONSTANT CURRENT **<u>JR/SR 2</u> <u>IEC</u>** BRIEF PULSE "ECT" DEVICE BASED ON CONDITIONAL-ER/RRC OF "96.8J AT 300Ω" and thus a 96.8J Ceiling with a 300Ω Maximum Impedance

VOLTAGE	POWER % @ Age	AGE Yrs	Ω Ohms	FREQUENCY (Hz)	DURATION (SECs)	CURRENT mAmps	ENERGY Joules	CHARGE mC
24	10	10	30	90	0.29	800	1.0	41.7
48	20	20	60	90	0.58	800	4.0	83.3
72	30	30	90	90	1.2	800	9.0	125.0
96	40	40	120	90	1.16	800	16	166.6
120	50	50	150	90	1.45	800	25	208.3
144	60	60	180	90	1.74	800	36	250.0
156	65	65	195	90	1.91	800	43	275.6
168	70	70	210	90	1.98	800	48	285.7
192	80	80	240	90	2.32	800	64	333.3
216	90	90	270	90	2.6	800	81	375.0
240	100	100	300	90	2.8	800	96.8J	403.2

(.001msec Pulse Width)

For both charts above, based on reported parameters, EO is derived from the formula: <u>EO = Charge x Current x Impedance</u>, and <u>EO = (Current squared) x Impedance x (hz x 2) x WL x Duration</u>. Duration is derived from: <u>Duration = Charge ÷ Current x (hz x 2) x WL</u>.

---

[409] Readouts depicted (for physicians) on the second generation MECTA devices range from one to approximately 100 maximum Joules.

Voltage or Impedance can be derived from Ohm's Law: Voltage = Current x Ω. Charge, EO, and Duration can be derived from Charge = EO ÷ Current x Impedance; Charge = Duration x Current x (hz x 2) x WL.

In sum, by reporting a **.403C Charge maximum**, a **240V maximum**, and maximum Durations of **2.0** and **2.8 Seconds** for each respective MECTA IEC BP device, MECTA indirectly reports a **96.8J maximum output** as well as an unlikely **300Ω maximum Impedance**,[410] in keeping with the minimal stimulus device charts above. Of course, as we shall see, both charts are wholly misrepresentative.

The Deliberate Engendering of the 100J Maximum Output World-Wide

In spite of appearances, like MECTA's unauthorized transmutation of the 1982 APA Standard, American, Canadian, and European manufacturers appear to have taken it upon themselves to interpret (by agreement) the 1989 IEC Standard in a manner permitting the gross surpassing of 100Js while reporting or strongly implying a circa 100J ceiling to the public, regulatory agencies, and even administering physicians. Like American BP devices, actual outputs (in joules) for IEC BP devices are never provided. While actual maximum Charge is often reported (though not in this case), the typical reporting of maximum Charge in tandem with an unexplicated ER-Output (in joules) results in the same false misconception of minimal stimulus outputs. This is because the correlation of actual maximum Charge with a circa 100J maximum output is a false correlation. [411] Indeed, there is ample evidence to suggest that manufacturers world-wide, act in concert to deliberately engender the impression of circa 100J ceilings for their second generation BP devices internationally.

In the case of MECTA, actual EO for IEC BP devices appears quite deliberately covered up through inaccurate reporting of maximum Voltage (Royal College of Psychiatry, p.125) suggesting a false maximum output of 96.8J; whereas, the more difficult to discern 130J derivative (based on the 30% cushion adjunct) is also an unexplained ER-output, as we shall see. [412] Both in America and internationally then, manufacturers appear to use various means of engendering false 100J ceilings through (1) bluntly reporting circa 100Js (i.e., Medcraft [413]), (2) through misleading reports of various electrical parameters such as Voltage, (3) though the creation of standards consistently depicting unexplicated 100J ERs, (4) through the ubiquitous reporting of unexplained 100J ERs [414] in lieu of actual outputs, (5) through deceptive depictions of Machine Readouts--both nationally and internationally--portraying circa 100 maximum joules, (6) through the reporting of actual maximum Charge in tandem with unexplained ERs misleadingly depicting 100 maximum Joules, (7) through the occasional reporting of ER Charge maximums and ER maximum Durations in lieu of actual maximum Charges and actual maximum Durations, and finally, (8) through failing to report actual outputs in joules relative to age, including overall maximum outputs (in joules). Together, these actions create the strong impression for regulatory agencies, the general public, the media, and even practicing physicians, that American and European Standards continue to limit what are actually second generation BP machines to about 100 maximum joules or minimal stimulus outputs internationally. In summation, because the "100J" maximum is the symbol of minimal stimulus output with Brief Pulse, ENR manufacturers strive to create this false impression on a world-wide basis.

---

[410] While we can put more than **300Ω** into the formula EO = (Current squared) x Impedance x (hz x 2) x WL x Duration, by doing so, we must increase Voltage in the formula: EO = Voltage x Current x (hz x 2) x WL x Duration. For example, EO = .8 x .8 x **400Ω** x 180 Pulses x .001 x 2.8 Sec = 129 Joules. However, we must now raise Voltage to **320V** to accommodate the 129 Joules. EO = **320V** x .8A x 180 Pulses x .001 x 2.8 Seconds = 129 Joules. While MECTA does report a 400Ω maximum for these devices, the increased Voltage necessary to do so directly contradicts MECTA's reported maximum of **240V** for both devices. In short, via the derived product of MECTA's reported maximum parameters in conjunction with 240V, MECTA indirectly reports for its IEC BP devices, a circa 100J maximum. Even with a 400Ω maximum Impedance, maximum output here is only 129 Joules.

[411] As we shall see, MECTA reports a false .403C for MECTA IEC BP devices which appear to be an ER to a false 173J maximum based on a false 400Ω maximum.130J/.403 = 173J/.540C.130J/300Ω = 173J/400Ω. .403C/300Ω = .540C/400Ω.

[412] MECTA continues to avoid reporting maximum Voltage and maximum EO to the FDA and the American public as well as to the ERA and the European public. EO = **240V** x .8A x 180 Pulses x .001 x 2.8 Seconds = 96.7J. EO = **240V** x .8A x 180 Pulses x .0014 x 2.0 Seconds = 96.7J.130J/300Ω = 217J/500Ω

[413] In the instance of Medcraft alone, the reported 100J ceiling for its B-25 BP device appears to be accurate. (See Medcraft B-25.)

[414] The APA Standard limits devices to between 100-110 Joules. Manufacturers illegally circumvented this Standard by instead reporting 100 Joule ERs.

Something Wrong

In fact, something seems wrong with the above charts depicting circa 100J maximums. Why would MECTA limit its IEC BP devices to a 300Ω maximum when the IEC allows a 500Ω maximum? The specious nature of MECTA's reporting becomes even more suspicious when we learn that MECTA follows its report of a 240V maximum (requiring a 300Ω maximum Impedance) with the reporting of a 400Ω maximum Impedance for both its IEC BP devices, a parameter which immediately alters maximum output to 129 maximum joules.

JR/SR 1 IEC BRIEF PULSE DEVICE
EO = .8A x .8A x **400Ω** x 180 Pulses x .001 Seconds x 2.8 Seconds = 129J

JR/SR 2 IEC BRIEF PULSE DEVICE
EO = .8A x .8A x **400Ω** x 180 Pulses x .0014 Seconds x 2.0 Seconds = 129J

Moreover, the new 400Ω Impedance maximum increases the reported maximum Voltage to 320V. Using Ohm's formula and the reported 400Ω maximum to derive the 320V maximum, we can use the Voltage oriented formula to determine the new maximum output of 129 joules.

Voltage = Current x Ω; 8A x **400Ω** = **320V.**

JR/SR 1 IEC BRIEF PULSE DEVICE
EO = .8 x **320 Volts** x 180 pulses x .0014 Seconds x 2.0 seconds = **129 Joules**.

JR/SR 2 IEC BRIEF PULSE DEVICE
EO = .8 x **320 Volts** x 180 Pulses x .001 Seconds x 2.8 Seconds = **129 Joules**.

Suddenly MECTA's IEC BP devices appear thusly:

EXPECTED *129J MECTA* 2nd GENERATION CONSTANT CURRENT **JR/SR 1 IEC**
BRIEF PULSE "ECT" DEVICE BASED ON CONDITIONAL-ER/RRC OF "129J AT 300Ω"
With a Reported 400Ω Maximum Impedance Reflective of the "Cushion Adjunct"

VOLTAGE	POWER % @ Age	AGE Yrs	Ω Ohms	FREQUENCY (Hz)	DURATION (SECs)	CURRENT mAmps	ENERGY Joules	CHARGE mC
32	10	10	40	40	.45	800	1.29	40.3
64	20	20	80	40	.90	800	5.16	80.6
96	30	30	120	60	.864	800	11.61	116.1
128	40	40	160	60	1.20	800	20.64	161.3
160	50	50	200	60	1.50	800	32.25	201.6
192	60	60	240	90	1.20	800	46.44	241.9
208	65	65	260	90	1.30	800	54.4	261.5
224	70	70	280	90	1.40	800	63.2	282.1
256	80	80	320	90	1.60	800	82.56	322.5
288	90	90	360	90	1.80	800	104.5	362.8
320	100	100	400	90	2.0	800	129J	403.2

(.001--.0014msec Pulse Width; only .0014 used in chart below)

The above parameters are deduced by the following: EO (BP) = Charge x Current x Impedance. Duration is based upon: Duration = Charge/Current x (hz x 2) x WL. Voltage = Ohm's Law: Voltage = Current x Ω. EO = Voltage x Current x (hz x 2) x WL x Duration. EO = (Current squared) x Impedance x (hz x 2) x WL x Duration.

Because MECTA directly reports to RCP a 400Ω maximum Impedance along with a 2.0 Second maximum Duration for its **JR/SR 1 IEC BP** device then, maximum Voltage cannot be 240 Volts as MECTA claims, but 320V. A 400Ω maximum Impedance along with the other maximum parameters reported by MECTA, as noted above, mathematically elicits 129 Joules. The 400Ω maximum Impedance reported by MECTA, therefore, must represent the 30% cushion aspect within the IEC Standard, or what appears to be a "130J at 300Ω" Conditional-ER/RRC with a 130J ceiling and a 400Ω maximum Impedance like the machine reflected in the chart above.

Again, because MECTA directly reports to RCP a 400Ω maximum Impedance along with a 2.8 Second maximum Duration for its **JR/SR 2 IEC BP** device, maximum Voltage cannot be 240V as MECTA claims, but once again, a 320V maximum. Moreover, a 400Ω Impedance maximum along with the other maximum parameters reported by MECTA once again elicits 129 Joules. Therefore, the 400Ω maximum reported by MECTA JR/SR 2, must also represent the 30% cushion aspect within the IEC Standard, or what appears to be a "130J at 300Ω" Conditional-ER/RRC with a 400Ω maximum such as the machine reflected in the chart below.

EXPECTED *129J MECTA* 2nd GENERATION CONSTANT CURRENT **JR/SR 2 IEC** BRIEF PULSE DEVICE "ECT" BASED ON CONDITIONAL-ER/RRC OF "129J AT 300Ω"
With a Reported 400Ω Maximum Impedance Reflective of the "Cushion Adjunct"

VOLTAGE	POWER % @ Age	AGE Yrs	Ω Ohms	FREQUENCY (Hz)	DURATION (SECs)	CURRENT mAmps	ENERGY Joules	CHARGE mC
32	10	10	40	90	0.3	800	1.29	40.3
64	20	20	80	90	0.6	800	5.16	80.6
96	30	30	120	90	0.81	800	11.61	116.1
128	40	40	160	90	1.12	800	20.64	161.3
160	50	50	200	90	1.4	800	32.25	201.6
192	60	60	240	90	1.68	800	46.44	241.9
208	65	65	260	90	1.82	800	54.4	261.5
224	70	70	280	90	1.96	800	63.2	282.1
256	80	80	320	90	2.24	800	82.56	322.5
288	90	90	360	90	2.52	800	104.5	362.8
320	100	100	400	90	2.8	800	129J	403.2

(.001 msec Pulse Width)

The above parameters are deduced thusly: EO is based upon: EO (BP) = Charge x Current x Impedance. Duration is based upon: Duration (BP) = Charge/Current x (hz x 2) x WL. Voltage = Ohm's Law: Voltage = Current x Ω. EO = Voltage x Current x (hz x 2) x WL x Duration. EO = (Current squared) x Impedance x (hz x 2) x WL x Duration. Charge = Duration x Current x (hz x 2) x WL; Charge = EO/Current x Impedance; EO = Charge x Current x Impedance.

MECTA's IEC machines now appear to be based on a circa "130J at 300Ω" Conditional-ER/RRC with a 130J ceiling or 1.3 MTTLOI for all age groups, yet within the minimal stimulus range. Such devices, as noted, seem to reflect the 30% cushion adjunct cited below, inconspicuously discoverable within the 1989 IEC Standard.

> The measured maximum output energy shall not deviate from the figures given in the accompanying documents by more than +/-30% for the load resistances specified in Sub-Section 6.8.3 [415] (International Electrotechnical Commission, 601-2-14, Section 8, 50.2, p.21).

But just like the seeming 100J maximum machines several charts above, once again, something seems amiss even with the circa 130J machines directly above. Again, we must ask ourselves--why would MECTA limit its overseas devices to 400Ω when the IEC Standard allows a 500Ω maximum? Our suspicions are strengthened that MECTA has once more underreported (typically via ER reporting) when we learn that Somatics IEC BP devices, the company which historically copies MECTA, definitively utilizes the full 500Ω for its second generation IEC device, as we shall shortly see.

IEC Standard of "130J at 300Ω" as a Pure-ER/RRC

Not surprisingly, as is its practice, MECTA appears to have reported not actual maximum parameters in utilizing the 30% cushion adjunct of circa "130J at 300Ω," but maximum ER parameters to underreport actual maximum outputs at unreported actual maximum Impedances, this, in spite of machine readouts depicting outputs of circa 100 maximum joules. One possibility is a 130J at 300Ω pure-ER/RRC to an actual 173J maximum at a 400Ω maximum Impedance so that MECTA devices emit a "true" 173J maximum.

---

[415] Load Resistances specified in subsection 6.8.3 are 100Ω, 200Ω, 300Ω, and 500Ω (International Electrotechnical Commission, 1989, p.11).

130J/300Ω = 173J/400Ω

But this hardly seems right, in that, in spite of MECTA's reporting, the IEC Standard, as noted, clearly permits a maximum 500Ω Impedance. Moreover, as also noted above, MECTA's twin sister, Somatics, does, in fact, utilize the maximum 500Ω Impedance allowed by the IEC.

Plainly, the actual maximum output allowed via a Pure-ER/RRC interpretation of the 1989 IEC Standard is 216.6J. If true, maximum outputs for the MECTA IEC BP devices must be at least circa 215 joules. [416]

130J/300Ω = XJ/500Ω; XJ = 216.6J

129J/300Ω = XJ/500Ω; XJ = 215J [417]

In short, the actual IEC Standard is plainly based on a ***"130J at 300Ω"*** Pure-ER/RRC, which must be derived by combining two separate components of the IEC Standard, (1) the obtrusive "100J at 300Ω" phrase, plus (2) the unobtrusive 30% cushion adjunct within the same IEC Standard. The two components must be pieced together to form the actual "130J at 300Ω" Pure-ER/RRC phrase, from which the IEC Standard is actually interpreted. The unnecessary dividing of the actual "130J at 300Ω" IEC pure-ER/RRC phrase into two component parts ("100J at 300Ω" plus the 30% cushion adjunct) indicates a concocted attempt to centralize and feature the "100J" figure for the purpose of reiteratively emphasizing the seeming 100J ceiling internationally associated with reduced output BP devices. Certainly, the concoction begs the question: "If '130J at 300Ω' is the actual phrase upon which the IEC Standard is based, "Why didn't the framers of the IEC Standard simply feature '130J at 300Ω'?" Moreover, why didn't they make clear that the inconspicuous "130J at 300Ω" phrase is intended to be a Pure-ER/RRC permitting about 217 maximum joules? Indeed, as we shall soon see, American manufacturers such as MECTA not only utilize the "130J at 300Ω" Pure-ER/RRC covertly "allowed" by the IEC Standard, but go so far as to tweak the phrase for the purpose of evincing even higher, never before reported Pure-ER/RRC phrases, such as "138J at 300Ω" in order that the IEC Standard perfectly meshes with the circa "100J at 220Ω" Pure-ER/RRC phrase utilized via the Mectan Transmutation. The purpose, of course, is secret enhancement of the IEC BP devices in the same manner second generation made-for-America BP devices are secretly enhanced. In fact, as we shall observe, it is a higher 138J at 300Ω Pure-ER/RRC phrase which MECTA both needed and utilized to internationally bridge the Mectan Transmutation with the IEC Standard, consequently, meshing MECTA IEC BP devices with MECTA made-for-America devices (101J/220Ω = 138J/300Ω) for the purpose of enhancing BP power globally. This meshing occurs in spite of the emphasis on the featured "100J" figure within the IEC Standard itself, just as it occurs in spite of the "100J" figure within the Mectan Transmutation to make the 100J figure paramount. Thus, while MECTA (indirectly) reports 96.8 Joules for MECTA IEC BP devices in seeming conformity with what appears to be a 100J IEC ceiling, in fact, the IEC Standard, given Pure-ER/RRC interpretation, actually allows a much higher unreported EO ceiling of 216.66 Joules. Moreover, MECTA tweaks even this covert standard allowing second generation MECTA IEC BP devices an even higher Pure-ER/RRC ceiling, as we shall now observe.

More Unreported Maximum Parameters

As noted, based on the IEC Standard of a Pure-ER/RRC of "130J at 300Ω" and MECTA's use of a "129J at 300Ω" Pure-ER/RRC in order to evince a possible 215J maximum for its second generation IEC BP devices, even a 215J maximum presents a slight problem for MECTA. First, however, let us discover the necessary parameter increases (relative to parameters actually reported by MECTA) needed to base MECTA IEC BP

---

[416] Note the triple Equivalent Ratio Maximum Output/Impedance to Actual Maximum Output/Impedance wherein 173J/400Ω acts as both Actual Maximum and ER maximum: 130J/300Ω = 173J/400Ω = 216J/500Ω.

[417] While MECTA utilizes the 130J at 300Ω Pure-ER/RRC cushion adjunct, MECTA has reported 400Ω in that this Impedance results in a 130J Pure-ER maximum. EO = (Current squared) x Impedance x (hz x 2) x WL x Duration: **JR/SR 1 IEC**: .8A x .8A x **400Ω** x 180 pulses x .0014 PW x 2.0 Sec. = 129J. 129J/300Ω = **215J**/500Ω; **JR/SR 2 IEC**: .8A x .8A x **400Ω** x 180 pulses x .001 PW x 2.8 Sec. = 129J. 129J/300Ω = **215J**/500Ω.

devices on a "129J at 300Ω" Pure-ER/RRC permitting the 215 maximum joules the standard actually allows (given a Pure-ER/RRC interpretation). Right away we can observe that in order to attain 215 joules, one or more parameters reported by MECTA must be increased. In fact, in order to derive the maximum "129J at 300Ω" Pure-ER/RRC MECTA needs to attain 215 joules, any number of parameters can be increased. For example, for the **JR/SR-2 IEC** BP device, Duration could be increased from the reported **2.8 Seconds** to an unreported **3.73 Seconds**, thusly:

JR/SR 2 IEC devices

ER-EO = .8 Amperes x .8 Amperes x **300Ω** x 180 Pulses x .001 Pulse Width x **3.73 Sec.** = **129.024 Joules**.

Actual-EO = .8 Amperes x .8 Amperes x **500Ω** x 180 Pulses x .001 Pulse Width x **3.73 Sec.** = **215 Joules**.

For the **JR/SR-1** IEC BP device, Duration could be increased from **2.0 Seconds** to **2.67 Seconds**, thusly:

JR/SR 1 IEC devices

ER-EO = .8 Amperes x .8 Amperes x **300Ω** x 180 Pulses x .0014 Pulse Width x **2.67 Sec.** = **129.024 Joules**.

Actual-EO = .8 Amperes x .8 Amperes x **500Ω** x 180 Pulses x .0014 Pulse Width x **2.67 Sec.** = **215 Joules**.

Maximum Charge rises accordingly to **.540C** (Charge = EO ÷ Current x Impedance; Charge = 215/6J ÷ .8 x 500Ω = .540C).

Another possible parameter increase allowing the IEC **JR/SR-2** to reach 215J might be an increased Pulse Width, from, for example, **.001** to **.00133** Seconds:

JR/SR 2 IEC devices

ER-EO = .8 Amperes x .8 Amperes x **300Ω** x 180 Pulses x **.00133** Pulse Width x **2.8 Sec.** = **129 Joules**.

Actual-EO = .8 Amperes x .8 Amperes x **500Ω** x 180 Pulses x **.00133** Pulse Width x **2.8 Sec.** = **215 Joules**.

In order for the IEC **JR/SR-1** to reach 215J, Pulse Width could be increased from a reported **.0014** to **.00187** Seconds:

JR/SR 1 IEC devices

ER-EO = .8 Amperes x .8 Amperes x **300Ω** x 180 Pulses x **.00187** Pulse Width x **2.0 Sec.** = **129 Joules**.

Actual-EO = .8 Amperes x .8 Amperes x **500Ω** x 180 Pulses x **.00187** Pulse Width x **2.0 Sec.** = **215 Joules**.

In fact, given that the 30% cushion statute for EO also includes a +/- 15% cushion for both Duration and Pulse Width (International Electrotechnical Commission, 1989, p.21), a combination of both Duration and Pulse Width enhancement is also possible. For instance, Duration and Pulse Width for the JR/SR 2 could be increased from the reported 2.8 Second maximum Duration and the reported .001 Second maximum Pulse Width to a 3.22 Second maximum Duration and a .00116 Second maximum Pulse Width.

JR/SR 2 IEC devices:

ER-EO = .8 Amperes x .8 Amperes x **300Ω** x 180 Pulses x **.00116** Pulse Width x **3.22 Seconds** = **129 Joules**.

Actual-EO = .8 Amperes x .8 Amperes x **500Ω** x 180 Pulses x **.00116** Pulse Width x **3.22 Seconds** = **215 Joules**. [418]

Similarly, Duration and Pulse Width for the JR/SR 1 could be increased from the reported 2.0 Second maximum Duration and the reported .0014 Second maximum Pulse Width to a 2.49 Second maximum Duration and a .0015 Second maximum Pulse Width.

JR/SR 1 IEC devices:

ER-EO = .8 Amperes x .8 Amperes x **300Ω** x 180 Pulses x **.0015** Pulse Width x **2.49 Seconds** = **129 Joules**.

Actual-EO = .8 Amperes x .8 Amperes x **500Ω** x 180 Pulses x **.0015** Pulse Width x **2.49 Seconds** = **215 Joules**.

In any case, if at least 215 joules is in actuality reached, MECTA appears to have misreported not only actual maximum Voltage and actual maximum Impedance, but one or more other maximum parameters as well. In brief, MECTA fails to report the increased parameter or parameters necessary to enhance output to the 216.6J output "allowed" by the 30% cushion statute, or more specifically, the 215J "allowed" (by the IEC Standard) for MECTA IEC BP devices generally. [419] We cannot know exactly which parameters were increased in that MECTA neglects to report the increases needed to take advantage of the thirty percent cushion statute [420] which also includes enhanced Charge. But we can be fairly certain that such increases do actually take place.

Even Higher

While we cannot know for certain which parameters MECTA enhanced so that its IEC BP devices could emit at least 215 maximum joules, we can be reasonably certain that the awkward figures in the above section are probably not viable. For example, increases in Duration to 3.22 and 2.67 seconds seem unwieldy. More importantly however, if we convert the IEC's covert "130J at 300Ω" Pure-ER/RRC phrase to an output based on the Americanized 220Ω, we attain a similar, but not perfectly equivalent "95J at 220Ω. "

130J at 300Ω = **95.3J/**220Ω

"Wouldn't it be much more convenient," MECTA may have reasoned, "if the IEC "Pure-ER/RRC" phrase were just a little higher, so that the phrase exactly matched our '101J at 220Ω' Pure-ER/RRC phrase upon which our second generation made-for-America BP devices are based? For that, we need only increase the implied "130J at 300Ω" Pure-ER/RRC phrase to a slightly illegal "138J at 300Ω" Pure-ER/RRC" phrase.

101J/220Ω = XJ/300Ω; X = 138J or 138J at 300Ω

---

[418] Statute 50.2 (the cushion statute) permits a 15% increase in PW and a 15% increase in Duration. In order to achieve approximately 215 Joules, therefore, a combination increase of Duration and PW is probable.

[419] ER: .3 x 100J = 30J + 100J = 130J; Actual: .3 x 166.66 = 50J + 166.6 = 216.6J.

[420] A similar rationale was utilized in the case of the MECTA D, emitting 140J for "exceptional cases only."

Is it possible then, that MECTA breached (by a few joules) even the IEC's secret "130J at 300Ω" Pure-ER/RRC in order to use a convenient "138J at 300Ω" Pure-ER/RRC resulting in its IEC devices reaching not the covert 216.6J IEC maximum, but a slightly higher, slightly illegal 230 maximum joules? [421]

138J/300Ω = **230J**/500Ω

MECTA Second Generation IEC BP Devices Based on a Secret "138J at 300Ω" Pure-ER/RRC

By using a secret "138J at 300Ω" Pure-ER/RRC, MECTA could achieve any of a number of advantages. "138J at 300Ω" is equivalent to the MECTA "101J at 220Ω" phrase (138J/300Ω = 101J/220Ω) used for its made-for-America devices. By reaching a phrase equivalent to that upon which MECTA second generation made-for-America BP devices are based, parameters for MECTA second generation IEC devices could be made to dovetail into parameters on which MECTA second generation made-for-America devices are constructed. In this way, the machines could remain essentially the same. But in order to reach a "138J at 300Ω" Pure-ER/RRC or secret "230J" maximum, MECTA would need to enhance one or more parameters even further, totally belying parameters MECTA reports to the Royal College of Psychiatry for its MECTA IEC BP devices. Any of a number of increases can suffice to reach the "138J at 300Ω" Pure-ER/RRC MECTA needed for its second generation IEC devices to dovetail into the outputs of its second generation made-for-America devices. For example, addressing MECTA's **JR/SR-2 IEC BP** device, the change might entail increasing the maximum Duration from the reported **2.8 Seconds**, not to an unreported **3.73 Seconds (to attain 215J)** but to an unreported **4.0 Seconds (to attain 230J):**

JR/SR 2 IEC devices

ER-EO = .8 Amperes x .8 Amperes x **300Ω** x 180 Pulses x .001 Pulse Width x **4.0 Sec.** = **138 Joules**.

Actual-EO = .8 Amperes x .8 Amperes x **500Ω** x 180 Pulses x .001 Pulse Width x **4.0 Sec.** = **230 Joules**.

For the **JR/SR-1 IEC** BP device, Duration would have had to be increased from the reported **2.0 Seconds**, not to an unreported **2.67 Seconds (to attain 215J)**, but to an unreported **2.85 Seconds (to attain 230J):**

JR/SR 1 IEC devices

ER-EO = .8 Amperes x .8 Amperes x **300Ω** x 180 Pulses x .0014 Pulse Width x **2.85 Sec.** = **138 Joules**.

Actual-EO = .8 Amperes x .8 Amperes x **500Ω** x 180 Pulses x .0014 Pulse Width x **2.85 Sec.** = **230 Joules**.

Durations of 4.0 and 2.85 Seconds suddenly seem much less wieldy than previous speculations and thus much more probable.

Too, maximum Charge suddenly rises to **.575C**, almost identical to that of MECTA's .576C second generation made-for-America BP devices.

---

[421] The IEC 30% cushion adjunct may have been added in response to more powerful second generation BP devices accommodated by the Mectan Transmutation in America. In essence, a Pure ER/RRC interpretation of the APA "70J/220Ω" = IEC "100J/300Ω," accommodated 200J made-for-America BP devices while the more expanded Mectan "100J/220Ω" = IEC "130J/300Ω," accommodated 260J made-for-America BP devices. (100J/300Ω = 200J/600Ω.130J/300Ω = 260J/600Ω). In that maximum IEC Impedance is 500Ω, further slight breaches or modifications became necessary, invisible changes which , in all probability, reflected continually increasing outputs.

Charge = EO ÷ Current x Impedance;
Charge = 230J ÷ .8 x 500Ω = **.575C**.
Charge = 138J ÷ .8 x 300Ω = **.575C**

Finally, testing for Voltage increases, we go from the 240V maximum MECTA reports to the RCP, all too suggestive of a circa "100J at 300Ω" Conditional-ER/RRC (with 100J ceiling), to an unreported 320V maximum accommodating a "129J at 300" Conditional-ER/RRC (with 129J ceiling), to an unreported 400 Volt maximum accommodating the IEC's factual "130J at 300Ω" Pure-ER/RRC (with 215J ceiling). However, the "130J at 300Ω" Pure-ER/RRC is yet based on unlikely 3.73 and 2.67 second maximum Durations respectively. Happily, 400V also accommodates an innovative never before reported, but much more probable "138J at 300Ω" Pure-ER/RRC facilitating a 230J ceiling for both its second generation IEC BP devices using much more likely 4.0 and 2.85 Second maximum Durations. Using Ohm's Law and a Voltage oriented formula for finding EO (Ohm's Law: Voltage = Current x Ω; EO = Voltage x Current x (hz x 2) x WL x Duration), we can test all of the above.

JR/SR 2 IEC devices:

V = Current x Ω; .8A x ***300Ω*** = **240V**.
EO = .8 Amperes x **240V** x 180 Pulses x .001 Pulse Width x 2.8 Seconds = **96.8J.**

V = Current x Ω; .8A x ***400Ω*** = **320V**.
EO = .8 Amperes x **320V** x 180 Pulses x .001 Pulse Width x 2.8 Seconds = **129.024J.**

V = Current x Ω; .8A x ***500Ω*** = **400V**.
EO = .8 Amperes x **400V** x 180 Pulses x .001 Pulse Width x 3.73 Seconds = **215J.**

V = Current x Ω; .8A x ***500Ω*** = **400V**
EO = .8 Amperes x **400V** x 180 Pulses x .001 Pulse Width x **4.0** Seconds = **230J.**

JR/SR 1 IEC devices:

V = Current x Ω; .8A x ***300Ω*** = **240V**.
EO = .8 Amperes x **240V** x 180 Pulses x .0014 Pulse Width x 2.0 Seconds = 96.8J.

V = Current x Ω; .8A x ***400Ω*** = **320V**.
EO = .8 Amperes x **320V** x 180 Pulses x .0014 Pulse Width x 2.0 Seconds = 129.024J.

V = Current x Ω; .8A x ***500Ω*** = **400V**.
EO = .8 Amperes x **400V** x 180 Pulses x .0014 Pulse Width x 2.67 Seconds = 215J.

V = Current x Ω; .8A x ***500Ω*** = **400V**.
EO = .8 Amperes x **400V** x 180 Pulses x .0014 Pulse Width x **2.85** Seconds = **230J**. [422]

Most likely and most conveniently then, a 400V maximum seems the most probable (for MECTA IEC BP devices) in that it is a very workable 50V decrease from the 450V maximum used for MECTA made-for-America BP devices, the necessary reduction to accommodate the IEC 500Ω Impedance maximum as opposed to the APA 600Ω Impedance maximum. Too, the 4.0 Second and 2.85 Second Duration are the most probable for

[422] Notice the triple ER Voltage/Impedance to actual Voltage/Impedance wherein 320V/400Ω is both an "Actual Voltage/Impedance and an ER Voltage/Impedance: "240V/300Ω = 320V/400Ω = 400V/500Ω. In essence, as is its practice, although MECTA claims to be reporting maximum parameters, it is actually reporting ER parameters, this time, in a series of three.

the JR2 and JR 1 IEC BP devices respectively. Of critical importance, moreover, is that the "138J at 300Ω" Pure-ER/RRC is the most likely Pure-ER/RRC phrase used for MECTA second generation IEC BP devices in that it is conveniently equivalent to the "101J at 220Ω" Pure-ER/RRC used for MECTA second generation made-for-America BP devices, making the transition from made-for-America to made-for-Europe devices both simple, cost effective, and very accommodating. Indeed, it is extremely accommodating to the same misleading 101J machine readout maximum MECTA made-for-America BP devices depict, as we shall see in a few moments.

138J/300Ω = 101J/220Ω

Note that MECTA's especially confusing ER Voltage/Impedance to actual Voltage/Impedance series: (240V/300Ω = 320V/400Ω = 400V/500Ω = 450V/562Ω. 450V/562Ω is the actual maximum Voltage/Impedance used for MECTA's second generation made-for-America BP devices. In brief, actual maximum Voltage and Impedance for MECTA's IEC BP devices are almost certainly 400V and 500Ω. Note again MECTA's ER-EO/Impedance to actual EO/Impedance series for its IEC devices: (129J/300Ω = 173J/400Ω = 215J/500Ω), none of which are actual. MECTA, in point of fact, almost certainly uses an unreported Equivalent Ratio EO/Impedance of 138J at 300Ω to derive an actual EO/Impedance maximum of 230J at 500Ω, that is, a Pure-ER/RRC of "138J at 300Ω" to derive actual "230J at 500Ω" maximums (138J/300Ω = 230J/500Ω). In essence, as is its practice, although MECTA claims to be reporting maximum parameters, it typically reports ER parameters, in this instance, a difficult to discern "129J at 300Ω" Pure-ER/RRC to evince "215J at 500Ω" (129J/300Ω = 215J/500Ω), which is then breached to accommodate an unreported "138J at 300Ω" pure-ER/RRC to evince an actual (138J/300Ω =) "230J at 500Ω" machine maximum. MECTA does this in order to easily transition its second generation made-for-America BP devices to second generation made-for-IEC BP devices. MECTA IEC Devices: 138J at 300Ω = 230J at 500Ω are now equivalent to Made-for-America Devices: (101J at 220Ω = 259J at 562Ω). In short: 138J/300Ω = 230J/500Ω = 101J/220Ω = 259J/562Ω. Ultimately then, second generation MECTA IEC BP devices, though slightly reduced in power from 259 to 230J, are the equivalent of second generation MECTA made-for-America BP devices:

230J/500Ω = 259J/562Ω

Secret Use of "138J at 300Ω" Pure-ER/RRC for MECTA Second Generation IEC BP Devices

We can now see that the 1989 IEC Standard actually "permits" a "130J at 300Ω" Pure-ER/RRC to allow for an actual 216.6J maximum output. But we can also see how MECTA breached the hidden "130J at 300Ω" Pure-ER/RRC IEC standard via a few minor infringements to create made-for-Europe devices equivalent to the transmuted "101J at 220Ω" Pure-ER/RRC which MECTA used for its second generation made-for-America devices.

To begin, while the true IEC Standard of a pure "130J at 300Ω" ER/RRC and the Mectan Transmutation of circa "100J at 220Ω" appear slightly disparate, in fact, they are almost synonymous. Certainly, the IEC Standard was ***never*** designed to be interpreted as a "***100J*** at 300Ω" Conditional-ER/RRC (with 100J ceiling), but rather (via manufacturers), as a "***130J*** at 300Ω" Pure-ER/RRC already almost equivalent to the Mectan phrase, "101J at 220Ω": (101J at 220Ω = 130J/**286Ω**; 130J at 300Ω = **95.3J/**220Ω). With but a slight infringement of the "130J at 300Ω" IEC standard then, that is, by slightly breaching the IEC's "130J at 300Ω" Pure-ER/RRC in order to reach a quietly illicit "138J at 300Ω" Pure-ER/RRC, MECTA IEC BP devices were made to dovetail into MECTA's second generation made-for-America BP devices. In short, the two Pure-ER/RRCs were now equivalent: 138J/300Ω = 101J/220Ω. The single difference between second generation MECTA made-for-America BP devices and second generation MECTA made-for-Europe BP devices is the 562Ω maximum Impedance used for MECTA's second generation made-for-America devices as opposed to the 500Ω maximum Impedance used for MECTA's IEC BP devices. In brief, while made-for-America second generation BP devices reach an unreported 259J ceiling, MECTA IEC BP devices reach an unreported 230J ceiling (101J/220Ω = **259J**/562Ω; 138J/300Ω = **259J**/562Ω; 101J/220Ω = **230J**/500Ω; 138J/300Ω = **230J**/500Ω). In any case both MECTA's made-for-America and made-for-Europe second generation BP devices now utilized ER/RRCs which are equivalent to each other and this was critical both for easy transition to market the devices in Europe and for depicting the same misleading machine readouts, as has been noted. Other than the obvious convenience of a “138J at 300Ω” Pure-ER/RRC, however, is there any additional evidence that MECTA indeed uses a “138J at 300Ω” Pure-ER/RRC for its second generation IEC BP devices? After all, MECTA not only neglects to provide such information, but underreports numerous parameters including Duration, Voltage, Charge, EO, and Impedance, all to suggest a circa 100J ceiling.

In fact, the "138J at 300Ω" Pure-ER/RRC from which actual machine parameters can be derived is well-founded in that the same methodology is used by Somatics to derive parameters for its second generation IEC BP device, the DGx, as we shall soon observe. This is highly relevant, in that, as we have already seen, an inviolable precedent exists regarding Somatics' imitation of MECTA with respect to output and enhancement. Specifically, as we shall soon see, Somatics' second generation made-for-Europe DGx IEC BP device is based upon a very similar also slightly illegal, but verifiable "136J at 300Ω” pure-ER/RRC, facilitating the delivery of a very similar 226J maximum output. Like MECTA's "138J at 300Ω” pure-ER/RRC then, Somatics' "136J at 300Ω” pure-ER/RRC directly dovetails into Somatics' second generation made-for-America Thymatron DG. Because Somatics consistently follows MECTA in power, output, and titration enhancement, we can be more than reasonably certain that the second generation Somatics IEC BP device is closely emulative of MECTA's IEC BP devices. Based upon the derivable Pure-ER/RRC used for the second generation Somatics IEC BP device, the DGx, that is, based on Somatics' enhancing of the IEC ER/RRC just enough for its IEC device to dovetail into the pure-ER/RRC upon which Somatics' made-for-America BP device, the DG is based, together with Somatics' unvaried record of closely emulating MECTA, we can realistically extrapolate MECTA's use of a similar Pure-ER/RRC enhancement in order to accomplish the same goal--allowing the Pure-ER/RRC upon which MECTA IEC BP devices are based to dovetail into the pure-ER/RRC upon which MECTA made-for-America BP devices are based. Thus, in that Somatics bases its second generation IEC BP device upon a verifiable "136J at 300Ω” Pure-ER/RRC dovetailing into its made-for-America device as we shall presently observe, we can be reasonably certain that MECTA bases its second generation IEC BP devices upon a very similar "138J at 300Ω” Pure-ER/RRC in order to accomplish the very same goal. [423]

Possible MECTA IEC BP Devices

As noted above, and as we shall soon see, Somatics uses a "136J at 300Ω" pure-ER/RRC to dovetail into the pure-ER/RRC upon which its second generation made-for-America BP device is based. Somatics does this, as we shall see, simply by retaining for its’ second generation Thymatron DGx IEC BP device, the same 4.0 second Duration used for its second generation made-for-America Thymatron DG device. MECTA's made-for-America JR/SR 2 device (second generation) also utilizes a 4.0 Second maximum Duration. Reflective of the Somatics practice then, in lieu of supplanting the reported 2.8 Second maximum Duration reported by MECTA with an unreported and unlikely 3.73 Second Duration to achieve an unreported 215J ceiling facilitating a “129J at 300Ω” Pure-ER/RRC for its MECTA IEC JR/SR 2 BP device, MECTA, like Somatics, very probably retains the same 4.0 second Duration utilized for its made-for-America (second generation) JR/SR 2 device. Similar to Somatics then, a 4.0 second maximum Duration results in the needed 230J maximum needed for its JR/SR 2 IEC BP device to perfectly dovetail into its made-for-America BP devices, an output very like that of the Somatics IEC BP device which emits a needed and verifiable 226 maximum joules (as we shall soon see) to accomplish the very same goal. In short, in lieu of the reported 2.8 second maximum Duration resulting in a “96.8J at 300Ω” Conditional-ER/RRC or an unreported 3.73 second maximum Duration resulting in a “129J at 300Ω” Conditional or Pure-ER/RRC, MECTA, like Somatics, probably retains for its JR/SR 2 IEC device the same 4.0 Second maximum Duration used for its second generation made-for-America JR/SR 2 device resulting in the necessary "138J at 300Ω” Pure-ER/RRC to create equivalency. Similar to the Somatics IEC BP device then, the retention of an unreported 4.0 Second maximum Duration for its made-for-Europe (second generation) JR/SR 2 facilitates an unreported Pure-ER/RRC of “138J at 300Ω” (slightly breaching the already invisible “130J at 300Ω” IEC cushion adjunct), enhancing the IEC JR/SR-2 to 230 maximum joules. Though not quite the power of its second generation made-for-America BP devices, as mentioned, the enhancement to

[423] While it is difficult to determine absolutely which of the two companies leads the other, it appears to be MECTA. In any case, we can conclude the two companies act collaboratively.

230J for its IEC JR/SR 2 is enough to facilitate, as we have hypothesized, a Pure-ER/RRC of "138J at 300Ω." The "138J at 300Ω" ER/RRC is equivalent to and thus able to dovetail into the "101J at 220Ω" Pure-ER/RRC upon which second generation made-for-America MECTA BP devices are based. This dovetailing creates unique manufacturer advantages as has been mentioned. Moreover, the "138J at 300Ω" Pure-ER/RRC, as noted, is reinforced by its similarity to Somatics identifiable "136J at 300Ω" Pure-ER/RRC, both phrases of which accomplish the same goal of dovetailing into second generation MECTA and Somatics made-for-America BP devices. Let us depict the possible 4.0 second, second generation JR/SR 2 IEC BP device below followed by corroborative formulations:

Possible Actual **2nd GENERATION** MECTA CONSTANT CURRENT **IEC JR/SR 2**
BRIEF PULSE ENR DEVICE BASED ON PURE-ER/RRC OF **"138J at 300Ω"** or **"101.2J at 220Ω"**

VOLTAGE	POWER % @ Age	AGE Yrs	Ω Ohms	FREQUENCY (Hz)	DURATION (SECs)	CURRENT mAmps	ENERGY Joules	CHARGE mC
40	10	10	50	90	0.4	800	2.30	57.6
80	20	20	100	90	0.8	800	9.22	115.2
120	30	30	150	90	1.2	800	20.74	172.8
160	40	40	200	90	1.6	800	36.86	230.4
200	50	50	250	90	2.0	800	57.6	288
240	60	60	300	90	2.4	800	82.94	345.6
260	65	65	325	90	2.6	800	97.34	374.4
280	70	70	350	90	2.8	800	112.9	403.2
320	80	80	400	90	3.2	800	147.5	460.8
360	90	90	450	90	3.6	800	186.48	518.4
400	100	100	500	90	4.0	800	230J	575

(**.001** sec Pulse Width)

Figures depicted on the JR/SR 2 IEC device above are speculative but probable. Charge equals that of the probable actual second generation made-for-America JR/SR 2. EO = Charge x Current x Impedance. Duration (BP) = Charge/Current x (hz x 2) x WL; Voltage = Ohm's Law: Voltage = Current x Ω. Charge = EO ÷ Current x Impedance. EO = Voltage x Current x (hz x 2) x WL x Duration.

Second Generation ***JR/SR 2*** IEC BP Device:

Impedance-oriented formula:
ER-EO JR/SR 2 IEC (**at 4.0 Sec**) = **.8 x .8 x 300Ω** x 180 Pulses x .001 x **4.0 Seconds** = **138 Joules** = (**138J at 300Ω** Pure -ER/RRC).

Voltage-oriented formula: (240V, just as 300Ω, is an ER figure)
ER-EO JR/SR 2 IEC (**at 4.0 Sec**) = .8 x **240V** x 180 Pulses x .001 x **4.0 Seconds** = **138 Joules** = (**138J at 240V** Pure-ER/RRC).

Pure-ER/RRCs to Actual Maximums for JR/SR 2 IEC (**at 4.0 Sec**):
138J/300Ω = ***230J/500Ω*** = (**230J true maximum**).
138J/240V = ***230J/400V*** = (**230J true maximum**).

Impedance-oriented formula:
Actual-EO JR/SR 2 IEC (**at 4.0 Sec**) = **.8 x .8 x 500Ω** x 180 Pulses x .001 x **4.0 Seconds** = **230 Joules**.

Voltage-oriented formula:
Actual-EO JR/SR 2 IEC (**at 4.0 Sec**) = .8 x **400V** x 180 Pulses x .001 x **4.0 Seconds** = **230 Joules**.

Note that the ER/RRC used for MECTA's second generation made-for-Europe JR/SR 2 above is now equivalent to the ER/RRC used for the second generation made-for-America JR/SR 2.

"138J at 300Ω" = "101.2J at 220Ω. "

Note too that the new maximum Charge of .575C is virtually identical to the .576C maximum Charge of the second generation made-for-America JR/SR 2. Thus, based upon Somatics' very similar second generation IEC BP device and the similitude of both MECTA and Somatics BP devices as well as their methodologies historically, the author speculates that the MECTA second generation JR/SR 2 IEC BP device is very possibly based on a **"138J at 300Ω" Pure-ER/RRC** facilitating a true maximum output of about **230J**. [424]

Now let us re-examine the second generation made-for-Europe MECTA **JR/SR 1** IEC BP device. As noted, MECTA reports a maximum Duration for this device of 2.0 Seconds. If, like the second generation **JR/SR 2 IEC** BP device above, the second generation **JR/SR 1 IEC** BP device has the same unreported enhanced maximum output of 230J, and like the made-for-America version, emits an ER/RRC equivalent to "101J at 220Ω," that is, a "138J at 300Ω" Pure-ER/RRC, then the maximum Duration of 2.0 Seconds reported by MECTA for the JR/SR 1 IEC BP device is almost certainly spurious. Simply by enhancing Duration for the JR/SR 1 IEC BP device from the 2.0 second maximum reported by MECTA, to a 2.85 second maximum, we can obtain the same needed 230J maximum output facilitating the same needed Pure-ER/RRC of "138J at 300Ω."

Possible Actual **2nd GENERATION** MECTA CONSTANT CURRENT **IEC JR/SR 1 BRIEF PULSE ENR DEVICE** BASED ON PURE-ER/RRC OF **"138J AT 300Ω"** or **"101.2J at 220Ω"**

VOLTAGE	POWER % @ Age	AGE Yrs	Ω Ohms	FREQUENCY (Hz)	DURATION (SECs)	CURRENT mAmps	ENERGY Joules	CHARGE mC
40	10	10	50	40	0.64	800	2.30	57.6
80	20	20	100	40	1.285	800	9.22	115.2
120	30	30	150	60	1.285	800	20.74	172.8
160	40	40	200	60	1.71	800	36.86	230.4
200	50	50	250	60	2.14	800	57.6	288
240	60	60	300	90	1.71	800	82.94	345.6
260	65	65	325	90	1.857	800	97.34	374.4
280	70	70	350	90	2.0	800	112.9	403.2
320	80	80	400	90	2.285	800	147.5	460.8
360	90	90	450	90	2.57	800	186.48	518.4
400	100	100	500	90	2.85	800	230J	575

(.001--.0014 sec Pulse Width; only 0014 used in chart above)

Except for maximum figures in bottom row (which are accurate), figures on the JR/SR 1 IEC device above are speculative but very possible. Charge now equals the probable actual made-for-America JR/SR 1. EO = Charge x Current x Impedance. Duration = Charge/Current x (hz x 2) x WL; Voltage = Ohm's Law: Voltage = Current x Ω. Charge = EO ÷ Current x Impedance. EO = Voltage x Current x (hz x 2) x WL x Duration.

Second Generation ***JR/SR 1*** IEC BP Device:

Impedance -oriented formula:
ER-EO JR/SR 1 IEC (at **2.85 Sec**)= **.8 x .8** x **300Ω** x 180 Pulses x .0014 x **2.85 Seconds** = **138 Joules** = (**138J at 300Ω** Pure-ER/RRC).

Voltage-oriented formula: (240V, just as 300Ω, is an ER figure)
ER-EO JR/SR 1 IEC (at **2.85 Sec**) = .8 x **240V** x 180 Pulses x .0014 x **2.85 Seconds** = **138 Joules** = (**138J at 300Ω** Pure-ER/RRC).

[424] This can be corroborated in an even stronger fashion with the examination of the SR/JR 2 *third generation* BP device (see third generation BP Devices) which appears to be an exact doubling of the probable 230 Joule second generation JR/SR 2 IEC BP device as we shall see (International Electrotechnical Commission, 1989, pp.124-125).

Pure-ER/RRCs to Actual Maximums for JR/SR 1 IEC (at **2.85 Sec**):
138J/300Ω = **230J/500Ω** (**230J maximum**).
138J/240V = **230J/400V** (**230J maximum**).

Impedance -oriented formula:
Actual-EO JR/SR 1 IEC (at **2.85 Sec**) = .8 x .8 x **500Ω** x 180 Pulses x .0014 x **2.85 Seconds** = **230 Joules**.

Voltage-oriented formula:
Actual-EO JR/SR 1 IEC (at **2.85 Sec**) = .8 x **400V** x 180 Pulses x .0014 x **2.85 Seconds** = **230 Joules**.

Unlike the 4.0 second maximum Duration most likely used for the second generation ***made-for-Europe JR/SR 2 IEC BP*** device which matches the 4.0 second maximum Duration of the ***second generation made-for-America JR/SR 2***, the 2.85 second maximum Duration most likely used here for the second generation ***made-for-Europe JR/SR 1 IEC BP device*** above does not match the 2.0 second maximum Duration used for ***MECTA's second generation made-for-America JR/SR-1***. This is only due, however, to the maximum 2.0 millisecond pulse width used for the ***second generation made-for America JR/SR 1*** as opposed to the maximum 1.4 millisecond pulse width used for the ***second generation made-for-Europe JR/SR-1***. The seeming inconsistency is resolved if we but multiply the probable 2.85 second maximum Duration used for the second generation IEC JR/SR-1 by its .0014 second PW (Pulse Width) and then multiply the 2.0 second maximum Duration used for the second generation made-for-America JR/SR-1 by its .002 millisecond PW to obtain the same (.0014 x 2.85 Seconds =; .002 x 2.0 Seconds =) .004 product. In essence, the Duration x Pulse Width product of the ***made-for-America second generation JR/SR 1 BP device*** is identical to the Duration x Pulse Width product of the ***made-for-Europe second generation JR/SR 1 BP device***. Not only do the MECTA devices mirror Somatics devices as we would expect, but all four second generation MECTA BP devices (the made-for-America JR/SR 1 and 2, and the made-for-IEC JR/SR 1 and 2) are now based on the same "138J at 300Ω" or "101 at 220Ω" pure-ER/RRC in that the two phrases are equivalent (138J/300Ω = 101.2J/220Ω). True to form, moreover, the second generation MECTA IEC BP machines are now very similar to the second generation Somatics IEC BP devices.[425] In short, both the second generation JR/SR 1 IEC BP device and the second generation JR/SR 2 IEC BP device not only appear to have surreptitious 230J maximums, but the probable "138J at 300Ω" pure-ER/RRC used for both second generation MECTA IEC BP devices now neatly dovetails into the of "101.2J at 220Ω" Pure-ER/RRC used for both second generation MECTA made-for-America BP devices (138J/300Ω = 101.2J/220Ω). This continental crossover mirrors Somatics continental crossover, each containing the same critical advantages. That the second generation MECTA IEC BP devices emit a probable 230 Joules as opposed to the circa 260 Joule maximums of second generation MECTA made-for-America BP devices, is again due to the lower 500Ω Impedance ceiling promulgated by the IEC Standard as opposed to the higher 600Ω Impedance ceiling allowed by the APA Standard. In virtually all other regards, the second generation made-for-Europe and made-for America MECTA BP devices are identical, a phenomenon only possible through equivalent Pure-ER/RRCs: (101.2J/220Ω = 259J/562Ω; 101.2J/220Ω = 230J/500Ω; 138J/300Ω = 230J/500; 138J/300Ω = 259J/562). Conveniently then, MECTA's second generation IEC BP devices, like those of Somatics as we shall soon see, appear to be but slightly modified second generation made-for-America MECTA BP devices.

Second generation JR/SR 1 and 2 IEC BP Devices--more Covert method of Enhancement

We can now be fairly certain that what are actually second generation MECTA IEC BP devices do indeed emit at least 230 maximum Joules and are but modified second generation made-for-America BP devices. The advantages are multifold. For one, modifications for second generation MECTA made-for-America devices

[425] We thus have a fairly cogent confirmation for the probable 2.85 Second Duration for MECTA's IEC JR/SR 1 BP device.

necessary for European sales become minimal and thus, as noted, extremely cost effective. But there is yet another essentially important advantage as we shall soon observe in more detail.

Other Possible Means of Reaching 230 Joules

While Somatics used and openly reported the same maximum Duration for its Somatics second generation IEC BP device as it did for its Somatics second generation made-for-America device in order to reach the necessary albeit unreported 226 Joule maximum to make the unreported ER/RRC of its IEC device equivalent to its made-for America device, MECTA may or may not have increased its reported Duration to accomplish the same goal. It is possible that MECTA feared that increasing of Duration was too overt. For example, in that MECTA manifestly reported a 2.0 Second maximum Duration for its JR/SR 1 IEC device, the blatant utilization of 2.85 Seconds might too conspicuously have belied the reported 2.0 Second maximum. Consequently, much more subtle methods of enhancing the MECTA IEC devices might have been used. One possibility is enhancement of the reported .0014 Second Pulse Width of MECTA's second generation made-for-Europe JR/SR 1 and, in fact, there is circumstantial evidence of just such a Pulse Width modification. Both MECTA's second generation made-for-America JR/SR 1 as well as MECTA's third generation JR/SR 1 device (as we shall eventually see) use and report a .002 Second maximum Pulse Width. It is possible, therefore, that the JR/SR 1-IEC BP device is enhanced not through increased Duration, but through the much more inconspicuous use of an augmented Pulse Width. Simply by increasing (and not reporting) the Pulse Width from the reported **.001--.0014** Seconds to an unreported but amplified **.001--.0020 Seconds,** MECTA could have enhanced the JR/SR 1-IEC BP device to the same unreported "138J at 300Ω" Pure-ER/RRC and 230 Joule maximum output needed. Indeed, by increasing Pulse Width in this manner, the reported maximum Duration of 2.0 Seconds need not have been altered. Simply by using an invisible .002 Second Pulse Width then, the made-for-Europe JR/SR 1 might appear thusly:

Probable Actual **2nd GENERATION** MECTA CONSTANT CURRENT **IEC**
JR/SR 1 BRIEF PULSE ENR DEVICE BASED ON PURE-ER/RRC OF
"138J AT 300Ω" or **"101.2J at 220Ω"**

VOLTAGE	POWER % @ Age	AGE Yrs	Ω Ohms	FREQUENCY (Hz)	DURATION (SECs)	CURRENT mAmps	ENERGY Joules	CHARGE mC
40	10	10	50	40	.45	800	2.30	57.5
80	20	20	100	40	.90	800	9.22	115.2
120	30	30	150	60	.864	800	20.74	172.8
160	40	40	200	60	1.20	800	36.86	230.4
200	50	50	250	60	1.50	800	57.6	288
240	60	60	300	90	1.20	800	82.94	345.6
260	65	65	325	90	1.30	800	97.34	374.4
280	70	70	350	90	1.40	800	112.9	403.2
320	80	80	400	90	1.60	800	147.5	460.8
360	90	90	450	90	1.80	800	186.48	518.4
400	100	100	500	90	2.0	800	230J	576

(modified to **.001--.002 sec** Pulse Width; only **.002** used in chart above)

Charge is based upon made-for-America JR/SR 1. Charge = EO/Current x Impedance. EO = Voltage x Current x (hz x 2) x WL x Duration. EO = Charge x Current x Impedance. Duration = Charge ÷ Current x (hz x 2) x WL; Voltage = Ohm's Law: Voltage = Current x Ω. [426]

For the above chart, in lieu of altering the reported Duration, the much less conspicuous Pulse Width is altered from the reported .0014 to .002. The result, however, is the same 230J device MECTA required. In any case, the same resultant "138J at 300Ω" Pure-ER/RRC yet dovetails into MECTA's second generation made-for America BP devices based on the same Pure-ER/RRC of "101J at 220Ω" (138J/300Ω = 101J/220Ω). Note the same .576C IEC Charge (as MECTA's second generation made-for- America BP devices).

---

[426] The second generation JR/SR 1--IEC BP device has an alleged minimal stimulus Duration of .5 Seconds. On the chart, a .45 Second minimal stimulus Duration is used to represent a 2.3 fold threshold titration level of 2.3 Joules for this age level. The discrepancy is negligible and may be due to a slightly lower than 50Ω Impedance depicted for the ten year old child.

Impedance -oriented formula:

ER-EO JR/SR 1 IEC (at **.002PW**) = .8 x .8 x **300Ω** x 180 Pulses x **.002** x **2.0 Seconds** = **138.24 Joules** = (**138J at 300Ω** Pure-ER/RRC)

Actual JR/SR 1 IEC (at **.002PW**) = .8 x .8 x **500Ω** x 180 Pulses x **.002** x **2.0 Seconds** = **230 Joules** = (**230J at 500Ω**)

Again, as we can see, Charge now equals that of MECTA's made-for-America JR/SR 1 BP device.

Duration x Current x (hz x 2) x WL = Charge
2.0 Sec. x .8A x 180 Pulses x .002 = .576C.

The same Pulse Width theory can be applied to the second generation JR/SR 2 IEC BP device, that is, a covert Pulse Width modification is also possible for the JR/SR 2 made-for-Europe BP device. In short, while it is almost certain that MECTA devises a surreptitious method of reaching circa 230 Joules and thus a **"138J AT 300Ω" pure-ER/RRC (equivalent to the "101.2J at 220Ω" pure-ER/RRC used for the second generation made-for-America JR/SR 2),** like the made-for-Europe JR/SR 1 above, MECTA may have avoided increasing Duration in that the increase may have felt too conspicuous. For example, MECTA blatantly reported a 2.8 Second maximum Duration for its second generation JR/SR 2 IEC BP device. While an increase in Duration (to 4.0 Seconds like that used for its second generation made-for-America JR/SR 2) achieves the desired enhancement up to 230J, a more subtle method could be a slight increase in maximum Duration together with a subtle enhancement of the almost invisible Pulse Width. Simply by increasing Duration from the reported 2.8 second maximum to a 2.85 Second maximum Duration (as the 30% enhancement aspect of the IEC Standard "allows"), and then increasing the Pulse Width from the reported .001 Seconds to an unreported .0014 Seconds, for instance, the second generation IEC JR/SR 2 could have been invisibly augmented to the same 230 Joule maximum and thus the same unreported "138J at 300Ω" Pure-ER/RRC as that most likely utilized by the JR/SR 1 IEC BP device. In fact, there is strong circumstantial evidence of just such a modification in that MECTA's third generation JR/SR 2 device (the enhanced sequel of the second generation JR/SR 2 IEC BP device--as we shall see), transitions to and, in fact, reports not a .001 Second Pulse Width, but a "new" **.001 to .0014** second maximum Pulse Width identical to the theoretical Pulse Width used below. The second generation JR/SR 2-IEC BP device then, may have contained (albeit unreported) the same.001--.0014 Pulse Width "eventually" used for MECTA's third generation JR/SR 2. This possible Pulse Width increase for the second generation JR/SR 2 IEC BP device is depicted on the chart below.

Probable Actual **2nd GENERATION** MECTA CONSTANT CURRENT **IEC JR/SR 2** BRIEF PULSE ENR DEVICE BASED ON PURE-ER/RRC OF **"138J AT 300Ω"** or **"101.2J at 220Ω"**

VOLTAGE	POWER % @ Age	AGE Yrs	Ω Ohms	FREQUENCY (Hz)	DURATION (SECs)	CURRENT mAmps	ENERGY Joules	CHARGE mC
40	10	10	50	90	0.286	800	2.30	57.6
80	20	20	100	90	0.571	800	9.22	115.2
120	30	30	150	90	0.857	800	20.74	172.8
160	40	40	200	90	1.14	800	36.86	230.4
200	50	50	250	90	1.43	800	57.6	288
240	60	60	300	90	1.71	800	82.94	345.6
260	65	65	325	90	1.857	800	97.34	374.4
280	70	70	350	90	2.0	800	112.9	403.2
320	80	80	400	90	2.285	800	147.5	460.8
360	90	90	450	90	2.57	800	182.89	518.4
400	100	100	500	90	2.85	800	230J	575

(modified to .001-**.0014** sec Pulse Width)

Charge is based upon Probable Actual made-for-America JR/SR 2. Charge = EO/Current x Impedance. EO = Voltage x Current x (hz x 2) x WL x Duration or EO = Charge x Current x Impedance. Duration = Charge ÷ Current x (hz x 2) x WL; Voltage is derived from Ohm's Law (Voltage = Current x Ω).

Impedance -oriented formula:
ER-EO JR/SR 2 IEC (at **.0014PW**) = .8 x .8 x **300Ω** x 180 Pulses x **.0014** x **2.85 Seconds** = **137.89 Joules** = (**138J at 300Ω** Pure-ER/RRC).

Actual JR/SR 2 IEC (at **.0014PW**)= .8 x .8 x **500Ω** x 180 Pulses x **.0014** x **2.85 Seconds** = **230 Joules** = (**230J at 500Ω**).

Duration x Current x (hz x 2) x WL = **Charge**
2.85 Sec x .8A x 180 Pulses x .0014 Sec. PW = **.575C.**

Once again, not only does this method achieve a "138J at 300Ω" Pure-ER/RRC for MECTA's second generation made-for-Europe BP JR/SR 2 device, equivalent to the "101J at 220Ω" Pure-ER/RRC upon which the second generation made-for-America JR/SR 2 is based, but maximum Charge for the second generation made-for-Europe BP device now equals that of the second generation made-for-America JR/SR 2. As noted, such a modification of the second generation made-for-Europe JR/SR 2 IEC BP device creating equivalency with made-for America devices, makes modification of the second generation MECTA made-for-America JR/SR 2 for European use extremely minimal and cost effective. Moreover, it minimizes transition to the third generation device, as we shall later see.

MECTA's ***Made-for-America*** *vs.* ***Made-for-Europe (IEC)*** *Second Generation BP Devices*

Assuming 230J maximum outputs for MECTA's second generation JR/SR 1 and 2 IEC BP devices, let's compare MECTA's 2nd generation ***made-for-America*** devices to MECTA's 2nd generation ***made-for Europe*** BP devices.

PROBABLE **ACTUAL** ***Made-for-America*** 2nd GENERATION CONSTANT CURRENT MECTA **JR/SR 1** BRIEF PULSE **ENR** DEVICE BASED ON ***PURE***-ER/RRC OF **"101.2J AT 220Ω"** (or **"138J AT 300Ω")**

VOLTAGE	POWER % @ Age	AGE Yrs	Ω Ohms	FREQUENCY (Hz)	DURATION (SECs)	CURRENT mAmps	ENERGY Joules	CHARGE mC
45	10	10	56.25	40	.5	800	2.88	64
90	20	20	112.5	40	.9	800	10.37	115.2
135	30	30	168.75	60	.9	800	23.33	172.8
180	40	40	225	60	1.2	800	41.47	230.4
225	50	50	281.25	60	1.5	800	64.8	288
270	60	60	337.5	90	1.2	800	93.31	345.6
292.5	65	65	365.63	90	1.3	800	109.51	374.4
315	70	70	393.75	90	1.4	800	127	403.2
360	80	80	450	90	1.6	800	165.89	460.8
405	90	90	506.25	90	1.8	800	209.95	518.4
450	100	100	562.5	90	2.0	800	259.2	576

.002 Sec. Pulse Width

Probable **Actual** ***Made-for-Europe*** 2nd GENERATION CONSTANT CURRENT MECTA **JR/SR 1** BRIEF PULSE **ENR** DEVICE BASED ON ***PURE***-ER/RRC OF **"138J AT 300Ω"** (or **"101.2J at 220Ω")**

VOLTAGE	POWER % @ Age	AGE Yrs	Ω Ohms	FREQUENCY (Hz)	DURATION (SECs)	CURRENT mAmps	ENERGY Joules	CHARGE mC
40	10	10	50	40	.45	800	2.30	57.5
80	20	20	100	40	.90	800	9.22	115.2
120	30	30	150	60	.864	800	20.74	172.8
160	40	40	200	60	1.20	800	36.86	230.4
200	50	50	250	60	1.50	800	57.6	288
240	60	60	300	90	1.20	800	82.94	345.6
260	65	65	325	90	1.30	800	97.34	374.4
280	70	70	350	90	1.40	800	112.9	403.2
320	80	80	400	90	1.60	800	147.5	460.8
360	90	90	450	90	1.80	800	186.48	518.4
400	100	100	500	90	2.0	800	230J	576

Modified to **.001--.002 sec.** Pulse Width; only **.002 sec.** used in chart below

Regardless of how the MECTA IEC BP devices reach 230J maximums, in comparing the probable second generation **JR/SR 1** made-for-Europe BP device (directly above) to the probable second generation JR/SR 1 made-for-America BP device (above that), we can now see that almost the only modification needed to transition from the made-for-America device to the made-for-Europe device is a reduction in Voltage from 450 to 400V. Except for slight adjustments in Duration wherein EO is slightly reduced due to the IEC's 500Ω maximum Impedance limit as opposed to the American 600Ω maximum Impedance as a result of which the IEC device has slightly lower EOs, all parameters remain almost unchanged, including Charge. This is the result of the 138J at 300Ω Pure-ER/RRC used for MECTA's **JR/SR 1** IEC device perfectly dovetailing into the 101J at 220Ω Pure-ER/RRC used for MECTA's **JR/SR 1** made-for-America device (138J/300Ω = 101.2J/220Ω). In short, almost the single adaptation needed to modify MECTA's 562Ω second generation made-for-America **JR/SR 1** to MECTA's 500Ω second generation made-for-Europe JR/SR 1, as noted, is a simple reduction in Voltage from 450 to 400V.

Similarly, the probable second generation **JR/SR 2** *made-for-Europe* BP device below (based on a 138J at 300Ω Pure-ERR/RRC) now perfectly dovetails into the second generation **JR/SR 2** *made-for-America* BP device below (based on a 101J at 220Ω Pure-ERR/RRC). Moreover, while Pulse Width and Duration differ between the second generation *made-for-Europe* **JR/SR 2** and the second generation *made-for-America* **JR/SR 2**, simple multiplication of the Pulse Width by maximum Duration produces the same virtual product (.0014 x 2.85 = ***.004***; .001 x 4.0 = ***.004***). The variation between the two JR 2s, in brief, is but superficial. Again, as a result of equivalent ER/RRCs (138J/300Ω = 101.2J/220Ω), virtually the single adaptation needed to modify the 562Ω second generation made-for-America JR/SR 2 BP device to the 500Ω second generation IEC JR/SR 2 BP device is a simple reduction in Voltage from 450 to 400V.

PROBABLE **ACTUAL** ***Made-for-America*** MECTA 2nd GENERATION CONSTANT CURRENT **JR/SR 2** BRIEF PULSE **ENR** DEVICE BASED ON ***PURE***-ER/RRC OF **"101.3J AT 220Ω"** (or **"138J AT 300Ω"**)

VOLTAGE	POWER % @ Age	AGE Yrs	Ω Ohms	FREQUENCY (Hz)	DURATION (SECs)	CURRENT mAmps	ENERGY Joules	CHARGE mC
45	10	10	56.25	90	0.5	800	3.24	72
90	20	20	112.5	90	0.8	800	10.37	115.2
135	30	30	168.75	90	1.2	800	23.33	172.8
180	40	40	225	90	1.6	800	41.47	230.4
225	50	50	281.25	90	2.0	800	64.8	288
270	60	60	337.5	90	2.4	800	93.31	345.6
292.5	65	65	365.63	90	2.6	800	109.51	374.4
315	70	70	393.75	90	2.8	800	127	403.2
360	80	80	450	90	3.2	800	165.89	460.8
405	90	90	506.25	90	3.6	800	209.95	518.4
450	100	100	562.5	90	4.0	800	259.2	576

.001 Sec. Pulse Width

PROBABLE **ACTUAL** ***Made-for-Europe*** MECTA 2nd GENERATION CONSTANT CURRENT **JR/SR 2** BRIEF PULSE **ENR** DEVICE BASED ON ***PURE***-ER/RRC OF **"138J AT 300Ω"** (or **"101.2J at 220Ω"**)

VOLTAGE	POWER % @ Age	AGE Yrs	Ω Ohms	FREQUENCY (Hz)	DURATION (SECs)	CURRENT mAmps	ENERGY Joules	CHARGE mC
40	10	10	50	90	0.286	800	2.30	57.6
80	20	20	100	90	0.571	800	9.22	115.2
120	30	30	150	90	0.857	800	20.74	172.8
160	40	40	200	90	1.14	800	36.86	230.4
200	50	50	250	90	1.43	800	57.6	288
240	60	60	300	90	1.71	800	82.94	345.6
260	65	65	325	90	1.857	800	97.34	374.4
280	70	70	350	90	2.0	800	112.9	403.2
320	80	80	400	90	2.285	800	147.5	460.8
360	90	90	450	90	2.57	800	182.89	518.4
400	100	100	500	90	2.85	800	230J	575

Modified to .001-**.0014** sec Pulse Width

In brief, as a result of equivalency, modification of second generation MECTA made-for-America BP devices to second generation made-for-Europe (IEC) BP devices becomes simple, minimal, and extremely "cost-effective."

Final Advantage--Machine Readouts

But perhaps the most important advantage with respect to the Pure-ER/RRC dovetailing of MECTA's second generation made-for-Europe devices with MECTA's second generation made-for-America BP devices is the enabling of virtually the same machine readouts in both instances. Remember, in reporting a 240V maximum, MECTA indirectly reports a 96.8J EO maximum for both its second generation made-for Europe BP devices--in essence, a circa 100J maximum output. This is tantamount to the 101J at 220Ω Conditional-ER/RRC with 101J ceiling that MECTA implies for its made-for-America BP devices. The circa 100J maximum is critical. Why, we might ask again, does MECTA report what seems to be a "100J at 300Ω" conditional-ER/RRC with circa 100J ceiling (for the IEC Standard) when it could simply have reported a 130J at 300Ω conditional-ER/RRC with 130J ceiling, still considered minimal stimulus? Almost certainly, MECTA reports circa 100J maximums for its made-for-Europe BP devices (via the false reporting of a 240V maximum) for the same reason MECTA utilizes the 101J figure for its made-for-America BP devices. Both refer to maximum machine readouts on all four second generation IEC and made-for-America second generation BP devices. Because the ER/RRC used for MECTA's made-for-Europe BP devices perfectly dovetail into MECTA's made-for-America BP devices (138J/300Ω = 101J/220Ω), MECTA is once again able to supplant all actual Impedances with a false 220Ω constant Impedance just as MECTA does for its made-for-America second generation BP devices. In short, both made-for-America and made-for-Europe second generation BP devices depict very similar Machine Readouts culminating in the same 101J maximum output, a depiction perpetuating the illusion of minimal stimulus output on a world-wide basis. It is only because all four devices are based on equivalent ER/RRCs (101J/220Ω = 138J/300Ω) that, using the same EO formula, MECTA is able to supplant the same false 220Ω constant for all age categories in all four second generation BP machine readout calculations both in the U. S. and abroad to depict virtually the same machine readouts for all age categories culminating in the same false maximum output of 101J.

MACHINE READOUTS BASED ON ONE FALSE 220Ω "CONSTANT" FOR ALL FOUR MECTA SECOND GENERATION BP DEVCIES

Below, all four second generation BP devices are presented as physicians and regulators see them, with minimal stimulus readouts as a result substituting "220Ω" for all actual Impedances.

JR/SR 1: Made-for-America and Made-for-Europe:

EO = Charge x Current x Impedance
EO = (Current squared) x Impedance x (hz x 2) x WL x Duration

EO = .576 x .8A x ***220Ω*** = **101.3J**
EO = .8 x .8 x ***220Ω*** x 180 Pulses x .002 x 2.0 Seconds = **101.3J**.

Made-for-America **MACHINE READOUTS BASED ON FALSE 220Ω IMPEDANCE FOR THE PROBABLE ACTUAL** 2nd GENERATION CONSTANT CURRENT MECTA **JR/SR 1** BRIEF PULSE ENR DEVICE BASED ON ***PURE***-ER/RRC OF **"101.3J AT 220Ω"** (or **"138J AT 300Ω"**)

VOLTAGE	POWER % @ Age	AGE Yrs	Ω Ohms	FREQUENCY (Hz)	DURATION (SECs)	CURRENT mAmps	ENERGY Readout	CHARGE mC
45	10	10	220	40	.5	800	11.26	64
90	20	20	220	40	.9	800	10.37	115.2
135	30	30	220	60	.9	800	30.41	172.8
180	40	40	220	60	1.2	800	40.55	230.4
225	50	50	220	60	1.5	800	50.68	288
270	60	60	220	90	1.2	800	60.83	345.6

292.5	65	65	220	90	1.3	800	65.89	374.4
315	70	70	220	90	1.4	800	70.96	403.2
360	80	80	220	90	1.6	800	81.1	460.8
405	90	90	220	90	1.8	800	91.2	518.4
450	100	100	220	90	2.0	800	101.3	576

.002 Sec. Pulse Width

Made-for-Europe **MACHINE READOUTS BASED ON FALSE 220Ω IMPEDANCE FOR THE PROBABLE ACTUAL** 2nd GENERATION CONSTANT CURRENT **MECTA JR/SR 1** BRIEF PULSE ENR DEVICE BASED ON ***PURE***-ER/RRC OF **"138J AT 300Ω"** (or **"101.2J at 220Ω"**)

VOLTAGE	POWER % @ Age	AGE Yrs	Ω Ohms	FREQUENCY (Hz)	DURATION (SECs)	CURRENT mAmps	ENERGY Readout	CHARGE mC
40	10	10	220	40	.45	800	10.12	57.5
80	20	20	220	40	.9	800	20.27	115.2
120	30	30	220	60	.9	800	30.41	172.8
160	40	40	220	60	1.2	800	40.55	230.4
200	50	50	220	60	1.5	800	50.68	288
240	60	60	220	90	1.2	800	60.83	345.6
260	65	65	220	90	1.3	800	65.89	374.4
280	70	70	220	90	1.4	800	70.96	403.2
320	80	80	220	90	1.6	800	81.1	460.8
360	90	90	220	90	1.8	800	91.2	518.4
400	100	100	220	90	2.0	800	101.3	576

modified to **.001--.002 sec** Pulse Width; only .0**02** used in above chart

JR/SR 2: Made-for-America and Made-for-Europe

EO = Charge x Current x Impedance
EO = (Current squared) x Impedance x (hz x 2) x WL x Duration

EO = .576 x .8A x ***220Ω*** = **101.3J**
EO = .8 x .8 x ***220Ω*** x 180 Pulses x **.001 x 4.0** Seconds = **101.3J**.

EO = .576 x .8A x ***220Ω*** = **101.3J**
EO = .8 x .8 x ***220Ω*** x 180 Pulses x **.0014 x 2.85** Seconds = **101.2J**.

Made-for-America **MACHINE READOUTS BASED ON FALSE 220Ω IMPEDANCE FOR THE PROBABLE ACTUAL** 2nd GENERATION CONSTANT CURRENT MECTA **JR/SR 2** BRIEF PULSE ENR DEVICE BASED ON ***PURE***-ER/RRC OF **"101.3J AT 220Ω"** (or **"138J AT 300Ω"**)

VOLTAGE	POWER % @ Age	AGE Yrs	Ω Ohms	FREQUENCY (Hz)	DURATION (SECs)	CURRENT mAmps	ENERGY Readout	CHARGE mC
45	10	10	220	90	0.5	800	12.67	72
90	20	20	220	90	0.8	800	20.27	115.2
135	30	30	220	90	1.2	800	30.41	172.8
180	40	40	220	90	1.6	800	40.55	230.4
225	50	50	220	90	2.0	800	50.68	288
270	60	60	220	90	2.4	800	60.83	345.6
292.5	65	65	220	90	2.6	800	65.89	374.4
315	70	70	220	90	2.8	800	70.96	403.2
360	80	80	220	90	3.2	800	81.1	460.8
405	90	90	220	90	3.6	800	91.2	518.4
450	100	100	220	90	4.0	800	101.3	576

.001 Sec. Pulse Width

Made-for-Europe **MACHINE READOUTS BASED ON FALSE 220Ω IMPEDANCE FOR THE PROBABLE ACTUAL IEC 2nd GENERATION CONSTANT CURRENT MECTA JR/SR 2** BRIEF PULSE ENR DEVICE BASED ON ***PURE***-ER/RRC OF **"138J AT 300Ω"** (or **"101.2J at 220Ω"**)

VOLTAGE	POWER % @ Age	AGE Yrs	Ω Ohms	FREQUENCY (Hz)	DURATION (SECs)	CURRENT mAmps	ENERGY Readout	CHARGE mC
40	10	10	220	90	0.286	800	10.13	57.6

80	20	20	220	90	0.571	800	20.27	115.2
120	30	30	220	90	0.857	800	30.41	172.8
160	40	40	220	90	1.14	800	40.55	230.4
200	50	50	220	90	1.43	800	50.68	288
240	60	60	220	90	1.71	800	60.83	345.6
260	65	65	220	90	1.857	800	65.89	374.4
280	70	70	220	90	2.0	800	70.96	403.2
320	80	80	220	90	2.285	800	81.1	460.8
360	90	90	220	90	2.57	800	91.2	518.4
400	100	100	220	90	2.85	800	101.3J	575

modified to .001-**.0014** sec Pulse Width

In brief, based on machine readouts which even administering physicians rely upon, all MECTA made-for-America and made-for-Europe second generation BP devices appear to emit the same minimal stimulus outputs for all age categories seemingly culminating in a 101J maximum output. [427] [428] Of course, because these readouts are wholly inaccurate, MECTA does not provide formulas containing actual Voltages and other parameters for calculating or deriving machine readouts, as such formulas would expose the inconsistencies. Indeed, the "100J" figure conspicuously published within the "100J at 300Ω" IEC Standard is not only arbitrary (like the figure within the "101J at 220Ω" Mectan Transmutation), but totally contrived, in that "100J" by any interpretation, is entirely inaccurate. We can be certain that the 100J figure is featured in standards and manufacturer reports (on both continents) to suggest circa 100J maximum outputs seemingly substantiated by circa 100J maximum machine readouts indicative of minimal stimulus. In brief, the aim of misleading or false parameters suggestive of spurious (circa) 100J maximums for all four MECTA second generation BP devices--those under the APA Standard and those under the IEC Standard--seemingly corroborated by maximum machine readouts of circa 100 Joules read even by administering physicians, is the creation of the false impression that what are actually second generation BP devices, continue to administer minimal stimulus outputs for all age categories. The impression, of course, is specious.

Higher Still

To this section should be added evidence that the second generation JR/SR **2** IEC BP device alone (as opposed to the second generation JR/SR 1 IEC) may eventually have transitioned into an even higher output device not of 230 Joules, but perhaps as much as 240 Joules. As we shall find in the section for third generation devices (see Volume 2), the **second generation** JR/SR-**1 IEC** device exactly doubles in output to constitute the **third generation** JR/SR-**1** device. On the other hand, the **third generation** JR/SR **2** IEC BP device (as we shall see) contains virtually all the parameters of the **second generation** JR/SR-**2 IEC** device except that the **third generation** JR/SR **2 IEC** device utilizes a 5.96 second maximum Duration. If the **second generation** JR/SR **1 IEC** device exactly doubles to form the third generation JR/SR 1, the second generation JR/SR 2 IEC may have further devolved at some point to utilize not a 2.85 second maximum Duration, but a **2.98 second** maximum Duration (2 x 2.98 = 5.96 Seconds) resulting not in a 230J maximum but a possible **240J maximum**. In short, somewhere along the way, the 230J second generation JR/SR **2** IEC device may have transitioned into a 240J device. If so, the Duration for the JR/SR **2 IEC** may have transitioned into an even higher **2.98 Seconds** (or some other increased parameter) resulting in a slightly higher Pure-ER/RRC not of "138J at 300Ω" but of "144J at 300Ω" (144J/300Ω = 240J/500Ω) tantamount to "105.6J at 220Ω" (144J/300Ω = 105.6J/220Ω"). Of course, it is also possible that MECTA simply increased the output of the the third generation JR/SR 2 at the point of its construction. Even so, we shall examine the possibility of a 240J JR/SR 2 IEC BP device.

[427] While the readouts do not reflect a uniform MTTLOI and are wholly inaccurate, because physicians have no access to relative threshold constants used by manufacturers, the inconsistent MTTLOI would not be noticeable even to administering physicians. Rather, the illusion of minimal stimulus outputs for all age categories culminating in a 100J ceiling is successfully created.

[428] Inaccurate parameters provided by MECTA for IEC BP devices derive a slightly disparate 96.8J as opposed to machine readouts of 101J, while the IEC Standard emphasizes "100J." To the casual onlooker, however, the small differences appear negligible.

Possible 240J Second Generation JR/SR 2 IEC BP Device:

Impedance -oriented formula using 300Ω ER:
ER-EO JR/SR 2 IEC (at **2.98 Sec**) = .8 x .8 x **300Ω** x 180 Pulses x .0014 x **2.98 Seconds** = **144 Joules** = (**144J at 300Ω** Pure-ER/RRC).

Voltage-oriented formula: (240V, just as 300Ω, is an ER figure)
ER-EO JR/SR 2 IEC (at **2.98 Sec**) = .8 x **240V** x 180 Pulses x .0014 x **2.98 Seconds** = **144 Joules** = (**144J at 240V** Pure-ER/RRC).

Pure-ER/RRCs to Actual Max for JR/SR 2 IEC (at **2.98 Sec**):
144J/300Ω = **240J/500Ω** (**240J maximum**).
144J/240V = **240J/400V** (**240J maximum**).

Impedance -oriented formula using actual 500Ω:
Actual-EO JR/SR 2 IEC (at **2.98 Sec**) = .8 x .8 x **500Ω** x 180 Pulses x .0014 x **2.98 Seconds** = **240 Joules**.

Voltage-oriented formula using actual 400V:
Actual-EO JR/SR 2 IEC (at **2.98 Sec**) = .8 x **400V** x 180 Pulses x .0014 x **2.98 Seconds** = **240 Joules**.

Thus, it is possible that the second generation JR/SR 2 IEC BP device transitioned at some point from an unreported 230J maximum to a 240J maximum, ever approaching the output emitted by MECTA second generation made-for-America BP devices (of 259 maximum joules).

At 240 Joules, the unreported charge for the second generation made-for-Europe JR/SR-2 (IEC) would necessarily have reached .600C, exactly half the Charge of the third generation JR/SR 1 (as we shall eventually see).

Charge = 240J/.8A x 500Ω = .600C.

If the JR/SR2 did evolve into a 240J device, supplanting all actual Impedances with the same false 220Ω would have resulted in the depiction not of a false 101J maximum output, but of a false 105J maximum output, still well within the bounds of what appears to be minimal stimulus output.

EO = Charge x Impedance x Amperage
EO = .600C x **220Ω** x .8A = **105.6J**

Such a device would look something like the following:

Approximate Actual CONSTANT CURRENT **JR/SR 2** BRIEF PULSE **IEC** ENR DEVICE
(2nd GENERATION)
BASED ON PURE-ER/RRC OF "**144J at 300Ω**" or "**105.6J at 220Ω**"

VOLTAGE	POWER % @ Age	AGE Yrs	Ω Ohms	FREQUENCY (Hz)	DURATION (SECs)	CURRENT mAmps	ENERGY Joules	CHARGE mC
40	10	10	50	90	0.298	800	2.40	60
80	20	20	100	90	0.595	800	9.60	120
120	30	30	150	90	0.893	800	21.6	180
160	40	40	200	90	1.19	800	38.4	240
200	50	50	250	90	1.49	800	60.0	300
240	60	60	300	90	1.79	800	86.4	360
260	65	65	325	90	1.94	800	101.4	390
280	70	70	350	90	2.08	800	117.5	420
320	80	80	400	90	2.38	800	153.6	480

360	90	90	450	90	2.67	800	194.4	540
400	100	100	500	90	2.98	800	240J	600

(Modified to .001--.0014 Sec. Pulse Width; only 0014 used in chart above)

Conclusion:

If the above speculations are correct, if MECTA's second generation JR/SR 1 IEC BP device emitted 230 maximum joules and the JR/SR 2 IEC device a 230 to 240J maximum output, then MECTA under reports, that is, fails to report not only actual maximum EO in joules, but actual maximum Voltage, actual maximum Impedance, actual maximum Duration, and actual maximum Charge for both its second generation IEC BP devices, under-reports which falsely suggest maximum outputs of between 100 and 130 maximum Joules. Actual parameter reporting is avoided by modern day BP manufacturers in that such information undermines the notion of improved safety (via reduced output), not only affecting Brief Pulse as a minimal stimulus device, but the viability of convulsion theory itself and thus the marketability of Brief Pulse, generally. Manufacturers may fear that accurate information revealing actual output and actual MTTLOI would warrant harsh criticism and potentially damaging publicity possibly leading to re-examination, more stringent regulations, and perhaps even abolition of the procedure generally. [429]

Thus, the “100J at 300Ω” phrase conspicuously published as the 1989 IEC Standard creates the suggestion of a “100J at 300Ω” conditional-ER/RRC, as noted, seemingly circumscribing output to circa 100 maximum Joules or minimal stimulus, a ceiling seemingly corroborated by circa 100J maximum machine readouts depicted on all second generation BP devices. In fact, like the Mectan Transmutation, MECTA's creative interpretation of the IEC Standard with the aid of additional, even less conspicuous adjuncts within the same standard, actually permits, as mentioned, a 130J at 300Ω pure-ER/RRC and thus an unreported 216.6J ceiling. Further, albeit slight breaches of the implicit 130J at 300Ω pure-ER/RRC may have facilitated an even higher "138J at 300Ω” pure-ER/RRC tantamount to the 101.3J at 220Ω pure-ER/RRC upon which second generation made-for-America MECTA BP devices are based. This equivalency conveniently bridges the output gap between American made made-for-America and American made-for-Europe BP devices facilitating an invisible and unreported maximum output of 230 joules or a 2.3 MTTLOI for all age categories with second generation IEC BP devices generally. It is no coincidence that the circa .576C maximum Charge which the "138J at 300Ω” pure-ER/RRC allows for second generation MECTA IEC devices, is equal to the .576C maximum Charge which the "101J at 220Ω” pure-ER/RRC facilitates for MECTA second generation made-for-America BP devices. (The same principle hold true for Somatics devices.)

Moreover, the equivalency of the MECTA’s "138J at 300Ω” made for Europe devices and MECTA’s "101J at 220Ω” made-for-America’s devices allows the supplanting of the same false 220Ω “constant” plugged into all second generation MECTA devices, resulting in the same 101J machine readout maximum displayed by all MECTA second generation devices both in America and Europe. As such, readouts for both made-for-America and made-for-Europe BP devices seem to corroborate the same approximate minimal stimulus outputs emitted by what appear to be first generation MECTA BP devices. Because MECTA's second generation IEC made-for-Europe JR/SR 1@2 IEC BP devices are the practical equivalents of MECTA second generation made-for America JR/SR 1@2 BP devices, moreover, necessary transition adjustments are minimized. Not surprisingly then, MECTA has never revealed either true maximum output in joules or true MTTLOIs for either its second generation made-for-America or second generation made-for-Europe BP devices. Neither has Somatics.

In fact, the double standard by which MECTA (and other BP manufacturers) report minimal stimulus on the one hand while secretly enhancing output on the other, ensures that regulatory agencies, consumers, physicians, (and media) alike remain ignorant of the actual power of second generation BP devices both in Europe and America, in fact, facilitating the false impression that (second generation) BP devices remain limited to circa 100 maximum Joules internationally. In short, the impression is created that second generation BP

---

[429] Outputs in excess of that necessary to induce adequate seizures are by definition excessive in that such outputs beyond that required to induce adequate seizures are allegedly superfluous. Unfortunately, “ECT” is not, nor ever has been based upon adequate seizure--long proven ineffective, but rather adequate amounts of electricity. It is due to this that manufacturers have gone to such great lengths to hide actual parameters together with any evidence of organic damage such as acknowledgement long term memory complaints as actual.

devices remain first generation BP devices, that second generation devices do not, in fact, exist. In sum, both MECTA and Somatics appear to have applied the same double standard in Europe and even Asia as they did in America, similarly suggesting minimal stimulus outputs for all age recipients while simultaneously more than doubling the MTTLOIs administered to these same recipients. In fact, the Mectan Transmutation enabled second generation made-for America MECTA BP devices to emit 259 joules and thus a 2.59 MTTLOI for all age groups while the IEC Standard enabled second generation made-for Europe MECTA BP devices to emit between 230 and perhaps 240 joules and thus a 2.3 to 2.4 MTTLOI for all age recipients. While we can only speculate regarding MECTA devices due to MECTA's withholding of information, we can be fairly certain that MECTA second generation made-for-Europe BP devices emit at least 230 joules. Consequently, these machines are no longer ECT devices at all, but ENR devices.

CHAPTER 35

Somatics and the 1989 IEC Standard: Somatics Figures EO for its IEC BP Device

By about 1989, BP device manufacturers under IEC auspices, totally ceased reporting actual ER/RRCs and maximum Energy Output in joules, making comparative outputs as well as comparative overall power of BP devices, extremely difficult to discern.

Nevertheless, in keeping with its' U. S. practices, unlike MECTA, the electrical parameters Somatics Incorporated reported to the Royal College of Psychiatry for its' IEC BP device--the Thymatron DGx--are actual (Royal College of Psychiatry, 1995, p.125). For example, Somatics not only accurately reported for its second generation made-for-Europe DGx Brief Pulse device, the true constant current of .9A, the true consistent pulse width of .001 Seconds, and the actual maximum Hertz of 70, but in contrast to MECTA, Somatics accurately reported for its made-for-Europe DGx the actual maximum Impedance of 500Ω, the machine's actual maximum Duration of 4.0 Seconds, the machine's actual maximum Charge of .504C, and the machine's actual maximum Voltage of 450V, making it factually possible to derive (indirectly at least) not only actual EO for the Thymatron DGx , but the unreported ER/RRC upon which the Somatics second generation DGx IEC BP device (marketed throughout Eurasia) is based. [430] Though not directly reported then, simply by plugging the reported maximum electrical parameters of the DGx into the Impedance-oriented formula for finding energy output for BP devices: <u>EO = Current squared x Impedance x Pulses x Pulse Width x Duration</u>, we can factually obtain for the Somatics' second generation DGx IEC BP device, it's unreported circa 227J maximum output:

EO = .9 x .9 x <u>500Ω</u> x 140 Pulses x .001 Pulse Width x 4.0 Seconds = <u>226.8 Joules</u>.

Moreover, working in reverse (in "deference" to MECTA), that is, by using the same formula and the same reported parameters, we can replace the DGx's actual maximum Impedance of "500Ω" (Royal College of Psychiatry, 1995, p.125) with a "300Ω" ER output (International Electrotechnical Commission, 1989, p.23) to accurately obtain the Pure-ER/RRC upon which the Somatics DGx IEC BP device is based.

ER-EO = .9 x .9 x <u>**300Ω**</u> x 140 Pulses x .001 Pulse Width x 4.0 Seconds = <u>**136 Joules**</u>. (Thus, the DGx Pure-ER/RRC = <u>**136J at 300Ω**</u>).

Consequently, it can be accurately determined that Somatics uses an unreported <u>"136J at 300Ω" Pure-ER/RRC</u> to derive an unreported maximum output of <u>226.7J</u> at the Thymatron DGx's actual maximum Impedance of <u>500Ω</u>.

<u>**136J/300Ω = 226.7J/500Ω**</u> [431]

---

[430] The Thymatron DG is produced for made-for-America consumption; whereas, the Thymatron DGx is the IEC model of the Thymatron DG marketed in the U.K. and other IEC-mandated countries. Eventually, for a time at least, Somatics adopted the DGx for universal use.

[431] XJ/300Ω = 226.66J/500Ω. <u>X = 136J</u>.136J/300Ω = XJ/500Ω <u>X = 226.66.1</u>36J/300Ω = 226.66J/500Ω.

Notably, in emitting approximately 227 maximum Joules, the DGx violates the "130J at 300Ω" Pure-ER/RRC maximum indirectly stipulated by the IEC Standard of 216.66 Joules (130J/300Ω = **216.6J**/500Ω). Somatics' application of a 136J at 300Ω Pure-ER/RRC, permitting 227 unreported Joules, is thus a moderate 10J violation of the IEC ceiling standard (227J - 217J = 10J) interpreted as a Pure-ER/RRC. In short, in emitting an unreported emission of approximately 227J, the Somatics' DGx IEC BP device, breaches the maximum output "permitted" by the inconspicuous Pure-ER/RRC maximum of the IEC Standard, by approximately ten joules.

__130J/300Ω__ = 216.66J/500Ω; 227-217= __10J__ (breach). [432]

Somatics, however, needs the 10J breach of the IEC Standard for an important purpose. Somatics urgently needs to base its second generation IEC BP device on a Pure-ER/RRC equivalent to the Pure-ER/RRC upon which its second generation made-for-America BP device is based--the Thymatron DG. In that the Thymatron DG is specifically based upon a known "99.7J at 220Ω" Pure-ER/RRC, not surprisingly, the "136J at 300Ω" ER/RRC upon which the made-for-Europe DGx is actually based is directly equivalent to the 99.7J at 220Ω upon which the DG is based, facilitating multiple advantages, as we have seen and shall observe in more detail shortly.

99.7J/220Ω = 136J/300Ω

Somatics' IEC Reporting Methodology vs. MECTA's IEC Reporting Methodology

Without doubt then, the second generation Somatics' DGx IEC BP device emits an unreported maximum of 227 Joules or a 2.27 MTTLOI for all age categories. In that Somatics inveterately imitates MECTA, we can now be reasonably confident that second generation MECTA IEC BP devices emit a very similar maximum output of about 230 Joules or about a 2.3 MTTLOI for all age categories (as noted above). To prove this point, let us suppose, for a moment, Somatics had underreported in the same manner as MECTA. In keeping with the Mectan method of seeming conformity to the seeming published IEC Standard of a "100J at 300Ω" conditional-ER/RRC with 100J ceiling, Somatics, as did MECTA, could have claimed to have limited its' IEC BP device--the Thymatron DGx--to a maximum Duration, not of its reported 4.0 Seconds, but 2.85 Seconds, suggesting the same circa 100J ceiling as did MECTA.

EO = .9 x .9 x 300Ω x 140 Pulses x .001 Pulse Width x 2.85 Seconds = 97 Joules. [433] [434]

Based upon the comparably reduced Duration of 2.85 Seconds and a .001 Second PW for the JR/SR 2, MECTA reports a spurious maximum Charge of .403C for its MECTA IEC BP devices (Royal College of Psychiatry, 1995, p.125). In fact, MECTA's reported maximum Charge of .403C can be derived from what appears to be a literal 96.8J at a literal 300Ω Impedance; whereas, MECTA actually reports an ER Charge.

MECTA Charge = 96.768 Joules ÷ .8 Amperes x 300Ω = .403 Coulombs.

Had Somatics, like MECTA, claimed to have used for the Somatics DGx, a similarly reduced Duration of 2.85 Seconds (tantamount to MECTA's reduced 2.8 Second Duration claim) as opposed to the DGx's actual

---

[432] The IEC Standard publishes "100J at 300Ω" but with the 30% cushion adjunct, the maximum is a "130J at 300Ω" ER/RRC permitting 216.66J. In the DGx's emission of 227J, a breach of 10J is committed. As we shall see, however, the DGx breaches its machine readouts of circa 100 maximum joules by about 117J.

[433] 1982 APA Standard appears to imply the reduction of electrical parameters to prevent surpassing 100J.

[434] In spite of appearances, both MECTA and Somatics' second generation devices, have always been and continue to remain extremely comparable (Cameron 1994).

reported 4.0 Second Duration, Somatics could have claimed a comparable maximum Charge of .359 Coulombs for its DGx [435] (Charge = Duration x Current x (hz x 2) x WL; Charge = EO/Current x Impedance).

Theoretical DGx Charge using a 2.85 Second maximum Duration =

2.85 Sec. x .9 Amperes x 140 Pulses x .001Sec. = **.359C**.
97 Joules ÷ (.9 Amperes x **300Ω**) = **.359 Coulombs**.

Moreover, just as MECTA claims but a 240V maximum based on a 300Ω maximum Impedance for its MECTA IEC BP devices, so Somatics could have claimed but a 270V maximum based on the same alleged 300Ω maximum.

Ohm's Law: Amperage and Impedance = Voltage

Somatics DGx IEC Device: .9A x 300Ω = **270V**
MECTA JR. SR 1@2 IEC Devices: .8A x 300Ω = **240V**

What if Somatics had next claimed a 400Ω maximum Impedance as did MECTA, reflective of the IEC Standard's inconspicuous but actual "130J at 300Ω" Pure-ER/RRC ceiling permitting an actual 216.6J ceiling (130J/300Ω = ***216.6J***/500Ω). However, if the 130J at 300Ω had been interpreted as a Conditional ER/RRC, a maximum 400Ω could suggest a false 129J maximum.

Somatics: .9A x .9A x **400Ω** x 140 pulses x .001PW x 2.85 Sec. = **129J**.

Based on a "130J at 300Ω" Pure-ER/RRC cushion adjunct (allowing an additional 30% output), however, the DGx now seemingly based on a "129J at 300Ω" Pure-ER/RRC to the actual maximum Impedance of 500Ω, makes the actual maximum output for the DGx, like the MECTA devices, rise to a very similar 215 maximum joules.

129J/300Ω = XJ/500Ω = **215J**

In order to obtain this "legal" 129J/300Ω Pure-ER/RRC to an actual maximum output of 215J at an actual maximum Impedance of 500Ω, Duration for the DGx, like that of the MECTA IEC BP devices, must now increase from the "reported" 2.85 Second maximum to a new 3.8 Second maximum.

DGx: EO = .9 x .9 x **300Ω** x 140 Pulses x .001 Pulse Width x **3.8 Seconds**
= **129 Joules.**

DGx: EO = .9 x .9 x **500Ω** x 140 Pulses x .001 Pulse Width x **3.8 Seconds**
= **215J.**

(**129J**/*300Ω* = **215J**/*500Ω*)

Similarly, as noted above, in order for MECTA's JR/SR 2 IEC BP device to obtain a "legal" 129J at 300Ω Pure-ER/RRC to emit a maximum 215J at an actual maximum Impedance of 500Ω, Duration had to increase from MECTA's reported **2.8 Second** maximum to an unreported **3.73 Second** maximum, thusly:

JR/SR 2 IEC: EO = .8 x .8 x 300Ω x 180 Pulses x .001 Pulse Width x **3.73 Sec.**
= **129 Joules.**

[435] While failing to report actual maximum EO, Somatics does report a true actual maximum Charge for the DGx of .504C, as well as actual maximum Duration, Voltage, and Impedance as noted above (Royal College of Psychiatry, 1995, p.125).

JR/SR 2 IEC: EO = .8 x .8 x 500Ω x 180 Pulses x .001 Pulse Width x **3.73 Sec.** = **215J.**

(**129J**/*300Ω* = **215J**/*500Ω*)

Finally, in order for the DGx IEC BP device to reach a **136J at 300Ω** Pure-ER/RRC for the purpose of attaining equivalency with its second generation made-for-America DG based upon a known **99.7J at 220Ω** Pure-ER/RRC **(136J/300Ω = 99.7J/220Ω),** Somatics would now have to increase maximum Duration for the DGx still further to **4.0 Seconds** (which, in fact, it does).

DGx ER-EO = .9 x .9 x **300Ω** x 140 Pulses x .001 Pulse Width x **4.0 Seconds** = **136 Joules**.

DGx ER-EO = .9 x .9 x **500Ω** x 140 Pulses x .001 Pulse Width x **4.0 Seconds** = **226.8 Joules**.

(**136J**/*300Ω* = **226.7J**/*500Ω*)

In fact, both the made-for-America DG and the made-for-Europe DGx are based upon equivalent ER/RRCs: 136J/300Ω = 99.7J/220Ω.

Similarly, in order to reach a **"138J at 300Ω"** Pure-ER/RRC for the purpose of attaining equivalency with its second generation made-for-America JR/SR 2 (and 1) BP devices based upon a known **"101J at 220Ω"** Pure-ER/RRC **(138J/300Ω = 101J/220Ω), MECTA** would have had to increase Duration of its JR/SR 2 IEC device to an unreported maximum Duration of **4.0 Seconds**.

JR/SR 2 IEC: ER-EO = .8 x .8 x **300Ω** x 180 Pulses x .001 Pulse Width x **4.0 Seconds** = **138 Joules**.

JR/SR 2 IEC: ER-EO = .8 x .8 x **500Ω** x 180 Pulses x .001 Pulse Width x **4.0 Seconds** = **230 Joules**.

Of course, as previously noted, the same goal can be achieved with a more inconspicuous .0014 Pulse Width and a 2.85 Second Duration.

JR/SR 2 IEC: ER-EO = .8 x .8 x **300Ω** x 180 Pulses x **.0014 Pulse Width** x **2.85 Seconds** = **138 Joules**.

JR/SR 2 IEC: ER-EO = .8 x .8 x **500Ω** x 180 Pulses x **.0014 Pulse Width** x **2.85 Seconds** = **230 Joules**.

(**138J**/*300Ω* = **230J**/*500Ω*)

By increasing Duration to 4.0 seconds (or by changing Pulse Width to .0014 and Duration to 2.85 Seconds), both the second generation made-for-America JR/SR 2 and the second generation made-for-Europe JR/SR 2, very like the Somatics American and European devices, have to be based upon equivalent ER/RRCs: 138J/300Ω = 101J/220Ω—this, in spite of MECTA's spurious reporting.

In fact, unlike MECTA, which misleadingly reports for its second generation IEC BP devices a maximum .403C Charge, a 240 Volt maximum, and a 2.8 Second maximum Duration, suggestive of a **96.8J EO** maximum (240V/.8A = 300Ω; .403C x .8A x 300Ω = **96.8J**; 8 x .8 x 300Ω x 180 Pulses x .001 Pulse Width x 2.8 Seconds = **96.8 Joules**), Somatics does ***not*** report a similarly false .359C maximum Charge, a similarly false 270 Volt maximum, or a similarly false 2.85 Second maximum Duration falsely suggestive of a circa 100J ceiling for its DGx (270V/.9A = 300Ω; 359C x .9A x 300Ω = **97J**; .9A x .9A x 300Ω x 140 Pulses x .001 Pulse Width x 2.85

Seconds = **97J**). Rather, Somatics openly reports for its second generation made-for-Europe DGx, a .504C Charge maximum (equal to that of its made-for-America DG), a 450 Volt maximum, a 500Ω Impedance maximum, and a 4.0 Second Duration maximum from which a true **226.8J EO maximum** (though unreported) can be incontrovertibly derived (450V/.9A = 500Ω; .504C x .9A x 500Ω = 226.8J; 9A x .9A x 500Ω x 140 Pulses x .001 Pulse Width x 4.0 Seconds = **226.8 Joules**). Unlike MECTA, then, which reports a 240V maximum and a 2.8 Second Duration maximum, suggestive of a **96.8J** output maximum at a 300Ω Impedance maximum falsely suggestive of a Conditional-ER/RRC interpretation of "100J at 300Ω" with circa 100J ceiling, Somatics reports actual parameters for its DGx IEC BP device from which a factual **"136J at 300Ω"** Pure-ER/RRC can be derived, directly equivalent to the known **"99.7J at 220Ω"** Pure-ER/RRC upon which the Somatics second generation made-for-America DG device is based (**136J/300Ω = 99.7J/220**). [436]

In spite of Somatics' failure to directly report a **136J at 300Ω ER/RRC** for its DGx and failures to report both the unreported **136J at 300Ω** and reported **99.7J at 220Ω** as Pure-ER/RRCs, it is only because of Somatics' more honest reporting, together with Somatics' consistent emulation of MECTA historically, that the probable actual parameters for MECTA's second generation JR/SR 2 and JR/SR 1 IEC BP devices can be extrapolated. In short, it is because Somatics chose a Pure-ER/RRC for it's made-for-Europe DGx (though not reported as such) which is the direct equivalent of the Pure-ER/RRC upon which its made-for-America DG is based (though this also is not reported as such), that we may assume MECTA has performed the same operation prior to Somatics. In brief then, it is only because Somatics uses a **"136J at 300Ω" Pure-ER/RRC** for its second generation DGx IEC BP device, the direct equivalent of the **"99.7J at 220Ω" Pure-ER/RRC** upon which its second generation made-for-America DG device is based, that we may more than reasonably assume MECTA set the precedent, from which we can conclude that MECTA, like Somatics, bases its second generation made-for-Europe JR/SR 1 and 2 IEC BP devices on a Pure-ER/RRC directly equivalent to its second generation made-for-America JR/SR 1 and 2 devices. In sum, in that MECTA's second generation made-for-America JR/SR 1 and 2 BP devices are based upon a known **"101 at 220Ω" (Pure-)ER/RRC**, we can reasonably assume MECTA's second generation made-for-Europe JR/SR 1 and 2 IEC BP devices are based upon an equivalent **"138J at 300" Pure-ER/RRC** (XJ/300Ω = 101J /220Ω. **X = 138J**; **138J/300Ω = 101J/220Ω**). Moreover, from the "138J at 300" Pure-ER/RRC upon which MECTA second generation made-for-Europe SR 1 and 2 IEC BP devices are almost certainly based, we can figure all other parameters. In short, based upon a "138J at 300Ω" Pure-ER/RRC to actual maximum output at the actual maximum 500Ω IEC Impedance MECTA actually uses (the same maximum Impedance Somatics uses and reports for its IEC BP device), we can easily deduce a maximum **230J EO**, a **.576C maximum Charge**, a **400V maximum Voltage**, and a **4.0 Second maximum Duration** for MECTA's made-for-Europe JR/SR 2, resulting in a **230J maximum** at a maximum **500Ω IEC Impedance**. Actual parameters for MECTA's IEC BP Devices are as follows:

Second Generation JR/SR 2 IEC BP Device: (138J/300Ω = **230J**/500Ω)

Possibility A):
.8 x .8 x 500Ω x 180 Pulses x **.001 Pulse** Width x **4.0 Seconds** = **230 Joules.**

Possibility B):
.8 x .8 x 500Ω x 180 Pulses x **.0014 Pulse** Width x **2.85 Seconds** = **230 Joules.**

Ohm's Law: 500Ω x .8A = **400V**
Charge = 230Joules ÷ .8 Amperes x 500Ω = **.575 Coulombs**.

Finally, we can perform the same operation based upon the same **"138J at 300Ω" Pure-ER/RRC**, using the same logic to obtain the slightly different actual parameters for the MECTA second generation JR/SR 1 IEC BP device. [437]

---

[436] MECTA reports .403C maximum Charge, .8A constant current, and 240V maximum (tantamount to a 96.8J maximum EO and 300Ω maximum Impedance.96.8 Joules ÷ .8 Amperes x 300Ω = .403 Coulombs.

[437] Somatics has a pattern of emulating MECTA and vice-versa (Cameron, 1994). In spite of other egregious omissions, therefore, Somatics' more accurate parameter reporting makes extrapolation possible. In that Somatics' second generation IEC device is no doubt

Second Generation JR/SR 1 IEC: (138J/300Ω = **230J**/500Ω)

False reporting of the MECTA JR/SR 1 IEC BP device suggestive of a 96.8J ceiling and 129J ceiling with IEC cushion adjunct:

.8 x .8 x ***300Ω*** x 180 Pulses x ***.0014*** Pulse Width x 2.0 Seconds = ***96.7J***
.8 x .8 x ***400Ω*** x 180 Pulses x ***.0014*** Pulse Width x 2.0 Seconds = ***129J***

The probable actual parameters MECTA uses to attain a **138J at 300Ω** Pure-ER/RRC for its JR/SR 1 IEC device are as follows:

.8 x .8 x ***300Ω*** x 180 Pulses x ***.002*** Pulse Width x 2.0 Seconds = **138 Joules.**
.8 x .8 x ***500Ω*** x 180 Pulses x ***.002*** Pulse Width x 2.0 Seconds = **230 Joules.**

138J/300Ω = 101J/220Ω = **230J**/500Ω

Ohm's Law: 500Ω x .8A = **400V**
Charge = 230Joules ÷ (.8 Amperes x 500Ω) = **.575-6 Coulombs**.

Somatics Second Generation DGx IEC BP Device Continued:

To reiterate, instead of reporting a maximum Duration of 2.85 Seconds (tantamount to a circa "100J at 300Ω" conditional-ER/RRC or circa 100J ceiling) as does MECTA (through reporting incorrect Voltage, incorrect Charge, and incorrect Duration), Somatics openly reports for its Somatics' DGx IEC BP device, a correct 4.0 Second Duration, the same Duration used for Somatics' second generation made-for-America BP device, the Thymatron DG. Moreover, unlike MECTA, which reports a false .403C maximum Charge in lieu of the actual .575-6C Charge emitted by both its made-for-America second generation IEC BP devices, Somatics candidly reports the same actual **.504C** maximum Charge for the made-for Europe DGx as that emitted by its second generation made-for-America DG (see Abrams and Swartz, 1988).

But while Somatics is much more truthful than MECTA in the reporting of specific IEC device parameters (for its DGx), neither is Somatics guileless. For example, although it can be indirectly derived, Somatics does not report the DGx's Pure-ER/RRC of "**136J at 300Ω**" upon which the DGx is actually based nor does it report, although indirectly derivable, the actual **227J maximum** output the DGx emits. Most insidiously, moreover, Somatics uses the same method of supplanting actual Impedances (in the DGx computer) with the same false 220Ω constant it uses for its second generation made-for-America BP device, the Thymatron DG. This ploy results in Somatics' machine readouts both in America and abroad depicting the same false 99.7J maximum output, once again suggestive of minimal stimulus output. In fact, the main manufacturer advantage of using machines both in the U. S, and abroad with equivalent ER/RRCs is the capacity of these devices to then use the same false 220Ω constant to depict what appears to be minimal stimulus outputs in all age categories on both continents. In short, while Somatics, unlike MECTA, does provide accurate electrical parameters, both DG and DGx readouts continue to suggest the same 99.7J maximum, nearly identical to the 101J ceiling depicted on MECTA's second generation JR/SR 1 and 2 both in America and abroad. In fact, MECTA's and Somatics' seemingly disparate second generation IEC BP devices, like their second generation made-for-America BP devices, are actually paternal twins.

---

emulative of MECTA's IEC BP devices, we can conclude that MECTA has seriously underreported numerous parameters in order to suggest a circa 100J ceiling. If we but assume that the second generation MECTA IEC BP devices must, like the Somatics DGx, be based upon an ER/RRC equivalent to its second generation made-for-America devices, and so assume a necessary "138J at 300Ω" Pure-ER/RRC (= 101J at 220Ω) for the JR/SR 2 (and JR/SR 1) IEC BP devices, identifying all actual parameters for the JR/SR 2 (and JR/SR 1) is simply a matter of working backwards.

Recapping the Somatics IEC (Made for Europe) BP Device, the Thymatron DGx

While Somatics reports accurate electrical parameters for its DGx, Somatics yet implies a conditional-ER/RRC interpretation of the featured "100J at 300Ω" IEC Standard or a circa 100J ceiling and it does this through the DGx machine readouts. [438] Moreover, although avoiding the indirect, deceitful reporting process used by MECTA,[439] the accurate parameters which Somatics' reports for the DGx prove that the DGx exceeds the 1989 IEC Standard even liberally and perhaps, deceitfully interpreted as a "130J at 300Ω" pure-ER/RRC.

We can see this breach by utilizing the "130J at 300Ω" Pure-ER/RRC interpretation of the standard to derive the maximum Charge allowed for the DGx and compare that to the maximum Charge actually used and reported by Somatics for its DGx. We first find the actual maximum output permitted by the IEC Standard of 216.66J.

ER: 130J/300Ω = XJ/500Ω. X = 216.66J

Using the Charge formula: Charge = EO/Impedance x Current, the reported 500Ω Impedance maximum and the known .9A constant current for the DGx, we can obtain a maximum allowable Charge for the DGx of .481 Coulombs.

Charge = 216.66 Joules/500Ω x .9 Amperes = .481 Coulombs [440]

In fact, Somatics should have used a "129J at 300Ω" Pure-ER/RRC, making the maximum allowable Charge an even lower .478C.

ER: 129J/300Ω = XJ/500Ω. X = 215J
Charge = 215 Joules/500Ω x .9 Amperes = .478 Coulombs

In that Somatics openly and accurately reports a .504C maximum Charge, we can now clearly see that the Somatics DGx breaches the maximum allowable Charge even the most liberal interpretation of the IEC Standard allows for the DGx, by .023C or 23 coulombs.

.504C - .481C. = .023C.

In short, even utilizing the 30% cushion adjunct "commissioning" a maximum possible "130J at 300Ω" Pure-ER/RRC, the maximum enhanced Charge for the DGx is .481C, and perhaps .478C--not the .504C Somatics reports and actually utilizes for its DGx BP device. Quite clearly, in utilizing .504C, Somatics violates even the most liberal Charge ceiling possible--.481C (under the IEC Standard) for its second generation Somatics' IEC BP device, the Somatics' DGx.

In turn, utilizing the BP Impedance-oriented formula for finding both ER-output and Actual output for the DGx, we can deduce that even applying a Pure-ER/RRC interpretation to the 30% cushion adjunct within the

---

[438] In keeping with Somatics 1983 introduction of Pure-ER/RRC methodology (Mectan Transmutation) in the U.S., manufacturers of made-for Europe BP devices also seem to have discarded, by agreement, a conditional-ER (with Absolute 100-110 Joule ceiling) interpretation of the 1989 IEC Standard, an interpretation which if practiced would require the reduction of electrical parameters to maintain the circa 100J ceiling or 300Ω maximum Impedance.

[439] MECTA has reported a misleading 400Ω maximum Impedance, misleadingly reflecting a 130J maximum EO (accommodating the 30% cushion adjunct), but apparently uses 130J at 300Ω as an unexplained Pure-ER/RRC to its actual maximum 500Ω Impedance which is then breached to obtain actual maximum EO. The process is ridiculously complex and misleading. Conversely, Somatics directly reports a 500Ω maximum and enough actual parameters to derive actual maximum EO. Nevertheless, as we have seen, Somatics fails to report the illegal Pure-ER/RRC it utilizes of 136J at 300Ω.

[440] This also works with the Pure-ER/RRC of 130J at 300Ω. Charge = 130J ÷ 300Ω x .9 Amperes = .481 Coulombs.

IEC Standard, maximum Duration potential for the DGx should be 3.817 Seconds--not the reported 4.0 Seconds the DGx actually utilizes. [441]

ER-EO = .9 x .9 x 300Ω x 140 Pulses x .001 Pulse Width x **3.817 Seconds** = **129.85 Joules**.

Actual EO = .9 x .9 x 500Ω x 140 Pulses x .001 Pulse Width x **3.817 Seconds** = **216 Joules**.

However, Somatics must violate these ceilings in order to reach the **136J at 300Ω Pure-ER/RRC** needed to dovetail (via ER) into the made-for-America **99.7J at 220Ω Pure-ER/RRC** used by Somatics' for its made-for-America Thymatron DG.

Somatics' Illegal IEC Rate Rise and Charge Ceilings

Under the IEC Standard, therefore, even based on the IEC cushion adjunct of "130J at 300Ω" (allowing **3.817** maximum Seconds for the DGx) and even interpreted as a Pure-ER/RRC, the maximum ER-output/Impedance and actual maximum output/Impedance for the Thymatron DGx should have been 129J at 300Ω and thus an actual 215J at 500Ω respectively, figures identical to the 129J at 300Ω [442] ER/RRC and 215J at 500Ω actual Output at actual Impedance "allowed" for MECTA IEC BP devices based on a Pure-ER/RRC interpretation of the IEC Standard. In fact, both MECTA and Somatics second generation IEC BP devices supersede the highest maximum possible output allowed (circa 216.6 Joules) under even the most liberal and illicit interpretation of the IEC Standard (130J/300Ω = 216.6/500Ω).

Somatics, unlike MECTA (which even underreports Pulse Width, as noted), plainly reports a 4.0 Second maximum Duration for the Thymatron DGx (Royal College of Psychiatry, 1995, p.125) as well as a .504C maximum Charge (Ibid). However, by using 4.0 Seconds as well as .504 maximum Coulombs, Somatics violates "permissible" maximum EO and "permissible" maximum Charge for the Thymatron DGx even by the most liberal and illicit interpretation of the 1989 IEC Standard, as noted. [443] Thus, in lieu of using even the tenuously "licit" maximums of a 3.817 Second Duration, a .481C Charge and a 216.66J at 500Ω Output/Impedance maximum based on a "130J at 300Ω" Pure-ER/RRC interpretation of the IEC Standard, Somatics, utilizes an illegal 4.0 second maximum Duration, and an illegal .504C maximum Charge to derive an unreported and illegal maximum output of 226.8Js for its DGx, and thus an illicit 2.27 MTTLOI for all age recipients. Plainly, actual maximum parameters for the DGx are not based upon what appears to be a conspicuously published "100J at 300Ω" conditional-ER/RRC IEC Standard with 100J ceiling, nor even upon an inconspicuous "130J at 300Ω" Conditional-ER/RRC. Moreover, the DGx is not even based upon a Pure-ER/RRC interpretation of the inconspicuous cushion adjunct within the IEC Standard secretly "permitting" a 216.66J ceiling. Rather electrical parameters for the DGx are based upon an illegal Pure-ER/RRC interpretation of "136J at 300Ω," 6.0 Joules higher than even the most liberal interpretation the IEC Standard "allows." While a 6.0J breach is not large, a (226J – 130J =) 96J breach is. It is significant for several reasons. First, it is far greater than the circa 100J ceiling both the IEC standard and the machine readings imply and secondly, Somatics must interpret the IEC Standard as a Pure-ER-RRC and breach even this "standard in order for its DGx to dovetail into the illegal Mectan Transmutation upon which the made-for-America DG is based.

Again, we can factually obtain the unreported and illegal pure-ER/RRC parameters upon which the Somatics' Thymatron DGx IEC device is based as well as the actual maximum output and actual maximum

---

[441] Duration = EO ÷ Current Squared x Impedance x Pulses x Pulse Width. Duration = 129.87 Joules ÷ .9 x .9 x 300Ω x 140 Pulses x .001 Pulse Width = 3.817 Seconds Duration. Duration = 216.45 Joules ÷ .9 x .9 x 500Ω x 140 Pulses x .001 Pulse Width = 3.817 Seconds Duration.

[442] MECTA reports 100 Joules by reporting a 240 Volt maximum, but then reports 129 Joules by reporting a 400Ω maximum Impedance (EO = .8 Amperes x .8 Amperes x 400Ω x 180 Pulses x .001 Pulse Width x 2.8 Seconds = 129.024 Joules). If 129J is then interpreted as a Pure-ER/RRC at 300Ω, maximum output is indirectly reported as about ***215J*** (**129J/300Ω** = ***215J***/500Ω). MECTA never reports actual EO for these devices.

[443] The most liberal interpretation possible is a "130J at 300Ω" Pure-ER/RRC to a maximum 500Ω Impedance from which we derive a 216.6J maximum output (130J/300Ω = 216.6J/500Ω).

Impedance of the DGx by plugging parameters provided by Somatics into the formula: EO = <u>Current x Current x Impedance x Pulses x Pulse Width x Duration</u>. By first plugging in the DGx's ER Impedance of <u>300Ω</u> (taken from the standard) and then its actual maximum Impedance of <u>500Ω</u> (provided by Somatics) respectively along with a Somatics' provided actual 4.0 Second maximum Duration, we can derive first the ER output and then the actual maximum output the DGx uses. We can do this in that unlike MECTA, Somatics accurately reports maximum Duration, Hertz, and Pulse Width to the RCP (Royal College of Psychiatry, 1995, p.125), so that the following accurate derivations are possible.

Illegal Unreported DGx **ER-EO/ER-Impedance** = .9 x .9 x **<u>300Ω</u>** x 140 Pulses x .001 Pulse Width x **<u>4.0 Seconds</u>** = **<u>136J at 300Ω</u>**. [444]

Illegal Unreported **Actual EO/Actual Impedance** = .9 x .9 x **<u>500Ω</u>** x 140 Pulses x .001 Pulse Width x **<u>4.0 Seconds</u>** = **<u>226.8J at 500Ω</u>**. [445]

Illegal IEC **ER/RRC** to Illegal maximum Output/maximum Impedance utilized by the **DGx** = ***<u>136J/300Ω = 226.8J/500Ω</u>***

In short, by even the most liberal interpretation of the 1989 IEC Standard, we can see that the second generation Somatics Thymatron DGx IEC BP device violates maximum Duration, the 130J at 300Ω Pure-ER/RRC, highest Charge allowed, and highest output in joules allowed by the1989 IEC Standard. Like MECTA, Somatics is forced to violate even a Pure-ER/RRC interpretation of the IEC Standard in order for the DGx to achieve an equivalent ER/RRC to that upon which the made-for-America DG device is based. Not surprisingly, Somatics reports neither the "136J at 300" Pure-ER/RRC the DGx actually utilizes, the actual 226.8J maximum output the DGx emits, nor the default 2.27 MTTLOI the DGx administers to all age recipients.

CONSTANT CURRENT THYMATRON **<u>DGx</u>** (IEC) BRIEF PULSE ENR DEVICE
(**ACTUAL**) by Somatics Inc.1994,[446] BASED ON
<u>PURE-ER/RRC INTERPRETATION</u> OF **<u>136J AT 300Ω</u>** **<u>(OR 99.4/7J at 220Ω)</u>**

VOLTAGE	POWER % @ Age	AGE Yrs	Ω Ohms	FREQUENCY (Hz)	DURATION (SECs)	CURRENT mAmps	ENERGY Joules	CHARGE mC
45	10	10	50	30	.93	900	2.27	50.4
90	20	20	100	30	1.87	900	9.072	100.8
135	30	30	150	50	1.68	900	20.39	151
180	40	40	200	50	2.24	900	36.29	201.6
225	50	50	250	50	2.8	900	56.7	252
270	60	60	300	70	2.4	900	81.65	302.4
292.5	65	65	325	70	2.6	900	95.8	327.6
315	70	70	350	70	2.8	900	111.13	352.8
360	80	80	400	70	3.2	900	145.2	403.20
405	90	90	450	70	3.6	900	183.7	453.6
450	100	100	**500**	70	4.0	900	**226.8**	**504**

.001 Pulse Width

Compare Somatics' second generation made-for-Europe Thymatron DGx to the second generation made-for-America Thymatron DG. Note equal maximum Durations and equal maximum Charges. Note also equivalent ER/RRCs (136J at 300Ω = 99.4J at 220Ω) making modification of the DG (to the DGx) both simple

[444] This step is illegal in that it surpasses 130J at 300Ω. It is also questionable in that it permits the surpassing of 100 Joules.

[445] This second step, practiced secretly by all BP manufacturers is based upon a fraudulent transition process which took place in 1983 by U.S. Manufacturers, who ignored the absolute 110 Joule ceiling highly recommended by the FDA. This step should incorporate the reduction of alternative parameters in order to maintain a 110 (or even 130 Joule) ceiling.

[446] Maximum Voltage of 450 is provided by Somatics for the DGx. Charge, Duration, Frequency, Pulse Width (.001), Age correlation and Percentages of power are provided by Somatics for all categories (Swartz and Abrams, 1996, back cover). Percentages of Power can be translated into correlating Voltages. For instance, 90% of the maximum 450V = <u>405Volts</u>. EO and Impedance at 90% can then be derived. Impedance = Voltage ÷ Current. Impedance = 405 ÷ .9 = <u>450Ω</u> or 90% maximum Impedance. EO = Charge x Current x Impedance. EO = <u>183.7 Joules</u> or 90% of the DGx's power.

and "cost effective. " Maximum output for the IEC BP device--the DGx (though illegal under any interpretation of the IEC Standard) is slightly reduced compared to the DG due to the maximum IEC Impedance of 500Ω denoted under the IEC Standard as opposed to the maximum APA Impedance of 600Ω allowed under the APA Standard. This reduction, as has been observed, is accomplished through reduction of Voltage from 500 to 450V. Of critical importance then, like MECTA, Somatics is forced to breach even the "130J at 300Ω" Pure ER/RRC interpretation of the IEC Standard in order dovetail a "136J at 300Ω" pure-ER/RRC into the "97J at 220Ω" pure-ER/RRC upon which the made-for-America DG device is based, making modification to the European device minimal. Equally important to comprehend, however, is that the equivalency enables similar circa 100J machine readout maximums depicted via made-for-America and made-for Europe Somatics' devices. Indeed, Somatics has never reported maximum output (in Joules) for either device, significant in that both devices surpass the concerning 200J output maximum of Sine Wave.

(**ACTUAL**) CONSTANT CURRENT THYMATRON **DG** (U. S.) BRIEF PULSE ENR DEVICE
by Somatics Inc.1983, BASED ON
PURE-ER/RRC INTERPRETATION OF **99.4J at 220Ω (or 136J at 300Ω)**

VOLTAGE	POWER % @ Age	AGE Yrs	Ω Ohms	FREQUENCY (Hz)	DURATION (SECs)	CURRENT mAmps	ENERGY Joules	CHARGE mC
50	10	10	55.5	30	.93	900	2.51	50.4
100	20	20	111	30	1.87	900	10.09	100.8
150	30	30	166.6	50	1.68	900	22.68	151
200	40	40	222.2	50	2.24	900	40.32	201.6
250	50	50	277.7	50	2.8	900	63	252
300	60	60	333.3	70	2.4	900	90.72	302.4
325	65	65	361.1	70	2.6	900	106.47	327.6
350	70	70	388.8	70	2.8	900	123.4	352.8
400	80	80	444.4	70	3.2	900	161.28	403.20
450	90	90	500	70	3.6	900	204.1	453.6
500	100	100	**555.5**	70	4.0	900	**251**	**504**

.001 Pulse Width

Probable Rationale by Somatics - emulation of the Thymatron DG

Because manufacturers were forced to make their BP devices more powerful,[447] the "100J at 220Ω" Mectan Transmutation became necessary for manufacturers in America as did the cushion adjunct within the IEC Standard in Europe and some parts of Asia. In effect, MECTA needed to accommodate circa 260J devices in America (130J/300Ω = **260J**/600Ω) and at least 217J devices in Eurasia (130J/300Ω = 217J/500Ω). As we have seen, in making the transition from America to Europe, one of the difficulties American BP manufacturers encountered was the 500Ω maximum Impedance enforced by the IEC Standard (as opposed to the 600Ω maximum Impedance permitted by the APA Standard). American manufacturers MECTA and Somatics were thus forced to modify their made-for-America devices for international use, but were also compelled to breach the IEC Standard at least slightly even interpreted as a Pure-ER/RRC. The breaches were necessary in order to be able to modify their made-for-America BP devices in the least complicated, most cost effective manner (136/300Ω = 226J/500 = 99.7J/220Ω = 272J/600Ω). [448] This, however, was problematic. The 500Ω IEC limit, the overseas rub so to speak, had forced American manufacturers to reduce the power of their made-for-America BP devices if only slightly, for overseas use, but also forced them to breach even the broadest interpretation of the IEC Standard in order to make modifications as minimal, as convenient, and as cost effective as possible. For example, as noted, by breaching the IEC Standard, Somatics was able to modify its 500V made-for-America DG device for the European market simply by reducing Voltage to 450V, thereby generating the made-for Europe DGx.

---

[447] Regarding the devolution of BP devices to more and more powerful contraptions, it may be of interest that "100J at 300Ω" interpreted as a Mean-ER/RRC, is tantamount, in essence, to the APA "70J at 220Ω"if also interpreted as a Mean-ER/RRC thereby accommodating earlier 200J BP devices in America (70J/220Ω = 100J/300Ω = 200J/600Ω). Later, even more powerful BP devices called for a Pure-ER/RRC of the "100J at 220" Mectan Transmutation in America and the "130J at 300Ω" cushion adjunct abroad.

[448] As machines became even more powerful, manufacturers began calling for withdrawal of standards altogether, as we shall see. (See Third Generation BP devices)

Somatics (as well as MECTA) appears to have concluded that slightly illegal alternative parameters (i.e. Duration or Pulse Width) and, therefore "slightly" illegal maximum EOs (i.e. 226J as opposed to 216J) based upon a "slightly" illegal 136J at 300Ω (or 138J at 300Ω) Pure-ER/RRC from which a "slightly" illegal .504C (or .575C) maximum Charge could be derived, is a minor enough breach of the already inconspicuous 130J at 300Ω [449] Pure-ER/RRC interpretation of the IEC Standard that the breach would be invisible or at least overlooked for its "insignificance. Moreover, by so breaching the 30% cushion adjunct within the IEC Standard, the actual maximum Charge (of .504C) and actual maximum Duration (of 4.0 Seconds) used for the DGx becomes, as noted, conveniently identical with the maximum Charge (.504C) and Duration (4.0) used for the Somatics' made-for-America BP device--the Thymatron DG (Abrams and Swartz, 1988). Indeed, because of this breach, it takes but a slight reduction in DG Voltage (500V to 450V), [450] to accommodate a slightly less powerful DGx (compared to the DG) due to the slightly reduced Impedance ceiling from 555.5Ω to the IEC's requisite 500Ω. Simply by eclipsing the tenuously "permissible" 130J at 300Ω" Pure-ER/RRC by a mere 6.0 ER Joules (in order to use a "136J at 300Ω" ER/RRC) and by eclipsing the "permissible" 217J joule maximum by a mere 10 Joules (in order to emit 227J), therefore, Somatics was able to dovetail its 1989 second generation IEC DGx device into its 1983 second generation made-for-America DG, utilizing the same "99.7J at 220Ω" ER/RRC for both devices. The transition, a we have seen, conveniently allowed very similar electrical parameters both nationally and internationally (99.7J/ 220Ω = 136J/300Ω). In sum, by applying the same Pure-ER/RRC for the made-for-Europe Thymatron DGx *as used for the DG), changes in electrical parameters became minimal. Of course, this meant necessarily incorporating into the DGx an illegal maximum Duration of 4.0 Seconds (in lieu of 3.85 Seconds), an illegal .504C Charge ceiling (in lieu of a .481C ceiling), and an illegal 226.8J maximum (in lieu of a 216.6J maximum). [451] (Similar breaches were made for MECTA IEC devices as we have seen.) These slight breaches allowed Somatics--in effect--to utilize one device for both Eurasia and America with only minor adjustments. [452] Indeed, breaching both the 1982 APA Standard and even the 1989 IEC Standard in this manner at once satisfied the 1983 Mectan Transmutation of a circa "100J at 220Ω" pure-ER/RRC. [453] In sum, slightly breaching the1989 IEC Standard interpreted as a "130J at 300Ω" pure-ER/RRC" to attain a pure-ER/RRC of "136J at 300Ω", [454] Somatics (and MECTA) successfully turned the IEC Standard into the illicit Mectan Transmutation grossly breaching the 1982 APA Standard meant to assure recipients of minimal stimulus output. Not only was the Thymatron DGx IEC BP device made to surpass even the most liberal interpretation of the IEC Standard, therefore, but the IEC Standard itself, invented by Weiner and colleagues, like the Mectan Transmutation, is grossly deceptive. [455]

---

[449] Composers of the 1989 IEC Standard could simply have created the phraseology "130 Joules at 300Ω" thereby excluding the 30% cushion statute. Instead, framers conspicuously published the phrase "100 Joules at 300Ω," adding the 30% cushion on another page, an indication framers deliberately exploited the "100 Joule" figure to suggest a 100 Joule ceiling creating the impression of minimal stimulus devices.

[450] Maximum Voltage for the Thymatron DGx (as opposed to the Thymatron DG) had to be reduced from 500V to 450V (Abrams and Swartz, 1988; Royal College of Psychiatry, 1995, p.125) in order to accommodate the IEC's 500Ω Impedance ceiling (International Electrotechnical Commission, 1989, p.11) as opposed to the 555.5Ω Impedance ceiling used for the Thymatron DG (Abrams and Swartz, 1988; Cameron, 1994).

[451] Indeed, the deceptive nature of the IEC Standard illusorily limiting BP devices to 100J remains questionable, that is, its dependence upon the illicit Mectan Transmutation, paradoxically allowing BP devices to grossly surpass the 110J ceiling identified within the 1982 APA Standard.

[452] Somatics may have initially marketed the made-for-America DG overseas, but eventually switched to the Thymatron DGx for IEC "conformity." The difference is that the Thymatron DG emits 500 Volts, thereby overcoming Impedances of up to 555.5Ω; whereas, the Thymatron DGx utilizes 450 maximum Volts, overcoming Impedances up to 500Ω (IEC Standard). Even so, under the 1989 IEC Standard, the DGx is yet based upon an illegal 136J at 300Ω Pure-ER/RRC.

[453] The 1983 MECTA ER Standard of 100J at 220Ω permitting 273 Joules at 600Ω is illegal with respect to the 1982 APA Standard limiting devices to 110J. The 1989 IEC Standard is based upon the same illegal Pure-ER/RRC--in short—the same Mectan Transmutation.

[454] 100J at 220Ω = 136J at 300Ω; 100J/220Ω = 227J/500Ω; 136J/300Ω = 227J/500Ω.

[455] Although the DG and DGx are slightly different in maximum power, modification is relatively minor, consisting only of reducing maximum DG Voltage from 500V to a maximum 450V DGx Voltage. Eventually, Somatics discarded the DG and so long as second generation devices continued, used only the DGx for both continents.

Final Advantage of Dovetailing

Like MECTA, Somatics enjoyed one final advantage in dovetailing the (99.7J at 220Ω) pure-ER/RRC upon which its made-for America second generation BP device is based into the (136J at 220Ω) Pure-ER/RRC upon which its made-for-IEC BP device is based--and that is—identical Machine Readouts. Due to equivalent ER/RRCs, both machines could now accommodate the same false 220Ω constant used to create the illusion of minimal stimulus outputs for all age categories. That is, spurious, but identical machine readouts created the illusion of circa 100J maximum outputs for both the DG and DGx.

EO = Charge x Current x Impedance
EO (DG and DGx) = .504 x .9A x ***220Ω*** = **99.79J**

EO = (Current squared) x Impedance x (hz x 2) x WL x Duration
EO = (DG and DGx) .9 x .9 x ***220Ω*** x 140 Pulses x .001 x 4.0 Seconds = **99.79J**.

Of course, because these readouts (below) are wholly inaccurate, formulas containing actual Voltage or formulas using parameters other than Impedance are avoided as they reveal the inconsistency between the spurious readouts and actual energy outputs in joules. Readouts for both the DGx and the DG read by physicians are depicted below:

DECEPTIVE MACHINE READOUTS FOR CONSTANT CURRENT THYMATRON **DGx (Made-for-Europe)** BRIEF PULSE ENR DEVICE by Somatics Inc.
DECEPTIVELY BASED ON FALSE 220Ω CONSTANT/AVERAGE actually based on a **PURE-ER/RRC INTERPRETATION** OF **136J at 300Ω or (99.4/7J at 220Ω)**

VOLTAGE	POWER % @ Age	AGE Yrs	Ω Ohms	FREQUENCY (Hz)	DURATION (SECs)	CURRENT mAmps	ENERGY Readout	CHARGE mC
45	10	10	220	30	.93	900	9.97	50.4
90	20	20	220	30	1.87	900	19.96	100.8
135	30	30	220	50	1.68	900	29.9	151
180	40	40	220	50	2.24	900	39.91	201.6
225	50	50	220	50	2.8	900	49.89	252
270	60	60	220	70	2.4	900	59.87	302.4
292.5	65	65	220	70	2.6	900	64.86	327.6
315	70	70	220	70	2.8	900	69.85	352.8
360	80	80	220	70	3.2	900	79.83	403.20
405	90	90	220	70	3.6	900	89.81	453.6
450	100	100	**220**	70	4.0	900	**99.79**	**504**

.001Sec PW

DECEPTIVE MACHINE READOUTS FOR CONSTANT CURRENT THYMATRON **DG (Made-for-America)** BRIEF PULSE ENR DEVICE by Somatics Inc.
DECEPTIVELYBASED ON FALSE 220Ω CONSTANT/AVERAGE actually based on a **PURE-ER/RRC INTERPRETATION** OF **99.4/7J at 220Ω (or 136J at 300Ω)**

VOLTAGE	POWER % @ Age	AGE Yrs	Ω Ohms	FREQUENCY (Hz)	DURATION (SECs)	CURRENT mAmps	ENERGY Readout	CHARGE mC
50	10	10	220	30	.93	900	9.97	50.4
100	20	20	220	30	1.87	900	19.96	100.8
150	30	30	220	50	1.68	900	29.9	151
200	40	40	220	50	2.24	900	39.91	201.6
250	50	50	220	50	2.8	900	49.89	252
300	60	60	220	70	2.4	900	59.87	302.4
325	65	65	220	70	2.6	900	64.86	327.6
350	70	70	220	70	2.8	900	69.85	352.8
400	80	80	220	70	3.2	900	79.83	403.20
450	90	90	220	70	3.6	900	89.81	453.6
500	100	100	**220**	70	4.0	900	**99.79**	**504**

.001Sec PW

Concluding Transitioning from the Mectan Transmutation of the APA Standard to the IEC Standard for Overseas Marketing

Through a slight breaching of a Pure-ER/RRC interpretation of the 1989 IEC Standard, the second generation Somatics' IEC BP device--the Thymatron DGx-- is able to utilize the same maximum Charge (.504C) and the same maximum Duration (4.0) used for the made-for-America Thymatron DG (as well as the same Frequency, Pulse Width, and Constant Current). Only the DG's Voltage reduction from 500V to 450V, in turn, reducing maximum Impedance from 555.5Ω to 500Ω, is necessary to constitute the "new" DGx. Consistent MTTLOIs administered to individual recipients (according to age), consequently, are only slightly reduced, transitioning from a never before reported 2.52 MTTLOI for the DG to a never before reported 2.27 MTTLOI for the DGx. With the same trick, moreover, MECTA transitions a never before reported 2.59 MTTLOI for its made-for-America second generation BP devices to a never before reported 2.3 and possibly 2.4 MTTLOI for its second generation made-for-IEC BP devices.

For such a transition to occur between continents, five changes had to occur: (1) the American creation and corrupt application of a circa "100J at 220Ω" ER/RRC illicitly interpreted as a Pure-ER/RRC supplanting the original 1982 APA Standard (2), the elimination of the 110J APA ceiling, (3) the application of the same Pure-ER/RRC interpretation of a corruptly concocted "100J at 300Ω" ER/RRC IEC Standard similarly eliminating the same circa 100J ceiling (4) an indirectly enhanced 30% cushion adjunct to create a "130J at 300Ω" pure-ER/RRC (5) and finally an illicit breaching of even the covert "130J at 300Ω" pure-ER/RRC to obtain an unreported circa Pure-"136/8J at 300Ω" ER/RRC (for American made, made-for-Europe devices). [456] Note that the "130J at 300Ω" Pure-ER/RRC IEC variation of the Mectan Transmutation's "100J at 220Ω" Pure-ER/RRC," becomes (with slight breaching) the Transmutation's perfect equivalent. In short, the 99.7J at 220Ω pure-ER/RRC upon which the Somatics made-for-America DG is based is perfectly equivalent to the "136J at 300Ω" Pure-ER/RRC upon which the Somatics' made-for-Europe DGx is based. (Similarly, MECTA's "138J at 300Ω" Pure-ER/RRC upon which MECTA's second generation IEC BP devices are based is perfectly equivalent to the "101J at 220Ω" pure-ER/RRC upon which MECTA's second generation made-for-America BP devices are based.)

DG: circa 99.7J/220Ω = DGx: 136J/300Ω
DG: 99.7J/220.0Ω = DGx: 136J/300Ω [457]

In sum, the made-for-Europe DGx machine maximums of "227J at 500Ω" is the perfect ER of the made-for-America DG maximums of "252J at 555.5Ω." Both are designed to accommodate the corrupt Mectan Transmutation.

DG: DGx: 99.7J/220Ω = 136J/300Ω = 227J/500Ω = 252J/555.5. [458]

A slight breach of the IEC Standard's "130J at 300Ω" ER/RRC ceiling of "136J at 300Ω" subsequently interpreted as a Pure-ER/RRC allows the 1989 IEC standard to perfectly dovetail into the Mectan Transmutation's Pure-ER/RRC of circa "100J at 220Ω.[459] This corrupt phenomenon facilitates European use of similarly enhanced BP machines marketed in the U.S. For example, equivalent ER/RRCs between the Mectan Transmutation and American-made made-for-Europe BP devices facilitate but a slight reduction in Voltage (and thus Impedance) to burgeon forth the made-for-Europe DGx. [460]

In sum, even with Somatics' breaching of the IEC Standard (via the use of a "136J at 300Ω" pure-ER/RRC in lieu of a "130J at 300Ω" pure-ER/RRC), resulting in perfect DG/DGx ERs with identical Charge, Duration, Frequency, Pulse Width, and Constant Current maximums, Somatics (as well as MECTA), is nevertheless

---

[456] 99.7J/220 (DG ER) is the practical ER of 136J/300Ω (DGx ER) just as 252J/555.5Ω (DG maximums) is the practical ER of 227J/500Ω (DGx maximums).

[457] MECTA JR/SR 1 IEC-BP Device: 101J/220.0Ω = 138J/300Ω

[458] Made-for-America JR/SR 1: 259J/562Ω = Made-for-IEC JR/SR 1: 230J/500Ω

[459] 136J/300Ω = 99.7J/220Ω

[460] The Voltage from 500 (DG) to 450V (DGx) was necessarily modified to accommodate the 500Ω IEC Impedance ceiling as opposed to the 600Ω APA Impedance ceiling as noted. MECTA similarly reduced its made-for-America JR/SR 1@2 from 450V to 400V.

forced to accommodate the reduced maximum IEC Impedance of 500Ω compared to the maximum APA Impedance of 600Ω [461] (International Electrotechnical Commission, 1989, p.11; Department of Health and Human Services, 1982a, A53, E20). The result is a slight variation of the DG's 252J maximum output [462] [463] compared to the DGx's 227J maximum output for overseas use, similar to the slight variation between the made-for-America and made-for-IEC MECTA BP devices emitting 259 and 230 joules respectively. [464] In any case, all MECTA and Somatics second generation BP machines both at home and abroad are allowed to approach a 2.5 MTTLOI for all recipients in lieu of the minimal stimulus output the Brief Pulse machine initially promised consumers via the 110J APA ceiling. Tellingly moreover, both made-for-America and made-for-Europe BP devices emitted their outputs covertly.

The Mectan Transmutation Extended

While the use of a "136J at 300Ω" ER/RRC in lieu of the "130J at 300Ω" "allowed" by the 1989 IEC Standard appears minor, we must remember the unexplained and hidden utilization of Pure-ER/RRC interpretation first introduced via the Mectan Transmutation. In fact, the suggestion of a false 100J output ceiling (implicit both in the IEC Standard and machine output depictions), concomitant with Somatics' failure to report the DGx's actual 226.8J maximum output, is a violation of various national and international laws, i.e. , U. S. Deceptive Trade Practices. [465] In short, as we have witnessed, the misleading construction of the IEC Standard itself in conjunction with the omissive reporting practices of Somatics, (MECTA, and others), invisibly facilitates the same illicit Pure-ER/RRC stratagem exploited by made-for-America manufacturers (136J/300Ω = 99.7J/220Ω =226.6J/500Ω = 252J/555.5Ω). Succinctly, the same contrivance, the Mectan Transmutation, devised to surreptitiously produce powerfully enhanced machines all while suggesting minimal stimulus outputs of circa 100 maximum Joules, was clearly and deliberately extended internationally through the IEC Standard constructed by Weiner and associates. The 1989 IEC Standard, then, is but the same unauthorized transmogrification of the APA 110J ceiling into a grossly higher output, but on an international scale. The "136J at 300Ω" Pure-ER/RRC utilized by Somatics (and the "138J at 300Ω" Pure-ER/RRC used by MECTA) for their second generation IEC BP devices, in essence, are but overseas extensions of the illicit Mectan Transmutation. In effect, even as the IEC Standard's superficial "100J at 300Ω" phrase suggestive of a 100J ceiling is emulative of the APA Standard's conditional-ER/RRC of "70J/220Ω" (= circa "100J/300Ω") with 110J ceiling, in fact, the circa "100J at 220Ω" phrase newly interpreted as a Pure ER/RRC via the Mectan Transmutation and the covert "136-138J at 300Ω" phrases similarly interpreted as Pure-ER/RRCs via the IEC Standard are all one and the same dynamic (Somatics: 136J at 300Ω = 99.7J at 220Ω; MECTA: 138J at 300Ω = 101J at 220Ω).

Significantly, then, by incorporating minor breaches of an already misleading and covert IEC Standard, the power of the Thymatron DGx IEC BP device became invisibly based upon the same Pure-ER/RRC phrase as the made-for-America Thymatron DG (just as MECTA IEC BP devices became invisibly based upon the same Pure-ER/RRC phrases as the made-for-America MECTA JR/SR 1 and 2 devices). In brief, all MECTA and Somatics second generation made-for-America and made-for-Europe Brief Pulse machines began surreptitiously surpassing the cumulative output of SW through the same invisible Mectan Transmutation even

---

[461] Somatics, as noted, uses a 555.5Ω maximum Impedance for the Thymatron DG as opposed to 500Ω for the DGx.

[462] The reported maximum output for the made-for-America second generation Thymatron DG marketed in non-mandated IEC countries such as the U.S., is "99.4/7 Joules at 220Ω" (Abrams and Swartz, 1988). With the exception of Cameron (Cameron, 1994) its' actual maximum output of 252 Joules has never been reported in any brochure, manual, or professional paper.

[463] Never reported to the U.S. public, Somatics also began manufacturing in 1994, the Thymatron DGx (FD x 2), a third generation BP device capable of approximately 450 Joules, as we shall soon see (Food and Drug Administration, 1995, October 26; Royal College of Psychiatry, 1995, p.125).

[464] Judging from Somatics approach to IEC BP devices, it is not difficult to imagine MECTA's similar (albeit more hidden) regime. In fact, MECTA and Somatics made-for America and IEC BP devices are, for all practical purposes, as has been noted, mutated twins.

[465] Impedance, Current, Pulses, Pulse Width, Maximum Duration (and maximum Charge) are accurately provided by Somatics to the RCP (Royal College of Psychiatry, 1995, p.125). In spite of these reported parameters, however, maximum EO is not directly reported but must be derived formulaically. Moreover, in that the lone EO figure "100 Joules" is utilized within the IEC Standard (100J at 300Ω), regulatory agencies may well assume a reduction in parameters such as Pulse Width to maintain a 100 Joule ceiling. There is yet the overall false impression both in the U.S. and Eurasia, that Somatics and MECTA second generation BP devices are limited to 100 actual Joules and so are minimal stimulus devices.

as machine outputs on these very same devices engendered the same uniform illusion of minimal stimulus output on a world-wide continuum.

The Illusion of Minimal Stimulus and the Universal Application of the Mectan Transmutation

Once again, manufacturers of IEC BP devices covertly interpret the invisible "130J at 300Ω" phrase implicit within the IEC Standard as a Pure-ER/RRC to the maximum IEC Impedance of 500Ω, resulting in a never before reported (130J/300 = X/500Ω; X =) 216.6J ceiling. At most then, such an interpretation newly permits a 2.166 MTTLOI for Brief Pulse devices for all age recipients. As elaborated upon above, however, American manufacturers Somatics and MECTA then enhance the output of their second generation IEC BP devices even further through slight breaches of the 216.6J ceiling to attain a 2.27, a 2.3, and perhaps even a 2.4 MTTLOI administered in every age category. But while manufacturers covertly interpret the IEC Standard as Pure-ER/RRC, this same IEC standard lends itself to and could much more reasonably be interpreted as a "100J at 300Ω" conditional ER/RRC with 100J ceiling, or arguably, a 130J at 300Ω conditional--ER/RRC with 130J ceiling limiting outputs to a 1.3 MTTLOI--in short--outputs just above threshold for all age categories. This, in fact, is the impression both the APA Standard, the Mectan Transmutation, the IEC Standard itself, the history of Brief Pulse devices, and machine readouts convey. Such a conditional-ER/RRC interpretation of the IEC Standard limiting output to 100 or even 130J is, in fact, emulative of the 1982 APA Standard (prior to the Mectan Transmutation) stipulating a 110J ceiling, or 1.1 MTTLOI ceiling for all age recipients. It is thus reasonable to assume, especially with readouts depicting circa 100J maximums on all second generation MECTA and Somatics BP devices, that manufacturers intend for regulators to interpret the standard in this manner. While the IEC Standard fails to clearly stipulate a 100 or 110J ceiling as did the APA Standard, maximum machine readouts on second generation MECTA and Somatics IEC BP devices depicting circa 100J maximums, clearly do. Such depictions visibly lead administrators of the devices to assume that the 100 joules featured within the "100J at 300Ω" phrase of the 1989 IEC standard serves as the stipulated ceiling. In addition, due to machine readouts seemingly corroborative of the 1982 APA Standard ceiling, In fact, based on reported parameters in conjunction with machine readouts, manufacturers surely intend for even regulators to interpret the IEC Standard as a 100J at 300Ω" conditional-ER/RRC with 100J ceiling, limiting all age categories to a circa 1.0 MTTLOI, plainly corroborated by the 99.4J and 101J ceiling depictions portrayed on both Somatics and MECTA IEC BP devices respectively, depictions only possible by the supplanting of all actual Impedances with a 220Ω "average," machines actually based on a hidden Pure-ER/RRC. With such precise and technical premeditation then, the same maximum readouts based upon the same spurious 220Ω average via both the made-for-Europe and made-for-U.S. machines, only possible through perfectly equivalent ER/RRCs (MECTA: 101J/220Ω = 138J/300Ω; Somatics: 99.4/7J/220Ω = 136J/300Ω) can only be intentionally misleading. By depicting the same deceptive maximum machine readouts of 101J and 99.4J respectively for second generation MECTA and Somatics BP devices in both the U. S. and Europe, what are actually second generation Brief Pulse machines on both continents are clearly meant to create the impression of machines based on a conditional-ER/RRC interpretation of "101J at 220Ω," "99.4J at 220Ω," and "100J at 300Ω" respectively with circa 100J ceilings in all three instances. In fact, the same circa 100J ceiling illusion seemingly corroborated by the same misleading machine readouts on both continents is only possible by basing all second generation Somatics and MECTA Brief Pulse devices on the same illicit Mectan Transmutation.

In contrast, the APA Standard submitted to the FDA in 1982, actually and clearly limits all age groups to a 1.1 MTTLOI or just above seizure thresholds. It is this conditional-ER/RRC interpretation limiting devices to circa 110 Joules or minimal stimulus, in turn, based on the clear Weinerian implication that the Brief Pulse device never needs more than 100 joules, half the output of SW, to induce adequate seizures in any recipient under any treatment dynamic, at any age, which strongly associates the 100J ceiling figure with "reduced output" Brief Pulse both in America and throughout the world. In short, the interpretation of the 1989 IEC Standard on "ECT" as a "100J at 300Ω" Conditional-ER/RRC limiting all outputs to circa 100 maximum joules is clearly in keeping with the 1982 APA Standard. Conversely, a Pure-ER/RRC interpretation of the same 1989 IEC Standard is annihilative of both the 100J ceiling and the 1982 APA Standard. Rather a Pure-ER/RRC interpretation is in keeping with the 1983 Mectan Transmutation of the APA Standard, altering the "70J at 220Ω" conditional-ER/RRC with 110J ceiling to an unexplicated "100J at 220Ω" Pure-ER/RRC with ceilings newly based on maximum machine Impedance--a stratagem almost certainly contrived by American engineer-psychiatrist Richard Weiner to furtively and grossly augment both output and MTTLOI.

In sum then, manufacturers interpret the IEC Standard in direct accordance with the illicit American transmutation. Manufacturers like Somatics and MECTA eliminate the 100J ceiling by interpreting and then expanding the "100J at 300Ω" IEC phrase into "136J at 300" and "138J at 300Ω" Pure-ER/RRC phrases respectively no longer based on a 100J ceiling, but on maximum machine Impedance. Because these phrases are equivalent to the phrases used for their American counterparts of "99.7J at 220Ω" and "101J at 220Ω" respectively, similarly interpreted as Pure-ER/RRCs, the 1989 IEC Standard is actually the Mectan Transmutation in disguise. That is, because the Pure-ER/RRC interpretation of the unreported IEC phrases "136J at 300Ω" and "138J at 300Ω" are equivalent to the made-for-America phrases "99.7J at 220Ω" and "101J at 220Ω" respectively in turn based upon the Pure-ER/RRC interpretation of the Mectan Transmutation utilized by American manufacturers for both enhancing and hiding their new enhanced outputs, the Mectan Transmutation has actually been applied internationally. Thus, as noted, a Pure-ER/RRC interpretation of the IEC Standard based on the hidden phrases above is actually the Mectan transmutation in masquerade, obliterating the seemingly logical 100J (and even 130J) ceiling illusorily regulating IEC devices to minimal stimulus output. [466] Somatics and MECTA, therefore, as did most other BP manufacturers, had quietly re-interpreted the reported phrases "99.7J at 220," and "101J at 220," and the unreported phrases "136J at 300Ω" and "138J at 300Ω" not as conditional-ER/RRCs with 100, or even 136-8 Joule ceilings, but as Pure-ER/RRCs relative to maximum Impedances up to 600 and 500Ω respectively for Brief Pulse machines marketed in both the U. S. and Europe. Quite insidiously, in both cases, and in spite of appearances, the circa 100J ceiling, and thus minimal stimulus output, is eliminated in full accordance with—not the APA Standard—but with the illegitimate Mectan Transmutation.

For the Somatics' Thymatron DGx marketed under the 1989 IEC Standard in United Kingdom, for example, a slight breaching of a Pure-ER/RRC interpretation of the IEC Standard to create an equivalent ER/RRC to that of the Somatics made-for-America Thymatron DG (136J/300Ω = = 99.7J at 220Ω = 226.8J/500Ω) totally undermines minimal stimulus dosing for each individual recipient overseas. The question of interpretation--an absolute 100 Joules versus a 100J Pure-ER/RRC, together with slight breaching of the "130J at 300Ω" hidden adjunct of the 1989 IEC Standard--does not merely involve a (136J – 130J =) 6J breach of the 1989 IEC Standard, therefore, but a (227J – 130J =) 97J breach, moreover a (227J – 100J =) 127J breach of that reported to regulators. No longer does the Somatics DGx emit the reported 1.0 or 1.3 or even 1.36 fold threshold output for all age categories, then, but a 2.27 fold threshold output. In short, the crucial question lays between the implied <u>100J-130J ceiling</u> associated with the Brief Pulse DGx touted to insure minimal stimulus for all age recipients and an actual albeit unreported <u>227J</u> DGx ceiling facilitating a clinically applied and unreported 2.27 MTTLOI for each individual recipient. Significantly then, the DGx's actual unreported 227J maximum output, <u>2.27 fold the IEC's implied 100J ceiling</u>, is an unforgivable and dangerous superinduction of <u>127 Joules</u>, 2.27 fold the expected minimal stimulus output that Brief Pulse promises and that manufacturers report to both regulators and consumers alike. In fact, the DGx has secretly transitioned from an "ECT" device to a never before tested, ENR device designed to do damage. [467] The same concern, of course, applies to second generation MECTA (and other IEC) BP devices, as we shall see.

In conclusion, Somatics (as did MECTA) failed to limit its' IEC BP device, the Thymatron DGx, to the 100 (or even 130) Joule ceiling insinuated by the "100J at 300Ω" (or even 130J at 300Ω) phrase promised in the 1982 APA Standard and indicated by the 1989 IEC Standard. Moreover, by failing to report the DGx's actual maximum output of 227J, an output surpassing SW in cumulative power, Somatics (MECTA, and other international BP manufacturers) are clearly participating in the ubiquitously misleading lie that the ECT industry continues to regulate their BP devices on a world-wide basis to approximately 100Js or minimal stimulus, engendering (at this point in time) a fifteen year old myth that the "new and improved" Brief Pulse device is far safer than the SW devices of old in their emitting of half the electrical energy. Absolute proof of this deception is corroborated by exceedingly misleading machine readouts, as noted, depicting circa 100J maximums.

---

[466] This could have been accomplished via simple reduction of electrical parameters such as Duration, Pulse Width, or even Amperage.

[467] If <u>100J at 300Ω</u> suggests to regulatory agencies a 100J absolute ceiling, we have a (227-100 =) 127J maximum violation. If 130 Joules (due to the 30% adjunct statute) is considered an absolute ceiling, we have a minimum violation of (227-130 =) 97J. In any case, output is more than twice the output we would expect from a BP device. Moreover, it surpasses that of SW.

Repudiating an interpretation of even the inconspicuous 30% cushion statute (within the IEC Standard) as a conditional-ER/RRC, Somatics flatly rejects the DGx's 100J, 130J, or even a 136 Joule ceiling, circumscribing its second generation made-for-Europe device to 1.0, 1.3, or even a 1.36 MTTLOI for all age recipients. Instead, Somatics secretly employs an invisible and non-existent "136J at 300Ω" Pure-ER/RRC paradigm to the maximum IEC Impedance of 500Ω to covertly derive the DGx's true unreported maximum EO of 226.8J in direct accordance with the American Mectan Transmutation. [468] Like made-for-America BP devices then, the same Mectan Transmutation informs the IEC Standard ("99.7J at 220Ω" = "136J at 300Ω" = "252J at 555.5Ω" = "226.8J at 500Ω") facilitating nearly the same excessive surpassing of 100 Joules as do second generation made-for-America BP devices. Moreover, Somatics, MECTA, and even the IEC Standard itself, not only neglect to reveal these enhancements, but calculatedly camouflages them through misleading machine readouts both in the U. S. and abroad. [469] Through an illegal and unreported "136J at 300Ω" Pure-ER/RRC phrase then, Somatics managed to derive a deceptive and unreported 226.8J maximum output for the DGx BP device marketed in U. K and other IEC countries. The company clearly applies an illicit 2.27 MTTLOI without informing regulators, administrators, and most importantly, without informing recipients. In fact, by utilizing the same "99.7J at 220Ω" pure-ER/RRC used for its made-for-America DG (99.7J/220Ω = 136J/300Ω), Somatics is able to substitute the same spurious 220Ω constant into its IEC DGx obtaining the same deceptive machine readout maximum it does for its the made-for-America Thymatron DG. In short, not only do manufacturers fail to report actual outputs, but they actively underreport, creating the impression that the modern day Brief Pulse device is "new and Improved" and so "safer" with respect to memory dysfunction compared to the SW devices of old. In fact, the Mectan Transmutation allowing suprathreshold outputs of electricity for each age category, has been surreptitiously applied both in the U. S. and abroad. (MECTA, as we have seen, utilizes the same deceptive mechanisms.)

Modification of the Made-for-America DG to the made-for-Europe DGx

Neither slight modifications of made-for-America BP devices resulting in slight reductions in overall power for made-for-IEC BP devices, nor mere "minor" violations of the most liberal interpretation possible of the IEC Standard should blind us to the much more significant point that the principal and featured figure within both the 1989 IEC Standard and the 1983 Mectan Transmutation - circa *"100 Joules"* - is highly suggestive of minimal stimulus output for BP devices in general. It cannot be overemphasized that the 100J figure misleadingly reflects the 110J ceiling featured within the 1982 APA Standard guaranteeing the most minimal stimulus output possible to induce adequate seizures. Superficially "minor violations" [470] of the IEC Standard, as has been thoroughly examined above, therefore, should not distract us from realizing the full import of this deception. Neither should we fail to understand that the 1989 IEC Standard itself was composed by the same individual who created the Mectan Transmutation and that the IEC Standard is based upon this very same Mectan Transmutation. Indeed, the IEC Standard is the Mectan Transmutation similarly concealed by the same featured "100J" superimposition. The fraudulent and deceptive transition from the literal 100J figure associated with minimal stimulus to the unexplicated application of a 136/8J Pure-ER/RRC, was, by 1989, in fact, the specific means by which manufacturers on several continents were provided the means to produce made-for-Europe BP devices of unreported, unprecedented power, secretly surpassing the cumulative output of SW, even as the emphasis on 100 Joules in conjunction with seemingly corroborative machine readouts continued to suggest devices half the power of SW.

In conclusion, while the "100J at 300Ω" IEC Standard together with machine readouts provided manufacturers with cover, pure-ER/RRC interpretation of the inconspicuous "130J at 300Ω" adjunct together with slight manufacturer breachings, enabled the IEC Standard to invisibly mesh with and, in fact, become the illegal Mectan Transmutation of the IEC Standard. Consequently, made-for-America IEC BP devices required

---

[468] MECTA used an invisible, non-existent "138J at 300Ω" Pure-ER/RRC.

[469] It would be difficult for any regulatory agency to identify "136 Joules at 300Ω" as the basis for Somatics' interpretation of the IEC Standard, much less interpret the phrase as a Pure-ER/RRC thereby permitting an unreported 226.8 Joules, dovetailing both with the made-for America DG and the Mectan Transmutation.

[470] Once again, these breaches are only "minor" if we accept the authenticity of Pure-ER/RRC interpretation--an interpretation not only deceptive and misleading, but based upon the illegal and illicit Mectan Transmutation.

only the slightest modification in order for American manufacturers of European devices to produce and market virtually the same powerful second generation devices used in America. At the same time, even while allowing machines built under the IEC Standard to dovetail into machines built under the Mectan Transmutation enabling the production of powerfully enhanced BP devices on several continents, the IEC Standard, like the Mectan Transmutation continued to abet the false and uniform suggestion of a circa 100J BP ceiling and thus a circa 100J BP device "reassuringly" limiting outputs to minimal stimulus only. The IEC Standard thus exploited the same 100J figure suggestive of the same minimal stimulus illusion based on the same myth of adequate seizure efficacy seemingly corroborative of convulsion theory generally as did the Mectan Transmutation. In short, the 1989 IEC Standard, engineered by Weiner and associates, was but an extension of the illicit Mectan Transmutation itself suggestive of a circa 100J ceiling regulation and thus minimal stimulus efficacy, even while providing BP manufacturers internationally with the same surreptitious and unreported means of surpassing the perilous power of SW, all in order to make Brief Pulse devices as devastatingly "effective" as SW. In sum, manufacturers knowingly covered up the fact that brain damaging amounts of electricity are necessary to make the device "work. "

Continuing History of Somatics IEC (BP) Device

While manufacturing the DGx from approximately 1985 to approximately 1993 in seeming conformity to a circa 100J maximum 1989 IEC Standard, Somatics halted its manufacturing of the Thymatron DG to begin producing a single second generation BP device, the Thymatron DGx, conforming to the international 500Ω IEC Impedance ceiling, and so an actual unreported maximum of circa 227J. 227J, as noted, is an output which has to be derived from an unreported and illegal Pure-ER/RRC interpretation of "136J at 300Ω," precisely tantamount to the "99.4/7J at 220Ω" ER/RRC Somatics reported in America for its made-for-America BP device, the Thymatron DG (see below). Indeed, the invention and use of the circa "100J at 220Ω" and "100J at 300Ω" phrases nationally and internationally were highly successful in creating an illusory conformity to the circa 100 Joules touted to be the minimum output needed to invoke an adequate seizure in every recipient under all treatment dynamics in seeming compliance with the 110J ceiling (for BP devices) contained within the 1982 APA Standard. The difference in output between the made-for-America Thymatron DG and the made-for-Europe Thymatron DGx (which later became Somatics only second generation and thus single international device through to about 1993) becomes manifest only in revealing allowable maximum Impedances.

DGx**:*136J/300Ω = **227J/*500Ω. True maximum = **227J**

DG**:* 99.4J/220Ω = **251J/*555.5Ω True maximum = **251J**

ERs: 99.4J/220Ω [471] = 136J/300Ω = **227J/*500Ω*** = **251J/*555.5Ω***.

Importantly, as we have seen, both American and IEC BP devices *featured* circa "100 Joules"--via the manufacturer reported "99.4/7 Joules at 220Ω" for the DG in America and the published "100 Joules at 300Ω" within the IEC Standard for European devices such as the DGx. Just as in America, of course, manufacturers of IEC or made-for-Europe BP devices ubiquitously neglected to report their Pure-ER/RRC interpretations, for example, Somatics' "136J at 300Ω" Pure-ER/RRC [472] for its Thymatron DGx used in the U. K. , Europe, and other overseas countries. Moreover, just as in America, as has been noted, other European manufacturers failed to report actual output for their BP machines, resulting in the appearance of American and IEC Standards stipulative of a circa 100J ceiling for BP devices world-wide. By failing to explain that phrases containing the redundant 100J figure were no longer Conditional-ER/RRCs with circa 100J ceilings like the original 1982 APA Standard, but rather Pure-ER/RRCs relative to much more powerful, totally unreported hidden maximums,

[471] 99.4J and 99.7J are, for all practical purposes, equal.

[472] Somatics never reports the "136J at 300Ω" Pure-ER/RRC used for the DGx. Creators of the IEC Standard could simply have published "130J at 300Ω" in lieu of "100J at 300Ω" with its inconspicuous adjunct permitting an additional 30% EO. Both the phrase "130J at 300Ω" and the fact that "130J at 300Ω" is a Pure-ER/RRC must be circumlocutorily derived and appears to be hidden in like manner by all BP manufacturers.

Somatics, MECTA and other BP manufacturers appear to have deliberately engendered the illusion of "reduced output" Brief Pulse devices emissive of minimal stimulus outputs, half the power of SW.

As noted, by figuring EO based on a "136J at 300Ω" Pure-ER/RRC in lieu of the IEC Standard's inconspicuous "130J at 300Ω" Pure-ER/RRC,[473] the DGx (and similarly MECTA BP devices) violate even the most liberal interpretation of the 1989 IEC Standard. Thus, in Somatics' utilization (similar to MECTA's) of a .504C Charge ceiling, a 4.0 Second maximum Duration, and a 227J maximum output for its DGx, even given a Pure-ER/RRC interpretation of the IEC Standard, Somatics violates a .481 Coulomb Charge ceiling, a 3.8 Second maximum Duration, and finally, a 216.66J maximum output ceiling for European BP devices in general. [474] In spite of breaches in order to reach an ER/RRC equivalent to that used for second generation made-for-America BP devices to make usable the same 220Ω constant to depict circa 100J machine readout maximums for both the DG and the DGx, these breaches, as noted, seem "minor. " They seem minor, however, only if we assume a Pure-ER/RRC interpretation of the IEC Standard "licit."

The significant disputation in need of examination as has been explained, is not whether the DGx (or MECTA SR 1 and 2 devices) slightly breach a Pure-ER/RRC interpretation of the IEC Standard, but whether a Pure-ER/RRC interpretation (versus a conditional-ER/RRC interpretation) is licit at all in light of the deceptive 100J ceiling interpretation strongly inferred by both the IEC Standard and the machines themselves. The pertinent question is: "Is it acceptable for manufacturers of IEC BP devices to allow parameters to reach outputs in accordance with a Pure-ER/RRC interpretation of the standard at all or should manufacturers have been forced to maintain a 100 or even a 130 Joule ceiling so maintain minimal stimulus outputs for all age categories. In sum, should BP machines under the IEC auspices have been allowed to reach unreported maximum outputs of between 227 and 240 Joules, surreptitiously surpassing in cumulative output, dangerously powerful SW machines of the past, or should the IEC Standard have been interpreted (as expected) in a manner restricting Brief Pulse machines to between 100 or even 130J Absolute Joules as the machine readouts infer? [475] The critical dialectic, in short, involves the dubious practice of interpreting the 1989 IEC Standard of "100J at 300Ω" and more inconspicuously, "130 Joules at 300Ω" as a Pure-ER/RRC and so with even slight breaching allowing up to 227J or a 2.27 MTTLOI? [476] So is the manufacturer interpretation, calculatingly disingenuous? Is, in fact, the Pure-ER/RRC interpretation of the IEC Standard's "100J at 300Ω" featured phrase (and "130J at 300Ω" unfeatured phrase) a deliberately corrupt stratagem to undermine minimal stimulus outputs via a deliberately deceptive standard? Moreover, can we then overlook contradictorily deceptive readouts suggestive of increased safety? Begrudgingly, the obvious answer to the first set of questions must be "Yes," and the last, a resounding "No." If, then, we must conclude that the IEC standard, its Pure-ER/RRC interpretation, and even the machine readouts of circa 100 maximum joules are intentionally deceptive, we must next ask, "Why?" Why would manufacturers deliberately harm recipients and lie to them about doing so?

Clearly, manufacturers' rendering of the 1989 IEC Standard as a Pure-ER/RRC is based upon and, in fact, is an extension of the 1983 Mectan Transmutation, a corruption of the American Psychiatric Association (APA) Standard initially presented to the FDA in 1982. Moreover, if the IEC Standard is nothing less than an extension of the Mectan Transmutation, that is, an extension of a U. S. BP manufacturers' conspiratorial, unreported and unauthorized transition from circa 100 Absolute Joules to an unexplained and unreported 100J Pure-ER/RRC in order to circumvent the 110J APA ceiling for the purpose of secretly facilitating outputs to suprathreshold dosages of electricity, [477] then a standard based on the same transmutation equally facilitating secret outputs must be equally corrupt. In short, we must conclude that all three mechanisms relating to the IEC Standard--1) the composition of the IEC standard itself, 2) manufacturer interpretation of the IEC Standard, and 3) deceptive machine readouts on second generation IEC BP devices, just like the three mechanisms regarding the Mectan

---

[473] ER, much less Pure-ER/RRC, is never mentioned within the IEC Standard - only the phrase "100J at 300Ω."

[474] Based upon a "130J at 300Ω" Pure-ER/RRC, the device should be confined to .481C., 3.8 Seconds maximum Duration and 216.66 maximum Joules (130J/300Ω = **216.66J**/500Ω). Instead the device is based upon an illegal "136J at 300Ω" Pure-ER/RRC.

[475] The same questionable methodology is initially used by MECTA (via the Mectan transmutation) for SR1@2 devices, followed by Somatics for the Thymatron DG. Rather than reducing alternative parameters such as Duration to maintain a 100J ceiling, Somatics began using maximum parameters derived from a new "99.4J at 220Ω" Pure-ER/RRC interpretation to unreported output at maximum machine Impedance of 555.5Ω. The result is an unreported maximum output - not of the expected 99.4J - but rather an unreported 252 maximum joules for the made-for-America Thymatron DG.

[476] An absolute or conditional interpretation of "100J at 300Ω" calls for the maintaining of 100J through the subsequent reduction of alternative parameters (i.e. Duration).

[477] The DGx has been marketed throughout the world.

Transmutation 1) the composition of the Mectan Transmutation itself, 2) manufacturer interpretation of the Mectan Transmutation, and 3) deceptive machine readouts for second generation made-for-America BP devices, all aim to accomplish the same end--surreptitiously enhanced outputs framed within the totally false impression of minimal stimulus emissions limited to around 100 maximum joules. Like the Mectan Transmutation's "100J at 220Ω" phrase then, it is the conspicuous "100J at 300Ω" phrase within the IEC Standard, subtly expanded to an implicit "130J at 300Ω" phrase, in turn expanded into unwritten and unreported "136J at 300Ω" and "138J at 300Ω" phrases subsequently interpreted as Pure-ER/RRCs of such precise specificity that they perfectly dovetail into the "99.4J at 220Ω" and "101J at 220Ω" phrases Somatics and MECTA exploit via the Mectan Transmutation that confirms the standard's corruption. This perfect dovetailing means that second generation made-for-Europe BP devices can be made comparable in power and parameter dynamics to made-for-America second generation BP devices manufactured in America. It is certainly no coincidence that both the American Mectan Transmutation and the IEC standard prominently feature the "100J" figure, emblematic of Brief Pulse minimal stimulus world-wide; it cannot be happenstance that manufacturers on both continents secretly re-interpret these phrases as Pure-ER/RRCs to paradoxically eradicate this same circa 100J ceiling for the sole purpose of facilitating much higher outputs; it cannot be chance that both second generation made-for-America Somatics and MECTA BP devices and their made-for-IEC Brief Pulse cousins all depict and display false circa 100J Readout maximums misleadingly scanned by practicing physicians, reinforcing the illusion of "100J" Brief Pulse devices generally. Indicative of safer reduced output machines, the standards, the reported outputs, and the machine readouts together continue to deceive professionals, regulators, and recipients alike on an international scale. In short, the manufacturers are lying to all three.

That both the Mectan transmutation of the APA Standard and the IEC Standard together with machine readouts are deceptive cannot be argued. Plainly, there is intent to deceive. Indeed, the misleading "100J at 220Ω" Mectan transmutation surreptitiously interpreted by American BP manufacturers as a Pure-ER/RRC, and the misleading "100J at 300Ω" IEC Standard surreptitiously expanded and also interpreted as a Pure-ER/RRC allowing outputs surpassing SW even as both superficially appear to limit BP devices to the same circa 100 Joules stipulated in the 1982 APA Standard, seemingly "corroborated" by 100J readout maximums on both Somatics and MECTA second generation BP devices nationally and internationally loudly bespeak of intent to deceive.

Not only do manufacturers deceptively interpret both the "100J at 220Ω" Mectan Transmutation and the "100J at 300Ω" IEC Standard as unexplicated Pure-ER/RRCs then, but both MECTA and Somatics breach the implicit "130J at 300Ω" phrase to specifically attain unreported "136J at 300Ω" and "138J at 300Ω" Pure-ER/RRCs for dovetailing into made-for-America devices in order to knowingly exploit the same Mectan Transmutation (136J/300Ω = circa 100/220Ω = 138J at 300Ω). [478] In making the case for deliberate deception, moreover, we must again emphasize that the featured IEC phrase "100J at 300Ω" appears to have been engineered by the same Richard Weiner who construed the circa "100J at 220Ω" Mectan phraseology newly and surreptitiously interpreted as a Pure-ER/RRC. Both transmute the APA 's 110J ceiling into never before now reported (in this manuscript) outputs well over 200 joules. In brief, both made-for-America and made-for-Europe devices are secretly based on the same illicit Pure-ER/RRC. Add to this, the simultaneous failure to report maximum EOs by virtually all BP manufacturers, underreported parameters reported to the RCP suggesting 100J maximums, the coincidental reporting of the "100J at 220Ω" and "100J at 300Ω" phrases in both America and Europe respectively, superficially emulative of the original 110J APA ceiling for BP devices, the expectation that BP is a reduced energy output device compared to SW, and finally blatant 100J maximum Machine Readouts on all second generation Somatics and MECTA made-for-America and made-for-IEC BP devices. Together, these facts indicate deliberate national and international deception regarding BP devices world-wide.

The "why" is obvious. Convulsive therapy is a myth. ECT devices, that is, devices inducing adequate grand mal seizures with the least amount of electricity possible, simply do not work. Indeed, to "work," machines must compromise or destroy an adequate percentage of neural pathways in the brain, specifically, as we have learned, in the left pre-frontal lobe, and this cannot be done with adequate seizures induced with the least amount of electricity possible. Indeed it can only be done with adequate, that is, with suprathreshold amounts of electricity (Perrin, 2012; Breggin, 1979; 2007). Only through adequate electricity, can machines successfully

---

[478] The difference in actual output for IEC versus made-for-America BP devices is due to maximum permissible Impedance (136J/300Ω = 100/220Ω = 227J/500Ω = 272J/600Ω).

effect not only a temporary anti-depressant effect, but the moderately enduring behavioral changes psychiatrists look for. This psychiatric principle is not a new one. But because the outdated means is clearly unsavory, indeed, because brain damage as treatment is unacceptable in this modern medical age, manufacturers have chosen to "protect" society from this understanding. In brief, manufacturers have chosen to cover up that ECT is not ECT at all, but rather ENR or Electro Neurotransmission Reduction--specifically, electro annihilation of enough neuro-transmitters to effect change. Certainly, modern Brief Pulse devices are no longer convulsive therapy devices at all, but rather consist of the deliberate application of suprathreshold dosages of electricity far superseding that required to induce adequate convulsions. Restated, modern Brief Pulse devices must destroy enough neural transmissions to affect mood, but more importantly, effect moderately enduring changes in behavior. What we appear to have with ENR, in effect, sadly to say, is a new variation of partial pre-frontal lobotomy. The main difference between surgical prefrontal lobotomy and ENR is that gray matter is not destroyed, only the neural pathways within the gray matter. While the immediate effect may be the same, therefore, there may be hope for ENR recipients in the regrowth of synaptic connections, but only after a very lengthy period of time. In any case, long term memory damage as a result of ENR now becomes comprehensible in that due to the necessary destruction of neural pathways and neural connections, cognitive dissonance is inescapable.

CHAPTER 36

Ectron Series 5A--Canadian and UK 2nd Gen. BP Devices: Ectron Figures EO for IEC-mandated UK

The main manufacturer of Canadian and English "ECT" devices is ***Ectron Incorporated***. As early as 1990 and perhaps earlier, Ectron began producing second generation Brief Pulse devices known as the "Series 5A" comparable in power not only to MECTA and Somatics second generation *made-for-Europe* (IEC) BP devices, but comparable in power even to MECTA and Somatics second generation *made-for-America* BP devices (Royal College of Psychiatry, 1995, pp.124-125). Like Somatics, the English/Canadian manufacturer Ectron, although similarly failing to report actual output in joules for its Series 5A, does, in fact, report enough of the 5A's actual parameters to deduce maximum output in Joules (Ibid). In keeping with U. S. practices, moreover, Ectron appears to have figured maximum output for its second generation Series 5A BP devices through the same furtive utilization of Pure-ER/RRC (to maximum Impedance) as American manufacturers, this, in spite of Canadian and British made Ectron machines falling exclusively under IEC auspices for marketing throughout Europe.

Like Somatics, Ectron accurately reports for its Series 5A: Amperage (.75A), Pulses (unidirectional--adjustable 30-70 per second), Pulse Width (.0022 Sec.), maximum Duration (6.0 Seconds), maximum Impedance (500Ω), and maximum Charge (.700C rounded up from .692C).

While Ectron fails to report maximum EO in joules, simply by using the formula: EO = Current squared x Impedance x Pulses x Pulse Width x Duration, and then by plugging in the reported Series 5A parameters including the actual "500Ω" IEC Impedance maximum accurately reported by Ectron for its Series 5A (Ibid 124), we can definitively determine a maximum output of 260 unreported joules for the Ectron Series 5A.

EO = .75 x .75 x 500Ω x 70 Pulses x .0022 Pulse Width x 6.0 Seconds = **260 Joules**.

By using the same formula: EO = Current squared x Impedance x Pulses x Pulse Width x Duration and the same reported Series 5A parameters with the exception of substituting the actual "500Ω" Impedance reported by Ectron with the "300Ω" figure (found in the 1989 IEC Standard), we can obtain the Pure-ER/RRC upon which the Ectron Series 5A is based:

EO = .75 x .75 x **300Ω** x 70 Pulses x .0022 Pulse Width [479] x 6.0 Seconds = **155.9 Joules**.[480]

Consequently, the pure-ER/RRC, upon which the Ectron 5A Series is based, is a clearly illicit ***"155.9J at 300Ω. "*** (As previously noted, even if we accept a Pure-ER/RRC interpretation, the maximum pure-ER/RRC

---

[479] Ectron BP devices are unidirectional using half as many pulses (70) as, for instance, Somatics (140). The difference is made up with Pulse Width - .0022 Seconds - more than twice that of Somatics' Thymatron DG or Thymatron DGx, both of which utilize .001 Seconds.

[480] This is (155.9/300Ω =) 114J at 220Ω.

allowed under the IEC Standard is an implicit "130J at 300Ω," permitting a furtive 216.6J maximum EO: **130J/300Ω = 216.6J/500Ω**.) Maximum output in joules for the Ectron Series 5A can now be reaffirmed through the Pure-ER/RRC application of "155.9J at 300Ω" with respect to actual maximum Impedance:

155.9J/300Ω = *XJ*/**500Ω**. **X = 260J**

In short, Ectron not only interprets the covert 1989 IEC Standard of "130J at 300Ω" as a Pure-ER/RRC, but similar to MECTA and Somatics, clearly uses an illegal "155.9J at 300Ω" Pure-ER/RRC surpassing not only the misleading "100J at 300Ω" phrase featured within the IEC Standard (even interpreted as a Pure-ER/RRC) but even the deducible, albeit implicit "130J at 300Ω" Pure-ER/RRC phrase derivable from the IEC Standard's thirty percent cushion adjunct.

As previously noted, Ectron reports and uses a maximum 6.0 Second Duration for its Series 5A. In order to comply with even the covert "130J at 300Ω" Pure-ER/RRC interpretation of the IEC Standard, Ectron should have reduced maximum Duration for its' Series 5A from the reported and actual 6.0 Seconds to 5.0 Seconds.[481]

EO = .75 x .75 x **300Ω** x 70 Pulses x .0022 Pulse Width x 5.0 Seconds = **130 Joules**.

Reducing maximum Duration to a hypothetical 5.0 Seconds, forces the Ectron Series 5A to adhere not only to the "130J at 300Ω" ER/RRC implicitly specified within the IEC Standard even interpreted as a Pure-ER/RRC, but to a derivable 216.6J EO ceiling also based on a Pure-ER/RRC interpretation.

EO = .75 x .75 x **500Ω** x 70 Pulses x .0022 Pulse Width x 5.0 Seconds = **216.6J**.

Confirmation of maximum allowable IEC output interpreted as a Pure-ER/RRC can again be affirmed through the direct use of the maximum "130J at 300Ω" phrase interpreted as a Pure-ER/RRC against the maximum IEC Impedance actually used for the Series 5A.

130J/300Ω = **216.66J/500Ω**. [482]

Using the Charge formula: Charge = EO ÷ Impedance x Amperage with the derivable Pure-ER/RRC maximum "allowed" by the IEC Standard ("130J at 300Ω"), we can additionally see that the maximum Charge for the Series 5A should have been reduced from the circa .700C actually used for the Series 5A to **.577C**. (Royal College of Psychiatry, 1995, p.124)

Charge = 130 Joules/300Ω x .75 Amperes = **.577 Coulombs**.

Through the Charge formula: EO = Charge x Impedance x Amperage, we can now derive what should have been the maximum allowable EO for the Series 5A (216.6J) using what should have been its maximum Charge (.577C), this, of course, based on Pure-ER/RRC.

Actual EO = **.577 Coulombs** x 500Ω x .75 Amperes = **216.6J**.

Completing the circle, based on the 30% cushion adjunct from which we derive the "130J at 300Ω" phrase implicit within the 1989 IEC Standard (still interpreted as a Pure-ER/RRC), we can again see that the Series

---

[481] Duration = EO/Current Squared x Impedance x Pulses x Pulse Width. Duration = 129.93 Joules ÷ .75 x .75 x 300Ω x 70 Pulses x .0022 Pulse Width = 5.0 Seconds Duration. Duration = 216.38 Joules ÷ .75 x .75 x 500Ω x 70 Pulses x .0022 Pulse Width = 5.0 Seconds Duration.

[482] The 216J maximum output here based on the "130J at 300Ω" cushion adjunct interpreted as a Pure ER/RRC is comparable to what should have been a 215J maximum for MECTA's IEC BP devices based on the same circa "130J at 300Ω" Pure-ER/RRC interpretation of the same IEC Standard.

5A device should have been limited to a maximum 5.0 Second Duration (in lieu of the 6.0 Second maximum Ectron actually utilizes).

EO (ER) = .75 x .75 x 300Ω x 70 Pulses x .0022 Pulse Width x 5.0 Seconds = **129.93 Joules**.

EO (Actual) = .75 x .75 x 500Ω x 70 Pulses x .0022 Pulse Width x 5.0 Seconds = **216.6 Joules**.

Thus, just as MECTA and Somatics fail to limit their second generation IEC BP devices to what should have been an absolute 216.6J maximum, even based on a Pure-ER/RRC, so Ectron similarly fails to limit its second generation BP device. Specifically, in lieu of a maximum Duration of 5.0 Seconds (derivable from a 130J at 300Ω Pure-ER/RRC interpretation of the IEC Standard), Ectron instead derives its' reported maximum Charge ceiling of approximately .700 Coulombs (Royal College of Psychiatry, 1995, p.124) from an illegal "155.9J at 300Ω" Pure-ER/RRC requiring a patently illegal (albeit reported) 6.0 second maximum Duration resulting in an illegal maximum Charge (for the Series 5A) of .692C (rounded up to and reported as .700Cs).

EO = .75 x .75 x **300Ω** x 70 Pulses x .0022 Pulse Width x 6.0 Seconds = **155.9 Joules**.

Charge = 155.9 Joules/300Ω x .75 Amperes = **.692 Coulombs**.

Maximum output for the Ectron BP Series 5A, then, is a highly illegal 260 unreported Joules as opposed to the 216.6J maximum "allowed" even under even the most liberal interpretation of the IEC Standard. To use the light-bulb analogy, the Ectron BP Series 5A at maximum output emits enough power to light up a 43 watt light-bulb for six full seconds against 500Ω of skull, skin, and brains. [483]

EO = .75 x .75 x 500Ω x 70 Pulses x .0022 Pulse Width x 6.0 Seconds = 260 Joules.

Hence, similar to MECTA's and Somatics' breach of the 1989 IEC Standard's potentially derivable Pure-ER/RRC maximum of "130J at 300Ω," Ectron's Series 5A uses a patently illegal (and unreported) Pure-ER/RRC of "155.9J at 300Ω," to emit an illicit Charge maximum of .692 Coulombs [484] derived from an illicit (but reported) 6.0 Second maximum Duration (Royal College of Psychiatry, 1995, p.124).

Just as MECTA and Somatics second generation IEC BP instruments fail to reduce electrical parameters in accordance with an anticipated conditional-ER/RRC interpretation of "100J at 300Ω" or even "130J at 300Ω," neither does the Ectron Series 5A reduce electrical parameters to limit outputs to a looked for 100, 130, or even 155.9 Joule ceiling. Rather than using a conditional-ER/RRC interpretation of the IEC Standard to minimize outputs to circa minimal stimulus--inducing adequate seizures at 1.0, 1.3, or even a 1.56 MTTLOI for all age levels as might be presumed--the Ectron Series 5A, bases its outputs on an illegal "155.9J at 300Ω" Pure-ER/RRC interpretation so that the Series 5A actually emits an unreported maximum 260 joules, in essence, an unreported 2.6 MTTLOI to every age recipient. The age-related relative threshold output constants are listed for reference below.

Age Related Thresholds; "Relative Constants"

10 year old male = 1.00J
20 year old male = 4.00J
30 year old male = 9.00J
40 year old male = 16.00J
50 year old male = 25.00J
60 year old male = 36.00J
65 year old male = 42.25J
70 year old male = 48.97J
80 year old male = 64.00J
90 year old male = 81.00J
100 year old male = 100.00J

---

483 260W ÷ 6.0 Sec = 43.3 Watts/Second. The analogy takes into account the interim between pulses.

484 Ectron reported a .700C maximum Charge (Royal College of Psychiatry, 1995, p.124).

Though non-existent, the following chart represents the expected, more or less minimal stimulus device with a 1.56 MTTLOI default administered in all age categories.

ANTICIPATED HYPOTHETICAL CONSTANT CURRENT **Series 5A** (IEC) BRIEF PULSE "ECT" DEVICE [485] BASED ON **Conditional-ER/RRC INTERPRETATION of 155.9J AT 300Ω**

VOLTAGE	POWER % @ Age	AGE Yrs	Ω Ohms	FREQUENCY (Pulses)	DURATION (SECs)	CURRENT mAmps	ENERGY Joules	CHARGE mC
37.5	10	10	50	30	.84	750	1.559	41.6
75	20	20	100	30	1.717	750	6.36	85
112.5	30	30	150	50	1.54	759	14.3	127
150	40	40	200	50	2.0	750	24.9	166
187.5	50	50	250	50	2.52	750	39.0	208
225	60	60	300	70	2.156	750	56.0	249
243.75	65	65	325	70	2.34	750	65.9	270
262.5	70	70	350	70	2.52	750	76.3	291
300	80	80	400	70	2.87	750	99.7	332
337.5	90	90	450	70	3.24	750	126.3	374
375	100	100	**500**	70	3.6	750	**155.9J**	**416**

.0022 Sec. PW

The following formulas are used to determine the variables for the above chart representing a non-existent, but expected minimal stimulus "ECT" device based on the expected Conditional-ER/RRC interpretation of the IEC Standard:

EO = **<u>1.599</u>** fold age threshold (see age related thresholds below)
Charge = EO ÷ 500Ω x .75 Amperes
Duration = Charge ÷ Current x (hz x 1) x WL
EO = .75 x .75 x Imp x Pulses x .0022 PW x Duration

Conversely, the chart below represents a "quasi-legal" pure-ER/RRC interpretation of the IEC Standard depicting an ENR device with a 2.17 MTTLOI for all age recipients. This device is also non-existent.

"LEGAL" HYPOTHETICAL CONSTANT CURRENT **Series 5A** (IEC) BRIEF PULSE "ENR" DEVICE [486] BASED ON **PURE-ER/RRC INTERPRETATION** OF **"130J AT 300Ω"**

VOLTAGE	POWER % @ Age	AGE Yrs	Ω Ohms	FREQUENCY (Pulses)	DURATION (SECs)	CURRENT mAmps	ENERGY Joules	CHARGE mC
37.5	10	10	50	30	1.17	750	2.166	57.8
75	20	20	100	30	2.34	750	8.7	116
112.5	30	30	150	50	2.1	759	19.5	173
150	40	40	200	50	2.8	750	34.7	231
187.5	50	50	250	50	3.5	750	54	288
225	60	60	300	70	3.0	750	78	347
243.75	65	65	325	70	3.25	750	91.5	375
262.5	70	70	350	70	3.5	750	106	404
300	80	80	400	70	4.0	750	138.6	462
337.5	90	90	450	70	4.5	750	175	519
375	100	100	**500**	70	5.0	750	**216.6**	**577**

.0022 Sec. PW

---

[485] Maximum Voltage is misreported as 225V. Actual maximum Voltage of 375V for the Series 5A is derivable via Ohm's Law: V = Amp x Imp: .75 x 500Ω = 375V. Maximum Charge, maximum Duration, maximum number of (unidirectional) pulses, Pulse Width (.0022), and Constant Current (.75 Amps) are provided by Ectron. Various Voltages are determined by percentage of age (out of 100 years) times maximum Voltage (375V), i.e.70 years = .70 x 375V = 262.5V. Various Impedances, i.e. Impedance at 70% can then be derived via Ohm's Law (Impedance = Voltage/Current): Impedance = 262.5V ÷ .75A = <u>350Ω</u> or 70% of 500Ω for 70 years old recipient (.7 x 500Ω = 350Ω). Various EOs delivered are figured via 1.559 fold minimal stimulus outputs (see table above), i.e. Minimal stimulus for 70 yr old = 48.97 Joules x 1.559 fold = 76.3J. Various Charges are derived via Charge = EO ÷ Current x Impedance, i.e.76.3J ÷ .75A x 350Ω = 291mC for 70 yr. old recipient.

[486] Maximum Voltage is misreported at 225V. Actual maximum Voltage of 375V for the Series 5A is derivable via Ohm's Law: V = Amp x Imp: .75 x 500Ω = 375V. Maximum Charge, maximum Duration, maximum number of (unidirectional) pulses, Pulse Width (.0022), and Constant Current (.75 Amps) are provided by Ectron. Various Voltages are determined through percentage of age (out of 100 years) times maximum Voltage (375V), i.e.70 years = 70% of 375V = 262.5V. Various Impedances, i.e. Impedance at 70% can then be derived via Ohm's Law (Impedance = Voltage/Current): Impedance = 262.5 ÷ .75 = <u>350Ω</u> for 70 years of age or .7 x 500Ω = 350Ω. Various EOs delivered are figured via 2.166 fold minimal stimulus outputs (see table above), i.e. Minimal stimulus for 70 yr old = 48.97 Joules x 2.166 fold = 106J. Various Charges are derived via Charge = EO ÷ Current x Impedance, i.e.106J ÷ .75A x 350Ω = 404mC for 70 yr. old recipient.

Formulas determining variables used in the above chart to depict the non-existent ENR device above are as follows:

EO = **2.166** fold age threshold (see age related thresholds above)
Charge = EO/500Ω x .75 Amperes
Duration = Charge/Current x (hz x 1) x WL
EO = .75 x .75 x Imp x Pulses x .0022 PW x Duration

The chart below depicts the illegal, even if we accept a pure-ER/RRC interpretation of the 1989 IEC Standard, Series 5A representing the actual ENR BP device with a 2.6 MTTLOI administered to all age recipients. In short, the chart below represents the actual second generation "ENR" device manufactured by the English/Canadian manufacturer, Ectron Inc.

ACTUAL CONSTANT CURRENT **Series 5A** (IEC) BRIEF PULSE "ENR" DEVICE by Ectron Inc. [487]
BASED ON an ILLEGAL **PURE-ER/RRC INTERPRETATION** OF "**155.9J AT 300Ω**"

VOLTAGE	POWER % @ Age	AGE Yrs	Ω Ohms	FREQUENCY (Pulses)	DURATION (SECs)	CURRENT mAmps	ENERGY Joules	CHARGE mC
37.5	10	10	50	30	1.4	750	2.59	69.3
75	20	20	100	30	2.76	750	10.4	136.67
112.5	30	30	150	50	2.52	759	23.4	208
150	40	40	200	50	3.36	750	41.6	277.3
187.5	50	50	250	50	4.2	750	65.0	346.67
225	60	60	300	70	3.6	750	93.6	416
243.75	65	65	325	70	3.91	750	110.0	451.3
262.5	70	70	350	70	4.2	750	127.3	485
300	80	80	400	70	4.8	750	166.4	554.66
337.5	90	90	450	70	5.4	750	210.6	624
375	100	100	**500**	70	6.0	750	**259.9**	**692**

.0022 Sec. PW

Formulas below are used to determine variables in the above actual ENR chart depicting the actual Ectron Series 5A:

EO = **2.59** fold age threshold (see age related thresholds above)
Charge = EO/500Ω x .75 Amperes
Duration = Charge/Current x (hz x 1) x WL
EO = .75 x .75 x Imp x Pulses x .0022 PW x Duration

Distribution of (unidirectional) pulse output per age is unreported by Ectron, thus the chart above is moderately speculative, but likely. In any case, the actual output of the Series 5A is 255.9J and the actual MTTLOI for all age categories is 2.59 threshold or a 2.59 MTTLOI. This second generation apparatus is no longer an "ECT" device, but like the second generation MECTA and Somatics BP devices, an "ENR" or adequate electricity device designed to compromise neurotransmitters in the left pre-frontal lobe.

False Equivalence of Charge to ER-Output (in Joules) with Ectron Series 5A

As noted, Charge would have had to be reduced to 346.66mC (at 500Ω) in order to limit the Ectron Series 5A device to an anticipated 130J conditional ceiling and .415 Coulombs (at 500Ω) [488] in order to limit output to a moderately excessive 155.9J conditional ceiling. Instead, the Ectron Series 5A skyrockets to almost 700mC (at

[487] Maximum Voltage is misreported at 225V. Actual maximum Voltage of 375V for the Series 5A is derivable via Ohm's Law: V = Amp x Imp: .75 x 500Ω = 375V. Maximum Charge, maximum Duration, maximum number of (unidirectional) pulses, Pulse Width (.0022), and Constant Current (.75 Amps) are provided by Ectron. Various Voltages are determined through by percentage of age (out of 100 years) times maximum Voltage (375V), i.e.70 years = 70% of 375V = 262.5V. Various Impedances, i.e. Impedance at 70% can then be derived via Ohm's Law (Impedance = Voltage/Current): Impedance = 262.5/.75 = 350Ω at 70 years of age or .7 x 500Ω = 350Ω. Various EOs delivered are figured via 2.6 fold minimal stimulus outputs (see table above), i.e. Minimal stimulus for 70 yr. old = 48.97 Joules x 2.6 fold = 127.3J. Various Charges are derived via Charge = EO ÷ Current x Impedance, i.e.127.3J ÷ .75A x 350Ω = 485mC for 70 yr. old recipient.

[488] Charge = 155.9 Joules ÷ 500Ω x .75 Amperes = .416 Coulombs. Charge = 130 Joules ÷ 500Ω x .75 Amperes = .3466 Coulombs

500Ω) facilitating its unreported 260 joule maximum output (Ibid). Confusingly, moreover, in spite of Ectron interpreting the 155.9J at 300Ω upon which the machine is based as a Pure-ER/RRC (in lieu of a conditional-ER/RRC) to the 260J at 500Ω maximums the machine actually elicits, the actual maximum Charge of approximately 700mC Charge can be derived using either the 155.9J at 300Ω Pure-ER phrase or the actual (unreported) Output/Impedance maximums of 260J at 500Ω.

Charge = 155.9 Joules/300Ω x .75 Amperes = .693 Coulombs.

Charge = 260 Joules/500Ω x .75 Amperes = .693 Coulombs. [489]

Similar to MECTA and Somatics devices, then, the .693C Charge maximum can be derived with either ER-output (155.9J) or actual maximum output (260 Joules), creating the same false equivalency between actual maximum Charge and what is actually an ER-output (of 155.9J) as do American BP devices. Once again, omission of actual output reporting in joules, leads to a confused and deceptive correspondence between the indirectly reported ER-output (here of 155.9Js) [490] and the directly reported actual maximum Charge (here of circa .700 Coulombs). This false correlation boosts the false assumption that Ectron and other manufacturers interpret the 1989 IEC Standard featured as a "100J at 300Ω" or implicitly derived "130J at 300Ω" conditional-ER/RRC with a 100 or even 130J ceiling with some slight breaching. [491] Assuming regulatory agencies even decipher enough of the indicatory information to derive what is actually a 155.9J ER-output, the Ectron Series 5A appears to breach the apparent maximum output of 130 Joules (permitted under a conditional-ER/RRC interpretation) by a relatively moderate 25.9 Joules (155.9J - 130J = 25.9J),[492] when in fact, the Ectron Series 5A breaches the anticipated conditional-ER/RRC interpretation of the 1989 IEC Standard not by 26 Joules, but by at least 130Js (260 Joules - 130 Joules = 130 Joules). In short, the unreported 260J maximum output emitted by Ectron's Series 5A BP device, surpassing even the potential 200J cumulative output of SW devices is, like MECTA and Somatics devices, virtually invisible.

But even interpreting the IEC Standard as a 130J at 300Ω Pure-ER/RRC, the Ectron Series 5A, as noted above, fails to conform to what should be a .578 Coulomb Charge ceiling, a 5.0 second maximum Duration, a 216.6J maximum, and a 2.166 MTTLOI. Instead, Ectron uses an illegal 155.9J at 300Ω Pure-ER/RRC, evincing an approximate .700 Coulomb Charge ceiling,[493] reflecting, as previously noted, an actual (but never before reported) maximum output of approximately 260 maximum Joules, a significant violation of the 1989 IEC Standard even interpreted as a Pure-ER/RRC.

Like MECTA and Somatics then, in spite of appearances, Ectron's second generation BP device, fails to emit a minimal stimulus output (of 1.0, 1.3 or even 1.59 fold threshold), but has instead devolved into an adequate electricity or ENR device emitting 260 maximum joules, emitting a 2.6 MTTLOI in every age category, surpassing even the cumulative output of SW.

Illegal

While Ectron does report most of the Series 5A electrical parameters accurately, Ectron ignores not only the published IEC "100 Joules at 300Ω" as a conditional-ER/RRC incorporative of a 100J ceiling [494] which indeed

---

[489] The legality of this step based on the Mectan Transmutation now practiced by all BP manufacturers, and utilizing in this instance, the same maximum Charge derived with a "155.9 Joules at 300Ω" ER phrase is both deceptive and questionable. Charge should drop correspondingly in order to maintain (in this instance) a slightly excessive, but still conditional 155.9J maximum output (EO = 500Ω x .75 Amperes x .4157 Coulombs = 155.9 Joules). Instead, Charge increases to accommodate a 260J ceiling.

[490] In this instance, the ER-output is the unexplicated, unreported, and remotely derived, implicit output of 155.9J, nevertheless suggestive of maximum output and so a spurious conditional-ER/RRC interpretation.

[491] It is quite possible that Ectron Series 5A devices depict a maximum output of 156 Joules similar to made-for-America BP devices. All that is necessary is the factoring in of a false 300Ω constant for the Machine Readouts similar to MECTA's 220Ω false constant.

[492] 155.9 Joules - 130 Joules = 25.9 Joules. (As noted in the above footnote, it is possible that machine readouts depict misleading outputs similar to MECTA BP devices.)

[493] Charge = EO/Current and Impedance. Charge = 100J/.75A x 300Ω = 444.4mC. Charge = 130J/.75A x 300Ω = 577.8mC. Charge = 155.9J/.75A x 300Ω = 693mC.

[494] In keeping with MECTA and Somatics, Ectron has discarded the absolute 100J ceiling interpretation.

is but a facade, but also ignores the implicit "130J at 300Ω" phrase as conditional-ER/RRC incorporative of a 130J ceiling. Moreover, it disregards even "155.9J at 300Ω" as a conditional-ER/RRC, even as a moderately breached 130J ceiling. Indeed, 155.9J may be spuriously depicted as a maximum machine readout, as we shall examine shortly. In addition, as we have seen, Ectron surpasses even the Pure-ER/RRC interpretation of "130J at 300Ω" "allowing" a 216.6J maximum. [495] Consequently, Ectron not only takes advantage of the 30% IEC cushion statute interpreted as a Pure-ER/RRC ("permitting" a 216.6J maximum), but like both MECTA and Somatics, breaches even this potential IEC maximum. As explained above, the Ectron Series 5A should at the least be limited to a .578 Coulomb Charge maximum, a 5.0 Second maximum Duration, and a 216J EO maximum at 500Ω. Instead, the Ectron 5A Series utilizes 6.0 full seconds and a circa .700 Coulomb Charge to evince a secret maximum EO of circa 260 Joules, breaching even a "130J at 300Ω" Pure-ER/RRC interpretation of the IEC Standard by 44 Joules (260J - 216J = 44J). In brief, the Series 5A is based upon a significantly illegal and unreported "155.9J at 300Ω" Pure-ER/RRC, facilitating a 44J higher output than that allowed even by the most liberal interpretation of the IEC Standard. With respect to the anticipated conditional-ER/RRC interpretation of the same "130J at 300Ω" cushion adjunct permitting a reasonable maximum of 130J, the never before reported 260J maximum emitted by Ectron's Series 5A is a full 130Js higher than the looked for conditional ceiling of 130J (260J - 130J = 130J). Finally, the machine emits a full 160Js more than the featured "100J at 300Ω" phrase logically interpreted as a conditional-ER/RRC, highly suggestive of the familiar 100J ceiling associated with minimal stimulus Brief Pulse.

Same American Inspired Methodology

Like both MECTA and Somatics, Ectron appears to have concluded that the actual maximum EO of the Series 5A--based upon a "155.9J at 300Ω" Pure-ER/RRC (from which its circa .700 Coulombs Charge can be derived [496])--is close enough to the IEC Standard's derivable "130J at 300Ω" (which manufacturers interpret as a Pure-ER/RRC) to be a relatively "insignificant" or at least "forgivable" breach (by regulatory agencies). In fact, eclipsing even a dubiously "permissible" Pure-ER/RRC maximum by a mere 26.0 Joules ("130Js at 300Ω" vs "155.9Js at 300Ω") and so secretly obtaining an unreported actual maximum output of circa 260J (in lieu of a possible IEC maximum of 216.38J) means that the Ectron Series 5A breaches an implied 100J IEC maximum by 160 Joules, a more subtly implied 130J IEC maximum by 130 Joules, and even the 216.6J maximum output based on a dubiously derived Pure-ER/RRC interpretation of the IEC Standard by about (260J - 216J =) 44 Joules.

Given the true Series 5A maximum output of 260 Joules then, like Somatics and MECTA, Ectron seems to rely upon invisibility or "forgiveness" for what might be argued a "mere" 44J breach (260J vs.216J) of the IEC Standard, and so Ectron seems to have gambled, a "modest enough violation" to escape reprimand. In fact, the never before reported and invisible 260J maximum output the Ectron Series 5A actually emits (and thus the 2.6 MTTLOI default administered to all age recipients) placed the English company in a position to compete with second generation made-for-America BP devices of comparably unreported outputs such as the 259J second generation made-for-America SR1 and 2 devices and the 252J Somatics' second generation made-for-America Thymatron DG device. Indeed, with an unreported 260J ceiling, Ectron was able to viably contend with the United States for a share of the world market (Somatics Incorporated, 1997b). Critically, however, what regulatory agencies never appear to have noticed is that manufacturers do not interpret the IEC Standard of "100J at 300Ω" or even "130J at 300Ω" absolutely, that is--as the expected Conditional-ER/RRC regulating BP output to an expected maximum of circa 100 or at most circa 130 maximum Joules. These figures create a 1.0 or 1.3 MTTLOI compared to which what appears to be a 155.9 Joule output maximum or a 1.56 MTTLOI for all age recipients might, indeed, seem somewhat "forgivable." Rather, just as American manufacturers transmuted the 110J ceiling of the APA Standard into a "100 at 220Ω" Pure-ER/RRC, English manufacturers such as Ectron transmuted the "100J at 300Ω" and even "130J at 300Ω" of the IEC Standard into a Pure-ER/RRC. In short, just as Americans transmuted the APA Standard by switching from an identifiable 110J ceiling to a ceiling based on maximum machine Impedance, Ectron, in lieu of interpreting the IEC Standard with an identifiable 100 or even 130J ceiling thereby guaranteeing minimal stimulus output for all age recipients,

[495] 100J/300Ω = 166.6J/500Ω; 130J/300Ω = 216.6J/500Ω.

[496] Charge = EO/Impedance x Amperage. Charge = 156 Joules / 300Ω x .75 Amperes = .693 Coulombs

decided, as did American manufacturers, to base maximum output on maximum machine Impedance. In brief, and as we have seen above, the IEC Standard interpreted as a Pure-ER/RRC is actually the Mectan Transmutation in costume. As such, together with some slight breaching, the unreported but derivable 259J Ectron device, means that Ectron furtively interprets the "155.9J at 300Ω" phrase it uses as a Pure-ER/RRC to maximum machine Impedance. Like the Mectan Transmutation, a pure-ER/RRC interpretation of the IEC Standard facilitates both an invisible but actual 260J maximum output for the Ectron Series 5A. This 260J maximum is neither a (156J – 130J =) **26J**, nor even a (155.9J – 100J =) **55.9J** breach (very possibly "corroborated" by spurious machine readout maximums), but similar to the Mectan Transmutation, a (260J - 130J =) **130J** to (260J - 100J =) **160J** breach. Like American made devices then, in spite of appearances, the Ectron Series 5A, is actually much more powerful than the most powerful SW device, compared to which Brief Pulse continues to be touted as a vast improvement by way of "reduced output. " In lieu of a minimal stimulus device emitting a 1.0, 1.3 or even 1.55.9 MTTLOI, as noted above, Ectron's Series 5A, like second generation made-for-America MECTA and Somatics BP devices, is clearly a second generation suprathreshold ENR device emitting an unreported 2.6 MTTLOI default to every age category.

Ectron Underreports

But did Ectron, like MECTA, really intentionally set out to deceive the European Regulatory Agency (ERA) and the International Electrotechnical Commission (IEC) by suggesting that its Series 5A BP device maximally emits a 155.9J output, that is, a 1.59 MTTLOI for all age recipients, and so yet an improvement over the 200J SW device? Like Somatics, as previously mentioned, Ectron accurately reports most electrical parameters with the exception of EO in joules. However, in one very important way, Ectron seriously misreports. Like MECTA, Ectron misreports maximum Voltage for the Series 5A as 225V (Royal College of Psychiatry, 1995, p.124).

In that we have the maximum electrical parameters of the Series 5A: .75A constant Current, 70 (unidirectional) Pulses, a 500Ω maximum Impedance, a .0022 Sec. Pulse Width, and a 6.0 Sec. maximum Duration and thus the actual maximum power of the Series 5A of 260 derivative joules, let us go back and observe how and what Ectron actually reports to the Royal College of Psychiatry and thus to the ERA and IEC (Ibid).

Because of Ectron's accurately reported parameters generally, we can, using the standard Impedance oriented formula for BP devices, definitively determine actual maximum power of the Series 5A.

EO = .75A x .75A x 500Ω x 70 Pulses x .0022 x 6.0 seconds = **259.9 Joules**.

Using Ohm's Law, we can determine actual maximum Voltage.

Ohm's law: Voltage = Current x Impedance.
Voltage = .750 Amperes x 500Ω = **375 Volts**.

Consequently, using the Voltage oriented formula for finding maximum power, we can affirm both the **375V** maximum as well as the circa **260J** maximum output for the Ectron Series 5A.

EO = .75 x **375 Volts** x 70 Pulses x .0022 x 6.0 seconds = **259.8J**.

However, Ectron does not report **375V**, but **225V** for its Ectron Series 5A. Like MECTA then, Ectron not only fails to report actual maximum Voltage, but abjectly misreports maximum Voltage. So why does Ectron blatantly report to the RCP and thus the ERA and IEC a maximum Voltage of **225V** for the Series 5A? (Royal College of Psychiatry, 1995, p.124).

Revealingly, if we substitute **225 Volts** (for the actual **375V**) into the above Voltage oriented formula for finding EO, we derive an EO not of the actual confirmable **259.8J**, but of **155.9 Joules**:

EO = .75 x **225 Volts** x 70 Pulses x .0022 x 6.0 seconds = **155.9J**.

In turn, **225 Volts** can be seen via Ohm's law to be the equivalent of **300Ω**.

Impedance = Voltage/Current: **225V**/.75A = **300Ω**.

Conversely, we can derive **155.9J** from the indirectly reported **300Ω**.

EO = .75 x .75 x **300Ω** x 70 Pulses x .0022 x 6.0 Seconds = **155.9J**.

We can plainly see that while Ectron, like Somatics, accurately reports most electrical parameters for its Series 5A such as a 500Ω maximum Impedance, like MECTA, Ectron not only fails to report the accompanying actual maximum Voltage, but reports (as maximum Voltage) a misleading **ER-Voltage instead**. In brief, Ectron falsely **reports the actual maximum Voltage at 500Ω as 225V**. In short, Ectron reports an unexplained ER-Voltage (of 225V) from which we derive (via the Voltage oriented formula) not the actual maximum output (of 260J), but an unexplicated and **misleading ER-output of 155.9J** which is then "mistaken" for maximum output.

EO = .75 x **225 Volts** x 70 Pulses x .0022 x 6.0 seconds = **155.9J**.

Only by re-substituting the unreported actual maximum Voltage of **375V**, can we derive the actual maximum output for the Series 5A.

EO = .75 x **375 Volts** x 70 Pulses x .0022 x 6.0 seconds = **259.9J**.

In just the way almost all BP manufacturers indicate lower EOs, Ectron, just as MECTA, **reports ER-Voltage as maximum Voltage**. Clearly, **225V is a pure-ER-Voltage at a pure-ER-Impedance of 300Ω** to **actual (unreported) maximum Voltage of 375V** at the **actual maximum Impedance of 500Ω**.

225V/300Ω = **375V/500Ω**

By reporting a maximum Voltage of 225V then, Ectron not only makes it difficult to determine actual maximum output, but similar to MECTA, has actively engendered the false impression that the Series 5A machine is limited to **155.9 maximum Joules**.

EO = .75 x **225 Volts** x 70 Pulses x .0022 x 6.0 seconds = **155.9J**.

Indirectly reporting a false maximum output of **155.9 Joules** for the Series 5A, is **thus erroneously suggestive of (more or less) minimal stimulus or just above threshold output,** a false suggestion which, based on the American paradigm, compels us to suspect **a false maximum machine readout for the Series 5A of 155.9J**. Such a pattern is similar to the misleading practices of both MECTA and Somatics apparently devised by American, Richard Weiner. Indeed, such a maximum machine readout (of 155.9J) can be accomplished in several ways, as we shall examine in a moment.

Ectron Underreporting Continued

To be clear, the maximum 225 Volts reported by Ectron for its Series 5A is not actual maximum Voltage, but--as noted above--an ER-Voltage corresponding to a pure-ER/RRC Output/Impedance of "155.9J at 300Ω. "

EO = .75 x .75 x **300Ω** x 70 Pulses x .0022 x 6.0 Seconds = **155.9J**.
EO = .75 x **225 Volts** x 70 Pulses x .0022 x 6.0 seconds = **155.9J**.

Like MECTA (which falsely reports to the RCP a 240V maximum), Ectron, in reporting a false 225V maximum, indirectly, but clearly indicates [497] a false maximum output of 155.9Js for the Ectron BP Series 5A, illustrating once more that BP manufacturers on a world-wide basis deliberately convey to regulatory agencies and the general public, the notion that BP devices continue to utilize much less output than they actually do. [498]

As is the common practice then, Ectron, like other BP manufacturers, fails to report its derivable 155.9J as a pure-ER-output (at a 300Ω pure-ER Impedance); in short, Ectron never reveals its indirectly reported 155.9J maximum as an ER output. [499] Thus Ectron utilizes a false 225V maximum and thus an unannounced 300Ω ER-Impedance in conjunction with the remaining actual maximum parameters of the Series 5A to suggest a 155.9J ceiling. Conversely, Ectron furtively replaces the *reported* 225V maximum with the actual *unreported* 375V maximum (tantamount to replacing the 300Ω ER-Impedance with the actual 500Ω maximum Impedance) to facilitate and administer the 5A's actual unreported maximum of 260 Joules. [500] In other words, as is the practice of manufacturers, Ectron implies one maximum output to the general public (155.9J) while utilizing another much higher maximum output (259.9J) to administer an unreported 2.6 MTTLOI to all recipients. By suggesting a conditional-ER/RRC interpretation (through the reporting of a false 225V maximum) but furtively interpreting the IEC Standard as a Pure-ER/RRC (thereby grossly surpassing an implied 100, 130, and even 155.9J ceiling), like MECTA and Somatics, Ectron circumvents the necessary Duration reductions required to maintain the implied 155.9J ceiling. Instead (as is the customary procedure), in applying a Pure-ER/RRC interpretation (i.e. the Mectan Transmutation) to the indirectly derived "155.9J at 300Ω" ER/RRC phrase, Ectron actually increases rather than decreases Duration (and thus Charge), [501] boosting the power of the Series 5A to a new, never before reported maximum output. In lieu of a seeming 1.59 MTTLOI for all recipients, consequently, the Ectron Series 5A actually utilizes a never-before-reported 2.6 MTTLOI for all age recipients.

Reported maximum EO of Series 5A (based on reporting of a 225V ER):
EO = .75 x **225 Volts** x 70 Pulses x .0022 x **6.0 sec.** = **155.9J**

Implied EO of Series 5A (based on reporting of a 300Ω ER):
.75A x .75A x **300Ω** x 70 Pulses x .0022 x **6.0 sec.** = **155.9 Joules**.

Anticipated 155.9J Maximum EO of Series 5A at **500Ω** interpreted conditionally and thus with a hypothetical 3.6 Second maximum output:
.75 x .75 x **500Ω** x 70 Pulses x .0022 Pulse Width x **3.6 sec.** = **155.9J**.
(Note the ***hypothetical*** reduction in Duration). [502]

---

[497] Just as a 300Ω ER-Impedance has replaced the actual maximum 500Ω Impedance in order to report what is actually an ER-EO for Ectron's Series 5A, U.S. manufacturers under the APA Standard, replace their actual 555.5-600Ω maximum Impedance with a "typical" 220Ω" or 220Ω ER-Impedance in order to report false 100 Joule maximums (Cameron, 1994).

[498] Though neglecting to report actual output in joules and depicting 99.4 maximum joules on its machine readouts for its DGx, Somatics alone reports true maximum Voltage (Royal College of Psychiatry, 1995, p.124-125).

[499] Ectron reports 155.9 Joules as maximum EO (which it isn't) by reporting 225 Volts as maximum Voltage (which it isn't). It then secretly interprets the 155.9J (derived at 225 Volts) as an ER output (at an ER Impedance of 300Ω) in order to secretly derive its true unreported maximum EO (at it true 500Ω maximum Impedance) of 259.8 Joules.

[500] Ectron seems to have deliberately created the false impression of a (more or less) minimal stimulus device. At the same time, should the actual 260J output ever come out (as it has here), Ectron might use the circuitous Pure-ER rationale to "claim" it indirectly reported it.

[501] Duration and Charge are not reduced to maintain the 100, 130, or even 155.9 Joule ceilings. Instead of decreasing, Duration and thus Charge, steadily increase up to 6.0 seconds and .700C, a Charge circa 2.5 times that required to induce adequate seizures for BL electrode placement and circa 5.0 times that required to induce adequate seizures with UL electrode placement. It is well known that adequate seizures for all recipients can be induced with 100 Joules or less (Department of Health and Human Services, 1982a, A53; E20).

[502] 225V is an ER tantamount to a 300Ω ER tantamount to 156J.375V is an actual maximum Voltage tantamount to an actual maximum 500Ω Impedance tantamount to actual maximum 260J.

Unreported but Actual Maximum EO of Ectron Series 5A at actual **375V**:
EO = .75 x **375 Volts** x 70 Pulses x .0022 x **6.0 sec.** = **259.9J**

Unreported but Actual Maximum EO Ectron Series 5A at actual **500Ω** and 6.0 second Duration:
.75A x .75A x **500Ω** x 70 Pulses x .0022 x **6.0 sec.** = **259.9J**. [503]

In brief, Ectron quietly re-interprets the 155.9J at 300Ω conditional-ER/RRC implicitly reported by Ectron (via a false 225V maximum) for its Series 5A as a Pure-ER/RRC to its true unreported maximum output and maximum Impedance of "260J at 500Ω," creating first one impression (a 1.56 MTTLOI) for the public while administering quite another (2.6 MTTLOI)--to all recipients to create the proverbial double standard.

155.9J/300Ω = 260J/500Ω.

If challenged, Ectron might claim that, in fact, it does report the actual 500Ω maximum Impedance (tantamount to a derivable 260 maximum joules) for its Series 5A. This, however, begs the question: "Why, in fact, does Ectron report a false 225V maximum tantamount to a derivable 300Ω and a derivable 155.9J maximum, which then directly contradicts the reported 500Ω maximum Impedance?" Indeed, by reporting a 225V maximum in conjunction with the actual 500Ω maximum Impedance, the impression of a 155.9J maximum output is strengthened, particularly if Ectron displays a 155.9J readout maximum on the machine itself. [504] In brief, the reporting of a 225V maximum in conjunction with a 500Ω maximum Impedance strongly suggests a 155.9J ceiling at 500Ω, a conditional--ER/RRC interpretation of the derivable "155J at 300Ω" phrase. [505] At the very least, Ectron's contradictory reporting results in a great deal of confusion while that which could clear up the confusion--the simple reporting of the actual 259.9J output maximum at 500Ω and thus a 2.6 MTTLOI emitted at every age category, never transpires.

In summary then, Ectron (like most other BP manufacturers) uses a Pure-ER/RRC interpretation of the 1989 IEC Standard in lieu of the anticipated Conditional-ER/RRC limiting output to the circa 100 Joules suggested by the IEC featured "100J at 300Ω" phrase, the implicit 130J ceiling suggested by the derivable "130J at 300Ω" phrase discoverable in the cushion adjunct, or the 155.9 joules deducible from the "155.9J at 300Ω" phrase derivable from the reported 225V maximum. In fact, Ectron's electrical parameters reflect an illegal "155.9J at 300Ω" Pure-ER/RRC, exceeding by almost (156J-130J =) 26 Joules even the IEC thirty percent EO cushion adjunct based on "130J at 300Ω" pure-ER/RRC. Indeed, the illegal "155.9J at 300Ω" interpreted as a Pure-ER/RRC (upon which the Ectron Series 5A is actually based) results in the illegal utilization of a .700 Coulomb Charge ceiling as well as an illegal 260J maximum output,[506] all in spite of which Ectron reports for its Series 5A a misleading 225 Volt maximum (Royal College of Psychiatry, 1995, p.124). The reporting of a 225V maximum, of course, suggests a misleading 155.9J maximum EO ceiling. Indeed, due to the actual Pure-ER/RRC interpretation which Ectron actually applies, the Series 5A device incorporates increasing Duration in lieu of the expected decreasing Duration needed to maintain an indirectly derivable 155.9J ceiling. In spite of a Series 5A 155.9J ceiling, inferred by the spurious reporting of a 225V maximum,

---

[503] Ectron reports a maximum Impedance of 500Ω to the RCP, which, if calculated, requires 375 Volts. In spite of this contradiction, Ectron reports a maximum of 225 Volts (tantamount to 300Ω or a 155.9J maximum), falsely suggesting that, in keeping with the 1982 APA Standard, alternative parameters are reduced, thereby maintaining 155.9J as maximum output. For instance, at 500Ω maximum, 155.9J could be maintained by reducing maximum Duration of 6.0 Seconds to 3.6 Seconds. EO = .75 x .75 x 500Ω x 70 Pulses x .0022 Pulse Width x 3.6 Seconds = 155.9J.

[504] The author is speculating.

[505] A "155.9J at 300Ω" conditional-ER/RRC interpretation incorporative of a 155.9J ceiling suggests a 1.56 MTTLOI at all age levels. This can mean that no more than 155.9J can be delivered to a 100 year old recipient, who seizes at a maximum of 100 joules but who may have an Impedance of 500Ω. In short, maximum output appears to be limited to 155.9J at 500Ω. The "100J at 300Ω" phrase then, appears to act merely as a conditional-ER/RRC indicative of gradient output with respect to age, but uniformly based on a 115.9J maximum output or 1.56 MTTLOI for every age recipient which is, of course, false. For context, the APA Standard depicts a "70J at 220Ω" true conditional-ER/RRC with true 110J ceiling.

[506] Even a Pure-ER/RRC interpretation based on a "130J at 300Ω" resulting in a 216.6J maximum output (130J/300Ω = 216.6J/500Ω) results in a .577 Coulomb Charge ceiling for the Ectron Series 5A devices. This ceiling is even lower, of course, if interpreted conditionally (with 130J ceiling).

therefore, Ectron actually increases Duration by using an actual, but unreported 375V maximum at an actual 500Ω maximum Impedance. This, as already noted, results in the illegal unreported EO maximum of 259.9J identified above. [507] This circa 260J EO maximum actually emitted by the Ectron Series 5A accomplishes Ectron's true aim of administering an unreported, default MTTLOI circa 2.6 times that necessary to induce an adequate grand mal seizure for every age recipient.

In Sum: Ectron Adopts the Secret U. S. Methodology Both to Hide and Grossly Surpass the 100 Joule Mark Needed to Induce Seizures in All Age Recipients

The featured phrase "100J at 300Ω" within the 1989 IEC Standard gives the impression of a conditional-ER/RRC incorporative of a 100J ceiling and thus minimal stimulus output for all age recipients. Like the 1982 APA Standard (clearly regulating BP devices to no more than 110 joules), in order to maintain threshold or minimal stimulus output for all age recipients, incremental reductions in Duration, as noted, would have to be applied. [508] In fact, the impression created by the featured "100J at 300Ω" IEC Standard as a Conditional-ER/RRC with 100J ceiling is ignored.

Instead, Ectron utilizes the same unlikely and unexplicated Pure-ER/RRC interpretation (eliminating the 100J ceiling) initiated in 1983 by American device makers MECTA and Somatics Inc. in America, an interpretation deemed "the Mectan Transmutation" (in this manuscript). Ignoring the anticipated Conditional-ER/RRC interpretation, therefore, the Series 5A neither maintains the logically implied 100J ceiling alluded to within the 1989 IEC Standard, nor the 130J ceiling (based upon the 30 percent cushion adjunct within the same standard), nor even the illegal 155.9J ceiling indirectly reported by Ectron for its Series 5A (through the 225V maximum report). All three maximum, of course, would require incremental reductions in Duration and correspondingly, Charge. In lieu of the 155.9J maximum output Ectron indirectly reports (via Voltage) for its Series 5A, [509] Ectron, similar to MECTA and Somatics, utilizes, as already noted, a 155.9J at 300Ω Pure-ER/RRC to an actual albeit unreported maximum EO of 260J at 500Ω. This Pure-ER/RRC (as opposed to a Conditional-ER/RRC) interpretation "permits" increasing rather than decreasing Duration and Charge, ultimately resulting in an actual maximum EO, as noted, of approximately 260 unreported joules for the Ectron BP Series 5A and thus, as pointed out, an unreported circa 2.6 MTTLOI for every age recipient.

155.9J/300Ω = 260J/500Ω.

The question regarding Ectron's breaching of the IEC Standard then, is not, as regulatory agencies may mistakenly believe, an illegal but somewhat forgivable 155.9J ceiling [510] as opposed to anticipated ceilings of 100 or even 130 maximum Joules, but rather a never before reported 260J maximum output versus 100 or 130 maximum Joules--grossly unacceptable breaches of between 160 and 130 Joules (260J - 100J = **160J**; 260J - 130J = **130J**). The evidence that a minimal stimulus impression is deliberately engendered for BP devices generally (i.e. MECTA's similarly based underreporting of maximum Voltage), suggests that Ectron and other European BP manufacturers on a world-wide basis, not only co-conspire with American manufacturers in omitting and actively covering up actual power of their modern day BP devices, but deliberately create the false impression of circa 100 maximum joules to falsely associate modern day Brief Pulse with minimal stimulus

---

[507] Once again, even permitting the very questionable manufacturers' interpretation of "130J at 300Ω" as a Pure-ER/RRC, actual maximum EO should not surpass 216J. Thus, by even the most liberal interpretation, Ectron violates the 1989 IEC Standard by 44 Joules (260J - 216J = 44J).

[508] Output would have to be restricted to 1.0 fold threshold or minimal stimulus, similar to the MECTA "C," thereby reflecting the 1982 APA Standard.

[509] Utilizing the 225 Volt maximum reported by Ectron for Series 5A along with other parameters reported by Ectron for BP Series 5A, we obtain an Absolute EO of 155.9 Joules. EO = .75A x 225V x 70 Pulses x .0022 PW x 6.0 Seconds = 155.9J. We are not told that 225V is but an ER Voltage and that actual maximum Voltage is 375V.

[510] An interesting side-note here, is that the B-24 SW by Medcraft, one of the most powerful SW devices ever manufactured, utilizes a typical 136 Joule maximum, approximately twenty Joules less than the Series 5A would emit even if interpreted conditionally although such maximums would occur in disparate age categories. (See B-24 in this manuscript.)

output. [511] Like American BP manufacturers then, the accurate maximum Charge reported by Ectron of circa .700C in tandem with an indirectly derivable ER-Energy Output of (in this instance) 155.9J, continues to bolster the false impression of minimal stimulus outputs well below that of SW. In fact, like American BP manufacturers, the Ectron Series 5A at circa 260 maximum joules not only emits power far in excess of the known and much publicized 100 minimum joules required to induce adequate seizures in even the most seizure recalcitrant Brief Pulse recipient, but, as we have seen, far in excess of SW--both factors of which BP manufacturers persistently and ubiquitously conceal.

Ectron's Earlier BP Devices--A Short History

To further buttress the argument that Ectron and other BP manufacturers not only hide actual output conspiratorially, but deliberately engender the false impression pf modern BP devices having much lower outputs than they actually do, let us briefly study the modern history of Ectron's previous BP devices in order that we might compare Ectron's modern history to the modern history of American BP devices.

In 1995, as already noted, Ectron reported to the RCP, false maximum Voltages of 225V not only for its Series 5A, but for all its BP devices, past and present (Royal College of Psychiatry, 1995, p.124). That 225V is inaccurate can be determined by figures derived from Ectron's accurately reported maximum Impedances, maximum Charges, and constant Currents for the entire series, that is, its initial Series 2/3, its subsequent Series 2+3+, the later Series 5, and finally, its subsequent second generation Series 5A (Ibid), which we have been examining. [512] For example, the accurately reported maximum Impedances for the Series 2/3, 2+3+, 5, and 5A are 450Ω, 450Ω, 500Ω, and 500Ω respectively (Ibid). Using Ohm's Law, the reported 225V maximums Ectron reports for its Series 2/3 and 2+/3+ are tantamount to a (Ohm's law: Impedance = V/Amperage. Impedance = 225V ÷ .85A =) 265Ω maximum Impedance, inconsistent with the actual maximum Impedances both reported and used by Ectron for these devices: 265Ω ≠ 450Ω. In fact, actual maximum Voltage, undermining the reported 225V, can also be determined through Ohm's Law: (Voltage = Amperage x Impedance; V = A x Ω; V = .85A x 450.) = **382V**. Thus actual maximum Voltage for Ectron's Series 2/3 and 2+/3+ is **382V**. Using Ohm's law once again, the reported 225V maximums reported for the Series 5 and 5A can be seen as untenable in that [513] the derived (Impedance = 225V ÷ .75A =) 300Ω maximums are inconsistent with the actual 500Ω maximum Impedance Ectron both reports and uses for its Series 5 and 5A: (300Ω ≠ 500Ω). Similarly moreover, also through Ohm's law, actual maximum Voltage for the Series 5 and 5A can be determined as (Voltage = Amperage x Impedance; .75A x 500Ω =) 375V (as opposed to the falsely reported 225V). Like MECTA's negligence, we can now be certain that Ectron fails to report actual maximum Voltages to the Royal College of Psychiatry and thus the IEC for its entire series (International Electrotechnical Commission). Rather, in reporting a spurious 225V maximum, Ectron is actually reporting ER-Voltages. [514] For

[511] While manufacturers have increasingly, out of necessity, begun to admit the need for greater than threshold dosages to be effective, the reasons they provide are spurious. Moreover, manufacturers yet hide the true power of their devices and even the degree of multifold dosing. Paradoxically, manufacturers continue to engender the false impression that BP devices have greatly reduced EO compared to SW.

[512] Ectron also accurately reports constant Amperages, maximum unidirectional pulses, maximum Charges, pulse widths, and maximum Durations. Amperages are reported as .85A for Series 2/3 and 2+/3+ and .75A for Series 5 and 5A respectively. Maximum unidirectional pulses are reported as 40, 55, 74, and 70 respectively. Maximum output Charges are reported as .255, .350, .400, and .700C respectively. Constant pulse widths are reported as .00125, .00125, .0022, and .0022 seconds respectively. Finally, maximum Durations are reported as 6.0, 6.0, 3.25, and 6.0 Seconds respectively (Royal College of Psychiatry, 1995, p.124).

[513] Ectron reports a .85A constant current for its 2/3 and 2+/3+ Series; whereas, it reports a .75A constant current for the more powerful 5 and 5A Series (Royal College of Psychiatry, 1995, p.124).

[514] In that Actual Charge is also provided by Ectron--.255C and .350C for the Series 2/3 and 2+3+ respectively and .400C and .700C for the Series 5 and 5A respectively, the inconsistency can be verified by comparing Voltage oriented formula for finding EO versus the Charge oriented formula for finding EO. Based upon the Charge-oriented formula for finding EO (which does not require Voltage: EO = Current x Impedance x Charge) and upon remaining parameters reported to RCP (Royal College of Psychiatry, 1995, p.124) the following actual maximum machine outputs can be derived. Series 2/3 = .850A x 450Ω x .255C = 97.5J. Series 2+/3+ = .850A x 450Ω x .350C = 133.9J. Series 5 = .750A x 500Ω x .400C = 150J. Series 5A = .750A x 500Ω x .700C (rounded) = 262.5J. Output inconsistencies for Ectron Series 5A of one or two Joules (compared to those derived with actual Voltages) are due to rounding of reported maximum Charge from .693 to .700 Coulombs.

example, using the reported 225V maximum for Series 2/3, 2+/3+, 5 and 5A, we derive (as noted above) not actual maximum Impedances at all, but for the Series 2/3 and 2+/3+, what is actually a 265Ω ER-Impedance and for the Series 5 and 5A, what is actually a 300Ω ER-Impedance. That these are ER-Voltages and ER-Impedances can be shown in relation to actual maximum Voltages and actual maximum Impedances.

Series 2/3 and 2+/3+: **225V/265Ω = 382V/450Ω**
Series 5 and 5A: **225V/300Ω = 375V/500Ω**

But what is the purpose of reporting an ER-Voltage for actual maximum Voltage while accurately reporting all other electrical parameters? Although we have already touched upon this issue, let us answer this question more definitively by determining ER-EOs (Equivalent Ratio-Energy Outputs) as opposed to actual maximum EOs for all four devices using first the reported ER-Voltages followed by actual unreported Voltages. For this, let us use the formula: EO = Current x Voltage x Pulse Width x Pulses x Duration.

Using the inaccurate or misleading 225V maximums along with accurately reported parameters, we obtain the following false outputs for the Series 2/3, 2+/3+, 5, and 5A:

Series 2/3: EO = .85A x **225V** x .00125 Sec. PW x 40 Pulses x 6.0 Seconds = ***57.3J***.
Series 2+/3+: EO = .85A x **225V** x .00125 Sec. PW x 55 Pulses x 6.0 Seconds = ***78.89J***.
Series 5: EO = .75A x **225V** x .0022 Sec. PW x 74 Pulses x 3.25 Seconds = ***89.28J***.
Series 5A: .75A x **225V** x .0022 Sec. PW x 70 Pulses x 6.0 Seconds = ***155.9J***.

In short, Ectron reports maximum EO for its 2/3, 2+/3+, 5, and 5A models as 57.3J, 78.89J, 89.28J, and, 155.9J respectively.

Of course, by replacing what are actually ER Voltages of 225V (from which we have derived ER-EOs) with actual Voltages, we obtain the actual albeit unreported EOs:

Series 2/3: EO = .85A x **382V** x .00125 Sec. PW x 40 Pulses x 6.0 Seconds = ***97.4J***.
Series 2+/3+: EO = .85A x **382V** x .00125 Sec. PW x 55 Pulses x 6.0 Seconds = ***134J***.
Series 5: EO = .75A x **375V** x .0022 Sec. PW x 74 Pulses x 3.25 Seconds = ***149J***.
Series 5A: .75A x **375V** x .0022 Sec. PW x 70 Pulses x 6.0 Seconds = ***260J***.

We now see the actual but unreported maximum EOs for the Ectron series **2/3**, **2+/3+**, **5**, and **5A**, as **97.4J**, **134J**, **149J**, and **260J** respectively.

In short, we have Ectron's pseudo versus actual history of first and second generation BP devices. Utilizing the false maximum (or ER) Voltages (of 225V) provided to RCP by Ectron (Ibid), we first obtained Ectron's indirectly reported maximum outputs for the Series 2/3, Series 2+/3+, Series 5, and finally Series 5A as **57.3J**, **78.89J**, **89.28J**, and **155.9J** respectively. Note how all machines except the Series 5A appear to fall under the 100J mark, while the 5A alone appears to breach the 1989 IEC ceiling of 130 Joules by a more or less "forgivable" twenty-six Joules. Thus, even the Series 5A yet appears improved (by virtue of reduced output) over the 200J SW device. All four appear to be "minimal stimulus" instruments or ECT devices, the most powerful emitting a 1.59 MTTLOI for all age groups. Use of unexplicated ER-Voltages as actual maximums in conjunction with (the remaining) actual maximum parameters makes the power progression of the Ectron series over time appear much less dramatic than it actually is. Conversely, the actual unreported maximum outputs derived with actual unreported maximum Voltages of 382V and 375V respectively, reveal actual power increases as **97.5J**, **134J**, **148.8J**, and **260 Joules** respectively.

Interestingly, in emitting an actual 97.5J maximum output, Ectron's 1981-1987 now defunct BP Series 2/3 corresponds to the "100J at 300Ω" statement contained within (the then soon to be published) 1989 IEC Standard if interpreted as a Conditional-ER/RRC, that is, if limited to 100 Joules. In any case, the Ectron Series 2/3 device was actually limited to circa 100 joules. Subsequently, the 1985 Ectron--now defunct--BP Series 2+/3+ in emitting an actual 134J maximum, corresponds (generally), to the legal 130J ceiling cushion adjunct (if interpreted conditionally) contained within the (then upcoming) 1989 IEC Standard. Following the Series 2+/3+, the 1985-1993 (now defunct) BP Series 5, emitted an actual 148.8J ceiling, a serious but still somewhat "forgivable" breach of the 130J ceiling maximum (again, if interpreted conditionally) of the same 1989 IEC Standard based on the 30% cushion adjunct. Finally, the1989 Series 5A, in emitting an actual unreported 260J maximum output, is totally out of compliance with any conditional-ER/RRC interpretation of the 1989 IEC Standard and any semblance of minimal stimulus. In short, the Series 5A is totally out of compliance with anything close to a 100J and even 130J ceiling. In observing the actual increasing EO of Ectron BP devices in general then (97.5J, 134J, 150J, 260J), Series 2/3 and Series 2+/3+ appear to conform to a conditional-ER/RRC interpretation of the 1989 IEC Standard whereas Series 5 (circa 150J) appears to be a somewhat "acceptable" breach. In sum, the first three series appear more or less minimal stimulus, more or less based on a 100J ceiling, and yet an improvement over the 200J SW device. In fact, the first three series might well be deemed first generation BP devices. The sudden jump in the unreported power of Ectron's Series 5A to 260Js, covered up by the false reporting of (an unexplained ER maximum of) 225 maximum Volts, actually surpasses SW. However, the false reporting of 225V which relinquishes a false 155.9J maximum output can only be unveiled via a Pure-ER/RRC interpretation of what is actually a "155.9J at 300Ω" ER phrase. In short, we must juxtapose this phrase against the actual maximum machine Impedance of 500Ω in order see the actual maximum EO used. That is, we have to see that, like the Mectan Transmutation, manufacturers, were interpreting the newly emerging IEC Standard as a Pure ER/RRC. In a word, the hidden and unreported output of the Series 5A is actually 2.6 fold minimal stimulus for all age recipients.

155.9J/300Ω = 260J/500Ω.

The Series 5A then, is a second generation BP device, and probably the first to be based on a Pure-ER/RRC interpretation of the 1989 IEC Standard (although breaching even that). It is, in short, the first to be figured via the Mectan Transmutation. Moreover, by substituting ER Voltages for actual Voltages, Ectron indirectly reports the same approximate 150J (vs.155.9J) maximum output for its Series 5A as it previously used for its Series 5. This Americanized method (of reporting ER figures) in lieu of actual figures, falsely suggesting the same relatively minor breach (of the IEC 130J ceiling) as that of the Series 5, engenders the misleading impression that the Series 5 and 5A are comparable in power when, in fact, the Ectron Series 5A has suddenly shot upwards in power by some 100 Joules, 1.73 times that of Ectron's previous Series 5 device. Succinctly, the Series 5A emits an astonishing and never before reported 260 unreported Joules, [515] increasing 110 Joules compared to its' immediate predecessor, the Series 5. Moreover, the Series 5A emits an unreported 2.6 fold the initial Series 2/3 which had apparently been restricted to an actual 100 maximum Joules, a history and cover-up remarkably similar to that of MECTA and Somatics BP devices in the U. S. Thus, like MECTA and Somatics, Ectron appears to cover up the actual 260J output of its Series 5A second generation BP device. Based on a breaching of the 1989 IEC Standard even interpreted as a never before explained, Pure-ER/RRC, Ectron instead appears (through the reporting of a 225V maximum) to suggest a relatively minor breaching of the 1989 IEC Standard interpreted as a Conditional-ER/RRC. In sum, Ectron wishes regulators to believe its Series 5A BP device emits a maximum 155.9J when, in fact, it actually emits a 260J maximum output.

Ectron and the Mectan Transmutation

By reporting unexplicated ER output in lieu of actual output, Ectron is utilizing the American double standard methodology, reporting a 155.9J output for the Series 5A (via the reporting of a false 225V maximum) while

[515] 260 ÷ 150 = 1.73.

surreptitiously utilizing <u>260 maximum Joules</u>. True maximum Voltage is never reported by Ectron. In essence, Ectron is utilizing the "Mectan Transmutation," switching (in this case from a Conditional-ER/RRC interpretation of "155.9J at 300"--tantamount to "225V at 300Ω"--indicative of a 155.9J ceiling) to a Pure ER/RRC interpretation of the same 155.9J at 300Ω (155.9J/300Ω = 260J/500Ω), thereby facilitating an actual (but never reported) 260J ceiling. In reporting a 225V maximum then, Ectron is reporting a 155.9J ceiling. Moreover, in reporting a 225V ceiling, Ectron is utilizing a 300Ω maximum Impedance for reporting purposes when, in fact, 300Ω, just as 225V, is not an actual maximum, but an <u>ER maximum</u>: (<u>225V/300Ω</u> = 375V/500Ω).

Series 5A:

Indirectly Reported False Maximum Output via ER-Voltage:
.75A x **<u>225V</u>** x 70 Pulses x .0022PW x 6.0 Seconds = **<u>155.9J</u>**.

Unreported True Maximum Output (via actual Voltage):
.75A x **<u>375V</u>** x 70 Pulses x .0022PW x 6.0 Seconds = **<u>260J</u>**.

(Ohm's law: Resistance = Voltage ÷ Amperage)

Reported ER maximum:
<u>225V</u> ÷ .75A = **<u>300Ω</u>**

Actual maximum:
<u>375V</u> ÷ .75A = **<u>500Ω</u>**

Reported maximum:
.75A x .75A x **<u>300Ω</u>** x 70 Pulses x .0022 x 6.0 **<u>sec.</u>** = **<u>155.9 Joules</u>**.

Actual maximum:
.75A x .75A x **<u>500Ω</u>** x 70 Pulses x .0022 x 6.0 **<u>sec.</u>** = **<u>259.9 Joules</u>**.

ER Voltage/Output to **Actual Maximum Voltage/Output**:
<u>225V</u>/**<u>156J</u>** = <u>375V</u>/**<u>260J</u>**

ER Output/Impedance to **Actual Maximum Output/Impedance**
<u>155.9J</u>/<u>300Ω</u> = **<u>260J</u>**/<u>500Ω</u>).

Ectron, like American companies, then, covers up the true power of the Series 5A by reporting ER maximums in lieu of actual maximums.

By indirectly reporting ER maximums as actual maximums (of 100J, 130J, 150J and 156J)-- like MECTA and Somatics, Ectron both engenders and maintains a totally false impression of actual power (and consequently, enhanced MTTLOI) not only for the Series 2/3, 2+/3+, and Series 5, but for the Series 5A. In fact, in reporting a false <u>225 Volt maximum</u> to the RCP, (like MECTA's reporting of a false <u>240V maximum</u> and thus a false <u>96.8J maximum</u> for its IEC device), Ectron indirectly albeit actively reports a 155.9J maximum for the Series 5A, abetting the notion, as noted above, that the 1989 IEC Standard is based on a Conditional-ER/RRC regulating devices to between 100-130Js (of which the Ectron Series 5A appears "to moderately breach" via a 155.9J ceiling). In brief, Ectron directly reports an ER-Voltage as actual maximum Voltage without so much as hinting that the derivable <u>155.9J</u> maximum is actually an ER output (of 155.9J at 300Ω) to actual maximum output (260J) at actual maximum Impedance (500Ω), ultimately, a never before reported circa 260 maximum Joules (155.9J/300Ω = <u>260J</u>/500Ω).

It is the wording and subtle construct of the 1989 IEC Standard, therefore, along with the absence of any explanatory clarification, which suddenly makes available to Ectron (and other BP manufacturers) both a Pure-ER/RRC interpretation--in lieu of a Conditional-ER/RRC interpretation--as well as a method of under-reporting power via ER reporting. [516] As such, manufacturers are able to repress the dramatic electrical energy enhancements BP devices have undergone internationally. Compare the age-related threshold outputs below to the probable actual Series 5A chart below that.

10 year old male = 2.60J ÷ 2.60 = **1.00J**
20 year old male = 10.41J ÷ 2.60 = **4.00J**
30 year old male = 23.40J ÷ 2.60 = **9.00J**
40 year old male = 41.60J ÷ 2.60 = **16.00J**
50 year old male = 65.00J ÷ 2.60 = **25.00J**
60 year old male = 93.60J ÷ 2.60 = **36.00J**
65 year old male = 110.00J ÷ 2.60 = **42.25J**
70 year old male = 127.30J ÷ 2.60 = **48.97J**
80 year old male = 166.40J ÷ 2.60 = **64.00J**
90 year old male = 210.60J ÷ 2.60 = **81.00J**
100 year old male = 260.00J ÷ 2.60 = **100.00J**

ACTUAL CONSTANT CURRENT **Series 5A** (IEC) BRIEF PULSE ENR DEVICE
by Ectron Inc. [517] BASED ON
PURE-ER/RRC INTERPRETATION of **155.9J at 300Ω (114J at 220Ω) or 2.6 MTTLOI**

VOLTAGE	POWER % @ Age	AGE Yrs	Ω Ohms	FREQUENCY (Pulses)	DURATION (SECs)	CURRENT mAmps	ENERGY Joules	CHARGE mC
37.5	10	10	50	30	1.4	750	2.59	69.3
75	20	20	100	30	2.76	750	10.4	136.67
112.5	30	30	150	50	2.52	759	23.4	208
150	40	40	200	50	3.36	750	41.6	277.3
187.5	50	50	250	50	4.2	750	65.0	346.67
225	60	60	300	70	3.6	750	93.6	416
243.75	65	65	325	70	3.91	750	110.0	451.3
262.5	70	70	350	70	4.2	750	127.3	485
300	80	80	400	70	4.8	750	166.4	554.66
337.5	90	90	450	70	5.4	750	210.6	624
375	100	100	**500**	70	6.0	750	**259.0**	**692**

.0022 Sec. PW

Distribution of (unidirectional) pulse output per age is unreported by Ectron, thus Frequency is moderately speculative in the above chart, but probable. In any case, the actual output of the Series 5A is 259.9J and the actual MTTLOI for all age categories is an unreported 2.6. Revealingly, Ectron appears to use the same relative constants used by American manufacturers.

Series 5A: .75A x **375V** x .0022 Sec. PW x 70 Pulses x 6.0 Seconds = ***260J***.

(See formulas below or in the footnote below for determining variables used in the above chart).

---

[516] The 225V reported as maximum by Ectron for Ectron BP devices (Royal College of Psychiatry, 1995, p.124) is actually a Pure-ER/RRC Voltage. Manufacturers' interpret the "100J at 300Ω" and the more difficult to discern, "130J at 300Ω" within the 1989 IEC Standard as Pure-ER/RRC, whereas regulatory bodies appear to interpret the same phrase/s as conditional-ER/RRC (combination ER/RRC//Absolute EO). Manufacturers such as Ectron and MECTA engender the Conditional-ER/RRC notion of the IEC Standard by indirectly reporting as maximums, what are actually unexplained ER-outputs, derived via unexplained and misreported ER-Voltages (in lieu of reporting actual outputs and actual Voltages).

[517] Maximum Voltage is misreported at 225V. Actual maximum Voltage of 375V for the Series 5A is derivable via Ohm's Law: V = Amp x Imp: .75 x 500Ω = 375V. Maximum Charge, maximum Duration, maximum number of (unidirectional) pulses, Pulse Width (.0022), and Constant Current (.75 Amps) are provided by Ectron. Various Voltages are determined by percentage of age (out of 100 years) multiplied by maximum Voltage (375V), i.e.70 years = .70 of 375V = 262.5V. Various Impedances, i.e. Impedance at 70% can then be derived via Ohm's Law (Impedance = Voltage ÷ Current): Impedance = 262.5V ÷ .75A = 350Ω or 70% of 500Ω = 350Ω. Various EOs delivered are figured via 2.6 fold minimal stimulus outputs (see table above), i.e. Minimal stimulus for 70 yr. old = 48.97J x 2.6 fold = 127.3J. Various Charges are derived via Charge = EO ÷ Current x Impedance, i.e.127.3J ÷ .75A x 350Ω = 485mC for 70 yr. old recipient.

Charge = Duration x Current x (hz x 2) x WL
Charge = EO/Current x Impedance
EO = Charge x Current x Impedance
Duration = Charge/Current x (hz x 2) x WL
EO = Voltage x Current x (hz x 2) x WL x Duration
EO = (Current squared) x Impedance x (hz x 2) x WL x Duration
Ohm's Law: Current = Voltage/Ω; Ω = Voltage/Current; Voltage = Current x Ω

Indeed, as noted earlier, even using actual Voltage, Ectron could have built an actual ECT machine with a 155.9J ceiling simply by reducing Duration. (See chart below.) Of course, this would have resulted in reduction of Charge as well.

ANTICIPATED BUT PURELY HYPOTHETICAL
CONSTANT CURRENT **Series 5A** (IEC) BRIEF PULSE ECT DEVICE
by Ectron Inc. [518] BASED ON
Conditional-ER/RRC INTERPRETATION OF **155.9J AT 300Ω or a 1.56 MTTLOI**

VOLTAGE	POWER % @ Age	AGE Yrs	Ω Ohms	FREQUENCY (Pulses)	DURATION (SECs)	CURRENT mAmps	ENERGY Joules	CHARGE mC
37.5	10	10	50	30	.84	750	1.559	41.6
75	20	20	100	30	1.68	750	6.23	83
112.5	30	30	150	50	1.50	759	14.0	124
150	40	40	200	50	2.0	750	24.9	166
187.5	50	50	250	50	2.52	750	39.0	208
225	60	60	300	70	2.156	750	56.0	249
243.75	65	65	325	70	2.34	750	65.9	270
262.5	70	70	350	70	2.52	750	76.4	291
300	80	80	400	70	2.87	750	99.8	332
337.5	90	90	450	70	3.24	750	126.3	374
375	100	100	**500**	70	3.6	750	**155.9J**	**416**

.0022 Sec. PW

Series 5A: .75A x **375V** x .0022 Sec. PW x 70 Pulses x 3.6 Sec. [519] = ***155.9J***.

AGE RELATED THREHOLD OUTPUTS X 1.56 SIMILAR TO THE OUTPUTS ABOVE

10 year old male = 1.00J **X 1.56** = **1.56**
20 year old male = 4.00J **X 1.56** = **6.24J**
30 year old male = 9.00J **X 1.56** = **14.04J**
40 year old male = 16.00J X 1.56 = 24.96J
50 year old male = 25.00J X 1.56 = 39.0J
60 year old male = 36.00J X 1.56 = 56J
65 year old male = 42.25J X 1.56 = 66J
70 year old male = 48.97J X 1.56 = 76.4J
80 year old male = 64.00J X 1.56 = 99.84J
90 year old male = 81.00J X 1.56 = 126.36J
100 year old male = 100.00J X 1.56 = 155.9J

---

[518] Maximum Voltage is misreported at 225V. Actual maximum Voltage of 375V for the Series 5A is derivable via Ohm's Law: V = Amp x Imp: .75 x 500Ω = 375V. Maximum Charge, maximum Duration, maximum number of (unidirectional) pulses, Pulse Width (.0022), and Constant Current (.75 Amps) are provided by Ectron. Various Voltages are determined by percentage of age (out of 100 years) times maximum Voltage (375V), i.e.70 years = 70% of 375V = 262.5V. Various Impedances, i.e. Impedance at 70% can then be derived via Ohm's Law (Impedance = Voltage ÷ Current): Impedance = 262.5 ÷ .75 = 350Ω at 70% or 70 years of age. Various EOs delivered are figured via 2.6 fold minimal stimulus outputs (see table above), i.e. Minimal stimulus for 70 yr old = 48.97 Joules x 1.56 fold = 76.4J. Various Charges are derived via Charge = EO ÷ Current x Impedance, i.e.76.4J ÷ .75A x 350Ω = 291mC for 70 yr. old recipient.

[519] Here, 3.6 Seconds replaces the actual 6.0 seconds emitted by the actual device.

False Readouts for the Ectron Series 5A

Factually, as already noted, the Series 5A emits a never before reported 259.9J maximum output and a 2.59 MTTLOI for all age categories. What is not entirely known is the readout depictions for the Series 5A. For example, MECTA and Somatics use a false 220Ω ER Constant to underreport actual EO readouts on their second generation BP devices. In that Ectron similarly reports to the RCP a misleading 225V ER maximum as actual maximum Voltage--a Voltage equivalent to a 300Ω ER Impedance, the possibility exists that Ectron similarly utilizes a false constant Impedance to display similar false readout depictions for its Series 5A. For example, Ectron may inject of a false 300Ω Impedance constant into the device's computer to obtain a maximum machine readout display of 155.9 joules as well as false readouts for all other machine displays as in the chart below. Note how Voltage, Pulses, Duration, Current, and Charge remain accurate, whereas, like Somatics and MECTA, Ectron's Impedance and thus EOs are wholly misrepresented. In fact, if EOs were actually limited to circa 155.9 Joules as in the chart below, though not depicted as such, all Charge outputs would have to be reduced as well. However, since Charge outputs are not actually reduced in correspondence to these false readouts, Charges remain actual and so do not actually reflect the false EO readouts. In any case, the result of a false 300Ω Impedance calculated into the machine's computer, provides the appearance of a reduced output Brief Pulse ECT device yet seemingly superior to "200J" Sine Wave devices.

ILLUSORY MINIMAL STIMULUS Ectron **Series 5A** (IEC) BRIEF PULSE "ECT" DEVICE WITH **FALSE CONSTANT IMPEDANCES OF 300Ω** SUGGESTIVE OF A "155.9J AT 300Ω" CONDITIONAL-ER/RRC AND SO A **FALSE 155.9J READOUT MAXIMUM**

VOLTAGE	POWER % @ Age	AGE Yrs	Ω Ohms	FREQUENCY (Pulses)	DURATION (SECs)	CURRENT mAmps	ENERGY Joules	CHARGE mC
37.5	10	10	**300**	30	1.4	750	**11.70**	69.3
75	20	20	**300**	30	2.76	750	**30.74**	136.67
112.5	30	30	**300**	50	2.52	759	**46.78**	208
150	40	40	**300**	50	3.36	750	**62.37**	277.3
187.5	50	50	**300**	50	4.2	750	**78**	346.67
225	60	60	**300**	70	3.6	750	**93.6**	416
243.75	65	65	**300**	70	3.91	750	**101.6**	451.3
262.5	70	70	**300**	70	4.2	750	**109**	485
300	80	80	**300**	70	4.8	750	**124.7**	554.66
337.5	90	90	**300**	70	5.4	750	**140.33**	624
375	100	100	**300**	70	6.0	750	**155.9**	**692**

.0022 Sec. PW

Impedance-Based Formula for Finding Maximum Output:
.75A. x .75A x **300Ω** x 70 Pulses x .0022 PW x 6.0 Sec. = **155.9J**.

Other possibilities exist. In that Ectron falsely reports a 225V ER maximum as actual maximum Voltage, Ectron may plug in a false 225 Volt constant--an ER Voltage as noted--into the machine's calculator (in lieu of a false 300Ω constant Impedance) resulting in the same false EO readouts, including the same false maximum output readout of 155.9 Joules. Note how Impedance, Pulses, Duration, Current, and Charge again remain accurate, whereas Voltage and thus EOs are false. As noted above, however, if EOs were actually limited to circa 155.9 Joules, all Charge outputs would have to be reduced as well and so the actual Charges depicted below, would be inaccurate. The result, in any case, is a seeming Brief Pulse device with seemingly minimal stimulus outputs (up to 155.9J) compared to that of Sine Wave.

ILLUSORY MINIMAL STIMULUS Ectron **Series 5A** (IEC) BRIEF PULSE ECT DEVICE BASED ON A **FALSE CONSTANT VOLTAGE OF 225V** SUGGESTIVE OF A "225V AT 300Ω" CONDITIONAL-ER/RRC WITH **FALSE 155.9J READOUT MAXIMUM**

VOLTAGE	POWER % @ Age	AGE Yrs	Ω Ohms	FREQUENCY (Pulses)	DURATION (SECs)	CURRENT mAmps	ENERGY Joules	CHARGE mC
225	10	10	50	30	1.4	750	**11.70**	69.3
225	20	20	100	30	2.76	750	**30.74**	136.67
225	30	30	150	50	2.52	759	**46.78**	208
225	40	40	200	50	3.36	750	**62.37**	277.3

225	50	50	250	50	4.2	750	**78**	346.67
225	60	60	300	70	3.6	750	**93.6**	416
225	65	65	325	70	3.91	750	**101.6**	451.3
225	70	70	350	70	4.2	750	**109**	485
225	80	80	400	70	4.8	750	**124.7**	554.66
225	90	90	450	70	5.4	750	**140.33**	624
225	100	100	500	70	6.0	750	**155.9**	**692**

.0022 Sec. PW

Voltage-Based Formula for Finding Maximum Output:
225V x .75A x 70 Pulses x .0022 PW x 6.0 Sec. = **155.9J**.

In sum, a false 300Ω constant or a false 225V constant, results in the same false readout maximums culminating in a misleading 155.9J maximum and the illusion of minimal stimulus or "ECT" similar to the illusory readouts on Somatics and MECTA second generation BP devices.

Finally, note how the same accurate maximum Charge of ***.692C*** can be derived using the ***ER***-Impedance maximum (of 300Ω) and an ***ER***-Output maximum (of 155.9J) just as the same ***.692C*** can be derived using the ***actual*** maximum Impedance (of 500Ω) and the **actual** maximum Output (of 259.9J). Exploiting this source of confusion can similarly result in the same misleading equivalence of a ***155.9J*** maximum output (which is but an ER maximum) with actual maximum Charge of ***.692C.***

EO ÷ Current x Impedance = Charge

155.9J ÷ .75A x 300Ω = 692mC.

259.9J ÷ .75A x 500Ω = 692mC.

Ectron History Continued

As already noted, Ectron, in 1995, reported all its BP devices (past and present) as having a 225 Volt maximum (Royal College of Psychiatry, 1995, p.124). In fact, the reported 225V maximum, as has been demonstrated above, is not an actual Voltage at all, but an ER-Voltage. [520] Interestingly, the ER-Voltage (225V) reported as an actual maximum Voltage in 1995 corresponds to a maximum ER-Impedance of 265Ω for the first two Ectron series: Series 2/3 and Series 2+/3+ (Ohm's Law: **225V**/.85A = **265Ω**). Actual Maximum Voltage--**382V**--can then be determined from the **450Ω** actual maximum Impedance reported for both series. (**225V/265Ω = XV/450Ω** = **382V**). In short, Series 2/3 and 2+/3+ are based upon a Pure-ER/RRC of **"225V at 265Ω"** to **Actual Maximum Voltage of 382V** at **Actual Maximum Impedance of 450Ω** (**225V/265Ω = 382V/450Ω**). Both the **ER Voltage (225V)** and **Actual Maximum Voltage (382V)** **for the 2/3 and 2+/3+ Series** can then be converted to **ER-EO** in **Joules (EO)** and **Actual Maximum EO in Joules:**

Series 2/3: **225V** x .85A x 40 Pulses x .00125PW x 6.0 Sec. = **57.3J (ER-EO)**;
Series 2/3: **382V** x .85A x 40 Pulses x .00125PW x 6.0 Sec. = **97.4J(Actual-EO)**;

Series 2+/3+: **225V** x .85A x 55 Pulses x .00125PW x 6.0 Sec = **78.9J (ER-EO)**;
Series 2+/3+: **382V** x .85A x 55 Pulses x .00125PW x 6.0 Sec= **134J (Actual-EO)**. [521]

---

[520] The actual reported 450Ω Impedances for BP Series 2/3 and Series 2+/3+ result in actual EOs of 97.5J and 134J respectively compared to ER-EO derived with 225V of 57.3 Joules and 78.89 Joules respectively. Series 2/3 (**ER**) EO = 225V x .85A x 40 Pulses x .00125PW x 6.0 Seconds = **57.3J**. Series 2/3 **Actual** EO = .85A x .85A x 450Ω x 40 Pulses x .00125PW x 6.0 Seconds = **97.5J**.**57.3J ≠ 97.5J**. Series 2+/3+ (**ER**) EO = 225V x .85A x 55 Pulses x .00125PW x 6.0 Seconds = **78.89J**. Series 2+/3+ **Actual** EO =.85A x .85A x 450Ω x 55 Pulses x .00125PW x 6.0 Seconds = **134J**.7**8.89J ≠ 134J**. The reported maximum 225Volts then, is actually ER Voltage.225V/265Ω = 382V/450Ω.225V/57.3J = 382V/97.5J.225/78.9J = 382V/**134J**. (Voltage may actually be 375V. The difference may be due to rounding).

[521] The reported maximum 225Vs is equivalent (ratio-wise) to an unreported 265Ω Impedance maximum for BP Series 2/3 and 2+/3+, not the reported actual maximum Impedance of 450Ω. We can obtain this ER-Impedance by plugging ER-Voltage and the known

Both **Series 5 and 5A** are based upon a Pure-ER/RRC of **"225V at 300Ω."** [522] **ER-Impedance** for Series 5 and 5A can be derived from Ohm's Law: (**225V** ÷ .75A = **300Ω**). Subsequently, the **Actual Maximum Voltage** of **375V** for Series 5 and 5A can be determined from the actual maximum **500Ω** Impedance reported for Series 5 and 5A: (**225V/300Ω = XV/500Ω = 375V**). Thus: **225V/300Ω = 375V/500Ω**. Both the ER Maximum Voltage and Actual Maximum Voltage for both Series 5 and 5A can then be converted to joules:

> **Series 5**: **225V** x .75A x 74 Pulses x .0022PW x 3.25 Sec. = **89.3J (ER-EO)**;
> **Series 5**: **375V** x .75A x 74 Pulses x .0022PW x 3.25 Sec. = **149J (Actual-EO)**.
>
> **Series 5A**: **225V** x .75A x 70 Pulses x .0022PW x 6.0 Sec. = **155.9J (ER-EO)**;
> **Series 5A**: **375V** x .75A x 70 Pulses x .0022PW x 6.0 Sec. = **259.9J (Actual-EO)**.

Once again, we see that the indirectly reported maximum EOs for all four Series--2/3; 2+/3+; 5; and 5A of **57.4J**, **78.9J**, **89J**, and **155.9J** --are not actual outputs at all, but **ER-Outputs** at **ER-Impedances**: **57.4J at 265Ω**, **78.89J at 265Ω**, **89.28 at 300Ω** and **155.9 at 300Ω** respectively. [523] For comparative purposes, we can further convert the Pure-ER/RRC figures for Series 2/3; 2+/3+ of 57.4J at 265Ω and 78.89J at **265Ω** to Pure-ER/RRC figures based on **300Ω** or 65J/300Ω, and 89.3J/300Ω respectively. [524] Pure-ER/RRC phrases for all four series can now be seen as: **65J at 300Ω**, **89.3J at 300Ω**, **89.28 at 300Ω** and **155.9 at 300Ω** suggestive of a **65J maximum for the Series 2/3**, an **89J maximum for the Series 2+/3+**, an **89J maximum for the Series 5**, and a **155.9J maximum for the Series 5A**, that is, an ER progression from **65J** to **89J** to **89J** to **155.9J**. Once more, we can now convert all these ER output maximums at ER Impedances into **actual maximum outputs** at **actual maximum Impedances**:

> **Series 2/3**: 65J/300Ω = **97.5J**/450Ω
> **Series 2+/3+**: 89.3J/300Ω = **134J**/450Ω
> **Series 5**: 89.28 at 300Ω = **149J**/500Ω
> **Series 5A**: 155.9 at 300Ω = **260J**/500Ω

In short, based upon the actual maximum Impedances used for these devices, we can confirm that the actual **unreported** maximum output progression for the Series 2/3; 2+/3+; 5; and 5A is ***97.5J***, ***134J***, ***149J***, and ***260J*** respectively, figures we have derived in another manner in a previous section.

Not surprisingly, the maximum ***97.5J*** output of the initial Series 2/3 indicates an original 100J ceiling similar to both the American-made MECTA "C" (emitting 108 maximum Joules) and the 1982 American APA Standard (stipulating a 110J ceiling). The ***134J*** Ectron Series 2+/3+, and perhaps even the ***149J*** Ectron Series 5, are very similar in actual maximum outputs to the American made 140J MECTA D-1, a continuation of "first generation BP devices" representing "slight" breaches of an original circa 100J ceiling, perhaps similarly justified via the "exceptionally seizure recalcitrant case" rationale. Most likely, the 97J Series 2/3 as well as the 134J Series 2+/3+ and perhaps even the 149J Series 5 were marketed before the 1989 IEC Standard influenced by the Mectan Transmutation went into effect . In all probability, moreover, Ectron's 97.5J Series 2/3

Constant Current of .850A (Ibid) for the Series 2/3 and 2+3+ into Ohm's law: Impedance = Volt/Current. Impedance = 225V/.85 = 265Ω. Then, through ER, we use the actual reported maximum Impedance for Series 2/3 and 2+/3+ of 450Ω (Ibid), to obtain actual maximum Voltage.225V/265Ω = XVoltage/450Ω; X = 382V. Actual maximum Voltage for Series 2/3 and 2+/3+ = **382V**.225V/XΩ = 382V/450Ω. ER Impedance = 265Ω; ER/RRC = 225V at 265Ω.

522 Ohm's Law: Impedance = Volt/Current. False maximum Voltage (actually an ER-Voltage) is reported as 225V for Series 5 and 5A (Royal College of Psychiatry, 1995, p.124). Reported Constant Current for Series 5 and 5A = .75A (Ibid). ER-Impedance = 225V/.75 = 300Ω. Actual maximum Voltage is found through ER: 225V/300Ω = XVoltage/500Ω; X = 375V.225V/XΩ = 375V/500Ω. Pure ER/RRC = 225V/300Ω. [The maximum Voltage for Series 2/3 and 2+/3+ above may also have been 375V (in lieu of 382V) similar to BP Series 5 and 5A. The negligible difference may be due to rounding].

523 Actual maximum outputs at actual maximum Impedances for Ectron Series 2/3, Series 2+/3+, Series 5, and Series 5A are as follows: **Series 2/3**: 57.4J/265Ω = 65J/300Ω = ***97.5J/450Ω***. **Series 2+/3+**: 78.89J/265Ω = 89.3J/300Ω = ***134J/450Ω***. **Series 5**: 89.28J/300Ω = ***148.8J/500Ω***. **Series 5A**: 155.9J/300Ω = ***260J/500Ω***.

524 57.4J/265Ω = 65J/300Ω, 78.89J/265Ω = 89.3J/300Ω.

and 134J Series 2+/3+ and perhaps even Ectron's 149J Series 5, like the 108J MECTA "C" and 140J MECTA "D-1", were all initially reported via their actual maximum outputs. Conversely, like MECTA with respect to its second generation JR/SR 2 (and 1) devices, Ectron seems to have stopped reporting maximum output (in joules) with the production of its ***260J*** second generation **5A Series**. Rather, similar to MECTA's actions, Ectron, in order to cover up this increase in power, begins reporting maximum ER outputs as actual maximum outputs, and even this only indirectly via ER Voltages.

Canada's/U. K. 's Ectron Series 5A: **155.9J**/300Ω = ***259.8J***/500Ω;
Made-for America MECTA JR/SR 2: **101.3J**/220Ω = ***259.2J***/562.5Ω.

What we see with respect to the history of Ectron devices then, is a progressively enhancing output series very similar to that of American BP devices and particularly MECTA BP devices, eventually culminating in a second generation BP device emitting an unreported 2.6 MTTLOI for all age categories. The similarity of the histories, the progressive output enhancements, what Ectron chooses to report and not report, in short, the coincidental suppression of second generation outputs for both Ectron and MECTA BP devices, all of which emit the same circa 260 Joule maximum output, and finally the actively deceptive illusion of reduced output through the use of near identical reporting strategies for these same second generation BP devices and in the same subsequent order, is remarkable.

As noted above then, like the 108J MECTA "C" and 140J MECTA "D-1" devices, the Series 2/3, 2+/3+, and perhaps even the Series 5, seem to have been initially reported via actual maximum outputs in joules of 97.5J, 134J, and 149J respectively. Like the history of American BP devices then, the circa 100J maximum output Brief Pulse device initially introduced through the Series 2/3 BP device in Canada and England, may have impressed some variation of the "ERA" (just as it did the FDA) as a newly regulated minimal stimulus mechanism, significantly improved over and thus very much safer than the unacceptably powerful 200J SW devices of the "past. " This favorable notion with the Series 2/3, which like the MECTA "C" device in America, almost certainly facilitated the approval and continued propagation of "ECT" in Canada and Great Britain (and perhaps even Eurasia) by virtue of "greatly reduced output" with Brief Pulse, may well have convinced some variation of the ERA (like the FDA) that despite the negative history with SW, "ECT" should not be banned, but rather continued into the final quarter of the twentieth century. To be clear, the continuation of "ECT" in Europe and Asia, just as it was in America, seems to have been based on the notion that the new Brief Pulse "ECT" device works with only enough electricity to induce the "necessary" grand mal seizure, that is, that the new Brief Pulse ECT device could elicit so-called "adequate seizures" with greatly reduced amounts of electricity, indeed half that of SW.

Ectron History Continued (2)

It should be no surprise that in converting the 97.5J maximum Series 3 from a "65J at 300Ω" conditional-ER/RRC to an Americanized "47.5J at 220Ω" conditional-ER/RRC with a circa 100J ceiling and thus 450Ω maximum (65J/300Ω = 47.5J/220Ω = 97J/450Ω), we find the Series 3 the circa equivalent of the later MECTA "C" conditional-ER/RRC of "59.2J at 220Ω" with circa 110J ceiling and thus circa 400Ω maximum (81J/300Ω = 59.2/220Ω = 108J/400Ω). In brief, we find similar Pure-ER/RRCs with similar maximum outputs suggesting an original Conditional ER/RRC standard similar to the 1982 APA Standard limiting outputs to 110J.

Ectron Series 3: ***47.5J/220Ω = 97J/450Ω***
MECTA C: ***59.2J/220Ω = 108J/400Ω***

In short, both Brief Pulse machines appear to have been initially limited to a circa 100J ceiling and thus threshold or minimal stimulus output for all age recipients in accordance with the 1982 APA Standard for Brief Pulse devices. [525]

---

[525] The APA Standard is comprised of a conditional ER/RRC of 70J at 220Ω and a 110J ceiling. The conditional 110J ceiling regulates BP devices to a 1.1 MTTLOI or just above threshold for all recipients. Using 220Ω to express the conditional-ER/RRC of a machine

Like the early American MECTA "C," then, the early Ectron Series 3, appears to have been limited to a circa 100J ceiling. Moreover, Ectron, like MECTA with its D-1 device, as we have seen, may have justified surpassing the 100J mark regarding the 134J and 140J maximums of its Series 2+/3+ and 5, as requisite for "exceptionally recalcitrant cases (seizure-wise)" only. [526] After all, like the MECTA "D" devices which emitted about 140J maximums, the Series 2+/3+ and the Series 5 which emitted 134 and 140J output maximums respectively, were yet below the 200J maximum of SW and so yet could be deemed "improvements. " In fact, in that they could all more or less be said to emit minimal stimulus outputs, they could, as mentioned, all be deemed first generation BP devices; in essence, they were "ECT" devices.

Prior to the 1989 IEC Standard, then, like American machines based on the 1982 APA Standard, English and Canadian Brief Pulse machines appear to have been designed to limit output to circa 100 maximum joules, guaranteeing minimal stimulus outputs in every age category. On the other hand, like the American devices, each series seems to have progressed in power, enhancing MTTLOIs comparable to American BP devices. Certainly, the production of the Ectron Series 5A with its indirect and unexplained ER reporting of a misleading 155.9J maximum output (via the reporting of a 225V ER Voltage) but which secretly emitted a maximum output of "260J at 500Ω" seems to represent a transition from some previous Conditional ER/RRC to the Pure-ER/RRC interpretation of the IEC Standard, in sum, the same Mectan Transmutation which had occurred in America. Indeed, it appears to be at this juncture that Ectron eliminates all actual output reporting in joules. Just as in America, then, with the manufacturing of second generation BP devices, the 100 Joule ceiling is altogether dropped even as the illusion of a 100J ceiling is maintained via ER reporting. It can be no coincidence that Ectron's false or misleading reporting of a 225V maximum for all four Ectron series, supplants the actual progression in power from ***97.5***, to ***134***, to ***149***, to ***260*** joules with a far more innocuous progression from **57.4**, to **78.9**, to **89**, to **155.9** joules respectively.

Ectron Continued--Failure of the "Adequate Seizure"

The evidence makes clear that European manufacturers, just as American manufacturers, soon discovered that the so-called adequate seizure is, in fact, inadequate, and that what the procedure actually requires to be "effective" is an adequate amount of electricity. Unfortunately, as we have seen, an enhanced amount of electricity is exactly what makes the procedure questionable, in short, damaging. With the failure of minimal stimulus Brief Pulse and thus the failure of the adequate seizure threatening to debunk convulsive therapy theory generally, the secret enhancement of Brief Pulse devices to make the machines "work," along with engineering of the 1989 IEC Standard to surreptitiously accommodate these enhancements, (an accomplishment influenced in main by American psychiatrist-engineer Richard Weiner and thus, not surprisingly, emulative of the Mectan Transmutation), Ectron and other made-for Eurasia Brief Pulse manufacturers, were forced to surreptitiously switch, just as American BP manufacturers had, from a Conditional-ER/RRC to a Pure ER/RRC interpretation of the 100J phrases. That is, companies such as Ectron were forced to switch from a Conditional-ER/RRC interpretation to a Pure-ER/RRC interpretation in order to seriously exceed the conditional circa 100J minimum required to elicit adequate seizures in all age recipients. Like American manufacturers then, it is this methodological transition from conditional to pure that enables both American and Eurasian Brief Pulse manufacturers to grossly but invisibly boost the output of what are actually second generation Brief Pulse devices. At the same time, however, both the Mectan Transmutation and the 1989 IEC Standard created a convincing counter-impression that all Brief Pulse devices were regulated to minimal stimulus output in all age categories. In short, not only did this Pure-ER/RRC stratagem make possible much higher actual outputs, but through featuring of the 100J ER figure in conjunction with machine readouts of circa 100 maximum joules, both the Mectan Transmutation and the 1989 IEC Standard were simultaneously able to maintain the proverbial illusion of the 100J ceiling.

While the 1989 IEC Standard featured the "100J" figure, therefore, like the Mectan Transmutation, it was the then new 1989 IEC Standard that launched Pure-ER/RRC interpretation overseas. As a result, like

---

with a 400Ω maximum limited to a 108 Joule ceiling, we simply set up: XJ/220Ω = 108J/400Ω. XJ = 59.2J, thus the conditional-ER/RRC expression for the MECTA C is "59.2J at 220Ω" with conditional ceiling of 108J.

[526] The rationale is a false one.100J is the minimum relative constant required to elicit an adequate seizure for any recipient under any treatment dynamic.

American manufacturers, Ectron and other Eurasian BP manufacturers were able to increase the output of their devices, while concurrently limiting device reporting to unexplained ER outputs not only for their newer second generation Brief Pulse devices, but even for their earlier first generation Brief Pulse devices in order to simulate reduced enhancements. Similar to American manufacturers then, the Canadian and English company Ectron, through the active and retroactive reporting of a misleading 225V ER Voltage as maximum for all its Brief Pulse devices, indirectly reports maximum EOs of **57.4J**, **78.9J**, **89J** [527] and **155.9J** [528] respectively for its BP Series, that is, for the 2/3, the 2+/3+, the 5, and the 5A which actually emit ***97.4J***, ***134J***, ***149J***, and ***260J*** maximums respectively. Due to the covert Pure-ER/RRC interpretation of the equally covert "130J at 300Ω" phrase concealed within the 1989 IEC Standard, then, manufacturers of made-for-Europe and perhaps even made-for-Asia BP devices secretly enhanced their BP devices to outputs similar to those manufactured in the U. S. under the Mectan Transmutation. In brief, the underpinned 100J phraseology within the 1989 IEC Standard, in conjunction with the 100J maximum output associated with and anticipated for Brief Pulse devices generally, at once made it possible for made-for-Eurasia BP device manufacturers to utilize the same misleading double standard of reporting heretofore available only to American BP manufacturers. [529] Total omission of actual output-reporting in joules, false equivalencies of actual maximum Charge with what were ER-outputs of circa 100 Joules, ER reporting of unremarkable machine parameters such as Voltage, and quite possibly, Machine Readouts depicting unexplicated or reverse-ER outputs falsely suggestive of circa 100J (or even 155.9J) maximums read and accepted by practicing physicians assured a successful coverup. As a result of unexplained Pure-ER/RRC interpretations both in America and overseas, therefore, the enormous power enhancement of BP devices such as the Ectron series which covertly increased from approximately 100 to approximately 260 maximum Joules, went entirely unobserved by Canadian and UK regulatory bodies. What appeared to be a series of relatively moderate power boosts in Ectron BP devices from 57.3Js to 78.89Js to 89.28Js, and finally to 155.9Js as noted, all seeming improvements over the 200J SW device, were actually , as noted, a series of much grosser enhancements, in the case of Ectron, 97.5Js to 134Js to 148.8Js to 260Js-- a devolution amazingly emulative--in sequence and power--of U. S. BP devices. Not surprisingly then, like American BP devices, the true power of these second generation Brief Pulse devices remained utterly undetected--until now.

Final Possibility

Finally, moreover, there is another possibility regarding misleading readouts on the Series 5A. While there is no doubt that the actual Ectron Series 5A emits a maximum output of about 259.9 joules or a 2.59 MTTLOI for all age recipients (***Series 5A***: .75A x **375V** x .0022 Sec. PW x 70 Pulses x 6.0 Seconds = ***260J***), probable skewed machine readouts read by physicians are likely based, as already noted, either on a false 225V or 300Ω constant indicating a false 155.9J ceiling. But because 155.9J at 300Ω is tantamount to 114J at 220Ω, the possibility also exists that Ectron, perhaps influenced by U. S. manufacturers MECTA and Somatics, replaced actual Impedances not with a false 300Ω or 225V constant, but with the same false 220Ω constant

---

[527] All parameters provided by Ectron for Series 5 are accurate with the exception of 225V (Royal College of Psychiatry, 1995, p.124). EO = .75A x 225V x .0022PW x 74 Pulses x 3.25 Seconds = 89.28 Joules. We can deduce that 225V is inaccurate from the fact that 225V is equivalent to 300Ω (Ohm's law: Impedance = V/Current. Impedance = 225V/.75 = 300Ω) and the fact that the reported 500Ω Impedance (Ibid) for the Series 5A results in an inconsistent EO of 150J compared to that derived with 225V of 89.28J. EO = .400C x .75A x 500Ω = 150J. We need 375V to obtain approximately 150J. EO = .75A x 375V x .0022PW x 74 Pulses x 3.25 Seconds = 149J. (The difference between 149J and 150J is due to rounding). That 225V is an ER can be verified directly: 225V/300Ω = 375V/500Ω.225V/90J = 375V/150J.90J/300Ω = 150J/500Ω.

[528] That 155.9J (based on a 225V ER) for the Series 5A is an ER can be verified in the same manner shown in the above footnote for the Series 5. Series 5A EO = .75A x 225V x .0022PW x 70 Pulses x 6.0 Seconds = 155.9 Joules. EO = .75A x 375V x .0022PW x 70 Pulses x 6.0 Seconds = 260 Joules.225V/300Ω = 375V/500Ω.225V/156J = 375V/260J.156J/300Ω = 260J/500Ω.

[529] MECTA reports 240V maximums to RCP for made-for-America second generation JR/SR 1@2 BP devices (Royal College of Psychiatry, 1995, p.125). In fact 240V appears to be an ER-Voltage equivalent to the 300Ω Pure-ER/RRC within the 1989 IEC Standard, in turn equating to the actual maximum Voltage and actual maximum Impedance for second generation made-for-America MECTA JR/SR 1@ 2 BP devices.240V/300Ω = 450V/562.4Ω. Too, the phrases "100J at 220Ω" and "100J at 300Ω" (then expanded to 130J at 300Ω) are both interpreted by manufacturers as Pure-ER/RRCs sans 100J ceilings.

used by American manufacturers so that a false maximum output with respect to machine readouts is depicted not as 155.9J, but an even lower 114J maximum. [530]

***ILLUSORY* MINIMAL STIMULUS <u>Ectron Series 5A</u>** (IEC) BRIEF PULSE ECT DEVICE
BASED ON FALSE CONSTANT OF 220Ω, **SUGGESTIVE OF A "114J AT 220Ω"**
CONDITIONAL-ER/RRC WITH **FALSE 114J MAXIMUM OUTPUT READOUT**

VOLTAGE	POWER % @ Age	AGE Yrs	Ω Ohms	FREQUENCY (Pulses)	DURATION (SECs)	CURRENT mAmps	ENERGY Joules	CHARGE mC
37.5	10	10	**220**	30	1.4	750	**11.4**	69.3
75	20	20	**220**	30	2.76	750	**22.6**	136.67
112.5	30	30	**220**	50	2.52	759	**34.3**	208
150	40	40	**220**	50	3.36	750	**45.7**	277.3
187.5	50	50	**220**	50	4.2	750	**53.4**	346.67
225	60	60	**220**	70	3.6	750	**68.6**	416
243.75	65	65	**220**	70	3.91	750	**74.4**	451.3
262.5	70	70	**220**	70	4.2	750	**80**	485
300	80	80	**220**	70	4.8	750	**91.6**	554.66
337.5	90	90	**220**	70	5.4	750	**103**	624
375	100	100	**220**	70	6.0	750	**114**	**692**

.0022 Sec. PW

Like the American-made devices, the readout math based on a false 220Ω constant only works with the Impedance oriented formula for finding EO (EO = Current squared) x Impedance x (hz x 2) x WL x Duration) wherein the false 220Ω constant can be plugged into the machine's calculator: .75A x .75A x ***220Ω*** x 70 Pulses x .0022WL x 6.0Sec. = **<u>114J</u>**. Using the actual 375 Volt maximum in the Voltage oriented formula for finding EO (EO = Voltage x Current x (hz x 2) x WL x Duration) reveals the inconsistency: ***375V*** x .75A x 70 Pulses x .0022WL x 6.0Sec = **<u>259.9J</u>**. In any case, the machine emits a secret 260J maximum and thus a 2.6 MTTLOI while readouts read by physicians are almost certainly skewed in some manner similar to that resulting in misleading readouts displayed on both MECTA and Somatics BP devices.

[530] We can convert Pure-ER/RRCs based on 300Ω for all four series to Pure-ER/RRCs based on 220Ω.6**<u>5J/300Ω = 47.6J/220Ω = 97.3J/450Ω</u>**, **<u>89.3J/300Ω =65.4J/220Ω = 134J/450Ω</u>** , **<u>89.28/300Ω =65.4J/220Ω = 149J/500Ω</u>** and **<u>155.9/300Ω = 114J/220Ω = 259J/500Ω</u>**. Based on 220Ω, unexplained ER output maximums for Series 2/3; 2+/3+; 5; and 5A might be falsely reported as **47.6J, 65.4J, 65.4J**, and **114J**. In any case, unreported actual maximum outputs for Series 2/3; 2+/3+; 5; and 5A are ***<u>97.5J</u>***, ***<u>134J</u>***, ***<u>149J</u>***, and ***<u>260J</u>*** respectively.

CHAPTER 37

The Medcraft B-25 Second Generation Brief Pulse Device and the Medcraft Transmutation

The B-25 by Medcraft [531] is another American made Brief Pulse device not to be confused with Medcraft's B-24 Sine Wave device. There is no mention of the B-25 device by the *Royal College of Psychiatry* in England, thus, the devices' main market seems to be the U.S., and in fact, there is reason to believe the device is a scant seller, generally. [532] Nevertheless, the machine is important for a number of reasons.

Medcraft introduced its B-25 BP device a year or so following the introduction of MECTA and Somatics Brief Pulse devices. In a successful attempt to skirt around FDA perusal of new devices, Medcraft claimed its B-25 BP device comparable to the already allowed second generation MECTA and Somatics BP devices allegedly based on the 1982 APA Standard. To make the argument for comparability, Medcraft reported its device to the FDA with the phrase, "99J at 220," almost identical to reports of "101.4J at 220" and 99.4J at 220" respectively submitted by MECTA and Somatics for their second generation BP devices. In that neither MECTA nor Somatics ever objected to Medcraft's claim of comparability, we might, in fact, argue that Medcraft leagued with both MECTA and Somatics in accepting the B-25 as a comparable device. Indeed, all three devices are described with the same approximate phrase, "100J at 220Ω." Below is MECTA's 510K pre-market application chart which MECTA submitted to the FDA, August 5, 1985 (Food and Drug Administration, 1985, K852069). FDA reviewer Harold Walder "confirmed" that at 220Ω, the following EOs are deliverable:

MECTA D-2 . . . . . **100.0J**,
MECTA SR1 . . . . . **101.4J**,
MECTA JR2 . . . . . **101.3J**,
MECTA SR1 . . . . . **101.4J**,
MECTA SR2 . . . . . **101.3J**,
Thymatron . . . . . **100.0J**.

On November 3, 1986, approximately one year later, Medcraft submitted to FDA reviewer Stephen M. Hinkley an exact duplicate of the above comparison chart (see Medcraft 510K pre-market submission application--File K860467B; Food and Drug Administration, 1986A, p.4), but with the inclusion of the B-25, again asserting that at 220Ω,[533] the following EOs are deliverable:

MECTA D-2 . . . . . **100.0J**,

[531] There does not appear to be a first generation Brief Pulse device by Medcraft. Nevertheless, we must label it "second generation" due to its overall power particularly in the younger age categories.

[532] **In** records from the Texas Reporting System covering the period from about 1990-2001, there is not a single Medcraft B-25 device in Texas hospitals; nor was there any purchase of a B-25 during this same period (Texas Department of Mental Health and Mental Retardation, 2001).

[533] The (220Ω) is handwritten (as is the entire chart) in a left-hand column in very small print.

MECTA SR1 . . . . . **101.4J**,
MECTA JR2 . . . . . **101.3J**,
MECTA SR1 . . . . . **101.4J**,
MECTA SR2 . . . . . **101.3J**,
Medcraft B-25 . . . . **99.0J**,
Thymatron . . . . . **100.0J**.

In short, Medcraft juxtaposed its B-25 device (Food and Drug Administration, 1986A, p.4) [534] with machines already on the market, specifically the Somatics' Thymatron (Food and Drug Administration, 1984),[535] the MECTA D-2, and the MECTA JR/SR 1 and 2 (Food and Drug Administration, 1985), all claiming to emit or limit output to circa "100J at 220Ω. " [536]

But are the machines indeed comparable? To begin, Medcraft Reports 99 Joules as its maximum EO for the B-25. If correct, this is curious, in that, though not reported as such, the early made-for-America second generation Thymatron emits 200 Joules, the early JR1@2 emit 200 Joules, and the later second generation Thymatron DG and MECTA JR/SR 1@2 BP devices, elicit maximums of at least 252 and 259 Joules respectively as has been previously demonstrated. Conversely, due to an unreported default circa 2.0 MTTLOI administered to all age groups with the early second generation Thymatron and MECTA devices and circa 2.5 MTTLOI with later second generation Somatics and MECTA BP machines, these devices, unlike the Medcraft B-25, never actually approach the 100J mark at 220Ω, in spite of their circa "100J at 220Ω" claims; nor are they limited to an actual 100J.

Indeed, discussion of the B-25 has been placed in its own distinct section here, in that, contrary to appearances and contrary to Medcraft's homonymic reporting phrase of "99J at 220Ω, the B-25 is unlike any other BP device manufactured either in America or Eurasia.

As noted, the 1989 IEC Standard, which applies to all devices manufactured for or marketed in Europe, provides a consistent but obscure criterion for BP (and all other made-for-Europe "ECT") devices, of "130 Joules at 300Ω" almost identical to the circa "100J at 220Ω" ER/RRC used for second generation made-for-America BP devices (130J/300Ω = 95J/220Ω). As noted earlier, manufacturers' secret interpretation of the 1989 IEC Standard as a Pure-ER/RRC (in lieu of a conditional-ER/RRC) permitting an unreported maximum EO of <u>216.67</u> Joules, like the Mectan Transmutation, enabled all makers of IEC BP devices to readily surpass 100 joules. On the other hand, (and in spite of international manufacturers typically breaching the hidden 216J maximum), a Pure-ER/RRC interpretation of the 1989 IEC Standard <u>does</u> at least *limit* BP devices under the 1989 IEC Standard to a maximum <u>216.67J</u> just as the Mectan Transmutation, at least limits made-for-America BP devices to a maximum <u>273J</u>. [537] [538] [539]

Manufacturers MECTA and Somatics, and possibly, Elcot [540]), the initiators of the Pure-ER/RRC transmutational methodology deemed the Mectan Transmutation, later used for IEC BP devices, newly

---

[534] See attachment to submission from FDA reviewer Stephen M. Hinkley, November 3, 1986, p.4, within Medcraft's 510K submission. (Food and Drug Administration, 1986A).

[535] Medcraft had not devised its B-25 at this time, while Somatics, like the MECTA devices, reported for its then new Thymatron (a precursor of the Thymatron DG) "100J at 220Ω."

[536] See submission from FDA reviewer Harold Walder, 8/5/85 within the MECTA's 510K submission application (Food and Drug Administration, 1985).

[537] In that IEC devices are limited to 500Ω maximum Impedance, applying the "130J at 300Ω" ER/RRC to 500Ω maximum Impedance, a maximum output for IEC devices of <u>216.6J</u> is obtained. (130J/300Ω = X/500Ω. <u>X = 216.67J</u>).

[538] 130J/300 = <u>XJ</u>/500Ω. X = <u>216.67J</u>. Even with manufacturer's transitional interpretation from "Conditional" to "Pure-ER/RRC," Ectron, the main Canadian and UK Manufacturer (as well as MECTA and Somatics), violate the enhanced <u>216.6J</u> EO ceiling for IEC devices, as has been shown.

[539] Made-for-America manufacturers' (possibly including Medcraft's) transition to a Pure-ER/RRC interpretation with the 1983 MECTA/Somatics phraseology "100 Joules at 220Ω" "permitting" up to <u>273J</u>, as well as made-for Eurasia Manufacturers' similar interpretation of the 1989 IEC Standard's inconspicuous "130 Joules at 300Ω" permitting up to <u>216.6 Joules</u>, result in extreme violations of the 1982 APA Standard limiting BP devices to <u>110 Absolute Joules</u>.

[540] While Elcot also reported "100 Joules at 220Ω," Elcot appears to have violated the maximum 273 Joule ceiling derivable at this ratio, and may, like Medcraft, have used the phrase "100J at 220Ω" merely to report maximum output at a specific Impedance. Elcot appears to have ignored any possible absolute ceiling either with respect to the APA Standard or a maximum output derived from ER/RRC.

interpreted the circa "100J at 220Ω" phrase as a Pure-ER/RRC (commonly described by American manufacturers as "100J at a 'typical' 220Ω"). The translation precipitately (and furtively) as noted, ushered in a new unreported American ceiling maximum (for second generation BP devices) of 273 maximum Joules (Cameron, 1994),[541] a gross albeit invisible 163J[542] violation of the 1982 APA Standard which plainly limits BP devices to 110 Joules maximum. In any case, both made-for-America and made-for-Europe BP devices appear to be based on MECTA's Pure-ER/RRC stratagem deemed the Mectan Transmutation. [543]

The U. S. manufacturer, Medcraft is the lone exception. To begin the discussion of the Medcraft B-25 Brief Pulse Device, Medcraft must first be credited with properly interpreting the APA Standard as limiting all BP devices to 110 maximum Joules. Unfortunately, this is not the entire story.

Continuing through to the present, Medcraft persists in making two "ECT" devices, the Medcraft B-24 SW (Sine Wave), compared to which Brief Pulse is an alleged improvement, and its more modern Medcraft Brief Pulse device, the B-25. In short, Medcraft has been manufacturing and marketing the B-24 SW since about 1950, and the B-25 Brief Pulse since about 1985 (Food and Drug Administration, 1986A). Thus, going back to the 1982 FDA investigation of ECT amidst avid criticism of SW, the B-25 Brief Pulse appears to have been launched into the modern-day BP era amongst the several new manufacturers introducing Brief Pulse devices--MECTA, Somatics, and Elcot. In short, closely following Brief Pulse manufacturers MECTA and Somatics, as well as the now defunct Brief Pulse manufacturer Elcot, and thus with what seemed like the immanent banning of SW, Medcraft engineered and introduced its own Brief Pulse device in order to remain viable within the "ECT" industry. In that MECTA and Somatics had managed to attain conditional FDA approval for their new Brief Pulse devices in alleged accordance with the 1982 APA Standard condoned by the Utah Biomedical Test Laboratory, not surprisingly, Medcraft reported to the FDA that its' own new BP device, the B-25, was the equivalent of MECTA and Somatics' BP devices. Medcraft did so by describing its B-25, as we have seen, in similar terms, i.e., the circa "100J at 220Ω" phraseology (Medcraft Corporation, 1986a)--reported by all new American manufacturers of made-for-America BP devices. [544] But, while all extant second generation MECTA, Somatics, and Medcraft Brief Pulse devices reported a circa "100J at 220Ω" phraseology and depicted circa 100J maximums via Machine Readouts, unlike MECTA, Somatics and even the now defunct Elcot, Medcraft alone appears to have actually limited its' B-25 BP apparatus to the 110J ceiling clearly portrayed in the 1982 APA Standard. In fact, Medcraft alone both reports and actually limits its Medcraft B-25 Brief Pulse to "99J at 220Ω," in fact, 99J at all Impedances, as we shall shortly see. As a result, in describing the machine's maximum output via fliers, only Medcraft does ***not*** and need ***not*** consistently add the contingency *"at 220Ω"* (Medcraft Corporation, 1986a) in that its reported 99 joules is, in fact, the machine's actual maximum output. Indeed, both in Medcraft manuals and submissions to the FDA, Medcraft unmistakably and outspokenly reports 99 Joules as the absolute maximum output for its B-25 (Food and Drug Administration, 1986A, 84, 160; Medcraft Corporation, 1986a; Medcraft Corporation, 1986b, 5, 19). [545] For example, in 1986, Medcraft reported to the FDA the following description of its B-25 Brief Pulse device.

> "Output Energy:" **0 to 99 joules** in 1 joule increments, operator selectable to +/- 10%. **Actual energy displayed** will be +/- 1% of the selected energy setting. (Food and Drug Administration, 1986A, p.160)

This description plainly contains the phrase *"0-99 Joules"* followed by the phrase *"actual energy displayed,"* in brief, clearly purporting a "99J" maximum output (within 1%) both on its machine readouts and in actuality. According to the 510K pre-market charts Medcraft submitted to the FDA in 1986, therefore, unlike MECTA and Somatics, Medcraft genuinely appears to limit its' B-25 BP device to an actual, literal 99 Joule ceiling (Food

---

541 Maximum FDA Impedance is 600Ω.100J/220Ω = 273J/600Ω.

542 273J - 110J = 163J violation. This method for surpassing the Standard, most probably invented by MECTA via the D-2 machine, followed or simultaneously by Somatics between 1983-1985, violates both the implied "70J at 220Ω" ER/RRC and the "100-110J" Absolute ceiling for BP devices depicted in the 1982 APA Standard.

543 The transmutation is the reinterpretation of the "70J at 220Ω" ER/RRC with conditional ceiling of 110J to an unconditional circa "100J at 220Ω" ER/RRC based on a 600Ω APA ceiling (100J/220Ω = 273J/600Ω). Perhaps a simpler way of looking at the change is the transition from a 110J ceiling to a 100J ER relative to maximum machine Impedance.

544 MECTA, Somatics, and Medcraft.

545 In essence, the "99J at 220Ω" reported by Medcraft, is not, like MECTA and Somatics BP devices, interpreted by Medcraft as a Pure-ER/RRC.

and Drug Administration, 1986A, pp.84, 60). Moreover, the B-25 genuinely appears to maintain its 99J ceiling via automatic incremental Duration reductions (as expected) inversely proportional to incremental increases in Voltage and Impedance (Medcraft Corporation, 1986b, p.19). [546] The Medcraft B-25, consequently, unlike second generation MECTA, Somatics, (and even Elcot) BP devices, as noted, earnestly conforms to the expected APA ceiling of 110 Absolute Joules plainly depicted within the 1982 APA Standard. Assuming adherence to the conditional-ER/RRC principle additionally found within the 1982 APA Standard (expanded by MECTA in 1985 from the original "70J at 220Ω" to "100J at 220Ω"), we would expect the B-25 to gradually increase in output to a 99J ceiling by age 100. Moreover, in that the 100 year old male is administered minimal stimulus threshold output at circa 100 Joules, we would expect outputs at all age levels to be minimal stimulus, that is, just at or above threshold output in accordance with the ER/RRC principle compelling a uniform MTTLOI applicable to all age categories. Based on the looked for conditional-ER/RRC [547] interpretation of the Medcraft B-25 reported as "99J at 220Ω" then, we would expect the B-25 profile, in conjunction with its 99J ceiling, to appear something like the profile below.

<u>THEORETICAL</u> CONSTANT CURRENT MEDCRAFT B-25 MINIMAL STIMULUS BRIEF PULSE DEVICE EMITTING THRESHOLD OUTPUTS IN ALL AGE CATEGORIES. THE PROFILE BELOW COMPLIES WITH BOTH THE (1) 110J CEILING SPECIFIED AND (2) THE "70J at 220Ω" CONDITIONAL-ER/RRC PRINCIPLE COMPRISING THE 1982 APA STANDARD [548]

VOLTAGE	POWER % @ Age	AGE Yrs	Ω Ohms	FREQUENCY (Hz)	DURATION (SECs)	CURRENT mAmps	ENERGY Joules	CHARGE mC
105	10	10	150	70	0.1	0.7	1.1	10.5
137	20	20	172	70	0.3	0.8	4.6	33.4
154	30	30	194	70	0.6	0.8	10.4	67.0
195	40	40	217	70	0.7	0.9	17.2	88.1
214	50	50	239	70	1.0	0.9	27.00	125.5
234	60	60	261	70	1.3	0.9	38.40	163.5
271	65	65	272	70	1.2	1.0	45.5	167.7
282	70	69	283	70	1.3	1.0	51.5	182.0
305	80	79	305	70	1.5	1.0	64.00	210
315	90	89	315	70	1.9	1.0	81.00	266
322	100	99	322	70	2.2	1.0	99J	307

PW .001 Seconds

The B-25 Chart above reflects knowns: various Constant Current Settings from 0.4 <u>to 1.0 Amperes</u>, constant Frequency of <u>140 Pulses</u> (70 Hz), constant Pulse Width of <u>.001</u>, and maximum Voltage of 325V (Food and Drug Administration, 1986A). Duration of from 0.0-6.0 Seconds and Frequency (140 Pulses) are non-selectable whereas EO (1-99 Joules) and constant Current (.4-1.0A) are selectable. The B-25 device above is set, as is possible with the B-25, to consistent minimal stimulus settings in all age categories, capping at 99J. Charge, Age, and Corresponding Voltages at these settings are probable. Charge, which Medcraft does not report, is derived formulaically. Note the exceptionally high Impedances in the 10 and 20 year old age categories (as reported by Medcraft) perhaps due to "ramping," as shall be investigated and the lower than normal Impedances in the 65 and over age categories (as reported by Medcraft), due to the 99J ceiling. The parameters above are based on a "67J at 220Ω" conditional-ER/RRC (XJ/220 = 99J/322Ω = 67J/220Ω) and a 99J ceiling, both in accordance with the 1982 APA Standard.

While the B-25 could indeed be set for the minimal stimulus outputs above, one odd anomaly exists. Strangely, as noted above, Medcraft reports minimal Impedance on the B-25 (for what appears to be the ten year old child) as 150Ω, a much greater Impedance than a ten year old child should normally invoke and particularly at the expected minimal stimulus output of 1.1J. Maximum Impedance, on the other hand, for what we must assume to be the 99 year old adult, is reported at between 325 and 350Ω, much less than the maximum Impedance depicted in this age category on MECTA and Somatics BP devices. The lower than normal maximum Impedance for the 99 year old (compared to second generation MECTA and Somatics devices) is comprehensible due to the B-25's actual 99 Joule ceiling, much lower than MECTA and Somatics. However, the atypically high Impedance for the ten year old is mysterious. In that the 99 year old at 99 Joules

---

[546] Unlike MECTA, Somatics, and Ectron, the author could not discover a loophole in Medcraft's reporting of the B-25 parameters. The B-25"s "99J" maximum appears genuine.

[547] Medcraft caps output at 99J; therefore, the ER/RRC is not "pure" but "Conditional."

[548] A BP device actually limited to 100 absolute Joules could be deemed (by the author), "1st generation." However, because Medcraft equates its actual BP device with MECTA and Somatics second generation BP devices, and because Medcraft, as we shall see, ignores ER/RRC, the actual B-25 is without doubt what we deem in this manuscript, a second generation BP device.

is administered at minimal stimulus just above threshold output intensity of a 1.0 or 1.1 MTTLOI, we would expect all age groups to receive the same uniform MTTLOI as seen on the chart above. If so, perhaps the unusually high Impedance for the ten year can be ascribed to the anomalous "ramping" mechanism subsumed into the B-25 device itself. But why is "ramping" even needed on the B-25? We shall investigate this phenomenon in a moment.

We should Keep in mind the joule oriented, perfect square, age-related relative constant thresholds below used by MECTA and Somatics.

10 year old male = 1.0
20 year old male = 4.00**J**
30 year old male = 9.00**J**
40 year old male = **16.00J**
50 year old male = **25.00J**
60 year old male = **36.00J**
65 year old male = **42.25J**
70 year old male = **48.97J**
80 year old male = **64.00J**
90 year old male = **81.00J**
100 year old male = **100.00J**

In that joules are selectable from 1-99J on the B-25, the machine's selector does indeed appear to have the mechanical capacity to select minimal stimulus output for all age groups on the B-25 as seen in the chart above. But to create the chart above and in accordance with what Medcraft tells us regarding output selection, let us suppose the Operator desires to emit just over minimal stimulus (just over 42.25J) for a 65 year old year old recipient. In order to emit just over minimal stimulus, the operator could select a circa 45.0 Joule maximum output for the 65 year old, whose theoretical Impedance on the chart above appears to be about 272Ω, much less than the 365Ω reached in this same age category with second generation MECTA and Somatics BP devices both of which administer default outputs well above threshold. The diminished Impedance on the B-25 in this older age category, as has already been noted, is no doubt due to the 99J ceiling, a ceiling in compliance with the 1982 APA Standard's proscribed 110J maximum; moreover, a ceiling both Somatics Inc. and MECTA Corp. discard (through pure-ER/RRC interpretation) whose machines, therefore, emit much greater output in these age categories due their circa 2.5 MTTLOI in every age category. Constant Current on the B-25 in this instance, might be selected at the 1.0A maximum (as seen in the chart above). As a result, Voltage for the 65 year old would be automatically set at 271V and Duration automatically programmed by the machine's computer to 1.2 Seconds in order to insure that up to, but no more than circa 45 Joules, or just above threshold is delivered to the 65 year old recipient. Charge can then be figured at 167.7mC. Hertz on the B-25 is a constant 70, that is, 140 Pulses, while Wave Length is a constant of 1.0 milliseconds (.001 Sec). Using the formula: EO = Voltage x Amperage x Hertz x Wave Length x Duration, we can verify the desired 45J minimal stimulus output (for this hypothetical device). This can be re-verified via the formula: EO = Amperage squared x Impedance x Hertz x WL x Duration. Finally, Charge, as noted, can be derived via the formula: EO ÷ Amperage x Impedance. (See Chart above.)

EO = 271V x 1.0A x 140 Pulses x .001WL x 1.2 Seconds = 45.6 Joules.

EO = 1.0A x 1.0A x 272Ω x 140 Pulses x .001WL x 1.2 Seconds = 45.6 Joules.

Charge = 45.6J/1.0A x 272Ω = .1677C.

Using the same methodology, we can now configure minimal stimulus outputs and the corresponding parameters for all other age groups.

For example, in order to emit minimal stimulus for the **10 year old**, that is, if the Operator selects a 1.0 Joule maximum output for the 10 year old whose Impedance, perhaps due to ramping, drops no lower than a 150Ω (according to Medcraft charts), a constant .7A Current might be selected. (See above chart). As a result, Voltage would be automatically set to 105V and emission time 0.1 Seconds. In spite of Medcraft's refusal to divulge specific output-age correlations, this appears to be in keeping with Medcraft charts. The result, in any case, is a little over 1.0 Joule, true minimal stimulus for what appears to be the 10 year old child. The Charge evinced is 10.5 millicoulombs:

EO = 105V x .7A x 140 Pulses x .001WL x 0.1 Seconds = 1.03 Joules.

EO = .7A x .7A x 150Ω x 140 Pulses x .001WL x 0.1 Seconds = 1.03 Joules.

Charge = 1.1J/.7A x 150 Ω = .0105C. (See theoretical chart above for age ten).

In order to emit just over what should be minimal stimulus for the **20 year old**, that is, if the Operator selects a circa 5.0 Joule maximum output for the 20 year old year old, for whom again, apparently due to ramping, Impedance may reach about 172Ω (as opposed to between 80 and 112Ω on second generation MECTA and Somatics BP devices), constant Current might be selected at about .8A maximum (see chart above). As a result, Voltage would automatically be set at 137V and emission time, 0.3 Seconds. The result is circa 5.0 Joules, which again, is just over minimal stimulus for the 20 year old recipient. Charge is now .0334C or 33.4 millicoulombs:

EO = 137V x 0.8A x 140 Pulses x .001WL x 0.3 Seconds = 4.6 Joules.

EO = 0.8A x 0.8A x 172Ω x 140 Pulses x .001WL x 0.3 Seconds = 4.6 Joules.

Charge = 4.6J/0.8A x 172Ω = .03343C. (See theoretical chart above for age 20).

In order to emit just over minimal stimulus for the **30 year old**, that is, if the Operator selects a circa 10.0 Joule maximum output for the 30 year old year old, the Impedance for whom begins to normalize at about 194Ω (as opposed to about 168Ω for the second generation made-for-America MECTA BP devices), a .8A constant Current might again be selected. As a result, Voltage would be automatically set at 154V and emission time, 0.6 Seconds. The result is a circa 10.0 Joule output, or just over minimal stimulus for the 30 year old recipient:

EO = 154V x 0.8A x 140 Pulses x .001WL x 0.6 Seconds = 10.4 Joules.

EO = 0.8A x 0.8A x 194Ω x 140 Pulses x .001WL x 0.6 Seconds = 10.4 Joules.

Charge = 10.4J/0.8A x 194Ω = .0670C. (See theoretical chart above for age 30).

In order to emit just over minimal stimulus for the **40 year old**, that is, if the operator selects a circa 17.0 Joule maximum output for the 40 year old year old, which once again normalizes to about 217Ω (as opposed to 225Ω on second generation made-for-America MECTA BP devices), constant Current would have to be selected at about .9A maximum. As a result Voltage is automatically set at 195V and emission time to 0.7 Seconds. The result is a circa 17.0 Joule output, again, just over minimal stimulus for the 40 year old recipient. Charge is 88mC.

EO = 195V x 0.9A x 140 Pulses x .001WL x 0.7 Seconds = 17.2 Joules.

EO = 0.9A x 0.9A x 217Ω x 140 Pulses x .001WL x 0.7 Seconds = 17.2 Joules.

Charge = 17.2J/0.9A x 217Ω = .08807C (See theoretical chart above for age 40).

In order to emit just over minimal stimulus for the **50 year old** whose Impedance on the B-25 appears to be about 239Ω, less than that reached in this same age category on second generation MECTA and Somatics BP devices, the operator should select a circa 26.0 Joule maximum output. In this instance, constant Current would probably have to be selected at about .9A maximum. As a result Voltage would automatically be set at 214V and emission time to 1.0 Seconds. The result is a circa 27.0 Joule output, which is just over minimal stimulus for the 50 year old recipient. Charge is 125.5mC.

EO = 214V x 0.9A x 140 Pulses x .001WL x 1.0 Seconds = 27.0 Joules.

EO = 0.9A x 0.9A x 239Ω x 140 Pulses x .001WL x 1.0 Seconds = 27.0 Joules.

Charge = 27J/0.9A x 239Ω = .1255C. (See theoretical chart above for age 50).

In order to emit just over minimal stimulus for the **60 year old**, that is, if the operator selects a circa 36.0 Joule maximum output for the 60 year old year old, whose maximum Impedance at about 261Ω is now much lower than on MECTA and Somatics BP devices in this category which emit about 335Ω, constant Current would probably have to selected at about 1.0A maximum. As a result Voltage would automatically be set at 234V and emission time to 1.3 Seconds. The result is a circa 38.0 Joule output, which is just over minimal stimulus for the 60 year old recipient. Charge is 163.5mC.

EO = 234V x 0.9A x 140 Pulses x .001WL x 1.3 Seconds = 38.4 Joules.

EO = 0.9A x 0.9A x 261Ω x 140 Pulses x .001WL x 1.3 Seconds = 38.4 Joules.

Charge = 38.4J/0.9A x 261Ω = .16347C. (See theoretical chart above age 60).

In order to emit just over minimal stimulus, the operator can select a circa 52.0 Joule maximum output for the **70 year old** recipient, whose Impedance at about 283Ω, continues to diminish compared to the 394Ω reached in this same age category with second generation MECTA and Somatics BP devices. The diminished Impedance is again entirely due to the 99J ceiling discarded by Somatics and MECTA which continue to emit 2.5 to 2.6 fold thresholds in all age categories. Constant Current in this instance, might be selected at about 1.0A maximum. As a result Voltage is automatically set at 282V and Duration to 1.3 Seconds in order to insure that circa 52 Joules is delivered. The result is a circa 52.0 Joule output, which is just over minimal stimulus for the 70 year old recipient. Charge is 182mC.

EO = 282V x 1.0A x 140 Pulses x .001WL x 1.3 Seconds = 51.5 Joules.

EO = 1.0A x 1.0A x 283Ω x 140 Pulses x .001WL x 1.3 Seconds = 51.5 Joules.

Charge = 51.5J/1.0A x 283Ω = .182C. (See theoretical chart above for age 70).

In order to emit just over minimal stimulus, the operator can select a circa 64.0 Joule maximum output for the **79-80 year old** recipient, whose Impedance is about 305Ω. Impedance in this age category for second generation MECTA and Somatics BP devices can reach up to 450Ω, about 150Ω higher than the B-25 in this age category. As noted previously, the diminishing Impedance is entirely due to the 99J ceiling discarded by Somatics and MECTA. Constant Current in this instance, might again be selected at about 1.0A maximum. As a result Voltage is automatically set at 305V and Duration to 1.5 Seconds in order to insure that circa 64 Joules is delivered. The result is a circa 64.0 Joule output, which is just over minimal stimulus for the circa 80 year old recipient. Charge is 210mC.

EO = 305V x 1.0A x 140 Pulses x .001WL x 1.5 Seconds = 64 Joules.

EO = 1.0A x 1.0A x 305Ω x 140 Pulses x .001WL x 1.5 Seconds = 64 Joules.

Charge = 64.0J/1.0A x 305Ω = .210C. (See theoretical chart above for age 80).

In order to emit just over minimal stimulus, the operator can select a circa 82.0 Joule maximum output for the **89-90 year old** recipient, whose Impedance is about 315Ω. Impedance in this age category for second generation MECTA and Somatics BP devices can reach around 506Ω, about 190Ω higher. As noted previously, the diminishing Impedance is entirely due to the 99J ceiling discarded by Somatics and MECTA which continues to deliver 2.5 to 2.6 fold thresholds in all age categories. Constant Current in this instance, might again be selected to about 1.0A maximum. As a result Voltage is automatically set at 315V and Duration to 1.9 Seconds in order to insure that circa 83 Joules is delivered. The result is a circa 83.0 Joule output, which is just over minimal stimulus for the circa 90 year old recipient. Charge is 266mC.

EO = 315V x 1.0A x 140 Pulses x .001WL x 1.9 Seconds = 83.8 Joules.

EO = 1.0A x 1.0A x 315Ω x 140 Pulses x .001WL x 1.9 Seconds = 83.8 Joules.

Charge = 83.8J/1.0A x 315Ω = .266C. (See theoretical chart above for age 90).

Finally, in order to emit just over minimal stimulus, the operator can select a circa 99.0 Joule maximum output for the **99 year old** recipient, whose Impedance is about 322Ω. If the operator further selects a 1.0A maximum Current, Voltage and emission time will automatically be selected at 322V and 2.2 Seconds respectively also in accordance with Medcraft B-25 charts. Not surprisingly, Impedance in this age category for second generation MECTA and Somatics BP devices reaches around 562Ω, about 237Ω higher. Clearly, the diminishing Impedance on the B-25 is entirely due to the 99J ceiling discarded by Somatics and MECTA whose second generation devices continue to deliver uniform 2.5 to 2.6 fold threshold outputs in all age categories. Constant Current in this instance, might again be selected at about 1.0A maximum. As a result Voltage is automatically set at 322V and Duration to 2.2 Seconds in order to insure that circa 99 Joules is delivered. The result is the maximum 99 Joules, which is minimal stimulus for the 99 year old male who seizes at about 99 Joules. Charge is figured at 307mC.

EO = 322V x 1.0A x 140 Pulses x .001WL x 2.2 Seconds = 99.0 Joules.

EO = 1.0A x 1.0A x 322Ω x 140 Pulses x .001WL x 2.2 Seconds = 99.0 Joules.

Charge = 99J/1.0A x 322Ω = .307C. (See theoretical chart above for age 99).

Thus, the B-25, as noted, appears to be able to maintain the absolute 99J output ceiling just as Medcraft claims, that is, the B-25 prevents outputs from exceeding 99Js, making the B-25 the single made-for-America second generation BP device in conformity with the 1982 APA ceiling Standard of 110 Absolute Joules. Moreover, if the B-25 also conforms to the expected "70J at 220Ω" (or even the later "100J at 220Ω") conditional-ER/RRC aspect of the 1982 APA Standard represented in the above chart, thereby gradually increasing output relative to increasing age (or Impedance) up to the APA 110J ceiling, adherence to the 1982 APA Standard is guaranteed.

If the theoretical chart above actually was the reality, and if Medcraft limited all outputs to the APA stipulated minimal stimulus outputs depicted in the theoretical chart above, the Medcraft B-25, like the MECTA "C," would be the perfect minimal stimulus ECT device, one in total compliance with the 1982 APA Standard (Department of Health and Human Services, 1982a, A53, E20). In short, the B-25 would be in compliance with both the expected conditional-ER/RRC interpretation of its reported "99J at 220Ω," guaranteeing diminishing emissions relative to diminishing age, and the 110J ceiling, guaranteeing a maximum, uniform 1.1 MTTLOI for all age categories, and thus the least amount of electricity possible to induce so-called adequate grand mal seizures in every age group. Unfortunately, this is not the reality.

Upon closer examination of the lengthy Medcraft charts (submitted by Medcraft to the FDA), we can see that while Medcraft, unlike MECTA and Somatics, does indeed recognize and implement for its B-25, the APA 110J maximum output ceiling, and so indeed appears to have interpreted the B-25's reported "99J at 220Ω" phraseology as incorporative of the 99J ceiling we would anticipate in a "99J at 220Ω" conditional-ER/RRC limited to 99J, the Medcraft B-25 does ***not*** appear to emit decreasing outputs with respect to decreasing age. That is, while acknowledging the 110J APA ceiling, Medcraft does ***not*** appear to recognize either the APA's "70J at 220Ω" or the later circa "100J at 220Ω" phrase as an ER/RRC of any sort, either conditional or pure. ER/RRC, remember, insures gradational decreases with respect to decreasing age and in conjunction with a 110J ceiling, and so a uniform 1.1 MTTLOI applied to all age recipients. In fact, unlike Somatics and MECTA, Medcraft ignores the ER/RRC principle altogether. Amazingly, unlike either MECTA or Somatics BP devices, the Medcraft B-25's 99J ceiling can be manually selected at even the lowest Impedance and thus applied to any age category, including the youngest. In brief, by ignoring ER/RRC, the machine can be made to reach its 99 Joule ceiling in even the lowest age category. While the Medcraft B-25 adheres to the looked for 99J ceiling, therefore, according to Medcraft charts, the B-25 can reach the maximum 99J both above and below 220Ω, and in fact, at the very lowest B-25 Impedance (apparently) of "150Ω. " By precipitously reaching 99Js at even the lowest B-25 Impedance level, then, Medcraft patently ignores both the APA's "70J at 220Ω" and even the later "100J at 220Ω" phrases as an ER/RRC of any sort, conditional or pure. [549] Unlike the anticipated minimal stimulus chart above culminating at a 99J ceiling only for the 100 year old recipient and so conforming to a conditional-ER/RRC and thus a gradual decrease in output relative to decreasing age, the actual B-25 incorporates no age-related gradation whatsoever. In short, the actual B-25 is capable of achieving its' 99J ceiling, as noted, in even the very youngest age category. So what does this mean?

Altogether ignoring the APA and Mectan phrases "70J at 220Ω," and "100J at 220Ω" respectively as ER/RRCs, but recognizing the 110J APA ceiling within the APA Standard, Medcraft properly interprets the newer "99J at 220Ω" phrase as incorporative of a 99J ceiling as noted, but, improperly (and surprisingly) allows this maximum 99J ceiling at every Impedance (or age) level. Instead of a gradual descension in output relative to descending age, maintaining minimal stimulus in every age category or limiting output relative to descending Impedance via even a pure-ER/RRC interpretation of "70 at 220Ω" or "100J at 220Ω," Medcraft, unlike MECTA and Somatics, has engineered the B-25 with the capacity to attain its' 99J ceiling potential in each age category. In lieu of even the "Pure-*ER/RRC*" variant applied by MECTA and Somatics then, Medcraft's interpretation of its Mectan-like phrase "99J at 220Ω," is what might be deemed a "*Pure-Ceiling.* " That is, unlike MECTA and Somatics' Pure-ER/RRC interpretation of "100J at 220Ω," Medcraft interprets its "99J at 220Ω" phrase as a 99J ceiling potential at all Impedance (age) levels. Thus, while incremental reduction in Duration may limit the B-25's overall ceiling to 99Js, thereby adhering or conforming to the 110J APA ceiling, alarmingly, Medcraft, unlike MECTA and Somatics BP devices, permits the B-25 to reach 99Js for even the ten year old child. In contrast, even third generation MECTA and Somatics BP devices, limit output for the ten year old recipient to five or six Joules.

In summation, second generation MECTA and Somatics BP devices contain gradual decreases in output in accordance with an ER/RRC and in accordance with a single uniform MTTLOI for all age categories, but unlike Medcraft's B-25, the later second generation Somatics and MECTA devices grossly surpass the 110J maximum specified within the 1982 APA Standard reaching between 252 and 260 maximum Joules and so between a 2.52 and 2.6 MTTLOI. Medcraft's B-25, on the other hand, though limiting output to a 99J maximum (in accordance with the 110J APA ceiling Standard), completely ignores ER/RRC (both conditional and pure) thus ignoring the implementation of a uniform MTTLOI. In brief, the B-25 machine fails to decrease outputs with respect to decreasing age, reaching 99Js and so a 99 MTTLOI in even the youngest age category. In short, outputs on MECTA and Somatics BP devices uniformly decrease with decreasing age but reach outputs up to 260J in the oldest age category, while the B-25 limits output to 99J but can emit this maximum output in even the youngest age category.

ACTUAL MEDCRAFT B-25 BP DEVICE

Medcraft's B-25, then, unlike MECTA and Somatics, adheres to a 99J absolute ceiling, but fails to apply its reported "99J at 220Ω" phrase as even a *pure* -ER/RRC. In short, Medcraft altogether ignores ER/RRC. In so doing, Medcraft's B-25 grossly violates electrical output "dosages" relative to age in accordance with the precept of ER/RRC, thereby violating the single consistent MTTLOI concept for Brief Pulse, particularly

[549] While MECTA and Somatics both surpass 100J, violating the 1982 Absolute ceiling, both manufacturers nevertheless appear to recognize ER/RRC, even illegally interpreting the "100J at 220Ω" as a *Pure*-ER/RRC. Medcraft ignores ER/RRC altogether.

dangerous at Impedances less than 220Ω (that is, in the younger age categories). Consequently, while the hypothetical B-25 minimal stimulus chart above represents the *anticipated* adherence to an ER/RRC of "70J at 220Ω" and even "100J at 220Ω" with conditional 99J overall ceiling in accordance with the 1982 APA Standard, and while, according to Medcraft, such minimal stimulus outputs could, in theory, be manually selected, the minimal stimulus chart above is illusory, as we shall eventually see. Quite conversely, utilizing the actual B-25 specs Medcraft reported to the FDA in 1986, the following chart represents actual possible settings of 99 maximum Joules at all age levels (Food and Drug Administration, 1986A), a chart factually reflective of the B-25's maximum potential revealing Medcraft's hidden Pure-Ceiling interpretation of its' featured "99J at 220Ω" phraseology. The chart below then, represents the actual maximum B-25 output potential of 99J at every Impedance (age) level.

ACTUAL CONSTANT CURRENT MEDCRAFT B-25 BRIEF PULSE DEVICE
BASED ON PURE-CEILING INTERPRETATION OF "99J AT 220Ω"
AT "ALLOWABLE" AND THUS POTENTIAL MAXIMUM SETTINGS
Medcraft Corp.1985 - 2000 (2nd GENERATION [550])

VOLTAGE	POWER % @ Age	AGE Yrs	Ω Ohms	FREQUENCY (Hz)	DURATION (SECs)	CURRENT mAmps	ENERGY Joules	CHARGE mC
150	10	10	150	70	4.71	1.0	99J	660
137	20	20	172	70	4.11	1.0	99J	575.6
154	30	30	194	70	3.65	1.0	99J	510
195	40	40	217	70	3.26	1.0	99J	456
214	50	50	239	70	2.96	1.0	99J	414
234	60	60	261	70	2.71	1.0	99J	379
271	65	65	272	70	2.6	1.0	99J	364
282	70	69	283	70	2.5	1.0	99J	350
305	80	79	305	70	2.31	1.0	99J	325
315	90	89	315	70	2.24	1.0	99J	314
322	100	99	322	70	2.2	1.0	99J	307

PW .001 Seconds

The B-25 Chart above reflects known parameters: in brief, various possible Constant Current Settings from .4 to 1.0 Amperes, a constant Frequency of 140 Pulses, a constant Pulse Width of .001 and maximum Voltage of circa 325V (Food and Drug Administration, 1986A). Duration, 0-6.0 Seconds and Frequency (140 Pulses) are non-selectable whereas EO (1-99 Joules) and constant Current (.4-1.0A) are selectable. (Actual Charge, though not provided by Medcraft, is derivable.)

The B-25 device chart above is set to maximum settings to derive the "allowable" maximum of 99J in all age categories. Charge, Age, and Corresponding Voltages are probable. Note the exceptionally high Impedances and Charges in the 10 and 20 year old age categories resulting (as we shall see) in grossly high MTTLOIs as opposed to the lower than normal Impedances and Charges in the 65 and over age categories both due to the 99J ceiling in all age categories. Remarkably, the B-25 is potentially more powerful than the B-24 SW in every age category with respect to MTTLOI potential.

In contrast to MECTA and Somatics Pure-ER/RRC interpretation of "100J at 220Ω," the B-25's Pure-Ceiling interpretation results in decreasing Charge and Duration relative to increasing age. This is due to the ceiling maximum of 99 Joules in even the oldest age category in accordance with the 1982 APA Standard. On the other hand, in potentially emitting 99Js at all Impedances as seen above, the B-25 can emit destructively excessive MTTLOIs in the younger age categories. Moreover, Charge, Voltage, Impedance, EO in Joules are all unacceptably high in the younger age categories.

In ignoring ER/RRC, the machine violates the principle of a single uniform MTTLOI for all age categories which should compel descending outputs with respect to descending age. Consequently, grossly high MTTLOIs are administered to recipients with low Impedances (i.e. the young). Outputs are so excessive in the younger age categories that the B-25 must incorporate a "ramping" mechanism to prevent external injury, a mechanism not extant in any other Brief Pulse device.

---

[550] A BP device actually limited to 99 absolute Joules would ordinarily be deemed "1st generation." However, because Medcraft equates this device with second generation MECTA and Somatics BP devices, and because Medcraft ignores ER/RRC, the B-25 must be categorized as a second (possibly even third) generation BP device.

Unique

With its 99J maximum, the B-25 is the only American second generation BP device to comply with the 110J ceiling regulation mandated within the 1982 APA Standard. Had the B-25 also adhered to the ER/RRC component of the same standard, a component necessitating a single uniform MTTLOI for all age categories and thus decreasing outputs with respect to decreasing age as do second generation MECTA and Somatics BP devices, the B-25 would be the only American BP device produced after 1985 to elicit minimal stimulus outputs at every age level. Adhering to both components means that the lowest common MTTLOI denominator on a device, that is, the lowest MTTLOI, in this instance, using maximum parameters which, for the B-25, is a circa 1.0 fold threshold titration level output administered to the 99 year old recipient-- [551] mandates the same 1.0 fold threshold for all other age categories. This method insures a uniform MTTLOI and (with the 99J ceiling) minimal stimulus output. In short, the ten year old would have to receive the same 1.0 fold threshold output as the 99 year old, which for the ten year old who seizes at 1.0J would mean 1.0J—not the 99 Joules (or 99 MTTLOI) possible under Medcraft's Pure-Ceiling interpretation. Because Medcraft does not acknowledge ER/RRC, however, and thus does not adhere to a uniform MTTLOI (as do MECTA and Somatics BP devices), the B-25 has the capacity to deliver 99 Joules to every age category. In brief, administrators of the B-25 are "free" to utilize not a single, but a variety of MTTLOIs.

The B-25, in sum, is limited to a 1.0 MTTLOI for the 99 year old recipient while simultaneously having the capacity to deliver a 99 MTTLOI to the ten year old child. In brief, because Medcraft ignores the ER/RRC component of the APA standard, the B-25 is allowed to deliver inconsistent Multifold Threshold Titration Level Output Intensities relative to age, a fact which makes the B-25 device dangerously unregulated. Stated differently, free from a uniform MTTLOI for all age categories, the B-25 has been engineered to ignore all decreasing power gradations with respect to decreasing age. In discarding the ER/RRC component of the APA Standard, therefore, the B-25 is free from administering a uniform MTTLOI to all age categories, thereby, allowing the B-25 to deliver not an equal MTTLOI, but equal amounts of electricity to all ages from 10 to 99 years, including maximum output. Specifically then, the machine is capable of delivering extremely dangerous MTTLOIs of electricity to the younger age categories. In fact, it is in order to emit its highest output of 99 Joules at even the lowest Impedances that the machine must be equipped with a "ramping" mechanism similar to the B-24's so-called "glissando," in an attempt to prevent external injury to the recipient (i.e. burns) due to sudden high dosages of electricity. In this respect, the alleged B-25 Brief Pulse is comparable in its delivery and effect to the B-24 SW, against which Brief Pulse was purported to be an improvement.

Comparing Medcraft's B-25 Brief Pulse Device to Medcraft's B-24 SW Device and other American-made Devices

Using the following parameter settings for the B-25: Pulse Width (.001Sec), Maximum Pulses (140), and Maximum Amperage (1.0A) together with various Voltages, various Impedances, and various Durations, the B-25 can be made to achieve 99J in all age groups as in the chart above, all of which can be confirmed with the following formulas: Different combinations of Voltage and Duration can be made to emit up to 99J in any age category:

1) EO = XV x 1.0A x 140 Pulses x .001WL x X Seconds = 99.0 Joules.

2) EO = 1.0A x 1.0A x XΩ x 140 Pulses x .001WL x X Seconds = 99 Joules.

Charge, based on various EOs and Impedances can be deduced using the formula below:

3) Charge = XJ ÷ 1.0A x XΩ = XCoulombs

---

[551] 99J for the 99J year old recipient who seizes at 99J: 99J ÷ 99J = 1.0 fold threshold.

SW, as has been noted, can in rare instances, reach up to 200 Joules, while the B-25 Brief Pulse is limited to half that output at 99J. On the other hand, the B-25 at maximum settings begins to surpass SW at maximum settings from about age 40 to 100.

B-24 SW at Maximum Settings in all Age Groups (Sans 1.0A Ceiling)
Vs.
B-25 BP at Maximum Settings in all Age Groups

AGE	B-24 SW at MAX SETTINGS	B-25 BP AT MAX SETTINGS
	Maximum Joules/Per Age Category	Maximum Joules/Per Age Category
10	**200J**	**99J**
20	**148J**	**99J**
24	**134J**	**99J**
30	**118J**	**99J**
40	**98.0J**	**99J**
50	**83.8J**	**99J**
60	**73.2J**	**99J**
65	**68.6J**	**99J**
70	**64.9J**	**99J**
80	**58.4J**	**99J**
90	**53J**	**99J**
100	**48.6J**	**99J**

Below, we can see that even in age categories wherein SW at maximum output surpasses the B-25 BP at maximum output, the B-25 at maximum output, in terms of MTTLOI, surpasses SW in every age category. Indeed, because the B-25 is not based on an ER/RRC, the MTTLOI has no regulatory consistency. These inconsistent MTTLOI potentials for the B-25 at various age groups can be determined simply by dividing the 99J maximum output achievable in each age group with the relative threshold output constant for that same age group. For example, the ten year old seizes at 1.0J. Consequently, 99J ÷ 1.0J = 99 fold threshold or a 99 MTTLOI. The 40 year old seizes at 16J, thus 99J ÷ 16J = 6.2 fold threshold or a 6.2 MTLLOI.

These MTTLOIs achievable with the B-25 BP can now be compared to the MTTLOIs achievable with the B-24 SW determined in an entirely different manner in a another section. [552] (See SW devices.)

Multifold Threshold Titration Level Output Intensities for B-24 SW at Maximum Settings in all Age Groups (Sans 1.0A Ceiling) Vs. B-25 BP at Maximum Settings in all Age Groups

AGE	B-24 SW at MAX SETTINGS	B-25 BP AT MAX SETTINGS
	MULTIFOLD THRESHOLD TITRATION LEVEL	*MULTIFOLD THRESHOLD TITRATION LEVEL*
10	***23.0 Fold***	***99.0 Fold***
20	***9.44 Fold***	***24.75 Fold***
24	***7.08 Fold***	***18.0 Fold***
30	***4.80 Fold***	***11.0 Fold***
40	***2.75 Fold***	***6.20 Fold***
50	***1.72 Fold***	***4.00 Fold***
60	***1.15 Fold***	***2.75 Fold***
65	***0.95 Fold***	***2.34 Fold***
70	***0.80 Fold***	***2.00 Fold***
80	***0.59 Fold***	***1.55 Fold***
90	***0.44 Fold***	***1.22 Fold***
99	***0.34 Fold***	***1.00 Fold***

---

[552] Relative constants do not apply to SW and so MTTLOI must be determined in another manner.

Note above that the B-24 SW at maximum settings can emit excessive dosages of electricity in younger age categories but is ineffective at ages 65 and older, that is, may not be powerful enough to elicit an adequate seizure in these older age groups denoted by darkened areas on bottom rows. (Outputs below 1.0 fold may not induce adequate seizures.) Now note how the B-25 BP at maximum settings surpasses SW with respect to MTTLOI in every age category. Though the B24 SW can emit a maximum of 200 Joules and the B-25 BP only 99 Joules (see below), due to greater efficiency and absence of an ER/RRC insuring gradation, the B-25 BP is even more powerful and more dangerous than the B-24 SW in most age categories. Thus, while the B-25 is limited to half that output (99J), due to the B-25's greater efficiency together with Medcraft's total disregard of ER/RRC, that is, disregard for descending outputs relative to descending age, we can see that the MTTLOI potential of the B-25 BP device is far greater than that of the B-24 SW.

Below are the two comparative charts melded together:

Multifold Threshold Levels and Maximum Output for B-24 SW at Maximum Settings in all Age Groups (Sans 1.0A Ceiling) Vs. B-25 BP at Maximum Settings in all Age Groups

AGE	B-24 SW at MAX SETTINGS	B-25 BP AT MAX SETTINGS	B-24 SW at MAX SETTINGS	B-25 BP AT MAX SETTINGS
	MULTIFOLD THRESHOLD TITRATION LEVEL	*MULTIFOLD THRESHOLD TITRATION LEVEL*	Max Joules/Per Age Category	Max Joules/Per Age Category
10	***23.0 Fold***	***99.0 Fold***	**200J**	**99J**
20	***9.44 Fold***	***24.75 Fold***	**148J**	**99J**
24	***7.08 Fold***	***18.0 Fold***	**134J**	**99J**
30	***4.80 Fold***	***11 Fold***	**118J**	**99J**
40	***2.75 Fold***	***6.2 Fold***	**98.0J**	**99J**
50	***1.72 Fold***	***4.0 Fold***	**83.8J**	**99J**
60	***1.15 Fold***	***2.75 Fold***	**73.2J**	**99J**
65	***.95 Fold***	***2.34 Fold***	**68.6J**	**99J**
70	***.80 Fold***	***2.0 Fold***	**64.9J**	**99J**
80	***.59 Fold***	***1.55 Fold***	**58.4J**	**99J**
90	***.44 Fold***	***1.22 Fold***	**53J**	**99J**
100	***.34 Fold***	***1.0 Fold***	**48.6J**	**99J**

Note how the B-25 is more powerful than the B-24 in cumulative output only from age 40 and older, but is more powerful regarding MTTLOI in every age group. This is an example of inverse exploitation of the much more efficient B-25 Brief Pulse device. Moreover, like the B-24, the B-25 is much more powerful in the younger age categories than in the older age categories regarding MTTLOI, but is nevertheless more than powerful enough to seize recipients 65-100 years of age, unlike SW. It is as if the B-25 is not designed as a reduced output device compared to SW, but to exploit the greater efficiency of Brief Pulse in order to enhance the MTTLOI and thus power of the B-24 SW both in the younger and older age categories. Maintaining a 99J ceiling as a means of reducing power here is illusory. By ignoring ER/RRC and thus a uniform MTTLOI insuring gradational outputs relative to Impedance (and thus age) and thus ignoring minimal stimulus outputs in all age categories, the B-25 Pure-Ceiling Brief Pulse device simply becomes a more powerful, more insidious rendition of the B-24 SW of old.

Note then, that like Medcraft's B-24 SW, Medcraft's B-25 BP device, because it ignores ER/RRC, delivers various, inconsistent MTTLOIs to the various age categories. Now let us compare the Medcraft B-24 SW, the Medcraft B-25 BP Pure-Ceiling device, and a later second generation MECTA IEC Pure-ER/RRC BP device, the JR/SR 2.

B-24 SW <u>Maximum</u> Settings in all Age Groups (Sans 1.0A Ceiling)
Vs.
B-25 BP <u>Maximum</u> Settings in all Age Groups
Vs.
2nd Gen. MECTA JR/SR 2 IEC BP <u>Default</u> Settings for all Age Groups

AGE	B-24 SW at MAX SETTINGS	B-25 BP AT MAX SETTINGS	2nd Gen MECTA JR/SR 2 IEC DEFAULT SETTINGS	B-24 SW at MAX SETTINGS	B-25 BP AT MAX SETTINGS	2nd Gen MECTA JR/SR 2 IEC DEFAULT SETTINGS
	MULTIFOLD THRESHOLD TITRATION LEVEL	*MULTIFOLD THRESHOLD TITRATION LEVEL*	*MULTIFOLD THRESHOLD TITRATION LEVEL*	Max Joules/Per Age Category	Max Joules/Per Age Category	Max Joules/Per Age Category
10	*23.0 Fold*	*99.0 Fold*	*2.3 Fold*	200J	99J	2.88
20	*9.44 Fold*	*24.75 Fold*	*2.3 Fold*	148J	99J	9.22
24	*7.08 Fold*	*18.0 Fold*	*2.3 Fold*	134J	99J	15
30	*4.80 Fold*	*11 Fold*	*2.3 Fold*	118J	99J	20.74
40	*2.75 Fold*	*6.2 Fold*	*2.3 Fold*	98.0J	99J	36.86
50	*1.72 Fold*	*4.0 Fold*	*2.3 Fold*	83.8J	99J	57.6
60	*1.15 Fold*	*2.75 Fold*	*2.3 Fold*	73.2J	99J	82.94
65	*.95 Fold*	*2.34 Fold*	*2.3 Fold*	68.6J	99J	97.34
70	*.80 Fold*	*2.0 Fold*	*2.3 Fold*	64.9J	99J	112.9
80	*.59 Fold*	*1.55 Fold*	*2.3 Fold*	58.4J	99J	147.5
90	*.44 Fold*	*1.22 Fold*	*2.3 Fold*	53.0J	99J	186.48
100	*.34 Fold*	*1.0 Fold*	*2.3 Fold*	48.6J	99J	230J

As noted above, maximum settings on the B-25 make the device more powerful than the B-24 in cumulative output only from age 40 and higher. However, the B-25 at maximum output is more powerful than the B-24 at maximum output regarding MTTLOI in every age category. Note how from age 10 to age 65, the B-25 at maximum settings is more powerful than the MECTA second generation SR/JR 2 IEC BP Device in both cumulative output and MTTLOI, while the second generation JR/SR 2 IEC BP device is more powerful than the B-25 in cumulative output and MTTLOI from age 65 and older. Note how the MECTA device is an improvement (MTTLOI-wise) over the B-24 SW only from age 10 to about age 40, after which the MECTA device surpasses the B-24. Regarding cumulative output, the second generation MECTA device surpasses SW at age 60 and above. (Third generation MECTA BP devices emit even higher EO as we shall see in Volume II). Finally, note the wild variation in MTTLOIs in both the B-24 and B-25 compared to the uniform MTTLOI of the MECTA (and Somatics--not represented) device due to Medcraft's ignoring of ER/RRC. All three of the above machines are ENR devices.

In brief, while the B-25's overall output is indeed limited to 99Js, the B-25 violates the APA Standard's ER/RRC principle ignoring a uniform MTTLOI meant to insure gradational outputs relative to age. In this sense, the B-25 emulates the B-24. In short, the B-25, similar to the B-24 permits its <u>99J maximum</u> at even the lowest B-25 Impedance (of a purported 150Ω) allowing 99J in even the youngest age category.

The B-25 vs Second Generation MECTA and Somatics BP devices with Respect to Multifold Threshold Titration Level Output Intensities

Normally, the modern day BP device evinces about 50Ω of Resistance or less for the ten year old child. In addition, the highest MTTLOI allowed by the 1982 APA Standard is 1.1 fold threshold. This is because the overall APA ceiling is a clearly delineated 110J. When we apply the 110J to the most seizure recalcitrant recipient--the 100 year old male--who never requires more than 100 joules to seize in any treatment setting, we obtain the 1.1 MTTLOI maximum implied by the 1982 APA Standard (110J ÷ 100J = 1.1 fold). In short, 1.1 fold becomes the lowest common denominator under the 1982 APA Standard, and so the highest MTTLOI allowed for any age category. Thus, no age group can receive more than a 1.1 MTTLOI, a reasonable regulation in that 1.1 fold threshold is just above the least amount of electrical energy required to induce a so called adequate grand mal seizure for all 100 year old recipients under any treatment dynamic, in essence, anyone at any time. Moreover, the 100 year old adult, according to the APA Standard, can never receive more than 110J just as the ten year old can never receive more than 1.1J. Indeed, the 110J ceiling in conjunction with the "70J at 220Ω" ER/RRC is the true impetus of the 1982 APA Standard, specifically created to regulate or limit ECT devices to the least amount of electricity possible to induce a grand mal seizure in any age category. In accordance with the APA standard, therefore, ten year old children, none of whom ever require more than 1.0 Joule to adequately seize with Brief Pulse, can ever be administered more than 1.1 maximum Joules (1.0J x 1.1 = 1.1J) just as 100 year old adults, none of whom ever require more than 100J to adequately seize with Brief Pulse can ever be administered more than 110 Joules (100J x 1.1 = 110J). The ER/RRC mechanism in conjunction with the 110J APA ceiling, in short, guarantees both minimal stimulus and adequate output for both the 100 year old adult and the ten year old child.

Because Medcraft fails to honor ER/RRC, that is, because Medcraft applies a Pure-ceiling (with no ER/RRC), the B-25's 99J output for the ten year old child breaches the 1.1J limit in this age group by (99 - 1.1 =) 97.9 Joules. In other words, the B-25 can administer (99J ÷ 1.1 =) 90 fold the maximum 1.1 MTTLOI permissible under the 1982 APA Standard. Conversely, second generation made-for-America MECTA and Somatics BP devices incorporate the APA ER/RRC concept, but ignore the APA 110J ceiling. In applying a Pure-ER/RRC (with no 110J ceiling), second generation MECTA and Somatics devices emit illegal maximum outputs of (101.4J/220Ω = XJ/562Ω; X =) **259J** and (99.7J/220Ω = XJ/555.5Ω; X =) **252J** respectively; well over the 110J ceiling, but albeit illegal outputs, a uniform 2.59 and 2.52 MTTLOI respectively for all age categories. In short, because MECTA and Somatics ignore the 110J APA ceiling, and because the 100 year old never requires more than 100 joules for the inducement of a grand mal seizure in any treatment setting, the uniform MTTLOI increases from a legal 1.1 to an illegal (259J ÷ 100J =) 2.59 and (252J ÷ 100J =) 2.52 MTTLOI. Applying these uniform intensities to the ten year old child then, made-for-America second generation MECTA and Somatics machines emit 2.59 and 2.52 Joules respectively to the ten year old, well above the APA standard's 1.1J. On the other hand, because MECTA and Somatics' devices incorporate the ER/RRC principle of the APA Standard, second generation MECTA and Somatics BP devices at least administer gradational outputs via the uniform 2.59 and 2.52 MTTLOI administered in every age category. In short, while MECTA and Somatics BP devices grossly surpass the 110J APA ceiling, they at least deliver gradational outputs relative to age. In contrast, while conforming to the 110J APA ceiling, because Medcraft ignores the ER/RRC principle, the B-25 can administer its 99J maximum even to the 10 year old child. This means the Medcraft device, while limited to 99J, can administer that 99J to all age categories, thereby, delivering a devastating 99 MTTLOI to the ten year old child, surpassing the APA 1.1 MTTLOI regulation (99J ÷ 1.1J =) 90 fold.

Without the Gradational Regulatory Mechanism of ER/RRC, the B-25 BP Remains Eerily Similar to the B24 SW

Upon close scrutiny of Medcraft's practice of allowing the B-25 to reach 99 Joules at all Impedances, we begin to see the insidiousness of Medcraft's Pure-Ceiling interpretation. MECTA and Somatics devices and what appear to be all other second generation BP devices, limit outputs to about 20 Joules at 150Ω and this for thirty--not ten year old--recipients. This is because, as already noted, unlike the Medcraft B-25 BP device, second generation MECTA and Somatics BP devices incorporate the ER/RRC principle within the APA Standard, the implementation of which requires a uniform MTTLOI applied to all age categories. Thus, while made-for-America second generation MECTA BP devices reach up to 259 Joules, grossly violating the 110J ceiling, because 259 Joules translates into a (259J ÷ 100J =) 2.59 MTTLOI for the 100 year old adult (the common denominator), the same 2.59 MTTLOI must be applied to all other age recipients as well. This means that while the 100 year old who seizes at 100J can be administered 259J on the MECTA device, the ten year old child who seizes at about 1.0 Joule can only be administered a default maximum of about (2.59 x 1.0J =) 2.59 Joules. Again, this is due to the mandatory application of a uniform (101.4J/220Ω = 259J/562; 259J ÷ 100J =) 2.59 MTTLOI applied both to the 100 year old adult and the ten year old child. In sum, second generation made-for-America MECTA BP devices emit gradational outputs based on the same 2.59 MTTLOI administered to every age recipient. In sum, while second generation Somatics and MECTA BP machines grossly surpass the 110J APA ceiling, unlike the B-25, both Somatics and MECTA devices adhere to the ER/RRC principle and thus a uniform MTTLOI insuring gradational output maximums relative to age. The Medcraft B-25, by contrast, while limiting output to a 99J ceiling, as noted, totally ignores the ER/RRC principle and thus uniform MTTLOI requirement. As a result, gradational outputs relative to age are lost. Unlike MECTA and Somatics BP devices, then, while the Medcraft B-25 guarantees minimal stimulus output (or 1.0 fold threshold) for 99 year old recipients, all of whom seize at or below a minimum output of 99 or 100 Joules, the B-25 can administer the same 99 joules to the ten year old child who seizes at about 1.0 Joule. In short, the ten year old child can be administered 99 times the minimum 1.0J electrical dosage at or below which all ten year old children seize.

Not only are MTTLOIs wildly inconsistent on the B-25 then, but the machine is alarmingly dangerous, as noted, to younger age recipients, more dangerous, possibly, than even the B-24-SW. Tellingly, the engineering of the B-25 is not only similar to the B-24 SW (as we shall see), but retains many of the same characteristics and hazards of the B-24. In fact, the B-24 SW appears to be incapable of seizing the most elderly recipients, while the B-25 can not only seize elderly recipients, but like the B-24, is insidiously dangerous to younger age individuals. Like the B-24, therefore, the B-25 elicits inconsistent MTTLOIs with respect to age, thereby eliciting menacingly perilous outputs for those under the age of about sixty. Thus, while MECTA and Somatics second generation BP devices grossly surpass the 110 Joule ceiling permitting circa 2.5 MTTLOIs in even the oldest age categories, by ignoring the ER/RRC and thus the application of a uniform MTTLOI for all recipients, the modern B-25 Brief Pulse device, like the B-24 SW of old, is similarly capable of eliciting destructively high MTTLOIs in the younger age categories.

Mystery Solved

But we still have a mystery to solve. According to Medcraft, the lowest Impedance for the B-25, which we must assume belongs to the ten year old child, is 150Ω, far higher than other BP devices. At maximum output, this higher than normal Impedance for the ten year old age (compared to MECTA and Somatics BP devices) might easily be explained by the extraordinarily high 99J output potential in this age category. But how do we explain the same extraordinarily high Impedance of 150Ω for the same ten year old child if the Selector can choose a true minimal stimulus setting of about 1.0J? In short, why doesn't the Impedance drop to somewhere around 50Ω like second generation MECTA and Somatics devices?

Explanation of Atypically High and Low Impedances on the B-25

So what causes the atypically high Impedances on the B-25 in the youngest age categories, the very lowest Medcraft reports of which is 150Ω (assumingly for the ten year old child), as opposed to the abnormally low Impedances in the older age groups, the very highest of which is only about 325Ω (for the 99 year old) both age categories of which follow the same ramping procedure? In short, why is the Impedance range for the B-25 between 150Ω and 325Ω compared to that of second generation MECTA and Somatics BP devices which range from about 50Ω-562Ω?

As noted, we can easily explain the abnormally high Impedance for the ten year old and the abnormally low Impedance for the 99 year old when both are administered the maximum output of 99 Joules. For example, administering of a MTTLOI of up to a 99 fold threshold requiring Amperage of up to 1.0A for the ten year old child is so excessive that "ramping" (the gradual build-up of Amperage over about .5 seconds until the target Amperage is reached before treatment begins) is necessary in order to avoid (according to Medcraft) injuring the child's skin.[553] The huge emission of up to 99 Joules at 1.0 Amp for the recipient with the lowest Resistance to electricity—the ten year old child—no doubt results in the simultaneous enhancement of resistance (Impedance). In short, an excessive MTTLOI of electricity requiring excessive Amperage triggers an equal and opposite reaction in the form of increased Impedance. Thus, at 99J, Impedance on the B-25 may shoot up abnormally for the ten year old child, from the typically initial 50Ω seen in MECTA and Somatics BP devices (requiring no ramping mechanisms) to an atypical 150Ω (or perhaps greater) on the B-25. On the other hand, the same 99 Joule maximum reached in the oldest age recipients whose Resistance to electricity is greatest, results in the diminishing of the MTTLOI (compared to MECTA and Somatics second generation BP devices)

[553] Ramping appears to be somewhat like gradually revving up an engine before it is put into gear in order to achieve maximum rpm at the earliest possible moment. Most, if not all other BP manufacturers appear to have abandoned this practice.

to only about 1.0 fold threshold or true minimal stimulus on the B-25, explaining the much lower maximum Impedance of 325Ω compared to the circa 555 and 562Ω maximum Impedances respectively invoked by second generation MECTA and Somatics BP devices (both of which emit uniform circa 2.5 MTTLOIs).[554] B-25 emissions of super-gross MTTLOIs (at maximum output) in the younger age categories compared to barely threshold (even at maximum output) in the very oldest age categories is the direct effect of Medcraft's failure to acknowledge the ER/RRC principle and thus failure to implement a uniform MTTLOI guaranteeing gradually diminishing outputs relative to gradually diminishing age. It is this failure to utilize a uniform MTTLOI for all age categories, thereby, allowing a 99 fold threshold output intensity for the ten year old child, but no more than a 1.0 fold threshold output intensity for the 99 year old adult, which explains the atypically high Impedances in the younger age categories and the atypically low Impedances in the older age categories using the same maximum output of 99J in both age categories.

But this does not account for the same atypically high Impedance (150Ω) for the ten year old at an alleged minimal stimulus setting of, for example, 1.0J. After all, according to Medcraft charts, the operator can set the B-25 to administer only 1.0 Joule of electricity if desired, thereby eliciting true minimum stimulus for the ten year old child. Is perhaps, the atypically high Impedance due to the addition of the "ramping" mechanism" taking place .46 seconds before "treatment"? In short, is it the electrical addition of "ramping" on the Medcraft B-25 administered prior to the main procedure, that is, the gradual increasing of Amperage until operator settings are reached, that accounts for the abnormally high Impedance in the 10 year old age category even at minimal stimulus settings?

To answer this question, let us re-create a minimal stimulus B-25 Chart. According to Medcraft, possible settings for the B-25 include a flexible selectable Constant Current ranging from .4 to 1.0 Amperes and selectable outputs from 1-99 Joules. In fact, Joule and Amperage selection are the only options for operator adjustment. Once set, the machine automatically emits the alleged operator selected 1 to 99 Joule output via any number of Duration/Constant Current combinations. The Duration ranging from 0 to 6.0 seconds, as noted, is "non-selectable by the operator. " Frequency on the B-25 is a never changing 70 Hertz (or 140 pulses) while Pulse Width is a constant .001 Seconds (see Medcraft Manuel). Mysteriously, as already noted, we are told that the lowest Impedance on the B-25 is 150Ω.

Succinctly then, Medcraft informs us that the B-25 Amperage can be Operator selected from .4 to 1.0 Amps and the EO (in joules) Operator-selected from 1-99 in one joule increments for any age group.

These facts appear to mean that nothing prohibits the operator from administering the maximum 99 Joules or what appears to be a 99 MTTLOI to the ten year old child. Set to minimal stimulus, however, Medcraft suggests that the B-25 automatically reduces Duration in order to administer a set electrical "dosage" of what seems to be just above threshold output for every age group. For example, the machine can supposedly be set, as noted, for 1.0 or circa 1.1 Joules for the ten year old child. Theoretically then, though not automatically or via default, the machine can be operator adjusted to administer true minimum output (1 to 99 Joules) or maximum output of 99J in every age category such as that depicted on the two charts below:

IMPROBABLE CONSTANT CURRENT B-25 BRIEF PULSE DEVICE as claimed by Medcraft Corp.1985 - 2000 ***adjusted for MINIMUM stimulus*** in all age categories. BASED ON PURE-CEILING INTERPRETATION OF "99J AT 220Ω" (2nd GENERATION)

VOLTAGE	POWER % @ Age	AGE Yrs	Ω Ohms	FREQ. (Hz)	DUR. (SECs)	CURRENT mAmps	ENERGY Joules	CHARGE mC	MTTLOI
60	10	10	150	70	0.3	0.4	1.1	16.8	1.1
67	20	20	168	70	1.17	0.4	4.4	65.5	1.1
93	30	30	185	70	1.53	0.5	9.9	107	1.1
102	40	40	203	70	2.48	0,5	17.6	173.4	1.1
132	50	50	220	70	2.47	0.6	27.5	208	1.1
143	60	60	238	70	3.29	0.6	39.6	277	1.1
179	65	65	255	70	2.77	0,7	46.2	259	1.1
191	70	70	273	70	2.87	0.7	53.9	282	1.1
232	80	80	290	70	2.71	0.8	70.4	330.4	1.1
277	90	90	308	70	2.55	0.9	89.1	321	1.1
325	100	98	325	70	2.18	1.0	99	304	1.1

---

[554] It is due to both to the longer period of time required to reach and overcome Impedance in the older age categories in turn due to their naturally higher Impedances, that the MTTLOI is so much less than that of younger recipients on the B-25 and the B-24..

.001 Second Pulse Width

PROBABLE CONSTANT CURRENT B-25 BRIEF PULSE DEVICE as claimed by Medcraft Corp.1985 - 2000 ***adjusted for MAXIMUM stimulus*** in all age categories. BASED ON PURE-CEILING INTERPRETATION OF "99J AT 220Ω. " (2nd GENERATION)

VOLTAGE	POWER % @ Age	AGE Yrs	Ω Ohms	FREQ. (Hz)	DUR. (SECs)	CURRENT mAmps	ENERGY Joules	CHARGE mC	MTTLOI
150	10	10	150	70	4.71	1.0	99	660	99
168	20	20	168	70	4.21	1.0	99	589	24.75
185	30	30	185	70	3.82	1.0	99	535	11
203	40	40	203	70	3.48	1.0	99	488	6.18
220	50	50	220	70	3.22	1.0	99	451	4
238	60	60	238	70	2.97	1.0	99	416	2.75
255	65	65	255	70	2.77	1.0	99	388	2.3
273	70	70	273	70	2.59	1.0	99	363	2.0
290	80	80	290	70	2.44	1.0	99	341	1.55
308	90	90	308	70	2.30	1.0	99	321	1.22
325	100	100	325	70	2.18	1.0	99	304	1.0

.001 Second Pulse Width

The question is then: "Why 150Ω for the ten year old child at a circa 1.0 or 1.1 MTTLOI or circa 1.0J output?" Moreover, why the same 150Ω Impedance for the same 10 year old at a 99 MTTLOI or circa 99J maximum output?

Ramping on the B-25

Medcraft, once again, tells us the B-25's lowest Impedance is 150Ω which we must assume belongs to the 10 year old child. Notice on the two charts above that both for the emission of 1.0 Joule or a 1.0 fold threshold output for the ten year old child (minimal stimulus) and 99 Joules or a 99 fold threshold output for the same ten year old child, the same atypically high Impedance of 150Ω occurs. This hardly seems logical. While, as we have noted, we might be able to explain a higher than normal Impedance at a maximum stimulus of 99 Joules for the ten year old child in terms of increased resistance due to excessive Amperage, how are we to explain the same high Impedance of 150Ω for the same ten year old child at a minimal stimulus setting of only 1.0 or 1.1J? Perhaps the atypically high Impedance for the ten year old child at minimal stimulus is due to the B-25 ramping mechanism utilized in all cases. Because ramping precedes all outputs for all recipients, the explanation of extraordinarily high Impedance due to ramping seems tenable. But is "ramping" really responsible for the irregular rise in Impedance in the younger age categories even at minimal stimulus output on the B-25? Conversely, is it the absence of ramping on second generation MECTA and Somatics BP devices which is responsible for the much lower circa 50Ω resistance in the same ten year old age category?

Plainly, ramping is necessary on the B-25 BP device in that, unlike MECTA and Somatics BP devices, Medcraft is the only Brief Pulse manufacturer to ignore ER/RRC, disregarding, thereby, a uniformly applied MTTLOI impelling gradational outputs relative to age-related Impedances. In fact, it is the ignoring of a uniform MTTLOI for all age levels, as already noted, which "permits" the B-25 to reach its 99J maximum in even the youngest age category. Because all ten year old children will seize at only 1.0 Joule, a 99 Joule output means an extraordinarily high 99 MTTLOI output requiring excessive Amperage and Voltage relative to age. In short, without "ramping," because the ten year old has almost no resistance to electricity, the sudden administering of a super suprathreshold titration level output intensity (of up to 99 fold threshold) would almost certainly injure the child, at the very least, burning the child's skin (see Medcraft manual). Thus, it is in order to prevent external injury from a sudden high Amperage, high Voltage, high Energy Output surge of electricity that a gradual building up of electricity is necessary on the B-25. In a later letter to the FDA dated August 27, 1986, Medcraft Representative James K. Seafort admits:

> "The use of a ramping technique in the B-25 is to allow time for the dynamic human Impedance to reach its terminal value prior to applying full voltage thus avoiding the use [of] excess power. The excess power results in the use of an excessively high Voltage and/or the potential for burning the skin at the point of contact with the current paddle probes. "

In short, even with increased Duration, in order to reach a 99 MTTLOI without injuring the young person's skin, etc., the machine must gradually build up to the extraordinarily high Amperage and Voltage required, in lieu of delivering the output "all at once. " Plainly, ramping on the B-25 is performed to avoid a precipitously high Amperage, high Voltage impact with (at least) the skin (if not the brain). In brief, only by "ramping," that is, only by gradually increasing the Amperage and Voltage applied to the recipient's skin, skull, and brain, can the very high--up to a 99 MTTLOI (for the ten year old child)--be administered safely with respect to skin. In any case, a 99 MTTLOI easily explains the atypically high Impedance in the ten year old category at maximum stimulus compared to second generation MECTA and Somatics BP devices, both of which are limited to a consistent circa 2.5 MTTLOI in all age categories including, the ten year old child. But while we have acknowledged that a 99 MTTLOI explains the atypically high Impedance of at least 150Ω with the administering of maximum stimulus or 99 Joules in even the ten year old age category, it does not explain, as noted, the same atypically high 150Ω Impedance with the administering of what should be minimal stimulus or 1.0 Joule (1.0 MTTLOI) in the same ten year old age category. Perhaps, as suggested earlier, the atypical 150Ω reached at only 1.0 or 1.1J in the ten year old category is due to the ramping used for all B-25 procedures. But, if ramping is responsible for increase Resistance up to 150Ω, shouldn't the 1.0J "treatment output" yet result in far less Impedance than a 99J "treatment output" administered to the same ten year old child? In short, even with ramping, why would the same ten year old child evince the same 150Ω resistance with the administering of both 1.0 and 99 Joules?

Ramping in the Older Age Categories on the B-25

Certainly, as noted, it is the B-25's relatively low circa 100 maximum Joules administered to the 100 year old recipient requiring up to 100J to adequately seize which results in the circa 1.0 MTTLOI (99J ÷ 100J = circa 1.0 MTTLOI) and thus atypically low 325Ω maximum machine Impedance. Conversely, it is the second generation MECTA and Somatics BP devices' relatively high circa 260J maximum administered to the same 100 year old recipient requiring up to 100J to adequately seize which results in the circa 2.6 MTTLOI (260JJ ÷ 100J = 2.6 MTTLOI) and thus much higher 555 to 562Ω maximum machine Impedance.

Moreover, because it can take up to 100 maximum Joules to induce an adequate seizure for a 100 year old adult on a Brief Pulse device as opposed to only 1.0 Joule to induce an adequate seizure for a ten year old child, the same circa 99 Joule output which is barely minimal stimulus for the 100 year old, as discussed, invokes a massive 99 MTTLOI for the ten year old child. Thus, as we have seen, it is a combination of high Resistance to electricity in the older age categories together with the limited 99J ceiling that explains the atypically low B-25 maximum Impedance for the 99 year old compared to the much higher Impedances reached by the same 99 year old recipient on second generation MECTA and Somatics BP devices. Thus, while second generation MECTA and Somatics BP devices are programmed to ignore the 110J APA ceiling in order to deliver a default circa 2.5 fold threshold output in the 100 year old age category, it is the B-25's adherence to the 110J APA ceiling that limits output to a 1.0 MTTLOI in the same age category. In short, we can safely conclude that it is the B-25's delivery of a minimal stimulus 1.0 MTTLOI to the oldest age recipient together with this recipient's inherently high Resistance to electricity that is responsible for the diminished maximum Impedance (of circa 325Ω) on the B-25 compared to the delivery of a circa 2.5 MTTLOI to the same age category that is responsible for the much higher maximum Impedances of 562 and 555Ω respectively on MECTA and Somatics second generation BP devices. Stated differently, second generation MECTA and Somatics devices emit between 252 and 260J maximum outputs, delivering consistent (circa) 2.5 MTTLOIs in the oldest age categories resulting in maximum Impedances of 562 and 555Ω respectively, while the B-25, limited to a 99J maximum output, delivers but a 1.0 MTTLOI (100J ÷ 100J = 1.0) to the same circa 100 year old adult resulting in a diminished maximum Impedance of circa 325Ω.

Clearly then, it is due to the naturally occurring much higher Resistance in the oldest age category in conjunction with a much lower 99J output on the B-25 in the same oldest age category which results in a much lower overall Impedance on the B-25 in the same oldest age category compared to MECTA and Somatics devices. Conversely, it is due to the same naturally occurring much higher Resistance in the oldest age category in conjunction with much higher 252-260J ceilings on MECTA and Somatics devices in the same oldest age category that results in a much higher overall Impedance on MECTA and Somatics devices in the same oldest age category.

Moreover, it is the naturally occurring much lower Resistance in the youngest age category in conjunction with the much higher 99J output compared to MECTA and Somatics devices which results in a much higher overall Impedance (150Ω) in the youngest age category on the B-25. Conversely, it is due to the same naturally occurring much lower Resistance in the youngest age category in conjunction with the much lower circa 2.5J MECTA and Somatics default output in the same youngest age category that results in a much lower Impedance in the same youngest age category on second generation MECTA and Somatics devices compared to the B-25.

Stated slightly differently, second generation MECTA and Somatics devices deliver uniform circa 2.5 MTTLOIs in all age categories from youngest to oldest, whereas, the B-25 can deliver up to a 99 MTTLOI in the youngest age category but never more than a 1.0 MTTLOI in the oldest age category. This explains the much higher 150Ω Impedance in the ten year old category at maximum output on the B-25 as opposed to the much lower 50Ω Impedance in the same ten year old age category on second generation MECTA and Somatics devices. This also explains the much lower 325Ω Impedance in the oldest category at the maximum 99J output on the B-25 as opposed to the much higher 555.5-562Ω Impedance in the same oldest category at the 252-260J output on second generation MECTA and Somatics devices. In short, at maximum B-25 output, the B-25 emits much higher outputs in the younger age categories and much lower output in the oldest age categories whereas second generation MECTA and Somatics devices emit much higher outputs in the oldest age categories and much lower outputs in the youngest age categories.

Ramping In the Younger Age Categories

But one mystery remains. Why when administered only 1.0J on the B-25 does the ten year old child reach the same 150Ω of resistance when administered 99J? Moreover, if it is indeed the ramping which is responsible for the increase in Impedance compared to MECTA and Somatics devices, why does the Impedance of the 99 year old remain comparatively low? In short, if ramping increases the Impedance of a ten year old from 50 to 150Ω even at 1.0J, why doesn't the same ramping mechanism increase the Impedance of the 99 year old from a relatively low 325Ω to some much higher Impedance? Instead, the B-25's maximum Impedance (circa 325Ω-350Ω) for the 99 year old is below the Impedance reached at minimal stimulus for the same 99 year old reached by original 108J MECTA "C. " So why does ramping so dramatically affect the ten year old's Impedance (reaching at least 150Ω) administered minimal stimulus output (of 1.0J) but doesn't affect the 99 year old whose Impedance remains a relatively low 325Ω in spite of ramping?

Let us examine the B-25's ramping dynamics. In a telephone conversation dated October 28, 1986 between an FDA Representative and Medcraft Representatives James K. Seafort and James Marquis, the FDA representative recorded the following assertions of Seafort and Marquis:

> ". . . during ramping of the stimulus [for the B-25], the current starts at 1% of the selected current and increases to the selected value in 460 millisecond[s]: (70 pulses). "

The same FDA representative next records Seafort's explanation regarding why the B-25 "ramping" mechanism is necessary and why it was engineered to replace the less desirable "glissando" mechanism of the B-24 SW.

> ". . . the B-24 has the capability of delivering a glissando ["ramping"] for a time period of .8 seconds. The maximum stimulus duration [on the B24] is 1 sec. Therefore, it is possible for the glissando to last for 80% of the stimulus duration or at low intensity settings the stimulus could be complete before glissando finished and it was possible in a situation like that [that] the patient would not get full treatment. . . . for these reasons the B-25 was designed differently. "

Based on Medcraft's comments to the FDA representative then, we can conclude that ramping on the B-25 is administered for a constant .46 Seconds tantamount to about 70 Pulses, and that during this period of time, ramping increases from 1% to 100% of the selected Amperage. Moreover, we can assume that "ramping" occurs in its entirety just prior to the main "treatment," and thus, in addition to each treatment administered on the B-25. Stated differently, actual treatment only begins upon completion of ramping which occurs over a constant .46 Seconds and only after the desired Amperage is reached. So how much additional output in Joules is emitted during the .46 Seconds of ramping which precedes each "treatment" and can this account for the high Impedance of even one joule administered to the ten year old child at minimal stimulus?

Ramping Converted to EO in Joules

Let us first experiment with "ramping" in the ten year old category wherein the maximum 99 Joules is administered and wherein Amperage may reach the full 1.0A. Clearly, 1.0A is not reached immediately, but only after .46 Seconds. In that the machine emits 140 pulses per second, over .46 seconds, 64.4 pulses are emitted in all (.46 Sec. x 140 pulses = 64.4 pulses). This is 14 pulses per .1 Seconds (.46Sec./64.4 pulses = .1Sec./X pulses; X = 14 pulses) and circa 8 pulses per the final .06 Seconds (.1/14 = .06/X pulses; X = 8.4 pulses). By creating a progression of output per every .1 seconds, we can simply add the outputs together to obtain an approximation of cumulative ramping output. We must also assume that Impedance rises to at least 150Ω (as noted earlier) over the .46 Seconds of ramping (as, according to Medcraft, 150Ω is the lowest Impedance utilized on the B-25). Let us also assume that during the first .1 Seconds, .2A is reached; the second .1 Seconds, .4A is reached; the third .1 Seconds, .6A is reached; the fourth .1 Seconds, .8A is reached; and the final .06 Seconds, 1.0A is reached.

Based on the formula: EO = Current squared x Impedance x (hz x 2) x WL x Duration, we can determine that in the first .1 Seconds, .00168J is emitted, the next .1 Second, .006J is emitted and so on to obtain an additional cumulative output of about .23J due to ramping for the ten year old child at maximum output.

.1 Second = .2A: .2A x.2A x 30Ω x 14pulses x .001 x .1 = .00168J
Voltage = Current x Ω; .2A x 30Ω = 6V is reached. Ω = V/Amperage; 6V/.2A = 30Ω.
.1 Seconds = .4A: . .4A x .4A x 60Ω x 14 pulses x .001 x .1 = .0061J
Voltage = Current x Ω; .4A x 60Ω = 24V is reached
.1 Seconds = .6A: .6A x .6A x 90Ω x 14 pulses x .001 x .1 = .045J
Voltage = Current x Ω; .6A x 90Ω = 54V is reached
.1 Seconds = .8A: .8A x .8A x 120Ω x 14 pulses x .001 x .1 = .108J
Voltage = Current x Ω; .8A x 120Ω = 96V is reached
.06 Seconds = 1.0A: 1.0 x 1.0A x 150Ω x 8 pulses x .001 x .06 = .072J
Voltage = Current x Ω; 1.0A x 150Ω = 150V is reached

The total output for the ramping alone set at maximum output (99 Joules and thus a 1.0A Amperage) for the ten year old child then, equals only about **.23 Joules** (.00168 + .0061 + .045 + .108 + .072 = **.23J**) or less than one quarter Joule so that the total EO at **maximum** output is (99J + .23J =) **99.23J**. Even a 200Ω Impedance would be negligible. Total output for ramping at **minimum** stimulus output for the ten year old will, of course, be even less or about (1.0J + .23J =) **1.23J**. In short, the atypical rise in Impedance to 150Ω or even 200Ω does not appear to be due to the additional EO emitted from ramping at either maximum output of 99J or minimum output of 1.0J. Not surprisingly then, at the atypically high 99 Joule output for the ten year old child, the atypically high Impedance of at least 150Ω must be due to the treatment output itself of 99J. In short, Impedance at maximum output seems to rise, not as a result of ramping (which appears to be negligible with respect to additional ramping output), but as a result of administering up to a 99 fold threshold output to the ten year old child who typically seizes at only 1.0J or less. In fact, given the extraordinarily high 99 MTTLOI, an even higher Impedance would not be surprising. [555] On the other hand, Impedance reaching 150Ω for the same ten year old child at a minimal stimulus output of only 1.0 or 1.1J or even 1.23J (which includes ramping) seems untenable. So if not due to ramping, what explains the extraordinarily high Impedance of at least 150Ω for the ten year old child administered 1.0J?

---

[555] Medcraft reveals no Impedance or EO correlation with age

Ramping In the Older Age Categories

Before examining the causality of high Impedance at low EO for the ten year old child, however, let us figure the B-25's maximum ramping output set at a maximum output of 99J, but this time for the oldest recipient, the 99 year old adult invoking the highest B-25 Impedance of circa 325Ω which, in fact, is extraordinarily low for this age recipient compared to second generation MECTA and Somatics BP devices. Using the same formula: EO = Current squared x Impedance x (hz x 2) x WL x Duration, but using higher Impedances due to the higher age category, we can approximate an additional **.519J** due to ramping.

.1 Second = .2A: .2A x.2A x 65Ω x 14pulses x .001 x .1 = .00364J
Voltage = Current x Ω; .2 x 65Ω = 13V is reached. Ω = V/Amperage; 13V/.2Amperage = 65Ω.
.1 Seconds = .4A: . .4A x .4A x 130Ω x 14 pulses x .001 x .1 = .029J
Voltage = Current x Ω; .4 x 130 = 52V is reached
.1 Seconds = .6A: .6A x .6A x 195Ω x 14 pulses x .001 x .1 = .098J
Voltage = Current x Ω; .6 x 195 = 117V
.1 Seconds = .8A: .8A x .8A x 260Ω x 14 pulses x .001 x .1 = .233J
Voltage = Current x Ω; .8 x 260 = 208V is reached
.06 Seconds = 1.0A: 1.0 x 1.0A x 325Ω x 8 pulses x .001 x .06 = .156J
Voltage = Current x Ω; 1.0 x 325 = 325V is reached

The total ramping output at maximum output for the 99 year old adult turns out to be only about (.00364 + .029 + .098 + .233 + .156 =) **.519 Joules** or about one half additional Joule adding up to about (99J + .519J =) **99.52J**. Even for the 99 year old adult then, ramping output remains negligible. Even substituting the maximum 325Ω into all the formulas above, we derive only about .64J, still negligible. For the circa 99 year old recipient then, we may now safely attribute the atypically diminished Impedance of 325Ω (compared to second generation MECTA and Somatics BP devices for this same age group) to the B-25's low 99J ceiling which for the 99 year old adult is but a 1.0 MTTLOI--barely minimal stimulus. Compare this with second generation MECTA and Somatics BP devices which administer a circa 2.5 MTTLOI or between 250 and 260 Joules (as opposed to the B-25's 99 Joules) for the same circa 100 year old adult. Impedance invoked by second generation Somatics and MECTA devices for the 100 year old category rises to between 555Ω and 562Ω respectively due to the much higher output administered (of between 259 and 260J) and thus much higher MTTLOI.

We can now eliminate ramping as much of a contributory factor explaining either extraordinarily high or extraordinarily low Impedances on the B-25. In short, for the ten year who receives a maximum 99J output or a 99 MTTLOI, we can now logically attribute the extraordinarily high Impedance of at least 150Ω or higher (compared to MECTA and Somatics devices) to the atypically high 99J or 99 MTTLOI alone administered in this age category. Moreover, for the 99 year old, we can also attribute the relatively diminished Impedance of 325Ω (compared to MECTA and Somatics devices) to the atypically low 99J ceiling or 1.0 MTTLOI in this age category. But, once again, how do we explain the extraordinarily high Impedance of at least 150Ω for the ten year old who receives a minimal stimulus dosage of 1.0J or a 1.0 MTTLOI output? Since ramping does not appear to account for the ten year old's abnormally high Impedance at minimal stimulus, what does?

Maximum Output on the B-25 Brief Pulse Device, the Absence of ER/RRC, and the Need for "Ramping. "

Before addressing the above question, let us first observe the varying MTTLOIs delivered by the B-25 at the maximum output of 99J in every age category and the unusual need for ramping. With no ER/RRC principle in place and thus no uniform MTTLOI applied to all age categories, we can see a pattern of descending MTTLOIs from greatest MTTLOI in the youngest recipient to least MTTLOI in the eldest recipient at the B-25's maximum output of 99J allowable in each age category. Simply by dividing the 99J maximum allowed in each age category by each age related relative threshold constant (for BP devices generally), we can determine the specific MTTLOI delivered by the B-25 in each age category at the maximum 99J output.

Age 10
1.0A x 1.0A x 150Ω x 140 pulses x .001 x 4.71 = **99J ÷ 1.0J = *99 MTTLOI*.**
(Voltage = Current x Ω 1.0 x 150Ω = 150V; Ω = V/Amperage; 150V/1.0A = 150Ω.)
Age 20
1.0A x 1.0A x 168Ω x 140 pulses x .001 x 4.21 = **99J ÷ 4.0 = *24.75 MTTLOI*.**
(Voltage = Current x Ω 1.0 x 168Ω = 168V)
Age 30
1.0A x 1.0A x 185Ω x 140 pulses x .001 x 3.82 = **99J ÷ 9.0J = *11 MTTLOI*.**
(Voltage = Current x Ω 1.0 x 185Ω = 185V)
Age 40
1.0A x 1.0A x 203Ω x 140 pulses x .001 x 3.48 = **99J ÷ 16J = *6.19 MTTLOI*.**
(Voltage = Current x Ω 1.0 x 203Ω = 203V)
Age 50
1.0A x 1.0A x 220Ω x 140 pulses x .001 x 3.22 = **99J ÷ 25J = *3.96 MTTLOI*.**
(Voltage = Current x Ω 1.0 x 220Ω = 220V)
Age 60
1.0A x 1.0A x 238Ω x 140 pulses x .001 x 2.97 = **99J ÷ 36J = *2.75 MTTLOI*.**
(Voltage = Current x Ω 1.0 x 238Ω = 238V)
Age 65
1.0A x 1.0A x 255Ω x 140 pulses x .001 x 2.97 = **99J ÷ 42.25J = *2.34 MTTLOI*.**
(Voltage = Current x Ω 1.0 x 255Ω = 255V)
Age 70
1.0A x 1.0A x 273Ω x 140 pulses x .001 x 2.77 = **99J ÷ 49J = *2.02 MTTLOI*.**
(Voltage = Current x Ω 1.0 x 273Ω = 273V)
Age 80
1.0A x 1.0A x 290Ω x 140 pulses x .001 x 2.59 = **99J ÷ 64J = *1.55 MTTLOI*.**
(Voltage = Current x Ω 1.0 x 290Ω = 290V)
Age 90
1.0A x 1.0A x 308Ω x 140 pulses x .001 x 2.44 = **99J ÷ 81J = *1.22 MTTLOI*.**
(Voltage = Current x Ω 1.0 x 308Ω = 308V)
Age 100
1.0A x 1.0A x 325Ω x 140 pulses x .001 x 2.18 = **99J ÷ 100J = *1.0 MTTLOI*.**
(Voltage = Current x Ω 1.0 x 325Ω = 325V)

POSSIBLE CONSTANT CURRENT B-25 BRIEF PULSE DEVICE as claimed by Medcraft Corp. 1985 - 2000 ***adjusted for MAXIMAL stimulus*** in all age categories. BASED ON PURE CEILING INTERPRETATION OF "99J AT 220Ω" (2nd GENERATION)

VOLTAGE	POWER % @ Age	AGE Yrs	Ω Ohms	FREQ. (Hz)	DUR. (SECs)	CURRENT mAmps	ENERGY Joules	CHARGE mC	MTTLOI
150	10	10	150	70	4.71	1.0	99	660	99
168	20	20	168	70	4.21	1.0	99	589	24.75
185	30	30	185	70	3.82	1.0	99	535	11
203	40	40	203	70	3.48	1.0	99	488	6.18
220	50	50	220	70	3.22	1.0	99	451	4
238	60	60	238	70	2.97	1.0	99	416	2.75
255	65	65	255	70	2.77	1.0	99	388	2.3
273	70	70	273	70	2.59	1.0	99	363	2.0
290	80	80	290	70	2.44	1.0	99	341	1.55
308	90	90	308	70	2.30	1.0	99	321	1.22
325	100	100	325	70	2.18	1.0	99	304	1.0

.001 Second Pulse Width

Instead of a uniform MTTLOI as in MECTA's and Somatics' devices, what we see with the B-25's maximum 99J output in every age category, is a descending MTTLOI, the youngest affected most with the highest MTTLOI, the eldest affected least, with the lowest MTTLOI. This, of course, is due to increasing age-related Resistance to electricity and the absence of the ER/RRC principle to insure a uniform MTTLOI and thus gradational outputs relative to age. Plainly, with an absurdly high 99 MTTLOI in the youngest age category, we can comprehend the necessity of ramping. While ramping itself may not greatly contribute to the overall EO elicited, the excess power required to deliver a 99 MTTLOI to the youngest age category requires it. Without ramping, the excessively high MTTLOI necessitating the precipitous delivery of excessively high Voltage and Amperage would result in external injury, the least of which is burning of the skin. Once again, in a formal letter to the FDA dated August 27, 1986, Medcraft representative James Seafort explains the "difference" between the "glissando" of the B-24 and "ramping" on the B-25.

> "The use of a current ramping technique in the B-25 was based on the use of a glissando control in the previous model B-24, which is a preamendment device. However, the technical basis for the two, although serving the same purpose are based on different technical reasons. In the B-24 device the constant supply of Voltage was glissandoed to prevent excessive muscle spasms and body contortions during the initial phase of the treatment. The use of a ramping technique in the B-25 is to allow time for the dynamic impedance to reach its terminal value prior to applying full voltage thus avoiding the use of excess power. The excess power results in the use of an excessively high voltage and/or the potential for burning the skin at the point of contact with the current paddle probes. "

In fact, while concluding before the "treatment" itself and, therefore not overlapping "treatment" as does "glissando," "ramping" on the B-25 Brief Pulse device is used for precisely the same purpose as "glissando" on the B-24 Sine Wave device--to reduce the sudden impact of excessively high MTTLOIs of electricity in order to avoid external injury. During the Sine Wave era, throughout much of which the B-24 SW (initially marketed in the 1950s) was utilized, recipients were neither anaesthetized nor injected with muscle relaxant and so "glissando" was used to prevent not muscle spasms and body contortions, but the breaking of teeth and bones. Currently, recipients in the United States at least, are almost always anaesthetized, injected with muscle relaxant (and hopefully "breathed") prior to and during "treatment" (as the muscle relaxant paralyzes the respiratory muscles). Consequently, the breaking of teeth and bones is no longer an issue. However, the same high excessive multifold threshold "dosages" of electricity yet utilized with the B-25 Brief Pulse in the younger age categories can still cause embarrassing external injuries, if no longer to bones and teeth (addressed via anesthetics and muscle relaxants) then at least to skin. Not only second, but even third generation MECTA and Somatics BP devices, as we shall see, use much less Voltage and EO and dramatically lower MTTLOIs in the younger age categories than the second generation B-25 is permitted to administer. The unsavory fact that the highest MTTLOI occurs in the youngest age group with Medcraft's B-25 BP device, is entirely due, as already noted, to Medcraft's failure to implement a uniform MTTLOI applicable to all age categories and this is due to Medcraft's failure to acknowledge ER/RRC or the gradational age-related output principle constituting one half the 1982 APA Standard. In brief, Medcraft does not acknowledge the common sense need for diminished output with respect to diminishing age-related resistance to electricity. The mere fact that "ramping" must be utilized at all, indicates unacceptably excessive electrical outputs, injurious not merely to skin, but brain. It is for this very reason, ironically, that SW devices such as the B-24 were to be replaced by the purportedly new era reduced-output constant current Brief Pulse device of the "future." The fact that, like the B-24 SW, inconsistent, unacceptably high MTTLOIs can yet be emitted with the B-25 Brief Pulse device, particularly in the youngest age categories, so that "ramping" like "glissando" is yet necessary to prevent external injury, is manifest proof that the B-25 is both dangerously unregulated and extremely harmful. That any Brief Pulse machine is allowed to emit a 99 MTTLOI of electrical energy, especially to children, and in spite of the 1982 APA Standard, is unconscionable. Such excessive outputs make a mockery of "standards," the notion of “regulation,” and any idea of Brief Pulse as a "safer reduced output" apparatus designed to replace the archaic excessively high emission devices of the past. It is telling that the same company which continues to make the B-24 SW device, has intentionally manufactured a Brief Pulse device similarly wanting, similarly inconsistent, and even more excessive than the B-24 SW upon which the B-25 BP was supposed to be an improvement via reduced output.

Minimal Stimulus on the B-25

So, while an atypically high 99J output for the ten year old child receiving an atypically high 99 MTTLOI may explain the child's atypically high Impedance of at least 150Ω (and probably more) on the B-25, how can a low 1.0 MTTLOI explain the same minimum 150Ω Impedance invoked in the same ten year old child receiving true minimal stimulus output?

But to be certain, let us figure ramping output over its .46 seconds in addition not to 99J but to an allegedly selectable 1.0J minimal stimulus output for the same ten year old child. For this we can use the lowest constant current of .4 Amps in lieu of the B-25's maximum 1.0A constant current even though we will continue to assume the same atypically high 150Ω Impedance.

Ramping, remember, is administered for a constant .46 Seconds tantamount to 70 Pulses. During the .46 seconds, ramping "gradually" increases from 1% to 100% of the selected .4A Amperage indirectly chosen through the selected output of 1.0J. In all cases, as we have learned, "ramping" is completed prior to actual "treatment. "

Based on the same formula: <u>EO = Current squared x Impedance x (hz x 2) x WL x Duration</u>, therefore, we can approximate the full following ramping output prior to an alleged operator-selected 1.0 Joule or true minimal stimulus output administered to the ten year old child, and we do so assuming the atypically high and inexplicable 150Ω minimum Impedance Medcraft reports. Here Voltage rises to a probable 60V in lieu of the 150V utilized at maximum stimulus (above) for the same ten year old child. [556]

.1 Second = .05A: <u>.05A x.05A x 30Ω x 14pulses x .001 x .1 = .000105J</u>
Voltage = Current x Ω; .05 x 30Ω = 1.5V
.1 Seconds = .1A: .1<u>A x .1A x 60Ω x 14 pulses x .001 x .1 = .00084J</u>
Voltage = Current x Ω; .1 x 60Ω = 6V
.1 Seconds = .3: <u>.2A x .2A x 90Ω x 14 pulses x .001 x .1 = .005J</u>
Voltage = Current x Ω; .2 x 90Ω = 18V
.1 Seconds = .4A: <u>.3A x .3A x 120Ω x 14 pulses x .001 x .1 = .015J</u>
Voltage = Current x Ω; .3 x 120Ω = 36V
.06 Seconds = .4A: <u>.4A x .4A x 150Ω x 8 pulses x .001 x .06 = .012J</u>
Voltage = Current x Ω; .4 x 150Ω = 60V

The total ramping output just prior to a minimal stimulus output of circa 1.0J for the ten year old child appears to be less than (.000105J + .00084J + .005J + .015J + .012J =) <u>**.033 Joules**</u> even using an atypically high 150Ω Impedance. Plainly, a cumulative (1J + .003J =) 1.033 Joules cannot be the cause of this atypically high 150Ω Impedance invoked at a minimal stimulus output of 1.0J for the ten year old child. Plainly, the addition of .033J is not the cause of the atypically high 150Ω Impedance emphasized by the fact that that while second generation MECTA and Somatics BP devices appear to administer default outputs of circa 2.5 Joules to the ten year old child, only about 50Ω is reached on MECTA and Somatics BP devices in this age category. [557] [558]

Why then, if not due to ramping, does Impedance for the ten year old child reach 150Ω at only 1.0 Joule? There appears to be only one viable explanation for the atypically high 150Ω Impedance at "minimum stimulus" output settings for the ten year old child and that is, output cannot be set at true minimal stimulus of 1.0J for the ten year old. In short, we must conclude that the B-25 does not allow a 1.0J output in the ten year old age category, that is, the B-25 appears to be restricted to much higher outputs in this age category. Thus, in spite

---

[556] From Voltage, we derive accompanying Impedance. Ohm's Law: Impedance = Voltage ÷ Amperage.60V ÷ .4A = 150Ω.

[557] Neither MECTA nor Somatics reveals age-related Impedances or age-related Voltages. However, maximum Impedance of 555.5Ω is revealed for the Thymatron DG from which we can derive maximum Voltage via Ohm's Law (.9A x 555.5Ω = 500V). Age-related Impedances for the MECTA and Somatics devices are thus speculatively based on age-related Voltages in turn based on age-related power percentages. For example, the ten year old appears to be administered 10% of the maximum 500V on the Thymatron DG. .1 x 500V = 50V. Impedance can then be derived from Ohm's Law (Impedance = Voltage ÷ Amperage).50V ÷ .9A = <u>55.55Ω</u> for the ten year old child.55.55Ω is also 10% of the maximum 555.5Ω Impedance.

[558] It should be pointed out that the APA Standard calls for Impedances of between 100 and 600Ω so that technically, "ECT" for the ten year old child should be prohibited since Impedance here is indeed less than 100Ω. Indeed, Texas has prohibited "ECT" for anyone 16 years of age or younger. There is some reason to believe, however, though less typical, that some few physicians indeed administer "ECT" in this age category (see "Ted Chabasinski" in Wikipedia).

of Medcraft's assertion that the operator may set output from 1-99 Joules, in fact, this does not appear to be permissible on the B-25 even in the younger age categories. After all, it is only logical that the machine does not allow a 1.0 Joule setting for a 100 year old recipient who may require up to 100J to seize. The default "minimal stimulus" output on the B-25 for the ten year old, in brief, must be a much higher output and a much higher MTTLOI than simply threshold or just above threshold (that is a 1.0 or 1.1 MTTLOI output). Just as the B-25 can be set to deliver a maximum 99J output for all recipients (including the ten year old child), and may be defaulted to 99J for the 100 year old recipient, there must be default "minimal stimulus outputs," in the younger age categories as well, that is, electrical emissions which cannot fall below a specific Energy Output. Tellingly, while Medcraft assures us that Impedances range from 150 to 325Ω, Medcraft representatives through recorded Medcraft letters to and conversations with FDA officials, make a very subtle but revealing statement. In FDA document K860467/E, for example, a letter to an FDA representative dated August 27, 1986 from Medcraft representative James K. Seafort, explains that during the last .06 seconds (of the.46 seconds) of ramping, if

> ". . . the circuitry detects an impedance of above 600 ohms or less than 100 ohms during the next 5-10 pulses, the B-25 will automatically shut down and will not allow a reapplication without resetting. Additionally, there is a lamp on the front panel marked "Impedance Hi/Lo" which lights when the impedance is outside the range of 100-600Ω" (see Medcraft letter to the FDA K860467/E).

Clearly then, the B-25 will simply not allow "treatment" if Impedance is above 600Ω or below 100Ω (and most likely below 150Ω). While the safety feature below 100Ω and above 600Ω is in accordance with the APA Standard, increasing output beyond a 1.1 MTTLOI in the ten year old age category so that Impedance rises to 100 or 150Ω, is not. Indeed, because the APA Standard disallows Impedances below 100Ω, second generation MECTA and Somatics BP devices invoking maximum Impedances of about 50Ω for the ten year old child should not be allowed, that is, administering "ECT" to a ten year old child should be "illegal." [559] The B-25 appears to repudiate outputs below 150Ω (according to Medcraft charts), but its seeming willingness to administer "ECT" to those in the younger age categories, plainly reveals that while the Operator can select a setting of, for example, 1.0 joule or true minimal stimulus for the ten year old child, the machine will not actually allow outputs which do not invoke at least 150Ω of Impedance. In order to accomplish this, therefore, the B-25 must administer the child a much higher than minimal stimulus output, also "illegal" under the 1982 APA Standard. That is, while the B-25 adheres to the APA Standard's prohibition of administering "ECT" to anyone with an Impedance below 100Ω, it adheres to this rule by breaking another, that is, it administers outputs well above the 1.1 MTTLOI implied by the 110J ceiling in conjunction with an ER/RRC. In short, because Medcraft ignores ER/RRC but adheres to the 110J ceiling, it solves the "problem" of administering "ECT" to the ten year old child, whose threshold Impedance is below 100Ω, by dramatically increasing the output delivered. [560] We must assume then, that the B-25 will only deliver electricity at Impedances of at least 150Ω requiring a much higher output than the 1.0J setting required for true minimal stimulus in the ten year old age category. In a word, the default outputs must be much higher than true minimal stimulus, particularly in the younger age categories. Because the B-25 appears to disallow Impedances lower than 150Ω in accordance with the APA Standard, then, the B-25 prohibits the delivery of the 1.0 or 2.0 Joules it takes to overcome the typical 35-50Ω of resistance required to seize a ten year old child. Rather, if the 150Ω "minimum" Impedance evinced by the B-25 is applicable to the ten year old child, this atypically high Impedance is indicative of a much higher default output for the same ten year old child than one or two joules, indeed, much higher than that utilized by second

---

[559] As noted previously, FDA never officially adopted the 1982 APA Standard as manufacturers never agreed to conform to it. It is for this reason, in fact, that FDA never allowed the "ECT" device itself out of Class III, those devices for which a standard either has not or cannot be written.

[560] MECTA and Somatics also breach the APA 1.1 MTTLOI ceiling, but much less dramatically, in the ten year old category. In any case, all three companies--MECTA, Somatics, nor Medcraft—should avoid administering "ECT" to a ten year old child in accordance with the 1982 APA Standard.

generation MECTA or Somatics BP devices (which, in fact, deliver 2.5 fold threshold outputs for all age groups, including, if applicable, the ten year old child). [561]

So what is the B-25's minimum default output setting for the ten year old child for whom Impedance rises to 150Ω? In that Medcraft carefully hides age-output information even to the FDA, we cannot know with certainty. What we can say with some certainty is that the B-25 does not elicit true minimal stimulus in the younger age categories such as those depicted earlier. We can be relatively certain of this in that 1.0 or 1.1J simply does not invoke a 150Ω Impedance in the ten year old child. Moreover, the same principle holds true for other younger age categories. Thus, based on a 150Ω minimum Impedance if applied to the ten year old child, we can intelligently speculate that on the B-25, minimal stimulus output In this age group must be at least 9 or 10 fold threshold, as seen below.

(MORE PROBABLE) ACTUAL CONSTANT CURRENT **B-25** BRIEF PULSE DEVICE by MEDCRAFT CORPORATION BASED ON PURE-CEILING INTERPRETATION OF "99J AT 220Ω" (2nd GENERATION) at *Minimal Stimulus*

Operator Selected Lowest Possible Outputs in All Age Categories

VOLTAGE	POWER % @ Age	AGE Yrs	Ω Ohms	FREQUENCY (Hz)	DURATION (SECs)	CURRENT mAmps	ENERGY Joules	CHARGE mC	MTTLOI
60	10	10	150	70	2.68	0.4	9	150	9
67	20	20	168	70	5.04	0.4	19	283	4.75
93	30	30	185	70	4.49	0.5	29	314	3.22
102	40	40	203	70	5.49	0.5	39	384	2.44
132	50	50	220	70	4.42	0.6	49	371	1.96
143	60	60	238	70	4.92	0.6	59	413	1.64
179	65	65	255	70	3.66	0.7	64	359	1.51
191	70	70	273	70	3.68	0.7	69	361	1.41
232	80	80	290	70	3.04	0.8	79	341	1.23
277	90	90	308	70	2.55	0.9	89	321	1.1
325	100	99	325	70	2.18	1.0	99	304	1.0

.001 Second Pulse Width

Note that "minimal stimulus" for the ten year old above is now represented as a more logical 9 (or 10) Joules and thus a 9 or 10 MTTLOI, accounting for the very high minimum Impedance of 150Ω. We can also speculate much higher "minimal stimulus" settings for the 20-80 year old categories as in chart above. Because there is no uniform MTTLOI on the B-25, note the descending MTTLOIs in the right hand column above, illogically decreasing with increasing age and increasing with decreasing age similar to the B-24 SW constant Voltage device.

Finally, this means we must also reevaluate the administering of maximum settings of 99J in all age categories. In lieu of 150Ω at 99J for the ten year old child, we now speculate 200Ω at 99J which yet culminates in a circa 325Ω maximum in the oldest age category.

(MORE PROBABLE) ACTUAL CONSTANT CURRENT **B-25** BRIEF PULSE DEVICE by MEDCRAFT CORPORATION BASED ON PURE-CEILING INTERPRETATION OF "99J AT 220Ω" (2nd GENERATION) at *Maximum Stimulus*

Operator Selected Maximum Outputs in All Age Categories

VOLTAGE	POWER % @ Age	AGE Yrs	Ω Ohms	FREQUENCY (Hz)	DURATION (SECs)	CURRENT mAmps	ENERGY Joules	CHARGE mC	MTTLOI
200	10	10	200	70	3.53	1.0	99	495	99
214	20	20	214	70	3.31	1.0	99	463	24.75
227	30	30	227	70	3.11	1.0	99	436	11
241	40	40	241	70	2.94	1.0	99	411	6.18
255	50	50	255	70	2.77	1.0	99	388	4
269	60	60	269	70	2.62	1.0	99	368	2.75
276	65	65	276	70	2.56	1.0	99	359	2.3
283	70	70	283	70	2.5	1.0	99	350	2.0

[561] Of course, it is possible that Medcraft's B-25 simply prohibits administering "ECT" to the ten year old child whose threshold Impedance is well below 100Ω and so should be excluded in accordance with the 1982 APA Standard, but given that there is no mention of this exception in Medcraft literature, this possibility is unlikely.

297	80	80	297	70	2.38	1.0	99	333	1.55
310	90	90	310	70	2.28	1.0	99	319	1.22
325	100	100	325	70	2.18	1.0	99	304	1.0

.001 Second Pulse Width

We can now logically assume that at a 99 MTTLOI in the youngest age category, Impedance must be even higher than 150Ω, affecting both Charge and Duration. Moreover, Impedance, Charge, and Duration for remaining age groups at 99J is affected accordingly. For example, at 99 Joules, we can intelligently speculate that Impedance rises to at least 200Ω in the ten year old category and that other maximum age-related Impedances at 99J are affected in kind.

In short, note on the chart above depicting a maximum output of 99J in all age groups, that Impedance for the ten year old child has increased to a more tenable 200Ω (as opposed to 150Ω) and may be even higher. Note also that due to the absence of ER/RRC, the non-uniform MTTLOI (in the right hand column) illogically increases with decreasing age and decreases with increasing age similar to the B-24 SW constant Voltage device.

Finally, note at maximum outputs above, the unusually lengthy Duration of 3.53 Seconds for the ten year old child, and the decreasing Duration with increasing age until the circa 100 year old receives the briefest Duration of only 2.18 Seconds. [562] Note too, the highest Charge of almost 500mC for the ten year old child as opposed to the lowest Charge of 304mC for the circa 100 year old adult, the consequence of a 99 MTTLOI for the ten year old child (at 99J) as opposed to a barely 1.0 MTTLOI for the 99 year old adult (at 99J), patterns quite the opposite of MECTA and Somatics BP devices. Finally, note the circa 9J minimum stimulus output for the ten year old on the minimal stimulus chart above this one, and the 99J maximum output on the maximum output for the same ten year old chart directly above. Instead of ranging from 1 to 99J then, the B-25 appears to emit more on the order of a 9 to 99J range for the ten year old child, now logically explaining the minimal 150Ω Impedance for the ten year old child at "minimum" B-25 output as well as at least 200Ω for the same ten year old child at maximum B-25 output.

Comparing Medcraft's B-25 Brief Pulse Device to Medcraft's B-24 SW Device

While the B-24 SW is capable of up to 200J of output, the much more efficient B-25 Brief Pulse device based on constant Current in lieu of the much less efficient Sine Wave device based on constant Voltage, can elicit a so-called adequate seizure with much less power and so a much lower MTTLOI than SW. But because of its greater efficiency, the Brief Pulse device can also be made to evince a much higher MTTLOI with much less power than SW. The B-25 is an example of evincing a much higher MTTLOI with much less power than SW or what might be called the inverse exploitation of Brief Pulse. Note how at maximum output, for instance, the B-25 Brief Pulse device can evince a 99 MTTLOI with 99 Joules in the ten year old age category as opposed to the B-24 Sine Wave device which takes 200 Joules to evince a circa 23 MTTLOI in the same ten year old age category. [563] Both outputs, of course, are unconscionable.

B-25 BP at Maximum Settings for all Age Groups

VOLTAGE	AGE Yrs	Ω Ohms	DURATION (SECs)	CURRENT mAmps	ENERGY Joules	CHARGE mC	MULTFLD THRESH
200	**10**	200	3.53	1.0	99	495	**99**
214	**20**	214	3.31	1.0	99	463	**24.75**
227	**30**	227	3.11	1.0	99	436	**11**
241	**40**	241	2.94	1.0	99	411	**6.18**
255	**50**	255	2.77	1.0	99	388	**4**
269	**60**	269	2.62	1.0	99	368	**2.75**
276	**65**	276	2.56	1.0	99	359	**2.3**
283	**70**	283	2.5	1.0	99	350	**2.0**

[562] The ten year old child should never be administered "ECT" as resistance is much too low in this age category. Indeed, a close reading of the 1982 APA Standard prohibits it. Because Medcraft ignores ER/RRC, however, the ten year old is not only administered "ECT" with the B-25, but the child suffers an exorbitant MTTLOI, indeed higher than any other age category.

[563] See section on SW for the figures derived in the SW Chart above.

297	**80**	297	2.38	1.0	99	333	**1.55**
310	**90**	310	2.28	1.0	99	319	**1.22**
325	**100**	325	2.18	1.0	99	304	**1.0**

B-24 SW at Maximum Settings for all Age Groups (*Not Limited* to 1.0A)

VOLTAGE	AGE Yrs	Ω Ohms	DURATION (SECs)	CURRENT mAmps	ENERGY Joules	CHARGE mC	MULTFLD THRESH
170	***10***	145	1.0	1.17	200	1.17	***23***
170	***20***	195	1.0	.870	148	.872	***9.44***
170	***30***	245	1.0	.694	118	.694	***4.80***
170	***40***	295	1.0	.576	98.0	.576	***2.75***
170	***50***	345	1.0	.493	83.8	.493	***1.72***
170	***60***	395	1.0	.430	73.2	.430	***1.15***
170	***65-100***		1.0				***No Seiz***

Comparing maximum settings for both devices above, the B-25 Brief Pulse appears to be more dangerous than the B-24 Sine Wave, emitting much higher MTTLOIs in all age categories although doing so with half the overall output. At maximum output, a 99 MTTLOI is possible on the B-25 solely due to Medcraft's denial of ER/RRC and the 1.1 MTTLOI maximum implicitly stipulated by the 1982 APA Standard.

Now let us compare the B-25 Brief Pulse to the B-24 SW at lowest output settings.

B-25 BP at "Minimum" Settings for all Age Groups

VOLTAGE	AGE Yrs	Ω Ohms	DURATION (SECs)	CURRENT mAmps	ENERGY Joules	CHARGE mC	MTTLOI
60	**10**	150	2.68	0.4	9	150	**9**
67	**20**	168	5.04	0.4	19	283	**4.75**
93	**30**	185	4.49	0.5	29	314	**3.22**
102	**40**	203	5.49	0.5	39	384	**2.44**
132	**50**	220	4.42	0.6	49	371	**1.96**
143	**60**	238	4.92	0.6	59	413	**1.64**
179	**65**	255	3.66	0.7	64	359	**1.51**
191	**70**	273	3.68	0.7	69	361	**1.41**
232	**80**	290	3.04	0.8	79	341	**1.23**
277	**90**	308	2.55	0.9	89	321	**1.1**
325	**100**	325	2.18	1.0	99	304	**1.0**

B-24 SW at "Maximum" Settings for all Age Groups (*Limited* to 1.0A) Possibly Used as "Minimal Stimulus."

VOLTAGE	AGE Yrs	Ω Ohms	DURATION (SECs)	CURRENT mAmps	ENERGY Joules	CHARGE mC	MTTLOI
100	***10***	145	1.0	.690	68.9	.690	***7.90***
150	***20***	195	1.0	.769	115	.769	***7.35***
170	***30***	245	1.0	.694	118	.694	***4.80***
170	***40***	295	1.0	.576	98.0	.576	***2.75***
170	***50***	345	1.0	.493	83.8	.493	***1.72***
170	***60***	395	1.0	.430	73.2	.430	***1.15***
170	***65-70***		1.0				***No Seiz***

Improbable B-24 SW at "Minimum" Settings for all Age Groups

VOLTAGE	AGE Yrs	Ω Ohms	DURATION (SECs)	CURRENT mAmps	ENERGY Joules	CHARGE mC	MTTLOI
70	***10***	100	0.1	.690	4.9	.07	***1.23***
120	***20***	150	0.1	.800	9.6	.113	***1.06***
140	***30***	205	1.0	.694	19	.166	***1.15***
170	***40***	260	0.3	.654	33.35	.196	***1.28***
170	***50***	320	0.5	.531	45.0	.266	***1.08***
170	***60***	390	0.9	.442	66.7	.392	***1.04***
170	***65-70***		1.0				***No Seiz***

At maximal machine settings limited to 1.0A, the B-24 and the B-25 are roughly comparable regarding MTTLOI, though once again, the B-25 emits less EO. (See section on Sine Wave for derived B-24 parameters.) Neither device approaches true minimal stimulus until about age 60, so that the dangerousness of one machine over the other is arguable. Certainly, studies have shown that unless Brief Pulse is utilized to induce adequate seizures at just above threshold output, the advantage of Brief Pulse's lower EO is lost (Squire and Zouzounis, 1986).

If the B-24 really can be manually set for true minimal stimulus, then at minimal stimulus settings, B-24 SW emits lower Energy Output than the B-25 up until about age 65. But this is odd. A Brief Pulse device should emit lower EO than SW even set at minimal stimulus. Certainly the MECTA "C" delivers less EO by half than minimal stimulus SW. Because the B-25 cannot actually be set for minimal stimulus, moreover, there is good reason to believe that neither can the B-24 SW. Indeed, there is every reason to indicate that the B-25 Brief Pulse has been made in the image of the B-24 SW. Unfortunately, Medcraft keeps the information needed to calculate the least amount of output the B-24 SW device is allowed to emit too close to the vest to speculate.

Although the B-25 is a Brief Pulse device limited to 99 Joules and the B-24 Sine Wave device capable of up to 200 Joules (when not confined to 1.0A), the B-25 constant current at maximum power is roughly as powerful as the B-24 at maximum stimulus. The proof of this manifests itself in the MTTLOIs with respect to the varying age categories (see above). Tellingly, the two devices, the B-24 Sine Wave and the B-25 Brief Pulse have very similar characteristics. Both utilize ramping. Both can emit grossly high MTTLOIs in the younger age categories. Both maximum output SW and the B-25 Brief Pulse have illogically descending MTTLOIs with youngest having the highest MTTLOI and oldest recipients having the lowest MTTLOI. Neither device appears designed for age categories over 60 or 65 years though the B-25 will induce seizures in the older age categories, whereas, the B-24 may not, even at maximum output. Finally, unlike MECTA and Somatics BP devices, neither the B-24 nor the B-25 has a uniform MTTLOI applicable to all age categories.

In fact, the B-25 at both minimum and maximum output appears oddly similar to the B-24. Indeed, the B-25, with its ramping mechanism, does not act like a Brief Pulse device at all, but rather like the SW devices of the past. Like the B-24, the B-25 BP educes exceptionally high outputs and exceptionally high MTTLOIs in the younger age categories up to about 45 years of age. Similar to the B-24, however, which does not appear powerful enough to induce an adequate seizure above sixty or sixty-five years of age, the more powerful B-25 can emit a 2.0 and 2.3 MTTLOI respectively in the 65 and 70 year old categories, which is a lower MTTLOI than that emitted in younger age categories and only just above threshold from ages 80-100. Both the B-24 and the B-25 can emit their highest outputs in the ten year old age category.

AGE RELATED THRESHOLD IMPEDANCES AND THRESHOLD OUTPUTS USING THE B-24 SW

AGE	Impedance Threshold (Ω)	Threshold Output in Joules
10	145	8.7
20	195	15.7
30	245	24.7
40	295	35.7
50	345	48.7
60	395	63.7

65	420	72.0
70	445	80.7
80	495	99.0
90	545	120
100	595	143

In brief, without ER/RRC to regulate output, no mathematical mechanism exists on the B-25 prohibiting a MTTLOI of up to 99 (fold threshold) even in the youngest age category and so like the B-24 and second generation MECTA and Somatics BP devices, the Medcraft B-25 Brief Pulse device is an ENR (Electro Neurotransmission Reduction) device in all instances from ages 10-40, may be Operator adjusted to become an ENR device from ages 50-70, and is an "ECT" device in all instances from ages from ages 80-100. Roughly as powerful as the B-24 SW, this pattern is similar to the B-24 which is an ENR device in all instances from ages 10-40, an "ECT" device in all instances from age 50-60, and may have difficulty inducing seizures at all from ages 65-100. In brief, both the B-24 and the B-25 appear to target recipients in the 10-40 year old age categories with excessive electrical energy. Neither has a uniform MTTLOI in that both ignore ER/RRC.

Is it possible, due to the trendy transition to Brief Pulse devices beginning about 1976, that Medcraft, with its specific physician clientele created its own peculiar version of a Brief Pulse device, the real purpose of which was not to improve upon SW (by virtue of reduced output), but rather to imitate and even enhance the power of the B-24 SW, specifically in the younger age categories? Did Medcraft sacrifice a uniform MTTLOI and thus the oldest age categories in order (like the B-24) to retain super gross MTTLOIs in the same younger age categories (as the B-24) from about age ten to forty and even fifty? In short, did Medcraft build its Brief Pulse device to retain and, in fact, augment what should have been the most undesirable characteristics of the B-24, but for which Medcraft had a specific physician patronage?

Was the B-25 then, Medcraft's attempt to "stay in the game" with FDA leaning towards Brief Pulse, while at the same time continuing to satisfy a specific group of physicians who demanded the B-24's virtually unregulated power in the younger to middle age categories? Did Medcraft contrive to escape detection merely by limiting overall output to 99 Joules in accordance with half the regulatory mechanism of the APA Standard while inconspicuously ignoring ER/RRC?[564] The irony is that in spite of FDA's impetus between 1976 and 1982 to replace SW with the more efficient reduced output Brief Pulse device, BP manufacturers never called for adoption of the 1982 APA Standard and so, perhaps to Medcraft's surprise and even delight, the standard never actually prohibited the B-24 Sine Wave as it was supposed to do. Consequently, the B-24 continues to be manufactured and marketed to this day, a fact which might account for the poor marketing record of the B-25 Brief Pulse Medcraft designed to replace it. [565] In brief, physicians who espouse the B-24 may simply have continued using it in lieu of the B-25 Brief Pulse device, as Brief Pulse manufacturers never compelled Medcraft to replace it through adoption of the 1982 APA Standard. In short, with the continuation of the B-24 SW, there appears to have been no urgent need for Medcraft to replace it with its B-25 Brief Pulse device.

In any case, it is neither the B-25's disarmingly low maximum Impedance of 325Ω in the oldest age category, nor the disarmingly low 99J ceiling in the oldest age category which should concern us. Rather, what should trouble us is the inconspicuously high "minimum" Impedance of 150Ω indicative of extremely high output levels in the lowest age categories, the presence of a ramping mechanism in a so-called modern day Brief Pulse device, and finally, Medcraft's failure to apply ER/RRC and thus the absence of gradation and of a uniform MTTLOI relevant to all age recipients. The questions we must ask of Medcraft's B-25 Brief Pulse Device are: "Why is the B-25's lowest Impedance which almost certainly applies to the ten year old recipient, so alarmingly high?" "Why is there no uniform MTTLOI applicable to all recipients?" and finally, "How is it possible that 99 Joules is permissible in the youngest age category wherein 1.0 Joule is enough to seize a child of ten?" Almost certainly, the answers lie within the unavoidable conclusion that Medcraft wants to retain the devastatingly high MTTLOIs in the younger age categories characteristic of the B-24 SW and that the chosen manner of accomplishing this feat with Brief Pulse was in the avoidance of an ER/RRC and so absence of a uniform MTTLOI impelling gradational age-related outputs relevant to all age categories. Indeed, ignoring ER/RRC allows MTTLOIs of such an enormous and disparate magnitude that just like the B-24, a "ramping"

[564] Both the MECTA "C" and the B-25 are limited to circa 100 joules. However, the "C" emits its circa 100J in the 100 year old age category; whereas, the B-25, similar to the B-24. Emits its 100J in the ten year old age category.

[565] In Texas reporting records, hospital purchases of the B-25 are virtually non-existent.

mechanism is required. In brief, both the beguiling 99J ceiling and the mollifying 325Ω maximum Impedance serve to cover up the truly devastating power and gross MTTLOI administered in the younger age categories by what is actually an unregulated and uncharacteristic Brief Pulse ENR device. Medcraft's reporting of a phrase similar to that reported for MECTA and Somatics, "99J at 220Ω," is quite misleading in that, for the B-25, this means reaching 99 Joules at all Impedances so that any notion of B-25 comparableness to MECTA and Somatics BP devices is blatantly deceitful. That the machine imitates and, in fact, enhances all those B-24 characteristics vehemently objected to by the original proponents of Brief Pulse, is cause for grave misgiving and frank trepidation with respect to Medcraft's so-called "safer" and "greatly improved" B-25 Brief Pulse device over SW.

How Medcraft Derives from the 1982 APA Standard its "99J at 220Ω" Pure-Ceiling Interpretation "Justifying" 99J at all Impedances for its B-25

As noted, Medcraft's reporting of "99J at 220Ω," in contrast with MECTA's and Somatics' almost identical reporting of "101J at 220Ω," and "99.4J at 220Ω" respectively are actually antithetically interpreted. Medcraft applies a Pure-Ceiling interpretation; whereas, MECTA and Somatics' apply a Pure-ER/RRC interpretation. While all three--Medcraft, MECTA, and Somatics made-for-America second generation BP devices--appear to prohibit output from surpassing *"100Js* specifically *at 220Ω,"* only MECTA and Somatics determine maximum output via Pure-ER/RRC, that is, output based on the pure-ER of their circa *"100J at 220Ω"* phrases to maximum machine Impedances of 562Ω and 555.5Ω respectively. Moreover, only MECTA and Somatics second generation BP devices (as opposed to Medcraft's B-25 Brief Pulse) utilize a uniform MTTLOI applicable to all age categories, i.e. a uniform 2.59 and 2.52 MTTLOI respectively for every age category. Consequently, at Impedances below 220Ω, second generation MECTA and Somatics devices (unlike the Medcraft B-25 device which can emit 99J at all Impedances) cannot emit their maximum outputs at all Impedances. Rather, outputs emitted by MECTA and Somatics' devices incrementally decrease with decreasing age and increase with increasing age. Indeed, outputs at Impedances at or under 220Ω are well below the 100J mark on second generation MECTA and Somatics devices. Conversely, outputs emitted from these same MECTA and Somatics' second generation BP devices at Impedances above 220Ω greatly surpass the 100J mark, up to, in fact, 259 and 252 Joules respectively, as mentioned. Moreover, unlike the Medcraft B-25, the MTTLOIs (of 2.59 to 2.52 fold threshold respectively) are uniform. Antithetically, the Medcraft B-25 limits, but also allows outputs at all Impedances of up to 99 Joules. Consequently, at Impedances under 220Ω, the B-25 outputs can emit up to 99 Joules in every age category, including the youngest. [566] On the other hand, B-25 outputs, unlike MECTA and Somatics second generation BP devices, are limited to 99 maximum Joules. Because of the 99J ceiling, therefore, outputs emitted at Impedances higher than 220Ω tend to be threshold while those emitted at Impedances below 220Ω tend to be excessive. Crucially then, because the same 99J output can be emitted at every age level on the B-25, the youngest recipient can receive a 99 fold threshold output, whereas, the oldest recipient is limited to circa 1.0 threshold at the same 99J output. This means that the B-25's MTTLOI varies wildly from a maximum 99 MTTLOI for the ten year old child to a circa maximum 1.0 MTTLOI output intensity for the 100 year old adult, the direct result of ignoring the ER/RRC aspect of the 1982 APA Standard.

Though reporting to the FDA what appears to be an analogous *"99J at 220Ω" phrase* to MECTA and Somatics' phrases of circa *"101J at 220" and "99.4J at 220Ω"*, Medcraft is the single made-for-America manufacturer of BP devices which, within advertising fliers, can and does report "99Js" as a ceiling without adding the contingency *"at 220Ω"* (Medcraft Corporation, 1986a). Consequently, in spite of its "99J at 220Ω" report to the FDA, Medcraft unequivocally depicts and, in fact, does limit its B-25 BP machine to a true 99J maximum output. [567] However, as already noted, unlike MECTA and Somatics, Medcraft's interpretation of "99J at 220Ω" is a 99J maximum not merely "at 220Ω" (Food and Drug Administration, 1986A, pp.84; 160), but

---

[566] According to the 1982 APA Standard, no recipient should receive a MTTLOI exceeding 1.1. Moreover, no one with an Impedance below 100Ω should be administered "ECT." As such, recipients at and under about sixteen years of age should never be administered "ECT." Resistance to electricity is simply too low in these age categories. Indeed, this is the law in Texas.

[567] MECTA and Somatics do not add the phrase "at 220Ω" to their second generation Machine Readouts, such as their circa 100J readout maximums. They do, however, juxtapose circa "100J" with the "at 220Ω" phrase in fliers, manuals, and in reporting to the FDA.

at all Impedances (both low and high). [568] Thus, unlike MECTA and Somatics, Medcraft interprets its "99J at 220Ω" as an unexplained Pure Output Ceiling--that is, 99J at all Impedances--below, at, and above 220Ω--thereby totally disregarding, as noted, the concept of ER/RRC. In sum, unlike MECTA and Somatics devices, as we have now seen, the Medcraft B-25 fails to apply a uniform MTTLOI to all age categories, that is, Medcraft circumvents the APA guarantee of descending outputs with respect to descending age (Food and Drug Administration, 1986A, p.99), particularly critical in the younger age categories.

But how does Medcraft justify its antithetical rendering of the APA Standard of 99J not only "at 220Ω" but at all Impedances, and thereby in every age category? Within Medcraft's 1986 510K FDA pre-market application, Medcraft gives this unusual explanation of the 1982 APA Standard (for BP devices). Medcraft states:

> We found section 5.1:4.3 of the APA standard misleading. The spec states, "The maximum energy output of the device shall not exceed 70 joules across a load of 220Ω, and shall not exceed 110 joules across the load range of 100 to 600 ohms." Since 220 ohms is between 100 & 600, the maximum energy should be 110 joules.
>
> (See Food and Drug Administration, 1986A, p.145)

In short, according to Medcraft, the APA phrase

> "110 joules across the load range of 100 to 600 ohms"

contradicts the APA phrase

> "70 joules across a load of 220Ω"

and is thus "misleading," in brief, according to Medcraft, a mistake. Medcraft reasons that the APA sentence,

> "The maximum energy output of the device shall not exceed 70 joules across a load of 220Ω "

should read:

> "The maximum energy output of the device shall not exceed 110 joules across a load of 220Ω."

Ignoring "70J at 220Ω" as an ER/RRC assuring gradational output maximums relative to age, then, Medcraft takes the term "220Ω" as emblematic of all Impedances (from 100 to 600Ω). Subsequently, Medcraft interprets the phrase "70J at 220Ω" as a 70J maximum output at all Impedances, except that, according to Medcraft's logic, the "70J" figure should "correctly" read "110 Joules. " Ultimately, Medcraft's statement,

> "Since 220 ohms is between 100 & 600, the maximum energy should be 110 joules,"

means that a maximum output of 110 Joules is allowed at all Impedances, regardless of age. Such an interpretation not only entails altering specific figures within the APA Standard, but illogically eliminates a uniform MTTLOI for all ages, thereby allowing a 110 MTTLOI for the ten year old child who seizes at 1.0J but no more than a 1.1 MTTLOI for the 100 year old adult who seizes at 100J. In effect, Medcraft's logic removes the ER/RRC principle from the APA Standard.

Medcraft next explains its specific choice of "99Js at 220Ω "

---

[568] In that the B-25 can literally emit a 99J maximum at all Impedances, Medcraft, as noted, does not interpret its report of "99J at 220Ω" as an ER/RRC. In essence, Medcraft interprets "99J at 220Ω" as a Pure-Ceiling of 99J at all Impedances, while MECTA and Somatics interpret the same phrase antithetically, that is, as a Pure-ER/RRC meaning an output ceiling relative to circa "100J at 220Ω" at maximum machine Impedance, for example, 99.4J/220Ω = 252J/555.5Ω and so age-related determinations based on, for example, a uniform 2.52 MTTLOI.

> APA standard calls for a limit of 70J of energy at 220 ohms of resistance. B-25 calls for a limit of 99J of energy at 220Ω. . . We chose 99 joules to be more consistent with the competition MECTA. The maximum energy for a MECTA unit at 220Ω is 101.4 joules. (Ibid, p.146)

Thus, Medcraft chooses "99J at 220Ω" in lieu of what allegedly could read "110J at 220Ω" (according to Medcraft) in order "to be more consistent with . . . MECTA. " That is, Medcraft chooses the phrase "99J at 220Ω" in that this phrase purportedly makes the Medcraft device more "comparable" to MECTA and Somatics second generation devices reported at "101J at 220Ω" and "99.4J at 220Ω" respectively. Very unlike MECTA (and Somatics) devices, however, Medcraft's B-25 device now allows (and is limited to) a maximum of 99 Joules at every age-related Impedance while MECTA and Somatics second generation BP devices allow 259 and 252 joules respectively, but only for the oldest recipient. In fact, MECTA and Somatics incorporate a uniform MTTLOI of 2.52 and 2.59 respectively for all age categories (on their second generation BP devices), guaranteeing gradational output with respect to age. For example, because of a uniform 2.59 MTTLOI for all age categories, MECTA's second generation device limits output to about 2.59 joules for the ten year old child and 259 joules for the 100 year old adult. Does Medcraft actually believe, then, that MECTA and Somatics second generation BP devices permit a maximum output of circa 100 Joules from the very lowest to the very highest Impedance (which they do not)? Or does Medcraft merely have its own private agenda?

How Medcraft Derives from the 1982 APA Standard its "99J at 220Ω" Pure-Ceiling Interpretation "Justifying" 99J at all Impedances for its B-25 . . . Continued

In declaring that the APA statements, "70 Joules at 220Ω" and ". . . shall not exceed 110 joules across the load range of 100 to 600Ω" should read, "110 Joules at all Impedances from 100 to 600Ω," Medcraft is declaring that the two pronged construction of the APA Standard, the "70J at 220" ER/RRC and the "110J" overall ceiling--are synonymous. In essence, Medcraft is asserting that ". . . [S]hall not exceed 110 joules across the load range of 100 to 600Ω" is a mere restatement of the "70J at 220Ω" phrase found within the APA Standard, but which should read as noted, "110J at 220Ω." Not only does Medcraft claim that "70J at 220Ω" should read "110J at 220Ω" then, but that this new made-up phrase "110J at 220Ω" should be interpreted to mean--"can reach 110 Joules at all impedances. " De-neutered of its' ER/RRC meaning, therefore, and thus the notion of descending outputs relative to descending age requiring a uniform MTTLOI applied to all age categories, Medcraft's newly contrived "110J at 220Ω" phrase becomes a redrafting and reinterpretation of the clear APA 110J ceiling phrase ". . . shall not exceed 110 joules across the load range of 100 to 600 ohms" to newly mean "can reach 110J at any Impedance between 100 to 600. "

Once again, then, dismissing what is certainly a "70J at 220Ω" ER/RRC (meant to assure gradational outputs relative to age), Medcraft reinterprets the "70J at 220Ω" phrase to mean a 70J ceiling at all Impedances between 100 and 600Ω, but claims that the "70J" figure is a mistake which should "correctly" read "110J at 220Ω" in turn meaning a "110J ceiling at all Impedances between 100 and 600Ω. " In sum, Medcraft interprets the newly "substituted" Medcraftian phrase "110J at 220Ω" to mean a potential "110J maximum output at every single Impedance. " Disregarding the fact that this is a contrasting interpretation, Medcraft subsequently chooses the more conservative "99J at 220" phrase to more closely resemble MECTA's "101J at 220Ω" and Somatics "99.4J at 220Ω" phrases. Totally unlike both MECTA and Somatics, however, Medcraft has entirely denuded its "99J at 220Ω" phrase of the critical ER/RRC principle within the APA Standard. Conversely, as already noted, Medcraft's "99J at 220" phrase is newly interpreted to mean "a 99J maximum output at each individual Impedance between 100-600Ω"--an unprecedented <u>Pure-Ceiling</u> construal of the 1982 APA Standard. Thus, in spite of Medcraft's seemingly analogous "99J at 220" phrase, seemingly equivalent to MECTA's and Somatics' "101J at 220Ω" and ' 99.4J at 220Ω" phrases, Medcraft's interpretation of its "99J at 220Ω" description of the Medcraft B-25, bears not the slightest resemblance to MECTA's and Somatics' interpretation of their almost identical "101J at 220Ω" and "99.4J at 220Ω" depictions of the second generation JR/SR 1 and 2 and second generation Thymatron DG and DGx respectively. [569]

Medcraft's surprising assertion, (corroborated by Medcraft charts found within Medcraft 510K files) that the APA phrase "70J at 220Ω" permits a maximum output of 70J at each age-related Impedance but which should really read "110J at 220Ω" or "110 joules across the load range of 100 to 600Ω" allowing a 110J maximum output at each age-related Impedance between 100 and 600Ω, starkly contrasts with MECTA and Somatics interpretation of the same APA Standard. According to Medcraft then, and as already noted, the maximum output at all Impedances purportedly derived from the phrase--"70J at 220Ω" (denuded of its ER/RRC meaning) should be "corrected" to "110J at 220Ω" meaning 110J at all Impedances. Subsequently, Medcraft "cautiously" chooses--"99J at 220Ω" [instead of "110J at 220Ω"] . . . to be more consistent with the competition, MECTA [and Somatics]. " Unlike MECTA and Somatics; however, Medcraft uniquely deciphers the common (circa) "100J at 220Ω" phrase (reported by all three manufacturers) to mean a circa 100J maximum at every individual Impedance, regardless of age.

In fact, Medcraft's curious construal of the 1982 APA Standard gleaned as "110J at 220Ω" from which Medcraft settles for "99J at 220Ω" interpreted as an absolute 99J output at all Impedances, makes little sense in light of the "70J at 220Ω" phrase actually found within the APA Standard. [570] Ignoring the "70J at 220Ω" phrase as an ER/RRC implementing gradational Impedance oriented, age-related outputs and replacing the APA phrase ". . .110 joules across the load range of 100 to 600Ω" with "110J at 220Ω" only to reinterpret the newly derived "110J at 220Ω" phrase as a 110J maximum output at all Impedances is neither logical nor regulatory. Where is the rationale in dispensing with the ER/RRC interpretation of the "70J at 220Ω" phrase, the presence of which compels diminishing outputs with respect to diminishing age in tandem with the 110J APA ceiling stipulation, forcing manufacturers to conform to a uniform 1.1 MTTLOI (minimal stimulus) in every age category? Where is the logic in depicting the APA phrase--"the maximum energy output of the device shall . . . not exceed 110 joules across the load range of 100 to 600 ohms"-- as a pure 110J ceiling at all Impedances regardless of age, totally ignoring the age-related Output/Impedance gradation principle via the APA's "70J at 220Ω" phrase interpreted as an ER/RRC?

Plainly, Medcraft's "110J at 220Ω" concoction is nowhere mentioned within the APA Standard, much less interpreted as a pure-110J ceiling allowing 110J at all Impedances meaning all age categories. What reasonable standard would allow a 110 MTTLOI for a ten year old child while at the same time limiting the 100 year old adult to a 1.0 MTTLOI? What kind of regulatory standard for "ECT" would discard graduated output relative to (age-related) Impedance, and replace it with wildly varying MTTLOIs from ages ten to 100, in fact MTTLOIs increasing with diminishing Impedances? [571]

*While Medcraft's recognition of the APA Standard's 110J maximum output is certainly a correct reading of the standard, why, other than as an ER/RRC compelling decreasing outputs in accordance with decreasing age-related Impedances and increasing outputs in accordance with increasing age-related Impedances, would the APA Standard include the independent phrase, "70J at 220Ω"? Certainly, the phrase at least delineates a 70J output maximum at 220Ω, indicating graduated outputs in direct accordance with a "70J at 220Ω" ER/RRC insuring gradational outputs with respect to increasing or decreasing age levels. Certainly too, the 110J ceiling is intended to further limit output not only by setting the overall ceiling, but by also setting a maximum uniform 1.1 MTTLOI for all age recipients (110J ÷ 100J = 1.1 MTTLOI). Not surprisingly, this 1.1 MTTLOI is the expected

---

[569] In that both MECTA and Somatics subscribe to an ER/RRC interpretation of the original "70J at 220Ω" phrase and interpret both their "101J at 220Ω" and "99.4J at 220Ω" phrases as ER/RRCs necessitating a uniform MTTLOI of circa 2.59 (101J/220Ω = 259J/562; 259J ÷ 100 = 2.59) and 2.52 (99.7J/220Ω = 252J/555.5Ω; 252J ÷ 100 = 2.52) respectively, MECTA and Somatics second generation BP devices, unlike Medcraft's B-25, never actually approach a literal 100J at 220Ω (see MECTA and Somatics second generation BP device charts). On the other hand, they grossly surpass the 110J APA ceiling.

[570] A "70J at 220Ω" and "110J at 220Ω" ER/RRC cannot sensibly exist simultaneously. Moreover, the existence of the 108J (maximum) "MECTA "C" presented to the FDA during the investigative period as well as overt statements made that seizures can be invoked in all cases with never more than 100J with BP (Department of Health and Human Services, 1982a, A53, E20), together with numerous other statements regarding the improvement of electroshock in terms of reduced output BP (Ibid, 1982a, p. A41, A44-A45) all within the 1982 APA Standard itself, affirm the Standard's original intent as a "70J at 220Ω" ER/RRC with conditional 110 Joule overall ceiling (Ibid, 1982a, A53, E20).

[571] The effect of this interpretation imitates the constant Voltage SW device in that as Current deteriorates with Constant Voltage, power and MTTLOI decreases with increasing age similar to the construct of the B-25. Conversely, the inability of the B-25 to be set at minimal stimulus suggests the same dynamic for the B-24 SW.

just above threshold output Utah recommended; in brief, the least amount of electricity required to induce a so-called "adequate grand mal seizure" in every age category. How and why would any rational standard ignore gradational outputs with respect to age by permitting the 110J overall ceiling in ever age category? Certainly, dismissing the ER/RRC principle associated with "70J at 220Ω" (or even "100J at 220Ω") entirely alters the APA Standard, in effect, deregulating the standard. Unquestionably, the second part of the Standard, the 110J ceiling is only intended for the highest age-related Impedance, thereby insuring a 1.1 MTTLOI not only for the 100 year old recipient, but for all age categories--in short, the ubiquitous application of minimal stimulus for all recipients, a construal both wholly corroborated by the 108J MECTA "C" as well as the independent conclusions of the Utah Biomedical Test Lab originally contracted by the FDA in 1976 (Grahn et al.). Even MECTA and Somatics, (though ignoring the 110J ceiling), while increasing the "70J at 220Ω" ER/RRC phrase to a circa "100J at 220Ω" interpret both the "70J at 220Ω" and circa "100J at 220Ω" phrases as ER/RRCs implementing gradational outputs with respect to age.

Clearly, the APA Standard contains two critical elements, 1) an ER/RRC of "70J at 220Ω," (later changed to circa "100J at 220Ω") and 2) a maximum overall ceiling of 110 Joules. The first component insures graduated outputs relative to age or age-related Impedances, the second a uniform 1.1 MTTLOI minimal stimulus output for each individual recipient (for which we need age-related threshold outputs). Where is the sense in Medcraft's newly juxtaposing the clear and singular "110J" ceiling with "220Ω" only to reinterpret the nascent "110J at 220Ω" phrase as a Pure "110J" ceiling at all Impedances (or age levels) from which Medcraft then "settles" on a Pure-99J (in lieu of a Pure-110J) ceiling at all Impedances (or age levels). All this, we are then supposed to believe creates parity with MECTA and Somatics BP devices, both of which interpret the standard in a completely antithetical manner with respect to totally antithetical devices. In sum, Medcraft's discarding of graduated output enabling the same maximum output of 99J for all age recipients is as absurd as it is perilous.

CHAPTER 38

Diverse Interpretations of the APA Standard

Regardless of motive, Medcraft plainly interprets the circa "100J at 220Ω" phrase used by all three American manufacturers of second generation Brief Pulse devices in an entirely different manner than that utilized by either MECTA or Somatics. While MECTA and Somatics recognize the ER/RRC concept inclusive of a uniform MTTLOI for all age categories, neither MECTA nor Somatics recognizes the plainly depicted 110J APA ceiling Standard. In contrast, while Medcraft recognizes the APA 110J ceiling standard, Medcraft ignores the ER/RRC principle (inclusive of a uniform MTTLOI for all recipients and thus gradational age-related outputs) depicted within the same APA Standard (as "70J at 220Ω" and later changed by MECTA to circa "100J at 220Ω").

More succinctly, MECTA and Somatics interpret the APA Standard's "70J at 220Ω with 110J ceiling" as a Pure-ER/RRC *(newly based on maximum machine Impedance thereby ignoring the 110J ceiling and so supplanting it with a 273J ceiling),* while Medcraft interprets the same "70J at 220Ω with 110J ceiling," as a 110J Pure-Ceiling *(that is, a 110J maximum at all Impedances), thereby dropping ER/RRC principle and thus the uniform MTTLOI meant to guarantee descending outputs with respect to descending Impedances.* (Of course, "70J at 220Ω" has been modified to "100J at 220Ω" as noted above.) Thus, while both interpretations allow gross surpassing of the APA standard, they do so in starkly contrasting ways.

Manufacturers Interpreting the 1982 APA Standard Antithetically: MECTA and Somatics vs. Medcraft

Albeit antithetically interpreting the APA Standard, both MECTA and Somatics as well as Medcraft have this in common. All three have managed to re-interpret the two part 1982 APA Standard for BP devices (the "70J at 220Ω" ER/RRC with conditional "110J" overall ceiling) into an explanation accommodating the singly devised phrase, circa *"100J at 220Ω.* "[572]

Via this compression, Medcraft ignores the APA ER/RRC adhered to by MECTA and Somatics, while MECTA and Somatics ignore the APA 110J ceiling adhered to by Medcraft. The commonsense purpose of the 1982 APA Standard is (1) to assure gradational outputs with respect to age via the 70J at 220Ω ER/RRC [573] and (2) to restrict all outputs to a uniform 1.1 MTTLOI via the overall 110J ceiling. In short, the aim is to regulate all Brief Pulse devices to minimal stimulus output in every age category. The first principle assures gradational output, the second, minimal stimulus. This interpretation is supported by the 1982 APA Standard itself, the history of the FDA investigation via the Utah Biomedical Test Laboratory conclusions, public outrage

---

[572] MECTA (and Somatics) somewhat overtly acknowledge replacing "70J at 220Ω" with "100J at 220Ω"; but reinterpret the new phrase as a Pure-ER/RRC, thereby eliminating the APA 110J overall ceiling. Medcraft acknowledges the 110J ceiling, but interprets the new "100J at 220Ω" phrase as a Pure-Ceiling, thereby eliminating the ER/RRC principle.

[573] The APA ER/RRC of "70J at 220Ω" (or later "100J at 220Ω" ER/RRC) means no more than 70J (or 100J respectively) can occur at 220Ω, and that at a lower Impedance, for instance 110Ω, only 35J (or 50J respectively) can occur. (70J/220Ω = XJ/110Ω. X = 35J; 100J/220Ω = XJ/110Ω. X = 50J). Output ceilings are thus gradationally proscribed via the ER/RRC principle. But this is only in general. To create uniformity, all recipients must receive the MTTLOI of the oldest recipient which is to be no greater than 1.1 according to the 110J ceiling of the APA Standard (110J ÷ 100J = 1.1 MTTLOI).

demanding the end of high dosage erratic SW, the much touted reduced output intent of Brief Pulse devices generally, the conspicuously repeated APA claims of BP's reduced output compared to SW, and Weiner's clearly depicted charts presented to the FDA in 1982 wherein Brief Pulse at a 100J maximum is represented as emitting half the 200J output of SW. Finally, the 108 Joule MECTA "C," limited to a consistent 1.08 MTTLOI (for all recipients) was presented to the FDA as the prototypical Brief Pulse device in full conformity to the straightforward two pronged directive comprising the 1982 APA Standard itself. Clearly, both the ER/RRC principle and the 110J overall ceiling are necessary to uniformly regulate machines to a minimal stimulus dosage of electricity in accordance with each individual's age-related Impedance. (For this, MECTA and Somatics utilize never before reported relative constants.) In brief, the two pronged 1982 APA Standard safeguards each individual recipient via the assurance of consistent, minimal stimulus titration level outputs of electricity, in essence, electrical doses limited to just above threshold for every age recipient. Both prongs are required. That is, even with the 110J ceiling in place, without additionally implementing the ER/RRC principle, individuals with low Impedances--younger individuals--could yet receive dangerously high MTTLOIs of electricity, whereas even with the ER/RRC principle in place, without additionally implementing the absolute 110J ceiling, individuals could yet receive electrical doses far in excess of minimal stimulus. Critically, 100 Joules is the prescribed minimum mark (identified by Weiner within the APA Standard) at which even the most seizure recalcitrant individual will "adequately seize" under any circumstances with Brief Pulse. On the other hand, without the 110J ceiling in place (slightly more than minimal stimulus), recipients could receive much higher than minimal stimulus output, electrical outputs in excess of that required to induce seizure. For example, MECTA and Somatics second generation BP devices, which ignore the 110J APA ceiling, administer circa 2.5 MTTLOIs to all recipients in lieu of the 1.1 fold threshold maximum (assuring adequate seizure at minimal stimulus output) prescribed by the APA Standard. Conversely, without an ER/RRC principle, even <u>with</u> the 110J ceiling in place, younger recipients particularly, could yet receive inconsistent MTTLOIs far in excess of minimal stimulus. For instance, the Medcraft second generation BP device limits output to 99J, but in ignoring the ER/RRC principle, yet has the capacity to administer a 99 MTTLOI to a ten year old child, (99J ÷ 1.0J =) 99 times threshold in lieu of what should be the 1.1 maximum MTTLOI prescribed by the APA Standard. In a word, only the "70J at 220Ω" ER/RRC principle in conjunction with the 110J ceiling comprising the whole of the 1982 APA Standard for Brief Pulse devices can insure inducement of an adequate grand mal seizure with the least amount of electricity possible in all age categories just as it was designed to do.

In essence, adherence to both prongs of what is actually an ingenious two-pronged 1982 APA Standard for BP devices, plainly containing an ER/RRC of "70J at 220Ω" with a conditional 110J ceiling, together insure that all recipients are guaranteed a 1.1 MTTLOI or the least amount of electricity possible to induce a grand mal seizure. For example, complete adherence to the standard means that machines must limit output to a ten year old child requiring one Joule for induction of a grand mal seizure to a 1.1 fold threshold output or 1.1 maximum Joules (1.1J ÷ 1.0J = 1.1 fold). By the same token, adherence means that machines must limit a 100 year old requiring up to 100 Joules for induction of a grand mal seizure to the same (110J ÷ 100J =) 1.1 fold threshold output or 110 maximum Joules guaranteeing an adequate seizure with the least amount of electricity possible.[574] In brief, the ingenious combination of an ER/RRC principle with 110J ceiling stipulation insures gradational outputs relative to age-related Impedance via a uniformly applied 1.1 MTTLOI (minimal stimulus) for all age levels. *Certainly the results of MECTA's and Somatics' partially correct, partially corrupt interpretation of the APA Standard as a Pure-ER/RRC with no 110J ceiling stipulation, and Medcraft's partially correct, partially corrupt interpretation of the same APA Standard as a Pure-110J Ceiling with no ER/RRC, support the standard's intended interpretation of applying both components at once--a "70J at 220Ω" ER/RRC insuring gradational outputs relative to age and a conditional 110J ceiling insuring a uniform 1.1 MTTLOI together regulating output to the least amount of electricity possible to guarantee an adequate seizure for each individual recipient.* The 1982 APA standard then, clearly compels minimal stimulus or just above threshold output for all age recipients, meaning the least possible amount of electricity necessary to induce a so-called "adequate" or "grand mal seizure" in each and every age category. In that the phrase "70J at 220Ω" limits devices to no more than 70J at 220Ω, common sense dictates gradational outputs in accordance with the ER of this same "70J at 220Ω" dictate. ER/RRC in conjunction with a 110 Joule overall ceiling, moreover, promotes further refinement

---

[574] In that the phrase "70J at 220Ω" limits devices to 70J specifically at 220Ω, common sense dictates not 70J at all Impedances, but a gradational ER/RRC output while the overall ceiling of 110J specifically limits MTTLOI to a 1.1 MTTLOI for all recipients or just above minimal stimulus. It is in exact accordance to this dual standard that the 108J MECTA "C" presented to the FDA was built.

of the ER/RRC, insuring uniform gradational outputs with respect to age via a consistent 1.1 MTTLOI for all age categories.

Plainly, the Standard's overall purpose in direct accordance with convulsion theory then, is to regulate electrical output in all age categories to just above threshold, in short, to the most minimum amount of electricity necessary to guarantee a so-called "adequate" grand mal seizure in every age category.

The 108J MECTA "C" introduced to the FDA as the new prototypically improved Brief Pulse Device (supplanting SW) was plainly engineered to conform to both components of the 1982 APA Standard. Indeed, both the standard and the MECTA "C" were presented to the FDA during the 1976-1982 investigation as the future of ECT. Clearly, the MECTA "C" exemplified the new Brief Pulse Device limiting all outputs to a consistent 1.08 MTTLOI in every age category in full compliance with the 1982 APA Standard. In effect, the MECTA C, in conformity with the 1982 APA Standard, satisfied authorities that the APA Standard both assured an adequate seizure while limiting electrical output to no more than just above threshold for each individual recipient. Indeed, it was manufacturers' failure to request adoption of the 1982 APA Standard as the official American standard that forced all "ECT" devices even today to remain in Class III FDA category in lieu of rising to Class I, those medical devices for which a standard can be written.

Because each of the two interpretations (one by MECTA and Somatics, one by Medcraft) is based on a partial aspect of the actual APA Standard each by itself incomplete, Medcraft's declared equivalency of its B-25 BP device to MECTA and Somatics second generation BP devices as well as MECTA's and Somatics' devices' alleged "equivalency" to the Medcraft B-25 BP is spurious. While *"101.4 and 99.4 Joules* respectively may be the maximum outputs permitted by second generation made-for-America "MECTA" (and Somatics) BP devices specifically at *220Ω, neither 101.4J nor 99.4 Joules"* is the overall ceiling for second generation MECTA or Somatics BP devices. Conversely, while 99Js may be the maximum output permitted by a second generation made-for-America Medcraft B-25 BP device specifically at *220Ω, "220Ω"* is certainly not the lowest or highest Impedance at which 99Js can be evinced on the Medcraft B-25. Not only is each respective interpretation by itself incomplete without the other, then, but each interpretation by itself permits gross violations the 1982 APA Standard in antithetical fashions.

Antithetical Interpretations Continued and What We Can Conclude

While all three manufacturers appear to have altered the APA phrase "70J at 220Ω" to circa "100J at 220Ω," Medcraft, as noted, unlike MECTA and Somatics, acknowledges a 110J ceiling but no ER/RRC (either conditional or pure) and thus no gradational output or uniform MTTLOI. In brief, because 99J is a pure ceiling maximum on the Medcraft B-25 BP device (a potential 99J at all Impedances) and not a "99J at 220Ω" ER/RRC, Medcraft fails to recognize relative ceilings according to age. The omission of the ER/RRC principle is of critical significance, principally at Impedances less than 220Ω (discernible in the younger age categories). Medcraft, as has been discussed, would have us believe that the APA Standard's "70J at 220Ω" ER/RRC (or even the newer circa "100J at 220Ω" interpreted as an ER/RRC) together with the "110J" overall ceiling can be adhered to via Medcraft's reported "99J at 220Ω" phrase interpreted as a *Pure*-99J-Ceiling, that is, 99J at all Impedances and thus all age categories. On the other hand, MECTA and Somatics, as we have seen, would have us believe that the same standard can be adhered to via their similarly reported phrases, "101J at 220Ω" and "99.4J at 220Ω" interpreted as *Pure*-ER/RRCs (that is, ER/RRC sans the 110J ceiling [575]), thereby permitting up to 259 and 252 maximum Joules respectively on their second generation devices. Because MECTA and Somatics ignore the 110J APA ceiling and thus the APA's prescribed 1.1 MTTLOI, their second generation devices are no longer confined to minimal stimulus (or 1.1 fold threshold); rather their second generation BP devices are set at 2.59 and 2.52 MTTLOIs, respectively. Conversely, in that MECTA and Somatics do acknowledge the ER/RRC principle, although not the 1.1 MTTLOI prescribed, both MECTA and Somatics machines apply a uniform MTTLOI for all age categories. In short, while grossly surpassing minimal stimulus or the prescribed 1.1 MTTLOI for all age categories with a 2.59 and a 2.52 MTTLOI respectively, outputs on second generation MECTA and Somatics devices are nevertheless both uniform and gradational (in accordance with age related

---

[575] Instead, MECTA and Somatics devices are based on the 600Ω Impedance maximum alone, specifically MECTA--562Ω and Somatics--555Ω.101J/220Ω = 259J/562Ω; 99.4J/220Ω = 252J/555Ω. These two manufacturers thus unofficially increase the ceiling from 110J to around 260J for second generation BP devices.

Impedances). In effect, while no recipient receives minimal stimulus, neither does any recipient receive more than the pre-set 2.59 and 2.52 MTTLOIs respectively from any second generation MECTA or Somatics BP device.

Factually, Medcraft's interpretation of the 1982 APA Standard and MECTA's and Somatics' interpretation of the same 1982 APA Standard are wholly antithetical. So what can we conclude, regarding this stark difference? First, we can ascertain that no Brief Pulse machine can violate either component of the APA Standard--neither the ER/RRC principle nor the 110J ceiling--without violating the Standard itself. That is, no Brief Pulse machine can violate either one of the components and adhere to the minimal stimulus regulatory aim the standard is designed to facilitate. So why do all three manufacturers circumvent the two pronged Standard? Why do they, or rather, why must they surpass minimal stimulus titration level output intensity when adequate grand mal seizures are plainly attainable with just above threshold outputs in all cases? The answer is clear. No machine can adhere to both components of the APA Standard--the ER/RRC principle and the 110 Joule ceiling--and be effective. This is because it is not the induction of grand mal seizures which render the "desired results." In short, in spite of the successful induction of grand mal seizures, minimal stimulus electrical output is simply unproductive.

Manufacturers, in brief, are forced to violate the 1982 APA standard in one way or the other to make the machines effectual, that is, in order to attain the "desired effects. " In other words, regardless of successful seizures, manufacturers must administer excessive non-minimal dosages of electricity to make “ECT” machines "work. " To achieve this, Medcraft gets around the minimal stimulus regulatory aim of the 1982 APA Standard by ignoring ER/RRC, while MECTA and Somatics get around the same regulatory aim by ignoring the 110J ceiling. Plainly, mere induction of a so-called "adequate" grand mal convulsion is ineffective. What is needed, embarrassingly enough, is adequate amounts of electricity. But if regulators or the public understood this, how could they avoid the logical conclusion that "convulsion theory" is wrong--that "convulsive theory" is spurious, that "convulsive theory" is myth? Indeed, functional "ECT" devices (BP or SW) do not, nor have they ever operated on the principle of "adequate convulsion." Rather, functional “ECT” machines operated, continue to operate, and have always operated on the principle of adequate amounts of electricity--first SW and now "souped-up" Brief Pulse devices. Is it any mystery, therefore, why manufacturers go to such great lengths to suppress the electro-oriented nature of their devices, why they continue to insist that "adequate convulsion" theory is correct? Manufacturers of these devices fully comprehend that adequate amounts of electricity make the devices not only "effective," but dangerously damaging. Based on hundreds of first hand recipient experiences (Cameron 1997; Frank; Andre) together with numerous electrical studies, only some of which are cited in this manuscript, we can safely conclude that all functional "ECT" [576] machines have been and continue to be based on "adequate amounts of electricity"--not adequate convulsion. The plain truth is--what are actually ENR machines, machine eliciting suprathreshold dosages of electricity--must damage their recipients to be "effective" (Friedman, 1942; Liberson, 1945a; 1945b; 1946, 1946, 1949; Ottosson, 1960; Wilcox, 1946; Breggin, 1979; 1991; 1998; Friedberg, 1971; 1976; Johnstone, 1992; Sament, 1983). Indeed, the facts force us to determine that all functional "ECT" devices, past and present, achieve efficacy via electrical damage to the brain. In sum, neither the B-24, the B-25, nor second generation MECTA and Somatics' BP devices are "ECT" devices at all, but rather ENR" devices (Perrin et al 2012).

Summing Up Second Generation BP Devices

To sum up then, Medcraft would have us suppose that the APA Standard contains no ER/RRC concept whatsoever--that the phrase “70J at 220Ω" is somehow a mistake so that any notion of ER/RRC is non-existent, that while the APA Standard clearly does limit BP devices to a maximum output of 110 Joules--this 110J ceiling is allowed at every age-related Impedance level! To rely on Medcraft's interpretation then, means no uniform MTTLOI and thus, no gradational output regulation relative to age within the 1982 APA standard. Instead, Medcraft would have us suppose that its *Pure*-Ceiling interpretation of its “99J at 220Ω” phrase permitting 99J at every Impedance level conforms to the APA Standard. MECTA and Somatics, on the other hand, claim conformity through the same circa “100J at 220Ω” phrase interpreted as a *Pure*-ER/RRC, that is, an

[576] Early devices based on minimal stimulus failed while minimal stimulus devices presented to the FDA between 1976 and 1982 are no longer utilized.

interpretation ignoring the clearly stated 110J ceiling, instead basing the ceiling on the 600Ω maximum Impedance allowed by the APA Standard. Thus, MECTA and Somatics would have us believe that their *Pure*-ER/RRC interpretation of their circa "100J at 220Ω" phrases permitting up to 272J conforms to the APA Standard. Unlike Medcraft then, MECTA and Somatics acknowledge a uniform MTTLOI and thus gradational output relative to age, but no 110J ceiling and thus no obligation to conform to minimal stimulus output. [577] [578] Conversely, Medcraft acknowledges a 110J ceiling, but no ER/RRC and thus no obligation to insure gradational outputs relative to age. In short, both circumvent minimal stimulus outputs, but in entirely different ways.

Medcraft's Pure-Ceiling interpretation then, is diametrically opposed to MECTA's and Somatics' Pure-ER/RRC interpretation, resulting in a divergently constituted B-25 Brief Pulse device compared to Somatics' second generation Thymatron DG (and DGx) and MECTA's second generation made-for-U. S. and made-for-Europe SR1 and SR2 BP devices. MECTA's and Somatics' Pure-ER/RRC interpretation (of the same standard) is, in turn, diametrically opposed to Medcraft's Pure-ceiling interpretation resulting in divergently constituted second generation BP devices compared to Medcraft's B-25 Brief Pulse device. Plainly, Medcraft's assertion that the B-25 is "substantially equivalent" to second generation MECTA and Somatics BP devices and vice-versa simply because all three report circa "100J at 220" phrases (Food and Drug Administration, 1986A, pp.4; 57) is specious. In fact, the notion that the Medcraft BP device is equivalent to MECTA and Somatics BP devices and vice-versa based on the reporting by all three American BP manufacturers of the same circa "100J at 220Ω" for their second generation BP devices is insidiously misleading.

Indeed, the common reporting by all three manufacturers of circa "100J at 220Ω" falsely suggests that both MECTA and Somatics limit their second generation BP devices to the same circa 100J maximum as the Medcraft B-25, and that Medcraft limits its B-25 device to gradational age-related outputs similar to MECTA and Somatics devices. Indeed, the only basis for equivalency between Medcraft's B-25 and Somatics and MECTA's second generation DG and SR1@2 respectively seems to be that all three second generation BP machines do not surpass *"100J at 220Ω,"* but this is the extent of any similarity. [579] Clearly, Medcraft's *"substantially equivalent"* statement together with MECTA's and Somatics' never contested acceptance of Medcraft's equivalency assertion, is bogus. In fact, the commonly stated circa "100J at 220" reports used by all three manufacturers actively engender the illusion that all three companies manufacture minimal stimulus second generation BP devices in perfect accordance with the 1982 APA Standard. In short, by Medcraft's using one prong of the standard and MECTA and Somatics the other prong, the illusion is created that that all three manufacturers utilize gradational outputs based upon a uniform MTTLOI and that all three limit their second generation BP devices to a 110J ceiling. Certainly, the illusion is created that that all three Brief Pulse manufacturers produce minimal stimulus machines confined to circa 100Js and a 1.1 MTTLOI.

In truth, Medcraft clearly ignores the ER/RRC principle and thus the gradational output stipulation facilitated by a uniform MTTLOI for all age recipients, just as MECTA and Somatics clearly ignore the 110J ceiling. None produce the minimal stimulus ECT machine the APA Standard calls for and which manufacturers promised to the FDA. Like two complementary bookends, the pseudo equivalency suggested by all three manufacturers' reporting the same circa "100J at 220Ω" phrase subtly conceals both MECTA's and Somatics' discarding of the 110J ceiling and Medcraft's discarding of the ER/RRC principle. No manufacturer interprets the circa "70J at 220Ω" (or the newer "100J at 220Ω) phrase as the conditional-ER/RRC with 110J ceiling clearly depicted within the 1982 APA Standard. In ignoring one or the other component of the plainly two-pronged Standard, that is, by avoiding incorporation of both prongs simultaneously, Medcraft's, MECTA's and Somatics' interpretations

---

[577] The Medcraft Pure-Ceiling interpretation is confirmed by Charts within the Medcraft Operation Manual providing us (at the B-25's maximum 1.0A constant current) 99J maximums not only at 220Ω, but at every Impedance level. This includes the lowest Impedance of a purported 150Ω, and the highest B-25 Impedance of a purported 350Ω (Food and Drug Administration, 1986A, p.113).

[578] Both MECTA and Somatics appear to recognize the APA's "70J at 220Ω" phrase as an ER/RRC, and the companies simply introduce a higher ER/RRC at a later date --"100J at 220Ω"(circa 1985). Though the newer higher ER/RRC is reported (by MECTA and Somatics) to the FDA, their *Pure*-ER/RRC interpretation along with the disappearance of the 110J ceiling is not reported; in fact, it is camouflaged. Unlike Medcraft; therefore, MECTA and Somatics conceal (or at least fail to report) maximum outputs. Medcraft, on the other hand, interprets the APA Standard itself as supporting a "110J at 220Ω"—interpreted not as an ER/RRC--but as a Pure 110J Ceiling at all Impedances.

[579] Because of the Pure-Ceiling interpretation, the B-25 can reach 99 Joules at 220Ω (as well as all other Impedances). Because Somatics and MECTA second generation BP devices are based on ER/RRC and thus a uniform MTTLOI, MECTA and Somatics BP devices, in spite of their circa "100J at 220Ω" reports, unlike Medcraft, do not even approach 100J at 220Ω.

allow the bypassing of the minimal stimulus regulatory principles mandated by the standard, that is, each interpretation enables bypassing of the least amount of electricity to induce the adequate seizure principle clearly compelled by the Standard and, in fact, each circumspection actively facilitates the suprathreshold electrical dosages both companies utilize in order to make their devices "work. " Indeed, each partial-interpretation enables a gross violation of the APA standard even as each complementary bookend conceals the inadequacy of the other. As a result, we must conclude that convulsion theory is false, that convulsive therapy is ineffective and thus mythological, and that these embarrassing details are concealed in what appears to be a conspiracy by all three American BP manufacturers to create the appearance of minimal stimulus devices even as the very opposite is true. In short, manufacturers go to great lengths to suppress the inconvenient fact that all so-called "ECT" devices "work" not via the induction of grand mal convulsion, but rather enough electrical output to damage the brain's neurotransmitters, that, like SW, all modern day Brief Pulse devices are no longer seizure-dependent, but rather electro-dependent apparatuses and as such, are not "ECT" devices at all, but rather ENR devices, the deliberate aim of which is reduction of neural transmissions in the left prefrontal lobe, as has been discussed.

Together

All three companies, as discussed, report circa "100J at 220Ω" for their second generation BP devices. Medcraft, as noted above, unlike MECTA and Somatics, limits its' B-25 BP device to an Absolute maximum of 99Joules. Conversely, neither Somatics nor MECTA interprets the condensed phrase circa "100J at 220Ω" as incorporative of a circa 100J ceiling. Rather, (albeit giving the false impression via Machine Readouts of similar 100J ceilings), both Somatics and MECTA interpret the circa phrase "100J at 220Ω" as a Pure-ER/RRC wholly violating the 110J ceiling depicted within the APA Standard. This is because a Pure-ER/RRC interpretation (as opposed to a Conditional-ER/RRC) bypasses the stipulated 110J APA ceiling, as discussed, by newly deriving maximum output from maximum machine Impedance, (i.e.1<u>01.4J/220Ω</u> = XJ/<u>562Ω</u>; X = <u>259J</u>). While a Pure-ER/RRC interpretation insures gradational outputs relative to age, therefore, the actual outputs delivered on a second generation Somatics or MECTA device grossly violate the 1.1 MTTLOI clearly implied within the APA Standard.

On the other hand, once the overall maximum output in Joules (in this case, 259J) is determined, the MTTLOI for that device can be derived simply dividing maximum overall output by 100J (the minimum output required to seize all 100 year old recipients in all circumstances). This process gives us the common (unreported) MTTLOI delivered by a particular MECTA or Somatics machine to all age recipients (i.e. 259J ÷ 100J = 2.59 MTTLOI). The MTTLOI (i.e. 2.59) is then multiplied by the relative threshold constant [580] for each age category to determine the default output delivered to each specific age category on that particular BP device. For example, 1.0J is the relative threshold constant for a ten year old child, thus the default output delivered to the ten year old by the JR/SR 1 and 2 is (1.0J x 2.59 =) <u>2.59J</u>.100J is the relative constant for a 100 year old adult, thus the default output delivered to the 100 year old adult is (100J x 2.59 =) <u>259J</u>.

Stated another way, the new Pure-ER/RRC interpretation (supplanting the original Conditional-ER/RRC) is a means of dispensing with the APA 110J ceiling and so supplanting a uniform (110J ÷ 100J =) 1.1 MTTLOI for all age categories with a much higher albeit uniform MTTLOI similarly applied to every age recipient. In brief, both MECTA and Somatics (both of which utilize Pure-ER/RRC) breach the 110J ceiling or 1.1 MTTLOI (minimal stimulus) prescribed by the 1982 APA Standard.

Medcraft, on the other hand, honors the 110J ceiling, but in altogether dispensing with ER/RRC, allows, if the Selector so chooses, 99J outputs in all age categories--from the youngest to the oldest. On the other hand, by honoring ER/RRC, MECTA and Somatics second generation BP devices confine emissions at less than 220Ω (younger age categories) to correspondingly decreasing outputs well below 100Js though allowing emissions at more than 220Ω (older age categories) to correspondingly increasing outputs well above 100Js. Both younger and older age categories, however, are administered a circa 2.5-2.6 MTTLOI.

In using a Pure-Ceiling interpretation, Medcraft confines outputs to 99 Joules at all Impedances greater than 220Ω (older age categories), but enables 99 Joules at all Impedances less than 220Ω (younger age

---

[580] Relative constants can be defined as the minimum outputs required to induce adequate seizures for every member of a particular age category.

categories). In so doing, Medcraft not only ignores gradationally increasing outputs in accordance with increasing age, but gradationally decreasing outputs in accordance with decreasing age. Indeed, there is no uniform MTTLOI. In sum, the Medcraft B-25 confines the 99 year old to a minimal stimulus output of 1.0 MTTLOI, while permitting a grossly unconscionable 99 MTTLOI or 99 fold threshold output to the ten year old child.

In conclusion, none of the three companies limits output to the 1.1 MTTLOI or the minimal stimulus output prescribed to and intended for all recipients by the 1982 APA Standard. Moreover, by all three companies concomitantly reporting circa "100J at 220Ω" to the FDA for their second generation BP devices, these companies create the false impression that not only are their devices comparable, but that all are confined to an overall ceiling output of circa 100 maximum joules delivered only to the 100 year old adult. Because all three report circa "100J at 220Ω," and because all three depict circa 100J maximum machine readouts, a strong illusion is created that all three honor both the APA 110J ceiling and the APA ER/RRC. In short, all appear to adhere to the conditional-ER/RRC with 110J ceiling stipulated in the 1982 APA Standard. In sum, a powerful impression is generated that all three companies confine machine outputs to a uniform 1.1 MTTLOI or minimal stimulus output in all age categories. Ultimately, not only is the illusion generated that all three manufacturers adhere to the 1982 APA Standard, but that all three Brief Pulse manufacturers produce reduced output ECT devices compared to SW. Nothing could be further from the truth. Indeed all three manufacturers produce adequate electricity or ENR devices designed to electrically and grossly diminish tens of thousands of neurotransmitters both within, and to and from, the left prefrontal lobe.

CHAPTER 39

Concrete Comparisons

Let us look at 100 and 10 year old recipients, comparing the the1982 APA Standard with Medcraft, MECTA, and Somatics second generation BP device emissions. Note how all manufacturers violate the 1.1 MTTLOI minimal stimulus stipulation of the 1982 APA Standard via spurious antithetical interpretations.

Actual 1982 APA Standard ("70J at 220Ω" Conditional-ER-RRC with 110J Ceiling)
***100 year old administered 110J maximum* (1.1 MTTLOI)** [581]
***10 year old administered 1.1J maximum* (1.1 MTTLOI)**

vs.

1) Medcraft B-25 (99J Pure-Ceiling--*No ER/RRC*)
***100 year old administered circa 99J default* (1.0 MTTLOI)**
***10 year old* administered circa *10J minimum* (10 MTTLOI)**
***10 year old* administered circa *100J maximum* (100 MTTLOI)** [582]

vs.

2) MECTA SR 2 ("101.4J at 220Ω" Pure-ER/RRC with 259J Ceiling)
***100 year old administered 259J default* (2.59 MTTLOI)**
***10 year old* administered 2.59J *default* (2.59 MTTLOI)** [583]

vs.

3) Thymatron DG ("99.4/7J at 220Ω" Pure-ER/RRC with 252J Ceiling)
***100 year old administered 252J default* (2.52 MTTLOI)**
***10 year old* administered 2.52J *default* (2.52 MTTLOI)**

---

[581] The 1982 APA Standard clearly confines all outputs in all age categories to a 1.1 MTTLOI or just above seizure output.
[582] Medcraft's B-25 BP violates the 1.1 minimal stimulus stipulation of the 1982 APA Standard, allowing a circa 10-100 MTTLOI to the ten year old child. Indeed, because the B-25 allows and confines all outputs in all age categories to 99 maximum joules, there is no uniform MTTLOI.
[583] MECTA and Somatics BP second generation BP devices violate the 1.1 minimal stimulus stipulation of the 1982 APA Standard, emitting 2.59 and 2.52 fold threshold respectively for all age categories, but in adhering to ER/RRC emit uniform MTTLOIs of 2.59 and 2.52 respectively (259J ÷ 100J = 2.59; 252J ÷ 100J = 2.52).

As can be seen in the examples above, MECTA and Somatics second generation BP devices ignore the maximum APA output ceiling of ***"110Js"*** or a 1.1 MTTLOI ceiling, instead, emitting 2.59 and 2.52 MTTLOIs respectively in all age categories, including the 100 year old category; whereas, Medcraft, in the same 100 year old age category, true to the 110J ceiling depicted in the 1982 APA Standard, confines its output to 99 Joules or minimal stimulus in this age category, but in ignoring ER/RRC allows an almost 100 MTTLOI in the youngest age category.

In brief, MECTA and Somatics second generation BP devices ignore the 110J ceiling, but acknowledge ER/RRC, breaching the 110J or 1.1 MTTLOI ceiling, though maintaining consistent 2.59 and 2.52 MTTLOIs in all age groups. The Medcraft B-25 ignores ER/RRC and thus a uniform MTTLOI, emitting wildly inconsistent suprathreshold outputs with respect to age, but in acknowledging the 110J APA ceiling, confines the oldest age category to a 1.0 MTTLOI, even while allowing a 99.0 MTTLOI in the youngest age category. None of the devices maintain the APA stipulation of minimal stimulus in all age categories, and so can no longer be deemed "ECT" devices. Rather all are ENR devices.

Below, see the second generation Medcraft B-25 based on a Pure-Ceiling interpretation of "99J at 220Ω" inclusive of a potential 99J ceiling at all Impedances. This odd interpretation ignores any uniform MTTLOI and thus gradational output relative to age.

ACTUAL (PROBABLE) CONSTANT CURRENT B-25 BRIEF PULSE DEVICE **Medcraft Corp.** 1985-2000 ***adjusted for maximum stimulus*** in all age categories.
BASED ON PURE-CEILING INTERPRETATION OF "99J AT 220Ω. " (2nd GENERATION)

VOLTAGE	POWER % @ Age	AGE Yrs	Ω Ohms	FREQUENCY (Hz)	DURATION (SECs)	CURRENT mAmps	ENERGY Joules	CHARGE mC	Non-Unif MTTLOI
200	10	10	200	70	3.53	1.0	99	495	99
214	20	20	214	70	3.31	1.0	99	463	24.75
227	30	30	227	70	3.11	1.0	99	436	11
241	40	40	241	70	2.94	1.0	99	411	6.18
255	50	50	255	70	2.77	1.0	99	388	4
269	60	60	269	70	2.62	1.0	99	368	2.75
276	65	65	276	70	2.56	1.0	99	359	2.3
283	70	70	283	70	2.5	1.0	99	350	2.0
297	80	80	297	70	2.38	1.0	99	333	1.55
310	90	90	310	70	2.28	1.0	99	319	1.22
325	100	100	325	70	2.18	1.0	99	304	1.0

.001 Second Pulse Width

In contrast to the MECTA and Somatics Pure-ER/RRC interpretation of "101J at 220Ω," the B-25's decreasing Charge and Duration above confines output, as expected, to 99 maximum Joules (in accordance with the APA Standard), but allows settings of up to 99 Joules for even the lowest Impedance or age category. In so doing, Medcraft violates both the implied and expected "70J at 220Ω" and even updated "100J at 220Ω" ER/RRC element of the APA Standard, thereby, ignoring a uniform MTTLOI and so age-related gradational outputs. As a result, the B-25, like the B-24 SW, is capable of emitting super suprathreshold dosages of electricity in the youngest age categories. So high is the MTTLOI potential in the younger age categories, that the B-25 must implement a "ramping" mechanism to prevent external injury.

Compare the B-25 Brief Pulse Device above set on maximum output in all age categories to the default outputs of the second generation made-for-America MECTA JR/SR 2 Brief Pulse Device below based on a Pure-ER/RRC interpretation of "101J at 220Ω" circumventing the APA 110J ceiling stipulation, but inclusive of a uniform MTTLOI (though much higher than the 1.1 MTTLOI indirectly stipulated under the APA Standard):

PROBABLE **ACTUAL** ***Made-for-America*** MECTA 2nd GENERATION CONSTANT CURRENT **JR/SR 2** BRIEF PULSE DEVICE BASED ON ***PURE***-ER/RRC OF **"101.3J AT 220Ω"** (or **"138J AT 300Ω"**) by **MECTA** Corp.1985

VOLTAGE	POWER % @ Age	AGE Yrs	Ω Ohms	FREQ (Hz)	DURATION (SECs)	CURRENT mAmps	ENERGY Joules	CHARGE mC	Uniform MTTLOI
45	10	10	56.25	90	0.5	800	3.24	72	2.59
90	20	20	112.5	90	0.8	800	10.37	115.2	2.59
135	30	30	168.75	90	1.2	800	23.33	172.8	2.59
180	40	40	225	90	1.6	800	41.47	230.4	2.59
225	50	50	281.25	90	2.0	800	64.8	288	2.59
270	60	60	337.5	90	2.4	800	93.31	345.6	2.59
292.5	65	65	365.63	90	2.6	800	109.51	374.4	2.59
315	70	70	393.75	90	2.8	800	127	403.2	2.59
360	80	80	450	90	3.2	800	165.89	460.8	2.59
405	90	90	506.25	90	3.6	800	209.95	518.4	2.59
450	100	100	562.5	90	4.0	800	259.2	576	2.59

.001 Sec. Pulse Width

As noted, the single commonality amongst MECTA, Somatics, and Medcraft second generation BP devices is that outputs do not surpass circa 100J specifically at 220Ω. Moreover, even this is not comparable. Unlike the Medcraft B-25 Brief Pulse Device, MECTA and Somatics second generation Brief Pulse Devices emit less than half the 99J output potential (of the B-25) at 220Ω, the result of conforming to a uniform MTTLOI for all age categories. On the other hand, note the 259J overall maximum emitted by the MECTA Brief Pulse device above (and 252 overall maximum of the Somatics DG device) compared to the 99J overall maximum of the Medcraft B-25 Brief Pulse device. [584] In short, the interpretation of the circa "100J at 220" phrase reported by Medcraft as opposed to the entirely disparate interpretation of the same circa "100J at 220Ω" phrase reported by MECTA and Somatics, make Medcraft's equivalency claims wholly spurious and MECTA's and Somatics' reticence, wholly suspicious. Clearly, Medcraft's equivalency claim to MECTA and Somatics devices is absurd. [585] Even so, by all three manufacturers reporting the same approximate "100J at 220Ω" phrase for their second generation BP devices in conjunction with all three reporting 100J maximums via Machine Readouts (two spuriously), the firm illusion is created that all second generation made-for-America BP devices are confined to the 110J ceiling in adherence to the 1982 APA Standard and that all these devices facilitate a gradational 1.1 MTTLOI relative to age also in accordance with the APA Standard. The illusion that all three companies produce minimal stimulus devices is indeed an enduring one, an Illusion regularly consumed by doctors, media, public general, and regulatory agencies alike. In short, by all three manufacturers reporting the same circa "100J at 220Ω" phrase, and by all three reporting circa 100J ceilings, the convincing suggestion is established that all three manufacturers produce devices based on a "100J at 220Ω" conditional--ER/RRC with 100 or 110J ceiling and thus age-related minimal stimulus gradational outputs in total conformity with the 1982 APA Standard. In brief, the overall impression of all three manufacturers reporting the same approximate phrase for their second generation BP devices is that all American made second generation BP devices conform to a 1.1 MTTLOI or minimal stimulus in all age categories. Indeed, two of the companies ignore the 110J ceiling while the other ignores ER/RRC. In fact, none are minimal stimulus Brief Pulse devices and none conform to the 1982 APA Standard.

Common Sense Interpretation of the 1982 APA Standard vs Oppositional Construals

MECTA and Somatics interpret the circa phrase "100J at 220Ω" as a **Pure-ER/RRC (sans 110J ceiling)** permitting unnecessarily high MTTLOIs in all age categories; Medcraft interprets the same circa phrase as a 99J **Pure-Ceiling (sans ER/RRC)** permitting not only inconsistent, but excessively high MTTLOIs at

---

[584] The 3.24J default output for the ten year old appears to be based on an anomalous 1.25J relative constant in lieu of the usual 1.0J (3.24J ÷ 2.59 = 1.25J) and thus an anomalous 3.24 MTTLOI in this age category instead of the 2.59 emitted for all other age categories on the MECTA JR/SR 2.

[585] While Medcraft confines its' B-25 to circa "100Js," all three manufacturers produce and market devices which emit outputs well above 100Js, MECTA and Somatics via souped up BP devices, and Medcraft, via the B-24 SW. (See the B-24 SW in this manuscript).

Impedances below 220Ω. Whereas MECTA and Somatics ignore the APA 110J ceiling allowing an excessive cumulative output of up to 260 joules, particularly striking in the older age categories, the Medcraft interpretation permits 99J at all Impedances enabling absurdly excessive MTTLOIs (up to 99 fold threshold) in the younger age categories. The new ceiling for MECTA and Somatics second generation BP devices permits a circa 2.5 MTTLOI for all age categories in lieu of the 1.1 MTTLOI indicated by the APA Standard (Food and Drug Administration, 1986A, p.145). The Medcraft B-25 on the other hand, has wildly varying MTTLOIs from a maximum 99 MTTLOI in the youngest age category to a maximum 1.0 MTTLOI in the oldest age category.

In sum, Medcraft ignores both the "70J at 220Ω" phrase within the APA Standard and even the later "100J at 220Ω" as an ER/RRC, thereby disregarding a uniform MTTLOI for all age categories and thus ignoring age-related gradational outputs. MECTA and Somatics, conversely, acknowledge the ER/RRC principle within the APA Standard, thus incorporating age-related gradation via a uniform MTTLOI, but grossly surpass the APA 110J ceiling more than doubling the 1.1 MTTLOI maximum indicated by the 1982 APA Standard. Thus, Medcraft violates the APA Standard in one way, MECTA and Somatics another.

In ignoring the ER/RRC principle of the APA Standard, the Medcraft B-25 device, as noted, can be set for a 99 MTTLOI in the youngest age category while in breaching the 110J APA ceiling, made-for-America second generation MECTA and Somatics devices emit up to 260 joules of cumulative output in the oldest age category. Whereas the Medcraft device must reach its 99J ceiling inordinately quickly relative to Impedance in the younger age categories (emitting far too much output in far too brief a period) thereby requiring ramping, second generation MECTA and Somatics devices, though uniform, emit more than two and a half times the APA's indicatory MTTLOI maximum in every age category. Contrariwise, the Medcraft B-25, like MECTA and Somatics BP devices, not only disregards the consistent 1.1 MTTLOI indicated by the APA Standard thereby failing to decrease outputs with decreasing age, but MTTLOI on the B-25 counterintuitively increases with decreasing age resulting in settings as perilously unregulated as the B-24 SW. Conversely, though administering a uniform MTTLOI in accordance with the APA Standard, second generation MECTA and Somatics BP devices emit circa 2.3 fold the 1.1 MTTLOI indicated by the Standard in every age category. Indeed, as already noted, default emissions of second generation MECTA and Somatics BP devices actually surpass the 200J cumulative output of SW.

Common sense dictates the proper interpretation of the 1982 APA Standard is as the standard indicates, a "70J at 220Ω" conditional-ER/RRC, compelling uniformly decreasing outputs relative to uniformly decreasing age in accordance with a conditional 110J overall ceiling specifically limiting all outputs to a 1.1 MTTLOI or just above threshold output in all age categories (Department of Health and Human Services, 1982a, A53, E20). Plainly, then, the heart of the 1982 APA interpretation is consistent with minimal stimulus induced adequate seizures in all age categories, in essence, the least amount of electricity possible to induce a so-called adequate grand mal seizure for every age recipient. This commonsense explanation of the APA Standard is based on the presence of a conditional--ER/RRC with clear 110J output ceiling, a ceiling incorporative of the oldest recipient--the 100 year old adult. Weiner himself, before the FDA, appears to tout Brief Pulse as never needing more than 100 maximum Joules to adequately seize any recipient. The disparate Medcraft vs. MECTA/Somatics dynamic then, clearly reflects partially adherent, partially deviant interpretations of the same 1982 APA Standard. Tellingly, the fact that these interpretations are directly oppositional is suppressed through manufacturer "equivalency" charts submitted by all three manufacturers (discoverable within 510K files submitted to the FDA). Indeed, contrasting interpretations of the 1982 APA Standard are artfully concealed through manufacturer reporting of the same (approximate) "100J at 220Ω" phraseology. The uniform reporting of the same circa "100J at 220Ω" phrase submitted by all three manufacturers, falsely suggestive of a uniform interpretation and, in fact, a uniform adherence to both the conditional-ER/RRC principle and the 110 Joule ceiling, therefore the 1982 APA Standard itself, appears deliberate, a supposition bolstered by Machine Readouts of circa 100 maximum joules depicted on all made-for-America second generation BP devices manufactured by all three companies, including the Medcraft B-25. These readouts are false with respect to two of the three manufacturers and misleading with respect to the third. Indeed, uniform depictions of circa 100J maximums in conjunction with uniform reports of circa "100J at 220Ω" submitted by all three American manufacturers of (second generation) BP devices, camouflage inconsistent, improper, half-licit, starkly divergent interpretations of the same 1982 APA Standard. Medcraft's partially correct, partially incorrect interpretation of the same APA Standard conforming to one-half the 1982 Standard, as opposed to MECTA's and Somatics' partially-correct, partially incorrect interpretation conforming to the other half of the same 1982 Standard, even while all three report virtually identical "100J at 220Ω" phrases and the same circa 100J maximum Machine Readout on all three American made second generation BP devices, strongly intimates conspiracy to conceal starkly conflicting construals of the same APA Standard in order to 1) covertly violate the standard and 2) cover up the violation. The false parity reporting of two wholly antithetical types of Brief Pulse devices based on two antithetical stratagems cannot have been generated but conspiratorially. Clearly, the APA Standard is composed of a single two pronged Standard guaranteeing just above threshold titration level outputs for all age categories, the aim of which is to regulate machines to the reliable induction of adequate convulsions with the least amount of electricity possible. Only through adherence to both prongs simultaneously, does the APA standard, originally designed by Weiner and originally condoned by FDA, insure adequate seizure "efficacy" with the greatest possible safety. In effect, the standard clearly regulates ECT devices to minimal stimulus, dependably induced adequate seizures. That each manufacturer interpretation is comprised of an opposing, complementary element of the standard itself while all three claim device equivalency bespeaks of intent to deceive. Such divergent stratagems each concealing what the other lacks, cannot have been but deliberately devised in order that all three manufacturers might covertly circumvent the APA Standard generally, each camouflaging the other's neglect to conform to both prongs simultaneously. [586]

The Illusion of "New and Improved"

It is Medcraft's, MECTA's, and Somatics' gross underreporting of what appears to be a "100J at 220Ω" conditional-ER/RRC with circa 100J ceiling seemingly corroborated with the reporting of circa "100J" machine Readout maximums, in short, the deceptive assertion of minimal stimulus by all three manufacturers' uniform reporting of a circa "100J at 220Ω" ER/RRC with circa "100J ceiling" that underpins the very good possibility of conspiratorial deception. It is this seemingly uniform reporting, in fact, which has actively engendered the illusion that all modern day American manufacturers of second generation BP adhere to both the ER/RRC principle and the 110J ceiling mandated by the 1982 APA Standard. In turn, it is the illusion that each manufacturer adheres to both prongs of the 1982 APA Standard and thus a maximum 1.1 MTTLOI, in short, minimal stimulus output in all age categories, which reinforces the long-held notion that the Brief Pulse device generally, remains a great improvement over SW by virtue of greatly reduced output, half that of the 200J SW device. In sum, it is the uniform reporting of circa "100J at 220Ω" by all three American manufacturers of second generation BP devices together with uniform 100J Readout depictions which has made the totally false notion of reduced Brief Pulse power so enduring. Finally, it is the misleading reporting of "100J at 220Ω" by all three manufacturers which has led to the ubiquitous belief that the use of Brief Pulse generally is an enormous improvement over the infamously, well known annihilative effects of Brief Pulse's predecessor, the ill-reputed Sine Wave device.[587]

Modern BP vs. SW

Because the pure-ER/RRC principle is incorporated into MECTA and Somatics' BP devices, the discarding of the 110J ceiling results in higher and higher cumulative outputs translating into higher and higher MTTLOIs for every individual recipient and this trend is ongoing with third generation Brief Pulse devices as we shall witness in Volume II. The anomaly of the Medcraft B-25 BP device in spite of its seemingly low 99J maximum output, because of its discarding of ER/RRC, constitutes a device almost as dangerous device as SW due to an even higher MTTLOI potential in the younger age categories. Because of partial (as opposed to whole) adherence to the APA Standard, in short, all modern day second generation and above BP devices not only fail to diminish dangerousness compared to SW, but in many cases, actually enhance dangerousness compared to SW by virtue of increased power and MTTLOI. Equally alarming is the continued utilization of SW devices (i.e. the Medcraft B-24) proffering no improvement over the devastating memory dysfunction associated with the same

---

[586] It is no coincidence that the one manufacturer, Medcraft, which holds its' BP device (the B-25) to 99 actual Joules, continues to produce and market the alleged 200J B-24 SW device.

[587] What have categorized the B-25 Brief Pulse device as second (and in some cases third) generation even though it is limited to a circa 100J maximum due to its high MTTLOI in some age categories. In fact, second generation MECTA and Somatics devices report the same circa 100J maximum (via Machine Readout maximums) while actually emitting more than two and a half times that output.

device introduced into the U. S. circa 1950 by Medcraft and no improvement over a similar device by the Ruben Reiter Company more than seven decades ago! (Cameron 1994). [588] [589] Certainly, the utilization of enhanced Brief Pulse devices by MECTA, Somatics, and Medcraft along with the continued utilization of the powerful B-24 SW by Medcraft supports the suspicion that the modern day Brief Pulse device was either ingenuously resurrected in order to bypass the FDA or was soon understood to be ineffective and so very quickly devolved into a much more powerful device, eliciting even higher Multifold Threshold Titration Level Output Intensities generally, than the SW device it was purported to have replaced.

Discrepant Interpretations of the 1982 APA Standard Continued

As noted, the APA Standard is actually based on a "70J at 220Ω" conditional-ER/RRC (limiting outputs generally to "70J at 220Ω" relative to outputs at all other Impedances up to 600Ω), but with an overall specific ceiling of 110 maximum Joules further refining gradational outputs to a uniform 1.1 MTTLOI maximum for all age categories. That is, the "70J at 220Ω" figure compels gradational outputs with respect to age (or Impedance) further refined to a 1.1 MTTLOI based on the conditional 110J APA ceiling as opposed to the 100J relative threshold constant for the most seizure recalcitrant recipient--the 100 year old male--the single category to which the 110J ceiling can be applied. Reiterated, because the MTTLOI must be uniform, a single MTTLOI must be applied to all age categories and that single uniform MTTLOI must be based on the lowest MTTLOI possible, here specifically the APA output ceiling of 110J divided by the 100J minimum output required to seize all recipients in the oldest old category. In short, no age recipient can be administered more than a (110J ÷ 100J =) 1.1 MTTLOI. [590] (Whatever MTTLOI is used for the 100 year old male for any specific Brief Pulse device must be used for all other age categories so long as the it is 1.1 or under.) This maximum 1.1 MTTLOI based on the 110J APA ceiling and the 100J threshold constant for the 100 year old male is the APA standard's guarantee that all treatments are to be confined to minimal stimulus (or just above seizure threshold) output in all age categories.

Though acknowledging the maximum 110J ceiling, Medcraft's interpretation of the APA Standard as a Pure-Ceiling, disregards the APA "70J at 220Ω" and even the newly devised "100J at 220Ω" as an ER/RRC phrase; instead, utilizing the 110J figure both within the APA Standard and within the newly coined phraseology, "100J at 220Ω" as a 100J ceiling at *all* Impedances. While Medcraft's recognition of the APA Standard's 110J ceiling conforms to the overall maximum output clearly stipulated within the APA Standard itself then, Medcraft's interpretation of the 110J APA ceiling as allowable at ***all*** Impedances (for which Medcraft then chooses 99J "to be more in accordance with MECTA")--is not only suspect, but insupportable. In brief, Medcraft's transmogrification of the APA "70J at 220Ω" conditional-ER/RRC with "110J" ceiling into a "99J at 220Ω" Pure-Ceiling (permitting 99J at all Impedances), thereby eliminating gradational output relative to age or Impedance, is regulatorily ridiculous. Indeed, Medcraft's elimination of any ER/RRC concept whatsoever, permits Medcraft's B-25 to reach its' 99J ceiling at all ages, including the very youngest. As a result, the B-25 can potentially emit much higher outputs in the younger age categories than either MECTA or Somatics second generation BP devices even without MECTA's or Somatics' recognition of the 110J ceiling. In brief, the B-25 can emit much more electricity and thus much more power much sooner and at much higher titration levels in the younger age categories than both MECTA and Somatics second generation BP devices.

Both MECTA and Somatics, on the other hand, while acknowledging both "70J at 220Ω" as well as the less licit "100J at 220Ω" phrase as the expected ER/RRCs they appear to be, ignore these phrases as ***Conditional***-ER/RRCs (limited to a 110J ceiling or 1.1 MTTLOI). Instead, MECTA and Somatics interpret them as ***Pure***-ER/RRCs with respect to maximum machine Impedances. Unlike Medcraft, therefore, both MECTA and Somatics acknowledge ER/RRC, but dismiss the 110J ceiling clearly specified within the APA Standard. MECTA's dismissal of the APA 110J ceiling via its interpretation of "70J at 220Ω" as a ***Pure***-ER/RRC is, like Medcraft's conflicting interpretation, extremely suspect. Indeed, MECTA's fantastic metamorphosis of the APA

---

[588] The Medcraft B-24 SW is virtually the same Medcraft SW device utilized in the U.S. since 1950 (Cameron 1994).

[589] The effect of eliminating ER/RRC even in spite of maintaining a 100J ceiling is excessive multifold threshold dosing for persons under 50 years of age.

[590] Manufacturers use relative threshold constants to determine uniform outputs with respect to age or Impedance and 100J is the relative threshold constant for the oldest recipient, the 100 year old male.

"70J at 220Ω" Conditional-ER/RRC with "110J" absolute ceiling guaranteeing a 1.1 MTTLOI or minimal stimulus output in all age categories, into a "100J at 220Ω" Pure-ER/RRC disposing of the "110J" ceiling, like Medcraft, effectively disposes of required minimal stimulus outputs in all age categories. Indeed, newly based on a Pure-ER/RRC interpretation of the newer "100J at 220Ω" phrase to the APA Impedance maximum of 600Ω in lieu of the standard's 110J ceiling, [591] [592] MECTA and Somatics give themselves transmutational "permission" to create second generation BP devices up to 273 maximum Joules or a 2.73 MTTLOI. This new never before reported ceiling covertly ushered in second generation Brief Pulse devices with default MTTLOIs up to 2.59 fold threshold in every age category.

Stark Contrast Continued

More succinctly, the MECTA/Somatics Pure-ER/RRC transmogrification, while retaining the ER/RRC aspect of the 1982 APA Standard and so uniform dissemination of gradational outputs with respect to age, nevertheless bypasses the Standard's 110J ceiling and so implied 1.1 MTTLOI or minimal stimulus guarantee in all age categories. Instead, MECTA newly raises the APA 110J APA ceiling to an unreported 273J and thus the 1.1 MTTLOI into a newly expanded 2.73 MTTLOI (100J/220Ω= 273J/600Ω) for all age categories. This starkly contrasts with the Medcraft interpretation of "99J at 220Ω" in which its BP device is limited to 99 absolute Joules, while discarding the ER/RRC aspect of the 1982 APA Standard, and so gradational output, thereby "allowing" its 99J ceiling to be administered to even the youngest recipients.

Thus, the Medcraft second generation BP device (unlike MECTA and Somatics second generation BP devices) is limited to 99J, more or less restricting outputs at Impedances greater than 220Ω, the older age categories, but permitting irresponsibly high outputs and thus super high MTTLOIs at Impedances less than 220Ω, in the younger age categories. In brief, MECTA and Somatics retain the ER/RRC concept of the APA Standard, but grossly surpass the APA 110J ceiling, so that their second generation devices deliver up to a 2.6 MTTLOI in lieu of the APA 1.1 MTTLOI maximum created to guarantee minimal stimulus output in all age categories, while Medcraft retains the 110J ceiling, but ignores the ER/RRC safeguard so that the younger age categories can be administered up to a 99 MTTLOI in lieu of the same APA 1.1 MTTLOI maximum created to guarantee minimal stimulus output in all age categories. Plainly, while these two interpretations are totally oppositional, neither MECTA/Somatics nor Medcraft adheres to the whole 1982 APA Standard, indeed, critically breaching in opposing manners the APA's minimal stimulus guarantee for all age categories. Without this minimal stimulus guarantee, the critical intention of the 1982 APA Standard fails.

Winding Up the B-25 Compared to other Second Generation Brief Pulse Devices

Let us accept the change of "70J at 220Ω" within the 1982 APA Standard to circa "100J at 220Ω. " At 150Ω, in accordance with a 99.4 ER/RRC application of approximately "99.4J at 220Ω," the Thymatron DG cannot emit more than a 68J output.

$$99.4J/220\Omega = XJ/150\Omega.\ X = 68 \text{ Joules.}$$

In fact, at 150Ω, the Thymatron DG emits an actual default maximum of 23 Joules (see Thymatron DG Chart). This lower EO is due to the refining influence of a uniform MTTLOI, in this instance a 2.52 MTTLOI multiplied by the aforementioned relative threshold constants in every age category. In contrast, at the same 150Ω, the B-25 can emit up to 99J, an ER/RRC transgression not only of the APA's "70J at 220Ω", but even of the more liberal "100J at 220Ω" ER/RRC, a breach of 51J and 32J respectively and an even greater breach

---

[591] Indeed FDA investigators Stephen M. Hinkley (Food and Drug Administration, 1986A) and Harold Walder (Food and Drug Administration, 1985) never seemed to recognize the breaching of the APA 110J ceiling or the fact and significance of dismissing ER/RRC. These kinds of oversights imply a lack of understanding of how the 1982 APA standard is supposed to work exacerbated by Weiner's ingenious aptitude for successfully confusing regulators.

[592] Conspicuous charts within the APA Standard itself point out the 100J ceiling of BP compared with the 200J ceiling of SW (Department of Health and Human Services, pp. G-3 - G-4).

given the refining influence of a uniform MTTLOI. [593] In creating the B-25's capacity to reach 99J at even the lowest B-25 Impedance of 150Ω; therefore, we can see that Medcraft has altogether dismissed any notion of ER/RRC, much less a uniform MTTLOI. Indeed, dispersant non-uniform MTTLOIs are administered to every age category.

In conclusion, while, the B-25 limits overall output to 99J, the B-25 is capable of reaching 99J far faster relative to Impedance than either MECTA or Somatics second generation BP devices, that is, the B-25 is capable of emitting far more output relative to Impedances below 220Ω than either MECTA or Somatics devices, the latter two of which adhere to ER/RRC and thus a uniform MTTLOI. Importantly then, the ER/RRC concept governs (a) gradation of power relative to age (b) maximum electrical dosage per individual recipient and (c) finally, degree of output over threshold (based on the refining influence of a uniform MTTLOI and the never before reported relative threshold "constants"). As ER/RRC increases from "70J at 220Ω" to "100J at 220Ω" for example, so does electrical EO over threshold, but only moderately. Thus, it is the ignoring of the 110J ceiling which permits gross increases in MTTLOI in both MECTA and Somatics devices. Nevertheless, the MTTLOI is consistent throughout all age categories in both MECTA and Somatics BP devices; whereas, there is no age-related MTTLOI uniformity administered with the Medcraft B-25 BP device. This is because the Medcraft B-25 dismisses ER/RRC altogether and so, as already noted, can deliver a 99 MTTLOI to the youngest age recipient (age ten) while only delivering a 1.0 MTTLOI to the oldest age recipient (age 100).

Medcraft attempts to explain the necessity of "ramping" on its B-25 as a different function than so-called "glissando" on its B-24 SW, plainly used to "soften the blow" of the otherwise precipitous power of the B-24, a device which can elicit dangerously high suprathreshold outputs to younger age recipients. On the B-25, what appears to be the same phenomenon for the same purpose is explained in Medcraft 510K pre-market submission files as a technique to prevent burning of the skin which, according to Medcraft, can allegedly occur at even low currents and low Voltages (Food and Drug Administration 1986A. pp 9-14. See letter to FDA from Medcraft Representative James K. Seafort). According to Medcraft, in short, "ramping" on the B-25 is supposedly used to prevent burning of the skin. The explanation is inadequate. No such technique is necessary with either MECTA or Somatics BP devices and, in fact, according to Weiner, the technique is both unnecessary and archaic. The absence of "ramping" or "glissando" in MECTA and Somatics BP devices can logically be attributed to gradationally distributed outputs on these devices with respect to age, in turn, based on a uniform MTTLOI for all age recipients. This dynamic is due to their acknowledgement of the ER/RRC precept facilitating gradational output relative to Impedance resulting in much lower output maximums for younger individuals than older Individuals. Conversely, as noted above, by discarding ER/RRC, the Medcraft B-25 can deliver its maximum output (of 99 Joules) to even the youngest recipient, a phenomenon eerily similar to the B-24 SW. It is clearly this ignoring of the APA ER/RRC concept, moreover, which necessitates "ramping," or "glissando" in light of the inordinately high suprathreshold outputs delivered in the younger age categories, giving credence to the suspicion that the B-25 Brief Pulse device is simply a more powerful re-make of the B-24. In short, the B-25 appears to contain many of the same features and problems of the B-24 except in Brief Pulse form. Indeed, the B-25, like the B-24, retains the capacity to deliver inordinately high outputs in the 10 to 40 year old age categories, a preference, perhaps, for a specific physician clientele. In sum, the "ramping" mechanism" of the B-25 in all likelihood, serves the same function as the "glissando" of the B-24 and for the very same purpose--gradually gliding into unusually high Voltages applied to recipients with unusually low Impedances. Clearly, the purpose of both is to prevent injury due to the precipitous elicitation of extremely high electrical outputs in the youngest age categories.

Indeed, only a B-25 Brief Pulse machine set at a "minimum" output of a probable circa 10 MTTLOI in the youngest age category can explain the much higher than ordinary 150Ω minimum Impedance for the ten year old child, just as only a 99 MTTLOI maximum can explain the higher probable 200Ω maximum Impedance for the same ten year child on the same B-25 Brief Pulse device. In a word, only the failure to adhere to uniform gradational outputs and thus the bypassing of the 1.1 MTTLOI stipulation can explain such unusually high Impedances for both "minimum and maximum settings in the youngest age category. In short, only very high outputs delivered to individuals with the very lowest Impedances can explain the unusually high Resistances in the younger age categories, necessitating ramping. After all, ten year old recipients can be made to seize at only about one joule on all constant current BP devices, rarely exhibiting more than about a 50Ω Impedance maximum. Indeed, the fact that the B-24 SW can elicit its 200J maximum in the ten year old age category and

---

[593] 70J/220Ω = XJ/150Ω X = 47.72J.99 - 47.72 = **51J**.100J/220Ω = XJ/150Ω X = 68J.99 - 68 = **32J**.

the B-25 BP its 99J maximum in the same ten year old category is a common feature of both the B-24 SW and the B-25 BP. At the same time, the 200J maximum output emitted by the B-24 SW as opposed to the 99J maximum output emitted by the B-25 BP is misleading. What must be taken into account is that the ten year old recipient may seize at about 8 Joules with the less efficient Sine Wave device as opposed to about 1.0 Joule with the much more efficient Brief Pulse device. As previously noted, this increase in Brief Pulse efficiency can be used to reduce the output and so the MTTLOI needed to elicit a so-called "adequate seizure" compared to SW. But it can also be exploited to increase the MTTLOI with much less total output than SW. Though using half the maximum output of SW; therefore, that is, in spite of the fact that the B-24 SW can elicit a potential 200 Joules as opposed to the B-25's 99 Joule maximum in the same ten year old age category, it is due to the greater efficiency and power of Brief Pulse that the ten year old child can be administered an even more unconscionable 99 MTTLOI with the B-25 BP device (at maximum output) than the (nevertheless unconscionable) 23 MTTLOI with the B-24 Sine Wave device (at maximum output). Indeed, it is due to the 1) Medcraft B-25's capacity to elicit its 99 Joule maximum output in even the youngest age category, and the 2) enhanced efficiency of the BP device over SW that the B-25 Brief Pulse device is able to elicit a much greater MTTLOI than the B-24 in every age grouping. In spite of the B-25 emitting a maximum of 99 Joules, half the output of the 200 Joule potential of the B-24 SW then, because the Medcraft B-25 Brief Pulse dismisses gradational output, the advantage of Brief Pulse as a reduced output device over SW is not only lost, but its' greater efficiency is exploited, actually enhancing the MTTLOI compared to SW in every age category. This is a clear example of the inverse application of Brief Pulse efficiency. Indeed, the B-25 performs all the undesirable activities of the B-24, except more powerfully (MTTLOI-wise) and thus as destructively. In brief, while all modern day Brief Pulse devices are perilous, the B-25, like the B-24 SW, is anomalously treacherous in the younger age categories, the B-25 BP at least as much as the B-24 SW.

In sum, all American made second generation Brief Pulse devices are dangerously suprathreshold and thus ENR (as opposed to ECT) devices, achieving their aim of adequate electricity in diversely opposing ways. While second generation MECTA and Somatics devices as well as Medcraft's B-25 Brief Pulse device all violate the 1982 APA Standard in order to circumvent the standard's minimal stimulus regulatory aim in all age categories, they do so in starkly disparate ways. Thus, while all made-for-America second generation Brief Pulse machines fail to adhere to the 1982 APA Standard, while all are dangerously suprathreshold, and while none are ECT or minimal stimulus devices, because the B-25 Brief Pulse device achieves its illicit power by violating one part of the APA standard and MECTA and Somatics Brief Pulse devices achieve their illicit power by violating a wholly different aspect of the APA standard, Medcraft cannot claim its B-25 Brief Pulse device comparable to second generation MECTA and Somatics Brief Pulse devices; neither can MECTA and Somatics claim their second generation Brief Pulse devices comparable to the B-25. On the other hand, both are designedly ENR devices.

CHAPTER 40

A Few Comparative Charts

The Chart below compares maximum settings on Medcraft's B-24 SW with maximum settings on Medcraft's B-25 BP. Note how the B-24 can reach 200 joules, but cannot maintain this power even at maximum settings due to deteriorating Amperage with respect to Impedance. The B-25, on the other hand, while not surpassing 100J, can, due to constant current, maintain its 99J output maximum regardless of increasing Impedances due to increasing age.

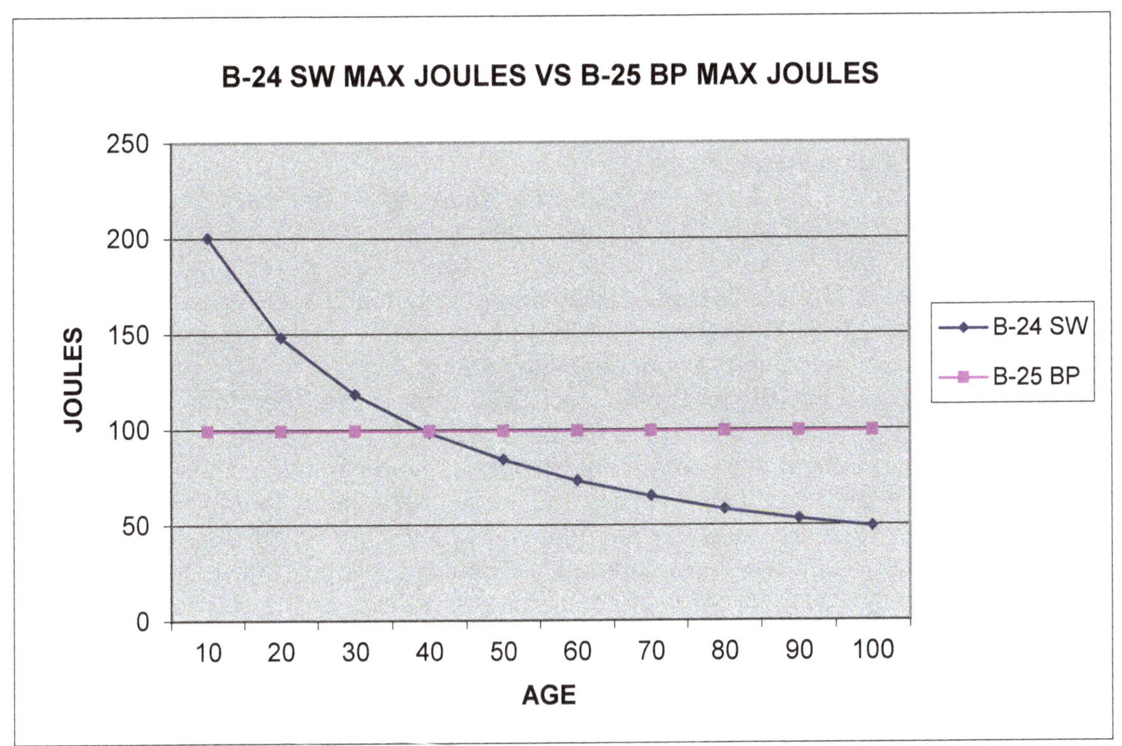

Now, on the chart below, observe the MTTLOIs for the B-24 SW and the B-25 BP both at maximum settings. In spite of the capacity of the B-24 SW to elicit 200J in the lowest age category, the B-25 BP surpasses the power of the B-24 SW with respect to MTTLOI in every age category.

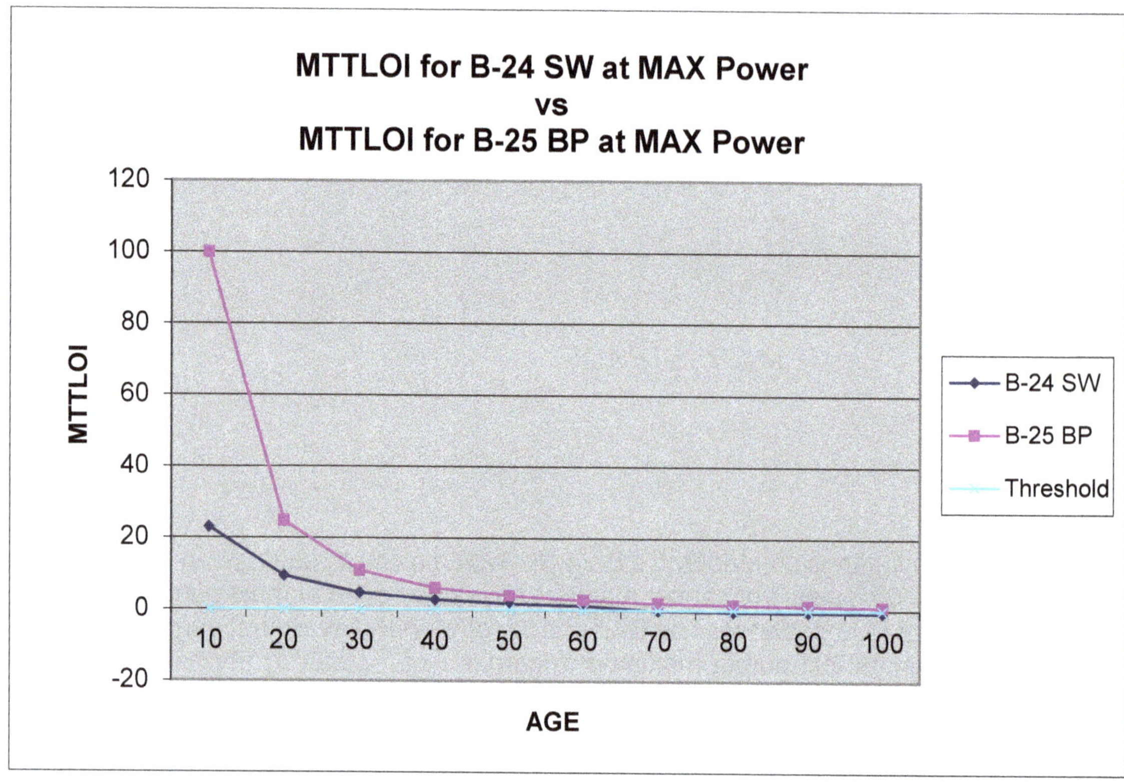

Medcraft, in building its B-25 Brief Pulse, appears to have created a device which though similar, is more efficient, more powerful, and more insidious than the B-24. In short, though technically Brief Pulse, the B-25 is but a more powerful version of the B-24 Sine Wave device.

For example, MTTLOIs for both for the B-24 and the B-25, are inconsistent, illogically decreasing with increasing age and increasing with decreasing age. Due to the constant current of a Brief Pulse device as opposed to the deteriorating current of SW; however, the B-25 can elicit a greater MTTLOI than the B-24 in every age category. Moreover, because of Medcraft's Pure-Ceiling interpretation of the APA Standard for Brief Pulse devices wherein Medcraft ignores ER/RRC, like the B-24 SW, no regulatory principle prohibits the B-25 BP from emitting the machine's maximum output in the youngest age category.

The effect of Medcraft's ignoring the ER/RRC principle for its B-25 Brief Pulse, therefore, is the B-25's potential for emitting electrical outputs incorporative of excessive MTTLOIs for those individuals with Impedances under 220Ω; that is, for younger age recipients, in fact, anyone under sixty years of age. Consequently, as noted, it is due to the B-25 capacity to emit output so quickly relative to Impedance, that is, its capacity to emit such high outputs at such low Impedances - that unlike any other Brief Pulse device, the B-25 BP device must integrate a "ramping" mechanism (a "gradual" 0.5 second glide or "glissando" up to the required Voltage before the actual "treatment"), in order to ameliorate the effects of the B-25's prodigiously precipitous power. [594] [595] Thus, because the B-25 is "allowed" to emit very high outputs, in fact, its highest output in the very youngest age category, like the B-24, a "ramping" or "glissando" mechanism must be used to soften the blow of abruptly excessive suprathreshold force, particularly for those with the lowest resistance to electricity--the younger age recipients. In sum, due to Medcraft's discarding of ER/RRC and so discarding of regulatory gradational age-related output maximums, the B-25, like the B-24, is capable of electrical dosages far in excess of minimal stimulus in the younger age categories. [596] Conversely, it is due to the discarding of

---

[594] The glissando on the B24 SW, added between .8 Seconds and 1.0 seconds to the 1.0 Second SW device, possibly adding (under remote circumstances, i.e. low Impedance) an additional 89 Joules.

[595] "Ramping" occurs before "treatment" begins; whereas, "glissando" can overlap "treatment," but that appears to be the single difference.

[596] Electrical dosing (amount of electrical output) used should decrease with decreasing age in that there is a direct correlation between increasing age and increasing resistance to electricity. Note how on the B-25 device, though never surpassing 99 joules, output can remain at the same 99J maximum for all age categories. As we can see, MECTA and Somatics devices utilize gradational age-related

the 110J APA ceiling, that MECTA and Somatics BP devices, unlike the B-25, emit excessive suprathreshold outputs in all age categories (though not as excessive as the B-25 in the younger age categories).

The following chart displays MECTA's uniform (and so gradational MTTLOIs) as opposed to the extreme disparate MTTLOIs (depicted here) at maximum settings for both the B-24 SW and the B-25 BP. Note how the B-25 BP does not look like MECTA BP devices, but is simply a more powerful form of the B-24 SW.

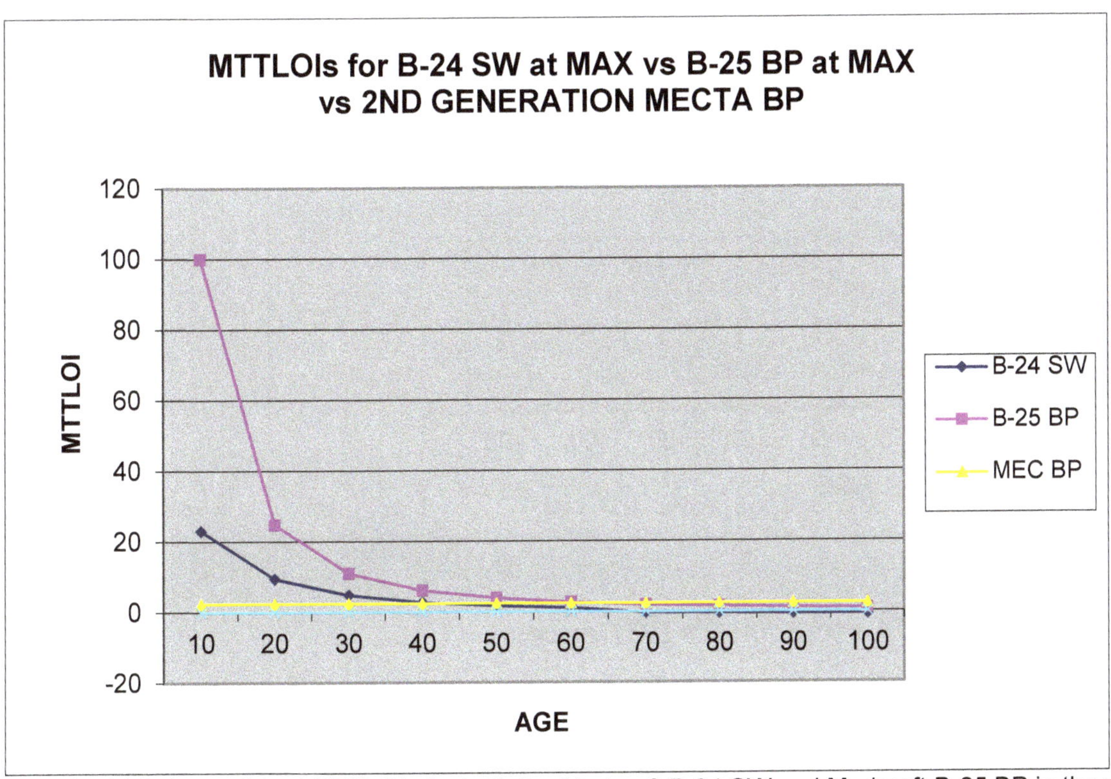

Note the high, inconsistent MTTLOIs for both the Medcraft B-24 SW and Medcraft B-25 BP in the younger age categories as opposed to second generation MECTA (and Somatics) BP devices which emit consistent default MTTLOIs of circa 2.5 in all age categories. Though the B-24 is more powerful than the B-25 with respect to overall output (100 versus 200 joules), the B-25 is more powerful than the B-24 with respect to MTTLOI. This is due to the inverse exploitation of the more efficient B-25 Brief Pulse device in conjunction with its violation of ER/RRC. Ironically, whereas the B-24 SW and B-25 BP are comparable; neither the B-24 SW nor the B-25 BP are comparable to MECTA (and Somatics) second generation BP devices.

B-25 vs second generation MECTA JR 1 and 2

The chart below displays how the B-25 BP device, ignoring ER/RRC, can be set at maximum output to deliver its 99J maximum to all age recipients (including the ten year old child) as opposed to the default settings of second generation MECTA (and Somatics) Brief Pulse devices which, though seriously surpassing the APA 110J ceiling, administer uniform gradational outputs with respect to age and so gradually rise in output relative to age.

---

outputs, but surpass the 110J ceiling, whereas, the B-25 device maintains the "110J" ceiling, but ignores ER/RRC. Both violate the APA Standard in oppositional manners.

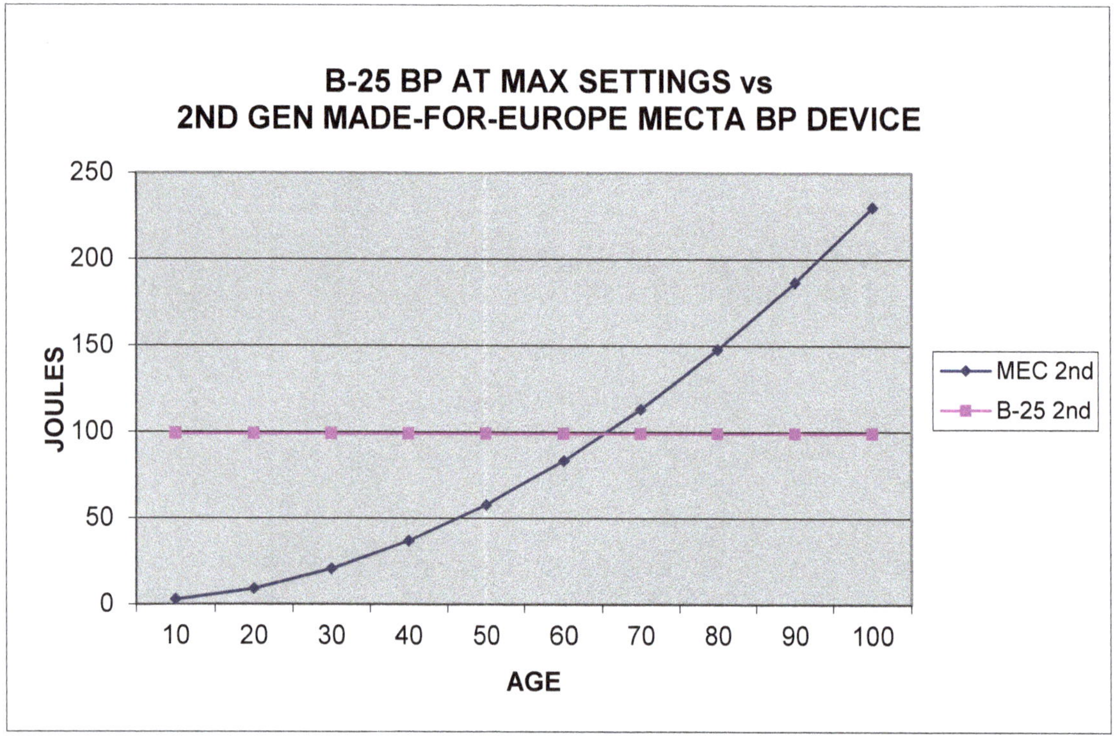

B-25 vs Second Generation MECTA and Somatics BP Devices

The following chart shows the gradational default outputs (in joules) of MECTA and Somatics 2nd generation BP devices circa 2.5 MTTLOI against the non-gradational outputs of the B-25 set for maximum output in all age categories. Note how MECTA and Somatics outputs gradually rise with age whereas the Medcraft device ignores ER/RRC with respect to age. Strangely, like the B-24, the B-25 administers unconscionable outputs in the lower age categories, becoming more and more impotent with increasing age.

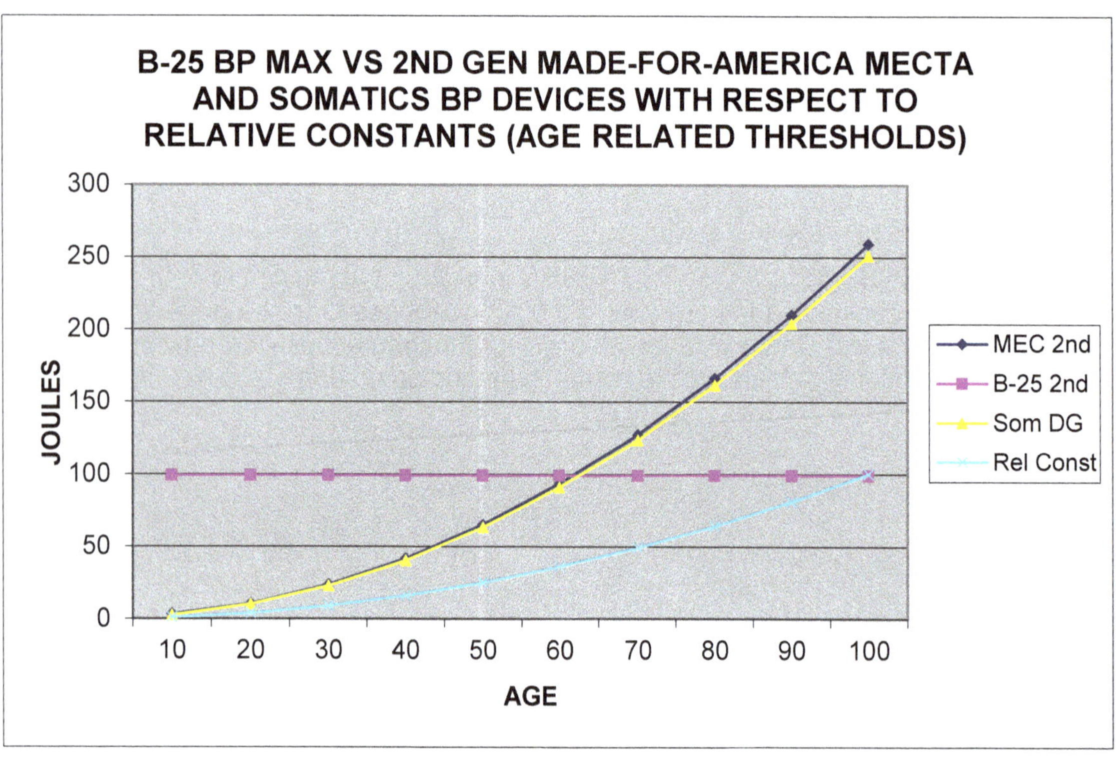

The following chart displays MECTA and Somatics uniform and so gradational MTTLOIs for their second generation BP devices as opposed to the extreme disparate MTTLOIs of Medcraft's B-25 Brief Pulse device.

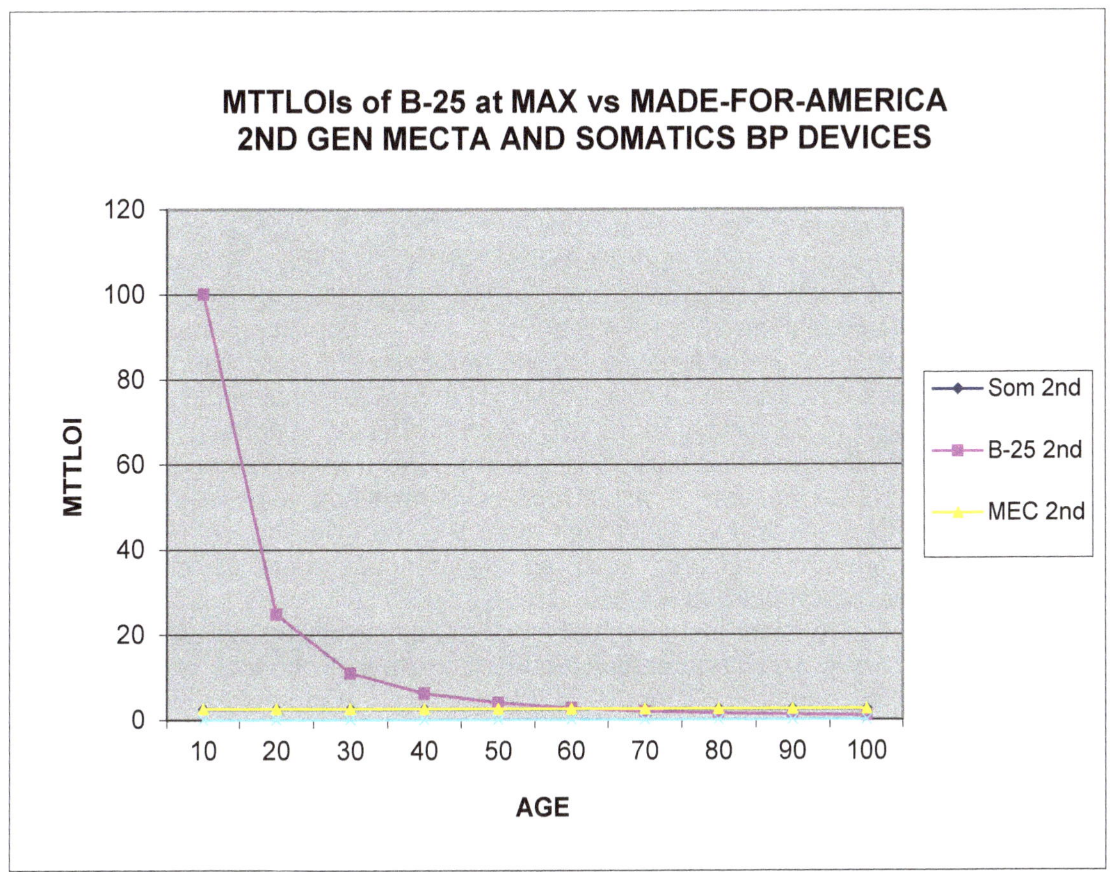

While MECTA and Somatics second generation BP devices utilize consistent 2.59 and 2.52 MTTLOIs respectively for all age categories, the inconsistent MTTLOI potentials of the B-25 in the younger age categories are so high (100 fold threshold at maximum settings in the ten year old age category) that the respective uniform MTTLOI for MECTA and Somatics second generation BP devices (deceptively) appear just above threshold on the above chart.

Conclusion: Medcraft's Pure 100J Ceiling Vs MECTA and Somatics Pure-ER/RRC Interpretation of the Same Reported "100J at 220Ω" Phrase for Second Generation Brief Pulse Devices

While the recognition by Medcraft of a 99J (albeit Pure) ceiling gives credence to the interpretation of the 1982 APA Standard's 110J ceiling and even suggests an interpretation of MECTA's newly devised phrase "100J at 220Ω" as incorporative of a circa 100J ceiling, unlike Medcraft, MECTA's and Somatics' interpretation of the same "100J at 220Ω" phrase as an ER/RRC (albeit Pure-ER/RRC), gives credence to the APA's "70J at 220Ω" as well as the later "100J at 220Ω" phrase as an ER/RRC. Medcraft, as noted, recognizes the Absolute ceiling of 110J, but ignores ER/RRC, grossly violating the APA Standard at Impedances below 220Ω, while MECTA and Somatics recognize ER/RRC within the same APA Standard, but ignore the 110J APA ceiling (manifestly surpassing the 110J ceiling at Impedances above 220Ω). Thus, Medcraft's violation consists in applying up to 99J at all Impedances (ages), even those below 220Ω, while MECTA and Somatics' violation consists in surpassing 110J. specifically at Impedances above 220Ω (thereby violating minimal stimulus output in all age categories). In sum, Medcraft violates the APA implied uniform MTTLOI while MECTA and Somatics violate the 110J ceiling. In short, both Medcraft and MECTA/Somatics, disparately violate the APA Standard, but violate it they do. In spite of these disparate violations, however, all three manufacturers report the same approximate "100J at 220Ω," spuriously implying a uniform 100J at 220Ω conditional-ER/RRC, uniform 110J maximum output, and thus uniform application of minimal stimulus output for all age categories. The explanation that the uniform reporting of "100J at 220Ω" merely describes maximum output at 220Ω justifies neither starkly conflicting interpretations nor stark violations of the APA Standard by all three manufacturers.

Indeed, uniform reporting of "100J at 220Ω" implying that all three manufacturers produce comparable second generation BP devices limited to the 110J maximum and a circa "100J at 220Ω" conditional-ER/RRC, that is, uniformly gradational outputs with a 110J cap and so a 1.1 MTTLOI minimal stimulus output in all age categories is shrewdly deceptive. Indeed, as discussed, it is an illusion bolstered by all three BP manufacturers depiction of circa 100 maximum Joules on their various second generation BP devices via maximum Machine Readouts. In fact, as has been discussed, only one company, Medcraft, adheres to the 110J ceiling (with its B-25 BP device) albeit a Pure Ceiling (meaning 99J maximums in all age groups) instead of Conditional ceiling (in which 99J is administered in the oldest category alone). Conversely, the other two manufacturers adhere to a "100J at 220Ω" ER/RRC, albeit Pure (based on maximum machine Impedance) instead of Conditional (with 100-110J overall ceiling). Succinctly, one of the interpretations (of the 1982 APA Standard) is based upon a 99J Pure-ceiling while the other is based on a "100J at 220Ω" Pure-ER/RRC. Tellingly, Medcraft's Pure-99J ceiling (sans ER/RRC) versus MECTA's and Somatics' Pure-ER/RRC (sans 110J ceiling) are perfectly antithetical, both of which, however, circumvent the 1982 APA Standard, even as both interpretations together create the overall false impression that all made-for-America second generation BP devices conform to the 1982 APA Standard as minimal stimulus devices limited to a 1.1 MTTLOI in all age categories. In short, the illusion of agreement creates the illusion of conformity to the APA Standard chiefly penned by Weiner and presented to the FDA in 1982. Stated differently, the illusion of uniform concurrence creates the illusion of conformity to the standard's minimal stimulus mandate. In actual fact, as we have now witnessed, the opposite holds true. The three companies' devices are only in agreement regarding the following: None of the three manufacturers' devices are based on adequate seizure; rather, all three manufacturers' devices, though in antithetically disparate fashions, are based on adequate amounts of electricity. All three manufacturers hide this truth in that numerous studies have shown that the degree of electricity administered over and above that necessary to induce an adequate seizure is directly proportional to the cognitive dissonance experienced by recipients, very likely to the amount of brain damage. It is for this very reason that a standard mandating minimal stimulus dosages of electricity and so minimal stimulus ECT devices via Brief Pulse was initially proposed under FDA auspices; indeed, minimal stimulus outputs in all age categories was the paramount idea behind a purported "new and improved" reduced output Brief Pulse device and so the regulatory mandate to elicit adequate seizures with the least amount of electricity possible. In short, it was to reduce or eliminate damage that a standard was ultimately proposed, a standard regulating the power of ECT devices to the induction of adequate grand mal seizures with the least amount of electricity possible. Such outputs were to be delivered, moreover, with reduced output Brief Pulse exclusively. In sum, the 1982 APA Standard was specifically designed to assure that ECT treatment for depression and other mental anomalies would only be performed with the reduced output and so much less dangerous, new and improved Brief Pulse device regulated to emitting the least amount of electrical energy possible to induce the adequate grand mal seizure. Unfortunately, because there is no therapeutic effect from a so-called adequate seizure, manufacturers either already knew or soon realized that it is adequate amounts of electricity alone that produces the looked for changes in mood and behavior psychiatrists look for. To remain in business then, manufacturers were forced to hide the true power of their devolved Brief Pulse devices. Indeed, the true, hidden aim of what are actually ENR (or adequate electricity) devices is quite simply, enough brain damage to achieve the looked for effect, an aim only achievable through "controlled," but nevertheless, sufficient amounts of electricity to accomplish the unsavory aim. In brief, to achieve the short term anti-depressant and somewhat longer term behavioral effect practitioners seek, the electrical "dosaging" of these machines has to be high enough to effectuate somewhat "controlled" damage to the brain. More scientifically stated, the electrical output of the modern Brief Pulse device must be high enough and prolonged enough to destroy or compromise enough synaptic connections in recipients' left pre-frontal lobe to effectuate the behavioral and mood altering result aimed at by practicing physicians (Perrin et al., p 5464), a process not always understood by the physicians themselves.

CHAPTER 41

MECTA, Somatics, and Medcraft--Machine Readouts

Regardless of arguments Somatics and MECTA might make to "justify" the Mectan Transmutation of the 1982 APA Standard's "70J at 220Ω" Conditional-ER/RRC with 110J ceiling into a "100J at 220Ω" Pure-ER/RRC with implicit 273J ceiling, almost tripling ceiling outputs and thus the MTTLOIs administered by second generation BP devices,[597] and regardless of what arguments Medcraft might make to "justify" its unique transmutation of the same "70J at 220Ω Conditional-ER/RRC with 110J ceiling into a Pure-110J-ceiling with no ER/RRC and so no uniform MTTLOI whatsoever, no explanation can adequately defend their mathematical manipulations. For example, there can be no plausible vindication of MECTA and Somatics [598] supplanting actual Impedance for an "average 220Ω" Impedance in every age category to misleadingly depict Machine Readouts from second generation BP devices as circa 100 maximum Joules. Neither can Medcraft adequately justify reporting its maximum output of 99 Joules, but failing to reveal the B-25's capacity to administer 99J in every age category, a tactic which misleadingly suggests the B-25 a reduced output device compared to SW. In fact, the B-25 can surpass SW in cumulative power from ages 40 to 100 and even the MTTLOI of SW in every age category. These deceptive tactics which make second generation MECTA, Somatics, and Medcraft BP devices appear to conform to the minimal stimulus stipulations of the 1982 APA Standard are indefensible. Finally, neither MECTA nor Somatics have made any objection to Medcraft's claim that its B-25 BP device is comparable to MECTA and Somatics second generation BP devices. Neither has Medcraft complained that MECTA and Somatics devices surpass the 110J APA ceiling. Partial adherence to the APA Standard together with misleading reporting by all three manufacturers is not only inordinately deceitful, and inordinately unethical, but inordinately injurious not only to recipients who agree or who are made to take the procedure based on such false and misleading information, but to family members and even administering physicians. Plainly, Machine Readouts of the same circa 100 Joule maximum by all three extant American BP manufacturers of second generation BP devices is suggestive not only of uniform conformity to the 1982 APA Standard, but of uniformly reduced output apparatuses designed to assure minimal stimulus outputs in all age categories.

The illusion of 100J maximum BP devices suggestive of minimal stimulus output in all age categories, clearly creates the perception that all three Brief Pulse manufacturers are creating much safer devices than SW under the auspices the APA Standard (Department of Health and Human Services, 1982a, pp. G3-G4). In fact, the one American manufacturer which actually does limit its BP device to approximately 100J--Medcraft—does so through elimination of ER/RRC and thus elimination of a uniform MTTLOI, delivering minimal stimulus output to but one single age category--the 100 year old adult. Indeed, why have none of the three Brief Pulse manufacturers called for the banning of the B-24-SW? In fact, Medcraft is the single manufacturer (both in America and the U. K.) which, in spite of its manufacturing of the B-25 Brief Pulse, continues to produce the same 200J SW device unabated. It can do so, moreover, in that neither MECTA nor Somatics nor Medcraft ever asked for the official adoption the 1982 APA Standard which called for the replacement of SW with Brief

---

[597] 100J/220Ω = 273J/600Ω. This interpretation allows MECTA and Somatics BP devices to emit more energy output than SW devices.

[598] In lieu of actual outputs at varying Impedances, machines, through the use of reverse ER, are made to readout EOs limited to circa 100J. For instance, the Thymatron DG reads out 99J even at an Impedance of 555.5Ω. The process occurs by the machine's automatically substituting 220Ω for the actual Impedance, thereby obtaining a misleading ER-Readout.251J/555.5Ω = XJ/220Ω. X = 99.4 Joules.

Pulse. Why, in fact, with so-called "safer" BP devices produced by all three manufacturers does Medcraft continue making and marketing its B-24-SW well into the twenty-first century?

To recap then, while Medcraft actually limits its B-25 to circa 100J (without clearly revealing the machine's capacity to elicit the maximum 99J in even the youngest age category), Somatics and MECTA devices emit outputs approaching 250J while spuriously reporting circa 100J maximums via misleading Machine Readouts. Both methods Pure-Ceiling and Pure-ER/RRC extremely deceptive as both intentionally circumvent the APA Standard's minimal stimulus regulatory aim. In light of this deception, let us focus for a moment on the Machine Readouts depicted on all American made second generation BP devices.

Machine Readouts

The B-25 alone [599] (of made-for-America second generation BP devices) though ignoring gradational age-related outputs, limits output to 99 Joules per the 1982 110J APA Standard stipulation. All other (later) second generation made-for-America BP devices, MECTA's SR1 @ 2 and Somatics' Thymatron DG, emit outputs up to 260 Joules. In spite of this, Readouts (perceived by physicians) on MECTA and Somatics (as well as Medcraft) second generation BP devices, deceptively depict approximately 100 maximum Joules--101.4J (MECTA), 99.4J (Somatics), 99 (Medcraft). Thus all three extant manufacturers of made-for-America second generation BP devices, devices roughly equivalent in dangerousness via extremely disparate breaches,[600] nevertheless depict uniform, extremely deceptive circa 100J maximum outputs on their second generation Brief Pulse machine Readouts. [601]

Machine Readouts on all second generation made-for-America BP devices, display ceilings of circa 100 maximum Joules. The three companies achieve these readouts either by an actual maximum emission of circa 100 Joules (Medcraft) while grossly violating a different regulatory dynamic, or by placing misleading information into the machines' computers so that the computers calculate and display all Readouts derived from a false constant Impedance of "220Ω" (MECTA and Somatics). Amazingly, this false 220Ω "constant" replaces all actual Impedances, in turn skewing machine readouts. MECTA's and Somatics' use of a misleading 220Ω constant results in what appear to be relatively uniform age-related Readouts up to about 100 maximum Joules. [602] The appearance of a maximum 100 Joules both in reporting circa "100J at 220Ω" and the circa "100J" depicted as maximum output via Machine Readouts by all three manufacturers, falsely suggest a Conditional-ER/RRC interpretation of the circa "100J at 220Ω" phrase reported by all three manufacturers, [603] that is, a "100J at 220Ω" conditional-ER/RRC incorporating a 100 or 110J overall ceiling in accordance with the APA Standard. Such an interpretation simulates the 1982 APA Standard of a "70J at 220Ω" ER/RRC with a conditional 110J ceiling, leaving regulatory agencies, physicians, the media, and certainly the public at large assuming actual 100J maximums and thus minimal stimulus outputs for all American made second generation BP machines. Re-stated, the assumption of a "100J at 220Ω" conditional-ER/RRC (with 100 or 110J ceiling) for all second generation BP devices implies a consistent MTTLOI of 1.0 or 1.1 in all age categories, deceptively engendering the notion of minimal stimulus output for all American made second generation BP devices. (This

---

[599] Almost certainly, the defunct Company Elcot, also violated the APA Rate Rise Ceiling.

[600] The B-25 is potentially more dangerous for persons under 65 compared to both the MECTA and Somatics devices which nevertheless appear equally dangerous for all age categories due to a uniformly excessive MTTLOI. This is due to the B-25's absence of ER/RRC and the absence of the 110J ceiling for MECTA and Somatics BP devices. On the B-25, potential MTTLOI decreases with increasing age, whereas, on the Somatics and MECTA devices, output increases with increasing age to maintain the MTTLOI. The excessive output is bot circumstances is due to increasing seizure resistance with increasing age and decreasing resistance with decreasing age.

[601] An argument can be made that the B-25 is the most dangerous amongst the three second generation BP devices it violates ER/RRC and so can emit a massive amount of electrical energy in the most vulnerable age category. Nevertheless, all second generation BP devices grossly exceed the power necessary to elicit adequate seizures, thus all should be considered dangerous and none should be considered convulsive therapy or ECT devices, but rather ENR devices based not on adequate seizure, but on adequate doses of electricity (Cameron, 1994).

[602] Like MECTA and Somatics, Ectron may utilize spurious Machine Readouts, but us not dealt with here.

[603] Medcraft (within closed 510K files and difficult to obtain MECTA manuals) claims to interpret its' reported "99J at 220Ω" to mean the B-25 elicits 99J specifically at 220Ω as well as a maximum 99J at all other Impedances.

includes not only American made, made-for America second generation BP devices, but American made, made-for-Europe second generation BP devices.

Plainly, the actual or misleading reporting of Machine Readouts limited to approximately 100J maximums juxtaposed with uniform reporting of circa "100J at 220Ω" by all three American BP manufacturers is deliberate, and thus conspiratorial. [604]

It must be pointed out that Medcraft overtly and directly reports a true maximum output of 99 Joules for its B-25 Brief Pulse, but, in fact, allows 99J at all Impedances up to its' 325Ω or possibly 350Ω maximum Impedance. However, while allowing a 99J maximum output potential at all machine Impedances, according to charts submitted by Medcraft (to the FDA), unlike MECTA and Somatics devices, Duration incrementally diminishes as Voltage and Impedance increase. This is necessary in order for the B-25 Brief Pulse device to maintain its 99J ceiling from youngest to oldest recipient (see Medcraft 510 K files). The Medcraft B-25 BP alone, then, (although ignoring ER/RRC) appears to contain accurate Readouts of between (a probable) 9.9 to 99 maximum joules. In order to fully appreciate the character of the B-25 BP device and the MECTA and Somatics BP devices, the never before reported relative age-related threshold constants manufacturers use for all modern day BP devices (including the B-25) are once again, listed below:

Age-Related Relative Threshold Constant x MTTLOI = Default Output (for the Thymatron DG)

10 year old male =	**1.00J**	**x 2.52 =**	**2.52J**
20 year old male =	**4.004J**	**x 2.52 =**	**10.09J**
30 year old male =	**9.00J**	**x 2.52 =**	**22.68J**
40 year old male =	**16.00J**	**x 2.52 =**	**40.32J**
50 year old male =	**25.00J**	**x 2.52 =**	**63.00J**
60 year old male =	**36.00J**	**x 2.52 =**	**90.72J**
65 year old male =	**42.25J**	**x 2.52 =**	**106.47J**
70 year old male =	**48.97J**	**x 2.52 =**	**123.40J**
80 year old male =	**64.00J**	**x 2.52 =**	**161.28J**
90 year old male =	**81.00J**	**x 2.52 =**	**204.10J**
100 year old male =	**100.00J**	**x 2.52 =**	**252.00J**

As noted, multiplying each relative constant by the MTTLOI gives us the default output emitted for that particular age category by that particular BP machine.

The B-25, as noted, is the single Brief Pulse device limited to an actual 99 Joules. Unlike MECTA and Somatics BP devices, however, this 99 Joules, as noted, can be emitted to any age recipient, including the ten year old child. Thus, the B-25's MTTLOIs are anything but gradational and anything but uniform. Indeed, the limiting of output to 99 Joules on the B-25 tends to camouflage supra-excessive dosing in the younger age categories. Thus, while the B-25 apparently depicts outputs via Machine Readouts accurately, it grossly supersedes ER/RRC safeguards stipulating gradational outputs in accordance with a uniform MTTLOI for all age recipients, thereby emitting both excessive and non-uniform MTTLOIs, particularly devastating, as noted above, in the younger age categories. [605]

In the chart below, in the first two columns, the B-25 maximum machine readouts are compared to actual maximum outputs used at all Impedances or ages. While the Machine readouts on the B-25 appear to be accurate, the correlating MTTLOIs seen here, have never been reported and so are not made available to practicing physicians. Indeed, based on relative constants, we can see the non-uniform, non-gradational MTTLOIs in the very right hand column for each age category.

---

[604] Medcraft never reveals MECTA and Somatics surpassing of 100 joules while neither MECTA nor Somatics reveals Medcraft's 99J emission in even the youngest age category.

[605] Medcraft, on charts within hard-to-access 510K files, reports for the B-25, 99J maximums at all Impedances - specifically - 150Ω, 220Ω and 350Ω, the lowest to the highest. These correlations appear to be actual (not merely abstract ERs) and if true (because ER/RRC is ignored) represent the exception relative to MECTA and Somatics.

B-25 (Maximum)

MACHINE READOUT	ACTUAL OUTPUT	AGE	ACTUAL MTTLOI
99 J	99 J	10	99
99 J	99 J	20	24.75
99 J	99 J	30	11
99 J	99 J	40	6.18
99 J	99 J	50	3.96
99 J	99 J	60	2.75
99 J	99 J	65	2.34
99 J	99 J	70	2.02
99 J	99 J	80	1.55
99 J	99 J	90	1.22
99 J	99 J	100	1.0

The MTTLOI is determined by dividing the 99J EO delivered in each respective age category by each age-related relative constant. For example, the relative constant for the 10 year old is 1.0 Joule. Therefore, (99J ÷ 1.0J =) 99 MTTLOI. The relative constant for the 50 year old in 25J. (99J ÷ 25J =) 3.96 MTTLOI. What might be considered true minimal stimulus or just above seizure threshold is only delivered to the 80, 90, and 100 year old age categories in the chart above and only the MTTLOI delivered to the 100 year old conforms to the 1982 APA Standard. All other outputs are excessive.

In the chart below, in the first two columns, the B-25 minimum machine readouts are compared to actual minimum machine outputs used at all Impedances or ages. Though far from actual minimal stimulus in the younger age categories, machine readouts once again appear accurate. However, once again, the excessive MTTLOIs seen here in the younger age categories have never been reported and so do not appear for practicing physicians.

B-25 (Minimum)

MACHINE READOUT	ACTUAL OUTPUT	AGE	ACTUAL MTTLOI
9 J	9 J	10	9
19 J	19 J	20	4.7
29 J	29 J	30	3.22
39 J	39 J	40	2.43
49 J	49 J	50	1.96
59 J	59 J	60	1.64
64 J	64 J	65	1.51
69 J	69 J	70	1.41
79 J	79 J	80	1.23
89 J	89 J	90	1.1
99 J	99 J	100	1.0

Even at the machine's minimum stimulus settings, true minimum stimulus or just above threshold only occurs In the 60-100 year old age categories and only the MTTLOI delivered to the 90 and 100 year old conforms to the 1982 APA Standard. All other outputs, even at the B-25 minimum settings, are excessive. Moreover, because physicians do not have access to the relative constants used by manufacturers, and because outputs do not exceed 100 Joules, physicians are unlikely to notice the excessive outputs.

The second generation MECTA JR/SR 1 @ 2 represented on the chart below depicts false machine readouts in the first column, suggestive of minimal stimulus. Compare these to actual outputs delivered by the MECTA device depicted in the second column. While ages ten to thirty read higher than they actually are, and the MTTLOI seems inconsistent, due to the readout maximum of 101 Joules, the advantage lies in the overall false impression of minimal stimulus or just above threshold output for all age categories. To be clear, the false readouts appear, while actual outputs do not. Moreover, neither the false nor the actual MTTLOIs seen below appear as readouts for physicians; neither has MECTA ever made them public. In short, physicians have access neither to the MTTLOI of the device nor the relative constants used by manufacturers. Consequently, because outputs do not appear to exceed 100 Joules, physicians have no way of identifying the excessive default outputs. On the other hand, note how closely the minimal stimulus outs of the B-25 match the Machine Readouts for both MECTA and Somatics second generation BP devices.

(2ND GENERATION)
MECTA JR/SR 1 @ 2

MACHINE READOUT	ACTUAL OUTPUT	AGE	FALSE MTTLOI	ACTUAL MTTLOI
10 J	02.59 J	10	10	2.59
20 J	10.37 J	20	4.95	2.59
30 J	23.33 J	30	3.33	2.59
41 J	41.47 J	40	2.56	2.59
51 J	64.80 J	50	2.04	2.59
61 J	93.31 J	60	1.69	2.59
66 J	109.51 J	65	1.56	2.59
71 J	127.00 J	70	1.45	2.59
81.1 J	165.89 J	80	1.27	2.59
91.2 J	209.95 J	90	1.13	2.59
101.4 J	259.20 J	100	1.01	2.59

Of the 256 possible readouts depicting outputs from 10-101.4 Joules above, eleven of the misleading readouts are shown above--all Reverse-ER outputs (left hand column), perhaps better understood as outputs based on a "220Ω average. " In short, MECTA machines display these outputs based on a false 220Ω "constant" in lieu of actual outputs based on actual Impedances (seen in column 2). The result is that JR/SR 1 @ 2 false output depictions of between 10-101.4 Joules are read and assumed accurate by practicing physicians. Note how the first three Machine Readouts surpass actual outputs while all other Machine Readouts are underreports. Even so, the advantage, as noted, lies in the 101J "maximum" creating the overall impression of minimal stimulus outputs. Note too how a machine Readout of 10 joules seems comparable to "minimal stimulus" on the B-25 making the two disparate machine appear almost identical. Note too, however, the "maximum" machine readout on the MECTA JR/SR1 @ 2 of 101.4J, as opposed to MECTA's actual maximum EO of 259J, never reported to regulators, physicians, the public general, or, most importantly, recipients themselves. Indeed, the actual unreported output violates the 1982 APA ceiling Standard by approximately (259.2 - 110J =) 149 Joules emitting a 2.59 MTTLOI to all age categories (as opposed to the APA 1.1 MTTLOI stipulated by the APA Standard). [606]

To understand how MECTA derives its Machine Readouts, let us use the formula: <u>EO = Amperage x Amperage x Impedance x Pulses x Wave Length x Duration</u>. Take the example of the 70 year old recipient. By using a <u>false 220Ω constant</u> (or "average") in lieu of the actual machine Impedance for the 70 year old of <u>393.75Ω</u> (see JR/SR 2 Chart for actual machine Impedances), the JR/SR 2 Machine Readout displays a false 71J default output (for the 70 year old) in lieu of the actual default output delivered of circa 127J. In short, 71J is but an ER-figure at an ER-Impedance in lieu of the actual output delivered at the actual Impedance used for this specific age category.

<u>Actual EO</u>: = .8 Amps x .8 Amps x <u>393.75Ω</u> x 180 Pulses x .001 Wave length x 2.8 Seconds = <u>127J</u>.

<u>Machine Readout</u>: = .8 Amps x .8 Amps x <u>220Ω</u> x 180 Pulses x .001 W. L. x 2.8 Secs = <u>71J</u>.

71J is the **Reverse-ER** of the **127J** actually emitted**:** **<u>XJ/220Ω = 127J/393.75Ω = X = 71J</u>**.
(We can also think of 71J as an output based on a 220Ω average in lieu of actual Impedance.)

<u>The second generation Somatics Thymatron DG below</u>, like second generation MECTA devices above, also depicts false Machine Readouts suggestive of minimal stimulus. Compare Machine Readouts to actual outputs delivered by the Somatics DG below. Once again, while ages ten to thirty read higher than they actually are, making the unreported MTTLOI spuriously inconsistent, again the advantage of readouts depicting a 99.7J "maximum," lies in the overall false impression of minimal stimulus or just above threshold

---

606 It is extremely likely that the MECTA JR/SR devices made for Europe depict the same Machine Readouts limited to circa 100 joules.

output for all age categories. Neither false nor actual MTTLOIs seen below appear as readouts for the observing physician; neither has Somatics ever made them public. In short, physicians have access neither to the MTTLOI of the device nor the relative constants used by manufacturers. Consequently, because readouts do not exceed 100 Joules, physicians have no way of identifying excessive default outputs emitted by the device, much less any idea how much above threshold these default outputs actually are.

(2ND GENERATION)
SOMATICS THYMATRON DG

MACHINE READOUT	ACTUAL OUTPUT	AGE	FALSE MTTLOI	ACTUAL MTTLOI
10 J	02.51 J	10	10	2.52
20 J	10.09 J	20	5	2.52
30 J	22.68 J	30	3.33	2.52
40 J	40.32 J	40	2.5	2.52
50 J	63.00 J	50	2.0	2.52
60 J	90.72 J	60	1.67	2.52
65 J	106.47 J	65	1.54	2.52
70 J	123.40 J	70	1.43	2.52
80 J	161.28 J	80	1.25	2.52
90 J	204.10 J	90	1.11	2.52
99.7 J	252.00 J	100	1.0	2.52

Like second generation MECTA devices, The THYMATRON DG above displays all machine readouts based on a false 220Ω constant in lieu of actual Impedances, falsely depicting 10-99.4 joules read by physicians. Eleven settings (left hand column)--all Reverse ERs--are shown in the first column above. Unreported Actual EOs--rounded to the nearest one hundredth--can be seen in the second column. Note, while the first three Readouts slightly surpass actual outputs, all remaining Readouts are underreports. Note too, however, that the 9J over-read for the ten year old makes the Somatics device seem almost identical to the B-25 device at "minimal stimulus. " Note also, that while the Somatics Thymatron DG depicts maximum output as 99.4 or 99.7J, actual maximum EO, a never before reported 252J, violates the APA 110J ceiling standard by approximately (252J - 110J =) 142 Joules emitting a never reported 2.52 MTTLOI in lieu of the APA required 1.1 MTTLOI maximum for all age categories. Note too, the same false readouts for the slightly less powerful DGx below compared to the slightly more powerful DG above. Neither the false nor the actual MTTLOIs have ever been reported, much less made available to observing physicians. Once again, physicians have access neither to the MTTLOI of the device nor the relative constants used by manufacturers. Consequently, because output depictions do not exceed 100 Joules, physicians have no way of identifying either the excessive default outputs or inconsistent MTTLOIs. Indeed, the spurious 99.4J "maximum" creates the Illusion of minimal stimulus in conformity with the 1982 APA Standard.

To understand how Somatics derives its Machine Readouts for the DG above, let us again use the formula: EO = Amperage x Amperage x Impedance x Pulses x Wave Length x Duration. Now let us again take the example of the 70 year old recipient. By using a false 220Ω "constant" in lieu of the actual 388.8Ω that the 70 year old actually evinces (see Chart of actual DG for the 70 year old), Somatics displays 70 Joules via the Machine Readout in lieu of the actual never reported 123.4 Joules actually emitted. In short, 70J is but an ER-output at an ER-Impedance in lieu of the actual output at the actual Impedance used for this age category.

Actual EO: = .9 Amps x .9 Amps x 388.8Ω x 140 Pulses x .001 Wave length x 2.8 Sec. = 123.45J.

Machine Readout: = .9 Amps x .9 Amps x 220Ω x 140 Pulses x .001 Wave length x 2.8 Sec. = 70J.

70J is the **Reverse-ER** of the **123.45J** actually emitted. **XJ**/220Ω = **123.4J**/388.8. **X = 70J.**

The second generation Somatics Thymatron DGx below, though slightly less powerful than the DG, displays the same false machine readouts as the DG, again suggestive of minimal stimulus. Compare Machine Readout outputs to actual outputs on the Somatics DGx device below. While ages ten to thirty read higher than they actually are, and the MTTLOI is inconsistent, once again the advantage lies in the overall false impression of a 99.4J maximum creating the illusion of minimal stimulus or just above threshold output for all age categories. Neither the false nor the actual MTTLOIs seen below appear as readouts for the physician; neither has Somatics ever made them public.

(2ND GENERATION)
SOMATICS THYMATRON DGx

MACHINE READOUT	ACTUAL JOULES	AGE	FALSE MTTLOI	ACTUAL MTTLOI
10 J	02.27 J	10	10	2.27
20 J	9.072 J	20	5	2.27
30 J	20.39 J	30	3.33	2.27
40 J	36.29 J	40	2.5	2.27
50 J	56.70 J	50	2.0	2.27
60 J	81.65 J	60	1.67	2.27
65 J	95.80 J	65	1.54	2.27
70 J	111.13 J	70	1.43	2.27
80 J	145.20 J	80	1.25	2.27
90 J	183.70 J	90	1.11	2.27
99.7 J	226.80 J	100	1.0	2.27

The THYMATRON DGx above displays readouts based on a false 220Ω constant displaying misleading Machine Readouts from 10-99.4/7 Joules read by physicians in lieu of actual outputs based on actual Impedances. Eleven readouts--all Reverse ERs--are shown (in the left hand column). All Actual EOs (2nd column) rounded to the nearest one hundredth are accurate though unreported. Note once again, while the first three Readouts in the first column slightly surpass actual outputs, all remaining Readouts are underreported giving the overall impression of just above threshold outputs in all age categories. Note, however, that the readouts in the first column emulate the Medcraft B-25 at "minimal stimulus" falsely suggesting that second generation MECTA, Somatics, and MECTA machines are extremely comparable. While the maximum Readout on the DGx above is about 99 joules, in fact, the actual unreported maximum EO of 226.8J violates the 110J APA ceiling standard by approximately (226.8J -110J =) 117 Joules and more than doubles the implied MTTLOI. Note too, in spite of the slightly more powerful outputs emitted by the DG above, that the same false machine readouts displayed on the DG are also displayed on the DGx.

To understand how Somatics derives its Machine Readouts for the DGx, let us again take the example of the 70 year old recipient. By using the false "constant" of 220Ω in lieu of an actual 350Ω evinced by the 70 year old (see Chart of actual DGx), the Somatics DGx displays 70 Joules on the Machine Readout in lieu of the 111.13 joules actually emitted. Due to the 99.4/7J readout maximum, the overall impression is minimal stimulus output for all age categories in accordance with the 1982 APA Standard. In short, once again, 70J is but an ER output at an ER Impedance in lieu of actual output emitted at the actual Impedance used in this age category.

Actual EO = .9 Amps x .9 Amps x 350Ω x 140 Pulses x .001 Wave length x 2.8 Sec. = 111.13J.

Machine Readout = .9 Amps x .9 Amps x 220Ω x 140 Pulses x .001 Wave length x 2.8 Sec. = 70J.

70J is the **Reverse-ER** of the **113J** actually emitted: **XJ/220Ω = 111.13J/350Ω. X= 70J.**

Comparing Medcraft B-25 Machine Readouts to MECTA and Somatics Machine Readouts

Note how the 9J (or 10J) minimum and 99J maximum readouts on the B-25 Medcraft emulate machine readouts on both MECTA and Somatics second generation BP devices, while, in fact, the Medcraft B-25 depicts actual outputs and MECTA and Somatics devices exhibit reverse-ER outputs calculated with a "220Ω" false "constant." The illusion of all three devices emitting virtually identical minimum (circa 10J) and maximum outputs (circa 100J) suggestive that all are comparable devices emitting minimal stimulus outputs in all age categories in accordance with the 1982 APA Standard bodes deception and conspiracy.

In fact, MECTA and Somatics BP devices emit default outputs from the youngest to the oldest categories of between 2.52 and 259 Joules both with a uniform 2.52 and 2.59 MTTLOI in all age categories while the B-25 emits between 9 and 99 Joules with a variety of MTTLOIs from 99 (youngest) to 1.0 (oldest). In short, the machines are starkly disparate. The illusion of comparableness is partly created by plugging a false constant Impedance of 220Ω into both Somatics and MECTA second generation machines, thereby supplanting actual default outputs with Reverse-ER outputs displayed on all MECTA and Somatics second generation Machine Readouts, Readouts comparable to actual outputs emitted by the B-25 at minimal settings. In short, it is the substitution of actual outputs with Reverse-ER outputs on second generation MECTA and Somatics devices compared to minimal settings on the B-25 which helps create the illusion of minimal stimulus outputs emitted by all second generation BP devices manufactured by all three American companies in all age categories in accordance with the 1982 APA Standard. The impression of similarity is further enhanced with the reporting of circa "100J at 220Ω" by all three manufacturers. However, the illusion of comparableness is exactly that--illusion. Below, compare B-25 minimum settings with MECTA and Somatics Reverse-ER Readouts on all second generation BP devices to see the illusion of similarity. Next, compare either B-25 minimum or maximum settings with the actual default outputs of second generation MECTA and Somatics devices to see the disparateness.

Machine Readouts for all Second Generation made-for-America BP Devices vs. Actual Outputs

AGE	B-25 min. **Actual**	MECTA **Readouts**	Somatics **Readouts**	B-25 max. **Actual**	MECTA **Actual**	Somatics **Actual**
10	9J	10J	10J	99J	2.59J	2.51J
20	19J	20J	20J	99J	10.4J	10.1J
30	29J	30J	30J	99J	23.3J	22.7J
40	39J	41J	40J	99J	41.5J	40.3J
50	49J	51J	50J	99J	64.8J	63J
60	59J	61J	60J	99J	93.3J	90.7J
65	64J	66J	65J	99J	109.5J	106.5J
70	69J	71J	70J	99J	127J	123.4J
80	79J	81J	80J	99J	165.9J	161.3J
90	89J	91J	90J	99J	210J	204.1J
100	99J	101J	99.4J	99J	259.2J	252J

As noted above, Minimum Machine Readouts on the B-25 together with Reverse-ER Machine Readouts on all second generation MECTA and Somatics BP devices create the illusion of similar just above threshold outputs in all age categories. This, in turn, is suggestive of adherence to the "70J at 220Ω" conditional-ER/RRC with 110J ceiling depicted via the 1982 APA Standard. In fact, the Medcraft B-25 can emit up to 99J in all age groups and so up to a 99 MTTLOI in even the youngest age category while MECTA and Somatics devices emit default outputs of 259 and 252 joules respectively and so a uniform 2.59 and 2.52 MTTLOI in all age categories respectively. Capable of emitting a 99 MTTLOI in the youngest age category, in short, the Medcraft B-25 has little in common with second generation MECTA and Somatics BP devices designed to emit default, uniform MTTLOIs of 2.59 and 2.52 respectively in every age category, all of which breach the 1.1 MTTLOI implied by the 1982 APA Standard.

In spite of Machine Readouts depicting circa 100J maximums on all second generation BP devices, therefore, Readout maximums of 101.4J and 99.4J on MECTA and Somatics devices respectively are not actual maximum outputs at all; whereas, the Medcraft depiction of its 99J maximum is actual, but in all age categories. [607] The MECTA and Somatics reported phrases of approximately "100J at 220Ω" are Pure-ER/RRCs with respect to maximum machine Impedances of 562 and 555Ω allowing ceiling outputs of 259.2J and 252J respectively. Antithetically, Medcraft's report of the same circa "100J at 220Ω" is a Pure-Ceiling and thus a literal 99J not only permitted at 220Ω, but at all Impedances or age categories. In short, the Medcraft B-25, as we have seen, can emit its 99J maximum in every age category. Put differently, in that the Medcraft B-25's "99J" maximum can be reached at all Impedances, Medcraft's reported "99J at 220Ω" is no way reflects

[607] Medcraft, on charts within hard-to-access 510K files, reports 99J maximums at all Impedances - specifically - 150Ω, 220Ω and 350Ω, the lowest to the highest B-25 Impedance. These correlations appear to be actual (not merely abstract ERs). Because ER/RRC is ignored, 99J at all Impedances represents a stark deviation with respect to MECTA and Somatics BP devices.

an ER/RRC compelling decreasing output with regard to decreasing age (as do MECTA and Somatics devices). Antithetically, the maximum Machine Readout of circa 100J on all American made second generation machines manufactured by all three American companies--Medcraft, MECTA, and Somatics--is actual only on the Medcraft device. On second generation MECTA and Somatics devices, the circa 100J "maximum" is but a reverse-ER. In spite of this, the reporting of the same circa "100J at 220Ω" phrase together with the same circa 100J Machine Readout maximum on all American-made second generation BP devices, helps create the powerful illusion of uniform, age-related minimal stimulus outputs emitted by all second generation BP devices made by all three American BP manufacturers. As such, all three deceptively appear to conform to the minimal stimulus requirements of the 1982 APA Standard. Succinctly then, comparable readouts of circa 100J maximums and comparable reports of circa "100J at 220Ω" falsely suggest a uniform "100J at 220Ω" conditional-ER/RRC incorporative of a circa 100 or 110J overall ceiling, in turn suggesting minimal stimulus or just above threshold outputs for all age recipients via all American made second generation BP devices. In short, all appear to conform to the 1982 APA Standard. The entire appearance, of course, is wholly Illusory.

The "coincidental" reporting, sans explanation, of the "100J" figure both nationally and internationally (circa the 110J ceiling contained within the 1982 APA Standard) is strongly associated with minimal stimulus output in all age categories. In fact, 100J used by Medcraft as a Pure-Ceiling and derived via Reverse-ER by MECTA and Somatics, allowing the Medcraft device to emit supra-gross outputs in the younger age categories, and MECTA and Somatics devices suprathreshold outputs in all age categories--is clearly conspiratorial.

Indeed, all three American manufacturers fail to report MTTLOI thereby generating the misleading impression that all American made second generation BP devices continue to retain the reduced output, minimal stimulus outputs they were initially touted to maintain, falsely suggesting that Brief Pulse is yet a major improvement over SW. In addition, the illusory effectiveness of minimal stimulus Brief Pulse shields the myth of convulsion theory itself; whereas, the actual power manufacturers utilize for their devices, clearly debunks the convulsion theory hypothesis.

Regulatory agencies, the public, academics via scholarly publications, and even practicing psychiatrists continue to believe that all second generation made-for-America BP devices are minimal stimulus apparatuses and thus greatly improved over SW (Department of Health and Human Services, 1982a, A53; E20; G3-G4). The reverse is true. In fact, uniform Machine Readouts of approximately "100J" and uniform reports of approximately "100J at 220Ω" by all three American BP manufacturers for their second generation BP devices are not only extremely misleading, but strongly suggestive of conspiracy. The truth is that neither the B-25 nor second generation MECTA and Somatics BP devices are "ECT" devices at all in that neither aim at adequate convulsion with the least amount electrical energy possible. Indeed all are electro-dependent in that none work on the premise of adequate convulsion efficacy, but rather efficacy of adequate amounts of electricity. Machines based on adequate doses of electricity in lieu of the least amount of electricity possible to induce the adequate convulsion can only have one purpose. That is, adequate doses of electricity can only serve to achieve what we shall generously deem controlled brain damage resulting in microscopic synaptic damage generally undetectable even via MRI, nevertheless, provable through Perrin-like prospective MRI neurotransmitter studies. In short, deliberate damage occurs to microscopic neurotransmitters as a result of excessive amounts of electrical output grossly reducing neurotransmissions, specifically within, and to and from the left pre-frontal lobe (Perrin et al., 2012).

The modern Brief Pulse device, just as the SW devices of the past then, actually reduce neurotransmissions through adequate amounts of electricity. That is, they are ENR or Electro Neurotransmission Reduction devices, the aim of which is reduction of neurotransmissions through electrical destruction of transmitters mainly in the recipient's left prefrontal lobe. With enough damage, with enough reduction, physicians are generally able to effect short term changes in mood in almost all recipients and (more or less) longer term changes in behavior in others. If forced to compare, the aim of ENR appears to most closely resemble a partial, pre-frontal lobotomy, but with more refined damage occurring on a much more microscopic level. Indeed, because gray matter is not actually destroyed as in the case of pre-frontal lobotomy, re-growth of neurons may be possible, but most likely, only after a considerable period of time.

The B-24 SW, an ENR device which can accomplish this same task from age 10 to about age sixty, appears to remain unchanged to the present and this is due to the failure to outright ban the B-24 in turn due to what appears to be a quiet agreement amongst all three manufacturers. Because both have hidden agendas, none have called for the B-24's discontinuation nor have any called for adoption of the 1982 APA Standard. It is because the B-24 is still in use today without APA or manufacturer objection that there appears to be no real pressure for Medcraft to aggressively market its B-25 Brief Pulse, really a new, more powerful form of the B-24. On the other hand, MECTA and Somatics devices, as Medcraft is no doubt aware, continue to devolve into more and more powerful Brief Pulse ENR devices, as we shall continue to see in Volume II in sections describing third, fourth, and even fifth generation Brief Pulse devices. Worth noting, all three manufacturers--Medcraft, MECTA, and Somatics--were represented from 1976-1982 and even more recently to the FDA by a single individual--electrical engineer, psychiatrist, APA Task Force President, primary author of the 1982 APA Standard itself, and finally, primary author of the current default international standard (as we shall see in Volume II)--Dr. Richard Weiner.

PART V

SECTION VII: "Safety" and "Efficacy" Studies

CHAPTER 42

Studies Comparing Brief Pulse to SW in Terms of Safety and Efficacy

Modern day comparative studies of "ECT" during what the author shall deem "the modern BP (Brief Pulse) era," include comparisons of BP to SW and a few prospective (before and after) studies with BP alone. Most, however, compare BP to SW, almost always showing equal efficacy and greater safety with BP. In fact, all the following comparative studies represent Brief Pulse as relatively harmless compared to SW, but equally effective, generating this now accepted conclusion in the literature.

Indeed, modern studies comparing BP with SW can be placed into two basic categories: 1) Safety and 2) Efficacy. Safety studies include investigation of memory and possible organic damage as a result of "ECT"; whereas, efficacy studies include the procedures' final outcomes, usually in terms of depression. Sometimes, a combination of cognitive and organic testing is used in one population. For example, the study tests for safety followed by a second study of the same population testing for efficacy. Thus, a single population is often divided into two separate studies authored by two mostly different teams of researchers, one evaluating safety, the other efficacy. For this reason, the studies sometimes overlap. A more than ample sampling of the studies listed below, which include prospective MRI publications, have been thoroughly evaluated by the author. To avoid repetition, it is the selected studies--those marked with stars—which have been analyzed and commented on by the author.

Safety Studies:

Cognitive Studies incorporate cognitive instruments for testing of memory retention and dysfunction, such as verbal and non-verbal memory loss, as well as retrograde and anterograde amnesia. These precedent setting cognitive studies include:

**Effects of electroconvulsive therapy upon brain electrical activity* (Weiner, Rogers, Davidson and Kahn,1986a)

**Evaluation of the central nervous system risks of ECT,* (Weiner, Rogers, Davidson, and Miller, 1982);

**Autobiographical amnesia with ECT: An analysis of the roles of stimulus wave form, electrode placement, stimulus energy, and seizure length* (Daniel, Weiner, and Crovitz, 1983);

**Cognitive consequences of low-dosage electroconvulsive*

therapy (Sackeim, Portnoy, Neeley, Steif, Decina, and Malitz,1986)

Effects of stimulus intensity and electrode placement on the efficacy and cognitive effects of electroconvulsive therapy. (Sackeim, Prudic, Devanand, Kiersky, Fitzsimmons, Moody, McElhuney, Coleman, and Settimbrino, 1993).

Organic Studies of the Brain testing for organic damage. Precedent setting organic studies include:

Prospective[608] EEG studies

**Autobiographical amnesia with ECT: An analysis of the roles of stimulus wave form, electrode placement, stimulus energy, and seizure length.* (Daniel, Weiner, and Crovitz, 1983);

**Effects of electroconvulsive therapy upon brain electrical activity.* (Weiner, Rogers, Davidson and Kahn, 1986a);

**Evaluation of the central nervous system risks of ECT.* (Weiner, Rogers, Davidson, and Miller, 1982);

**Effects of stimulus parameters on cognitive side effects, in electroconvulsive therapy.* (Weiner, Rogers, Davidson, and Squire, 1986b),

Retrospective CT scans

Computer Tomographic Scans in ECT-patients. (Kolbeinson, Arnaldson, Peturrson, and Skulason, 1986);

**Structural abnormalities in cerebral cortex of chronic schizophrenic patients* (Weinberger, Torrey, Neophytides, and Wyatt, 1979b),

Prospective CT scans [609]

**Electroconvulsive therapy and cerebral computed tomography: A prospective study.* (Bergsholm, Larsen, Rosendahl, and Holsten, 1989),

Restrospective MRI scans

**Leukoencephalopathy in elderly depressed patients for ECT.* (Coffey, Figiel, Djang, Cress, Saunders, and Weiner, 1988b);

**Subcortical hyperintensity on magnetic resonance imaging: a comparison of normal and depressed elderly subjects.* (Coffey, Figiel, Djang, Weiner, 1990a);

Electroconvulsive therapy of depression in patients with white matter hyperintensity. (Coffey, C. E. , Hinkle, Weiner, Nemeroff, Krishnan, Varia, and Sullivan, 1987a);

Quantitative cerebral anatomy in depression: A controlled

---

[608] "Prospective" means testing before and after the procedure; "retrospective" means testing only after the procedure.

[609] While both SW and BP have been utilized in CT and MRI scans, such scans do not usually compare SW with BP, but rather compare the brain to itself retrospectively or prospectively. There is but a single partially prospective MRI (and CT) study comparing SW with BP to be discussed later within this report.

magnetic resonance imaging study. (Coffey, Wilkinson, Weiner, Parashos, Djang, Webb, Figiel, and Spritzer, 1993);

Subcortical hyperintensities on magnetic resonance imaging: Clinical correlates and prognostic significance in patients with severe depression. (Hickie, Scott, Mitchell, Wilhelm, Austin, and Bennett, 1995);

**Cortical magnetic resonance imaging changes in elderly inpatients with major depression.* (Rabins, Pearlson, Aylward, Kumar, and Dowell, 1991);

Structural brain abnormalities in bipolar affective disorder: Ventricular enlargement and local hyperintensities. (Swayze, Andreasen, Alliger, Ehrhardt, and Yuh, 1990).

<u>Prospective MRI scans</u>

**MR imaging prior to and following electroconvulsive therapy in patients with major affective disorders.* (Braffman, Grossman, McCallister, Price, Gyulai, Atlas, Hackney, Goldberg, Bilaniuk, and Zimmerman, 1988);

**Effects of ECT on brain structure: A pilot prospective magnetic resonance imaging study.* (Coffey, Figiel, Djang, Sullivan, Herfkens, and Weiner, 1988a);

**Cerebral and brain stem changes after ECT revealed by nuclear magnetic resonance imaging.* (Mander, Whitfield, Smith, Douglas, and Kendell, 1987);

**Brain anatomic effects of electroconvulsive therapy: A prospective magnetic resonance imaging study.* (Coffey, Weiner, Djang, Figiel, Soady, Patterson, Holt, Spritzer, and Wilkinson, 1991b);

**A preliminary magnetic resonance imaging study of ECT-treated depressed patients.* (Pande, Grunhaus, Aisen, and Haskett, 1990);

**Time course of cerebral magnetic resonance changes after electroconvulsive therapy.* (Scott, Douglas, Whitfield, and Kendell, 1990). [610]

**Electroconvulsive therapy reduces frontal cortical connectivity in severe depressive disorder.* (Perrin, Merz, Bennett, Currie, Steele, Reid, and Schwarzbauer, 2012).

<u>Non-Prospective Animal Studies-modern</u>

**Absence of biological lesions in primate models of ECT and magnetic seizure therapy.* (Dwork, Arango,

[610] Note the dearth of autopsy studies (in the BP Era, from 1976 forward) and, as pointed out by Dr. Peter Breggin (1991), the total absence of animal studies. Both Dr. Friedberg (1976; 1977) and Dr. Breggin (1979; 1991) pointed out that many researchers discovered brain damage in such studies. In the BP era, detractors from Friedberg and Breggin claimed staining techniques, antiquated methodology, i.e. lack of oxygenation, and high dosing invalidate findings in animals and autopsied humans (Devanand, Dwork, Hutchinson, Bolwig, and Sackheim, 1994). Nevertheless, advocates of "ECT" in the new BP era have not included any new such experiments in modern safety studies.

Underwood, Ilievski, Rosoklija, Sackeim, and Lisanby 2004).

Efficacy Studies:

These studies are primarily composed of Cognitive and Subjective testing for effective outcomes of the procedure usually with respect to depression.

Self-Rating Scales for measuring the anti-depressant effect include:

Hamilton Depression Rating Scale (HDRS)

Effects of electroconvulsive therapy upon brain electrical activity (Weiner et al, 1986a);

**Efficacy of ECT in the treatment of depression: Wave form and electrode placement considerations.* (Welch, Weiner, Weir, Cahill, Rogers, Davidson, Miller, and Mandel, 1982, p.32);

**The Efficacy of Electroconvulsive Therapy: Dose-Response Interractions With Modality* (Malitz, Sackeim, Decina, Kanzler, and Kerr, 1986)

Zung Self-Rating Depression Scale (SDS)

**Effects of stimulus parameters on cognitive side effects, in electroconvulsive therapy.* (Weiner, Rogers, Davidson, and Squire, 1986b, p.317);

Montgomery and Asberg Depression Rating Scale (MADRS)

Is old-fashioned electroconvulsive therapy more efficacious?: A randomized comparative study of bilateral brief-pulse and bilateral sine-wave treatments. (Scott, Rodger, Stocks, and Shering, 1992, p.361);

Subjective Observation by Clinicians

**Efficacy of ECT in the treatment of depression: Wave form and electrode placement considerations.* (Welch et al. , 1982);

Rating Tests for Patient Improvement from Clinician Viewpoint -

Brief Psychiatric Rating Scale (BPRS).

**Effects of stimulus parameters on cognitive side effects, in electroconvulsive therapy.* (Weiner, Rogers, Davidson, and Squire, 1986b, p.317);

Other Efficacy criteria not encompassed in the manuscript include:[611]

Manageability of Patients

Efficacy and safety of induced seizures (EST) in man. (Fink, 1978, p.5);

Length of Stay in Hospital

Effects of stimulus parameters on cognitive side effects, in

[611] Manageability, Length of Stay, and Marketability - third person perspectives of efficacy related to insurance - are not encompassed within this article, nor other less common efficacy tests, i.e. comparison of ECT to Placebo, Drug Therapy, Psychotherapy, Simulated ECT, or Subconvulsive Treatments. Nevertheless, the same principles uncovered within this report apply.

electroconvulsive therapy. (Weiner, Rogers, Davidson, and Squire, 1986b, p.318);

Successful Versus Non-successful Marketing of "ECT" Devices to Hospitals and Clinicians

The Molac-II - an alternating current electroshock therapy machine incorporating a new principle. (Impastato, Berg, and Gabriel, 1957, p.381)

ECT: Sham statistics, the myth of convulsive therapy, and the case for consumer misinformation. (Cameron, 1994, p.188);

Comparison of "ECT" to Placebo

Differential response of hospitalized depressed patients to somatic therapy. (Greenblatt, Grosser, and Wechsler, 1964);

Drug Therapy

Comparative efficacy of anti-depressant drugs and placebo in relation to electric shock treatment. (Greenblatt, Freeman, Meshorer, 1966);

Psychotherapy

Prognosis in psychiatry. (Appel, Meyers, and Sheflin, 1953);

Simulated ECT

A controlled comparison of simulated and real ECT in depressive illness (Lambourn and Gill, 1978) and

Subconvulsive Treatments

Evaluation of convulsive and subconvulsive shock therapies utilizing a control group. (Ulett, Smith, and Gleser, 1956).

Careful evaluation of the selected studies amongst those above show several interesting and revealing phenomena. To begin, there are two basic means of administering Brief Pulse. The first is true minimal stimulus (just above seizure threshold) wherein Brief Pulse is indeed greatly advantageous to SW regarding safety or memory dysfunction, but wherein Brief Pulse is not as effective as SW from a clinical standpoint (as we shall see). The second is multifold threshold dosing wherein the memory advantage over SW is lost (as we shall see), but wherein Brief Pulse is as or more effective than SW.

The findings of the author's evaluations are simple. Upon careful analysis, the author has discovered that almost all these precedent setting Brief Pulse safety studies along with the precedent setting Brief Pulse efficacy studies, appear to have been conducted at minimal stimulus or just above threshold output, not at the clinically applied multifold threshold outputs actually utilized in the field. In short, almost none of the Brief Pulse safety studies and almost none of the Brief Pulse efficacy studies are based upon the much higher default settings of Brief Pulse devices used in the field. Consequently, almost none of the Brief Pulse safety studies and almost none of the Brief Pulse efficacy studies above are representative of the Brief Pulse ENR devices actually utilized in the field.

In short because the above studies are almost wholly performed at minimal stimulus, none of these precedent-setting Brief Pulse safety studies dismiss the possibility of cognitive or organic damage as a result of the much more powerful Brief Pulse procedures administered in the field.

Moreover, because Brief Pulse multifold threshold output in lieu of minimal stimulus is required and used for efficacy in the field, almost none of the above precedent-setting minimal stimulus Brief Pulse efficacy studies showing equal or greater efficacy with minimal stimulus BP compared to SW are reliable.

Finally, damage, as Perrin shows us in 2012, occurs mainly on a neuronal level and so is not directly visible even with MRI. Tellingly, as we shall see, the evidence fails to show efficacy for any length of time without this neuronal damage (Perrin et al., 2012).

CHAPTER 43

Non-MRI Comparative Studies Showing Safety and Efficacy of Brief Pulse

Study No.1
"Evaluation of the Central Nervous System Risks" - by Weiner et al, 1982.

This is a fairly early study performed before the introduction of the later second generation MECTA SR-1 and SR-2 Brief Pulse devices,[612] both of which are set at two and one half times threshold (via charge and EO in joules) with BL-"ECT" and five times threshold with UL-"ECT" for all age settings (Beale et al. , 1994). The study uses prospective (before and after) EEG and prospective cognitive instruments to test for memory damage with BP compared to SW. The study compares SW to BP using UL (unilateral electrode placement) ECT. It also compares SW to BP using BL (bilateral electrode placement) ECT, comparing all four combinations (SW-UL, SW-BL, BP-UL, BP-BL). Comparing SW to BP is a common theme of many of the Weiner-Coffey-Sackeim comparative studies. While neither the electrical parameters nor any method for determining adequate number of treatments is provided, the study unquestionably compares just above threshold or minimal stimulus BP to SW--not the suprathreshold Brief Pulse outputs used in the field by modern day second generation BP devices. By way of verification, there is an efficacy portion of this study by Welch et al. , entitled *Efficacy of ECT in the treatment of depression: Wave form and electrode placement considerations (Welch at al. , 1982).* The Welch study, simultaneously published with Weiner's safety study, is based on the same treatment and same treatment population. Welch verifies the use of minimal stimulus or just above threshold output Brief Pulse in asserting:

> . . [P]ulse stimulation required less total energy to trigger a seizure, generally 50% or less than the energy required for sine wave stimulation. (Welch et al. , 1982, p.32)

The use of 50% or less energy than SW is not true of clinically applied dosages emitted by modern day MECTA and Somatics BP devices. Indeed, in spite of the probable use of a modern Brief Pulse device, the minimal stimulus Brief pulse outputs used in the above two studies were manually titrated for threshold. Welch clearly tells us:

> Estimated minimum threshold dosage was given, and if a patient failed to seize, the stimulus was repeated at sufficiently higher Joules to produce a seizure. (Welch et al. , 1982, p.32)

Clearly the manual titration method for determining minimal output (to induce adequate seizures) is used here in lieu of the default outputs deferred to In the field, that is, initial sub-convulsive dosages are utilized in the study with the aim of administering all dosages as close to just above threshold as possible. It is well known that minimal stimulus Brief Pulse output with BL ECT is half that of SW.

---

[612] While Weiner denies affiliation with MECTA Corporation, Weiner exclusively utilizes MECTA devices throughout his publications. As well, he aided in editing the MECTA manual, and appears in MECTA's video-taped information for doctors and patients. He was virtually the single spokesperson for all American manufacturers during the 1976-1982 FDA hearings.

It is not surprising, then, that the Weiner portion of the study, which is the prospective comparative investigation for cognitive and organic damage (Weiner et al. ,1982) shows less EEG slowing with UL-Brief Pulse (requiring the least electricity) than with UL-Sine Wave (even at alleged SW threshold dosing). Moreover, at minimal stimulus Brief Pulse, we are not particularly surprised to see that BL-Brief Pulse is slightly superior even to UL-Sine Wave and of course, to BL-Sine Wave. Neither are we surprised at similar results regarding retrograde and anterograde amnesia scores (> = superior to): UL-BP > BL-BP > UL-SW > BL-SW. BL-Brief Pulse, we are informed, is administered (not surprisingly) at 50% less electrical output than BL-Sine Wave in these studies.

The complementary efficacy study by Welch--referred to above--specifically entitled: "Efficacy of ECT in the Treatment of Depression: Wave Form and Electrode Placement Considerations" (Welch et al. , 1982), is, of course, the efficacy portion of the same study. Most studies at this time utilized the Hamilton Depression Rating Scale (HDRS) for measuring efficacy (regarding the effect on depression) and Welch's evaluation is no exception. Administered blindly, the evaluator determined equal efficacy for UL-BP compared to UL-SW, as well as equal efficacy with BL-BP [613] and BL-SW. Furthermore, the rater found all UL ECT more effective than all BL ECT (with respect to depression), but conceded that while UL ECT appeared more (or at least equally) effective to BL ECT, the (not surprisingly) better cognitive functioning finding following UL ECT (due to less electricity) may have clouded the results.

While safety results denoting the superiority of BP (at minimal stimulus) compared to SW (also allegedly at minimal stimulus) are no surprise, the efficacy results of this same study (Welch et al. , 1982) declaring BP (at minimal stimulus) equally effective to SW are not only surprising, but later studies directly contradict such findings (Malitz, Sackeim, Decina, Kanzler, and Kerr, 1986). It was soon understood, in fact, that UL-BP at just above threshold is not as effective (with respect to patient efficacy from a clinical perspective) as UL-SW, BL-BP or BL-SW. In fact, while these earlier studies (i.e. Weiner et al, 1982; Welch et al.1982), seemed to prove brief pulse superiority both in safety and efficacy compared to SW, it is now known that the Brief Pulse efficacy portion (at just above threshold) established a false precedent in "the literature" for both UL-BP and BL-BP. This became clear in 1994, when Beale discovered that what were actually second generation BP devices were administering default outputs of 2.5 fold threshold for BL ECT and 5.0 fold threshold for UL ECT for all age categories (Beale, 1994). Thus, it was with the 1994 Beale study that concrete evidence suggested that even BL-BP administered at minimal stimulus is much less effective than BL-SW administered at "minimal stimulus." In fact, in later calling for more powerful BP devices, Sackeim, Abrams, and even Weiner all conceded that both minimal stimulus UL-BP and minimal stimulus BL-BP are more or less therapeutically useless or weak (See Weiner's comments in International Electrotechnical Commission, 1997, Dec 26, p.5; see third generation BP devices in Volume II).

It wasn't until 1986, however, four years following the Weiner study above, that newer studies began informing readers that UL-BP at just above threshold is not as effective (Malitz, Sackeim, Decina, Kanzler, and Kerr, 1986). But it was not until 1994 that a study appeared suggesting that neither was BL-BP effective at just above threshold in that second generation BP devices were delivering default outputs of 2 and 1/2 times threshold for BL-BP in actual clinical practice (Beale, 1994), outputs which had been ongoing since the introduction of these later second generation BP devices approximately 1985. Even following 1994, however, numerous earlier comparative studies such as the Weiner and Welch studies above, continued to engender the strongly entrenched publicly disseminated idea that all modern day BP devices both emit and are effective at a much lower Energy Output than SW, and that modern BP devices, therefore, are much safer than the SW devices of the past by virtue of reduced output. Indeed, alleged documentation touting that BL-Brief Pulse at just above threshold is equally effective to standard BL-Sine Wave became so replete throughout the literature via comparative (BP to SW) studies before 1994, that even today these same fallacious assertions remain embedded as lore within the public psyche, implicit "truisms" to be accepted without question in spite of the continually proliferating power of modern day BP devices many more times as powerful as SW in most age categories. The false assumption of minimal stimulus BL-Brief Pulse efficacy in conjunction with the Brief Pulse

[613] Declarations of equal efficacy with minimal stimulus BL-BP compared to standard BL-SW are nevertheless replete throughout almost all modern-day comparative BP to SW studies. The false assertion of minimal stimulus BL-BP efficacy in conjunction with the fact that minimal stimulus BP can be delivered at half the Energy Output of standard SW is the single strongest justification for BP superiority to SW, and the main argument by which BP manufacturers convinced FDA and National Psychiatric Organizations to endorse modern day BP as safe and effective. It is from these endorsements, based on these misleading studies, that media has falsely spread the idea that modern day BP is kinder and gentler by virtue of delivering much less Energy Output than the older SW devices.

capacity to induce so-called adequate seizures at half the Energy Output of SW, continues to remain the single strongest justification for alleged BP superiority (over SW) even today. Moreover, though false, reduced output continues to remain the chief argument by which BP manufacturers in conjunction with National Psychiatric Organizations such as the Royal College of Psychiatry (Royal College of Psychiatry, 1977), the American Psychiatric Association (American Psychiatric Association Task Force on ECT, 1978) , and the Canadian Psychiatric Association (Canadian Psychiatric Association, 1981) convinced their respective regulatory agencies, i.e. the FDA and the ERA to allow modern "ECT" into the latter part of the twentieth century and beyond (Department of Health and Human Services, 1982a, p.3). It is these initial endorsements of Brief Pulse, based on the spurious minimal stimulus studies denoted in this section, in fact, which convinced media that the modern day BP device is an improved, kinder and gentler device, emitting much lower Energy Output than the older and more malevolent SW devices of the past. There is, of course, no acknowledgement by MECTA, Somatics, or Medcraft that from about 1982, American BP devices began newly delivering pre-set suprathreshold dosages of electricity with even higher cumulative Energy Outputs than SW devices generally or that the reason these devices had to increase in power was the necessity of suprathreshold dosing (for both BL and UL "ECT") in order to make the Brief Pulse device "work. " Indeed, the actual power of modern day Brief Pulse devices, is a well-kept manufacturers' secret.

Study No.2

"A double blind controlled comparison of the therapeutic effects of low and high energy electroconvulsive therapies"--by Robin and Tissera 1982.

If the false notion of UL minimal stimulus efficacy was inadvertent in these earlier studies, the myth certainly should have been exploded in light of Robin and Tissera's 1982 study, "A double blind controlled comparison of the therapeutic effects of low and high energy electroconvulsive therapies" which in the same year the Weiner and Welch studies were published, clearly revealed that it is electrical dosage--not convulsion or convulsion alone--which influences efficacy for all forms of ECT. Testing the anti-depressant effect of 56 recipients of all ages with low Brief Pulse dosages, high Brief Pulse dosages, and SW dosages, the authors concluded ". . . that the quantity of current, as well as the induction of a convulsion, is relevant to therapeutic outcome with ECT" (Robin and Tissera, 1982, abstract).

It was not until 1986, however, that the necessity of suprathreshold dosages of electricity for even UL-BP efficacy was fully acknowledged by the main proponents of "ECT," although cited as an exception, that is, proponents yet maintained BL-BP efficacy at minimal stimulus. Suddenly, UL-Brief Pulse was deemed "dose-sensitive" so that a two-fold threshold electrical dose was required to make the procedure effective as opposed to "non-dose-sensitive" BL-Brief Pulse, which was yet held to be effective at just above threshold output. Thus, in spite of Robin and Tissera's 1982 study identifying the necessity of suprathreshold dosing for all forms of ECT in order to make Brief Pulse effective, proponents of Brief Pulse continued to intimate that BL-Brief Pulse could be effectively administered at minimal stimulus or just above threshold output. The spurious assertion of previous studies claiming UL-Brief Pulse effective at just above threshold was explained as the "accidental overlooking of what were actually suprathreshold dosages administered with UL-ECT," utilized in these earlier studies. Apparently, the effective two fold threshold outputs administered with UL-ECT in the earlier studies had been "accidentally reported" as just above threshold (Malitz et al. , 1986). [614] On the other hand, the just above threshold BL Brief Pulse output actually used in these studies was yet deemed as effective as BL-SW which required two-fold the electrical energy of Brief Pulse to induce an adequate convulsion. In this way, Brief Pulse could yet be claimed safer than SW by virtue of reduced output, at least with BL-Brief Pulse ECT, contradicted not only by Robin and Tissera, but by the suprathreshold default outputs utilized by Brief Pulse devices today, fully exposed in this manuscript. Indeed, even at the publication date of the journal articles discussed here, manufacturers MECTA and Somatics were already administering at least two and one half times threshold with BL-Brief Pulse for all age categories with their new second generation Brief Pulse

[614] Malitz explains the equal efficacy of minimal stimulus UL-BP-ECT with Bl-BP-ECT in the Lambourn and Gill study (1978) in this manner: UL-BP-ECT had been administered at the same dosage as minimal stimulus BL-BP-ECT. However, since UL-BP-ECT can induce seizures at half the output of BL-BP-ECT, researchers had failed to take into account the fact that UL-BP-ECT had actually been administered at twice threshold, accounting for its equal efficacy.

machines in order make the procedure effective. Indeed, by 1986 all major academic proponents of "ECT" had begun calling for (what were actually) even more powerful third generation BP devices, emitting even more enhanced suprathreshold dosages of electricity than second generation BP devices in order to make the BP device more effective. In fact, if we are to believe the results of the efficacy studies here as honest, we might be forced to conclude the Hamilton Depression Rating Scale (HDRS) defective. In short, the HDRS instrument used in these early comparative studies which determined minimal stimulus BL-BP effective at threshold (regarding depression), like the UL-ECT results, had to have been either defective, incorrectly applied, skewed, or that other criteria such as behavioral modification simply did not occur. In brief, if BL-Brief Pulse-ECT is effective at minimal stimulus as testing with the HDRS concluded, why did manufacturers begin producing more and more powerful BP devices emitting higher and higher multifold threshold dosages of electricity? One possibility is that the HDRS, as a subjective measurement, may not have taken into account the well-known placebo effect. Another possibility is that efficacy regarding depression may have been extremely short lived or, as noted above, efficacy in the field may be defined as something other than anti-depression, i.e. patient management. A third possibility might be that, although the HDRS is allegedly administered blind, researchers may have wanted minimal stimulus BP output to be effective and were somehow able to identify groups through subtly manifest clues. In fact, even as the 1982 Welch at al. efficacy portion of the study sums up its conclusions, the 1982 Weiner et al. safety portion of the study sums up its conclusions by referring to the much earlier Ottoson study (Ottoson et al, 1960), suggesting that minimal stimulus Brief Pulse is both safe and effective. Welch at al. assert:

> Ottoson’s (1960) milestone work indicated that a generalized grand mal seizure is the essential component of the treatment and that other variables such as mode of stimulus and severity of side effects were unrelated to ultimate efficacy. [615] (Welch et al. , 1982, p.33)

The above assertion, that seizure is the essential component of "ECT" though ideologically desirable, has today, been thoroughly destroyed (Robin and Tissera 1982, Squire and Zouzounis, 1986 Cameron, 1994, Wilcox, Liberson, Impastato et al. , 1957, Beale et al. , 1994; Cameron, 2023, this manuscript). Nevertheless, the reference to Ottoson underpins Welch’s, Weiner's, and other Clinician-Researcher’s zealous, almost religious conviction regarding the viability of convulsive theory itself, the whole hypothesis of which depends upon just above threshold efficacy, the attainability of which has become an elusive, fifty year obsessional pursuit by numerous ECT Researchers in a field over which Ottoson was a kind of Guru. That Ottoson was wrong must have been and must yet be unbearable to such enthusiasts, similar to the resistance which diehard Freudians experienced at the ideological waning of psychoanalysis (Masson, 1984). Such enthusiasm, in any case, may account for much of the recalcitrant denial, absurdly contradictory rationalizations, and out and out cover-ups regarding the inefficacy of just above threshold seizures together with the obvious cognitive side-effects accompanying the unfortunate, but necessary suprathreshold dosing required of modern day Brief Pulse in order to make the device "work. " It is the insistence upon a failed bygone procedure that in theory seemed to approach so near to a true ameliorative, that explains in part the almost fanatical, irrational recalcitrance of convulsive therapy zealots blindly insisting upon the treatment's viability rather than perforce, coming to terms with the unfortunate fact [616] that convulsion theory is untenable or in a word--mistaken (Cameron 1994). [617]

---

[615] d’Elia, Ottosen, and Stronmerg (1983) publish a similar statement: “An optimal therapeutic effect depends on the occurrence of a generalized, tonic-clonic seizure. . . On the other hand, supraliminal stimulation does not enhance the therapeutic effect. The organic syndrome, however, as measured by retrograde and anterograde dysmensia, is aggravated by supraliminal stimulation. The aim is therefore to induce generalized seizure activity with a minimum of electrical energy.”

[616] If the theory of convulsive therapy really worked, it would work with adequate convulsion--period.

[617] The religious zealotry of convulsive therapy enthusiasts in conjunction with clinicians and family members whose sole aim is management and control irrespective of injury, is matched only by the fervor of organizations whose constituency is composed of those having experienced injury as a result of “ECT” (Psychee, CTIP, CUBES, ECT Anonymous, NAPA-- the movement). Such organizations though often short-lived, continue to emerge, often engaging in various attempts to limit or ban the procedure world-wide (California 1982, Texas 1993, 1995, 1997, 2007). Deeply opposing convictions on both sides continue to stage one of the most embittered long-term sociological-medical struggles in modern day history.

Study No.3

"Autobiographical Amnesia with ECT: An Analysis of the Roles of Stimulus Wave Form, Electrode Placement, Stimulus Energy, and Seizure Length" (Daniel et al. , 1983).

This publication is another of the precedential comparative safety studies, a number of which include Weiner as one of the authors. This study prospectively tests for cognitive and (through EEG) organic dysfunction before and following "ECT. "

Employing a common theme, this specific study again compares various combinations of SW to BP, again utilizing UL and BL electrode placement. The study contains 22 persons tested for subsequent memory defects. Here we are given the general names of the devices compared--MECTA versus Medcraft's B-24. Too, we are provided some electrical parameters for the respective devices. From the parameters, the Brief Pulse MECTA device is once again, most likely a "C" or "D" apparatus, a first generation BP device, and this can also be determined from the year of the study. (The "C" had a maximum output of 108J and the "D" 140J). We are not given specific doses applied, nor are we told how an "adequate number of seizures" in the study is determined. Nevertheless, we are given minimal and maximal parameters for both devices (MECTA--800 mA, 60-70 pulse pairs/sec. , .75-1.5 millisecond pulse widths, 1.0-2.0 second duration; Medcraft--140-170 V, 60 Hz, and .4-1.0 seconds duration). From this, we can derive MECTA parameters emitted between twenty and thirty actual joules and Medcraft parameters of between 40 and 75 Joules, roughly twice that of BP. [618]

That the MECTA parameters are once again threshold amounts is never in question, especially in light of the MECTA ("C") capability of slightly over 100 Joules maximum. (The "C" and "D" were basically defaulted for minimal stimulus using BL-ECT.) Moreover, Daniel et al. go to the trouble of measuring actual Joules (though they never give us the figure) with a "custom-made watt-second meter" (Daniel et al., 1983, p.122) and we are informed that "sinusoidal stimulation [SW] delivered more Joules of electrical energy than did pulse stimulation . . . ."

Again, there is no surprise that at just above threshold or minimal stimulus Brief Pulse output, the researchers discover from prospective memory tests that BL-BP is safer than BL-SW and that UL-BP is safer than UL-SW. Once again, we see that it is from precedential studies such as these, comparing minimal stimulus BP with "threshold" SW (using at least twice the output of BP) that both clinicians in the field and the American Public become convinced that modern day BP is safer than SW by virtue of BP's lower energy emission. Once again, then, we see the precedent setting study with Brief Pulse performed only at minimal stimulus, not the second generation BP devices actually utilized in the field.

Safety and Efficacy Studies Continued

The next three comparative safety studies were conducted in 1986, and in spite of Robin and Tissera's break-through 1982 publication showing that efficacy, particularly BP efficacy is related to electrical dosage and not convulsion, the 1986 comparative studies continue to test and compare SW with BP at just above threshold. In fact, American manufacturers Somatics and MECTA had by this time already begun marketing the Thymatron DG and SR 2 series respectively pre-set at more than 2.5 times threshold (in EO and Charge) for BL "ECT" and more than five times threshold for UL "ECT," suprathreshold dosages undetected by physician administrators (due to deceptive machine readouts emulating minimal stimulus). While the second generation Somatics' device had a dial the administrator could set in accordance with the recipient's age, the second generation MECTA SR1 device "titrated" from a chart, both of which, unbeknownst to administrators, facilitated multifold dosages exceeding two and one half times threshold (with BL "ECT"). Safety studies, as already noted, misleadingly based on adequate convulsion, continued at minimal stimulus.

---

[618] Maximum current for the Medcraft's SW device may be approximately 1.410 peak at .1 seconds and 1000 mA at 1.0 seconds (Department of Health and Human Services, 1982a, p. A10). Weiner has informed us that threshold for SW devices is approximately twice that of BP (Weiner et al, 1980; Welch et al, 1982); he does not, however, inform us that this ratio is true only when BP is administered at minimal stimulus.

Study No.4
"Cognitive consequences of low-dosage electroconvulsive therapy" (Sackeim et al, 1986).

The first of these 1986 studies is a Sackeim et al. safety study called "Cognitive consequences of low-dosage electroconvulsive therapy" published in Annals New York Academy of Sciences (462, 326- 340). The study compares BL to UL electrode placement for Brief Pulse (Sackeim, Portnoy, Neeley, Steif, Decina, and Malitz, 1986), utilizing various memory tests to evaluate the cognitive effects of--once again--just above threshold ECT. The study is double blind and in that only a MECTA device is used, probably a "C" or "D;" all recipients are administered BP only. Cognitive tests are used for discovering deterioration in memory and other kinds of cognitive functions, thus the study can be categorized as a "safety" study. The study moreover, makes it quite clear that its single purpose is to evaluate UL and BL (Brief Pulse) modalities at (just above) threshold. In short, it is another Brief Pulse minimal stimulus study.

> ECT stimulus dosage was titrated for each patient to just above seizure threshold using a method of limits paradigm. (Sackeim et al. , 1986, p.328)

The paradigm referred to above is that of initial sub-convulsive treatment titrated up to threshold in order to induce seizure as close to threshold as possible (p.328-329). According to the results, UL, not surprisingly, is superior to BL in most areas of memory recovery, but allegedly, following minimal stimulus BL and UL ECT, the BL and UL rate equally in retrograde and anterograde neutral face recognition (p.335). Sackeim utilizes his findings to disagree with "Squire's earlier findings (Squire, Slater, and Miller, 1981) as well as other studies, that bilateral ECT produces greater retrograde memory disturbance for information processing . . . " (p.335). In typical fashion, however, Sackeim utilizes his BP findings to confirm BP superiority over SW findings in other studies.

> In our view, the most compelling findings of these data are the absence of cumulative deterioration in postictal [after seizure] measures over the course of treatment. As noted earlier, with traditional forms of ECT administration [SW], 13 of 16 studies demonstrated deterioration effects. . . . The magnitude of deficits did not increase over the course of ECT. [619] (Ibid, p.336)

In short, Sackeim concludes that all forms of BP ECT are superior to all forms of SW ECT, that there is not the cumulative deterioration with BP that there is with SW. Sackeim goes even further, claiming actual memory improvement with BP ECT.

> [T]he only significant cumulative change in these data was improvement for nonsense shape recognition. This improvement pertained for the most part to patients who showed strong clinical response to ECT. This provides some additional support for the suggestion of Fromm-Auch that clinical recovery with ECT is associated with enhanced right hemisphere cognitive processing. (Ibid, p.336)

Sackeim's findings for BP include the following:

> With respect to retrograde and anterograde neutral face recognition, we observed equivalence with the modalities [UL and BL]. (Ibid, p.336)

> The claim that depression [- not ECT -] is associated with a difficulty in the acquisition of information was supported . . . . (Ibid, p.338)

---

[619] This, of course, is another proof of BP wave form superiority over SW, (albeit BP at threshold).

> . . . [F]our days following the last ECT . . ., [a]cquisition of memory returned to pretreatment baseline (p.338). . . [P]atients showed at post treatment no change in their capacity to acquire information. (Ibid, p.339)

Thus, Sackeim concludes that minimal stimulus BP-BL-ECT is just as safe as minimal stimulus BP-UL-ECT (in spite of BP-UL-ECT being administered at half the dosage of BP-BL-ECT), that it is depression which causes memory loss-not BP-ECT, and finally that BP-ECT in no way negatively affects memory following the procedure.

Sackeim makes clear that his study is based on low dosage (or minimal stimulus) output for both forms of BP ECT, stating:

> Under standard administration techniques in which all patients receive the same absolute dosage, dosage in excess of threshold is likely to be greater with unilateral than with bilateral ECT. (Ibid)

In short, this is one of the first studies to test just above threshold for both UL and BL Brief Pulse ECT, as opposed to "absolute dosage" (in previous BP studies) meaning minimal stimulus for BL ECT but the same dosage [as BL ECT] for UL ECT. In that BP-UL-ECT produces seizures at half the output of BP-BL-ECT, an absolute or equal dosage for both BL and UL results in UL being administered at twice the threshold dosage of BL ECT. A just above BL threshold output for a forty year old man at about forty Joules, for example, at the same forty Joules for the same man administered UL ECT amounts to a two-fold threshold output with UL ECT in that threshold dosage with UL ECT might be about 20 Joules [instead of 40 joules]. In fact, both MECTA and Somatics via their second generation BP devices respectively utilize absolute dosage regarding BL and UL ECT, pre-set by MECTA via age Chart and pre-set by Somatics via the "Dial-a-Dosage" Method. Moreover, not only do persons in a particular age (and gender) category receive the same or absolute dosage with BL and UL ECT on second generation BP devices, but unlike the study, titration levels for second generation BP devices are pre-set at more than 2.5 fold threshold with BL ECT and thus more than 5.0 fold threshold with UL ECT--a fact not known by academics in general until about 1994. Thus, in 1986, when this minimal stimulus Sackeim study was published, physician administrators had no reason to believe Brief Pulse BL-ECT was being administered in the field at any titration level other than just above threshold. Consequently, while Sackeim appears to be encouraging more accurate threshold dosing with (Brief Pulse) BL "ECT" in this 1986 study (Sackeim, Portnoy, Neeley, Steif, Decina, and Malitz, 1986), that is, as close to threshold as possible with both BL and UL ECT, professionals in the field had no idea that the pre-calibrated titration level outputs they were administering via Somatics and MECTA second generation BP devices were actually set not at minimal stimulus, but at a more than 2.5 fold threshold titration level with BL ECT and thus more than a 5.0 fold threshold titration level with UL ECT. In spite of these facts, which both Sackeim and Weiner as close manufacturer affiliates must have or should have been keenly aware, the allusion to low dosage ECT in the study clearly substantiates the study's performance at minimal stimulus, and thus reduced electrical outputs compared to SW. Clearly, researchers in this Sackeim Brief Pulse safety study make every attempt to remain as close to threshold as possible with both BL (and UL) ECT, the safety results of which are thus based on BP minimal stimulus, contradicting that used in actual clinical practice.

So many aspects and nuances of BP are defended via threshold demonstration within these modern day comparative studies, it is disconcerting to think that not until 1994, as noted above, did a single study (Beale 1994) reveal that second generation MECTA and Somatics BP devices, were, in fact, administering suprathreshold dosages of at least 2.5 times threshold with BP-BL-ECT and at least 5.0 times threshold with BP-UL-ECT and in fact, by 1994, third generation BP devices were beginning to be manufactured based on twice the threshold output of second generation BP devices (see third generation BP devices in Volume II). In sum, virtually all positive safety conclusions regarding BP, as we shall continue to see, are based on minimal stimulus outputs. There is little doubt, therefore, that both the public and regulatory agencies world-wide, and even administering physicians have been and continue to be misled by the false picture these multifarious minimal stimulus safety studies have painted of modern day BP devices.

Study No.5
"The Efficacy of Electroconvulsive Therapy: Dose-Response Interactions With Modality" (Malitz, Sackeim, Decina, Kanzler, and Kerr, 1986)

"The Efficacy of Electroconvulsive Therapy: Dose-Response Interactions With Modality" (Malitz, Sackeim, Decina, Kanzler, and Kerr, 1986) is the separately published efficacy portion of the same study entitled, "Cognitive consequences of low-dosage electroconvulsive therapy" by Sackeim, Portnoy, Neeley, Steif, Decina, and Malitz, 1986, above. While two of the authors of the efficacy portion are new, three of them, Sackeim, Malitz, and Decina, also authored the safety portion. The efficacy portion ("The Efficacy of Electroconvulsive Therapy: Dose-Response Interactions with Modality") of the two complementary studies then, as does the safety portion, tests BL and UL at threshold, in short minimal stimulus with Brief Pulse. There are 52 subjects and as before, only a MECTA Brief Pulse Device is used (p.58). Once again, then, there is no question that all treatments are titrated to threshold or minimal stimulus and that all recipients receive Brief Pulse. Similar to the above study, the authors' revealing premise is that 35 previous studies denoting UL ECT as equally effective to BL ECT had been, in fact, incorrectly performed in that the UL portion of all 35 studies had used the same (or absolute) dosage for UL ECT as that titrated for minimal stimulus BL ECT. In short, due to the lower threshold output of BP-UL-ECT (half that of BP-BL-ECT), BP-UL-ECT recipients which, in all the previous studies, had been administered the same electrical dose as BP-BL-ECT, had "accidentally" been administered well above threshold, thus giving the false impression that "minimal stimulus" BP-UL-ECT was equally effective to minimal stimulus BP-BL-ECT. In other BP studies as well, instead of titrating for BP-UL-ECT threshold separately, the same electrical dosage administered for minimal stimulus BP-BL-ECT had been used for BP-UL-ECT. The momentous revelation (and concession) in this efficacy study then, is that minimal stimulus BP-UL-ECT is, in fact, not effective at threshold (or minimal stimulus) and, therefore, admittedly requires suprathreshold dosing to be effective. The equally momentous implication, moreover, is that BP-BL-ECT is absolutely effective at just above threshold or minimal stimulus (which, as we have already seen via the power of second generation BP devices, is similarly spurious).

Again, the Hamilton Rating Depression Scale (HRDS) is the main mode for testing of efficacy in this study. The study is double-blind. The titration method administered for both BL and UL is described below.

> A methods of limits procedure was used to titrate dosage to just above seizure threshold. (Malitz et al. , 1986, p.58)

As noted above, then, the sub-convulsive titration method titrates to just above threshold output for each individual treatment (p.58), in brief, minimal stimulus output for both BP-BL and BP-UL-ECT.

This 1986 study is important as noted because it claims to be the first study to correctly identify UL as ineffective at just above threshold, a premise of anomaly which numerous future studies would exploit in demanding more and more powerful BP devices. [620] The equal efficacy of UL with BL-BP-ECT reported in 1982 by Welch (Welch et al. , 1982) and others (American Psychiatric Association, 1978; d'Elia and Raotma, 1975; Fink, 1979) was now admittedly based upon an error wherein accidental suprathreshold dosages had been unintentionally administered with BP-UL-ECT in all previous studies. Just above threshold BP-UL-ECT, then, is suddenly "discovered" or acknowledged in this 1986 study, to be only about half as effective at threshold as BL-BP-ECT at threshold (Malitz et al. , 1986, p.60). Minimal stimulus BL-BP-ECT (just above threshold bilateral brief pulse), however, is yet deemed extremely effective in this efficacy study, allegedly averaging a 70% reduction in depression on the Hamilton Depression Rating Scale (HDRS) and over 70% Efficacy relative to the number of subjects (p.60). The study thus concludes:

---

[620] Unbeknownst to administering psychiatrists in the field, for at least one year prior to this paper's publication, device manufacturers MECTA and Somatics had begun pre-setting their second generation BP devices to automatically administer BP-UL-ECT recipients at least five times threshold outputs. While Somatics did eventually begin "informing" purchasers (of their devices) that UL was set for two and one half times threshold on the Age-Dosage dial (Abrams and Swartz, 1988, p.28), implying that BP-BL-ECT was set for just above threshold, it was not until 1994 that a single independent study revealed that BP-UL-ECT recipients were actually receiving a 5.0 fold threshold dosage on second generation BP devices and that BP-BL-ECT recipients were receiving a 2.5 fold threshold dosage (Beale 1994).

> At titrated, relatively low dosage, bilateral [BP] ECT was a powerful antidepressant treatment. At titrated relatively low dosage, right unilateral ECT was therapeutically weak. (Malitz, 1986, p.61)

Henceforth, we are informed by manufacturers that BP-*UL*-ECT, unlike BP-*BL*-ECT, is "dose sensitive" and that BP-*UL*-ECT alone, therefore, must be administered at suprathreshold (multifold threshold stimulus) levels in order to be effective. Consequently, while minimal stimulus BP-*UL*-ECT is deemed *ineffective* at [just above] threshold, the Malitz study and other studies to follow, continue to indicate or assume BP-*BL*-ECT effective at [just above] threshold output or minimal stimulus. In short, "dose-sensitive" BP-*UL*-ECT is deemed anomalous in requiring multifold threshold dosing, specifically two fold threshold dosing for efficacy. Based on these new findings then, and to simplify pre-set electrical dosing for administering physicians, the second generation Somatics Thymatron DG device began featuring an "easy to use set-to-age" dial while second generation MECTA devices relied upon an "easy to use" chart methodology. In that BP-*UL*-ECT seizures can be induced at half the output of BP-*BL*-ECT seizures and in that BP-*BL*-ECT is yet assumed to be effective at just above threshold at this point, practitioners were given the distinct impression that using the simple "set-to-age-dial" technique on the Thymatron DG and the simple age-related chart settings on MECTA devices, BP-*BL*-ECT was being administered at just above threshold output while at the same dosage and thus same age setting, BP-*UL*-ECT was being administered at twice threshold in order to be effective. In short, simply dialing to the age of the individual or using the same age-related chart setting for both BP-*UL*-ECT and BP-*BL* ECT (as was recommended by both Somatics and MECTA respectively), practitioners believed BP-*BL*-ECT was being administered at minimal stimulus and BP-*UL*-ECT (at the same or absolute dosage) was being administered at twice fold threshold. In fact, unbeknownst to practitioners, as already noted, by dialing the age of the individual on the second generation Somatics device or using the settings via MECTA's age-related chart, BP-*BL*-ECT was actually being administered at a circa 2.5 fold threshold output on second generation BP devices while BP-*UL*-ECT (at the same electrical dosage) was being administered a circa 5.0 fold threshold output (Beale et al. , 1994). This 2.5/5.0 fold occurrence, ongoing since about 1983, would not be discovered as noted, until 1994, when an independent research team (ibid) would eventually uncover the phenomenon (Beale et al. , 1994). In brief, BP-*BL*-ECT on second generation MECTA and Somatics BP devices had been set--not to just above threshold as practitioners believed--but to a circa 2.5 fold threshold titration level output for BP-*BL*-ECT and thus a circa 5.0 fold threshold titration level output for BP-*UL*-ECT. This information in fact, suggests that manufacturers had secretly known for years that both forms of BP ECT had to be administered with multifold threshold titration level outputs in order to be effective. The significance of this information is that the secret agent of efficacy in "ECT" is not seizure, but electricity and that manufacturers sought to cover it up.

While researchers Robin and Tissera (1982) alone showed early on that both BL-BP and UL-BP are ineffective at just above threshold, no other study before the 1994 Beale study (that the author of this manuscript has been able to locate) ever provided any indication that not just UL-"ECT," but both BL-BP and UL-BP were being administered at suprathreshold titration levels. Certainly, no literature until the 1994 Beale study ever revealed that BP-BL-ECT had actually been being administered via second generation MECTA and Somatics BP devices at doses at least two and one half times threshold since about 1983 and certainly since 1985, at least a year before the publication of the 1986 Malitz study. The myriad of comparative studies juxtaposing SW with BP during this period deeming minimal stimulus BP-*BL*-ECT equally effective to SW-*BL*-ECT, simply do not explain the increasing power of the Brief Pulse device beyond minimal stimulus with BP-*BL*-ECT. At the same time, beginning about 1980, it is not surprising to find that virtually all claims of BP safety superiority to SW are based on studies showing BP seizures achievable at half the electrical dosage of standard SW, resulting in less cognitive dissonance. So, if safety is improved with minimal stimulus Brief Pulse and Brief Pulse is equally effective to SW, why were Brief Pulse manufacturers secretly enhancing the power of their machines? Morover, why do modern day MECTA and Somatics BP devices no longer administer just above threshold outputs for either BL or UL "ECT." Indeed, none of these comparative studies conclude that BP-BL-ECT (like BP-*UL*-ECT) is ineffective at (just above) threshold output--in fact, the efficacy portion of these studies maintain quite the opposite--that BP-BL-ECT is effective at just above threshold. Certainly, none of these studies take into account that in the field, default outputs administered with both BP-*BL*-ECT and BP-*UL*-ECT were and are no longer administered at minimal stimulus. In fact, it was not until the 1986 Sackeim, Malitz, and Decina safety and efficacy studies mentioned here, that any psychiatric literature at all declared even BP-*UL*-

ECT ineffective at (just above) threshold. [621] Undeniably, over thirty-five previous studies claim BP-*UL*-ECT effective at threshold. In any case, regulatory bodies appear to have accepted the Malitz "discovery" of BP-UL-ECT "dose-sensitivity" (meaning UL inefficacy at threshold) as a legitimately new understanding of BP-*UL*-ECT and that thirty-five previous studies had simply "erred" in their conclusions.[622] As for the public as well as regulators, and as manufacturers would have it, the "discovery" of UL "dose sensitivity" appeared far too arcane to be significant. After all, physicians administered the great majority of BP-ECT bilaterally. Because it was assumed that BP devices still automatically defaulted the most dominant form of "ECT"--BP-BL-ECT—to just above seizure threshold, then, UL inefficacy was dismissed as irrelevant and the much publicized reduced dosing aspect of Brief Pulse compared to SW remained the accepted narrative (NIMH; Fodero, Kellner). [623] It was due to the assumption that BP-BL-ECT was yet effectively administered at just above threshold output then, that the so-called discovery of BP-UL-ECT "dose sensitivity" did not become of paramount relevance to physicians, regulatory bodies, media, or the public general. The fact that both UL and BL BP ECT might be ineffective at threshold and that both were being administered at suprathreshold outputs was to remain undisclosed for at least another ten years, and only then, revealed obliquely and somewhat vaguely as we shall soon see. [624] In fact, manufacturers were slowly acclimating the public to the same higher levels of electrical power for which SW had been condemned between 1976 and 1982.

In any case, due to the 1986 Malitz efficacy portion of the study above, BP-UL-ECT administered at minimal stimulus had at long last been identified as *ineffective,* but "*anomalous.*" The thirty-five previous BP-UL-ECT studies showing BP-UL-ECT as effective at just above threshold had simply been "flawed." Evidently, effective BP-UL-ECT had "unknowingly" been administered not at just above threshold, but at twice threshold in lieu of the minimal stimulus reported. Apparently, even the 1987 American Psychiatric Association Task Force report on ECT, a major disseminator of minimal stimulus UL-Brief Pulse "efficacy" [625] had been mistaken (*The 1987 Electroconvulsive therapy: Task force report 14)*. Never mind that between 1976 and 1982, APA had given FDA the impression that a the "new and improved" Brief Pulse device was effective with both BL and UL ECT at half the output required for SW.

Concomitantly, moreover, the same Malitz efficacy study which had revealed minimal stimulus BP-*UL*-ECT inefficacy, continued with an alleged double-blind application of the HDRS, to find minimal stimulus BP-*BL*-ECT "effective" at threshold, results now known to be highly dubious (see third generation BP devices in Volume II). It would not be until 1994, however, about the time Beale et al. (1994) published findings of pre-set suprathreshold titration levels with BL and UL ECT of 2.5 and thus 5.0 fold threshold respectively on what were actually second generation MECTA and Somatics BP devices, that Somatics Incorporated would acknowledge the need of suprathreshold BP-*BL*-ECT dosing in order to achieve BL efficacy. Petrides and Fink's discovery that default outputs on (what was actually a second generation) Somatics device could actually induce adequate seizures set to half the age of the recipient (the HAAS method), sent advocate-experts of Brief Pulse clamoring to inform fellow professionals, that the need for BL suprathreshold dosing "as stated by the 1990 APA Task Force" had been understood all along, that it was only through mistaken context that BP-*BL*-ECT dosing had been correlated with age-related minimal stimulus on (second generation) BP devices. Indeed, dialing 100 (on the Somatics device) for the 100 year old adult suggesting 100 Joules with BL ECT, actually administered about 250 Joules on the Thymatron DG. The discovery of HAAS (Half Age Stimulation Strategy),

---

[621] In that BP device manufacturers had surreptitiously administered suprathreshold dosing with UL since at least 1980 and with BL since at least 1983, the introduction of the necessity of BP-UL-ECT here may have been a planned gradual transition for public and academic digestion of the ubiquitous need for suprathreshold dosing. BP-UL-ECT, first acknowledged here, in 1986 to require suprathreshold dosing in order to be effective, may have been the first step in a three step process to introduce this concept. The second step might have been the gradual acceptance of suprathreshold dosing for BL as well, which begins to be acknowledged by about 1994. The third step is total deregulation of BP and other ECT devices in order to administer suprathreshold dosing far in excess of even that of SW. Certainly the necessity of BP-UL-ECT is exploited in the call for more and more powerful BP devices. The third step may represent passive public acceptance of what might be considered the new psychosurgery.

[622] The few premonitory studies experimenting with multifold threshold BP-BL-ECT at this time claimed only a faster response time--not greater efficacy.

[623] During 1998 hearings in Texas on ECT, one misinformed psychiatrist explained to the Texas Legislature how the Energy Output of BP devices is limited to that of a "nine volt battery."

[624] About 1997, Weiner will claim the need for twice threshold BP-BL-ECT on the basis that threshold can increase 100% over a treatment course. This, however, does not explain why third generation BP devices already extant at that time, emit almost 5.0 fold threshold for BP-BL-ECT, a fact manufacturers have hidden to date for several decades.

[625] The report also claims just above threshold BL-Brief pulse efficacy.

therefore, led pro-ECT experts to accuse each other of committing a "contextual fallacy." For Instance, in a 1997 Petrides and Fink (1997) article entitled: "Clinical common sense versus theoretical correctness" Harold Sackeim, closely associated with MECTA, accuses Petrides and Fink's explanation of Somatics' Dial-a-matic as the source of spreading a "BP-BL efficacy fallacy" forcing Petrides and Fink to defend their assertions. Petrides and Fink respond:

> Dr Sackeim . . . states that we assume a close correlation between age and threshold (on BP devices due to the popular use of the Dial-a-matic age titration method), and refers to several studies reporting a weak correlation between the two variables. . . . These studies used some form of titration to calculate a correlation between age and an estimated threshold. We did not claim a close correlation between age and threshold, but a close correlation between HASS (Half Age Stimulation Strategy) estimates and DTM (Dose Titration Methods). (Petrides and Fink, 1997, p.41)

Sackeim seems to have been suggesting that the erroneous assumption of pre-fixed minimal stimulus BL-BP-ECT on the Somatics device (similar to the charts on MECTA devices) may have been due to the popular "Dial-a-matic to age titration method" in which the physician simply dialed the age of the recipient and pressed a button. That is, Sackeim is suggesting that administrators may have mistaken age for Joule output (EO) due to misleading explanations or a misunderstanding [626] that dialing the age to 100 for a 100 year old adult was only assumed to be a setting of 100 Joules, or that dialing to 50 for a fifty year old adult was only assumed to be fifty Joules, roughly tantamount to minimal stimulus output. (Actually, this "mistaken assumption" by administrators of the device is hardly surprising in that maximum machine readouts on second generation BP devices clearly but falsely depict 100 maximum Joules). In fact, dialing to age 100 actually set the machine for about 250 unreported Joules, dialing to age fifty about 150 unreported Joules, etc. Petrides, and Fink respond, by claiming that they never implied BL-ECT default outputs at minimal stimulus on these (second generation BP) devices, that instead they had actually asserted a close correlation not between age and output but between HASS estimates and DTM estimates. (HASS, as noted above, is the method of setting the dial to half the age of the recipient from which adequate seizures appear to have been to be invariably elicited). In short, Petrides, and Fink claim to have asserted a close correlation between half age settings and minimal stimulus--not actual age settings and minimal stimulus. A correlation between half age settings (i.e. dialing to age 50 for a 100 year old adult) and minimal stimulus is not surprising, of course, in that the dial-a-matic on the made-for-America Somatics second generation BP device (as well as the MECTA chart instructions) is actually set, as we have seen, for 2.5 times threshold with BL ECT and, in fact, the HASS method somewhat uncovered this fact. Indeed, HASS or half age outputs are shown to be only slightly greater than DTM (the method for titrating up to just above threshold by beginning with sub-convulsive dosages, in short, minimal stimulus). In fact, no such admission regarding either the need for BL suprathreshold dosages or default settings of 2.5 fold threshold for BP-BL-ECT (and thus 5.0 fold for BP-UL-ECT) was ever made public either in the 1990 Task Force Report or in any other literature before Beale (1994; see also Cameron, 1994). Succinctly, pre-fixed BL suprathreshold dosing automatically pre-calibrated on second generation BP devices was not reported anywhere in the literature until 1994 (Beale), approximately ten years subsequent to the marketing of made-for-America second generation BP devices--the Thymatron DG and MECTA SR 1 and 2 BP devices. Moreover, the respective circa 2.5 fold 5.0 fold BL and UL ECT default titration levels for MECTA and Somatics second generation BP devices were never reported by manufacturers at all until independent researchers discovered them in 1994 (Beale et al.1994). While no manufacturer or ECT proponent was ever reprimanded for either the protracted "confusion" over both UL and BL inefficacy or the fact that "ECT" in the field at default outputs is not administered at threshold, the question remains: if the necessity of suprathreshold dosing for both BL and UL ECT was initially known and understood by manufacturer-affiliated researchers such as Sackeim, Weiner, and Fink, and if there was no cover-up regarding suprathreshold dosing with second generation BP devices, how do these same researchers and manufacturers account for virtually all BP safety studies having been conducted at minimal stimulus. i.e., the Malitz safety and efficacy studies above? Moreover, if BL-Brief Pulse is effective at minimal

---

[626] This "mistake" is hardly surprising in that maximum machine readouts on second generation BP devices clearly but falsely depict 100 maximum Joules.

stimulus as asserted by these "safety and efficacy" studies, why unreported default outputs of 2.5 fold threshold on second generation MECTA and Somatics devices?

Study No.6
"Effects of Stimulus Parameters on Cognitive Side Effects" (Weiner et al. , 1986)

Another 1986 comparative safety published by Weiner et al. (Weiner, Rogers, Davidson, and Squire, 1986b), entitled, "Effects of Stimulus Parameters on Cognitive Side Effects" may be one of the more important of the comparative studies in that it categorically identifies SW devices as brain damaging. [627]

The study typically compares SW with BP as well as BL and UL electrode placements with various combinations of each. Machines used are a MECTA BP device versus the Medcraft B-24 SW. Adequate number of treatments is determined by the attending physician. The study is prospective, testing before ECT, 2-3 days after final ECT, and again at six months for "long-term" follow-up. There are 53 subjects as well as a Control of 21 subjects, 39 and 13 respectively of whom were tested again at six month follow-up. Memory and EEG prospective testing was utilized to measure safety, while the Hamilton Depression Rating Scale (HDRS), as well as the Brief Psychiatric Rating Scale (BPRS), the Zung Self-Rating Depression Scale (SDS), and a discharge summary rating was used for rating efficacy. Thus, although EEG results are published separately for these subjects under "Effects of electroconvulsive therapy upon brain electrical activity" (Weiner et al.1986a) both safety and efficacy are tested under the one study "Effects of Stimulus Parameters on Cognitive Side Effects" (Weiner et al 1986b).

This is an especially intriguing study in that Larry Squire, well known for his retrograde memory studies of "ECT" recipients wherein permanent amnesic gaps are identified, teams up with one of the world's strongest advocates of BP-ECT, Richard Weiner. Right away, we are told:

> Specific initial stimulus parameters of each device were chosen to be relatively equivalent with respect to seizure threshold. [628] (p.316)

"Stimulus parameters" adjusted to "seizure threshold" once again denotes minimal stimulus BP (and SW) which apparently includes minimal stimulus UL-ECT. Moreover, just above threshold output is confirmed in the separately published EEG portion of this study, "Effects of electroconvulsive therapy upon brain electrical activity," wherein the threshold titration method is specifically described (Weiner et al. , 1986a, p.271).

We are further informed that SW stimuli is: ". . . associated with 2.6 times stimulus energy (joules), 3.1 times the applied charge (coulombs), and 6.9 times the mean current [629] [630] (coulombs per second) as that associated with pulse stimuli" (p.317).

---

[627] The negative findings and the inclusion of well-respected researcher Larry Squire, one of the more objective, unbiased investigators in the field, appears to be no coincidence.

[628] The idea is to come as close as possible to just above threshold for each recipient with each device—both BP and SW.

[629] Even ignoring the one Ampere APA limit, the normal maximum peak current of the Medcraft device, though high, does not exceed 1.410 mAmps and is usually lower than this (Department of Health and Human Services, 1982a, pp. A9-A10; see section in this manuscript on SW). In fact, if the Medcraft was limited to a floor of 200 ohms Resistance as Weiner suggests, by Ohm's Law, the B-24 would never surpass 850 mAmps of current, comparable to MECTA's current. But even if lower impedances are allowed, such as in the rare circumstance of 120 ohms wherein 1.410 mAmps could be reached, the dramatically deteriorating current of constant voltage devices could fall as low as 425 mAmps (400 ohms) at the end of one second maximum duration even at a maximum voltage of 170 volts, less than half the current of BP. Moreover, even at SW threshold dosages, the dramatically deteriorating current of constant voltage devices concomitant with increasing impedances, yet results in much less overall Energy Output in Joules than voltage increasing, constant current BP devices administered at clinically applied suprathreshold dosages. That this is so can be deduced by the fact that even if 3.1 fold (maximum) Joules of SW compared to BP are needed to induce adequate seizures, the Energy Output in Joules is immediately regained by BP by the up to seven fold Joules (maximum) that BP at clinically applied dosages exceeds EO at BP-threshold. This can result in a BP Energy Output two and one half to three times that required for SW-threshold.

[630] In 1982, Weiner informed the FDA that maximum current on a SW device is 1.410 Amps (Department of Health and Human Services, 1982a, pp. A9-A10; see section in this manuscript on SW). MECTA devices normally emit a constant current of .8Amps.6.9 times the constant current of the MECTA device would be 5.52 Amperes (.8 x 6.9 = 5.52), an awesome wallop, if true. It would be interesting to know how Weiner derived such a figure. Did Weiner simply attach the two electrodes to an ammeter wherein, except

Given that BP threshold can mean half (or less) the electrical dosage of (even just above threshold) SW, it is certainly not surprising to find minimal stimulus BP superior to SW in all safety concerns.

Not unexpectedly then, in terms of anterograde (short term) memory 2-3 days after final ECT, we find that UL is superior to BL, and BP is superior to SW. Again, not unexpectedly, BL (in general) and SW recipients (in general) showed the greatest deficits (in that these required higher electrical outputs to reach seizure threshold) performing far worse than Controls. BL-SW recipients, of course, were clearly "the most impaired" (p.318) whereas the UL-BP group did not differ from Control (showing no deficits). Of course, UL ECT, as we have learned, is ineffective at threshold. All other groups in the study were impaired. One interesting finding, however, was that in tasks requiring non-dominant right brain functioning, i.e. figure reproduction, the UL (BP and SW) subjects (shocked on the non-dominant side) could not be well differentiated from BL (BP and SW) subjects respectively while Controls outperformed them both. In short, tasks requiring brain functioning on the hemisphere UL-ECT recipients were administered ECT, did not score better than BL-ECT recipients administered ECT to both sides of the brain.

In terms of retrograde (or long term) memory functioning 2-3 days after final shock, similar findings were reported. Given minimal stimulus BP versus (minimal stimulus) SW, minimal stimulus BP outperforms minimal stimulus SW, predictable results in that less EO (electrical energy) is required for minimal stimulus BP than minimal stimulus SW.

> By six months, anterograde (short term) memory functions allegedly return to normal. (p.320)

Some retrograde (long term) memory functions also return to normal by six months.

But surprisingly, and perhaps due to the presence of Squire, we see something very significant and contradictory to the above findings, at least regarding retrograde amnesia, something not identified in any previous Weiner-Sackeim comparative study.

Self-ratings of memory functioning co-variated (that is, were not consistent) with actual memory scores 2-3 days following ECT, indicating recipients believed their memories to have improved at this point, when, in fact, their memories had gotten much worse. Moreover, instead of relating to actual objective memory scores, feelings of improved memory directly correlated with either an actual or placebic anti-depressant effect, an effect recipients either actually experienced as a result of "treatment" or believe they experienced as a result of "treatment" (p.320). In other words, anti-depressant effects seemed to correlate not to actual improved memory (which had actually gotten worse), but to *feelings* of improved memory. In short, feelings of memory improvement, instead of correlating to actual memory scores (which had deteriorated), instead correlated to participants' belief they had received "treatment" and participants' belief that this "treatment" had improved their memories.

But just as amazingly and for the first time in any Weiner-Sackeim comparative study, the study differentiates between positive and negative results not merely between BP and SW but between BL and UL ECT in general, that is for both BP at minimal stimulus and SW at minimal stimulus. The study states:

---

for the ammeter, there is no resistance at all-- no human or animal skull to traverse--but perhaps an ammeter only? A constant current BP machine, given the same test, will not surpass .8A under any circumstances. But such a test is highly deceptive in that the current on a SW constant voltage device, unlike a constant current BP device, is totally dependent upon Resistance. In fact, in order to obtain 5.52 Amperes on the SW device, the floor resistance even at maximum voltage, would have to be only 30 Ohms (Ohm's law), about that of an ammeter. A 30Ω resistance is an unrealistic possibility with even a small animal, much less a human skull. Comparing BP to SW with an ammeter only is highly deceptive in that while a BP device maintains its constant current of .8A even with 30Ω of Resistance, it also maintains .8A at 500 or even 600Ω of Resistance whereas, SW devices cannot overcome such Resistances. At high resistances, therefore, the BP device utilizes many more times the EO of a SW device. The comparison is reminiscent of analogies to the amperage elicited from 9 volt battery to light the tiny inside bulb of an automobile which the author heard offered by untutored Psychiatrists during testimony in the Texas Legislature. While amperages as high or even higher than amperages with BP ECT devices are indeed possible with small batteries, achieving such amperage is possible only with virtually no resistance. Quite obviously, a far greater power source than a 9 volt battery is needed to complete a circuit of electricity which must overcome the resistance of a human's skull, brain, blood, and tissue. Because of such misleading analogies, Energy Output in Joules is the best measure of the machines' power—not amperage or charge. In fact, the difficulty of such deception with EO, is the very reason BP manufacturers have now shied away from reporting in EO (Joules).

> The percentage of initial items not recalled at both the two to three day post-ECT and six month post-ECT test sessions revealed a greater impairment for BL subjects than either UL subjects or control subjects. These differences were significant even when partitioning on the basis of stimulus waveform (p.320). . . The above results represent provocative evidence for what amounts to objective personal memory losses lasting at least six months with BL, but not with UL ECT and represents the first time such a differential effect has been reported. (p.321)

In other words, memory of initial responses before BL-ECT, had simply not returned even after six months. Importantly, this included recipients of both BL-BP-ECT (at minimal stimulus!) as well as BL-SW-ECT (at minimal stimulus). To corroborate these findings, subjects were shown their initial responses before ECT. Unlike UL recipients (BP and SW) or Control groups, BL recipients (BP and SW) could not recognize their own initial responses. The total memory of important autobiographical items had simply disappeared--permanently! [631] The study concludes with:

> This strengthens the likelihood that the observed findings represent a true persistent deficit with BL ECT. (p.322)

To be clear, true persistent deficits occurred with both BP-BL-ECT and SW-BL-ECT. The study then uses the recipients' friends and relatives to corroborate the persistent memory loss, concluding:

> It was, in fact, found that corroborated items . . . showed at least as much persistent forgetting . . . as was observed without the use of external corroboration. (p.323) [632]

In short, the memory loss found through cognitive testing was indeed corroborated through friends and relatives.

But perhaps the most astounding revelation--contradicting the earlier conclusions that anterograde and retrograde memory functions returned to normal after six months--is that even six months later, recipients still believed their memory recall for autobiographical items had improved when, in fact, they remained far worse on the objective testing (p.323). Moreover, the anti-depressant effect measured by HRDS continued to correlate with the belief that memory had improved. The study concludes with the assertion that individuals who were experiencing an anti-depressant effect believed their memories had improved when, in fact, they had gotten far worse, a fact which according to the study:

> . . . suggests that the [memory loss] findings are in fact organic rather than functional, and is supported by a number of highly significant correlations between acute objective memory test changes and acute EEG abnormalities. (p.323)

The rather conspicuous correlation between impairment and anti-depression goes unmentioned in the study, a correlation which clearly suggests a relationship between efficacy and impairment. In fact, such a relationship appears corroborative of the organic euphoria theory espoused by Breggin (1979, p.173-177), that is, damage creates a temporary euphoria so that "damage is the cure" (Breggin, 1991, p.198). In short, the unspoken correlates of permanent memory loss (with respect to autobiographical data), concomitant EEG brain abnormalities, and concomitant anti-depressant effects, seem to indicate a direct relationship between so-called therapeutic efficacy (the anti-depressant effect) and brain damage.

Of equal import, the same study—"Effects of Stimulus Parameters on Cognitive Side Effects" (Weiner, Rogers, Davidson, and Squire, 1986b)--eliminates possible memory damage from drugs on the basis that UL subjects would have been just as susceptible to findings of memory damage as a result of drugs and yet were

---

[631] The findings are corroborative of the famous Janis studies (Janis, 1950).

[632] BL recipients had permanently forgotten 35% of base-line items compared to 15% for Controls (p.323), a 20% increase in persistent loss. Among other implications, the findings indicate that long-term forgetting with respect to ECT is not merely a function of depression, but rather a true iatrogenic deficit, that is, a result of the treatment itself.

not affected (at least on tasks requiring the side not "treated"). Consequently, organic damage from BL-ECT appears highly probable and this includes not only SW-BL-ECT, but BP-BL-ECT even at minimal stimulus.

Amazingly, then, the 1986 study with both Larry Squire and Richard Weiner, "Effects of Stimulus Parameters on Cognitive Side Effects" (ibid) through both retrograde memory tests and prospective EEG measurements, appears to confirm the long-term autobiographical damage complained of by "ECT" recipients for some fifty years, damage adamantly and persistently denied by modern day manufacturers.

In spite of concrete findings of damage with both SW and BP, however, Weiner's EEG follow-up study six months later "Effects of electroconvulsive therapy upon brain electrical activity" (Weiner, Rogers, Davidson, and Kahn, 1986a), which does not include Squire, somewhat vaguely concludes, that once "the effects of stimulus intensity per se (energy, current, and charge) upon objectively assessed memory function were evaluated," SW alone was found to be the culprit. Thus, in spite of both BP and SW showing long-term autobiographical memory loss, the study, "Effects of Stimulus Parameters on Cognitive Side Effects" (Weiner, Rogers, Davidson, and Squire, 1986b) apparently by way of addendum, concludes with:

> [T]he relatively low-energy stimuli present with the pulse wave form may lie below a cutoff for intensity-related effects upon memory performance with ECT and, furthermore, that only the higher energy sine-wave stimulus (see footnote 29) is able to exceed this cutoff in an appreciable number of cases. (p.323)

In short, (according to Weiner at al.), BP is simply too minimal in energy output (compared to SW) to have caused any irreversible (memory) damage. In sum, damage from minimal stimulus BL-BP-ECT is simply denied. Moreover, according to the EEG results reported in Weiner's separately published EEG follow-up over the same population, "Effects of electroconvulsive therapy upon brain electrical activity" (Weiner, Rogers, Davidson, and Kahn, 1986a), researchers assert that acute slowing had generally dissipated by six months. [633] The subtle implication, however, is that some (less acute) slowing may have persisted, suggesting at least some degree of irreversible EEG change. In the EEG portion of the follow-up, Weiner et al. are careful to note that the "three individuals with the greatest amount of residual slowing [six months post "ECT"] had all received sine wave bilateral "ECT" (Weiner, Rogers, Davidson, and Kahn, p.277). While SW is no doubt inferior to minimal stimulus BP regarding both EEG slowing and cognitive deficits, this unsurprising fact does not countermand the long term retrograde memory loss for both BL-BP and BL-SW recipients identified via immediate post cognitive testing still present six months following the procedure.

But even if there had been no memory loss regarding BP-ECT, it is important to remind the reader that BP in these studies is once again performed at just above threshold output in spite of the fact that no minimal stimulus BP is administered in the field via second generation MECTA and Somatics BP devices. Untested clinically applied dosages of BP at Energy levels far in excess of those tested here and, in fact, far in excess of SW are administered every day with modern day BP devices throughout the world (see Third Generation BP Devices in Volume II). Moreover, if even minimal stimulus BP can create at least some long term retrograde memory loss, what might be the effects BP-ECT at Energy Outputs grossly exceeding those used in the two studies above?

Regarding the efficacy portion of *Effects of Stimulus Parameters on Cognitive Side Effects* (Weiner, Rogers, Davidson, and Squire, 1986b), once again we are asked to believe that based on all three anti-depressant scales, (BP) results were equivalent (to SW) both at 2-3 days (short term) and at six months (long-term) for all forms of treatment, regardless of electrode placement or wave-form.

> All groups, including controls, were equivalent with regard to baseline HDRS . . . and degree of acute [short term] improvement in HDRS, BPRS, and Zung SDS over the course of treatment. . . . No intergroup differences were found in terms of HDRS, BPRS, and Zung SDS change scores between baseline and six-month post-ECT testing, all of which continued to show evidence of improvement. . . . These findings together suggest an apparent acute therapeutic equivalence on the basis of both electrode placement and stimulus waveform (p.318).

---

[633] Note Squire's absence in the follow-up.

In short, in accordance with Weiner's impetus, the study dubiously asserts that minimal stimulus Brief Pulse (UL and BL) is just as effective as (UL and BL) SW. The finding of "no intergroup differences" with respect to efficacy, that is, between minimal stimulus BP and SW, as has already been noted, conflicts with both earlier and later studies even by ECT advocates themselves calling for more power based upon BP inefficacy. For example, according to the earlier well-respected Robin and Tissera study, BP is only as effective as SW when BP is administered at suprathreshold dosages (Robin and Tissera 1982), but in which case, Squire and Zouzounis found that suprathreshold BP also creates the same cognitive deficits as SW (Squire and Zouzounis 1986). Given that almost all BP today is clinically applied at suprathreshold levels of electricity automatically administered by second, third generation, and possibly even fourth generation BP devices, the above findings in Weiner's 1986 Weiner studies asserting that minimal stimulus BP is as effective as standard or even minimal stimulus SW is extremely suspect. Such conclusions directly conflict with the above Robin and Tissera study (1982) clearly and convincingly identifying efficacy as a product of electrical dosage alone. Indeed, they conflict with later calls for more powerful Brief Pulse devices, generally.

It may well be that HDRS as well as other subjective rating scales are not capable of ferreting out placebo from actual efficacy, that research conclusions are simply not objectively evaluated here or even that the findings actually suggest the anti-depressant effect is indeed connected to damage. After all, perhaps the most critical finding within the Weiner studies above is that the anti-depressant effect directly correlates with the ***belief*** of memory improvement even though no such improvement occurs, but, in fact, has worsened.

Perhaps inspired by the Weiner at al. studies above, Squire and Zouzounis (1986) the very same year, attempt to repeat a Weiner safety study comparing BP with SW, but with one difference. Unlike all the previous safety studies, Squire and Zouzounis test for safety (via memory dysfunction) at suprathreshold BP dosages. The results contradict all previous safety studies with BP, all of which had been performed at threshold or minimal stimulus. The Squire and Zouzounis study finds that truly efficacious (suprathreshold) dosages of BP clearly attenuate safety and are no safer than SW; BP is only safer when delivered at just above threshold or minimal stimulus, but is not truly effective at those outputs. What we seem to be able to conclude from the above studies then, is that while minimal stimulus BP causes less damage than minimal stimulus SW due to the reduction in electrical output, even minimal stimulus BP causes at least some long term damage. Moreover, while minimal stimulus BP causes less damage, minimal stimulus Brief Pulse is not as effective as minimal stimulus SW (which uses twice the electricity). In short, the anti-depressant effect picked up by the HDRS, BPRS, and Zung with minimal stimulus Brief Pulse appears to be directly related to the recognition one has been administered "treatment" followed by the belief that one has gotten better, reflected by the false belief that memory has improved. In short, even with less damage as a result of Brief Pulse minimal stimulus as opposed to SW minimal stimulus, the anti-depressant effect with Brief Pulse may be partially euphoric due to "minor" damage and partially placebic in nature. To what degree minimal stimulus BP efficacy actually equals minimal stimulus SW efficacy then, is difficult to discern. However, a lack of Brief pulse efficacy at minimal stimulus or desire for greater efficacy explains manufacturers decision to increase the power of BP via second and later, third generation BP devices. Moreover, it is important to understand that the Weiner studies here asserting greater safety with BP than SW, that is, less memory disturbance and greater cognitive functioning are once again performed at minimal stimulus BP as opposed to the suprathreshold BP dosages of electricity actually administered in the field.

Study No.7
"Seizure Threshold in Electroconvulsive Therapy, (Sackeim et al.,1987)

This 1987 Sackeim study, the final safety study we shall evaluate, is composed of ECT administered to 52 recipients with a Brief Pulse MECTA device and, once again, clearly at minimal stimulus. Sackeim (et al.) tells us, "In this study, we deliberately administered subconvulsive intensities to determine the dosage necessary to elicit seizure" (Sackeim et al.1987, p 358). Thus, the sub-convulsive method of attaining as close to threshold as possible with both BL and UL ECT and even with respect to male and female is used for both BP and SW, as opposed to the absolute or equal emissions previously used with both BL and UL, a method (according to Sackeim), often leading to unnecessarily high suprathreshold dosing. In short, Sackeim implies that equal or absolute dosages of electricity were previously utilized with both BL and UL ECT with both BP and SW with little or no discretion regarding sex, age, weight, etc. Sackeim concludes that:

> . . . an outcome of this variability is that . . . patients with low thresholds can receive in each treatment session stimulus, intensities that may be several thousand percent in excess of their thresholds. To the extent that a dosage above threshold contributes to adverse cognitive side effects, the traditional practice may unnecessarily increase the magnitude of these side effects. (Sackeim et al.1987, p 358)

Sackeim appears to be increasing physicians' awareness of the indiscriminate use of electrical emissions emanating from SW and even BP in order that future users of Brief Pulse strive to use true minimal stimulus in all instances to reduce the cognitive side effects.

Thus Sackeim points out the superiority of BP minimal stimulus over SW at minimal stimulus. However, while Sackeim's observation is certainly true of young children receiving absolute doses on constant voltage SW devices compared to minimal stimulus BP devices, Sackeim fails to mention that SW devices are often too weak to induce seizure in older recipients, whereas, modern day BP devices by virtue of their ability to maintain a constant current regardless of increasing Impedances, often use outputs far in excess of that utilized by constant voltage SW devices.

But Sackeim also fails to inform the reader that, in spite of his emphasis on the "responsible" use of minimal stimulus Brief Pulse, that second generation MECTA BP devices in use at this time and, in fact, the one utilized by Sackeim in this very study, emit default outputs of circa 2.5 fold threshold with BL-ECT and circa 5.0 fold threshold with UL "ECT," which Sackeim circumvents through manual titration. Indeed, the default outputs of what were actually second generation BP devices were not known to the general public at this time and so not reported until 1994 (Beale 1994; Cameron 1994) and even then only obliquely. Rather than using the default outputs of the second generation MECTA BP device, in short, Sackeim manually titrates for minimal stimulus.

In fact, Sackeim seems to falsely suggest that what are actually second generation BP devices in use at this time, deliver minimal stimulus outputs with BL ECT so that the single fault with BP strategies is in using the same electrical dose administered to males and females of the same age and that both BL and UL ECT are delivered with the same absolute output. Quite counterintuitively, moreover, Sackeim subsequently points out that threshold output with BP-BL-ECT can increase as much as 87% over a treatment course (Ibid p 358), asserting, "The increase in seizure threshold observed over the course of treatment was a highly consistent finding" (Ibid p 359). Revealingly, it is this rationale that is eventually used to justify increasing the power of what are actually second generation BP devices to third generation BP devices, as we see in Volume II. Indeed, Sackeim .even expands upon the second great rationale for increasing BP power.

> There are preliminary indications that low-dosage techniques may not be as efficacious as traditional forms of ECT administration, particularly with unilateral electrode placement. Unfortunately, no information is presently available concerning the extent that dosage should exceed seizure threshold to maintain strong therapeutic results. If and when a therapeutic dosage window is determined, titration strategies may be designed to administer doses that exceed the threshold by fixed amounts (e. g. , 50%). (Sackeim et al.1987, p 359)

Thus, beneath his concern for suprathreshold outputs, Sackeim lays the groundwork for increasing BP-BL-"ECT" and BP-UL-"ECT" with "doses that exceed the threshold by fixed amounts," thereby calling for more powerful BP machines, generally. In claiming that seizure threshold can increase by as much as 87% for BP-BL-ECT and because "there are [new] preliminary indications that low-dosage techniques may not be as efficacious as traditional forms of ECT administration," i.e. Sine Wave, Sackeim is vying for outputs at least twice that of minimal stimulus, even with BP-*BL*-ECT and 5.0 fold threshold with UL-ECT, default outputs already delivered by the second generation BP device he is using. Thus, in spite of his close association with MECTA, Sackeim fails to inform us that the very MECTA BP machine he is operating in the study already administers default outputs greater than the circa 2.5 fold threshold with BL-ECT and greater than circa 5.0 fold threshold with UL-ECT he is indirectly suggesting, indeed, more than enough to accommodate alleged rising thresholds of 100% and so already more than enough to obtain "strong therapeutic results" with both BL and UL Brief Pulse "ECT." In fact, by ignoring the existence of the second generation BP device he is using, Sackeim is actually vying for third generation BP devices, twice as powerful as second generation BP devices as we shall witness in Volume II. In sum, Sackeim would have us believe that what are actually the second generation BP devices manufactured at this time, BP machines in the field are eliciting the minimal stimulus he uses in his study, thereby justifying the unpublished 2.5/5.0 fold power output of the already extant unreported second generation BP devices of which he must certainly have been aware. Even more insidiously, Sackeim's arguments attempt to "justify" not only the unreported second generation BP devices which are already being manufactured and used in the field at this time, but even more powerful third generation BP devices, as we shall see in Volume II. This manufacturer stratagem, with which we shall grow familiar in Volume II, is entirely contingent upon the false notion that what were aware actually second generation BP devices such as that used by Sackeim in this very study, were pre-set for minimal stimulus output with BL-ECT. Sackeim, in short, is using a second generation MECTA BP device which he must know is already pre-set to more than 2.5 and 5.0 fold threshold BL/UL "ECT" respectively, and which he hand-titrates to minimal stimulus to "prove" greater safety with Brief Pulse compared to SW. In short, Sackeim would have us believe he is working with a first generation BP device.

CHAPTER 44

Non-prospective Comparative MRI and CT Studies

Bio-psychiatry has provided us with a myriad of MRIs and CT scan studies. Most of these studies are not related to ECT or psychotropic drug damage, but rather attempt to identify certain parts of the brain reflective of specific psychiatric disorders. Upon examining the literature, as did the Utah Biomedical Test Laboratory during the 1976-1982 FDA Investigation (Grahn, 1976; Grahn et al. , 1977), however, the most apparent and striking finding, is possibly the almost ubiquitous damage and abnormal structural findings discovered by such MRI and CT investigations in those who had a history of psychiatric hospitalizations, including those administered ECT. Damage discovered on CT and MRI scans include ventricular enlargement and focal volume loss in the temporal lobes (Shelton, and Weinberger, 1986), cerebellar atrophy (Nasrallah, Coffman, and Olson, 1989), subcortical (Rabins et al. , 1991), white matter hyperintensity (Bradley et al. , 1984; Coffey,1987a), amygdala-hippocampal and cortical atrophy (Coffey et al. , 1993, p.11), sulcal widening (Coffey et al. , 1993, p.11; Dolan et al.), frontal lobe atrophy, and cerebral hemisphere asymmetry (Hauser, Altshuler, Berrittini, Dauphinais, Gelernter, Pos, 1989). Utilizing MRI, percentages of discoverable damage within psychiatrically treated populations in these studies range from 70 to 94 percent (Pande et al. , 1990; Coffey, Weiner, Djang, Figiel, Soady, Patterson, Holt, Spritzer, Wilkinson, 1991b, p.1014). Indeed, both retrospective and prospective MRI studies comparing pre and post BP-ECT, find structural damage in the pre-MRIs (Pande et al. ,1990; Coffey et al. , 1991b).

Bio-psychiatrists conducting these MRI (and CT) studies most often explain these pre-CT and pre-MRI abnormalities as causes or manifestations of schizophrenia (Shelton and Weinberger, 1986; Swayze, Andreasen, Randall, Ehrhardt, and Yuh, 1990), depression (Coffey, Wilkinson, Weiner, Parashos, Djang, Webb, Figiel, and Spritzer, 1993; Dolan, Calloway, Thacker, and Mann, 1986) or other so-called affective disorders (Kellner, Rubinow, Gold, and Post, 1983; Sackheim, Prohovnik, Moeller, Brown, Apter, Prudic, Devanand, and Mukherjee, 1990), in short, alleged biological manifestations of mental illnesses. [634] While it is sometimes acknowledged that such changes might be attributable to either psychiatric drug usage (Coffey, Figiel, Djang, and Weiner, 1989; Dupont, Jernigan, Butters, Delis, Hesselink, Heindel, and Gillin, 1990) or previous bouts of "ECT" [635] (Coffey et al. ,1992, p.13), the favored offender is "mental illness. "

In any case, since almost all these MRI and CT studies are of previously hospitalized patients, a serious bio-psychiatric problem arises--the treatment itself as a source of damage. In short, both drugs and/or ECT cannot be ruled out as the embarrassing cause for some, if not most of this damage. Indeed, so ubiquitous is the prescribing of psychiatric drugs to hospitalized mental patients, that the possibility of long-term damage due to these prescriptions cannot be eliminated. Proponents of "ECT," on the other hand, through cognitive and EEG studies (see above) and in the last fifteen years, through a handful of CT and MRI retrospective and prospective studies, the most modern of which utilize Brief Pulse, have dismissed ECT as a possible source of

---

[634] Changes found within the context of a study are usually ascribed to aging (Bradley, Waluch, Brandt-Zawadzki, Yardley, and Wyckoff, 1984; Coffey, Weiner, Djang, Figiel, Soady, Patterson, Holt, Spritzer, Wilkinson, 1991b; Hickie, Scott, Mitchell, Wilhelm, Austin, and Bennett, 1995;)

[635] Damage due to prior ECT is typically explained away in these prospective MRI studies by no new structural changes after a series of BP (Coffey, 1991b; Coffey et al., 1993., Rabins, Pearlson, Aylward, Kumar, and Dowell, 1991; Swayze, Andreasen, Alliger, Ehrhardt, and Yuh, 1990).

damage. Consequently, in that we have examined several important cognitive and EEG studies, let us now examine several important MRI and CT scan studies. First, let us examine the non-prospective MRI and CT studies (following ECT) most often used for dismissing ECT as a possible source of damage (Devanand et al, 1994).

Prior to the first prospective (before and after) MRIs for BP-ECT, there are three to five main studies dismissing ECT as the source of irreversible brain damage discovered on CT scans and MRIs of previously treated psychiatric patients. These studies include "Structural brain abnormalities in bipolar affective disorder: Ventricular enlargement and local hyperintensities" (Swayze et al. , 1990), "Cortical magnetic resonance imaging changes in elderly inpatients with major depression" (Rabins et al, 1991), "Leukoencephalopathy in elderly depressed patients for ECT" (Coffey, Figiel, Djang, Cress, Saunders, and Weiner, 1988b), "Subcortical white matter hyperintensity on magnetic resonance imaging: Clinical and neuroanatomic correlates in the depressed elderly" (Coffey and Weiner, 1989) and "Structural brain abnormalities in the depressed elderly" (Coffey, 1991a). Amongst the several retrospective studies we examine, serious methodological flaws are discoverable in each of them.

Study No.8
"Leukoencephalopathy in elderly depressed patients for ECT," (Coffey et al. 1988b).

This retrospective [636] MRI study, which includes Weiner as one of the authors, and which is often used to dismiss ECT as a source of damage, uses MRI and CT scans to examine previously hospitalized patients in the older age category. After discovering hyperintensities (areas of the brain containing lesions) in almost all the brains of these depressed patients, the study points out that only 18% of all these previously hospitalized patients had received ECT. The researchers conclude that ECT could not have been the cause of the discovered damage (found in these recipients) since there was damage in many of the non-ECT recipients as well. Unfortunately, this particular study offered no Control Group, that is, a group of never hospitalized persons. Thus, the retrospective finding of no ECT damage based on findings of ubiquitous damage in virtually all previously hospitalized patients, is far from conclusive.

Continuing with the examination of the same retrospective MRI study (following ECT) by Coffey et al. , *Leukoencephalopathy in elderly depressed patients for ECT* (1988b), which as noted, includes Weiner as one of the authors, the stimulus dosing strategy described regarding Brief Pulse ECT following MRI (Coffey et al. , 1988b, p.146), is referred to as "moderately suprathreshold" [637] which appears to be just that--barely above threshold, as expected. Within the retrospective study here, Coffey refers us to yet another of his studies (which also includes Weiner as author), "Augmentation of ECT seizures with caffeine" *(*Coffey et al. , 1987b) for the stimulus strategy utilized in his later 1988(b) non-prospective MRI study. Not only is the stimulus strategy to which he refers the (Dose) Titration Method, and not the automated Age-Dosage Method used in the field, but the referenced study (Coffey et al. ,1987b) is actually concerned with lowering seizure threshold through the use of caffeine, hardly a suprathreshold issue. The referenced study, "Augmentation of ECT Seizures with Caffeine," voices Coffey's concern with the rise in seizure threshold throughout a course of ECT and the use of caffeine to successfully suppress increasing threshold throughout the ECT course. In the study, Coffee et al. inform the reader that a MECTA "C" or . . . Thymatron is used. The MECTA "C" is a known minimal stimulus Brief Pulse device never exceeding a default output of more than 1.08 MTTLOI or just above seizure threshold output for any age category while the Thymatron is an early second generation Somatics BP device with default settings of 2.0 fold threshold in every age category. In both cases, however, Coffee et al. manually titrate for minimal stimulus, despite the utilization of later more powerful second generation MECTA and Somatics Brief Pulse devices used in the field at this time eliciting default outputs of circa 2.5 fold threshold with BL ECT and circa 5.0 fold threshold outputs with UL ECT in every age category. We must assume from the reference and the referenced study itself that during this period, Coffey believed threshold seizures with BL-BP ECT desirable

---

[636] Retrospective study, in this instance, refers to the event (here, the possible cause of the damage) which occurs here before the evaluation as opposed to a prospective study which evaluates both before and after the event (that is, the possible cause of the damage).

[637] Moderately threshold as opposed to barely threshold, has since come to mean two and one half times threshold for BL and approximately five times threshold for UL. At the time of the 1988 study; however, which refers to a 1987(b) study (Coffey, Weiner, Hinkle, Cress, Daughtry, and Wilson, 1987b), the term actually meant barely over threshold (Coffey et al., 1987b, p.639).

and effective and that his non-prospective MRI study, "Leukoencephalopathy in elderly depressed patients for ECT" (1988b) following ECT is thus performed at just above threshold. As such, we can reliably assume that Coffey's prospective MRI studies finding no new damage with BP were indeed conducted at just above threshold output or minimum stimulus in lieu of the much higher outputs administered in the field.

Study No.9
"Subcortical hyperintensity on magnetic resonance imaging: a comparison of normal and depressed elderly subjects" (Coffey et al.1990a).

This later Coffey et al. (1990a) study (which includes Weiner as one of the authors once again), offers the missing control group (of non-previously hospitalized patients) for a similar older age category. In the newer retrospective MRI scan study, we again see that almost all persons in this age category--both persons with no history of psychiatric treatment and persons with a history of psychiatric treatment--commonly display damage discoverable on MRIs. Obviously, some changes occur with age and this is one of the given explanations. But we also discover, from a comparison with the never-psychiatrically hospitalized Control Group, that damage in previously hospitalized psychiatric patients is much more severe than the damage seen in the non-previously hospitalized group. Thus, the initial Coffey (1988b) study had failed to differentiate between normal damage of elder populations and the more severe damage associated with past treatment groups. The fact that the first study used subjects belonging to an umbrella category of older age patients with hospitalization histories wherein severe organic findings were common in both ECT and non-ECT recipients fails to take into account damage due to psychiatric drugs which may have masked damage caused by ECT, thereby nullifying the study's conclusion that damage cannot be attributed to ECT. In short, the group in the first study of previously hospitalized patients without a never-hospitalized Control group, is revealed by the second study with a never-hospitalized Control group, to have had much more severe damage than those without a history of psychiatric treatment. Because the entire previously-hospitalized group contained both ECT and non-ECT and because all recipients had all been treated with psychiatric drugs, the first study fails to differentiate between damage caused by psychiatric drugs, damage caused by a combination of ECT and drug therapy, and damage caused by ECT alone. Thus ECT as a source of damage is not eliminated in either the earlier study (with no Control Group) or the later study wherein the more severe damage found in previously hospitalized recipients might well have been a result of drugs, a combination of ECT and drugs, or ECT alone. The more severe ubiquitous damage found in previously hospitalized patients, in short, may well have masked damage due to ECT alone. In brief, because the findings in the second study reveal more severe damage in individuals with psychiatric histories, neither study eliminates the prospect of damage caused by ECT. In fact, while the finding that damage is more severe in patients with a history of psychiatric hospitalizations may be the result of mental illness--such a finding may also be the result of iatrogenic injury due to psychiatric treatment itself. Not only do these MRI retrospective studies fail to eliminate the possibility of damage due to ECT, therefore, but they open up the possibility of damage due to psychiatric treatment generally.

Study No.10
"Cortical magnetic resonance imaging changes in elderly inpatients with major depression" (Rabins et al. , 1991)

This is another of the commonly cited retrospective MRI studies, which attempts to eliminate ECT as a source of damage. This study is also conducted within the older age category of psychiatrically treated patients. The study points out that among depressed patients, those who had previously received ECT did not manifest damage which was worse than other psychiatrically treated persons. Once again, however, there is no Control Group of Depressed older patients who had never been hospitalized or treated. Thus, damage which may have been caused by psychiatric drugs is inextricable from damage which may have been caused by ECT. This study too fails to eliminate psychiatric drugs, a combination of psychiatric drugs and ECT, or ECT alone as factors generating the more severe damage discernable in older psychiatrically treated patients compared to individuals of the same age who have never been hospitalized or treated. [638] Too, we do not know if the former ECT recipients were treated with minimal stimulus, the higher default titration outputs of second generation BP devices, or SW. In fact, elderly patients who had been previously hospitalized and administered "ECT" may well have been the recipients of SW. Finally, these studies are not prospective, that is, these are not comparisons of non-previously treated individuals before ECT with the same individuals following ECT. In short, although damage is identified, none of the retrospective MRI studies eliminate the possibility of damage due to ECT. At most, these studies merely point out that almost all psychiatrically treated older subjects display more severe damage than non-psychiatrically treated older individuals in the same age category, a fact which not only does not eliminate the possibility of damage due to ECT, but raises the possibility of psychiatrically induced, iatrogenic injury, generally.

Conflicting Studies

Retrospective and pre-MRI and CT damage findings are not without conflicting conclusions. An equal number of modern retrospective MRI and CT studies have found direct correlations between ECT and brain damage. Such studies include (a) Andreasen, Ernhardt, Swayze, Alliger, Yuh, Cohen, and Ziebell (1990); (b) Calloway, Dolan, Jacoby, and Levy, (1981); (c) Weinberger, Torrey, Neophytides, Wyatt (1979a); and (d) Weinberger Torrey, Neophytides, and Wyatt (1979b).

(a) “Magnetic resonance imaging of the brain in schizophrenia” (Andreasen et al.1990) utilizes MRI for an ECT treated population of twenty to correlate ECT treatments with lateral ventricular volumes, in short, brain damage. The results are convincing, but not conclusive in that **no** non-ECT recipient controls are utilized. Moreover, the study contains no differentiation between BP and SW treated recipients.

(b) “ECT and cerebral atrophy: a computed tomographic study” by Calloway et al. (1981), utilizes CT scans to report that among a population of older psychiatrically treated individuals, frontal lobe atrophy (sulcal widening) is remarkably more common among those who have been administered ECT (68%-ECT as opposed to 27%-non-ECT). In short, brain matter is diminished in a much larger percentage of those who had experienced “ECT.” Results are convincing in that the differences were discovered amongst the same older population--that is, older previously hospitalized individuals. These findings contradict the retrospective Coffey-Weiner and Rabins et al. (1991) studies above. Once again, however, there is no differentiation between BP and SW treated recipients.

(c) “Lateral cerebral ventricular enlargement in chronic schizophrenia” by Weinberger et al. (1979a) utilize CT scans among a group of psychiatrically treated individuals to find those who had been administered ECT with larger ventricular brain ratios compared to those who had never received ECT; in short, ECT recipients had more damage. But while differences between ECT and non-ECT recipients are found amongst the same population of psychiatrically treated individuals, no differentiation is made between older and younger psychiatrically treated individuals. Thus, while results are convincing, they are not conclusive. Once more, moreover, no differentiation is made between BP and SW treated recipients.

(d) “Structural abnormalities in cerebral cortex of chronic schizophrenic patients” by Weinberger et al. (1979b), utilize CT in another psychiatrically treated population study to discover that cortical atrophy is remarkably more common among those who had been administered ECT than in those who had not been administered ECT (53%-ECT as opposed to 17%-non-ECT). But while differences between ECT and non-ECT recipients are found amongst the same population of psychiatrically treated individuals, once again, no differentiation is made between older and younger psychiatrically treated individuals. Consequently, results, though convincing,

[638] The earlier Coffey et al. (1990a) study (which included Weiner) only introduced the control group in an attempt to associate organic manifestations with psychiatrically depressed patients, in short, organic syndrome with “mental illness.”

cannot be considered conclusive. Once again, moreover, there Is no differentiation between BP and SW treated recipients.

While the above four studies identify damage in ECT recipients, none utilize controls of non-psychiatrically treated individuals. Nevertheless, in three of the four studies, psychiatrically treated non-ECT recipients are compared to psychiatrically treated ECT recipients so that, unlike the Coffey et al. (1988b; 1990a) and Rabins et al. , (1991) studies, convincing differences between ECT and non-ECT recipients are, in fact, identified. While it is now known that in older populations of non-psychiatrically treated individuals, damage of a less severe nature is common, the 1981 Calloway study discovers differences between ECT and non-ECT recipients amongst the same older population of previously hospitalized individuals and this finding is convincing. Unfortunately, the types of machines used are not mentioned so that the Calloway study (as well as the Weinberger studies) based on the years they were conducted (1981 and 1979 respectively), may be damning of SW alone. The 1990 Andreasen study may well have included BP, but does not specify; moreover, it fails to use controls either of non-ECT recipients or non-previously hospitalized individuals of the same age category.

CHAPTER 45

Prospective MRI and CT Studies "Proving" Safety and Efficacy of Brief Pulse

Although a strong case had been made for brain damage caused by SW at this point, the stage was now set for seemingly incontrovertible proof of damage, moderate damage, or no damage at all with the newer, allegedly safer BP devices. The question which yet remained to be definitively settled was: "Does modern BP ECT eliminate cognitive dissonance or brain damage?" An incontrovertible answer seemed possible by use of the newest most sensitive of technologies together with the most unassailable of studies-- purely prospective MRI scans--a simple before and after picture. A handful of these seemingly decisive studies emerged, upon which the entire issue of Brief Pulse safety compared to SW seems to have been weighed, balanced, and ultimately determined (Devanand, Dwork, Hutchinson, Bolwig, and Sackheim, 1994). The final outcome of these studies was that little or no structural damage is discoverable following BP-ECT. But let us evaluate these "decisive" prospective MRI studies, which seemingly settled this issue, particularly minimal stimulus.

Problematically, as already noted, almost all prospective MRI studies, that is, comparisons of pre and post BP and SW, find structural damage in the pre-MRIs (Pande et al. ,1990). Researchers conducting these MRI (and CT) investigations, as also noted above, often explain these pre-MRI abnormalities as schizophrenia (Shelton and Weinberger, 1986; Swayze, Andreasen, Randall, Ehrhardt, and Yuh, 1990), depression (Coffey, Wilkinson, Weiner, Parashos, Djang, Webb, Figiel, and Spritzer, 1993; Dolan, Calloway, Thacker, and Mann, 1986), aging (Bradley, Waluch, Brandt-Zawadzki, Yardley, and Wyckoff, 1984; Hickie, Scott, Mitchell, Wilhelm, Austin, and Bennett, 1995), and other affective disorders (Kellner, Rubinow, Gold, and Post, 1983; Sackheim, Prohovnik, Moeller, Brown, Apter, Prudic, Devanand, and Mukherjee, 1990)--biological manifestations of mental illnesses. Although it is sometimes acknowledged--usually as a side-note--that such changes might be attributable to either psychiatric drugs (Coffey, Figiel, Djang, and Weiner, 1989; Dupont, Jernigan, Butters, Delis, Hesselink, Heindel, and Gillin, 1990) or previous ECT[639] (Coffey et al. ,1992, p.13), the latter two possibilities have generally been dismissed, as noted, through the modern retrospective studies showing ubiquitous damage in almost all pre-ECT scans. Most of the modern prospective MRIs, as we shall see, do not compare BP to SW, but rather, as is fitting, compare pre and post BP-ECT scans. The following prospective studies we shall examine, allegedly find--not without exception--no new structural damage following BP ECT.

We have been observing how cognitive testing as well as EEG safety (and efficacy) testing for BP has been administered almost exclusively at threshold--a therapeutically ineffective or only mildly effective procedure--but which produces relatively little or no manifest physiological damage. Since many of these minimal stimulus studies included Weiner--and Weiner is also included in a number of the MRI studies done in tandem with Coffey, we might suspect that MRIs regarding BP ECT conducted by Coffey and Weiner (Coffey et al. , 1988a; Coffey et al. , 1989; Coffey et al. , 1993) are also performed at threshold. In fact, as we shall see, these studies typically employ either the HASS (Half Age Stimulus Strategy) or sub-convulsive Dose Titration Method--not the more "effective," but much more damaging clinically applied dosages employed through the automated Age-Dosage method used with MECTA and Somatics second generation BP devices. Not

---

[639] Previous ECT damage is explained away either by methodologically flawed non-prospective or pre-ECT MRIs and CT scans or by these same prospective MRI studies which allegedly show no structural changes after a series of BP (Coffey, 1991a; Coffey et al., 1991b; Coffey et al., 1993., Rabins, Pearlson, Aylward, Kumar, and Dowell, 1991; Swayze, Andreasen, Alliger, Ehrhardt, and Yuh, 1990.)

surprisingly, in short, we will discover that virtually all the prospective MRI scans are performed at minimal stimulus, ingenuous, in that, one might expect Weiner, who actually edited the MECTA manuals, to have been aware of the default suprathreshold electrical dosages automatically administered by second generation BP devices at this time of these studies. That the MRI prospective studies utilize minimal stimulus is not questioned by any regulatory agency, however, in that most of the MRI prospective studies were conducted before 1994--the year Beale et al. (1994) finally revealed that MECTA and Somatics BP devices were actually set for two and one-half times threshold with BL and 5.0 fold threshold with UL. It was not until 1994, moreover, that Cameron (1994) first revealed the preponderant power of BP devices compared to SW. All literature before about 1994, we should recall, reported BL-BP "ECT" effective at just above threshold outputs--outputs typically using much less Energy and power than SW. Moreover, it was yet assumed at this time, that all ECT worked by inducing an adequate seizure. Accordingly, it was yet assumed Brief Pulse effective at minimal stimulus, and therefore regulated to minimal stimulus. Indeed, Readouts, on MECTA and Somatics BP devices as we have seen, (falsely) corroborated these assumptions. Naturally, almost all BP safety studies designed to prove greater BP safety, including prospective MRI BP safety studies, were performed at minimal stimulus.

Numerous retrospective studies associating ECT with brain damage as well as dissociating ECT with damage, and particularly in previously hospitalized patients, revealed that brain damage often exists even prior to ECT, damage which might be attributable to any number of sources, e. g. aging, mental illness, drug treatment, and/or previous ECT treatment. For this reason, results both pro and con continued to remain dubious. Fairly clear EEG evidence implicated SW as a source of brain damage but the critical question remained: "Does the "new and improved" BP-ECT cause brain damage, so that if prior damage is identified, is there any new damage following BP-ECT? Prospective CT and (most especially) prospective MRI studies seemed the definitive method by which to answer this yet unresolved question, the answer to which would either redeem or condemn the modern day ECT industry--and by modern is meant--the Brief Pulse devices of today.

Specific Prospective MRI and CT Studies "Proving" Safety and Efficacy of Brief Pulse

There are only about seven actual prospective MRI and CT studies of ECT in existence--(Mander at al. , 1987), (Pande et al. , 1990), (Scott et al. , 1990), (Braffman et al. , 1988), (Coffey, Weiner at al.1988a), (Coffey, Weiner et al.1991b), and (Perrin et al. 2012). All except the last find little or no damage following "ECT. " But how reliable are these studies? Let us now examine them in detail.

Study No.11
"Cerebral and brain stem changes after ECT revealed by nuclear magnetic resonance imaging" (Mander, Whitfield, Smith, Douglas, and Kendell, 1987)

"Cerebral and brain stem changes after ECT revealed by nuclear magnetic resonance imaging" is a prospective MRI study of fourteen individuals receiving a mixture of Brief Pulse UL and Brief Pulse BL electrode placement. A control is used for effects of anesthesia, but the post-scans encompass very short-term follow-ups--from immediately after the individual recovers from anesthesia to no more than 24 hours post treatment. Individuals have a mean of only 5.4 treatments total administered 2.4 times per week. The devices used are an English made CC-100 and a MECTA BP device. No electrical parameters are mentioned, nor titration methodology. While the MECTA device is a Brief Pulse, the CC-100 machine type is unknown, but may be an early BP device limited to 100 Joules indicative of minimal stimulus. Moreover, the MECTA device is not identified and may even be a MECTA "C" minimal stimulus BP device. Consequently, minimal threshold and even primarily UL placement (permitting the lowest minimal stimulus) cannot be ruled out. The emphasis here is not on tissue damage, but rather volumetric changes immediately before and after ECT. [640] Mander clearly showed that significant, if temporary changes, did occur during the period tested and concluded:

> It is unlikely that these T1 changes represent inflammation or brain damage, since they are reversed so quickly. It is known that ECT produces a temporary breakdown of the blood-brain barrier (BBB) and

[640] Ventricles are the spaces in center of the brain. Widening of these ventricles suggests shrinkage or atrophy of the brain.

> that this is probably due to the concomitant increase in blood pressure (Bolwig, and Westergaard, 1977a) and cerebral blood flow (Bolwig, Hertz, Paulson, Spotoft, and Rafaelsen, 1977b). It is also known that repeated convulsions at short intervals produce cerebral oedema (Laursen et al, 1985). It has been shown that macromolecules leak into cerebral tissue during the temporary breakdown of the BBB induced by ECT (Bolwig and Westergaard 1977a). This would cause an increase in the relative osmotic pressure of the brain. After restoration of the BBB, movement of water from blood vessels into the tissues would therefore occur, and this would provide an explanation for the rise in T1 over time. . . . [T]he possibility that the observed changes in T1 are induced by the electrical stimulus rather than by the subsequent convulsive activity in the brain cannot be excluded. (Mander et al, p.71)

While Mander finds no permanent damage, he does show persistent significant short term trauma even at what may have been relatively low dosage output even with the initial treatment. No long-term study is carried out. Importantly, however, minimal stimulus brief pulse dosing is likely.

Study No.12
"A preliminary magnetic resonance imaging study of ECT-treated depressed patients" by (Pande, Leon, Grunhaus, Aisen, and Haskett, 1990)

"A preliminary magnetic resonance imaging study of ECT-treated depressed patients" is a prospective MRI study of seven women. In the pre-treatment MRIs, Pande et al. legitimately find damage (multiple areas of hyperintensity mainly in periventricular white matter) in 70% of the seven ECT recipients, but fail to eliminate the possibility of damage due to a previous history of ECT and/or drugs. The researchers denote neither the number of treatments administered nor any "adequate" number (of treatments) methodology. There is no long-term follow-up. No electrical parameter, dosage, titration method, titration level, or device identification is provided. This Pande et al. prospective study utilizes UL-ECT only, indicating that the team sought and titrated for the lowest electrical dosage possible. Based on the publication year (1990) and the journal of publication (*Biological Psychiatry*), the most likely device is a MECTA or Somatics BP apparatus. Threshold dosages of UL-ECT with Brief Pulse are likely. In short, the least damaging of all ECT methodologies--minimal stimulus BP-*UL*-ECT, emitting the smallest (and least effective) electrical dose possible to reach adequate seizure threshold may have been used. Not too surprisingly then, the study finds no visible change from pre-treatment to post-treatment MRI. In that the experiment was most likely carried out with Brief Pulse minimal stimulus outputs, this study does not eliminate the possibility of new damage as a result of BP ECT administered in the field, i.e. via Brief Pulse default outputs of circa 2.5 fold threshold for BP-BL-ECT and 5.0 fold threshold for BP-UL-ECT or greater.

Study No.13
"Time course of cerebral magnetic resonance changes after electroconvulsive therapy" (Scott, Douglas, Whitfield, and Kendell, 1990).

"Time course of cerebral magnetic resonance changes after electroconvulsive therapy" evaluates prospective MRIs on twenty individuals. Post-treatment MRI was administered very shortly after the procedure--25 minutes following ECT. Scott's findings repeat Mander's 1987 study above, but with more detail--breakdown of the blood brain barrier, oedemia, and what appears to be an eventual reversal of these phenomena. There is no long-term follow-up. The study is somewhat tainted as a result of mixed electrode placement--about one-half UL and one-half BL ECT--especially in that the team provides neither titration method nor titration levels. We are only given by way of machine identification, maximum parameters of a MECTA device, which by its' electrical description is either a "C" or "D" BP model BP, an early minimum stimulus Brief Pulse device. Judging from the mixed use of UL and BL electrode placement, seizure duration (a 5-48 second mean), relatively small number of procedures (2-7), and finally the probable use of a "C" or "D" BP device while far more powerful (MECTA) BP devices were available in the field at this time, the study is almost certainly carried out with minimal stimulus or threshold dosages of electricity. Consequently, these results are again not clinically applicable, in that they are not representative of BP administered in the field. Both MECTA and Somatics at this period, marketed BP devices with greatly enhanced power compared to the "C" or even "D" device--about 2.0 to 2.6 fold the power respectively of the older MECTA "D" or "C" BP models used here. Neither the "C" nor "D" was automatically calibrated for suprathreshold dosing and are first as opposed to second generation BP devices. [641] Once again, this prospective MRI study appears to have examined the least damaging dosages possible, utilizing just above threshold BP. [642] Once more then, the study which finds temporary reversible brain trauma fails to eliminate longer term damage as a result of clinically administered BP ECT in the field.

Study No.14

"MR imaging prior to and following electroconvulsive therapy in patients with major affective disorders" (Braffman et al. , 1988).

"MR imaging prior to and following electroconvulsive therapy in patients with major affective disorders" is another referenced MRI prospective study and which is included in Devanand et al. 's 1994 review of animal, CT, and MRI studies on ECT. The study claims to be an MRI prospective study, but exists only as an abstract--most probably a talk delivered at the Hospital affiliated with the University of Pennsylvania. No titration method, number of treatments, electrode placement, long-term follow-up, or Control Group information is provided. From pre-treatment to post-treatment ECT, according to the study, no brain changes occur. It is not possible to evaluate this study based on available information. Minimal number of procedures, UL, and BP minimal threshold dosage cannot be ruled out. Once again, therefore, the study does not eliminate the possibility of brain damage as a result of clinically administered BP ECT.

Study No.15

"Electroconvulsive therapy and cerebral computed tomography: A prospective study" (Bergsholm et al., Bergsholm, Larsen, Rosendahl, and Holsten, 1989).

"Electroconvulsive therapy and cerebral computed tomography: A prospective study" is one of the more sophisticated CT investigations in that it is prospective and has a long-term follow-up. This is a fairly good study, but has a number of obvious limitations. The study is of 40 recipients, who receive a rather large number of treatments (from 3 to 46) with long average seizure durations (the longest mean in one patient, age 65, is 3.0 minutes--and the longest individual seizure in a 37 year old woman--6.5 minutes). Even so, the study utilizes minimal stimulus UL electrode placement apparently with Brief Pulse, the technique requiring the least electrical dosage possible and known to create the fewest cognitive deficits. Tellingly, UL-ECT is now known to be therapeutically useless at just above threshold. That Bergsholm applies just above threshold dosage only, is verified by his reference to the stimulation technique he utilizes. He tells us "the stimulus was delivered by optimal technique," for which he refers us to two referenced studies, one by d'Elia, Ottosson, and Stromberg (1983), and a second by Gordon (1981). Both d'Elia (d'Elia, 1970; d'Elia and Raotma, 1975) and Ottoson (Ottoson, 1960) were proponents and believers in the efficacy of convulsion at minimal dosage (as opposed to efficacy due to adequate electrical dosage) and, therefore, were strong proponents of minimal stimulus. Ottoson, though mistaken, misled numerous practitioners and researchers by claiming that seizure alone--not electricity--was the therapeutic agent in ECT and that threshold convulsion is effective. D. Gordon (1981), another staunch believer in minimal stimulus seizures, wrote such articles as "Electroconvulsive therapy with minimal hazard" (1982). It was Gordon who rediscovered in the present age, the induction of adequate grand

---

[641] The newer second generation BP devices during this period, as has been noted, were pre-calibrated for at least 2.5 fold threshold for BL and 5.0 fold threshold UL ECT. Even if Scott et al. utilized second generation BP devices, the team almost certainly hand-titrated outputs for minimal stimulus.

[642]Neither is the number of treatments (2-7) a representative "course."

mal seizures via low electrical dosages (1980), convinced that high doses of electricity cause irreversible brain damage (1982). [643]

In their study, Bergsholm at al. inform us that stimulus is delivered by a German made Siemons Konvulsator-622 [644] with intermittent volleys of 4 unidirectional 50 waves/sec quarter sine-wave/three-quarter BP pulses of 5 ms. (.005 seconds) duration and 95 ms. intervals between the volleys. The study continues to inform us that the stimulus duration is initially 4.0 seconds (resulting in a current duration of .5 seconds [645]), but is often increased to 6 seconds and occasionally to 8 seconds during the ECT series. The peak value, he tells us, is 800 mA and in a few treatments, 900 mAmps. The approximate amount of electrical energy we are told, is 16-96 Joules with a stimulus duration of 3-6 seconds and an assumed electrode impedance of 200Ω. [646]

Second generation American BP devices by MECTA and Somatics which had already been marketed for four years at the time of the study (1989), delivered a comparable constant current of between 800 and 900 mAmps utilizing an assumed impedance of 220Ω and could be made to emit comparable EOs to those depicted above. [647] While duration trains appear long in this study, it should be understood that with long duration trains with BP (interrupted) output need not be excessive if recipients are manually titrated to threshold (Cameron, 1994). Medcraft's B-25 BP device, for instance, utilizes up to 6.0 seconds of electricity and yet emits no more than 100 Joules. [648] While second generation made-for-America Somatics and MECTA BP devices utilize up to 4.0 seconds and are extremely powerful at pre-set, suprathreshold quantities of electricity, the machines are also extremely versatile [649] and can deliver just above threshold dosages of electricity if recipients are manually titrated for minimal stimulus in lieu of default age-related outputs. [650] In short, the machines can be made to induce adequate seizures at low electrical doses. It is a confusing fact that BP devices can deliver suprathreshold dosages far in excess of standard SW or dosages far below that of SW, depending upon age of recipient and method of titration. The long duration trains in this study, therefore, need not indicate suprathreshold dosing. [651] In the Bergsholm CT study, therefore, given the 16-96 Joule range, and that the study is a research project destined for publication, researchers almost certainly titrated for minimal stimulus, in lieu of using the default outputs administered in the field.

The German made Siemens Konvulsator--in this study at least--utilizes Direct Current (DC) in lieu of the more powerful AC option. DC, at equal frequency and wave length is only half as powerful as the AC typically utilized by all American manufacturers (Cameron, 1994). The Siemens Konvulsator, just as Elcot's American-made MF-1000, appears to have had adjustable AC/DC current and thus would have been set for half-power

---

643 Gordon did not realize that this same cycle of events had been traversed by Wilcox and Liberson in the 1940s and 1950s who also found that just above threshold convulsions--while no doubt safer as well as adequate with respect to seizure duration and intensity—were nevertheless, in essence, therapeutically useless (Cameron, 1994).

644 Apparently, this is a German made Brief Pulse device made by Siemens Healthineers AG located in Erlangen, Germany. Bernd Montag is the CEO of this multibillionaire dollar company with 45,000 employees world-wide. The company manufactures myriad electrical medical devices.

645 BP is interrupted current; therefore, 25 pulses for 4.0 seconds at .005 pulse width equals .5 seconds of actual current duration (25 pulses x 4.0 seconds x .005 sec pulse width = .5 seconds).

646 Information provided of 50 waves or pulses per second is misleading.50 waves x .005 seconds (wave length) x 4.0 seconds = 1.0 second actual current flow--not .5 second current flow. Most likely, the number of alternating current waves (AC) is 50 per second and thus the number of unidirectional or direct current waves (DC) is 25; consequently we divide 50 by two for unidirectional current.25 x .005 x 4.0 = .5 second current duration. The maximum output of 96J which the study reports is probably a combination of an .8A current, and a 6.0 second duration train. .8A x .8A x 200Ω x 25 pulses x .005 sec. WL x 6.0 second duration = 96J. The different combinations used are no doubt a result of manually titrating for minimal stimulus.

647 Energy Output machine readouts of 100 maximum Joules for made-for-America second generation BP devices were misleading, in that calculations were based upon an artificially absolute Resistance of 220Ω. The machines were actually capable of emitting about 250 Joules maximum. The Siemens Konvulsator was probably at least as powerful as second generation American BP devices--perhaps more so. At true minimal stimulus, however, that is, if hand titrated for minimal stimulus, interrupted (BP) current on these devices can induce low output levels limited to a true maximum of 100 Joules and this appears to be the case here.

648 Unfortunately, Medcraft allows the full 100 joules to be administered in even the ten year old age category which may or may not be the case here. Regardless, outputs appear to be hand titrated for minimal stimulus in the study investigated here.

649 SW devices typically have ten settings. Modern BP devices have between 100 and 256 settings (see Thymatron DGx and the defunct Elcot for 100 settings and MECTA devices for 256 settings).

650 Certainly manual titration is utilized almost exclusively in published studies as opposed to "in the field" where almost all recipients are administered default age-related outputs.

651 Longer durations with half-power (DC in lieu of AC) may, depending upon age, yet be minimal threshold.

(or DC) in the Bergsholm study (Bergsholm, p.568). The fact that current appears to change in the Bergsholm study indicates that the machine could be set at varying constant currents. Finally, in spite of the one-quarter sine wave, three quarter brief pulse make-up of the pulse itself, the interrupted current makes the wave essentially brief pulse. [652] In short, this study is based on unilaterally administered minimal stimulus brief pulse. In spite of long seizures, therefore, and what appears on the surface to be intensive ECT, the Bergsholm CT prospective study is based on unilateral minimal stimulus brief pulse dosages of electricity [653] known to be the least cognitively and organically damaging. Such outputs are therapeutically ineffective and almost never utilized in actual clinical practice.

Indeed, the exceptionally long seizures in this study appear to have been induced--not by a stronger current or higher electrical dosage--but through hyperventilation-induced hypocapnia [654] (Bergsholm et al. , p.570). Dosages are individually and manually titrated (16-96 Joules) with varying duration trains for varying age and gender-different subjects. (The 96 Joule maximum is typically a clear indication of minimal stimulus so long as an ER/RRC is implemented limiting output with respect to age). Titrating for minimal stimulus, of course, is the antithesis of the automated Age-Dosage Method pre-set for two and one half times threshold with BL-ECT and five times threshold with UL-ECT in second generation made-for-America MECTA and Somatics BP devices, dosages clinically applied throughout most of America as well as most of the world during this period.

In addition to the unrepresentative UL, minimal stimulus, BP utilized in the study, the study is not blind; that is, raters are aware which are pre and which are post scans. Moreover, thirteen pre-damaged patients are identified. We are then informed that eight patients had received ECT previously. However, we are not told whether or not the eight previous ECT recipients are among the pre-damaged thirteen or whether or not or there is overlapping. Nevertheless, this 1989 CT study is important in that it contains the first long-term prospective follow-up (5-10 months later) with both CT or MRI. In conclusion, the Bergsholm et al. study claims no new damage--except for one older patient. One sixty-nine year old man has a "questionable dilation of the left temporal horn," which became apparent via the long-term follow-up six months later. (Bergsholm et al. , p.569). Bergsholm et al. attribute this to aging, late-onset depression, "imminent dementing disorder," and/or "hypertension" rather than ECT (p.569). The study concedes that for aging individuals, "a similar CT follow-up would have been necessary in matched controls of depressed patients not given ECT" (p.569). Another shortcoming of the study is the CT scan itself. CT is, of course, inferior to MRI and Bergsholm et al. flatly state: "If ECT can induce neuronal damage, this is probably too subtle to be discovered by CT" (p.570). Ultimately, regardless of its prospective nature and regardless of its long-term follow-up, the Bergsholm study is based on therapeutically useless unilaterally administered minimal stimulus brief pulse ECT, leaving us with findings which are of little practical value with respect to the question of potential organic damage as a result of the clinically applied suprathreshold dosing utilized by the BP devices amid the modern era.

Studies apparently find temporary brain trauma with minimal stimulus administered UL and even BL Brief Pulse ECT. It may be no coincidence that efficacy results are not satisfactory in that the anti-depressant effect as well as behavioral modification may be similarly short lived. Indeed, there is a suggestion in these studies in light of the need for more powerful second and third generation BP devices, that where damage is temporary, so is efficacy.

---

[652] The so-called Sine wave is not inherently more destructive than BP, nor is the Brief Pulse (or Wave) inherently safer than SW. What makes the SW potentially destructive is simply the unnecessarily high energy output of uninterrupted current compared to BP. When interrupted, however, SW is as inherently safe as BP and, in fact, might then be deemed BP. BP is thus safer due to lower output as a result of the interrupted current. Moreover, the constant current feature of the modern day BP device makes the machine more efficient, facilitating adequate seizures at comparatively lower outputs. What can make BP potentially destructive, on the other hand, is the electrical compensation utilized to deliver multi-threshold dosages of electricity. In so doing, the constant current feature of BP makes the machine potentially more powerful than SW, particularly, at higher resistances.

[653] By contrast, Calloway et al.'s 1981 retrospective CT study of 41 bilaterally administered ECT recipients, *ECT and cerebral atrophy: a computed tomographic study* (Calloway et al., 1981), and which also utilized a long-term follow-up, discovered frontal lobe atrophy associated with "ECT."

[654] Hypocapnia is defined as less than the normal level of carbon dioxide in the blood, facilitated in this instance perhaps, with the incorporation of pure oxygen.

Study No.16
"Effects of ECT on brain structure: A pilot prospective magnetic resonance imaging study" (Coffey, Weiner et al.1988a)

"Effects of ECT on brain structure: A pilot prospective magnetic resonance imaging study" is a pilot of the later main Coffey, Weiner et al. study "Brain anatomic effects of electroconvulsive therapy: A prospective magnetic resonance imaging study" (Coffey, Weiner, Djang, Figiel, Soady, Patterson, Holt, Spritzer, Wilkinson, 1991b), the first true prospective MRI study with long-term follow-up. This 1988 pilot study is conducted blind on 9 persons--five women and four men. None had received ECT previously. Seven receive BP from a Model "C" MECTA Brief Pulse device and two from a SW Medcraft device (the B-24). Importantly, six of the nine recipients (67%) show pre-MRI damage, which includes cortical atrophy in five of the recipients and/or foci of periventricular and deep white matter lesions in another (Coffey at al. , 1988a). [655] Coffey et al. (1988b) explain this damage as possible multiple sclerosis in one case and ischemic changes secondary to atherosclerosis of the medullary arteries in the five others (p. 703). [656] Importantly, all recipients are titrated at approximately just above threshold seizure.

> A moderately suprathreshold stimulus dosing strategy was employed: 1) parameters for each of the devices were chosen empirically to elicit seizures of at least 30 seconds' duration in the first ECT in over 80% of the cases, and 2) stepwise increases in stimulus intensity of at least 30% were employed in cases of brief or missed seizures or seizures of rapidly declining duration. (Coffey at al. , 1988a)

While this method (as opposed to sub-convulsive doses incrementally increased) is a slightly different means of titrating for just above threshold for the purpose of avoiding the necessity of re-stimulation, the titration method employed is yet aimed at minimal stimulus output. [657] Neither of these just above threshold titration methods, however, are representative of the common chart and set-to-age dosage method clinically employed via second generation BP devices extant at this time which emitted two and one-half times threshold with BL-ECT and five times threshold with UL-ECT by default. Both SW and BP devices in the study are set for minimal stimulus. While the continuity of sine wave compared to the intervalic nature of brief pulse generally suggests higher output with SW, a major weakness of the study is that we are never informed which individuals receive SW and which BP. This lack of discrimination is puzzling in that without this determination, potential damage cannot be associated with respective devices. [658] One explanation for the failure to distinguish may be the age category of the recipients. While BP minimal stimulus output is dramatically reduced in younger age categories compared to SW minimal stimulus, SW grows progressively weaker in older age recipients (with higher Impedances). By contrast then, in the older age categories, due to the constant current feature of BP, even minimal stimulus BP can surpass the output of SW (see SW devices in this manuscript). Moreover, judging from the high percentage pre-MRI damage, all recipients appear to fall within the older age category. As a result, SW minimal stimulus output in this study may not differ dramatically from BP minimal stimulus output, and in some age categories, SW may even emit less power than BP. In short, disparity between SW and BP outputs in this particular age category may not be significant.

---

[655] White matter lesions have been identifiable with MRIs whereas, CT scans seem to have missed them (Coffey, 1991a.; Coffey, C.E. and Weiner, 1989; Coffey, Figiel, Djang, Weiner, 1990b).

[656] In spite of the fact that none had a pervious history of ECT, all had been psychiatrically treated with drug therapy. There is yet no study eliminating the possibility of drug damage nor does the existence of such damage negate ECT damage. Regardless of how such damage occurred, the high percentages of pre-treatment MRI damage findings, raises the possibility that many psychiatrically treated individuals end up suffering from organic brain syndrome due to treatment. If so, should these persons continue to receive psychiatric treatment (which may be worsening the condition) or a more conventional form of medical treatment?

[657] The MECTA "C" administered just above threshold outputs (or "moderately suprathreshold") for BL ECT as opposed to second generation BP devices in the field at this time delivering at least double the outputs delivered by the "C." As such, sub-convulsive doses incrementally increased may have the method used with SW as opposed to the MECTA "C" already set at default outputs of just above threshold.

[658] The opposite is true regarding efficacious BP dosages, in that second generation BP devices far surpass standard SW for ages of about forty and above.

Another weakness in this prospective MRI pilot study is that the study offers no long-term follow-up; all post-treatment scans occur only 2-3 days after completion of the series. Moreover, in that the scans occur more than twenty-four hours after the final ECT, evidence of oedema and breakdown of the Blood Brain Barrier are no longer evident (Mander et al. , 1987; Scott et al. , 1990). Finally, we are told neither how many treatments are administered nor what method is utilized for determining an "adequate number of treatments." Despite minimal stimulus, one subject "develops a marked delirium associated with background slowing of the EEG and focal slowing in the temporal area" (Coffey et al. , 1988a, p.703). Treatment is stopped in this case and delirium is said to have cleared. MRI continues to read "normal" in this instance, in spite of the abnormal EEG and, in fact, the study concludes with findings of no MRI changes in any of the recipients. Nevertheless, in four of six patients, there is a nonsignificant trend toward higher VBRs (Ventricle Brain Ratio) [659] after the course of ECT (p.704).

For these four subjects--representing 67% of the total population--the mean VBR before ECT is 8.65/+-3.57, the mean VBR after ECT 8.97/+-3.30. [660] In short, brain matter appears to have diminished. The study attributes the increase in ventricle size [661] to subtle differences in head tilt and recommends a more reliable measure of ventricle size, specifically "quantitative assessment from contiguous coronal sections through the entire ventricular system" (p.704). Nevertheless, what appears to be subtle new atrophy not previously manifest via less sensitive EEG and CT scan, is suddenly and for the first time visible on the first prospective MRI, a finding which cannot nor should not be readily dismissed. Amazingly, both BP and SW recipients received only minimal stimulus. Moreover, while there is no differentiation found between BP and SW in this study, due to the age category tested, the lack of output disparity between minimal stimulus BP and minimal stimulus SW might be expected. In any case, four recipients show VBR reduction; only two received SW. As noted, no long-term follow-up is conducted so that Coffey et al. (1988b) are compelled to state:

> It would have been possible to miss structural brain changes that could theoretically have taken longer to evolve. (p.704)

Long term follow-up is important as even recipients who believe they have benefited short-term, may later complain bitterly regarding the long-term effects of ECT (Cameron, 1997; Andre, 1991; Janis 1952). Significantly, the above pilot study (Coffey et al. , 1988b) represents virtually "the first prospective investigation in humans of brain MRI, that is, the first before and after MRI study regarding a course of ECT" (p.701). While findings in the first prospective MRI study of what appear to be mild brain atrophy are dismissed as "subtle differences in head tilt," these findings are, in fact, noteworthy in that this same atrophy repeats in the main study wherein only minimal stimulus Brief Pulse is used. While results are somewhat tainted in this pilot study in that both SW and BP devices are utilized, emphasis must again be placed on the fact that seven of the nine subjects are treated with minimal stimulus Brief Pulse, unlike the suprathreshold Brief Pulse doses used in the field, a fact of which Weiner cannot have been unaware.

Study No.17
"Brain anatomic effects of electroconvulsive therapy: A prospective magnetic resonance imaging study" (Coffey, Weiner, Djang, Figiel, Soady, Patterson, Holt, Spritzer, Wilkinson, 1991b)

"Brain anatomic effects of electroconvulsive therapy: A prospective magnetic resonance imaging," is the main study following the pilot above and (if seen as an extension of the above pilot) is among the first prospective MRI studies ever conducted. Moreover it is one of only two prospective MRI studies containing long-term follow-up scans. Importantly, only a MECTA SR1 is utilized, meaning this is a prospective MRI study of Brief Pulse only.

Once again, the extremely critical question arises, "Did researchers stimulate at just above threshold in this study, utilizing the sub-convulsive dose titration method (or perhaps HASS), or did they stimulate at the

[659] Increased Ventricle-Brain ratio may indicate mild atrophy.
[660] In short, the ventricles (spaces between brain matter) got larger and the brain matter smaller.
[661] The ventricles are major spaces within the brain.

suprathreshold dosages utilizing the default Age-Dosage method applied in the field, the outputs of which were discovered by Beale to be 2.5 and 5.0 fold BL and UL threshold titration levels respectively? Not unexpectedly, of course, Coffey, Weiner, et al. (1991b, p.1051) tell us:

> The standard bifrontotemporal [662] ECT stimulus electrode technique was used. The stimulus was administered by a brief-pulse ECT device (MECTA SR1), and stimulus dosage variables were adjusted to elicit seizures of at least 25 seconds by standard electroencephalographic criteria. (Coffey, Weiner, et al. , 1991b, p.1051)

Coffey has just described manual titration, that is, manually identifying and administering (just above) threshold dosages. In short, the electrical dosage delivered is adjusted for each individual recipient until a so-called adequate seizure can be elicited. Thus, we may assume that while this prospective study is performed using bilateral ECT, and although it is conducted with a second generation BP device, the study is nevertheless conducted at therapeutically ineffectual just above threshold dosages rarely used in actual clinical practice. The method typically used by practitioners in the field, the automatic set to age and chart method eliciting 2.5 fold threshold outputs with BL ECT, therefore, has once again been supplanted with manual titration for minimal stimulus output.

For information regarding the stimulus method used here, Coffey et al. (1991b) refer us to two Sackeim studies (Sackeim et al, 1987a; Sackeim, 1987b). Sackeim is known for efficacy studies, but in the referenced articles, Sackeim performs safety studies in which Sackeim is more concerned with cognitive dysfunction than efficacy. His alleged consideration in both referenced studies is that due to individuation of seizure thresholds, use of set electrical amounts (i e. automated Age-Dosage method normally used with second generation BP devices), may result in some recipients receiving dosages far in excess of threshold. [663] Within the referenced articles, consequently, Sackeim endorses the sub-convulsive dose titration method to discover just above threshold outputs for each individual, in short, minimal stimulus. In the first referenced study, Sackeim states,

> This procedure involved the deliberate administration of subconvulsive intensities throughout the treatment course to determine the minimal intensity required to elicit seizure. (Sackeim et al, 1987a, p.252) [664]

The abstract of the same Sackeim study states:

> Seizure threshold, defined as the minimal dosage necessary to elicit adequate generalized seizure, was determined throughout the course of electroconvulsive therapy. (Sackeim et al, 1987a, p.249)

The abstract of the second Sackeim study entitled "Seizure Threshold in Electroconvulsive Therapy" (1987b) referenced in the 1991 Coffey prospective study, states:

> In a random-assignment trial to unilateral right and bilateral electrode placements, electroconvulsive therapy (ECT) stimulus intensity was titrated to just above seizure threshold for each of 52 patients. (Sackeim, 1987b, p.355)

There is no doubt that in all the Coffey MRI studies (and almost all other serious MRI studies), including the 1991 Coffey study we are currently evaluating ("Brain anatomic effects of electroconvulsive therapy: A prospective magnetic resonance imaging study"), that Coffey et al. titrate for just above threshold only--not the suprathreshold dosages clinically applied with second and third generation BP devices at this time both in

---

[662] There has never been a prospective MRI study utilizing UL-"ECT" at suprathreshold dosages.

[663] In short, the automated age-dosage pre-set method is too broad and individuals with lower thresholds may be receiving unnecessarily high dosages.

[664] In typical fashion, using the justification that UL alone requires suprathreshold dosages and thus more electricity than is currently available to be efficacious for some older patients, Sackeim manages to make a circuitous and paradoxical argument for more powerful devices.

America and throughout the world. Tellingly, studies such as the important Coffey study we are evaluating are the sole sources of information upon which practitioners derive conclusions regarding possible damage as a result of Brief Pulse ECT.

To continue, Coffey's 1991 prospective MRI study is comprised of 35 previously psychiatrically treated individuals, fifteen of whom previously had ECT. To be consistent, Coffey et al. administer the ECT entirely bilaterally. The team uses three MRI scans, one before, one 2-3 days post a course of ECT, and one six months later. The study is at least partially blind (several raters blind--several raters not blind) but unfortunately, there is no Control Group of non-previously psychiatrically treated individuals. Finally, we are told the "total number of ECT treatments . . . [is] determined by each patient's physician and . . . [is] based on therapeutic response" (Coffey et al. , 1991b, p.1015).

In pre-ECT imaging, 14 (40%) show cortical atrophy, 13 (37%) lateral ventricular enlargement, 33 (94%) periventricular hyperintensity, 27 (77%) deep white matter hyperintensity, 12 (34%) foci of subcortical hyperintensity in the deep gray nuclei (basal ganglia and thalamus), and eight (23%) foci of subcortical hyperintensity in the deep gray nuclei in the midpons. (Obviously, there is some overlapping.) How much of these pre-ECT abnormalities are age-appropriate and would also appear in so-called "normal" or non-psychiatrically treated populations shall be discussed later.

Of the 35 initial recipients, four refuse further participation (and thus do not participate in the long-term follow-up), one becomes pregnant, and one dies of a stroke (2.9%). Thus, 29 of the original 35, participate in the long-term follow-up.

In that short-term follow-up is performed 2-3 days following the course of treatment, manifestations of breakdown in blood brain barrier and oedemia are no longer visible. Subtle changes in ventricular volume attributable either to head tilt or very mild atrophy which appeared in the pilot prospective study (Coffey et al.1988a) have inspired a change in measurement technique--quantitative assessment from contiguous coronal sections through the entire ventricular system. In spite of this, subtle changes in volume at six month follow-up appear again. For example, we are told that in the case of the frontal lobes, there is an increase (in the adjunct lateral ventricles) of "only" .6%. [665] We are told that results for other regions can be interpreted similarly. The team comments:

> From these narrow confidence intervals, we can be reasonably certain that the effect of ECT on regional brain volume is quite small if, in fact, there is any effect at all. (Coffey et al. , 1991b, p.1016)

Coffey et al. then justify the reappearance of these changes thusly:

> Although we failed to find evidence of changes in brain volume after ECT, this does not mean that such changes did not or could not have occurred, since even modern brain imaging technologies have certain inherent limitations. . . . Measurement error may arise . . . as a result of subject movement during the imaging process. Such movement was difficult to eliminate even with headholders, and it was our impression that this factor likely accounted for the small amount of variability observed in our serial MR imaging volume measurement. (Ibid, p.1018)

Additionally, long-term follow-ups reveal new increases in subcortical hyperintensity (lesions) in five (17.24%) [666] out of the now 29 recipients. This is an especially important finding in that this is virtually the first prospective ECT MRI long-term follow-up in history. Coffey et al. (1991b) attribute these changes to progressive cerebrovascular disease (Ibid, p.1019), stating:

---

[665] Increases in ventricular volume (the large spaces within the brain) again suggest mild atrophy.

[666] A 1995 non-prospective MRI study (Hickie et al., 1995) indicated that abnormal damage in psychiatrically-treated recipients was especially prevalent in older persons. Over half of all ECT recipients are 65 and over (Texas and California Reporting Systems). This may be due to a combination of more fragile older brains in conjunction with higher doses of electricity required to induce seizures. Older brains are also more susceptible to psychotropic drugs.

> Since these neurologic changes were not present 2 to 3 days after ECT, it is unlikely that they were related to the therapy. (Ibid)

Nevertheless, Coffey et al. concede:

> Still, it is difficult to interpret with certainty worsening of brain MRI imaging abnormalities after ECT in the absence of control data describing the natural course of such brain abnormalities. (Ibid)

Since numerous abnormalities were identified pre-ECT, a control of same age non-psychiatrically treated individuals (or even of non-participant previously psychiatrically treated individuals) would have been of critical importance in identifying new age-appropriate abnormalities as opposed to new abnormalities as a result of ECT. In conclusion, possible subtle ventricular enlargement in addition to subcortical hyperintensity (lesions) in five (17.24%) of the 29 recipients appear at the six month follow-up. While these changes are underplayed or attributed to other causes, ECT damage cannot be ruled out and, in fact, seems probable. This is particularly interesting in that recipients were administered Brief Pulse only, and only at minimal stimulus.

Study No.18
"Quantitative cerebral anatomy in depression: A controlled magnetic resonance imaging study" (Coffey, Wilkinson, Weiner, Parashos, Djang, Webb, Figiel, and Spritzer, 1993)

In 1993, in yet another Coffey-Weiner et al. MRI study entitled "Quantitative cerebral anatomy in depression: A controlled magnetic resonance imaging study," researchers utilize just such a Control--76 non-psychiatrically treated individuals and compare them to 48 psychiatrically-treated individuals including 19 psychiatrically-treated persons from the 1991 MRI ECT prospective study immediately above (Coffey et al, 1991b). While no new ECT is administered in this study, the 48 psychiatrically treated individuals have been referred for ECT (and are thus considered severely depressed). Seventeen [667] of these 48 individuals with psychiatric histories (in this 1993 study) had ECT on a previous occasion, none less than six months preceding the study. MRIs of the 76 non-psychiatrically treated individuals were then compared to MRIs of the 48 psychiatrically-treated individuals awaiting ECT. The researchers conclude:

> In summary, inpatients who were referred for ECT of severe depression were found to have smaller frontal lobe volumes [7.2%] and a greater prevalence of subcortical hyperintensity [lesions] on MRI than normal control subjects. (Coffey et al.1993, p.14)

In that only about 35% of the psychiatrically-treated group (all of whom were referred for ECT) were previous "ECT" recipients, the research team attributes the greater damage in the psychiatrically treated group (as did researchers to changes found following ECT in the 1991 prospective study)--to depression, aging, affective disorder or some other unknown cause such as cerebrovascular disease. In short, since greater damage was found in the entire group of psychiatrically treated individuals (compared to the non-psychiatrically treated group) and only part of the psychiatrically treated group had received ECT, the team contends that something other than ECT must have caused the damage. Since the entire group were considered depressed, the team suggests:

> [The] relationship between structural brain changes and late age-onset psychiatric illness . . . might be the first manifestations of a brain degenerative disorder. (Coffey et al.1993)

---

[667] Why the number of individuals--17--who had histories of ECT in this study does not match the 19 psychiatrically treated individuals included from the 1991 study, all of whom received ECT, is not known. Perhaps two of these individuals were among the few who dropped out of the study or perhaps the disparity is a simple typo.

In short, the team determines that the greater damage discovered in the psychiatrically treated group may be the organic manifestation of mental illness, that is, depression manifesting itself organically. That ECT is the source of damage is dismissed on the basis that not all of the psychiatrically treated group had received ECT.

Contraindicating these conclusions, however, is a smaller comparison within the main comparison. The team compared previous MRIs taken of the subgroup who had received ECT in the 1991 (or some other) study with the new MRIs (of the same subgroup) taken for the 1993 study. Comparing earlier MRI scans taken of 22 individuals most of whom were scanned following the 1991 six month follow-up study, with new MRIs of the same 22 recipients referred for ECT in the 1993 study, the team found that in this particular sub-group: "No [new] changes in parenchymal or ventricular volumetric measures were observed," in brief, no new brain damage had occurred. As a result of this observation, the authors deduce:

> [O]ur data therefore provide no evidence that these MRI abnormalities are reversible in patients with depression. (Ibid).

In short, what the authors seem to be claiming is that not only did ECT not produce damage in these 22 (or any other) individuals, but that the previous ECT stopped the progress of any further organic deterioration (evidently as a result of mental illness). The team is indirectly suggesting then, that what the comparative MRIs of the ECT recipients show is that while ECT is not capable of reversing the damage (allegedly caused from depression, etc.), ECT may have stopped any further deterioration.

The conclusion is laughable. Firstly, the 22 individuals who previously received ECT are again being referred for ECT and, therefore, must again be severely depressed (and thus "mentally ill"). If depression or "mental illness" is recurring, and if mental illness causes or manifests itself through organic damage, where is the new damage in the recurrent "mentally ill" patients? In fact, the observation that there is no new brain damage in these previous ECT recipients, strengthens the probability that what appeared to be new frontal lobe atrophy originally discovered in the prospective 1988 and 1991 MRI studies, both 2-3 days (Coffey et al. ,1988) and six months following ECT (Coffey et al, 1991b), as well as new subcortical hyperintensity (new lesions) discovered by prospective MRI six months post ECT in the 1991 study (Coffey et al. , 1991b), is not the result of degenerative disease exacerbated or caused by mental illness at all, but rather, is directly attributable to ECT. Certainly if degenerative disease or mental illness was the culprit, new damage would have appeared in these cross-over recipients. The fact that no new ECT had been administered and no new damage is found clearly implicates ECT.

Once again, moreover, the fact that more severe damage is found amongst recipients who had been administered either psychiatric drugs alone or psychiatric drugs and ECT, simply implicates psychiatric drugs and ECT as the source of the more severe damage. While damage discovered in psychiatrically treated individuals is neither normal nor age-appropriate in non-psychiatrically treated individuals and so may be indicative of an organically manifested mental illness, it is just as likely if not more so, that the damage is the result of iatrogenic (treatment induced) injury, generally. Indeed, new frontal lobe atrophy and subcortical hyperintensity found in the first short and long-term prospective MRI follow-up studies in history (1988; 1991b), and no new damage occurring without new ECT in the 1993 study, clearly implicates ECT as the source of damage. In short, specific new damage following ECT in both the 1988 and 1991 MRI studies, and no new damage in previously damaged ECT recipients who had received no new ECT treatment as seen in the 1993 study, unquestionably point toward closed head injury due to "ECT. "

Of vital importance then, all these prospective MRI studies were conducted with Brief Pulse and at minimal stimulus outputs only. Thus, post-MRI findings of new damage following BP ECT compared to pre-MRI screenings in which this damage was not present, findings previously indiscernible with CT scans or EEG, but which become manifest in both short and long-term follow-ups of just above threshold BP ECT is concerning. In sum, no new damage found in ECT recipients who had not received new ECT, as opposed to new damage found following new BP ECT is the first picture-proof evidence of structural brain damage following BP ECT in spite of minimal stimulus induced BP seizures. [668] While investigators may dispute interpretations of the

[668] It should be noted that [regarding the MRI] the hippocampus area was combined with another region of the brain "to insure reproducibility of measurement . . . [so that] it is possible that subtle atrophic effects . . . may be obscured when that structure is combined with other adjacent structures in the same region (Coffey et al, 1991b, p.1018)." This seems inexcusable in the case of ECT wherein memory is strongly associated with the hippocampus alone and wherein electrodes are placed directly over this area (Breggin,

relatively few MRI prospective studies which appear skewed in favor of researchers who may not wish to discover damage, one indisputable fact remains--all these studies were conducted with minimal stimulus BP output. If these are the results of minimal stimulus BP ECT, what will prospective MRI studies reveal with the clinically applied outputs delivered from second, and third (and even fourth and fifth) generation BP devices, double and triple (and even quadruple) the outputs used in the above studies? (See third generation BP devices in Volume II).

Finally, we must evaluate the 2012 prospective MRI study by Perrin et al, "Electroconvulsive therapy reduces frontal cortical connectivity in severe depressive disorder," the best of the prospective MRI studies. However, we shall defer discussion of this critical study until the end of this section.

Study No.19: Retrospective (following ECT) MRI Study on Monkeys
"Absence of biological lesions in primate models of ECT and magnetic seizure therapy" (A. J. Dwork, V. Arango, M. Underwood, Boro Ilievski, G. Rosoklija, H. Sackeim, and S. Lisanby, 2004)

Although non-prospective, one later MRI study (2004) must be examined as a result of the greater than minimal stimulus output used to test for organic damage in twelve Macaca mullata (rhesus monkeys) following ECT. In short, this is a modern day non-prospective MRI brain study of rhesus monkeys. This non-prospective MRI study, which purports as the title implies, the "Absence of biological lesions in primate models of ECT and magnetic seizure therapy" was conducted by A. J. Dwork, V. Arango, M. Underwood, Boro Ilievski, G. Rosoklija, H. Sackeim, and S. Lisanby (Dwork et al.2004). Published in the American Journal of Psychiatry in 2004, the abstract states:

> The authors present preliminary findings from the first nonhuman primate neuropathological study of ECT to use perfusion fixation and adequate controls . . . . " (Dwork et al. , 2004, Abstract)

Indeed this is perhaps the first ECT animal study performed since the 1950s. The study was designed to quell the findings of early animal studies in which cell death and structural brain damage were identified following ECT in cats and other primates, and even autopsied humans. Repudiating the early animal ECT studies in a 1994 rebuttal, Sackeim and others attribute damage seen in the early animal studies to staining techniques (performed on the sacrificed brains of animals) and other "antiquated methodologies" such as lack of oxygenation and high dosing during ECT treatment itself (Devanand, Dwork, Hutchinson, Bolwog, and Sackheim, 1994). That the earlier studies were almost certainly conducted with SW in lieu of BP is significant. This 2004 MRI monkey study includes two of the 1994 repudiators (of the earlier animal studies)--A. J. Dwork and Harold Sackeim. The brief for the 2004 monkey study states:

> Twelve Macaca mullata received 6 weeks of daily ECT, magnetic seizure therapy, or anesthesia alone. After perfusion fixation, [669] their brains were examined while masked to intervention. Results: No identified lesions were attributable to the interventions. Cortical and hippocampal immunoreactivity for glial fibrillary acidic protein (an astrocytic marker) was most intense in the group that received ECT. Conclusions: This small but rigorous primate study supports the view that ECT does not produce histological lesions in the brain and provides the first comparable safety data on magnetic seizure therapy. (Devanand, Dwork, Hutchinson, Bolwog, and Sackheim, 1994)

Eight of the rhesus monkeys in this study were administered either ECT or magnetic seizure therapy [MST] "at [precedentially] 2.5 times each individual monkey's seizure threshold" and thus, although not a human

---

1979, pp.118-119; Friedberg, 1977; Press, Amaral, and Squire, 1989). Moreover, an excellent technique by Press et al. (1989) would have allowed singular perusal of the hippocampal region.

[669] Perfusion fixation, according to the later researchers, is a more advanced method of preservation and preparation.

experiment, may represent the first identifiable MRI multifold threshold "safety" study in history. [670] Of the twelve monkeys, then, four were administered ECT, four MST,[671] and four sham ECT (as a control). No pre-MRIs were administered. The monkeys were subsequently sacrificed and their brains examined. Of the four administered magnetic seizure therapy, one was found to have pathological changes in the cerebral cortex "consistent with acute hypoxia . . . " allegedly "too pathologically acute to be linked with magnetic seizure therapy or accompanying anesthesia. " Of the four sham treated monkeys, one was seen to have "eosinophilia in a few of the neurons in the CA1 region," a finding "compatible with pathological change" also allegedly "too pathologically acute to be linked with . . . accompanying anesthesia. " [672] Of the four monkeys administered ECT, no lesions were found. On the other hand, all four of the ECT administered monkeys exhibited intense "hippocampal immunoreactivity for glial fibrillary acidic protein. "

The team's conclusion as noted above was that, "This small but rigorous primate study supports the view that ECT does not produce histological lesions in the brain. " In that only a Brief Pulse machine was used on the lesion free ECT treated monkeys, a significant implication is that SW (as a result of higher dosage) may [673] have contributed to the damage found in the earlier studies; whereas, BP induced seizures even at multifold threshold outputs, do not result in the cell death or lesions (identified in the earlier animal studies).

Close scrutiny of this 2004 study is warranted. Of the four monkeys seized with magnetic seizure therapy . . . at 2.5 times an individual monkey's seizure threshold "approximating high doses of bilateral ECT in patients," the finding in one of the MST seized monkeys of "pathological changes in the cerebral cortex" cannot be assumed to have existed prior to the magnetic seizure therapy in that the study is not prospective, that is, no MRI scan was administered before the MST procedures. Moreover, while we are told that the 2.5 fold threshold output magnetic seizure therapy was administered with a "custom repetitive stimulator with enhanced output" (Magstim Company Limited, Whitland, South East Wales, U. K.), no actual power parameters are provided in the study. Regarding the four ECT treated monkeys, we are again informed that "bilateral ECT. . . [was] administered at 2.5 times an individual monkey's seizure threshold, approximating high doses of bilateral ECT in patients." Moreever, we are informed that "ECT was delivered with a "Spectrum 5000Q (MECTA Corp. , Lake Oswego, Ore)," a Brief Pulse--in lieu of a SW—instrument. Once again, however, no (electrical) parameters are provided.

Of critical relevance here is that adult male rhesus monkeys (Macaca mullata) average about 53 cm in length or about 20.9 inches (1.74 feet) and weigh on average 7.7kg or about 16.9 pounds, about the size of an adult male cat. Female adult rhesus monkeys (Macaca mullata) average about 47 cm in length or about 18.5 inches (1.54 feet) and weigh on average 5.3kg or about 11.7 pounds, about the size of a female adult cat. The weight of a human being is roughly related to the amount of energy output utilized via ECT devices. For instance, due to disparity in resistance, on Brief Pulse devices, the least amount of electricity is utilized for a ten year old child (typically the youngest and smallest recipient), whereas, the greatest amount of electricity is employed for the 100 year old adult. On most modern BP devices, for instance, the made-for-America second generation JR/SR 2 BP device which utilizes a default 2.5 fold threshold with BL ECT for all age categories, the typical Impedance for a ten year old child may be about 50Ω; whereas, the typical Impedance for a 100 year old adult may be about 560Ω. Just above threshold output for the ten year old child on modern BP devices, that is, the output required with BP devices to overcome seizure resistance for all ten year old children with BL ECT is about 1.04 Joules while just above threshold output on modern BP devices for even the most seizure recalcitrant 100 year old adult with BL ECT is about 104 Joules. Thus, for the ten year old child, about 2.6 Joules of output is utilized on the made-for-America second generation JR/SR 2 to emit a 2.5 fold threshold titration level, whereas, for the 100 year old adult, about 260 Joules is utilized to elicit the same 2.5 fold threshold titration level output intensity. In short, while both receive 2.5 fold threshold outputs, electrical output on modern day BP devices for the much larger 100 year old adult is 100 fold that of the much smaller ten year old child.

---

[670] A few (non-MRI) multifold threshold studies on humans had been performed, but tested for efficacy, not safety—allegedly resulting in faster, not greater efficacy. Studies at this time still claimed minimal stimulus efficacy.

[671] Seizures can be elicited with enhanced magnetism via an MRI machine and some studies have been conducted via this instrumentation.

[672] While no ECT was administered to the sham group, they were anaesthetized.

[673] According to the study, damage in early animal studies may have been a result of high dosage SW, antiquated staining techniques, and/or lack of oxygenation.

A normal ten year old human male child weighs about 100 pounds, a female human child about 85 pounds. An adult rhesus male monkey, as noted previously, weighs about 17 pounds, an adult female about 12 pounds. Thus the ten year old human child is between five and eight times heavier than the adult rhesus (100 ÷ 12 = 8.33; 85 ÷ 17 = 5). In that Impedance generally decreases with decreasing size and weight, electrical outputs for the rhesus monkey may have been as low as .5 Joules or less, even for a 2.5 fold threshold output level of BL ECT, outputs so low that a 2.5 fold threshold titration level of about .5 Joules compared to a just above threshold titration level of about .2 Joules may approach insignificance.

Unlike BP, SW output is dependent upon Impedance, that is, for constant current SW devices, the lower the Impedance, the higher the Amperage and so potential output. It is not surprising then, that constant voltage SW ECT administered to small animals sacrificed in the 1950s (i.e. cats and rats) with similarly low (or even lower) Impedances resulting in inordinately high amperages (and consequently high doses of electricity) resulted in brain impairment far exceeding that of animals with similarly low Impedances administered constant current ECT even at 2.5 fold threshold titration levels (see SW devices in this manuscript). A maximum dosage SW output administered to a ten year old child, for example, due to the relatively low Impedance, can reach as high as 200 Joules, (200J ÷ 2.65J =) 75 fold the 2.65 Joules reached by a 2.5 fold threshold titration level of BP for the same ten year old child. On the other hand, due to BP's ability to maintain constant current at even extremely high Impedances compared to SW's extremely diminished current at the same high Impedances, a 2.5 MTTLOI with a BP device administered to a 100 year old adult (with the highest human Impedance), may be as much as 5.4 fold maximum SW output delivered to the same 100 year old adult. [674] The disparity between BP and SW becomes even more exaggerated in the case of small animals with Impedances far less than that of the ten year old child (typically the youngest and smallest human recipient exhibiting the lowest Impedance amongst humans). [675] In short, comparing small animals with low Impedances administered high dosage SW to small animals with low Impedances administered even a 2.5 fold threshold output of BP is misleading, the picture only half painted. The complete portrait must include animals or humans with high (not merely low) Impedances in which case the machines reverse roles; BP becomes much more powerful in the older age categories, and much more detrimental than SW. There are as yet no prospective MRI safety studies using the default outputs of modern day BP devices administered to adult humans (or even human children) who weigh much more and so have much higher Impedances than small animals such as rats, cats, and even the relatively tiny rhesus monkey. Prospective MRI studies based on the default outputs administered every day to human beings in the field via modern day BP devices will almost certainly prove as devastating as early SW devices.

While authors of the 2004 monkey study purport that "2.5 times an individual monkey's seizure threshold" approximates "high doses of bilateral ECT in [human] patients," then, BP outputs used on humans in the field may at times approach 1000 times that of the BP output used on the small low resistant animal subjects employed here (480 Joules ÷ .5 J = 960 [676]). Moreover, while made-for-America second generation BP devices administer a default output of 2.5 fold threshold using BL ECT for all age ECT recipients, the titration levels for third generation BP devices (extant at the time of this study) double that of second generation BP devices while potential (and now legal) fourth generation BP devices have doubled that of third generation BP devices (See third generation BP devices in Volume II). Indeed, the four monkeys in this study are administered ECT via the "MECTA Spectrum 5000Q which is at least a third generation BP device. MECTA third generation BP devices administer between a 4.6 and 4.8 MTTLOI of BL ECT to human beings (see third generation BP devices in Volume II), a fact which tells us (not surprisingly) that the four ECT monkey recipients administered a 2.5 fold threshold titration level, were titrated manually. In lieu of the almost 5.0 MTTLOI default output typically administered in the field by the Spectrum 5000Q (for human BL ECT recipients), the monkeys, in addition to being small, receive only half the titration level clinically administered to humans by the same machine. While

---

674 A ten year old child has a titration threshold of about 1.06 Joules on a BP device; 2.5 x 1.06J = 2.65 Joules. The same child has about an 8.6J threshold with SW and due to the low Impedance (145Ω for SW) at maximum SW output, can receive up to 200 Joules on a SW device.200J ÷ 2.65J = 75.27 (See SW Devices in this manuscript). While a 100 year old male has about a 595Ω Impedance on a SW device, due to the high Impedance, a SW device can only emit about 48 Joules (not enough to reach threshold); on the other hand, a BP device emitting a 2.5 multifold threshold output, in maintaining its constant current, emits about 260 Joules (as did second generation made-for-America MECTA BP devices) for the same 100 year male.260J ÷ 48J = 5.4 (See SW Devices in this manuscript).

675 Ten years old is generally the youngest age group administered electroshock. It is illegal in fact, to administer ECT in Texas to anyone under the age of sixteen.

676 One MECTA third generation BP device delivers about 480 Joules to a high Impedance 100 year old human male. Compare this to perhaps .5 maximum Joules used on small rhesus monkeys in this 2004 Sackeim study.

it is true that output is relative to Impedance, that is, the monkeys receive small electrical dosages in accordance with their low Impedances, the small monkeys here may have had exceedingly low Impedance thresholds; in short, in spite of the 2.5 fold dosing, the monkeys may have received very low, not "high electrical dosing." As noted above, moreover, the tiny rhesus monkeys were not even administered the 4.6 to 4.8 fold default outputs administered to humans in the field with the same Spectrum 5000Q. This latter fact is perplexing given that Harold Sackeim, an expert in MECTA BP ECT devices and one of the study's main authors, must have been aware of the default titration level outputs administered every day by this same apparatus to human beings. Should experimental animals whose brains were sacrificed in order to test for brain safety in human beings receive half the titration level of that typically administered to people by this very same device?

Even had the tiny monkeys been administered the default titration levels normally utilized with the Spectrum 5000Q, however, due to the monkeys' low Impedance thresholds, threshold outputs may have been so low that even the alleged 2.5 fold threshold titration output administered to the monkeys may have been insignificant. That we are provided neither electrical parameters nor primate Impedances, therefore, seriously undermines the study. The Impedance levels of rhesus monkeys (weighing between 12 to 17 pounds) may have been so much lower than even the lowest Impedances known in human beings (typically 100 pound, ten year old children as this is typically the youngest age administered ECT) that the 2004 monkey experiment may amount to little more than another BP study once again based on minimal stimulus output. Neither are we told, moreover, whether or not the monkeys are titrated before each individual treatment, or merely once before the entire series. Weiner (another advisor to MECTA Corporation) purports, as we shall see later, a 100% rise in threshold over a treatment course, which if true, means that monkeys titrated only once before the series (as opposed to each individual "treatment"), would have been administered just above threshold by the end of the treatment course.

In spite of the extremely low electrical output utilized on these monkeys, one outcome of the four ECT administered monkeys is worth noting. While no actual lesions appear, the study admits a statistically significant effect of treatment on diffuse glial fibrillary acidic protein immunoreactivity in the superior frontal gyrus . . . where immunoreactivity was the greatest in the ECT group [for all four monkeys] and the least in the sham group. In conclusion, the study states: "Diffuse glial fibrillary acidic protein immunoreactivity in the superior gyrus, the amygdala, and the hippocampus was greatest in ECT-treated monkeys, probably indicating widespread astrocytic activation . . . . " The authors explain this as "a transient reaction to neuronal excitation" and that similarly, "spreading depression does not cause neuronal injury but temporarily stimulates glial acidic protein expression in the rat. " Shortly following publication of the study, however, a letter to the Editor from well-known neurologist John Friedman was published in the American Journal of Psychiatry suggesting that diffuse glial fibrillary acidic protein immunoreactivity is, in fact, indicative of brain damage. The authors shot back with a follow-up Letter to the Editor entitled "Dr. Dwork and Colleagues Reply," stating:

> Dr. Friedberg contends that our demonstration of increased immunoreactivity for glial fibrillary acidic protein after ECT in a nonhuman primate model indicates that ECT resulted in brain damage. Although glial fibrillary acidic protein can be increased with neuronal injury or cell death, it is also increased with a variety of other conditions not involving brain damage including . . . (1) [spreading constriction of blood vessels] and subconvulsive transcranial magnetic stimulation (2). . . . Had neuronal injury occurred during the treatments, we would have seen histological evidence of both acute . . . and subacute . . . damage to the neurons themselves. We saw neither. (Devanand, Dwork, Hutchinson, Bolwog, and Sackheim, 1995)

The authors do admit, however,

> It is impossible to prove the negative and we cannot rule out the possibility that the observed increase in glial fibrillary acidic protein immunoreactivity was due to neuronal damage. (Ibid)

The study was not prospective; thus, the fact that one of four monkeys administered magnetic seizure therapy showed pathology "consistent with acute hypoxia," cannot rule out injury due either to anesthesia or the magnetic seizure therapy itself. Because no electrical parameters are provided in the ECT group, no final conclusions can be drawn. This is critical in that based on the height and weight of the primates utilized, the author suspects inordinately low dosages of electricity tantamount to minimal stimulus, that is, wherein the 2.5 fold threshold titration level becomes insignificant. As a result, the fact that "diffuse glial fibrillary acidic protein immunoreactivity in the superior gyrus, the amygdala, and the hippocampus was greatest in ECT-treated monkeys not only does not rule out the formation of lesions in ordinary practice on humans, but, in fact, suggests that the clinically applied higher doses of electricity administered with present-day second, third, and possibly even fourth and fifth generation BP devices utilized on humans, like the higher dosages of electricity utilized in earlier animal studies with SW, do, in fact, result in some gross damage such as lesions, sulcal widening, and even more importantly, neuronal death (see Perrin et al., 2012). The fact that even the electrical dosages used on primates one sixth the size of human children in this study administered at half the titration level administered to human beings by this very same device results in diffuse glial fibrillary acidic protein immunoreactivity in the superior gyrus, the amygdala, and the hippocampus certainly suggests damage at higher outputs and higher titration levels and most certainly damage on a micro level as we shall soon see. The flagrant fact that potential BP machines capable of titration levels more than twice that of even third generation BP devices are now "legal" in the U. S. and abroad (see Volume II), that the monkeys received inordinately low dosages of electricity due to inordinately low Impedances, that the study is not prospective, that the titration level used in the study is only half that typically used on human beings, and finally that increased immunoreactivity for glial fibrillary acidic protein was discovered in the four ECT treated monkeys seriously undermines the study's conclusion that " . . . the ECT-treated monkeys. . . [show no] pathological findings" as a result of ECT. Of the tens of thousands of "treatments" administered each year in the U. S. alone, the simple fact remains that no prospective MRI study utilizing modern day BP devices at the clinically applied dosages of electricity administered to human beings in the field has ever been performed. That older adult humans receiving the greatest electrical dosing--not only receive at least twice the MTTLOI of that utilized in the study, but in some cases electrical outputs approaching one thousand (or more) fold that administered to the tiny rhesus monkeys in the 2004 primate study above, clearly suggests a study performed at minimal stimulus outputs as opposed to that actually administered in the field to human beings. [677]

---

[677] The primates may have been administered as little as .5 Joules of maximum output. In spite of the possible 2.5 fold threshold output that .5 Joules may represent, this is yet one thousandth of the circa 500 Joule output administered to a 100 year old human male with the same third generation Spectrum 5000Q BP device used in the study (but which in the field delivers 4.6 to 4.8 multifold threshold titration levels).

CHAPTER 46

Conclusion of Safety and Efficacy Studies

In conclusion, virtually all those safety studies (testing for cognitive and organic damage) and many efficacy studies, (particularly those conjoined to safety studies) which have found BP both "safe and effective," have been conducted at minimal stimulus outputs, that is, just above threshold only. In short, neither long-term efficacy nor the alleged absence of organic and cognitive damage is proven with these studies in that they are not representative of clinically applied dosages of electricity with BP devices in the field. Indeed, even subtle positive indications of damage at minimal stimulus is extreme cause for alarm.

Findings of effectiveness with respect to depression in efficacy portions of early BP vs. SW studies conducted with BP minimal stimulus are suspect given that minimal stimulus BP, except for the placebo effect, has long been known to be therapeutically deficient and this can be shown via the revealed power of third and even second generation BP devices. Almost all studies utilizing the most sensitive medical instrument for brain scan--MRI--to date including prospective MRI studies have been conducted at minimal stimulus or much lower doses of electricity than that clinically administered in the field. This is significant in that third generation BP devices are capable of emitting up to 500 Joules of energy, almost two and a half times as powerful as the most powerful SW output ever delivered to humans. Indeed, third generation outputs reach twice the power of second generation BP devices while potential fourth and fifth generation BP devices can legally emit even higher maximum outputs, a we shall soon observe in Volume II. In spite of the administering of manually titrated minimal stimulus or extremely low doses of electricity in almost all ECT safety studies, moreover, at least subtle damage attributable to ECT has been indicated through both cognitive instruments and by the single prospective MRI study with long-term follow-up. This is concerning in that no prospective MRI study has ever been conducted at clinically applied dosages for either second or third generation Brief Pulse devices, much less potential, now "legal," fourth or fifth generation BP devices. (See Third Generation BP Devices in Volume II). In any case, it is almost exclusively these unrepresentative minimal stimulus or low dosage Brief Pulse studies which form the basis of the powerfully misleading impression of BP as both safe and effective, so much so, in fact, that relatively few others of this kind have ever been conducted, despite the increasing power and default titration levels administered with the latest BP devices in the field. In fact, the more representative albeit rare studies, i.e. the single cognitive study performed at clinically applied suprathreshold dosages with second generation BP devices (Squire and Zouzounis, 1986) clearly indicates no safety advantage over SW, a study, unfortunately, relatively ignored in the wake of myriad undepicted minimal stimulus experiments contradicting Squire and Zouzounis. In sum, the most optimistic outcomes of safety studies indicate reversible brain trauma at minimal stimulus outputs, whereas the most optimistic outcomes of efficacy studies suggest only temporary "effectiveness" with minimal stimulus. In short, the evidence suggests efficacy is not enduring when trauma or brain damage is readily reversible, illuminating the true aim of the much more powerful later BP devices. Had the safer minimal stimulus output levels truly corresponded with efficacy, surely manufacturers would have accepted and conformed to the 1982 APA Standard thereby maintaining Brief Pulse minimal stimulus outputs as opposed to the surreptitious enhancements of the later BP devices. Instead, even as Brief Pulse devices become more and more powerful in the field, studies used to convince the public of greater BP safety compared to SW continue to be those based on BP devices manually titrated to minimal stimulus or just above threshold outputs and so continue to mislead. Indeed, it is the false impression of simultaneous safety and efficacy engendered with these same misinformed or disingenuous minimal stimulus studies, that is responsible for FDA tolerance of BP manufacturers freely promoting what are yet untested suprathreshold devices on the open market. Certainly, manufacturers' failure to solicit official adoption of the 1982 APA Standard bespeaks of the inability of manufacturers to create efficacious "ECT" devices with even a modicum of "safety," that is, wherein benefit outweighs risk. In short, Brief Pulse "ECT" devices regulated to minimal stimulus induced adequate seizures conforming to the 1982 APA Standard have actually been replaced by adequate electricity apparatuses much more properly deemed "ENR" devices. Quite unfortunately, manufacturers' creation, utilization, and power cover-up of their suprathreshold BP devices indicate that the damage effectuated by these later BP devices and the relatively enduring "effectiveness" they actuate are one and the same event. In sum, all evidence suggests that modern day Brief Pulse machines are knowingly and deliberately made to damage recipients.

Illuminating Brief Pulse Studies

Perhaps the two most illuminating modern studies of Brief Pulse devices before the 2012 Perrin et al. experiment were those conducted by Robin and Tissera (1982) and Squire and Zouzounis (1986). While the former established that efficacy is related to electrical dosage--not convulsion, the latter established that efficacious dosages of BP attenuate safety making BP at higher than just above threshold dosages no safer than SW; in short, BP is only safer when delivered at just above threshold outputs wherein it is, in essence, ineffective. In 1994, as noted earlier, the Beale et al. study (1994) revealed that the pre-set Charge outputs (and thus pre-set Energy Outputs as shown in this manuscript) in both MECTA and Somatics second generation BP devices are two and one-half fold minimal stimulus for BL electrode placement and thus 5.0 fold minimal stimulus for UL electrode placement. In the same year, Cameron's (1994) paper revealed that modern day BP devices are, in fact, generally more, not less powerful than SW devices of old in that as the present manuscript reveals, modern day BP devices no longer emit minimal stimulus, but suprathreshold default doses of electricity in all age categories. These four studies together--Robin and Tissera, Squire and Zouzounis, Beale et al., and Cameron--powerfully contradict both the safety and efficacy findings of the BP studies above, virtually all of which are preformed not at clinical outputs, but at minimal stimulus, the misleading results of which almost alone have established the misleading conception that the modern BP device is far safer and just as effective as the more antiquated SW device of the "past." Notably, many of what are actually studies based on BP minimum stimulus output, include Richard Weiner as co-author. BP safety studies based on convulsion alone, that is, on minimum stimulus outputs (although rarely identified as such) include virtually all of the prospective cognitive, EEG, CT and MRI studies. Almost no modern prospective organic safety study on humans has been performed at the clinically applied dosages typically emitted by modern BP devices in the field and none with extant third generation BP devices (see Volume II). [678] In fact, the electrical compensation of modern day BP devices which deliver consistent suprathreshold electrical dosages to all age levels via constant never diminishing currents, results in clinically applied outputs equaling or surpassing standard SW outputs in most instances, making modern day BP apparatuses and the titration levels they reach the most powerful and excessive in "ECT" history. Astoundingly, the organic effects of clinically applied electrical dosing with the most modern day BP devices have never been examined. Minimal or low dosage stimulus studies claiming to have settled safety concerns regarding modern day BP apparatus compared to SW are unintentionally ingenuous at best and wholly fraudulent at worst.

Efficacy Cancels Out Safety

BP devices, so Weiner tells us in an oversimplified paradigm within the Task Force Report containing the 1982 APA Standard, can induce seizures at generally one half the Energy Output of standard SW. But BP, it is now recognized, requires at least twice and usually two and one half times threshold dosage to be effective even

[678] Even the negative findings of Robin and Tissera, and Squire and Zouzounis were not based on the level of electrical dosing emitted by current BP devices.

with bilateral "ECT. " This means that a 100 year old man can have an "adequate" seizure with BP at X number of Joules, half that required with SW, but to make the BP "treatment" effective for even a moderate length of time, X Joules must then be multiplied at least two and one half times X, that is, administered at least two and one-half times the Energy Output needed to induce the so-called "adequate" seizure. In essence, the output required to induce an adequate seizure with BP is (more or less) reduced to half to conduct (virtually all) BP safety tests) compared to SW. But this same BP output must be multiplied at least two and one half fold in actual clinical practice (the titration level at which second generation BP devices are pre-set) in order to make the procedure with BP actually "work." [679] The concept exploited here is the spurious notion of "convulsive therapy," the premise upon which virtually all BP safety (and efficacy) testing has been performed. In fact, the modern "ECT" device is not a "convulsive therapy" apparatus at all, but an adequate electricity apparatus wherein convulsion is but an unavoidable, in fact, "convenient" side-effect. Indeed, it is adequate electrical dosing--not adequate seizure--upon which the actual procedure, Electro Neurotransmission Reduction, is actually based. No great insight is required to see the contradiction in terms, a critical inconsistency given that extant third generation BP devices double the titration level of second generation BP devices even as potential fourth generation BP devices double the titration level of extant third generation BP devices as we shall soon see in Volume II. It is almost inconceivable that tens of thousands of individuals receive "ECT" treatments each year via second, third, (and possibly even fourth) generation BP devices, given that no safety studies, and certainly no prospective MRI studies have ever been conducted at actual default outputs, that is, the clinically applied electrical dosages actually administered by what are actually modern day Brief Pulse ENR devices in the field. Incredibly, virtually all BP safety (and efficacy) studies have been unrepresentatively performed at minimal stimulus only, much, much lower outputs than that administered in actual practice to thousands of people daily.

In short, most of the BP safety tests compare "threshold" doses of SW against threshold dosages of BP--that is, safety (and efficacy) studies are performed at threshold doses wherein BP requires "half" the output of SW to induce an adequate seizure.[680] Electrical dosing with Brief Pulse is thus (generally) reduced by half compared to SW to demonstrate increased safety (and supposedly equal efficacy) in safety and efficacy studies, but commonly surpasses SW in order to make BP effective in the field. As mentioned, perhaps with the exception of the Perrin study (2012), no prospective "safety study" (attempting to demonstrate reduced cognitive or organic damage) has ever been conducted on humans using clinically applied doses administered in the field with ENR. Given the facts regarding the devolution (increase in power) of BP devices from one generation to the next, no complex reasoning is required to see that safety and efficacy cannot occur simultaneously with machines pre-calibrated to either equal or in most instances, surpass the EO of SW in order to be effective, at which point the superior safety factor of Brief Pulse compared to SW entirely disappears. Succinctly, with the exception of Perrin, no human prospective MRI safety study has ever been conducted on humans at the clinically applied BP dosages constituting what is actually "Electro Neurotransmission Reduction."

But Isn't BP at Electrical Dosages Equal To or Surpassing that of SW still Safer than SW?

BP, Weiner assures us within the 1982 APA Standard, utilizes circa one half the energy output of SW to induce an adequate seizure. BP, on the other hand (and as has now been acknowledged by Weiner and others), requires (at least) 2.0 to 2.5 fold threshold (even with BL placement) in order to be effective (apparently in terms of even a moderately enduring anti-depressant effect, and perhaps correspondingly, enduring behavioral modification).

In short, "effective" Energy Output doses emitted by default from modern-day BP devices, at least equals, and, in fact, typically supersedes the energy output emitted by SW (depending upon age and Impedance). This supersession occurs both due to the constant current aspect of BP (wherein Voltage automatically increases to overcome increasing Impedances) compared to the decreasing current of standard SW (until diminishing Current eventually fails to overcome the increasing Impedance altogether), but also due to the multi-threshold

---

[679] Tellingly, the results of the single safety study, a primate inquiry in which BP titration levels are multiplied 2.5 fold, is suggestive of brain damage (**Friedberg**).

[680] It is quite possible that the Medcraft-24 SW, cannot be reduced even to what might be considered minimal stimulus SW outputs.

output required to make BP effective. That is, in spite of SW being less efficient than BP so that SW requires more output to induce an adequate seizure, BP requires output surpassing threshold by at least 2.0 fold to make the procedure as effective as SW. In fact, though an adequate seizure with SW requires twice the output of BP to induce an adequate seizure, SW current diminishes with increasing Impedance; whereas the more powerful BP Current remains constant with increasing age in spite of increasing Resistance. In short, BP current remains constant over relatively long durations, delivering a consistent Multifold Threshold Titration Level Output Intensity throughout the entire age spectrum (Cameron, 1994), whereas, SW current weakens with increasing Resistance. Indeed, SW, though exceedingly powerful for low resistance recipients, is often too weak to be effectively utilized for patients sixty-five and over. SW, in fact, becomes so weak at the sixty-five and older age juncture that oftentimes a seizure cannot be obtained in these age categories (see SW devices in Volume II). Thus at 2.0 to 2.5 times threshold to make the procedure effective, except for the youngest age categories wherein Resistance is exceedingly low, BP current is actually much more powerful than SW. Indeed, the effort to create a more efficient machine to capture the sixty-five and over market lost with the weaker more inefficient SW current, may, in fact, have been Medcraft's chief motivation for producing not a less powerful device with BP as has been advertised, but rather a more powerful apparatus (the B-25)--by which the inherent constant current mechanism constitutive of all Brief Pulse devices seizes any age category regardless of advancing age. Add to this the necessity of consistent multifold threshold dosing with MECTA and Somatics BP devices in the field to make the procedure effective as opposed to the inconsistent Multifold Threshold Titration Level Output Intensities over the entire age spectrum with the Medcraft B-25 and the surpassing power of MECTA and Somatics BP over SW generally, suddenly comes into focus.

CHAPTER 47

Machine Readouts in Joules are Misrepresentative

But if modern BP devices are actually more powerful generally than SW, why haven't the preponderant levels of Energy Output (in Joules) been identified as such in modern BP devices? The answer is simple. Manufacturers have covered up the information. Beginning with second generation BP devices, readouts of Energy Output in Joules, as noted, beginning with MECTA and Somatics BP devices misrepresent actual output. The phenomenon occurs with the artificial incorporation of a 220Ω constant (representing "average" Impedance) into computer generated calculations of second generation MECTA and Somatics BP machines resulting in misleading readouts culminating in false 100 Joule maximums, an arithmetical tactic which artificially reduces actual Energy Output depictions by as much as 150% (250J actual - 100J max readout = 150J ÷ 100J max readout = 150%). Thus, the preponderant levels of energy actually being utilized in the field of up to about 250J (for second generation BP devices) which can only be derived using actual age-related Impedances (in lieu of a 220Ω "average") disappear from view. In short, the increase in power from first to second generation BP devices becomes invisible, a strategy for which BP manufacturers have been wholly accountable. Indeed, the question must be asked: "Is it mere coincidence that almost all American safety studies have been hand titrated to minimal stimulus outputs of 100J or less, the same deceptive readout maximum on all second generation MECTA and Somatics BP devices, just under the 110J ceiling the 1982 APA Standard stipulates, or is this "coincidence," deliberate? The answer is apparent in understanding that these same manufacturers adopted the even newer tactic of eliminating the use of Joules altogether, in order to increase machine output even further with later even more powerful third generation BP devices surpassing 450 maximum joules which we shall soon see in Volume II. Very relevantly then, by 1990, with the production of third generation BP devices, manufacturers switched from "average" EOs in joules to charge parameters alone, which though actual, are not only much less accessible to the lay public, but to regulatory agencies as well in that Charge reporting (without accompanying EO in Joules) can be highly misleading, as we shall observe in more detail. (See third generation BP devices in Volume II). In any case, the final switch makes comparison of modern BP devices to SW as well as to previous BP devices--both of which had been heretofore measured in Joules--virtually impossible. [681] In fact, a comparison of actual Energy Outputs of BP versus actual Energy Outputs of SW as shall be seen in Volume II, reveals that BP devices are the most powerful in "ECT"

---

[681] In an unfortunate conflict of interests, FDA has relied almost entirely upon electrical engineer and psychiatrist Richard Weiner, closely associated with device manufacturers for whom Weiner has been almost the sole spokesperson in communicating with the FDA. As a result, manufacturers of third generation BP devices now report electrical dosages in millicoulombs or Charge in lieu of Joules or Energy Output, which, while "accurate," can nonetheless be misleading (see Third generation BP Devices in this manuscript); whereas, reporting in Joules, much more consistently representative of the true overall power of BP devices throughout several machine generations, was abandoned with the marketing of third generation BP devices. Utilization of the "220Ω average" (probably invented by Weiner), results in the false impression of minimal stimulus outputs for what are actually second generation BP devices emitting circa 2.5 fold minimal stimulus in all age categories with BL ECT and circa 5.0 fold threshold in all age categories for UL ECT, a fact undiscovered until 1994 (Beale et al.). The tactic successfully hid the fact that output from second generation BP devices is often well over the 110 Joule APA ceiling purported as the safe maximum by BP manufacturers of both first and second generation BP devices and as recommended by the FDA Advisory Committee during the 1976-1982 FDA hearings. Indeed, a 100J maximum for Brief Pulse was alleged by Weiner in his early depiction of BP as half as powerful as SW and therefore "twice as safe."

history. Even when reported in a misleading combination of Joules and Charge as were second generation BP devices, the following charts reveal how the false constant impedance of "220Ω" (utilized in output depictions on second generation BP devices) results in the appearance of spurious minimal stimulus readouts (outputs 110J and under) for second generation BP devices. Note in the chart below, once again, the false correlation between actual Charge and the reputed EO Readouts for the made-for America second generation BP device, the Thymatron DG. Compare these outputs to the actual Energy Outputs (in Joules) emitted by this same Brief Pulse machine in the chart following the one directly below for the same second generation Thymatron DG.

MISLEADING EO Readouts Based on a False 220Ω "Average" Impedance on Somatics' 2nd Generation Thymatron DG

VOLTAGE	POWER % Device	AGE Yrs	FALSE CONSTANT (Ω) Ohms	FREQUENCY (Hz)	DURATION (SECs)	CURRENT mAmps	AVER. EO READOUTS Joules	ACTUAL CHARGE mC
25	5	5	220	30	.47	900	5.02	25.2
50	10	10	220	30	.93	900	9.94	50.4
75	15	15	220	30	1.40	900	14.9	75.6
100	20	20	220	30	1.87	900	19.99	100.8
125	25	25	220	30	2.33	900	24.91	126
150	30	30	220	50	1.68	900	29.93	151
175	35	35	220	50	1.96	900	34.92	176.4
200	40	40	220	50	2.24	900	39.91	201.6
225	45	45	220	50	2.52	900	44.90	226.8
250	50	50	220	50	2.8	900	49.90	252
275	55	55	220	70	2.20	900	54.89	277.2
300	60	60	220	70	2.4	900	59.87	302.4
325	65	65	220	70	2.6	900	64.86	327.6
350	70	70	220	70	2.8	900	69.85	352.8
375	75	75	220	70	3.0	900	74.84	378
400	80	80	220	70	3.2	900	79.83	403.2
425	85	85	220	70	3.4	900	84.82	428.4
450	90	90	220	70	3.6	900	89.81	453.6
475	95	95	220	70	3.8	900	94.80	478.8
500	100	100	220	70	4.0	900	99.80	504

Compare resulting "average" Energy Outputs above based on an "average" 220 Ohm to the chart below utilizing actual Resistances and so actual EOs. Ω = refers to resistance of the skull, brain, and blood brain barrier to electricity.

Actual Impedances and Actual but Unreported EOs on the same Second Generation Thymatron DG by Somatics

VOLTAGE	POWER % Device	AGE Yrs	TRUE IMPED (Ω) Ohms	FREQUENCY (Hz)	DURATION (SECs)	CURRENT mAmps	TRUE EO READOUTS Joules	ACTUAL CHARGE mC
25	5	5	27.7	30	.47	900	.63	25.2
50	10	10	55.5	30	.93	900	2.51	50.4
75	15	15	83.3	30	1.40	900	5.67	75.6
100	20	20	111	30	1.87	900	10.09	100.8
125	25	25	138.8	30	2.33	900	15.72	126
150	30	30	166.6	50	1.68	900	22.68	151
175	35	35	194.4	50	1.96	900	30.87	176.4
200	40	40	222.2	50	2.24	900	40.32	201.6
225	45	45	250	50	2.52	900	51.03	226.8
250	50	50	277.7	50	2.8	900	63	252
275	55	55	305.5	70	2.20	900	76.23	277.2
300	60	60	333.3	70	2.4	900	90.72	302.4
325	65	65	361.1	70	2.6	900	106.47	327.6
350	70	70	388.8	70	2.8	900	123.48	352.8
375	75	75	416.6	70	3.0	900	141.75	378
400	80	80	444.4	70	3.2	900	161.28	403.2
425	85	85	472.2	70	3.4	900	182.07	428.4

450	90	90	500	70	3.6	900	204.12	453.6
475	95	95	527.7	70	3.8	900	227.43	478.8
500	100	100	555.5	70	4.0	900	252	504

For even greater clarity, note Misleading Readouts resulting from an average 220Ω Impedance juxtaposed with Actual Outputs resulting from actual Impedances below:

Second Generation Thymatron DG Brief Pulse Constant Current Device

Compare Energy Output Readouts in Joules Based On False 220 Ohm "Average" Impedance with Actual Energy Outputs in Joules Based on Actual Impedances

False Average 220Ω Impedance used by Manufacturers	False EO (Joules) Readouts Derived from False 220Ω Impedance Average	AGE	Actual Impedances (Ω)	Actual but Unreported EOs (Joules) Derived From Actual Impedances (Ω)
220	5.02	5	27.7	.63
220	9.94	10	55.5	2.51
220	14.9	15	83.3	5.67
220	19.99	20	111	10.09
220	24.91	25	138.8	15.72
220	29.93	30	166.6	22.68
220	34.92	35	194.4	30.87
220	39.91	40	222.2	40.32
220	44.90	45	250	51.03
220	49.90	50	277.7	63
220	54.89	55	305.5	76.23
220	59.87	60	333.3	90.72
220	64.86	65	361.1	106.47
220	69.85	70	388.8	123.48
220	74.84	75	416.6	141.75
220	79.83	80	444.4	161.28
220	84.82	85	472.2	182.07
220	89.81	90	500	204.12
220	94.80	95	527.7	227.43
220	99.80	100	555.5	252

First two columns show Energy Output Readouts based on a 220 ohm false constant Impedance. As a result, the second column reflects the illusion of minimal stimulus. 4th column shows actual Impedances and the 5th column shows actual but unreported outputs. [682] Actual unreported outputs are approximately 2.5 times (not the readouts, but) actual minimal stimulus.

Now Compare the Minimal Stimulus Readout Illusion Based On Misleading 220 Ohm "Average" in the 2nd Column to Actual Minimal Stimulus at which Most Safety Studies Have Been Performed in the 3rd Column to Actual Default Energy Outputs Delivered in the Field Based on Actual Impedances in the 4th Column below.

---

[682] Voltage and Current are known variables provided by Somatics (Abrams and Swartz, 1988). Dynamic Resistances (4th column) are derived by Ohm's Law: (Resistance = Voltage/Current). Actual Energy Outputs are derived from formula: Joules (Energy Output) = (current squared [.9 x .9]) x impedance (Ω) x (Hz x 2) x wave length (.001) x Duration (see Thymatron chart in previous section).

Second Generation Thymatron DG Brief Pulse Constant Current Device

AGE	Illusion of Minimal Stimulus Based on Machine Readouts Derived from a 220Ω Impedance "Average"	**True Minimal Stimulus at which Most Safety Tests Have Been Performed**	**Actual, Unreported EOs (Joules) Applied by Default with the 2nd Generation Thymatron DG**
5	5.02	.535	.63
10	9.94	1.007	2.51
15	14.9	2.52	5.67
20	19.99	4.03	10.09
25	24.91	6.55	15.72
30	29.93	9.06	22.68
35	34.92	12.6	30.87
40	39.91	16.13	40.32
45	44.90	20.67	51.03
50	49.90	25.2	63
55	54.89	31	76.23
60	59.87	36.8	90.72
65	64.86	42.58	106.47
70	69.85	49.4	123.48
75	74.84	57	141.75
80	79.83	64.5	161.28
85	84.82	73.05	182.07
90	89.81	81.6	204.12
95	94.80	91.2	227.43
100	99.80	100.8	252

Second Generation MECA JR/SR 2 Brief Pulse Constant Current Device

AGE	Illusion of Minimal Stimulus Based on Machine Readouts Derived from a 220Ω Impedance "Average"	**True Minimal Stimulus at which Most Safety Tests Have Been Performed**	**Actual, Unreported EOs (Joules) Applied by Default with the 2nd Generation MECTA JR/SR 2**
5	**5.0**	.535	1.3
10	10	1.007	2.59
15	15	2.52	6.48
20	20	4.03	10.37
25	25	6.55	16.8
30	30	9.06	23.33
35	35.5	12.6	32.4
40	41	16.13	41.47
45	46	20.67	53.1
50	51	25.2	64.8
55	56	31	79
60	61	36.8	93.31
65	66	42.58	109.51
70	71	49.4	127
75	76.05	57	146
80	81.1	64.5	165.89
85	86.2	73.05	188
90	91.2	81.6	209.95
95	96.3	91.2	234
100	101.4	100.8	259.2

Spurious BP outputs based on false 220Ω constants or "averages" are misleadingly similar to manually titrated BP minimal stimulus outputs used for almost all safety studies with Brief Pulse vs SW. In short, false readouts derived and depicted in this manner on second generation BP devices falsely emulate minimal stimulus dosages in turn generating the illusion that all BP devices emit greatly reduced outputs compared to SW. As a result, actual minimal stimulus outputs have been utilized in virtually all comparative Brief Pulse vs

SW safety studies in lieu of actual default outputs used in the field leading to nonscientific conclusions regarding the safety of clinically applied BP.

Meaningful scientific results, of course, should be based on clinically applied default doses administered in the field. Instead, sometimes through no fault of the researcher, threshold doses of SW generally twice threshold doses of BP are unrepresentatively compared in numerous "safety studies." While threshold seizures with a standard SW device are generally effective in terms of short term depression and behavior management, but cognitively undesirable, threshold seizures with BP, though more cognitively desirable, appear to be ineffective for any appreciable period of time. Thus, meaningful safety studies should compare efficacious doses of SW with efficacious or clinically applied doses of BP with respect to safety--not manually titrated minimal stimulus BP. Indeed, the facts suggest that neither efficacious doses of SW nor efficacious doses of BP are cognitively desirable in that both compromise memory, reflective of neuronal diminishment (Squire and Zouzounis 1986; Perrin et al.2012). In short, at the point the procedure becomes effective with either BP or SW, benefit no longer outweighs risk in that the "treatment" is damaging.

Threshold outputs manually titrated on the Thymatron DG BP compared to unreported clinically applied doses, reveal several interesting points. First, the Brief Pulse delivered in the field (in the U. S.) is at least 2.5 fold minimal stimulus in terms of energy output (EO) or Joules with BL "ECT" and 5.0 fold minimal stimulus with UL "ECT. " Secondly, true to the original 1982 findings presented to the FDA by both the Utah Biomedical Test Laboratory and apparently, by Weiner himself, no more than 100 Joules is ever required with BP to induce adequate seizures in even the most seizure resistant recipient--the 100 year old male. Readouts appearing on MECTA and Somatics second generation BP devices, create the false impression that these devices emit just above threshold dosages, so that researchers titrate for minimal stimulus on safety studies, a phenomenon which has deluded both doctors and lay public alike since at least 1976. In brief, while Machine Readouts limited to circa 100 Joules are illusory, it is actual minimal stimulus dosages--doses actually limited to 100 Joules and less--which have been utilized in virtually all safety tests for Brief Pulse via manual titration.

Third Generation (introduction to Volume II)

Safety Tests, including MRI, performed at just above Threshold (1.1 Fold)
Compared to Clinically Applied Dosages 2.5 and 4.54 Fold Threshold
Emitted in the Field (ages 10-99) by the
THYMATRON DG Second Generation **Somatics** BRIEF PULSE DEVICE (1983)
and the
SYSTEM IV Third Generation **Somatics** BRIEF PULSE DEVICE (1995)

1.1 x Threshold Minimal Stimulus EO (Joules) Safety-Tested Here	2.5 x Threshold Clinically Applied EO (Joules) Never Tested for Safety	4.54 Threshold Clinically Applied EO (Joules) Never Tested for Safety
1.007	2.51	4.54
4.03	10.09	18.14
9.06	22.68	40.78
16.13	40.32	72.58
25.2	63	113.4
36.28	90.72	163.3
42.58	106.47	191.6
49.4	123.4	222.26
64.5	161.28	290.4
81.6	204.1	367.4
100.8	251	454

Safety Tests, including MRI, performed at just above Threshold (1.1 Fold) Compared to Clinically Applied Dosages 2.59 and 4.6 Fold Threshold Emitted in the Field (ages 10-100) by **JR/SR 2** Second Generation **MECTA** BRIEF PULSE DEVICE (1985) and the **JR/SR 1** Third Generation **MECTA** British Brief Pulse IEC BP Device (1995)

1.1 x Threshold Minimal Stimulus EO (Joules) Safety-Tested Here	2.59 x Threshold Clinically Applied EO (Joules) Never Tested for Safety	4.54 Threshold Clinically Applied EO (Joules) Never Tested for Safety
1.04	2.59	5.76
4.15	10.37	18.43
9.33	23.33	41.47
16.59	41.47	73.73
25.92	64.8	115.2
37.32	93.31	165.88
43.8	109.51	194.68
50.8	127	225.8
66.36	165.89	295
83.98	209.95	373
100.8	259.2	460

For BP devices, human safety testing has occurred almost exclusively at threshold doses wherein BP outperforms SW. [683] However, BP is only effective at suprathreshold dosing of at least 2.5 times minimal stimulus, which generally surpasses SW in cumulative output. Allegedly, minimal stimulus BP can induce so-called adequate seizures at half the output of SW so that 200 overall Joules is required with SW versus 100 overall Joules of BP. In the section on Medcraft's B-24 SW, we learned that, while SW depicted by Weiner of up to 200 Joules has been shown to engender severe cognitive difficulties, clinically applied doses of BP reach between 230 and 480 Joules, though in disparate age categories compared to SW. Thus, while BP devices do administer their electrical doses over a longer period of time than SW, BP, beyond minimal stimulus, has been shown to lose its safety advantage specifically at suprathreshold dosages of 2.5 fold minimal stimulus (with BL ECT) and beyond, imitating SW in morbidity or memory dysfunction (Squire and Zouzounis 1986). Alarmingly, third generation BP devices double the output of second generation BP devices (for all age recipients). Almost no safety testing at either 2.5 or circa 5.0 multifold threshold doses has ever been studied in human beings.

In brief, positive claims with respect to cognitive or memory dysfunction using MRI, EEG, CT, and memory gages have almost all been performed at just above threshold output on Human Subjects. Clinically applied doses (2.5 and 5.0 fold EO in Joules for BL ECT) have never been safety tested for human beings. [684] Indeed, third generation BP devices currently in use, circa doubling the output of second generation BP devices, have never been tested for safety either on animal or human subjects. Instead, second and third generation BP devices set for default outputs of circa 2.5 and 5.0 fold threshold with BL "ECT" have been manually titrated down to minimal stimulus when testing for safety on humans. The single BP animal study allegedly performed at 2.5 fold threshold with BL ECT due to the diminutive size of the animal subjects, appears to have been performed at such low outputs that, in essence, the study was performed at minimal stimulus so that results cannot be compared to 2.5 fold outputs used in the field on humans.

In conclusion, almost no second and no third generation BP devices have ever been tested for safety at the clinically applied doses applied to human beings. Almost all have been safety tested at minimal stimulus outputs in which case they outperform SW with respect to safety but not efficacy, at least with respect to duration. At clinically applied doses, which equal or surpass SW in output in most age categories and at which point efficacy occurs, BP loses its safety advantage over SW, and this has been corroborated both by Robin

---

[683] A single non-prospective monkey study with alleged 2.5 fold BP threshold dosing was based on too few monkeys (four) and with undenoted electrical outputs. Based on the size and weight of rhesus monkeys, the outputs used in the study were almost certainly too low for doubling to be of any significance. For all practical purposes, the study appears to have been but another minimum stimulus study.

[684] In fact, the results of the only studies performed at 2.5 fold threshold in humans, i.e. Robin and Tissera, Squire and Zouzounis, directly contradict minimal stimulus findings, including the 2004 monkey study (Dwork et al.2004).

and Tissera (1982) and Squire and Zouzounis (1986). Spurious Readouts on second generation BP devices only emulate minimal stimulus, while virtually all safety testing has been carried out at actual minimal stimulus. At actual default clinically applied 2.5 and 5.0 fold minimal stimulus electrical dosages with BL "ECT," no actual safety testing on humans has ever been performed. Finally, no prospective Cognitive, EEG, CT, MRI or memory testing for the safety of second or third generation BP devices has been performed at the clinically applied outputs for either. (Even Perrin uses 2.0—not 2.5--fold threshold as we shall see). Potential fourth and fifth generation BP devices provide even greater doubt (See Volume II).

Because of manufacturer cover-up, some researchers in the field have been legitimately deluded into believing that all BP devices induce seizures at just above threshold and so, ironically, have been fastidious in manually titrating to just above threshold in determining cognitive and organic deficits as a result of BP "ECT." A few researchers, moreover, and one in particular, Richard Weiner, appear to have deliberately misled both the public and the psychiatric industry in general regarding the power of modern day BP devices. Psychiatrist, electrical engineer, Chairman of the American Psychiatric Association Committees on ECT, and spokesperson for virtually every American "ECT" manufacturer in North America, most critically during the 1976-1982 FDA hearings on ECT, Richard Weiner has worked closely with MECTA Corporation in editing technical MECTA manuals regarding various MECTA Brief Pulse devices and has even headed international committees with respect to international standards pertaining to BP devices, particularly (See Volume II). Instrumental in generating both formal and informal "ECT" standards (i.e. the 1982 APA Standard, the Mectan Transmutation which covertly allows manufacturers to build Brief Pulse devices two and a half times the ceiling the APA Standard allows, and finally, as we shall see, the current de facto international standard on ECT) permitting and camouflaging multifold threshold titration level output intensities for third, and possibly fourth and fifth generation BP devices utilized throughout the world, Weiner is well versed in the technical make-up and power of both Brief Pulse and SW "ECT" devices. It is for these reasons that the inadvertency of minimal stimulus outputs used in the numerous safety studies on ECT for humans, many of which are Weiner related, must be doubted. Such minimal stimulus safety studies, we must remember, were conducted even amidst the period that both MECTA and Somatics second generation BP devices were secretly delivering default outputs 2.5 fold minimal stimulus with BL placement and a 5.0 fold minimal stimulus with UL placement for all age categories, studies, though unrepresentatively based on minimal stimulus, continue to portray the benignity of the modern day "ECT" Brief Pulse device even today. Indeed, even more powerful fourth and even fifth generation BP devices are legal under the Weiner de facto standard as we shall soon see in Volume II, the actual existence of which cannot be identified under the latest Weiner de facto standard.

CHAPTER 48

The Most Credible Prospective MRI Study (ENR and How ENR Works)

Finally, in March of 2012, the most credible of the MRI studies, "Electroconvulsive therapy reduces frontal cortical connectivity in severe depressive disorder" by Perrin et al., was published in the formidable PNAS journal (Proceedings of the National Academy of Sciences of the United States). The study is credible for several reasons. First, the study is prospective (before and after), composed of nine participants averaging 46.8 years, administered "ECT" twice weekly for an average of about 8.3 treatments. Second, MTTLOI is identified at twice seizure threshold which is closer, if not quite as high as that administered by default with second generation BP devices. (Seizure thresholds are first determined "using standard stimulus dosing techniques"). Third, electrode placement is both identified and consistent, all receiving "bilateral . . . ECT electrode placement." Fourth, the machine is identified as (the second generation) Thymatron DGx made by Somatics. Thus, we know that all recipients receive Brief Pulse and that the MTTLOI is two-fold threshold. This is of interest in that the Thymatron DGx (Perrin et al. , p 5468) has a default output of about 2.3 fold threshold for all age categories, not a 2.0 fold threshold per recipient so that "treatments" are either hand-titrated or rounded down. In any case, the study is not performed at minimal stimulus. Moreover, the study is complex, scientific, and completely data driven, containing specific and highly accurate information comparing pre-"ECT" and post-"ECT" neuronal interconnectivity of the brain. The authors state:

> In the present study, we examined the impact of ECT on [neuronal] connectivity in nine patients successfully treated for severe depressive disorder by comparing functional connectivity in the whole brain before and after therapy using MRI. (Perrin et al. , 2012, p.5466)
>
> To identify statistically significant changes in functional connectivity between pre- and posttreatment data, a unique method referred to as cortical hub and related network topology . . . analysis was used, which consisted of two stages. First, for each subject and each condition (i.e. , pre- and post-ECT treatment), maps of the average global connectivity, also known as weighted global connectivity (WGC), were calculated from the components . . . of the corresponding correlation matrices . . . . To obtain statistically significant differences in the WGC between pre- and posttreatment data on a voxel-by-voxel [685] basis, a nonparametric permutation test . . . was used . . . . (Ibid, p 5468-9)

While the authors put a positive spin on the results, the findings are revealing.

> A cluster of 12 voxels exhibited a significant decrease in the WGC [Weighted Global Connectivity] . . . posttreatment . . . . The significant cluster of voxels identified during the first

---

[685] A voxel can be thought of as a small cubic area of space, in this case, small mapped areas of the brain

stage of the analysis was used as a seed region to determine the associated functional brain networks (i.e. , the brain areas to which the seed region was functionally connected before and after ECT treatment). . . . . Two correlation maps, showing connectivity with the seed region pre- and post-ECT treatment, were created. . . . . These correlation maps were then converted to binary connectivity maps . . . . Finally, the two binary pre- and posttreatment connectivity maps were combined into a single parametric map . . . . " (Ibid, p 5469)

The authors incontrovertibly "show that ECT alters the functional architecture of frontal systems by strongly down-regulating connectivity in key circuits implicated in mood disorder" (Ibid, p 5466). Moreover, this loss of connectivity occurs mainly in the "left dorsolateral prefrontal cortical region," in brief, the left prefrontal lobe, "where the average global functional connectivity was considerably decreased after ECT treatment" (Ibid).

To be sure, the authors see this loss in brain connectivity as positive since it is accompanied by positive findings on the "Montgomery Asberg Depression Rating Scale" (Ibid). In short, the treatment is considered "successful" in that all recipients score "less depressed. " The Perrin study, according to its authors, gives credence to the theory that mood related disorders are related to brain "hyperconnectivity," suggesting that the dramatic decrease in brain connectivity found following "ECT" is remedial. What the authors fail to discuss is how brain connectivity is decreased, in short, the probable electrical destruction of tens of thousands of neuronal connectors as a direct result of "ECT," indeed, as a direct result of excessive electricity.

What the authors in this study are not aware of, of course, is manufacturer suppression of information regarding the tremendous power of modern day Brief Pulse devices, figures manufacturers have withheld from both the lay public and practicing professionals. One reason for this is that, in spite of the rare titrating of a 2.0 fold threshold output (with BL ECT) for all recipients within the Perrin MRI study, the Thymatron DGx never depicts more than 101 maximum joules when, in fact, the device emits a maximum 230 maximum joules. In spite of Perrin et al.'s important findings and in spite of the rare 2.0 fold threshold output for all recipients in this study, then, the authors no doubt subscribe to the adequate convulsion theory of "ECT," and so may not recognize the critical element in the study--excessive electrical output. They would have no idea, for example, that in lieu of the rare two fold threshold output at which their recipients are (evidently) manually titrated, the DGx emits a default 2.3 fold threshold output for all age recipients (with BL ECT). Nor would they have been aware that a third generation Somatics BP device manufactured subsequent to the DGx emits a default circa 4.6 fold threshold output with BL "ECT" for all age recipients (See "Third Generation Devices" in Volume II). In fact, the authors seem to have inadvertently discovered the elusive results not of adequate convulsion, but of adequate amounts of electricity on which these devices are actually based, indeed, emitted by design, and by which these BP devices actually work. In any case, the authors avoid discussing the possibility that while these "treatments" may have indeed produced an anti-depressant effect (and perhaps accompanying behavior modification), that the price for this diminished depression may well be irreversible or, at least, relatively long term memory damage reflective of brain damage (for what else can we call a conspicuous and sudden reduction of neuro-connectivity), a detail that virtually all "ECT" manufacturers have denied for some sixty years or more. Indeed, manufacturers themselves know all too well both how their devices work and what the aim of their devices actually is, an aim convincingly, even if accidentally, substantiated by the Perrin prospective MRI study. Certainly, manufacturers themselves, those who actually make these devices are fully aware that convulsion alone has little or no lasting "therapeutic effect," and that their machines must emit much more electricity than that required to induce an adequate seizure in order to make the devices "work" which as the Perrin study reveals for the first time, is directly due to recipients' inordinate physical reduction in neurotransmissions due to the inordinate physical reduction of neurotransmitters. In short, just as so many recipients have so long known from personal experience, and just as psychiatrist Peter Breggin has so often proclaimed, "damage is the treatment," damage long since manifesting itself via ubiquitous long-term memory dysfunction. Perrin et al. are simply the first to definitively identify the specific organic occurrence behind it. [686] (Remember too, that recipients can have an initial anti-depressant effect both from damage and because they think their memories improved though they are not.) In any case, Perrin et al. successfully identify the mechanism behind "ECT"--loss of neuronal transmitters. The researchers are successful for three main

---

[686] Even MRI studies have shown subtle changes, but because the dynamic occurs on a neuronal level, too microscopic even for MRI to physically identify, it was not until the Perrin et al. method of identifying pre and post neuronal connectivity, that diminishment in neuronal connectivity was actually identified following "ECT."

reasons; first they performed a prospective MRI study; second they examined recipients receiving at least two fold threshold outputs in lieu of minimal stimulus, and third, they mapped pre and post changes on a neuronal level.

But what specifically does the authors' description, "down-regulating connectivity in key circuits" mean? Quite literally, "down-regulating connectivity in key circuits" translates into the destruction of neurotransmitters and so the reduction of neurotransmissions mainly in the left prefrontal lobe, in brief, the devastation of thousands, if not millions of left pre-frontal lobe neuronal synaptic connections. Indeed the brain is comprised of billions of neurons, in turn comprised of pre-synaptic, post synaptic connectors. The delicate nature of the billions of microscopic dendritically laced neurons essential to the billions of electro-chemical connections comprising brain functionality can be clearly compromised or destroyed through a high enough load, i.e., a surge of electric current. That damage occurs from excessive electrical output has long been known through numerous scholarly studies (cited in this manuscript) regarding the application of high electrical current through the brain. Indeed, electrical damage studies were the very impetus behind the 1982 APA standard requiring minimal stimulus induced adequate seizures for all age recipients and which FDA encouraged manufacturers to adopt. In short, the 1982 APA standard guaranteed minimal stimulus output, meaning, only enough electricity to induce an adequate seizure with the so-called "ECT" device. Astonishingly, we must conclude that the destruction of neurons through simple electrical overload, is exactly what the modern day ENR BP device--as is the more archaic SW device--designed to do. Moreover, it is only through the destruction of enough neurotransmitters and so enough neurotransmissions that the temporary anti-depressant effect appears to occur. Indeed, it is solely due to the inextricably direct relationship between the amount of electricity, the amount of electrical damage, and any semblance of enduring "efficacy," that manufacturers have gone to such great lengths to hide. In brief, they deliberately hide the degree of electrical output emitted by their Brief Pulse machines. What the Perrin study inadvertently substantiates for the first time then, is not only damage, but the nature of the damage and its direct relationship to "efficacy. "

Implied Rationale

The implied rationale behind the application of "ECT" in the Perrin article is that patients who suffer from "mood disorder," have the "abnormal" condition of hyperconnectivity of the brain, the logical cure for which must be reduction of this "hyperconnectivity" through the reduction of neurotransmitters. But the assumption that so-called "depressed patients" suffer from a physical "hyperconnectivity" of the brain is a dangerous one in that the abnormal hyperconnective brain theory is fraught with speculation and assumption. In short, the notion that activity is abnormally excessive in depressed individuals, really only reveals hyperactivity, not hyperconnectivity. What is needed then is a reduction in hyperactivity--not reduction in brain connectivity. Indeed, the "different kind of brain" notion is the core rationale behind racism and eugenics. Moreover, it is the type of rationale used to justify psychosurgeries of the past such as those of the 1950s. The Perrin study even makes such an allusion, asserting that ". . . reductions in functional connectivity observed here encompass the region lesioned in anterior cingulotomy for severe treatment-resistant depressive disorder . . . " (Ibid, p 5467).[687] Indeed, the aim of cingulotomy is to severely reduce connectivity.

But there is another very important finding in the Perrin study and this is that the inordinate reduction in connectivity following "ECT" which Perrin discovered, occurs mainly, if not almost exclusively within the left prefrontal lobe.

> A comparison of pre- and posttreatment connectivity data revealed a significant and unexpectedly restricted cluster of voxels [sections] in and around the *left* dorsolateral prefrontal cortex (D*L*PFC) region . . . where the average global functional connectivity was considerably decreased after ECT treatment. . . . The impact of ECT on global functional connectivity change (as opposed to the many reported widespread effects on other aspects of brain function)

[687] Burr holes in the skull were drilled and lesions made in the brain through heated electrodes until dorsal nexus was either severed or compromised.

> appears remarkably restricted and lateralized, limited to an area within the left DLPFC . (Perrin et al.2012)

So why, even though Alternating Current (AC) is equally applied to both sides of the brain, does the reduction in connectivity occur primarily in the left prefrontal lobe and not the right prefrontal lobe, indeed, a reduction between the left prefrontal lobe and other parts of the brain so profound, that between 35 and 100 percent of the connections appear to stop working following "ECT"? (See the 2012 Perrin study). The explanation may be found in another very similar, but unrelated MRI brain mapping study in which "ECT" is not a component. In the 2012 similar MRI brain mapping study entitled "Connectivity of prefrontal cortex predicts cognitive control and intelligence" by Cole et al. (2012), the Cole team concludes:

> Control of thought and behavior is fundamental to human intelligence. Evidence suggests a [left] frontoparietal brain network implements such cognitive control across diverse contexts. . . . [that] . . . components of this network might coordinate control of other networks. [In short, the left] lateral prefrontal cortex (LPFC) [exclusively] . . . was found to . . . exhibit high global connectivity [with other parts of the brain]. . . . suggest[ing] [that] LPFC is a global hub . . . implement[ing] control processes central to human intelligence. (Cole et al. , 2012)
>
> We . . . examin[ed] GBC [Global Brain Connectivity] correlations . . . in all brain voxels [sections]. Remarkably, only a single significant region was identified . . . the LPFC [Left Pre-Frontal Cortex] region . . . suggest[ing] . . . GBC [Global Brain Connectivity] . . . was specific to [the] LPFC [Left Pre-Frontal Cortex]. (Ibid)
>
> . . . the present results might seem to suggest left LPFC is the 'seat of intelligence. ' (Ibid)
>
> Our results provide novel evidence that left LPFC supports cognitive control and intelligence via a unique mechanism involving extensive global connectivity . . . suggest[ing] a reconceptualization of LPFC as a functional hub that uses its brain wide influence to facilitate cognitive control and intelligence. (Ibid)
>
> One possibility, based on Miller and Cohen's (2001) model of LPFC function, is that LPFC acts as a “flexible” hub, able to flexibly shift its connectivity with a variety of [other] task-relevant regions according to task demands. Within this conceptualization, resting state fMRI GBC likely reflects the number of possible routes that LPFC can use during tasks to reconfigure connectivity. (Ibid)
>
> This may reflect a particular architecture for a flexible neural system underlying human intelligence. (Ibid)

In essence, all roads, that is, all GBC [Global Brain Connectivity] leads to the LPFC, very possibly the hub of the entire brain. Almost horrifyingly, this might explain why the LPFC is the most exclusively affected area of the human brain following the excessive emission of Alternating Current into both brain hemispheres equally via "ECT. " In short, regardless of what part of the brain is "shocked," all the electric current via neuro connectors makes its way back to the LPFC, so that it is the LPFC which incurs the chief damage. Indeed, rather than suggesting that hyperconnectivity in the LPFC is abnormal and should be reduced, the Cole et al. study, suggests that the more connections the LPFC has with the rest of the brain, the greater that individual's intelligence.

While all human beings suffer from depression, some severely, and while all human beings endure the assailing mental chatter of the mind very possibly reflected through hyperactivity of the brain, certainly the first treatment tool should not be the destruction of physical neuronal connectors, but the mere reduction of hyperactivity and this via a tool that has been available to us for thousands of years--varying forms of meditation. In any case, no recipient should be forced to submit to or be misled into undergoing a procedure which physically destroys functional connectivity of what may be the hub of the entire human brain. That is, no one should be deceptively, much less forcibly subjected to a modern form of psychosurgery via ENR (Electro Neuro transmission Reduction) through which excessive or "adequate" doses of electrical output result in gross reduction of brain connectivity quite possibly resulting in irremediable degradation of that connectivity. Certainly, no one should be administered such a procedure without being fully informed of the aim, purpose, and consequences of ENR, which is quite plainly, considerable physical reduction of functional connectivity within, and to and from, the left prefrontal frontal lobe with other parts of the brain. Quite bluntly, the aim of ENR through excessive induction of electricity--appears to be controlled brain damage--specifically the annihilation of a goodly percentage of neuro connectors constituting the left pre-frontal lobe. Indeed, the aim of Electro Neurotransmission Reduction appears most similar to partial pre-frontal lobotomy with this important difference. It is not gray matter which is physically destroyed, but neuro-connectors within the gray matter. Indeed, because gray matter is not destroyed as with the original partial pre-frontal lobotomy, there yet remains the hope supported by some scientific evidence, that compromised or even destroyed connections can eventually regenerate over time [688] (Gould et al.1999). The information these neurons contained may never be recovered, but the potential to store new information and make new connections may eventually return. Nevertheless, the loss, once discovered can be devastating, much like a stroke victim discovering he or she has lost the ability to read. Amazingly, because of the cover-up surrounding how "ECT" works and how much electricity is used, that is, because manufacturers insist it works by way of "therapeutic convulsions" invoked with small relatively harmless amounts of electricity as opposed to adequate amounts of electricity deliberately designed to annihilate tens of thousands of connections, electroshock has been accepted as "standard treatment" in most states. Indeed, even coerced "ECT" following mental health hearings is fairly common in at least 48 of the 50 United States. [689] It goes without saying, that no human being in any civilized society today should be forced to undergo a partial prefrontal lobotomy via electricity, or more specifically, electro neuro transmission reduction merely because it may be accompanied by a temporary antidepressant effect, a delusional belief (at least for a time) that memory has improved and most importantly, the often overlooked societal justification for the procedure, desirable changes in behavior. In sum, what family members and society achieve from imposing “ECT” on loved ones and/or plaintive members of society often suffering from some sort of overwhelm, is fewer complaints, the modern equivalent of greater tractability. Indeed, following a powerful enough procedure, recipients sometimes grow silent , not due to memory improvement, but ironically, due to much greater memory dysfunction. This “silence” was the looked for effect of psychosurgery. Ultimately, of course, no human being should be subjected through either deception or force to the destruction of his or her left pre-frontal connections or what might be deemed a partial left prefrontal neuronectomy (LPFN) simply to silence his or her complaints. This method of silencing satisfies not so much the individual recipient him or herself as third parties, in brief, some variation of societal demand. Indeed, all psychosurgery aims at reducing brain capacity in order to control mood and behavior and ENR is no exception. The physiological findings of diminished connections discovered by the Perrin study in conjunction with the unexpected power of what are actually ENR devices containing surprisingly high outputs over threshold no longer based on adequate seizure but rather adequate doses of electricity point to one conclusion. To make the procedure "work," manufacturers have long understood that what are actually modern day "ENR" devices only work through damaging amounts of electrical energy in order deliberately designed to reduce brain connectivity. In sum, ENR is a modern day form of psychosurgery, in effect, what might be deemed a partial left prefrontal neuronectomy (LPFN), information which manufacturers have understood and covered up for well over seventy-five years.

---

688 Brain studies on monkeys proved that, with intellectual stimulation, neuronal regrowth does occur.

689 Texas, and to a lesser extent California, due to citizen advocacy groups, are the major exceptions.

Works Cited

Abrams, R. (1996). ECT stimulus parameters as determinants of seizure quality. *Psychiatric Annals,* 26(11), 701-704.

Abrams, R. (1988). *Electroconvulsive therapy*. Oxford, New York: Oxford University Press.

Abrams, R. (1992). *Electroconvulsive therapy*. Oxford, New York: Oxford University Press.

Abrams, R., and Swartz, C. (1988). *ECT instruction manual.* Lake Bluff, Illinois: Somatics, Inc.

Abrams, R., and Swartz, C. (1985). *Thymatron instruction manual.* Lake Bluff, Illinois: Somatics, Inc.

Abrams, R., Taylor, M.A., Faber, R., Tso, T.O.T., Williams, R.A., and Almy, G. (1983). Bilateral vs. unilateral electroconvulsive therapy: Efficacy in meloncholia. *American Journal of Psychiatry*, 140, 463-465.

Alexander, L., (1953). *Treatment of mental disorder.* Philadelphia: W.B. Saunders.

Alexander, L., and Lowenbach, H. (1944). Experimental studies on electro-shock treatment. *Journal of Neuropathology and Experimental Neurology, 3,* 139-171.

American Psychiatric Association. (1979, July 9). Letter to Acting Commissioner Sherwin Gardner from Medical Director of American Psychiatric Association Melvin Sabshin, M.D. *Department of Health and Human Services*, Hearing Clerk's Office, 5600 Fishers Lane, Rockville, Maryland 20857, Rm 4-65, HFA-305; 78N; C00010/ANS, HFK-1, K-571, 7902883.

American Psychiatric Association. (1990). *The practice of electroconvulsive therapy: Recommendations for treatment, training, and privileging. Task Force on ECT.* Washington, D.C.: American Psychiatric Association.

American Psychiatric Association. (1992). *American Psychiatric Association fact sheet: Electroconvulsive therapy (ECT)* [three page flyer]. Washington, D.C.: American Psychiatric Association.

American Psychiatric Association - Draft (1999). *The practice of electroconvulsive therapy: Recommendations for treatment, training, and privileging. Second Edition (Completely Revised) A Task Force Report of the American Psychiatric Association.* Washington, D.C.: American Psychiatric Association.

American Psychiatric Association Task Force on ECT (1978). *Electroconvulsive therapy: Task force report 14.* Washington D.C.: American Psychiatric Association.

Andre, L., (2009) *Doctors of Deception—What They Don't Want You to Know about Shock Treatment.* New Brunswick: Rutgers University Press.

Andre, L., (1991). *Electroshock as head injury.* Unpublished manuscript, Committee For Truth In Psychiatry, 13 St. Marks (7-F), New York, New York 10003.

Andre versus Somatics et al. (1987). New York State Supreme Court, New York, New York, File Number 9220-87.

Andreasen, N.C., Ernhardt, J.C., Swayze, V.W., Alliger, R.J., Yuh, W.T.C., Cohen, G., and Ziebell, S. (1990). Magnetic resonance imaging of the brain in schizophrenia. *Archives of general Psychiatry*, 47, 35-44.

Appel, K.E., Meyers, J., and Sheflin, A. (1953). Prognosis in psychiatry. *Archives of Neurological Psychiatry*, 70, 459-468.

Association for the Advancement of Medical Instrumentation. (1998). *"8th Annual International Standards Conference on Medical Devices."* [six page information flyer]. Arlington, Virginia: Association for the Advancement of Medical Instrumentation.

Association for the Advancement of Medical Instrumentation. (1998, February 4). Letter from Nick Tongston to members of the IEC/SC 62D and IEC/SC 62D/WG 2 committee. Subject: Vote on review of IEC 60601-2-14, Ed.1, Medical electrical equipment - Part 2: Particular requirements for the safety of electroconvulsive therapy equipment. Ballot Deadline: 25 March 1998.

Bayles, S.; Busse, E.W., and Ebaugh, F.G. (1950). "Square waves (BST) versus sine waves in electroconvulsive therapy." *American Journal of Psychiatry,* 107, n.p.

Beale, M.D., Kellner, C.H., Pritchett, J.T., Bernstein, H.J., Burns, C.M., and Knapp, R. (1994). Stimulus dose-titration in ECT: A 2-year clinical experience. *Convulsive Therapy* , 10(2), 171-176.

Bergsholm, P., Larsen, J.L., Rosendahl, K., and Holsten, F. (1989). Electroconvulsive therapy and cerebral computed tomography: A prospective study. *Acta Psychiatria Scandanavia*, 80, 566-572.

Blachley, P. (1976a). New developments in electroconvulsive therapy. *Diseases of the Nervous System*, 37, 356-358.

Blachley, P. H., (1976b). (Ed.) *Convulsive Therapy Bulletin.,* 1(3), City not known: Publisher not known.

Blachley, P., Denney, D., and Fling, J.L. (1974). A new stimulus generator and recorder for electroconvulsive therapy. *Unpublished Manuscript*. (Cited in Grahan, A.R., Jerhrich, J.L., Couvillon, L.A., and Moench, L.G., 1977, p. 98).

Blachley, P., Denney, D., and Fling, J.L. (1976?). Engineering and electrical considerations necessary for safe apparatus for electroconvulsive therapy. *Unpublished Manuscript.* (Cited in Grahn et al, 1977, p. 33).

Blachley, P., and Gowing, D. (1966). Multiple monitored electroconvulsive treatments. *Comprehensive Psychiatry*, 7, 100-109.

Bolwig, T.G., Westergaard, E. (1977a). Acute hypertension causing blood-brain barrier breakdown during epileptic seizures. *Acta Neurologica Scandinavia, 56*, 335-342.

Bolwig, T.G., Hertz, M.M., Paulson, O.B., Spotoft, H. and Rafaelsen, O.J. (1977b). The permeability of the blood-brain barrier during electrically induced seizures in man. *European Journal of Clinical Investigations,* 7, 87-93.

Bradley, W.G., Waluch, V., Brandt-Zawadzki, M., Yardley, R.A., and Wyckoff, R.R. (1984). Patchy perventricular white matter lesions in the elderly: A common observation during NMR imaging. *Noninvas Imaging*, 1, 35-41.

Braffman, B.H., Grossman, R.I., McCallister, T., Price, T.P.R., Gyulai, L., Atlas, S.W., Hackney, D.B., Goldberg, H.I., Bilaniuk, L.T., and Zimmerman, R.A. (1988). MR imaging prior to and following electroconvulsive therapy in patients with major affective disorders. *American Journal of Neuroradiology (Abstracts)* , 9, 1933.

Breggin, P.R. (1979). *Electroshock: Its brain disabling effects*. New York: Springer Publishing Company.

Breggin, P.R. (1991). *Toxic Psychiatry*. New York. St. Martin's Press.

Breggin, P.R. (1998). Electroshock: Scientific, ethical, and political issues. *International Journal of Risk & Safety in Medicine*, 11, 5-40.

Breggin, P.R. (2007). Brain disabling treatments in psychiatry: Drugs, Electroshock, and the psychopharmaceutical complex. New York: Springer Publishing Company.

Breggin, P.R. (2007). ECT damages the brain: Disturbing news for patients and shock doctors alike. *Ethical Human Psychology and Psychiatry,* 9(2), 83-86.

Calloway, S.P., Dolan, R.J., Jacoby, R.J., and Levy, R. (1981). ECT and cerebral atrophy: a computed tomographic study. *Acta Psychiatric Scandanavia,* 64, 442-445.

Cameron, D.G. (1979). *How to survive being committed to a mental hospital.* New York: Vantage Press.

Cameron, D.G. (1994). ECT: Sham statistics, the myth of convulsive therapy, and the case for consumer misinformation. *Journal of Mind and Behavior,* 15, 177-198.

Cameron, D.G. (1997). *Horror Stories from the mental health system: ECT: 200 cases of permanent memory loss, volumes 1 and 2.* unpublished manuscripts.

Cameron, D.G. (1998). *EST: Morbidity and Mortality with Suprathreshold Dosing.* unpublished article.

Canadian Psychiatric Association, (1981), Quote - march 20, *Psychiatric News*,16(6), 7, 15.

Carney, M.W.P., and Sheffield, B.F. (1974). The effects of pulse ECT in neurotic and endogenous depression. *British Journal of Psychiatry,* 125, 91-94.

Cerletti, U. and Bini, L. (1938). Un nuevo motodo di shockterapie "l'elettro-shock." *Boll. Acad. Med. Roma*, 64, 136-138.

Chabasinski, Ted. (2022, October 24). Mad in america. *Science, Psychiatry, and Social Justice.*

Chamberlin, J. (1977). *On our own: Patient controlled alternatives to the mental health system.* New York: Hawthorne.

Coffey, C.E., Hinkle, P.E. Weiner, R.D., Nemeroff, C.B., Krishnan, K.R.R., Varia, I. and Sullivan, D.C. (1987a). Electroconvulsive therapy of depression in patients with white matter hyperintensity. *Biological Psychiatry*, 22, 629-636.

Coffey, C.E., Weiner, R.D., Hinkle, P.E., Cress, M., Daughtry, G., and Wilson, W.H. (1987b). Augmentation of ECT seizures with caffeine. *Biological Psychiatry*, 22, 637-649.

Coffey, C.E., Figiel, G.S., Djang, W.T., Sullivan, D.C., Herfkens, R.J., and Weiner, R.D. (1988a). Effects of ECT on brain structure: A pilot prospective magnetic resonance imaging study. *American Journal of Psychiatry,* 145, 701-706.

Coffey, C.E., Figiel, G.S., Djang, W.T., Cress, M., Saunders, W.B., and Weiner, R.D. (1988b). Leukoencephalopathy in elderly depressed patients for ECT. *Biological Psychiatry*, 24, 143-161.

Coffey, C.E. and Weiner, R.D. (1989). Subcortical white matter hyperintensity on magnetic resonance imaging: Clinical and neuroanatomic correlates in the depressed elderly. *Journal of Neuropsychiatry and Clinical Neurosciences*, 1, 135-145.

Coffey, C.E., Figiel, G.S., Djang, W.T., Weiner, R.D. (1990a). Subcortical hyperintensity on magnetic resonance imaging: a comparison of normal and depressed elderly subjects. *American Journal of Psychiatry,* 147, 187-189.

Coffey, C.E., Figiel, G.S., Weiner, R.D., and Saunders, W.B. (1990b). Caffeine augmentation of ECT. *American Journal of Psychiatry, 147,* 579-85.

Coffey, C.E., and Weiner, R.D. (1990c). Electroconvulsive therapy: An update. *Hospital and Community Psychiatry, 41(5),* 515-520.

Coffey, C.E. (1991a). Structural brain abnormalities in the depressed elderly. In: P. Hauser (Ed.), *Brain imaging in affective disorders* (pp. 89-111). Washington, D.C.: American Psychiatric Press.

Coffey, C.E., Weiner, R.D., Djang, W.T., Figiel, G.S., Soady, S.A.R., Patterson, L.J., Holt, P.D., Spritzer, C.E., Wilkinson, W.E. (1991b). *Brain anatomic effects of electroconvulsive therapy: A prospective magnetic resonance imaging study*. Archives of General Psychiatry, 48, 1013-1021.

Coffey, C.E., Wilkinson, W.E., Weiner, R.D., Parashos, I.A., Djang, W.T., Webb, M.C., Figiel, G.S., and Spritzer, C.E. (1993). Quantitative cerebral anatomy in depression: A controlled magnetic resonance imaging study. *Archives of General Psychiatry*, 50, 7-16.

Coffey, C.E., Lucke, J., Weiner, R.D., Krystal, A.D., and Aque, M. (1995). Seizure threshold in electroconvulsive therapy (ECT) II: The anticonvulsant effect of ECT. Biological Psychiatry, 37, 777-778.

Cole, M.W., Yarconi. T., Repovs, G., Anticevic, & A., Braver, T. (2012). Global Connectivity of prefrontal cortex predicts cognitive control and intelligence. *Journal of Neuroscience, Jun 27, 32*(26): 8988-8999.

Coleman, L. (1984). *The reign of error.* Boston: Beacon Press.

Cook, L.C. (1940). Has fear any therapeutic significance in convulsion? *Journal of Mental Science, 40,* 414.

Council of the European Communities (June 14, 1993). Council, directive 93/42/EEC of 14 June 1993 concerning medical devices . *Official Journal of the European Communities. 12(7),* L169/2-L169/43.

Cronholm, B., and Ottosson, J.O. (1963). Ultrabrief stimulus techniques in ECT. II. Comparative studies of therapeutic effects and memory disturbances in treatment of endogenous depression with the Elther ES apparatus and Siemens Konvulsator III. *Journal of Nervous and Mental Diseases, 137,* 268-276.

Daniel, W.F., Weiner, R.D., and Crovitz, H.F. (1983). Autobiographical amnesia with ECT: An analysis of the roles of stimulus wave form, electrode placement, stimulus energy, and seizure length. *Biological Psychiatry*, 18(1), 121-126.

Davies, R.K., Detre, T.P., Egger, M.D., Tucker, G.J., and Wyman, R.J. (1971). Electroconvulsive therapy Instruments - should they be reevaluated?. *Archives of General Psychiatry*, 25, 97-99.

d'Elia, G. (1970). Unilateral electroconvulsive therapy. *Acta Psychiatria Scandanavia (Supplement)*, 215.

d'Elia, G., Ottosen, J.-O., and Stronmerg L.S. (1983). Present practice of electroconvulsive therapy in scandinavia. *Archives of General Psychiatry*, 40, 577-581.

d'Elia, G., and Raotma, H. (1975). Is unilateral ECT less effective than bilateral ECT? *British Journal of Psychiatry*, 126, 83-89.

Delmas-Marsalet, P.L. (1942). L'electro-choc par courant continu. *Comptes rendus des Seances. Societe de Biologie et de ses Filiales et Associees (Paris)*, 136, 551-553.

Department of Health and Human Services, (1982a). *Petition to reclassify*. Silver Spring, Maryland: Food and Drug Administration.

Department of Health and Human Services, (1982b). *Summary minutes, seventh meeting, neurological section, respiratory and nervous system device panel.* Silver Spring, Maryland: Food and Drug Administration.

Department of Health and Human Services, (1982c). *Open public hearing regarding reclassification of ECT.* Silver Spring, Maryland: Food and Drug Administration.

Devanand, D.P., Dwork, A.J., Hutchinson, M.S.E., Bolwig, T.G., and Sackheim, H.A. (1994). Does ECT alter brain structure? *American Journal of Psychiatry*, 151, 957-970.

Dolan, R.J., Calloway, S.P., Thacker, P.F., and Mann, A.H. (1986). The cerebral cortical appearance in depressed subjects. *Psychological Medicine*, 16, 775-779.

Dunn, A., Giuditta, A., Wilson, J.E., and Glassman, E. (1974). The effect of electroshock on brain RNA and protein synthesis and its possible relationship to behavioral effects. In M. Fink, S. Kety, and J. McGaugh (Eds.), *Psychobiology of convulsive therapy* (pp. 185-197). New York: Wiley.

Dupont, R.M., Jernigan, T.L., Butters, N., Delis, D., Hesselink, J.R., Heindel, W., and Gillin, J.C. (1990). Subcortical abnormalities detected in bipolar affective disorders using magnetic resonance imaging: clinical and neuropsychological significance. *Archives of General Psychiatry*, 47, 55-59.

Dwork, A.J., Arango, V., Underwood, M., Ilievski, B., Rosoklija, G., Sackeim, H. A., and Lisanby, S. H. (2004). Absence of histological lesions in primate models of ECT and magnetic seizure therapy. *The American Journal of Psychiatry*, 161(3): 576-78.

Dwork, A.J., Arango, V., Underwood, M., Ilievski, B., Rosoklija, G., Sackeim, H. A., and Lisanby, S. H. (2005). Dr. Dwork and colleagues reply. *The American Journal of Psychiatry*, 162: 196.

Echlin, F.A. (1942). Vasospasm and forced cerebral ischemia. *Archives of Neurological Psychiatry, 47*, 77-96.

Elcot Incorporated. (1993). Microprocessor-Controlled, MULTI-FUNCTION ECT Units[flyer]. New York, New York: Elcot Incorporated.

Essman, W.B. (1968). Electroshock-induced retrograde amnesia in seizure-protracted mice. *Psychobiological Reports, 22*, 929-935.

Farmer, F. (1973). *Will there really be a morning?* New York: Putnam.

Field, E. (1964). *The white shirts.* Los Angeles: Tasmania Press.

Fink, M., and Kahn, R.L. (1957). Relation of EEG delta activity to behavioral response in electroshock. *Archives of Neurological Psychiatry*, 78, 516-525.

Fink, M. (1957). *A unified theory of the action of physiodynamic therapies.* Journal of Hillside Hospital, 6, 197-206.

Fink, M. (1978). Efficacy and safety of induced seizures (EST) in man. *Comprehensive Psychiatry*, 19(1), 1-18.

Fink, M. (1979). Convulsive therapy: Theory and practice. New York: Raven Press.

Fink, M. (1997). ECT update. *(Internet).* http://www.mhsource.com/edu/psytimes/p970439.html.

Fink, M., Kahn, R.L., and Green, M. (1958). Experimental process of the electroshock process. *Diseases of the Nervous System*, 19, pp. 113-118.

Fodero, L. (1993, July 19). With reforms in treatment, shock therapy loses shock. *New York Times*, p. A1, A16.

Food and Drug Administration. (1978, November 28). *Federal Register*, pp. 55729-30.

Food and Drug Administration. (1979, May 29). Neurological section: Respiratory and nervous systems devices panel (public meeting). Department of Health, Education, and Welfare.

Food and Drug Administration. (1979, September 4). Neurological devices: Classification of electroconvulsive therapy devices. *Federal Register*, Volume 44, Number 172, 21 CFR Part 882, Docket Number 78N-1103.

Food and Drug Administration. (1984). Electroconvulsive Therapy Devices - 510K. *Somatics Incorporated Premarket Notification Submission: Reference K843923. Product: Electroconvulsive Therapy Device, Thymatron.* Center for Devices and Radiological Health. Food and Drug Administration, Rockville MD 20857.

Food and Drug Administration. (1985). Electroconvulsive Therapy Devices - 510K. *MECTA Corporation Premarket Notification Submission: Reference K852069. Product: Electroconvulsive Therapy Device, MECTA D; JR/SR1; JR/SR2.* Center for Devices and Radiological Health. Food and Drug Administration, Rockville MD 20857.

Food and Drug Administration. (1986A). Electroconvulsive Therapy Devices - 510K. *Medcraft Corporation Premarket Notification Submission: Reference K860467. Product: Electroconvulsive Therapy Device, B-24; B-25.* Center for Devices and Radiological Health. Food and Drug Administration, Rockville MD 20857.

Food and Drug Administration. (1986B). Electroconvulsive Therapy Devices - 510K. *Elcot Incorporated Premarket Notification Submission: Reference K863815. Product: Electroconvulsive Therapy Device, Model MF-1000.* Center for Devices and Radiological Health. Food and Drug Administration, Rockville MD 20857.

Food and Drug Administration. (1990, September 5). Neurological devices: Proposed rule to reclassify the electroconvulsive therapy device intended for use in treating severe depression. *Federal Register*, Volume 55, Number 172, 21 CFR Part 882, Docket Number 82P-0316, pp. 36578-36590.

Food and Drug Administration. (1995, August 14). Order for Certain Class II Devices; Submission and Effectiveness Information; Notices. *Federal Register*, Volume 60, No. 156, Part III, Docket Number 94N-0417, pp. 41986-41989.

Food and Drug Administration. (1995, October 26). (Substantially Equivalent Letters For Some 510(k)'s). *Somatics, Incorporated Premarket Notification Submission: Reference K945120. Product: Electroconvulsive System, Model: Thymatron 2000. Product Code: GXC.* Center for Devices and Radiological Health. Food and Drug Administration, Rockville MD 20857.

Food and Drug Administration. (1996, September 18). (Substantially Equivalent Letters For Some 510(k)'s). *MECTA Corporation Premarket Notification Submission: Reference K960754. Product: Spectrum 5000Q, 5000M, 4000Q, 4000M. Product Code: 84GXC* . Center for Devices and Radiological Health. Food and Drug Administration, Rockville MD 20857.

Food and Drug Administration. (1997, March 6). (Substantially Equivalent Letters For Some 510(k)'s). *MECTA Corporation Premarket Notification Submission: Reference K965070. Trade Name: SpECTrum 5000 and 4000 ECT Devices. Product Code: 84GXC* . Center for Devices and Radiological Health. Food and Drug Administration, Rockville MD 20857.

Frank, L.R. (1978). (Ed.) *The history of shock treatment.* San Francisco: Frank.

Freeman, C.P.L. and Kendell, R.E. (1980). (Interviews with patients in Scotland from one to two years after routine ECT in 1976): Part 1, ECT: Patients' experiences and attitudes. *British Journal of Psychiatry,* 137, 8-16.

Friedberg, J. (1976). *Shock treatment is not good for your brain.* San Francisco: Glide Publications.

Friedberg, J. (1977). Shock treatment, brain damage, and memory loss: A neurological perspective. *American Journal of Psychiatry,* 134(9), 1010-1014.

Friedberg, J. (200**5**). Dr. Friedberg retorts. *The American Journal of Psychiatry,* 162: 196.

Friedman, E. (1942). Unidirectional electrostimulated convulsive therapy. *American Journal of Psychiatry,* 99, 218-223.

Friedman, E., Wilcox, P.H., and Reiter, R.M. (1942). Electrostimulated convulsive doses in intact humans by means of unidirectional currents. *Journal of Nervous and Mental Disease,* 96, 56-63.Gangadhar, B.N., Janakiramaiah, N., Dutt, D.N., and Motreja, S. (1997). Strength symmetry index: A measure of seizure adequacy in ECT. *Convulsive Therapy,* 13(1), 18-24.

Glen, M., and Weiner, R. (1983). *Electroconvulsive therapy: A programmed text.* Washington, D.C.: American Psychiatric Press.

Glueck, B.C., Reiss, H., and Bernard, L.E. (1957). Regressive electric shock therapy. *Psychiatric Quarterly*, 31, 117-135.

Gordon, D. (1982). Electroconvulsive therapy with minimal hazard. *British Journal of Psychiatry, 141,* 12-18.

Gotkin, J. and Gotkin, P. (1974). *Too much anger, too many tears: A personal triumph over psychiatry.* New York: Quadrangle.

Gould, E., Reeves, A.J., Fallah, M., Tanapat, P., Gross, C.G., & Fuchs, E. (1999). Hippocampus neurogenesis in adult Old World primates. *Proceedings National Academy of Science, USA (96)*9, 5263-5267.

Grahn, A.R. (1976, October 15). *Summary of presentation to FDA Neurology Panel: Study of Electroconvulsive Therapy device: Safety and Efficacy,* FDA Docket Number 78N-1103, Contract 223-74-5253, Task Order Number 22, Utah Biomedical Test Laboratory. Utah: University of Utah Research Institute, 520 Wakara Way, Salt Lake City, Utah, 84108.

Grahn, A.R., Jerhrich, J.L., Couvillon, L.A., and Moench, L.G. (1977). *Final Report (Revision A): A Study of Safety and Performance for ECT Devices*, TR 226-001, December 15, Utah Biomedical Test Lab. Utah: University of Utah Research Institute, 520 Wakara Way, Salt Lake City, Utah, 84108.

Greenblatt, M. (1977). Efficacy of electroconvulsive therapy in affective and schizophrenic illness. *American Journal of Psychiatry,* 134, 1001-1005.

Greenblatt, M., Freeman, H., and Meshorer, E. (1966). Comparative efficacy of anti-depressant drugs and placebo in relation to electric shock treatment. In: M. Rinkel (Ed.), *Biological treatment of mental Illness*, (574-594) New York: L.C. Page.

Greenblatt, M., Grosser, G.H., and Wechsler, H. (1964). Differential response of hospitalized depressed patients to somatic therapy. *American Journal of Psychiatry*, 120, 935-943.

Hauser, P., Altshuler, L.L., Berrittini, W., Dauphinais, Gelernter, J., and Pos, R.M. (1989). Temporal lobe measurement in primary affective disorder by magnetic resonance imaging. *Journal of Neuropsychiatry and Clinical Neuroscience,* 1, 128-134.

Hickie, I., Scott, E., Mitchell, P., Wilhelm, K., Austin, M-P. and Bennett, B. (1995). Subcortical hyperintensities on magnetic resonance imaging: Clinical correlates and prognostic significance in patients with severe depression. *Biological Psychiatry,* 27, 151-160.

Hordern, A., Burt, C.G., and Holt, N.F. (1965). *Depressive states.* Springfield, IL: Charles C. Thomas.

Hotchner, A.E. (1966). *Papa Hemmingway.* New York: Random House, pp. 291-335.

Imlah, N.W., Ryan, E., and Harrington, J.A. (1965). The influence of antidepressant drugs on the response to electroconvulsive therapy and on subsequent relapse rates. *Neuropsychopharmacology,* 4, 438-42.

Impastato, D. (1957). Prevention of fatalities in electroshock therapy. *Diseases of the Nervous System*, 18, 34-75.

Impastato, D., Berg, S., and Gabriel, A.R. (1957). The Molac-II - an alternating current electroshock therapy machine incorporating a new principle. *Journal of Nervous and Mental Disease*, 125, 380-384.

International Electrotechnical Commission. (1977, 1988). *International Standard: Medical electrical equipment: Part 1: General requirements for safety: IEC 601-1.* Bureau de la Commission Electrotechnique Internationale, 3, rue de Varambe, Geneve, Suisse.

International Electrotechnical Commission. (1989). *Medical electrical equipment. Part 2: Particular requirements for the safety of electroconvulsive therapy equipment. CEI/IEC International Standard, 601-2-14.* Bureau de la Commission Electrotechnique Internationale, 3, rue de Varambe, Geneve, Suisse.

International Electrotechnical Commission. (1991). *International Standard: Medical electrical equipment: Amendment 1 (to 1988), Part 1: General requirements for safety: IEC 601-1.* Bureau de la Commission Electrotechnique Internationale, 3, rue de Varambe, Geneve, Suisse.

International Electrotechnical Commission. (1997, Dec 26). Document Dispatch Advice Note. Subcommittee 62D. Vote on Review of IEC 60601-2-14. Review of International Standard. Comments on 62D/201/CD from the United States National Committee. Revision of IEC 60601-2-14, Ed.2, Part 2-14: Particular requirements for the safety of electroconvulsive therapy equipment. *International Electrotechnical Commission*, 1211 Geneva 20, Switzerland.

Isenberg, K.E., Dinwiddle, S.H., Heath, A.C. (1996). Effect of stimulus parameters on seizure threshold and duration. *Convulsive Therapy,* 12, 68. Abstract.

Janis, I. (1950). Psychologic effects of electric convulsive treatments (I, II, III, post treatment amnesia). *The Journal of Nervous and Mental Disease*, 3, 360-397; 469-489.

Johnstone, L. (1992). Is the use of ECT a non-issue for psychologists? *Clinical Psychology Forum*, 30-31.

Kay, D.W., Fahy, T., and Garside, R.F., (1970). A seven-month double-blind trial of amitriptyline and diazepam in ECT-treated depressed patients. *British Journal of Psychiatry,* 150, 112-114.

Kellner, C.H. (1994, February 2). *Electroshock with Susan Spencer* [television interview]. In C. Lasiewicz [Producer], 48 Hours. New York: CBS.

Kellner, C.H., Rubinow, D.R., Gold, P.W., and Post, R.M. (1983). Relationship to cortisol hypersecretion to brain CT scan alterations in depressed patients. *Psychiatry Residence*, 8, 191-197.

Kesey, K. (1962). *One flew over the cuckoo's nest.* New York: Viking.

Kolbeinson H., Arnaldson, O.S., Peturrson, H. and Skulason, S. (1986). Computer Tomographic Scans in ECT-patients. *Acta Psychiatrica Scandinavica,* 73, 28-32.

Krystal, A.D., Weiner, R.D., and Coffey, C.E. (1995). The ictal EEG as a marker of adequate stimulus intensity with unilateral ECT. *Journal of Neuropsychiatry,* 7, 295-303.

Krystal, A.D., Weiner, R.D., and Gasseert, D. (1996). The relative ability of three ictal EEG frequency bands to differentiate ECT seizures on the basis of electrode placement, stimulus intensity, and therapeutic response. *Convulsive Therapy,* 12, 13-14.

Krystal, A.D., Weiner, R.D., and McCall, W.V. (1993). The effects of ECT stimulus dose and electrode placement on the ictal electroencephalogram: An intra-individual cross-over study. *Biological Psychiatry,* 34, 759-767.

Laing, R. D. (1967). *The politics of experience and the bird of paradise.* United Kingdom. Penguin Press.

Lambourn, J., and Gill, D.A. (1978). A controlled comparison of simulated and real ECT in depressive illness. *British Journal of Psychiatry*, 133, 514-519.

Lapon, L. (1986). *Mass murderers in while coats.* Springfield, Massachusetts: Psychiatric Genocide Research Institute.

Leiknes, Keri Ann at al. (2012) *Contemporary use and practice of electroconvulsive therapy worldwide.* Brain and Behavior, 2(3), 283-344.

Lewis, S. (1922) *Babbitt.* United States: Harcourt, Brace and Company.

Liberson, W.T. (1945a). Study of word association processes, part II: Reactions to "average emotional" and "average neutral" words in normal and abnormal populations. Effects of electric convulsive therapy. *Digest of Neurology and Psychiatry, 13,* pages unknown.

Liberson, W.T. (1945b). Time factors in electric convulsive therapy. *Yale Journal of Biological Medicine*, 17, 571-578.

Liberson, W.T. (1946). Physiological basis of electric convulsive therapy. *Connecticut State Medical Journal,* 10, 754-756.

Liberson, W.T. (1948). Brief stimulus therapy. *American Journal of Psychiatry* , 105, 28-39.

Liberson, W.T. (1949). Review of psychiatric progress. 1948. Electroencephalography. *American Journal of Psychiatry, 105,* 503-505.

MacQueen, G. et al. (2007). The long term impact of treatment with electroconvulsive therapy on discrete memory systems in patients with bipolar disorder. *Journal of Psychiatry and Neuroscience,* 32(4), 241-249.

Malitz, S., Sackeim, H.A., Decina, P. (1979). ECT in the clinical treatment of major affective disorders: Clinical and basic research issues. *Psychiatric Journal of the University of Ottawa, 7,* 126-134.

Malitz, S., Sackeim, H.A., Decina, P., Kanzler, M., and Kerr, B. (1986). The efficacy of electroconvulsive therapy: dose response interactions with modality. *Annals of the New York Academy of Sciences*, 462, 56-64.

Mander, A.J., Whitfield, D.M.K., Smith, M.A., Douglas, R.H.B., and Kendell, R.E. (1987). Cerebral and brain stem changes after ECT revealed by nuclear magnetic resonance imaging. *British Journal of Psychiatry*, 151, 69-71.

Mangaoang, M.A. and Lacey, J.V. (2007). Cognitive rehabilitation assessment and treatment of persistent memory impairments following ECT. *Advances in Psychiatry,* 13, 90-100.

Marks, J. (1979). *The Search For The Manchurian Candidate. The CIA and Mind Control.* New York: New York Times Books.

Masson, J.M. (1984). *The Assault On Truth* . New York: Farrar, Straus, and Giroux; Toronto: Collins Publishers.

McCall, W.V., Reid, S., Rosenquist, P., Foreman, A., and Kiesow-Webb, N. (1993). A reappraisal of the role of caffeine in ECT. *American Journal of Psychiatry,* 150, 1543-1545.

McGaugh, J.L. and Alpern, H.P. (1966). Effects of electroshock on memory: Amnesia without convulsions. *Science, 152,* 665-666.

MECTA Corporation. (1987). *Health information network for hospitals and professionals* [video]. Lake Oswego, Oregon: MECTA Corporation.

Medcraft Corporation. (1984). *Medcraft B24III, Electroconvulsive Therapy Instrument* [flyer]. Darien, Connecticut: Medcraft Corporation.

Medcraft Corporation. (1986a). *Medcraft B25 Electroconvulsive Therapy Instrument* [flyer]. Darien, Connecticut: Medcraft Corporation.

Medcraft Corporation. (1986b). *Operation/Maintenance Manual B-25: Electroconvulsive Therapy Device.* Darien, CT: Medcraft Corporation.

Mellish, R.G. (1998). E-mail communication. Medical Devices Agency, Elephant and Castle, London, SE1 6TQ.

Mindham, R.H., Howland, C., and Shepherd, M. (1973). An evaluation of continuation therapy with tricyclic antidepressants in depressive illness. *Psychological Medicine,* 3, 5-17.

Nasrallah, H.A., Coffman, J.A., and Olson, S.C. (1989). Structural brain-imaging findings in affective disorders: an overview. *Journal of Neuropsychiatry Clinical Neuroscience,* 1, 21-26.

National Institutes of Mental Health and Center for Mental Health Services. (1994). Treatment methods: Biomedical therapies: Electroconvulsive treatment (ECT). *Decade of the Brain: A Consumer's Guide to Mental Health Services,* NIH Publication No. 94-3585, pp. 15-16.

Nobler, M.S., Sackeim, H.A., and Solomou, M. (1993). EEG manifestations during ECT: Effects of electrode placement and stimulus intensity. *Biological Psychiatry,* 34, 321-330.

Offner, F. (1946). Stimulation with minimum power. *Journal of Neurophysiology*, 9, 387-390.

Ottosson, J.O. (1960). Experimental studies on the mode of action of electroconvulsive therapy. *Acta Psychiatrica Scandanavia* (Supplement 145), 30, 1-141.

Pande, A.C., Grunhaus, L.J., Aisen, A.,M., and Haskett, R.F. (1990). A preliminary magnetic resonance imaging study of ECT-treated depressed patients. *Biological Psychiatry*, 27, 102-104.

Perrin et al. (2012). Electroconvulsive therapy reduces frontal cortical connectivity in severe depression disorder. *PNAS* , 109(14), 5464-8.

Perry, P., and Tsuang, M.T. (1979). Treatment of unipolar depression following electroconvulsive therapy. Relapse rate comparisons between lithium and tricyclic therapies following ECT. *Journal of Affective Disorders,* 1, 123-129.

Petrides, G., and Fink, M. (1996). The "half-age" stimulation strategy for ECT dosing. *Convulsive Therapy*, 12(3), 138-136.

Petrides, G., and Fink, M. (1997). Clinical common sense versus theoretical correctness. *Convulsive Therapy*, 13(1), 41-43.

Philpot, M., Collins, C., Trivedi, P., Treloar, A., Gallacher, S., and Rose, D. (2004). Eliciting users' views of ECT in two mental health trusts with a user-designed questionaire. *Journal of Mental Health,* 13(4), 403-413.

Plath. S. (1971). New York: Harper and Roe.

Press, G.A., Amaral, D.G., and Squire, L.R. (1989). Hippocampal abnormalities in amnesic patients revealed by high-resolution magnetic resonance imaging. Hippocampal abnormalities in amnesic patients revealed by high-resolution magnetic resonance imaging. *Nature*, 341, 54-57.

Proctor, L.D., and Goodwin, B.A. (1943). Comparative electroencephalo-graphic observations following electroshock therapy using raw 60 cycle alternating and unidirectional fluctuating current EEG. *American Journal of Psychiatry, 99,* 525-530.

Rabins, P.V., Pearlson, G.D., Aylward, E., Kumar, A.J., and Dowell, K. (1991). Cortical magnetic resonance imaging changes in elderly inpatients with major depression. *American Journal of Psychiatry*, 148, 617-620.

Read, John, and Bentall, Richard. (2010). The effectiveness of electroconvulsive therapy: A literature review. *Epidemiologia e Psichiatria,* 19(3), 333-347.

Reed, K. (1988). Electroconvulsive therapy: A clinical discussion. *Psychiatric Medicine, 6,* 29.

Rice, M. (1982). *Testimony of Marilyn Rice concerning the American Psychiatric Association's petition to reclassify ECT devices from class III to class II for presentation at hearings of neurological panel, FDA, on Nov 4-5, 1982.* In: Department of Health and Human Services, Silver Spring, Maryland: Food and Drug Administration. (pp. 82P-0316-TS003).

Robin, A., and De Tissera, S. (1982). A double blind controlled comparison of the therapeutic effects of low and high energy electroconvulsive therapies. *British Journal of Psychiatry*, 141, 357-366.

Rose, D. et al. (2003). Patient perspective on electroconvulsive therapy: Systematic review. *British Medical Journal,* 326, 1363-1365.

Royal College of Psychiatry. (1977). Memorandum on the use of ECT. *British Journal of Psychiatry*, 131, 261-272.

Royal College of Psychiatry. (1995). *The ECT handbook: Second report of the Royal College of Psychiatrists' Special Committee on ECT. Council report 39.* London: Royal College of Psychiatrists.

Sackeim, H.A. (1991). Are ECT devices underpowered? *Convulsive Therapy,* 7, pp. 233-6.

Sackeim, H.A. (1997) Comments on the "half-age" method of stimulus dosing. *Convulsive Therapy*, 13(1), 37-40.

Sackeim, H.A., Decina, P., Portnoy, P., Neeley, P., and Malitz, S. (1987a). Studies of dosage, seizure threshold, and seizure duration in ECT. *Biological Psychiatry*, 22, 249-268.

Sackeim, H.A., Decina, P., Prohovnik, I., and Malitz, S. (1987b). Seizure threshold in electroconvulsive therapy: Effects of sex, age, electrode placement, and number of treatments. *Archives of General Psychiatry*, 44, 355-360.

Sackeim, H.A., Debanand, D.P., and Prudic, J. (1991). Stimulus intensity,seizure threhold, and seizure duration: Impact on the efficacy and safety of electroconvulsive therapy. *Psychiatric Clinic North America,* 14, 803-843.

Sackeim, H.A., Luber, B., Katzman, G.P. (1996). The effects of electroconvulsive therapy on quantitative electroencephalograms. Relationship to clinical outcomes. *Archives of General Psychiatry,* 53(9), 814-824.

Sackeim, H.D., and Malitz, S. (1987c). Seizure threshold in electroconvulsive therapy: Effects of sex, age, electrode placement, and number of treatments. *Archives of General Psychiatry*, 44, 355-360.

Sackeim, H.A., Portnoy, S., Neeley, P., Steif, B.L., Decina, P., and Malitz, S. (1986). Cognitive consequences of low-dosage electroconvulsive therapy. *Annals New York Academy of Sciences,* 462, 326- 340.

Sackeim, H.A., Prohovnik, I., Moeller, J.R., Brown, R.P., Apter, S., Prudic, J., Devanand, D.P., and Mukherjee, S. (1990). Regional cerebral blood flow in mood disorders. *Archives of General Psychiatry,* 47, 60-70.

Sackeim, H.A., Prudic, J., Devanand, D.P., Kiersky, J., Fitzsimmons, L., Moody, B.J., McElhiney, M.C., Coleman, E.A., and Settembrino, B.A. (1993). Effects of stimulus intensity and electrode placement on the efficacy and cognitive effects of electroconvulsive therapy. *Journal of the American Medical Association,* 328(12), 839-846.

Sackeim, H.A., and Weiner, R.D. (1993). *MECTA Instruction Manual, SR and JR Models.* Lake Oswego, Oregon: MECTA Corporation.

Sament, S. (1983). In favor of wider ECT ban. *Clinical Psychiatry News,* 11.

Satcher, David (August 16,1999). Adults and Mental Health. *Surgeon General's Report - Draft, p 4-45.*

Scott, A.I.F., Douglas, R.H.B., Whitfield, A., and Kendell, R.E. (1990). Time course of cerebral magnetic resonance changes after electroconvulsive therapy. *British Journal of Psychiatry*, 156, 551-553.

Scott, A.I.F., Rodger, C.R., Stocks, R.H., and Shering, P.A. (1992). Is old-fashioned electroconvulsive therapy more efficacious?: A randomized comparative study of bilateral brief-pulse and bilateral sine-wave treatments. *British Journal of Psychiatry,* 160, 360-364.

Seager, C.P., and Bird, R.L., (1962). Imipramine with electrical treatment in depression - a controlled trial. *Journal of Mental Science,* 108, 704-707.

Sheline, Yvette I., Price, Joseph L., Yan, Zhizi, and Mintun, Mark A. (2010). Resting-state functional MRI in depression unmasks increased connectivity between networks via the dorsal nexus. *PNAS,* 107 (24) 11020-11025.

Shelton, R.C., and Weinberger, D.R. (1986). X-ray computerized tomography studies in schizophrenia; A review and synthesis. In: H.A. Nasrallah and D.R. Weinberger (Eds.), *The neurology of schizophrenia. Handbook of schizophrenia* (1, 207-250). Amsterdam, the Netherlands: Elsevier Science Publishers.

Small, J.G., and Small, I.F. (1981). Electroconvulsive therapy update. *Psychopharmocology Bulletin*, 17, 29-42.

Somatics Incorporated. (1993a). *"Just Set To Patient's Age and Treat."* [two page information flyer]. Lake Bluff, Illinois: Somatics Incorporated.

Somatics Incorporated. (1993b). *The Only ECT Instrument that Determines Seizure Length.* [eight page information flyer]. Lake Bluff, Illinois: Somatics Incorporated.

Somatics Incorporated. (1997a). *Setting The ECT Stimulus By Age* [flyer], Lake Bluff Illinois: Somatics Incorporated.

Somatics Incorporated. (1997b). *Somatics, Inc.: Makers of the Thymatron: Distributors.* http://www.thymatron.com/distribu.htm Internet: Lake Bluff Illinois: Somatics, Inc.

Somatics Incorporated. (1998). "Upgrade To The Only Integrated ECT System: Thymatron DGx by Somatics." [eight page information flyer]. Lake Bluff, Illinois: Somatics Incorporated.

Somatics Incorporated. (1999). "Advanced ECT: Just Became a Lot Easier to Give: Thymatron IV™ by Somatics." [eight page information flyer]. Lake Bluff, Illinois: Somatics Incorporated.

Squire, L. (1986). Memory functions as affected by electroconvulsive therapy. *Annals of the New York Academy of Sciences*, 462, 307-313.

Squire, L.R., and Chace, P.M., (1975). Memory functions six to nine months after electroconvulsive therapy. *Archives of General Psychiatry,* 32, 1557-1564.

Squire, L., and Slater, P.C. (1983). Electroconvulsive therapy and complaints of memory dysfunction: A prospective three-year follow-up study. *The British Journal of Psychiatry*, 142, 1-8.

Squire, L., Slater, P.C., and Miller, P.L. (1981). Retrograde amnesia and bilateral electroconvulsive therapy: Long-term follow-up. *Archives of General Psychiatry*, 38, 89-95.

Squire, L., and Zouzounis, J.A. (1986). ECT and memory: Brief pulse versus sine wave. *American Journal of Psychiatry,* 143(1), 596-601.

Sterling, Peter. (2000). ECT damage Is easy to find If you look for it. *Nature*, 403, 242.

Stone. G. (1994, November 14). When prozac fails . . . electroshock works. *New York* (Magazine), 55-59.

Sulzbach, W., Tillotson, K.J., Guillemin, V., and Sutherland, G.F. (1943). A consideration of some experiences with electric shock treatment in mental diseases, with special regard to various psychosomatic phenomena and to certain electrotechnical factors. *American Journal of Psychiatry,* 99, 519-524.

Susko, M. (1991). *Cry of the invisible.* Baltimore, Montreal: Conservatory Press.

Swartz, C.M., and Abrams, R. (1996). *ECT instruction manual.* Lake Bluff, Illinois: Somatics, Inc.

Swayze, V.W., Andreasen, N.C., Alliger, R.J., Ehrhardt, J.C., and Yuh, W.T.C. (1990). Structural brain abnormalities in bipolar affective disorder: Ventricular enlargement and local hyperintensities. *Archives of General Psychiatry*, 47, 1054-1059.

Szasz, T. (1974). *The myth of mental illness.* New York: Harper and Row.

Texas Department of Mental Health and Mental Retardation. (2001). *ECT Equipment Registration History.* Austin, Texas: Texas Department of Mental Health and Mental Retardation.

Tresise and Stenhouse, (1968). ECT phases with and without anaesthesia: a preliminary statistical study. *British Journal of Psychiatry*, 114, 1383-1386.

Ulett, G.A., Smith, K., and Gleser, G.C. (1956). Evaluation of convulsive and subconvulsive shock therapies utilizing a control group. *American Journal of psychiatry*, 112, 795-802.

Underwriters Laboratories, Incorporated. (1997). *UL Services For Medical Devices Manufacturers: Worldwide Conformity Assessment For the Medical Equipment Industry.* [eight page brochure]. New York, New York: Underwriters Laboratories, Incorporated.

United States v Karl Brandt (1946-1949). Nuremberg Code: Permissible medical experiments: Trials of war criminals before the Nuremberg military tribunals under control council law 10, Volume 2, 181-182. Washington: U.S. Printing Office.

Valentine, M., Keddie, K.M.G., and Dunne, D. (1968). A comparison of techniques in electroconvulsive therapy. *British Journal of Psychiatry,* 114, 989-996 .

von Meduna, L. (1938). General discussion of cardiazol therapy. *American Journal of Psychiatry,* 94, 46.

Weaver, L.A., Ives, J.O., Williams, R., and Nies, A. (1977). A comparison of standard alternating current and low-energy brief pulse electrotherapy. *Biological Psychiatry*, 12, 525-543.

Weaver, L.A., Ravaris, C.L., Rush, S., and Paananen, R. (1970; 1971). Final report: Sequential and other parameters of electroshock treatment. *Department of Psychiatry, Department of E.E. Instrument and Model Facility.* University of Vermont. (Unpublished).

Weinberger, D.R., Torrey, E.F., Neophytides, A.N., and Wyatt, R.J. (1979a). Lateral cerebral ventricular enlargement in chronic schizophrenia. *Archives of General Psychiatry*, 36, 735-739.

Weinberger, D.R., Torrey, E.F., Neophytides, A.N., and Wyatt, R.J. (1979b). Structural abnormalities in cerebral cortex of chronic schizophrenic patients. *Archives of General Psychiatry*, 36, 935-939.

Weiner, R.D. (1979). The psychiatric use of electrically induced seizures. *American Journal of Psychiatry*, 136, 1507-1517.

Weiner, R.D. (1980), ECT and seizure threshold: Effects of stimulus waveform and electrode placement. *Biological Psychiatry*, 15, 225-241.

Weiner, R.D. (1988). The first ECT devices. In M. Fink (Ed.), *Convulsive therapy* (pp. 50-61). New York: Raven Press, Ltd.

Weiner, R.D. (1997). Stimulus dosing with ECT: To titrate or not to titrate - that is the question. *Convulsive therapy,* 13(1), 7-9.

Weiner, R.D., Rogers, H.J., Davidson, J.R.T., and Kahn, E.M. (1986a). Effects of electroconvulsive therapy upon brain electrical activity. *Annals New York Academy of Sciences*, 462, 271-281.

Weiner, R.D., Rogers, H.J., Davidson, M.B., and Miller, R.D. (1982). Evaluation of the central nervous system risks of ECT. *Psychopharmacology Bulletin*, 18(1), 29-31.

Weiner, R.D., Rogers, H.J., Davidson, J.R.T., and Squire, L.R. (1986b). Effects of stimulus parameters on cognitive side effects, in electroconvulsive therapy. *Annals New York Academy of Sciences*, 462, 315-325.

Welch, C.A. Weiner, R.D., Weir, D., Cahill, J.F., Rogers, H.J., Davidson, M.B., Miller, R.D., and Mandel, M.R. (1982). Efficacy of ECT in the treatment of depression: Wave form and electrode placement considerations. *Psychopharmocology Bulletin*, 18(1), 31-34.

Wilcox, P.H. (1946). Brain facilitation, not brain destruction, the aim in electroshock therapy. *Diseases of the Nervous System*, 7, 201-204.

Wilson, I.C., Vernon, J.T., Guin, T., Sandifer, M.G. (1963). A controlled study of treatments of depression. *Journal of Neuropsychiatry,* 4, 331-337.

www.ingramcontent.com/pod-product-compliance
Lightning Source LLC
Chambersburg PA
CBHW051748200326
41597CB00025B/4485

* 9 7 9 8 9 8 8 1 2 8 0 0 7 *